Strategies & Tactics for the MBE 2

(Multistate Bar Exam)

Third Edition

Steven L. Emanuel, J.D.

Founder & Editor in Chief, Emanuel Bar Review

Member, NY, CT, MD, and VA bars

To contact Customer Service, e-mail customer.service@wolterskluwer.com, call 1-800-234-1660, fax 1-800-901-9075, or mail correspondence to:

> Wolters Kluwer Law & Business
> Attn: Order Department
> PO Box 990
> Frederick, MD 21705

Printed in the United States of America.

1 2 3 4 5 6 7 8 9 0

ISBN 978-1-4548-7313-6

This book is intended as a general review of a legal subject. It is not intended as a source for advice for the solution of legal matters or problems. For advice on legal matters, the reader should consult an attorney.

About Wolters Kluwer Legal & Regulatory US

Wolters Kluwer Legal & Regulatory US delivers expert content and solutions in the areas of law, corporate compliance, health compliance, reimbursement, and legal education. Its practical solutions help customers successfully navigate the demands of a changing environment to drive their daily activities, enhance decision quality and inspire confident outcomes.

Serving customers worldwide, its legal and regulatory portfolio includes products under the Aspen Publishers, CCH Incorporated, Kluwer Law International, ftwilliam.com, and MediRegs names. They are regarded as exceptional and trusted resources for general legal and practice-specific knowledge, compliance and risk management, dynamic workflow solutions, and expert commentary.

SUMMARY OF CONTENTS

TABLE OF CONTENTS

CIVIL PROCEDURE
CIVIL PROCEDURE QUESTIONS BY TOPIC

CHAPTER I
JURISDICTION AND VENUE

CHAPTER 2

LAW APPLIED BY THE FEDERAL COURTS

CHAPTER 3

PRETRIAL PROCEDURES

CHAPTER 4

JURY TRIALS

CHAPTER 5

MOTIONS

CHAPTER 6

VERDICTS AND JUDGMENTS

CHAPTER 7

APPEALABILITY AND REVIEW

CONSTITUTIONAL LAW

CONSTITUTIONAL LAW QUESTIONS BY TOPIC

CHAPTER 1

THE SUPREME COURT'S AUTHORITY
AND THE FEDERAL JUDICIAL POWER

CHAPTER 2

POWERS OF THE FEDERAL GOVERNMENT; THE SEPARATION OF POWERS

CHAPTER 3

TWO LIMITS ON STATE POWER: THE DORMANT COMMERCE CLAUSE AND CONGRESSIONAL ACTION

CHAPTER 4

INTERGOVERNMENTAL IMMUNITIES; INTERSTATE RELATIONS

CHAPTER 5

THE DUE PROCESS CLAUSE

Chapter 6

EQUAL PROTECTION

Chapter 7

MISCELLANEOUS CLAUSES

CHAPTER 8

THE "STATE ACTION" REQUIREMENT; CONGRESS'S ENFORCEMENT OF THE CIVIL WAR AMENDMENTS

CHAPTER 9

FREEDOM OF EXPRESSION

CHAPTER 10

FREEDOM OF RELIGION

Chapter 11

JUSTICIABILITY

CONTRACTS

CONTRACTS QUESTIONS BY TOPIC

Chapter 1

OFFER AND ACCEPTANCE

CHAPTER 2

CONSIDERATION

CHAPTER 3

PROMISES BINDING WITHOUT CONSIDERATION

CHAPTER 4

MISTAKE

CHAPTER 5

PAROL EVIDENCE AND INTERPRETATION

CHAPTER 6

CONDITIONS, BREACH, AND OTHER ASPECTS OF PERFORMANCE

CHAPTER 7

ANTICIPATORY REPUDIATION AND OTHER ASPECTS OF BREACH

CHAPTER 8

STATUTE OF FRAUDS

CHAPTER 9

REMEDIES

<small>CHAPTER 10</small>

CONTRACTS INVOLVING MORE THAN TWO PARTIES

<small>CHAPTER 11</small>

IMPOSSIBILITY, IMPRACTICABILITY, AND FRUSTRATION

CHAPTER 12
MISCELLANEOUS DEFENSES

CRIMINAL LAW AND PROCEDURE
CRIMINAL LAW QUESTIONS BY TOPIC

CHAPTER 1
ACTUS REUS AND *MENS REA*

CHAPTER 2

RESPONSIBILITY

CHAPTER 3

JUSTIFICATION AND EXCUSE

CHAPTER 4

ATTEMPT

CHAPTER 5

CONSPIRACY

CHAPTER 6

ACCOMPLICE LIABILITY AND SOLICITATION

CHAPTER 7

HOMICIDE AND OTHER CRIMES AGAINST THE PERSON

CHAPTER 8

THEFT CRIMES

CRIMINAL PROCEDURE QUESTIONS BY TOPIC

CHAPTER 4

CONFESSIONS AND POLICE INTERROGATION

CHAPTER 5

LINEUPS AND OTHER IDENTIFICATION PROCEDURES

CHAPTER 6

FORMAL PROCEEDINGS

EVIDENCE

EVIDENCE QUESTIONS BY TOPIC

CHAPTER 1

BASIC CONCEPTS

CHAPTER 2

CIRCUMSTANTIAL PROOF: SPECIAL PROBLEMS

CHAPTER 3

EXAMINATION AND IMPEACHMENT OF WITNESSES

CHAPTER 4

HEARSAY

CHAPTER 5

HEARSAY EXCEPTIONS AND EXCLUSIONS

CHAPTER 6

PRIVILEGES

CHAPTER 7

REAL AND DEMONSTRATIVE EVIDENCE, INCLUDING WRITINGS

CHAPTER 8

OPINIONS, EXPERTS, AND SCIENTIFIC EVIDENCE

CHAPTER 9

BURDENS OF PROOF, PRESUMPTIONS, AND OTHER PROCEDURAL ISSUES

CHAPTER 10

JUDICIAL NOTICE

REAL PROPERTY

REAL PROPERTY QUESTIONS BY TOPIC

CHAPTER 1

ADVERSE POSSESSION

CHAPTER 2
FREEHOLD ESTATES

CHAPTER 3
FUTURE INTERESTS

CHAPTER 4
CONCURRENT OWNERSHIP

CHAPTER 5

LANDLORD AND TENANT

CHAPTER 6

EASEMENTS AND SERVITUDES

CHAPTER 7

LAND SALE CONTRACTS, MORTGAGES, AND DEEDS

CHAPTER 8

RECORDING ACTS

CHAPTER 9

RIGHTS INCIDENT TO LAND

TORTS

TORTS QUESTIONS BY TOPIC

CHAPTER 1

INTENTIONAL TORTS AGAINST THE PERSON

CHAPTER 2

INTENTIONAL INTERFERENCE WITH PROPERTY

CHAPTER 3

DEFENSES TO INTENTIONAL TORTS

CHAPTER 4

NEGLIGENCE GENERALLY

CHAPTER 5

ACTUAL AND PROXIMATE CAUSE

CHAPTER 6

JOINT TORTFEASORS

Chapter 7

DUTY

Chapter 8

OWNERS AND OCCUPIERS OF LAND

Chapter 9

DAMAGES

CHAPTER 10

VICARIOUS LIABILITY

CHAPTER 11

STRICT LIABILITY

CHAPTER 12

PRODUCTS LIABILITY

CHAPTER 13
NUISANCE

CHAPTER 14
DEFAMATION

PREFACE

Thank you for buying this 3d edition of *Strategies & Tactics for the MBE 2* (which I'll refer to as "*S&T II*"). This book's sole purpose is to help you excel on the MBE.

Here's how I prepared this book, and why I think it will help you:

- For this book, I've selected over 500 MBE-format questions. A small percentage of these questions also appear in our companion volume, *Strategies & Tactics for the MBE*, published in 2019 in its 7th edition (which I'll refer to as "*S&T I*").[1] The substantial majority of the questions in the present book are **actual past** MBE questions released by the MBE's drafters.

- I've put the questions into a **subtopic-by-subtopic hierarchy**. So, for instance, within Contracts, suppose you wanted to review just questions dealing with the Parol Evidence Rule. You'd look in the Table of Contents for the Contracts portion, then the Chapter on Parol Evidence, then the part called "II. SITUATIONS WHERE PAROL EVIDENCE RULE DOES NOT APPLY," then the sub-part called "A. Existence of a condition on effectiveness of contract." In that sub-part, you'd find multiple questions turning on this sub-issue, i.e., the effect of an oral provision that the writing won't become effective until some condition (e.g., "My architect's approval") has been satisfied.

- Because I've arranged the questions by subtopic, you can **spot the "hot topics"** on the MBE by seeing where the questions are **clustered**. So, for instance, if you're studying the Parol Evidence Rule, you could see at a glance—by the number of questions devoted to it—that the examiners like to focus on fact patterns where the Parol Evidence Rule does *not* apply.

- I **personally wrote and edited the answers** to each question in the book.

- For nearly all answer explanations, I tell you not just why the right choice is right, but also **why each wrong choice is wrong**. During my many years of helping students prepare for the MBE, I've learned that the MBE examiners exploit a pool of common student misconceptions over and over. So focusing on why a given wrong choice from a past question is wrong will help you a lot in spotting the examiners' use of that same trap on your actual exam.

- My discussion of each answer choice is **extensively researched and annotated.** When I did this research, I was often surprised to learn intricacies of law that I hadn't been aware of before. And one thing I can promise you based on my review of over 1,200 past MBE questions: when the MBE drafters write a question, they look carefully at Restatements, treatises, technical statutory provisions (e.g., subtleties of UCC Article 2 that you probably never covered in class), semi-obscure court decisions, and other authorities. The MBE is a very technical exam, and to do your best on it you need choice-by-choice analysis that focuses on the same authorities as those the drafters rely on; that's what I've given you here.

---

[1]Unlike the prior (2d) edition of this book, the current edition includes a major section on Civil Procedure. Because Civil Procedure was only recently (in 2015) added to the MBE, the NCBE has released relatively few Civil Procedure MBE questions. I have attempted to deal with this scarcity—while simultaneously trying to give you a sense of how actual past Civil Procedure MBE questions are distributed across the various Civ Pro subtopics—by repeating in this book nearly all of the Civ Pro questions that appear in *S&T I*. But apart from the Civil Procedure section, very few of the questions in this book also appear in *S&T I*. Even counting Civil Procedure, the substantial majority of all questions in this book are different from those in *S&T I*.

- Some of the questions are ones to which the National Conference of Bar Examiners (the drafters of the MBE) has released its own "annotations." But the answer discussions in this book are my own independently-researched ones, and I believe that my analysis is generally **significantly more complete** than the ones released by the National Conference of Bar Examiners.

All of these questions and answers have been used by hundreds of bar-prep students in major markets as part of Emanuel Bar Review materials. These students then passed their state's bar exam at a rate ten percentage points higher than the state-wide average.[2]

I would like to express my deep thanks to Barbara Lasoff, my publishing colleague, for her work on this edition.

Good luck on the MBE. I hope this book helps.

Steve Emanuel
Larchmont, NY
January 2020

---

[2]Based on passage rate of students who used Emanuel Bar Review materials in California and New York for bar exams in 2008 and 2009

CIVIL PROCEDURE

CIVIL PROCEDURE QUESTIONS BY TOPIC

Introductory Note: A line beginning in the form "**Question *n***" (e.g., a line starting "Question 13") indicates that the full text of a question is about to follow. Each full-text question appears only once, and is placed within whatever sub-topic in my judgment best captures the principal subject matter covered by the question. Full-text questions are numbered 1, 2, and so forth up to [100].

In addition, there are many references of the form "**See Question *n***" (e.g., "See Question 15"); these are *cross references* to the previously-mentioned full-text questions. There is no limit to the number of cross references there may be to a single full-text question. When a cross reference appears within a given sub-topic, this means that at least one correct or incorrect choice to the question raises issues falling within that sub-topic. At the end of a "See Question *n*" reference, you will see a reference to one or more choices; this means that the particular choice(s) listed raises an issue falling within the sub-topic where the reference is placed. To take a real-life example, suppose that underneath the following sub-topic:

2. Amount-in-controversy requirement in federal-question cases

there is the following cross reference:

See Question 1 [Choices (B) and (C)]

This cross reference would mean, "Consult the question whose full text occurs as Question 1. You will find that Choices (B) and (C) to this question raise issues involving the amount-in-controversy requirement in federal-question cases. Therefore, for help on this amount-in-controversy topic, you may wish to consult, within the Answer to Question 1, the explanation of why each of Choice (B) and (C) is or isn't correct."

CHAPTER 1

JURISDICTION AND VENUE

I. FEDERAL SUBJECT MATTER JURISDICTION

A. Federal-question jurisdiction

1. Federal-question jurisdiction generally

Question 1

A woman brought suit in State A federal district court against the company she worked for, claiming that it had failed to promote her on account of her gender, in violation of a federal employment-discrimination statute. The woman is a citizen of State A; the company is a corporation incorporated in State B, with its headquarters in State C and with most of its employees working at the office in State A where the woman works. The relief sought by the suit consisted solely of $46,000 in back pay. Two months after the company timely filed its answer, and while discovery was still pending, the company made a motion to dismiss the suit for lack of subject-matter jurisdiction. Will the federal court grant the motion?

(A) Yes, because the company is a citizen of several states, one of which is the same as the woman's state of citizenship.

(B) Yes, because although there is diversity of citizenship, the amount in controversy requirement is not met.

(C) No, because the woman's claim arises under federal law.

(D) No, because the company waived its objection by failing to assert it either in its answer or in a motion made before it served its answer.

2. **Amount-in-controversy requirement in federal-question cases**

3. **Federal question as negating the relevance of whether there is diversity**

4. **Does the federal question appear on the face of the well-pleaded complaint?**

5. **Additional party in case, who is not a defendant or plaintiff as to the federal-question claim**

B. Diversity jurisdiction

1. **Garden-variety diversity jurisdiction, between citizens of different states**

a. **Complete diversity normally required**

b. **Circumstances under which citizenship of defendant matters**

c. **Time as of which diversity must exist**

Question 2

Company is a for-profit corporation that at the time of the relevant transactions was incorporated in and headquartered in State A. Company hired Partnership, a two-partner general partnership of the state where it was organized, to redesign its computer system so as to improve security. Partnership's two members were and are citizens of State B and State C respectively. After the contract work was done, the system was hacked by unknown persons, causing Company to sue Partnership for breach of contract in federal district court for State A. The suit sought damages in excess of $75,000. Partnership did not initially challenge subject-matter jurisdiction. During discovery, and after the time to make threshold objections had passed, Partnership learned that Company had reincorporated in State B during the course of the lawsuit.

Partnership now moves to dismiss the action for lack of subject-matter jurisdiction. How should the court resolve the motion?

(A) The court should deny the motion because it was made too late.

(B) The court should grant the motion, dismiss the action, and sanction Company for having withheld information pertinent to jurisdiction.

(C) The court should deny the motion because the court has subject-matter jurisdiction.

(D) The court should remand the matter to State A state court to be tried there.

See Question 5 [Choices (A) and (C)]

See Question 37 [Choice (B)]

d. Diversity involving corporations

Question 3

Plaintiff, a State A citizen, worked in a plant in State A operated by Defendant, a company that manufactures radioactive materials used exclusively by the federal government. Defendant is incorporated in State B, but conducts all of its day-to-day operations (including all manufacturing, shipping, accounting, and sales-generation activities) at the State A plant. Defendant's corporate officers all work from a small office in State C, from which they direct, control, and coordinate the company's activities. Plaintiff was injured by radiation burns from radioactive materials he was handling at the State A plant, due to a fellow employee's negligent removal of a warning sign on the materials.

Plaintiff sued Defendant for negligence in a State A state court (located in State A's capital city of Cap City) for $100,000. The complaint alleged that under *respondeat superior,* Defendant was liable to Plaintiff for his personal injuries caused by the fellow employee's negligence. Defendant timely removed the action to the federal district court located in Cap City. Defendant then filed an answer in the federal court denying liability, citing (correctly) a federal statute that gives any defense contractor an affirmative defense to any federal-law-based or state-law-based negligence claim by an employee if the claim is premised on the *respondeat superior* doctrine.

Now, in the State A federal court, Plaintiff opposes the removal and moves to have the case transferred back to the State A state court where it was originally filed. Should the federal court grant Plaintiff's transfer motion?

(A) Yes, because the fact that Defendant conducts its day-to-day operations in, and maintains its inventory in, State A causes it to be a citizen of that state, nullifying Defendant's right of removal.

(B) No, because Defendant is a citizen solely of States B and C and Plaintiff is a citizen of State A, thereby creating complete diversity and satisfying all requirements for Defendant to have a right to remove to the State A federal court.

(C) Yes, because Plaintiff is a citizen of State A and Defendant is a citizen of both State A and State C, preventing the required complete diversity from existing and nullifying Defendant's right of removal.

(D) No, because the case presents a federal question, thereby entitling Defendant to remove whether or not it is a citizen of State A, in whose state courts the action was originally filed.

See Question 12 [Choices (A) and (B)]

See Question 4 [Choices (A), (B), and (C)]

See Question 1 [Choice (A)]

e. Diversity involving trusts or estates

Question 4

A doctor, a citizen of State A, went to shop at a factory outlet for computers located in that state. The outlet was operated by a corporation that makes computers and sells them throughout the U.S. While at the outlet, the doctor fell down the stairs in a poorly-lit stairwell, hit his head, and died instantly. The doctor died intestate, leaving only one relative and heir, his son, who is a citizen of State B. The son procured from the State B courts an order appointing him as the doctor's personal representative for purposes of bringing any wrongful-death action on behalf of the doctor's estate. The son then commenced a wrongful death action for negligence in the State B courts for $1 million against the corporation; the complaint listed the plaintiff as being the son suing "as personal representative of" the estate of the doctor and stated that the son was a citizen of State B.

The corporation then removed the suit to the federal district court located in State B, and in its removal petition asserted that there was diversity of citizenship. The corporation's headquarters are located in a 2,000 square foot office in State A, from which all 3 officers of the corporation supervise the corporation's activities. Three-quarters of the corporation's employees work in a 200,000 square-foot plant located in State C, at which all of the computers made and sold by the corporation are manufactured. The corporation is incorporated in State D, where it has no employees or operations. All required pleadings were served several months ago, and the son has not opposed the removal.

You are the clerk for the federal judge sitting in State B who has been assigned the suit. The judge asks you for advice about how she should resolve any issue that may exist relating to the court's subject-matter jurisdiction over the case. You should tell her that her court

(A) has jurisdiction and may hear the case, because the son is a citizen of State B and the corporation is a citizen of States C and D only, thereby creating complete diversity.

(B) has jurisdiction and may hear the case, because the son is a citizen of State B and the corporation is a citizen of State D only, thereby creating complete diversity.

(C) does not have jurisdiction and may not hear the case, because the doctor was a citizen of State A at his death and the corporation is a citizen of States A and D, thereby preventing complete diversity from existing.

(D) may hear the case whether or not complete diversity exists, because the son has by now waived any objection based on lack of subject-matter jurisdiction.

f. Diversity involving partnerships and other unincorporated associations

Question 5

Three years ago, a limited partnership as plaintiff brought a suit, stated to be based on the alienage variety of diversity, against the defendant, a corporation, in federal court for the district of State A. The defendant corporation was and is a citizen of State A, since it was incorporated in that state and has its principal place of business there. The partnership was and still is organized under the law of Canada, with its principal place of business also in Canada. At the time the suit was filed, the partnership consisted of a general partner (a corporation that was solely a citizen of Canada) and ten limited partners, all individuals. Eight of the limited partners were citizens of Canada; two were citizens of State A.

Last year, after discovery had been completed but the case not yet tried, the two limited partners who were citizens of State A left the partnership because they sold their interests to the other limited partners, and under the partnership agreement were thus required to leave the partnership. (This sale and exit happened for reasons unrelated to the lawsuit.)

This year, after a one-month trial, the jury rendered a verdict in favor of the plaintiff partnership. The next day, before any judgment had been entered, the defendant corporation moved to have the action dismissed for lack of subject matter jurisdiction, in that there had not been complete diversity of citizenship between the parties at the time the suit was filed three years ago.

Should the district court grant the defense motion and dismiss the suit for lack of subject-matter jurisdiction?

(A) Yes, because at the time suit was commenced the partnership was a citizen of both Canada and State A, preventing the existence of complete alienage diversity between the partnership and the corporation.

(B) Yes, so long as the court does not believe that the defendant learned or should have learned of the two limited partners' State A citizenship prior to the start of the trial.

(C) No, because the two limited partners' exit from the partnership prior to the start of trial was a timely cure for any lack of subject-matter jurisdiction that might otherwise have existed.

(D) No, because a partnership is deemed to be a citizen of the place where it was formed, plus the place of its principal place of business, so there was complete alienage diversity jurisdiction at the time the suit was filed.

Question 6

Plaintiff is an insurance company that is incorporated in State A and has its principal place of business in State B. It provides liability insurance coverage for automobile accidents. Plaintiff wrote a liability policy on Driver, a State C resident, the face value of which was $1 million. (This was the maximum amount Plaintiff would be committed to pay for claims against Driver arising out of multiple accidents in any single six-month policy period.) Plaintiff then received claims filed by seven different individuals against Driver, all of whom were involved in different car accidents in which the other driver was Driver during a single six-month policy period. Four of the claimants are citizens of State C; two of the claimants are citizens of State D; and the seventh is a citizen of State B. All had brought suits in various state courts against Driver (who was and is insolvent) and received default judgments that total $2 million. Under relevant state-law insurance principles, Plaintiff is responsible to pay the full amount of these judgments, subject to the $1 million aggregate policy limit.

Plaintiff has filed a statutory interpleader action in State C federal district court to determine which of the claimants, if any, should receive payment under Driver's insurance policy and how much each should receive. Plaintiff has caused service to be made on each of the seven claimants. One claimant, a citizen of State C, has moved to have the interpleader action dismissed for lack of subject-matter jurisdiction.

Should the court grant the motion to dismiss the interpleader action for lack of subject-matter jurisdiction?

(A) Yes, because complete diversity does not exist between Plaintiff and the seven claimants.

(B) No, because two or more claimants are citizens of different states and the amount in controversy exceeds the statutory amount.

(C) Yes, because although diversity-of-citizenship is present, the amount in controversy is less than $5 million, the statutory amount for high-stakes, multi-state disputes.

(D) Yes, because the competing claims do not have a common origin and do not arise out of the same transaction.

See Question 15 [Choice (A)]

g. **Diversity not relevant to state-court actions**

See Question 21 [Choice (D)]

2. Alienage jurisdiction

See Question 47 [Choice (D)]

3. Devices to create or destroy diversity

Question 7

Plaintiff is a State A corporation that rents stage equipment for use in theatrical performances. Defendant is a small theater group that entered into a rental agreement with Plaintiff. Defendant is incorporated in State A and its main theater is in that state. Defendant's latest show was a box office failure. Defendant has been unable to pay Plaintiff the annual rental fee, and Plaintiff wanted to compel payment by means of a federal-court suit.

Therefore, Plaintiff assigned its interest in the rental agreement for "one dollar" to Lawyer, an individual who lives and works in nearby State B. By separate agreement, Lawyer agreed that if he litigated or settled the assigned claim, he would pay Plaintiff two-thirds of any recovery he received, "solely as a bonus." Under State A law, an assignment is legal "when made for valid consideration, even if only for a nominal amount."

After the assignment, Lawyer sued Defendant in diversity in federal district court for the District of State A, alleging breach of the rental agreement. Defendant has moved to dismiss the action for lack of subject-matter jurisdiction. Assuming the amount-in-controversy is satisfied, the district court should

(A) grant the motion because diversity jurisdiction is not available if any defendant is a citizen of the state in which the federal court sits.

(B) deny the motion, because Lawyer and Defendant are citizens of different states, and the assignment was legal under state law.

(C) grant the motion, because the assignment was collusively made for the purpose of creating diversity of citizenship.

(D) deny the motion, because Defendant and Lawyer are citizens of different states, and Lawyer has a sufficiently large economic stake in the outcome to motivate him to vigorously litigate the suit.

4. Amount in controversy requirement in diversity cases

Question 8

A statute passed by the legislature of State A, the "Employee Check Act," or "ECA," provides that if five or more persons work in the state for a given employer, the employer may pay them by check only if the employer offers the employees a free method of cashing the check within one mile or less of the workplace. The statute also provides a flat damages award of $1,000 per employee for each check as to which the employer violates the ECA.

A brokerage firm with many employees in State A failed to comply with the statute. Twenty employees of the firm, each of whom was given payroll five checks in violation of the ECA, joined as co-plaintiffs in a non-class-action suit against the brokerage firm filed in the State A state courts; each plaintiff asserted a claim for $5,000. The brokerage firm promptly filed a notice removing the action to the local federal court for State A. Ninety days after the firm filed the notice of removal, all plaintiffs jointly filed a motion to remand the case to the State A court from which it had been removed, on the grounds that the case did not satisfy the relevant amount-in-controversy requirement.

Should the court grant the plaintiffs' motion to remand the case?

(A) No, because the federal supplemental jurisdiction statute permits the court to aggregate all of the plaintiffs' claims since they all derive from a common series of transactions, and when aggregated the claims are collectively worth in excess of $75,000.

(B) No, because by case law the claims here may be aggregated for amount-in-controversy purposes since they arise from a common series of transactions, and when aggregated the claims are collectively worth in excess of $75,000.

(C) No, because the plaintiffs waived their right to request remand when more than 30 days passed following the brokerage firm's filing of its notice of removal.

(D) Yes, because by case law the fact that the claims are not for a single right in which all plaintiffs have a common interest prevents the claims from being aggregated for amount-in-controversy purposes.

Question 9

Husband, Wife, and Child, all citizens of State A, ate a can of soup that turned out to be contaminated. Each suffered food poisoning that resulted in permanent neurological damage. Defendant, a food company in State B, processed and distributed the can of soup. Husband, Wife, and Child sued Defendant in a federal district court in State A. Defendant has moved to dismiss the complaint for lack of subject-matter jurisdiction. He concedes that the parties are citizens of diverse states, but argues that the complaint does not meet the amount-in-controversy test. Assume that all allegations in the choices below regarding the amount of plaintiffs' damages are made in good faith, and that it is not "legally certain" that any plaintiff has suffered smaller damages than he or she alleges. Assume also that as to each choice, there are no allegations regarding the amount of damages other than those mentioned in the choice.

How should the court resolve the motion?

(A) The court should grant the motion if the complaint alleges that: (i) Husband suffered $60,000 in personal damages; (ii) Wife suffered $50,000 in personal damages; and (iii) Child suffered $40,000 in personal damages.

(B) The court should deny the motion if the complaint alleges that each family member suffered $40,000 in personal damages, because supplementary jurisdiction applies.

(C) The court should grant the motion if the complaint alleges that (i) Husband suffered $40,000 in personal damages and $40,000 for loss of consortium; and (ii) Wife and Child each suffered $40,000 in personal damages.

(D) The court should deny the motion if the complaint alleges that Husband and Wife each suffered $40,000 in personal damages, because their claims are based on a common and undivided interest.

See Question 90 [Choice (C)]

See Question 8 [Choice (B)]

5. Federal court's power to abstain from hearing certain cases qualifying for diversity jurisdiction

Question 10

Husband and Wife, American citizens, were married in State A and then moved, together with their two children, to State B. After a number of years, Husband relocated to State C, where he now works, insures his car, and votes. He decided to end his marriage and sued Wife for divorce in federal district court for the district of State B. In addition to a divorce decree, he sought joint custody of the children and a court order that each parent would contribute $25,000 per year for the next ten years to support the children.

Wife has now moved to dismiss the State B federal-court action for lack of subject-matter jurisdiction. The court should

(A) deny the motion because diversity jurisdiction is present.

(B) remand the action to a state court in State B, since that is where Husband should have brought it.

(C) transfer the action to the state courts of State A, where the marriage took place.

(D) decline to exercise jurisdiction even if the case meets the requirements for diversity jurisdiction.

C. Supplemental jurisdiction ("SJ")

   1. SJ generally

   2. SJ where the "anchor claim" is based solely on diversity

      a. SJ asserted as to claims by an original defendant against an original plaintiff (i.e., counterclaims)

         See Question 18 [Choices (A) and (B)]

      b. SJ asserted as to a third-party claim by an original defendant (i.e., a third-party plaintiff) against a third-party defendant

         Question 11

Plaintiff is a widow whose husband was killed in an accident while working for Defendant, a construction company. Plaintiff is a citizen of State A. Defendant is incorporated in and has its principal place of business in State B. Plaintiff brought a diversity action against Defendant in federal district court for State A, asserting that the accident was caused in part by Defendant's negligent maintenance of certain equipment owned by Defendant; the suit sought $100,000 in damages. Defendant immediately filed a third-party claim against Distributor, seeking $100,000 in damages and alleging that if Defendant were to be found liable to Plaintiff, Distributor would be liable to Defendant for having leased to Defendant the defective equipment that caused the accident. Distributor is incorporated in State A and has its principal place of business there. Plaintiff then amended her complaint to assert a defective-product claim directly against Distributor; the claim sought $100,000 in damages.

Defendant and Distributor have now moved to dismiss the claims against them based on lack of subject-matter jurisdiction. That is, (1) Defendant has moved to dismiss Plaintiff's negligence claim, and (2) Distributor has moved to dismiss both of the claims against it, i.e. Defendant's third-party claim and Plaintiff's direct claim. The court should dispose of these motions by

(A) granting all of the motions.

(B) granting only Distributor's motion as to both claims against it.

(C) granting only Distributor's motion, and only as to Plaintiff's claim against it.

(D) granting only Defendant's motion.

         See Question 41 [Choice (A)]

      c. SJ asserted as to a claim by third-party defendant against anyone

         Question 12

A shop owner domiciled in State A sued a distributor in a federal district court in State A for breach of a contract. The shop owner sought $100,000 in damages for allegedly defective goods that the distributor had provided under the contract. The distributor is incorporated in State B, with its principal place of business in State C. The distributor brought in as a third-party defendant the wholesaler that had provided the goods to the distributor, alleging that the wholesaler had a duty to indemnify the distributor for any damages recovered by the shop owner. The wholesaler is incorporated in State B, with its principal place of business in State A.

The wholesaler has asserted a $60,000 counterclaim against the distributor for payment for the goods at issue, and the distributor has moved to dismiss the counterclaim for lack of subject-matter jurisdiction.

Should the motion to dismiss be granted?

(A) No, because the wholesaler's and the distributor's principal places of business are diverse.

(B) No, because there is supplemental jurisdiction over the wholesaler's counterclaim.

(C) Yes, because there is no diversity of citizenship between the distributor and the wholesaler.

(D) Yes, because there is no diversity of citizenship between the shop owner and the wholesaler.

d. SJ asserted as to claim by the original plaintiff against a third-party defendant

See Question 11 [Choices (A), (B), and (C)]

e. SJ and the amount in controversy, when multiple Ps' claims are aggregated

See Question 9 [All Choices]

See Question 8 [Choices (A) and (D)]

3. SJ where the "anchor claim" raises a federal question

a. SJ for a state-law claim that's closely related to the anchor claim, and the state-law claim is against the same defendant as the anchor claim

b. SJ for a state-law claim that's closely related to the anchor claim, and the state-law claim is against an additional party (i.e., one is not a defendant to the anchor claim) who is not diverse with the plaintiff(s)

Question 13

Plaintiff was born in State A and has lived there her entire life. For the last 20 years she worked as a data-entry operator for Employer, a corporation incorporated in, and with its principal place of business in, State B. Employer announced one day that it was outsourcing its data-entry operations and gave Plaintiff the choice between transferring to a lower-paying job and being fired. Plaintiff refused the transfer and was fired. Plaintiff believed that Employer had discriminated against her because of her age. She therefore brought a lawsuit against Employer and Manager, the controlling shareholder of Employer who, Plaintiff believed, made the decision to force her to choose between being fired or taking the lower-paying job. Manager, an individual, lives and works in State A.

The complaint contained two claims. The first claim was against Employer alone and asserted that Employer had violated the federal Age Bias Act (ABA), which provides, "No employer shall discriminate on the basis of age." The second claim was against both Manager and Employer; it alleged that (1) Employer breached Plaintiff's employment contract, a clause of which said that Employee could only be fired for "repeated unwillingness or inability to perform the essential functions of the job"; and (2) Manager used his control of Employer to cause Employer to breach the contract, thereby himself committing the tort of interference with contract.

Plaintiff filed her lawsuit in a federal district court located in State A. Both claims seek more than $100,000 in damages against each party. Manager has moved to dismiss the claim against him for lack of subject-matter jurisdiction. How should the court resolve the motion?

(A) The court should deny the motion because the court can exercise federal-question jurisdiction over Manager since the ABA claim arises under a federal statute.

(B) The court should deny the motion because it can exercise federal diversity jurisdiction over Manager.

(C) The court has power to hear the claim against Manager since that claim is closely related to a federal-question claim in the case, and there is no reason for the court to exercise its discretion not to hear the claim against Manager.

(D) The court should grant the motion because Manager is a pendent party over whom the court cannot exercise jurisdiction on these facts.

4. Situations in which the court considers whether to use its discretion to decline to exercise otherwise-available SJ

Question 14

A jogger was stopped by a police officer, who thought the jogger matched the description of a burglar being sought by the police. The officer arrested the jogger, handcuffed her, and brought her to the police station, where the charges were dismissed as a case of mistaken identity. The jogger, a citizen of State A, brought a civil suit against the officer (also a citizen of State A) in State A federal court. The suit contained two claims: (1) a common-law claim for false arrest based on State A tort law; and (2) a claim that the officer's stop of the jogger and his excessive force against her was a denial of her federal civil rights made under color of law, thereby entitling her to recover damages under a federal statute known as "§ 1983." The State A statute of limitation for the false-arrest claim is two years from the arrest; the federal statute of limitations on the §1983 claim is four years.

The officer asserted various defenses, one of which (asserted solely in response to the § 1983 claim) was the defense of qualified immunity. By the time the parties completed discovery, nearly three years had elapsed since the arrest. At the close of discovery, the officer moved for summary judgment on the §1983 claim based on his immunity defense. The judge granted the motion, and therefore dismissed the § 1983 claim with prejudice. The officer then moved to have the false-arrest claim dismissed on the grounds that the court now lacked subject-matter jurisdiction over that claim due to the dismissal of the § 1983 claim. The jogger opposed the dismissal, pointing out (correctly) that discovery was complete, and that the court and litigants had devoted significant time to the issues raised by the false-arrest claim. The jogger also expressed the fear that if the court dismissed the claim, she might be time-barred from refiling it in State A court. Which of the following best summarizes how the federal court should rule on the officer's motion to dismiss the false-arrest claim?

(A) The court must dismiss the false-arrest claim regardless of whether the claim could be refiled in State A, because the court's dismissal of the § 1983 claim deprived that court of subject-matter jurisdiction to hear the false-arrest claim.

(B) The court must try the false-arrest claim, because supplemental jurisdiction applies to that claim, and the court does not have discretion to decline to exercise that jurisdiction.

(C) The court has discretion whether to dismiss the false-arrest claim or try it, and if it dismisses, federal law guarantees the jogger 30 days to refile the claim in State A court.

(D) The court must dismiss the false-arrest claim, but federal law guarantees the jogger 30 days to re-file the claim in State A court.

See Question 13 [Choice (C)]

D. Removal to the federal courts

1. Requirement that the federal court to which removal is made would have had subject-matter jurisdiction over the action had it initially been filed in that court

Question 15

Plaintiff owns and resides in a house in State A and has no plans to move. He ordered a garden hose for $100 by telephone from a catalogue distributed by Defendant, a garden-supply company that is incorporated in State A and has its principal place of business there. The garden hose turned out to have a defective nozzle, and while Plaintiff was watering his garden a flood developed, ruining his garden. Plaintiff was angry, and therefore posted disparaging comments about Defendant on an online discussion board. Plaintiff also sued Defendant in State A state court on a breach-of-warranty theory to recover the purchase price plus consequential damages for his lost garden, for a total of $5,000. Defendant filed a counterclaim alleging violation of a federal statute entitled the "Federal Trade Libel Law" (the FTLL), which provides: "Any false or disparaging online statement made about a business that conducts online sales or sales by mail shall be per se actionable in state or federal court, and the disparaged business shall be entitled to recover from the maker of the statement, without proof of pecuniary harm, statutory damages of $10,000 for each day in which said statement is publicly accessible online." Defendant's counterclaim alleged that Plaintiff's disparaging statement appeared online for ten days, and the company therefore sought $100,000 in damages. Defendant then removed the action to federal court for the district of State A. Plaintiff now seeks to have the case remanded to State A state court.

Should the federal district court remand the action or any part of it?

(A) No, because the federal court has power to hear Defendant's counterclaim.

(B) No, because the federal court may exercise federal-question jurisdiction over the counterclaim, and supplemental jurisdiction extends to cover Plaintiff's claim.

(C) Yes as to the entire action, because the removal was not proper.

(D) Yes as to Plaintiff's state-law claim, but the court may and should retain jurisdiction over Defendant's federal counterclaim.

2. What party or parties may remove?

a. Requirement that the removing party must be a defendant

Question 16

A woman sued her former employer in state court, asserting age and sex discrimination claims under both state and federal law. The woman's attorney had recently been embarrassed in court by the judge to whom the case was assigned. Wishing to avoid difficulties with the judge, the woman's attorney promptly removed the case to federal court on the basis of federal-question jurisdiction. The employer's attorney has timely moved to remand.

How is the federal court likely to proceed?

(A) Remand the entire case.

(B) Remand the state claims but keep the federal claims.

(C) Retain the case to avoid the risk of bias and impropriety in having it proceed before a judge who has shown clear hostility toward the woman's attorney.

(D) Retain the case, because it was timely removed and the woman alleges federal claims.

b. Requirement that the removal not be made by a citizen of the state where the action is pending, if no federal question is present

See Question 15 [Choices (B) and (C)]

See Question 3 [Choices (A) and (B)]

3. To what court may the action be removed?

4. When should some or all claims be remanded to the state court?

See Question 16 [Choices (A) and (B)]

See Question 2 [Choice (D)]

E. Time for raising objection to lack of subject-matter jurisdiction, and waiver of such objections

II. PERSONAL JURISDICTION

A. Requirement of minimum contacts between D and the forum state

1. The requirement of "minimum contacts" generally

Question 17

Plaintiff is a franchisor of brake-repair services for automobiles. Plaintiff's headquarters are in State A, a state located in the southwestern part of the U.S. Plaintiff issues franchises for the operation of local brake-repair stores to franchisees located in all 50 states, as well as in 20 foreign countries. Defendant, an individual with considerable business sophistication, was and is a citizen and resident of Canada. After meeting with Plaintiff's two-person Canadian sales office regarding his desire to buy a franchise from Plaintiff, Defendant negotiated for six months to complete the purchase. The franchise was to be located in eastern Canada, about 2,000 miles from Plaintiff's State A headquarters. Most negotiations occurred by telephone and email, with Defendant participating from his home in Canada and Plaintiff from its State A headquarters. During that period, Plaintiff's only connections with State A were that he travelled twice to Plaintiff's headquarters for face-to-face negotiating sessions, and on one of those trips also attended a three-day "prospective franchisee training session" there. Defendant then signed his copy of the final contract in Canada, and Plaintiff signed its copy in State A.

The contract said that any disputes would be "resolved according to the laws of State A," and said nothing about in which court(s) a suit on the contract could be brought. The contract also required Plaintiff to support Defendant's efforts as to sales, marketing, finance, and operations, and indicated that most such support work by Plaintiff would be done by employees working from Plaintiff's headquarters. After signing the contract, Plaintiff never travelled to State A, and never did any business in the state, or with State A parties, other than having some dealings by telephone with Plaintiff's personnel located in the state.

After Defendant failed to make required payments of monthly franchise fees, Plaintiff brought a breach-of-contract action against Defendant based on diversity in federal district court for State A. The State A long-arm grants the State A courts personal jurisdiction to hear all disputes concerning contracts, if one party to the contract is an individual or business located in State A, and if such exercise of personal jurisdiction "would be consistent with the due process limits imposed by the U.S. Constitution." Before filing an answer to the suit, Defendant made a timely motion that the court lacked personal jurisdiction over him. The trial court denied the motion. Defendant tried the case on the merits, lost, and then appealed the adverse judgment to the appropriate federal Court of Appeal on the grounds that the trial court erred in concluding that it had personal jurisdiction over Defendant.

Should the federal Court of Appeals reverse the judgment and dismiss the case for lack of personal jurisdiction?

(A) No, because by raising and losing the jurisdiction question and then continuing to trial on the merits, Defendant waived the right to raise the jurisdiction issue on appeal.

(B) No, because Defendant should have anticipated being required to defend an action in State A, making it not unfair to require him to do so.

(C) Yes, because although Defendant had minimum contacts with State A, it would violate traditional notions of fair play and substantial justice to require him to defend this suit in State A.

(D) Yes, because Defendant did not voluntarily avail himself of the privilege of doing business in State A, thereby preventing him from having minimum contacts with that state.

2. **The "purposeful availment" standard**

  See Question 30 [Choice (B)]

  See Question 90 [Choice (B)]

  See Question 17 [Choice (D)]

3. **The requirement that it not be "fundamentally unfair" to require D to defend in the forum state**

  See Question 17 [Choices (B) and (C)]

4. **The requirement of minimum contacts with the forum state when the suit is in federal court, and includes a federal-question claim**

  See Question 23 [Choice (D)]

5. **Consent as a basis for personal jurisdiction**

  Question 18

  Plaintiff, an individual residing in State A, owns and operates a retail store in that state. Plaintiff, for use in the store, licenses security software from Defendant, a corporation specializing in security technology with its principal place of business in State B and incorporated in State C. Despite the software, hackers broke into Plaintiff's financial system. Plaintiff sued Defendant in a state court in State C for breach of contract, choosing that forum because of the three plausible fora, State C had the longest statute of limitations. After a trial, Plaintiff lost on the merits; the state court held that Plaintiff's own faulty installation of the software was the sole proximate cause of the vulnerability to hackers.

  Plaintiff then filed a second lawsuit against Defendant, this time in federal court for the district of State C, and based on diversity jurisdiction. (Other than filing the pair of lawsuits, Plaintiff has had no contacts with State C.) This second suit essentially repeated the breach-of-contract claim that was held invalid in the first suit. Defendant in its answer raised the affirmative defense of claim preclusion. Defendant also asserted a counterclaim alleging that Plaintiff's filing of multiple lawsuits constituted the tort of wrongful use of civil proceedings; the counterclaim alleged that this tort had caused Defendant to suffer pecuniary loss (in the form of lost business profits) in excess of $75,000.

  Plaintiff has now moved to dismiss the counterclaim for (1) lack of personal jurisdiction over him; and (2) failure to properly serve him, in that no summons was served with the counterclaim (a factually-correct allegation). The court should

  (A) deny the motion because a compulsory counterclaim does not require an independent basis for personal jurisdiction over the plaintiff.

  (B) grant the motion because a permissive counterclaim requires an independent basis for personal jurisdiction over the plaintiff.

  (C) grant the motion on the grounds that Defendant failed to properly serve Plaintiff.

  (D) deny the motion because Plaintiff has effectively consented to the court's exercise of personal jurisdiction over him.

B. General jurisdiction — special requirements for

Question 19

A plaintiff domiciled in State A brought a wrongful death action in a federal court in State A against a State B parent corporation and one of its foreign subsidiaries. The plaintiff alleged that a tire manufactured by the subsidiary in Europe had caused his wife's death in an automobile accident in Europe.

The parent corporation does significant business throughout the United States, including in State A. The subsidiary conducts no business and has no employees or bank accounts in State A. The subsidiary manufactures its tires for the European market, but 2% of its tires are distributed in State A by the parent corporation. The subsidiary has moved to dismiss for lack of personal jurisdiction.

Should the court grant the subsidiary's motion?

(A) No, because 2% of the subsidiary's tires entered State A through the stream of commerce.

(B) No, because of the general personal jurisdiction established over the parent corporation.

(C) Yes, because the accident did not occur in the United States.

(D) Yes, because the subsidiary lacks continuous, systematic, and substantial contacts with State A.

Question 20

An insurer is incorporated in State A, and has had its principal place of business there for many years. Ten years ago, the insurer sold a disability insurance policy to a surgeon. At the time the surgeon purchased the policy, the surgeon was a resident of State A, and all communications and activities regarding the purchase occurred in State A. Last year, the surgeon moved to State B. The insurer has had for some time a small office in State B, from which it markets insurance policies to State B residents; these policies account for about 10% of the insurer's worldwide revenues. When the insurer's website (run from State A) receives an inquiry from a State B resident, the insurer refers the inquiry to the company's State B office.

The surgeon now claims that for the last six months he has been disabled and is entitled to disability benefits from the insurer. The insurer has refused to pay, on the grounds that the policy lapsed eight months ago for non-payment. Prior to the surgeon's demand for disability payments, the insurer took no actions in State B concerning the policy, except to send the surgeon bills for premiums at his new State B address once it received a change-of-address notice from him. Last month, the surgeon filed suit against the insurer in State B court, alleging that the insurer's failure to make the disability payments was a breach of their contract. Under the State B long-arm statute, a State B resident bringing a contract action in the State B courts may make service on an out-of-state corporate defendant by causing a summons and complaint to be personally served upon the CEO or other officer of the defendant wherever in the United States that officer can be found. (The State B courts will exercise personal jurisdiction over an out-of-state corporate defendant in such a suit brought so long as such jurisdiction would not violate the U.S. Constitution.) The process server hired by the surgeon handed the summons and complaint to the insurer's CEO at the CEO's home in State A; the suit named only the insurer, not the CEO.

One week after the insurer's CEO received the summons on behalf of the insurer, the CEO happened to travel to State B for a one-day conference on an unrelated matter. While he was in State B, he was handed a summons and complaint in a divorce action brought against him in the State B courts by his long-estranged wife. The two had been married decades ago in State A, and the wife had moved to State B a few years ago. Until the one-day conference, the CEO had not visited—or done any activity connected to—State B at any time in the last ten years. By coincidence, the divorce suit was assigned to the same State B judge as the surgeon's suit against the insurer.

The CEO and the insurer, in their respective suits, have each made timely motions in State B court to have the suit against each dismissed for lack of personal jurisdiction; each defendant argues that the court's exercise of such jurisdiction over that defendant would violate the Due Process Clause of the Fourteenth Amendment. How should the court rule on the two motions?

(A) Grant the motion as to both suits.

(B) Deny the motion as to both suits.

(C) Grant the motion as to the suit against the insurer, but deny the motion as to the suit against the CEO.

(D) Grant the motion as to the suit against the CEO, but grant the motion as to the suit against the insurer.

1. General jurisdiction based on residency

Question 21

Plaintiff, a State A corporation, has sued Defendant, an individual, in State B state court. Defendant was served at his home in State B. The suit, based on State E law, sought money damages. The suit contended that Defendant breached a contract to convey a piece of State E real estate to Plaintiff, thereby depriving Plaintiff of the benefit of his bargain. The terms of the contract were negotiated face-to-face in State C by Plaintiff's CEO and by Defendant; the next day, after a final document had been created, the document was signed by Defendant while he was in State D. No activities connected with the contract occurred in State B.

Defendant has timely moved to dismiss the suit for lack of personal jurisdiction over him. State B's statute governing jurisdiction permits the exercise of jurisdiction "to the full extent allowed under the United States Constitution." Should the State B court grant Defendant's motion?

(A) Yes, because the cause of action does not arise out of or relate to Defendant's contacts within State B, the forum state.

(B) Yes, because when a claim arises out of breach of a contract to convey real estate, only the state in which the real estate is located has jurisdiction.

(C) No, because the state in which a defendant resides may exercise general jurisdiction regardless of the nature of the cause of action.

(D) No, because the plaintiff and defendant are citizens of different states, permitting the court to exercise diversity jurisdiction over the suit.

2. General jurisdiction based on presence in the forum state at the time of service

See Question 20 [All Choices]

C. Specific jurisdiction—requirements for

1. Minimum contacts always required

See Question 47 [Choice (C)]

See Question 76 [Choice (D)]

D. *In Rem* and *Quasi in Rem* jurisdiction

Question 22

Plaintiff is an individual who lives in State A. While on holiday in State B, he bought an antique map from Defendant, a corporation that deals in art, and whose principal place of business is in State B. The map turned out to be a counterfeit, and Plaintiff filed a diversity suit against Defendant in federal district court for the Northern District of State A. The action alleged breach of contract, misrepresentation, and fraud, and sought $100,000 in damages. Before filing suit, Plaintiff learned from the Internet that Defendant advertised the fact that "We frequently visit the West Coast, including State A, to show our inventory." Plaintiff also learned that Defendant owned a storage facility in State A valued at $95,000. A State A long-arm statute ("Statute 1") authorizes service in a State A state court action by registered mail to any person found in the U.S. outside of State A, if such service would be consistent with the Due Process Clause of the Fourteenth Amendment. Another State A statute ("Statute 2") provides: "The courts of this state have authority, consistent with the Due Process Clause of the Fourteenth Amendment, to exercise *quasi in rem* jurisdiction based on attachment of the defendant's tangible or intangible property located within this state." No federal statute bears on the use of *quasi in rem* jurisdiction on facts such as those presented in Plaintiff's suit.

Plaintiff did not attempt to obtain personal jurisdiction over Defendant by using Statute 1, because he was not aware of that statute's existence. Instead, he served Defendant by attaching the storage facility, and asserting *quasi in rem* jurisdiction under authority of Statute 2. (He was willing to take the risk that he might get a judgment for the full $100,000 sought, but be able to realize only $95,000 by having the storage facility seized and sold to satisfy the judgment.)

Defendant has now moved to dismiss the action for lack of personal jurisdiction over it. How should the district court resolve the motion?

(A) The court should grant the motion because Plaintiff has not made reasonable efforts to use the service-by-registered-mail provisions of Statute 1 to establish *in personam* jurisdiction.

(B) The court should deny the motion because Plaintiff was entitled to use Statute 2 to establish quasi in rem jurisdiction and met the requirements of that statute.

(C) The court should grant the motion because no federal statute or rule authorizes *quasi in rem* jurisdiction in lawsuits filed in federal court.

(D) The court should grant the motion because the attached assets are not related to Plaintiff's claim against Defendant.

See Question 21 [Choice (B)]

E. How to raise a challenge to the lack of personal jurisdiction

1. Motion to dismiss for lack of personal jurisdiction under Rule 12(b)(2)

a. Preservation of right to appeal denial of the dismissal motion

See Question 17 [Choice (A)]

F. Special procedural contexts raising the issue of personal jurisdiction

1. Class actions

See Question 48 [Choice (D)]

2. Situations where nationwide service of process may be authorized

Question 23

Plaintiff is a construction company. Plaintiff is incorporated in State A and operates in that state as well as in State B. Defendant is an Internet-based company that is incorporated in

State C. Plaintiff has brought suit, alleging that Defendant defrauded Plaintiff in violation of a federal statute called the Internet Commercial Fraud Act (ICFA). Section 1 of the ICFA creates a federal private right of action for anyone defrauded in a commercial transaction conducted over the Internet. Section 2 of the statute authorizes suit to be brought in the federal court located anywhere in plaintiff's state of principal residence (which in the case of a corporate plaintiff includes the plaintiff's state of incorporation); Section 3 allows service in an ICFA action "on the defendant in any U.S. state in which the defendant may be found"; and Section 4 says that in ICFA suits the court will be deemed to have personal jurisdiction over the defendant regardless of the nature of the defendant's contacts with the plaintiff's state of principal residence.

Plaintiff's complaint, filed in federal district court in State A, asserted that an employee of Plaintiff working out of Plaintiff's State A office purchased a computer online from Defendant; that Defendant knew the order came from that State A office; that Defendant knew the computer was defective; and that Defendant shipped the computer as requested to Plaintiff's State B office. The State B long-arm statute allows nationwide service of process upon, and personal jurisdiction over, any defendant who "voluntarily and knowingly ships any item of tangible personal property into this state."

After Plaintiff filed the suit, Plaintiff's sole effort to make service on the Defendant was to have the summons and complaint handed to the CEO of Defendant while the CEO was visiting State D to attend a technology conference. Defendant has never sold a computer to a State D resident.

Has Plaintiff established personal jurisdiction over Defendant for purposes of this ICFA claim?

(A) Yes, because the ICFA statute and the Federal Rules of Civil Procedure, taken together, authorize the service that occurred here, and the State A federal court's exercise of jurisdiction would not offend due process.

(B) Yes, because service in federal-question suits may be made anywhere in the United States where the defendant may be found, and in this case the Defendant could be found wherever the CEO was at the moment of service.

(C) Yes, because a federal court will exercise personal jurisdiction where service and personal jurisdiction would be allowed by the long-arm of the state where the federal court sits, and the State B long-arm would apply to these facts.

(D) No, because the Defendant does not have minimum contacts with State A and the exercise of personal jurisdiction over the Defendant in the State A federal courts would therefore violate the Defendant's due process rights.

III. SERVICE OF PROCESS AND NOTICE

A. Service of Process

1. Methods of accomplishing service

a. Service on an individual

Question 24

A university student, a citizen of State A, believes that her university violated federal law when it eliminated funding for the women's varsity volleyball team. She has sued the university, a nonprofit corporation located and incorporated in State B, and the university's athletic director, a citizen of State B, in federal court in State B.

What is the best method of serving the defendants?

(A) Service as required by State B's rules of civil procedure.

(B) Service by a process server's leaving copies of the summons and complaint with secretaries in the respective offices of the athletic director and the university president.

(C) Service by emailing copies of the summons and complaint to the athletic director and the university president.

(D) Service by the student herself on the athletic director and the university president.

Question 25

A novelist sued her accountant, an individual, in a federal-court diversity action based on breach of contract. The novelist, who is a citizen of State A, brought the suit in that state's federal court. After the novelist filed the complaint, she instructed a process server to serve the summons and complaint personally on the accountant at what a recent check of the accountant's business website check showed to be his business address, 123 Main Street, Suite 101, in City, State B. Unbeknownst to the novelist, the accountant had moved his office to a different location in City one month before and had neglected to update his website with the new address.

The process server arrived at Suite 101 in the 123 Main Street office building and asked the receptionist there if the accountant was present to receive papers. The receptionist replied that the accountant had moved, but mentioned that she would be seeing him the next day; she therefore offered to take the papers and give them to the accountant. The process server agreed, leaving the papers with the receptionist, who as promised gave the papers to the accountant the next day.

The accountant then immediately filed a timely answer, in which he raised the defense of improper service. The provisions of State A and State B regarding valid methods of service are identical to the ones set forth for federal courts in the Federal Rules of Civil Procedure.

Should the court dismiss the complaint for improper service?

(A) Yes, because although the papers were left with a person of suitable age and discretion, this was done at a location that was no longer the accountant's usual place of business.

(B) Yes, because no federal or relevant state statute allows service on an individual by leaving papers with a person of suitable age and discretion at that person's usual place of business.

(C) No, because the process server left the papers with a person of suitable age and discretion at what the accountant represented to the world to be his usual place of business.

(D) No, because the accountant waived any objection to improper service by asserting the defense in an answer instead of by a motion made before the answer.

Question 26

A musician, who lived in State A, was a member of a touring rock band. On a day the musician was away from State A, an envelope sent "first class, certified, return receipt requested" via the U.S. Postal Service mail arrived at his residence. The envelope contained a summons and complaint for an action being brought against the musician by an accountant. The summons and complaint stated on their face that the action was for breach of contract and was being brought in federal court for the district of State B, which was the accountant's state of residence. The suit was properly based on diversity and met the jurisdictional amount. The musician had authorized his fiancée to accept mailed letters and packages he might receive and to sign receipts for them. Therefore, the fiancée signed the delivery receipt for the envelope and handed the receipt to the mail carrier. The musician never answered or otherwise responded to the summons or complaint, and the court in due course entered a $1.7 million default judgment against him.

Two years after the entry of judgment, the musician happened to discover on the Internet that the default judgment against him had been entered. He immediately moved under FRCP Rule 60 to have the judgment set aside as void because proper service had never been made on him. At a judicial hearing on his motion, the musician testified that he had seen the original sealed certified-mail envelope on his desk when he returned from his trip, but had never opened it because he thought it related to some other completed business transaction. The accountant's lawyer did not contest this factual testimony. At the time of the original mailing, neither the law of State A nor the law of State B authorized in-state service of process on an individual by means of certified mail (or, indeed, by any means other than personal service).

Should the federal judge set aside the default judgment as requested by the musician?

(A) Yes, but only if the judge finds that the musician was not negligent in failing to open the certified letter envelope.

(B) Yes, because the judgment was void due to lack of proper service on the musician.

(C) No, because the musician did not make his motion until more than one year had elapsed from the entry of the default judgment.

(D) No, because the musician had authorized his fiancée to sign for mail, causing her receipt of the envelope to constitute valid service on the musician.

   b. Service on a corporation

   See Question 24 [Choices (B) and (C)]

2. **Territory within which service may be made — use of the local state long-arm to determine where and how service may be made in a federal-court action**

   See Question 23 [Choice (C)]

3. **Territory within which service may be made — third-party claims**

   See Question 41 [Choice (B)]

4. **Deadline for objecting to improper service**

   See Question 25 [Choice (D)]

5. **Request by plaintiff that defendant waive service**

   Question 27

   Plaintiff, an individual who is a citizen of State A, wanted to bring a diversity suit against Defendant, a corporation incorporated and with its headquarters in State B. The suit alleged that some years ago, Defendant committed fraud on Plaintiff. On July 1, Plaintiff filed the civil fraud complaint against Defendant with the federal district court located in State A. On July 5, Plaintiff sent, by first-class mail, a package containing the following documents to Defendant ("c/o President") at Defendant's headquarters address in State B: (1) a copy of the complaint; (2) two copies of a form (appended to a copy of FRCP 4) by which Defendant could by signing agree to waive service of a summons; and (3) a prepaid means for Defendant to return a signed copy of the waiver form. The mailing also included a notice to Defendant stating that the suit had been commenced and requesting that Defendant waive service of a summons by signing and returning a copy of the waiver form by no later than 30 days after the July 5 mailing date. The notice-and-request met all requirements set forth in Federal Rule 4(d)(1).

In order to determine whether Plaintiff satisfied the statute of limitations, it has become important to know *the earliest date* as of which all events needed for the complaint to be deemed served via the waiver method had occurred. The earliest date as of which service in the action will be treated as complete would be

(A) July 5, by virtue of Plaintiff's act of mailing the package to Defendant.

(B) August 10, if on that day Plaintiff, not having received from Defendant the signed waiver form or any communication, filed a sworn statement with the court stating that Defendant had not submitted the requested signed waiver within the 30 days specified in the waiver request.

(C) August 20, if on that day Plaintiff received from Defendant a return of the signed waiver form.

(D) August 22, if on that day Plaintiff filed the signed waiver form with the court, after having received it from Defendant on August 20.

B. Notice

1. Constitutional requirements as to

Question 28

Plaintiff lives in State A. He bought hiking equipment from Defendant, a catalog retailer that is incorporated in, and has its headquarters in, State B. Plaintiff, from his home in State A, selected his purchase from a copy of Defendant's hard-copy catalog; he then placed his order by telephone to a sales agent working out of Defendant's State B headquarters. 20% of Defendant's annual sales are made by mail-order and Internet-order to customers who live in State A. However, Defendant has no employees or agents physically located in State A. The hiking equipment turned out to be defective, and Plaintiff decided to sue Defendant in State A state court for a refund.

Before filing the suit, Plaintiff looked on the Internet and located Defendant's published street address in State B. However, Plaintiff did not serve a copy of the summons and complaint on Defendant either by mail or hand-delivery to that State B address. Instead, Plaintiff discovered a State A statute providing that "Service for an action in this state may be made upon a nonresident company that is registered to do business in this state by means of hand-delivery of the summons and complaint to the State A Secretary of State at the Secretary's official address in Capital City, State A." Plaintiff therefore served Defendant by having his agent hand-deliver a copy of the summons and complaint to the State A Secretary of State as provided in the statute. It is unclear what additional actions, if any, were taken by either Plaintiff or the Secretary of State to attempt to give Defendant actual notice of the suit.

Defendant did not appear in the action, and a default judgment was entered against it by the State A court last year. Defendant now seeks to have the default judgment re-opened, and the suit dismissed for improper service; Defendant claims not to have received actual notice of the suit until this year. (The statute of limitations ran on December 31 of last year, so if the court finds that Defendant was not validly served prior to December 31, Plaintiff will not be able to re-serve Defendant.) Defendant does not dispute that it is registered to do business in State A, but claims that whatever service occurred did not comport with the Due Process Clause of the Fourteenth Amendment.

The following choices list, in estimated ascending order of the likelihood that they would have given Defendant actual notice of the suit, various additional steps that might have been taken to notify Defendant of the suit. Which choice represents the additional step(s) beyond service on the Secretary of State that would be the LEAST likely-to-be-effective notice steps that would nonetheless have been sufficient to give Defendant constitutionally-sufficient notice of the suit?

(A) No other acts calculated to give notice to Defendant were required, because service was constitutionally sufficient as soon as Plaintiff hand-delivered the summons and complaint to the state official.

(B) Notice published in a newspaper of general circulation widely distributed through State B would have sufficed (if done in addition to the delivery of the summons and complaint to the state official).

(C) A mailing of the summons and complaint to Defendant at its last-known address, by either Plaintiff or the Secretary of State, would have sufficed (if done in addition to the delivery of the summons and complaint to the state official).

(D) Only hand delivery of the summons and complaint by Plaintiff or his agent to Defendant's published address in State B would have sufficed (even if there had been delivery of the summons and complaint to the state official), given that Plaintiff knew that published address.

IV. VENUE

A. Venue generally

1. Districts in which venue is proper

See Question 30 [Choice (A)]

B. *Forum non conveniens* — dismissal based on

1. Requirements for dismissal based on *forum non conveniens*

See Question 30 [Choice (C)]

2. Use of *forum non conveniens* dismissal when alternative forum is a non-U.S. jurisdiction

Question 29

Plaintiff, a company that manufactures pencils, is organized under the laws of China and has its operating plant and management office in that country. It bought wood pulp from Defendant, a corporation incorporated and located in State A. The sales contract provided that "the laws of China will govern any dispute that might arise between the parties pertinent to this agreement." Defendant was late in delivering the wood pulp, and Plaintiff sued Defendant in State A federal district court. Plaintiff has no office or agents in the United States, and the contract was negotiated and executed through the Internet.

Defendant has moved to dismiss the action under the doctrine of *forum non conveniens* on the ground that the case should be heard in a court in China. How should the court resolve the motion?

(A) The court should grant the motion because the requirements of the federal "transfer of venue" statute are satisfied.

(B) The court should deny the motion if a court in China will apply law less favorable to Plaintiff than will the Delaware district court.

(C) The court should grant the motion if it determines that China is an appropriate alternative forum for the lawsuit.

(D) The court has a duty to first establish that it has jurisdiction before deciding the motion to dismiss.

C. Transfer for convenience

1. To judicial district where the action "might have been brought"

Question 30

A small commercial airplane crashed in State A. The passengers and pilot, all citizens of State B, were killed in the crash. The airline that owned and operated the airplane is incorporated and has its maintenance facilities and principal place of business in State C.

One day before the statute of limitations on their claims would have run, the estates of the pilot and each of the passengers filed a wrongful death action against the airline in federal court in State A. The airline was served one week later and wants to prevent the State A federal court from hearing the action.

Which of the following motions is most likely to accomplish the airline's goal?

(A) A motion to dismiss the action for improper venue.

(B) A motion to dismiss the action for lack of personal jurisdiction.

(C) A motion to dismiss the action under the doctrine of forum non conveniens.

(D) A motion to transfer the action to a federal court in State C.

Question 31

A bakery incorporated and headquartered in State A had a dispute with a mill incorporated and headquartered in State B over the quality of the flour the mill had delivered to the bakery. The bakery sued the mill in a federal court in State A for breach of contract seeking $100,000 in damages.

The contract between the bakery and the mill contained a clause designating State B courts as the sole venue for litigating disputes arising under the contract. Under precedent of the highest court in State A, forum-selection clauses are unenforceable as against public policy; under U.S. Supreme Court precedent, such clauses are enforceable.

The mill has moved to transfer the case to a federal court in State B, citing the forum-selection clause in the parties' contract and asserting the facts that the flour was produced in State B and that the majority of likely witnesses are in State B.

Is the court likely to grant the mill's motion?

(A) No, because State A law treats forum-selection clauses as unenforceable.

(B) No, because the mill should have instead filed a motion to dismiss for improper venue.

(C) Yes, because federal common law makes the forum-selection clause controlling.

(D) Yes, because federal law governs transfers of venue, and it would be more convenient for the witnesses and parties to litigate the claim in State B.

Question 32

Purchaser is an individual who lives in State A and operates a factory in State B. He entered into a contract with Seller, a company incorporated in State C. The contract provided that goods purchased under the contract were to be delivered from Seller's warehouse in State D to Purchaser's factory in State B. Seller failed to deliver the goods on time, and Purchaser brought a diversity suit against Seller in federal court for the District of State A. Soon after the case was filed (but after the statute of limitations for bringing such an action had expired), Purchaser moved for a change of venue to the Western District of State B, the district in which Purchaser's factory was located. Seller opposed the transfer. Assume that the court has concluded that litigating in the Western District of State B would be more convenient over-all for the parties and the witnesses, considered as a group, than litigation in the District of State A.

How should the district court resolve the transfer motion?

(A) Grant the motion, so long as Purchaser could initially have brought the action in the Western District of State B.

(B) Deny the motion, because Purchaser, having chosen the action's original venue, waived the right to request a transfer of the action.

(C) Deny the motion, because changes of venue, even in the federal system, may not cross state boundaries if the suit is based solely on diversity of citizenship.

(D) Dismiss the action if the court concludes that the District of State A was not a district in which venue was ever proper.

a. No transfer to state court

See Question 10 [Choices (B) and (C)]

2. Significance of forum-selection clause

See Question 31 [Choices (B) and (C)]

D. Procedure for asserting venue-related objections

Question 33

Plaintiff owns and operates a restaurant located in State A. Defendant, a citizen of State B, works as a freelance restaurant reviewer for a website. After eating at Plaintiff's restaurant, Defendant published a highly critical online review of it. On July 1, Plaintiff filed an action for libel in federal district court for State C (the state in which Plaintiff resides) based on diversity jurisdiction. On August 1, Defendant served an answer, in which he made a general denial. On October 1, Defendant suddenly realized the State C district court was not a proper venue for the action under the appropriate federal statute. Which of the following choices describes Defendant's best opportunity to raise the venue objection on October 2 and the court's appropriate response to that objection?

(A) Defendant can move to amend his answer to include the venue defense, at which point the court will have discretion whether to dismiss the action if the court agrees that venue was improper.

(B) Defendant can make a motion to dismiss based on the venue objection, at which point the court will have discretion whether to dismiss the action if the court agrees that venue was improper.

(C) Defendant can make a motion to dismiss based on the venue objection, at which point the court must as a jurisdictional matter dismiss the action if the court agrees that venue was improper.

(D) Defendant has waived the venue objection and therefore cannot raise that objection by any method.

LAW APPLIED BY THE FEDERAL COURTS

I. STATE LAW IN FEDERAL COURT (INCLUDING *ERIE v. TOMPKINS* PROBLEMS)

A. Situations in which the state law in question is "substantive," so that *Erie* applies

Question 34

A skydiver was injured in a skydiving accident in State A when his parachute opened late. The skydiver brought a product liability suit, based on diversity, against the manufacturer of the parachute in State A federal court. At trial, one of the issues was the extent of the skydiver's injuries. The skydiver's lawyer offered into evidence that the hospital that treated the skydiver for his injuries billed him $200,000 for care, and that this amount was paid in full by the skydiver's health insurance carrier on his behalf. The manufacturer's lawyer did not contest the accuracy or reasonableness of the hospital's bill. Nor did the manufacturer offer evidence that any person other than itself was fully or partly at fault. The case was submitted to the jury without any motion having been made by either side. The jury returned a verdict of $100,000, and the judge entered judgment for this amount.

Under the relevant law of State A, a state trial judge is encouraged to use the "additur" technique where appropriate, i.e., to conditionally grant a new trial in response to a verdict for an amount markedly lower than that shown by the clear weight of the evidence; the grant is conditional in the sense that the new trial will be canceled if the defendant agrees to pay an amount specified by the trial judge as being the minimum justified by the evidence. After the disappointing verdict in the federal action, the skydiver's lawyer asked the judge by motion either (1) to issue an additur under which the manufacturer would be given a choice between undergoing a new trial solely on the issue of damages (with liability deemed decided in the first trial) or agreeing to pay $200,000 in damages; or (2) alternatively, to issue judgment as a matter of law for $200,000.

Assume that the district judge believes that the weight of the evidence clearly shows that the skydiver has sustained at least $200,000 of damages—the amount of the hospital bill—for injuries that would be compensable under State A's case law on tort damages. Which of the following represents the ruling the judge is most clearly authorized to make on the skydiver's alternative motions?

(A) The court may award judgment as a matter of law (JML) for $200,000, so long as the skydiver made his JML motion for within 28 days after the entry of the judgment for $100,000.

(B) The court may award additur as proposed by the skydiver, because additur represents a substantive legal rule of State A that should be applied by the federal court sitting in diversity.

(C) The court may not award additur as proposed by the skydiver, because additur may be applied only in federal-question cases, not in cases based solely on diversity.

(D) The court may not apply additur as proposed by the skydiver, because to do so would violate the defendant's jury trial rights under the Seventh Amendment.

1. Use of state-law conflict-of-law principles in a federal-court action

Question 35

A landscaper who was a citizen of State A bought a lawn mower produced in State B by a manufacturer incorporated and headquartered in State B. While the landscaper was doing a job in State C, he was badly injured when the mower rolled over his foot. The landscaper brought a $1 million strict product liability action in diversity against the manufacturer in State C federal court, based on the allegedly defective design of the mower.

States A, B, and C all impose slightly different tests for determining whether a product's design should be deemed defective. Which of the three states' substantive test for determining whether a design is defective should the federal court apply?

(A) The design-defect test used by the State C courts in cases involving only State C's tort laws, because State C is where the federal court sits.

(B) The design-defect test developed by the federal courts for use in claims arising under federal statutes.

(C) The design-defect test of the state whose design-defect law the State C courts would apply if the suit had been filed in the State C court system.

(D) The design-defect test developed by whichever of the three states the federal court believes has the strongest interest in having its own substantive laws apply to this controversy.

Question 36

Plaintiff, a corporation incorporated and headquartered in State A that manufactures office supplies, purchased wood pulp from Defendant, a corporation incorporated in State B and headquartered in State C. The sales contract required Defendant to deliver the pulp to Plaintiff's factory in State A on or before May 1 and was silent about which state's law should govern in case of a dispute between the parties. Defendant delivered the pulp 45 days late, after which Plaintiff sued Defendant in federal district court in State B, invoking diversity jurisdiction. The complaint alleged breach of contract and sought damages in excess of $75,000. Defendant moved to dismiss the complaint for failure to state a claim. Defendant argued that the judge was required to apply State B law to the case and pointed out (correctly) that a State 2 statute, the Grace Period for Deliveries Act (GPDA), provides that "Every supply contract is deemed to permit the vendor to deliver goods up to 60 days after the date specified in the contract." Plaintiff opposed the motion and argued that the court should apply generally federal common-law principles. Assume that federal common-law principles—such as those applicable to contracts involving the federal government—do not provide for a grace period analogous to that of the GPDA.

Is the federal district court required to apply the GPDA to the dispute?

(A) No, because a federal court sitting in diversity is required to apply federal common-law principles to this dispute.

(B) Yes, because State B is the state of Defendant's incorporation, so its law governs the interpretation of any contract to which the company is a party.

(C) Yes, so long as the highest court of State B has held that the GPDA applies to a supply contract of the sort involved in this dispute.

(D) Yes, so long as a State B state court would apply the GPDA to this contract dispute if the case were being heard in that court.

2. State procedural rules that nonetheless reflect a strong state substantive policy

Question 37

A plumber who lived in State A had surgery in a hospital, which was operated by a non-profit corporation incorporated and located in State A. A serious infection set in, which the plumber believed was negligently handled by the hospital. After partly recovering, the plumber moved permanently to State B. Then, shortly before expiration of State A's two-year statute of limitations on medical malpractice claims, the plumber brought a $300,000 diversity action for malpractice against the hospital in the federal district court located in State A.

The legislature of State A has enacted a statute providing that before any medical malpractice suit may be filed in the State A courts against a hospital located in that state, the claimant must first send a "notice of claim" to the hospital stating the claimant's intent to sue and the nature of the claimed malpractice; only after waiting for 60 days following the giving of this notice is the claimant permitted to file the malpractice suit in the state A courts. The purpose of the notice-of-claim provision is to give the hospital the chance to investigate and negotiate a settlement before a malpractice suit is publicly filed, thereby reducing the cost of hospital malpractice insurance by encouraging lower-cost settlements. In the case of the plumber's federal suit, the hospital's lawyer noticed that the plumber had not given a notice of claim prior to filing that suit.

The hospital has now, in a timely manner, moved the State A federal court to dismiss the case. The motion makes two arguments for dismissal: (1) because diversity of citizenship is lacking; and (2) because the federal court must enforce the notice-of claim requirement, thus requiring it to dismiss for failure to state a claim for which relief may be granted. The federal judge should

(A) allow the suit to proceed, because there is diversity, and the notice-of-claim provision is a procedural rule that is therefore not binding on the federal court.

(B) dismiss the suit, because the plumber was a citizen of State A at the time the malpractice claim arose, preventing him from having diversity of citizenship as to the hospital.

(C) dismiss the suit, because the notice-of-claim requirement is sufficiently bound up with the substantive rights of the parties that the federal court must enforce that requirement since the State A courts would do so.

(D) dismiss the suit, because the court must apply the State A notice-of-claim rule as long as there is a non-trivial chance that the decision on whether to apply that rule will be outcome-determinative.

3. State procedural rules that are outcome-determinative

See Question 37 [Choice (D)]

B. Situations in which the state law in question is purely procedural, so that *Erie* does not apply

See Question 37 [Choice (A)]

PRETRIAL PROCEDURES

I. PRELIMINARY INJUNCTIONS AND TEMPORARY RESTRAINING ORDERS

A. Preliminary injunctions

1. Requirements for granting

Question 38

Plaintiff, an environmental activist in State A, was concerned that extensive lakeshore development would destroy vegetation that fish need in order to spawn. Defendant was a wealthy individual who owned a 3-acre parcel of undeveloped shoreline in State A, which she had started to develop into a single-family residence for herself. The plans Defendant filed with the local municipality showed that she intended to plant a lawn to a point within five feet of the shoreline. A federal statute, the Fish Protection Act (or "FPA"), provides, "Because overdeveloped shorelines are harmful to fish, owners of shoreline property are strongly encouraged to maintain a 30-foot strip of natural vegetation between the shoreline and the part of their grass or lawn nearest the shoreline." Plaintiff sued Defendant in federal court for State A on a claim based on the FPA; the lawsuit asked the court to permanently enjoin Defendant from planting a lawn within the 30 feet of her property nearest the shoreline. Plaintiff also made a motion for a preliminary injunction against such planting until the case could be tried on the merits. Defendant has now opposed the motion for preliminary injunction.

Which statement best expresses how the federal court should decide Plaintiff's motion?

(A) The court should grant the motion, because damages will never be able to repair the injury that the environment will suffer if the fish cannot spawn due to Defendant's illegal development of her property.

(B) The court should grant the motion, because otherwise Defendant will develop the land without the necessary buffer and the public interest will be hurt.

(C) The court should deny the motion, because money damages will be sufficient to remedy a violation of the Fish Protection Act.

(D) The court should deny the motion because Plaintiff is unlikely to succeed on the merits.

B. Temporary restraining orders

II. PLEADINGS

A. Pleadings generally

1. The complaint

a. The "plausibility" standard for pleading a cause of action

See Question 39 [Choice (B)]

b. Pleading special matters (e.g., fraud)

Question 39

Plaintiff owns a luncheonette called the Healthy Home. Defendant runs a company that sells baked goods that it labels as "organic." Plaintiff entered into a contract with Defendant for the weekly delivery of organic oatmeal cookies. After several such deliveries, Plaintiff learned that the "organic" cookies were really repackaged highly-processed cookies that Defendant bought in bulk from a foreign wholesale company. Plaintiff sued Defendant in federal court, alleging diversity jurisdiction. The complaint included a proper jurisdictional statement and alleged that (1) Defendant entered into a contract with Plaintiff to weekly deliver 30 pounds of organic oatmeal cookies; and (2) Defendant instead knowingly delivered non-organic cookies; (3) Defendant consequently engaged in fraud. The complaint made no other statements regarding Defendant's conduct or state of mind.

Before answering, Defendant moved to dismiss the complaint for failing to state a claim. The court will most likely

(A) grant the motion because the complaint fails to plead Defendant's alleged special matters.

(B) deny the motion because Defendant has not shown that Plaintiff can prove no set of facts in support of the fraud claim.

(C) deny the motion because Defendant was required to move for judgment on the pleadings.

(D) grant the motion because the complaint improperly joins a contract claim with a tort claim.

2. **The answer**

   a. **Defenses that are "affirmative defenses"**

      See Question 47 [Choice (A)]

   b. **Defenses that are not affirmative defenses**

      See Question 68 [Choice (C)]

   c. **When and how to present defenses — "in the responsive pleading" vs. by motion**

      See Question 43 [Choice (D)]

   d. **Deadline for raising certain defenses**

      See Question 33 [All Choices]

3. **The reply**

   See Question 68 [Choice (A)]

4. **Third-party practice**

   Question 40

   A construction company was incorporated and headquartered in State A. A distributor (a corporation that was a citizen of State B) was in the business of distributing asphalt used in the construction of residential driveways. The construction company placed a large order for asphalt with the distributor, and the distributor failed to deliver the product on time. The construction company sued the distributor in diversity in State A federal court for breach of contract, claiming losses of more than $3 million from the delay.

   The distributor then impleaded a trucker that it had hired to ship the products in question to the construction company. In the distributor's third-party complaint against the trucker, the distributor alleged that the trucker "is or may be liable" to the distributor if the distributor were found liable to the construction company.

   Which of the following defenses, if supported by the facts, may the trucker properly assert?

   (A) The construction company could not recover directly against the trucker.

   (B) The distributor may seek to implead the trucker only after, not before, a judgment is entered in the construction company's suit against the distributor.

(C) The court lacks venue over the distributor.

(D) The statute of limitations has lapsed on the construction company's claim against the distributor.

Question 41

A messenger, who is a citizen of State A, drove his truck onto a construction site in State A in order to deliver a package. There were a number of other vehicles on the site. The messenger's truck was hit from the rear by one of these vehicles, injuring the messenger. He sued an electrician (a citizen of State B), alleging that the electrician had negligently driven the vehicle, a van, that hit the messenger's truck. The suit, seeking $100,000 in damages, was based on diversity and was filed in State A federal court. The electrician filed an answer denying that he had driven the vehicle that had hit the messenger's truck.

Eleven days after the electrician served his answer, he also served a third-party impleader complaint against a plumber (a citizen of State B) who had been driving a truck on the same site; that complaint alleged that it was the plumber whose truck hit the messenger, and that if there was anyone whose negligence caused the accident, that person was the plumber. The electrician made personal service of the third-party complaint on the plumber by having the summons and complaint handed to the plumber while the plumber was doing a multi-week project at a job site in State C, at a location 80 miles from the State A federal courthouse where the messenger-electrician suit was pending. No provision of State A law would permit service of process on a defendant found at the State C job site for a complaint in the State A courts on facts analogous to the facts of the electrician-plumber complaint here.

The plumber would like to try to get the third-party ("TP") complaint against him dismissed by the federal court. Which of the following arguments offers the plumber the best chance of achieving that result?

(A) The court does not have subject-matter jurisdiction to adjudicate the TP complaint, because the electrician and the plumber are both citizens of State B.

(B) The court does not have personal jurisdiction over the plumber for purposes of adjudicating the TP complaint.

(C) The electrician did not serve the TP complaint within the "of right" time limit for such service and did not obtain leave of court as required for a TP complaint served after expiration of that "of right" time limit.

(D) The TP complaint fails to state a valid third-party claim.

5. **Requirement that the Real Party in Interest be named in the complaint**

Question 42

A six-year-old child, while playing on the sidewalk in front of his parents' home, was run over by a motorcyclist. The motorcyclist, a recent college graduate, was visiting his aunt and uncle, who lived next door to the child and his family. The motorcycle was owned by the aunt and uncle, and the motorcyclist had borrowed it without their permission or knowledge. The child's family intends to file a federal lawsuit based on diversity, seeking recovery for the child's injuries on account of the motorcyclist's negligence. Which of the following statements is correct about the parties to the action?

(A) The child must be listed as the plaintiff, because he is the real party in interest.

(B) A guardian or parent of the child may be listed as the plaintiff, without the need to include the child as a plaintiff.

(C) The motorcyclist's insurance carrier must be joined as a defendant because it is the real party in interest on the defense side.

(D) The motorcyclist's aunt and uncle must be joined as co-defendants because they will be either primarily or secondarily liable.

B. Amended and supplemental pleadings

1. Deadline for amending as of right

Question 43

Plaintiff brought a diversity suit in federal court against Defendant. The suit claimed that several years previously, Defendant, an individual, had breached a contract to deliver certain food colorings to Plaintiff, also an individual, for use in Plaintiff's bakery. Plaintiff filed the complaint with the district court on March 1. On March 3, Plaintiff requested by mail that Defendant waive service, and Defendant did so by returning the waiver form on March 10. On March 15, Defendant served his answer, which consisted solely of a general denial. On April 20, Defendant first realized that he probably had a valid defense based on the statute of limitations. Defendant's lawyer decided not to ask Plaintiff to consent to Defendant's immediate filing of an amended answer that would include the limitations defense.

Which of the following statements best describes whether and how Defendant may, on April 20, assert the limitations defense?

(A) Defendant may assert the defense by amending his answer as of right, because due to his having signed the waiver his original time to answer has not yet run.

(B) Defendant may not assert the defense by amending his answer unless he receives leave of court to do so, because more than 21 days have passed since Defendant's service of his original answer, and that answer did not require a responsive pleading.

(C) Defendant may not assert the defense by amending his answer unless he receives leave of court, because his filing of an answer that did not contain an affirmative defense in his answer resulted in his automatic waiver of that defense and left him without the ability to amend as of right.

(D) Defendant may, as of right, make a motion asserting the defense.

2. Waiver of the right to amend a pleading

See Question 43 [Choice (C)]

3. Situations in which the amended pleading relates back to the date of the original pleading

Question 44

On January 1 three years ago, Defendant, a technology company, hired Plaintiff, a technology specialist, on a one-year contract terminable only for cause. The parties agreed that any dispute was to be governed by the substantive law of State A. Three months after the contract began, Defendant fired Plaintiff on April 1 for what Plaintiff believed was no cause at all. The statute of limitations on a contract action, according to State A's laws, is three years, and was therefore about to expire on April 1 of this year. Consequently, on March 15 of this year, Plaintiff filed a diversity action against Defendant in federal district court for State A alleging that the firing breached her contract. On June 1 of this year, Plaintiff remembered that on May 1 three years ago (i.e., 30 days after the firing), Defendant wrongfully interfered with Plaintiff's ability to take a new job (also in State A) that another potential employer had offered her by falsely telling the new employer that Defendant had recently fired Plaintiff for cheating on her expense account.

Therefore, on June 2 of this year, Plaintiff amended her suit to add a new state-law claim: that by telling this lie, Defendant tortiously interfered with Plaintiff's new employment contract. The statute of limitations for tortious interference in State A is also three years; therefore, if the new tortious-interference claim had been a separate action, it would have become time-barred in the courts of State A on May 1 of this year.

Defendant has now moved in federal court to have the tortious-interference claim dismissed as time-barred. Under the procedural law of State A, when an existing complaint is amended, the doctrine of "relation back" applies for statute of limitations purposes if and only if any newly-added claims (1) arise out of the same conduct, transaction, or occurrence as set out in the original pleading *and* (2) are supported by the same or nearly-same legal theory as at least one claim set out in the original pleading.

If Defendant's motion succeeds, which of the following is the most likely legal explanation for that success? In evaluating each choice, assume that any *factual* allegation contained in that choice is correct (though do *not* necessarily assume that any *legal* conclusion the choice draws from that fact is correct).

(A) Under State A law, the relation-back rule does not permit relation back.

(B) The tort claim rests on a legal theory different from that of the original contract claim.

(C) The tort claim arose out of a different transaction or occurrence than the original contract claim.

(D) Plaintiff unduly delayed in amending her complaint.

III. RULE 11

See Question 57 [All choices]

IV. JOINDER OF PARTIES AND CLAIMS, INCLUDING CLASS ACTIONS

A. Joinder of parties

1. Joinder of plaintiffs

2. Joinder of defendants

a. Persons who must be joined if feasible

See Question 84 [Choice (A)]

See Question 42 [Choice (D)]

3. Intervention

Question 45

A mail clerk domiciled in State A slipped and fell on ice that had formed near the loading dock of the building in State B where the clerk's State B employer leased space for its headquarters. The building was owned and operated by a State C corporation. As a result of the fall, the clerk was injured and the employer's expensive computer he was carrying was badly damaged.

The clerk sued the building owner for negligence in a federal district court in State B, seeking $100,000 in personal-injury damages. The employer has filed a timely motion to intervene, asserting an $80,000 negligence claim against the building owner for the damage to its computer.

Is the court likely to grant the employer's motion to intervene?

(A) No, because although the employer has an interest in the clerk's action, that interest is not likely to be impaired in the employer's absence.

(B) No, because the clerk chose not to join the employer as a co-plaintiff in his action.

(C) Yes, because the employer is an indispensable party.

(D) Yes, because the employer's claim shares common questions of law and fact with the clerk's action.

4. Interpleader

Question 46

Plaintiff is an insurance company incorporated and headquartered in State A. It issued a liability insurance policy to Defendant, a company incorporated and headquartered in State B that operates an interstate bus line. A bus driver employed by Defendant crashed into a car on an interstate highway in State B. More than a dozen individuals, both drivers and passengers, were seriously injured. Under the policy, Plaintiff insured Defendant for claims aggregating up to $3 million arising from any accidents occurring during the one-year policy period where a single driver was at the wheel of a bus owned by the Defendant.

Ten of the injured parties brought individual negligence suits against Defendant in various state courts. Two of the claimants are citizens of State A, three are citizens of State B, and the remaining five are citizens of States C, D, E, F, and G, respectively. The individual claims were for sums between $10,000 and $3 million. Plaintiff then filed a statutory interpleader action in federal court in State B. The interpleader action purported to join all ten state-court claimants (each of whom was individually personally served in his or her home state).

As part of the interpleader action, Plaintiff requested that the federal court enjoin each claimant from trying to collect any amounts from Plaintiff under the policy in the separate state-court actions (though Plaintiff did not ask that the claimants be enjoined from seeking judgments against Defendant in those state-court actions). The ten claimants have hired a lawyer to represent them jointly in the interpleader action. The lawyer seeks to have the interpleader action dismissed on procedural grounds so that the ten state-court suits could proceed unimpeded.

Which of the following statements best summarizes how the federal court should dispose of one or both requests of the parties (i.e., Plaintiff's request for injunctions and the claimants' joint request for dismissal of the interpleader action)?

(A) The court must dismiss the entire interpleader suit if complete diversity does not exist between Plaintiff and all of the claimants.

(B) The court must dismiss from the interpleader suit any claimant whose individual claims, when aggregated together, do not total at least $75,000 in value.

(C) The court must dismiss the interpleader suit if Plaintiff fails to either deposit the $3 million policy limit in cash with the court or to furnish a bond in that amount, after being ordered by the court to do so.

(D) Even if the court properly declines to dismiss the interpleader suit, the court may not issue the injunctions against continuation of the state-court actions.

See Question 6 [All Choices]

B. Joinder of claims, generally

1. Counterclaims

a. Compulsory counterclaims

Question 47

A pedestrian domiciled in State A was crossing a street in State B when he was hit by a car driven by a citizen of a foreign country. Both the pedestrian and the driver suffered injuries.

The pedestrian filed a negligence action against the driver in a federal district court in State B, seeking $100,000 in damages. The driver believes that the pedestrian was crossing the street illegally and is therefore responsible for the accident. The driver seeks an attorney's advice on how best to respond to the action. Assume that State B is a contributory negligence state.

How should the attorney advise the driver to respond?

(A) File an answer raising the affirmative defense of contributory negligence and asserting a counterclaim for negligence, seeking damages for the driver's injuries.

(B) File an answer raising the affirmative defense of contributory negligence and move for judgment on the pleadings.

(C) Move to dismiss for lack of personal jurisdiction, because the driver is not a citizen of State B.

(D) Move to dismiss for lack of subject-matter jurisdiction, because the driver is not a U.S. citizen.

b. Permissive counterclaims

C. Class actions

1. Requirements for case to be certified as a federal class action

Question 48

Plaintiff, a black woman, has long worked as a data-entry clerk for Defendant, a sizable corporation with many small corporate offices spread throughout the United States When Plaintiff applied for a promotion and was denied it, she concluded that she had been passed over based on a combination of her gender and race, and that such discrimination against black women was widespread throughout the company. She filed a class action lawsuit in federal court for the district of State A, in which her particular office of Defendant was located. The suit alleged that Defendant's hiring and promotion policies violated Title I of a federal anti-employment-discrimination statute. Title I prohibits an employer from disfavoring an applicant in the hiring or promotion process, as a matter of intentional corporate policy, on account of the applicant's gender or race.

The suit defined the class as consisting of every black woman who was denied an initial clerical job or a promotion to such a job, on account of her gender and race, by Defendant, over a ten-year period. The suit alleged that Defendant, at any given time, has nearly 100 low-level managers (few of whom are black women), that each such manager is given substantial discretion in hiring or promoting clerks who would report to that manager, and that many of the managers have intentionally discriminated against black women. Plaintiff framed the suit as a Rule 23(b)(3) class action and sought compensatory damages and back pay for each of what she estimated as 100 class members. The suit listed Plaintiff as the sole named class member. The suit estimated that individual class members' claims would each have a value ranging from $40,000 to $200,000 and would in the aggregate total at least $4 million in value.

Discovery has been completed, and Defendant now wishes to oppose certification of the class. Each of the following choices represents a legal objection that Defendant is considering making to class certification, based upon a factual assertion. For each objection, assume that the federal judge concludes that the factual assertion on which the objection is based is true. Which of the objections is most likely to lead the court to grant Defendant's motion to deny the requested class certification?

(A) The class as defined includes only 100 clerical workers or applicants, a number so small that a class action is not clearly superior to individual actions.

(B) Because the mental states of nearly 100 managers who made individual hiring and promotion decisions are in issue, there are no questions of law or fact common to all class members that predominate over questions involving only individual class members.

(C) The overall amount claimed to be in controversy does not exceed $5 million.

(D) Nearly all of the 100 putative class members other than Plaintiff live outside State A, the state in which the federal court hearing the dispute is located, causing the court to lack personal jurisdiction over these absent class members.

2. Interlocutory appeals of trial court orders granting or denying class action certification

Question 49

Five homeowners who took out mortgage loans from a large bank filed a putative class action in federal court against the bank in which the five served as named plaintiffs. Each of the five was either black or Hispanic, and they claimed that the bank had engaged in a pattern of charging black and Hispanic mortgage borrowers higher fees than Caucasian borrowers, in violation of a federal statute prohibiting such discrimination. The suit sought certification of a plaintiff class consisting of many thousands of black and Hispanic homeowners who had taken out mortgages from the bank. In response to the bank's objection to certification of this class, the district court denied certification, ruling that the proposed class action did not satisfy FRCP 23(a)(2)'s requirement that there be "questions of law or fact common to the class." The judge indicated that she was, however, willing to allow the five named members to proceed to trial on their individual claims.

Because the plaintiffs' lawyer took the case only on the assumption that certification of a class would permit the lawyer to receive adequate fees upon success, the lawyer is unwilling to go forward with the individual claims without a large retainer, which the five named claimants are unable or unwilling to advance. The five, and their lawyer, would like to make an immediate appeal of the district court's denial of certification. Which of the following best describes the named plaintiffs' right to make such an immediate appeal?

(A) The court of appeals does not have jurisdiction to hear the immediate appeal, so the denial cannot be appealed until a final judgment has been entered on the individual plaintiffs' claims after a trial.

(B) The court of appeals has discretion whether to allow the immediate appeal, provided that promptly following the trial court's denial of certification, the named plaintiffs file a petition for permission to appeal.

(C) The named plaintiffs have a right to take the immediate appeal, provided that promptly after the trial court's denial of certification, they file a notice of appeal.

(D) The district court has discretion to allow the immediate appeal if the judge believes that without such an appeal, the denial of certification will effectively sound the "death-knell" of the suit because the small size of the five individual claims would make a non-class trial financially unfeasible.

V. DISCOVERY, DISCLOSURE AND SANCTIONS

A. Discovery generally

1. The parties' Rule 26(f) discovery planning conference

Question 50

The attorney for a plaintiff in an action filed in federal district court served the defendant with the summons, the complaint, and 25 interrogatories asking questions about the defendant's contentions in the case. The interrogatories stated that they were to be answered within 30 days after service.

The defendant is likely to succeed in obtaining a protective order on which of the following rounds?

(A) Interrogatories are only proper to discover facts, not contentions.

(B) Interrogatories may not be served until an answer to the complaint is filed.

(C) Interrogatories may not be served until the parties have conferred to arrange for initial disclosures and prepare a discovery plan.

(D) The interrogatories exceed the number permitted without permission from the court or an agreement between the parties.

2. The scope of discovery, generally

Question 51

Plaintiff heads a company that sells photography equipment. Defendant, an individual who owns a film school, bought 500 cameras from Plaintiff. Defendant received the cameras but refused to pay, insisting that the goods did not meet industry standards. Plaintiff sued Defendant in federal district court for breach of contract, invoking the court's diversity jurisdiction. Plaintiff knows from publicly available sources that Defendant has purchased studio lighting from a particular lighting company. Plaintiff wants to find out, through discovery, whether Defendant also defaulted on that contract.

Which statement best describes whether Plaintiff may get discovery about any contract between Defendant and the lighting company?

(A) Plaintiff may, during a deposition of Defendant, ask about the lighting contract so long as the information is not privileged, is relevant to a claim or defense in the case, and is proportional to the needs of the case.

(B) Plaintiff may not, during a deposition of Defendant, ask about the lighting contract if the answer would not be admissible at trial.

(C) Plaintiff may propound interrogatories to the lighting company asking about the company's contracts with Defendant, if that information would be relevant to a claim or defense in the case.

(D) Plaintiff is entitled to receive a copy of the lighting contract as a part of automatic initial disclosure from Defendant.

3. Earliest time at which discovery is permitted

Question 52

Company manufactures off-road recreational vehicles. Driver owns a vehicle manufactured by Company. Driver was injured while driving the vehicle on the highway. A state trooper was called and arrived at the scene of the accident. Driver has informed Company that he intends to file a federal action, based on diversity jurisdiction, for injuries caused by the car's alleged product-design defects; Driver claims that the vehicle accelerated when it was supposed to brake, and as a result it rolled into a ditch.

Company now wants to find out whatever the state trooper knows about the accident. Company has filed a verified petition with the federal district court in the district in which the accident occurred, asking the court to issue an order granting Company permission to depose the state trooper. The petition does not specify any particular topics to be covered in the deposition.

Should the court issue the requested order?

(A) No, because in federal civil practice a party may not take discovery from a nonparty before the commencement of a lawsuit.

(B) No, because a party may take discovery before a suit is commenced only if the request is accompanied by a draft complaint against the party from whom discovery is sought.

(C) Yes, because a party to an anticipated federal civil suit may depose a non-party witness who is believed to be in possession of information that is relevant to a claim or defense that is expected to be raised in the suit.

(D) No, because a party may not take discovery before the commencement of a federal lawsuit absent a special need to preserve testimony.

4. Various types of discovery

a. Interrogatories

See Question 50 [Choices (A), (B), and (D)]

See Question 51 [Choice (C)]

b. Depositions

Question 53

Plaintiff, a black woman, worked for a bookstore owned by Defendant, a large corporation with stores in many states. The bookstore where Plaintiff worked was in State A. Plaintiff's supervisor, the store manager, passed her over for a promotion. Believing she had been passed over because of her race and/or gender, Plaintiff sued Defendant in federal district court for State A, alleging discrimination in violation of federal employment-discrimination statutes. The complaint has survived a motion to dismiss.

Plaintiff's lawyer now wants to depose a man who was Plaintiff's colleague at the store, where the colleague served as a cashier; the lawyer believes the colleague has knowledge of the circumstances under which Plaintiff was passed over for the promotion. The colleague, who has since left the employ of Defendant, now works and lives in State B, at a location 200 miles from the federal courthouse in State A where the suit is pending; he rarely travels more than 50 miles from his present home and place of business. Plaintiff's lawyer wishes to depose the colleague in person at the lawyer's office, which is next door to the State A federal courthouse. Can the lawyer require the colleague to attend the deposition at this office, assuming the lawyer will choose a date when the colleague has no conflicting appointments and assuming that the lawyer pays the colleague's reasonable expenses of travelling to the deposition?

(A) Yes, but only if the lawyer issues a subpoena.

(B) Yes, and the lawyer may do so by means of a notice of deposition.

(C) Yes, so long as the lawyer demonstrates good cause for not holding the deposition in State B at a location within 100 miles of the colleague's home or place of business.

(D) No, because the colleague is not a party or an officer of a party.

c. **Orders for medical examinations**

Question 54

Plaintiff, while a pedestrian, was struck by a truck owned by Defendant, a corporation in the business of making local deliveries. The truck was driven by Driver, a full-time employee of Defendant. Since Plaintiff and Defendant were citizens of different states, Plaintiff brought a diversity suit in Defendant's home state against Defendant for negligence, seeking more than $75,000 in damages. Plaintiff elected not to make Driver (who left Defendant's employ soon after the accident) a co-defendant. Defendant served an answer denying liability on the grounds that the accident occurred because Driver had a sudden epileptic seizure that neither Driver nor Defendant could have foreseen.

Plaintiff then served on Defendant a motion under FRCP 35 to compel Defendant to produce Driver for a physical examination to be conducted by a physician identified in the motion papers. In support of the motion, Plaintiff asserted that the examination was necessary in order for Plaintiff's attorneys to assess the accuracy of Defendant's assertion that the accident was caused by a seizure. Defendant opposed the motion.

The district court hearing the suit should rule on Plaintiff's motion by

(A) granting the discovery request because a physical examination is relevant to at least one claim or defense in the action.

(B) denying the discovery request because Driver no longer works for Defendant and is thus not under Defendant's legal control.

(C) denying the discovery request unless the court finds that Plaintiff has shown good cause for the examination.

(D) granting the request and, if Defendant does not produce Driver for the examination, treating Defendant's failure as a contempt of court.

B. **E-Discovery**

C. **Documents that are non-discoverable on account of privilege or work-product immunity**

1. **Privilege**

2. **Work-product immunity**

Question 55

The plaintiff, while driving on April 2, was injured in a collision with a car driven by the defendant. The plaintiff believed that the defendant had gone through a stop sign. The police officer at the scene did not perform a sobriety test, but the plaintiff thought she smelled liquor on the defendant's breath. The plaintiff brought a negligence suit against the defendant in State A state court. The plaintiff's lawyer then engaged a private investigator to try to find out whether the defendant had been drinking prior to the accident.

The investigator located a musician who had the status of "friend" of the defendant on a particular social media website. The investigator conducted an interview with the musician, at which she told the investigator that on April 3, the defendant had posted a message on the social media website in which he said "I had a few beers yesterday and then got into a car accident, but fortunately the dumb cop didn't make me walk a white line." The musician then at the investigator's request wrote a handwritten statement with these facts, signed it, and handed it to the investigator, who gave it to the plaintiff's lawyer. The plaintiff's lawyer plans to call the musician at trial to testify about the defendant's admission of drinking, and plans to use the statement either in its case in chief, or to rehabilitate that testimony if the defendant claims on cross-examination that the musician's testimony is a recent fabrication.

The defendant, during discovery, made a demand for the production of any written statements in the possession of the plaintiff or her attorney by any person with knowledge relevant to the accident. The plaintiff's lawyer submitted a "privilege log" to the defendant, mentioning the musician by name, and stating that the musician had given a written statement to the plaintiff's legal team about a matter relevant to the accident; but the plaintiff's lawyer refused to produce the statement itself on the grounds that it was protected by work-product immunity. The defendant has now moved for a court order compelling production of the statement on the grounds that any work-product immunity should not prevent production on these facts. State A follows the Federal Rules of Civil Procedure on all matters relevant to discovery.

Should the court grant the defendant's motion to compel the plaintiff to produce the statement?

(A) Yes, because the defendant is entitled to a copy of his own prior admissions regarding the action or its subject matter.

(B) Yes, because the statement contains only the musician's own words and does not reveal any mental impressions or legal theories of the plaintiff's legal team.

(C) No, because the defendant and his attorney have not demonstrated that they cannot obtain their own statement from the musician that would be substantially equivalent to the one being sought.

(D) No, because the use the plaintiff intends to make of the statement at trial, if it's used at all, will be solely to enhance the musician's credibility as a witness.

D. Automatic disclosure

1. Where automatic disclosure is or isn't applicable

Question 56

Plaintiff, an individual who lives and works in State A, was visiting State B. While crossing the street, he was struck by a car driven by Defendant, a citizen of State B. Plaintiff was seriously injured and brought a diversity suit for negligence against Defendant in federal court for the district of State B for $200,000. Plaintiff would like to obtain, during the discovery process, as much information as possible about any liability insurance coverage that Defendant may have that would cover a judgment that Plaintiff receives in the suit. Also, Plaintiff would like to obtain that information with as little effort as possible. The following statements about what information Plaintiff is entitled to, and under what procedure, are arranged in descending order of their desirability from Plaintiff's perspective. Which one represents the MOST DESIRABLE (and thus earliest-listed) outcome to which Plaintiff is entitled?

Plaintiff is entitled to . . .

(A) a copy of the policy, without Plaintiff's being required to make any discovery request for it.

(B) a copy of the policy, upon Plaintiff's submission of a proper request for document production.

(C) the name of the insurance company and the policy limits, upon Plaintiff's submission of an interrogatory to Defendant asking for this information.

(D) no information about any such policy, unless Plaintiff establishes good cause for believing that the information would be relevant to a claim or defense in the case.

See Question 51 [Choice (D)]

2. Exception for material to be used at trial, but "solely for impeachment"

See Question 55 [Choices (B) and (C)]

E. Sanctions for conduct regarding pleadings or discovery

Question 57

A teacher who was suffering from abdominal pain agreed to be operated on by a surgeon who practiced in State A. Immediately after the operation, the teacher developed a pelvic infection, which she suspected was the result of negligence by the surgeon during the operation. The teacher then consulted a tort lawyer, who urged that the teacher retain her to bring a federal diversity action in State A federal district court against the surgeon for medical malpractice.

The lawyer prepared a complaint that in its first count alleged malpractice. Without consulting the teacher, the lawyer added a second count alleging that the surgeon, in his advertising to the public, had made various false advertising claims (e.g., that he graduated from State A University Medical School), and that these false claims constituted a "pattern of racketeering activity" in violation of a State A anti-racketeering criminal statute. The teacher read the draft complaint, understood merely that it was a suit for "medical malpractice," did not know what was meant by "pattern of racketeering activity," and authorized the lawyer to file the complaint. The lawyer signed the complaint and brought the action.

During discovery, it became clear that (1) the lawyer's only reason for believing the surgeon had made false advertising claims was hearsay passed on to the lawyer by a colleague (and the lawyer did not check with the Medical School, which would immediately have confirmed that the surgeon really *did* graduate from the School); (2) the claims of false advertising were in fact themselves all false; and (3) the lawyer had previously made virtually the same racketeering allegations in a state-court malpractice suit against the same surgeon on behalf of a different client, which allegations had been dismissed on summary judgment as being both legally and factually completely without merit. Defense counsel therefore drafted a motion reciting the above facts about the racketeering count and seeking as a Rule 11 sanction an award against both the teacher and her lawyer of the attorney's fees actually spent by the surgeon in defending against the count. Defense counsel followed proper procedures for filing and serving the motion.

Assume that the federal court has now concluded that the motion's allegation that there was no factual or legal basis for the racketeering count was correct. The court, in response to the defense motion for attorney's fees as a sanction under Rule 11

(A) may order that the surgeon be reimbursed for the defense attorney's fees, with the teacher to be vicariously liable for the reimbursement if the teacher's lawyer does not pay.

(B) may order that the teacher reimburse the surgeon for the defense attorney's fees, because the teacher should have known that she did not have actual knowledge about whether there was evidentiary support for the racketeering charge.

(C) may not order the teacher's lawyer to reimburse the surgeon for the defense attorney's fees, because Rule 11 sanctions, if monetary, must take the form of fines paid to the court.

(D) may order that the teacher's lawyer reimburse the surgeon for the defense attorney's fees even if the lawyer honestly believed the racketeering count was supported by evidence, if the court finds that the lawyer failed to make reasonable inquiries into whether there was factual support for the count.

Question 58

A pedestrian, while crossing the street, was seriously injured when she was hit by a car driven by a messenger. The day after the accident, she started a lengthy period of medical treatment. Shortly after the accident, she sued the messenger for negligence in a federal diversity action in State A. As a part of automatic disclosure, the pedestrian provided the name and contact information of both the doctor who examined her in the emergency room and of the physician who treated her during her long period of recuperation. During discovery, the messenger requested that the pedestrian produce all medical records kept by any doctor or hospital relating to any injuries allegedly suffered by the pedestrian as a consequence of the accident. The pedestrian's counsel produced certain records, but these did not include any handwritten notes taken by the treating physician over the 18-month treatment period. At trial, the treating physician was called as part of the pedestrian's direct case; the pedestrian's lawyer authenticated 70 pages of handwritten notes he had made during the various treatment sessions, and the lawyer offered these into evidence under an appropriate exception to the hearsay rule.

The messenger's lawyer then objected to the admission of the notes; the lawyer pointed out that detailed analysis of the notes would be needed for the lawyer to adequately cross-examine the physician and argued that the court should exclude the notes from evidence because they were not produced during discovery. In a sidebar conference, the pedestrian testified in response that she had not learned of the existence of the treatment notes until the prior week. The trial judge will most likely

(A) rule that the notes may not be excluded without the defendant's first making a motion for sanctions.

(B) rule that the notes should not be excluded unless the messenger shows that his case will be prejudiced if the pedestrian is permitted to use the notes as evidence without her having made timely disclosure of them.

(C) rule that the notes should not be excluded if the judge believes that the pedestrian had learned about the notes only the prior week, since in that event the failure to produce the notes would be substantially justified.

(D) rule that the notes must be excluded unless the judge believes that the failure to produce them is now harmless.

Question 59

A driver was injured when her Model X car suddenly swerved off the road and hit a tree. The driver sued the car's manufacturer in federal district court based on diversity; the suit claimed that the steering wheel failed on account of a manufacturing defect, causing the swerve. At an appropriate time, the driver's lawyer submitted a Rule 34 request that the manufacturer produce in hard copy form all accident reports submitted to the manufacturer during the prior 15 years by any owner of any make or model car manufactured by the company, if the owner alleged that the accident may have been due to a product defect, whether of the steering wheel or any other part of the vehicle. Within the time allowed for a response, the manufacturer submitted a written response to the request: (1) stating that it would make available for inspection all accident reports in which the owner mentioned a possibility that the accident was caused by a steering-wheel defect; but (2) objecting to the request as it related to reports of possible defects of components other than the steering wheel, on the grounds that the burden and expense of identifying and producing such documents was not proportional to the needs of the case, and vastly outweighed the document's relevance to the driver's claim.

After the driver's lawyer received this response, she made no attempt to contact the manufacturer's lawyer. Instead, the driver's lawyer made a motion in the court where the action was pending, seeking an order to compel the manufacturer to produce the accident reports as to which the manufacturer had made its objection. The court gave both sides the opportunity to be heard both with respect to the merits of the driver's motion, as well as with respect to any sanctions against the losing party (whichever party that turned out to be) that might be appropriate in the circumstances. Which of the following is the most legally accurate statement about what sanctions the court may, must, or may not issue after it decides the motion on the merits?

(A) If the court wholly denies the motion, the court must order the driver (and/or her lawyer) to pay the manufacturer's attorney's fees incurred in opposing the motion, if the court believes that the motion was not substantially justified and that such a fee award would not be unjust.

(B) If the court wholly denies the motion, the court has discretion whether or not to order the driver (and/or her lawyer) to pay the manufacturer's attorney's fees incurred in opposing the motion, except that the court may not order such a fee award if the court believes that the motion was substantially justified or that such a fee award would not be unjust.

(C) If the court wholly denies the motion, the court may not order the driver (and/or her lawyer) to pay the manufacturer's attorney's fees incurred in opposing the motion, regardless of whether the motion was substantially justified, because the manufacturer did not move for a protective order before the driver made her motion to compel discovery.

(D) If the court wholly grants the motion, the court has discretion whether or not to order the manufacturer (and/or its lawyer) to pay the driver's attorney's fees, if the court concludes that the manufacturer's objection was not substantially justified.

See Question 68 [Choice (B)]

See Question 2 [Choice (B)]

VI. ADJUDICATION WITHOUT A TRIAL

See Chapter 5 (Motions), Parts I and II

VII. PRETRIAL CONFERENCE AND ORDER

A. The Pretrial conference

1. Deadline for holding the pretrial conference

See Question 63 [Choices (C) and (D)]

JURY TRIALS

I. RIGHT TO A JURY TRIAL

A. The Seventh Amendment right to a jury trial

1. Trial of legal and equitable claims in same case so as to protect the right to a trial jury

Question 60

A football team entered into a ten-year lease with a city for use of the city's athletic stadium. Five years into the lease, the team threatened to leave the stadium and move to another city.

The city sued the team in federal court, seeking a permanent injunction to prevent the team from breaching its lease and leaving. In its answer, the team included a counterclaim seeking $10 million in damages for losses caused by the city's alleged failure to properly maintain the stadium, as the lease required. The team demanded a jury trial on the counterclaim.

The city moved to try its claim for a permanent injunction before the trial on the team's counterclaim. The team objected and moved that the jury trial of its counterclaim be held before the trial of the city's injunction claim.

How should the court rule on the parties' motions?

(A) The court should first hold a jury trial of the team's counterclaim, and then a nonjury trial of the issues remaining in the city's claim.

(B) The court should first hold a nonjury trial of the city's claim without giving binding effect to its findings or conclusions in the later jury trial of the team's counterclaim.

(C) The court should first hold a nonjury trial of the city's claim, and then a jury trial of the issues remaining in the team's counterclaim.

(D) The court should schedule a jury trial of both the city's claim and the team's counterclaim.

Question 61

Until she was fired, a cook worked in a restaurant owned by a corporation. The cook sued the corporation in federal court, alleging that her firing violated a federal statute forbidding intentional discrimination against employees on the basis of gender. In her suit, the cook asked for an order that she be reinstated to her job, plus money damages as compensation for the firing. The cook also timely asked for a jury trial on the issues of liability and damages, but conceded that under court rules the decision about reinstatement would have to be made by the judge. During jury selection, the two sides each used one peremptory challenge during the course of seating the first 10 members of a proposed 12-member jury of whom 6 were men and 4 were women. Then, as to the next prospective Jurors, XX and YY (who if accepted would fill the final two seats, and who were both women), the plaintiff approved these jurors, but the defendant's lawyer announced that she wanted to use her final two peremptory challenges on them, giving as her only explanation that, "I'm sure these two ladies would be fair, but I think that on average males will be more sympathetic to my client's position than women will be." The judge is now prepared to decide two motions before him:

Motion 1: The defendant corporation has moved to have the facts bearing on "Did the defendant discriminate against the plaintiff on gender grounds?" tried first. Then, it argues, the judge should immediately decide whether the defendant discriminated, and if so, whether the defendant should be ordered to reinstate the plaintiff. After that, the motion says, if the court found that discrimination occurred, the jury should be asked to decide on the amount of damages. The plaintiff opposes this motion, saying that the jury should first decide whether there was discrimination, and if so, decide what damages to award; only then should the judge decide on reinstatement.

Motion 2: The plaintiff has moved to have the defendant's peremptory challenges to potential jurors XX and YY disallowed, on the grounds that allowing these challenges would violate the excluded jurors' equal protection right not to be disqualified from a jury on account of their gender and that the plaintiff has standing to assert these jurors' rights.

The court will most likely rule on the two motions by

(A) denying Motion 1 and granting Motion 2.

(B) granting Motion 1 and denying Motion 2.

(C) granting both motions.

(D) denying both motions.

2. Use of additur or remittitur as violation of Seventh Amendment right to a jury trial

See Question 34 [Choice (D)]

See Question 74 [Choice (D)]

B. The need to make a demand for a jury trial

1. Deadline for making the demand

Question 62

A retailer brought a federal diversity action against an architect, alleging fraudulent misrepresentations in the architect's design of the retailer's store. The complaint did not include a jury demand.

The architect timely moved to dismiss the action for failure to state a claim; he did not file an answer. Twenty days after being served with the motion, the retailer amended the complaint to add a defamation claim based on the architect's recent statements about the retailer in a local newspaper. In the amended complaint, the retailer demanded a jury trial on both claims.

Has the retailer properly demanded a jury trial?

(A) No, because the retailer filed the demand more than 14 days after service of the motion to dismiss.

(B) No, because the retailer filed the demand more than 14 days after service of the original complaint.

(C) Yes, but on the defamation claim only, because the original complaint did not contain a jury demand.

(D) Yes, on both claims, because the architect had not answered the original complaint when the retailer filed the amended complaint with the jury demand.

Question 63

A screenwriter wanted to bring a federal lawsuit for copyright infringement against a movie studio that he believed had copied elements of his unpublished screenplay. He consulted a lawyer, who agreed to bring the case. The lawyer drafted a complaint, signed it, and filed it with the court. At about the same time, the screenwriter and the lawyer agreed that a jury would probably be more sympathetic to the screenwriter's claim than would be a judge, so they tentatively decided to demand a jury trial on the infringement claim. However, the lawyer and the screenwriter also decided that it would be best to postpone making the jury-trial demand as long as possible, since later events in the case, including the attitude of whatever judge was assigned, might cause them to change their mind and prefer a bench trial instead of a jury trial.

The following times for the screenwriter to demand a jury trial are arranged in anticipated chronological order, with the earliest-to-occur listed first. Which choice represents the LATEST stage at which the screenwriter can serve a demand on the studio for a jury trial while being confident that his demand will not be deemed to have been waived?

(A) At the same time as the summons and complaint are served on the studio.

(B) Within 60 days after the studio serves its answer, if the answer does not contain a counterclaim.

(C) On or before the date on which the parties' lawyers conduct their initial case-planning conference required by FRCP 26(f).

(D) On or before the date on which the first pretrial conference in the case occurs.

II. SELECTION AND COMPOSITION OF JURIES

A. Number of jurors

1. Minimum number of jurors at start of trial

See Question 64 [Choices (C) and (D)]

2. Minimum number of jurors needed when the verdict is rendered

Question 64

A man filed a federal diversity action against a bus company, seeking damages for injuries he had sustained in an accident while riding a bus owned by the company. The man demanded a jury trial.

After the parties' attorneys examined the prospective jurors and exercised their challenges, six jurors and two alternate jurors were chosen. During the trial, two jurors became ill and were replaced by the alternate jurors. At the conclusion of the trial, a third juror also became ill, and the court excused that juror.

The parties' attorneys stipulated to the return of a verdict from a five-person jury. The jury then deliberated and returned a verdict for the company. The man timely filed a motion for a new trial, arguing that the five-person jury was not large enough to return a verdict.

Should the court grant the motion?

(A) No, because the court properly excused the three jurors due to illness.

(B) No, because the parties stipulated to a verdict from a jury of fewer than six jurors.

(C) Yes, because there must be at least six jurors on a federal civil jury.

(D) Yes, because there must be at least 12 jurors on a federal civil jury.

B. Unanimity of jurors in reaching a verdict

C. Jury selection

1. Excuse of prospective juror for cause

a. Excuse generally

See Question 64 [Choice (A)]

b. Excuse on account of juror bias

Question 65

A consumer was driving a car late at night when the headlights went out, causing the consumer to run off the road and hit a tree, injuring him badly. The consumer brought a product liability suit in diversity against the car's manufacturer, a large publicly-traded corporation. The suit alleged that the headlight system failed on account of a defective design. The consumer demanded a jury trial.

During voir dire, one prospective juror testified that he owned $100 of publicly-traded stock in the defendant manufacturer. Under questioning by the judge, the prospective juror said that she was confident that her stock ownership would not interfere with her ability to be impartial in the case. The consumer's lawyer has challenged the prospective juror for cause. Should the judge dismiss the juror for cause?

(A) No, because the juror's financial stake is sufficiently small that it would not affect the ability of an average juror to be impartial.

(B) Yes, because there is a presumption that any direct financial relationship between a juror and a party will impair the juror's ability to be impartial.

(C) Yes, so long as there is at least one other potential juror in the pool who would not be challengeable for cause.

(D) No, so long as the judge believes the juror's testimony that she can be impartial.

2. Excuse of prospective juror by means of peremptory challenge

See Question 61 [All Choices]

III. REQUESTS FOR AND OBJECTIONS TO JURY INSTRUCTIONS

A. Requests for jury instructions

See Question 67 [Choice (B)]

See Question 66 [Choice (C)]

B. Objections concerning jury instructions

1. Need to make objection in order to preserve issue

See Question 67 [Choice (D)]

a. Exception where court has rejected the request in a definitive ruling

See Question 66 [Choice (D)]

2. Deadline for making objection

Question 66

Before the close of evidence in a federal negligence trial, the defendant submitted a proposed jury instruction on contributory negligence. Before instructing the jury, the judge informed the parties of the instructions she would give, which did not include the defendant's contributory negligence instruction or any instruction on contributory negligence. Neither party objected, either then or after the judge had given the instructions. The jury returned a verdict for the plaintiff, and the judge entered judgment on the verdict.

The defendant would like to appeal the verdict on the ground that the judge should have instructed the jury on contributory negligence.

Has the defendant preserved the issue for appeal?

(A) No, because the defendant failed to object after the judge gave the instructions to the jury.

(B) No, because the defendant failed to object after the judge informed the parties of the instructions she would give.

(C) Yes, because the defendant submitted a proposed instruction on contributory negligence.

(D) Yes, because the judge's failure to give the defendant's contributory negligence instruction amounted to a ruling on the instruction.

See Question 67 [Choice (C)]

3. Plain error exception when objection deadline is missed

Question 67

A worker was injured when a machine he was using on the job malfunctioned. The worker brought a federal diversity action against both the machine's manufacturer and the company responsible for the machine's maintenance. At trial, the worker submitted a proposed jury instruction on negligence. The court did not accept the proposed instruction and instead gave a negligence instruction that the worker's attorney believed was less favorable and legally incorrect. The attorney did not object to the negligence instruction before it was given. The jury returned a verdict for the defendants.

The worker has moved for a new trial on the ground that the court's negligence instruction was improper.

What argument has the best chance of persuading the court to grant the motion?

(A) Issues of law can be raised at any time.

(B) The court's negligence instruction was incorrect and the worker's objection to it was preserved when he submitted his proposed negligence instruction.

(C) The court's negligence instruction was plain error that affected the worker's substantial rights.

(D) The need for a formal objection to a judicial ruling in order to preserve an argument has been eliminated in the Federal Rules of Civil Procedure.

MOTIONS

I. PRETRIAL MOTIONS

A. Motions addressed to face of pleadings

1. Motions for judgment on the pleadings

See Question 47 [Choice (B)]

See Question 39 [Choice (C)]

2. Motions to strike from a pleading

Question 68

A purchaser filed a federal diversity action against a seller, alleging breach of contract. The seller answered the complaint and included as a separate defense an allegation that the purchaser had brought and lost a similar contract claim against a different seller three years earlier, and that this history represented a pattern of filing frivolous lawsuits. The purchaser believes that the earlier lawsuit was factually completely different from the current one and is therefore irrelevant.

What is the purchaser's best response to the seller's answer?

(A) File a reply that includes a denial of the separate defense.

(B) Move for sanctions against the seller for asserting a frivolous defense.

(C) Move to amend the complaint to add allegations about the differences between the lawsuits.

(D) Move to strike the separate defense as irrelevant.

B. Motions to dismiss, under Rule 12(b)

1. Waiver of certain defenses by failure to raise them in a timely way

See Question 33 [All Choices]

C. Motions for summary judgment

1. Summary judgment motions generally

See Question 72 [Choice (A)]

2. Burden imposed on movant

a. Burden imposed on movant, generally

See Question 71 [Choice (C)]

b. Burden imposed on movant, where witness credibility is at issue

Question 69

A broker who was an African American male worked for a brokerage company. The broker applied to be promoted to supervisor, but the company's sole owner awarded the promotion to a white male who worked in the same office. The broker quit and then sued the company in federal court for violating a federal statute prohibiting intentional racial discrimination in employment. The complaint quoted several detailed conversations that the broker claimed to have overheard in the office, in which the owner said he would never promote the plaintiff or any other African American as a supervisor because blacks rarely have managerial talent. The company filed a general denial.

Shortly thereafter, the company moved for summary judgment on the grounds that there was no evidence that the owner's decision to pass over the broker for the promotion was caused by racial animus. In support of the motion, the company submitted an affidavit from the owner in which he stated, "I never made any of the statements imputed to me in the complaint; all of those supposed statements are lies the plaintiff is telling in order to coerce me into settling this suit." The broker's lawyer, who was out-of-state tending to a dying parent, failed to submit papers in opposition to the motion within the allowable time.

The trial judge granted summary judgment in favor of the defendant. The full text of the judge's opinion was as follows: "Because the plaintiff failed to submit papers in opposition to the motion, I will treat all statements made by the defendant and its owner as undisputed. Therefore, I find that the plaintiff has come forward with no evidence which would be sufficient to allow a reasonable jury to find that the plaintiff has carried his burden of proving that he was passed over on account of his race."

The broker has appealed the grant of summary judgment. Will the Court of Appeals likely reverse the grant of summary judgment?

(A) Yes, because the owner's moving papers established that the broker's credibility was a central issue that must be resolved during a trial rather than as a matter of law.

(B) Yes, because the complaint contained detailed factual allegations that, if believed by a jury, would justify a finding that the defendant violated the plaintiff's federal rights.

(C) No, because the broker's failure to submit papers in opposition to the motion meant that there was no sworn affidavit as required to support the factual allegations of the complaint.

(D) No, because the broker's failure to submit papers in opposition to the motion constituted a default, entitling the judge to treat the defendant's uncontested allegations as true.

3. Burden imposed on nonmovant

a. The burden on the nonmovant, generally

Question 70

A patient filed a medical malpractice action against a hospital in federal court, alleging that hospital staff had failed to diagnose the patient's cancer based on an X-ray that had been taken at the hospital. The patient's cancer was diagnosed six months later, based on the same X-ray, when the patient sought a second opinion. In the interim, the cancer had spread.

Fact and expert discovery have been completed in the action. The hospital has moved for summary judgment. In support of its motion, the hospital has submitted a memorandum identifying facts that it claims are not in dispute. It has also cited and attached supporting exhibits, including a report from the hospital's radiologist, who found no signs of cancer on the X-ray.

What is the best way for the patient to raise a genuine dispute of material fact?

(A) Submit a report from the patient's expert radiologist contradicting the findings in the report of the hospital's radiologist.

(B) Submit an affidavit from the patient's attorney detailing his conversations with the patient's expert radiologist.

(C) Submit an affidavit from the patient's expert radiologist with findings that contradict the report of the hospital's radiologist.

(D) Submit the patient's medical records showing the patient's current cancer diagnosis.

See Question 71 [Choice (B)]

See Question 69 [Choices (B), (C), and (D)]

b. **The burden when facts are unavailable to the nonmovant**

Question 71

A construction worker sued an insulation manufacturer in federal court, claiming that he had developed a chronic health condition as a result of 20 years of exposure to the manufacturer's insulation at his work sites. The manufacturer answered, denying all liability and stating that it had never supplied its insulation to the worker's employer.

The worker's attorney deposed the manufacturer's president, and the manufacturer's attorney deposed the worker. Immediately thereafter, the manufacturer moved for summary judgment on the ground that the worker had no evidence showing that the insulation had ever been used by the worker's employer.

What would be the worker's best response to the motion for summary judgment?

(A) Argue that more time is needed for additional discovery to show the manufacturer's liability, and attach a declaration describing the desired discovery.

(B) Argue that the motion should be denied, because a central issue in the case will be the manufacturer's credibility on the question of its distribution of the insulation, and only a jury can decide questions of credibility.

(C) Argue that the motion should be denied, because the manufacturer failed to attach any evidence to its motion to show that the insulation was not used by the worker's employer.

(D) Make a cross-motion for summary judgment arguing that the manufacturer has introduced no evidence to show that its insulation did not harm the worker.

II. MOTIONS FOR JUDGMENT AS A MATTER OF LAW ("JML")

A. Pre-verdict JML motions (a/k/a "motion for directed verdict")

1. Standard for granting a JML motion, under FRCP 50(a)(1)

Question 72

A railroad worker's widow brought a wrongful death action in federal court against the railroad, claiming that its negligence had caused her husband's death. At trial, the widow offered the testimony of a coworker of the husband. The coworker testified that he had seen the rail car on which the husband was riding slow down and the cars behind it gain speed. The coworker also stated that he later heard a loud crash, but did not turn around to look because loud noises were common in the yard. Three other railroad employees testified that no collision had occurred.

At the close of the evidence, the railroad moved for judgment as a matter of law, which was denied, and the case was submitted to the jury. The jury returned a verdict for the widow.

The railroad has made a renewed motion for judgment as a matter of law.

What standard should the court apply to determine how to rule on the motion?

(A) Whether the evidence revealed a genuine dispute of material fact supporting the widow's claim.

(B) Whether the verdict is against the weight of the evidence.

(C) Whether the widow presented a scintilla of evidence to support the verdict.

(D) Whether there is substantial evidence in the record to support the verdict, resolving all disputed issues in the widow's favor.

See Question 73 [Choice (A)]

2. Deadline for making the JML motion

Question 73

A retailer brought a federal diversity action against a wholesaler, alleging breach of contract and fraudulent misrepresentation. After the parties presented their evidence at trial, the court instructed the jury on the law. Neither party filed a motion for judgment as a matter of law before the case went to the jury.

The jury found for the retailer on both claims. After the court entered judgment on the verdict, the wholesaler moved for a new trial and for judgment as a matter of law, arguing that the evidence was insufficient to support the jury verdict on either claim. The court acknowledged that there had been problems with some of the evidence, but it denied the motions. The wholesaler appealed, challenging the sufficiency of the evidence.

Should the appellate court consider the wholesaler's challenge?

(A) No, because a determination of the sufficiency of the evidence is solely within the jury's province.

(B) No, because the wholesaler did not raise the sufficiency-of-the-evidence issue in a motion for judgment as a matter of law before the case went to the jury.

(C) Yes, because the challenge was raised and ruled on by the trial court before the wholesaler filed the appeal.

(D) Yes, because, as the trial court acknowledged, the wholesaler has strong arguments on the challenge.

See Question 34 [Choice (A)]

See Question 74 [Choice (A)]

B. Post-verdict motion for JML (a/k/a Judgment Notwithstanding the Verdict or "JNOV")

III. POSTTRIAL MOTIONS

A. Motions for a new trial

1. Standard for granting the new-trial motion

See Question 72 [Choice (B)]

2. Deadline for making the motion

See Question 75 [Choice (A)]

See Question 34 [Choice (A)]

3. Motion for new trial on some (rather than all) of the issues

See Question 74 [Choice (C)]

4. Remittitur as a substitute for granting a new trial

Question 74

A photographer lent 200 of his photographic prints to a museum to be featured in an upcoming exhibit. The museum agreed to return all prints in the same condition as it received them. Due to staff error, the museum instead sent the prints to a recycling bin, where they were compressed beyond recognition. The photographer sued the museum in federal court for breach of contract, alleging diversity jurisdiction, and sought to recover the market value of the 200 prints. The evidence presented to the jury showed that none of the photographer's photo prints throughout his career had ever sold for more than $500 a print. No motions were made by either side before the case went to the jury. The jury returned a verdict of $1 million. The judge mentally agreed with the jury that the museum ought to be held liable but believed that the jury's award reflected an arithmetic error and that the jurors had intended to issue a verdict of $100,000 in damages rather than $1 million.

After judgment was entered on the jury's verdict for the photographer, the museum made a motion for judgment as a matter of law, by which it asked the judge to set the judgment at $100,000 rather than $1 million. What action can the judge take, if any, that is procedurally proper, is not wasteful of judicial resources, and will correct the judgment to or near the $100,000 that the judge believes the jury intended?

(A) The judge should grant the museum's motion and enter judgment for $100,000.

(B) The judge on her own initiative should conditionally order a new trial unless the photographer agrees to a reduction of the damages to $100,000, an amount set by the court.

(C) The judge on her own initiative should order a new jury trial solely on the issue of damages.

(D) The judge must deny the museum's motion because the Seventh Amendment requires that the judge accept the jury's damage award without adjustment.

B. Motions for relief from judgment

Question 75

A plaintiff sued a defendant in federal court for injuries arising out of an accident involving the parties. The plaintiff alleged and presented evidence at trial demonstrating that her injuries had left her legs permanently paralyzed. The jury found in favor of the plaintiff and awarded her $5 million in damages. Two months after the court entered judgment, the defendant was given a videotape made that day showing the plaintiff jogging with her doctor.

What is the best way for the defendant to seek relief from the judgment?

(A) Move for a new trial or in the alternative for remittitur to reduce the award in light of the shortened duration of the plaintiff's injuries.

(B) Move for relief from the judgment on the ground that the judgment was based on the jury's mistaken belief that the plaintiff's injuries would be permanent.

(C) Move for relief from the judgment on the ground that the plaintiff committed a fraud in obtaining damages for permanent injuries.

(D) Move for relief from the judgment on the ground that there is newly discovered evidence that the plaintiff's injuries were not permanent.

VERDICTS AND JUDGMENTS

I. DEFAULTS AND DISMISSALS

A. Default judgments

1. Default judgments generally

2. Proper service as a pre-condition to a default judgment

See Question 26 [All Choices]

3. Notice requirements for entry of default judgment

Question 76

A company incorporated and headquartered in State A sued a plumber domiciled in State B in a federal court in State A, alleging that the plumber had negligently installed pipes in a manner that resulted in $250,000 in damage to the company's headquarters building. In response to the complaint, the plumber filed a motion to dismiss for lack of personal jurisdiction. The court denied the motion. Thereafter, the plumber did not file an answer or any other response to the company's action.

Sixty days after the court's order denying the motion to dismiss, the company asked the clerk to enter default, and the clerk did so. The company applied to the court for the entry of a default judgment and notified the plumber three days before the default judgment hearing. After an *ex parte* hearing in which the court received evidence on the damages amount, the court entered a default judgment for the full amount sought. Ten days later, the plumber filed a motion to set aside the default judgment.

Is the court likely to grant the plumber's motion?

(A) No, because the court could fix the amount of damages even without hearing the plumber's evidence.

(B) No, because the plumber failed to plead or otherwise defend against the company's action.

(C) Yes, because the plumber was not given adequate notice of the hearing on the company's application for the entry of a default judgment.

(D) Yes, because the State A federal court lacked personal jurisdiction over the plumber as a State B citizen.

4. Entry of the default judgment by the clerk vs. by the judge

Question 77

A student published a highly critical written online review of a college course she attended taught by a professor; the review claimed that the professor delivered false information and handed out written materials that she had plagiarized. The professor filed a complaint for defamation against the student in federal court based on diversity; the complaint described in detail the student's statements and how they were false. The suit sought $100,000 in damages for "intangible injury to the plaintiff's professional reputation," and also sought "reasonable attorney's fees." The professor's lawyer arranged for proper personal service of the summons and complaint, but the student never answered the complaint or took any other action regarding the suit. After several months passed, the clerk of the court noted on the court's docket that the student had defaulted and sent a letter to the student's last known address warning that a default judgment would be entered against her if she did not object within 30 days. After the 30-day period passed without an objection, the professor's lawyer applied in writing to have the clerk enter a default judgment for $110,000 against the student; the application was accompanied by an affidavit from the professor saying that she had suffered $100,000 in loss as claimed in the complaint, plus had incurred legal fees (documented in the affidavit) of $10,000.

Is the clerk authorized to enter the requested $110,000 judgment against the student?

(A) No, because only the judge may enter such a judgment, and only after having made an independent determination of what would constitute a reasonable amount of damages and attorney's fees in the circumstances.

(B) No, unless the clerk conducts an evidentiary hearing, as the result of which the clerk concludes that $100,000 is a reasonable estimate of the damages actually suffered by the professor from the defamation and that $10,000 was actually and reasonably spent by her on legal fees.

(C) Yes, because once the professor requested the entry of the judgment and submitted an affidavit stating that the sum due was $110,000, the clerk was required to enter judgment for that amount without further notice to the student.

(D) Yes, but only if the professor's lawyer or the clerk serves the student with at least seven days advance written notice that the clerk will conduct an evidentiary hearing as to the amount of damages and the clerk then conducts such a hearing based on which the clerk concludes that the $110,000 is a reasonable estimate of the professor's damages and attorney's fees.

B. Dismissals

1. Voluntary dismissals

a. Time within which the dismissal motion must be made

See Question 78 [Choices (B) and (C)]

b. The two-dismissal rule

Question 78

A plaintiff filed an action in federal district court and served the defendant with the summons and complaint. The defendant moved to dismiss the complaint for failure to state a claim.

Instead of opposing the motion to dismiss, the plaintiff voluntarily dismissed the action and filed a new action, alleging the same claims but also addressing the pleading defects outlined in the defendant's motion to dismiss. The defendant then moved to dismiss the second action, and the plaintiff again voluntarily dismissed the second action instead of filing opposition papers.

The plaintiff then filed a third action, alleging the same claims but also including additional allegations that were responsive to the defendant's second motion. The defendant has moved to dismiss the third action; the plaintiff opposes the motion.

Is the court likely to grant the defendant's motion?

A) No, because the plaintiff has promptly and diligently attempted to address the pleading defects.

(B) No, because the plaintiff voluntarily dismissed each previous action before the defendant filed an answer or moved for summary judgment.

(C) Yes, because the plaintiff failed to seek a court order dismissing the second action.

(D) Yes, because the plaintiff's previously dismissed actions asserting the same claims operate as an adjudication on the merits.

II. JURY VERDICTS—TYPES AND CHALLENGES

III. JUDICIAL FINDINGS AND CONCLUSIONS

A. Requirement that judge make findings of fact and conclusions of law

Question 79

A manufacturer sued a buyer in federal court for failing to make timely payments under the parties' sales contract. The case was tried to the court solely on documentary evidence. Immediately after the close of the evidence, the judge announced from the bench, "Judgment shall be entered for the manufacturer," and judgment was so entered. The buyer has appealed the judgment.

What is the buyer's best argument for persuading the appellate court to reverse the judgment?

(A) The judgment is clearly erroneous because it was based solely on documentary evidence.

(B) The manufacturer was required to file proposed findings and conclusions before the trial court ruled.

(C) The trial court erred because it announced the judgment without giving the parties an opportunity to submit proposed findings and conclusions.

(D) The trial court erred by not providing findings and conclusions.

See Question 92 [Choice (C)]

IV. EFFECT OF JUDGMENTS

A. Which jurisdiction's preclusion rules apply

1. First judgment is by a state court

Question 80

An individual investor purchased stock through a company's stock offering. When the price of the stock plummeted, the investor sued the company in a state court in State A, claiming that the company's offering materials had fraudulently induced him to purchase the stock and seeking $25,000 in damages.

A university that had purchased the company's stock through the same offering sued the company in federal court in State B, claiming that the offering materials violated federal securities laws and seeking $1 million in damages.

The individual investor's suit proceeded to trial. The state court ruled that the company's offering materials contained false information and awarded the investor a $25,000 judgment. The university immediately moved for partial summary judgment in its federal action against the company, arguing that the state court judgment bound the federal court on the issue of whether the company's offering materials contained false information.

Neither State A nor State B permits nonmutual issue preclusion.

Should the court grant the university's motion?

(A) No, because State A does not permit nonmutual issue preclusion.

(B) No, because the federal court sits in a state that does not permit nonmutual issue preclusion.

(C) Yes, because federal law permits nonmutual issue preclusion.

(D) Yes, because the issue of whether the materials contained false information was actually litigated and necessarily decided.

Question 81

A plaintiff filed a tort action in state court but then failed to prosecute the action. The defendant moved to dismiss the action, and the court granted the motion in an order that stated: "The defendant's motion to dismiss is granted, and this action is dismissed with prejudice." The court accordingly entered judgment for the defendant.

The plaintiff then filed the same claim against the defendant in federal court, invoking diversity jurisdiction. The defendant has asserted the defense of res judicata (claim preclusion) in its answer.

Should the federal court give preclusive effect to the state court judgment?

(A) No, because the judgment was entered by a state court, not a federal court.

(B) No, because the state court did not rule on the merits in its dismissal.

(C) Yes, because a dismissal with prejudice operates as a judgment on the merits.

(D) Yes, because a judgment for failure to prosecute operates as a judgment on the merits under the Federal Rules of Civil Procedure.

2. First judgment is by a federal court

Question 82

A car manufacturer produced a car that was sold nationwide. Problems with the car's brakes allegedly caused several accidents and injuries. Two individual buyers of the car each filed a class action, in different states, against the manufacturer, asserting the same products liability claims on behalf of all buyers nationwide. One class action was filed in federal court and the other was filed in state court.

The parties in the federal action reached a court-approved settlement, and the court entered judgment dismissing the action with prejudice.

The manufacturer's attorney has moved to dismiss the state court action on the basis of res judicata (claim preclusion).

Should the state court look to federal or state law to decide the effect of the judgment?

(A) Federal law, because the judgment was entered in federal court.

(B) Federal law, because the judgment was the result of a nationwide action governed by the federal class action rule.

(C) State law, because the judgment is being asserted in a state court.

(D) State law, because there is no general federal common law and preclusion is a common-law doctrine.

B. Claim preclusion (a/k/a merger and bar)

1. The requirement that the "same claim" be present in the second suit

a. Personal-injury claim and property-damage claim arising out of the same transaction

Question 83

In State A, an accountant got into a taxi cab owned by a company that employed the driver as a full-time driver. During the trip, the cab collided with a truck whose driver sped away and was never located. The accountant brought a negligence suit in a State A court known as a "city court," whose jurisdiction was limited to claims not to exceed $250,000, but whose procedures were otherwise identical to those of the State A courts of general jurisdiction. The suit was solely against the cab driver, and the relief sought was $20,000 to compensate for property damage caused during the collision to a framed oil painting that the accountant owned and was carrying with her in the cab. After the resulting jury trial, the jury returned a verdict in favor of the cab driver, and the judge entered final judgment.

The accountant then brought a $200,000 negligence suit in a State A court of general juris-diction against the company that owned the cab, for personal injuries the accountant had sus-tained in the same collision. The company moved to dismiss the suit on account of the earlier judgment in favor of the cab driver. Will the court dismiss the suit on this ground?

(A) Yes, based on the doctrine of issue preclusion (or "collateral estoppel").

(B) Yes, based on the doctrine of claim preclusion (or "res judicata").

(C) No, because the cab company would not have been bound had the judgment in the earlier suit been in favor of the accountant.

(D) No, because the first suit was in a court of limited jurisdiction, making any form of preclu-sion unfair to the accountant.

b. The requirement that the plaintiff have been able to seek the same remedy in the first action as he is seeking in the second action

See Question 83 [Choice (D)]

c. The requirement that the party seeking the benefit of claim preclusion (or that party's privy) in the second action must have been a party to the first action

Question 84

Plaintiff, a citizen of State A, purchased a used car from Defendant, a corporation that is a cit-izen of State B, in a transaction that occurred in State B. At the time of the sale, Plaintiff did not know that the car had defective brakes. While driving the car in State A, Plaintiff crashed into a taxi, owned and driven by Taxi Driver (a citizen of State B), which was going faster than the speed limit. Plaintiff brought a diversity action against Defendant in federal district court for the Eastern District of State B for personal injuries and property damage suffered by Plaintiff in the crash; Plaintiff's theory was that Defendant committed fraud on her (as defined under State B common-law principles) by knowingly concealing the condition of the brakes, and that the fraud was the proximate cause of Plaintiff's damages. A jury awarded Plaintiff the full $100,000 she sought, but Plaintiff was unable to collect because Defendant went bankrupt.

Plaintiff then sued Taxi Driver in a separate diversity action in federal district court for the Southern District of State A, again for $100,000, for the same personal injury and property damage sustained by Plaintiff in the crash. Taxi Driver raised the affirmative defense of claim preclusion, arguing that any claim Plaintiff might have had against Taxi Driver should have been asserted as part of the State B action since Plaintiff's claim against Defendant and her claim against Taxi Driver arose out of a single episode. Since Plaintiff failed to assert the claim against Taxi Driver, Taxi Driver argued, that claim became merged into Plaintiff's successful judgment against Defendant, and may no longer be asserted. Taxi Driver has therefore moved for summary judgment on the basis of this claim-preclusion theory.

Which statement provides the best explanation of how the State A federal court should resolve Taxi Driver's motion?

(A) The federal court should grant the motion because once Plaintiff chose to bring any suit in State B concerning the accident, Plaintiff was required to sue all parties involved in accident in that first action.

(B) The federal court should grant the motion under the transactional test for claim preclusion.

(C) The court should deny the motion because Taxi Driver was not a party to the State B action.

(D) The court should deny the motion because the judgment of the State B court will not be final until all appeals have been concluded.

2. **The requirement that the judgment in the first action be valid and final in order to have claim-preclusive effect on the second action**

    See Question 84 [Choice (D)]

C. **Issue preclusion (a/k/a collateral estoppel)**

1. **The requirement that the issue have been "actually litigated"**

    See Question 80 [Choice (D)]

    See Question 83 [Choice (A)]

D. **"Mutuality" in both Claim and Issue Preclusion**

    See Question 83 [Choice (C)]

E. **What is included in the prior "judgment" for purposes of the preclusion rules?**

Question 85

An engineer worked for many years for a manufacturer of auto airbags. The engineer's job was both to design, and to evaluate the safety of, the manufacturer's airbag inflation systems. Three years ago, the engineer quit and began giving paid expert testimony against the manufacturer in civil suits brought by consumers who said they had been injured when airbags made by the manufacturer had detonated prematurely; the engineer testified that based on his own experience working for the manufacturer, the airbags in question were defectively designed.

The manufacturer responded to this testimony by suing the engineer in State A state court, alleging that his testimony unfairly disclosed the manufacturer's trade secrets. The manufacturer and the engineer then settled this suit. As part of the settlement, both parties asked the State A judge to enter an injunction prohibiting the engineer from "giving testimony, by deposition or trial testimony, in any personal injury suit brought in any American state or federal court against [the manufacturer] concerning [the engineer's] knowledge of the design of manufacturer's airbag systems." The judge entered the requested injunction.

Shortly thereafter, a consumer was injured in a car crash in State B when an airbag system made by the manufacturer allegedly failed to inflate properly in the consumer's car. The consumer brought a diversity action based on product liability against the manufacturer in federal district court for State B. The consumer's lawyer issued a subpoena to compel the engineer to testify about his personal knowledge of the design of the airbag at issue in the consumer's case.

The state courts of State B have said in past opinions that the state has a strong public interest in ensuring that potential witnesses with knowledge of pertinent matters not be barred from testifying to that knowledge on account of confidentiality agreements between the witness and another private party. The manufacturer has now asserted in the federal court action that under the relevant federal full faith and credit statute, the federal court has a duty to exclude any testimony by the engineer about matters covered by the injunction, including the engineer's knowledge about the manufacturer's airbag designs.

Should the federal court grant the manufacturer's request to exclude the engineer's testimony?

(A) No, because the application of full faith and credit principles must yield to any strong countervailing public-policy interest on the part of State B, and admitting the engineer's testimony here would serve such a public-policy interest held by that state.

(B) No, because the admissibility of evidence is not governed by full faith and credit principles.

(C) Yes, because the principles of claim preclusion embodied in the federal full faith and credit statute require a State B federal court to enforce the injunction issued by the State A court even if a State B state court would not issue such an injunction on comparable facts if the suit were pending in that court.

(D) Yes, so long as the federal court believes that the State A judge who issued the injunction would on request modify it to allow the engineer to obey the subpoena and give the testimony sought here.

APPEALABILITY AND REVIEW

I. AVAILABILITY OF INTERLOCUTORY REVIEW

A. Situations in which interlocutory review (review without a final judgment) is or may be available

1. Orders involving injunctions

Question 86

Two days before his home was to be sold at a foreclosure sale, a homeowner obtained a temporary restraining order (TRO) in federal court that prevented his lender from proceeding with the sale for 14 days or until a preliminary injunction hearing could take place, whichever was sooner. When a preliminary injunction hearing could not be scheduled within the original 14-day period, the court extended the TRO for another 30 days.

The lender appealed the court's order extending the TRO. The homeowner has moved to dismiss the appeal.

Is the appellate court likely to dismiss the appeal?

(A) No, because a TRO is immediately appealable.

(B) No, because the 30-day extension makes the TRO equivalent to a preliminary injunction and therefore appealable.

(C) Yes, because a TRO is not appealable under the interlocutory appeals statute.

(D) Yes, because there is no final judgment from which an appeal may be taken.

2. Situations involving the "collateral order" doctrine (including orders granting or denying claims of civil immunity)

See Question 88 [Choice (D)]

See Question 89 [Choice (C)]

3. Judges' discretion to allow an interlocutory appeal

See Question 49 [All Choices]

See Question 88 [Choices (A) and (B)]

See Question 90 [Choices (B) and (D)]

II. THE FINAL JUDGMENT RULE

A. The final judgment rule generally

Question 87

A patient domiciled in State A sued a surgeon domiciled in State B in a federal court in State A, alleging claims for malpractice. The surgeon moved to dismiss the action for lack of personal jurisdiction. The court denied the motion and set discovery cutoff and trial dates.

The surgeon has appealed the denial of the motion.

Should the appellate court hear the merits of the surgeon's appeal?

(A) No, because the appellate court lacks jurisdiction over the appeal.

(B) No, because the district court's decision on jurisdiction is final.

(C) Yes, because a contrary appellate decision could terminate the action.

(D) Yes, because the surgeon's personal-jurisdiction challenge raises a constitutional question.

Question 88

A man who owned riverfront property sued an upstream factory in federal court for polluting the river, seeking injunctive relief and $250,000 in damages. The factory moved for summary judgment on the ground of res judicata (claim preclusion), arguing that the man had sued on and lost an identical claim one year before. The court denied the motion.

The factory has asked its attorney's advice as to whether it may appeal the court's denial of summary judgment in order to avoid an expensive trial.

What advice should the attorney give?

(A) The factory may appeal if the appellate court finds that the case involves a controlling question of law upon which the courts are divided.

(B) The factory may appeal if the trial court certifies that there is no just reason for delay.

(C) The factory may not appeal until after a trial on the merits or other disposition resulting in a final judgment.

(D) The factory may not appeal, because the denial of summary judgment is a collateral order.

B. Situations in which appeal is allowed despite the lack of a final judgment

> **See Question 86 [Choice (D)]**

C. Situations in which appeal is not allowed because there is no final judgment, and no exception to the requirement of a final judgment applies

1. Temporary restraining orders

> **See Question 86 [Choices (A) and (C)]**

2. Grants or denials of motions for summary judgment

a. Denials of summary-judgment motions, generally

Question 89

An animal-rights protester joined others in carrying a picket sign on the front steps of a U.S. Army facility in which, the protesters claimed, the Army was conducting experiments that abused monkeys. A military police officer employed by the Army arrested the protester for trespassing and forcibly handcuffed him. The protester brought a federal civil suit against the officer for violation of a federal statute making a person civilly liable for violating another person's constitutional rights under color of federal or state law (in this case, for violating the protester's Fourth Amendment rights).

After discovery and before trial, the officer made two motions: (1) a motion for summary judgment on the grounds that his behavior was objectively reasonable and was therefore not a substantive violation of the protester's constitutional rights; and (2) a motion to dismiss the claim based on the judge-made doctrine of qualified immunity, under which a government official has civil immunity from trial if he reasonably though incorrectly believes that his conduct is lawful.

The district court denied both motions on the grounds that it could not be said as a matter of law that the protester would not be able to establish the officer's civil liability at trial. The judge then ordered a trial. The officer immediately appealed the rulings denying each of his motions. The protester now argues in the Court of Appeals that neither ruling is properly appealable until after the case has been tried. How should the Court of Appeals rule as to the timeliness of the appeals of the two rulings?

(A) Neither the summary judgment ruling nor the immunity ruling is properly appealable now.

(B) Both of the rulings are properly appealable now.

(C) The immunity ruling is appealable now, but the summary judgment ruling is not.

(D) The summary judgment ruling is appealable now, but the immunity ruling is not.

b. Grants of partial summary judgment

Question 90

Defendant, a corporation that manufactures automobile tires, entered into a long-term sales contract with Plaintiff, a company that distributes used cars. Plaintiff, dissatisfied with the quality of Defendant's tires, filed a diversity action in federal court against Defendant. The complaint alleged three claims: breach of warranty, strict liability, and breach of contract. On April 1, the district court granted Plaintiff's motion for partial summary judgment (judgment only as to the contract claim) and ordered a trial on the two remaining claims. The court's opinion granting the partial summary judgment said nothing about whether the judgment was deemed final or whether there was any reason to allow an immediate appeal from it.

On April 15, Defendant filed a motion in the appropriate federal court of appeals, asking that court to hear an immediate appeal of the grant of partial summary judgment. On April 25, Plaintiff filed a written consent to this appeal—he did so in the hopes that if he won that appeal, Defendant would immediately settle the contract claim without a trial in return for Plaintiff's dropping the other two claims.

Assuming that the appeals court desires to hear the immediate appeal, does that court have jurisdiction to do so?

(A) Yes, because the grant of partial summary judgment is a final judgment.

(B) Yes, because the grant of partial summary judgment, although an interlocutory order, may be immediately appealed in the discretion of either the trial or appeals court.

(C) No, because the grant of partial summary judgment here was an interlocutory order from which no immediate appeal is possible.

(D) No, because the parties did not file their consent to the appeal within ten days of the court's entry of its order.

3. Miscellaneous situations

See Question 87 [Choice (D)]

III. DEADLINE FOR FILING NOTICE OF APPEAL

Question 91

A consumer brought a diversity suit against a baker in State A federal district court, alleging that the baker made a defectively dangerous croissant that contained glass fragments that injured the consumer. The complaint asserted that the baker made the croissant at his sole proprietorship in State B, sold the croissant to a State B wholesaler, who sold it to a restaurant in State A, where the consumer bought it, ate it, badly cut his mouth, and had to be hospitalized for nearly a week. The suit sought $100,000 in damages.

The baker appeared in the action via his lawyer and filed an answer consisting solely of a general denial. The baker did not attend the trial and relied on his lawyer to conduct the trial without calling witnesses and relying solely on the lawyer's cross-examination of the consumer's witnesses. The trial evidence showed that the baker had never travelled to State A, sold all items he baked solely to wholesalers located in State B, and did no advertising outside of State B. On June 1, the jury awarded $55,000 to the consumer for various categories of damages.

The baker made a post-trial motion to set aside the verdict on various grounds, including lack of jurisdiction; the motion was denied by the judge on July 1. On July 15, the judge had the court clerk file a judgment against the baker for $55,000, and notice of the entry of judgment was sent to the baker's lawyer.

On September 20, the baker via his lawyer filed a notice of appeal with the clerk of the district court. The notice of appeal correctly listed the parties and the judgment being appealed from, and the parties then timely submitted briefs to the federal Court of Appeals for the circuit encompassing State A. The baker based his appeal on two errors: that the district court had lacked subject-matter jurisdiction due to the award of less than $75,000, and that the court lacked personal jurisdiction over him because he did not have minimum contacts with State A.

How will the Court of Appeals likely rule in the appeal?

(A) The court will dismiss the appeal because it lacks jurisdiction, whether or not the district court had subject matter and personal jurisdiction over the action.

(B) The court will reverse the judgment, because the district court lacked personal jurisdiction over the baker.

(C) The court will reverse the judgment, because the district court lacked subject matter jurisdiction over the action.

(D) The court will affirm the judgment, because the baker waived both of the jurisdiction-related defenses at the district-court level.

IV. THE SCOPE OF REVIEW

A. Review of bench trials

1. The "clearly erroneous" rule

Question 92

A construction contractor brought a breach of contract claim in federal court against a homeowner who had hired the contractor to build an apartment over an existing garage. The action turned on the scope of the work covered by the contract. The contractor and the homeowner were the only witnesses at the bench trial, and they strongly disagreed about the scope of the work. At the end of the trial, the judge stated findings of fact on the record but never issued a written opinion. Neither party objected to the findings. The judge found in favor of the homeowner, and the contractor appealed.

Is the appellate court likely to overturn the findings?

(A) No, because the appellate court must give due regard to the trial judge's opportunity to determine witness credibility.

(B) No, because the contractor failed to object to the findings when the judge stated them in open court.

(C) Yes, because a judge must set forth findings of fact in a written opinion or memorandum of decision.

(D) Yes, because there were disputed issues of fact at trial.

See Question 79 [Choice (A)]

See Question 93 [Choice (B)]

B. Review of jury trials

Question 93

A driver was badly injured when her car ran off the road for unknown reasons and hit a tree, and the car's airbags did not inflate. The driver sued the manufacturer in a federal diversity action for product liability, alleging that there was a defect in the airbags' inflating mechanism. At the jury trial, the plaintiff's lawyer offered testimony by two other consumers that the airbags in their cars, which were the same model and manufacturer as the driver's car, also failed to trigger during collisions. The manufacturer's lawyer objected to the evidence, arguing (without factual contradiction from the plaintiff) that the speed and other circumstances in the two witnesses' collisions had not been shown to be substantially similar to those of the present case, creating a large risk that these witnesses' testimony would mislead the jury and be unfairly prejudicial to the defense.

The trial judge allowed the two witnesses to testify, and the jury returned a verdict in favor of the plaintiff. The manufacturer appealed; one of its arguments on appeal was that the two witnesses' testimony about their airbags' failure should have been excluded as irrelevant, misleading, and highly prejudicial.

What standard will the appeals court use in evaluating this argument?

(A) An "abuse of discretion" standard.

(B) A "clearly erroneous" standard, applied while giving due regard to the trial court's opportunity to judge the proposed witnesses' credibility.

(C) A "de novo" standard, giving no special deference to the trial court's decision to admit the evidence.

(D) A "harmless error" standard, requiring reversal unless the reviewing court believes that the evidence ruling was not only erroneous but probably changed the trial's outcome.

CIVIL PROCEDURE ANSWERS

Answer 1

The correct choice is **(C),** because the fact that the suit arises under a federal statute means that there is no minimum amount in controversy and that the presence or absence of diversity is irrelevant. When you are told that the defendant has moved to dismiss for "lack of subject-matter jurisdiction," you know that the motion can be successful only if the defendant demonstrates one of two defects in the suit: (1) that there was neither diversity of citizenship nor a "federal question claim"; or (2) that there was an amount in controversy requirement applicable to the type of suit in question, which amount was not satisfied. Here, neither of these potential defects exists, so the motion will be denied.

As to (1), start with the basic idea that the federal courts have original jurisdiction over two broad categories of claims: (a) those involving "diversity of citizenship" (or its close cousin "alienage" jurisdiction, which we'll ignore here); and (b) those raising what is loosely referred to as a "federal question." Here, the case falls into category (b): 28 U.S.C. § 1331, entitled "Federal Question," gives the federal district courts "original jurisdiction of all civil actions arising under the Constitution, *laws*, or treaties *of the United States*."

Section 1331 means that if the plaintiff's claim is based upon a federal statute (which is of course a "law . . . of the United States"), there is subject-matter jurisdiction under § 1331, regardless of which states or countries the parties are citizens of. Since the woman's suit is based on a federal employment-discrimination statute, § 1331 gives the court federal-question jurisdiction, and you can and should ignore entirely the citizenship of the parties.

But what about potential defect (2), failure to meet an amount-in-controversy requirement? The very modest "trick" in this question, if there is one, is that *there is no minimum amount-in-controversy requirement for federal-question suits.* So while the "matter in controversy" in a suit based solely on *diversity* must exceed $75,000 in value (see 28 U.S.C. § 1332(a)), a suit raising a federal question may proceed even if the matter is worth, say, $1, or involves an intangible stake with no specific financial value (e.g., a request for an injunction).

Therefore, when you analyze this question, as soon as you can see that the complaint raises on its face an allegation that the defendant violated a federal statute, you can be confident that the court has subject-matter jurisdiction over the claim regardless of the parties' citizenship and regardless of the amount at stake.

Choice (A) is wrong, for two different reasons: (1) As explained in Choice (C), the citizenship of the parties never matters at all for purposes of determining the existence of subject-matter jurisdiction in a federal-question suit; and (2) this choice incorrectly states the rule that would apply if the parties' citizenship *were* relevant. A corporation is deemed to be a citizen both of its state of incorporation and the state in which it has its "principal place of business," which is considered to be the location from which the company's officers direct business affairs (generally, and in this case, the company's "headquarters"); it is not the case that a corporation is also a citizen of the state in which it has a majority of its employees. Therefore, the defendant here is not a citizen of State A (just of States B and C), which means that there *would* be complete diversity between plaintiff and defendant if the case were based on diversity rather than the existence of a federal question.

Choice (B) is wrong, because, as discussed in the analysis of Choice (C), where the plaintiff's claim raises a federal question (as it does here), there is no amount in controversy requirement, and the existence or non-existence of diversity of citizenship is irrelevant.

Choice (D) is wrong, because an objection to lack of subject-matter jurisdiction can never be waived. It's true that there are *some* objections to matters involving jurisdiction, service, venue, or the like that will be waived if the defendant fails to assert them in either a pre-answer motion or in the answer itself. See FRCP 12(h), saying that the four defenses listed in Rule 12(b)(2)-(5) (lack of personal jurisdiction, improper venue, insufficient process, and insufficient service of process) are waived if the party fails to make them in either a "responsive pleading" (here, the answer) or in a timely motion made before the responsive pleading.

But because the drafters of the FRCP feared that allowing the federal district courts to hear a case for which there was no subject-matter jurisdiction would exceed the limited powers given to the federal judiciary by the Constitution, the FRCP provide that the defense of lack of subject-matter jurisdiction is *never* waived. (Indeed, Rule 12(h)(3) says that "if the court determines *at any time* that it lacks subject-matter jurisdiction, the court *must dismiss* the action.")

Answer 2

The correct choice is **(C),** because subject-matter jurisdiction is determined based on the facts regarding citizenship on the day that the lawsuit is commenced. *Changes* in a party's citizenship post-commencement *do not affect* the court's jurisdiction unless they suggest that a party acted in bad faith. See *Grupo Dataflux v. Atlas Global Group, LP*, 541 U.S. 567 (2004). Thus, although a defect in subject-matter jurisdiction can be raised at any time during a lawsuit, and even for the first time on appeal, the federal court does not lose subject-matter jurisdiction over the action because of changes in the citizenship of an existing party that occurred after the commencement of the suit.

Here, the court properly exercised diversity jurisdiction over the suit when it was filed. See 28 U.S.C. § 1332(a). Diversity jurisdiction requires a showing of complete diversity—meaning that no plaintiff may be a citizen of a state that is also the state of citizenship of any defendant. A corporation is a citizen of the state(s) in which it is incorporated and of the state in which it has its principal place of business; so in this problem, Company was a citizen of State A (and only State A) at the moment the action was filed. See 28 U.S.C. § 1332(c); *Hertz Corp. v. Friend,* 559 U.S. 77 (2010). A partnership is an unincorporated association and is deemed to be a citizen of every state in which any member of the partnership is a citizen. See *Carden v. Arkoma Associates,* 494 U.S. 185 (1990). Since neither of the partners on the date of the commencement of the suit was a citizen of State A (Company's sole state of citizenship on that date), the requirement of complete diversity was satisfied on that date. And the fact that Company's own state of citizenship changed after the date the suit was filed (so that Company then became a citizen of the same state as one partner of Partnership) did not trigger the need to re-evaluate the existence of diversity.

(A) is wrong, because objections to lack of subject-matter jurisdiction are never waived. In the federal system, objections to lack of subject-matter jurisdiction are never waived and can thus be raised at any time during the lawsuit and even for the first time on appeal. See FRCP 12(h)(3): "If the court determines at any time that it lacks subject-matter jurisdiction, the court must dismiss the action." See also *Capron v. Van Noorden,* 6 U.S. 126 (1804). (So if the district court lacked jurisdiction as of the time of the commencement of the suit, the court would have an obligation to dismiss the lawsuit if it later discovered this lack.) However, as discussed in the treatment of Choice (C), diversity jurisdiction did exist at the time of the commencement of the suit, and no change in one party's citizenship post-commencement could divest the court of subject-matter jurisdiction. Therefore, the motion to dismiss should be denied not because it was made too late, but because it is incorrect on the merits.

(B) is wrong, because there is no subject-matter jurisdiction problem, and in any event sanctions would not be appropriate here. As to the absence of a subject-matter jurisdiction problem, the existence of subject-matter jurisdiction is determined as of the moment the case is filed, and a post-filing change in the citizenship of a party cannot divest jurisdiction that existed at the time of filing, as is more fully explained in the discussion of Choice (C). As to sanctions, sanctions would be warranted, with appropriate notice, if the party in question had violated its obligations of pleading in good faith (see FRCP 11) or had violated its obligations to comply with the discovery rules (see FRCP 37). But the mere fact that Company changed its state of incorporation after the filing of the action does not indicate bad faith in pleading, and Company's failure to tell the court about the change after it occurred does not indicate bad faith either (especially given that the change didn't in fact affect the existence of jurisdiction).

(D) is wrong, because no remand was called for (or even authorized) on these facts. Remand to a state court is a procedural step that would be appropriate only if plaintiff had originally filed the action in state court and defendant had improperly removed it. In this case, the action was filed as an original matter in federal court; therefore, remand would not be an option even if subject-matter jurisdiction did not exist. Rather, if subject-matter jurisdiction did not exist, the appropriate course of action would be for the district court to dismiss the suit, not to remand it to state court. (And in any event, as discussed in Choice (C), subject-matter jurisdiction does exist.)

Answer 3

The correct choice is **(B)**, because there is complete diversity of citizenship, and Defendant is not a citizen of the state where the action was filed. In those cases where Congress has chosen to allow a defendant to remove a state-court action to federal court, the removal is "of right"—if the pre-conditions for removal are met, the court does not have discretion to send the case back to state court. Thus 28 U.S.C. § 1441(a) says that unless Congress has specifically said otherwise, "any civil action brought in a State court of which the district courts of the United States have original jurisdiction, may be removed by the defendant or the defendants, to the district court of the United States for the district and division embracing the place where such action is pending." Here, since Plaintiff brought suit in state court in Cap City, State A, Defendant had the right to remove the case to the federal district court in the district that includes Cap City, so long as (1) Congress didn't expressly impose a limitation on removal that would apply to these facts; and (2) the federal district court here would have had "original jurisdiction" had the case been initially filed in that federal court. Both of these requirements are satisfied here.

Because the claim asserted by Plaintiff is a state-law tort claim, any federal-court jurisdiction over the claim would have to be based on diversity of citizenship (not on the presence of a federal question). For the court to exercise diversity jurisdiction, both citizenship and amount-in-controversy requirements must be met. See 28 U.S.C. § 1332. In particular, the citizenship of *all* plaintiffs must be diverse from the citizenship of *all* defendants—a rule known as the requirement of **complete diversity**. Since Plaintiff is a citizen of State A, the required complete diversity is present if and only if Defendant is *not* a citizen of State A.

The fact that defendant not only operates a factory in State A but does all of its day-to-day manufacturing in State A might lead you to guess that defendant would be considered to be a citizen of that state. But such a guess would be *incorrect*. Under 28 U.S.C. § 1332(c), the citizenship of a corporation includes the state in which it is incorporated and the state in which it has its principal place of business. The Supreme Court has held that the principal place of business of a corporation is the state from which the company's high level officers, such as the chief executive officer, the treasurer, and the secretary, direct the corporation's decisions—the so-called "nerve center test." See *Hertz Corp. v. Friend*, 559 U.S. 77 (2010). Since all of Defendant's corporate officers direct the corporation's affairs from their office in State C, only State C, not State A, is the Defendant's principal place of business under *Hertz*, making the Defendant's State A-based factory operations irrelevant to the citizenship issue. Therefore, Defendant is a citizen of both State C and State B (its state of incorporation) but not of State A. That, in turn, means that there is complete diversity of citizenship—the sole plaintiff is not a citizen of any of the two states in which Defendant is a citizen.

As to the requirement that there not exist any provision by which Congress explicitly took away the removal right of a defendant in the position of Defendant, there is no such provision.

Choice (A) is wrong, because Defendant is not in fact a citizen of State A. As is more fully explained with respect to Choice (B), a corporation is deemed to be a citizen only of its state of incorporation and the state in which it has its principal place of business. "Principal place of business" has been defined by the Supreme Court as the place from which the corporations-level officers control business, which in this case is Texas. So the fact that day-to-day operations all took place in State A is not sufficient to make Defendant a citizen of State A, making Choice (A) factually incorrect. (If Defendant *were* a citizen of State A, however, the outcome predicted by this choice—removal not allowed—would be correct for two reasons: (1) there would not be the required complete diversity of citizenship between Plaintiff and Defendant, thereby depriving the federal court of original jurisdiction since there is no federal question present; and (2) even if there *were* diversity, under 28 U.S.C. § 1441(b)(2), a case based solely on diversity may not be removed if any defendant is a citizen of the state where the action was originally brought.)

Choice (C) is wrong, for the same reason (A) is not correct; the choice incorrectly asserts that Defendant is a citizen of State A. See the more extensive discussion of why Defendant is not a citizen of State A in the treatment of Choices (A) and (B) above. (If Defendant *were* a citizen of State A, this choice would be correct, though no more correct than Choice (A) would be as well.)

Choice (D) is wrong, because it is factually incorrect; the claim does not fall within the federal courts federal-question jurisdiction. If Plaintiff's claim *did* present a federal question, this choice would be correct; Defendant would have the right to remove even if it *was* a citizen of State A, the state where the action was originally brought by plaintiff. But here, Plaintiff has alleged negligent infliction of harm, which is a state-law claim. It's true that Defendant has raised an *affirmative defense* that is based on federal law. But under *Louisville & Nashville R.R. Co. v. Mottley*, 211 U.S. 149 (1908), a claim will fall within the federal court's federal-question jurisdiction only if the claim "arises under" a federal constitutional provision or federal statute, and this fact must appear on the face of the (well-pleaded) complaint—it's not enough that the federal question is raised in the answer or raised by a defense that is certain to be litigated. Therefore, the fact that Defendant has already raised an appropriate affirmative defense based on a federal statute is not enough to convert the claim into one raising a federal question, and jurisdiction will have to be premised solely on diversity of citizenship.

Answer 4

The correct choice is **(C),** because the suit is deemed to be between the doctor and the corporation, who are both citizens of State A. For jurisdiction to be based on diversity, the diversity must be *"complete."* That is, it must be the case that no plaintiff is a citizen of the same state as any defendant. Determining whether there is diversity here requires you to answer two different questions: (1) Whose citizenship counts when a ***personal representative*** sues on behalf of an ***estate,*** and (2) of what state(s) is a ***corporation*** deemed to be a citizen?

As to problem (1), the answer is given quite specifically in a federal statute. According to 28 U.S.C. § 1332(c)(2), "The **legal representative** of the **estate of a decedent** shall be deemed to be a citizen **only of the same state as the decedent**[.]" So here, the fact that the son is domiciled in State B is irrelevant—given that the son is bringing suit here as the legal representative of the estate of his father the doctor, § 1332(c)(2) requires that the son be deemed to be a citizen of State A, since that was the state of citizenship of the doctor at the moment of his death. (For purposes of applying § 1332(c)(2), the "decedent" is deemed to be a citizen of whatever state he was domiciled in **at the moment of his death**, which in the case of the doctor is State A.)

Now, as to problem (2), how to determine the citizenship of a corporation is specified in almost the same place as the citizenship of an estate. 28 U.S.C. § 1332(c)(1) says that a corporation is deemed to be a citizen of both of the following, if they are different: (a) the state in which the corporation was **incorporated**; and (b) the state in which the corporation "has its **principal place of business**." Place (a) is easy; the facts tell you the corporation was incorporated in State D. But what is the state in which the corporation here "has its principal place of business"?

The Supreme Court has given guidance on the meaning of this term in *Hertz Corp. v. Friend*, 559 U.S. 77 (2010), by applying the so-called ***"nerve center" test***. That is, a corporation's "principal place of business" is "best read as referring to the place where a **corporation's officers direct, control, and coordinate the corporation's activities**." In practice, the Court said in *Hertz*, this will normally be "the place where the corporation **maintains its headquarters**— provided that the headquarters is the actual center of direction, control, and coordination, i.e., the 'nerve center'." Here, the nerve center is clearly State A, since the facts tell you that State A is not only the state in which the corporation's "headquarters" are located, but the state from which all the officers of the corporation supervise the corporation's activities. Because the "nerve center" test is used, the fact that three quarters of the corporation's employees work in State C, and all of the corporation's products are made in that state, is irrelevant. In sum, the corporation here is a citizen of both State D (its state of incorporation) and State A (its state of principal place of business, i.e., the state of its "headquarters," from which its executives supervise the business).

Since the plaintiff is deemed to be a citizen of State A (because that was the doctor's state of domicile at his death), and the defendant is a citizen of both State A and State D, the same state (State A) is represented on both sides of the suit. And that is enough to destroy the required complete diversity. Furthermore, as discussed more extensively in the treatment of Choice (D) below, the federal court must refuse to hear the case once it realizes that the required complete diversity is absent, even if no litigant has raised the subject-matter-jurisdiction issue.

Choice (A) is wrong, because it misstates the relevant citizenship on both sides of the suit. On the plaintiff side of the equation, the relevant citizenship is that of the decedent (the doctor), not that of the nominal plaintiff (the son as personal representative). See the discussion of Choice (C) above for why this is the case. And on the defendant side, the corporation, in addition to being a citizen of the state of incorporation (State D), is deemed a citizen of its headquarters location (State A), and not the state where most employees work and most production occurs (i.e., not State C). This, too, is discussed further in the treatment of Choice (C) above.

Choice (B) is wrong, because like Choice (A), it misstates the relevant citizenship on both sides. On the plaintiff side, it's the citizenship of the decedent, not the personal representative, that counts. On the defendant side, while it's true that the corporation is a citizen of State D (its state of incorporation), the choice incorrectly fails to list State A as the second state of which the corporation is deemed a citizen; it's a citizen of State A because that's the state in which the corporation's principal place of business (i.e., its headquarters) is located.

Choice (D) is wrong, because lack of federal subject-matter jurisdiction is never waived. Many defenses are deemed waived if not promptly asserted. That's true even of the defense that the court lacks *personal* jurisdiction over the defendant. (See Rule 12(h)(1), saying that the defense of lack of personal jurisdiction is among those waived if the defendant doesn't raise it by either making a timely motion under Rule 12(b) or asserting it as part of his answer.) But there is a different rule for the defense of lack of *subject-matter* jurisdiction: Rule 12(h)(3) says that ***"If the court determines at any time that it lacks subject-matter jurisdiction, the court must dismiss the action."*** So the son's failure to raise this defense prior to the completion of the pleadings is irrelevant—the judge has no choice but to dismiss the action for lack of subject-matter jurisdiction "sua sponte" (on her own). And that would be true even if, say, the trial was already complete, and even if the reason the lack of jurisdiction wasn't discovered before then was because, say, one of the parties fraudulently concealed the lack.

Answer 5

The correct choice is **(A),** because a partnership is deemed to be a citizen of the state or foreign country of EACH of its partners, and the existence of diversity is to be determined as of the time the suit is filed. First, let's figure out the citizenship of the plaintiff, a limited partnership. A limited partnership—like other artificial entities such as general partnerships, labor unions, and business trusts (but not corporations) — is considered an "unincorporated association." And the rule has always been that an unincorporated association, for diversity purposes, is deemed to be a citizen of ***every state or nation in which any member of the association is a citizen***. See *Carden v. Arkoma Assocs.,* 494 U.S. 185, 195-196 (U.S. 1990), involving exactly our present question of the citizenship of a limited partnership, where the Supreme Court said that "[D]iversity jurisdiction in a suit by or against the [artificial] entity depends on the ***citizenship of . . . 'each of its members[.]'***"

Therefore, if the plaintiff limited partnership as of a particular moment had as its partners a general partner that was a citizen of Canada, eight individuals as limited partners who were citizens of Canada, and two individuals as limited partners who were citizens of State A, the limited partnership as a whole would be deemed to have been a citizen of both Canada and State A at that time. (The only type of artificial entity to which a different rule for determining citizenship applies is the standard "corporation," whose place of incorporation and principal place of business are the *only* sources of citizenship—in other words, the citizenship of the individual stockholders is irrelevant. And that different rule exists only because Congress expressly so provided, in 28 U.S.C. § 1332(c)(1).)

The second rule you need to know to solve this problem is that the relevant time for measuring a litigant's citizenship is the ***moment the complaint was filed***, not some later moment such as the commencement of the trial. As the Supreme Court put it in *Grupo Dataflux v. Atlas Global Group, L.P.,* 541 U.S. 567, 570-571 (2004), "It has long been the case that . . . 'the jurisdiction of the court depends upon the state of things at the time of the action brought.' . . . This time-of-filing rule . . . measures all challenges to subject-matter jurisdiction premised upon diversity of citizenship against the state of facts that existed at the time of filing—whether the challenge be brought shortly after filing, after the trial, or even for the first time on appeal."

The Supreme Court in *Grupo Dataflux* explicitly rejected even a modest proposed exception to this general rule, under which if neither the parties nor the judge *raised* the lack-of-diversity problem until after a jury verdict had been rendered, and due to intervening developments the litigants became completely diverse before the verdict was rendered, the court could treat subject-matter jurisdiction as existing and preserve the verdict. So in *Grupo Dataflux*, where the factual situation was virtually identical to the one in our question (the only two limited partners who had the same citizenship as the defendant had left the partnership between the moment of filing and the start of trial), the Supreme Court nonetheless concluded that the general rule—existence of diversity is determined at the moment of filing, and changes in any litigants' citizenship post-filing are irrelevant—should apply and required that the case and the jury verdict be dismissed.

So here, these two rules combine to make it be the case that *the federal court does not have subject-matter jurisdiction over the case.* In suits in which one of the parties is a citizen of a foreign nation, diversity jurisdiction would have to be of the "alienage" variety, specified in 28 U.S.C. § 1332(a)(2). Section 1332(a)(1) provides for jurisdiction in suits that are between "citizens of a State and citizens or subjects of a foreign state" (as long as the citizen of the foreign state is not also a permanent resident in the same U.S. state as any opposing party). Since the defendant corporation here is deemed a citizen of State A (remember, a corporation is a citizen of any state in which it was incorporated, plus the state of its principal place of business, which is the state from which its executives direct the company's business), diversity is measured as of the moment of filing, and the requisite complete diversity could exist only if no partner in the plaintiff limited partnership was a citizen of State A.

Thus, the fact that two of the limited partners in the plaintiff, as of the moment the suit was filed, were citizens of State A means that the requisite complete diversity between the plaintiff limited partnership and the defendant corporation *never existed.* The fact that the citizenship of the limited partnership changed after filing and before commencement of the suit (by the exit of the two State A limited partners), making the partnership a citizen solely of Canada, is *irrelevant.* It would also be irrelevant (if it were true, which we don't know) that the defendant knew of the lack-of-diversity problem at all times and purposely tried to play "heads I win, tails you lose" by waiting until after the verdict and deciding that it would point out the diversity problem only if it lost at trial.

You should keep in mind one other rule about determining diversity that might sound inconsistent with the above "time of filing controls" rule, but that the Supreme Court has found to be distinguishable from the time-of-filing rule. If after filing of the suit and before judgment, *the lineup of the litigant parties changes*, in that an existing plaintiff or defendant leaves the suit, or a new party joins the suit, we *do* analyze the existence of diversity immediately after the change.

So, for instance, suppose P (a citizen of State A) files suit against D1 (a citizen of State A) and D2 (a citizen of State B), based solely on diversity. Then, after both Ds object to the lack of the required complete diversity, P voluntarily dismisses her claim against D1, and continues only against D2. In this situation, assuming that D1 is not an indispensable party, the suit *may* continue, because the change of party "cures the lack of complete diversity." The Supreme Court has decided that this "change in the party lineup" situation is conceptually different from the "change in the citizenship of a continuing party" scenario posed by our problem—in the former, the change in citizenship due to the change in the party lineup dictates a re-evaluation of the existence of diversity post-change, whereas in the latter, the change in the citizenship of a continuing party does not dictate a re-evaluation. See *Grupo Dataflux,* supra, making this distinction between the two situations.

Choice (B) is wrong, because the state of the defendant's knowledge or motive concerning the diversity issue is irrelevant. This choice asserts that the critical fact is whether the defendant knew (or at least should have known) that there was a lack of the required diversity prior to the start of trial. But the state of the defendant's knowledge is completely irrelevant here. As is more fully discussed in the analysis of Choice (A), the only critical issue is whether the requisite diversity existed at the moment the suit was filed; if diversity was not present then, then even if the defendant knew about the problem and remained silent in the hopes of getting a "free bite at the apple" (i.e., planned to try the case and raise the diversity issue only if it lost at trial), no rule prevented the defendant from using this tactic.

Choice (C) is wrong, because a lack of diversity as of the moment the suit was filed cannot be cured by a later change to a party's citizenship. As is discussed in the analysis of Choice (A), the existence of diversity is determined by looking at the parties' citizenship at the moment the suit is filed. If as of that moment there is an overlap between the state(s) of which any plaintiff is a citizen and the states of which any defendant is a citizen, that overlap prevents the requisite diversity from existing no matter what happens post-filing. But distinguish this situation from one in which there are multiple parties on one side, and as the result of post-filing changes in the lineup of the parties (e.g., a party is dismissed from the case) there is a change in citizenship; in this new situation, the existence of diversity is determined by looking at the new lineup (though the citizenship of each of the remaining parties is still measured as of the initial filing)—thus, if P is diverse with D1 but not diverse with D2 as of filing, the problem can be cured by dropping D2. (For more about that scenario, see the last paragraph discussing Choice (A) above.)

But the "change of party lineup" scenario in the prior sentence is the *only* situation in which a post-filing change relating to diversity can matter. If the party lineup *doesn't* change—and the only thing that changes post-lineup is the citizenship of a continuing party—that change never affects the diversity analysis. So here, where the suit has continued to be solely between the original limited partnership plaintiff and the original corporate defendant, the fact that two limited partners of the plaintiff departed post-filing (thereby converting the partnership from being a citizen of both Canada and State A to a citizen only of Canada) does *not* "cure" the lack of subject-matter jurisdiction, as this choice says it does.

Choice (D) is wrong, because it is an incorrect statement of the rules for determining the citizenship of a partnership. As is more fully discussed in the treatment of Choice (A), the only "artificial entity" whose citizenship is determined without reference to the citizenship of the constituent members or owners is a true corporation (as to which Congress has specially provided that the citizenship of the stockholders is to be ignored). For a limited partnership (as well as for other types of "unincorporated associations," like labor unions, general partnerships, business trusts, etc.), the judge-made rule is and has always been that the entity is deemed a citizen of every state and/or foreign nation of which any constituent member is a citizen. So if, as is the case here, a limited partnership has as its partners a general partner and multiple limited partners, it must be the case that none of this whole set of partners may be a citizen of the same state or nation as any defendant.

Answer 6

The correct choice is **(B),** because it states the correct rule and applies it properly to the facts. Interpleader is a joinder device that allows a person who faces multiple and possibly conflicting claims to property to resolve all claims in one proceeding. Interpleader can be used when the property is a "common fund," making it a very useful procedural device in the insurance context. In the federal system a stakeholder can use one of two different interpleader mechanisms: *statutory* interpleader, under 28 U.S.C. § 1335, or *rule* interpleader, under FRCP 22. Statutory interpleader eases the subject-matter jurisdictional requirements in a way that Rule interpleader does not. The question tells you that the stakeholder has commenced a statutory interpleader action. The statute, 28 U.S.C. § 1335(a), applies when *"[t]wo or more adverse claimants, of diverse citizenship* . . . , are claiming or may claim to be entitled to . . . *money or property"* that the stakeholder has in its "custody or possession . . . of the value of *$500* or more." The action that Plaintiff has commenced here easily meets the requirements of statutory interpleader. First, statutory interpleader's watered-down diversity requirements are met; the statute requires only "minimal" diversity, i.e., requires only that two or more of the adverse claimants be citizens of different states (versus the usual requirement of complete diversity as between all plaintiffs and all defendants). Since there are at least two "adverse claimants" that are of different citizenship from each other (e.g., a State B claimant and a State C claimant), that's enough to create minimal diversity. (In other words, it's irrelevant that Plaintiff, the stakeholder, is a citizen of State B given that its principal place of business is there and that one claimant is also a citizen of State B.) Second, the watered-down amount-in-controversy requirement is also met, because the value of the fund (here, $1 million) *exceeds $500*.

Choice (A) is wrong, because the rule of diversity that it applies does not apply to federal statutory interpleader. *The federal statutory interpleader mechanism provides an exception to the usual rule of complete diversity.* That is, as long as there is diversity between two or more of the adverse claimants, diversity under the federal interpleader statute is met. (See the language of 28 U.S.C. § 1335(a), quoted in the discussion of Choice (B) above.) The fact that the individual commencing the interpleader action—the stakeholder who is in custody of the property, here, Plaintiff—is not diverse from all the claimants is irrelevant. See *State Farm Fire & Casualty Co. v. Tashire*, 386 U.S. 523, 530-531 (1967).

Choice (C) is wrong, because the amount-in-controversy requirement that it mentions is irrelevant. There *is* a context in which the amount in controversy must be $5 million or more, but that context involves *class actions*; under the Class Action Fairness Act (CAFA), embodied in 28 U.S.C. § 1332(d), any class action in which at least $5 million is in controversy meets the jurisdictional amount, and the requirement of diversity is satisfied as long as at least one member of the plaintiff class is diverse with at least one defendant. But here, since the action is not a class action, this choice is not correct.

Choice (D) is wrong, because the rule of joinder that it applies is irrelevant to federal statutory interpleader actions. It is true that many federal joinder rules limit joinder to claims that share common facts or law and that are therefore likely to arise from a common origin or from the same transaction. See, e.g., Fed. R. Civ. P. 24(b)(A)(B) (permitting permissive intervention by "anyone . . . who . . . has a claim or defense that shares with the main action a common question of law or fact"). But statutory interpleader is not one of the joinder devices that requires that the claims have a common origin or arise out of a single transaction. In fact, statutory interpleader specifically authorizes the court to maintain the action "although the titles or claims of the conflicting claimants *do not have a common origin, or are not identical*." 28 U.S.C. § 1335(b). What is critical is the fact that the claims to be resolved "are *adverse to and independent of one another*." Id. And when the stakeholder is confronted by competing demands for payment by beneficiaries under insurance policies, the "adverse and independent claims" requirement is satisfied.

Answer 7

The correct choice is **(C),** because it recognizes that diversity jurisdiction cannot be created through the collusive assignment of a claim. Had Plaintiff not assigned the claim to Lawyer, diversity jurisdiction would not be present in a lawsuit filed by Plaintiff against Defendant, because Plaintiff and Defendant are citizens of the same state, State A. See 28 U.S.C. §1332(a). So the issue is whether Plaintiff's assignment of its claim to Lawyer, a citizen of State B, creates diversity jurisdiction (since if Lawyer is viewed as now being the true plaintiff, he is diverse with Defendant).

The answer is "no," because of a statute enacted by Congress to deal with exactly this sort of scenario. 28 U.S.C. § 1359 provides that a "district court shall not have jurisdiction of a civil action in which any party, by *assignment* or otherwise, has been *improperly or collusively made or joined to invoke the jurisdiction of such court*." One of the circumstances in which the courts are especially likely to find that an assignment was collusive is where "the assignee *merely functions as a collection agent* for the assignor[.]" F,K&M (5th Ed.), § 2.7, p. 42. Here, notice that Lawyer (1) has not paid any of his own money (beyond the token $1) as compensation for the assignment; (2) will do all the work of collecting the debt; and (3) holds as his only economic interest the possibility of receiving one-third of the amount collected (a fairly standard fee-split in contingent-fee debt-collections cases). So a court would almost certainly conclude that Lawyer is merely *functioning as a collection agent* for the assignor, bringing the case squarely within § 1359. See, e.g., *Kramer v. Caribbean Mills*, 394 U.S. 823, 824 (1969) (assignment held collusive where assignee paid $1 for the assignment and at the same time promised to pay back to the assignor 95% of any net recovery on the assigned claim).

Choice (A) is wrong, because the rule that it relies upon is not accurate. Diversity jurisdiction may be invoked by a plaintiff even in a suit against a defendant who is a citizen of the state in which the federal court sits. The exception to which this choice seems to pertain applies only in *removal* cases; a defendant who is sued in the state courts of his state of residence may not remove the suit to that state's federal court on the basis of diversity jurisdiction. See 28 U.S.C. § 1441(b)(2). Here, the action was filed in federal court as an original matter, so the ban on removal by an in-state defendant is irrelevant.

Choice (B) is wrong, because the relevant test here for the purpose of determining federal diversity jurisdiction is whether the assignment is impermissibly collusive, not whether it is valid under state law. As discussed in the context of Choice (C), 28 U.S.C. § 1359 prohibits a district court from exercising diversity jurisdiction if the requisite diversity is brought about (by assignment or otherwise) "improperly or collusively." The factual issue of whether the joinder here was collusive is a matter of federal, not state, law—so the fact that the assignment may have been effective or legal under State A law is irrelevant to whether § 1359 applies.

Choice (D) is wrong, because the assignment is collusive under 28 U.S.C. § 1359 and therefore does not create diversity jurisdiction. The likely vigor of Lawyer's representation will not cure the fact that the assignment here was collusive and done for the purpose of manufacturing diversity.

Answer 8

The correct choice is **(D)**, because multiple plaintiffs are not permitted to aggregate their claims to meet the jurisdictional amount unless they are suing to enforce their common interest in a single undivided right. First, pay attention to the obvious fact that here, *no single plaintiff* has claims aggregating more than $75,000. (If one plaintiff *did* have claims aggregating more than $75,000 against a single defendant, that would pose a very different situation, discussed at the end of this discussion of Choice (D).) It has long been the case that where no single plaintiff has claims against any defendant for more than the jurisdictional amount, the court will not combine the dollar amounts of multiple plaintiffs' claims for purposes of determining whether more than the jurisdictional amount is at stake, except in the uncommon situation where all plaintiffs share a "single title or right." See, e.g., *Snyder v. Harris,* 394 U.S. 332, 334-335 (1969): "[T]he separate and distinct claims of *two or more plaintiffs cannot be aggregated* in order to satisfy the jurisdictional amount requirement. Aggregation has been permitted *only* (1) in cases in which *a single plaintiff seeks to aggregate two or more of his own claims against a single defendant* and (2) in cases in which *two or more plaintiffs* unite to enforce a *single title or right in which they have a common and undivided interest*."

The "single title or right [with] a common and undivided interest" standard is very rarely met—an example where it would be met is that four individuals are each bequeathed an "undivided interest" in a piece of property (so that if the plaintiffs all sued a defendant over title to the property, the amount-in-controversy requirement would be satisfied if the property was worth more than $75,000, even if no one person's interest would be worth $75,000 if the property were partitioned). The fact that the defendant may have committed the "same" wrong towards each plaintiff by violating a single rule of law in the same way at the same time, is *not* enough to give the plaintiffs the requisite "single undivided title or right" status. So here, the fact that the brokerage firm violated the ECA statute by the same type of act, at the same time, as to each employee would not be enough to permit aggregation of their claims.

Note, however, that where there is *at least one plaintiff* whose own claim (or claims) against a single defendant is/are valued at *more than $75,000*, the doctrine of *supplemental jurisdiction*, as enacted in 28 U.S.C. § 1367 and then interpreted by the U.S. Supreme Court in *Exxon Mobil Corp. v. Allapattah Services, Inc.*, 545 U.S. 546 (2005), applies. In that situation, supplemental jurisdiction *does* permit the federal court to hear the claims of certain other plaintiffs with claims that are transactionally related to the "main" plaintiff's claim, even though each of these "minor" plaintiffs has less than $75,000 at stake—and that's true whether the way the multiple plaintiffs are together in the case is via a class action or via a Rule 20 joinder. So on our facts, if one employee had received 76 checks so that his claims against the firm amounted to $76,000, the court *would* have supplemental jurisdiction to hear the transactionally related claims of the other 19 employees, each of whom had less than $76,000 at stake. In other words, the key point here is that *no single plaintiff* has claims against any defendant totaling more than $75,000.

But nothing in the supplemental jurisdiction statute changes the main "no-aggregation-of sub-$75,000-plaintiffs" result we've been discussing above—supplemental jurisdiction can *only* kick in when there is at least one single plaintiff-vs-defendant pairing as to which there is both diversity and more than $75,000 at stake.

Choice (A) is wrong, because supplemental jurisdiction does not apply to the situation in which no single plaintiff has more than $75,000 at stake. As is further explained in the discussion of Choice (D) above, the supplemental jurisdiction statute (28 U.S.C. § 1367(a)) does not apply where no single plaintiff has claims against a single defendant aggregating more than $75,000. And that's true even though the various plaintiffs have claims that all derived from the same transaction or series of transactions (which is the case here). (But if at least one employee had claims totaling more than $75,000 against the defendant, then the court *could* use supplemental jurisdiction to hear the other employees' claim as well, assuming these other plaintiffs were diverse with the defendant.)

Choice (B) is wrong, because it is an incorrect statement of how the case law of aggregation has developed. As is further explained in the discussion of Choice (D) above, Supreme Court cases like *Snyder v. Harris,* 394 U.S. 332, 334-335 *(1969)* have expressly rejected the argument that where multiple plaintiffs have claims arising out of the same transaction or series of related transactions, aggregation of the various claims should be permitted for purposes of determining whether the $75,000 amount-in-controversy requirement is satisfied. It is only in the very unusual case where all plaintiffs have a common or undivided interest in a "single right" that the dollar value of each plaintiff's interest may be aggregated in determining whether the $75,000 requirement is satisfied.

Choice (C) is wrong, because an objection to the court's lack of subject-matter jurisdiction is never waived. Where the defendant has improperly removed from state to federal court, the plaintiff or plaintiffs normally have a limited time in which to move to have the case remanded back to state court: 28 U.S.C. § 1447(c) says that "A motion to remand the case on the basis of any defect other than lack of subject matter jurisdiction must be made *within 30 days after the filing of the notice* of removal[.]" But where the motion is based upon the lack of subject-matter jurisdiction, the next sentence of § 1447(c) shows that there's no time limit: "If at any time before a final judgment it appears that the district court lacks subject matter jurisdiction, the case shall be remanded." (And notice that the remand can happen even if no party moves for it—so if the federal judge suddenly notices the lack of, say, complete diversity or amount-in-controversy, the judge not only may but *must* remand the case no matter how far it has proceeded on the merits, as long as final judgment has not yet been entered.)

Answer 9

The correct answer is **(A),** because it correctly applies the rule that aggregation is ordinarily not allowed where no single plaintiff meets the jurisdictional amount. When no single plaintiff's claim independently meets the amount-in-controversy requirement for diversity jurisdiction, *multiple plaintiffs may not meet the amount-in-controversy requirement by aggregating the value of their claims unless their claims are "common and indivisible,"* which the tort claims of the plaintiffs are not. Article III of the U.S. Constitution does not impose any amount-in-controversy requirement on the grant of diversity jurisdiction (see Article III, § 2), but Congress has always imposed such a minimum-dollar requirement in the federal statute that authorizes diversity jurisdiction. The current statute requires that the amount exceed "the sum or value of *$75,000*, exclusive of interest and costs." 28 U.S.C. § 1332(a). When a lawsuit involves multiple plaintiffs, and each plaintiff's claims are separate and distinct from the claims of the others (not "common and indivisible"), *at least one plaintiff must by him/herself have claims that meet the statutory requirement.* (If one plaintiff's claims *do* meet the statutory requirement, the claims of the other plaintiffs can be heard under the discretionary doctrine of supplemental jurisdiction, assuming the other requirements of the statute are met. See 28 U.S.C. § 1367; *Exxon Mobil Corp. v. Allapattah Services, Inc.,* 545 U.S. 546 (2005).) Here, since no plaintiff independently has claims aggregating $75,000 or more, and since each plaintiff's claims are separate and distinct from the others' claims, aggregation is not allowed and the entire case must be dismissed.

Be attentive as to why plaintiffs' claims here would *not* be considered *"common and indivisible."* Claims are considered to be common and indivisible *only where, "if one plaintiff were to fail to collect his share, the remaining plaintiffs would collect a larger share." Durant v. Servicemaster Co. Trugreen, Inc.,* 147 F. Supp. 2d 744, 749 (E.D. Mich. 2001). Such claims typically involve a *shared interest in a property title* or in a status of entitlement. A series of individual torts, even when arising from the same contaminated product, do not come within this definition; in torts, each plaintiff is suing for the harm he or she individually suffered—the co-plaintiffs are not suing to recover part of a shared interest.

Choice (B) is wrong, because it incorrectly applies the amount-in-controversy requirement for diversity jurisdiction. Under the federal statute, a court may exercise diversity jurisdiction only if the claim exceeds the value of $75,000. See 28 U.S.C. § 1332(a). Here, no individual plaintiff meets that requirement, because each party's claim is valued only at $40,000. Moreover, the plaintiffs may not aggregate their claims to meet the amount-in-controversy requirement because their claims are not common and indivisible; as discussed in the second paragraph of Choice (A) above, each plaintiff's claims are considered to be separate and distinct from the claims of the other plaintiffs, even though all claims arise out of the same transaction or occurrence. And supplementary jurisdiction does not apply, because that doctrine applies only where at least one plaintiff's claim(s) independently meet subject-matter-jurisdictional requirements (in which case other claims by other parties may often be added even though they don't independently meet jurisdictional requirements); here, there is no plaintiff whose claim(s) independently meet subject-matter-jurisdictional requirements.

Choice (C) is wrong, because it incorrectly applies the amount-in-controversy requirement for diversity jurisdiction. As explained with respect to Choices (A) and (B), the diversity statute permits the exercise of jurisdiction only "where the matter in controversy exceeds the sum or value of $75,000, exclusive of interest and costs." 28 U.S.C. § 1332. *An individual plaintiff may aggregate all claims against a single defendant, whether or not the claims are transactionally related.* Here, Husband's two claims against Defendant together aggregate $75,000 or more, so he is deemed to meet the amount-in-controversy requirement. Once that happens, supplemental jurisdiction permits the other two plaintiffs to remain in the action, since their claims and Husband's are all "so related" (since they arise out of the same basic occurrence, joint consumption of a single can of soup) as to form one "case or controversy," the standard for triggering the availability of supplemental jurisdiction under 28 U.S.C. § 1367(a). Since this choice grants a dismissal to Defendant, it's wrong.

Choice (D) is wrong, because it's wrong as a factual matter. If Husband's and Wife's claims were in fact all based on a "common and undivided interest," this choice would be correct, as is explained in Choice (A): When multiple plaintiffs have claims based on a common and undivided interest, all claims by all plaintiffs based on that interest may be aggregated together for amount-in-controversy purposes. But as explained in the second paragraph of the discussion of Choice (A), the claims of Husband and Wife are not based on such a common and undivided interest.

Answer 10

The correct choice is **(D),** because even though the case probably falls within the court's diversity jurisdiction, federal courts will *abstain* from exercising such power when the lawsuit pertains solely to divorce and child custody. Usually, a federal court is required to exercise subject-matter jurisdiction over a state-law claim if the individual parties are citizens of different states and the amount in controversy is satisfied. However, the U.S. Supreme Court has long recognized an exception as a matter of policy in diversity actions for suits that *seek a divorce decree, an alimony award, or a child-custody determination.* "The rationale for this limitation is that family relations are uniquely a matter of state policy and state interest, with which the federal courts should not interfere." F,K&M (5th Ed.), § 2.5, p. 29. See also *Ankenbrandt v. Richards*, 504 U.S. 689 (1992). The Constitution does not mandate this limitation; rather, the Court has based the limitation on the history and statutory language of the grant of diversity jurisdiction. Since what Husband is seeking is precisely these three types of domestic-relations orders, the district court must obey the Supreme Court's policy determination by declining to exercise diversity jurisdiction even if it is present.

Choice (A) is wrong, because the court won't hear the case regardless of whether diversity exists. As explained with respect to Choice (D), the Supreme Court has decided that federal courts should decline to exercise their diversity jurisdiction in cases that seek a divorce decree, an alimony award, or a child-custody determination. So whether or not the requirements of diversity are met here (which they probably are), this choice, by implying that the court should hear the case, is not correct.

Choice (B) is wrong, because it incorrectly assumes that a federal court can remand an action when a party moves to dismiss the action for lack of subject-matter jurisdiction. Remand is a procedure that applies only in removal situations; the procedure requires the federal court to transfer an action back to state court when defendant has improperly removed an action from state court to federal court. See 28 U.S.C. § 1441. Since the case here was never filed in state court and was never "removed," the federal court cannot "remand" it to that (or any) court.

Choice (C) is wrong, because a federal court can't "transfer" a case to a state court. Although it is true that the district court will exercise discretion and decline to exercise diversity jurisdiction in a suit that pertains to divorce, alimony, or child custody, a federal court does not have power to "transfer" a federal lawsuit to the court of a different system, including the court of a state system in the United States. The transfer rules that apply in federal district court allow a district court to change the venue of an action, including by transferring the suit to another federal court that sits in a state different from the one in which the transferor court sits. See 28 U.S.C. § 1404. However, apart from the special case of a remand to the original court of an improperly-removed action (see Choice (B) above), a federal court may not transfer a federal suit to a state court, whether it is a court of the state where the federal court sits or a court of some other state.

Answer 11

The correct choice is **(C),** because Plaintiff's claim against Distributor is not within the court's diversity jurisdiction, supplemental jurisdiction cannot be exercised over Distributor, and the facts do not suggest that any other jurisdictional basis is available.

When faced with a multi-party and multi-claim action, it helps to diagram the action:

Plaintiff (State A) v. Defendant (State B)
(main action)

↓ (plus)

Defendant (State B) v. Distributor (State A)
(third-party claim under FRCP 14(a)(1))

↓ (plus)

Plaintiff (State A) v. Distributor (State A)
(direct claim under FRCP 14(a)(3))

Here, Plaintiff is seeking to sue Distributor, who has been joined in the action as a third-party defendant. See FRCP 14. However, in order to bring a claim against a third-party defendant, the court must be able to exercise subject-matter jurisdiction. One form of subject-matter jurisdiction is ordinary diversity jurisdiction under 28 U.S.C. § 1332(a), by which the court can hear the case if the plaintiff and the defendant are "citizens of different States" and "the matter in controversy exceeds the sum or value of $75,000 exclusive of interests and costs." 28 U.S.C. § 1332(a)(1). Since Plaintiff and Distributor are citizens of the same state (State A), ordinary diversity jurisdiction is not present as between them.

The Plaintiff-vs-Distributor claim could *still* be heard if that claim fell within a second type of jurisdiction, *supplemental jurisdiction*. But the Plaintiff-vs-Distributor claim does *not* qualify for supplemental jurisdiction. That's because 28 U.S.C. § 1367(b) says that when the anchor claim (here, Plaintiff-vs-Defendant) is grounded in *diversity* jurisdiction, there is *no* supplemental jurisdiction over any claim "by plaintiffs against *persons made parties* under Rule *14*, 19, 20, or 24 of the Federal Rules of Civil Procedure. . . ." 28 U.S.C. § 1367(b). In federal actions, third-party claims are governed by Rule 14; the defendant's right to claim against the third-party-defendant is covered by 14(a)(1), and the original plaintiff's right to claim against the third-party-defendant is covered by 14(a)(3).

In other words, in this case Distributor is a "person made party under Rule 14," and as such, § 1367(b) says that there is no supplemental jurisdiction over any claim "by [a] plaintiff against [that] person made party under Rule 14." So Plaintiff's third-party claim against Distributor is not supported by either basic diversity or supplemental jurisdiction and must be dismissed.

On the other hand, the court *has* subject-matter jurisdiction over both (1) Plaintiff's original claim against Defendant; and (2) Defendant's third-party claim against Distributor. As to (1), Plaintiff and Defendant are citizens of different states, so that's an easy situation for ordinary diversity. As to (2), since Plaintiff and Distributor are not diverse (and "complete diversity" is ordinarily required), Distributor's presence in the case (to defend against Defendant's third-party claim against him) might be viewed as destroying the required complete diversity. But the Defendant-vs-Distributor claim *does* fall within the court's *supplemental* jurisdiction. That happens because of 28 U.S.C. § 1367(a), the main provision creating supplemental jurisdiction. Section 1367(a) says that in general, "[i]n any civil action of which the district courts have original jurisdiction, the district courts shall have **supplemental jurisdiction** over **all other claims that are so related to claims in the action within such original jurisdiction that they form part of the same case or controversy** under Article III of the United States Constitution . . . . Such supplemental jurisdiction shall **include claims that involve the joinder or intervention of additional parties**."

Since the court started by having jurisdiction over the Plaintiff-vs-Defendant "anchor" claim, supplemental jurisdiction included any claim that was "so related" to the Plaintiff-vs-Defendant claim as to be part of the "same case or controversy" as the Plaintiff-vs-Defendant claim. And since Defendant's third-party claim against Distributor ("If I'm liable to Plaintiff, you have to indemnify me because you caused the accident by leasing defective equipment") arose out of the **same accident** as the one giving rise to the anchor claim (Plaintiff-vs-Defendant), the third-party claim is easily **sufficiently closely-related to the anchor claim** as to make the two claims part of the **same "case or controversy"** (as that term is used in Article III of the U.S. Constitution).

Finally, there is no provision, in § 1367 or elsewhere, that specifically withholds supplemental jurisdiction as to a third-party claim by the original defendant against the third-party defendant. Therefore, that third-party claim stays in the case. Indeed, this type of claim — a garden-variety third-party claim by the original defendant against a third-party defendant, claiming indemnification or contribution as to the main claim — is the prototypical claim that Congress had in mind when it drafted the clause of § 1367(a) allowing supplemental jurisdiction over "claims that involve the joinder or intervention of additional parties."

Choice (A) is wrong, because, of the three claims in the case, the *only* claim that lacks subject-matter jurisdiction is Plaintiff's claim against Distributor, for the reason described in the explanation to Choice (C). Diversity jurisdiction exists over Plaintiff's claim against Defendant because both parties are citizens of different states and the amount-in-controversy requirement is met. And as is discussed more fully in the explanation of Choice (C), supplemental jurisdiction exists over Defendant's third-party claim against Distributor. So the fact that Distributor and Plaintiff are not diverse does not oust the district court of power to hear the anchor claim or the third-party claim. Since the court will grant the dismissal motion only as to the Plaintiff-v-Distributor claim, this choice's statement that all three motions should be granted is incorrect.

Choice (B) is wrong, because Distributor's motion to dismiss Defendant's third-party claim for lack of subject-matter jurisdiction should not be granted. When the anchor claim (here, Plaintiff's claim against Defendant) is grounded in diversity jurisdiction, federal law permits the exercise of supplemental jurisdiction over a third-party claim brought by Defendant against a party joined by FRCP 14, as is more fully explained as to Choice (C). So Distributor's motion will be granted only as to Plaintiff's claim against it, not as to Defendant's "main" third-party claim against it.

Choice (D) is wrong, because the court may exercise diversity jurisdiction over Plaintiff's claim against Defendant. The complaint alleges that the parties to the main claim are citizens of different states (Plaintiff is a citizen of State A and Defendant is a citizen of State B) and that the amount in controversy exceeds $75,000; therefore, both conditions of diversity jurisdiction are present. See 28 U.S.C. § 1332(a)(1). Consequently, Defendant's motion to dismiss Plaintiff's complaint will be denied. (Furthermore, the court will grant Distributor's motion to dismiss Plaintiff's claim against it, making this choice doubly wrong.)

Answer 12

The correct choice is **(B)**, because supplemental jurisdiction applies to claims by third party defendants, since they are not "plaintiffs."

There is no claim in the case that raises a federal question, since all claims are based on contract. Therefore, subject-matter jurisdiction will have to be based on diversity. When a litigant is a corporation, that corporation is deemed to be a citizen of both: (1) the state in which it is *incorporated*; and (2) the state in which it has its *"principal place of business."* 28 U.S.C. § 1332(c)(1). Therefore, in this case the distributor is a citizen of both State B (its state of incorporation) and State C (the state where it has its principal place of business). And the wholesaler is a citizen of both State B (state of incorporation) and State A (principal place of business).

The diversity that is required is so-called *"complete diversity,"* i.e., no two parties on opposite sides may be citizens of the same states. Here, since both the distributor and the wholesaler are treated as being citizens of State B, the required complete diversity is absent; thus if there were no special doctrine available, there would be no diversity available to support the wholesaler's counterclaim against the distributor (or, for that matter, to support the distributor's third-party interpleader claim against the wholesaler).

However, there *is* a special doctrine available to give the court jurisdiction over the counterclaim: the doctrine of *supplemental jurisdiction*. Supplemental jurisdiction is conferred by 28 U.S.C. § 1367(a), which states that (subject to some important exceptions):

> "[I]n any civil action of which the district courts have original jurisdiction, the district courts shall *have supplemental jurisdiction* over *all other claims that are so related to claims in the action* within such original jurisdiction that they *form part of the same case or controversy* under Article III of the United States Constitution. Such supplemental jurisdiction shall include *claims that involve the joinder or intervention of additional parties.*"

Here, the wholesaler's counterclaim against the distributor relates to payment for the very goods that are the subject of the original shop-owner-versus-distributor claim; therefore, the counterclaim is clearly *"part of the same case or controversy"* as the original claim; that's enough to bring the counterclaim (which happens to be a compulsory counterclaim) within § 1367(a)'s general grant of supplemental jurisdiction. However, there is one more major obstacle that the counterclaim will have to avoid in order to be covered by supplemental jurisdiction: § 1367(b) specifically denies supplemental status to certain claims by parties that are *acting as plaintiffs*. Section 1367(b) says that there shall *be no supplemental jurisdiction over:*

> "claims *by plaintiffs* against persons made parties under *Rule 14,* 19, 20 or 24 of the Federal Rules of Civil Procedure, or over claims *by persons proposed to be* joined *as plaintiffs* under Rule 19 of such rules, or seeking to *intervene as plaintiffs* under Rule 24 of such rules [if there is no independent diversity or amount in controversy for the claim]."

But § 1367(b) doesn't pose a problem here, because the wholesaler's counterclaim is not deemed to be a claim *"by [a] plaintiff,"* since the wholesaler has been brought into the case as a Rule 14 third-party defendant (i.e., one who is a "nonparty who is or may be liable to [a defending party in the original action] for all or part of the claim against [the original defending party]"). See W,M,C&F, v. 13D, § 3567.2, pp. 376-77: "[I]t is clear that a defendant or third-party defendant does not become a 'plaintiff' for purposes of § 1367(b) by asserting a claim."

What about the fact that the wholesaler's counterclaim is for just $60,000, i.e., for less than the $75,000 amount in controversy? That, too, doesn't matter: § 1367's grant of supplemental jurisdiction applies to eliminate *both* the requirement of complete diversity *and* the amount in controversy requirement.

Choice (A) is wrong, because the fact that the wholesaler and the distributor's principal places of business are diverse does not eliminate the incomplete diversity caused by the fact that these two parties are both incorporated in State B. As we discuss more extensively in Choice (B), a corporation is deemed to be a citizen of *both*: (1) the state in which it is incorporated; and (2) the state in which it has its "principal place of business." Since the wholesaler and the distributor are both incorporated in State B, they are non-diverse. Therefore, the fact that they have different states of principal place of business is not enough to create diversity between them.

Choice (C) is wrong, because the absence of diversity between the distributor and the wholesaler does not matter, given the availability of supplemental jurisdiction. It's true that there is not the required complete diversity between the distributor and the wholesaler, since each is deemed to be a citizen of its state of incorporation, State B. (For a discussion of the fact that "complete" diversity is required, see the explanation in Choice (B).) However, the absence of the required complete diversity doesn't matter, because supplemental jurisdiction is available, as described in Choice (B).

Choice (D) is wrong, because the lack of diversity between the shop owner and the wholesaler doesn't matter, given that the motion involves only the counterclaim by the wholesaler against the distributor. It's true that the wholesaler and the shop owner are non-diverse (since each is a citizen of State A). But this fact is irrelevant, since there is no claim by the wholesaler against the shop owner, and diversity is to be analyzed on a claim-by-claim basis. What matters under the present motion is whether the court has subject-matter jurisdiction over the wholesaler's counterclaim against the distributor, and the shop owner's citizenship does not matter on that issue. (Furthermore, the lack of diversity as between the wholesaler and the distributor does not matter, because of the availability of supplemental jurisdiction; see the explanation of Choice (B).)

Answer 13

The correct choice is **(C),** because supplemental jurisdiction applies. This situation illustrates a situation in which (1) the district court has power to exercise *supplemental jurisdiction* and (2) there is no reason for the court to use its discretion to decline to exercise that power. Supplemental jurisdiction is authorized under a federal statute, 28 U.S.C. § 1367. Under the key portion of that statute, § 1367(a), when a federal court has original jurisdiction over a claim, the court has supplemental jurisdiction over "all other claims that are *so related to claims in the action* within such original jurisdiction that *they form part of the same case or controversy* under Article III of the United States Constitution." Then, the last sentence of § 1367(a) goes on to say that § 1367(a)'s grant of supplemental jurisdiction "shall include claims that involve the *joinder* or intervention of *additional parties.*" In those cases where § 1367(a) gives the district court power to exercise supplemental jurisdiction, the court then has the power to "decline to exercise supplemental jurisdiction" if any of the special factors set out in § 1367(c) is present.

Here, the court has original jurisdiction over the ABA claim against Employer, since that claim "arises under" federal law, namely the ABA statute. The breach-of-contract claim against Employer and Manager is in turn related to the ABA claim, because both claims concern the conditions of Plaintiff's firing. § 1367(a) therefore gives the court power to exercise supplemental jurisdiction over the state-law claim, including any "additional" party added on account of that state-law claim. But, as noted above, the court may *decline to exercise* that supplemental jurisdiction if any of the special factors listed in § 1367(c) is present. Factors listed in § 1367(c) include: that the state-law claim (against Manager and Employer) involves a novel or complex state law issue; that the state-law claim "substantially predominates" over the federal claim; that the federal claim has been dismissed; or that there are some "exceptional circumstances" that present a compelling reason for declining jurisdiction.

Here, none of the discretionary factors seems to tilt against the exercise of power: the contract claim is not novel or complex; that claim is not likely to predominate over the federal law claim; and, so far the federal claim has not been dismissed. Finally, there seem to be no exceptional circumstances or compelling reasons to deny supplemental jurisdiction. Therefore, there is no reason for the court to decline to exercise the supplemental jurisdiction that it has over the state-law claim (and over all parties to that claim).

Choice (A) is wrong, because the claim against Manager does not itself arise under federal law. Plaintiff's claim against *Manager* does not arise under the ABA or, indeed, under *any* federal statute, preventing jurisdiction over that claim from being present under the statute granting federal-question jurisdiction, 28 U.S.C. § 1331. Plaintiff's claim against Manager is a garden-variety state-law contract claim, and no federal issue is alleged as part of the well-pleaded complaint relating to that claim (a requirement for federal-question jurisdiction made clear by *Louisville & Nashville R. Co. v. Mottley*, 211 U.S. 128 (1908), as well as by 28 U.S.C. § 1331). This choice reaches the right outcome (motion denied, because the court has subject-matter jurisdiction), but reaches it on incorrect reasoning by asserting that the reason the court has jurisdiction for the claim against Manager is "since the ABA claim arises under a federal statute." (The correct choice would have to somehow point to supplemental jurisdiction, which Choice (C) does.)

Choice (B) is wrong, because it incorrectly applies the test for federal diversity jurisdiction. Federal courts can invoke diversity jurisdiction to adjudicate claims alleged to be valued at more than $75,000 between citizens of different states. See 28 U.S.C. § 1332. Both Plaintiff and Manager are citizens of the same state, State A, so diversity of citizenship is not present. Remember that for diversity jurisdiction, **complete** diversity is required—no plaintiff may be a citizen of the same state as any defendant. So the fact that there is diversity as between the sole plaintiff and *one* of the defendants to the state-law claim (Employer) is not enough to give the court diversity jurisdiction over that state-law claim.

Choice (D) is wrong, because the court can exercise jurisdiction over Manager, based on supplemental jurisdiction and the power to add additional parties pursuant to that jurisdiction. Federal statute authorizing the exercise of supplemental jurisdiction explicitly provides that the scope of such jurisdiction "shall include claims that involve the *joinder* or intervention of *additional parties.*" (See the last sentence of 28 U.S.C. § 1367(a).) There are certain exclusions to supplemental jurisdiction (specified in § 1367(b)) that apply when the anchor claim is based solely on diversity jurisdiction. But the anchor claim here (the ABA claim) is based on a federal question, not solely diversity, so these exclusions don't apply.

Answer 14

The correct choice is **(C),** because supplemental jurisdiction applies, but the court has discretion to decline to exercise that jurisdiction because all claims over which the court had original jurisdiction have been dismissed.

The key to this question is to recognize that whether the court may (or indeed must) decide the state-law false-arrest claim depends entirely on whether and how the doctrine *of supplemental jurisdiction* applies. The mechanics of supplemental jurisdiction are laid out in great detail in 28 U.S.C. § 1367, and everything you need in order to answer this question can be found somewhere in sub-sections (a) through (d) of § 1367. First, let's look at sub-section (a), which contains the main language granting the federal courts supplemental jurisdiction over a claim that could be sued on if it were the only claim in the suit:

> "(a) Except as provided in subsections (b) and (c) or as expressly provided other-wise by Federal statute, in any civil action of which the district courts have *original jurisdiction*, the district courts shall have *supplemental jurisdiction* over *all other claims that are so related to claims in the action within such original jurisdiction that they form part of the same case or controversy* under Article III of the United States Constitution. Such supplemental jurisdiction shall include claims that involve the joinder or intervention of additional parties."

Here, the federal court has (or, more accurately, it *had*, at the time the suit was filed) "original jurisdiction" over the § 1983 claim, since that is a federal question claim (i.e., it arises under a federal statute). So the above-quoted language means that the court also has "supplemental jurisdiction" over "all other claims that are so related to" the §1983 claim that the other claims "form part of the same case or controversy" as the §1983 claim. Where the "anchor claim" (here, the § 1983 federal-question claim) shares the same *"common nucleus of operative facts"* as the "other claim" in question (here, the state-law false-arrest claim), that's clearly a sufficiently close relationship to make the two claims part of the "same case or controversy." Here, both claims arise out of a single episode or transaction (the arrest and handcuffing of the plaintiff by the defendant), so the two claims share a "common nucleus of operative facts," and the false-arrest claim therefore satisfies § 1367(a) and triggers supplemental jurisdiction unless something in § 1367(b) or (c) changes this result.

Sub-section (b) (i.e., 28 U.S.C. § 1367(b)) doesn't apply here—that sub-section applies only to cases where the only reason the "anchor claim" falls within the court's "original jurisdiction" is because of *diversity*; here, the § 1983 claim is a federal-question claim, so we can ignore § 1367(b) entirely. Sub-section (c), however, not only applies, but is key to solving our question; here's what that section provides:

> "(c) The district courts may *decline to exercise supplemental jurisdiction* over a claim under subsection (a) if —
>
> (1) the claim raises a novel or complex issue of State law,
>
> (2) the claim substantially predominates over the claim or claims over which the district court has original jurisdiction,
>
> (3) *the district court has dismissed all claims over which it has original jurisdiction*, or
>
> (4) in exceptional circumstances, there are other compelling reasons for declin-ing jurisdiction."

As you can see, (3) above—"the district court has *dismissed all claims* over which it has original jurisdiction"—fits our situation exactly, since the only claim over which the court ever had original jurisdiction was the § 1983 claim, and that claim has now been dismissed. Therefore, § 1367(b)(3) says that the judge "may decline to exercise supplemental jurisdiction" over any remaining claim. And Choice C correctly indicates that the court has such discretion.

But what about the last phrase of Choice C, that "federal law guarantees the jogger 30 days to refile the claim in State A court"? Well, sub-section (d) of § 1367 says that:

> *"The period of limitations for any claim asserted under subsection (a),* and for any other claim in the same action that is voluntarily dismissed at the same time as or

after the dismissal of the claim under subsection (a), *shall be tolled while the claim is pending and for a period of 30 days after it is dismissed unless State law provides for a longer tolling period.*"

The state-law false-arrest claim is a "claim asserted under subsection (a)" (i.e., it's a claim that triggers subsection (a)'s grant of supplemental jurisdiction). Therefore sub-section (d) provides that the statute of limitations for that state claim will be "tolled" not only for the whole time the claim was "pending" (i.e., while the federal action was pending), but also for a minimum of 30 days after the federal court dismisses the claim, to give the jogger this period in which to re-file in State A court. (If State A would grant a *longer* tolling period, the jogger would get that longer time—but § 1367(d) guarantees her *at least* the 30 days.) Normally, federal law wouldn't lengthen the statute of limitations for a state-law claim asserted in state court, but under the Supremacy Clause and the Necessary and Proper Clause, Congress has the power to do so in the exercise of Congress' power over the federal judiciary, and it has chosen to use that power to guarantee, to any claimant whose claim has been dismissed from the federal action based on the court's discretion, the time to refile in state court. Therefore, Choice (C) correctly indicates that the judge has discretion whether or not to hear the now standalone false arrest claim, and that the jogger will have at least 30 days to refile in state court if the judge declines to exercise that discretion. (By the way, on these facts, the judge could plausibly go either way on the dismissal decision: Generally, federal courts will dismiss the remaining state claim if all federal claims have been dismissed before the start of trial; but if the judge believes that both sides have expended significant resources in getting the surviving state-court claim(s) ready for trial, and one party affirmatively desires to have the federal court try the surviving claim, the court may well accede to that request in the interest of judicial efficiency.)

Choice (A) is wrong, because the federal court has supplemental jurisdiction over the surviving state-law claim and may choose to exercise that discretion. As is described in detail in the discussion of Choice (C) above, the fact that the federal court had original jurisdiction over the federal-question § 1983 claim at the time the suit was filed was enough to give the court supplemental jurisdiction over the transactionally related state-law false arrest claim; and that remained true even after the § 1983 claim was dismissed. This choice, by saying that the federal court "must" (rather than "may") dismiss the state-law claim, is thus legally incorrect.

Choice (B) is wrong, because the federal court *does* have discretion to decline to exercise supplemental jurisdiction over the state-law claim.

This choice correctly states that supplemental jurisdiction applies to the state-law false-arrest claim; the reason this is true is extensively discussed in the treatment of Choice (C). But this choice is exactly wrong in asserting that the court lacks discretion *to decline to exercise* that jurisdiction. As the discussion of Choice (C) indicates, § 1367(b)(3) gives the court discretion to dismiss the supplemental-jurisdiction claim(s) once all claims falling within the court's original jurisdiction (here, the § 1983 claim) have been dismissed.

Choice (D) is wrong, because the court has discretion about whether to dismiss, or instead try, the false-arrest claim. As is described in the treatment of Choice (C) above, the federal court has discretion either to try the false-arrest claim or dismiss it. Therefore, this choice is legally incorrect in saying that the court "must" dismiss the false-arrest claim. However, the second clause in this choice is exactly correct; if the court *does* dismiss the claim, § 1367(d) guarantees the jogger at least 30 days after dismissal to refile that claim in State A court (and the jogger would have a longer period in which to refile if State A law would grant her such a longer period under the circumstances).

Answer 15

The correct choice is **(C),** because it recognizes that the removal here was improper. The removal was improper for two reasons. First, ***when the federal court would have lacked original jurisdiction over the plaintiff's claim, removal is not proper.*** Second, even if original subject-matter jurisdiction (based on diversity) over the plaintiff's original claim *had* existed, ***an in-state defendant cannot remove when jurisdiction is based solely on diversity***. And as to each of these two reasons, the presence of Defendant's counterclaim does not change the analysis. Let's take each of these steps in turn.

First, an action can be removed to federal court only if, as an original matter, the federal courts would have had subject-matter jurisdiction had the plaintiff initially filed the suit in federal court instead of state court. (See 28 U.S.C. § 1441, saying that the state-court action is removable only if the action is one as to which "the [U.S.] district courts . . . have original jurisdiction[.]")

A plaintiff can file suit in a federal court if either (i) there are grounds for federal-question jurisdiction (see 28 U.S.C. § 1331), or (ii) diversity jurisdiction is present (see 28 U.S.C. § 1332) (as well as if there is some other jurisdictional basis that is not relevant to this problem). Here, there are no grounds for federal-question jurisdiction because plaintiff has asserted solely a ***state-law*** breach-of-warranty claim and has not asserted any claim arising under federal law. Therefore, the suit could have been filed in federal court only if diversity jurisdiction would have been available for that warranty claim. Diversity jurisdiction requires both complete diversity of citizenship as between all plaintiffs and all defendants, plus satisfaction of the amount-in-controversy requirement. (See 28 U.S.C. § 1332(a).) Neither condition is met here. The citizenship requirement is not met because both the Plaintiff and the Defendant are citizens of State A. (The Plaintiff, who owns a home in State A, would be considered a citizen of that state based on his domicile plus his intent to remain. Defendant is incorporated in, and has its principal place of business in, State A, and therefore is considered to be a citizen of that state. See 28 U.S.C. § 1332(c); *Hertz Corp. v. Friend*, 559 U.S. 77 (2010).) Moreover, the amount-in-controversy requirement for suits based solely on diversity is met only by a claim that exceeds $75,000, and Plaintiff's claim is for less than that amount. Therefore, the federal district court could not have exercised original subject-matter jurisdiction over Plaintiff's claim, making removal improper, and requiring that the court remand the case to state court.

Second, even if diversity jurisdiction *were* present, the federal removal statute ***bars a defendant who is a citizen of the state where the action is pending from removing if diversity is the sole basis for subject-matter jurisdiction***. (See 28 U.S.C. § 1441(b)(2).) Here, Defendant is a citizen of State A, the state in which the state-court action is pending, and so Defendant is automatically barred from removing the litigation to federal court.

Finally, does the analysis change if Defendant's counterclaim arises under federal law (i.e., would qualify for "federal question jurisdiction" if it were sued on alone)? The answer is ***"no."*** Federal-question jurisdiction over a claim is available only if (i) an issue of federal law appears on the face of the well-pleaded complaint, (ii) the federal issue is actually disputed and substantial, and (iii) that issue's resolution by the federal court would not disturb the allocation of judicial business as between the federal and state courts. See *Gunn v. Minton*, 133 S. Ct. 1059 (2013). So Defendant's counterclaim would indeed fall within the federal court's federal-question jurisdiction ***if it were brought as a separate federal action***. However, the fact that federal-question jurisdiction would exist over the *counterclaim* had it been filed in an independent lawsuit is irrelevant to the removal issue — the case is removable only if the ***plaintiff's complaint*** independently meets the requirements for removal. See, e.g., *Mortgage Electronic Registration Systems, Inc. v. Malugen*, 2012 WL 1382265, *8 (M.D. Fl.

2012) ("[t]he law is well settled that federal claims raised in a counterclaim may not serve as a basis for removal jurisdiction").

Choice (A) is wrong, because it makes an incorrect assertion of law. As explained with respect to Choice (C), removal jurisdiction exists only if the district court could have exercised subject-matter jurisdiction over the suit had it been filed as an original matter in the federal, rather than the state, court. (See 28 U.S.C. § 1441.) In determining whether subject-matter jurisdiction as an original matter exists, the district court is required to look *solely at the complaint*, and not to the answer or the notice of removal. The Plaintiff's well-pleaded complaint did not raise any federal question. Furthermore, two factors prevent the requirements for diversity jurisdiction from being met (no diversity between Plaintiff and Defendant, and lack of amount-in-controversy). Thus, regardless of whether the district court could have exercised subject-matter jurisdiction over Defendant's federal-law counterclaim, jurisdiction would not exist over the suit as an original matter, and this fact means that the federal court must remand the case to the state court from which it was (improperly) removed.

Choice (B) is wrong, because it misapplies the rules for diversity jurisdiction and for removal jurisdiction. As is explained with respect to Choice (C), removability is judged by whether the main complaint (the Plaintiff's original claim) could have been brought originally in federal court. And the complaint here could not have been brought, because it is not supported by either complete diversity or federal-question jurisdiction. And even if the Plaintiff's claim could have been brought in federal court, a defendant who is a citizen of the state where the action is pending may not remove, according to 28 U.S.C. § 1441(b).

Choice (D) is wrong, because it misapplies the rule governing removal of a non-removable state-law claim and a removable federal claim. Under 28 U.S.C. §§ 1441(c)(1) and 1441(c)(2), if a civil action includes both a claim arising under federal law (a "removable federal claim") and "a claim not within the original or supplemental jurisdiction of the district court" (a "non-removable claim," usually one based on state law), then the entire matter may be removed to district court, but the district court shall *sever* the non-removable state law claims and remand them "to the State court from which the action was removed." Id. While this might appear to match the circumstances of the problem here, it doesn't. That's because Plaintiff's complaint did *not* include both a non-removable state-law claim and a removable federal claim, as required under 28 U.S.C. § 1441(c)(1)-(2). Rather, Plaintiff's complaint contained *only* a state-law claim that could not have qualified for diversity jurisdiction (because the citizenship and amount-in-controversy requirements were not met), and that was therefore not removable. (Defendant's assertion of a removable federal claim in the form of a counterclaim is irrelevant, because that claim was not part of the original civil action. As discussed at the start of this paragraph, even partial removal is allowed solely when there is at least one claim *by the plaintiff* as to which the federal courts would have had original jurisdiction.) As a result, the district court must remand the entire action.

Answer 16

The correct choice is (A), because only a defendant may remove a case to federal court. The procedures for removing an action from state to federal court are specified in a statute, 28 U.S.C. § 1441. Section 1441(a) says that except in situations where Congress provides a different rule, "any civil action brought in a State court of which the district courts of the United States have original jurisdiction, *may be removed by the defendant or the defendants,* to the district court of the United States for the district and division embracing the place where such action is pending." The key phrase for our purposes here is "removed *by the defendant*"—nothing in § 1441 gives a *plaintiff* the right to remove. Since the question tells us that it is the plaintiff (the woman) whose lawyer has purported to remove the case, removal is improper. See W,M,C&S, vol. 14B, § 3721, pp. 43-44: "a plaintiff cannot remove a state court action even when he or she could have commenced the action in a federal court[.]"

A different provision, 28 U.S.C. § 1447(c), specifies how a party who wants to undo an improper removal should go about getting the removal nullified: "A motion to **remand the case** on the basis of any defect other than lack of subject matter jurisdiction must be made **within 30 days after the filing of the notice of removal** under section 1446(a)." The facts tell us that the defendant's motion to remand is "timely," so the court should (and will) remand the case back to the state court where it was initially filed. As to whether the remand should be of the entire case (rather than just the state-law claims), a court would likely interpret §§ 1441(a) and 1447(c) as meaning that since removal by a plaintiff is always improper (even as to claims that would have been properly removable by the defendant), the entire case must (or at least should) be remanded. (See the discussion of Choice (B) for more about this issue.)

Choice (B) is wrong, because the entire removal, since done by the plaintiff, was improper, and the court therefore has no statutory authority to keep even the federal claims. As we discuss more fully in Choice (A), the federal removal statute, 28 U.S.C. § 1441, gives only defendants, not plaintiffs, the right of removal. Therefore, when (as here) the plaintiff purports to remove an entire case that consists of both state-law and federal-law claims, and the defendant timely moves for remand, the *entire case* is one over which the federal court does not have jurisdiction. Therefore, the federal court should remand *all* claims, since no act by any party ever gave the federal court jurisdiction over any of those claims.

When the examiners drafted this choice, they may have been trying to trick you into thinking of the one scenario in which the federal must remand state-law claims while keeping (and deciding) the federal-law claims; but the provision governing this scenario does not apply here. The provision is 28 U.S.C. § 1441(c), which reads as follows:

"(c) *Joinder of Federal law claims and State law claims.*

   (1)   If a civil action includes —

         (A)   a **claim arising under the Constitution, laws, or treaties of the United States** (within the meaning of section 1331 of this title [28 U.S.C. § 1331]) [i.e., a *federal-question claim*], and

         (B)   a claim **not within the original or supplemental jurisdiction of the district court** . . .,

         the **entire action may be removed** if the action would be removable without the inclusion of the claim described in subparagraph (B).

   (2)   **Upon removal** of an action described in paragraph (1), the district court shall **sever** from the action all claims described in paragraph (1)(B) and **shall remand the severed claims to the State court** from which the action was removed. Only defendants against whom a claim described in paragraph (1)(A) has been asserted are required to join in or consent to the removal under paragraph (1)."

So if the action had been properly removed (i.e., by the *defendant*), and if the state-law claim had neither qualified for diversity jurisdiction (which would have required that the woman and the employer be citizens of different states) nor been within the supplemental jurisdiction of the court (which would have required that the state and federal claims be so factually related that they were "part of the same case or controversy" as per the supplemental jurisdiction statute, 28 U.S.C. § 1367(a)), then this choice would have been correct: the federal court would be required to remand the state claims while keeping the federal claims. But § 1441(c) would almost certainly be interpreted to refer *only* to a case where the initial removal was proper;

since removal by a plaintiff is never permitted, it's highly unlikely that the court would conclude that § 1441(c) ever comes into play.

Choice (C) is wrong, because it ignores the fact that since a plaintiff cannot remove, the case was never properly removed in the first place. The federal removal statute, 28 U.S.C. § 1441, is the only general source of removal jurisdiction. And as we discuss in Choice (A), § 1441 only allows defendants, not plaintiffs, to remove. If the requirements of § 1441 are not met (and they are clearly not met here), then the federal court simply does not have jurisdiction to "retain the case," regardless of whether there is a risk that a remand would result in the case being heard by a state-court judge who is demonstrably hostile towards the plaintiff's attorney.

Choice (D) is wrong, because it ignores the fact that the case was never properly removed in the first place, since a plaintiff cannot remove. As we discuss more extensively in Choice (A), the federal removal statute simply does not allow removal by a plaintiff. And that is true even if the plaintiff's removal notice is "timely" (i.e., within the 30-day time limit imposed by § 1446(b)), and even if the case involves a federal claim.

Answer 17

The correct choice is **(B),** because Defendant's voluntary contacts with State A in connection with the contract were sufficiently great as to constitute "minimum contacts" and to render it not unfair to require Defendant to defend an action related to the contract in that State.

For the forum state to have personal jurisdiction over the defendant for purposes of a suit relating to activities occurring in the forum state, it must as a general rule be the case that (a) the defendant had "minimum contacts" with the forum state; and (b) it would not be "fundamentally unfair" to require the defendant to defend suit in the forum state. See *Burger King Corp. v. Rudzewicz,* 471 U.S. 462 (1985).

The facts of this problem are quite close to those of *Burger King,* supra, where the Supreme Court found both that the defendant had "minimum contacts" with the forum state (the plaintiff franchisor's home state) and that it would not be unfair to make him defend a franchise-agreement-related suit there. In *Burger King,* unlike here, the defendant didn't even travel to the franchisor's forum-state headquarters state to receive training (or for anything else), but his prospective partner did so. Also in *Burger King,* the defendant understood (as Defendant here understood) that much of the franchisor's contractually obligated work to support the defendant, and the regulation by the franchisor of the defendant's performance under the franchise agreement, would occur from the franchisor's forum-state headquarters. Finally, as is the case here, the franchise agreement in *Burger King* specified that the law of the forum state (the franchisor's home state) would apply.

The Supreme Court therefore held in *Burger King* that the defendant had "established a substantial and continuing relationship with [the franchisor's forum-state] headquarters, received fair notice from the contract documents and the course of dealing that he might be subject to suit in [the forum state], and . . . failed to demonstrate how jurisdiction in that forum would otherwise be fundamentally unfair[.]" Thus, the Supreme Court concluded, it did not "offend due process" for the forum state to exercise jurisdiction over him for an action on the franchise agreement.

Here, given that Defendant had the same basic forum-state contacts as the defendant did in *Burger King,* but also traveled twice to the forum state before signing the agreement, a court would almost certainly conclude that (1) Defendant had minimum contacts with State A, and (2) it would not be "fundamentally unfair" to require Defendant to defend a suit relating to the franchise agreement in State A.

It's important to note, by the way, that the suit here was on a claim that arose from the Defendant's activities ***connected with the forum state*** (i.e., from a contract whose negotiation included the trips by Defendant to the forum state, and the performance of which from plaintiff's side would be done mostly in the forum state). In other words, the suit here was based on *"specific jurisdiction,"* the label applied to suits on claims related to whatever in-forum-state activities the defendant may have had. That's why all that was required for personal jurisdiction over Defendant was minimum contact with the forum state and a lack of "unfairness" in requiring Defendant to come to the forum state to defend an action. Suppose, however, that the suit had involved a claim having nothing to do with whatever connections Defendant had with the forum state — for instance, suppose Plaintiff's claim in State A federal court was a libel action claiming that Defendant had, in Canada, published a libel about some other business owned by Plaintiff in Mexico, having nothing to do with the brake-repair business or with Defendant's franchise agreement.

In this hypothetical example, personal jurisdiction would have to have been what is called *"general jurisdiction"* (jurisdiction not relating to the defendant's forum-state-connected activities). And the Supreme Court has required **much greater voluntary contacts** between the defendant and the forum state for general jurisdiction than for specific jurisdiction; for instance, if Defendant had been a corporation, a suit based on general jurisdiction could have been brought against it only if Defendant was "found in" State A, defined as being either incorporated in State A or with its principal place of business in State A.

So when you analyze a problem requiring you to decide whether the defendant can be required to defend an action in a particular jurisdiction, first check whether the suit relates to defendant's activities connected to the forum state, so that you'll know whether to apply the easy-to-satisfy minimum-contact standard for specific jurisdiction, or instead the hard-to-satisfy "found in the forum state" standard for general jurisdiction.

Choice (A) is wrong, because when the defendant properly seeks dismissal for lack of jurisdiction and loses, the right to raise the issue on appeal is preserved. A defendant is permitted — indeed, encouraged — to assert the defense of lack of personal jurisdiction in a federal court case by making a motion on that ground before serving an answer. See Rule 12(b)(2). That's what the facts tell you that Defendant did here. Once a defendant has raised the jurisdiction objection in this way and loses, he does not forfeit or waive the right to argue on direct appeal that the district court was incorrect in denying the motion.

For clarification, though, distinguish the situation here (where the defendant is trying in a *direct* appeal to contest the trial court's denial of his lack-of-jurisdiction defense) from the quite different *"collateral attack"* scenario. In this second scenario, the defendant raises the jurisdiction defense in the first action, loses, and then either tries the case and loses, or defaults immediately after losing on the jurisdiction argument; then, we'll assume, because the defendant has no assets in the state where the initial suit took place, the plaintiff "sues on the judgment," i.e., brings a second suit to "enforce" the judgment in a place where the defendant *does* have assets, such as his home state. Now, when the defendant argues in the second suit (the one brought to enforce the earlier judgment) that the first court lacked personal jurisdiction, this is called a "collateral attack."

In the collateral-attack scenario, the defendant *does* have a fatal waiver problem; merely by having raised the jurisdiction defense in the first action and losing, the defendant will be found to have already had and used his chance to litigate the jurisdiction issue, so the second court will not permit him to re-litigate this issue by way of collateral attack. But that's not a problem in our question, since Defendant is re-raising the jurisdiction issue in his direct appeal from the judgment.

Choice (C) is wrong, because requiring Defendant to defend the case in State A on these facts would not violate traditional notions of fair play and substantial justice. This choice is partially correct, in the sense that it correctly suggests that there may be cases in which the defendant has just enough "minimum contacts" with the forum state to make it not a violation of his due process rights to force him to defend in the forum state, but in which these contacts are so attenuated, and the burden on the defendant to having to defend in the forum state so great, that the court will decide that it would "offend 'traditional notions of fair play and substantial justice'" for the court to exercise jurisdiction over him. See *Asahi Metal Indus. Co. v. Superior Court,* 480 U.S. 102 (1987), where the Court found that in the very unusual facts there (involving impleader of a foreign corporation as a third-party defendant, followed by a settlement of the main claim between the original plaintiff and the third-party plaintiff), it would be unfair for the forum-state court to require the third-party defendant to defend the case.

But this choice is incorrect in asserting that the case here is one of those unusual situations—here, Defendant's trips to the forum state, his understanding that the other party to the contract would perform extensive services from its headquarters in the forum state, and his voluntary agreement to a contract that provided that forum-state law would apply, taken together, mean that it would *not* "offend traditional notions of fair play and substantial justice" to require Defendant to defend in the forum state.

Choice (D) is wrong, because Defendant *did* voluntarily avail himself of the privilege of doing business in State A. It's true that after the signing of the contract, Defendant never took any voluntary action directed at State A, beyond dealing with some of Plaintiff's personnel based there. But that fact is not inconsistent with a conclusion that Defendant "voluntarily avail[ed] himself of the privilege of doing business" in State A. On facts very similar to the ones here, the Supreme Court in *Burger King Corp. v. Rudzewicz* (see the discussion of Choice (B) above) found that the defendant's limited contacts with the forum state—the headquarters state of the plaintiff/franchisor—were enough to constitute "purposeful availment" of the privilege of doing business relating to the forum state. (For instance, the defendant in *Burger King* knew that the services provided to him by the plaintiff under the contract would be rendered from the forum state, and he agreed that the forum state's substantive laws would govern any dispute about the contract.)

So on our facts, it's clear that Defendant would be found to have purposely availed himself of the privilege of doing business connected with State A sufficient to give him minimum contacts with that state.

Answer 18

The correct choice is **(D)** because Plaintiff consented to personal jurisdiction by filing the counterclaim. A plaintiff's *filing of a lawsuit* is treated as *consent by the plaintiff* to personal jurisdiction in the forum for any counterclaim. *Adam v. Saenger,* 303 U.S. 59, 67-68 (1938). As the Supreme Court has explained, deeming the plaintiff to have consented to personal jurisdiction in the forum in which he has elected to sue "is the price which the state may exact as the condition of opening its courts to the plaintiff" and is consistent with the requirements of the Due Process Clause. Id. Therefore, when Plaintiff chose to bring the second suit in federal district court for State C, he availed himself of the benefits of litigating in State C. By doing that, Plaintiff effectively waived any objection to personal jurisdiction over him by the courts in State C (whether state or federal courts) with respect to the counterclaim. And that waiver is effective even though Plaintiff might have successfully asserted lack of personal jurisdiction had Defendant brought a separate and independent suit against him in the state or federal courts of State C for the same wrongful-civil-proceedings claim that Defendant is now asserting via the counterclaim.

Choice (A) is wrong, because it relies on an irrelevant legal rule. A compulsory counterclaim is a claim made by any party against an opposing party that "arises out of the transaction or occurrence that is the subject matter of the opposing party's claim." FRCP 13(a)(1)(A). And where a federal court has jurisdiction of an "anchor" claim by the plaintiff against the defendant, the court will also have "supplemental jurisdiction" over closely-related claims; a compulsory counterclaim (since by hypothesis it arises out of the same transaction or occurrence as the main claim) will *always* be sufficiently closely related to the main claim as to fall within the court's supplemental jurisdiction. But supplemental jurisdiction is relevant only as a means of curing a problem with *subject-matter jurisdiction* (e.g., lack of complete diversity in a case founded solely on diversity, or failure to meet the amount-in-controversy requirement). Supplemental jurisdiction **cannot cure a lack of personal jurisdiction over the defendant to the counterclaim**. Since this choice says that the presence of a compulsory counterclaim can cure what would otherwise be a lack of personal jurisdiction over the Plaintiff, the choice is incorrect as a matter of law — the cure comes not from the fact that a compulsory counterclaim is involved, but from the fact that Plaintiff, by suing, is deemed to consent to the court's personal jurisdiction over him for *any* counterclaim, compulsory or permissive (as discussed in the treatment of Choice (D) above.)

Choice (B) is wrong, because it relies on an irrelevant legal rule. A permissive counterclaim is defined as a counterclaim that does not arise out of the same transaction or occurrence as the opposing party's claim. See FRCP 13(b). Unlike a compulsory counterclaim, *a permissive counterclaim requires an independent basis of subject-matter jurisdiction.* And most (though not all) federal courts have held that the doctrine of supplemental jurisdiction, now codified in 28 U.S.C. § 1367, doesn't change this rule. See W&K (7th Ed.), § 79, p. 573. But the entire issue of whether the counterclaim here is permissive or compulsory is irrelevant to whether there is *personal* jurisdiction over the defendant to the counterclaim (i.e., over the original plaintiff) — even if the counterclaim here were compulsory, that fact would have no bearing on the existence of personal jurisdiction. (See the discussion of Choice (A) above.) Therefore, since this choice says that the presence of a permissive counterclaim is what creates — or at least fails to cure — a lack of personal jurisdiction over the Plaintiff, the choice is incorrect. (The cure to the lack of personal jurisdiction comes from the fact that Plaintiff, by suing, is deemed to consent to the court's personal jurisdiction over him for *any* counterclaim, as discussed in the treatment of Choice (D) above.)

Choice (C) is wrong, because it misstates the procedure for asserting a counterclaim. A party asserts a counterclaim either by **pleading the counterclaim in an answer** or by **raising it as a reply to a prior-asserted counterclaim**. In either scenario, no summons is required. See *Schnabel v. Lui*, 302 F.3d 1023, 1036 (9th Cir. 2002) ("Because the Third Amended Complaint stated claims in the nature of compulsory counterclaims, no service of summons was necessary to effect personal jurisdiction.").

Answer 19

The correct choice is **(D)**, because it correctly states and applies the standard for determining when an out-of-the-forum-state corporation has sufficient contacts with the forum state to support general, rather than merely specific, jurisdiction.

To solve this problem — and indeed to solve almost any question that raises the issue "Can the forum state constitutionally exercise personal jurisdiction of an out-of-state corporation?" — you will at the outset have to decide whether (1) *"specific"* jurisdiction will suffice for the suit in question; or (2) instead, *"general"* jurisdiction will be needed. *Specific* jurisdiction refers to the jurisdiction needed to hear a suit that **arises out of the defendant corporation's activities in the forum state**. *General* jurisdiction refers to the jurisdiction needed to hear a suit that **does not** arise out of the defendant corporation's in-forum-state activities; the ties between the out-of-state corporation and the forum state must be **much greater** for general jurisdiction than for specific jurisdiction.

Here, notice that the dismissal motion concerns personal jurisdiction over the subsidiary, not the parent, corporation. And yet, the subsidiary has very few contacts with State A: you're told that (1) the subsidiary "conducts no business and has no employees or bank accounts in State A"; and (2) what caused the accident (in Europe) was a tire made by the subsidiary in Europe (and thus not in State A). Indeed, the *only* connection the subsidiary has with State A is that when the subsidiary makes (in Europe) its tires for the European market, 2% of those tires end up being distributed in State A, with the distribution carried out by the parent, not the subsidiary. Since the suit concerns an accident that occurred in Europe—not in State A—the only way the State A courts can constitutionally exercise jurisdiction over the subsidiary is if the subsidiary's contacts with State A are **sufficiently great as to qualify for general (not just specific) jurisdiction.**

How great must the subsidiary's contacts with State A be to qualify for general jurisdiction? The answer given by the Supreme Court in a 2011 case (whose facts are almost the same as the facts of this question) is that the out-of-state corporation must have **"continuous and systematic general business contacts"** with the forum state. *Goodyear Dunlop Tires Operations, S.A. v. Brown*, 564 U.S. 915 (2011). (A later case, *Daimler AG v. Bauman*, 134 S. Ct. 746 (2014), says that except in extraordinary cases, this "continuous and systematic contacts" test will only be satisfied if the corporation is either **incorporated** in the forum state or **has its principal place of business** in the forum state.) Choice (D) recites this standard; and since the indirect distribution of 2% of the subsidiary's output of tires into State A does not come even close to meeting the "continuous and systematic contacts" standard, the choice correctly reflects that the subsidiary will win by virtue of not having the requisite level of contacts with State A.

Choice (A) is wrong, because the fact that 2% of the subsidiary's tires entered State A through the stream of commerce does not suffice for *general* jurisdiction, even though it probably would suffice for *specific* jurisdiction. As we discuss in connection with Choice (D), for the State A courts to have personal jurisdiction over the subsidiary for this accident claim, the jurisdiction would have to be *general* rather than specific, since the suit does not arise out of any in-forum-state activities by the subsidiary. Consequently, the subsidiary's motion should be granted unless the subsidiary's contacts with State A are continuous, systematic and substantial. The subsidiary's contacts fall far short of this standard.

Even if the *subsidiary itself* had knowingly and directly shipped 2% of its tires into State A, it's very doubtful that the continuous / systematic standard would be met (since a post-*Goodyear* case, *Daimler AG v. Bauman*, says that normally that standard will be med only if the corporate defendant is incorporated in the forum state or has its principal place of business there). But in reality, we have the further fact that it was the *parent*, not the subsidiary, that carried out the distribution of 2% of the subsidiary's tires into State A; the mere fact that the subsidiary stood by while the parent caused 2% of the tires to enter State A through the stream of commerce would certainly not be enough of a volitional act by the subsidiary to satisfy the continuous-and-systematic standard.

Choice (B) is wrong, because the issue that matters is the type of personal jurisdiction that State A can establish over the *subsidiary*, and even if the state had general jurisdiction over the parent (which it probably doesn't), that fact would be irrelevant to the issue of jurisdiction over the subsidiary. The facts say that the parent is a "State B corporation." This phrasing probably means that the parent is incorporated in State B, and has its principal place of business there (or at least not in State A). As we discuss in Choice (D), under *Daimler AG v. Bauman* a corporation that is neither incorporated in the forum state nor has its principal place of business there will not, except in extraordinary cases, fall within the general jurisdiction of the forum state. So the premise of this choice—that State A has general jurisdiction over the parent—is almost certainly false.

But even if State A *does* have general jurisdiction over the parent, that fact would be irrelevant to whether that state has the required general jurisdiction over the *subsidiary*—there is no legal principle under which the personal-jurisdiction status of a parent will be passed through to a subsidiary, assuming that standard corporate formalities are observed (e.g., the two entities maintain separate records, bank accounts, etc.) Since the subsidiary is far from having the continuous-and-systematic contacts with State A that would be required for the state to have general jurisdiction over it, this choice cannot be correct.

Choice (C) is wrong, because even though the accident did not occur in the United States, State A would still be able to exercise jurisdiction over the subsidiary if the subsidiary had the continuous-and-systematic contacts with State A required for personal jurisdiction. First, in deciding the relevance of where the accident occurred, the only distinction that matters is between an accident occurring in State A and one occurring outside of state A; there is no relevant difference between an accident occurring in the U.S. (but not in State A) and an accident occurring in a foreign nation. Next, the fact that the accident did not occur in State A is not necessarily fatal to State A's ability to exercise personal jurisdiction over the subsidiary; but this fact *does* trigger a requirement that the subsidiary's contacts with State A be systematic and continuous, so as to qualify for general jurisdiction. And, as is explained in Choice (D), the subsidiary's contacts with State A fall far short of meeting this standard. So this choice states the right outcome, but gives an incorrect reason for that outcome.

Answer 20

The correct choice is **(C),** because the CEO's in-state presence at the time of service sufficed for personal jurisdiction over him, but the insurer's contacts with the state were not sufficient to allow for "general jurisdiction" over it. Let's take the two suits one at a time.

Suit against the insurer: The first thing to notice is that the suit against the insurer involves a particular policy sold by it, and that all activities connected with that sale occurred in State A, during the time the surgeon/insured was a State A resident. Furthermore, in the years since the policy has been in force, no activities by the insurer in connection with the policy have occurred in State B, beyond the fact that the insurer has corresponded with the surgeon at his State B address and has received premiums sent by him from that address. Therefore, the suit brought by the surgeon against the insurer in State B—since the suit does not arise out of the insurer's State B activities or contacts—will have to be based on *"general"* jurisdiction rather than "specific" jurisdiction.

When a suit is brought against an out-of-state corporation and is based on general jurisdiction, it's been clear since a 2011 Supreme Court decision that the corporation must have contacts with the forum state that are so " 'continuous and systematic' as to render [the corporation and its affiliates] *essentially at home* in the forum State." *Goodyear Dunlop Tires Operations, S.A. v. Brown*, 131 S. Ct. 2846 (2011). Then, in the later case of *Daimler AG v. Bauman*, 134 S. Ct. 746 (2014), the Court said that in determining whether a corporation is "essentially at home" in the forum state, the corporation must (except in an "exceptional case") either (1) have its *principal place of business* in the forum state or (2) be *incorporated* in that state. Here, the insurer is neither incorporated in State B nor has its principal place of business there. And there is nothing in the case that would dictate treating any connection between the insurer and State B as sufficiently "extraordinary" to merit deviating from this rule requiring either in-forum-state incorporation or in-forum-state principal place of business. So under *Goodyear* and *Daimler*, it would violate the insurer's federal due process rights to be required to defend in State B a suit that has no real connection with that state beyond the fact that the plaintiff now lives there (i.e., a suit based on general jurisdiction). The State B judge will therefore dismiss the suit for lack of personal jurisdiction.

Divorce suit: Now, let's turn to the divorce suit against the CEO. Ever since *Pennoyer v. Neff*, 95 U.S. 714 (1877), the Supreme Court has recognized that if an individual who doesn't reside in the forum state voluntarily enters the state and is ***served with process there***, the state may exercise personal jurisdiction over him without violating his due process rights, even if the defendant has absolutely no other contacts with the forum state. And more recently, in *Burnham v. Superior Court*, 495 U.S. 604 (1990), the Supreme Court decided a case involving precisely the issue here: Because D had voluntarily visited the forum state and been served with process in a divorce suit brought there by his estranged wife, the forum state had personal jurisdiction over him regardless of whether he had any connection whatsoever with the forum state beyond this one visit. So in light of *Burnham*, there is no due process impediment to the State B court's exercising personal jurisdiction over the CEO for purposes of issuing a divorce decree (or, indeed, for any other purpose that would require the court to exercise personal jurisdiction over him).

Choices (A), (B), and (D) are not the best responses, because each of them reaches the wrong conclusion as to at least one of the two motions.

Answer 21

The correct choice is **(C)**, because in-state residence is a recognized basis for the exercise of general jurisdiction, and its use is constitutional under the federal Due Process Clause. The Supreme Court has long held that it does not violate due process for a state to exercise personal jurisdiction over any cause of action against a ***resident of that state***, whether or not the claim is related to the defendant's in-state activities. (That is, "general jurisdiction"—jurisdiction for all claims, whether related to in-state activities or not—is allowed against residents of the forum state.) See *Goodyear Dunlop Tires Operations, SA v. Brown*, 131 S. Ct. 2846 (2011). It is true that personal jurisdiction may only be exercised by a state court if a state statute permits such jurisdiction in the type of situation in question. But you're told that State B's jurisdiction statute does so (since it extends the state's personal jurisdiction as far as the U.S. Constitution allows). Indeed, this statute is typical of many state jurisdictional statutes.

Choice (A) is wrong, because it is based on a rule of law about the exercise of personal jurisdiction that is legally incorrect. A state court can exercise "specific jurisdiction"—that is, jurisdiction over a plaintiff's claim that arises out of or relates to defendant's in-state contacts—even if the defendant is *not* a resident of the forum state. However, *the converse is not true*; that is, the fact that the suit does *not* relate to any in-forum-state activities does not automatically mean that jurisdiction is improper. Rather, a court can always exercise "general jurisdiction" (i.e., "all-purpose" jurisdiction over suits that do not involve in-state activities) in some circumstances. And one of those circumstances where general jurisdiction is always allowed is where the defendant is ***domiciled in the forum state***, as is the situation here. See *Goodyear Dunlop Tires Operations, SA v. Brown*, 131 S. Ct. 2846 (2011).

Choice (B) is wrong, because it contains an incorrect statement of law. It's true that only a court in the state in which property is located can exercise *"in rem"* jurisdiction regarding that property. But here Plaintiff is seeking money damages for breach of contract, so the court is being asked to act *"in personam,"* not *"in rem."* (Only a suit to determine the property's *status*, such as who properly holds title, would be *"in rem."*) And the court will have *in personam* jurisdiction—assuming defendant does not consent to jurisdiction or waive any defect—only if the exercise of jurisdiction satisfies the tests of ***minimum contacts and reasonableness*** articulated in such decisions as *World-Wide Volkswagen v. Woodson*, 444 U.S. 286 (1980). It's true that the location of the property here would be *one* of the factors to be considered on the issue of reasonableness. But the fact that the property is located outside the forum state would ***not by itself automatically make exercise of jurisdiction unreasonable***, as this choice suggests it would. (Indeed, the fact that Defendant *resides* in the forum state would automatically have the opposite effect, i.e., suffice to make the exercise of jurisdiction automatically *reasonable*.)

Choice (D) is wrong, because diversity of citizenship is an irrelevant concept on these facts. Diversity of citizenship is a condition of *subject-matter jurisdiction* for actions brought in *federal* court, as authorized by 28 U.S.C. § 1332. So the existence (or non-existence) of diversity of citizenship is irrelevant here for two reasons: (1) the concept never applies to a *state* court suit; and (2) even in a federal court, diversity jurisdiction would not be relevant to a motion to dismiss based on lack of "personal jurisdiction." See FRCP 12(b)(2). (For diversity to be relevant, the plaintiff's complaint would have to be based solely upon diversity — not the existence of a federal question — and the motion would have to be one asserting lack of "subject-matter jurisdiction," not lack of "personal jurisdiction.")

Answer 22

The correct choice is **(A),** because it explains why Plaintiff has not met the requirements for use of federal *quasi in rem* jurisdiction. FRCP 4(n) allows the use of *quasi in rem* jurisdiction in a federal lawsuit, but only in special circumstances where personal jurisdiction over the defendant cannot readily be obtained in the district where the plaintiff plans to bring the action. Rule 4(n)(2) says that "On a *showing that personal jurisdiction over a defendant cannot be obtained in the district where the action is brought by reasonable efforts to serve a summons* under this rule, the court may assert jurisdiction over the defendant's *assets found in the district*." (The reference to "this rule" refers to the entirety of FRCP 4, which includes 4(e) and 4(k)(1); those two sub-sections, when taken together, would allow service in the U.S. outside of State A on any defendant if State A's long-arm would allow the exercise of personal jurisdiction.)

So if Plaintiff had been able to "show[] that personal jurisdiction over [Defendant] cannot be obtained in [N.D. State A] by reasonable efforts to serve a summons under [FRCP 4]," Plaintiff would indeed have been entitled to assert *quasi in rem* jurisdiction based on attachment of "defendant's assets found in the district" (the storage facility). But the facts, by citing Defendant's Internet statement that its personnel often visit State A to solicit business, indicate that Defendant has the "minimum contacts" with State A that would suffice for the state to exercise personal jurisdiction over Defendant. (And Statute 1 is a long-arm that would suffice to let State A exercise that jurisdiction.) In other words, it is clearly *not* the case that "personal jurisdiction over [Defendant] cannot be obtained in [N.D. State A] by reasonable efforts to serve a summons," and indeed Plaintiff has not even tried to make the showing that it is the case. So FRCP 4(n)(2) doesn't apply, and there is no other provision allowing *quasi in rem* jurisdiction in this type of case either. (If there *were* a federal statute that authorized *quasi in rem* jurisdiction for the type of case in question, FRCP 4(n)(1) would allow that statute to serve as the basis for *quasi in rem* jurisdiction; but the facts tell you that there is no such federal statute.)

Choice (B) is wrong, because compliance with Statute 2 is not sufficient to establish a basis for the federal court's exercise of *quasi in rem* jurisdiction.

As explained in Choice (A), Plaintiff must show that personal jurisdiction cannot be obtained over Defendant "in the district where the action is brought by reasonable efforts to serve a summons." FRCP 4(n)(2). And Plaintiff has not even tried to make this showing, nor could he do so successfully, given Defendant's more-than-minimum contacts with State A.

Choice (C) is wrong, because it misstates the rules governing when a federal court can exercise *quasi in rem* jurisdiction. As explained in Choice (A), a federal court *is* permitted to exercise *quasi in rem* jurisdiction over property located in the district upon a showing that due process is satisfied and that the requirements of FRCP 4(n)—mainly the unavailability of *in personam* jurisdiction—are satisfied. This choice, by asserting that no federal statute or rule *ever* authorizes *quasi in rem* jurisdiction in federal lawsuits, states a rule that is incorrectly broad (even though the choice reaches the correct conclusion).

Choice (D) is wrong, because it misstates the constitutional principles governing the exercise of *quasi in rem* jurisdiction. An action *quasi in rem* seeks to impose a monetary judgment on the defendant. Property is attached as a basis for the court's power and as a means to secure any eventual judgment that the plaintiff obtains. One use of *quasi in rem* jurisdiction is to adjudicate the rights of ownership of particular persons to the attached property. The other use is to obtain a basis for jurisdiction. In the latter use, the property that is attached is **unrelated to the subject matter** of the lawsuit. Here, Plaintiff is using *quasi in rem* jurisdiction for that latter purpose, to secure jurisdiction. So the fact that the storage facility is unrelated to his contract and other claims against Defendant does not matter. (Notice, by the way, that if Defendant does not make a general appearance in the suit, the very nature of *quasi in rem* jurisdiction means that Defendant's exposure to liability will be capped at the value of the property that is attached—in this case, $95,000.)

Answer 23

The correct choice is **(A),** because nationwide service of process was permissible in this situation. **FRCP 4(k)(1)** lists several situations in which serving a summons "establishes personal jurisdiction over a defendant" for a federal-court suit. Rule 4(k)(1)(C) covers one of these situations by saying that service of the summons will establish personal jurisdiction "when **authorized by a federal statute**." The purpose of FRCP 4(k)(1)(C) is to allow Congress to add special rules of service, and special rules for ascertaining whether the federal court has personal jurisdiction over the defendant, for particular statutes. This allows a defendant to be served and subject to the federal court's personal jurisdiction without regard to whether the defendant has minimum contacts with the state where the federal court sits; so Congress can even provide for **"nationwide service of process"** for a particular category of federal suits. That's what Congress has done here in Section 2 of the IFCA—Congress has said that even if the defendant has no connection with the state where the federal court hearing the IFCA claim is located (in this case, State A), personal service on the defendant that occurs anywhere within the United States will suffice to establish personal jurisdiction.

Keep in mind that even when Congress uses its power to authorize nationwide service for a particular type of federal claim, the exercise of that power in the case at hand must still **comport with constitutional due process**. See, e.g., *Hogue v. Milodon Eng'g, Inc.*, 736 F.2d 989, 991 (4th Cir. 1984) ("Where . . . Congress has authorized nationwide service of process . . . so long as the assertion of jurisdiction over the defendant is **compatible with due process**, the service of process is sufficient to establish the jurisdiction of the federal court over the person of the defendant."). Notice that the final clause of Choice (A) correctly refers to this requirement. But is this choice also correct in asserting that the due process requirement is satisfied on these facts? Consider these points: (1) Congress has the express power under the Constitution's Commerce Clause to regulate interstate transactions; (2) Congress has a strong interest in providing a local forum for anyone who is harmed by the sort of interstate Internet-based fraud that the IFCA is directed against (rather than, say, requiring the person harmed to sue in the fraudster's home state); and (3) as Defendant knew when it took Plaintiff's order, the order by the Plaintiff originated from Plaintiff's State A office. Therefore, it does not seem especially unfair to Defendant to require it to defend in State A a suit arising out of an order that as Defendant knew originated in State A. In any event, it's unlikely that a court would hold that any unfairness is great enough to constitute a violation of Defendant's due process rights. And that's true even though Defendant shipped the computer to a non-forum state (State B).

Choice (B) is wrong, because it incorrectly states applicable law. It is *not* true that in all federal-question suits, service may be made anywhere in the U.S. where the defendant may be found. Rather, on our present facts, nationwide service is permissible *only* because Congress took the trouble to specify for ICFA suits in particular that service may be made nationwide. If Congress had merely drafted the ICFA to create a federal civil cause of action, and had not said anything about where suit on such a claim could be brought, nationwide service—as conditionally allowed by FRCP 4(1)(k)(C)—would *not* apply. (Service might still be valid under some *other* provision of the federal rules, but this choice specifically, and incorrectly, relies on the availability of nationwide service.)

Choice (C) is wrong, because the rule that it recites does not apply to these facts. It's true that a federal court will exercise personal jurisdiction where service and personal jurisdiction would be allowed by the long-arm *of the state where the federal court sits*. See FRCP 4(k)(1)(A), so stating. But Choice (C) is a trick; the state whose long-arm is quoted is State B (and the computer was indeed shipped into State B), but the state where the federal court is sitting is *State A*, not State B, so it's State A's long-arm, assuming one existed, that would apply. (If the suit were pending in State B federal court, this choice would be correct—Rule 4(k)(1)(A) allows the plaintiff to rely on the local state long-arm even if the suit is based on a federal question rather than on diversity.)

Choice (D) is wrong, because it relies on an incorrect legal premise. It's true that in a case based solely on *diversity*, the defendant's lack of minimum contacts with the state where the federal court is based might well prevent the federal court from hearing the case, because it may well be a due process violation to force the defendant to defend a state-law-based action if it has no minimum contacts with the state where the federal court sits. (It's possible that Congress could constitutionally authorize the exercise of personal jurisdiction by a federal court sitting in diversity even in this circumstance of no-contacts-with-the-forum-state, but that issue has never been decided by the Supreme Court. In any event, it's clear that as a matter of *practice*, federal courts won't hear diversity actions where the long-arm of the state where the federal court sits wouldn't allow a state-court suit on analogous facts.) But the Supreme Court has never held that minimum contacts with the state where the federal court sits are necessary if the suit is based in part on *a federally-created right of action* (i.e., the suit is a "federal question suit"). And, in fact, in those instances where Congress has authorized *nationwide service of process* for a particular type of federally-created claim (as it not infrequently does), it's *often* the case that the defendant does not have minimum contacts with the state where the federal court is hearing the case. Since Choice (D) says that the Defendant's lack of minimum contacts with State A makes it an automatic due process violation for the State A federal court to hear this federal-question case, it's wrong as a matter of law.

Answer 24

The correct choice is **(A)**, because Rule 4 allows use of any method of service that would be valid in a state-court suit in the state where the federal court sits. Keep in mind that we need a method of service that will work both for an individual (the athletic director, or "AD") and a corporation (the university). As to the *individual*, FRCP 4(e)(1) allows service by a method that would suffice under the law of the state where the federal court is located. That section says that, as a general rule:

> "[A]n individual . . . may be served in a judicial district of the United States by:
>
> (1) *following state law for serving a summons* in an action brought in *courts of general jurisdiction in the state where the district court is located*[.]"

Since the action is pending in State B federal court, Rule 4(e)(1) means that the AD may be served by any means that would be adequate for a State B civil suit.

As to the *corporation*, we have to combine two parts of Rule 4 to see how any method that would be allowed by State B's civil procedure rules would suffice. First, Rule 4(h) says that as a general matter:

"[A] domestic or foreign *corporation* . . . must be served:

(1) in a judicial district of the United States [as opposed to service in a foreign country]:

(A) in the manner *prescribed by Rule 4(e)(1) for serving an individual* or

(B) [provision omitted.]"

Second, as we've just seen in the case of service on the AD, Rule 4(e)(1) says that any method of service that would be valid under the law of the state where the district court sits will be valid. So putting 4(h)(1)(A) and 4(e)(1) together, service on the university (a corporation, even though it's a non-profit corporation) will be valid if done in a way that would be valid for serving an individual under State B's rules for serving individuals.

Therefore, Choice (A)'s compact reference to "service as required by State B's rules" accurately covers both the service-on-an-individual and service-on-a-corporation situations presented by the question.

Choice (B) is wrong because a "secretary" is not an agent authorized by law to receive process for either an individual or a corporation. This choice fails to work for either an individual (the AD) or a corporation (the university). As to an individual, assuming the authorized-by-state-law method (see Choice (A)) is not being used, Rule 4(e)(2) gives these three alternatives:

"(A) delivering a copy of the summons and of the complaint *to the individual personally*;

(B) leaving a copy of each at the *individual's dwelling or usual place of abode* with someone of *suitable age and discretion who resides there*; or

(C) delivering a copy of each to an *agent authorized by appointment or by law* to receive service of process."

Leaving the papers with the AD's secretary at the AD's office doesn't match up with any of these three options because: (A) requires delivery to the "individual personally," not to someone who might act on the individual's behalf; (B) requires delivery to the individual's "dwelling," not office (assuming the dwelling and the office are not the same, as is clearly the case for a university athletic director); and (C) requires delivery to an agent "authorized by appointment or by law to receive service of process," and there is no reason to believe that a secretary in the AD's office has been authorized either by appointment (i.e., by act of the AD) or by law (i.e., by some legal principle) to act as the AD's agent for this purpose.

As to service on a corporation (the university), then, again assuming that the authorized-by-state-law method (see Choice (A)) is not being used, and assuming that the service is being made within the U.S., Rule 4(h) gives only one method, specified in 4(h)(1)(B):

"by delivering a copy of the summons and of the complaint to an *officer*, a managing *or* general *agent,* or any other *agent authorized by appointment or by law* to receive service of process[.]"

A secretary in the office of a corporation's president is clearly not an "officer" of the corporation absent some special fact saying so. And the secretary is not a "managing or general agent" of the corporation, again in the absence of some special fact saying so. Finally, as with the AD's secretary, there is no reason to believe that a university president's secretary has been authorized either by appointment (i.e., by act of the university) or law (i.e., by some legal principle) to act as the university's agent for this special purpose. So Choice (B) fails as to both the AD and the university.

Choice (C) is wrong, because service by email is never an authorized method under the FRCP. Again, we'll assume that we are not going to rely on the service-according-to-state-law method (see Choice (A)); therefore, even though it's possible that State B's civil procedure rules allow email service, that possibility is not enough to make Choice (C) correct, since that choice, by failing to mention state law, has to work regardless of what state law says. So for service on the AD (an individual), we're left with Rule 4(e)(2)'s three methods (quoted in the discussion of Choice (B) above). None of these three methods mentions email as a possibility. Similarly, for the University (a corporation), the single method specified in Rule 4(h)(1)(B) (quoted in the discussion of Choice (B)), calling for personal delivery on an officer or a certain type of agent, does not mention email.

Choice (D) is wrong, because service may not be made by a party. The Federal Rules allow a very wide variety of persons to serve a summons and complaint. But the *only* class of persons who are *not* permitted to make service (apart from persons under the age of 18), are *parties*. See Rule 4(e)(2): "Any person who is at least 18 years old and *not a party* may serve a summons and complaint."

Answer 25

The correct choice is **(B)**, because where the defendant being served is an *individual*, the papers may not be left at the person's usual place of business. This question is mildly tricky because it involves service of process on an individual who is in business, so in a sense it falls half-way between the situation of service on an individual arising out of a non-business matter (e.g., an auto accident) and the situation of service on a corporation arising out of a business matter. The key insight is to know that when an *individual* is being served, even if the individual *operates a business*, he or she cannot be served by leaving the papers with a *third person* found at the individual's usual place of business (at least assuming that there is no special provision of state law that allows this).

Let's review the FRCP provisions governing service on an individual found within the United States. These provisions are given in Rule 4(e). Since we can't conclude that a particular form of service was invalid unless we look at *all* the allowable methods, we have to look at the full text of 4(e):

> "(e) Unless federal law provides otherwise, an *individual*—other than a minor, an incompetent person, or a person whose waiver has been filed—may be served in a judicial district of the United States by:
>
> (1) following state law for serving a summons in an action brought in courts of general jurisdiction in the state where the district court is located or where service is made; or
>
> (2) doing any of the following:
>
> > (A) delivering a copy of the summons and of the complaint *to the individual personally*;
> >
> > (B) *leaving a copy* of each at the individual's *dwelling or usual place of abode* with *someone of suitable age and discretion who resides there*; or
> >
> > (C) delivering a copy of each to an *agent* authorized by appointment or by law to receive service of process."

So, putting aside for the moment the possibility that state law may supply an additional method, if the plaintiff is relying only on the federal methods specified in Rule 4(e)(2), then other than handing the papers to the "individual personally" (4(e)(2)(A)) or to an authorized "agent" (4(e)(2)(C)), the only way service can be made by leaving the papers with someone other than the individual being served is by leaving them at the individual's ***dwelling or usual place of abode*** with ***someone of suitable age and discretion who resides there.*** In other words, there's no way to make service by showing up at the individual's usual ***place of business*** and leaving the papers with a co-worker or employee of the individual defendant. So on our facts, even if the accountant still worked at the 123 Main Street address, and even if the receptionist who took the papers was the accountant's employee, the service would *still* have been improper under Rule 4(e)(2).

Notice that 4(e)(2)(C) allows service on an individual without regard to the location (and thus possibly allows service at the person's place of business) if the papers are left with "an ***agent*** authorized by ***appointment or by law*** to receive service of process." But this provision is interpreted pretty narrowly; unless the defendant has, according to common-law "agency" principles, conferred on the third person the power to accept service (and merely conferring the general power to "act as my assistant when I'm not around" would *not* be sufficient), a co-worker or employee of the individual would not count as an agent. Here, where the defendant doesn't even work at those premises any more, and there's nothing to suggest that he has authorized the receptionist to act on his behalf to receive papers, the receptionist would certainly not be an "agent authorized by appointment or by law to receive service of process."

There's one last possibility that you have to rule out before you can be confident that the service method here was improper. Under Rule 4(e)(1), if either State A (the "state where the district court [in which the suit is pending] is located") or State B (the state "where service is made") had passed a statute allowing service on an individual by leaving the papers with a third person at the individual's place of business, that state provision would have made the service here valid. But the facts tell you that States A and B have no method-of-service provisions beyond those provided directly by the FRCP (i.e., those listed in 4(e)(2)), so this escape-hatch allowing the use of state-law service methods is not available to save the method used here.

Choice (A) is wrong, because it reaches the right result but on incorrect legal reasoning. This choice suggests that the only reason service was invalid was that the accountant was no longer using 123 Main St. as his usual place of business at the time the service occurred. But as the analysis of Choice (B) above demonstrates, federal law does not allow service on an individual by leaving papers with a third person at the individual's place of business (or, indeed, any location other than the individual's "dwelling or usual place of abode"), even if that place of business is current. So even if the accountant customarily showed up at 123 Main St. as his place of business every day, service would still have been improper, making this choice a much less good explanation of the result than Choice (B).

Choice (C) is wrong, both because it reaches the incorrect result and because it does so by an incorrect legal analysis. As the analysis of Choice (B) above demonstrates, federal law does not allow service on an individual by leaving papers with a third person at the individual's place of business. So even if the 123 Main St. address were the accountant's actual place of business (rather than merely being a place he falsely identified on his website as being his place of business), the service here would still have been improper.

Choice (D) is wrong, because it is based on an incorrect legal rule about when a waiver of the right to object to improper service occurs. It's certainly true that under federal law, a defendant can easily be found to have waived, by mere inaction, his right to object to improper service. The relevant provisions are found in FRCP 12. Rule 12(b)(5) effectively gives a defendant a choice of two ways of raising the defense of "insufficient service of process": (1) by raising the defense in that defendant's "responsive pleading" (which is of course the answer) or (2) by motion. And Rule 12(h)(1) says that the defenses listed in Rule 12(b)(2)-(5) (which as just noted include the 12(b)(5) "insufficient service of process" defense) are waived if made in neither a pre-answer Rule 12 motion nor in the answer itself. But the facts here tell you that after receiving the papers from the receptionist, the accountant "immediately" filed an answer that included the insufficient-service defense. "Immediately" implies that the accountant did not file a Rule 12(b) motion prior to the answer (which, if he had so filed without raising the insufficient-service defense as part of the motion, *would* have been an automatic waiver), so by raising the defense in his answer the accountant properly and timely asserted it.

In other words, this choice, by suggesting that the insufficient-service defense must be made by a pre-answer motion rather than in the answer itself, is making an incorrect statement of law. (But keep in mind that if the accountant had made a Rule 12(b) motion for any other reason—such as, say, a 12(b)(6) motion for failure to state a claim on which relief can be granted—his failure to assert the insufficient-service objection as part of that 12(b) motion *would* have resulted under Rule 12(h)(1)(A) in a waiver of the objection, so that it could no longer later be asserted as part of even a timely-filed answer.)

Answer 26

The correct choice is **(B)**, because the default judgment was void for invalid service, and the court must therefore set aside the judgment. Solving this problem requires multiple steps. Probably the best way is to start at the "back end," by first looking at whether there is a procedural mechanism whereby the court can be induced to consider setting aside the judgment. Where a judgment has become final (as it is here), the mechanism for relief is given in FRCP 60(b). 60(b) says that "On motion and just terms, the court *may relieve a party* or its legal representative *from a final judgment*, order, or proceeding for the following reasons," and then lists six categories of reasons, of which the fourth is because "the judgment is void." So if the musician can show that the judgment is "void," he will be entitled to have it set aside under Rule 60(b).

All federal courts agree that if a court enters an *in personam* judgment against the defendant without the court's having personal jurisdiction over the defendant, the judgment is void. See, e.g., *Combs v. Nick Garin Trucking*, 825 F.2d 437, 442 (D.C. Cir. 1987) ("Of course, an *in personam* judgment entered without personal jurisdiction over a defendant is void as to that defendant."). All courts also agree that where the requirements for effective service of process on a defendant have not been met (and have not been waived by the defendant), the court does not gain personal jurisdiction over that defendant. See id. at 442: "[S]ince service of process is the means by which a court asserts jurisdiction to adjudicate the rights of a party, it is uniformly held that a judgment is void where the requirements for effective service have not been satisfied." So the musician will be entitled to have the default judgment set aside as void if he can show that service of process on him was not effective (assuming he is not found to have waived service).

The valid procedures for making service of a summons and complaint on an ***individual*** within the United States are forth in FRCP 4(e), which reads as follows:

"(e) Unless federal law provides otherwise, an ***individual***—other than a minor, an incompetent person, or a person whose waiver has been filed—may be served in a judicial district of the United States by:

(1) ***following state law for serving a summons*** in an action brought in courts of general jurisdiction in the state where the district court is located or where service is made; or

(2) doing *any of the following*:

    (A) *delivering* a copy of the *summons and of the complaint* to the *individual personally*;

    (B) *leaving a copy of each at the individual's dwelling or usual place of abode with someone of suitable age and discretion who resides there*; or

    (C) delivering a copy of each to an agent authorized by appointment or by law to receive service of process."

Here, the facts tell you that the two states whose law might apply (State A, where the service is being attempted, or State B, where the federal court hearing the suit is located) do not have laws allowing any possibly relevant method of service, such as service by mail. Therefore, Rule 4(e)(1)'s grant of the right to make service by "following state law for serving a summons" does not apply here. Consequently, you know that if service here was valid, it would have to have been done pursuant to Rule 4(e))(2), which lists three methods (in 2(A), (B), and (C) respectively, quoted above) that are always available based on "federal law," regardless of whether they are allowed under state law.

But all three of these methods (service on the individual defendant personally, service by leaving a copy at the defendant's dwelling with an adult co-resident, and service by delivery to an agent) require "in person" delivery. That is, although Rule 4(e)(2) doesn't expressly say that the delivery must be "in person" as opposed to, say, by registered mail, courts have universally interpreted the Rule to require in-person service. So the attempted service here, in which the mails were used, does not meet the requirements for any of the three branches of Rule 4(e)(2).

Now, it so happens that the federal courts recognize — and, indeed, encourage — litigants to use an alternative non-physical-service notification method, namely the "request for waiver of service" method authorized by Rule 4(d), in which a copy of the summons and complaint can be sent by "first-class mail or other reliable means," together with a request that the defendant waive personal service. But even when a plaintiff attempts to use the request-for-waiver method, the attempt does not eliminate the need for personal service unless the defendant *signs and returns the waiver form* (and the plaintiff files the signed form with the court).

Here, it's clear that even if the envelope that was sent to the musician met the standards for a Rule 4(d) request for waiver (which it probably did not, since there is no mention in the facts of a waiver form or a pre-paid method for the defendant to return it), the musician *never signed and returned any form.* Therefore, no waiver-of-service ever occurred.

Putting it all together, there never occurred either a valid service or a valid waiver of the need for service. Consequently, the federal court never gained personal jurisdiction over the musician, and the default judgment against him was a nullity. Therefore, the court can — and, indeed, must — assert its power to set aside "void" judgments. (By the way, strictly speaking, this result would be true even if the musician had actually opened the envelope and learned of the suit in a timely way; however, the fact that the musician asserts — without proof to the contrary — that he never received actual notice of the suit until recently, makes it even easier for the court to conclude that it never had personal jurisdiction over him.)

Choice (A) is wrong, because service was improper even if the musician was negligent in failing to open the envelope. As is discussed more extensively as to Choice (B) above, the sending of the summons and complaint by certified mail was not a valid way to carry out service under these circumstances. And, according to most courts, that would be true even if the musician had in fact opened the envelope and learned of the suit in a timely manner. But certainly, the mere fact that the musician was negligent in failing to open the letter would not be enough to convert the mail service into a valid method of service, assuming that the musician did not in fact gain timely actual knowledge of the suit.

Choice (C) is wrong, because the musician's right to move to set aside the default was not limited to a one-year period. It's true that for some types of relief from a judgment available under Rule 60, there is a one-year time limit. Rule 60(c)(1) says that, "A motion under Rule 60(b) must be made within a reasonable time — and for reasons (1), (2), and (3) no more than a year after the entry of the judgment or order or the date of the proceeding." But relief from a judgment because it is "void" is made for reason (4) in 60(b), not reasons (1), (2), or (3). Therefore, there is no one-year limit, though the motion must be made "within a reasonable time." Here, where the facts tell you that the musician made his motion "immediately" after discovering the judgment's existence, the "within a reasonable time" requirement would certainly be deemed satisfied (at least assuming that there is no contrary evidence that the musician unreasonably ignored other evidence of the judgment's existence, and nothing in the facts here suggests that there was such evidence).

Choice (D) is wrong, because whatever authority the fiancée might have been given would not be relevant to papers that were attempted to be served by mail. There can indeed be situations, as this choice suggests, in which it matters whether the summons and complaint were or were not left with a person whom the defendant had "authorized" to receive them. In particular, where the plaintiff is relying on federal-law-based rather than state-law-based methods of service, Rule 4(e)(2)(C) make service valid if it is accomplished by "delivering a copy of [the summons and complaint] to an agent authorized by appointment or by law to receive service of process." (And at least some cases say that "by law" can include an authorization that occurs pursuant to the common-law of agency, whereby the defendant might confer on, say, a family member actual authority to accept papers on his behalf.) But 4(e)(2)(C), like the other two branches of 4(e)(2), applies only where the papers are hand-delivered by a person purporting to make service.

Here, where the papers arrived via the U.S. Postal Service, the fact that the defendant might have authorized someone else to "receive service of process" will not be enough to make the mail service valid merely because the mail carrier handed the document to that authorized person.

Answer 27

The correct choice is **(D),** because it correctly applies the federal rule governing a request for a waiver of service. Under the waiver-of-service procedure laid out in Federal Rule 4(d)(1), a plaintiff can send "by first-class mail or other reliable means" notice to a corporate (or for that matter an individual) defendant of the commencement of the suit and request that the defendant "waive service of a summons." Then, if the defendant complies with the request by signing and returning the waiver form to the plaintiff, the plaintiff can file the waiver with the court and avoid having to make service. See Rule 4(d)(4), entitled "Results of Filing a Waiver": "When the plaintiff *files a waiver*, proof of service is not required and *these rules apply as if a summons and complaint had been served at the time of filing the waiver*."

But the request-for-waiver process does not obviate the need for actual service *unless and until the plaintiff receives the signed waiver and files it with the court.* See the Advisory Committee Notes to the 1993 Amendments on Rule 4: "[i]f the waiver is not returned *and filed*, ... the action will not otherwise proceed until formal service of process is effected." See also *Cambridge Holdings Group, Inc. v. Federal Insurance Company,* 489 F.3d 1356 (D.C. Cir. 2007): "if the defendant does not waive, the rule does not suggest that service is nonetheless effective." So service was not deemed complete until Plaintiff filed the signed return with the court on August 22.

Choice (A) is wrong, because it misstates the requirements for the waiver-of-service procedure to be proper. As is more fully described in the treatment of Choice (D) above, the waiver procedure does not result in the complaint's being deemed served unless and until the plaintiff has received back from the defendant the signed waiver and filed it with the court.

Choice (B) is wrong, because it misstates how the waiver-of-service procedure works. It's true that according to Rule 4(d)(1)(F), the plaintiff, when he mails the defendant a request for waiver of service, is not required to give the defendant more than 30 days in which to sign and return the form to the plaintiff. But once the plaintiff does that, the fact that the defendant does not comply with the request within the allotted 30 days does not entitle the plaintiff to file a statement with the court or otherwise treat the requirement of service as having been satisfied.

Indeed, *there is no period of time so lengthy that the defendant's failure to return the requested signed form is deemed to be a waiver of service.* Unless and until the defendant returns the signed form and the plaintiff files the form with the court, service is not deemed to have been carried out—so by declining to sign, the defendant can effectively require the plaintiff to make actual service. (The only "teeth" contained in the Rule 4(d)(1) request-for-waiver mechanism is that if the defendant does not grant the waiver, the court is *required* to make the defendant pay for the plaintiff's expenses in making service, as well as plaintiff's attorney's fees for any motion that plaintiff makes in order to collect the service expenses.)

Choice (C) is wrong, because it misstates the point at which the waiver-of-process mechanism substitutes for actual service. Plaintiff's receipt of the signed waiver form from the defendant is certainly a *necessary* condition to Plaintiff's ability to avoid making service, but that receipt is *not* also a *sufficient* condition for that ability—the need for actual service on defendant is not extinguished unless and until Plaintiff files the signed waiver with the court. See the explanation of Choice (D) for more about this process.

Answer 28

The correct choice is (C), because service on an in-state agent followed by mail notice meets due process requirements. Constructive notice to an out-of-state defendant made through service on a state official "appointed by law" to fulfill that function is constitutionally adequate if authorized by a state statute, so long as notice by mail is also required to be given to the defendant. See *Hess v. Pawloski*, 274 U.S. 352 (1927). The Due Process Clause of the Fourteenth Amendment requires that defendant receive notice of an action before the court can proceed. The requirement of notice is in addition to, not a substitute for, the requirement that a court have personal jurisdiction over defendant. Although personal in-hand service to defendant has traditionally been required in most situations, alternative forms of notice will satisfy Due Process if they are *"reasonably calculated, under all the circumstances,* to apprise interested parties of the pendency of the action and afford them an opportunity to present their objections." *Mullane v. Central Hanover Bank & Trust Co.*, 339 U.S. 306 (1950).

The Supreme Court has implicitly held on various occasions that a scheme in which an out-of-state individual or business is deemed to appoint an in-state official as agent for service of process meets due process requirements, provided that the state official is required to notify the defendant that the action has commenced. See, e.g., *Wuchter v. Pizzutti*, 276 U.S. 13, 18-19 (1928), in which the Supreme Court discussed the question "whether a statute, making the Secretary of State the person to receive the process, *must*, in order to be valid, contain a provision making it reasonably probable that *notice of the service on the Secretary will be communicated to the non-resident defendant* who is sued." The Court answered "yes" to the question, but in so doing indicated by negative implication that if the service-on-the-Secretary-of-State scheme *does* include a requirement that the state official in turn give notice of service to the non-resident defendant, the scheme *is constitutionally adequate.* Since Choices (A) and (B)—each of which mentions steps less likely than mail notice to give the non-resident actual notice—are constitutionally insufficient for the reasons discussed below as to those choices, Choice (C) is the "least effective" method that still meets the requirements of due process.

Choice (A) is wrong, because mere service on the Secretary was not reasonably calculated to result in the defendant's timely receipt of actual notice of the suit. In *Wuchter v. Pizzutti*, 276 U.S. 13, 18-19 (1928), the Supreme Court asked itself "whether a statute, making the Secretary of State the person to receive the process, ***must***, in order to be valid, contain a provision making it reasonably probable that ***notice of the service on the Secretary will be communicated to the non-resident defendant*** who is sued." The Court then answered this question in the ***affirmative***, reasoning that "where the service of summons is limited to a service on the Secretary of State or some officer of the state, without more, it will be entirely possible for a person injured to sue any non-resident he chooses . . . [leaving] open . . . a clear opportunity for the commission of fraud[.]" Therefore, the Court concluded, such a provision not calling for the Secretary to notify the non-resident defendant "is not a reasonable provision, and . . . would certainly be ***depriving a defendant of his property without due process of law.***"

Choice (B) is wrong, because newspaper publication does not satisfy the requirement that the best reasonably-available notice method be used. The Supreme Court has held that "[t]he means [of notice] employed must be such as one desirous of ***actually informing*** the absentee might ***reasonably adopt*** to accomplish it." *Mullane v. Central Hanover Bank & Trust Co.*, 339 U.S. 306, 314-315 (1950). In the case of a defendant whose name and address are known to the plaintiff, or can be determined with reasonable diligence, *Mullane* holds that ***publication will not suffice***, and that nothing less than notice by mail to that address will be adequate. Cf. F,K&M (5th Ed.) § 3.20, p. 176. Since Plaintiff has learned Defendant's street address, mere publication (even together with service on the Secretary of State) will not suffice—either Plaintiff or the Secretary must give at least mail notice to Defendant.

Choice (D) is wrong, because Choice (C)—calling for mail notice—is a less-good method that will nonetheless be constitutionally sufficient. The question asks you to choose the LEAST effective notice method listed that will nonetheless be constitutionally adequate. For the reasons discussed as to Choice (C), the mail notice listed in that choice is sufficient to satisfy due process. Therefore, Choice (D) is not the least effective method that is nonetheless constitutionally sufficient.

Answer 29

The correct choice is **(C),** because it properly applies the federal-court standard governing a motion to dismiss on grounds of *forum non conveniens* when the plaintiff is not a U.S. citizen. The doctrine of *forum non conveniens* authorizes a trial court, in its ***discretion***, to decline to exercise jurisdiction and to dismiss the action in favor of an alternative forum if that forum is adequate. The decision to grant such a motion is governed by a number of public and private considerations, including which state or country's substantive law will govern the case, the forum state's interest in trying the case, the location of witnesses, and the burdensomeness of jury duty. See *Gulf Oil Corp. v. Gilbert*, 330 U.S. 501 (1947). A foreign plaintiff's forum choice is ***not entitled to deference*** (see *Piper Aircraft Co. v. Reyno*, 454 U.S. 235 (1981)), and the key question is whether an alternative forum that would be adequate to hear the claim is available.

Here, the contract for sale specifies that the laws of China will govern any dispute between the parties, which suggests (but does not dictate) that the remedy offered by a Chinese forum is not "clearly inadequate or unsatisfactory"; if the federal court decides that the suit may indeed appropriately be tried in China, the court may use its discretion to dismiss so that the case may be tried there. Id. at 254. If the federal judge here cannot find any strong reasons to honor Plaintiff's forum choice (and none are apparent from the facts as presently stated), the court should exercise its discretion to grant the motion, leaving Plaintiff to re-file the case in China.

Choice (A) is wrong, because the federal statute does not allow transfer to a foreign court. The federal transfer-of-venue statute, 28 U.S.C. § 1404, permits either plaintiff or defendant to move to transfer an action that is pending in a federal district court to *any other district in the United States* "[f]or the convenience of parties and witnesses, in the interest of justice." Transfers under § 1404 can be made *only between different federal district courts*, not to a foreign court. Furthermore, transfer under the statute does not result in a *dismissal* of the action, just a transfer (and the facts tell you that Defendant is seeking to *dismiss* the action). Plus, Defendant is urging that the action would be better heard in China (not in some other federal district court). So the use of § 1404 would be inappropriate for two distinct reasons — the lack of a transfer and the fact that the proposed alternative forum is not another federal district court. Thus, although this choice reaches the correct outcome (that the motion should be granted), its reliance on the transfer-of-venue statute as the reason for granting the motion is incorrect.

Choice (B) is wrong, because it misstates the standard used in a federal case to decide whether an action should be dismissed on grounds of *forum non conveniens*. The motion is directed to the district court's discretion, and it is not an abuse of discretion to grant such a motion even if the grant will result in an unfavorable change in the law for the plaintiff. This principle is illustrated by the Supreme Court's decision in *Piper Aircraft Co. v. Reyno*, 454 U.S. 235 (1981), where plaintiff (an American administratrix representing the estates of foreign individuals killed in an airplane crash in Scotland) opposed a *forum non conveniens* dismissal on the ground that Scotland, the alternative forum, would apply law less favorable to plaintiff (for example, by refusing to apply strict tort liability). The Supreme Court rejected this argument, holding that a change in law would defeat such a motion only when the remedy in the alternative forum is "so clearly inadequate or unsatisfactory that it is no remedy at all." Id. at 254. Here, the parties themselves contracted to be bound by the law of China, so it would be difficult for Plaintiff to argue that the law is inadequate.

Choice (D) is wrong, because jurisdiction is not a pre-condition to the court's power to dismiss for *forum non conveniens*. The Supreme Court has made clear that district courts have authority to dismiss a federal action on grounds of *forum non conveniens* without first determining that they have jurisdiction over the case. See *Sinochem Intern Co. Ltd. v. Malaysia International Shipping Corp.* 549 U.S. 422, 435-436 (2007) ("[W]here subject-matter jurisdiction or personal jurisdiction are difficult to determine, and *forum non-conveniens* weighs heavily in favor of dismissal, the court properly takes the less burdensome course."). So there is no bright-line rule stating that a federal court must first consider dismissal on jurisdictional grounds before reaching the question of *forum non conveniens*.

Answer 30

The correct choice is **(D)**, because 28 U.S.C. § 1404(a) allows the court to transfer the case to a federal district where the case "might have been brought," if the convenience of the parties and witnesses would thereby be served. 28 U.S.C. § 1404(a) says:

> "For the convenience of parties and witnesses, in the interest of justice, a district court may transfer any civil action to *any other district or division where it* might *have been brought* or to any district or division to which all parties have consented."

First obstacle: Assuming that fewer-than-all plaintiffs here consent to the transfer, the first obstacle the airline's § 1404(a) transfer motion will have to surmount is to show that the district of State C is a district in which this suit "*might have been brought*." This "might have been brought" requirement means that the district of State C must be: (1) in a state that would have had *personal jurisdiction* over the defendant; and (2) a district in which *venue* would originally have been proper.

As to (1) (personal jurisdiction), State C is both the airline's state of incorporation and its state of principal place of business, either of which would be enough to give State C personal jurisdiction over the airline (in fact, enough for "general" jurisdiction for all claims, not just "specific" jurisdiction limited to State-C-related claims).

As to (2) (venue), 28 U.S.C. § 1391(b) says that venue is proper in "(1) a judicial district in which ***any defendant resides***, if all defendants are residents of the State in which the district is located." 28 U.S.C. § 1391(c)(2) then says that an entity such as a corporation, if a defendant, "shall be deemed to reside . . . in any judicial district in which such defendant is subject to the court's personal jurisdiction with respect to the civil action in question." Since (as we've just seen), the airline will be subject to the personal jurisdiction of State C's courts for this (or any) suit, the airline is deemed to reside in the district of State C. Thus both prongs of the "district in which the suit might have been brought" requirement are satisfied as to State C.

Second obstacle: The second obstacle that the airline's § 1404(a) transfer motion will have to surmount is that the transfer to State C federal court must be "for the convenience of parties and witnesses" and "in the interest ***of justice.***" As to the convenience of the *parties*, this factor favors the transfer, since none of the plaintiffs' decedents (nor, presumably, the executors of those decedents' estates) resided in State A, and there is no indication that the airline, as a party, has any connection with State A. By contrast, the transferee state, State C, is the sole state of citizenship of the airline, so the transfer would increase the convenience of at least one party (the airline) while not being less convenient for any other party.

As to the convenience of *witnesses*: in this sort of suit, the testimony of eyewitnesses to the crash (all of whom would have to be ground-based, since the pilot and passengers were all killed) will likely not bear very much on who was at fault. Therefore, the convenience of eye-witnesses residing in State A near the crash scene will not be much of a factor cutting against transfer. By contrast, to the extent that poor maintenance of the aircraft, poor training of the pilot, or other airline-related causes are relevant to determining fault, these witnesses are more likely to be based at the airline's State C facilities, so that the convenience of these witnesses cuts in favor of transfer.

Third (and final) obstacle: Lastly, as to the "interests of justice," this factor does not seem to weigh very much either in favor of or against transfer.

In sum, the airline has a decent chance (though by no means a certainty) of establishing that the § 1404(a) factors cut in favor of the transfer; that chance—which would lead to a success-ful motion—is clearly greater than the chance that the airline's personal-jurisdiction motion (Choice (B), discussed below) will succeed, making Choice (D) the best answer.

Choice (A) is wrong, because there is "place of events" venue in State A. 28 U.S.C. § 1391(b)(2) makes venue proper (for both diversity and federal-question cases) in "a judicial district in which a substantial part of the events or omissions giving rise to the claim occur[.]" In a wrongful death claim against an airline arising out of a crash, the judicial district where the crash occurred is surely a district in which "a substantial part of the events or omissions giv-ing rise to the claim occurred." Therefore, at least assuming that State A has only one judicial district, venue is proper in that district, since we know the crash occurred there. (If we knew for sure that there were two or more judicial districts in State A, and that the crash occurred in, say, the Northern District while the suit was brought in the Southern District, then venue in the Southern District would not be proper. But there is no indication in the facts that there is more than one judicial district in State A.)

Choice (B) is wrong, because the airline may have minimum contacts with State A. The com-plaint here arises out of an occurrence in the forum state, State A, since that's where the crash, and the allegedly wrongful deaths, occurred. Therefore, the State A federal court will have personal jurisdiction over the airline as long as the airline can be said to have "minimum contacts" with state A. Those contacts will exist so long as it can be said that the airline has "*purposefully avail[ed] itself* of the *privilege of conducting activities* within the forum State." (*J. McIntyre Machinery, Ltd. v. Nicastro*, 131 S. Ct. 2780 (2011) [plurality opinion, but joined on this point by a majority].)

The problem is that we are not given enough facts to know whether the airline's relationship with State A meets this "purposeful availment" requirement. The mere fact that the flight crashed in state A would not be enough to constitute "purposeful availment" by the airline of the privilege of doing business in the state (since all flights by the airline might have been scheduled so as to neither start nor end in State A, merely to overfly the state, except for the unintended crash in State A). But suppose, however, that the airline conducted regularly scheduled flights from or to a location in state A — in that event, the airline clearly *would* be found to have purposely availed itself of the privilege of doing business in the state, in which case the airline's motion to dismiss for lack of personal jurisdiction would fail.

Since we simply don't have enough information to know whether the personal-jurisdiction motion will succeed or fail, Choice (B) is not the choice "most likely" to succeed, given the high likelihood that the transfer motion in Choice (D) will succeed.

Choice (C) is wrong, because the federal courts will transfer the action — not dismiss it based on *forum non conveniens* — where another federal court is a more convenient forum.

Where the more-appropriate forum is another American (rather than foreign) court, the federal courts do not dismiss the case under the *forum non conveniens* doctrine, as they might have done before the enactment of the federal transfer-of-venue provision, 28 U.S.C. § 1404(a). See *American Dredging Co. v. Miller*, 510 U.S. 443 (1994), saying that as a consequence of the adoption of § 1404(a), "the federal doctrine of *forum non conveniens* has continuing application only in cases where the alternative forum is abroad."

Answer 31

The correct choice is **(D)**, because a federal statute allows transfer to another federal district for the convenience of the parties, and the court will ordinarily view the parties' forum-selection clause as demonstrating the parties' mutually-agreed-upon view of where suit would be most convenient. The federal statute that governs when and how a case may be transferred for reasons of convenience is 28 U.S.C. § 1404. Section 1404(a), the main provision, reads as follows:

> "For the convenience of parties and witnesses, in the interest of justice, a district court may transfer any civil action to any other district or division where it might have been brought or to any district or division to which all parties have consented."

Since the parties agreed in their contract that any suits should be brought in courts located in State B, any federal court located in State B is in a "district . . . to which all parties have **consented**," as that phrase is used in 28 U.S.C. 1404(a). Therefore, the court should apply § 1404(a) so as to transfer the action as the mill requests, so long as that transfer would be "for the convenience of parties and witnesses, in the interests of justice[.]"

In fact, in a case posing facts similar to these, the Supreme Court has decided that the court *must* normally treat a valid forum-selection clause as **binding** on the issue of which forum is most convenient for the parties: "[W]hen parties agree to a forum-selection clause, they **waive** the right to challenge the preselected forum as inconvenient or less convenient for themselves or their witnesses . . . [T]he practical result is that *forum-selection clauses should control except in unusual cases*." *Atlantic Marine Constr. Co. v. U.S. Dist. Ct.*, 571 U.S. 49 (2013).

Therefore, the federal court should treat the clause designating the courts located in State B as being dispositive on the issue of convenience; the court should thus transfer the case there without making its own determination of where the litigation would be most convenient for the parties and witnesses.

Choice (A) is wrong, because what State A says about the enforceability of forum-selection clauses is irrelevant. This is not an *Erie*-type situation, in which the common law of the state where the federal court sits needs to be consulted; that's because there is a federal statute (28 U.S.C. § 1404(a)) that deals precisely with the issue in question, i.e., whether a transfer for convenience of the parties should be granted. Therefore, only the federal statute—and cases construing it (such as the *Atlantic Marine* case referred to in the discussion of Choice (D))—should be consulted, and any state-law policy (or for that matter statute) of State A is irrelevant.

Choice (B) is wrong, because venue was not "improper" in State A, and a motion to transfer for convenience, not a motion to dismiss on account of improper venue, was the correct procedure for the mill to follow. This choice is designed to fool you into thinking that the mill should have used the federal statute allowing dismissal for improper venue. There is indeed such a statute: 28 U.S.C. § 1406(a) says that "The district court of a district in which is filed a case *laying venue in the wrong division or district shall dismiss*, or if it be in the interest of justice, transfer such case to any district or division in which it could have been brought." So if the bakery's filing of the case in State A had constituted a choice of a "wrong" venue, § 1406(a) would have been the correct provision under which the mill should have made its motion for dismissal (or, perhaps, transfer to State B).

But the Supreme Court has held that § 1406(a)'s reference to a "wrong" district means merely a district that is not made a proper place for the suit *according to the venue statute* (28 U.S.C. § 1391)—"If the federal venue statutes establish that suit may be brought in a particular district, a *contractual bar* [in a forum-selection clause] *cannot render venue in that district 'wrong.'*" *Atlantic Marine Constr. Co. v. U.S. Dist. Ct.*, 571 U.S. 49 (2013). Therefore, State A was not a "wrong" district for venue, and § 1406(a) is not the provision that the mill should have used—rather, the mill correctly used § 1404's transfer-for-convenience provision.

Choice (C) is wrong, because there is a statute on point, making federal common law irrelevant. Like *state* common law in an *Erie*-type case (i.e., a diversity case where state common law supplies the relevant substantive rule and must be followed by the federal court), *federal* common law *matters only where there is no federal statute or regulation governing the issue*. If there were no relevant statute, *and* if federal common law made forum-selection clauses controlling on the issue of transfer (it's not clear whether there is such law), then this choice might be correct. But, as we discuss in connection with Choice (D), there *is* a federal statute dealing with transfers of venue (28 U.S.C. § 1404), and that statute has been interpreted by the Supreme Court in *Atlantic Marine,* supra, to mean that a forum-selection clause in the parties' contract amounts to an agreement by them that the designated forum is more convenient than any alternative forum. Therefore, there is no scope for federal common law to apply.

Answer 32

The correct choice is **(A),** because transfer based on convenience is allowed to any district where the action might have originally been brought. The general federal change-of-venue statute, 28 U.S.C. § 1404(a), permits the district court to *transfer* "any civil action to any other district or division *where it might have been brought,*" on consideration of *"the convenience of parties and witnesses, in the interest of justice."* The statutory language "where it might have been brought" has been interpreted to require, at the least, that transfer be to a district in which *venue would have been proper*. (Some courts *also* require that the transfer be to a district from which personal jurisdiction over the defendant could be asserted, which in a diversity case might mean that transfer cannot be made to a district in a state with which the defendant did not have minimum contacts.) In any event, you don't have to interpret the precise meaning of the phrase "where it might have been brought" to evaluate Choice (A), since that choice echoes the phrase by adding the condition that plaintiff "could initially have brought the action" in W.D. State B. Since the facts tell you to assume that the court has found that litigation in W.D. State B would be more convenient overall than litigation in State A, § 1404(a)'s requirement that the transferring judge consider the "convenience of parties and witnesses" is also satisfied.

Choice (B) is wrong, because it misstates the governing law on the right to transfer an action. A plaintiff may move to transfer an action despite the fact that plaintiff chose the action's initial venue. The transfer statute "says nothing about affording plaintiffs different treatment from defendants," *Ferens v. John Deere Co.*, 494 U.S. 516, 522 (1990), and transfer under the general federal venue statute is not limited to defendants. Thus, Plaintiff is free to seek to change the venue of the action even though he was the one who made the original choice of where to sue.

Choice (C) is wrong, because it misstates the relationship of venue to state boundaries in the federal system even when the federal court sits in diversity jurisdiction.

Although it is true that individual circuits and districts in the federal system generally do not cross state boundaries, there is nothing in the federal change-of-venue provisions that prohibits a transfer across state lines. And that is true whether the action is based solely on diversity or involves a federal-question claim. (Notice, by the way, that a party who seeks to transfer an action from one district to another, when the districts are in different states, will not get the benefit of a change in law; the transferee court must apply the law of the transferor court. See *Van Dusen v. Barack*, 376 U.S. 612 (1964) and *Ferens v. John Deere Co.*, 494 U.S. 516 (1990).)

Choice (D) is wrong, because the fact that venue wasn't proper does not require the court to dismiss the action. The court in which the case was originally brought *may transfer it to another district, even if venue was improper in the original (transferor) court.* In that situation, the correct statutory procedure to use is not the generally used § 1404(a) (discussed in Choice (A) above), but a special provision for cases in which the original choice of venue is improper, 28 U.S.C. § 1406. Section 1406 lets the original court make the transfer (assuming venue in the transferee district is proper and that convenience will be served), even though because of the venue error that original court could not have heard the action over the defendant's objection.

Answer 33

The correct choice is **(D)**, because it recognizes that Defendant has *waived* the defense of improper venue by failing to include it when he filed a responsive pleading. Rule 12(b) lists seven special defenses that may be asserted by motion; one of these is "improper venue," listed in Rule 12(b)(3). Rule 12(h) then says that each of these seven defenses is waived by a party's "failing to either (i) make [the defense] by motion under [Rule 12]; or (ii) include it in a responsive pleading or in an amendment allowed by Rule 15(a)(1) as a matter of course." We know by negative implication from the facts that Defendant did not raise the venue defense by a Rule 12 motion. Therefore, Defendant will be deemed to have waived the defense unless he included it either in "a responsive pleading" or in "an amendment allowed by Rule 15(a)(1) as a matter of course." As to raising it in a responsive pleading, Defendant's only "responsive pleading" so far has been his answer, and the facts tell us that he did not include the venue defense in that answer. So Defendant's only hope for avoiding losing the defense by waiver is if the Rules permit him to include it in "an amendment allowed by Rule 15(a)(1) as a matter of course." But Rule 15(a)(1)(A) says that where the pleading to be amended will not require a responsive pleading (which is the situation here), the pleader's time to amend as a matter of course expires 21 days after the pleader served the pleading. So on August 21, Defendant's time to amend his answer as a matter of course expired. Thus by now (October 2), he has no way to avoid the waiver that Rule 12(h) says has occurred.

Choice (A) is wrong, because Defendant can no longer amend his answer. As this choice suggests, under some circumstances a defendant who has answered without including a venue defense might be able to amend the answer to include that defense. But as is discussed more fully in the treatment of Choice (D), for the amendment to include the addition of a venue defense, the amendment must be one that is allowed "as a matter of course" (rather than by leave of court), and Defendant's power to amend as a matter of course ended on August 21, 21 days after he served his original answer. Therefore, Defendant does not have the power to place the issue of whether the action should be dismissed for lack of venue in front of the court.

Choice (B) is wrong, because Defendant can no longer make a motion to dismiss based on the venue objection. When Defendant was first served with the complaint, a motion by him to dismiss for improper venue would have been proper: Under FRCP 12(b), a party may assert various defenses by motion, including a motion under 12(b)(3) to dismiss for improper venue. However, as is discussed more fully in the explanation of Choice (D), once defendant served his answer without including the venue defense, he waived his right to assert the defense by motion. See Rule 12(h)(i). So the court will not have discretion to dismiss the action for improper venue even if the court concludes that venue was improper.

Choice (C) is wrong, because Defendant has waived his right to make a motion based on the venue objection. As is described in the explanation to both Choice (D) and Choice (B), when Defendant filed an answer that did not include the venue defense, he waived his right to assert that defense by motion. Therefore, the court is not authorized to dismiss the action for lack of venue, even if the judge is satisfied that venue was improper. Unlike a lack of subject-matter jurisdiction, a lack of venue is not deemed "jurisdictional," so the federal court has power to hear the case even though the case was brought in a district where venue did not lie.

Answer 34

The correct choice is **(B),** because the *Erie* doctrine requires the federal court to follow the substantive policy embedded in the additur technique. The principle embodied by *Erie v. Tompkins*, 304 U.S. 64 (1938) is that when a federal court is sitting in diversity, the court must apply *state*—not federal—substantive law. So the issue here is whether State A's common-law rule allowing a trial judge to use the "additur" conditional-new-trial technique if the judge believes a jury verdict to be manifestly and excessively low is a "substantive" principle that is binding on the federal judge.

It's very likely that the Supreme Court would hold that State A's endorsement of the additur technique represents an attempt by the state to achieve the substantive goal of ensuring that jury verdicts are not unreasonably low. The Supreme Court has never expressly decided whether *Erie* doctrine applies to additur, but the Court *has* decided a case involving a closely analogous state-law technique for controlling the size of jury verdicts. In *Gasperini v. Center For Humanities, Inc.*, 518 U.S. 415 (1996), the Court had to decide whether a federal judge sitting in diversity must apply a New York statute under which the trial judge should order a new trial if the jury's award "deviates materially from what would be reasonable compensation." The Court held that the answer was yes: Although the statute may have had a procedural aspect, the state was pursuing the obviously substantive goal of controlling the size of jury verdicts, so the federal court was required to follow a similar policy of ordering a new trial if the jury verdict was a material deviation from compensation that would be reasonable.

Here, by recognizing additur, State A is, similarly, pursuing the substantive objective of using conditional new trial orders to make sure that a clearly-inadequate jury verdict does not stand. Therefore, the federal court should (and indeed under *Erie must*) pursue the same objective.

There is an additional complication in this case: The Seventh Amendment guarantees a litigant in a federal trial a right to a jury trial, and there is some older Supreme Court precedent suggesting that use of additur may violate the Seventh Amendment by leading the judge to award a damage amount greater than was ever awarded by the jury. But as is discussed more fully in the treatment of Choice (D) below, use of additur in the circumstances here would be very unlikely to be found to be a violation of the Seventh Amendment, because the $200,000 hospital-bill payment was not genuinely in dispute.

Choice (A) is wrong, because the movant must, as a pre-condition to a post-verdict motion for judgment as a matter of law, make the motion at the close of evidence. The making of a motion for judgment as a matter of law or "JML" (the federal equivalent of the common-law motion for "JNOV," or "judgment notwithstanding the verdict") is governed by FRCP 50(a). Rule 50(a)(2) says that "A motion for judgment as a matter of law may be made at any time *before the case is submitted to the jury*." In other words, by negative implication once the case is submitted to the jury, the motion is no longer timely. Assuming that the motion was timely made, then after the jury hands down a verdict with which the movant is unhappy, Rule 50(b) says that "No later than 28 days after the entry of judgment . . . The movant may file a *renewed* motion for judgment as a matter of law[.]"

Here, the facts tell you that the case was submitted to the jury "without any motion having been made by either side"—therefore, you know that the skydiver did not move for JML before the case was sent to the jury and that he therefore lost the right to make (or renew) such a motion after the verdict. (But if the skydiver *had* moved for JML before the case went to the jury, this choice would be correct: The skydiver would have had 28 days after entry of the judgment in which to renew his JML motion, and the court would have been justified in granting the motion—i.e., awarding judgment for $200,000—since that amount would be correct as a matter of law in the sense that there would have been uncontested proof of the $200,000 in hospital-bill damages.)

Choice (C) is wrong, because it states a legally-incorrect rule. The case for using additur is actually weaker in federal-question cases than in diversity cases. That's because in a federal question case, *Erie* doctrine is irrelevant, so there's no state-law substantive policy that the federal court might be required to implement, as would arguably be the situation in a diversity case where the relevant state law encourages the use of additur to prevent unreasonably low jury verdicts. But in any event, this choice is wrong in asserting that additur may not be applied in diversity cases, as is explained in the discussion of Choice (B).

Choice (D) is wrong, because the use of additur here would be the equivalent of a grant of summary judgment on damages and would therefore not invade the province of the jury. It's true that in an old case, the Supreme Court seemed to hold that the use of additur violated the plaintiff's Seventh Amendment right to a jury trial. That case was *Dimick v. Schiedt*, 293 U.S. 474, 486-487 (1935), in which the majority said that "where the verdict is too small, an increase by the court [by use of additur] is a bald addition of something which in no sense can be said to be included in the verdict," thereby violating the right of the *plaintiff* (not the defendant) to have a jury determine the correct damage amount. It's not at all clear that *Dimick* would turn out the same way today, i.e., that the present Supreme Court would find *any* use of additur to be a violation of the Seventh Amendment.

But in any event, the lower federal courts have, post-*Dimick*, always recognized that there is no Seventh Amendment problem with the use of additur in one particular situation: that in which the trial demonstrates that if the defendant is liable at all, he is liable for at least some particular amount *as proven by the uncontested evidence*. See, e.g., *Roman v. Western Manufacturing, Inc.*, 691 F.3d 686, 702 (5th Cir. 2012): "[T]he constitutional rule against additur is not violated in a case where the jury ha[s] properly determined liability and there is *no valid dispute as to the amount of damages*. In such a case the court is in effect simply *granting summary judgment* on the question of damages."

That's the situation here: The jury has found liability (a defective product that caused the injury), and the manufacturer never contested the skydiver's evidence that the hospital bill for the resulting injuries totaled $200,000 and was paid. Therefore, the trial judge's use of additur — i.e., the judge's grant of a new trial conditioned upon the manufacturer's refusal to agree to pay $200,000 — was functionally no different from the judge's granting post-trial summary judgment of $200,000 as the amount of damages about which there was no genuine issue of law or fact; and no court would consider a grant of summary judgment to be a violation of a litigant's Seventh Amendment right to jury trial.

Answer 35

The correct choice is **(C)**, because in a diversity action, the federal court must follow the conflict-of-laws principles of the state in which the federal court sits. The underlying claim here is based on state law of product liability. In that situation, there is no federal statute or rule that governs what test is to be used in determining whether the product's design was defective (and the product would have to be defective in order for the landscaper to recover). Since there is no federal statute or rule on point, the case is governed by the basic rule of *Erie v. Tompkins*, 304 U.S. 64 (1938), that the federal court must follow the state's substantive law. The question then becomes, *which* state's substantive law must the federal court follow?

The answer has always been, since soon after *Erie* itself was decided, that the federal court must follow the substantive law of whichever state the state court where the federal court sits would follow had the case been filed in state court. In other words, the federal court must *follow the conflict of laws principles of the state in which the federal court sits*. See *Klaxon Co. v. Stentor Co.*, 313 U.S. 487, 496 (1941), a diversity case filed in Delaware federal court: "The conflict of laws rules to be applied by the federal court [sitting] in Delaware must conform to those prevailing in Delaware's state courts." (If the federal court were free to make its own conflict-of-laws decision about which state's substantive law to apply, then the plaintiff could "forum shop" between the state and federal courts in a particular state, by picking whichever court she thought would use a conflicts rule that would lead to use of the most favorable-to-the-plaintiff substantive law, thereby defeating *Erie*'s anti-forum-shopping purpose.)

Choice (A) is wrong, because it leads to the wrong result in those cases where State C's conflict principles would lead that state to apply another state's design-defect test. If State C's conflict principles would cause State C to use, say, the design-defect test applied by the state where the product was designed and manufactured (State B), then this choice would result in the federal court's using a different substantive rule than would be used by the courts of the state where the federal court sits (State C). And, for the reasons discussed in the analysis of Choice (C) above, such an approach would encourage plaintiffs to forum-shop. The correct approach is for the federal court to use the conflict-of-law rules of the state where the federal court sits, rather than necessarily the substantive law of that state.

Choice (B) is wrong, because *Erie* principles require a federal court sitting in diversity to apply state, not federal, substantive law. It is probably true that there are design-defect standards developed by the federal courts for use in suits where the federal law supplies the rule of decision (e.g., in a suit by a member of the Armed Forces who is injured by a defective product purchased by the military from the company now being sued). But the basic principle behind *Erie* doctrine is that where the right sued upon is created by a state, a federal court hearing a suit on that right is required to consult state law, not federal common-law principles developed in connection with analogous federally-created rights.

Choice (D) is wrong, because it is not up to the federal court to select what it thinks is the best conflict-of-laws approach to the controversy. *Erie* requires that a federal court sitting in diversity apply "state substantive law." The object of *Erie* doctrine is principally to ensure that insofar as the outcome of a suit is dependent on substantive rules, a diversity suit should reach the same outcome as a suit brought in the courts of the state where the federal court sits, so as to reduce forum-shopping. The Supreme Court has interpreted this rationale to require that the federal court apply the conflict-of-laws rule of the state where the federal court sits, rather than permitting the federal court to use "federal conflict-of-law principles," which might include the federal judge's own judgment about which state has the strongest interest in having its substantive law apply. This "follow state conflict-of-laws principles" approach was announced by the Supreme Court in *Klaxon Co. v. Stentor Co.*, 313 U.S. 487, 496 (1941) (quoted in Choice (C) above), and has remained good law despite some criticisms.

Answer 36

The correct choice is **(D),** because a federal district court sitting in diversity in a particular state is required to apply the ***same rule of decision*** as a state court sitting in that same state would apply. This means that if the State B ***conflict-of-law rule*** requires a State B state court to apply the GPDA to the dispute, a federal court sitting in State B is required to as well. This result follows indirectly from *Erie Railroad Co. v. Tompkins*, 304 U.S. 64 (1938), in which the Supreme Court held that in the absence of federal statutory law on point, a federal district court sitting in diversity must follow the common-law decisions as well as state statutes and state constitutional rules of the state where the federal court sits. More directly, the Court held post-*Erie* in *Klaxon Co. v. Stentor Electric Mfg. Co.*, 313 U.S. 487 (1941) that the *Erie* doctrine requires a federal district court sitting in diversity to apply not only the substantive rules of decision of the state in which it sits but ***also that state's choice-of-law (i.e., conflicts) rules***. (The *Klaxon* rule has the advantage that it ***discourages the parties from forum shopping***. Thus a plaintiff will not get the benefit of a different substantive rule by filing in a federal court for State X rather than in a State X state court; likewise, a defendant will not get the benefit of a different substantive rule by removing the action from a state court to a federal court in that same state.)

Choice (D), by making the federal court's decision on whether to apply the State B statute turn on whether the State B courts would apply the statute to this same dispute, correctly expresses the *Klaxon* choice-of-law-based rule. Under that rule, for instance, if the State B courts would apply State A rather than State B substantive contracts principles to this dispute because delivery was to occur in State A and/or because the Plaintiff was a citizen of State A, then the federal court would also be free to disregard the State B statute.

Choice (A) is wrong, because this choice ascribes to the federal court a power it does not have. Under a long-standing federal statute called the Rules of Decision Act, 28 U.S.C. § 1652, a federal court is required, in the absence of a contrary federal statute or rule, to apply "the laws of the several states," which are to be treated as "rules of decisions" in federal civil actions. The phrase "the laws of the several states" has long been interpreted to include a state's statutes. (*Erie v. Tompkins* expanded the meaning of the phrase to include a state's *judicial* decisions in the category of "laws of [a] state." But even pre-*Erie*, a state's statutes were always treated as being part of that state's laws.) Here, there is no federal statute or rule governing the issue. So even if the federal court thinks that federal "common law" (the body of non-statutorily-focused decisions by federal judges on analogous issues) would supply a good rule for deciding the issue of whether Defendant's delay constituted a material breach, the Rules of Decision Act requires the court to defer to any State B statute on point, if the State B courts would apply that statute to the case at hand in a state-court suit. Since Choice (A) ignores the effect of the Rules of Decision Act, it is not the correct answer.

Choice (B) is wrong, because the rule it states does not apply to the facts. The state of incorporation is relevant to determining the *citizenship of a corporation* for purposes of determining whether diversity jurisdiction exists under 28 U.S.C. § 1332. But the citizenship of the defendant corporation here is not directly relevant to the issue of what body of law should control on the substantive issue of whether the Defendant has materially breached the contract. In determining whether to apply state law to a dispute, the federal diversity court in the first instance must look to the *choice-of-law rule* of the state in which the federal court sits—whichever state's substantive law would be applied by the state where the federal court sits, the federal court must apply that state's law. So here, the question is, "Under State B's choice-of-law rules, which state's substantive contracts law—State A or State B—would be applied by the State B courts, if the State B courts were hearing this case?" State B's choice-of-law rules might or might not give weight to the Defendant's state of incorporation; and if State B *wouldn't* consider that state of incorporation as part of the state's choice-of-law analysis, the federal court may not do so either. So Choice (B), by implying that the federal court must use the substantive law of the Defendant's state of incorporation, makes an incorrect statement of law.

Choice (C) is wrong, because it incorrectly imposes a condition on the federal court's duty to apply the State B statute. Under the federal Rules of Decision Act, 28 U.S.C. § 1652, a federal court, assuming no federal statute or rule applies, is required to apply state law to resolve the dispute before it. So the federal court here, where no federal statute or rule applies, must apply the relevant State B law—first, the State B choice-of-law rule (State B's method of deciding which state's substantive law should apply), and then, the substantive law of State B if that's the body of law the State B courts would apply on these facts. When the federal court carries out this task of ascertaining state law, it of course looks to any decisions by the state's highest court, so the federal court here would indeed look to see what State B's highest court has to say about the choice-of-law issue and thus about whether the GPDA would apply to this suit. But *whether or not the highest state court has ruled*, the federal court is not free to disregard the GPDA if it believes State B's trial courts would choose to apply that statute to the dispute before it. Since Choice (C) suggests that the federal court must apply the GPDA *only* if the highest court of State B has held that the statute applies to this sort of dispute, the choice places an incorrect limit on the federal court's duty to apply the GPDA.

Answer 37

The correct choice is **(C),** because the State A notice-of-claim rule expresses a strong state substantive policy that must be respected by the federal court under *Erie* principles. When a federal court hears a claim based solely on state law (i.e., a diversity case), the doctrine of *Erie v. Tompkins,* 304 U.S. 64 (1938), requires the federal court to apply any state statutes, rules, or judicial decisions that are mostly substantive, but not state-law principles that are essentially procedural. However, before you can even know whether *Erie* doctrine applies to a particular set of facts, you have to first determine whether there is a valid *federal rule or statute governing the matter in question*, which if applied would be *inconsistent* with the state principle; if there is, the federal rule or statute *must be applied*, and *Erie* never even gets triggered. (Notice that this is one of the tricky things about applying *Erie* doctrine—you first have to *know* that there doesn't exist any federal rule or statute conflicts with the state rule in question, and to do that you in turn theoretically have to know "everything" about which federal rules and statutes exist! But for MBE purposes, you can usually safely *assume* that there is no such inconsistent federal principle unless you specifically recall it from studying the FRCP or the core Civil Procedure provisions of Title 28 of the U.S. Code, or the examiners call the conflict to your attention somehow.)

In this case, there is *no federal statute or rule applicable to these facts* that would be inconsistent with having the federal court honor the state notice-of-claim requirement. Therefore, this is indeed a situation in which classic *Erie* analysis is required.

The question then becomes, does the state-law requirement of notice-of-claim embody a sufficiently strong state *substantive interest* that *Erie* principles require the federal court to defer to state law by applying that requirement? The extent to which the state rule is *outcome-determinative* is an important part of the analysis. That's because "[W]here a federal court is exercising jurisdiction solely because of the diversity of citizenship of the parties, the *outcome* of the litigation in the federal court *should be substantially the same*, so far as *legal rules determine the outcome* of a litigation, as it would be if tried in a State court." *Guaranty Trust Co. v. York*, 326 U.S. 99, 109 (1945). Otherwise, the federal courts will be encouraging *"forum shopping,"* in which one party (sometimes the plaintiff, and sometimes the non-resident defendant deciding whether to remove a state-filed case to federal court) gets the chance to choose between having the case heard in state court or having it heard it a federal court located in that same state, based on which one will give him better odds of winning.

Here, the choice to apply or not apply the state notice-of-claim rule is *quite strongly outcome-determinative*: If the rule is applied, the plumber doesn't even get a chance to have his claim heard at all; without the rule, the plumber may well win. The notice-of-claim requirement is similar to a state statute of limitations rule, and the Supreme Court has long held that such limitations rules are highly outcome-determinative and must be applied by courts sitting in diversity. Thus, in *Guaranty Trust v. York*, supra, the Supreme Court held that a federal court sitting in diversity must apply the state statute of limitations because the federal court "cannot afford recovery if the right to recover is made unavailable by the State[.]"

But the fact that the choice between state and federal court would be somewhat outcome-determinative is *not the sole factor* the federal court must consider. Beyond considering the degree to which following the state law (or not doing so) will be outcome-determinative, the federal court must perform a type of *interest-balancing*; the court must weigh the *strength of the state's interest* in using its rule to *affect the substantive rights of the parties* against the strength of the federal judicial system's interest in *applying uniform procedures nationally*.

Here, that interest balancing cuts in favor of *applying State A's notice-of-claim rule*. The facts tell you that the object of the notice-of-claim requirement was to reduce malpractice claims and thus the cost of malpractice insurance; this is a strongly substantive goal, one tied up with parties' rights beyond how the actual litigation will be conducted. So the state interest in having its policy applied by the federal courts is quite strong. Conversely, there is no strong federal interest in having nationally uniform procedures that would be jeopardized by applying the notice-of-claim rule in just those states that have such a rule. So the federal-versus-state interest-balancing analysis, like the outcome-determinative analysis, cuts strongly in favor of requiring the federal court to apply the state's notice-of-claim rule.

Therefore, *Erie* principles almost certainly require the federal court to dismiss the suit because that's what the State A courts would do.

Choice (A) is wrong, because the notice-of-claim provision is not a mere procedural rule and is therefore binding on the federal court. While the notice provision is in a sense "procedural" (it deals with the "procedures" for bringing a malpractice claim against the hospital), that label is not dispositive when the federal court is deciding whether *Erie* principles require that the state rule be followed. As is more fully described in the discussion of Choice (C) above, the decision whether to apply the state rule is heavily outcome-determinative, and the state has manifested a strong interest in using its rule to pursue the substantive state interest in reducing malpractice insurance rates. Therefore, the court must apply the state notice rule, making this choice legally incorrect. (And given that fact, the issue of whether diversity exists is irrelevant.)

Choice (B) is wrong, because it misstates the time as of which a party's state citizenship is to be determined for diversity purposes. It's true that if the plumber and the hospital had both been citizens of State A at the relevant time, there would be no diversity. But the time as of which each party's citizenship is to be determined is the ***moment the suit is filed***, not the moment the cause of action arose. See *Freeport-McMoRan, Inc. v. K. N. Energy, Inc.*, 498 U.S. 426, 428 (1991), referring to "the well-established rule that diversity of citizenship is assessed at the time the action is filed." Here, the plumber's state of citizenship (i.e., his state of "domicile") changed when he moved permanently from State A to State B. Once that happened, he became diverse with the hospital, and remained so at the moment he filed the suit, which is what counts for jurisdiction purposes. (Also, as long as his move was intended to be permanent, the fact that it may have been motivated in part by a desire to be able to sue the hospital in diversity is irrelevant.)

Choice (D) is wrong, because it gives an unduly simplistic explanation of why the federal court must follow the state notice-of-claim rule. It's true that the degree to which the federal court's decision to follow or not follow the state rule might affect the outcome of the suit is *one* of the factors that the federal court must consider in deciding whether *Erie* principles require the court to apply the state rule. *But it's not the only factor.* As the Court said in *Hanna v. Plumer*, 380 U.S. 460, 466-67 (1965), " 'Outcome-determination' analysis was never intended to serve as a talisman."

As is discussed more extensively in the analysis of Choice (C) above, even where there is *some* chance that the decision on whether to follow the state rule will affect the outcome, the federal court need not follow the state rule if the state's choice of rule does not manifest a strong substantive policy, and requiring the federal court to follow the state rule would significantly interfere with a strong federal interest in having uniform national procedures.

So while this choice correctly predicts the outcome (that the case must be dismissed because the plumber did not follow the state notice rule), it explains the reason for that outcome less precisely than does Choice (C).

Answer 38

The correct choice is **(D)**, because it correctly recognizes that Plaintiff's motion for preliminary injunctive relief will not succeed due to the fact that the federal statute upon which it is based is advisory, not mandatory. A court will issue a preliminary injunction only if the person seeking it shows that she is ***likely to succeed on the merits*** and can also demonstrate three additional factors: (1) the likelihood of irreparable injury if provisional relief is not granted; (2) a balance of hardships in favor of the movant; and (3) a showing that the requested relief is in the public interest. See *Winter v. Natural Resources Defense Council, Inc.*, 555 U.S. 7, 20 (2008). A preliminary injunction is never awarded as of right; it is an equitable order and viewed as "an extraordinary remedy that may only be awarded upon a clear showing that the plaintiff is entitled to such relief." Id.

Plaintiff cannot show that she will succeed on the merits, because the FPA does not create a mandatory duty on waterfront homeowners to refrain from lawn-planting in the buffer zone—it merely recommends that they do so. Because Plaintiff's likely success on the merits is a necessary condition for a preliminary injunction, her failure to prove likely success on the merits ends the analysis. (The other three conditions would only become relevant if Plaintiff showed a likelihood that she would succeed on the merits.)

Choice (A) is wrong, because the rule it states, while accurate, is insufficient to support the granting of preliminary relief. It is true that preliminary injunctive relief is available only on a showing of *irreparable* harm, meaning harm that cannot be remedied through the payment of money damages. And this choice plausibly suggests that during the pendency of the suit, Defendant may well over-develop her land, impede spawning, and cause damage that cannot be remedied through the payment of money. However, the likelihood of irreparable harm means merely that *one* of the four requirements for an injunction has been met. Given the fact that Plaintiff can't meet the other three requirements (because she can't show she's likely to succeed on the merits, as described in the treatment of Choice (D) above), the court must deny the injunction.

Choice (B) is wrong, because as with Choice (A), the rule that it states is insufficient to support the granting of preliminary relief. The possibility that an injunction may be in the public interest is only one of the four necessary conditions before a preliminary injunction may be granted. So while it's true that the district court, before *granting* preliminary relief, would be required to consider whether the order will serve the public interest, the fact that Plaintiff is unlikely to succeed on the merits (as described in Choice (D)) means that the four conditions can't all be satisfied and that the motion must be denied.

Choice (C) is wrong, because although the answer correctly states the expected outcome of the request for the preliminary injunction, it misidentifies the most likely reason for the denial. It's true that, as this choice indicates, a preliminary injunction is an equitable form of relief and is available only when money damages will not be able to compensate for the harm (making the harm irreparable). But it's far from clear on these facts that an award of money will indeed be sufficient to remedy the harm—perhaps an award of damages would be enough to adequately remediate the harm prospectively, in that the award could pay for removal of the lawn, so that any interim damage to fish would be minor and temporary. In any event, this choice refers to a "violation" of the FPA, and the advisory nature of the FPA means that planting by Defendant would not be a "violation." A far more compelling reason for the court to deny the motion is Plaintiff's failure to show likely success on the merits, for the reason described in the analysis of Choice (D).

Answer 39

The correct choice is **(A),** because the complaint alleges fraud and so is required to plead the particulars of the fraud. FRCP 9(b) requires that, "[i]n ***alleging fraud*** or mistake, a party must ***state with particularity the circumstances constituting fraud*** or mistake." Here the complaint includes only the conclusory allegation that Defendant, by delivering non-organic cookies, engaged in fraud. Courts interpret the special pleading rules for fraud to require that the complaint allege the relatively-precise misconduct that constitutes the fraud. Generally this heightened pleading requirement is met when the complaint alleges the "who, what, when, where, and how" of the fraudulent representation. See, e.g., *Lerner v. Fleet Bank, N.A.*, 459 F.3d 273 (2d Cir. 2006) (to meet the requirements of FRCP 9(b) when fraud is alleged, "the complaint must: (1) specify the statements that the plaintiff contends were fraudulent, (2) identify the speaker, (3) state where and when the statements were made, and (4) explain why the statements were fraudulent"). Here, the allegations of the complaint do not meet this standard because they do not specify when and where Defendant made the fraudulent statements, how Plaintiff knows that the statements were untrue, or how Plaintiff knows that any falsity was intentional (i.e., how/why Plaintiff believes that Defendant knew of the falsity when it made the statement, or at least when it shipped the merchandise). Moreover, most courts say the allegations of fraud must include specific facts giving rise to a "strong inference" of fraud, whereas the complaint here contains only a bare assertion that fraud occurred.

Choice (B) is wrong, because it relies on a pleading standard that the Supreme Court no longer applies. Prior to 2007, the Court held that a complaint should not be dismissed for failure to state a claim "unless it appears beyond doubt that the plaintiff can prove no set of facts in support of his claim which could entitle him to relief." *Conley v. Gibson*, 355 U.S. 41, 45-46 (1957). But in *Bell Atlantic Corp. v. Twombly*, 550 U.S. 544, 554-563 (2007), the Court "retired" the *Conley* formulation, and announced a new *"plausibility"* standard for when to dismiss a federal-court complaint for failing to state a claim; *Twombly* "require[s] that the allegations in the complaint must allege facts showing that recovery [is] not merely 'conceivable' but that it [is] 'plausible.' " F,K&M (5th Ed.), s. 5.9. See also the post-*Twombly* decision in *Ashcroft v. Iqbal,* 556 U.S. 662, 684 (2009) (held, a federal complaint must state a "plausible" claim, and "threadbare *recitals of the elements* of a cause of action, supported by *mere conclusory statements*, do not suffice" to meet the requirement of plausibility.) Choice (B), by asserting that the motion must be denied unless defendant has shown that there is "no set of facts" that plaintiff could prove that would be sufficient to show fraud, adheres to the now-abandoned *Conley* standard rather than to the current standard by which the motion will be granted if the court determines that plaintiff's allegations are "conclusory" and not "plausible."

Choice (C) is wrong, because a party is never required to move for a judgment on the pleadings and, in any event, such a motion is available only after the pleadings are "closed." FRCP 12(c). In contrast, a motion to dismiss for failure to state a claim is filed prior to any responsive pleading, and thus prior to any motion for judgment on the pleadings. See FRCP 12(b) ("A motion asserting any of these defenses [including a motion under 12(b)(6) for "failure to state a claim upon which relief can be granted"] must be made before pleading if a responsive pleading is allowed.") The pleadings are closed only after an answer has been filed. See FRCP 7(a). Here, since the facts say that Defendant has not yet answered, it's clear that Defendant was not required to move for judgment on the pleadings.

Choice (D) is wrong, because under federal pleading rules, a plaintiff *may* join a tort and a contract claim in one lawsuit and, indeed, may join "as many claims as it has against an opposing party." FRCP 18(a). The federal joinder rules are broad and do not restrict the joinder of claims even if they relate to different transactions or depend on different legal theories.

Answer 40

The correct choice is **(D),** because a third-party defendant may assert against the plaintiff any defenses that the third-party plaintiff has to the plaintiff's claim. Once a person is brought in as a third-party defendant, Rule 14(a)(2)(C) says that that person "may assert against the plaintiff any defense that the third-party plaintiff has to the plaintiff's claim[.]" By allowing the third-party defendant to raise defenses that the third-party plaintiff might have failed to raise, the Rule 14(a)(2)(C) "protects the impleaded third-party defendant where the third-party plaintiff *fails or neglects to assert a proper defense* to the plaintiff's action." *Lindner v. Meadow Gold Dairies, Inc.*, 515 F. Supp. 2d 1141, 1149 (D. Haw. 2007) (quoting Advisory Committee Notes to 1946 Amendments to FRCP 14(a)). While it is unclear from the fact pattern whether a statute of limitations defense would be meritorious, the trucker is entitled to assert it as a way of showing that he has no third-party liability.

Choice (A) is wrong, because it's irrelevant for impleader whether the third-party defendant is or could be directly liable to the original plaintiff. Impleader does not require that the third-party defendant be liable directly to the original plaintiff; rather, it requires that the third-party defendant "is or may be liable" to *the original defendant*. Impleader thus is based on the *theory of derivative or secondary liability.* "It is well established that a defendant may, as third-party plaintiff, implead a party that the plaintiff could not sue directly, [so that] the claim against the third-party defendant inur[es] to the benefit of the third-party plaintiff and not to the original plaintiff." *Parks v. United States*, 784 F.2d 20, 24 (1st Cir. 1986).

So here, even though it is probably true as a matter of substantive law that the construction company could not recover directly against the trucker (because the trucker's promise of performance ran only to the benefit of the distributor, and the construction company was not an intended third-party beneficiary of that promise), this would be completely irrelevant to the key issue in the third-party suit of whether the trucker is liable to the distributor. Consequently, the court will not permit the trucker to raise as a defense that the construction company couldn't recover directly against the trucker.

Choice (B) is wrong, because impleader does not have to await judgment on the main claim. Federal Rule 14(a)(1) allows impleader against a party who "is or *may be liable*" to the third-party plaintiff, and this use of "may be" indicates that the impleader claim is permitted before the third-party plaintiff's liability has been determined by the court in the main action. In other words, the Rule does *not* require that the court first adjudicate the third-party plaintiff's liability. (In fact, Rule 14's strong preference that impleader occur very early in the litigation of the main claim is demonstrated by the last sentence of Rule 14(a)(1), which says that if the third-party plaintiff will be filing the third-party complaint "more than 14 days after serving its original answer," the third-party plaintiff must move to obtain leave of court to allow this later-than-usual filing.)

Choice (C) is wrong, because although the federal rule permits a third-party defendant to assert most defenses that the third-party plaintiff may have against the original plaintiff, there is an exception for "personal defenses" like venue. As is discussed more fully in the explanation of Choice (D) above, as a *general* rule the third-party defendant may assert against the original plaintiff any defense that the third-party plaintiff would have to the original plaintiff's claim. But the federal courts have recognized an exception to this general rule for any defense held by the third-party plaintiff that is classified as a *"personal defense,"* and venue (like lack of personal jurisdiction and improper service) is one of these personal defenses. See W,M&K (3d Ed.), Vol. 6, § 1457, p. 518: "[T]he third-party defendant may not object to the court's lack of personal jurisdiction over the defendant . . . [or] its lack of venue over the original action . . . even if the original defendant has not waived these defenses . . . . These matters are considered the original defendant's personal defenses and are therefore not available to the third-party defendant."

Answer 41

The correct choice is **(D),** because a third-party complaint is proper only where any liability it alleges would be derivative of the main plaintiff's claim against the third-party plaintiff. First, let's take care of several pieces of nomenclature: The electrician's claim against the plumber is a "third-party complaint"; the electrician is the "third-party plaintiff" (or "TPP"), and the plumber is the "third-party defendant" (or "TPD").

Now, then: The mechanism by which a third-party plaintiff may bring a third-party complaint against a third-party defendant is specified by FRCP 14. Rule 14(a)(1) says that "A defending party may, as third-party plaintiff, serve a summons and complaint on a nonparty ***who is or may be liable to it for all or part of the claim against [the third-party plaintiff].***" So the Rule 14 impleader procedure applies where, and only where, the third-party plaintiff is alleging that the third-party defendant "is or may be liable to [the third-party plaintiff] *for all or part of the claim against"* that third-party plaintiff.* In other words, the third-party complaint must assert some sort of ***derivative*** liability, whereby the TPD is alleged to be liable *not directly* to the original plaintiff, but *to the TPP* in the event that the TPP is found liable to the original plaintiff. See W,M&K (2d Ed.): "A third-party claim may be asserted under Rule 14(a) only when the third party's liability is in some way *dependent on the outcome of the main claim* or when the third party is *secondarily liable to defendant*."

Consequently, one type of claim that *cannot* be made in the form of a Rule 14 third-party claim is a so-called "claim" (which is really a "defense" rather than a claim) of the form, "If any party is liable to the main plaintiff, it's X, not me." See, e.g., *Toberman v. Copas,* 800 F. Supp. 1239, 1242 (M.D. Pa. 1992): "A theory that another party is the correct defendant is not appropriate for a third party complaint."

And that's what's going on here: The electrician is claiming that the driver who hit the messenger (the messenger being the original plaintiff) is not the electrician, but rather the plumber, so that only the plumber, not the electrician, could possibly be liable to the messenger. This claim is not a valid third-party claim, because any liability that the plumber might have for negligent driving is *completely separate* from the electrician's conduct and does not derive from any liability that the electrician might have to the messenger.

Since the claim is not a valid third-party claim, the court should (indeed must) dismiss the third-party complaint under Rule 12(b)(6) for failure to state a claim on which relief can be granted.

Choice (A) is wrong, because if the electrician-vs-plumber complaint here were an otherwise-valid third-party complaint, the doctrine of supplemental jurisdiction would remove any subject-matter jurisdiction problem. Supplemental jurisdiction is granted by 28 U.S.C. § 1367. § 1367(a) says that "in any civil action of which the district courts have *original jurisdiction*, the district courts shall have *supplemental jurisdiction* over *all other claims that are so related to claims in the action within such original jurisdiction that they form part of the same case or controversy* under Article III of the United States Constitution. Such supplemental jurisdiction *shall include claims that involve the joinder or intervention of additional parties*." So if the original claim by the plaintiff against the defendant falls within the district court's "original jurisdiction," then a third-party claim falls within supplemental jurisdiction as long as that third-party claim is "so related to" the original claim(s) that the original claim and the third-party claim can be said to be "part of the same case or controversy" for Article III constitutional purposes. And because of the derivative nature of a valid third-party claim (i.e., the fact that by definition it derives from the defendant's liability to the original plaintiff), the third-party claim will virtually *always* be "so related" to the main claim as to make them part of the "same case or controversy," as § 1367(a) requires.

In other words, *as a practical matter a valid Rule 14 third-party claim will virtually always fall within the court's supplemental jurisdiction.* See W,M,C&F (3d Ed.), Vol. 13D, § 3567.1, p. 347: "[I]mpleader claims routinely satisfy § 1367(a) because they concern the ultimate liability for the very transaction that is the basis of the underlying suit." Therefore, if the electrician's claim against the plumber were a valid third-party claim under Rule 14 (which it isn't), the applicability of supplemental jurisdiction under 28 U.S.C. § 1367(a) would mean that the fact that the electrician and the plumber are not diverse to each other would be irrelevant. That makes Choice (A) incorrect as an argument for why the court should dismiss the third-party complaint.

Choice (B) is wrong, because the "100-mile bulge" provision of Rule 4(k)(1)(B) gives the court personal jurisdiction over the plumber.

Rule 4(k)(1) says that "Serving a summons or filing a waiver of service establishes personal jurisdiction over a defendant: . . . (B) who is a *party joined under Rule 14* or 19 and is *served within a judicial district of the United States and not more than 100 miles from where the summons was issued*[.]" This is the so-called *"100-mile bulge" provision*, which grants a federal court personal jurisdiction over a third-party defendant if that party can be found and served within a 100-mile radius of the courthouse in which the federal court hearing the case sits. And that's true even if the third-party defendant does not have minimum contacts (or, indeed, *any* contacts whatsoever) with the state where the action is pending, as long as that third-party defendant has minimum contacts with the state where he was served.

The service on the plumber here meets this requirement, because: (1) the underlying case is pending at the federal courthouse located in State A; (2) service of the third-party complaint was made in person on the plumber at a place in State C less than 100 miles from the State A federal courthouse; and (3) the facts tell you that the plumber was performing a multi-week project at the site in State C where he was served, enough of a contact with State C to constitute the constitutionally-required minimum contacts with State C.

So if the complaint were a valid third-party complaint as defined in Rule 14, the 100-mile bulge provision would apply, furnishing the State A federal court with personal jurisdiction over the plumber and making this choice an incorrect argument for why the claim against the plumber should be dismissed.

Choice (C) is wrong, because service of the complaint on plumber was quick enough to meet the "of right" requirements. FRCP 14, in addition to specifying what types of claims may be made by impleader, specifies the time limits for making service of a Rule 14 impleader claim. Rule 14(a)(1) starts by articulating the general principle that "A defending party may, as third-party plaintiff, serve a summons and complaint on a nonparty who is or may be liable to it for all or part of the claim against [the third-party plaintiff]." Then, the next sentence of 14(a)(1) says, "But the third-party plaintiff must, by motion, obtain the court's leave *if it files the third-party complaint more than 14 days after serving its original answer*[.]"

Reading these first two sentences of Rule 14(a)(1) together, the scheme is that as long as the defending party serves the third-party complaint within 14 or fewer days after that defending party served its "original answer," no leave of court is required (i.e., the third-party claim can be served "of right"). The facts here tell you that the electrician served his purported third-party complaint against the plumber 11 days after the electrician had served his original answer to the messenger's complaint. So the service of the third-party complaint occurred less than 14 days after service of the original answer, obviating the need for the electrician to obtain leave of court. That means that the electrician's failure to get leave of court is not a reason for dismissing the third-party claim.

Answer 42

The correct choice is **(B),** because a suit may be brought on behalf of a minor by a parent or guardian. Federal Rule of Civil Procedure 17(c)(1) says that "The following representatives may sue or defend on behalf of a *minor* or an incompetent person: (A) a *general guardian* . . . or (D) a like fiduciary." Rule 17(c)(2) then says that "A minor or an incompetent person *who does not have a duly appointed representative* may sue *by a next friend or by a guardian ad litem*." So in this case, assuming that neither parent has been appointed to be a "general guardian" for the child (i.e., his guardian for all legal purposes), either parent can file suit as a "next friend" of the child, as authorized by 17(c)(2). "A next friend is one who, without being [a] regularly-appointed guardian, represents an infant plaintiff." *Till v. Hartford Acc. & Indem. Co.*, 124 F.2d 405, 408 (10th Cir. 1941). So the suit would be captioned "[Parent] as next friend of [Child] v. Motorcyclist."

Not only is the parent *permitted* to appear as the named plaintiff/next friend, but under the Federal Rules there *must* be some competent adult who is given responsibility for protecting the interests of the minor if the suit is brought solely in the name of the minor. That's because the final sentence of Rule 17(c)(2) (which follows the sentence quoted above) says that "The court ***must appoint a guardian ad litem — or issue another appropriate order*** — to protect a minor or incompetent person who is unrepresented in an action." So it's very likely that the court will either require that the child's parent be the named plaintiff as a "next friend" or insist that the parent or someone else with the child's welfare at heart be named as a guardian *ad litem* (i.e., guardian for the limited purposes of protecting the child's interest in the litigation).

Choice (A) is wrong, because the rule that it asserts — that the plaintiff in a lawsuit must be the real party in interest — is correct in most situations, but not correct in the special situation where the party in interest is a minor. Federal Rule 17 (which is in fact entitled "Real Party in Interest") begins by announcing the general rule that "An action must be prosecuted in the name of the real party in interest." But Rule 17 then goes on to list various exceptions to this rule. One exception is that a "guardian" is among several types of people all of whom "may sue in their own names without joining the person for whose benefit the action is brought." Rule 17(a)(1)(C). So if the child's parent or some other adult had been appointed as the child's guardian for all purposes, the guardian *would* be allowed to bring suit in his own name. Furthermore, Rule 17(c)(1) says that "A minor or an incompetent person who does not have a duly appointed representative may sue by a next friend or by a guardian ad litem." So even if, say, no one had been appointed a general guardian for the child, the child's parent could in effect appoint himself or herself "next friend," and bring suit in his/her name as authorized by 17(c)(1). So Choice (A), by saying that the child must be named as plaintiff because he is the real party in interest, is simply wrong.

Choice (C) is wrong, because the insurance carrier is not in fact a "real party in interest." First, as a matter of nomenclature, under the FRCP, the phrase "real party in interest" refers *only* to people on the ***plaintiff*** side of the action, not those on the defense side. So even if there were some rule requiring that the insurance carrier be made a defendant, that result would not be correctly explained by saying that the carrier was a "real party in interest."

More substantively, there simply is no procedural rule in the federal system that would require the joinder of the insurer as a party at all. It's true that in some circumstances, a party must be joined — whether as a plaintiff or as a defendant — because that party's presence in the action is required in order for the court to do justice in the action. See FRCP 19. But a party is a required party only if one of several quite specific fact patterns exists: either (1) in that party's absence, the court cannot accord complete relief among the existing parties, or (2) the person alleged to be required to be joined claims an interest related to the action's subject and that person is so situated that not joining the person may "impair or impede the person's ability to protect the interest" or "leave an existing party subject to a substantial risk of incurring double, multiple, or otherwise inconsistent obligations because of the interest." FRCP 19(a)(1)(B). Here, the motorcyclist's insurance carrier does not fit into any of these categories: First, the carrier's absence does not prevent complete relief among the existing parties. Second, the carrier does not have an interest that needs to be protected in the current lawsuit, because the motorcyclist's liability can be determined without assessing his insurance situation. Finally, there is no person already a party (and the only plausible "already present" party would be the motorcyclist) who would be subjected to double, multiple, or otherwise inconsistent obligations — the motorcyclist will be entitled to have the insurer pay any judgment and/or legal expense up to the policy limits, even if the carrier is not joined.

Choice (D) is wrong, because the underlying rule of liability that it asserts is not legally correct. Whether a party must be joined in a lawsuit is governed by the rules determining who is a required party, and those rules are set out in FRCP 19. Even if the aunt and uncle were joint tortfeasors with the motorcyclist, "[i]t has long been the rule that it ***is not necessary for all joint tortfeasors to be named as defendants in a single lawsuit.***" *Temple v. Synthes Corp.,*

Ltd., 498 U.S. 5, at 7 (1990). The Advisory Committee Notes to the 1966 amendments to Rule 19(a) state that "a tortfeasor with the usual 'joint-and-several' liability is merely a ***permissive*** party to an action against another with like liability." Therefore, it is up to the child (or his lawyer or guardian) to decide whether to make permissive joinder of the aunt and uncle.

Furthermore, as a matter of substantive tort law, it's not at all clear that the aunt and uncle would indeed be primarily or secondarily liable as this choice asserts. Since they didn't give the motorcyclist permission to use the cycle or even know that he was planning to do so, they can't be primarily liable for, say, negligent entrustment. And unless there existed a somewhat unusual state statute making them strictly or vicariously liable for damage done by a vehicle or instrument they owned, they would not have secondary liability.

Answer 43

The correct choice is **(B),** because it correctly states the standard that governs amendment under the federal rules when a responsive pleading omits an affirmative defense. Under the fairly liberal amendment procedure of Federal Rule 15, a party (call that party "*A*," and the opposing party "*B*" for clarity) may amend his pleading ***once as a matter of right*** in either of these two situations: (1) within ***21 days of when A served his original pleading*** (see Rule 15(a)(1)(A)) or (2) if *A*'s pleading was one that required a ***responsive pleading*** by *B*, within ***21 days*** of when B either (i) ***served that responsive pleading*** or (ii) made a ***motion*** under Rule 12(b), (e), or (f) (with the 21 days starting on whichever of two events mentioned in (i) and (ii) happened earlier) (see Rule 15(a)(1)(B)).

In our situation, Defendant's answer did not assert any counterclaims. Therefore, the service of that answer did not require a "responsive pleading" (the way, for instance, an answer that included a counterclaim would have required that Plaintiff filed an answer to the counter-claim). Since no responsive pleading was required, the scenario covered in sub-section (2) in the prior paragraph (the situation governed by Rule 15(a)(1)(B)) does not apply. Consequently, the only scenario in which defendant had a period in which to amend "of right" was the scenario covered in sub-section (1) above, the garden-variety scenario in which Defendant had the right to amend once if he acted within the 21 days following his service of his original answer (with that original service having happened on March 15).

Therefore, once 21 days passed after March 15 (i.e., once April 7 or thereabouts arrived), Defendant ***lost the right to amend even once as of right.*** So by April 20, defendant was in a position where he could amend only "with the opposing party's written consent or the court's leave." (Rule 15(a)(2).) Since we know from the facts that Defendant did not request (and thus did not receive) Plaintiff's consent to the amendment, the only route left to Defendant was to seek the court's permission to amend. (And, by the way, Rule 15(a)(2) says that "the court should ***freely give leave*** when justice so requires"; since the case is still in its early stages, and there is no apparent prejudice to Plaintiff that would result from an amendment, the court is very likely to grant the leave to amend if asked to do so.)

Choice (A) is wrong, because it misstates the timing requirement of the federal rule with respect to amendment. A party has an ***automatic right to amend his or her pleadings, but only if 21 days have not elapsed since service of the paper.*** See FRCP 15(a). Putting aside special provisions for the situation in which that party's pleading required a responsive plead-ing (not applicable here), once 21 days passed from when Defendant filed his original answer on March 15, Defendant could *only* amend by successfully requested leave of court. (See more about this in the discussion of Choice (B) above.)

It's true that Defendant, as one who granted a requested waiver of service, was *originally* entitled to 60 days from the day Plaintiff sent the waiver request (i.e., until about May 3) in which to answer, a time period that has still not elapsed. But once Defendant filed his first answer, the relevant time limit became 21 days after that filing, not the originally available 60-days-following-service-of-waiver-request; that's why a defendant should take care before filing a first version of his or her answer.

Choice (C) is wrong, because the doctrine of waiver does not operate in the automatic manner described in this choice. It's true that, generally, a defendant's failure to plead an affirmative defense, such as the statute of limitations, will *eventually* act as a waiver of that defense. However, a party that fails to include an affirmative defense in its answer may **amend** the answer as of right if 21 days have not passed since service of that answer (and may also amend on consent of the opposing party or with leave of court). So Choice (C), by saying that Defendant's failure to include the defense in his answer constituted an "automatic" waiver that could not be cured by amendment-of-right, is legally incorrect.

Choice (D) is wrong, as a matter of law. There *are* certain defenses that may be asserted by motion rather than as part of the answer; they are the seven defenses specified in Rule 12(b)(1)-(7), which include lack of subject-matter or personal jurisdiction, failure to state a claim on which relief can be granted, etc. But unless a defense is one of the seven special ones listed in 12(b)(1)-(7), the defense may *only* be asserted as part of the answer, not by motion. The statute of limitations is not one of the seven, so it may not be asserted by motion. (Indeed, statute of limitations is an "affirmative defense," and as such must, according to Rule 8(c)(1), be affirmatively stated in the "responsive pleading" filed by the one asserting it, which in this case is the answer.)

Answer 44

The correct choice is **(C)**, because it recognizes that an ***untimely amended claim*** will ***"relate back"*** to the date of the original pleading ***only if it arises out of the same transaction or occurrence as the original claim.*** The facts tell you that the tort claim would be time-barred if it were brought as a new state-court action. The federal courts in diversity cases are required to treat a state-law-based claim as time-barred if it would be time-barred in a state-court action. Therefore, the tort claim will also have to be time-barred in the federal diversity action unless there is some procedural rule that allows the tort claim to "relate back" to the earlier-filed contract claim. In federal actions — whether ones asserting federal-question claims or state-law claims asserted in diversity — the availability of the relation-back doctrine is controlled by Rule 15(c).

Assuming that all defendants to the newly-asserted claim are ones who were named in the previously-filed claims (and that's the situation here, where only Defendant is named in both the old contract claim and the new tort claim), Rule 15(c)(1) recognizes two situations in which relation back will apply. 15(c)(1) says that:

> "An ***amendment*** to a pleading ***relates back to the date of the original pleading*** when:
>
> (A) the ***law that provides the applicable statute of limitations allows*** relation back; [or]
>
> (B) the ***amendment asserts a claim or defense that arose out of the conduct, transaction, or occurrence set out*** — or attempted to be set out — in the ***original pleading***[.]"

As to 15(c)(1)(A), the "law that provides the applicable statute of limitations" is, of course, the substantive law of State A, since the new claim is based on state tort law. The facts tell you that under State A law, "relation back" applies where the new and old claim not only arise out of the same conduct or transaction but are supported by identical or near-identical legal theories. Here, the old claim is a pure breach-of-contract claim, and the new claim is a pure tort claim, so it is very unlikely that the federal court would find that State A law would allow relation back in this circumstance.

This fact means that Plaintiff's only hope of getting relation back applied will have to come from convincing the court that the requirements of 15(c)(1)(B) are satisfied here — i.e., that the breach-of-contract claim and the tortious-interference claim arise out of the same "conduct, transaction or occurrence." Plaintiff is unlikely to succeed in convincing the court of this. But *you don't have to decide whether plaintiff will succeed* with that argument — you just have to realize that *if* we start from the assumption that Defendant wins on its motion (i.e., gets the tort claim dismissed as time-barred), the only one of the four choices that asserts a legal theory that would deliver a victory to Defendant is the choice that turns on whether both claims involved the same conduct or transaction. Because of 15(c)(1)(B), a conclusion by the court that they involve different conduct/transactions will deliver a victory to defendant; and as we'll see in the discussion of the other choices, none of those makes a legal argument that could deliver a victory to Defendant.

Choice (A) is wrong, because it misstates the significance of the law of State A. As discussed in Choice (C) above, Rule 15(c)(1) allows the pleader to get the benefit of relation back if either of two standards is satisfied, one of which (given in 15(c)(1)(A)) is that in a diversity case, the law of the state that supplies the rule of decision would allow relation-back. So if State A law allowed relation back on these facts, Plaintiff would get the benefit of relation back here, without any need to consider the other (federal-law) standard listed in 15(c)(1). But the converse is not true — even if the law of the state that supplies the rule of decision doesn't allow relation back, the pleader gets the benefit if the test of 15(c)(1)(B) (the old claim and new claim arose out of the same transaction or occurrence) is satisfied. Choice (A) asserts that Defendant automatically wins (i.e., there's no relation back) if State A law doesn't allow relation back; since Plaintiff could still win based on same-transaction-or-occurrence even if State A law didn't allow relation back, Choice (A) is legally incorrect.

Choice (B) is wrong, because a difference in legal theory between the two claims does not necessarily prevent relation back from operating. Remember that regardless of what the relevant state law says about the availability of relation back, Rule 15(c)(1)(B) says that Plaintiff can get the benefit of relation back based *solely* on whether the old claim and the new claim arise out of the same transaction or occurrence. In other words, for purposes of meeting the 15(c)(1)(B) federal standard, there is no requirement that the old claim and the new claim be based on the same legal theory. Since Choice (B) says that a difference in legal theory would cause Defendant to win (i.e., would cause relation back not to apply), that choice is legally incorrect.

Choice (D) is wrong, because any delay by Plaintiff in amending would be irrelevant to the issue of whether relation back is allowed. It's true that in some circumstances, a federal court may use its discretion to deny leave to amend a pleading because the pleader delayed his attempt to amend unduly and without good cause. However, the issue here is solely the one raised by Defendant on its motion; whether the tort claim is *time-barred*, i.e., foreclosed by the statute of limitations. Any delay by the Plaintiff in amending would not bear on whether the statute of limitations has run — only successful use of the relation-back doctrine will allow plaintiff to avoid being time-barred, and a delay by plaintiff in amending will not prevent use of relation back if the requirements imposed by Rule 15(c)(1) for that doctrine are otherwise satisfied. See *Arthur v. Maersk, Inc.*, 434 F.3d 196, 203 (3d Cir. 2006) ("There is no allowance in Rule 15(c) for inquiry into a party's delay in moving for leave to amend.").

Answer 45

The correct choice is **(D)**, because it states the standard for permissive intervention. First, note that the employer's claim against the building owner independently meets federal subject-matter jurisdiction requirements: (1) the employer is a citizen of State B and the building owner is a citizen of State C, so there is complete diversity between them; and (2) the claim is for more than $75,000, thus meeting the amount in controversy requirement for diversity actions.

Everything else you need in order to answer this question is contained on the face of Rule 24, covering intervention. The Rule distinguishes between intervention of *right* (covering situations in which the court *must* allow the intervention) and *permissive* intervention (covering situations in which the court has *discretion* about whether to permit the intervention). 24(b), which covers permissive intervention, says that "(1) On timely motion, the court *may permit* anyone to intervene who: . . . (B) has a claim or defense that *shares with the main action a common question of law or fact*."

Since both the clerk's personal injury claim and the employer's property-damage claim assert that it was negligent for the building owner not to correct the icy condition of the ground near the loading dock, the employer's claim "shares with the main action" (i.e., with the clerk's claim) a "common question of law or fact," namely whether it was indeed negligent for the owner not to clear the icy condition. That's enough to trigger permissive intervention under 24(b)(1)(B).

It's not clear that the district court *will* allow the intervention; but where the "common question of law or fact" requirement is met, the district court *usually* grants the motion for intervention, on the theory that doing so best conserves scarce judicial resources. In any event, the question asks you to say not what the court "will do" but merely what the court's "likely" response to the intervention request will be; Choice (D) is the best prediction of that response.

Choice (A) is wrong, because for permissive intervention there is no requirement that absent intervention, the would-be intervener's interest would likely be impaired. In this choice, the examiners are trying to trick you into thinking of intervention *of right* rather than permissive intervention. Intervention *of right* requires a risk that without the ability to intervene, the would-be intervenor's ability to protect her own interest will be impaired. As Rule 24(a)(2) puts it, intervention of right — that is, intervention that the district court *must* (not just "may") allow — is present where the would-be intervenor "claims an *interest relating to the property or transaction that is the subject of the action*, and is so situated that *disposing of the action may as a practical matter impair or impede the movant's ability to protect its interest*, unless existing parties adequately represent that interest."

So if the question were asking you whether the court "must" permit intervention, this choice would be correct (since the court "must" allow intervention only if the facts qualify for intervention of right, which these facts do not). But here, the question is asking you only whether the court is "likely" to allow intervention. And in a fact pattern like the one here — where it's not just the case that *some* claim or defense in the proposed intervention would share *some* common question of law or fact with a claim in the main action, but rather the case that the *only* claim in the main action and the only claim in the intervening action share a common question — the district court is likely to grant the motion even though it's not required to do so.

Choice (B) is wrong, because the fact that the clerk chose not to join the employer as a co-plaintiff in the clerk's action is completely irrelevant to the issue of intervention. As we discuss in the analysis of Choice (D), all that is required for the court to have discretion under Rule 24(b)(1)(B) to allow intervention (i.e., for the case to be one that's proper for *permissive* intervention rather than one giving the intervenor the power of intervention as of *right*) is that the proposed intervenor "has a claim or defense that shares with the main action a common question of law or fact." And the fact that the proposed intervenor satisfies this "shares with the main action a common question" does not in turn mean that the clerk was required to join the employer as a co-plaintiff.

(It probably *is* the case that the clerk and the employer *could* have jointly decided to sue as co-plaintiffs, since Rule 20(a)(1), part of Rule 20 on "permissive joinder," says that two or more persons "may join in one action as plaintiffs if: (A) they assert any right to relief . . . severally . . . with respect to or arising out of the same transaction, occurrence, or series of transactions or occurrences; and (B) any question of law or fact common to all plaintiffs will arise in the action." But the fact that the clerk and employer didn't exercise their right to join as co-plaintiffs does not mean that the employer lost its right to seek permissive intervention.)

Choice (C) is wrong, because (1) the employer is *not* an indispensable party; but (2) there is no requirement that in order to be a proper situation for permissive intervention, the would-be intervenor must be an indispensable party. Rule 19(a) identifies certain situations in which a person who is not currently part of the action is "required to be joined if feasible." Within that category, Rule 19(b)(2) identifies the possibility of a third person who is not now a party (call her "X") whose presence going forward is so important that if the limits on service of process or subject-matter jurisdiction prevent X from being made a party on one or the other side of the action, the court determines that "in equity and good conscience," it is better to dismiss the action than to continue the action without X. If X is such a party (colloquially called an "indispensable party"), Rule 19(b)(2) effectively requires the court to dismiss the action rather than proceeding without X's (impossible-to-achieve) presence.

But on our facts here, there is no reason to believe that the employer is a Rule 19(a) person who is "required to be joined if feasible," let alone reason to believe that the employer is one who is so important to the action that in its absence, the suit should be dismissed rather than pursued without it. But as we discuss in Choice (D), the employer meets the much easier-to-satisfy test for permissive intervention (a common question of law or fact between the main claim and the intervenor's claim). Therefore: (1) the employer is not an "indispensable party" (one in whose absence the case is better dismissed than proceeded with); but (2) the fact that the employer is not an indispensable party comes nowhere close to preventing the case from being one where the employer is likely to succeed in being granted permissive intervention.

Answer 46

The correct choice is **(C),** because it recognizes the special requirements imposed on a stake-holder in a statutory interpleader action. Interpleader is a procedure that allows a party — called the stakeholder — *to join in one lawsuit all claimants to whom he is or might be liable.* Federal law recognizes two different kinds of interpleader actions: "*Rule 22*" interpleader (see FRCP 22) and "*statutory*" interpleader (see 28 U.S.C. § 1335). Although the procedures serve the same purpose — to enable a party to avoid the risk of multiple and conflicting liability — statutory and rule interpleader differ in their procedural requirements.

Statutory interpleader requires that the plaintiff **deposit the stake** "into the registry of the court . . . or [furnish a] bond payable to the clerk of the court in such amount and with surety as the court or judge may deem proper." 28 U.S.C. § 1335(a)(2). In the situation in which the stake is an insurance policy sought by multiple claimants who assert claims that aggregate more than the policy limit, the court will normally require that cash or a bond for the full policy limit (here, $3 million) be deposited. If the court issues such an order (as it will almost certainly do here) and Plaintiff declines to post that amount in cash or via a surety bond, the court will lack subject-matter jurisdiction over the interpleader action and will have no choice but to dismiss the action. See, e.g., *United States Fire Insurance Co. v. Asbestospray, Inc.,* 182 F.3d 201, 210 (3d Cir.

1999) ("A proper deposit or bond is a jurisdictional prerequisite . . . . The stakeholder . . . must deposit the largest amount for which it may be liable in view of the subject matter of the controversy." (By the way, *Rule 22* interpleader does *not* have an explicit deposit or bond requirement.)

Choice (A) is wrong, because it misstates the subject-matter jurisdiction requirements for a statutory interpleader action. ***Statutory interpleader requires only diversity of citizenship between any two of the claimants—what is known as "minimal diversity."*** The statute explicitly provides that subject to a special amount-in-controversy requirement, "[t]he district court shall have original jurisdiction of any action of interpleader . . . ***if [t]wo or more adverse claimants, of diverse citizenship*** as defined in subsection (a) or (d) of section 1332 of this title, ***are claiming*** or may claim to be entitled to such money or property . . . ." 28 U.S.C. § 1335(a)(1). The U.S. Supreme Court has recognized that this statutory provision requires only " 'minimal diversity,' that is, diversity of citizenship between two or more claimants, without regard to the circumstance that other rival claimants may be co-citizens." *State Farm Fire & Casualty Co. v. Tashire*, 386 U.S. 523, 530 (1967).

Since the facts tell you that there are at least two claimants of diverse citizenship (more precisely, that the claimants include citizens of seven different states, State A through State G), you know that the requirement of minimal diversity is satisfied here. Contrary to the statement in Choice (A), the citizenship of the *stakeholder* (here, Plaintiff) is ***irrelevant*** to this determination—so it wouldn't matter, say, if every claimant but one was a citizen of State A, the same state of citizenship as Plaintiff.

Choice (B) is wrong, because it misstates the special amount-in-controversy requirement that applies to statutory interpleader in a diversity suit. ***Statutory interpleader requires only that a claim of at least $500 be in controversy, as measured by the stake.*** See 28 U.S.C. § 1335(a) ("The district courts shall have original jurisdiction of any civil action of interpleader . . . filed by any person . . . having in his . . . custody or possession money or property of the value of $500 or more. . . ."). By contrast, in "Rule 22" interpleader, the amount-in-controversy must exceed $75,000 if the suit is based solely on diversity.

Choice (D) is wrong, because it misstates the federal court's power to issue the requested injunction. The whole purpose of statutory interpleader is to protect the stakeholder from multiple and/or inconsistent judgments. And that purpose would be defeated if the federal court hearing the interpleader suit couldn't ***enjoin the claimants*** from trying to collect the stake in other lawsuits, whether federal or state ones. Therefore, 28 U.S.C. § 2361 provides that as part of any statutory interpleader action, "a district court may issue its process for all claimants and ***enter its order restraining them from instituting or prosecuting any proceeding in any State or United States court affecting the . . . obligation*** involved in the interpleader action[.]" (But this language does not authorize the federal court to enjoin the individual state-court suits from continuing against *Defendant*. So the claimants can continue to litigate in their state-court suits whether Defendant is liable, and for how much; what the claimants *can't* do in the state-court suits is to try to collect from Plaintiff, the insurer, insurance proceeds to cover any judgment against Defendant.)

Answer 47

The correct choice is **(A)**, because it is the only one of the choices that proposes actions that have a real chance of success. This is one of the rare MBE questions in which you cannot confidently arrive at the correct choice without eliminating each of the other choices first—that's because all three of the other choices involve motions which, if successful would terminate the action in the driver's favor, but in fact none of these motions will succeed. We'll discuss why each motion fails in our discussion of the choice that raises the motion. For now, let's briefly analyze why the answer proposed in this choice meets procedural requirements.

First, let's consider whether this choice is correct in proposing that the answer raise "the affirmative defense of contributory negligence." Affirmative defenses, as the name implies, are defenses as to which the party asserting the defense (typically but not always the defendant) has an affirmative obligation to raise the defense in her answer—she is not free to remain silent in her answer, and then "spring" the defense at trial. FRCP 8(c)(1) says that "In *responding to a pleading,* a party *must affirmatively state* any avoidance or affirmative defense," and then goes on to list nearly 20 defenses that it classifies as affirmative ones, a list that includes contributory negligence. Here, the driver's answer is a "respon[se] to a pleading" (the complaint), so the driver was not only entitled, but required, to raise contributory negligence as a defense.

Now, let's look at this choice's statement that the driver should "assert[] a counterclaim for negligence, seeking damages for the driver's injuries." As with the affirmative defense of contributory negligence, the counterclaim for negligence is something that the driver is not merely permitted, but *required*, to assert as part of her answer. Rule 13(a) says that:

> "(a) *Compulsory Counterclaim.*
>
> > (1) *In General.* A pleading *must state as a counterclaim* any claim that—at the time of its service—the pleader has against an opposing party if the claim:
> >
> > > (A) *arises* out of the *transaction or occurrence* that is the *subject matter of the opposing party's claim*; and
> > >
> > > (B) [omitted because not relevant here]"

Here, the driver's counterclaim for negligence arose out of the same "transaction or occurrence" (the accident) as the pedestrian's claim against the driver. Therefore, under Rule 13(a)(1)(A), the driver's counterclaim was a compulsory one, which the driver was *required* to assert as part of her pleading (her answer)—if the driver did not assert it as part of her answer, she would lose the right to assert it in a future action. (See Adv. Comm. Note 6 to Rule 13: "If the action proceeds to judgment without the interposition of a counterclaim as required by subdivision (a) of this rule, the counterclaim is barred.")

Choice (B) is wrong, because judgment on the pleadings is not appropriate given that there is a factual issue about whether the pedestrian was negligent. The portion of this choice that suggests filing "an answer raising the affirmative defense of contributory negligence" is perfectly appropriate, as is discussed in Choice (A). But the portion suggesting that the driver "move for judgment on the pleadings" is *not* procedurally correct.

The procedural problem is that judgment on the pleadings is appropriate only where the pleadings disclose that there are no genuine issues of material fact in the case. See W&M (2004 Ed.), v. 5, § 1368, pp. 238-242: "[T]he district court should not dismiss the complaint [under Rule 12(c)] unless it appears beyond doubt that *the plaintiff can prove no set of facts* that would entitle him or her to relief under the governing substantive law." Furthermore, "[F]or purposes of the court's consideration of the Rule 12(c) motion, *all of the well pleaded factual allegations in the adversary's pleadings are assumed to be true* and *all contravening assertions in the movant's pleadings are taken to be false*. Thus, in effect, the party opposing the motion has the benefit of all possible favorable assumptions." Id. at pp. 230-237.

Here, the state of the pleadings clearly does not satisfy these requirements for judgment on the pleadings: the pedestrian is implicitly contending that he was not contributorily negligent, and the driver's assertion (in the affirmative defense in the answer) that the pedestrian *was* contributorily negligent must, for purposes of the dismissal motion, be taken to be false. In other words, when the court makes the required inferences, it will certainly not be the case that the pedestrian "can prove no set of facts that would entitle him to relief" (Id. at pp. 238-242.)

Choice (C) is wrong, because the State B federal court can exercise personal jurisdiction (of the "specific" variety) over the driver for this accident that occurred in State B, even though the driver does not live in that state. For the State B federal court to dismiss the pedestrian's suit for lack of personal jurisdiction, it would have to be the case that the defendant (the driver) did not have such minimum contacts with State B for it to be consistent with due process for the State B courts to exercise jurisdiction over that defendant. But it's well-established that when a person (here, the driver) *commits a tort while in the forum state*, the forum state does *not* violate due process by exercising personal jurisdiction over that person, at least for purposes of a suit arising out of the in-state tort. In other words, states may constitutionally exercise "specific jurisdiction" over out-of-state defendants who commit an in-state tort, i.e., jurisdiction for purposes of a suit arising out of the tort. And given that the state courts of State B may constitutionally exercise personal jurisdiction over the driver as an alleged in-state tortfeasor, so may the *federal* court located in State B exercise such jurisdiction.

Since we know that the State B courts may exercise specific jurisdiction over the driver as an alleged State B tortfeasor, it follows that the federal court may similarly exercise that jurisdiction, and the motion to dismiss for lack of personal jurisdiction will fail even though the driver is not a citizen (or even resident) of State B.

Choice (D) is wrong, because subject-matter jurisdiction of the "alienage" variety is available. This suit does not involve a federal question, because the pedestrian's negligence cause of action arises under state law, not federal law. Therefore, the basis for subject-matter jurisdiction will have to be some form of diversity jurisdiction. It's true that "conventional" diversity—which in a two-party case requires a citizen of one state to be suing a citizen of a different state—is not present here, because the driver is a citizen of a foreign country, not of any American state. But there is a second, less-common, form of diversity jurisdiction, known as *"alienage" jurisdiction*. Alienage jurisdiction is conferred by 28 U.S.C. § 1332(a)(2), which gives the federal district courts jurisdiction of civil actions (assuming more than $75,000 is at stake) that are between "*citizens of a State and citizens or subjects of a foreign state*[.]" Alienage jurisdiction exists here, since on one side we have the pedestrian, who is domiciled in State A (making him a "citizen" of State A for diversity purposes) and on the other side we have the driver, who the facts says is a "citizen of a foreign country." Therefore, it is not the case that the driver's lack of U.S. citizenship causes subject-matter jurisdiction to be lacking.

Answer 48

The correct choice is **(B),** because for a 23(b)(3) class action, common issues of law or fact must predominate. The facts tell you that the case has been brought as a (b)(3) action, which is both the most common kind of class action and the only type whose principal object can be the award of compensatory damages. (In other words, where the plaintiff representing the class is mainly interested in obtaining compensation for the members, a (b)(3) action is usually the only realistic alternative.) But as 23(b)(3) says in its initial words, a (b)(3) is suitable where (and only where), among other factors, "the court finds that the *questions of law or fact common to class members predominate* over any questions affecting only individual members."

Here, the facts tell you that Title I only prohibits *intentional* race or gender discrimination. The facts also tell you that there are nearly 100 low-level managers who each made his or her own decision about whether to hire or promote a particular class member. Therefore, for the fact-finder to decide which of the plaintiffs had her Title I rights violated by Defendant (and even ignoring the further issue of damages), the fact-finder would have to consider the relevant manager's mental state concerning *separately* as to each hiring decision, in order to determine whether the class member was indeed intentionally discriminated against by her manager. Therefore, it's unlikely that the trial judge can or will conclude that questions of law or fact *"common to class members"* will indeed **predominate** over these intent-focused issues that will have to be resolved on a per-claimant basis. See, e.g., *Wal-Mart Stores, Inc. v. Dukes*, 131 S. Ct. 2541, 2561 (2011), noting that in the employment-discrimination class suit there, the corporate defendant would have to be given the chance to "demonstrate that [each] *individual applicant* was denied an employment opportunity for lawful reasons," thereby preventing common issues from predominating over individual issues. In any event, the question asks you to choose the objection that is *most likely* to succeed for Defendant, and while the argument here might not succeed, it is the only one that offers even a decent possibility of success.

Choice (A) is wrong, because it's not likely that the 100 potential class members will be found insufficiently non-numerous. It's true that according to Rule 23(a)(1), no class action (i.e., regardless of whether the action is brought under 23(b)(1), (b)(2), or (b)(3)) may be certified unless the court concludes that "the class is so numerous that joinder of all members is impracticable[.]" There is no hard and fast rule on how large the class must be to meet this requirement. Classes as small as 14 members have been found sufficient to meet the numerosity requirement, although generally the class must include at least forty members. See *Consolidated Rail Corp. v. Town of Hyde Park*, 47 F.3d 473, 483 (2d Cir. 1995). Here, where there are about 100 potential class members, it's unlikely that the court would find that the number of members is so small as to be disqualifying. In any event, the common-question objection cited in Choice (B) is far more likely to succeed than the numerosity objection here.

Choice (C) is wrong, because it states a rule that is irrelevant to these facts. It's of course true that class actions, like all actions filed in federal court, must satisfy subject-matter jurisdiction requirements. But here, the complaint alleges a violation of a federal statute, making this a "federal question" class action rather than a class action based solely on diversity. And in federal question suits, jurisdiction does not require the showing of any amount in controversy (see 28 U.S.C. § 1331), and that's just as true with respect to class actions as in individual actions. If you were attracted to this choice, you might have been thinking of the one situation in which the availability of a class action *does* depend on at least $5 million being at stake: Under the Class Action Fairness Act or CAFA (embodied in 28 U.S.C. § 1332(c)(2) and (3)), a state-law-based class action in which at least one class member is of citizenship diverse to at least one defendant, the amount in controversy is satisfied if at least $5 million is at stake in the aggregate, even if no single claim would meet the ordinary $75,000 amount-in-controversy requirement. But since the suit here is based on a federal question, CAFA never comes into play, and there is no amount in controversy requirement at all.

Choice (D) is wrong, because the rule that it recites is not correct. In a class action, the court must be able to exercise personal jurisdiction over *defendant*. However, there is **no requirement that the court determine whether it could exercise personal jurisdiction over the class members**. See *Phillips Petroleum Co. v. Shutts*, 472 U.S. 797 (1985). Thus, even if the class members have no connection to the state in which the district court sits, the court is not thereby prevented from hearing the case. (There might be some due process problems if the absent class members who had no contacts with the forum state were nonetheless bound by a negative outcome in the suit, after those members were denied a chance to opt out from the suit. But in a (b)(3) action, such as the one here, absentees are always given the right to opt out, so there would be no problem in binding a class member who did not opt out, even if that member had never had any contacts with State A, where the class suit is proceeding.)

Answer 49

The correct choice is **(B),** because FRCP 23(f) gives the court of appeals discretion to allow the appeal if the plaintiffs petition for permission to appeal within 14 days after the trial judge entered her order denying certification. This question, like most MBE Civil Procedure questions, can be reliably answered solely by looking at the text of the relevant rule or statute. In this case, the relevant provision is FRCP 23(f). (Remember that Rule 23 sets out most details regarding how and when federal class actions are permitted.) The first sentence of 23(f) says that "A court of appeals *may permit an appeal from an order granting or denying class-action certification* under this rule if a petition for permission to appeal is filed with the circuit clerk within 14 days after the order is entered." The Advisory Committee's Notes to Rule 23(f) make it clear that this provision gives *full discretion* to the Court of Appeals—the court can hear, or reject, the immediate appeal for any reason or no reason.

Choice (A) is wrong, because it incorrectly asserts that the court of appeals does not have jurisdiction to hear the immediate appeal even if it wishes to do so. As the discussion of Choice (B) makes clear, FRCP 23(f) gives the court of appeals complete discretion to hear the immediate appeal, so long as the named plaintiffs file their petition to appeal with that court within 14 days of the entry of the trial court's denial of certification. In other words, the court of appeals has jurisdiction to hear the appeal if it wishes to do so; this choice, by asserting that the court does not have jurisdiction, is flatly incorrect.

Choice (C) is wrong, because it incorrectly asserts that the plaintiffs may immediately appeal as of right. As the discussion of Choice (B) shows, FRCP 23(f) leaves it to the court of appeals to decide, in its discretion, whether to hear the immediate appeal. Choice (C), by asserting that the named plaintiffs have a "right" to take the appeal if they file promptly, is inconsistent with Rule 23(f). (To look at it another way, federal appeals are generally allowed as of right only after the entry of a "final judgment" in the case. Here, where the trial judge is willing to have the case go forward to trial on the five named plaintiffs' individual claims, no final judgment has yet been entered; the order denying certification is not viewed as a "final judgment" for this purpose.)

Choice (D) is wrong, because the trial judge does not have the power to allow the immediate appeal, at least for the reasons stated in the choice. In limited circumstances, a federal district judge has the power to in effect *urge* the court of appeals to hear an interlocutory appeal. 28 U.S.C. § 1292(b) says:

> "When a district judge, in making in a civil action an order not otherwise appealable . . . , shall be of the opinion that such order involves a *controlling question of law* as to which there is *substantial ground for difference of opinion* and that an immediate appeal from the order may materially advance the ultimate termination of the litigation, he shall *so state in writing* in such order. The Court of Appeals which would have jurisdiction of an appeal of such action may thereupon, in its discretion, permit an appeal to be taken from such order, if application is made to it within ten days after the entry of the order[.]"

But there are at least two reasons why Choice (D) is not correct despite § 1292(b): (1) that section applies only where the district judge believes that her order (in this case, the denial of class certification) involves a "controlling question of law as to which there is substantial ground for difference of opinion," and there's nothing in the facts to indicate that the judge believes that this "ground for difference of opinion" requirement is satisfied (and the fact that denial will sound the "death knell" of the suit is not at all the same concept); and (2) even if the district judge *does* invoke § 1292(b) in a written order, this fact doesn't automatically bring about an interrogatory appeal—it's still within the complete *discretion* of the Court of Appeals to hear or not hear the appeal. (But as a practical matter, if the named plaintiffs here were able to convince the trial judge to include a § 1292(b) statement in the order, that statement would materially increase the odds that the Court of Appeals would exercise its discretion to hear the immediate appeal.) Therefore, Choice (D) is not the best response.

Answer 50

The correct choice is **(C)**, because no discovery may happen until the parties have conferred in the manner this choice describes. FRCP 26(d)(1) says that as a general rule, "A *party may not seek discovery* from any source before *the parties have conferred* as required by Rule 26(f)[.]" So until the parties have conferred (which Rule 26(f)(1) says must usually occur "as soon as practicable"), neither party may request any sort of discovery, a prohibition that implicitly includes the serving of interrogatories. Rule 26(f)(2) then describes the tasks that the parties must perform during the 26(f) conference, two of which are to "make or arrange for the [initial] disclosures required by Rule 26(a)(1)" and to "develop a proposed discovery plan." Since Choice (C) refers to a conference that will include arranging for "initial disclosures" and preparing "a discovery plan," the choice correctly echoes two of the major tasks that must occur during the Rule 26(f) conference.

Choice (A) is wrong, because it states a limitation on interrogatories that does not exist. Rule 33(a)(2), on the scope of interrogatories, says that "[a]n interrogatory may relate to any matter that may be inquired into under Rule 26(b)." Rule 26(b) in turn says (in 26(b)(1)) that parties may obtain discovery "regarding any nonprivileged matter that is relevant to any party's claim or defense and proportional to the needs of the case[.]" In other words, nothing in Rule 26(b)(1) on discovery generally, or in Rule 33 on interrogatories in particular, makes questions about the other party's "contentions" off-limits. Indeed, to the extent that the word "contentions" in this question means "contentions about law or the application of law to fact," the second sentence of Rule 33(a)(2) expressly makes this choice's assertion about contentions incorrect, by saying, "An interrogatory is *not objectionable* merely because it asks for an opinion or *contention* that relates to fact or the application of law to fact[.]"

Choice (B) is wrong, because it states a limitation on interrogatories that does not exist. It may well be true that *usually*, interrogatories won't be served until after the defendant has answered, due to a combination of the fact that (1) the defendant must normally answer within 21 days after service, assuming the defendant did not waive service (see Rule 12(a)(1)(A)(i)) and did not make a Rule 12(b) motion; and (2) interrogatories can't be served until the Rule 26(f) initial conference has occurred, something that in most instances will not occur within 21 days following service. But there is no *requirement* that interrogatories be delayed until the answer has been filed, so long as Rule 26(d)(1)'s no-discovery-before-a-26(f)-conference principle (see Choice (C)) is not violated.

Choice (D) is wrong, because the maximum number of interrogatories has not been exceeded here. This choice correctly suggests that there is a maximum on the number of interrogatories that may be served unless the court gives permission or the parties so agree. But that limit is *exactly 25*, the number served here. See Rule 33(a)(1), saying that absent permission by the court, one party may serve on another "no more than 25 written interrogatories, including all discrete subparts."

Answer 51

The correct choice is **(A),** because it correctly reflects the general scope of discovery. Here is the FRCP's basic statement about what information may be obtained in discovery:

> "Unless otherwise limited by court order, the scope of discovery is as follows: Parties may obtain discovery regarding any nonprivileged matter that is *relevant to any party's claim or defense and proportional to the needs of the case*[.]"

Rule 26(b)(1), first sentence. (Notice, by the way, that the material has to be relevant to a "claim or defense in the case" — it's not enough that the material, though not directly relevant to any claim or issue, might reasonably *lead* to discovery of information that *is* relevant to a claim or issue.) So unless Plaintiff can show that the contract between Defendant and the lighting company somehow has bearing on Plaintiff's own claim (e.g., by helping to establish a pattern in which defendant intentionally orders goods and then refuses to pay), Plaintiff won't be entitled to the information, since it relates to a contract between different parties than does the contract presently in dispute.

Choice (B) is wrong, because it states a requirement that does not in fact exist. The last sentence of Rule 26(b)(1) says that "Information within this scope of discovery [defined in the prior sentence of the Rule] ***need not be admissible in evidence to be discoverable***." So as long as Defendant's answer would somehow be relevant to a claim or defense—relevant in the sense of making some proposition of fact or law more or less likely to be true then without the answer—the fact that the answer would not be directly admissible (e.g., because of some technical evidence rule like hearsay) is irrelevant.

Choice (C) is wrong, because ***an interrogatory may not be used to obtain information from a nonparty***. The "only to parties" limitation on the use of the interrogatory is clear from the language of the Federal Rule on interrogatories. The Rule is actually entitled "Interrogatories ***to Parties***," and says that "[a] party may serve ***on any other party*** no more than 25 written interrogatories" FRCP 33(a)(1). There is no analogous provision allowing for interrogatories to non-parties. Court decisions confirm that interrogatories may not be directed at a nonparty. See, e.g., *Lehman v. Kornblau*, 206 F.R.D. 345, 346 (E.D.N.Y. 2001) ("any interrogatories . . . served on non-parties are a nullity."). Since the choice refers to interrogatories "to the lighting company," and since there's no indication that the lighting company is a party to Plaintiff's case, the choice is incorrect.

Choice (D) is wrong, because it misapplies the standard that governs automatic initial discovery under FRCP 26(a)(1)(ii). Disclosure without a request or court order is required under the federal discovery rules as to all documents "that the disclosing party has in its possession, custody, or control and ***may use to support its claims or defenses***, unless the use would be solely for impeachment." FRCP 26(a)(1)(ii). So unless the document is one that the disclosing party (here, Defendant) thinks it may use in motions or at trial during the case, that party has no duty to make automatic disclosure of the document. Here, it is highly unlikely that Defendant will rely in any way on its contract with the lighting company to support its defenses in the present case—how would that contract plausibly help Defendant (though it could conceivably *hurt* Defendant, by showing a pattern of fraud)? Therefore, Defendant has no obligation to furnish a copy of the contract (or even to allude to its existence) as part of automatic initial disclosure. (Then, if Defendant later were to change its mind and try to use the contract as part of its case, that use would be prohibited unless Defendant could show that its earlier failure to disclose was "substantially justified or was harmless." FRCP 37(c)(1).)

Answer 52

The correct choice is **(D),** because the federal discovery rules recognize only one situation in which a person may be permitted to conduct discovery before any suit involving that person has been filed; that's the situation in which, under Rule 27, a person may seek a court order to ***"perpetuate testimony."*** Under the Rule 27 procedure, a person "who wants to perpetuate testimony about any matter cognizable in a United States court" may, even before any suit has been filed, file a "verified petition" showing, among other things:

> "(A) that the petitioner ***expects to be a party*** to [a federal-court action] but cannot presently bring it or cause it to be brought;
>
> (B) the subject matter of the expected action and the petitioner's interest;
>
> (C) the ***facts*** that the petitioner ***wants to establish*** by the proposed testimony and the ***reasons to perpetuate it***; . . .
>
> (E) the name, address, and expected substance of the testimony of each deponent."

Rule 27(a)(1).

Courts have interpreted Rule 27 as applying only where a delay in discovery (e.g., a delay until the case is filed and the usual post-filing discovery methods can be used) is *likely to result in a loss of evidence*. See, e.g., *Ash v. Cort*, 512 F.2d 909 (3d Cir. 1975). The facts here supply no reason to believe that if Company has to wait until Plaintiff files the expected suit and Company can use ordinary discovery methods, the state trooper's testimony is likely to become lost or unavailable. (For instance, Company does not allege that the state trooper is ill or planning soon to leave the country or that he plans to destroy or conceal evidence.)

Furthermore, Company has not specified any "facts that [it] wants to establish by the proposed testimony" (let alone any "reasons to perpetuate" that testimony) as 27(a)(1)(C) requires; it simply wishes to learn more about the accident. So Company has not met the requirements for the Rule 27 pre-filing deposition procedure, and there is no other procedure in the federal rules allowing for discovery before a case has been filed.

Choice (A) is wrong, because it asserts a legal rule that is broader than the actual rule. As discussed in the explanation for Choice (D) above, FRCP 27 explicitly allows for a deposition before commencement of a suit, as long as the party seeking discovery can show that it expects a suit to be brought, and that the testimony it seeks is at risk of being lost or destroyed. So although Choice (A) reaches the right outcome (that the request should be denied), the choice cites an absolute ban on taking discovery from nonparties before commencement of a suit, and no such ban exists.

Choice (B) is wrong, because is misstates the requirements of the relevant federal rule. A party seeking pre-complaint discovery must, according to Rule 27, file a *verified petition* with the district court, as explained in the discussion of Choice (D). But Rule 27 does not require that a draft complaint be attached to the petition, only that the petitioner show that it expects to be a party in a lawsuit. Thus, though Company's request should be denied, it is not for this reason, but rather the reason given in Choice (D).

Choice (C) is wrong, because no rule of the sort cited exists. If a suit *had already been filed*, this choice would be essentially correct in stating what information Company could obtain via a deposition of the non-party state trooper. (Note, however, that even then, the formulation in Choice (C) is a little too broad; Rule 26(b)(1), in addition to requiring that the information be relevant to a claim or defense, also requires that the information be "proportional to the needs of the case[.]") But where, as here, no case has yet been filed, discovery is narrowly limited to the situation in which there is a special need to "perpetuate testimony," as covered in the discussion of Choice (D).

Answer 53

The correct choice is **(D),** because one who is not a party or an officer of a party cannot be required to travel to be deposed if the deposition is more than 100 miles from the deponent's residence, place of business, or where he regularly transacts business. First, non-parties may be deposed only if they are first subpoenaed. Second, the places to which the non-party may be required to travel for a deposition are strictly limited by FRCP 45(c)(1), which provides that

> "A subpoena may command a person to attend a trial, hearing, or deposition only as follows:
>
> (A) *within 100 miles* of where the person *resides, is employed, or regularly transacts business in person*; or
>
> (B) *within the state* where the person resides, is employed, or regularly transacts business in person, if the person
>
> > (i) is *a party or a party's officer*; or
> >
> > (ii) is commanded to attend a trial and would not incur substantial expense."

So under Rule 45(c)(1)(A) and (B), if the person to be deposed is not a "party or a party's officer," that person may only be required to attend the deposition in a place covered by sub-paragraph (A), not one covered by sub-paragraph (B). That is, the person can be required only to travel "within 100 miles of where the person resides, is employed, or regularly transacts business in person[.]"

The facts tell you that the colleague (the person to be deposed) no longer works for Defendant, so the colleague cannot be an "officer" of the only party that is an entity rather than an individual (Defendant). And the facts also tell you that the colleague lives and works 200 miles away from the State A federal courthouse (and thus 200 miles from the deposing lawyer's office, since the office is next door to that courthouse). Lastly, the facts (laboriously) tell you that the colleague rarely travels more than 50 miles from his home and business, so you can infer that the lawyer's office is not within the 100-mile radius of any place the colleague "regularly transacts business in person." In sum, you can be confident that the deposing lawyer's office is not a place covered by Rule 45(c)(1)(A), and is therefore not a place to which this non-party can be compelled to travel.

Choice (A) is wrong, because the colleague's attendance at the specified place for deposition cannot be compelled even by a subpoena. As is more fully discussed in the analysis of Choice (D) above, the deponent is a non-party and therefore cannot be required to take the more-than-100-mile trip to the lawyer's office. (But this choice is partially correct in the sense that it accurately implies that even if the specified deposition site *were* within the 100-mile-radius of the deponent's home or workplace, a subpoena, not a mere notice of the deposition, would be required since the deponent is a non-party, and a notice of deposition may be used only as to a party. See the Advisory Committee Note to 2013 Amendments to Rule 45: "Depositions of parties, and officers, directors, and managing agents of parties, need not involve use of a subpoena.")

Choice (B) is wrong, because the colleague can't be required to make the trip at all, let alone be required to do so by means of a notice of deposition rather than subpoena. First, as is discussed in the analysis of Choice (D), the place of deposition is beyond the 100-mile-radius of the deponent's home or office, which represents the limit of the distance a deponent can be required to travel if the deponent is neither a party nor the officer of a party. Second, as is described in the parenthetical portion of the discussion of Choice (A), where the deponent is a non-party, attendance to a proper place for deposition must be compelled by a subpoena, not a mere notice of deposition.

Choice (C) is wrong, because not even "good cause" would support requiring the colleague to travel more than 100 miles to the lawyer's office. As is explained more fully in the analysis of Choice (D), if the deponent is neither a party nor the officer of a party, the deponent cannot be required to travel more than 100 miles from his residence, workplace, or place where he routinely transacts business. And that's true no matter how much "good cause" there is for holding the deposition outside the 100-mile radius. Furthermore, the fact that the deposition will be in state in which the deponent resides, works, or routinely does business in person, is *irrelevant* if the deponent is not a party or the officer of a party. (Where the deponent *is* a party or the officer of a party, then according to Rule 45(c)(1)(B), the deponent *may* be compelled to attend a deposition anywhere in the state in which he resides, works, or routinely transacts business, even if this would require a more-than-100-mile trip.)

Answer 54

The correct choice is **(B)**, because Rule 35 orders for medical examinations may be rendered only against parties or those under a party's control. FRCP 35(a)(1) specifies which persons may be ordered to undergo a physical or mental examination: "The court where the action is pending may **order a party** whose mental or physical condition — including blood group — is in controversy to submit to a physical or mental examination by a suitably licensed or certified examiner. The court has the same authority to *order a party* to produce for examination *a person who is in its custody or under its legal control.*"

The facts tell you that Driver is not a party to the action. And while Plaintiff might point to Driver's status as an employee of Defendant at the time of the accident in support of an argument that Driver is "under [Defendant's] legal control," this argument would almost certainly fail—the facts tell you that Driver is *no longer employed* by defendant, so he is no longer under Defendant's "legal control" even if he was under that control while employed. (Furthermore, it's doubtful that even if Driver *were* still employed by Defendant, this would be enough to put him under Defendant's "legal control." The courts have interpreted the sole purpose of the "under legal control" clause as being to help in cases where a parent or guardian is suing to recover for injuries to a *minor*; the clause "allows the court to order that the parent or guardian makes a good faith effort to produce the minor for examination." *Scharf v. U.S. Atty. Gen.*, 597 F.2d 1240, 1244 (9th Cir. 1979). That purpose obviously does not apply here.)

Choice (A) is wrong, because Rule 35 does not authorize in order to compel a non-party to submit to a physical or mental examination, even if the examinee's medical condition is relevant to a claim or defense in the action. As is more fully discussed in the treatment of Choice (B) above, only a party (or a person under the legal control of a party) may be the subject of a Rule 35 order.

Choice (C) is wrong, because the court would be required to deny the discovery request even if the plaintiff *had* shown good cause for the examination. It's true that even in the core situation to which Rule 36 applies—a request for an order compelling a party to submit to a physical or mental examination—the person requesting the order must show good cause. See Rule 35(a)(2)(A), which provides that the order for an examination may be made "only *on motion for good cause* and on notice to all parties and the person to be examined." But a showing of good cause is necessary *but not sufficient* for the order—no matter how strong the movant's need is for a physical examination of a non-party, Rule 35 does not authorize the court to order that examination. By implying that a showing of good cause would justify the court in ordering the examination, Choice (C) incorrectly states how Rule 35 works.

Choice (D) is wrong, because it misstates the rule that applies to requests for physical examinations. As is discussed in Choice (B), Rule 35 authorizes the court to order a party to produce a non-party for examination only if that party has "legal control" over the non-party, a situation that does not exist here, since Driver no longer works for Defendant.

Answer 55

The correct choice is **(C)**, because the defendant has not made the showing required to overcome the qualified work-product immunity that applies on these facts. Rule 26 confers a limited immunity from discovery (colloquially called *"work-product immunity,"* though that term is not used by the FRCP) for materials prepared in anticipation of litigation. The main provision that does this is the first sentence of Rule 26(b)(3)(A): "Ordinarily, a party *may not discover documents and tangible things that are prepared in anticipation of litigation or for trial by or for another party or its representative* (including the other party's attorney, consultant, surety, indemnitor, insurer, or agent)." But the Rule goes on to explain that this immunity is limited, in the sense that even materials that are prepared in anticipation of litigation may be discovered if (i) the materials otherwise meet the requirements for discoverability set out in Rule 26(b)(1) (i.e., they are "nonprivileged matter that is relevant to any party's claim or defense and proportional to the needs of the case"), and (ii) the party seeking discovery "shows that it has *substantial need* for the materials to prepare its case and *cannot, without undue hardship, obtain their substantial equivalent by other means.*"

Let's see how these work-product provisions apply to the musician's statement here. First, the statement certainly falls within the broad definition of work-product given by the first sentence of Rule 26(b)(3)(A), in that it is a "document *prepared in anticipation of litigation* or for trial by or *for another party or its representative* (including the other party's attorney, consultant, surety, indemnitor, insurer, or agent)." This is so because: (1) the document was prepared for a "representative" of "another party," since the investigator is a "consultant" to, or "agent of" (either of which statuses count as being a "representative" of) the plaintiff; and (2) the investigator was hired to find the musician and take her statement after the plaintiff had filed suit, and it's clear from context that the plaintiff's lawyer's purpose in trying to get the statement was to prepare for trial.

Therefore, the plaintiff will be entitled to keep the statement out of discovery unless the defendant makes two showings:

(i) "that it has *substantial need* for the materials to prepare its case" and

(ii) that it (the defendant) "cannot, *without undue hardship*, obtain their *substantial equivalent by other means*."

The courts have held that the party seeking discovery bears the burden of production and persuasion as to both of these showings.

The defendant might be able to make showing (i), that he has "substantial need" for the statement to prepare his case. He can plausibly argue that by the plaintiff's own assertion, the statement contains something the musician knows about the case, and if so, the defendant will be materially helped by learning what that information is, so he can counter or explain it at trial. (It's not clear that the defendant will succeed in making this showing, but he's at least got a plausible chance of doing so.)

But it's very *unlikely* that the defendant can make showing (ii), that he "*cannot, without undue hardship, obtain their substantial equivalent by other means*." That's because the privilege log has given the defendant the identity of the musician, and the defendant has not demonstrated why his legal team can't simply approach the musician on its own and ask her to tell them the contents of the statement. Nor has the defendant indicated that the defense team has already tried and failed to get this information from the musician. The courts have generally held, in cases where a party tries to obtain witness statements given to the other party, that unless the party seeking discovery shows that it *has already made significant efforts to get equivalent information* from the witness and failed, that party has failed to carry its burden of making the requisite showing of inability to get the "substantial equivalent by other means." (Later in the case, if the defendant shows that his team approached the musician for the information, was rejected, tried to get the information by deposing the musician and failed, this showing might now be enough to show the required inability to obtain equivalent materials.)

Choice (A) is wrong, because the statement being sought here is not a copy of the defendant's own prior admissions. This choice is referring to an actual provision of the discovery rules, but misapplies that provision. Rule 26(b)(3)(C) says that "Any party or other person may, on request and without the required showing, *obtain the person's own previous statement* about the action or its subject matter." So if what the defendant were seeking is a copy of a statement he had directly made to the plaintiff's investigator about, say, his sobriety at the time of the accident, the defendant *would* be entitled to that disclosure. But the sentence just quoted does *not* apply to a statement made by someone other than the person seeking disclosure, which statement in turn quotes a statement made by the seeking party.

And that's what's happening here; the statement being sought is the musician's statement, and the fact that the musician is repeating something said by the defendant is not enough to make the 26(b)(3)(C) "own previous statement" applicable to this disclosure request by the defendant. (If it were the *musician* who was seeking to make the plaintiff's team give the musician a copy of her own signed statement, the musician *would* be entitled to use 26(b)(3)(C), and she could then pass that copy on to the defendant—but the defendant does not have standing to make the request on his own.)

Choice (B) is wrong, because the fact that it cites does not have the legal consequence that the choice asserts it to have. This choice correctly draws a distinction between the words spoken by an occurrence witness (in this case, "the musician's own words"), and what's usually called "opinion work product" (here, "mental impressions or legal theories" of the plaintiff's legal team). As is more fully discussed in the last paragraph of the explanation of Choice (C) above, "opinion work product" is indeed absolutely protected, whereas ordinary "factual" work product (like the musician's own words) gets only qualified immunity, which can be overcome by a suitable showing of need. But for the reasons explained in the treatment of Choice (C), even the qualified immunity applicable to the musician's own statement would not be overcome on these facts—so the distinction between qualified and absolute immunity that this choice is referring to does not produce the outcome that the defendant would be granted the requested discovery.

Choice (D) is wrong, because how the plaintiff intends to use the statement is irrelevant to the outcome of the motion. This choice in effect asserts that where an item of work product would only be used by the discovering party for a credibility-related purpose, that fact makes a difference to whether the item is discoverable. Actually, it's true that in *some* circumstances, the fact that the item will or will not be used solely for its effect on witness credibility *is* relevant; but the facts here do not involve such a circumstance. Two provisions of Rule 26 say that an item that would otherwise be discoverable will not be discoverable if it is expected to be used at trial *"solely for impeachment."* For example, Rule 26(a)(3)(A) requires one party to make automatic disclosure shortly before trial to the other of certain types of materials (e.g., the names of witnesses expected to be called at trial, or the contents of documents), but says that the disclosure is not required where the evidence will be used at trial *"solely for impeachment."* So if the *only* way in which the plaintiff were planning to use the musician's out-of-court signed statement (or, for that matter, the musician's live testimony repeating the contents of the statement) were as a method of impeaching the defendant's anticipated trial testimony that "I did not have anything to drink," this choice would correctly articulate a reason the plaintiff could decline to release the statement.

But here, the statement's likely use by plaintiff is *not* just for impeachment—it would be admissible (and the plaintiff would probably want to use it) as substantive evidence that the defendant was drunk, a use that would apply even if the defendant never took the stand. So while this choice correctly states the outcome of the motion—that the court will deny the motion to compel—it does so for a reason that would probably not apply under these circumstances.

Answer 56

The correct choice is **(A),** because the federal discovery rules make the disclosure of insurance agreements a subject of mandatory initial disclosure without a discovery request. Under Rule 26(a)(1)(A)'s provisions governing "initial disclosure," a party must, *"without awaiting a discovery request*, provide to the other parties" various items. One of those items (specified in 26(a)(1)(A)(iv)) is "for inspection and copying . . . *any insurance agreement* under which *an insurance business may be liable to satisfy all or part of a possible judgment* in the action or to indemnify or reimburse for payments made to satisfy the judgment." As with the other mandatory initial disclosures, the copy of the insurance policy must normally be provided by the insured early in the case, at or within 14 days after the parties hold a Rule 26(f) mandatory conference in which they plan for discovery and discuss settlement.

Choice (B) is wrong, because Plaintiff need not make the request. As is discussed more fully in the treatment of Choice (A) above, Defendant must furnish Plaintiff with a copy of the policy "without awaiting a discovery request[.]" Rule 26(a)(1)(A), including 26(a)(1)(A)(iv).

Choice (C) is wrong, because Plaintiff is entitled to receive a copy of the full insurance policy. The question asks you to select the choice that represents the largest amount of relevant information to which Defendant is entitled and specifies that the choices are in descending order of the amount of information covered. Since Choice (A) correctly says that Plaintiff is automatically entitled to a copy of the full policy, and that's more information than just the name of the insurer and the policy limits, Choice (A) is correct and Choice (C) is not.

Choice (D) is wrong, because Plaintiff is entitled to the full policy, and without any showing of relevance. This choice hints at a correct statement about the scope of discovery in federal suits: that as a normal matter, a party may obtain discovery only of information that is "relevant to any party's claim or defense and proportional to the needs of the case[.]" (Rule 26(b)(1). And, it will often be the case that liability insurance is not relevant to any claim or defense in the case (and will usually not be admissible as evidence, in part for that reason). But the federal rules reflect a policy decision that the existence and terms of a defendant's liability insurance coverage have such large practical implications for the plaintiff that the former should be compelled to disclose the full details of that coverage early in the case, and even without a request.

Answer 57

The correct choice is **(D),** because Rule 11 sanctions are available against a lawyer who fails to make reasonable inquiries, even if the lawyer behaves in good faith. FRCP 11 specifies the obligations imposed on a lawyer who submits a pleading to a court, as well as the sanctions that are available if the lawyer does not discharge these obligations. Rule 11(a) requires that where a party is represented, at least one lawyer of record must sign the pleading (which happened here). Then, 11(b) specifies that when a lawyer signs or files the pleading, that lawyer "certifies that to the best of the [lawyer's] knowledge, information, and belief, *formed after an inquiry reasonable under the circumstances*," certain things are true. One of the propositions that the lawyer is deemed to certify is that "the *factual contentions have evidentiary support* or, if specifically so identified, will likely have evidentiary support after a reasonable opportunity for further investigation or discovery" (11(b)(3)).

Since there's no indication in the facts here that the complaint identified the racketeering allegations as needing further investigation or discovery in the future in order to be supported by evidence, the lawyer's filing of the pleading containing those allegations constituted his certification that, to the best of the lawyer's present knowledge, information, and belief, those racketeering allegations (e.g., the allegation that the surgeon falsely advertised where he had gone to medical school) currently *"have evidentiary support."* Unverified hearsay based on a rumor passed to the lawyer by another lawyer (and without any attempt to perform an easily-done fact-check) would not be considered "evidentiary support" of those allegations. Therefore, the court can and should easily determine that by making the factually-false racketeering allegations, the lawyer violated the "evidentiary support" certification imposed by Rule 11(b)(3).

Furthermore, Rule 11(b)(2) says that the lawyer is also certifying a belief, again "formed after an inquiry reasonable under the circumstances," that "the *claims*, defenses, and other legal contentions are *warranted by existing law* or by a nonfrivolous argument for extending, modifying, or reversing existing law or for establishing new law." Since the facts tell us that the lawyer had previously made these same racketeering allegations against the same surgeon on behalf of a different malpractice client in a state proceeding, and that that court had dismissed the allegations as meritless, the federal court seems justified in concluding that the lawyer's reusing the same allegations against the same defendant in a different court violates this "warranted by existing law" certification.

The next sub-issue is whether, even if the teacher's lawyer had an "honest" but erroneous belief that the racketeering count was "supported by evidence" and "warranted by existing law," that good-faith but unreasonable belief insulates the lawyer against sanctions. The answer is "no," at the least where the lawyer arrives at her honest belief without having performed the "*inquiry* reasonable under the circumstances" that Rule 11(b) requires. As one court put it, "[W]e must inquire whether [the attorney] *would have been aware* that [the claim] was frivolous if she had conducted a reasonable inquiry. If an attorney has failed to conduct a reasonable inquiry into the matter, then the court is obligated to impose sanctions *even if the attorney had a good faith belief that the claim was sound*." *In re Mroz*, 65 F.3d 1567, 1573 (11th Cir. 1995). That's the situation here: The teacher's lawyer knew he was relying only on hearsay as to the racketeering matters and that he had made no independent attempt to check the underlying facts (a check that would have immediately disclosed that at least the medical school attendance allegation was false); therefore, even if the attorney had a "good faith belief that the claim was sound" (which is questionable), that belief would not insulate him from Rule 11 sanctions.

Finally, there is a sub-issue about whether, given that some sort of Rule 11 sanction was appropriate, requiring reimbursement of the defendant's attorney's fees spent in combating the frivolous count is an appropriate form of sanction. The answer is yes, in the circumstances. It's true that, in general, Rule 11 reflects a preference that a monetary sanction be paid to the court, not the movant, in most circumstances. Thus, the Advisory Committee Note to the 1993 Amendments to Rule 11 say that "[s]ince the purpose of Rule 11 sanctions is to deter rather than to compensate, the rule provides that, if a monetary sanction is imposed, it should ordinarily be paid into court as a penalty." But the Rule itself says, in 11(c)(4), that "The sanction may include . . . if imposed on motion and *warranted for effective deterrence*, an order *directing payment to the movant of part or all of the reasonable attorney's fees* and other expenses *directly resulting from the violation*." Here, the fact that the lawyer had already made the same false allegations in a different suit and has repeated them here suggests that an award of attorney's fees is indeed "warranted for effective deterrence"; also, the award that's being sought is limited to the attorney's fees spent by the surgeon on rebutting the wrongfully-asserted racketeering claim, not rebutting the plaintiff's entire case, so it's fair to say that the fees being sought are ones "directly resulting from the violation."

Choice (A) is wrong, because nothing in Rule 11 allows the court to make the client vicariously liable for a sanction that is imposed on the lawyer without any wrongdoing by the client. You have to read this choice carefully to see exactly what it's asserting. The choice does not assert that the judge should find the teacher herself in violation of any Rule 11 obligation; it merely asserts that sanctions should be awarded against the lawyer and that the client should be made vicariously liable as a "back-up" source of payment. But nothing in Rule 11 authorizes the court to make the client vicariously liable for a sanction imposed against the lawyer—and, indeed, vicarious liability would be inconsistent with Rule 11's general approach, which focuses mainly on *lawyer* misconduct rather than client misconduct.

Choice (B) is wrong, because it relies on a factual assertion about the teacher's state of mind that, even if true, would not by itself justify the conclusion that the teacher violated Rule 11. The scheme of Rule 11 generally favors sanctions against attorneys, not against the client when the client is represented by an attorney. There are exceptions, but none applies here. As is described in the analysis of Choice (D) above, the wrongdoing here has two components:

(1) a lack of belief, formed after reasonable inquiry, that the "factual contentions" of the racketeering claim "have evidentiary support" (a violation of Rule 11(b)(3)); and

(2) a lack of belief, again formed after reasonable inquiry, that the "claims [of racketeering] are warranted by existing law" (a violation of Rule 11(b)(2)).

As to component (2), the violation of 11(b)(2), Rule 11 specifically prohibits the judge from imposing a sanction on the client (since 11(c)(5) says that "The court must not impose a monetary sanction: (A) against a represented party for violating Rule 11(b)(2)." (The idea is that it's up to the lawyer, not the client, to form a belief, after reasonable inquiry, that the claims are "warranted by existing law.") And here, where the facts tell you that the teacher did not even know what the complaint meant by "a pattern of racketeering activity," it would be especially inappropriate to sanction the teacher.

As to component (1) (that the claim had "evidentiary support") the facts indicate that the racketeering claim was invented by the lawyer, not the client, and that the client did not supply any factual background at all relating to the supposed advertising falsehoods that were alleged to constitute racketeering. Therefore, any wrongdoing in connection with the frivolous racketeering claim was solely that of the lawyer, not the client, and nothing in Rule 11 authorizes sanctions against the client in this "innocent client" scenario.

To put it another way, it is simply not the case, as this choice says it is, that Rule 11 sanctions can be imposed on a client merely because the client "should have known that she did not have actual knowledge about whether there was evidentiary support" for the claim in question. See, e.g., *Byrne v. Nezhat,* 261 F.3d 1075, 1118 (11th Cir. 2001), a case on facts similar to those in this question; the court held that the client could not be sanctioned because there was no evidence that the client "knew the complaint filed on her behalf was factually or legally baseless," and no evidence that she had "provided false information to her attorneys, thereby facilitating a factually groundless complaint." That's equally the case in our question.

Choice (C) is wrong, because it misstates what Rule 11 provides. It's true that Rule 11, and the Advisory Committee Notes to it from the 1993 Amendments, say that *ordinarily*, if the sanctions are monetary, the payment should take the form of a fine paid to the court. But this is not a hard-and-fast rule; if the court believes that deterrence will be better accomplished by an award of attorney's fees payable to the movant who has incurred the expense of defending against the frivolous claim, such a fee award is permitted. For more about this, see the last paragraph in the explanation of Choice (D) above.

Answer 58

The correct choice is **(D),** because the plaintiff was under an obligation to correct and supplement her disclosure, and the sanction for the failure to do so is exclusion of the evidence. First, the treatment notes were documents that the pedestrian was required to provide at the beginning of the case, without a request for them, according to the automatic-disclosure provisions of Rule 26(a)(1)(A). That's because 26(a)(1)(A)(ii) requires a party to provide "a copy . . . of *all documents* . . . that the *disclosing party has in its possession, custody, or control* and *may use to support its claims* or defenses, unless the use would be solely for impeachment[.]" It's true that most if not all of these notes did not yet exist at the moment the pedestrian was required to make initial disclosures (since the 18-month treatment period probably continued past the time of this disclosure). However, Rule 26(e) says that a party who has made a Rule 26(a) automatic disclosure "*must supplement or correct its disclosure* or response: (A) in a timely manner if the party learns that in some material respect the disclosure or response is incomplete or correct . . ." And the facts tell you that the pedestrian is now "using" these notes as evidence in support of her claim, making the notes fall within this duty-to-supplement-automatic-disclosure category. So the pedestrian was required to supplement her prior disclosure by furnishing the notes once they came into existence. (As is discussed more fully in Choice (C), it's very unlikely that the court will find that the pedestrian's ignorance of the notes was reasonable on these facts, and therefore unlikely that the court will conclude that her failure to supplement was excusable.)

Since the pedestrian and her lawyer were required to furnish the notes in a timely way, the only question is whether the remedy for the non-disclosure should include excluding the notes as evidence in support of the pedestrian's case. The issue is dealt with directly by Rule 37(c)(1): "If a party *fails to provide information* or identify a witness as required by Rule 26(a) or (e), the party is *not allowed to use that information* or witness to *supply evidence* on a motion, at a hearing, or *at a trial*, unless the failure was *substantially justified or is harmless*." Since what the pedestrian is trying to do is precisely what Rule 37(c)(1) is talking about—to use as evidence at a trial material that she was required to produce by the combination of Rule 26(a)'s automatic-disclosure requirements and Rule 26(e)'s requirement to supplement prior Rule 26(a) disclosures—the judge is not only permitted, but required, to exclude the evidence unless the judge makes an affirmative determination that the failure was "substantially justified or is harmless." As to the "harmless" possibility, Choice (D) already covers this possibility by adding the escape hatch that exclusion won't be required if the judge believes the failure to be harmless (which is an unlikely outcome, since the messenger's lawyer will be entitled to cross-examine the maker of the notes, and it's unlikely that, say, a brief continuance will be enough to undo that lawyer's inability to make up for the loss of an adequate time to study 70 pages of detailed notes). And although this choice does not refer to the possibility that the judge might conclude that the failure was "substantially justified," it's very unlikely that where a patient/litigant undergoes many treatment sessions for injuries that are the subject of the litigation, that patient and her lawyer are "substantially justified" in not bothering to inquire whether the treating physician has taken notes during the course of the treatments.

Choice (A) is wrong, because it inaccurately states the procedure for sanctioning a party who has failed to supplement prior disclosures. The federal discovery rules provide that a sanction is *automatic* if a party fails to provide information (or to identify a witness) as required by the combination of the Rule 26(a) initial duty to make disclosure and the Rule 26(e) duty to supplement such disclosures as time passes; the wronged party is not required to make a prior motion for sanctions in this situation. See the text of FRCP 37(c)(1), quoted in the final paragraph of the discussion of Choice (D) above, which sets exclusion as the sanction while making no reference to the need for a motion by the wronged party.

Choice (B) is wrong, because it incorrectly imposes a requirement that prejudice be shown. FRCP 37(c)(1) says that a party who fails to correct or supplement its prior disclosures as required under Rule 26(e) may not use that evidence at trial "unless the failure was substantially justified or is harmless." This language does not require the wronged party to show that he or she would be prejudiced if the non-disclosed materials were permitted to be used as evidence. Courts have, rather, concluded that under Rule 37(c)(1) *the burden is on the party facing the sanction* "to demonstrate that the failure to comply . . . is substantially justified or harmless." *Torres v. City of Los Angeles*, 548 F.3d 1197, 1213 (9th Cir. 2008).

Choice (C) is wrong, because the pedestrian's ignorance of the notes' existence would not "substantially justify" the lack of disclosure. It's true that the automatic sanction imposed by Rule 37(c)(1) for non-disclosure—exclusion of the material from use as evidence by the wrongdoer—does not apply where the lack of disclosure "was substantially justified or is harmless." But here, the pedestrian's contention that she did not know about the notes of the treating physician will almost certainly be found not meet to this standard. Courts interpreting this 37(c)(1) language have concluded that a party who does not actually know of the existence of the material, but who *should* reasonably have been aware of it, is not "substantially justified" in failing to disclose it. See, e.g., *Arthur v. Atkinson Freight Lines, Corp.*, 164 F.R.D. 19, 20 (S.D.N.Y. 1995), a similar case in which plaintiff and her counsel claimed to have been unaware until the eve of trial of the existence of a medical report in plaintiff's doctor's possession: "[Rule 26(e)] place[s] a duty on a party to turn over not only proper materials of which he is aware, but also those of which he reasonably *ought* to have been aware."

Answer 59

The correct choice is **(A),** because if the court denies the motion under the circumstances described in this choice, Rule 37(a)(5)(B) leaves the court no choice but to make the attorney's fee award.

Before we look at the attorney's-fees-as-sanctions issue, it's worth examining the procedural correctness of the *manufacturer's* conduct: Notice that the manufacturer raised its objection to the document-production request but then took no other affirmative acts to shield itself from the request. The manufacturer *could* have taken the affirmative step of seeking a "protective order" from the trial court, as authorized by Rule 26(c)(1). But the manufacturer was not *required* to take this step, and did not expose itself to any serious "extra" sanctions by not seeking the order and instead waiting for the driver to move to compel discovery (since the manufacturer faced the same risk of sanctions if its refusal to produce was held to be wrongful whether the court's holding came in response to the manufacturer's motion to protect or in response to the driver's motion to compel).

Once the driver moved for an order compelling the document production, the motion was governed by Rule 37. More specifically, Rule 37(a)(3)(B) says that

> "A party seeking discovery may move for an order compelling an answer [or] production[.] This motion may be made if: . . . (iv) a party *fails to produce documents* . . . as requested under Rule 34."

But Choice (A) tells you to assume that the court "wholly denies" the motion. (Such a denial is a very plausible holding for the court to make on these facts: Rule 26(b)(1) says that "Parties may obtain discovery regarding any nonprivileged matter that is relevant to any party's claim or defense and *proportional to the needs of the case*, considering the importance of the issues at stake in the action, the amount in controversy, the parties' relative access to relevant information, the parties' resources, the importance of the discovery in resolving the issues, and *whether the burden or expense of the proposed discovery outweighs its likely benefit*." Requiring the manufacturer to supply documents about accidents having no apparent connection to steering wheel problems is just the sort of large-scale and time-consuming request that a court might well decide was wholly disproportional to the "needs of the case.")

So we need to know how Rule 37 deals with sanctions in the event the court denies the motion to compel. That issue is dealt with by Rule 37(a)(5)(B), which says:

> "If the motion [to compel discovery] is denied, the court *may* issue any protective order authorized under Rule 26(c) and *must*, after giving an opportunity to be heard, *require the movant, the attorney filing the motion, or both to pay the party or deponent who opposed the motion its reasonable expenses incurred in opposing the motion, including attorney's fees*. But the court must not order this payment if the motion was substantially justified or other circumstances make an award of expenses unjust."

The key word in the above-quoted passage is the word "must" in the middle of the first sentence—that word means that if the court wholly denies the motion, the court has **no choice** but to "require the movant [and/or her lawyer] to pay the party . . . who opposed the motion its reasonable expenses incurred in opposing the motion, including **attorney's fees**[,]" unless the special circumstances spelled out in the second sentence are present. But here, Choice (A) tells you to assume that the court "believes that the motion was not substantially justified and that such a fee award would not be unjust," thus making it clear that none of the special conditions that would relieve the court of its obligation (and even its authority) to order payment of the expenses as a sanction exist here. So Choice (A), by emphasizing that an order that the driver pay the manufacturer's attorney's fees incurred in opposing the motion to compel is not discretionary but mandatory on the part of the court, is legally correct.

Choice (B) is not the best response, because it incorrectly says that the court has discretion to order or not order the driver to reimburse the attorney's fees. As is discussed more fully in the treatment of Choice (A) above, if the court wholly denies the motion to compel, and neither of the special circumstances in the second sentence of Rule 37(a)(5)(B) (e.g., "the motion was substantially justified") is present, the court "must" (not "may") order that the motion's opponent be reimbursed for its reasonable expenses, including attorney's fees, incurred in opposing the motion. So Choice (B), by indicating that even where the special circumstances are not present, a reimbursement order is only discretionary, is legally incorrect.

Choice (C) is not the best response, because the sanction of expense-reimbursement was not dependent on the manufacturer's having made a motion for a protective order. It's true that the manufacturer had the *right* to seek a protective order against being required to produce the objected-to documents. (For more about this right, see the first paragraph in the discussion of Choice (A) above.) But such a motion for a protective order was **optional** on the manufacturer's part—the manufacturer was free to instead do nothing (beyond noting its objection, and its reasons for making that objection, in a timely response to the production request), and wait for the requesting party (the driver) to make her own motion to compel. And nothing in Rule 37(a)(5)(B)'s procedures regarding sanctions in the event the motion to compel is wholly denied makes those sanctions weaker or less available because the opponent of the motion never sought a protective order. (The overall approach of Rule 37—applicable whether the motion to compel succeeds or fails—is that "the loser pays" the winner's litigation expenses in making or opposing the motion.) So Choice (C), by asserting that the manufacturer's failure to seek a protective order prevents the court from awarding sanctions to that party, relies on a wholly-irrelevant fact, and is flatly incorrect.

Choice (D) is not the best response, because the driver's failure to try to resolve the dispute without court action would eliminate any right the driver might otherwise have to recover sanctions if she prevailed on the motion. This choice is a bit tricky, because its wrongness stems from the non-occurrence of an event the significance of which would be apparent only if you knew a particular detail about how Rule 37 limits the award of sanctions to a successful movant. First, notice that of the four choices this is the only one that assumes that the driver has *succeeded* in her motion. Therefore, sanctions are governed by Rule 37(a)(5)(A), which says that

> *"If the motion is granted—or if the disclosure or requested discovery is provided after* the motion was filed—the court must, after giving an opportunity to be heard, require the party or deponent whose conduct necessitated the motion, the party or attorney advising that conduct, or both to **pay the movant's reasonable expenses incurred in making the motion, including attorney's fees**. But the court must not order this payment if:
>
>   (i) *the movant filed the motion before attempting in good faith to obtain the disclosure or discovery without court action*; (ii) the opposing party's

nondisclosure, response, or objection was substantially justified; or (iii) other circumstances make an award of expenses unjust."

In analyzing Choice (D), the key provision in the above language is subsection (i): the court not only *isn't required* to award sanctions to the victorious movant, but is *forbidden* to award her sanctions, if "the movant filed the motion **before attempting in good faith to obtain the disclosure or discovery without court action[.]"** The facts tell us that "After the driver's lawyer received this response, she made no attempt to contact the manufacturer's lawyer. Instead, the driver's lawyer made a motion. . . ." If the driver's lawyer brought the motion without even trying to contact her adversary, she couldn't have "attempt[ed] in good faith to obtain the . . . discovery without court action." And by failing to try to resolve the matter without court intervention, she deprived the judge of even the power—let alone the obligation—to award her any expense reimbursement as a sanction in the event she prevailed on the motion to compel. Therefore, Choice (D)—by asserting that the court would have power to award the driver attorney's fees assuming the manufacturer's objection was not "substantially justified"—is legally incorrect.

Answer 60

The correct choice is **(A)**, because that's the best way to ensure that the team's Seventh Amendment right to a jury trial on its counterclaim is fully prepared. The Seventh Amendment to the U.S. Constitution provides that "in suits **at common law** . . . the **right of trial by jury shall be preserved[.]"** (Federal Rule 38(a) implements this Amendment, by saying that "the right of trial by jury as declared by the Seventh Amendment . . . is preserved to the parties inviolate.") The Amendment's reference to "preserv[ing]" the right as to "suits at common law" means that there is a right to a jury trial in federal cases only as to issues that, had they been raised in a suit brought just before the 1791 adoption of the Bill of Rights (and thus the Seventh Amendment), would have been treated as being "at common law" (i.e., "legal") rather than "at equity" (i.e., "equitable"). **A request for an injunction is always treated as equitable**; therefore, the city's request for an injunction is equitable (and thus does not trigger a right by either party to have the case heard by a jury). But the team's **counterclaim, since it seeks money damages, is "legal,"** and thus triggers a right—on the part of either litigant—to **demand a jury trial,** a right that the team has correctly made.

If the court were to hold a nonjury trial of the city's claim for an injunction before holding a jury trial on the team's counterclaim, then by operation of various doctrines (discussed in Choices (B) and (C) below), the team's Seventh Amendment right to have all issues germane to its counterclaim decided by a jury might be impaired as a practical matter. Therefore, as the Supreme Court has long held in cases involving both legal and equitable claims, to preserve the trial right as completely as possible, if at all feasible **the court must hold a jury trial on the legal claim(s) before holding a nonjury trial on the equitable claims.**

The Court so held in *Beacon Theatres v. Westover*, 359 U.S. 500 (1959), involving a scenario quite similar to the one in this question, i.e., one in which P sued D for a permanent injunction against certain conduct by D, and D counterclaimed for money damages (and demanded a jury trial on the counterclaim) for P's conduct relating to the same core set of facts. The Court held that the court must conduct a jury trial on D's counterclaim before holding a nonjury trial on P's request for a permanent injunction.

Applying the *Beacon Theatres* rationale here requires that the court first hold a jury trial on the team's legal counterclaim, then a nonjury trial on the city's request for a permanent injunction.

Choice (B) is wrong, because holding the bench trial first would violate the principle laid down by the Supreme Court in *Beacon Theatres v. Westover*. As we discuss in Choice (A), a Supreme Court case, *Beacon Theatres v. Westover*, says that when a case will involve both a legal claim and an equitable claim arising from somewhat overlapping facts, the court must hold the jury trial on the legal claim first if at all feasible, in order to protect the Seventh Amendment rights of the party who has made a proper demand for a jury trial (here, the team) on that legal claim.

It's true that Choice (B), by specifying that the nonjury trial on the city's injunction claim be held first but "without giving binding effect to its findings or conclusions in the later jury trial," would partly mitigate any damage to the team's jury trial right on its later-to-be-tried legal counterclaim, since there would be no mandatory collateral estoppel effect from the earlier nonjury trial. But events in the earlier trial might still adversely affect the team's jury trial prospects. For instance, the team would likely need to cross-examine the city's witnesses during the bench trial about the negotiations for and administration of the lease; those witnesses would therefore have an unfair advance look at the questions the team would probably be asking on cross (for a second time) during the later jury trial.

Consequently, the trial court needs to follow the bright-line rule laid down in *Beacon Theatres*: if at all feasible (and it *is* feasible here), the jury trial on the team's counterclaim must be held first.

Choice (C) is wrong, because holding the bench trial first would violate the principle laid down by the Supreme Court in *Beacon Theatres v. Westover*. As we discuss in Choice (A), a Supreme Court case, *Beacon Theatres v. Westover*, says that when a case will involve both a legal claim and an equitable claim arising from somewhat overlapping facts, the court must hold the jury trial on the legal claim first if at all feasible, in order to protect the Seventh Amendment rights of the party who has made a proper demand for a jury trial (here, the team) on that legal claim. Even more so than in Choice (B), the procedure proposed in this choice is likely to lead to a practical impairment of the team's right to benefit from a jury trial on its counterclaim. That's mainly because the rules of issue preclusion (i.e., collateral estoppel) will mean that where an issue that was actually and necessarily litigated in the first trial is relevant to the second trial, the party who lost on that issue in the first trial will be estopped from re-litigating that issue during the second, jury, trial.

For instance, the team might well choose to defend against the city's request for an injunction against the move by arguing, "You [the city] materially breached the lease by repeatedly failing to maintain the stadium, and that breach entitled us to cancel the lease, so that we have a right to move immediately." If that's the team's only defense, and the judge in the bench trial finds for the city, then the team will be collaterally estopped from reasserting that same breach by the city in the second, nonjury, trial on its counterclaim for money damages from that breach; that result would obviously constitute a serious practical impairment to the team's Seventh Amendment right to an (effective) jury trial on that counterclaim.

Choice (D) is wrong, because neither party has a right to receive (or an obligation to undergo) a jury trial on the city's injunction claim. As we discuss more fully in Choice (A), the Seventh Amendment guarantees a right to a jury trial only on claims that are legal rather than equitable. Federal Rule 38, in Sub-paragraphs (a) and (b), implements this guarantee; but under the Federal Rules neither party has a right to a jury trial on an equitable claim. Since this choice calls for a jury trial on the city's equitable claim (which seeks an injunction against the move), the choice calls for a jury trial in a situation where such a trial is not authorized by federal procedure.

Answer 61

The correct choice is (**A**), because these rulings are both required to protect various constitutional rights.

First, let's consider Motion 1. If a federal-court claim is one that would have been "at common law" at the time the Seventh Amendment was adopted in 1791, that Amendment guarantees the plaintiff the right to have the claim heard by a jury. Where a federal court suit involves both a "legal" claim (roughly speaking, one that in 1791 would have been a claim "at common law") and an "equitable" claim (one that could not have been brought "at common law" in 1791, and thus would have had to be brought before a court of equity), various Supreme Court decisions require the federal judge to manage trial of the case so that the plaintiff's right to have the legal claim heard by a jury is not impaired. Because of the rules of "former adjudication" (claim preclusion and collateral estoppel), safeguarding the plaintiff's practical ability to have the legal claim heard by a jury generally requires that any issue of law or fact that is common to the legal and equitable claims be tried *first* to (and decided by) the jury — only then may the judge decide the equitable claims. See *Beacon Theatres, Inc. v. Westover*, 359 U.S. 500 (1959), so holding. Here, this principle means that since the cook has a Seventh Amendment right to have a jury determine whether her firing was a gender-discriminatory act and, if so, what compensatory damages she is entitled to, the jury must decide these two issues before the judge may rule on whether the cook is also entitled to an order reinstating her at her job. (Furthermore, whichever way the jury rules on whether the defendant discriminated, the rules of former adjudication mean that the trial court probably has to accept and apply that ruling in deciding the reinstatement issue.) So the motion, which asks the court to make the first ruling on whether there was discrimination and, if so, on whether reinstatement is required, cannot be granted without violating the cook's Seventh Amendment right to have her damages claim decided by a jury.

Now, let's look at <u>Motion 2</u>. The Supreme Court has held repeatedly that neither state nor federal courts may permit a private litigant (or for that matter a government litigant) to use peremptory challenges to exclude civil jurors on the basis of either their race or their gender — allowing such challenges violates the excluded jurors' equal protection rights, and the opposing litigant is given standing to assert these rights. See, e.g., *J. E. B. v. Alabama Ex Rel. T. B.*, 511 U.S. 127, 146 (1994): "[T]he Equal Protection Clause prohibits discrimination in jury selection on the basis of gender, or on the assumption that an individual will be biased in a particular case for no reason other than the fact that the person happens to be a woman or happens to be a man"; *Edmonson v. Leesville Concrete Co.*, 500 U.S. 614 (1991): Even in civil litigation, allowing racially-discriminatory peremptory challenges constitutes state action because the government-run court system becomes a party to the discrimination.

It is usually not easy for one party to demonstrate that the other party has indeed used its peremptory strikes in a race- or gender-discriminatory way. But the facts here are so egregious that the challenger (the cook) will succeed with her motion. To make a challenge to the discriminatory use of peremptory challenges, the challenger must first show a "pattern" of discriminatory peremptory strikes; the two strikes here, coupled with the defendant's bald-faced (and tactically stupid) explicit reference to gender as being the reason, will be enough to satisfy this first step. If the defendant had succeeded in giving a "facially neutral" explanation for the strikes (i.e., one that avoided expressly referring to gender as the reason for the strikes, such as an explanation like "I didn't like the way either juror refused to look me in the eye when I was questioning her"), then the burden would have shifted to the cook to show that this neutral explanation was a mere pretext. But here, where the defendant has not even been able to come up with a facially-neutral-though-unconvincing explanation, the judge should deny the peremptory strikes out-of-hand, without even shifting back on the cook the burden of showing pretext.

Choices (B), (C), and (D) are all wrong, because each reaches the wrong outcome as to at least one of the two motions (and (B) gets *both* outcomes wrong).

Answer 62

The correct choice is **(D)**, because the time limit on making a jury demand on any issue is 14 days after the last pleading directed to that issue, and the last pleading directed to both the fraud and defamation claims would have been an answer, which had not yet been served when the jury demand was made. The time for making a demand for jury trial is specified in Rule 38(b), which reads as follows:

> "(b) *Demand.* On any issue triable of right by a jury, a party **may demand a jury trial** by:
>
> > (1) *serving* the other parties with a written demand—which may be included in a pleading—**no later than 14 days after the last pleading directed to the issue is served**; and
> >
> > (2) *filing* the demand in accordance with Rule 5(d)."

So the time limit for the retailer to demand a jury trial on any given issue was "14 days after the last pleading directed to that issue [was] served." Since both of the claims here were by a plaintiff against the original defendant, the "last pleading directed to [each] issue" was an answer. The facts make it clear that by the time the retailer made its demand for jury trial: (1) the architect had not yet filed an answer to the original complaint; and (2) the retailer had incorporated its jury trial demand in the amended complaint (something that's expressly allowed by 38(b)(1)'s "may be included in a pleading" language), so that the demand occurred before the architect could possibly have answered the amended complaint.

Therefore, we know that no answer to either the original complaint or the amended one had ever been filed by the time the retailer made the jury demand in the amended complaint. Thus the demand came before the "last pleading directed to [either] issue" could have been served. That made the demand timely as to both issues.

Choice (A) is wrong, because only the "last pleading" directed to an issue—not a dismissal motion directed to that issue—can start the running of the jury-demanding party's 14-day clock. Rule 38(b) (quoted in full in the discussion of Choice (D)) says that a jury trial demand on an issue must be made "no later than 14 days after the last pleading directed to the issue is served." When (as here) a plaintiff raises an issue in a complaint against the original defendant, the "last pleading directed to the issue" will be the defendant's answer. And that's true even where (as here) the defendant makes a motion to dismiss prior to answering—the motion is not the "last pleading directed to" the issue in the claim that the defendant is seeking to dismiss, and therefore the plaintiff's 14-day time limit on requesting a jury trial does not start to run when the motion is made.

Choice (B) is wrong, because only the "last pleading" directed to an issue—not the complaint raising that issue—can start the running of the jury-demanding party's 14-day clock. Rule 38(b) (quoted in full in the discussion of Choice (D)) says that a jury trial demand on an issue must be made "no later than 14 days after the last pleading directed to the issue is served." When (as here) a plaintiff raises an issue in a complaint against the original defendant, the "last pleading directed to the issue" will be the defendant's answer, and only when the answer is served will be plaintiff's 14-day limit on serving the jury-trial demand start to run. Since this choice effectively asserts that the plaintiff's demand for jury trial on the fraud must have started upon "service of the original complaint," the choice misstates how and when the plaintiff's 14-day time limit starts to run.

Choice (C) is wrong, because nothing in the FRCP requires a complaint raising an issue to contain a jury demand—a plaintiff's time to demand a jury trial on an issue does not even start to run until the defendant answers. Rule 38(b) (quoted in full in the discussion of Choice (D)) says that a jury trial demand on an issue must be made "no later than 14 days after the last pleading directed to the issue is served." Where a plaintiff raises an issue in an original complaint (in this case, the issue of fraud), the plaintiff's time to demand a jury trial would not expire until 14 days after the defendant files an answer (the "last pleading directed to the [fraud] issue"). This choice, by effectively asserting that the filing of the original complaint without a jury demand somehow caused the plaintiff's right to later make such a demand to be waived, is inconsistent with Rule 38(b)'s "14 days after the last pleading" rule.

Answer 63

The correct choice is **(A),** because it is the only one of the choices that is guaranteed to occur early enough in the case that there could be no waiver of the right to make the jury-trial demand. The time for demanding a jury trial in federal actions is specified in FRCP 38. Rule 38(b) says that a party may demand a jury trial on any issue triable by right by a jury, if the demanding party does so by "(1) serving the other parties with a written demand—which may be included in a pleading—no later than 14 days after the last pleading directed to the issue is served[.]" (The party must also then file the demand with the court within "a reasonable time after service"; see the combination of Rules 38(b)(2) and 5(d)(1).) Since Rule 38(b) allows the demand to be "included in a pleading," this choice states a method and time for serving the demand that is guaranteed not to exceed the "no later than 14 days after the last pleading" deadline. And this method also turns out to be the latest stage that's guaranteed to be timely, since the other three choices may involve missing the deadline.

Choice (B) is wrong, because the time it specifies may fall after the appropriate deadline. As is noted in the explanation of Choice (A), a party's right to demand a jury trial on an issue ends unless service of the demand is made "no later than 14 days after the last pleading directed to the issue is served." This choice requires you to assume that the answer does not contain a counterclaim, since on that assumption the answer *is* the "last pleading directed to the issue [of infringement]." On that assumption, the screenwriter's time to serve the demand will end 14 days after the studio serves its answer on him. Since Choice (B) purports to give the screenwriter 60 days after service of the answer, it overstates the amount of time available.

Choice (C) is wrong, for the same reason that (B) is not the best response. The parties are required by Rule 26(f) to hold a conference at which they discuss the claims, possibilities of settlement, initial disclosure, etc. "as soon as practicable." This conference may—and in the majority of cases will—occur more than 14 days after service of the last pleading. Therefore, if as this choice suggests the screenwriter waits until the conference to serve his demand for jury trial, he cannot count on his demand still being timely.

Choice (D) is wrong, for the same reasons that (B) and (C) are incorrect. Rule 16 sets out the procedures by which the judge will hold one or more pretrial conferences. Normally, the judge will not even issue a scheduling order until after he or she has received a report by the parties outlining their discovery plan, which Rule 26(f) requires them to prepare. And the discovery plan cannot possibly be filed with the court until sometime after the discovery conference between the parties, referred to in Choice (C), has occurred. Since as is explained in the discussion of Choice (C) the day of the discovery conference will itself be too late for service of the jury trial demand, the date on which the judge holds the initial pretrial conference is guaranteed to fall even further past the deadline for filing of the jury-trial demand.

Answer 64

The correct choice is **(B),** because although the jury trial must start with at least six jurors, the parties' later stipulation to accept a verdict of less than six will be enforced

This question is easily resolved by consulting just two sentences in Rule 48. First, 48(a) says that "A jury *must begin with at least 6* and *no more than 12 members*, and each juror must participate in the verdict unless excused under Rule 47(c)." (Rule 47(c) says that "During trial or deliberation, the court may excuse a juror for good cause.") Here, of course, this sentence was satisfied, since: (1) six jurors (as well as two alternates) were seated; and (2) when the two jurors became ill, the court properly excused them for good cause under Rule 47(c).

Second, Rule 48(b) deals with what happens if fewer than six jurors are left to deliver the verdict: "*Unless the parties stipulate otherwise*, the verdict must be **unanimous** and must be returned by a *jury of at least 6 members."* So here, once the third ill juror was excused, either party would have been free to cause a mistrial by refusing to stipulate to the return of a verdict from fewer than six jurors. But, of course, both parties' attorneys *did* stipulate to a verdict from a five-person jury (and this stipulation was binding on each party), so under Rule 48(b) the verdict was valid.

Choice (A) is wrong, because the fact that the court properly excused the three jurors would not by itself have been enough to make the less-than-six-juror verdict proper. As we discuss more extensively in Choice (B), not only must a jury trial begin with at least six jurors, but if the jury shrinks to fewer than six (even if due to excuse for a proper cause like illness), the verdict will not be proper unless both parties stipulate to accept it. Since this choice asserts that the proper excuse of the three jurors due to illness was *by itself enough* to lead the court to deny the motion, the choice gives an incorrect explanation for the correct outcome.

Choice (C) is wrong, because although a federal civil trial must *start* with at least jurors (and the parties are not free to stipulate otherwise), a verdict *rendered* by fewer than six is proper if both parties stipulate to accept it. As we discuss more extensively in Choice (B), Rule 48(a) says that the trial must start with at least six jurors, but Rule 48(b) says that if the number then shrinks below six, the verdict is still proper if—and only if—both parties stipulate to accept it. So while this choice is correct if it is read to mean that the federal civil jury must have at least six jurors at the outset, it is not correct in implying that at least six must *remain* to deliver the verdict even if the parties stipulate to accept a verdict from fewer than six.

Choice (D) is wrong, because it is not the case that there must be at least 12 jurors on a federal civil jury, even at the outset of the trial. At common law, juries typically had to have 12 members. But Rule 48(a) changes this, by saying merely that at the outset of the trial, the jury must have at least six and no more than 12 members. So this choice is incorrect, even as a statement about the minimum required size at the moment the trial commences (and it's even further from correct as a statement of the minimum number of jurors required at the moment the verdict is delivered).

Answer 65

The correct choice is **(B),** because the federal courts presume that a direct financial relationship between a juror and a party will interfere with the juror's ability to be impartial. Most American courts, including the federal system, apply a *per se* presumption that a prospective juror who owns even a small amount of stock in a party must be discharged for cause. See, e.g., *Chestnut v. Ford Motor Company*, 445 F.2d 967, 971-972 (4th Cir. 1971): "That a stockholder in a company which is a party to a lawsuit is incompetent to sit as juror is so well settled as to be black letter law." In fact, most state and federal courts hold that a trial judge's refusal to strike a juror for cause who owns any stock at all in a party is reversible error. Id.

In the federal system, there is no statute or Federal Rule that expresses this presumption—it is merely a policy applied as a matter of judge-made law. But the strength of the policy is demonstrated in an analogous area in which there *is* a federal statute that imposes a similar *per se* restriction: 28 U.S.C. § 455(b)(4) requires a federal *judge* to disqualify himself from any case in which he, his spouse, or his minor child residing in the judge's household has a financial interest in a party (including even a small amount of publicly-traded stock in the party). In fact, the presumption of conflict is so strong that under § 455(e), the judge may not participate in the case even if both parties are willing to *waive* the disqualification.

Choices (A), (C), and (D) are all wrong, because each of them is flatly inconsistent with the *per se* rule discussed in Choice (B) that any ownership stake by a juror in a party, no matter how small, and no matter how convincing the juror's testimony that she can be impartial, is automatically grounds for disqualifying the juror for cause.

Answer 66

The correct choice is **(B)**, because the defendant's right to object was waived once the judge gave the instructions to the jury. The FRCP's procedures governing jury instructions are set out in Rule 51, a surprisingly intricate multi-part rule. Although the fact pattern here is pretty simple, it turns out that in order to answer this question confidently (and to distinguish among several plausible choices), you need to have an understanding of *all four sub-paragraphs* of Rule 51. And as we'll see, there was at least one occasion on which the defendant's lawyer was required to act affirmatively in order to preserve his client's right to object, and the lawyer catastrophically failed to take that act.

First, let's look at sub-paragraph (a) of 51, which governs how and when a party should *request* particular jury instructions that he would like the judge to give; here's the full text of 51(a):

"(a) *Requests*.

(1) *Before or at the Close of the Evidence.* At the ***close of the evidence*** or at any earlier reasonable time that the court orders, a party may ***file and furnish*** to every other party written ***requests for the jury instructions it wants the court to give***.

(2) *After the Close of the Evidence.* ***After*** the close of the evidence, a party may:

(A) file requests for instructions on ***issues that could not reasonably have been anticipated by an earlier time*** that the court set for requests; and

(B) ***with the court's permission***, file ***untimely requests*** for instructions on any issue."

The defendant properly complied with this "Requests" provision; we know this because the facts start by telling us that "before the close of evidence" the defendant "submitted a proposed jury instruction" on the issue in question, contributory negligence. So far, so good for the defendant: the defendant timely put the court on notice of the instruction he wanted (and if he hadn't ***done*** so, once the evidence closed any objection based on the court's failure to instruct on contributory negligence would already have been waived unless the court in its discretion gave permission for an "untimely request.")

Next to become relevant are sub-paragraphs (b) and (c) of Rule 51, which deal with how the court should handle ***instructions*** ((b)) and how the parties should handle any objections they have ((c)). Here's how these two parts read:

"(b) *Instructions*. The court:

(1) must inform the parties of its proposed instructions and proposed action on the requests before instructing the jury and before final jury arguments;

(2) ***must give the parties an opportunity to object*** on the record and out of the jury's hearing before the ***instructions and arguments are delivered***; and

(3) may instruct the jury at any time before the jury is discharged.

(c) *Objections.*

    (1) *How to Make.* A party who **objects to** an instruction or the **failure to give an instruction** must **do so on the record**, stating distinctly the matter objected to and the grounds for the objection.

    (2) *When to Make.* An objection is **timely** if:

    (A) a party **objects at the opportunity provided** under Rule 51(b)(2); or

    (B) a party was **not informed** of an instruction or action on a request before that opportunity to object [i.e., before the Rule 51(b)(2) opportunity], and the party **objects promptly after learning** that the instruction or request will be, or has been, given or refused."

Then, 51(d) specifies when an error as to jury instructions may be **considered on appeal:**

"(d) *Assigning Error; Plain Error.*

    (1) *Assigning Error.* A party **may assign as error:**

    (A) an error in an instruction **actually given**, if that party **properly objected**; or

    (B) a **failure to give an instruction**, if that party **properly requested it** and—unless the court rejected the request in a **definitive ruling** on the record—**also properly objected**.

    (2) *Plain Error.* A court may consider a **plain error** in the instructions that has **not been preserved** as required by Rule 51(d)(1) if the error **affects substantial rights**."

Let's go through how sub-paragraphs 51(b), (c) and (d) apply here. First, before the judge instructed the jury, 51(b)(1) required her to "inform the parties of [the court's] proposed instruction." The judge complied; although she did not explicitly point out that she was declining to give the defendant's proposed instruction on contributory negligence, she was not **required** to do so—it was up to the defendant to notice that his proposed instruction on this point was being declined. The judge was also required, by 51(b)(2), to "give the parties an opportunity to object on the record . . . before the instructions and arguments [were] given"; the facts don't say explicitly that the judge did this, but you should assume from context that the judge followed this requirement (since if she had not done so, the facts would almost certainly have told you this explicitly).

Once the judge told the parties of her proposed instruction and gave each side a chance to object, the **defendant** was required to **act immediately** on that opportunity; we know this because 51(c)(2) says that "an objection is timely if: (A) a party objects **at the opportunity provided under Rule 51(b)(2)**; or (B) [a situation not applicable here]." The "opportunity provided under Rule 51(b)(2)" is, as we've just seen, the opportunity to object that is given once the judge has told both sides about her proposed instructions. We know that the defendant failed to take that opportunity, since the facts tell us that "neither party objected, either then or after the judge had given the instructions" (though an objection made *after* the judge delivered the instruction to the jury would have been *too late*, according to the phrase ". . . before the instructions . . . are delivered" in 51(b)(2).)

Now, to see exactly what the consequences were of the defendant's failure to object before the judge delivered the instructions to the jury, we need to do a close review of sub-paragraph (d)(2). The supposed error here is not covered by (d)(1)(A) (which covers only an instruction "actually given"), but by (d)(1)(B) (which covers "a failure to give an instruction")—the **defendant** is saying, "I properly asked for a contributory negligence instruction, and the judge erred in not giving it." (d)(1)(B) says that the party will be deemed to "assign as error" the failure to give an instruction only if that party satisfies *two* distinct requirements:

(1) he "properly requested" the instruction (meaning he requested it at or before the close of evidence, as required by 51(a)(1)); *and*

(2) he "also ***properly objected***" (meaning, in effect, "objected in a timely way once it was clear that the judge would give the jury instructions that did not include the requested one")—though requirement (2) does not apply if "the court rejected the request in a definitive ruling on the record[.]"

Here, the defendant satisfied requirement (1), by requesting the contributory instruction at or before the close of evidence. But the defendant ***completely failed to satisfy requirement (2),*** that he have "properly objected." For him to have "properly objected," he would have had to make a "timely" objection, and as we saw above, 51(b)(2) makes an objection timely only if it is made at the time the court "give[s] the parties an opportunity to object on the record . . . before the instructions . . . are given."

Therefore, even though the defendant timely *requested* the contributory negligence instruction, his ***failure to make an objection on the record*** once he knew that the court was proposing not to give the requested instruction—and ***before the court actually gave instructions that didn't include the requested one***—51(d)(1)(B) made this lack of a timely objection a failure to "assign as error" the lack of the desired instruction. (It's true that under 51(d)(2), the appellate court might still consider the lack of the requested instruction, but only if that lack was a "plain error" that "affects substantial rights"—however, the question doesn't ask you whether the appeals court could possibly consider the issue; it asks you whether the defendant "preserved the issue for appeal," and it's clear that because of the ***failure*** to object, the defendant did not do so.)

You probably won't remember this whole welter of procedural rules in the heat of trying to answer a question like this in the prescribed 1 2/3 minutes. Here's a conceptual *shortcut* that may help you intuit the correct behavior by the lawyer who's seeking a particular instruction: Because errors in jury instructions are very costly to correct after the fact (since a new trial will typically be required), we want to incentivize each party to make absolutely certain to give the trial judge a ***"final warning"*** about any instruction error the judge seems to be about to make. Therefore, even if a party has already timely requested a particular instruction, if the trial judge indicates (by giving the parties an advance look at her proposed instructions) that she won't be giving the requested instruction, the requesting party must immediately ***repeat the request*** in the form of an ***objection*** on the record—that way, the judge will receive one "last clear chance" (to use a phrase from the bygone days of contributory negligence) to avoid error by giving the requested instruction.

Choice (A) is wrong, because an objection after the judge gave the instructions to the jury would have been too late to preserve the issue for appeal. As we discuss further in connection with Choice (B), Rule 51(c)(2) says that an objection concerning jury instructions is, ordinarily, "timely [only] if: (A) a party objects at the opportunity provided under Rule 51(b)(2)[.]" The opportunity provided under 51(b)(2) occurs when the court gives the parties "an opportunity to object on the record . . . ***before the instructions . . . are delivered[.]***" So as soon as the court delivered the instructions to the jury, the defendant had already missed his chance to make the required pre-delivery-to-the-jury objection. Since this choice suggests that had the defendant objected after the judge gave the instructions to the jury the objection would still have been timely, the choice gives an incorrect explanation for the correct outcome.

Choice (C) is wrong, because the defendant's submission of a proposed instruction to the judge was a necessary, but not sufficient, condition for the defendant to preserve for appeal the judge's failure to give the instruction. It's true that the defendant submitted a proposed instruction on contributory negligence; indeed, given that the submission occurred "before the close of evidence," the submission was timely under Rule 51(a)(1) (which says that a party may request particular jury instructions "at the close of the evidence or at any earlier reasonable time that the court orders)." But making a timely submission of the proposed instruction is **not the only procedural step** a party requesting a particular instruction is required to take. As we discuss more extensively in Choice (B), even where a party submits a proposed jury instruction, if the judge indicates that the instructions she proposes to give will not include the requested one, then under 51(c)(2)(A) the party **must make an objection** "at the opportunity provided under Rule 51(b)(2)," i.e., the opportunity given **before the court gives the proposed instructions to the jury.**

Once the defendant failed to make a pre-delivery-to-the-jury objection "on the record, stating distinctly the matter objected to and the grounds for the objection" (51)(c)(1)), the objection was **waived** for purposes of the appeal, even though the defendant had properly and timely requested the instruction earlier.

Choice (D) is wrong, because for purposes of preserving an issue for appeal, the judge's failure to give the requested instruction did not "amount[] to a ruling on the instruction." This choice actually hints at a true and relevant provision buried within Rule 51, but the stringent conditions for application of that provision are not satisfied here. As we discuss in Choice (B), Rule 51(d)(1) specifies how and when a party is to "assign as error" rulings in connection with jury instructions. 51(d)(1) deals with how to assign two separate types of errors: (1) where there is "an error in an instruction actually given" (51(d)(1)(A)); and (2) where what is being assigned as error is "a failure to give an instruction" (51(d)(1)(B)).

What we're dealing with here, of course, is situation (2), since the defendant is claiming that the court failed to give a particular instruction. In this scenario 2, 51(d)(1)(B) says that the party will be deemed to have properly assigned as error the failure to instruct "if that party properly requested [the instruction] and—**unless the court rejected the request in a definitive ruling on the record**—[the party] also properly objected." Here, the defendant "properly requested" the instruction before the close of the evidence. Therefore, under the phrase in between the dashes above, the defendant's failure to "properly object" would not have been fatal *if* "the court [had] rejected the request in a definitive ruling on the record."

But there *was* no "definitive ruling on the record" here; the judge merely omitted the defendant's requested instruction when she told the litigants what instructions she would be giving, and this sort of "implied *rejection*" doesn't count as a "definitive ruling." Therefore, the defendant's failure to object was not the sort of "definitive ruling on the instruction" that would have been required for Choice (D) to be a correct response.

Answer 67

The correct choice is **(C)**, because the worker's failure to object in a timely way to the instruction, something that would normally be fatal, is excused because the instruction was **plain error** affecting the worker's substantial rights. Ordinarily, a litigant who is unhappy with an instruction given by the trial judge **must object** before the case goes to the jury. The procedures for handling jury instructions are laid out in Rule 51. Rule 51(a)(1) says that "At the close of the evidence . . . a party may file . . . **written requests for the jury instructions** it wants the court to give." Then, Rule 51(b)(1) says that the court "**must inform the parties of its proposed instructions** and proposed action on the [parties'] requests [for instructions] before instructing the jury[.]" And Rule 51(b)(2) specifies that once the court has informed the parties of its proposed instructions, the court must also "give the parties an *opportunity to object on the record* and out of the jury's hearing *before the instructions and arguments are delivered[.]*" Rule 51(c)(2), governing when objections are to be made, says that "An objection is timely if: (A) a party objects *at the opportunity provided under Rule 51(b)(2)*; or (B) [a situation not relevant here]." And 51(d)(1) says that, in the ordinary situation, "A party may assign as error: (A) an error in an instruction actually given, if that party properly objected[.]"

Putting all this together to see how it applies to this case, here's what we have:

(1) The trial judge was required by 51(b)(1) to "inform the parties of its proposed action on the [worker's] request[ed instruction] before instructing the jury" (we know that the trial judge did this, because the facts tell us that the court "did not accept the proposed instruction"), and by 51(b)(2) to "give the parties an *opportunity to object on the record* and out of the jury's hearing *before the instructions and arguments [were] delivered[.]*"

(2) We know that the worker did not take this 51(b)(2) opportunity to object (since we're told that the worker "did not object to the negligence instruction before it was given").

(3) The worker's failure to object at this pre-instruction moment would normally constitute a failure to make a "timely" objection, since to be timely 51(c)(2)(A) says the objection must be made "at the opportunity provided under Rule 51(b)(2)" (i.e., before the instruction is given).

(4) By 51(d)(1)A), a party may normally assign as error "an error in an instruction actually given, if that party properly objected[.]"

(5) Here, the worker's failure to object to error in the "instruction actually given" was not "proper," because the objection was not "timely" under step (3) above.

So the worker is out of luck unless some extenuating circumstance—not covered in the above analysis—intervened to save the worker from the usual effects of not objecting in a timely way.

Fortunately for the worker, Rule 51(d)(2), entitled "Plain Error," furnishes just such an extenuating circumstance for the worker. 51(d)(2) says that "A court may consider *a plain error* in the instructions that has *not been preserved as required* by Rule 51(d)(1) if the error *affects substantial rights.*" That language precisely tracks Choice (C).

Choice (A) is wrong, because it's not true that "issues of law can be raised at any time." When the issue of law concerns the correctness of an instruction to the jury, Rule 51 contains quite precise provisions about when and how objections are to be made; in all but unusual circumstances, these provisions (summarized in the discussion of Choice (C)) require that an objection be made before the instruction is given to the jury.

Choice (B) is wrong, because it's not the case that "the worker's objection [to the instruction] was preserved when he submitted his proposed negligence instruction." It's true that, under Rule 51(a)(1), at the close of the evidence the worker was permitted to file "written requests for the jury instructions it wants the court to give." It's also true that the worker timely made such a request. And, finally, it's true that the judge said he would not give the instruction requested by the worker. But it is *not* at all true that the worker's submission of a proposed objection—followed by the trial court's rejection of that proposal—was enough to "preserve" the objection. Rather, as is detailed in Choice (C), the worker received—and was required to immediately use—an "*opportunity to object on the record* and out of the jury's hearing *before the instructions and arguments [were] delivered*" (51(b)(2) and 51(c)(2)(A)).

Choice (D) is wrong, because it's not true that the need for a formal objection to a judicial ruling, in order to "preserve an argument," has been eliminated in the FRCP. There are some respects in which the Federal Rules of both Civil Procedure and Evidence are less formal—when it comes to preserving an objection or argument for appeal—than older law was. But as Choice (C) describes at length, when it comes to objecting to a particular set of jury instructions, Rule 51 is quite precise and demanding about how and when a formal objection must be made in order to preserve the issue for appeal. (There's a good reason for this precision: a jury trial is an expensive resource, and we want to minimize the chances that the resource will be wasted on account of an instruction the judge proposes to give, which the judge might have reconsidered had she been presented with a party's reason for *not* giving that instruction.)

Answer 68

The correct choice is **(D)**, because Rule 12(f) allows a party to move to strike from a pleading an "insufficient defense" or any "immaterial . . . matter." Rule 12(f) governs motions to strike matter from a pleading. The rule reads as follows:

> "*Motion to Strike.* The court may **strike** from a pleading an **insufficient defense** or any redundant, **immaterial**, impertinent, or scandalous **matter**. The court may act:
>
> (1)   on its own; or
>
> (2)   on motion **made by a party either before responding to the pleading** or, if a response is not allowed, within 21 days after being served with the pleading."

Since the purchaser's objection to the defense based on the earlier lawsuit is that that lawsuit is irrelevant, the purchaser is basically arguing that the defense is legally invalid on these facts. So the purchaser has a good argument that the defense is an "insufficient" one, and should therefore be "stri[cken] from [the] pleading" under 12(f). Alternatively, the defense can be viewed as containing "immaterial . . . matter," which would also allow it to be stricken. Finally, a procedural aspect: if the purchaser does what this choice posits—makes a motion to strike prior to filing an answer—the motion will be *timely* according to 12(f)(2), since it will be "on motion made by a party . . . before responding to the pleading" from which the defense is to be stricken.

Choice (A) is wrong, because absent a court order, a ***reply is not permitted*** in response to an answer that does not contain a counterclaim. Rule 7(a) is the source for determining what pleadings are allowed. 7(a) reads as follows:

> "Only these pleadings are allowed:
>
> (1)   a complaint;
>
> (2)   an answer to a complaint;
>
> (3)   ***an answer to a counterclaim designated as a counterclaim***;
>
> (4)   an answer to a crossclaim;
>
> (5)   a third-party complaint;
>
> (6)   an answer to a third-party complaint; and
>
> (7)   ***if the court orders one, a reply to an answer***."

This list makes it clear that there are only two situations in which a person (typically but not necessarily a plaintiff) will need to submit an "answer to an answer," also known as a "reply":

(1)   where the pleading by the other party (typically a defendant) contains ***"a counterclaim designated as a counterclaim"*** (Rule 7(a)(3)); and

(2)   where the ***court orders*** a "reply to an answer" (7(a)(7)).

In other words, by negative implication, the plaintiff is never required—or even permitted—to file a response to a defense asserted in the defendant's answer where the defense is not labelled a counterclaim and there is no relevant court order.

Neither of the two special situations requiring/allowing a reply—described in the prior paragraph—applies here. As to situation (1), the seller's allegation about the purchaser's prior contract claim is, you're told, "included as a separate defense…", which informs you that it is ***not*** labeled as a counterclaim. As to (2), there is no indication that the court has "order[ed] . . . a reply to an answer."

Therefore, not only is the purchaser not *required* to file a reply (or, indeed, *any* responsive pleading), but she is not even *permitted* to file one. So what Choice (A) posits—the filing of a "reply that includes a denial of the separate defense"—cannot be even an acceptable tactic by the purchaser, let alone the purchaser's "best response" to the seller's answer.

Choice (B) is wrong, because (1) it would not be proper to assess sanctions against the seller, rather than against the seller's attorney; and (2) a successful request for sanctions will require proof of everything that a motion-to-strike would require, plus additional elements, for little incremental benefit to the purchaser. Notice that this Choice (B) posits that the purchaser should "move for sanctions *against the seller…*" not "sanctions *against the seller's lawyer.*" As to reason (1) above: Rule 11 sanctions are generally awarded against the *lawyer* who signs the pleading, not the client (except in the unusual case where either the client has no lawyer, or there is evidence that the client lied to her lawyer about the underlying facts cited in the pleading, making the client the better target of a sanctions motion). Since the allegedly-irrelevant defense shows no hint of being based on a lie by the seller to the seller's attorney, the court is unlikely to view the party, rather than her lawyer, as being deserving of sanctions.

As to reason (2): any problem with the irrelevant language in the defense can be better taken care of directly via a motion to strike (as discussed in Choice (D)). In any event, the sanctions motion couldn't be granted without the court first deciding the underlying issue in the purchaser's favor, i.e., that the matter in the defense was indeed irrelevant. So bringing the sanctions motion will simply add to the purchaser's burden of persuasion (e.g., by requiring her to show financial loss from the inclusion of the irrelevant material), with little likely incremental benefit to the purchaser even if the motion is successful.

Choice (C) is wrong, because no pleading directed to the irrelevant defense is allowable here, whether by amendment or by any other method. The material in the answer about the prior lawsuit constitutes at best a defense, not a counterclaim. Therefore, as we discuss further in Choice (A), no responsive pleading (e.g., a "reply"), is even allowed, let alone required. Doing what Choice (C) posits—amending the complaint to explain why the material about the prior lawsuit is legally irrelevant—is an even-less-appropriate response than is the filing of a reply, since the purpose of the complaint is to state the pleader's claims, not to explain why the defendant's defenses are without merit.

Answer 69

The correct choice is **(A),** because issues of credibility will almost never be suitable for summary judgment, and the defendant's papers establish that credibility is a key issue here. The standards for granting summary judgment are set out in FRCP 56, which says that the court "shall grant summary judgment if the movant shows that there ***is no genuine dispute as to any material fact*** and the ***movant is entitled to judgment as a matter of law.***" Since the defendant company is not disputing the fact that the company promoted someone else rather than the plaintiff, the only real issue in the case is whether the company's (i.e., its owner's) reason for doing so was racially discriminatory.

The basis for the defendant's claim that it is entitled to judgment as a matter of law is that the only potential evidence cited by the plaintiff about the defendant's racially-discriminatory mental state—the quotations recited in the complaint—are "lies." In other words, the defendant's own affidavit in support of the summary judgment motion ***puts the plaintiff's credibility*** (as well as the owner's actual intent) ***in issue*** and suggests that the defendant will win at trial only if the plaintiff's expected admissible testimony is found not to be credible. In general, summary judgment is not a suitable vehicle for disposing of a case where a witness's credibility—especially as to matters of mental state (such as intent to lie or intent to discriminate)—is central. See, e.g., W,M&K (3d Ed.), Vol. 10A, § 2727, p. 485: "[I]f the evidence contained in the moving party's affidavit raises *subjective questions* such as *motive, intent, or conscience*, there may have to be a trial inasmuch as *cross-examination is the best means of testing the credibility* of this kind of evidence." See also the Advisory Committee Note to the 1963 amendment of Rule 56: "Where an issue as to a material fact *cannot be resolved without observation of the demeanor of witnesses in order to evaluate their credibility*, summary judgment is not appropriate."

Furthermore, as is discussed more fully in the analysis of Choice (C) below, the plaintiff's failure to submit an affidavit or other sworn testimony in opposition to the motion does not entitle the court to treat the company's factual allegations in the motion papers as undisputed, if the motion papers *themselves* show that there is a disputed factual issue. Here, the reference in the owner's affidavit to the plaintiff's "lies" shows that the plaintiff's credibility, as well as the owner's state of mind, are genuinely disputed issues that will require trial.

Choice (B) is wrong, because the factual allegations of the complaint, no matter how detailed, cannot themselves rebut the movant's claim that there is no available evidence that would permit the plaintiff to carry her burden of production at trial. This choice essentially asserts that the detailed factual allegations in the complaint here are sufficient by themselves that if they are believed, they would rebut the defendant's claim that there is no "genuine dispute as to any material fact." But that assertion is unduly broad, and is contradicted by something in Rule 56(c). Rule 56(c)(2) says that "A party may object that the material cited to . . . dispute a fact cannot be *presented in a form that would be admissible in evidence*." This means that if the papers in support of the motion (here, the defendant's submission) contain evidence that if uncontradicted would demonstrate that there is no genuine dispute of material fact, the non-movant will lose on the motion unless he can point to *"admissible evidence"* that if believed would put some fact into dispute.

The plaintiff's pleadings here are not themselves "admissible evidence," so factual allegations in the pleadings—unless they're specifically shown to be embodied in admissible evidence—can't create a genuine issue. The reason that the appeals court will reverse is *not* that the pleadings themselves can be enough to create a genuine dispute of material fact—the reason is that the *defendant's affidavit* demonstrates (by putting the plaintiff's credibility at issue) that there will be an issue, plaintiff's credibility, that cannot be resolved as a matter of law.

Choice (C) is wrong, because in this situation no sworn affidavit was required to be submitted by the plaintiff. There are certainly situations in which the nonmovant's failure to submit an affidavit will cause the nonmovant to have summary judgment entered against him. But here, as is discussed further in Choice (A), the owner's affidavit *itself* shows the existence of a genuine dispute (plaintiff's credibility) that cannot be resolved except by a trial. Because that is so, the plaintiff survives the motion even without having submitted an affidavit. But if the fact pattern were one in which there were no issues of mental state or credibility (e.g., a suit to collect on a negotiable instrument), the nonmovant's failure to submit an affidavit or any other piece of admissible evidence *would* likely be fatal—it's only the fact that the defendant inadvertently injected a credibility issue that allows the plaintiff here to avoid summary judgment without having submitted an affidavit or other admissible piece of evidence.

Choice (D) is wrong, because there is no such thing as an automatic "default" in response to a motion for summary judgment. The Advisory Committee Note on the 2010 amendments to Rule 56 says that "summary judgment cannot be granted by *default* even if there is a complete failure to respond to the motion[.]" Rather, the court may grant summary judgment only "if *the motion and supporting materials*—including the facts considered undisputed—*show that the movant is entitled to it*[.]" (Rule 56(e)(3)). In other words, the mere fact that the nonmovant (the plaintiff) here didn't file papers in opposition to the motion does not mean that every fact asserted by the movant should be accepted as undisputed by the court—the judge was required to examine all evidence called to the court's attention, including the *movant's own affidavit* (with its accusation that the plaintiff was lying), and to notice that that affidavit itself demonstrated the existence of a triable issue (the credibility of the plaintiff). Given that the judge was required to review this evidence from sources other than the plaintiff, no submission by the plaintiff in opposition to the motion was required in order for the plaintiff to be entitled to have the motion denied.

Answer 70

The correct choice is **(C)**, because the affidavit will be based on personal knowledge, will set out facts that would be admissible at trial, and will show that there is a genuine dispute about whether the original hospital X-ray contained signs of cancer.

The patient's response to the hospital summary judgment motion must raise a genuine dispute of material fact, and must do so according to the procedural rules set out in Rule 56. Rule 56(c)(1), which sets out the general procedures for supporting factual positions made by either the movant on a summary judgment motion or by the adversary, reads as follows (edited to show only the parts that most directly apply here):

"(c) Procedures.

(1) Supporting Factual Positions. A party asserting that a fact . . . **is genuinely disputed** must **support the assertion by**:

(A) *citing to particular parts of materials in the record*, including depositions, documents, electronically stored information, *affidavits* or declarations, stipulations (including those made for purposes of the motion only), admissions, interrogatory answers, or other materials; or

(B) showing that the *materials cited* [by the other side] *do not establish the absence* . . . of a genuine dispute[.]"

Let's see how this excerpt from Rule 56(c)(1) applies to our facts here. First, the hospital is asserting various facts that it claims are not in dispute; one of these facts (the key one) is that the hospital X-ray that led the hospital staff not to diagnose the patient's cancer does not show any signs of cancer. (This is key, because if that X-ray indeed doesn't show any signs of cancer, hospital staff could not have been negligent in failing to diagnose the plaintiff's cancer.)

Now, it's up to the patient to "assert[] that a fact . . . is genuinely disputed" (see the beginning of 56(c)(1)), and the patient must therefore "support the assertion" by either the method prescribed in 56(c)(1)(A) or the one prescribed in 56(c)(1)(B). The submission proposed by Choice (C)—submission of an affidavit from the plaintiff's expert radiologist contradicting the findings in the report of the hospital's radiologist—qualifies by combining both of these methods.

First, the affidavit from the plaintiff's expert radiologist, once it is submitted on plaintiff's behalf, becomes a "particular part[] of materials in the record, including . . . affidavits or declarations" (56(c)(1)(A)). Then, this affidavit "show[s] that the materials cited [by the hospital] do not establish the absence . . . of a genuine dispute" (56(c)(1)(B)); that's because the materials cited by the hospital (the report from the hospital's radiologist, claiming that the hospital X-ray shows no signs of cancer) are directly rebutted by the plaintiff's expert radiologist's affidavit (claiming that the same hospital X-ray does show signs of cancer, since Choice (C) says that the plaintiff's expert's affidavit contains "findings that contradict the report of the hospital's radiologist.")

There is additional language in Rule 56(c) that bears on the appropriateness of the affidavit from the plaintiff's expert radiologist. Rule 56(c)(4) says:

> "(4) *Affidavits or Declarations*. An **affidavit** or declaration used to support or oppose a motion must be **made on personal knowledge, set out facts that would be admissible in evidence**, and show that the affiant or declarant is competent to testify on the matters stated."

Here, the plaintiff's expert radiologist is making his affidavit "on personal knowledge" (since he's describing what he himself sees on the hospital X-ray). And he is "set[ting] out facts that would be admissible in evidence" (namely, his expert testimony about how his reading of the X-ray "contradict[s] the report of the hospital's radiologist") — there would be no hearsay or other admissibility problems with the expert's giving testimony echoing what he is currently saying in his affidavit.

In sum, the expert's affidavit meets all the requirements of Rule 56(c) for supporting the plaintiff's assertion that a fact (what the X-ray disclosed about whether plaintiff had cancer) "is genuinely disputed."

Choice (A) is wrong, because a "report" is not one of the types of items that may be used in support of a party's opposition to a motion for summary judgment. As we discuss more extensively in Choice (C), Rule 56(c) spells out what types of materials a party may use in support of, or opposition to, a motion for summary judgment. Here, the patient needs to show why there is a genuine dispute about whether the original hospital X-ray shows signs of cancer. Rule 56(c)(1), edited to apply to the patient's situation, says that:

> "A party asserting that a fact . . . is *genuinely disputed* must *support the assertion by*:
>
> (A) *citing to particular parts of materials in the record*, including depositions, documents, electronically stored information, *affidavits* or declarations, stipulations (including those made for purposes of the motion only), admissions, interrogatory answers, or other materials; *or*
>
> (B) showing that the materials cited [by the hospital] do not establish the absence . . . of a genuine dispute[.]"

A "report" (which is what Choice (A) proposes) is not one of the types of "materials in the record" that 56(c)(1)(A) contemplates.

Furthermore, 56(c)(4) says that "An affidavit or declaration used to support or oppose a motion must be made on personal knowledge, set out facts that would be admissible in evidence, and show that the affiant or declarant is competent to testify on the matters stated." The implication of 56(c)(4) is that a "report," since it's not an "affidavit or declaration," can't be used to "oppose a motion," and doesn't show that the "affiant or declarant is competent to testify" (since a report doesn't have an "affiant or declarant.")

Choice (B) is wrong, because to the extent the affidavit covers the key issue of what the X-ray shows, the affidavit is not "made on personal knowledge," consists of inadmissible hearsay, and does not show that the affiant would be "competent to testify on the matters stated." To combat the motion, the patient needs to establish, by proper means, that there is a genuine issue of material fact about whether the hospital X-ray shows signs of cancer. As we discuss more fully in Choices (C) and (A), Rule 56(c)(4) says that "An affidavit or declaration used to support or oppose a motion must be made on personal knowledge, set out facts that would be admissible in evidence, and show that the affiant or declarant is competent to testify on the matters stated."

The affidavit here, which needs to demonstrate a genuine issue about what the X-ray shows, would have to do that by containing statements about the affiant's own "personal knowledge."

But the affidavit here (by the lawyer) does not demonstrate the affiant's personal knowledge about what the X-ray shows, since the affidavit merely details the attorney's "conversations with the patient's expert radiologist," and it's the expert radiologist who knows what the X-ray shows.

Similarly, the main "fact" set out in the affidavit is only "what the expert radiologist told me the X-ray shows" (not what the X-ray actually shows), and this "fact" would not be admissible in evidence because it consists of hearsay.

Finally, the affidavit does not show that "the affiant . . . is competent to testify on the matters stated," because the affiant (the lawyer), who lacks first-hand knowledge on the key matter at issue (what the X-ray shows), is not "competent to testify" on that matter.

Choice (D) is wrong, because the patient's current cancer diagnosis is not the key fact at issue in the motion—the key factor is whether the hospital X-ray showed signs of cancer.

The thrust of the hospital's summary judgment motion is that there is no genuine issue of fact about whether the hospital X-ray showed signs of cancer; if no reasonable jury could conclude that the X-ray showed such signs, the plaintiff cannot possibly establish that the no-cancer diagnosis premised on that X-ray was negligent. Therefore, to successfully oppose the motion, the plaintiff will need to (in the words of Rule 56(c)(1)) either "cit[e] to particular parts of materials in the record" (56(c)(1)(A)) or "show[] that the materials cited [by the hospital] do not establish the absence . . . of a genuine dispute" (56(c)(1)(B)). This choice, by calling for submission of the patient's current medical records, ensures that those medical records will be "materials in the [court] record."

But those medical records—since they are being cited only to demonstrate that the plaintiff is currently diagnosed with cancer—do not speak at all to the key issue, which is whether the original hospital X-ray showed cancer. Nor do these current medical records meet the requirement of 56(c)(1)(B)—these current records don't show that the "materials cited" by the hospital, i.e., the report from the hospital's radiologist finding no signs of cancer on the original X-ray, "do not establish the absence . . . of a genuine dispute." (Only an item in the record tending to show that there is a genuine dispute about whether the original hospital X-ray showed signs of cancer could satisfy either 56(c)(1)(A) or (c)(1)(B).)

Answer 71

The correct choice is **(A)**, because Rule 56 expressly allows the court to defer ruling on the motion when more discovery might produce evidence showing a genuine issue of material fact. Rule 56(d) says that:

> "(d) *When Facts Are Unavailable to the Nonmovant.* If a nonmovant **shows by affidavit or declaration** that, **for specified reasons**, **it cannot present facts essential to justify its opposition**, the court may: …
>
> (2) **allow time to obtain affidavits or declarations or to take discovery**; …"

Here, the essence of the manufacturer's summary judgment motion is that there is no evidence showing that the worker's employer ever used insulation made by the manufacturer. The employer (a non-party) is the most likely source of information about whether this insulation was used by the employer, and we know that the worker hasn't had a chance to seek that information from the employer (since the facts tell us that the only discovery has been in the form of each party deposing the other).

Therefore, so long as the worker's declaration says that the desired discovery would consist of requests to the employer for information (whether in the form of depositions, document requests or other) about whether insulation from the manufacturer was ever used during the time the worker worked for the employer, the declaration will meet the requirement of Rule 56(d) that the nonmovant come forward with "specified reasons" about why discovery will supply the nonmovant with "facts essential to justify its opposition" to the motion.

Choice (B) is wrong, because the worker has the burden of producing enough evidence on the distribution issue that a jury could reasonably find for the worker on this point, and the mere *possibility* that the jury might find the manufacturer's testimony on the point not credible does not satisfy this burden.

The party moving for summary judgment initially has the burden of coming forward with a showing that there is "no genuine dispute as to any material fact" (the phrase used in Rule 56(a)). How the movant can do this depends on which party will have the burden of persuasion at trial. In the common scenario where the burden of persuasion at trial will be on the *non*-moving party (which is the scenario here), the movant may bear her initial production burden by *either* (1) submitting affirmative evidence that negates an essential element of the nonmovant's claim or (2) demonstrating to the court that the nonmovant does not seem to have any evidence that would suffice to establish each element of the nonmovant's claim. Once the movant has done either of these things, the burden then *shifts* to the nonmovant to point out to the court specific admissible evidence showing that the movant is wrong, i.e., evidence that if believed will legally suffice to let the nonmovant carry his burden of persuasion at trial. Cf. *Celotex Corp. v. Catrett*, 477 U.S. 317 (1986) (dissent on the merits by Justice Brennan, but agreeing with the majority as to how the burden of production shifts).

When this burden-shifting mechanism of summary judgment is applied to these facts, it becomes clear that at the summary judgment stage, the possibility that the credibility-focused tactic used by the worker in this choice might convince the jury to disbelieve the manufacturer's testimony *will not be enough* to allow the worker to escape summary judgment now. At trial, the worker, like any plaintiff bringing a strict tort liability action against a manufacturer of a toxic substance, will bear the burden of persuasion on every element of his *prima facie* case, including the burden of showing that the manufacturer was probably the source of the substance that caused the plaintiff's harm. The manufacturer, as the party moving for summary judgment, bore the initial burden of production, i.e., the burden of showing that as to at least one element of the worker's *prima facie* case (here, the source of the injury-causing insulation), there is "no genuine dispute as to any material fact." The manufacturer carried this burden by using the second method described in the prior paragraph, i.e., by calling to the court's attention the apparent absence of any evidence in the record to date that, even if believed by a jury, and even if coupled with all inferences favorable to the worker that could plausibly be drawn from any record-evidence to date, would justify the jury in finding that the manufacturer probably made the illness-causing insulation.

Once the manufacturer carried this burden of production, the **burden shifted to the worker** to come forward with a **specific item of admissible evidence** rebutting the manufacturer's showing, i.e., evidence that if believed would tend to show that the worker's illness was probably caused by exposure to insulation made by the manufacturer. If the worker were to make *only* the credibility-based argument given by this choice, the worker will **not have carried** this burden-of-production that has been shifted to him. That is, the worker must come forward with some piece of *affirmative* and specific evidence that the defendant made the insulation in question; it's not enough for the worker to argue, in substance, "I will put the president of the manufacturer on the stand, and when he or she denies that the company made the insulation in question, I will rely on the possibility that the jury may find this testimony not worthy of belief." (If this type of credibility-focused hypothetical "evidence" were sufficient to block summary judgment, summary judgment would be largely stripped of its function, which is to terminate meritless claims before trial.)

Choice (C) is wrong, because the manufacturer was not required to "attach [some] evidence to its motion to show that the insulation was not used by the worker's employer," given that the ultimate burden of persuasion on the issue of who made the insulation used by the worker's employer will be on the worker, not the manufacturer.

It's true that under Rule 56(a), the party moving for summary judgment must "show[] that there is no genuine dispute as to any material fact" regarding the claim at issue. And when the motion concerns a claim as to which the *moving party* will bear the burden of persuasion at trial (not very common), the movant will indeed typically need to "support the assertion" (that there is no genuine dispute) by "citing to particular parts of materials in the record, including depositions, documents, electronically stored information, affidavits or declarations . . . or other materials." Rule 56(c)(1)(A).

But in the usual situation in which, as here, the motion concerns a claim on which the *non*movant will bear the burden of persuasion at trial, nothing in Rule 56 requires the movant to cite to or attach any particular evidentiary materials. Instead, Rule 56(c)(1) allows the movant to support her assertion by two alternative methods, one of which is by reviewing the record in order to show that the **nonmovant won't be able to establish** at least one fact that's essential to the nonmovant's claim.

Here's how 56(c)(1) reads when language not applicable to our scenario is stripped out:

> "A party asserting that a **fact cannot be . . . genuinely disputed** must support the assertion by
>
> (A) **citing to particular parts of materials in the record** ... or
>
> (B) showing that **the materials cited do not establish** the . . . presence of a **genuine dispute** [as to that fact], or that an **adverse party cannot produce admissible evidence** to support the fact."

Here, the manufacturer is (1) asserting the "fact" (a negative fact) that it did not make the insulation that caused the worker's illness; and (2) asserting that there is no genuine dispute about this negative fact. And it is complying with 56(c)(1) by using both method (A) and method (B).

As to (A), the manufacturer is (or at least we can reasonably presume that it is) referring to "particular parts of materials in the record," namely, the full texts of the two depositions. And as to (B), the manufacturer is "showing that the materials cited" (the depositions) "do not establish the . . . presence of a genuine dispute" about whether the manufacturer made the injury-causing insulation, in that the depositions are completely silent about who made the insulation in question. Also as to (B), the manufacturer is saying that "an adverse party" (the worker) "cannot produce admissible evidence to support" the opposite fact (that the manufacturer's insulation *did* cause the injury), as demonstrated by the absence of any evidence in the record so far—depositions or otherwise—supporting the manufacturer's having made the insulation.

Therefore, the manufacturer has done enough to shift back to the worker the burden of producing evidence that would justify a reasonable jury in finding that the manufacturer more likely than not made the insulation that harmed the worker. Thus to the extent that Choice (C) says that the motion should be denied, the choice fails to take account of this burden-shifting, and of how shifting works to the manufacturer's benefit.

Choice (D) is wrong, because a cross-motion will not remedy the problem with the worker's lack of evidence.

Any cross-motion by the worker for summary judgment would have to meet the same requirements as if the worker were the only one making a motion (i.e., as if the worker were making a standalone "motion for summary judgment" rather than a "cross-motion" for that relief). If the worker were the movant, he would bear the burden of showing, by reference to "particular parts of materials in the record" (56(c)(1)) that as to *each* element of his strict product liability claim, there is no "genuine dispute as to any material fact." Even if the worker were trying to obtain just "partial" summary judgment—summary judgment on the limited issue of whether the manufacturer's insulation was the cause of harm to the worker—the worker's motion would at the very least have to show, from specific admissible materials in the record, that a reasonable jury would have no choice but to conclude that the manufacturer made the injury-causing insulation.

But the argument cited by this choice—that the manufacturer "has introduced no evidence to show that its insulation did not harm the worker"—does not come close to constituting the required showing that the manufacturer certainly made the insulation. That's because, at trial, if there is no evidence either way on whether the manufacturer made the injury-causing insulation, the worker as the bearer of persuasion on the "who made the insulation?" question will lose.

Answer 72

The correct choice is **(D)**, because it best reflects the "legally sufficient evidence" standard set forth in FRCP 50(a)(1). FRCP 50(a)(1) sets out the general standard that the federal trial judges to use in deciding whether to grant judgment as a matter of law ("JML") in a jury trial:

> "If a party has been fully heard on an issue during a jury trial and the court finds that a reasonable jury would ***not have a legally sufficient evidentiary basis*** to find for the party on that issue, the court may: . . . (B) grant a motion for ***judgment as a matter of law*** against the party on a claim . . . that, under the controlling law, can be maintained . . . only with a favorable finding on that issue."

Choice (D) does not quite echo the key phrase "a legally sufficient evidentiary basis" used by Rule 50(a)(1). But this choice, by saying that the railroad's motion will fail if there is "substantial evidence . . . to support the verdict, resolving all disputed issues in the [non-movant's] favor," tracks the more-specific standard that the Supreme Court has said is to be used when Rule 50(a)(1) is applied. See *Reeves v. Sanderson Plumbing Prods.*, 530 U.S. 133 (2000): "[I]n entertaining a motion for judgment as a matter of law, the court should review all of the evidence in the record. In doing so, however, the court must ***draw all reasonable inferences in favor of the nonmoving party***, and it may not make credibility determinations or weigh the evidence."

Choice (A) is wrong, because it states the standard for ruling on a motion for summary judgment. Rule 56(a) says that a motion for summary judgment should be granted "if the movant shows that there is ***no genuine dispute as to any material fact*** and the movant is entitled to judgment as a matter of law." Therefore, if the question involved the railroad's motion for summary judgment prior to the trial, this choice would more-or-less correctly state the standard. But where the fact pattern involves a post-verdict motion for JML, the correct standard needs to be one that relies only on the legal sufficiency of evidence that was ***actually presented*** to the jury, not one that also includes admissible evidence that was available to the nonmovant (the widow) but that her lawyer chose not to present.

Choice (B) is wrong, because it states a ground for granting a new trial, not a motion for judgment as a matter of law. Rule 59(a)(1) says that after a jury trial, the federal district court may "grant a new trial . . . for any reason for which a new trial has heretofore [i.e., before the adoption of the FRCP in 1938] been granted" in federal civil cases. One of the reasons for which federal judges have always had the power to grant a new trial is that the verdict was against the weight of the evidence. W,M&K (2012 Ed.), § 2806, p. 80. But the circumstances under which the judge may reverse the jury's verdict have always been more limited than those for which the judge may grant a new trial: "On a motion for new trial the trial judge may consider the credibility of witnesses and the weight of the evidence; on a motion for judgment as a matter of law, the judge may not." W&M (2008 Ed.), § 2531, pp. 477-478.

Choice (C) is wrong, because the presence of a "scintilla" of evidence in support of the verdict does not prevent the granting of the motion. In the usual case where the nonmovant (here, the widow) had the burden of production on one or more issues, the judge may grant the motion for JML as long as the nonmovant did not produce enough evidence to justify a reasonable jury in finding for her on each of those issues, even if the nonmovant produced a "scintilla" (a very small amount) of evidence on each of the issues. See W&M (2008 Ed.), § 2524, pp. 248-257: "[T]he federal courts do not follow the extremely restrictive rule that a mere scintilla of evidence in support of the nonmoving party is enough to create an issue for the jury and, consequentially, on a denial of a rule 50 motion the question is not whether there is literally no evidence supporting the party against whom the motion is directed but whether there is evidence upon which the jury might reasonably find a verdict for that party."

Answer 73

The correct choice is (**B**), because a motion for judgment as a matter of law must be made ***before the case goes to the jury.*** Judgment as a matter of law in a jury trial is governed by FRCP 50. Rule 50(a)(2) says that "A motion for judgment as a matter of law may be made at any time before the case is submitted to the jury." If a party makes a timely motion under Rule 50(a)(2), then (assuming the trial judge doesn't grant the motion before submitting the case to the jury), after the jury reaches a verdict that same movant "may file a *renewed* motion for judgment as a matter of law and may include an alternative or joint request for a new trial[.]" Rule 50(b). But as the reference to a "renewed" motion suggests, if the party did *not* move for judgment as a matter of law before the case went to the jury, that party has **waived** the right to ask for judgment as a matter of law post-verdict.

Choice (A) is wrong, because the right to move for judgment as a matter of law must initially be made before the case goes to the jury. It is *not* true that, as this choice asserts, "a determination of the sufficiency of the evidence is solely within the jury's province." After all the evidence has been submitted in a federal jury trial, on a motion by the defendant the trial judge is free (1) to conclude that the plaintiff has not submitted sufficient evidence for a reasonable jury to find for the plaintiff; and therefore (2) to "take the case from the jury" on the grounds of insufficient evidence (a type of judgment as a matter of law).

What prevents the wholesaler's challenge to the sufficiency of the evidence from being heard here is not the sanctity of the "jury's province," but the procedural rule (discussed in Choice (B)) that the wholesaler's failure to make its motion for judgment as a matter of law before the case went to the jury caused a waiver of the right to make the motion post-verdict.

Choice (C) is wrong, because the fact that the judge ruled on the challenge before the wholesaler filed the appeal does not save the wholesaler from its failure to make its motion before the case went to the jury. The fact that the wholesaler raised its challenge (and received a rejection of that challenge) before the wholesaler filed the appeal does not help the wholesaler. The wholesaler's fundamental problem is that it failed to raise its challenge before the case went to the jury (a requirement discussed in Choice (B)), and that failure is fatal to both (1) any right to raise the challenge post-verdict by motion for judgment as a matter of law; and (2) any right to appeal the trial judge's rejection of the post-verdict motion.

Choice (D) is wrong, because the trial judge's acknowledgment that the wholesaler had strong arguments is irrelevant. As with Choice (C), the wholesaler's fundamental problem is that it failed to raise the challenge before the case went to the jury (a requirement discussed in Choice (B)). Once the wholesaler made that error, nothing that happened post-verdict (including the trial judge's acknowledgment of "problems with some of the evidence") would have enabled the wholesaler to appeal the judge's rejection of the post-verdict motion.

Answer 74

The correct choice is **(B),** because the district judge has discretion to use this "remittitur" device. The museum has not moved for a new trial (which is what it probably should have done). But even without a motion by one of the parties, Rule 69(d) gives the trial judge the right to order a new trial on her own: "No later than 28 days after the entry of judgment, the court, ***on its own***, may ***order a new trial for any reason that would justify granting one on a party's motion***." So we have to determine whether the excessiveness of the verdict here is a "reason that would justify granting [a new trial] on a party's motion." Rule 59(a)(1) gives the answer, by saying that "The court may, on motion, grant a new trial on all or some of the issues—and to any party—as follows: (A) after a jury trial, for ***any reason for which a new trial has heretofore been granted in an action at law in federal court***[.]" This reference to reasons for which new trials have "heretofore been granted in an action at law in federal court" means that if the reason for a new trial is one that the common-law courts would have recognized as valid before the 1938 enactment of the FRCP, the reason will suffice for a new trial under Rule 59.

One of the best-established reasons for granting a new trial is that the verdict is ***greatly excessive***—sometimes the phrase used to describe such a verdict is that it is so large that it "shocks the conscience." Since there is good reason to believe that a verdict calculated by valuing each of the photographer's 200 prints at ten times the highest amount ($500) that he had ever sold a print for during his career is greatly excessive, the judge would be entitled to avoid this excess award by ordering either an entirely new trial on liability and damages or a new trial just on the issue of damages. But by long-standing federal practice, federal trial judges are permitted, instead of unconditionally ordering a new trial, to issue a "conditional new trial order," which is what we have here; that is, the trial judge orders a new trial (either on all issues or just damages) but agrees that the new trial need not take place if the plaintiff is willing to consent to a reduction of the verdict to a lesser amount that the judge believes is justified by the evidence. (This "conditional new trial order" device is often called a "***remittitur***.") See, e.g., *Kirsch v. Fleet Street, Ltd.*, 148 F.3d 149, 165 (2d Cir. 1998) (district judge may enter a conditional order of remittitur, "compelling a plaintiff to choose between reduction of an excessive verdict and a new trial.")

Choice (A) is wrong, because the museum's motion does not meet the procedural requirements for a motion for a judgment as a matter of law. The facts tell you that the nature of the motion made by the museum post-verdict is that it is a motion for "judgment as a matter of law" (a/k/a a "JML" motion). The procedures governing JML motions are set out in FRCP 50. Of critical importance, Rule 50(a)(2) says that "A motion for judgment as a matter of law may be made at any time ***before the case is submitted to the jury.***" Then, if the court does not grant the motion before submitting the case to the jury, and the jury comes back with a verdict that the movant views as unfavorable, the movant may "file a ***renewed motion*** for judgment as a matter of law[.]" Courts have interpreted this language as meaning, by negative implication, that if the would-be movant does not make any JML motion before the case is submitted to the jury, the movant has ***waived his right to do so after the verdict.*** Here, the facts tell you that "No motions were made by either side before the case went to the jury," so you know the museum waived its right to make a JML motion. (Indeed, you should have interpreted the very fact that the statement of facts bothered to specify the lack of any pre-verdict motions as a signal that a post-verdict JML motion might be coming, and if made, would be found to have been made too late.) So due to the absence of a pre-verdict version of the motion, the JML motion referred to in this choice is one that the judge may not grant, no matter how much the judge thinks that justice would be well served if it could be granted. (By the way, Rule 50 does not give the trial judge the right to issue judgment as a matter of law *sua sponte*, i.e., without a motion having been made for it.) But as is discussed in the treatment of Choice (B), the judge can achieve much the same result as a grant of JML at a reduced amount by using the remittitur or "conditional new trial" order mentioned in that choice.

Choice (C) is wrong, because it is wasteful of judicial resources and therefore not the "best" alternative. What's proposed by this choice is that the judge grant a partial new trial. FRCP 59(a)(1) indeed allows the judge to do this, by giving her the right to grant, on motion, "a new trial on all *or some* of the issues[.]" But the question asks you to choose the procedurally-available alternative that will avoid being "wasteful of judicial resources," and the partial new trial will waste resources by requiring the impaneling of a whole new jury to decide the damages issue from scratch. The device of remittitur, i.e., conditional grant of new trial, mentioned in Choice (B), is a better approach because it will avoid such waste if the photographer accepts the reduction — and if he doesn't accept, the consequent new trial on damages won't be any more wasteful than if such a new trial had been unconditionally ordered as mentioned in this Choice (C).

Choice (D) is wrong, because it misstates the current state of Seventh Amendment jurisprudence. The Seventh Amendment guarantees the litigants in federal trials brought "at law" (as opposed to "in equity") the right to a jury trial. Part of the Seventh Amendment is the so-called *"re-examination clause,"* which says that "no fact tried by a jury, shall be otherwise re-examined in any Court of the United States, than according to the rules of the common law." The re-examination clause would be violated by the court's overturning of a jury verdict for reasons that would not have been permitted "at common law" as that law existed in 1789, when the Seventh Amendment was enacted. But the Supreme Court has held that a grant of a new trial on grounds of the excessiveness of the verdict (as well as the use of a conditional new trial order or remittitur) were permitted at common law, and therefore do not normally violate the Seventh Amendment. So this choice, by saying that the museum's motion for judgment as a matter of law would violate the Seventh Amendment, is legally incorrect. (The court is indeed not permitted to grant the motion — but as is discussed in the analysis of Choice (A), the reason is that the museum didn't make the motion before the case was submitted to the jury, not that the granting of the motion would violate the Seventh Amendment.)

Answer 75

The correct choice is **(C)**, because Rule 60(b)(3) expressly allows the court to order relief from a final judgment that was procured by fraud. Rule 60 specifies circumstances under which the court can grant relief from a judgment or order. Rule 60(b) lists various substantive grounds for relief from a judgment. Most pertinent here is 60(b)(3), which authorizes the court to relieve a party "from a final judgment . . . for the following reasons: . . . (3) *fraud* (whether previously called intrinsic or extrinsic), misrepresentation, or misconduct *by an opposing party*[.]"

Cases interpreting 60(b)(3) as applied to allegations of fraud say that the movant must show, *by "clear and convincing evidence*," that the opposing party engaged in a fraud that "*prevented* the movant from *fully and fairly presenting its case*." *Harley v. Zoesch*, 413 F.3d 866 (8th Cir. 2005). The videotape certainly appears to be clear and convincing evidence that the plaintiff has not been permanently paralyzed. Furthermore, although it's *possible* that the plaintiff's present ability to jog is due to an unforeseen recovery after the trial, the shortness of time between the judgment and the videotape (just two months) strongly suggests that fraud at trial, rather than an unexpected recovery, is what occurred.

Also, the videotape here is a type of evidence that defendant probably couldn't have gotten in time for the trial—it's unlikely that the plaintiff would have jogged before trial knowing that she might be subject to surveillance; therefore, plaintiff's fraudulent concealment of her true physical status certainly seems to have directly prevented the defendant from "fully and fairly" presenting a highly material aspect of its case, plaintiff's paralysis or lack thereof.

Choice (A) is wrong, because the time for a motion for a new trial has already expired. Rule 60, discussed in the analysis of Choice (C), does not apply here, because Rule 60 only allows for "relief from a judgment," not for the granting of a new trial. The procedure under which the district court could order a new trial is prescribed by Rule 59. Here, we don't need to go into sorts of reasons that might suffice under Rule 59 for the granting of a new trial; that's because the time for making a motion for new trial under Rule 59 *has already expired*. Rule 59(b) says that "[a] motion for a new trial must be filed *no later than 28 days after the entry of judgment*." Here, we're told that the defendant received the videotape "two months after the court entered judgment." Therefore, we know that even if the defendant made its new-trial motion on the same day it received the videotape, the motion would be made more than 28 days post-judgment, and thus too late.

Choice (B) is wrong, because the jury's "mistaken belief" about a factual matter is not the sort of ground for which the Federal Rules authorize relief from a judgment. As we discuss more extensively in the analysis of Choice (C), the Rule that allows a party to seek relief from a judgment is Rule 60. Nothing in Rule 60 allows for relief from a judgment merely because the judgment stems from the jury's factually-incorrect conclusion about an issue in the case. It's true that Rule 60(b)(1) allows the court to relieve a party from a judgment by reason of "mistake, inadvertence, surprise, or excusable neglect." But 60(b)(1)'s reference to a "mistake" is interpreted to mean a mistake by a litigant or a lawyer, not a mistake by the finder of fact. If a party believes that the judgment stems from the jury's mistaken finding of fact, the proper remedy is for the party to make a timely Rule 59 motion for a new trial; and as discussed in connection with Choice (A), the defendant's time for making such a motion has already expired.

Choice (D) is wrong, because a motion for relief based on newly discovered evidence requires that the evidence have been in existence at the time of trial. It's true that Rule 60, which recognizes various grounds for granting relief from a judgment, mentions as a valid ground "newly discovered evidence that, with reasonable diligence, could not have been discovered in time to move for a new trial under Rule 59(b)." (Rule 60(b)(2).) But cases interpreting both Rule 60(b)(2) and Rule 59(b) hold that "the evidence must have been *in existence at the time of the trial.*" W,M&K, vol. 11, § 2859, p. 387. Here, the evidence—the videotape—did not come into existence until two months after the judgment was entered.

Answer 76

The correct choice is **(C)**, because 7 days' advance written notice of the hearing was required, given that the company's claim was not for a sum certain. The procedure for entering a default judgment is given by Rule 55, and varies depending on whether the plaintiff's claim is or is not "for a *sum certain* or a sum that can be *made certain by computation*." Where the plaintiff's claim *is* one that is or can be made certain, Rule 55(b)(1) says that the clerk of the court can (indeed must) enter the judgment, *with no hearing, and thus no advance notice to the defendant, required.* But where the plaintiff's claim is *not* one that is, or can by computation be made, for a sum certain, then Rule 55(b)(2) says that it's up to the court (not the clerk), to enter judgment, which may only be done *following a hearing* that in some scenarios requires *advance written notice to the defendant*.

Here, even if it's undisputed (due to the plumber's failure to answer) that the plumber's negligence caused at least *some* damage to the company's building, the dollar value of that damage is *not* "a sum certain or a sum that can be made certain by computation." (Rather, the court will need to conduct a hearing to "determine the amount of damages"; see Rule 55(b)(2)(B).) In cases where such a hearing is required, here's what 55(b)(2) says about whether—and how much—advance notice is required:

> "If the party against whom a default judgment is sought *has appeared personally or by a representative*, that party or its representative must be *served with written notice of the application at least 7 days before the hearing.*"

Recall that earlier in the case, the plumber "filed a motion to dismiss for lack of personal jurisdiction"; that motion constituted an "appear[ance] personally or by a representative." Once the plumber did this, the company was then required to *give at least seven days' advance written notice* of the hearing on the company's application for a default judgment. But the plumber received only *three days' notice*; that made the entire *ex parte* hearing on the amount of damages procedurally defective.

Given the lack of sufficient notice, Rule 60(b) comes to the plumber's rescue, by saying that "On motion and just terms, the court *may relieve a party . . . from a final judgment* . . . for the following reasons: (1) *mistake*, inadvertence, surprise, or *excusable neglect*; . . . (4) the judgment is *void*; . . . or (6) *any other reason that justifies relief.*" The lack of advance notice here probably makes the judgment "void," but if not, is very likely to be an "other reason that justifies relief." Thus as far as 60(b) is concerned, the court is authorized to set aside the judgment.

There is, however, one other procedural hurdle that the plumber will have to surmount: the timeliness of his motion. Rule 60(c)(1) says that a Rule 60(b) motion to set aside a judgment "must be *made within a reasonable time*[.]" But here, since the plumber filed his motion just ten days after entry of the judgment, the court will almost certainly conclude that he acted "within a reasonable time."

Choice (A) is wrong, because (1) it's not true that the court can accurately fix the amount of damages without hearing the plumber's evidence; and (2) therefore, the plumber, having appeared in the action, was entitled to seven days advance notice. As we discuss more fully in Choice (C), the test given by Rule 55(b)(1) for whether the plaintiff's claim is what the common law calls a "liquidated" amount is whether the claim "is for a sum certain or a sum that can be made certain by computation[.]" An example of a sum that "can be made certain by computation" is a claim for payment on a promissory note that contains a stated rate of interest—the total due on any given day can be made certain by computation, with no need for "evidence" outside the document. But the amount of damages suffered by the plaintiff to its headquarters building is not something that can be fixed by mere "computation"—for instance, there's likely to be an issue of whether the plaintiff made reasonable efforts to select the lowest-cost qualified bidder to do the repairs.

Given that the plaintiff's claim is not for a sum that is, or by computation can be made to be, a "sum certain," then Rule 55(b)(2) says that the plumber—as one who "has appeared personally or by a representative"—was entitled to seven days written notice before a hearing. Therefore, it is not the case that the court had authority to "fix the amount of damages even without hearing the plumber's evidence," as this choice posits.

Choice (B) is wrong, because the plumber was entitled to seven days advance notice of the default hearing, even though he failed to plead or otherwise defend against the company's suit. As we discuss more fully in Choice (C), given (1) the fact that the plaintiff's claim is not for a sum certain; and (2) the fact that the plumber appeared in the action by moving to dismiss for lack of personal jurisdiction, the plaintiff could obtain a default judgment only by applying to the court for that relief, and giving the plumber seven days advance notice of the court hearing on that application. In other words, the plumber was entitled to the seven days' notice despite his having failed to "plead or otherwise defend," and the lack of the required notice gave him the right to make a probably-successful Rule 60 motion to have the judgment set aside.

Choice (D) is wrong, because (1) the federal court had personal jurisdiction over the plumber, and (2) the plumber's right to relief from the judgment stems from his failure to receive the required advance for notice, not from any lack of personal jurisdiction over him. It's true that the plumber is domiciled in State B, but is being sued in State A. So there is potentially an issue as to whether the State A federal court has personal jurisdiction over the plumber—in a diversity case (which is what we have here, given the absence of a federal question), the State A federal court will have personal jurisdiction over a State B citizen only if the State A state courts could constitutionally (i.e., without violating the due process clause) exercise personal jurisdiction over that State B citizen. But here, the suit is based on the plumber's having done allegedly-negligent work, in person, on the plaintiff's State A headquarters; it's well-established that a state *has specific jurisdiction* to hear a claim alleging that the defendant *committed a tortious act in that state*. Therefore, this choice states the correct outcome, but based on incorrect reasoning: the federal court had jurisdiction over the plumber, but the plumber was entitled to seven days advance notice of the hearing, which he failed to receive.

Answer 77

The correct choice is **(A)**, because under the federal rules, only the court can enter a default judgment if plaintiff's claim is not "for a sum certain or a sum that can be made certain by computation." One key factor that determines how and when a default judgment may be entered is whether the claim can be considered for a "sum certain"—when the claim meets this definition, entry of a default judgment for that amount is essentially ministerial, whereas if the sum is not certain, the procedure is far more complex and a judge's participation is required. The entry of default judgments is governed by FRCP 55. Rule 55(b)(1) (entitled "By the Clerk"), says that "If the plaintiff's claim *is for a sum certain or a sum that can be made certain by computation*, the clerk—on the plaintiff's request, with an affidavit showing the amount due—*must enter judgment for that amount* and costs against a defendant who has been defaulted for not appearing and who is neither a minor nor an incompetent person." So at least where the defendant never answers or otherwise "appears" in the suit, if the claim is for a "sum certain" (or for a sum that "by computation" can be made certain), *no involvement by the judge* is necessary, and the clerk of the court not only may but "must" enter judgment for that amount at the plaintiff's request, as long as the plaintiff submits an affidavit showing the amount due. So if, on our facts here, the professor's claim met the requirements for a "sum certain," the answer to the question would be yes, the clerk could enter judgment without further action by anyone (making Choice (C) correct).

However, the professor's claim here is definitely *not* one "for a sum certain or a sum that can be made certain by computation." A claim is not for a sum certain "unless there *is no doubt as to the amount* to which a plaintiff is entitled as a result of the defendant's default." *KPS & Assocs. v. Designs by FMC, Inc.,* 318 F.3d 1, 19-20 (1st Cir. 2003). Or, as the idea is sometimes put, the claim must be for some sort of *"liquidated amount."* Examples of sums certain include a suit to enforce another court's money judgment and a suit on a promissory note—in those situations, the damages can be "determined without resort to extrinsic proof[.]" Id. Here, the professor is claiming damages for "intangible harm" to her reputation, and it cannot be said that there is "no doubt" about what the proper amount is (even assuming liability), or that the amount can be determined without resort to proof other than that contained in the complaint or the professor's affidavit. Furthermore, where the plaintiff seeks attorney's fees, those fees are virtually never deemed to constitute an "amount certain," even if the claim being sued on *is* for such an amount.

Once it's clear that the claim is not for "a sum certain or a sum that can be made certain by computation," the method for entering a default judgment is completely different than the clerk-administered method mentioned above for sum-certain claims. Now, the situation is governed by Rule 55(b)(2) (entitled "By the Court"). Under that section, "the party must ***apply to the court*** for a default judgment." If the defendant has "appeared" in the action (which the student here did not do), seven days advance notice has to be given to the defendant before the court (i.e., the judge) can conduct any hearing. The judge then determines the appropriate amount for the judgment. In doing so the court "may" (but is not required to) "conduct hearings" in order to "determine the amount of damages." Even when the judge decides that the hearing is not necessary, the judge will typically make a careful review of the pleadings, affidavits, documentary evidence submitted by the plaintiff, etc., to make a reasonable estimate of the actual damages. In other words, the judge does not simply reason that since the complaint was not answered, the allegations in it about damages must be taken at face value. So Choice (A) is an accurate statement about the steps that the judge will have to go through before entering a default judgment on the professor's claim.

Choice (B) is wrong, because it is not within the clerk's authority to conduct the type of evidentiary hearing described. If the claim here were for a "sum certain," then as described in the explanation of Choice (A), the clerk could, indeed would be required to, enter judgment—but that would happen without any evidentiary hearing or even examination of evidence. But the claim here is *not* for a sum certain, so the job of fixing the amount of the judgment must be handled by the judge, not the clerk. And when the judge does this, the judge is permitted—though not required—to conduct an evidentiary hearing of the sort described in this choice.

Choice (C) is wrong, because the claim was not for a sum certain. Under Rule 55(b)(1), if the claim was "for a sum certain or a sum that can be made certain by computation," then the clerk could indeed enter judgment automatically and without notice to the student, as suggested in this choice (at least assuming that the student was neither a minor nor an "incompetent person," and that she had never appeared in the action). But as discussed in the analysis of Choice (A), the claim here does not meet the definition of "sum certain." Therefore, the ministerial procedure carried out by the clerk, as described in this choice, is not available.

Choice (D) is wrong, because it incorrectly gives a role to the clerk as hearing officer and incorrectly requires notice to the student. This choice is correct in suggesting that there are some scenarios in which a seven-day notice has to be given to the defendant in advance of a hearing at which the amount of damages will be set, but the present fact pattern is not such a scenario. Rule 55(b)(2) says that in cases in which the claim is not for a sum certain (so that the judge will have to determine the appropriate judgment amount), seven days advance notice of any hearing by the judge must be given to the defendant if the defendant "has appeared personally or by a representative" previously in the action. But there are two reasons why this advance-notice provision does not apply in the way suggested by this choice: First, the facts tell you that the student never appeared in the action (so she is not entitled to any notice at all) and second, this choice refers to an evidentiary hearing that will be conducted by the clerk, but in reality if an evidentiary hearing is to be conducted (which will happen only where the claim is not for a sum certain) the hearing is conducted by the *judge*, not the clerk. So as is correctly stated in Choice (A), any evidentiary hearing will be conducted by the judge (and it will be in the judge's discretion whether to conduct a true hearing or to simply review documentary evidence), and no advance notice to the student will need to be given if there *is* going to be a hearing.

Answer 78

The correct choice is **(D),** because these facts trigger ***the "two dismissal" rule***, by which two voluntary dismissals of the same or related claims cause the second to operate as an adjudication on the merits. The fact pattern here doesn't tell you the ground on which the defendant has based her dismissal motion, so you first have to figure out what the defendant's most plausible ground for dismissal would be, and then figure out whether the defendant can prevail on the basis of that ground. As soon as you see that the fact pattern involves three actions that have all involved the same claims by the plaintiff, that's a strong clue that the defendant's best argument for dismissal will somehow involve the fact that the plaintiff has already dismissed not one but two prior suits raising the same claims.

Normally, early in a case the plaintiff can voluntarily dismiss an action without having that dismissal act as an adjudication on the merits. This result comes from Rule 41(a)(1) (entitled "Voluntary Dismissal By the Plaintiff"). First, 41(a)(1)(A)(i) says that the plaintiff may voluntarily dismiss by filing "a notice of dismissal before the opposing party serves either an answer or a motion for summary judgment." And the first sentence of 41(a)(1)(B) says that such a voluntary dismissal is normally "without prejudice." But the next sentence of 41(a)(1)(B) adds a very important exception to this general without-prejudice rule: "But if the plaintiff *previously dismissed any federal- or state-court action based on or including the same claim,* a notice of *dismissal operates as an adjudication on the merits*." That's the so-called *"two dismissal rule."*

Here, the plaintiff's *first* dismissal was governed by the first sentence of 41(a)(1)(B), making that dismissal without prejudice. But the *second* dismissal gets a different treatment. You're told that this second action "alleg[ed] the same claims" as the first action. That's enough to trigger 41(a)(1)(B)'s two-dismissal rule. (The fact that the second complaint tried to "address[] the pleading defects outlined in the defendant's [prior] motion to dismiss" does not stop the second complaint from being "based on or including" the same claim(s) as the first). Since the second dismissal operated as an adjudication on the merits, that gave the defendant the winning argument that the *third* suit must be dismissed on the pleadings because it is barred by claim preclusion.

Choice (A) is wrong, because the plaintiff's prompt and diligent attempt to address the pleading defects does not prevent the two-dismissal rule from applying. This choice is wrong because Choice (D) is right—the two-dismissal rule of 41(a)(1)(B) does not recognize any exception based on the plaintiff's prompt or diligent attempts to address pleading defects that have come to light in either of the prior two (now dismissed) actions.

Choice (B) is wrong, because the fact that the plaintiff dismissed each previous action before the defendant answered or moved does not prevent the two-dismissal rule from applying. This choice confuses a "necessary" and a "sufficient" condition for dismissal. It's true that under 41(a)(1)(A), any voluntary dismissal—even the first one involving a given claim—will be valid if, and only if, the notice of dismissal occurs "before the opposing party serves either an answer or a motion for summary judgment." But the need to dismiss before the defendant answers or moves for summary judgment is merely a *necessary* condition—not a *sufficient* one—for the dismissal to be without prejudice. That's because the plaintiff must *also* fulfill a second condition, that the same claim not have already been voluntarily dismissed twice. As discussed more fully in Choice (D), the two-dismissal rule caused the plaintiff's second dismissal to operate on the merits, even though both the first and second dismissals were filed before the defendant either answered or moved for summary judgment.

Choice (C) is wrong, because the plaintiff's failure to seek a court order of dismissal is irrelevant. It's true that in some circumstances, a plaintiff cannot voluntarily dismiss the action, and must instead request and obtain a court order. Thus Rule 41(a)(2) says that except where the plaintiff complies with Rule (41)(a)(1), "an action may be dismissed at the plaintiff's request only by court order, on terms that the court considers proper." So, for instance, if the defendant had already answered, then the plaintiff would have been required to obtain a court order. But here, the plaintiff dismissed the second action before an answer or motion for summary judgment occurred, so no court order was required. Therefore, this choice reflects the correct outcome—third action dismissed—but fails to give a correct explanation for the result (which is that the two-dismissal rule applies).

Answer 79

The correct choice is **(D)**, because the trial court is required to make findings and conclusions even if the case is tried solely on documentary evidence. FRCP 52(a)(1) says that "In an action tried on the facts without a jury . . . , the *court must find the facts specially and state its conclusions of law separately.*" So the trial judge erred when she ordered judgment entered without having first made findings of fact and conclusions of law (which could have been done either orally or in writing). The judge's failure to do this is reversible error; see W&M (2008 Ed.), § 2577, p. 290: "[T]he court of appeals may vacate the judgment and remand the case to the district court for findings if the trial court has failed to make findings when they are required by the rule [Rule 52.]"

The fact that the case was tried solely based on documentary evidence, with no witnesses, does not matter—even in such a case, the appeals court needs to understand what facts the trial judge derived from the documentary evidence, and what rules of law the judge applied to those facts, so that the appeals court can fulfill Rule 52(a)(6)'s requirement that "[f]indings of fact, whether based on *oral or other evidence*, must not be set aside unless clearly erroneous[.]" (The reference in 52(a)(6) to "other evidence," i.e., non-oral evidence, exists precisely to make sure that the appeals court follows the clearly-erroneous rule even as to findings made from documentary evidence, something that that court cannot do if there are no trial-court findings in the record.)

Choice (A) is wrong, because a judgment based only on documentary evidence does not thereby become clearly erroneous. This choice asserts that a judgment that is "based solely on documentary evidence" is, ipso facto, "clearly erroneous." But this is simply false: there is no rule or principle rendering a judgment based only on documentary evidence automatically "erroneous," let alone "clearly erroneous."

The examiners may have been using the phrase "clearly erroneous" in this choice to trick you into focusing on Rule 52(a)(6) governing appeals, which says in its entirety that "[f]indings of fact, whether based on oral or other evidence, must not be set aside unless clearly erroneous, and the reviewing court must give due regard to the trial court's opportunity to judge the witnesses' credibility." You might think that this requirement that the reviewing court "must give due regard to the trial court's opportunity to judge the witnesses' credibility" somehow casts doubt on whether a bench trial in which there *are* no witnesses whose credibility is to be judged can avoid being clearly erroneous. But this reference to witness credibility doesn't mean what this choice implies it means. 52(a)(6) merely says that *if* there were witnesses called during the trial, the trial judge's opportunity to judge the credibility of those witnesses is to be given "due regard" by the appeals court. In a case (like this one) where there are documents and no witnesses, the appeals court is still required to accept the trial judge's findings of fact unless they are clearly erroneous, but the absence of witnesses certainly doesn't cause the trial judge's findings to be clearly erroneous, as this choice implies.

Choice (B) is wrong, because there is no requirement that either party file proposed findings or conclusions before the judge rules. Rule 52, which is the sole source of the requirement that the judge in a bench trial must make findings and conclusions, makes no reference to the concept of "proposed" findings and conclusions. Nothing in Rule 52 or anywhere else requires a party to "file proposed findings and conclusions before the trial court rule[s]," as this choice asserts.

Choice (C) is wrong, because there is no requirement that the judge give the parties an oppor-tunity to submit proposed findings and conclusions before the judge announces the judg-ment. Rule 52 simply does not recognize the concept of "proposed" findings and conclusions, whether put forth by the judge or by the parties. A party does in fact get the opportunity to object to the court's findings and conclusions, but this opportunity happens *after* the trial judge has made its findings and conclusions and then entered judgment. After judgment has been entered, Rule 52(b) gives each party 28 days to make a motion asking the judge to amend her findings, as well as amend the judgment.

Answer 80

The correct choice is **(A)**, because federal courts may not give greater issue-preclusive effect to a state-court judgment than that state's own courts would give to that judgment. An import-ant federal statute, 28 U.S.C. § 1738, governs whether and when a federal court must or may give full faith and credit to the prior judgment of a state court. The statute says that state-court judgments "shall have the same full faith and credit in every [federal] court . . . as they have . . . in the courts of such State . . . from which they are taken." So if State A had chosen to *apply* nonmutual issue preclusion, then under 28 U.S.C. § 1738 the federal court would have been required to follow State A's policy, and similarly apply nonmutual issue preclusion here (thus giving the university the benefit of partial summary judgment as it has requested).

But the converse is also true: the Supreme Court has interpreted § 1738 to mean that if a state would *not* give preclusive effect to a particular judgment rendered by that state's courts, then the federal court is also *forbidden* to give the judgment preclusive effect (whether the case involves claim preclusion or issue preclusion). See *Johnson v. De Grandy*, 512 U.S. 997 (1994): "[A] federal court **gives no greater preclusive effect to a state-court judgment** than the **state court itself would do.**"

Choice (B) is wrong, because the issue preclusion law of the state where the federal court sits is irrelevant. As we discuss in Choice (A), a federal statute requires the court to give a state-court judgment the same preclusive effect (if any) as that judgment would have in the courts of the state that rendered it. So on these facts, what matters is whether the state that rendered the judgment (here, State A) would give it nonmutual issue-preclusive effect. The issue-preclusive policies of the courts of the state where the federal court happens to sit are irrelevant. (Even if you didn't know the exact rule, you should have been able to eliminate this choice, because the federal suit involves a right given by federal substantive law [the federal securities laws], not by state law since this is not a diversity case, and the *Erie v. Tompkins* principle would not apply so as to give any significance to the common law of the state where the district court happens to sit.)

Choice (C) is wrong, because by a federal statute, the federal court here must follow state, not federal, law on whether nonmutual issue preclusion applies. As we discuss in Choice (A), a federal statute requires the federal court to give a state-court judgment the same pre-clusive effect (if any) as that judgment would have in the courts of the state that rendered it. Therefore, even if it is true that as a matter of general policy, "federal law permits nonmutual issue preclusion" (which *is* true in this type of situation), where the prior judgment is from a state court the federal statute makes the federal policy irrelevant.

Choice (D) is wrong, because State A has chosen not to apply nonmutual issue preclusion even where the issue was "litigated and necessarily decided," and the federal court must fol-low State A's approach. It's true that, as this choice suggests, issue preclusion (i.e. collateral estoppel) will virtually never apply to a factual issue unless that issue was actually litigated and decided, and the decision was necessary to the verdict. But this trio of criteria for issue preclusion are merely "necessary," *not* "sufficient," for issue preclusion to apply. That is, State

A (like many states) has chosen not to apply nonmutual issue preclusion even to issues that *were* actually litigated and necessarily decided. And as explained in Choice (A), once State A made that choice, a federal statute requires the federal court to apply the policy choice of State A regarding the judgment's issue-preclusive effect.

Answer 81

The correct choice is **(C),** because a federal statute requires the federal court to give the judgment the same preclusive effect that the courts of the state that rendered the judgment would give to it. A federal statute, 28 U.S.C. § 1738, refers to the "[t]he records and judicial proceedings of any court" of "any State . . . of the United States[.]" The statute then says that "[s]uch . . . records and judicial proceedings . . . shall have the **same full faith and credit in every court within the United States** . . . as they have by law or usage in the courts of such State . . . from which they are taken." Since the phrase "every court within the United States" includes the federal district courts, the effect of § 1738 is to require that **once a state court issues a judgment, any federal district court is required to give that judgment the same effect** — including the **same preclusive effect** — as the judgment would have in the **state courts of the rendering state.**

Consequently, whatever the judgment's merger-and-bar (i.e., "claim preclusion") effect, as well as its collateral estoppel (i.e., "issue preclusion") effect in the rendering state, the judgment must be given that same effect by the federal court. And that's true even though the rendering state's courts would give the judgment a lesser or greater effect than the federal courts would, by general common-law principles, give to a similar judgment rendered by a sister federal court.

Applying § 1738 to these facts: once the state court dismissed the action, and said that the dismissal was "with prejudice," the federal court was required to give the judgment that same claim-preclusive effect. And that's true even if, for instance, a federal court hearing the first version of the tort action would not have dismissed for failure to prosecute, or would have dismissed for failure to prosecute but without prejudice.

Choice (A) is wrong, because when a judgment is entered by a state court, a federal court must give that judgment the same preclusive effect it would have in the courts of the rendering state. As we discuss in Choice (C), 28 U.S.C. § 1738 requires any federal court to give a state-court judgment the same effect — including the same preclusive effect — as the judgment would have in the courts of the rendering state. Therefore, when this choice asserts that the fact that the judgment was entered by a state court relieves the federal court of the obligation to apply claim preclusion, the choice is flatly inconsistent with § 1738.

Choice (B) is wrong, because (1) the courts of the rendering state would apply claim preclusion even though the rendering court did not rule on the merits, and therefore (2) the federal courts must similarly apply claim preclusion. As we discuss more extensively in Choice (C), 28 U.S.C. § 1738 requires any federal court to give a state-court judgment the same effect — including the same preclusive effect — as the judgment would have in the courts of the rendering state. Here, we're told that the state court has declared that its dismissal of the action is "with prejudice." This means that all courts in the state will treat that judgment as having claim-preclusive effect, i.e., as barring the plaintiff from bringing the suit again.

Since the state courts would not regard the absence of a ruling on the merits as a factor that would negate the dismissal's claim-preclusive effect, neither may the federal courts regard this factor as blocking the dismissal from having a claim-preclusive effect. (In any event, even according to general federal principles, *claim*-preclusion [merger and bar] can apply even where the first judgment is made without there having been any ruling on the merits — it's *issue*-preclusion, i.e., collateral estoppel, that generally requires that the issue have been actually litigated and necessary to the outcome.)

Choice (D) is wrong, because what the FRCP would provide about the effect of a judgment for failure to prosecute is irrelevant here; it's the effect that the courts of the rendering state would give to the judgment that matters. As we discuss in connection with Choice (C), a federal statute requires the federal court to give an earlier state-court judgment the same claim-preclusive effect that that judgment would have in the courts of the rendering state. Consequently, it's irrelevant whether the FRCP would supply a different claim-preclusion rule had the earlier judgment been made by a federal court.

By the way, Choice (D) is correct in the limited sense that a judgment for failure to prosecute, if rendered by a federal court, *would* normally operate as a judgment on the merits. See Rule 41(b).

Answer 82

The correct choice is **(A)**, because the preclusive effect of a federal court judgment is determined by the law of the court that rendered that judgment.

There is a good general rule that applies with few exceptions: ***the law of the court that renders a judgment determines what preclusive effect that judgment should have in another court.*** Since the question is asking you to specify which law (state or federal) applies to determine the effect of this federal-court judgment, applying the general rule here means that you should apply the body of law that would be used by the federal court that dismissed the action. And the federal court that issued the dismissal, if it had to decide what the effect of the dismissal would be, would be applying "federal law." See Rest. 2d of Judgments, § 87: "Federal law determines the effects under the rules of res judicata of a judgment of a federal court."

Choice (B) is wrong, because the fact that the federal action was nationwide, and/or was "governed by the federal class action rule," is irrelevant to determining what body of law should be consulted in deciding the federal judgment's preclusive effect. As we discuss more extensively in Choice (A), the rule is that when a federal court issues the first judgment, the body of law that is to be consulted in determining the preclusive effect of that judgment is federal law (just as, if the first judgment came from a state court, that state's body of law would be looked to when a state court in a different state—or a federal court sitting in the same or a different state—had to decide the preclusive effect of the first judgment). This choice correctly says that the state court should look to "federal law" to decide the preclusive effect of the earlier federal-court judgment. But the choice is not correct in its explanation of *why* this is so—the reason is not because the earlier action was a "nationwide action governed by the federal class-action rule," but rather because of the simple fact that the earlier judgment was entered in a federal court.

Choice (C) is wrong, because it's the law of the court that ***rendered the first judgment*** that is to be consulted in determining the first judgment's preclusive effect. As we discuss in Choice (A), the preclusive effect of a judgment is what the court that rendered the judgment says should be the judgment's preclusive effect. Since the earlier judgment was entered in federal court, it's the federal law of preclusion that must be followed by the state court now. The fact that the judgment's preclusive effect is now being litigated in state court has no bearing on what that preclusive effect is.

Choice (D) is wrong, because there *is* federal common law on the issue of which system's body of law should be consulted to determine the preclusive effect of a federal-court judgment, and that federal common law must be applied by the state court here. As we discuss more extensively in Choice (A), the rule is that when a federal court issues the first judgment, the body of law that is to be consulted in determining the preclusive effect of that judgment is federal law. It may be more or less true that, as this choice asserts, "there is no *general* federal common law." But there *is* certainly federal common law on the specific issue of "what system's body of law determines what the effect of a federal judgment should be?" And that body of federal common law (i.e., judge-made law) has long been recognized by the federal courts as specifying that—whatever the precise rule for determining the preclusive effect of a federal-court judgment may be—it's *federal principles*, not, say, the preclusion law of the state where the federal court that rendered the judgment sits, that must be consulted to determine the preclusive effect of the federal judgment.

Answer 83

The correct choice is **(B),** because situations involving derivative liability represent an exception to the general rule preventing a stranger to the first action from invoking the benefits of claim preclusion. "Claim preclusion" involves twin doctrines, the doctrines of "*merger*" and "*bar*." Depending on whether the plaintiff wins or loses the first suit, either merger or bar will prevent a second litigation by that plaintiff on the same claim. If the plaintiff wins the first suit (i.e., gets a favorable judgment against the defendant), "merger" prevents the plaintiff from bringing a second suit on the claim against the same defendant; if the plaintiff loses the first suit, "bar" prevents her from bringing a second suit on the claim against the same defendant. Obviously here, the two actions are not against the same defendant, so neither "merger" nor "bar" would seem to apply, but as we'll soon see, to analyze some scenarios we have to first figure out whether merger or bar would apply had the second suit been against the same plaintiff as the first suit.

Here, the judgment in the first suit by the plaintiff (the accountant) was against her; therefore, she would be "barred" from bringing another suit on the "same claim" against the cab driver. See Rest. 2d Judgments, § 19: "A valid and final personal judgment rendered in favor of the defendant *bars another action* [against that defendant] *by the plaintiff on the same claim*."

But we next have to figure out whether a suit by the accountant against that same defendant (the cab driver) for her personal injuries would be deemed to be on the "same claim" as the first suit for property damage. The answer is "yes." That's because modern courts nearly always apply a "transactional" test for determining whether two suits involve a single claim, and the transactional test would be satisfied here. Here's how the Restatement of Judgments 2d defines the dimensions of a claim for purposes of the doctrines of merger or bar:

> "(1) When a valid and final judgment rendered in an action extinguishes the plaintiff's claim pursuant to the rules of merger or bar . . . , the *claim extinguished* includes *all rights of the plaintiff to remedies against the defendant* with respect to *all or any part of the transaction, or series of connected transactions, out of which the action arose*.
>
> (2) What factual grouping constitutes a 'transaction,' and what groupings constitute a 'series,' are to be determined pragmatically, giving weight to such considerations as *whether the facts are related in time, space, origin, or motivation*, whether they *form a convenient trial unit*, and whether their treatment as a unit *conforms to the parties' expectations or business understanding or usage*."
>
> Rest. 2d of Judgments § 24.

Where both suits involve a single physical accident, courts almost universally treat *property damage and personal injuries from that accident* as both involving a single claim. Thus, Rest. 2d Judgments, Illustration 1 to § 24, reaches exactly this conclusion: "*A* and *B*, driving their respective cars, have a collision injuring *A* and damaging his car. The occurrence is single, and so is *A*'s claim. If *A* obtains a judgment against *B* on the ground of negligence for the damage to the ***car***, he is prevented by the doctrine of merger from subsequently maintaining an action for the ***harm to his person***." So in our question, the accountant has a single claim covering both property damage to her painting and injuries to her person, and the judgment against her in the property-damage suit would cause her to be "barred" from bringing a personal-injury suit against the same defendant, the cab driver.

Then, a separate rule of law provides that where one person (call him *A*) is vicariously responsible for the conduct of another person (*B*), then if an injured person sues *B,* the merger or bar consequences are normally the same for purposes of a second suit by the injured person against *A* as they would be for a second suit against the original defendant *B*. Here's how Rest. Judgments 2d, § 51, expresses the rule:

> "If two persons have a relationship such ***that one of them is vicariously responsible for the conduct of the other***, and an action is brought by the injured person ***against one of them***, the judgment in the action has the following preclusive effects against the injured person in a subsequent action against the other.
>
> (1) A judgment against the injured person that ***bars him from reasserting his claim against the defendant in the first action extinguishes any claim he has against the other person responsible for the conduct unless:***
>
> > (a) The claim asserted in the second action is based upon ***grounds that could not have been asserted*** against the defendant in the first action; or
> >
> > (b) The judgment in the first action was ***based on a defense that was personal*** to the defendant in the first action."

Here, under the common-law principle of *respondeat superior*, the cab company was vicariously responsible for negligent conduct of its employee, the cab driver, that occurred during the course of the employment. Therefore, unless one of the two exceptions mentioned in (a) and (b) of Rest. 2d § 51 above applies, when the accountant sued the driver and lost on the property claim her personal injury suit against the cab company would be barred exactly the same way her personal injury suit against the driver would be barred (since the property damage and personal injury suits involved a single claim, as we saw above). And neither of the exceptions applies here; the claim for personal injuries could have been asserted as part of the initial suit in city court, and there was no plausible defense that could have been asserted by the cab driver in the first suit that would have been "personal" to him and inapplicable to the company as vicariously liable for the driver's negligence.

In sum, the accountant's personal injury suit against the company is barred by the judgment against her in the property suit, just as any personal injury suit by her against the cab driver would have been barred by that same judgment. And since the doctrine of "bar" is a species of claim preclusion, Choice (B) is the correct explanation for why the judge would dismiss the suit.

Choice (A) is wrong, because collateral estoppel would not apply since we cannot say what issues were actually litigated and decided in the first suit. "Issue preclusion" (a/k/a "collateral estoppel") applies to prevent re-litigation of an issue only when the issue (whether of fact or law) is "***actually litigated*** and determined . . . and the determination is ***essential to the judgment***." Rest. 2d Judgments, § 27. Here, the cab company might argue that the judgment against the accountant in the first suit demonstrates that the cab driver must not have been negligent, because otherwise judgment would have been for the accountant in at least some amount. But that argument wouldn't work: collateral estoppel applies only where we can say ***authoritatively*** that the issue in question was actually litigated and that that determination was essential to the judgment—doubts about what happened in the first suit get resolved against the use of preclusion. Here, the jury might have issued its verdict against the accountant because it found that the painting wasn't damaged at all, or that the damage did not come from the collision but from some conduct by the accountant or a third-party—in other words, we simply don't know that the jury in fact rested its verdict on a finding that the cab driver was not negligent.

Since we can't say that the first judgment rested on a factual finding of non-negligence by the driver, the court will not use collateral estoppel at all. So this choice reaches the correct result (dismissal granted), but based on incorrect legal reasoning (use of collateral estoppel instead of claim preclusion).

Choice (C) is wrong, because the mutuality principle it implicitly refers to would not apply in this situation of vicarious liability. Traditionally, a party to the second suit who was a "stranger" to the first suit was prevented from gaining the benefit of either claim preclusion or issue preclusion on the theory that the stranger could not have been bound by an favorable result in the first suit, so the concept of "mutuality" dictated that the stranger not be given the benefit of a favorable result either. Modern courts no longer have an absolute rule against nonmutual use of either claim preclusion or issue preclusion, so even if the company would not have been bound by any judgment *against* its employee in the first suit, this fact would not automatically prevent the company from obtaining the *benefit* of claim preclusion or issue preclusion if those doctrines otherwise applied.

For the reasons discussed in the analysis of Choice (B), the fact that the cab company would be vicariously liable for on-the-job negligence by its driver means that the cab company is not treated as a "stranger" to the first action, and therefore will be able to get the benefit of claim preclusion even in a jurisdiction that would otherwise forbid nonmutual use of claim preclusion as a general matter.

Choice (D) is wrong, because the fact that the first court was of limited jurisdiction is irrelevant on these facts. In some circumstances, the fact that the first suit is in a court of limited jurisdiction or whose procedures are significantly limited may indeed make it unfair to bind the loser to the results of that first suit for purposes of a second suit in a court that does not have the limitation. Thus, Rest. 2d of Judgments, § 26, says that the usual rules of merger and bar do not apply where "(c) The plaintiff was unable to . . . seek a certain remedy . . . in the first action because of *the limitations on the subject matter jurisdiction of the courts* . . . and the plaintiff desires in the second action to . . . seek that remedy or form of relief[.]" So, for instance, if the "city court" had had a cap on available damages lower than the combined property and personal-injury damages that the accountant was seeking, that fact might have been enough to prevent the accountant's failure to add the personal-injury claim to the first suit from barring her second suit. But here, the two claims together sought only $220,000 (i.e., less than the $250,000 limit on the city court's cap on recovery), so this rationale would not apply to give the accountant a "second bite at the apple."

Answer 84

The correct choice is **(C),** because it accurately states and applies the rule that only parties to the first action (or their "privies") may receive the benefit of claim preclusion in a second action.

Claim preclusion is a judicially-created doctrine that bars the re-litigation of a claim raised in a prior suit. The basic rule of claim preclusion is that a person will receive both the benefit and the burden of a valid and final judgment from one suit ("Suit 1"), for purposes of another suit ("Suit 2"), *if only if that person was a party to Suit 1.* In other words, both federal and state courts universally follow the rule that *neither the benefit nor the burden of claim preclusion applies to a "stranger" to the first action.* Since Taxi Driver was not a party to Plaintiff's initial suit against Defendant, Plaintiff's potential claim against Taxi Driver was not "merged into" Plaintiff's judgment against Defendant, just as that claim wouldn't have been "barred" had the judgment in the first suit gone in favor of Defendant rather than Plaintiff.

Note that in some rare cases, there may be a such a *close pre-existing legal relationship* between a party to Suit 1 (call him X) and a person who is absent from Suit 1 but present in Suit 2 (call him Y) that it's fair to give Y the benefit (and charge him with the burden) of the result in Suit 1. (In this situation, X and Y might be called "proxies" or "privies" for each other.) But no such close pre-existing relationship exists here between Defendant and Taxi Driver, so the court will not find that Plaintiff's failure to join Taxi Driver in the suit against Defendant caused Plaintiff to lose her right to bring the separate suit against Taxi Driver. (Or, to put it another way, there was no principle that required Plaintiff to join Defendant and Taxi Driver as co-defendants in a single action arising out of the same episode, even if it was the case that no jurisdictional or other procedural reasons would have prevented such a joinder.)

Choice (A) is wrong, because the rule that it states does not apply to the problem. Taxi Driver was not a "party to be joined if feasible" in the State B action as that term is defined in FRCP 19 (entitled "Required Joinder of Parties"); therefore, he was not required to be joined in the lawsuit. Aside from situations in which Rule 19 requires joinder, *the rules of claim preclusion do not* (with very few exceptions, none applicable here) *require a claimant to join in one lawsuit all parties to the transaction*. Thus, Plaintiff was not required to join Taxi Driver in his original lawsuit. As is described further in the discussion of Choice (C), Taxi Driver was a stranger to the lawsuit between Plaintiff and Defendant and therefore cannot invoke the benefits and is not bound by the burdens of the judgment in that earlier lawsuit.

Choice (B) is wrong, because the rule that it mentions does not apply on these facts. If Plaintiff had had two different claims *against Defendant* arising out of the same transaction, and Plaintiff had asserted only one of those claims against Defendant in the first action, Plaintiff would indeed probably now be precluded from bringing a separate suit against Defendant on the second claim (assuming that no procedural rule would have prevented Plaintiff from bringing both claims in a single proceeding). And this choice would be correct in asserting that whether Plaintiff was required to join both claims against Defendant in a single suit would be determined based on a "transactional test," i.e., on whether both claims arose out of the same transaction. But the transactional test has no relevance to a situation in which a plaintiff brings one claim against one defendant in Suit 1 and a different claim against *a different defendant* in Suit 2 — the mere fact that different defendants are involved is enough to prevent the transactional test from applying (and the plaintiff won't be precluded from bringing the second suit against the second defendant, as further described in Choice (C)).

Choice (D) is wrong, because the rule it states is not pertinent. Whether or not the State B judgment is final, it cannot be raised as a bar by Taxi Driver because he is not a party to that judgment. It's true that *as between the same parties*, a judgment must be valid and final to have claim preclusive effect. But the finality of the judgment in the first action is irrelevant on the issue of whether that judgment is binding in favor of, or against, a *stranger* to the first action who is now a party to the second action. So although this choice correctly states that the court will deny the motion, the choice is incorrect in citing the possible lack of finality of the first judgment as the reason for the denial.

Answer 85

The correct choice is **(B)**, because full faith and credit principles do not require a court to apply procedural rules of another court that has rendered a judgment.

When a state court has rendered a judgment, whatever obligation is imposed on a federal court to honor and enforce that judgment derives not from the U.S. Constitution's "Full Faith &

Credit Clause" (which only requires a *state* court to honor another state's judgments), but from a federal statute. That statute, 28 U.S.C. § 1738, says that the "records and judicial proceedings of any court of any . . . State . . . shall have *the same full faith and credit in every [federal] court* as they have by law or usage in the courts of [the rendering] State[.]" But the present question doesn't involve enforcement of a typical out-of-state judgment (say, an award of money damages); rather, it involves an issue of *admissibility of evidence*. And to answer the question, you have to decide whether the federal full faith and credit statute requires the State B federal court to refuse to allow the engineer's testimony if the State A courts would so refuse on account of the injunction. The answer to that question is not completely obvious just looking at the text of the federal statute.

However, precisely this issue of statutory interpretation has come before the U.S. Supreme Court, and the Court held unanimously that the full faith and credit statute does *not* require the federal court to honor any rule of evidence-admissibility imposed by such an injunction. The facts here are modeled on *Baker v. General Motors Corp.*, 522 U.S. 222 (1998), in which all nine Justices agreed that a Missouri federal court hearing a consumer suit against G.M. was not required by the full faith and credit statute to exclude evidence from a former G.M. engineer merely because a Michigan state court had entered an injunction against the engineer barring him from giving testimony against G.M. in any third-party suit. The Court in *Baker* agreed that the full faith and credit statute would require non-Michigan courts to honor the *true res judicata effects* of the Michigan judgment in the same way that the Michigan courts themselves would honor those effects; so, for instance, since as the result of the Michigan settlement and injunction G.M. and the engineer would be prevented from bringing new suits against each other for the claims that were resolved in the Michigan settlement, the Missouri federal court would similarly be required not to hear such a suit brought by one of those parties against the other. But full faith and credit principles did *not* allow Michigan to preclude other states from hearing suits brought by *strangers* to the Michigan litigation, or to tell these other states what *procedural rules* they should follow in such "stranger" suits. Therefore, the Court held, Michigan "lacks authority to *control courts elsewhere* by precluding them, in *actions brought by strangers to the Michigan litigation*, from *determining for themselves what witnesses are competent to testify* and *what evidence is relevant and admissible* in their search for the truth."

That principle applies here: The suit in State B federal court was brought by a stranger to the State A litigation and injunction, and the concept of full faith and credit does not require the federal court (or indeed *any* state or federal court outside of the State A state-court system) to apply a rule or policy of evidence admissibility or witness competence just because that rule would be followed in the State A courts.

By the way, it's important to note that on our facts here (as in *Baker*, supra), the "stranger" to the first litigation (i.e., the injured consumer who had nothing to do with the earlier suit) is the one trying to bring about the engineer's testimony, by means of a subpoena. If instead the issue arose because the engineer wanted to *volunteer* to testify on behalf of the stranger/consumer, then in all probability the federal court *would* have to "honor" the State A injunction, by holding that the State A suit, settlement, and injunction had definitively foreclosed the engineer's own right to volunteer testimony.

Choice (A) is wrong, because the reason the federal court need not exclude the testimony has nothing to do with the strength or existence of any policy interest on the part of State B. This choice correctly states the outcome (that the federal court does not have to exclude the engineer's testimony even if the State A courts would do so in a comparable suit). But the choice reaches this correct result by incorrect legal reasoning. As is discussed more fully in the treatment of Choice (B), the full faith and credit statute simply does not require the federal courts to follow the evidence-admissibility or witness-competence rules of State A. And that's true whether the state in which the federal court sits (here, State B) has a countervailing policy in favor of making testimony available, or not—in fact, even if the State B courts would choose, for policy reasons, to honor the State A "no testimony" ruling, the federal court is free to follow federal procedures and policies for determining whether to enforce the subpoena and admit the engineer's testimony.

Choice (C) is wrong, because the full faith and credit statute does not require the State B federal court to enforce the injunction in the way this choice asserts. This choice articulates the argument actually made by G.M. in the *Baker* case (see Choice (B)), that the full faith and credit statute requires the federal court to "enforce" the earlier state court injunction by refusing to hear the engineer's testimony. But the Supreme Court unanimously rejected this argument in *Baker*—the full faith and credit principle, the Court said, does *not* extend to the point of requiring the second court to follow the first court's litigation procedures, such as matters of witness competency and evidence admissibility.

Choice (D) is wrong, because the likely willingness of the State A judge who originally entered the injunction to modify it is irrelevant. As is discussed more extensively in connection with Choice (B), the full faith and credit statute does not require the federal court to support the policy embodied in the State A judge's decision to impose an injunction on future testimony by the engineer. So even if the federal judge is certain that the State A judge would ***not***, in the event of a new State A action brought by a stranger against the manufacturer, consent to modify the injunction to allow the engineer's testimony to be subpoenaed by the stranger, the State A judge's unwillingness to compel the testimony would not prevent the federal judge from making his or her own independent decision about whether to enforce the subpoena and allow the testimony.

Answer 86

The correct choice is **(B)**, because, under Rule 65(b)(2), a TRO cannot last more than 28 days; the Supreme Court has held that an order lasting longer than 28 days, even if labeled by the judge as a "TRO," is to be treated as an immediately-appealable preliminary injunction. To really "solve" this question (as opposed to making a quasi-guess), you need to combine knowledge of a particular Federal Rule with knowledge of a semi-obscure Supreme Court case interpreting that Rule. To begin with, Rule 65(b) governs how and when a federal court may issue a TRO. In part because TROs are normally issued *ex parte* (i.e., without prior notice to the adverse party), the Rule limits such orders to a very short duration; Rule 65(b)(2) says that a TRO "expires at the time after entry—***not to exceed 14 days***—that the court sets, unless before that time the court, for good cause, ***extends it for a like period*** or the adverse party consents to a longer extension."

In other words, putting the phrase "not to exceed 14 days" together with the phrase "extends it for a like period," **the TRO cannot last, even with an extension, more than 28 days.** Yet here, we're told that due to the difficulty in scheduling a preliminary injunction proceeding within the original 14 days, the court extended the TRO for another 30 days, i.e., **a total of 48 days.** As we'll see in a moment, this extension had a profound effect on the lender's right to take an immediate appeal.

At the most general level, a federal litigant has ***no*** right to take an ***"interlocutory" appeal***, i.e., an appeal from an order that is not embodied in a final judgment. (This is the "final judgment rule"; see 28 U.S.C. § 1291, giving the federal courts of appeal jurisdiction of appeals "from all final decisions of the district court.") TROs do not fall within any exception to the final judgment rule, so they are not appealable. But ***preliminary injunctions*** are a quite different matter; the most important single exception to the final judgment rule is given by 28 U.S.C.

§ 1292(a)(1), which gives the courts of appeal jurisdiction to hear appeals from "interlocutory orders" of the district courts, where the order is one "*granting*, continuing, modifying, refusing or dissolving *injunctions*, or *refusing to dissolve* or modify *injunctions*[.]" Therefore, if the order here is properly treated as being in essence a preliminary injunction rather than a true TRO, the order is one "*granting . . . [an] injunction*" (or refusing to dissolve a previously-granted injunction), *and is thus immediately appealable.*

It turns out that the Supreme Court has held that where an order labeled "TRO" is allowed to remain in force for more than 28 days without the consent of the adverse party, the order is indeed one that should be treated as a preliminary injunction, making the order immediately appealable. The Court so held in *Sampson v. Murray*, 415 U.S. 61 (1974). There, the lower federal appeals court had held that (as the Supreme Court later characterized the holding), "a temporary restraining order [that is] continued beyond the time permissible under Rule 65 must be treated as a preliminary injunction"; the Supreme Court said that "this analysis is correct."

Although *Sampson* didn't involve the immediate appealability of such an injunction, the lower federal courts have held that the case stands for the proposition that when an order extends beyond the 28-day maximum, it follows that the order is immediately appealable as an injunction. See, e.g., *Nutrasweet Co. v. Vit-Mar Enters.*, 112 F.3d 689 (3d Cir. 1997). So Choice (B), by reasoning that "the 30-day extension makes the TRO equivalent to a preliminary injunction and therefore appealable," is exactly correct.

Choice (A) is wrong, because in the usual situation, a TRO is not immediately appealable. As we discuss more fully in Choice (B), an order that's labeled as a "TRO," and that does not extend beyond the 28-day maximum allowable as-extended duration set out in Rule 65(b)(2), does not qualify for any exception to the usual rule that decisions not embodied in a final judgment may not be appealed. It's only because the order here was extended beyond the 28-day maximum, making the order the equivalent of a preliminary injunction, that the order was immediately appealable.

Choice (C) is wrong because, although it's true that a "real" TRO is not immediately appealable by statute, the order here, as extended, was no longer correctly viewed as a TRO. As we discuss more fully in Choice (B), an order that is not only labeled as a TRO, but meets the procedural requirements for being one, does not fall within the limited class of orders that are immediately appealable under the interlocutory appeals statute, 28 U.S.C. § 1292. But once the order here was extended beyond the 28-day limit for TROs, Supreme Court precedent dictates that the order be treated as an order granting a preliminary injunction, which *is* immediately appealable under § 1292.

Choice (D) is wrong because the order here was properly treated as a grant of a preliminary injunction, a grant that qualifies for an immediate appeal despite the absence of a final judgment. It's true that there is no final judgment in the case. And it's also true that normally, no appeal can be made unless there has been a final judgment. But orders granting or denying injunctions represent a major exception to the general rule prohibiting appeals where there has been no final judgment. And the "trick" here is that the order, once it was extended beyond the 28-day maximum for TROs, was required to be treated as a grant of an injunction, making the order appealable.

Answer 87

The correct choice is (**A**), because there has not been a final judgment entered in the case. 28 U.S.C. § 1291 implements what is known as the *"final judgment rule"*: "The courts of appeals . . . shall have jurisdiction of appeals from *all final decisions* of the district courts of the United States[.]" In other words, with a few exceptions, only decisions that are "final" are appealable. A good brief statement of when a decision is "final" is this: "A 'final decision' generally is one which **ends the litigation on the merits** and leaves nothing for the court to do but execute the judgment." *Catlin v. U.S.*, 324 U.S. 229 (1945). By this standard, the denial of the motion here is certainly not final, because the litigation has not been "end[ed] on the merits." There are a small number of situations in which an *interlocutory* appeal (i.e., an appeal from a *non*-final judgment) is allowed—principally cases involving injunctions—but none of those situations applies here.

Notice, by the way, that even though the key to answering this question is the fact that there is no "final judgment," Choice (A) is correct despite not mentioning the word "final." Presumably, the examiners declined to use the word "final" or the phrase "final judgment" in the choice because they thought this would make the choice too obviously-correct. But the choice is certainly correct: the final-judgment rule is a **matter of jurisdiction**, so that even if the appeals court thought that judicial efficiency would be better served by hearing an immediate appeal in this case, the court does not have jurisdiction to do this (barring a couple of special circumstances not relevant here).

Choice (B) is wrong, because the district court's decision on jurisdiction is not final. As we discuss more fully in Choice (A), a decision is not deemed final—for purposes of the final judgment rule—unless it "ends the litigation on the merits." The trial court's denial of the motion here certainly has not ended the case on the merits, since at the very least, discovery will now be conducted.

Choice (C) is wrong, because it states an incorrect standard for appealability. As we discuss more fully in Choice (A), the final judgment rule says that ordinarily, appeals may be taken only from final judgments. A judgment is normally "final," and thus appealable, only if it ends the case on the merits. So in any case in which the trial judge's order has not ended the case on the merits, it is *irrelevant* to the issue of appealability that were the Court of Appeals to reverse, the litigation would be ended on the merits.

Choice (D) is wrong, because it relies on an irrelevant factor. The surgeon's challenge may or may not raise a constitutional question. (If the objection is based on lack of minimum contacts, it indeed poses a constitutional question; but if it is based on, say, the plaintiff's failure to make service in a manner sufficient to confer personal jurisdiction, no constitutional question would be present.) But there is no rule or doctrine that allows an immediate appeal from an otherwise non-appealable order merely because the order rejects a claim based on the federal Constitution.

Answer 88

The correct choice is (**C**), because the denial of summary judgment is not a final judgment, and there is no applicable exception to the general rule that only final judgments may be appealed from. The basic grant of jurisdiction to the federal courts of appeal occurs in 28 U.S.C. § 1291, which says that those courts have jurisdiction of appeals from "all **final decisions** of the district courts[.]" So unless the situation falls within an exception to § 1291, once you've determined that what's being appealed from is not a "final decision," you know that no appeal is timely right now. (This general rule is commonly referred to as the *"final judgment"* rule.)

Once you've determined that there has been no final judgment in the case, there are only two significant exceptions that you need to make sure don't apply. One is the exception involving decisions about *injunctions*, given in 28 U.S.C. § 1292(a)(1). That section allows an immediate appeal from "[i]nterlocutory orders of the district courts . . . granting, continuing, modifying, refusing or dissolving *injunctions*, or refusing to dissolve or modify *injunctions*[.]"

The present case clearly does not involve a request for an injunction. The other exception you need to rule out is given by 28 U.S.C. § 1292(b), which applies where the district court certifies that its order involves a "controlling question of law" that meets certain requirements; there is no such certification in this case, as we discuss more fully in connection with Choice (A).

Choice (A) is wrong, because it does not correctly state the procedure allowing an interlocutory appeal in certain cases involving cases presenting a controlling question of law as to which there are differences of opinion.

In this choice, the examiners have picked out a real exception that allows an interlocutory appeal, but they have misstated the requirements for that exception. 28 U.S.C. § 1292(b) reads as follows:

> "When a district judge, in making in a civil action an order not otherwise appealable under this section, shall *be of the opinion that such order involves a controlling question of law as to which there is substantial ground for difference of opinion* and that an *immediate appeal from the order may materially advance the ultimate termination of the litigation, he shall so state in writing* in such order. The Court of Appeals which would have jurisdiction of an appeal of such action may thereupon, *in its discretion, permit an appeal to be taken* from such order, if application is made to it within ten days after the entry of the order[.]"

This choice fails to match up to the requirements for the § 1292(b) exception in three respects:

(1) the choice fails to say that the right of immediate appeal is contingent upon the existence of an *order by the district judge* (not on a finding by the court of appeals) stating that the case involves a controlling issue of law on which there is substantial ground for differences of opinion;

(2) the choice fails to say that the district court's order would have to state also that "an immediate appeal from the order *may materially advance the ultimate termination* of the litigation"; and

(3) the choice fails to note that even if the order did meet the requirements referred to in (1) and (2), the court of appeals would still have to *choose to exercise its discretion* to allow the appeal.

So the "controlling question of law" exception of § 1292(b) does not apply in the way that Choice (A) posits.

Choice (B) is wrong, because it does not correctly state the certification that the district court would have to make in order for an exception to the final judgment rule to apply. There is indeed a certification that the trial court may make that might lead to the factory's having a right to make an immediate appeal. This is the certification described in 28 U.S.C. § 1292(b) (quoted in Choice (C)), in which the trial judge expresses a belief that her order "involves a controlling question of law as to which there is substantial ground for difference of opinion[.]" But this choice, with its reference to a certification "that there is no just reason for delay," does not come even close to matching the requirements of § 1292(b) (or any other exception to the final judgment rule).

Choice (D) is wrong, because the order here is not a "collateral order." There is indeed something called the "collateral order" doctrine, by which an order that does not dispose of the merits of the case but that constitutes a final disposition of some "collateral matter" may be immediately appealed. For instance, suppose a state statute requires that in a shareholders derivative action, the plaintiff must post a certain amount of security to guarantee that if the plaintiff ultimately loses on the merits and is then held liable for defendants' attorneys fees, the needed funds will be available. Suppose further that the trial judge, in a federal-court diversity action containing state-law-based shareholders derivative action claims, decides at the outset that the state security-posting statute does not apply. If that decision is final, it will be immediately appealable under the collateral order doctrine, even though trial on the merits has not yet occurred. (See *Cohen v. Beneficial Indus. Loan Corp.,* 337 U.S. 541 (1949).) But here, *there is no "collateral" order in the case*—the denial of summary judgment is an order regarding the merits of the case, not regarding some matter that is independent of the merits. So the collateral order doctrine has no application.

Answer 89

The correct choice is **(C)**, because only the decision on the immunity motion falls within an exception to the final-judgment rule. As a general rule, only "final judgments" may be appealed from the federal district court to the federal Court of Appeals. Thus 28 U.S.C. § 1291 gives the Court of Appeals jurisdiction over "appeals from all final decisions of the district courts of the United States[.]" There are a few situations in which an "interlocutory" appeal—i.e., an appeal from a lower-court decision that has not yet been embodied in a final judgment—is allowed in the federal system. But unless the decision falls within one of this handful of exceptions (mostly, decisions granting or denying injunctions), the decision is not appealable if there has not yet been a final judgment in the case.

Here, the trial judge has denied both motions and has set the case for trial. So you should be able to infer that there has been no final judgment in the case. Therefore, the problem boils down to determining whether either of the two rulings here falls within one of the rare exceptions to the general principle that interlocutory appeals—appeals from decisions that have not led to a final judgment—are usually not allowed.

Let's look first at the denial of the officer's motion for summary judgment on the "objectively reasonable" contention. Motions for summary judgment—like motions for other dispositions that would end the case, like Rule 12(b)(6) motions for dismissal for failure to state a claim—are part of the category called "motions to dismiss." And the denial of a motion to dismiss is virtually *never* a final judgment. See W, M&C (2d Ed.), Vol. 15A, § 3914.6 ("Orders refusing to dismiss an action are almost always not final.") Since there is nothing about the present denial of summary judgment that would bring it within one of the rare situations allowing an interlocutory appeal, the court's refusal to grant summary judgment was not properly appealable. That being the case, the Court of Appeals has no choice—it *must*, as a jurisdictional matter, refuse to review the correctness of the denial, even if both parties would like the court to conduct the review now.

Now, let's look at the other ruling, the trial court's denial of immunity to the defendant officer. Denials of motions for governmental immunity are one of the rare situations in which an interlocutory appeal may be allowed.

Under the ***"collateral order"*** doctrine, certain orders are characterized as "final" for appeal purposes, even though they don't terminate any part of the action; where the collateral order doctrine is or may be applicable, the only "finality" required is that the lower court "have made its final determination of the ***matter in question***." W,M&C (2d Ed.), Vol. 15A, § 3911, p. 329. A collateral order that meets this definition of finality can be immediately appealed if: (1) the matter is separate from (i.e., "collateral to") the merits of the claim being pursued; (2) the matter is too important to be denied appellate review entirely; and (3) deferring appeal until entry of a final judgment in the whole case would prevent the eventual review from being "effective" in the circumstances. Id. at p. 330; *Cohen v. Beneficial Indus. Loan Corp.*, 337 U.S. 541 (1949).

Trial-court decisions denying a defendant's claim of governmental immunity often satisfy the requirements of the collateral order doctrine, and that is the case here:

(1) the issue of whether the officer is entitled to immunity for his official acts is quite distinct from the issue of whether he actually violated the protester's constitutional rights (since immunity at least sometimes applies to a situation in which, were there no immunity, the defendant would be liable for such a violation);

(2) a grant of immunity here would be completely outcome-determinative (the case would end), so the issue is too important to deny the officer forever a right to appellate review; and

(3) governmental immunity, where it applies, confers on the defendant not just freedom from ultimate liability, but also freedom from the burden of having to **prepare for and go through a trial**, so forcing the defendant to wait until after trial to appeal the denial of immunity would make eventual review "ineffective," thereby denying him this core "avoidance of trial" benefit.

Note that the claim here is for "qualified immunity," i.e., immunity that applies unless the defendant's actions violated the plaintiff's rights under "clearly established law." So when the court denied the defendant's motion asserting that he had qualified immunity, this was a collateral order that met the above requirements for immediate appealability, at least as to "the purely legal [issue] of whether the facts alleged by the plaintiff . . . support a claim of violation of clearly established law." *Mitchell v. Forsyth*, 472 U.S. 511 (1985). (In other words, the appeals court will *avoid* reviewing the highly fact-intensive issue of whether the defendant actually and reasonably believed that his conduct was lawful; the court will review only the purely legal/pleadings-driven issue of whether the plaintiff has alleged facts that *if proven* at trial would constitute a violation of a clearly established legal right.)

Choices (A), (B), and (D) are wrong, because each is in some way directly inconsistent with the analysis in (C) (that the immunity ruling is appealable now, but the summary judgment ruling is not appealable until there has been a final judgment).

Answer 90

The correct choice is **(C),** because it accurately recognizes that partial summary judgments are normally not final and that the judgment here does not fall within any exception that would make the judgment here final. Federal courts of appeal "have jurisdiction of appeal from all **final decisions** of the district courts of the United States" (28 U.S.C. § 1291). But the appeals courts do **not** have jurisdiction to hear appeals from **non-final** orders, except for a few special situations specified in 28 U.S.C. § 1292 (most importantly, cases involving injunctions), none of which exists here. So the Court of Appeals has power to hear the appeal *only* if the district court's grant of partial summary judgment (i.e., its judgment on the contract claim) is deemed to be a final judgment rather than an interlocutory order.

FRCP 54(b) deals with the finality of claims in actions presenting more than one claim by stating the general rule that "any order or other decision, however designated, that adjudicates fewer than all the claims . . . does not end the action." However, 54(b) recognizes one exception to this "no final judgment" rule: "[T]he [district] court may direct entry of a final judgment as to one or more, but fewer than all, claims or parties only if the court expressly determines that there is no just reason for delay[.]"

Here, the facts tell you that the district court's order granting the partial summary judgment was silent about "whether the judgment was deemed final, or whether there was any reason to allow an immediate appeal from it." From this, you can infer that the district court did not "expressly determine that there [was] no just reason for delay," the pre-condition for the partial summary judgment to be deemed final.

Since the partial judgment was not final and did not fall within any special exception to the general rule stating that appeals from non-final judgments are not allowed in federal practice, the court of appeals does not have jurisdiction to hear the appeal even if it would like to do so.

Choice (A) is wrong, because the grant of partial summary judgment is normally not a final judgment. As is described more fully in the discussion of Choice (C) above, under FRCP 54(b) an entry of judgment on fewer than all claims is not deemed final unless the district court "expressly determines that there is no just reason for delay" (which didn't happen here). Since Choice (A) says that the grant of partial summary judgment is automatically a final judgment, this choice is an incorrect statement of law (and also incorrectly predicts the outcome).

Choice (B) is wrong, because immediate appellate review is not available on the facts presented. Federal law under 28 U.S.C. § 1292(b) allows for appeals of interlocutory orders only in limited circumstances, none of which applies on the present facts. Since Choice (B) asserts that grants of partial summary judgment are immediately appealable at the discretion of the appeals court — and implies that that's true whether or not the district court took any action to make the judgment immediately appealable — Choice (A) is wrong as a matter of law.

Choice (D) is wrong, because although there is a rule which makes an appeal filed within ten days a relevant fact, the rule does not apply in the present situation. Under 28 U.S.C. § 1292(b), if a district court includes in an otherwise non-appealable order a statement that the order involves a "controlling question of law as to which there is substantial ground for difference of opinion and that an immediate appeal from the order may materially advance the ultimate termination of the litigation," the court of appeals may, "in its discretion" permit an appeal. In that special circumstance, the appealing party must apply for leave to appeal within ten days of when the district court entered its order. 28 U.S.C. § 1292(b). Here, however, the facts tell you that the District Court said nothing about an immediate appeal, so the special situation referred to in the prior sentence could not have arisen, making the presence or absence of a consent to appeal within ten days irrelevant to this problem.

Answer 91

The correct choice is **(A),** because the baker's notice of appeal was filed too late, and the lateness divested the Court of Appeals of jurisdiction. Federal Rule of Appellate Proc. 4(a)(1)(A) says that as a general rule, in a civil case a "notice of appeal" must be "be filed with the district clerk *within 30 days after entry of the judgment* or order appealed from." The facts tell you that the judgment for $55,000 was filed on July 15. Therefore, once 30 days passed, it was too late for the baker to file his notice of appeal. There are a few exceptions to this strict 30-day filing period, but none applies here. For instance, an extension can be given by the trial judge if the party seeking to appeal makes a motion for the extension no more than 30 days after the end of the 30-day-of-right period; but even that 30 day period in which to move for an extension ended on September 15. So by September 20, the baker's time to file a notice of appeal had passed, and the failure to timely file such a notice is "jurisdictional" — that is, neither the district court nor the Court of Appeals has the power to excuse the lateness even if it wants to (putting aside the special case where the would-be appellant shows that he never got notice of the entry of the judgment, not something that he can show here).

Therefore, the Court of Appeals will have no choice but to dismiss the late-filed appeal. And that's true even in situations where the would-be appellant would have had a good chance of demonstrating on appeal that the district court lacked subject-matter jurisdiction (an objection that is never deemed waived as long as the case is alive). Once the time for filing a notice of appeal has passed, the case is over, even for purposes of determining that there was never valid subject-matter jurisdiction in the first place. (In any event, as is discussed in the treatment of Choice (C) below, the lower court *did* have subject-matter jurisdiction.)

Choice (B) is wrong, both because the appeal was not timely filed, and because the baker had waived any objection to personal jurisdiction. On the underlying facts, there is a relatively good chance that the baker would have been able to establish that his contacts with State A were so slight that he would not have been found to have "purposely availed himself" of the opportunity to do business in the state, making the State A federal court's exercise of personal jurisdiction over him a denial of due process. (The resolution of this issue would depend on just how the court applied the "stream of commerce" theory, under which a defendant who knowingly puts an article into interstate commerce may be found to have minimum contacts with the place where the article ends up causing injury; application of the test depends on subtleties of the particular facts, including how much of the defendant's product went into the forum state, what the defendant knew about the likelihood that an article would find its way to that state, etc.) But for this question, you don't have to decide how the minimum contacts issue would have been decided had it been properly raised; that's because the baker waived any lack of personal jurisdiction by neither making a pre-answer motion raising that defense nor including the defense in his answer. So even if the baker had timely filed his notice of appeal, he would still have been found to have waived the personal-jurisdiction objection, and would not be permitted to re-litigate the objection as part of his appeal.

Choice (C) is wrong, in part because the district court had subject-matter jurisdiction over the action. The facts tell you that the baker's objection to lack of subject-matter jurisdiction is based on the fact that the jury's award was for less than $75,000, and $75,000 is the minimal amount-in-controversy requirement for diversity cases. But an action will not be dismissed based on failure to meet the amount-in-controversy requirement unless it is clear **at the moment of filing** that **to a legal certainty**, more than $75,000 cannot be in issue. Here, where the claim is for personal injuries that led to a hospital stay, it certainly cannot be said as a legal certainty that no jury could reasonably award more than $75,000. So the fact that the **ultimate judgment** awarded by the jury was less than the jurisdictional amount does not mean that the case failed to satisfy the requirement. In any event, this choice is also wrong because the appeal was not timely filed (as discussed in Choice (A)), so no reversal would have been possible even if, in fact, the district court had lacked subject-matter jurisdiction.

Choice (D) is wrong, both because there could not have been a waiver of the subject-matter jurisdiction defense and because the lack of a timely notice of appeal would prevent the appeals court from affirming the judgment. Unlike an objection to lack of personal jurisdiction, an objection to lack of subject-matter jurisdiction is *never* waived—as long as the case is still alive (i.e., there has not been a final judgment entered from which any appeal is now time-barred), either party can raise the objection, and the district court or Court of Appeals must dismiss the case if it notices the lack of subject-matter jurisdiction on its own. So this choice, by saying that "both" of the jurisdiction-related defenses were waived at the district-court level, incorrectly describes how a subject-matter jurisdiction objection would be treated. Furthermore, the Court of Appeals can "affirm" the judgment of the lower court only if the appeal is properly before the appellate court; here, where the notice of appeal was not timely filed, the Court of Appeals never got jurisdiction over an appeal, and is not in a position to "affirm" the judgment. All the Court of Appeals can do is to dismiss the improperly-asserted appeal, leaving the judgment in place.

Answer 92

The correct choice is **(A)**, because FRCP 52(a)(6) allows the appellate court to set aside findings of fact *only if they are "clearly erroneous,"* and requires that court to give "due regard to the trial court's opportunity to *judge the witnesses' credibility."*

This is one situation in which the relevant Federal Rule gives a precise answer to the problem, with essentially zero need for you to resolve any problem of interpretation. Rule 52(a)(6) reads as follows:

> *"Findings of fact,* whether based on oral or other evidence, *must not be set aside unless clearly erroneous,* and the reviewing court *must give due regard to the trial court's opportunity to judge the witnesses' credibility."*

So in order for the appeals court to overturn the "findings" here (i.e., the single conclusion that the scope of work was what the homeowner argued it was), two things would have to be true: (1) the findings were "clearly erroneous"; and (2) in deciding that the findings were indeed clearly erroneous, the appellate court reached that conclusion despite giving "due regard to the trial court's opportunity to judge the witnesses' credibility." Here, it's very unlikely that either—let alone both—of these conditions would be decided in favor of the appellant/contractor.

As to (1), since this was a classic "he said / she said" scenario—just two opposing witnesses, and no indication why one be more believable than the other—there is no apparent reason why the appellate court should determine that the trial judge's factual conclusion was "clearly erroneous." And as to (2), the proof consisted of just two opposing witnesses (and apparently no relevant documents), so the case comes down to which of the two witnesses should be believed. This is a matter in which the credibility of those witnesses would be vital, and as to which the trial judge's opportunity to see the witnesses face-to-face and to judge their credibility by (in part) their demeanor while on the stand would also be vital. Therefore, the trial judge's superior opportunity to judge witness credibility is likely to have been crucial, a fact that cuts even more strongly in favor of the appellate court's not setting aside the findings.

Choice (B) is wrong, because in a case tried without a jury, nothing requires a party to object to the judge's findings of fact as a pre-condition to an appeal that seeks to overturn those findings. As in the (correct) Choice (A), this choice can be fully evaluated based solely on the explicit language of a Federal Rule. Rule 52 as a whole governs findings and conclusions in non-jury trials. A sub-section, Rule 52(a)(5), says that in such a bench trial, "A party may later *question the sufficiency of the evidence* supporting the findings, *whether or not the party requested findings, objected to them*, moved to amend them, or moved for partial findings." This section quite precisely fits the scenario posed by this choice:

(1) we're not told explicitly the grounds for the contractor's appeal, but since we're told that the scope-of-work issue was the only issue in the case, and we're asked whether the appellate court will "overturn the findings," it must be the case that the appeal is an attempt to overturn the trial result based on "sufficiency of the evidence supporting the findings" (since there's no other plausible ground that would lead to an overturning of the findings); and

(2) given that what the contractor is trying to do on appeal is to question the sufficiency of the evidence supporting the findings, 52(a)(5) tells us that the contractor may do so "whether or not [the contractor] requested findings [or] objected to them[.]"

Choice (C) is wrong, because, although the trial judge was required to make findings of fact, she was not required to put those findings in a written opinion or memorandum of decision. Again, a sub-section of Rule 52 directly disposes of the issue raised by this choice. Rule 52(a)(1)'s first sentence says that in a non-jury trial, the court "must find the facts specially[.]" But the next sentence says: "The findings . . . may be *stated on the record* after the close of the evidence or may appear in an opinion or a memorandum of decision filed by the court." The Advisory Committee Notes to the 1983 amendment to Rule 52 (which is when the "may be stated on the record" language was added) says that the purpose of the amendment was "to provide explicitly that the district judge may make the findings of fact and conclusions of law required in nonjury cases *orally*." So this choice, by stating that the findings must be put into a writing, is flatly inconsistent with the language of 52(a)(1).

Choice (D) is wrong, because the fact that there were disputed issues of fact at trial does not by itself strip the appellate court of the authority to reverse the findings of fact for being against the weight of the evidence. In federal bench trials (as in jury trials), the losing party is permitted to appeal on the grounds that the verdict was against the weight of the evidence. It's true that the Federal Rules try to avoid having the appellate court act as a substitute finder of fact as to disputed issues; this is done mainly by Rule 52(a)(6)'s provision that the findings of fact must not be set aside unless "clearly erroneous," and that the appellate court must "give due regard to the trial court's opportunity to judge the witnesses' credibility." But there is no provision anywhere in the Rules that prohibits the appellate court from setting aside findings of fact merely because those findings involved "disputed issues of fact at trial," as this choice posits. (Indeed, if there *were* a rule or principle preventing reversals as to any factual issue that was disputed at trial, Rule 52(a)(6)'s statement that the appellate court must "give due regard to the trial court's opportunity to judge the witnesses' credibility" would be unnecessary, since witnesses' credibility really matters only as to disputed issues.)

Answer 93

The correct choice is **(A),** because the evidence issue here required balancing various factors that are left to the discretion of the trial judge. This is a Civil Procedure question, not an Evidence question, but the solution nonetheless depends on the technical rule of evidence that applies to this particular admissibility issue. The manufacturer's objection to the evidence would have to have been based on FRE Rule 403, which says that "The court may exclude relevant evidence if its *probative value* is *substantially outweighed* by a danger of one or more of the following: *unfair prejudice*, confusing the issues, *misleading the jury*, undue delay, wasting time, or needlessly presenting cumulative evidence."

Since Rule 403 requires the trial judge not only to estimate the "probative value" of the evidence (which in turn depends on an assessment of all other evidence in the case dealing with the same issue), but also to "weigh" that probative value against a whole range of hard-to-quantify dangers (like prejudice and juror confusion), the trial judge is in a much better position to make this complex assessment than is the reviewing court. Therefore, Rule 403 gives *wide discretion to the trial judge* about whether to admit or exclude the evidence, and the appellate court will reverse *only if the judge has clearly "abused" that discretion*, a very hard standard for the appellant to satisfy. See, e.g., *Rigby v. Beech Aircraft Co.,* 548 F.2d 288, 293 (10th Cir. 1977): "The [Rule 403] task of balancing the probative value of evidence against danger of confusion of the issues is one for which the trial judge, because of his familiarity with the full array of evidence in the case, is particularly suited."

Choice (B) is wrong, because the standard to which it refers applies to a judge's findings of fact in a non-jury case, not to the ruling on evidence at issue here. If the phrasing of this choice seemed familiar to you, you were not imagining things. FRCP 52 governs the procedures for bench trials; Rule 52(a)(1) says that the judge must "find the facts specially," and then put those findings into the record. Then, Rule 52(a)(6) goes on to say that these "[f]indings of fact, whether based on oral or other evidence, must not be set aside [on appeal] *unless clearly* *erroneous*, and the ***reviewing court must give due regard to the trial court's opportunity to judge the witnesses' credibility*.*" So as you can see, this "clearly erroneous" standard applies only to appellate review of the "findings of fact" made by the judge sitting without a jury — it does not apply to review of the judge's decision on evidentiary matters.

Choice (C) is wrong, because the standard to which it refers applies only to certain issues of pure law. Appellate courts give greater or lesser deference to the trial judge's rulings depending on how fact-intensive the ruling under review is. A "de novo" review is a review taken from scratch, i.e., from the same position as the trial judge would have been in. De novo review tends to occur only when the main issue is how the law applies to a given set of facts. See, e.g., F,K&M (5th Ed.), § 13.4, p. 603: "The fullest scope of review, not surprisingly, is for errors of law; the appellate court will decide questions of law de novo." The issue here, which requires the court to consider how the jury is likely to react to a mass of factual evidence, is not considered the sort of purely-legal issue that is suitable for de novo review. (As you would guess, de novo review involves the appellate court's giving virtually no deference to the trial judge's familiarity with the case or her opportunity to see the demeanor of the witnesses; the issue here is at the other end of the spectrum in terms of the degree of deference which the appeals court should and will give to the trial court's initial decision.)

Choice (D) is wrong, because this choice does not list a standard, but rather a method of judging whether one or more errors justify a reversal on appeal. The question asks you to specify the "standard" for evaluating the manufacturer's argument that the judge committed error in allowing the testimony. That is, the question asks you to describe the test that the appellate court will use to determine whether the judge's ruling was an error at all. The concept of "harmless error" deals with a separate issue — whether, on the ***assumption that a ruling was erroneous***, the error was ***sufficiently grave*** that the judgment below cannot be affirmed. Even when the appellate court decides that a particular ruling or set of rulings was incorrect, that court will not reverse (i.e., order a new trial, or a judgment for the other party) if the court believes that the error was ***unlikely to have changed the outcome of the trial***. Here, given the large degree of deference given by the appellate court to a trial court's ruling on a Rule 403 "probative value" objection, the appellate court would probably not find error at all (i.e., would find that the trial judge did not "abuse his discretion"), so the court would never even *get to* the question of whether any error that may have occurred was harmless. So, in short, this choice is incorrect in saying that "harmless error" specifies a "standard" by which the appellate court will evaluate whether the trial judge's ruling was correct.

CONSTITUTIONAL LAW

CONSTITUTIONAL LAW QUESTIONS BY TOPIC

CHAPTER 1

THE SUPREME COURT'S AUTHORITY AND THE FEDERAL JUDICIAL POWER

I. THE SUPREME COURT'S AUTHORITY AND THE FEDERAL JUDICIAL POWER

A. Supreme Court review of state court decision

1. "Independent and adequate state grounds"

a. Violation of both state and federal constitutions

Question 1

A state constitution provides that in every criminal trial "the accused shall have the right to confront all witnesses against him face to face." A defendant was convicted in state court of child abuse based on testimony from a six-year-old child. The child testified while she was seated behind one-way glass, which allowed the defendant to see the child but did not allow the child to see the defendant. The defendant appealed to the state supreme court claiming that the inability of the witness to see the defendant while she testified violated both the United States Constitution and the state constitution. Without addressing the federal constitutional issue, the state supreme court reversed the defendant's conviction and ordered a new trial. The state supreme court held that "the constitution of this state is clear, and it requires that while testifying in a criminal trial, a witness must be able to see the defendant." The state petitioned the United States Supreme Court for a writ of certiorari.

On which ground should the United States Supreme Court DENY the state's petition?

(A) A state may not seek appellate review in the United States Supreme Court of the reversal of a criminal conviction by its own supreme court.

(B) The decision of the state supreme court was based on an adequate and independent state ground.

(C) The Sixth Amendment to the United States Constitution does not require that a witness against a criminal defendant be able to see the defendant while the witness testifies.

(D) The state supreme court's decision requires a new trial, and therefore it is not a final judgment.

Question 2

Plaintiff challenged the constitutionality of a state tax law, alleging that it violated the Equal Protection Clauses of both the United States Constitution and the state constitution. The state supreme court agreed and held the tax law to be invalid. It said: "We hold that this state tax law violates the Equal Protection Clause of the United States Constitution and also the equal protection clause of the state constitution because we interpret that provision of the state constitution to contain exactly the same prohibition against discriminatory legislation as is contained in the Equal Protection Clause of the Fourteenth Amendment to the United States Constitution."

The state sought review of this decision in the United States Supreme Court, alleging that the state supreme court's determination of the federal constitutional issue was incorrect.

How should the United States Supreme Court dispose of the case if it believes that this interpretation of the federal Constitution by the state supreme court raises an important federal question and is incorrect on the merits?

(A) Reverse the state supreme court decision, because the equal protection clause of a state constitution must be construed by the state supreme court in a manner that is congruent with the meaning of the Equal Protection Clause of the federal Constitution.

(B) Reverse the state supreme court decision with respect to the Equal Protection Clause of the federal Constitution and remand the case to the state supreme court for further proceedings, because the state and federal constitutional issues are so intertwined that the federal issue must be decided so that this case may be disposed of properly.

(C) Refuse to review the decision of the state supreme court, because it is based on an adequate and independent ground of state law.

(D) Refuse to review the decision of the state supreme court, because a state government may not seek review of decisions of its own courts in the United States Supreme Court.

Question 3

A baseball fan had a fierce temper and an extremely loud voice. Attending a baseball game in which a number of calls went against the home team, the fan repeatedly stood up, brandished his fist, and angrily shouted, "Kill the umpires." The fourth time he engaged in this conduct, many other spectators followed the fan in rising from their seats, brandishing fists, and shouting, "Kill the umpires."

The home team lost the game. Although no violence ensued, spectators crowded menacingly around the umpires after the game. As a result, the umpires were able to leave the field and stadium only with the help of a massive police escort.

For his conduct, the fan was charged with inciting to riot and was convicted in a jury trial in state court. He appealed. The state supreme court reversed his conviction. In its opinion, the court discussed in detail decisions of the United States Supreme Court dealing with the First Amendment Free Speech Clause as incorporated into the Fourteenth Amendment. At the end of that discussion, however, the court stated that it "need not resolve how, on the basis of these cases," the United States Supreme Court would decide the fan's case. "Instead," the court stated, "this court has always given the free-speech guarantee of the state's constitution the broadest possible interpretation. As a result, we hold that in this case, where no riot or other violence actually occurred, the state constitution does not permit this conviction for incitement to riot to stand."

The United States Supreme Court grants a writ of certiorari to review this decision of the state supreme court. In this case, the United States Supreme Court should

(A) affirm the state supreme court's decision, because the fan's ballpark shout is commonplace hyperbole that cannot, consistently with the First and Fourteenth Amendments, be punished.

(B) remand the case to the state supreme court with directions that it resolve the First and Fourteenth Amendment free-speech issue that it discussed in such detail.

(C) dismiss the writ as improvidently granted, because the state supreme court's decision rests on an independent and adequate state law ground.

(D) reverse the decision of the state supreme court, because incitement to violent action is not speech protected by the First and Fourteenth Amendments.

B. Supreme Court's jurisdiction

Question 4

A federal statute provides that the United States Supreme Court has authority to review any case filed in a United States court of appeals, even though that case has not yet been decided by the court of appeals.

The Environmental Protection Agency (EPA), an agency in the executive branch of the federal government, issued an important environmental rule. Although the rule had not yet been enforced against them, companies that would be adversely affected by the rule filed a petition for review of the rule in a court of appeals, seeking a declaration that the rule was invalid solely because it was beyond the statutory authority of the EPA. The companies made no constitutional claim. A statute specifically provides for direct review of EPA rules by a court of appeals without any initial action in a district court.

The companies have filed a petition for a writ of certiorari in the Supreme Court requesting immediate review of this case by the Supreme Court before the court of appeals has actually decided the case. The EPA acknowledges that the case is important enough to warrant Supreme Court review and that it should be decided promptly, but it asks the Supreme Court to dismiss the petition on jurisdictional grounds.

The best constitutional argument in support of the EPA's request is that

(A) the case is not within the original jurisdiction of the Supreme Court as defined by Article III, and it is not a proper subject of that court's appellate jurisdiction because it has not yet been decided by any lower court.

(B) the case is appellate in nature, but it is beyond the appellate jurisdiction of the Supreme Court, because Article III states that its jurisdiction extends only to cases arising under the Constitution.

(C) Article III precludes federal courts from reviewing the validity of any federal agency rule in any proceeding other than an action to enforce the rule.

(D) Article III provides that all federal cases, except those within the original jurisdiction of the Supreme Court, must be initiated by an action in a federal district court.

II. CONGRESS'S CONTROL OF FEDERAL JUDICIAL POWER

A. Limits on judicial power imposed by Congress

Question 5

Assume that Congress passed and the President signed the following statute:

> "The appellate jurisdiction of the United States Supreme Court shall not extend to any case involving the constitutionality of any state statute limiting the circumstances in which a woman may obtain an abortion, or involving the constitutionality of this statute."

The strongest argument against the constitutionality of this statute is that

(A) Congress may not exercise its authority over the appellate jurisdiction of the Supreme Court in a way that seriously interferes with the establishment of a supreme and uniform body of federal constitutional law.

(B) Congress may only regulate the appellate jurisdiction of the Supreme Court over cases initially arising in federal courts.

(C) the appellate jurisdiction of the Supreme Court may only be altered by constitutional amendment.

(D) the statute violates the Equal Protection Clause of the Fourteenth Amendment.

Question 6

Which of the following acts by the United States Senate would be constitutionally IMPROPER?

(A) The Senate decides, with the House of Representatives, that a disputed state ratification of a proposed constitutional amendment is valid.

(B) The Senate determines the eligibility of a person to serve as a senator.

(C) The Senate appoints a commission to adjudicate finally a boundary dispute between two states.

(D) The Senate passes a resolution calling on the President to pursue a certain foreign policy.

CHAPTER 2
POWERS OF THE FEDERAL GOVERNMENT; THE SEPARATION OF POWERS

I. POWERS OF THE THREE FEDERAL BRANCHES

A. Powers of the three branches

1. Congress's powers

a. Federal property

Question 7

The National Ecological Balance Act prohibits the destruction or removal of any wild animals located on lands owned by the United States without express permission from the Federal Bureau of Land Management. Violators are subject to fines of up to $1,000 per offense.

After substantial property damage was inflicted on residents of a state by hungry coyotes, the state legislature passed the Coyote Bounty Bill, which offers $25 for each coyote killed or captured within the state. A National Forest, owned by the federal government, is located entirely within that state. Many coyotes live in the National Forest.

Without seeking permission from the Bureau of Land Management, a hunter shot several coyotes in the National Forest and collected the bounty from the state. As a result, he was subsequently tried in federal district court, convicted, and fined $1,000 for violating the National Ecological Balance Act. The hunter appealed his conviction to the United States court of appeals.

On appeal, the court of appeals should hold the National Ecological Balance Act, as applied to the hunter, to be

(A) constitutional, because the Property Clause of Article IV, Section 3, of the Constitution authorizes such federal statutory controls and sanctions.

(B) constitutional, because Article I, Section 8, of the Constitution authorizes Congress to enact all laws necessary and proper to advance the general welfare.

(C) unconstitutional, because Congress may not use its delegated powers to override the Tenth Amendment right of the state to legislate in areas of traditional state governmental functions, such as the protection of the property of its residents.

(D) unconstitutional, because Congress violates the Full Faith and Credit Clause of Article IV when it punishes conduct that has been authorized by state action.

2. President's powers

a. Status as CEO of the U.S., and power to issue "Executive Orders"

Question 8

The President issued an executive order in an effort to encourage citizens to use the metric (Celsius) system of temperatures. Sec. 1 of the executive order requires the United States Weather Bureau, a federal executive agency, to state temperatures only in Celsius in all weather reports. Sec. 2 of the executive order requires all privately owned federally licensed radio and television stations giving weather reports to report temperatures only in Celsius. No federal statute is applicable.

Is the President's executive order constitutional?

(A) Sec. 1 is constitutional, but Sec. 2 is not.

(B) Sec. 2 is constitutional, but Sec. 1 is not.

(C) Sections 1 and 2 are constitutional.

(D) Sections 1 and 2 are unconstitutional.

b. Power to issue pardons

Question 9

Congress passed a bill prohibiting the President from granting a pardon to any person who had not served at least one-third of the sentence imposed by the court which convicted that person. The President vetoed the bill, claiming that it was unconstitutional. Nevertheless, Congress passed it over his veto by a two-thirds vote of each House.

This act of Congress is

(A) constitutional, because it was enacted over the President's veto by a two-thirds vote of each House.

(B) constitutional, because it is a necessary and proper means of carrying out the powers of Congress.

(C) unconstitutional, because it interferes with the plenary power of the President to grant pardons.

(D) unconstitutional, because a Presidential veto based upon constitutional grounds may be overridden only with the concurrence of three-fourths of the state legislatures.

3. The federal judiciary's powers

Question 10

In 2003, a man was appointed to a tribunal established pursuant to a congressional act. The tribunal's duties were to review claims made by veterans and to make recommendations to the Veterans Administration on their merits. Congress later abolished the tribunal and established a different format for review of such claims. The man was offered a federal administrative position in the same bureau at a lesser salary. He thereupon sued the government on the ground that Congress may not remove a federal judge from office during good behavior nor diminish his compensation during continuance in office. Government attorneys filed a motion to dismiss the action.

The court should

(A) deny the motion because of the independence of the federal judiciary constitutionally guaranteed by Article III.

(B) deny the motion, because the man has established a property right to his federal employment of the tribunal.

(C) grant the motion, because the man lacked standing to raise the question.

(D) grant the motion, because the man was not a judge under Article III and is not entitled to life tenure.

II.   THE FEDERAL COMMERCE POWER

A. Does the activity in question "substantially affect" commerce?

Question 11

A federal statute prohibits the sale or resale, in any place in this country, of any product intended for human consumption or ingestion into the human body that contains designated chemicals known to cause cancer, unless the product is clearly labeled as dangerous.

The constitutionality of this federal statute may most easily be justified on the basis of the power of Congress to

(A) regulate commerce among the states.

(B) enforce the Fourteenth Amendment.

(C) provide for the general welfare.

(D) promote science and the useful arts.

Question 12

"Look-alike drugs" is the term used to describe nonprescription drugs that look like narcotic drugs and are sold on the streets as narcotic drugs. After extensive hearings, Congress concluded that the sale of look-alike drugs was widespread in this country and was creating severe health and law enforcement problems. To combat these problems, Congress enacted a comprehensive statute that regulates the manufacture, distribution, and sale of all nonprescription drugs in the United States.

Which of the following sources of constitutional authority can most easily be used to justify the authority of Congress to enact this statute?

(A) The spending power.

(B) The Commerce Clause.

(C) The general welfare clause.

(D) The enforcement powers of the Fourteenth Amendment.

Question 13

Congress wishes to enact legislation prohibiting discrimination in the sale or rental of housing on the basis of the affectional preference or sexual orientation of the potential purchaser or renter. Congress wishes this statute to apply to all public and private vendors and lessors of residential property in this country, with a few narrowly drawn exceptions.

The most credible argument for congressional authority to enact such a statute would be based upon the

(A) general welfare clause of Article I, Section 8, because the conduct the statute prohibits could reasonably be deemed to be harmful to the national interest.

(B) Commerce Clause of Article I, Section 8, because, in inseverable aggregates, the sale or rental of almost all housing in this country could reasonably be deemed to have a substantial effect on interstate commerce.

(C) enforcement clause of the Thirteenth Amendment, because that Amendment clearly prohibits discrimination against the class of persons protected by this statute.

(D) enforcement clause of the Fourteenth Amendment, because that Amendment prohibits all public and private actors from engaging in irrational discrimination.

B. **The Tenth Amendment as a limit on Congress's power**

Question 14

A federal law provides that all motor vehicle tires discarded in this country must be disposed of in facilities licensed by the federal Environmental Protection Agency. Pursuant to this federal law and all proper federal procedural requirements, that agency has adopted very strict standards for the licensing of such facilities. As a result, the cost of disposing of tires in licensed facilities is substantial. The state of East Dakota has a very large fleet of motor vehicles, including trucks used to support state-owned commercial activities and police cars. East Dakota disposes of used tires from both kinds of state motor vehicles in a state-owned and -operated facility. This state facility is unlicensed, but its operation in actual practice meets most of the standards imposed by the federal Environmental Protection Agency on facilities it licenses to dispose of tires.

Consistent with United States Supreme Court precedent, may the state of East Dakota continue to dispose of its used tires in this manner?

(A) No, because a state must comply with valid federal laws that regulate matters affecting interstate commerce.

(B) No, because some of the tires come from vehicles that are used by the state solely in its commercial activities.

(C) Yes, because some of the tires come from vehicles that are used by the state in the performance of core state governmental functions such as law enforcement.

(D) Yes, because the legitimate needs of the federal government are satisfied by the fact that the unlicensed state disposal scheme meets, in actual practice, most of the federal standards for the licensing of such facilities.

Question 15

A member of a state legislature is prosecuted in federal court for a violation of the Federal Securities Act arising out of the activities of a state-owned corporation. The legislator's defense includes a claim that the alleged wrongful acts were committed in the course of legislative business and are immune from scrutiny.

Which of the following is the strongest constitutional argument supporting the legislator?

(A) Because of doctrines of federalism, federal law generally cannot be applied to state legislators acting in the course of their official duties.

(B) State legislators enjoy the protection of the Speech and Debate Clause of the U.S. Constitution.

(C) A federal court must follow state law respecting the scope of legislative immunity.

(D) To apply the Federal Securities Act to state legislators would violate the Due Process Clause.

1. Tenth Amendment not a source of state authority

Question 16

Widgets are manufactured wholly from raw materials mined and processed in the state of Green. The only two manufacturers of widgets in the United States are also located in that state. However, their widgets are purchased by retailers located in every state. The legislature of the state of Green is considering the adoption of a statute that would impose a tax solely on the manufacture of widgets. The tax is to be calculated at 3% of their wholesale value.

Which of the following arguments would be LEAST helpful to the state in defending the constitutionality of this proposed state tax on widgets?

(A) At the time widgets are manufactured and taxed they have not yet entered the channels of interstate commerce.

(B) The economic impact of this tax will be passed on to both in-state and out-of-state purchasers of widgets and, therefore, it is wholly nondiscriminatory in its effect.

(C) Because of the powers reserved to them by the Tenth Amendment, states have plenary authority to construct their tax system in any manner they choose.

(D) A tax on the manufacture of widgets may be imposed only by the state in which the manufacturing occurs and, therefore, it is not likely to create the danger of a multiple tax burden on interstate commerce.

III. THE TAXING AND SPENDING POWERS

A. The taxing power

1. The taxing power generally

Question 17

In order to reduce the federal deficit, Congress enacted a statute imposing a 5% national retail sales tax. The tax was levied upon all retail sales in the United States and applied equally to the sales of all kinds of goods.

Is this tax constitutional as applied to retail sales of newspapers?

(A) Yes, because it is within Congress's power to tax.

(B) Yes, because the tax is necessary to serve the compelling interest of balancing the federal budget.

(C) No, because retail sales taxes are within the taxing power of the states.

(D) No, because the imposition of a tax on the sale of newspapers violates the freedom of the press.

2. Validity of tax that has a regulatory purpose or effect

a. Adverse economic consequences no problem

Question 18

The Sports Championship Revenue Enhancement Act is a federal statute that was enacted as part of a comprehensive program to eliminate the federal budget deficit. That act imposed, for a period of five years, a 50% excise tax on the price of tickets to championship sporting events. Such events included the World Series, the Super Bowl, major college bowl games, and similar championship sports events.

This federal tax is probably

(A) constitutional, because the compelling national interest in reducing the federal budget deficit justifies this tax as a temporary emergency measure.

(B) constitutional, because an act of Congress that appears to be a revenue raising measure on its face is not rendered invalid because it may have adverse economic consequences for the activity taxed.

(C) unconstitutional, because a 50% tax is likely to reduce attendance at championship sporting events and, therefore, is not rationally related to the legitimate interest of Congress in eliminating the budget deficit.

(D) unconstitutional, because Congress violates the equal protection component of the Fifth Amendment by singling out championship sporting events for this tax while failing to tax other major sporting, artistic, or entertainment events to which tickets are sold.

b. No relation needed between activity taxed and how funds are spent

Question 19

In order to provide funds for a system of new major airports near the ten largest cities in the United States, Congress levies a tax of $25 on each airline ticket issued in the United States. The tax applies to every airline ticket, even those for travel that does not originate in, terminate at, or pass through any of those ten large cities.

As applied to the issuance in the United States of an airline ticket for travel between two cities that will not be served by any of the new airports, this tax is

(A) constitutional, because Congress has broad discretion in choosing the subjects of its taxation and may impose taxes on subjects that have no relation to the purpose for which those tax funds will be expended.

(B) constitutional, because an exemption for the issuance of tickets for travel between cities that will not be served by the new airports would deny the purchasers of all other tickets the equal protection of the laws.

(C) unconstitutional, because the burden of the tax outweighs its benefits for passengers whose travel does not originate in, terminate at, or pass through any of the ten largest cities.

(D) unconstitutional, because the tax adversely affects the fundamental right to travel.

B. Spending power

1. Spending to achieve the general welfare

Question 20

A newly enacted federal statute appropriates $100 million in federal funds to support basic research by universities located in the United States. The statute provides that "the ten best universities in the United States" will each receive $10 million. It also provides that "the ten best universities" shall be "determined by a poll of the presidents of all the universities in the nation, to be conducted by the United States Department of Education." In responding to that poll, each university president is required to apply the well-recognized and generally accepted standards of academic quality that are specified in the statute. The provisions of the statute are inseverable.

Which of the following statements about this statute is correct?

(A) The statute is unconstitutional, because the reliance by Congress on a poll of individuals who are not federal officials to determine the recipients of its appropriated funds is an unconstitutional delegation of legislative power.

(B) The statute is unconstitutional, because the limitation on recipients to the ten best universities is arbitrary and capricious and denies other high-quality universities the equal protection of the laws.

(C) The statute is constitutional, because Congress has plenary authority to determine the objects of its spending and the methods used to achieve them, so long as they may reasonably be deemed to serve the general welfare and do not violate any prohibitory language in the Constitution.

(D) The validity of the statute is nonjusticiable, because the use by Congress of its spending power necessarily involves political considerations that must be resolved finally by those branches of the government that are closest to the political process.

C. The taxing and spending powers taken together

Question 21

The strongest constitutional basis for the enactment of a federal statute requiring colleges and universities receiving federal funds to offer student aid solely on the basis of need is the

(A) police power.

(B) war and defense power.

(C) power to tax and spend for the general welfare.

(D) power to enforce the Privileges or Immunities Clause of the Fourteenth Amendment.

IV. THE WAR, TREATY AND FOREIGN AFFAIRS POWERS

A. The treaty power

Question 22

With the advice and consent of the Senate, the President entered into a self-executing treaty with a foreign country. The treaty provided that citizens of both nations were required to pay whatever torts damages were awarded against them by a court of either nation.

A man and a woman who were U.S. citizens and residents of the same state were traveling separately in the foreign country when their cars collided. The foreign court awarded the woman a judgment for $500,000 in damages for her injuries from the accident.

In federal district court in their home state, the woman filed suit against the man to enforce the judgment. The man filed a motion to dismiss for lack of jurisdiction.

Should the court grant the motion to dismiss?

(A) Yes, because the citizenship of the parties is not diverse.

(B) Yes, because the traffic accident was a noncommercial transaction outside interstate commerce.

(C) No, because the case falls within the federal question jurisdiction of the court.

(D) No, because the treaty power is plenary and not subject to judicial review.

V. THE SEPARATION OF POWERS

A. Separation of powers generally

1. President can't make the laws

a. Delegation by Congress to the Executive Branch

Question 23

Congress passed a statute directing the United States Forest Service, a federal agency, to issue regulations to control campfires on federal public lands and to establish a schedule of penalties for those who violate the new regulations. The statute provided that the Forest Service regulations should "reduce, to the maximum extent feasible, all potential hazards that arise from campfires on Forest Service lands." The Forest Service issued the regulations and the schedule of penalties directed by Congress. The regulations include a rule that provides for the doubling of the fine for any negligent or prohibited use of fire if the user is intoxicated by alcohol or drugs.

Which of the following is the best argument for sustaining the constitutionality of the Forest Service's rule providing for the fines?

(A) The executive branch of government, of which the Forest Service is part, has inherent rule-making authority over public lands.

(B) The rule is issued pursuant to a valid exercise of Congress's power to delegate rule- making authority to federal agencies.

(C) The rule is justified by a compelling governmental interest in safeguarding forest resources.

(D) The rule relates directly to law enforcement, which is an executive rather than legislative function, and hence it does not need specific congressional authorization.

2. Presidential Commissions

Question 24

The vaccination of children against childhood contagious diseases (such as measles, diphtheria, and whooping cough) has traditionally been a function of private doctors and local and state health departments. Because vaccination rates have declined in recent years, especially in urban areas, the President proposes to appoint a Presidential Advisory Commission on Vaccination which would be charged with conducting a national publicity campaign to encourage vaccination as a public health measure. No federal statute authorizes or prohibits this action by the President. The activities of the Presidential Advisory Commission on Vaccination would be financed entirely from funds appropriated by Congress to the Office of the President for "such other purposes as the President may think appropriate."

May the President constitutionally create such a commission for this purpose?

(A) Yes, because the President has plenary authority to provide for the health, safety, and welfare of the people of the United States.

(B) Yes, because this action is within the scope of executive authority vested in the President by the Constitution, and no federal statute prohibits it.

(C) No, because the protection of children against common diseases by vaccination is a traditional state function and, therefore, is reserved to the states by the Tenth Amendment.

(D) No, because Congress has not specifically authorized the creation and support of such a new federal agency.

3. The veto power, and Congress's power to override it

Question 25

An appropriations act passed by Congress over the President's veto directs that one billion dollars "shall be spent" by the federal government for the development of a new military weapons system, which is available only from a particular arms manufacturer. On the order of the President, the secretary of defense refuses to authorize a contract for the purchase of the weapons system. The manufacturer sues the secretary of defense, alleging an unlawful withholding of these federal funds.

The strongest constitutional argument for the arms manufacturer is that

(A) passage of an appropriation over a veto makes the spending mandatory.

(B) Congress's power to appropriate funds includes the power to require that the funds be spent as directed.

(C) the President's independent constitutional powers do not specifically refer to spending.

(D) the President's power to withhold such funds is limited to cases where foreign affairs are directly involved.

4. Appointment and removal of executive personnel

Question 26

A federal statute with inseverable provisions established a new five-member board with broad regulatory powers over the operation of the securities, banking, and commodities industries, including the power to issue rules with the force of law. The statute provides for three of the board members to be appointed by the President with the advice and consent of the Senate. They serve seven-year terms and are removable only for good cause. The other two members of the board were designated in the statute to be the respective general counsel of the Senate and House of Representatives Committees on Government Operations. The statute stipulated that they were to serve on the board for as long as they continued in those positions.

Following all required administrative procedures, the board issued an elaborate set of rules regulating the operations of all banks, securities dealers, and commodities brokers. A securities company, which was subject to the board's rules, sought a declaratory judgment that the rules were invalid because the statute establishing the board was unconstitutional. In this case, the court should rule that the statute establishing the board is

(A) unconstitutional, because all members of federal boards having broad powers that are quasi-legislative in nature, such as rulemaking, must be appointed by Congress.

(B) unconstitutional, because all members of federal boards exercising executive powers must be appointed by the President or in a manner otherwise consistent with the Appointments Clause of Article II.

(C) constitutional, because the Necessary and Proper Clause authorizes Congress to determine the means by which members are appointed to boards created by Congress under its power to regulate commerce among the states.

(D) constitutional, because there is a substantial nexus between the power of Congress to legislate for the general welfare and the means specified by Congress in this statute for the appointment of board members.

5. Congress's power to regulate executive branch members' job performance

Question 27

A woman is cited for contempt of the House of Representatives after she refused to answer certain questions posed by a House Committee concerning her acts while serving as a U.S. ambassador. A federal statute authorizes the attorney general to prosecute contempts of Congress. Pursuant to this law, the House directs the attorney general to begin criminal proceedings against the woman. A federal grand jury indicts the woman, but the attorney general refuses to sign the indictment.

Which of the following best describes the constitutionality of the attorney general's action?

(A) Illegal, because the attorney general must prosecute if the House of Representatives so directs.

(B) Illegal, because the attorney general must prosecute those who violate federal law.

(C) Legal, because ambassadors are immune from prosecution for acts committed in the course of their duties.

(D) Legal, because the decision to prosecute is an exclusively executive act.

TWO LIMITS ON STATE POWER: THE DORMANT COMMERCE CLAUSE AND CONGRESSIONAL ACTION

I. THE DORMANT COMMERCE CLAUSE

A. Dormant Commerce Clause generally

1. As a prohibition on protectionism

Question 28

A toy manufacturer that has its headquarters and sole manufacturing plant in the state of Green developed a "Martian" toy that simulates the exploration of Mars by a remote-controlled vehicle. It accurately depicts the Martian landscape and the unmanned exploratory vehicle traversing it. The toy is of high quality, safe, durable, and has sold very well. Other toy manufacturers, all located outside Green, developed similar toys that are lower in price. These manufacturers have contracts to sell their Martian toys to outlets in Green. Although these toys are safe and durable, they depict the Martian landscape less realistically than the toys manufactured in Green. Nevertheless, because of the price difference, sales of these toys have cut severely into the sales of the Martian toys manufactured in Green. The Green legislature subsequently enacted a law "to protect the children of Green from faulty science and to protect Green toy manufacturers from unfair competition." This law forbids the sale in Green of any toy that purports to represent extraterrestrial objects and does not satisfy specified scientific criteria. The Martian toy manufactured in Green satisfies all of these criteria; none of the Martian toys of the competing manufacturers meets the requirements.

Is the Green law constitutional?

(A) No, because it abrogates the obligations of the contracts between the other toy manufacturers and their Green outlets who have agreed to sell their Martian toys.

(B) No, because it imposes an undue burden on interstate commerce.

(C) Yes, because it deals only with a local matter, the sale of toys in Green stores.

(D) Yes, because the state's interest in protecting the state's children from faulty science justifies this burden on interstate commerce.

Question 29

Small retailers located in the state of Yellow were concerned about the loss of business to certain large retailers located nearby in bordering states. In an effort to deal with this concern, the legislature of Yellow enacted a statute requiring all manufacturers and wholesalers who sell goods to retailers in Yellow to do so at prices that are no higher than the lowest prices at which they sell them to retailers in any of the states that border Yellow. Several manufacturers and wholesalers who are located in states bordering Yellow and who sell their goods to retailers in those states and in Yellow bring an action in federal court to challenge the constitutionality of this statute.

Which of the following arguments offered by these plaintiffs is likely to be most persuasive in light of applicable precedent?

The state statute

(A) deprives them of their property or liberty without due process of law.

(B) imposes an unreasonable burden on interstate commerce.

(C) deprives them of a privilege or immunity of national citizenship.

(D) denies them the equal protection of the laws.

2. As a prohibition on unduly burdensome regulations

Question 30

In recent years, several large corporations incorporated and headquartered in a state have suddenly been acquired by out-of-state corporations that have moved all of their operations out of the state. Other corporations incorporated and headquartered in the state have successfully resisted such attempts at acquisition by out-of-state corporations, but they have suffered severe economic injury during those acquisition attempts.

In an effort to preserve jobs in the state and to protect its domestic corporations against their sudden acquisition by out-of-state purchasers, the state legislature enacts a statute governing acquisitions of shares in all corporations incorporated in the state. This statute requires that any acquisition of more than 25% of the voting shares of a corporation incorporated in the state that occurs over a period of less than one year must be approved by the shareholders of record of a majority of the shares of the corporation as of the day before the commencement of the acquisition of those shares. The statute expressly applies to acquisitions of in-state corporations by both in-state and out-of-state entities. Assume that no federal statute applies. Is this state statute constitutional?

(A) No, because one of the purposes of the statute is to prevent out-of-state entities from acquiring corporations incorporated and headquartered in the state.

(B) No, because the effect of the statute will necessarily be to hinder the acquisition of in-state corporations by other corporations, many of whose shareholders are not residents of the state and, therefore, it will adversely affect the interstate sale of securities.

(C) Yes, because the statute imposes the same burden on both in-state and out-of-state entities wishing to acquire a corporation in the state, it regulates only the acquisition of in-state corporations, and it does not create an impermissible risk of inconsistent regulation on this subject by different states.

(D) Yes, because corporations exist only by virtue of state law and, therefore, the negative implications of the Commerce Clause do not apply to state regulations governing their creation and acquisition.

3. As a prohibition on discrimination against foreign commerce

Question 31

In response to massive layoffs of employees of automobile assembly plants located in the state of Ames, the legislature of that state enacted a statute which prohibits the parking of automobiles manufactured outside of the United States in any parking lot or parking structure that is owned or operated by the state or any of its instrumentalities. This statute does not apply to parking on public streets.

Which of the following is the strongest argument with which to challenge the constitutionality of this statute?

(A) The statute imposes an undue burden on foreign commerce.

(B) The statute denies the owners of foreign-made automobiles the equal protection of the laws.

(C) The statute deprives the owners of foreign-made automobiles of liberty or property without due process of law.

(D) The statute is inconsistent with the Privileges or Immunities Clause of the Fourteenth Amendment.

II. CONGRESSIONAL PRE-EMPTION AND CONSENT; THE SUPREMACY CLAUSE

A. The Supremacy Clause and federal pre-emption

1. Direct conflict

a. Where Congress forbids and the state allows

Question 32

Congressional hearings determined that the use of mechanical power hammers is very dangerous to the persons using them and to persons in the vicinity of the persons using them. As a result, Congress enacted a statute prohibiting the use of mechanical power hammers on all construction projects in the United States. Subsequently, a study conducted by a private research firm concluded that nails driven by mechanical power hammers have longer-lasting joining power than hand-driven nails. After learning about this study, the city council of the city of Green enacted an amendment to its building safety code requiring the use of mechanical power hammers in the construction of all buildings intended for human habitation.

This amendment to the city of Green's building safety code is

(A) unconstitutional, because it was enacted subsequent to the federal statute.

(B) unconstitutional, because it conflicts with the provisions of the federal statute.

(C) constitutional, because the federal statute does not expressly indicate that it supersedes inconsistent state or local laws.

(D) constitutional, because the long-term safety of human habitations justifies some additional risk to the people engaged in their construction.

b. Conflict between federal and state aims

Question 33

The United States Department of the Interior granted the plaintiff the food and drink concession in a federal park located in the state of Purple. The plaintiff operated his concession out of federally owned facilities in the park. The federal statute authorizing the Interior Department to grant such concessions provided that the grantees would pay only a nominal rental for use of these federal facilities because of the great benefit their concessions would provide to the people of the United States.

The legislature of the state of Purple enacted a statute imposing an occupancy tax on the occupants of real estate within that state that is not subject to state real estate taxes. The statute was intended to equalize the state tax burden on such occupants with that on people occupying real estate that is subject to state real estate taxes. Pursuant to that statute, the Purple Department of Revenue attempted to collect the state occupancy tax from the plaintiff because the federal facilities occupied by the plaintiff were not subject to state real estate taxes. The plaintiff sued to invalidate the state occupancy tax as applied to him.

The strongest ground upon which the plaintiff could challenge the occupancy tax is that it violates the

(A) Commerce Clause by unduly burdening the interstate tourist trade.

(B) Privileges or Immunities Clause of the Fourteenth Amendment by interfering with the fundamental right to do business on federal property.

(C) Equal Protection of the Laws Clause of the Fourteenth Amendment because the tax treats him less favorably than federal concessionaires in other states who do not have to pay such occupancy taxes.

(D) Supremacy Clause of Article VI and the federal statute authorizing such concessions.

Question 34

Road Lines is an interstate bus company operating in a five-state area. A federal statute authorizes the Interstate Commerce Commission (ICC) to permit interstate carriers to discontinue entirely any unprofitable route. Road Lines applied to the ICC for permission to drop a very unprofitable route through the sparsely populated Shaley Mountains. The ICC granted that permission even though Road Lines provided the only public transportation into the region.

Foley is the owner of a mountain resort in the Shaley Mountains, whose customers usually arrived on vehicles operated by Road Lines. After exhausting all available federal administrative remedies, Foley filed suit against Road Lines in the trial court of the state in which the Shaley Mountains are located to enjoin the discontinuance by Road Lines of its service to that area. Foley alleged that the discontinuance of service by Road Lines would violate a statute of that state prohibiting common carriers of persons from abandoning service to communities having no alternate form of public transportation.

The state court should

(A) dismiss the action, because Foley lacks standing to sue.

(B) direct the removal of the case to federal court, because this suit involves a substantial federal question.

(C) hear the case on its merits and decide for Foley because, on these facts, a federal agency is interfering with essential state functions.

(D) hear the case on its merits and decide for Road Lines, because a valid federal law preempts the state statute on which Foley relies.

2. **Congressional pre-emption**

   a. **Where there is federal occupation of the field**

      i. **Pre-emption of state common law**

Question 35

Lee contracted with Mover, an interstate carrier, to ship household goods from the state of Green to his new home in the state of Pink. A federal statute provides that all liability of an interstate mover to a shipper for loss of or damage to the shipper's goods in transit is governed exclusively by the contract between them. The statute also requires the mover to offer a shipper at least two contracts with different levels of liability. In full compliance with that federal statute, Mover offered Lee a choice between two shipping agreements that provided different levels of liability on the part of Mover. The more expensive contract provided that Mover was fully liable in case of loss or damage. The less expensive contract limited Mover's liability in case of loss or damage to less than full value. Lee voluntarily signed the less expensive contract with Mover, fixing Mover's liability at less than the full value of the shipment.

Mover's truck was involved in an accident in the state of Pink. The accident was entirely a product of the negligence of Mover's driver. Lee's household goods were totally destroyed. In accordance with the contract, Mover reimbursed Lee for less than the full value of the goods. Lee then brought suit against Mover under the tort law of the state of Pink claiming that he was entitled to be reimbursed for the full value of the goods. Mover filed a motion to dismiss.

In this suit, the court should

(A) dismiss the case, because the federal statute governing liability of interstate carriers is the supreme law of the land and preempts state tort law.

(B) dismiss the case, because the contractual relationship between Lee and Mover is governed by the Obligation of Contracts Clause of the Constitution.

(C) deny the motion to dismiss, because the Full Faith and Credit Clause of the Constitution requires that state tort law be given effect.

(D) deny the motion to dismiss, because it is unconstitutional for a federal statute to authorize Mover to contract out of any degree of liability for its own negligence.

3. Where there is no conflict between the federal and state schemes

Question 36

Radon is a harmful gas found in the soil of certain regions of the United States. A statute of the state of Magenta requires occupants of residences with basements susceptible to the intrusion of radon to have their residences tested for the presence of radon and to take specified remedial steps if the test indicates the presence of radon above specified levels. The statute also provides that the testing for radon may be done only by testers licensed by a state agency. According to the statute, a firm may be licensed to test for radon only if it meets specified rigorous standards relating to the accuracy of its testing. These standards may easily be achieved with current technology; but the technology required to meet them is 50% more expensive than the technology required to measure radon accumulations in a slightly less accurate manner.

The United States Environmental Protection Agency (EPA) does not license radon testers. However, a federal statute authorizes the EPA to advise on the accuracy of various methods of radon testing and to provide to the general public a list of testers that use methods it believes to be reasonably accurate.

WeTest, a recently established Magenta firm, uses a testing method that the EPA has stated is reasonably accurate. WeTest is also included by the EPA on the list of testers using methods of testing it believes to be reasonably accurate. WeTest applies for a Magenta radon testing license, but its application is denied because WeTest cannot demonstrate that the method of testing for radon it uses is sufficiently accurate to meet the rigorous Magenta statutory standards. WeTest sues appropriate Magenta officials in federal court claiming that Magenta may not constitutionally exclude WeTest from performing the required radon tests in Magenta.

In this suit, the court will probably rule in favor of

(A) WeTest, because the Full Faith and Credit Clause of the Constitution requires Magenta to respect and give effect to the action of the EPA in including WeTest on its list of testers that use reasonably accurate methods.

(B) WeTest, because the Supremacy Clause of the Constitution requires Magenta to respect and give effect to the action of the EPA in including WeTest on its list of testers that use reasonably accurate methods.

(C) Magenta, because the federal statute and the action of the EPA in including WeTest on its list of testers that use reasonably accurate methods are not inconsistent with the more rigorous Magenta licensing requirement, and that requirement is reasonably related to a legitimate public interest.

(D) Magenta, because radon exposure is limited to basement areas, which, by their very nature, cannot move in interstate commerce.

B. Consent by Congress to the state regulatory scheme

Question 37

A state legislature conducted an investigation into a series of fatal accidents in the state involving commercial trucks with trailer exteriors made of polished aluminum. The investigation revealed that the sun's glare off of these trucks blinded the drivers of other vehicles. The state's legislature then enacted a law prohibiting commercial trucks with polished aluminum trailer exteriors from traveling on the state's highways.

Litigation over the state law resulted in a final decision by the United States Supreme Court that the law impermissibly burdened interstate commerce and, therefore, was unconstitutional. Congress later enacted a statute permitting any state to enact a law regulating the degree of light reflectiveness of the exteriors of commercial trucks using the state's highways.

Is this federal statute constitutional?

(A) No, because the U.S. Supreme Court has already determined that state laws of this type impermissibly burden interstate commerce.

(B) No, because Article III vests the judicial power in the federal courts, the essence of judicial power is the ability to render a final judgment, and this statute overrules a final judgment of the federal Supreme Court.

(C) Yes, because Article I, Section 8 grants Congress authority to enact statutes authorizing states to impose burdens on interstate commerce that would otherwise be prohibited.

(D) Yes, because Article I, Section 8 grants Congress authority to enact statutes for the general welfare, and Congress could reasonably believe that state laws regulating the light reflectiveness of the exteriors of trucks promote the general welfare.

Question 38

A federal statute provides that the cities in which certain specified airports are located may regulate the rates and services of all limousines that serve those airports, without regard to the origin or destination of the passengers who use the limousines.

The cities of Redville and Greenville are located adjacent to each other in different states. The airport serving both of them is located in Redville and is one of those airports specified in the federal statute. The Redville City Council has adopted a rule that requires any limousines serving the airport to charge only the rates authorized by the Redville City Council.

Airline Limousine Service has a lucrative business transporting passengers between Greenville and the airport in Redville, at much lower rates than those required by the Redville City Council. It transports passengers in interstate traffic only; it does not provide local service within Redville. The new rule adopted by the Redville City Council will require Airline Limousine Service to charge the same rates as limousines operating only in Redville.

Must Airline Limousine Service comply with the new rule of the Redville City Council?

(A) Yes, because the airport is located in Redville and, therefore, its city council has exclusive regulatory authority over all transportation to and from the airport.

(B) Yes, because Congress has authorized this form of regulation by Redville and, therefore, removed any constitutional impediments to it that may have otherwise existed.

(C) No, because the rule would arbitrarily destroy a lucrative existing business and, therefore, would amount to a taking without just compensation.

(D) No, because Airline Limousine Service is engaged in interstate commerce and this rule is an undue burden on that commerce.

Question 39

The United States Congress enacted a federal statute providing that any state may "require labeling to show the state or other geographic origin of citrus fruit that is imported into the receiving state." Pursuant to the federal statute, a state that produced large quantities of citrus fruit enacted a law requiring all citrus fruit imported into the state to be stamped with a two-letter postal abbreviation signifying the state of the fruit's origin. The law did not impose any such requirement for citrus fruit grown within the state. When it adopted the law, the state legislature declared that its purpose was to reduce the risks of infection of local citrus crops by itinerant diseases that have been found to attack citrus fruit. A national association of citrus growers sued to have the state law declared unconstitutional. The association claims that the law is prohibited by the negative implications of the Commerce Clause of the Constitution.

Which of the following is the best argument in favor of the state's effort to have this lawsuit dismissed?

(A) Any burden on interstate commerce imposed by the state law is outweighed by a legitimate state interest.

(B) Congress has the authority to authorize specified state regulations that would otherwise be prohibited by the negative implications of the Commerce Clause, and it has done so in this situation.

(C) The state law does not discriminate against out-of-state citrus growers or producers.

(D) The state law furthers a legitimate state interest, the burden it imposes on interstate commerce is only incidental, and the state's interest cannot be satisfied by other means that are less burdensome to interstate commerce.

CHAPTER 4

INTERGOVERNMENTAL IMMUNITIES; INTERSTATE RELATIONS

I. TAX AND REGULATORY IMMUNITIES

A. Several types of immunities

1. Federal immunity from state regulation

Question 40

A federally owned and operated office building in the state of Red is heated with a new, pollution-free heating system. However, in the coldest season of the year, this new system is sometimes insufficient to supply adequate heat to the building. The appropriation statute providing the money for construction of the new heating system permitted use of the old, pollution-generating system when necessary to supply additional heat. When the old heating system operates (only about two days in any year), the smokestack of the building emits smoke that exceeds the state of Red's pollution-control standards.

May the operators of the federal office building be prosecuted successfully by Red authorities for violating that state's pollution control standards?

(A) Yes, because the regulation of pollution is a legitimate state police power concern.

(B) Yes, because the regulation of pollution is a joint concern of the federal government and the state and, therefore, both of them may regulate conduct causing pollution.

(C) No, because the operations of the federal government are immune from state regulation in the absence of federal consent.

(D) No, because the violations of the state pollution-control standards involved here are so *de minimis* that they are beyond the legitimate reach of state law.

Question 41

The United States Department of Energy regularly transports nuclear materials through Centerville on the way to a nuclear weapons processing plant it operates in a nearby state. The city of Centerville recently adopted an ordinance prohibiting the transportation of any nuclear materials in or through the city. The ordinance declares that its purpose is to protect the health and safety of the residents of that city.

May the Department of Energy continue to transport these nuclear materials through the city of Centerville?

(A) No, because the ordinance is rationally related to the public health and safety of Centerville residents.

(B) No, because the Tenth Amendment reserves to the states certain unenumerated sovereign powers.

(C) Yes, because the Department of Energy is a federal agency engaged in a lawful federal function and, therefore, its activities may not be regulated by a local government without the consent of Congress.

(D) Yes, because the ordinance enacted by Centerville is invalid because it denies persons transporting such materials the equal protection of the laws.

II. THE FULL FAITH AND CREDIT CLAUSE

A. Effect of Clause

1. Obligation of second state to enforce collection of money judgment issued by first state

Question 42

The state of Red sent three of its employees to a city located in the state of Blue to consult with a chemical laboratory there about matters of state business. While in the course of their employment, the three employees of Red negligently released into local Blue waterways some of the chemical samples they had received from the laboratory in Blue.

Persons in Blue injured by the release of the chemicals sued the three Red state employees and the state of Red in Blue state courts for the damages they suffered. After a trial in which all of the defendants admitted jurisdiction of the Blue state court and fully participated, plaintiffs received a judgment against all of the defendants for $5 million, which became final.

Subsequently, plaintiffs sought to enforce their Blue state court judgment by commencing a proper proceeding in an appropriate court of Red. In that enforcement proceeding, the state of Red argued, as it had done unsuccessfully in the earlier action in Blue state court, that its liability is limited by a law of Red to $100,000 in any tort case. Because the three individual employees of Red are able to pay only $50,000 of the judgment, the only way the injured persons can fully satisfy their Blue state court judgment is from the funds of the state of Red.

Can the injured persons recover the full balance of their Blue state court judgment from the state of Red in the enforcement proceeding they filed in a court of Red?

(A) Yes, because the final judgment of the Blue court is entitled to full faith and credit in the courts of Red.

(B) Yes, because a limitation on damage awards against Red for tortious actions of its agents would violate the Equal Protection Clause of the Fourteenth Amendment.

(C) No, because the Tenth Amendment preserves the right of a state to have its courts enforce the state's public policy limiting its tort liability.

(D) No, because the employees of Red were negligent and, therefore, their actions were not authorized by the state of Red.

2. Where first state's judgment constitutes an error of law

Question 43

A man bought an antique car from a car dealer in State A. Under State A law, a person who buys from such a dealer acquires good title, even if the property was stolen from a previous owner. The man showed the car at an antique car show in State B. A woman recognized the car as having been stolen from her. Under State B law, a person whose property is stolen may reclaim it, even if the current possessor is an innocent purchaser. The woman sued the man in a State B court to reclaim the car. The man defended, claiming that he had good title under the law of State A. Nevertheless, the State B court applied State B law, and the woman prevailed. The man did not appeal. The sheriff gave the woman possession of the car. Several months later, the woman drove the car to State A. The man brought a new suit against the woman, claiming that the State B court in the prior suit should have applied the State A law, which protected innocent purchasers. The woman appeared and moved to dismiss the suit.

What should the State A court do?

(A) Apply the federal law of sale of goods, because the car has moved in interstate commerce.

(B) Apply the State A law, because the car is currently located in State A.

(C) Dismiss the suit, because the State A court must give full faith and credit to the State B judgment.

(D) Remove the case to federal court, because the car has moved in interstate commerce, and therefore the case raises a federal question.

CHAPTER 5
THE DUE PROCESS CLAUSE

I. SUBSTANTIVE DUE PROCESS — ECONOMIC AND SOCIAL WELFARE REGULATION

A. Economic and social welfare regulation

1. Easy test to satisfy

Question 44

A state statute requires each insurance company that offers burglary insurance policies in the state to charge a uniform rate for such insurance to all of its customers residing within the same county in that state. So long as it complies with this requirement, a company is free to charge whatever rate the market will bear for its burglary insurance policies.

An insurance company located in the state files suit in federal district court against appropriate state officials to challenge this statute on constitutional grounds. The insurance company wishes to charge customers residing within the same county in the state rates for burglary insurance policies that will vary because they would be based on the specific nature of the customer's business, on its precise location, and on its past claims record.

In this suit, the court should

(A) hold the statute unconstitutional, because the statute deprives the insurance company of its liberty or property without due process of law.

(B) hold the statute unconstitutional, because the statute imposes an undue burden on interstate commerce.

(C) hold the statute constitutional, because the statute is a reasonable exercise of the state's police power.

(D) abstain from ruling on the merits of this case until the state courts have had an opportunity to pass on the constitutionality of this state statute.

II. SUBSTANTIVE DUE PROCESS — REGULATIONS AFFECTING FUNDAMENTAL RIGHTS

A. Abortion

1. Requirement of parental consent where patient is a minor

Question 45

A state statute requires, without exception, that a woman under the age of 18 notify one of her parents at least 48 hours before having an abortion. A proper lawsuit challenges the constitutionality of this state statute.

In that suit, should the court uphold the constitutionality of the statute?

(A) No, because a 48-hour waiting period is excessively long and, therefore, it imposes an undue burden on a woman's right to procure an abortion.

(B) No, because the state law does not provide a bypass procedure that would allow a court to authorize a minor to obtain an abortion without prior parental notification under appropriate circumstances.

(C) Yes, because parents' rights to supervise their minor daughter's health care outweighs any individual right she may have.

(D) Yes, because such parental notification and waiting-period requirements do not impose an undue burden on a minor's right to procure an abortion.

2. Public funding of abortion

Question 46

A state statute prohibits the use of state-owned or state-operated facilities for the performance of abortions that are not "necessary to save the life of the mother." That statute also prohibits state employees from performing any such abortions during the hours they are employed by the state.

A woman was in her second month of pregnancy. She sought an abortion at a state-owned and state-operated hospital. The woman did not claim that the requested abortion was necessary to save her life. The officials in charge of the hospital refused to perform the requested abortion solely on the basis of the state statute. The woman immediately filed suit against those officials in an appropriate federal district court. She challenged the constitutionality of the state statute and requested the court to order the hospital to perform the abortion she sought. In this case, the court will probably hold that the state statute is

(A) unconstitutional, because a limit on the availability of abortions performed by state employees or in state-owned or state-operated facilities to situations in which it is necessary to save the life of the mother impermissibly interferes with the fundamental right of the woman to decide whether to have a child.

(B) unconstitutional, because it impermissibly discriminates against poor persons who cannot afford to pay for abortions in privately owned and operated facilities and against persons who live far away from privately owned and operated abortion clinics.

(C) constitutional, because it does not prohibit a woman from having an abortion or penalize her for doing so, it is rationally related to the legitimate governmental goal of encouraging childbirth, and it does not unduly burden the voluntary performance of abortions by private physicians in private facilities.

(D) constitutional, because the use of state-owned or state-operated facilities and access to the services of state employees are privileges and not rights and, therefore, a state may condition them on any basis it chooses.

III. PROCEDURAL DUE PROCESS

A. Process required

1. Stage at which hearing must be provided

Question 47

A state statute declares that after five years of continuous service in their positions all state employees, including faculty members at the state university, are entitled to retain their positions during "good behavior." The statute also contains a number of procedural provisions. Any state employee who is dismissed after that five-year period must be given reasons for the dismissal before it takes effect. In addition, such an employee must, upon request, be granted a post-dismissal hearing before an administrative board to seek reinstatement and back pay. The statute precludes any other hearing or opportunity to respond to the charges. That post-dismissal hearing must occur within six months after the dismissal takes effect. The burden of proof at such a hearing is on the state, and the board may uphold the dismissal only if it is supported by a preponderance of the evidence. An employee who is dissatisfied with a decision of the board after a hearing may appeal its decision to the state courts. The provisions of this statute are inseverable.

A teacher who had been employed continuously for seven years as a faculty member at the state university was dismissed. A week before the dismissal took effect, she was informed that she was being dismissed because of a charge that she accepted a bribe from a student in return for raising the student's final grade in her course. At that time she requested an immediate hearing to contest the propriety of her dismissal.

Three months after her dismissal, she was granted a hearing before the state administrative board. The board upheld her dismissal, finding that the charge against her was supported by a preponderance of the evidence presented at the hearing.

The faculty member did not appeal the decision of the state administrative board to the state courts. Instead, she sought a declaratory judgment in federal district court to the effect that the state statute prescribing the procedures for her dismissal is unconstitutional.

In this case, the federal district court should

(A) dismiss the suit, because a claim that a state statute is unconstitutional is not ripe for adjudication by a federal court until all judicial remedies in state courts provided for by state law have been exhausted.

(B) hold the statute unconstitutional, because the Due Process Clause of the Fourteenth Amendment requires a state to demonstrate beyond a reasonable doubt the facts constituting good cause for termination of a state employee.

(C) hold the statute unconstitutional, because a state may not ordinarily deprive an employee of a property interest in a job without giving the employee an opportunity for some kind of pre-dismissal hearing to respond to the charges against that employee.

(D) hold the statute constitutional, because the Due Process Clause of the Fourteenth Amendment entitles state employees who have a right to their jobs during good behavior only to a statement of reasons for their dismissal and an opportunity for a post-dismissal hearing.

EQUAL PROTECTION

I. ECONOMIC AND SOCIAL LAWS—THE "MERE RATIONALITY" TEST

A. Applies where government makes a classification

Question 48

A realty company acquired a large tract of land upon which it developed a mobile home subdivision. The tract was divided into 60 lots, appropriate utilities were installed, and a plat of the entire tract, including a Declaration of Restrictions, was properly drawn and recorded. The Declaration of Restrictions included the following: "3. Ownership and/or occupancy are restricted to persons 21 years of age or over; one family per lot." As the separate lots were sold, the deed to each lot included the following provision: "As shown on recorded plat [properly identified by page and plat book reference] and subject to the restrictions therein contained." One of the lots was purchased by a carpenter, who now resides in a mobile home on the lot together with his wife and two children, aged 11 and 13. Other lot owners in the subdivision brought action against the carpenter to enjoin further occupancy by the children under 21 years of age. If judgment is for the carpenter, the issue that most likely will determine the case will be whether

(A) the mobile home is treated as personalty or realty.

(B) the restriction constitutes an unlawful restraint on alienation.

(C) enforcement of the restriction is considered a violation of the Equal Protection Clause of the Fourteenth Amendment of the U.S. Constitution.

(D) the terms of the restriction are expressly repeated verbatim in the carpenter's deed.

B. Non-suspect, non-fundamental rights (economic and social legislation)

1. "Grandfather clause" as rational classification

Question 49

A city has had a severe traffic problem on its streets. As a result, it enacted an ordinance prohibiting all sales to the public of food or other items by persons selling directly from trucks, cars, or other vehicles located on city streets. The ordinance included an inseverable grandfather provision exempting from its prohibition vendors who, for 20 years or more, have continuously sold food or other items from such vehicles located on the streets of the city.

A retail ice cream vendor qualifies for this exemption and is the only food vendor that does. A yogurt company is a business similar to the ice cream company, but the yogurt company has been selling to the public directly from trucks located on the streets of the city only for the past ten years. The yogurt company filed suit in an appropriate federal district court to enjoin enforcement of this ordinance on the ground that it denies the yogurt company the equal protection of the laws.

In this case, the court will probably rule that the ordinance is

(A) constitutional, because it is narrowly tailored to implement the city's compelling interest in reducing traffic congestion and, therefore, satisfies the strict scrutiny test applicable to such cases.

(B) constitutional, because its validity is governed by the rational basis test, and the courts consistently defer to economic choices embodied in such legislation if they are even plausibly justifiable.

(C) unconstitutional, because the nexus between the legitimate purpose of the ordinance and the conduct it prohibits is so tenuous and its provisions are so underinclusive that the ordinance fails to satisfy the substantial relationship test applicable to such cases.

(D) unconstitutional, because economic benefits or burdens imposed by legislatures on the basis of grandfather provisions have consistently been declared invalid by courts as per se violations of the Equal Protection Clause of the Fourteenth Amendment.

2. Non-suspect classes

a. Status as convicted criminal

Question 50

A city zoning ordinance requires anyone who proposes to operate a group home to obtain a special use permit from the city zoning board. The zoning ordinance defines a group home as a residence in which four or more unrelated adults reside. An individual applied for a special use permit to operate a group home for convicts during their transition from serving prison sentences to their release on parole. Although the proposed group home met all of the requirements for the special use permit, the zoning board denied the individual's application because of the nature of the proposed use. The individual sued the zoning board seeking declaratory and injunctive relief on constitutional grounds.

Which of the following best states the appropriate burden of persuasion in this action?

(A) Because housing is a fundamental right, the zoning board must demonstrate that denial of the permit is necessary to serve a compelling state interest.

(B) Because the zoning board's action has the effect of discriminating against a quasi-suspect class in regard to a basic subsistence right, the zoning board must demonstrate that the denial of the permit is substantially related to an important state interest.

(C) Because the zoning board's action invidiously discriminates against a suspect class, the zoning board must demonstrate that denial of the permit is necessary to serve a compelling state interest.

(D) Because the zoning board's action is in the nature of an economic or social welfare regulation, the individual seeking the permit must demonstrate that the denial of the permit is not rationally related to a legitimate state interest.

II.   SUSPECT CLASSIFICATIONS, ESPECIALLY RACE

A. Classifications based on race

Question 51

The United States government demonstrated that terrorist attacks involving commercial airliners were perpetrated exclusively by individuals of one particular race. In response, Congress enacted a statute imposing stringent new airport and airline security measures only on individuals of that race seeking to board airplanes in the United States.

Which of the following provides the best ground for challenging the constitutionality of this statute?

(A) The Commerce Clause of Article I, Section 8.

(B) The Due Process Clause of the Fifth Amendment.

(C) The Privileges and Immunities Clause of Article IV.

(D) The Privileges or Immunities Clause of the Fourteenth Amendment.

1. Requirement that discrimination be purposeful

a. Peremptory jury challenges

Question 52

The executive director of an equal housing opportunity organization was the leader of a sit-in at the offices of a real estate management company. The protest was designed to call attention to the company's racially discriminatory rental practices. When police demanded that the director desist from trespassing on the company's property, she refused and was arrested. In her trial for trespass, the prosecution peremptorily excused all non-whites from the jury, arguing to the court that even though the director was white, minority groups would automatically support her because of her fight against racism in housing accommodations.

If the director is convicted of trespass by an all-white jury and appeals, claiming a violation of her constitutional rights, the court should

(A) affirm the conviction, because the director was not a member of the class discriminated against.

(B) affirm the conviction, because peremptory challenge of the non-whites did not deny the director the right to an impartial jury.

(C) reverse the conviction, because racially based peremptory challenges violate equal protection of the law.

(D) reverse the conviction, because the director was denied the right to have her case heard by a fair cross-section of the community.

III. MIDDLE-LEVEL REVIEW (GENDER, ILLEGITIMACY AND ALIENAGE)

A. Classifications based on gender

Question 53

A public high school has had a very high rate of pregnancy among its students. In order to assist students who keep their babies to complete high school, the high school has established an infant day-care center for children of its students, and also offers classes in child care. Because the child-care classes are always overcrowded, the school limits admission to those classes solely to students at the high school who are the mothers of babies in the infant day-care center.

A male student at the high school has legal custody of his infant son. The school provides care for his son in the infant day-care center, but will not allow the male student to enroll in the child-care classes. He brings suit against the school challenging, on constitutional grounds, his exclusion from the child-care classes.

Which of the following best states the burden of persuasion in this case?

(A) The student must demonstrate that the admission requirement is not rationally related to a legitimate governmental interest.

(B) The student must demonstrate that the admission requirement is not as narrowly drawn as possible to achieve a substantial governmental interest.

(C) The school must demonstrate that the admission policy is the least restrictive means by which to achieve a compelling governmental interest.

(D) The school must demonstrate that the admission policy is substantially related to an important governmental interest.

IV. FUNDAMENTAL RIGHTS

A. Voting rights

1. Fifteenth Amendment

Question 54

Twenty percent of the residents of Green City are members of minority racial groups. These residents are evenly distributed among the many different residential areas of the city. The five city council members of Green City are elected from five single-member electoral districts that are nearly equally populated. No candidate has ever been elected to the city council who was a member of a minority racial group.

A group of citizens who are members of minority racial groups file suit in federal district court seeking a declaratory judgment that the single-member districts in Green City are unconstitutional. They claim that the single-member districting system in that city diminishes the ability of voters who are members of minority racial groups to affect the outcome of city elections. They seek an order from the court forcing the city to adopt an at-large election system in which the five candidates with the greatest vote totals would be elected to the city council. No state or federal statutes are applicable to the resolution of this suit.

Which of the following constitutional provisions provides the most obvious basis for plaintiffs' claim in this suit?

(A) The Thirteenth Amendment.

(B) The Due Process Clause of the Fourteenth Amendment.

(C) The Privileges or Immunities Clause of the Fourteenth Amendment.

(D) The Fifteenth Amendment.

B. Ballot access

1. Where ballot restriction may be unfair to new parties or independent candidates

Question 55

A state has a statute providing that an unsuccessful candidate in a primary election for a party's nomination for elected public office may not become a candidate for the same office at the following general election by nominating petition or by write-in votes.

A woman sought her party's nomination for governor in the May primary election. After losing in the primary, the woman filed nominating petitions containing the requisite number of signatures to become a candidate for the office of governor in the following general election. The chief elections officer of the state refused to certify the woman's petitions solely because of the above statute. The woman then filed suit in federal district court challenging the constitutionality of this state statute.

As a matter of constitutional law, which of the following is the proper burden of persuasion in this suit?

(A) The woman must demonstrate that the statute is not necessary to achieve a compelling state interest.

(B) The woman must demonstrate that the statute is not rationally related to a legitimate state interest.

(C) The state must demonstrate that the statute is the least restrictive means of achieving a compelling state interest.

(D) The state must demonstrate that the statute is rationally related to a legitimate state interest.

Question 56

A state statute permits a person's name to appear on the general election ballot as a candidate for statewide public office if the person pays a $100 filing fee and provides proof from the State Elections Board that he or she was nominated in the immediately preceding primary election by one of the state's two major political parties. It also permits the name of an independent candidate or a candidate of a smaller party to appear on the general election ballot if that person pays a filing fee of $1,000, and submits petitions signed by at least 3% of the voters who actually cast ballots for the office of governor in the last state election. The state maintains that these filing requirements are necessary to limit the size of the election ballot, to eliminate frivolous candidacies, and to help finance the high cost of elections.

Historically, very few of the state's voters who are members of racial minority groups have been members of either of the two major political parties. Recently, a new political party has been formed by some of these voters. Which of the following constitutional provisions would be most helpful to the new political party as a basis for attacking the constitutionality of this statute?

(A) The First Amendment.

(B) The Thirteenth Amendment.

(C) The Fourteenth Amendment.

(D) The Fifteenth Amendment.

C. Necessities

1. Education as a necessity

Question 57

Public schools in a state are financed, in large part, by revenue derived from real estate taxes imposed by each school district on the taxable real property located in that district. Public schools also receive other revenue from private gifts, federal grants, student fees, and local sales taxes. For many years, the state has distributed additional funds, which come from the state treasury, to local school districts in order to equalize the funds available on a per-student basis for each public school district. These additional funds are distributed on the basis of a state statutory formula that considers only the number of students in each public school district and the real estate tax revenue raised by that district. The formula does not consider other revenue received by a school district from different sources.

The school boards of two school districts, together with parents and schoolchildren in those districts, bring suit in federal court to enjoin the state from allocating the additional funds from the state treasury to individual districts pursuant to this formula. They allege that the failure of the state, in allocating this additional money, to take into account a school district's sources of revenue other than revenue derived from taxes levied on real estate located there violates the Equal Protection Clause of the Fourteenth Amendment. The complaint does not allege that the allocation of the additional state funds based on the current statutory formula has resulted in a failure to provide minimally adequate education to any child.

Which of the following best describes the appropriate standard by which the court should review the constitutionality of the state statutory funding formula?

(A) Because classifications based on wealth are inherently suspect, the state must demonstrate that the statutory formula is necessary to vindicate a compelling slate interest.

(B) Because the statutory funding formula burdens the fundamental right to education, the state must demonstrate that the formula is necessary to vindicate a compelling state interest.

(C) Because no fundamental right or suspect classification is implicated in this case, the plaintiffs must demonstrate that the funding allocation formula bears no rational relationship to any legitimate state interest.

(D) Because the funding formula inevitably leads to disparities among the school districts in their levels of total funding, the plaintiffs must only demonstrate that the funding formula is not substantially related to the furtherance of an important state interest.

MISCELLANEOUS CLAUSES

I. THE "TAKING" CLAUSE

A. The "Taking" Clause generally

1. Taking vs. regulation

Question 58

A company that operated a supermarket wanted to expand the size of the building it owned that housed the supermarket, by adding space for a coffeehouse. The company's building was located in the center of five acres of land owned by the company and devoted wholly to parking for its supermarket customers.

City officials refused to grant a required building permit for the coffeehouse addition unless the company established in its store a child care center that would take up space at least equal to the size of the proposed coffeehouse addition, which was to be 20% of the existing building. This action of the city officials was authorized by provisions of the applicable zoning ordinance. In a suit filed in state court against appropriate officials of the city, the company challenged the child care center requirement solely on constitutional grounds. The lower court upheld the requirement even though city officials presented no evidence and made no findings to justify it other than a general assertion that there was a shortage of child care facilities in the city. The company appealed. The court hearing the appeal should hold that the requirement imposed by the city on the issuance of this building permit is

(A) constitutional, because the burden was on the company to demonstrate that there was no rational relationship between this requirement and a legitimate governmental interest, and the company could not do so because the requirement is reasonably related to improving the lives of families and children residing in the city.

(B) constitutional, because the burden was on the company to demonstrate that this requirement was not necessary to vindicate a compelling governmental interest, and the company could not do so on these facts.

(C) unconstitutional, because the burden was on the city to demonstrate that this requirement was necessary to vindicate a compelling governmental interest, and the city failed to meet its burden under that standard.

(D) unconstitutional, because the burden was on the city to demonstrate a rough proportionality between this requirement and the impact of the company's proposed action on the community, and the city failed to do so.

II. *EX POST FACTO* LAWS

A. Constitutional prohibition

1. Applies to penal regulations only

Question 59

A doctor, a resident of the city of Greenville in the state of Green, is a physician licensed to practice in both Green and the neighboring state of Red. The doctor finds that the most convenient place to treat her patients who need hospital care is in the publicly owned and operated municipal hospital of the city of Redville in the state of Red, which is located just across the state line from Greenville. For many years the doctor had successfully treated her patients in that hospital. Early this year she was notified that she could no longer treat patients in the Redville hospital because she was not a resident of Red, and a newly adopted rule of the Redville hospital, which was adopted in conformance with all required procedures, stated that every physician who practices in that hospital must be a resident of Red.

Which of the following constitutional provisions would be most helpful to the doctor in an action to challenge her exclusion from the Redville hospital solely on the basis of this hospital rule?

(A) The Bill of Attainder Clause.

(B) The Privileges and Immunities Clause of Article IV.

(C) The Due Process Clause of the Fourteenth Amendment.

(D) The Ex Post Facto Clause.

III. BILLS OF ATTAINDER

Question 60

Two tenured professors at a state university drafted a new university regulation prohibiting certain kinds of speech on campus. Students, staff, and faculty convicted by campus tribunals of violating the regulation were made subject to penalties that included fines, suspensions, expulsions, and termination of employment. The regulation was widely unpopular and there was a great deal of public anger directed toward the professors who drafted it. The following year, the state legislature approved a severable provision in the appropriations bill for the university declaring that none of the university's funding could be used to pay the two professors, who were specifically named in the provision. In the past, the professors' salaries had always been paid from funds appropriated to the university by the legislature, and the university had no other funds that could be used to pay them.

If the professors challenge the constitutionality of the appropriations provision, is the court likely to uphold the provision?

(A) No, because it amounts to the imposition of a punishment by the legislature without trial.

(B) No, because it was based on conduct the professors engaged in before it was enacted.

(C) Yes, because the Eleventh Amendment gives the state legislature plenary power to appropriate state funds in the manner that it deems most conducive to the welfare of its people.

(D) Yes, because the Full Faith and Credit Clause requires the court to enforce the provision strictly according to its terms.

THE "STATE ACTION" REQUIREMENT; CONGRESS'S ENFORCEMENT OF THE CIVIL WAR AMENDMENTS

I. STATE ACTION

A. "State involvement" doctrine

1. Entanglement or entwinement as a form of state involvement

Question 61

Insurance is provided in a particular state only by private companies. Although the state insurance commissioner inspects insurance companies for solvency, the state does not regulate their rates or policies. A particular insurance company charges higher rates for burglary insurance to residents of one part of a county in the state than to residents of another section of the same county because of the different crime rates in those areas.

A resident of that county was charged the higher rate by the insurance company because of the location of her residence. The resident sues the insurance company, alleging that the differential in insurance rates unconstitutionally denies her the equal protection of the laws.

Will the resident's suit succeed?

(A) Yes, because the higher crime rate in the resident's neighborhood demonstrates that the county police are not giving persons who reside there the equal protection of the laws.

(B) Yes, because the insurance rate differential is inherently discriminatory.

(C) No, because the constitutional guarantee of equal protection of the laws is not applicable to the actions of these insurance companies.

(D) No, because there is a rational basis for the differential in insurance rates.

II. CONGRESSIONAL ENFORCEMENT OF CIVIL RIGHTS

A. Congress's power to reach private conduct

1. Thirteenth Amendment

a. "Badges of slavery"

Question 62

A proposed federal statute would prohibit all types of discrimination against black persons on the basis of their race in every business transaction executed anywhere in the United States by any person or entity, governmental or private.

Is this proposed federal statute likely to be constitutional?

(A) Yes, because it could reasonably be viewed as an exercise of Congress's authority to enact laws for the general welfare.

(B) Yes, because it could reasonably be viewed as a means of enforcing the provisions of the Thirteenth Amendment.

(C) No, because it would regulate purely local transactions that are not in interstate commerce.

(D) No, because it would invade the powers reserved to the states by the Tenth Amendment.

FREEDOM OF EXPRESSION

I. GENERAL THEMES

A. Analysis of content-based government action

1. "Viewpoint neutrality" not enough

Question 63

The Federal Family Film Enhancement Act assesses an excise tax of 10% on the price of admission to public movie theaters when they show films that contain actual or simulated scenes of human sexual intercourse.

Which of the following is the strongest argument against the constitutionality of this federal act?

(A) The act imposes a prior restraint on the freedom of speech protected by the First Amendment.

(B) The act is not rationally related to any legitimate national interest.

(C) The act violates the equal protection concepts embodied in the Due Process Clause of the Fifth Amendment because it imposes a tax on the price of admission to view certain films and not on the price of admission to view comparable live performances.

(D) The act imposes a tax solely on the basis of the content of speech without adequate justification and, therefore, it is prohibited by the Freedom of Speech Clause of the First Amendment.

II. TIME, PLACE AND MANNER REGULATIONS

A. Three-part test for time, place and manner regulations

Question 64

The owner of a milk container manufacturing firm sought to focus public attention on the milk packaging law of a state in order to have it repealed. On a weekday at 12:00 p.m., he delivered an excited, animated, and loud harangue on the steps of the state capitol building in front of the main entryway. An audience of 200 onlookers, who gathered on the steps, heckled him and laughed as he delivered his tirade. The owner repeatedly stated, gesturing expressively and making faces, that "the damned milk packaging law is stupid," and that "I will strangle every one of those damned legislators I can get hold of because this law they created proves they are all too dumb to live." After about 15 minutes, he stopped speaking, and the amused crowd dispersed.

There are three relevant statutes of the state. The first statute prohibits "all speech making, picketing, and public gatherings of every sort on the Capitol steps in front of the main entryway between 7:45 a.m.– 8:15 a.m., 11:45 a.m.–12:15 p.m., 12:45 p.m.–1:15 p.m., and 4:45 p.m.–5:15 p.m., on Capitol working days."

If the owner is prosecuted under the "Capitol steps" statute and defends on constitutional grounds, which of the following best describes the proper burden of proof?

(A) He would have to prove that the state did not have a rational basis for enacting this statute.

(B) He would have to prove that the state did not have a compelling need for this statute or that it had less restrictive means by which it could satisfy that need.

(C) The state would have to prove that it had a rational basis for enacting this statute.

(D) The state would have to prove that it had a compelling need for this statute and that there were no less restrictive means by which it could satisfy that need.

III. DEFAMATION AND INVASION OF PRIVACY

A. Other state-law tort claims as possible First Amendment violation

Question 65

Roberts, a professional motorcycle rider, put on a performance in a privately owned stadium during which he leaped his motorcycle over 21 automobiles. Spectators were charged $55 each to view the jump and were prohibited from using cameras. However, the local television station filmed the whole event from within the stadium without the knowledge or consent of Roberts and showed the film in its entirety on the evening newscast that day. Roberts thereafter brought suit to recover damages from the station for the admittedly unauthorized filming and broadcasting of the act. The television station raised only constitutional defenses.

The court should

(A) hold against Roberts, because the First and Fourteenth Amendments authorize press coverage of newsworthy entertainment events.

(B) hold against Roberts, because under the First and Fourteenth Amendments news broadcasts are absolutely privileged.

(C) find the station liable, because its action deprives Roberts of his property without due process.

(D) find the station liable, because the First and Fourteenth Amendments do not deprive an entertainer of the commercial value of his or her performances.

IV. OBSCENITY

A. Regulating secondary effects of adult speech

1. Regulation of red-light districts

Question 66

A city has an ordinance that prohibits the location of "adult theaters and bookstores" (theaters and bookstores presenting sexually explicit performances or materials) in residential or commercial zones within the city. The ordinance was intended to protect surrounding property from the likely adverse secondary effects of such establishments. "Adult theaters and bookstores" are freely permitted in the areas of the city zoned industrial, where those adverse secondary effects are not as likely. A storekeeper is denied a zoning permit to open an adult theater and bookstore in a building owned by him in an area zoned commercial. As a result, the storekeeper brings suit in an appropriate court challenging the constitutionality of the zoning ordinance.

Which of the following statements regarding the constitutionality of this city ordinance is most accurate?

(A) The ordinance is valid, because a city may enforce zoning restrictions on speech-related businesses to ensure that the messages they disseminate are acceptable to the residents of adjacent property.

(B) The ordinance is valid, because a city may enforce this type of time, place, and manner regulation on speech-related businesses, so long as this type of regulation is designed to serve a substantial governmental interest and does not unreasonably limit alternative avenues of communication.

(C) The ordinance is invalid, because a city may not enforce zoning regulations that deprive potential operators of adult theaters and bookstores of their freedom to choose the location of their businesses.

(D) The ordinance is invalid, because a city may not zone property in a manner calculated to protect property from the likely adverse secondary effects of adult theaters and bookstores.

Question 67

A city zoning ordinance contains provisions restricting places of "adult entertainment" to two specified city blocks within the commercial center of the city. These provisions of the ordinance define "adult entertainment" as "live or filmed nudity or sexual activity, real or simulated, of an indecent nature."

A promoter proposes to operate an adult entertainment establishment outside the two-block area zoned for such establishments but within the commercial center of the city. When his application for permission to do so is rejected solely because it is inconsistent with provisions of the zoning ordinance, he sues the appropriate city officials, seeking to enjoin them from enforcing the adult entertainment provisions of the ordinance against him. He asserts that these provisions of the ordinance violate the First Amendment as made applicable to the city by the Fourteenth Amendment. In this case, the court hearing the promoter's request for an injunction would probably hold that the adult entertainment provisions of the city zoning ordinance are

(A) constitutional, because they do not prohibit adult entertainment everywhere in the city, and the city has a substantial interest in keeping the major part of its commercial center free of uses it considers harmful to that area.

(B) constitutional, because adult entertainment of the kind described in these provisions of the city ordinance is not protected by the free speech guarantee of the First and Fourteenth Amendments.

(C) unconstitutional, because they prohibit in the commercial area of the city adult entertainment that is not "obscene" within the meaning of the First and Fourteenth Amendments.

(D) unconstitutional, because zoning ordinances that restrict freedom of speech may be justified only by a substantial interest in preserving the quality of a community's residential neighborhoods.

V. FREEDOM OF ASSOCIATION, AND DENIAL OF PUBLIC BENEFITS OR JOBS

A. Denial of public benefit or job

1. Denial of license

Question 68

A city ordinance requires every operator of a taxicab in the city to have a license and permits revocation of that license only for "good cause." The taxicab operator's licensing ordinance conditions the issuance of such a license on an agreement by the licensee that the licensee "not display in or on his or her vehicle any bumper sticker or other placard or sign favoring a particular candidate for any elected municipal office." The ordinance also states that it imposes this condition in order to prevent the possible imputation to the city council the views of its taxicab licensees and that any licensee who violates this condition shall have his or her license revoked.

A driver, who is a holder of a taxicab operator's license, decorates his cab with bumper stickers and other signs favoring specified candidates in a forthcoming election for municipal offices. A proceeding is initiated against him to revoke his taxicab operator's license on the sole basis of that admitted conduct. In this proceeding, does the driver have a meritorious defense based on the U.S. Constitution?

(A) No, because he accepted the license with knowledge of the condition and, therefore, has no standing to contest it.

(B) No, because a taxicab operator's license is a privilege and not a right and, therefore, is not protected by the Due Process Clause of the Fourteenth Amendment.

(C) Yes, because such a proceeding threatens the driver with a taking of property, his license, without just compensation.

(D) Yes, because the condition imposed on taxicab operators' licenses restricts political speech based wholly on its content, without any adequate governmental justification.

2. Speech critical of superiors or otherwise inappropriate

a. Where speaker is in a non-policy-making role

Question 69

A clerical worker has been employed for the past two years in a permanent position in the Public Records Office of a county. The clerk has been responsible for copying and filing records of real estate transactions in that office. The clerk works in a nonpublic part of the office and has no contact with members of the public. However, state law provides that all real estate records in that office are to be made available for public inspection.

On the day an attempted assassination of the governor of the state was reported on the radio, the clerk remarked to a coworker, "Our governor is such an evil man, I am sorry they did not get him." The clerk's coworker reported this remark to the clerk's employer, the county recorder. After the clerk admitted making the remark, the county recorder dismissed him stating that "there is no room in this office for a person who hates the governor so much."

The clerk sued for reinstatement and back pay. His only claim is that the dismissal violated his constitutional rights.

In this case, the court should hold that the county recorder's dismissal of the clerk was

(A) unconstitutional, because it constitutes a taking without just compensation of the clerk's property interest in his permanent position with the county.

(B) unconstitutional, because in light of the clerk's particular employment duties his right to express himself on a matter of public concern outweighed any legitimate interest the state might have had in discharging him.

(C) constitutional, because the compelling interest of the state in having loyal and supportive employees outweighs the interest of any state employee in his or her job or in free speech on a matter of public concern.

(D) nonjusticiable, because public employment is a privilege rather than a right and, therefore, the clerk lacked standing to bring this suit.

b. Where speech interferes with speaker's job performance

Question 70

A city ordinance makes the city building inspector responsible for ensuring that all buildings in that city are kept up to building code standards, and requires the inspector to refer for prosecution all known building code violations. Another ordinance provides that the city building inspector may be discharged for "good cause." The building inspector took a newspaper reporter through a number of rundown buildings in a slum neighborhood. After using various epithets and slurs to describe the occupants of these buildings, the building inspector stated to the reporter: "I do not even try to get these buildings up to code or to have their owners prosecuted for code violations because if these buildings are repaired, the people who live in them will just wreck them again." The reporter published these statements in a story in the local newspaper. The building inspector admitted he made the statements.

On the basis of these statements, the city council discharged the building inspector.

Is the action of the city council constitutional?

(A) Yes, because the statements demonstrate that the building inspector has an attitude toward a certain class of persons that interferes with the proper performance of the obligations of his job.

(B) Yes, because the building inspector is a government employee and a person holding such a position may not make public comments inconsistent with current governmental policy.

(C) No, because the statements were lawful comments on a matter of public concern.

(D) No, because the statements were published in a newspaper that is protected by the First and Fourteenth Amendments.

VI. SPECIAL PROBLEMS OF THE MEDIA

A. Media's right of access to government-held information

Question 71

A state enacted a statute providing for the closure of the official state records of arrest and prosecution of all persons acquitted of a crime by a court or against whom criminal charges were filed and subsequently dropped or dismissed. The purpose of this statute is to protect these persons from further publicity or embarrassment relating to those state proceedings. However, this statute does not prohibit the publication of such information that is in the possession of private persons.

A prominent businessman in the state was arrested and charged with rape. Prior to trial, the prosecutor announced that new information indicated that the charges should be dropped. He then dropped the charges without further explanation, and the records relating thereto were closed to the public pursuant to the statute. A newspaper in the state conducted an investigation to determine why the businessman was not prosecuted, but was refused access to the closed official state records. In an effort to determine whether the law enforcement agencies involved were properly doing their duty, the newspaper filed suit against appropriate state officials to force opening of the records and to invalidate the statute on constitutional grounds. Which of the following would be most helpful to the state in defending the constitutionality of this statute?

(A) The fact that the statute treats in an identical manner the arrest and prosecution records of all persons who have been acquitted of a crime by a court or against whom criminal charges were filed and subsequently dropped or dismissed.

(B) The argument that the rights of the press are no greater than those of citizens generally.

(C) The fact that the statute only prohibits public access to these official state records and does not prohibit the publication of information they contain that is in the possession of private persons.

(D) The argument that the state may seal official records owned by the state on any basis its legislature chooses.

FREEDOM OF RELIGION

I. THE ESTABLISHMENT CLAUSE

A. Three-part test

1. Incidental benefit to religion not fatal

Question 72

A city operates a cemetery pursuant to a city ordinance. The ordinance requires the operation of the city cemetery to be supported primarily by revenues derived from the sale of cemetery lots to individuals. The ordinance further provides that the purchase of a cemetery lot entitles the owner to perpetual care of the lot, and entitles the owner to erect on the lot, at the owner's expense, a memorial monument or marker of the owner's choice, subject to certain size restrictions. The ordinance requires the city to maintain the cemetery, including mowing the grass, watering flowers, and plowing snow, and provides for the expenditure of city tax funds for such maintenance if revenues from the sale of cemetery lots are insufficient. Although cemetery lots are sold at full fair market value, which includes the current value of perpetual care, the revenue from the sale of such lots has been insufficient in recent years to maintain the cemetery. As a result, a small amount of city tax funds has also been used for that purpose.

A group of city taxpayers brings suit against the city challenging the constitutionality of the city ordinance insofar as it permits the owner of a cemetery lot to erect a religious memorial monument or marker on his or her lot.

Is this suit likely to be successful?

(A) No, because only a small amount of city tax funds has been used to maintain the cemetery.

(B) No, because the purpose of the ordinance is entirely secular, its primary effect neither advances nor inhibits religion, and it does not foster an excessive government entanglement with religion.

(C) Yes, because city maintenance of any religious object is a violation of the Establishment Clause of the First Amendment as incorporated into the Fourteenth Amendment.

(D) Yes, because no compelling governmental interest justifies authorizing private persons to erect religious monuments or markers in a city-operated cemetery.

II. THE FREE EXERCISE CLAUSE

A. Generally-applicable laws

1. State need not tolerate serious impairment of important state interest

Question 73

Members of a religious group believe in Lucifer as their Supreme Being. The members of this group meet once a year on top of Mt. Snow, located in a U.S. National Park, to hold an overnight encampment and a midnight dance around a large campfire. They believe this overnight encampment and all of its rituals are required by Lucifer to be held on the top of Mt. Snow. U.S. National Park Service rules that have been consistently enforced prohibit all overnight camping and all campfires on Mt. Snow because of the very great dangers overnight camping and campfires would pose in that particular location. As a result, the park superintendent denied a request by the group for a permit to conduct these activities on top of Mt. Snow.

The park superintendent, who was known to be violently opposed to cults and other unconventional groups had, in the past, issued permits to conventional religious groups to conduct sunrise services in other areas of that U.S. National Park.

The group brought suit in federal court against the U.S. National Park Service and the superintendent of the park to compel issuance of the requested permit.

As a matter of constitutional law, the most appropriate result in this suit would be a decision that denial of the permit was

(A) invalid, because the Free Exercise Clause of the First Amendment prohibits the Park Service from knowingly interfering with religious conduct.

(B) invalid, because these facts demonstrate that the action of the Park Service purposefully and invidiously discriminated against the group.

(C) valid, because the Establishment Clause of the First Amendment prohibits the holding of religious ceremonies on federal land.

(D) valid, because religiously motivated conduct may be subjected to nondiscriminatory time, place, and manner restrictions that advance important public interests.

Question 74

As a part of the practice of the religious beliefs of a small cult of Satan worshippers, the worshippers' high priest was required to sacrifice a cat to the glory of Satan after a live dissection of the animal in which it endured frightful pain. In the course of such religious sacrifice, the priest was arrested on the complaint of the local Humane Society and charged under a statute punishing cruelty to animals. On appeal, a conviction of the priest probably will be

(A) sustained on the grounds that belief in or worship of Satan does not enjoy constitutional protection.

(B) sustained on the grounds that sincere religious belief is not an adequate defense on these facts.

(C) overturned on the grounds that the constitutionally guaranteed freedom of religion and its expression was violated.

(D) overturned on the grounds that the beliefs of the cult members in the need for the sacrifice might be reasonable, and their act was religious.

JUSTICIABILITY

I. STANDING

A. Cases not based on taxpayer or citizen status

1. Requirement of an "injury in fact"

Question 75

An ordinance of a city requires that its mayor must have been continuously a resident of the city for at least five years at the time he or she takes office. The plaintiff, who is thinking about running for mayor in an election that will take place next year, will have been a resident of the city for only four and one-half years at the time the mayor elected then takes office. Before he decides whether to run for the position of mayor, the plaintiff wants to know whether he could lawfully assume that position if he were elected. As a result, the plaintiff files suit in the local federal district court for a declaratory judgment that the five-year-residence requirement is unconstitutional and that he is entitled to a place on his political party's primary election ballot for mayor. He names the chairman of his political party as the sole defendant but does not join any election official. The chairman responds by joining the plaintiff in requesting the court to declare the residence requirement invalid.

In this case, the court should

(A) refuse to determine the merits of this suit, because there is no case or controversy.

(B) refuse to issue such a declaratory judgment, because an issue of this kind involving only a local election does not present a substantial federal constitutional question.

(C) issue the declaratory judgment, because a residency requirement of this type is a denial of the equal protection of the laws.

(D) issue the declaratory judgment, because the plaintiff will have substantially complied with the residency requirement.

B. Third-party standing

Question 76

City police officers shot and killed the plaintiff's friend as he attempted to escape arrest for an armed robbery he had committed. The plaintiff brought suit in federal district court against the city police department and the city police officers involved, seeking only a judgment declaring unconstitutional the state statute under which the police acted. That newly enacted statute authorized the police to use deadly force when necessary to apprehend a person who has committed a felony. In his suit, the plaintiff alleged that the police would not have killed his friend if the use of deadly force had not been authorized by the statute.

The federal district court should

(A) decide the case on its merits, because it raises a substantial federal question.

(B) dismiss the action, because it involves a nonjusticiable political question.

(C) dismiss the action, because it does not present a case or controversy.

(D) dismiss the action, because the Eleventh Amendment prohibits federal courts from deciding cases of this type.

II. RIPENESS

A. A reasonable probability of harm required

Question 77

The legislature of the state of Gray recently enacted a statute forbidding public utilities regulated by the Gray Public Service Commission to increase their rates more than once every two years. Economy Electric Power Company, a public utility regulated by that commission, has just obtained approval of the commission for a general rate increase. Economy Electric has routinely filed for a rate increase every 10 to 14 months during the last 20 years. Because of uncertainties about future fuel prices, the power company cannot ascertain with any certainty the date when it will need a further rate increase; but it thinks it may need such an increase sometime within the next 18 months.

Economy Electric files an action in the federal district court in Gray requesting a declaratory judgment that this new statute of Gray forbidding public utility rate increases more often than once every two years is unconstitutional. Assume no federal statute is relevant.

In this case, the court should

(A) hold the statute unconstitutional, because such a moratorium on rate increases deprives utilities of their property without due process of law.

(B) hold the statute constitutional, because the judgment of a legislature on a matter involving economic regulation is entitled to great deference.

(C) dismiss the complaint, because this action is not ripe for decision.

(D) dismiss the complaint, because controversies over state-regulated utility rates are outside of the jurisdiction conferred on federal courts by Article III of the Constitution.

III. THE ELEVENTH AMENDMENT AND SUITS AGAINST THE STATES

A. The Eleventh Amendment generally

1. Congress can't override

a. Exception for Congress's use of power to enforce the post-Civil-War amendments

Question 78

A federal statute enacted pursuant to the power of Congress to enforce the Fourteenth Amendment prohibits any state from requiring any of its employees to retire from state employment solely because of their age. The statute expressly authorizes employees required by a state to retire from state employment solely because of their age to sue the state government in federal district court for any damages resulting from that state action. On the basis of this federal statute, a retiree who had worked for State X sues the state in federal district court. State X moves to dismiss the suit on the ground that Congress lacks authority to authorize such suits against a state.

Which of the following is the strongest argument that the retiree can offer in opposition to the state's motion to dismiss this suit?

(A) When Congress exercises power vested in it by the Fourteenth Amendment, Congress may enact appropriate remedial legislation expressly subjecting the states to private suits for damages in federal court.

(B) When Congress exercises power vested in it by any provision of the Constitution, Congress has unlimited authority to authorize private actions for damages against a state.

(C) While the Eleventh Amendment restrains the federal judiciary, that Amendment does not limit the power of Congress to modify the sovereign immunity of the states.

(D) While the Eleventh Amendment applies to suits in federal court by citizens of one state against another state, it does not apply to such suits by citizens against their own states.

CONSTITUTIONAL LAW ANSWERS

All cases cited are U.S. Supreme Court cases unless otherwise noted.

Answer 1

Choice **(B)** is correct. The Supreme Court may not review a judgment by the highest court of a state if that judgment is supported entirely by state law and is wholly independent of the interpretation and application of federal law. In this case, although the defendant claimed a violation of the Sixth Amendment of the U.S. Constitution, the state supreme court based its decision entirely on the state constitution without addressing the federal constitutional issue.

(A) is wrong because the Supreme Court *may* review a judgment of the highest court of a state reversing a criminal conviction, if the state high court's decision turns on a question arising under federal law. (But what happened here was that the state court decision was based entirely on state, not federal, law.)

(C) is wrong for two reasons. First, the Sixth Amendment right of a criminal defendant (even in a state-court rather than federal-court proceeding) to confront the witnesses against him *does* usually include the right to view the witness, so this choice is wrong as a matter of law. Second, the Supreme Court would not reach even the merits of the defendant's Sixth Amendment claim, for the reason stated in (B) above.

(D) is wrong because, although the Supreme Court may only review final judgments and decrees from the highest state courts, this judgment qualifies because it finally settled the confrontation issue (i.e., that issue would not arise again on re-trial, so the present petition provided the U.S. Supreme Court with its only opportunity to review the confrontation issue).

Answer 2

Choice **(B)** is correct. Although the state supreme court made a finding about what the state constitution required, this decision was not truly "independent" of federal constitutional law, because the facts make it clear that the state court was first determining what the federal Constitution required, and only then concluding that the state constitution required the same thing. Therefore, the Supreme Court can and should correct the state court's error in federal constitutional law. Once the Supreme Court has done this, it should then remand in order to give the state court the opportunity to conclude, after further reflection, that the state constitution's ban on discriminatory legislation goes further than the federal ban.

Choice (A) is wrong as a pure matter of law: Even where provisions of a state and the federal Constitution contain identical language, the state court is always free to interpret the state constitution as imposing different requirements than the apparently-identical federal provision.

Choice (C) is wrong because, for the reasons described above, the state court's decision was not in fact based on an adequate and independent state ground.

Choice (D) is wrong as a pure matter of law: Nothing prevents a state government from seeking review of the decisions of its own courts in the U.S. Supreme Court, as long as the decision poses some serious question of federal law.

Answer 3

Choice **(C)** is correct, because the decision for the fan was reached entirely on state grounds. The Supreme Court may hear a case from a state only if the state court judgment turned on federal grounds. The Court must refuse jurisdiction if it finds adequate and independent non-federal grounds to support the state decision. To be "adequate," the non-federal grounds must be fully dispositive of the case. To be "independent," the state court's interpretation of the state provision must be based on the court's own reasoning about state law, not based in whole or part on the state court's conclusion about what federal law provides.

Here, the state grounds mentioned by the state supreme court were "adequate" to support the decision, because that court's decision was based entirely on its own practice of giving the broadest possible interpretation to the state constitution's free-speech guarantee. The state grounds were "independent" because, although the state court discussed in detail the Supreme Court's First and Fourteenth Amendment decisions, the state court specifically stated that its determination was independent of how the Supreme Court would decide the federal constitutionality of the statute. Because there were both adequate and independent state grounds, the Court can and should dismiss the writ of certiorari as improvidently granted.

(A) is wrong because it is an incorrect statement of the law. First, the Court may not hear the case at all, for the reason given in the discussion of Choice (C) above. But even if the Court did hear the case, Choice (A) would not explain what the Court should do. One of the categories of speech unprotected by the First Amendment is "fighting words"—that is, words that are likely to induce the person to whom they are addressed to commit an immediate act of violence. (To constitute "fighting words" it is not enough that the speaker's words make the listeners angry; an incitement to immediate violence is required.) The fan's ballpark shout could constitutionally be punished under this "fighting words" doctrine, because it tended to incite the other spectators to violence.

(B) is wrong because the state court's decision was reached on independent state grounds. The Court may not hear the case due to the presence of an independent and adequate state ground, as described in the discussion of Choice (C) above. Therefore, the Court does not have jurisdiction to issue a "remand" (which is itself an exercise of federal jurisdiction, and thus inappropriate here).

(D) is wrong because the Court does not have jurisdiction. The Court may not hear the case due to the presence of an independent and adequate state ground, as described in the discussion of Choice (C) above. Therefore, the Court does not have jurisdiction to reverse the state court decision. (If the Court *did* have jurisdiction, because the state court had rested its decision partly or fully on federal-constitutional grounds, then Choice (D) *would* be a correct statement of what the Supreme Court should do, since incitement to violent action is not protected speech, under the "fighting words" doctrine.)

Answer 4

Choice **(A)** is correct, because no lower court has yet reached a decision in the case. The best argument in support of the EPA's request that the Supreme Court dismiss the petition on jurisdictional grounds is that the case is within neither the Court's original nor appellate jurisdiction. *Original jurisdiction:* Under Article III, § 2, the Supreme Court has original jurisdiction in (and only in) all cases affecting ambassadors, other public ministers and counsels, and those in which a state shall be a party. The case here does not involve any of those categories, so original jurisdiction does not exist.

Appellate jurisdiction: Article III, § 2, also provides that in those cases arising under the Constitution, by an Act of Congress, or by treaty, the Supreme Court shall have appellate jurisdiction. It's true that, as the facts tell us, a federal statute gives the Supreme Court the authority to review any case filed in a U.S. court of appeals, even though that case has not yet been decided by the court of appeals. But that statute presumes a decision by a lower court, which hasn't yet happened in this case. Indeed, for the Supreme Court to hear this case, in the absence of any lower-court decision, would not be an exercise of "appellate" jurisdiction at all—there is no decision being appealed from.

(B) is wrong because the answer is an inaccurate statement of what Article III provides. Article III, § 2, provides that in addition to cases arising under the Constitution, the Supreme Court shall have appellate jurisdiction in cases arising relating to an act of Congress or a treaty. So insofar as this choice says that the Supreme Court's appellate jurisdiction extends "only" to cases "arising under the Constitution" (and implies that there is no jurisdiction over cases arising under federal statutes), it's flatly wrong.

(C) is wrong because the answer is an inaccurate statement of the law. Article III, § 2, limits federal court jurisdiction to "cases" and "controversies" and so the federal courts may not issue "advisory opinions" (i.e., opinions giving advice about particular legislative or executive action, when no party is before the court who has suffered or imminently faces specific injury). Federal courts can, however, issue declaratory judgments, where the court is not requested to award damages or an injunction, but rather is requested to state what the legal effect would be of proposed conduct by one of the parties. Because an action for declaratory judgment would be within federal courts' Article III power, yet such an action would not be an "action to enforce the rule," Choice (C) is wrong.

(D) is wrong because the answer is an inaccurate statement of the law. This choice states that all federal cases not falling within the Supreme Court's original jurisdiction must be "initiated by an action in federal district court." This is simply an untrue statement. For example, the Court may hear a case originally filed with and heard by a U.S. court of appeals, if Congress authorizes this arrangement.

Answer 5

Choice (**A**) is correct. In cases not falling within the Supreme Court's original jurisdiction (e.g., cases in which a state is a party), the Supreme Court has "appellate Jurisdiction, both as to Law and Fact, with such Exceptions, and under such Regulations as the Congress shall make." (Article III, Sec. 2, Cl. 2.) So Congress, acting under this clause, has the power to regulate (including limit) the appellate jurisdiction of the Supreme Court. However, the Court held in *U.S. v. Klein* that Congress cannot use this power to specify jurisdiction as a "mean to an end" to make a particular substantive question come out a certain way. Choice (A) best captures this limitation, by suggesting that Congress was attempting to freeze then-current abortion law and to prevent a future Supreme Court from developing constitutional law in this area as the Court sees fit. This argument might not succeed, but it is the only choice that could even theoretically work.

(B) is simply wrong—Congress can under Article III, Sec. 2, Cl. 2 regulate the appellate jurisdiction of the Supreme Court whether the case originally arose in federal court or state court (and the only significance of where the case arose is that in those rare cases falling within the original jurisdiction of the Supreme Court itself, no "appellate jurisdiction" is necessary, so that there is no appellate jurisdiction which Congress might limit.)

(C) is also simply wrong—as discussed in (A) above, Article III, Sec. 2, Cl. 2 lets Congress, acting without a constitutional amendment, change the appellate jurisdiction of the Supreme Court.

(D) is wrong because the Fourteenth Amendment's Equal Protection Clause protects only against classifications made by state governments, and if there is any classification being made here (doubtful), it is being made by Congress, not a state.

Answer 6

Choice (**C**) is correct. Art. III, Sec. 2, says that the federal judicial power extends "to controversies between two or more States." Art. III, Sec. 3 then says that "in all cases . . . in which a State shall be a Party, the supreme Court shall have original jurisdiction." That same article says that the Supreme Court's "appellate jurisdiction" shall be "with such exceptions, and under such regulations as the Congress shall make." There is no similar provision allowing

Congress to make exceptions to (i.e., restrictions on) the Supreme Court's original jurisdiction, so Congress can't restrict the Supreme Court's original jurisdiction. Since a boundary dispute between two states is a dispute in which "a State shall be a Party," since the Supreme Court has original jurisdiction over cases involving a party, and since Congress is not authorized to limit the Supreme Court's original jurisdiction, it follows that Congress cannot "adjudicate finally" (i.e., remove the Supreme Court's right to adjudicate) the boundary dispute.

Choice (A) is wrong because, under *Coleman v. Miller* (1939), the House and Senate together *do* have the right (indeed, the exclusive right) to determine whether a disputed state ratification of an amendment is valid.

Choice (B) is incorrect because the Senate *does* have the power to determine the eligibility of its members—Art. I, Sec. 5, Cl. 1 says that "each House shall be the judge of the Elections, Returns, and *Qualifications* of its own Members."

Choice (D) is wrong because Art. I, Sec. 7, Cl. 3 says that "Every Order, *Resolution*, or Vote to which the Concurrence of the Senate and House of Representatives may be necessary . . . shall be presented to the President of the United States[.]" This clause implicitly gives each House the power to adopt resolutions; a resolution will not become law unless signed by the President, but the clause means that either House's adoption of a resolution is proper.

Answer 7

Choice (**A**) is correct. Art. IV, Sec. 3, Cl. 2 gives Congress the power to "make all needful Rules and Regulations respecting the Territory or other Property belonging to the United States[.]" Since the National Forest is federally-owned property, this clause gives Congress the power to pass regulations governing it. Under the Supremacy Clause, those regulations would take precedence over any conflicting state regulations, such as the right to kill coyotes implied by the state bounty bill.

(B) is wrong because it suggests that there is an independent congressional power to act to advance "the general welfare." This is not so—there's a power to "*tax and spend* . . . for the general welfare," but that's not what's at issue here (because Congress is doing pure regulating, not taxing or spending).

(C) is wrong because if Congress has been given an explicit power in a certain area (here, the power to regulate on federal lands), Congress can indeed override whatever right the state might otherwise have to legislate in areas of traditional state governmental functions.

(D) is wrong because the Full Faith and Credit Clause does not block Congress from punishing conduct that has been authorized by a state; the Clause merely requires one state to enforce every other state's judgments.

Answer 8

Choice (**A**) is correct. Sec. 1 of the executive order is constitutional, because the President, as the chief executive officer of the U.S. government, has authority to direct the actions of federal executive agencies, so long as the President's directives are not inconsistent with an act of Congress. (The facts state that there is no applicable statute here.) Sec. 2 of the executive order is unconstitutional. At least as a general rule, the President does not have authority to direct the actions of persons outside the executive branch unless the President's direction is authorized by an act of Congress. There are no circumstances presented in the facts (such as a sudden attack on the U.S.) that might justify an exception to this general rule.

(B), (C), and (D) are wrong because each is inconsistent with the above analysis.

Answer 9

Choice is **(C)** correct. The President's pardon power is indeed plenary. Therefore, when Congress purported to place conditions on that power, those conditions were ineffective. For the same reason, Choices (A), (B), and (D) are wrong. (By the way, Choice (D) is also grossly incorrect as a statement of the law of vetoes: Where the President vetoes a bill passed by Congress, Article I, Sec. 7, Cl. 2 says that the veto can be overwritten by a two-thirds vote of both Houses. There is no procedure by which the concurrence of three-fourths of state legislatures can act as an overriding method.)

Answer 10

Choice is **(D)** correct, because it correctly identifies the central reason why the motion to dismiss should be granted: the man was not a federal judge, and thus was not entitled to life tenure.

As these facts state, federal judges, serving on federal courts created pursuant to Article III of the Constitution, are entitled to lifetime tenure and undiminished pay. Had the man been a federal judge, he would have been entitled to both these benefits. However, the man wasn't a federal judge; instead, you're told he served on a tribunal created by Congress. Problematically, Congress can create tribunals under Article I of the Constitution, and can create lower federal courts under Article III.

The difference between a tribunal and a court depends on the functions served; a tribunal is legislative in nature, and a court is adjudicative. Here, the functions of the tribunal were legislative, and as a result the man wouldn't enjoy the Article III privileges of a federal judge. Instead, he'd serve at the pleasure of Congress.

Thus, the motion to dismiss should be granted, because the man could prove no set of facts under which he'd be entitled to life tenure, an Article III privilege. Since Choice (D) recognizes this, it's the best response.

(A) is wrong, because the man is not an Article III judge, and thus there's no issue under Article III; and even if there were an Article III issue, (A) misstates the law. Congress in fact has considerable power with regard to Article III courts. Under Article III, § 1, of the Constitution, the federal judicial power is "vested in one Supreme Court, and in such inferior Courts as the Congress may from time to time . . . establish." Congress cannot only create new, inferior courts, but it can regulate the appellate jurisdiction of federal courts under Article III, § 2. Thus, the federal judiciary could hardly be characterized as "independent," contrary to what Choice (A) states.

In any case, the man was not an Article III judge. Instead, he was a member of a legislative tribunal created by Congress. While it's true that federal judges cannot be removed from office during good behavior, nor can their pay be cut, this would not apply to the man. Instead, he was appointed by Congress and Congress could remove him as it sees fit. Since (A) doesn't recognize that the man wasn't a judge, it's not the best response.

(B) is wrong, because the man had no property right in his federal employment. With the words "property right," Choice (B) suggests that the man's removal, without some form of fair hearing, constitutes a due process violation. When the effect of a governmental activity amounts to a deprivation of a property interest or right, there's a potential due process problem. While "property" needn't necessarily be actual, tangible land or chattels, it requires at least interests already acquired in specific benefits. As far as governmental employment is concerned, the existence of a "property" interest in continued employment is determined under applicable federal, state, or municipal law. Thus, the statute creating the job, or the employment contract, or a clear understanding must provide for termination only "for cause." Here, there's no indication that the man's employment was anything other than at the pleasure of Congress. He served only as a member of a tribunal, not as a federal judge, so the lifetime employment and prohibition of salary diminution applicable to federal judges wouldn't apply to him.

Even if the man *had* a property right in his employment, this wouldn't determine that his dismissal involved a due process violation. Instead, he'd have to establish that he wasn't granted a fair hearing pursuant to his dismissal. Here again, there are no facts under this question to indicate this. Since (B) incorrectly focuses on a due process issue when none are indicated under these facts, it's not the best response.

(C) is wrong, because the man *did* have standing to challenge his dismissal. In order to press a claim, a party must have standing. Standing requires that the governmental action challenged must have caused or is imminently likely to cause, an injury to the party seeking review. Here, the man was removed from his job, so he clearly suffered an injury. While his claim isn't *valid,* since he wasn't a federal judge, this doesn't address the threshold question of whether or not he has standing. Since (C) doesn't recognize this, it's not the best response.

Answer 11

Choice (**A**) is correct. The key point is that Congress can use its commerce powers to regulate even entirely *intrastate* transactions, on the theory that such transactions are being regulated as part of a broader regulation of interstate transactions, and excluding purely intrastate transactions from the overall scheme would be unwieldy. So, for instance, Congress here can forbid a farmer's sale, at a roadside stand adjacent to his farm, of a tomato that he had raised, where the farmer sprayed a cancer-causing substance produced inside that same state onto the tomato—even though this is an entirely intrastate transaction, it is still a "commercial" transaction, and can be regulated pursuant to Congress's broader interstate-commerce regulatory scheme.

(B) is wrong for several reasons; most importantly, the Fourteenth Amendment protects only against various conduct (e.g., denials of equal protection and due process) involving "state action," and while Congress has the power to enforce that Amendment by appropriate legislation, Congress here is not focused on attempting to prohibit any state from violating the Amendment.

(C) is wrong because there is no general congressional power to "provide for the general welfare"; there is only a power to *tax and spend* for the general welfare.

(D) is similarly incorrect because there is no general congressional power to "promote science and the useful arts"; there is only the limited power in Art. I, Sec. 8, Cl. 8 to "promote the progress of science and useful arts" by "securing for limited times to authors and inventors the exclusive right to their respective writings and discoveries" (i.e., the power to issue *patents* and *copyrights*).

Answer 12

Choice (**B**) is correct. All of the activities being regulated by Congress here—manufacturing, distribution and sale of drugs—pertain to commerce. Therefore, Congress's power to regulate commerce is an ample source of authority for the regulatory scheme here. That is true even though the overall objectives being sought by Congress—the protection of health and the enforcement of law at the local level—are arguably "local" concerns traditionally left to the states.

(A) is wrong because the congressional statute here is essentially regulatory, and does not involve significant spending of federal funds.

(C) is wrong because there *is* no "general welfare" clause in the sense of a freestanding congressional power to legislate for the general welfare; there is, instead, only the power to tax and spend to achieve the general welfare, and Congress is not doing meaningful taxing or spending in the regulation at issue here.

(D) is wrong because the Fourteenth Amendment protects only against various conduct (e.g., denials of equal protection and due process) involving "state action," and while Congress has the power to enforce that Amendment by appropriate legislation, Congress here is not focused on attempting to prohibit states from violating the Amendment; for instance, there is no indication that Congress is trying to prevent the states from discriminating in the sale of nonprescription drugs or from denying anyone due process as to such drugs.

Answer 13

Choice (**B**) is correct, because the "substantial effect on commerce" rationale has been accepted by the Supreme Court. For instance, in *Wickard v. Filburn* (1942), the Court held that Congress could regulate even the consumption of wheat on the farm where it was produced, because such intrastate uses, when aggregated, had a substantial effect on interstate commerce. The same principle would apply here: (1) the rental or sale of property is clearly "commercial"; and (2) even a local ("intrastate") sale or rental of property would indirectly affect interstate commerce (e.g., by substantially affecting the demand for housing-construction materials from out of state).

Note that this question does *not* raise the same commerce problem as *N.F.I.B. v. Sebelius* (2012), where the Court said that the commerce power doesn't allow Congress to require someone who is *not presently in the market* for an interstate good or service to buy or sell such a good or service. Here, the statute implicitly applies only to one who is already proposing to rent or sell housing property, and all the statute does is to prevent the seller or landlord from engaging in certain types of discrimination in choosing the other party. But suppose Congress instead passed a statute saying, "Anyone who has a vacant housing unit that is suitable for habitation must make good faith efforts to rent it to the first financially qualified applicant for no more than $x per square foot per year." This statute *would* run afoul of *N.F.I.B.* (i.e., would be beyond Congress's commerce powers), because Congress would be forcing someone not already in the "be a landlord" market to enter that market.

(A) is wrong, because Congress has no power to regulate for the general welfare. Article I § 8 gives Congress the power to "tax and spend" for the general welfare, but that's not what's happening here — what's happening here is pure regulation.

(C) is wrong, because the Thirteenth Amendment almost certainly cannot be used to protect against sexual-orientation discrimination. The Thirteenth Amendment expressly protects against slavery. Its enforcement clause has been interpreted to allow Congress to legislate against the "badges of slavery," and to prohibit even private actors from practicing racial discrimination. The Court has never held that the Amendment may be used outside of the racial area. It's possible (though not certain) that Congress could rely on the Amendment to prohibit private discrimination on the basis of ethnicity and national origin in addition to race, since these are similar to racial discrimination. But it's very unlikely that the Amendment can be used to bar private discrimination on grounds so distinct from slavery as sexual orientation.

(D) is wrong, because it is a misstatement of law. The Equal Protection Clause of the Fourteenth Amendment bars discrimination only when there is *state action*. When a purely

private actor practices discrimination, Congress's Fourteenth Amendment § 5 remedial powers do not permit it to prohibit that discrimination. So, although Congress could probably rely
on its § 5 powers to prohibit public entities (states and cities, for instance) from discriminating
on grounds of sexual orientation, if there was evidence such entities had frequently committed
such discrimination in the past, Congress cannot do so with respect to purely private discrimination. See, e.g., *U.S. v. Morrison* (2000) (Congress can't use its Fourteenth Amendment § 5
powers to let victims of gender-motivated violent crimes sue in federal court).

Answer 14

Choice (A) is correct. The federal law on tire disposal was a proper exercise of Congress's
power to regulate interstate commerce, so the law was validly enacted. The fact that Congress
has chosen to regulate the actions of state governments does not prevent an otherwise-valid
statute from being constitutional. There is one major exception—the Tenth Amendment prevents Congress from "commandeer[ing] the legislative processes of the states" by directly
compelling states to enact or enforce a federal regulatory program [*New York v. U.S.*] But
here, although Congress is regulating the states, it is not forcing the states to enact or enforce
any federal regulatory program (merely forcing the states to obey the federal program in the
state's own internal operations), so the exception does not apply.

Choice (B) is wrong because, although it reaches the correct conclusion, it does so for the
wrong reasons; even if none of the tires came from vehicles used by the state in commercial
activities, the federal regulation would still be valid.

Choice (C) is wrong because Congress has power to regulate interstate commerce in a way
that binds the states, and there is no exception to this power for regulation of "core state governmental functions" (although as noted above, if Congress were actually ordering the state to
enact or enforce a regulatory program, this *would* be beyond Congress's commerce powers).

Choice (D) is wrong because the fact that the unlicensed state disposal facility meets most
federal standards is irrelevant; Congress has the power to insist that the state strictly obey the
federal requirement that only licensed disposal facilities be used.

Answer 15

Choice (A) is correct, because it recognizes that federalism is the basis of the legislator's
strongest argument. Under the Tenth Amendment, the states and the people retain all rights
not delegated to the United States by the Constitution. Here, the Federal Securities Act would
have been passed pursuant to Congress's broad commerce power. While that power is broad,
it's not absolute. The concept of state sovereignty under the Tenth Amendment would mean
that *some* state functions are outside the scope of Congress's commerce power. The state's
legislative functions could well be outside the ambit of federal regulation. While this isn't an
airtight argument, it's the best of the four possibilities, making (A) the best response.

(B) is wrong, because the Speech and Debate Clause does not apply to state legislators. Under
Article I, § 6, of the Constitution, members of Congress enjoy immunity "for any Speech or
Debate in either House." The immunity covers only "legislative acts," which include those
matters that form "an integral part of the deliberative and communicating processes" of
Congress. This provision does not apply to the states, and thus the legislator could not use
it as an argument. Even if he *were* a federal legislator, it's unlikely that the source of the
prosecution—a Federal Securities Act violation—could be considered "legislative business." In any case, the central reason this argument is not good for the legislator is that he isn't
covered by speech and debate immunity as a state legislator. Since (B) doesn't recognize this,
it's not the best response.

(C) is wrong, due to operation of the Supremacy Clause. Under the Supremacy Clause, found in Article VI, § 2, of the Constitution, federal law takes precedence over inconsistent state laws. That's the essence of the issue here. Congress would have power to legislate concerning securities under its commerce power, thus making the Federal Securities Act valid. Thus, any state law contradicting the federal act would be invalid. In fact, under these facts there is no indication of any state law concerning legislative immunity. Under the Supremacy Clause, it doesn't matter — as long as Congress has the power to legislate in an area, even if a state has the power to legislate in that area as well, the federal law will control. (Note that this is only true where the power is *concurrent* — that is, held by both the federal and state governments.) Since Choice (C) ignores the application of the Supremacy Clause, it's not the best response.

(D) is wrong, because such an application would not constitute a due process violation. When the effect of a governmental activity amounts to the deprivation of a property interest or right, there's a potential due process problem. However, that's not what the legislator's immunity argument is about. Due process has nothing to do with immunity; it has to do with fair process when a right or privilege is limited. Thus, what's at issue here is not whether the legislator's rights or privileges were fairly limited, but whether he's immune from prosecution altogether; as a result, there's no due process issue. Since (D) doesn't recognize this, it's not the best response.

Answer 16

Choice (**C**) is correct. If this tax scheme has a problem, the problem is likely to have to do with the fact that Green is imposing a tax on widgets that are shipped throughout the U.S., and that tax may be a burden on commerce. The Tenth Amendment does not solve this problem for Green—if Green is unduly burdening commerce, the Tenth Amendment won't save it. And it's certainly inaccurate to say that the states "have plenary authority to construct their tax system in any manner they choose"—for instance, if a state intentionally designs its tax system so as to put most of the burden on out-of-staters who derive some revenue from customers in the state and who don't vote in state elections, the scheme would clearly violate the dormant commerce clause.

(A), (B), and (D) each arguably helps the state rebut the plaintiff's argument that the tax is an undue burden on commerce and that it thus violates the dormant commerce clause. Therefore, each of these arguments might help the state.

Answer 17

Choice (**A**) is correct, because Congress has plenary power to raise revenue through taxes. Article 1, § 8, of the Constitution provides that Congress may levy taxes for the purpose of raising revenue. In general, the only limitation on a generally applicable tax is that it must be designed to raise revenue. Whether or not the tax has incidental effects on a particular industry is an irrelevant consideration. Since a 5% national retail sales tax would certainly raise funds, and the freedom of the press is not being curtailed because the tax is generally applied to all sales, the tax is constitutional, both as written, and as applied to the newspapers.

(B) is wrong, because strict scrutiny does not apply to the taxing and spending powers. Congress's power under the Constitution to raise funds through taxes is limited only by the concern of whether the tax is designed to raise revenue, rather than to affect an otherwise unconstitutional goal. Here, it is obvious that a national retail sales tax would raise funds. There is no indication in the law that seeks to target newspapers, nor is there disproportionate impact since the tax is levied on all retail sales. If you chose this response, you were probably thinking that strict scrutiny applies to certain types of decisions that restrict free speech.

However, since this tax in no way targets the newspapers, or any other form of speech, First Amendment analysis is not needed.

(C) is wrong, because it mistakes the law. The Constitution permits Congress to enact this national sales tax since doing so would be an exercise of the taxing and spending power in Article 1, § 8. The Constitution does not prohibit states from enacting their own sales taxes, but it also does not prohibit Congress from doing so as well. In general, the only limitation on a generally applicable tax is that it must be designed to raise revenue. Whether or not the tax has incidental effects on a particular industry is an irrelevant consideration. Since a 5% national retail sales tax would certainly raise funds, and the freedom of the press is not being curtailed because the tax is generally applied to all sales, the tax is constitutional, both as written, and as applied to the newspapers.

(D) is wrong, because the tax is not targeting newspapers. Article 1, § 8, of the Constitution provides that Congress may levy taxes for the purpose of raising revenue. In general, the only limitation on a generally applicable tax is that it must be designed to raise revenue. Since this tax in no way targets the newspapers, or any other form of speech, First Amendment analysis is not needed. Since a 5% national retail sales tax would certainly raise funds, and the freedom of the press is not being curtailed because the tax is generally applied to all sales, the tax is constitutional, both as written, and as applied to the newspapers.

Answer 18

Choice **(B)** is correct; a federal tax that will raise revenue is not rendered invalid by virtue of the fact that it has regulatory consequences, including a lessening of demand for the product or activity being taxed. (That's true, by the way, whether or not Congress intended that lessening of demand.)

(A) is incorrect because the tax would be valid as a revenue-raising measure even in the absence of a compelling national interest.

(C) is incorrect for the same reason that Choice (B) is correct—as long as the tax is on its face a revenue-raiser, it does not even have to be rationally related to some broader federal interest like deficit-reduction (and in any event the tax probably *is* rationally related to deficit-reduction even though sporting attendance may go down—the rational-relation test is very easy to satisfy, and you should beware of any choice that requires you to conclude that a means chosen by government is not rationally related to a particular governmental goal).

(D) is incorrect because where, as here, a legislative classification involves economics and does not implicate any suspect class or fundamental right, equal protection is satisfied as long as the classification is rationally related to the achievement of some legitimate governmental objective; here, the objective is revenue-raising, and the fact that other similar activities are spared the tax does not prevent the tax from being rationally-related to that objective.

Answer 19

Choice **(A)** is correct. This choice accurately restates the fundamental rule about Congress's power to tax: As long as Congress can rationally be said to be pursuing the general welfare (not a meaningful constraint), Congress can pick pretty much any activity it wishes as the subject of taxation, and can then spend the funds for a purpose that has no relation to the activity taxed. So here, the fact that Congress is taxing trips that do not involve the 10 large cities, and then spending the funds solely for the benefit of passengers whose travel does involve those 10 cities, makes no difference.

(B) is wrong because, although the main conclusion is correct (that the tax is constitutional), giving an exemption for cities that would not be served would certainly not deny any other purchasers equal protection. In the case of economic regulation not involving a suspect class or fundamental right, the classification scheme merely needs to withstand easy-to-satisfy mere-rationality review, and giving an exemption for travel between cities not involving the new airports would certainly pass this easy test.

(C) is wrong because the burden/benefit analysis used here would not be the proper test for a federally-imposed tax; the burden/benefit analysis would be a proper way to analyze a *state* regulation that might burden interstate travel and thus violate the dormant commerce clause, but the regulation here is not by a state.

(D) is wrong because, while the Supreme Court has occasionally recognized a fundamental "right to travel" for equal protection purposes, these cases have involved what would better be called the right to "migrate interstate," (e.g., the right to change one's state of residence and still receive welfare benefits), not the right to take a trip from one state to another.

Answer 20

Choice (C) is correct. Although Congress, when it spends, must spend "for the general welfare," this test is extremely easy to satisfy—as the choice correctly states, all that is required is that the spending be "reasonably deemed to serve the general welfare," and that it not violate some specific constitutional ban (e.g., the Establishment Clause's ban on spending for the purpose of advancing religion). Since Congress could rationally have believed that rewarding the "best universities" would promote the country's general welfare, and that determining the "ten best" by this kind of vote was a rational way to go about attaining that end, the spending is constitutional.

(A) is wrong because the statute here is an acceptable exercise of legislative delegation: Congress has made it reasonably clear to the Dept. of Education what they are to do, and how they are to do it, so there is no "unconstitutional delegation" despite the fact that non-federal officials will be somehow involved in the process.

(B) is wrong, because when a governmental classification does not involve a suspect or semi-suspect class or fundamental right, equal protection requires only a rational relation between the means chosen and a legitimate governmental objective, and the means and end here meet this easy-to-satisfy standard. (To put it another way, limiting the money to the "top ten," and picking the top ten this way, are *not* "arbitrary and capricious" methods.)

(D) is wrong because the mere fact that Congress's use of its spending power is being challenged does not make the matter a nonjusticiable political question.

Answer 21

Choice (C) is correct, because it offers a federal power to which a need-based student aid program is rationally related. The welfare power addresses the federal government's power to collect taxes and spend money for all matters of national concern. In implementing this power, Congress *can* impose any reasonable conditions on the states as a prerequisite to participating in federal spending programs. Here, student aid will have a general beneficial effect on the welfare of the country. Requiring that the aid be distributed on the basis of need is a reasonable condition to place on such a program. As such, the welfare power provides a strong constitutional basis for the statute.

Incidentally, the reason that this problem requires some thought is that education is traditionally a *state* function. Congress can only pass laws rationally related to its enumerated powers (e.g., defense, interstate commerce, etc.). As this question indicates, Congress can use its spending power to indirectly achieve objectives it couldn't achieve directly pursuant to its regulatory powers (as long as it doesn't violate any independent constitutional limitations, like due process). By relying on the Welfare Clause, Choice (C) overcomes the problem that education is a state function, making it the best response.

(A) is wrong, because there is no federal police power, and the question here addresses a federal statute. Under the police power, a state enactment is a valid means of achieving a legitimate state interest where the public health, safety, welfare, and morals is involved. There is no federal equivalent of the police power, although Congress can achieve many of the same ends through valid use of its powers. (For instance, Congress can use its commerce power to regulate the use of interstate channels, thus prohibiting interstate transport of stolen property, misbranded goods, lottery tickets, and the like.) Since Choice (A) doesn't recognize this, it's not the best response.

(B) is wrong, because the war and defense power would not provide a basis for a statute of this sort. Congress gets its war and defense power from Article I, § 8, of the Constitution, under which it can declare war, raise and support armed forces, and, in general, administer those forces. The types of regulations Congress could pass under the war power include conducting a draft, instituting economic controls in wartime, excluding people from sensitive areas, and confiscating the property of enemies. In order to be upheld under an enumerated power, a statute must be rationally related to the power, or a necessary and proper means of effectuating that power. A need-based student aid program has no obvious connection with the war power, and as such the war power wouldn't provide a strong constitutional basis for the legislation. Since (B) states otherwise, it's not the best response.

(D) is wrong, because the Privileges or Immunities Clause of the Fourteenth Amendment is not a source of constitutional power for the federal government. The Privileges or Immunities Clause of the Fourteenth Amendment voids those state enactments that clearly infringe privileges enjoyed by U.S. citizens. It is construed narrowly, typically being restricted to fundamental rights that are shared in common by all U.S. citizens, namely:

1. The right to travel freely from state to state;

2. The right to petition Congress for redress of grievances;

3. The right to vote for national officers;

4. The right to assemble peaceably; and

5. The right to discuss matters of national legislation.

Thus, the Clause would not provide a means by which to *support* the constitutionality of a need-based student aid program. The Clause *limits* the power of the *states*, but is not a source of power for the *federal* government.

Since (D) doesn't recognize this, it's not the best response.

Answer 22

Choice (**C**) is correct, because the district court has jurisdiction over claims arising under treaties. In order to fall within the subject-matter jurisdiction of the federal district courts, there must be either diversity jurisdiction or federal question jurisdiction. Since we are told that the man and woman in this problem were residents of the same state, there is no diversity jurisdiction. However, there is federal question jurisdiction, since Article III, § 2, of the Constitution provides that "[t]he judicial power shall extend to all cases, in law and equity, arising under this Constitution, the laws of the United States, *and treaties made*, or which shall be made, under their authority." Since the basis for the woman's suit is the treaty that requires citizens to pay tort judgments awarded by the foreign court, the suit involves a "federal question" and is within the district court's jurisdiction.

(A) is wrong, because the suit raises a federal question. In order to fall within the subject-matter jurisdiction of the federal district courts, there must be either diversity jurisdiction or federal question jurisdiction. Since we are told that the man and woman in this problem were residents of the same state, there is no diversity jurisdiction. However, there is federal question jurisdiction, since Article III, § 2, of the Constitution provides that "[t]he judicial power shall extend to all cases, in law and equity, arising under this Constitution, the laws of the United States, *and treaties made*, or which shall be made, under their authority." (Emphasis added.) Since the basis for the woman's suit is the treaty that requires citizens to pay tort judgments awarded by the foreign court, the suit involves a "federal question" and is within the district court's jurisdiction.

(B) is wrong, because the Commerce Power applies to Congress, not the federal judiciary. The federal district court will have jurisdiction over the woman's suit because the suit arises under a treaty of the United States, and thus raises a "federal question." If you selected this choice, you are probably thinking that since the traffic accident was not a commercial transaction, Congress could not pass a law governing the accident because the Commerce Power does not reach it. This line of reasoning makes two errors. First, whether or not Congress could legislate an issue is an entirely distinct question from whether the federal courts have jurisdiction over a suit, which requires only that either diversity or federal jurisdiction applies. Second, it erroneously implies that the Commerce Power is the only power under which Congress may legislate. This is not the case, as Article I, § 8, provides several other enumerated powers of the legislative branch. (Although none of these other powers would allow Congress to legislate in this arena, that fact does not make Choice (B) any more correct.)

(D) is wrong, because it is irrelevant. The scope of the President's power to enter into treaties (with the advice and consent of the Senate) is very broad. However, that information does not inform the question asked, which is whether the federal district court has subject-matter jurisdiction to hear the woman's claim. In this case, the district court will have subject-matter jurisdiction because the woman's claim involves a federal question. Article III, § 2, of the Constitution provides that "[t]he judicial power shall extend to all cases, in law and equity, arising under this Constitution, the laws of the United States, *and treaties made*, or which shall be made, under their authority." (Emphasis added.) Since the basis for the woman's suit is the treaty that requires citizens to pay tort judgments awarded by the foreign court, the suit involves a "federal question" and is within the district court's jurisdiction.

Answer 23

Choice **(B)** is correct. Congress can only delegate powers it possesses, so you first have to determine whether Congress itself has power to regulate federal lands. The answer is "yes," because Art. I, Sec. 8, Cl. 17 gives Congress power to regulate federal lands. Next, you have to determine whether Congress validly delegated this power that it possesses. Here, too, the answer is "yes." Congress may delegate rule-making authority to federal agencies through statutes that set concrete objectives for the agency, and that list adequate criteria for carrying out those objectives. The Supreme Court has been very deferential in applying these "concrete objectives" and "adequate criteria" requirements. The objective being pursued here (control of campfires on federal lands) is quite concrete, and the criteria specified by Congress for achieving that objective (use of a penalty schedule for rule violators) seem quite adequate. Therefore, the statute's provision of authority to the Forest Service would likely be held to satisfy the requirements.

(A) is incorrect, because the executive branch does not have inherent rule-making authority over public lands. The only source of federal power to regulate public lands is the grant in Art. I, Sec. 8, Cl. 17, to *Congress* to regulate such lands, as discussed above. So the executive's rule-making authority over public lands comes from delegation by Congress, not from any inherent authority.

(C) is wrong because the compelling nature of the government's regulatory interest is neither necessary nor sufficient to justify the Forest Service's regulation. The constitutional requirement is merely that the regulation be pursuant to a valid act of Congress, and that it not violate any specific constitutional prohibition. Since the act is a valid exercise of Congress's power to regulate federal lands, and since the delegation was validly done (as described in (B) above), that's the end of the matter, and the strength of the federal interest never becomes relevant.

(D) is wrong because, although law enforcement is an executive function, the constitutional exercise of that function requires that the executive act pursuant to congressional authorization provided by law.

Answer 24

Choice (**B**) is correct. The setting up of a presidential advisory commission, such as the one here, falls within the President's executive powers—nothing in the facts indicates that the commission will have legislative or judicial powers, so the commission is a proper delegation by the President of his executive power. As to funding: Congress has the right to earmark specified federal monies to be spent as the President shall determine. Therefore, nothing about this arrangement violates any constitutional provision.

(A) is wrong, because the President does *not* have "plenary power to provide for the health, safety, and welfare of the people. . . ." For instance, the President does not have power to spend federal money for what he determines to be the health needs of "the people." This answer ignores both the source of the President's authority (which is limited to the executive power, that is, the power to see that the laws are carried out) and the need for all funding to be appropriated by Congress.

(C) is wrong because it incorrectly states the effect of the Tenth Amendment. The Tenth Amendment states that the powers not delegated to the federal government by the Constitution, and not prohibited to the states, are reserved to the states. The Tenth Amendment has relatively little force today as a limit on federal power. (About the only force it has as a limit on federal powers is to prevent Congress from directly forcing the states to enact or enforce federal policies.) The Amendment does not mean that the federal government may not exercise power over a "traditional state function." So the fact that vaccination has traditionally been a function handled by the states does not mean that the Tenth Amendment bars the federal government from taking action with respect to vaccinations.

(D) is wrong, because Congress does not need to authorize the creation of a temporary commission. An Advisory Commission on Vaccination is not a new federal agency—it is an advisory group, set up for a specific purpose and having a temporary existence. The President does not need congressional approval to create such an organization. Nor has Congress prohibited its creation (which if it had happened might bar creation of the Commission) because, as the facts state, no federal statute authorizes or prohibits this action.

Answer 25

Choice (**B**) is correct, because it's the only choice that addresses the central issue under these facts, impoundment, and offers a solid argument for the arms manufacturer. "Impoundment" is the President's refusal to spend funds appropriated by Congress. The rule is that the President does not have the power to refuse to spend funds that were appropriated with an express mandate from Congress that the funds be spent. *Kendall v. United States* (1838). Here, Congress mandated that the billion dollars "shall be spent" for the weapons system; thus, the

President *must* authorize the contract for purchase of the system. (Note, incidentally, that the Supreme Court has decided only that the President may not impound funds that Congress has *expressly mandated* be spent; where Congress merely appropriates without an express "you must spend" direction to the President, the Supreme Court has never decided whether the President may impound.)

(A) is wrong because Congress's passing an appropriation over a veto does not by itself require the President to spend the appropriated funds. A veto occurs when the President refuses to sign a bill passed by Congress. Congress can override a presidential veto with a two-thirds vote of both Houses. The President's power to impound does not depend on whether the bill became law because the President signed it, or because Congress overrode the President's veto. Rather, as noted in Choice (B) above, the Court has held that the President does not have the power to impound funds that were appropriated with an express mandate from Congress that the funds be spent, a rule that does not depend on the exact process by which the law appropriating the funds became law.

(C) is wrong because the argument it makes would not authorize the President to withhold spending funds appropriated by Congress. It's true that Congress holds the enumerated power to tax and spend for the general welfare. The President, on the other hand, has the power to enforce laws, which includes carrying out spending programs authorized by Congress once those programs become law (either because the President signed the bill authorizing the program, or because Congress passed the bill over the President's veto). However, this choice doesn't specifically address whether the President can refuse to spend funds appropriated by Congress; the answer is that he cannot so refuse, at least where Congress "directs" that he spend the funds, a situation best addressed by Choice (B).

(D) is wrong, because the President's power of impoundment does not turn on the subject matter of the legislation. It's true that the President holds broad powers with respect to foreign affairs, and it's possible that, since the spending here involves a weapons system, the President's power to spend or not spend would control. But even if it *did*, this certainly wouldn't be a good argument for the arms manufacturer, which would be trying to argue that the President has no power to withhold spending funds Congress appropriated, and in this question you're looking for the manufacturer's best argument. This choice ignores the central issue under these facts: the President's right of impoundment, i.e., his right to refuse to spend funds appropriated by Congress. Choice (B) correctly deals with that issue.

Answer 26

Choice **(B)** is correct, because Congress cannot constitutionally designate two members of this board. Under the Appointments Clause, the President, not Congress, is given the power to appoint federal officers. So Congress itself may not make any appointments of federal officers (defined as federal officials who exercise executive power). The statute here endowed the board with broad rule-making powers. In *Buckley v. Valeo* (1976), the Court held that rule-making is an executive function, so that the members of a board or agency with rule-making powers are federal officers who must be appointed by the President. So here, the fact that two of the board's five members are directly designated by Congress violates the Appointments Clause.

(A) is wrong because the powers here are not "quasi-legislative." Congress may make its own appointments of persons to exercise powers that are essentially of an investigative or informative nature — such powers *would* be "quasi-legislative." But where the appointee's powers are essentially rule-making rather than investigative, this is an executive function, not a legislative function. Consequently, as described in Choice (B) above, it is the President, not Congress, that has the right of appointment. So this choice is correct that the statute is unconstitutional on account of separation-of-powers problems, but incorrect about what those problems are.

(C) is wrong because although the Necessary and Proper Clause gives the Congress the power to *create* the board, it does not give Congress the power to appoint the board's members. It's true that where Congress is exercising one of its enumerated powers, it may enact any law which is "necessary and proper for carrying into execution" that power. So Congress can regulate the securities and banking industries pursuant to its commerce power, and it can enact laws to carry out that regulation. But as explained in the discussion of Choice (B), the Appointments Clause means that the power to appoint members of the board (who are exercising rulemaking authority and are thus "federal officers") falls to the President under the Appointments Clause. Nothing in the Necessary and Proper Clause overcomes this Appointments-Clause problem.

(D) is wrong because (1) it ignores the Appointments-Clause problem described in the discussion of Choice (B); and (2) it falsely indicates that Congress has a free-standing power to pass laws that are for the "general welfare." As to (1), the Appointments Clause, as interpreted by the Court, means that "Officers of the United States" must be appointed by the President, not Congress. The board members here are exercising rule-making powers, which makes them executive-branch members (i.e., "federal officers), so the fact that two of them are appointed by Congress violates this Clause. As to (2), the general welfare clause, Article 1, § 8 states that Congress shall have the power to lay and collect taxes, to pay debts and to provide for the common defense and the general welfare. This clause gives Congress the substantive power to tax and appropriate money. But it does not confer on Congress a free-standing power to regulate to achieve the general welfare. So Congress's general welfare power is irrelevant to the constitutionality of the regulatory statute here.

Answer 27

Choice (**D**) is correct, because it recognizes that the attorney general is not subject to direction from Congress as to whom to prosecute. Law enforcement is an exclusively executive power. The President is the only source of executive power, under Article II, § 1, of the Constitution. He can, of course, delegate those executive functions to others in the executive branch. The attorney general is the chief law enforcement official. He can prosecute criminal activity as he sees fit, and in his discretion, he can choose not to do so, as a general rule. Since Choice (D) recognizes this, it's the best response.

(A) is wrong, because the attorney general is not subject to any orders from the legislative branch. The President is the only source of executive power, under Article II, § 1, of the Constitution. Many of his duties are delegated to others within the executive branch, including the attorney general, the chief law enforcement official. The law enforcement function is an *exclusively* executive branch power. Thus, Congress enjoys *no* law enforcement powers, and could not direct the attorney general to prosecute anyone. Since (A) doesn't recognize this, it's not the best response.

(B) is wrong, because it misstates the law. Law enforcement is an exclusively executive power. The President is the only source of executive power, under Article II, § 1, of the Constitution. He can, of course, delegate those executive functions to others in the executive branch. The attorney general is the chief law enforcement official. He can prosecute criminal activity as he sees fit, and in his discretion, he can choose not to do so, as a general rule. Since (B) states that the attorney general *must* prosecute all federal law violators when, in fact, prosecution is generally discretionary, (B) is not the best response.

(C) is wrong, because the woman's immunity from prosecution for acts committed in office would be *irrelevant* as to whether the attorney general must prosecute her for contempt. When someone does not comply with a congressional investigation, contempt is the appropriate punishment. Here, the woman's contempt charge is due to her failure to answer questions posed during a congressional investigation, *not* due to any wrongdoing in the course of her duties.

Instead, the reason the attorney general needn't prosecute is that law enforcement is exclusively an *executive* function, and thus the House of Representatives, as part of the *legislative* branch, can't order the attorney general to prosecute. Since (C) doesn't recognize this, it's not the best response.

Answer 28

Choice **(B)** is correct. The Commerce Clause gives Congress the power to regulate commerce among the states and, by negative implication, restricts the regulatory power of the states with respect to interstate commerce. Any state law that has a substantial effect on interstate commerce must not be protectionist (i.e., must not benefit in-state interests at the expense of out-of-state interests) or otherwise impose an undue burden on interstate commerce. A state law that discriminates against interstate commerce is protectionist unless it serves a legitimate local interest that cannot be served by nondiscriminatory legislation. By barring the sale in Green of the Martian toys manufactured in other states, the state law here has a substantial negative effect on interstate commerce. Although the law does not explicitly discriminate against the out-of-state toy manufacturers, it has a purely discriminatory effect against them, and the state has less discriminatory alternatives available to protect the legitimate interests cited in the law (e.g., better public education about the nonsensicality of extraterrestrialism). The state law therefore violates the negative implications of the Commerce Clause.

(A) is wrong because, while it is true that the Green law is unconstitutional, this answer misstates the basis for this conclusion. The Contracts Clause (Article I, Section 10, Clause 1 of the Constitution) does not forbid state laws affecting contractual relations between private parties so long as they are reasonably related to a legitimate state interest. Because the courts typically defer to state regulations of private contracts as reasonable, the statute at issue here is not likely to be found unconstitutional under the Contracts Clause.

(C) is wrong because the fact that the matter being regulated is arguably a "local matter" is not a defense to a dormant commerce clause claim, if the state's form of regulation discriminates against out-of-state producers. So the fact that education is arguably a "local" state matter won't protect the obviously-protectionist statute here.

(D) is wrong because it is not a defense to protectionist legislation (i.e., legislation that intends to protect in-state economic interests at the expense of out-of-staters, or has that clear effect) that the state is also attempting to achieve some otherwise-permissible state objective. So here, although the state's interest in protecting children from faulty science is legitimate, that interest does not justify the law's intentional discrimination against out-of-staters where the state has less discriminatory alternatives available to protect that interest (e.g., better science education).

Answer 29

Choice **(B)** is correct. This is a classic case of protectionism: The in-state retailers have persuaded the legislature to strengthen the in-staters' economic position vis-à-vis out-of-state retailers (since small in-state retailers now get an advantage that small out-of-state retailers don't get, and get an unearned cost-equality with large out-of-state retailers). So out-of-state retailers are being discriminated against (treated less favorably by virtue of their out-of-state status). This sort of protectionism is virtually a per se violation of the dormant commerce clause, and is certainly an undue burden on commerce.

(A) is wrong because economic regulation that does not involve a suspect class or fundamental right (and the regulation here involves neither) will receive only mere-rationality review under the Due Process Clause, and the measure here would pass that review.

(C) is wrong because the privileges and immunities of "national" (as opposed to state) citizenship are guaranteed by the Fourteenth Amendment, Sec. 1; that Privileges or Immunities Clause, however, would not protect the plaintiffs here because only a few rights have been recognized as rights of national citizenship for purposes of the Clause (e.g., the right to travel physically from state to state, to move from state to state, and to vote in national elections), and the right of an out-of-stater to be free of economic discrimination is not one of them. (The plaintiffs might win with an argument based on Art. IV's P&I Clause, which protects against discrimination by a state against out-of-staters; however, that Clause doesn't protect the rights of "national citizenship," but rather, the rights of state citizenship.)

(D) is wrong because economic regulations that do not involve a suspect or semi-suspect class or fundamental right receive only easy-to-satisfy mere-rationality review under the Equal Protection Clause, and the statute here would pass that review (since the legislature could reasonably have believed that its citizens would fare better, overall, if small local retailers were not at a disadvantage to large out-of-state retailers).

Answer 30

Choice (C) is correct, because the state's statute does not violate the dormant commerce clause, in that it neither unduly burdens, nor intentionally discriminates against, out-of-state economic interests. Under the dormant commerce clause, a regulation will be valid if it: (1) does not intentionally discriminate against out-of-state competition to benefit local economic interests; and (2) is not unduly burdensome, in that the incidental burden on interstate commerce does not outweigh the legitimate local benefits produced by the regulation. The statute here is constitutional because it passes both tests. As to the first test: Although the statute seeks to benefit local economic interests, it does not discriminate against out-of-state competition in the method it employs to protect domestic corporations. That is so because the statute, by requiring that any acquisition of more than 25% of the voting shares of a corporation incorporated in the state be approved by the holders of record of a majority of the corporation's shares, imposes exactly the same burden on both in-state and out-of-state entities wishing to acquire an in-state corporation.

The second requirement is that the regulation not be "unduly burdensome" to interstate commerce. The statute here regulates only the acquisition of in-state corporations, and there is no obvious large burden on out-of-staters that want to acquire in-state corporations. Since only corporations incorporated in the state are covered by the statute, one important form of undue burden—the inconsistent state-by-state regulation of a corporation incorporated in another state—does not occur. Thus, the second prong of the test is satisfied.

The act here is similar to one upheld by the Court against Commerce Clause attack in *CTS Corp. v. Dynamics Corp. of Amer.* (1987) (statute making it harder to acquire a corporation incorporated in the state upheld because, "to the limited extent that the Act affects interstate commerce, this is justified by the State's interests in defining the attributes of shares in its corporations and in protecting shareholders.")

(A) is wrong because dormant commerce clause attacks generally won't succeed unless the plaintiff shows either a discriminatory intent (less-favored treatment of out-of-staters than in-staters) or an "undue burden" on commerce. (See the discussion of Choice (C) above.) The mere fact that one of the regulation's purposes is to prevent out-of-staters from doing something unsatisfactory won't be enough, if in-staters are also prevented (since then there is no discrimination).

(B) is wrong because the presence of an "adverse effect" on an interstate market does not suffice for a violation of the dormant commerce clause. As is discussed more fully in the treatment of Choice (C) above, a plaintiff in a dormant commerce clause case must generally show either discrimination against interstate commerce, or a "substantial burden" on it. (B), by making the test be whether there is any sort of "adverse effect" at all, is not the right test.

(D) is wrong because it's an incorrect statement about what the dormant commerce clause prohibits. It's true that corporations exist only by virtue of state law. It's also true that a state probably has greater freedom in how it regulates its own domestic (i.e., state-chartered) corporations than in some other areas of regulation. But an anti-takeover statute, even if applied only to state-chartered targets, would still violate the dormant commerce clause if it discriminated against—i.e., treated less favorably—out-of-state acquirers than in-state acquirers (for instance, by requiring a higher percentage of target stockholders to approve an out-of-state takeover than a domestic takeover). So when (D) says that the "negative implications of the commerce clause" (an accurate way to refer to the dormant commerce clause) "do not apply to state regulations governing [domestic corporations'] creation and acquisition," the choice is not stating the law correctly.

Answer 31

Choice **(A)** is correct. Ames is making foreign cars materially less attractive to Ames residents, so residents are likely to buy fewer of them. Therefore, Ames is discriminating against foreign imports and in favor of U.S.-made cars. Since such a rule would clearly be held to be an undue burden on "domestic" interstate commerce if it were applied to the parking of cars made in U.S. states other than Ames, it will found to be an undue burden here, since restraints on foreign commerce are if anything scrutinized more strictly than restraints on domestic interstate commerce.

(B) is wrong because this is an economic regulation not involving a suspect class or fundamental right (there's no fundamental right to park in state-operated parking facilities), so it will be upheld as long as it's rationally related to achievement of a legitimate state objective; the measure here would meet this easy-to-satisfy test, since it's at least rational to believe that making it harder to park will cut down on the number of foreign cars sold in Ames and thus make in-state-produced cars more economically viable.

(C) is wrong, because (1) it's not clear that a person has *any* liberty or property interest in being able to park in a state-owned facility; and (2) even if there is such an interest, the interest is not "fundamental" (parking in state-owned facilities has not been held to be a fundamental right for due process purposes—only some privacy/autonomy-related rights have this status), so the measure would merely need to satisfy the easy rational-relation test, which it does.

(D) is wrong because the Fourteenth Amendment's Privileges or Immunities Clause protects only the rights of "national citizenship," and the right to park in a state-owned facility is certainly not a right of national citizenship.

Answer 32

Choice is **(B)** is correct. This is a relatively easy case in which Congress is forbidding action X (use of mechanical power hammers) and the state is purporting to allow that very same action X. So this is about as simple a case of preemption by operation of the Supremacy Clause as could be imagined.

(A) is wrong because where federal and state rules conflict, the Supremacy Clause causes the state regulation to be invalid even if it was enacted subsequent to the federal rule.

(C) is wrong because state rules that directly conflict with federal rules are invalid even though the federal pronouncement does not expressly indicate that it supersedes inconsistent state or local laws.

(D) is wrong because whether or not a state regulation might represent a better balance of risk and reward than a directly-conflicting federal regulation, the state law must yield on account of the Supremacy Clause.

Answer 33

Choice **(D)** is correct. The federal concession statute, by requiring a nominal rental on account of the great public benefit from concessions, shows a federal intent to keep the total occupancy costs for concessionaires low. The state occupancy tax has the effect (and purpose) of making occupancy costs higher for the affected taxpayers than it would otherwise be. This fact is coupled with the fact that the state is singling out taxpayers on non-state-taxed property, including federally-owned property, so the interference with federal interests is especially acute. Therefore, a court might well hold that the state law so undermines the federal purposes as to be invalid under the Supremacy Clause. The court would not *necessarily* reach this conclusion, but this is the most powerful of the four arguments.

(A) is wrong because the occupancy tax does not discriminate against interstate commerce (since the effect on tourists from inside Purple is the same as on out-of-state tourists), and it is unlikely that subjecting the plaintiff to the same overall level of taxation as businesses located in state-taxable facilities would be found to be an "undue burden."

(B) is wrong because the Fourteenth Amendment's Privileges or Immunities Clause protects only certain very limited rights of "national citizenship" (mostly the right to travel from state to state), and the Clause has never been interpreted to protect a "fundamental right to do business on federal property." (It's true that the Privileges and Immunities Clause of Art. IV protects the fundamental right to pursue one's business or profession, but the examiners have tried to trick you here by using the Fourteenth Amendment's Privileges or Immunities Clause, not the Art. IV Clause.)

(C) is wrong because the Fourteenth Amendment Equal Protection Clause protects only against a given state's unfair classification of multiple persons, not against one state's treating a person less favorably than other states treat similarly-situated persons. (Also, any classification being done by Purple here does not involve a suspect or semi-suspect class or a fundamental right, so the classification merely has to be rationally related to the achievement of a legitimate state objective, and the occupancy tax here meets this easy-to-satisfy standard.)

Answer 34

Choice **(D)** is correct. There is a *direct conflict* between the federal and state regulations in this case, and it is impossible for the regulated party (Road Lines) to obey both regulations simultaneously. That is, the ICC has expressly permitted Road Lines to drop its route, and the state statute appears to prohibit Road Lines from dropping the route. Since the federal action is constitutional (it falls within Congress's commerce power), under the Supremacy Clause the federal action preempts the state action.

(A) is wrong, because Foley *does* have standing. It's true that the ICC, in taking the challenged action (letting Road Lines drop the service), was not intending to affect Foley and probably was not even aware of Foley's interest in the matter. But since Foley would suffer imminent and concrete economic harm from the challenged action, and since the injury he would suffer will be at least somewhat different from that suffered by every local resident, Foley has standing even though the challenged action was not directed at him.

(B) is incorrect because the state court does not have power to order a removal to the federal courts. There is no process by which a state court judge (rather than the defendant) can compel a pending state-court case to be removed to the federal courts. And that's true whether the case falls within the state court's jurisdiction or not. So the case will not be removed unless the defendant takes action to remove it.

(C) is wrong because (1) there is probably no constitutional rule that prevents the federal government from interfering with any "essential state function"; and (2) even if there were such a rule, it's highly unlikely that such an interference is happening here (since the federal government is merely allowing a private party to do something, not, for instance, ordering the state to change or eliminate any state function).

Answer 35

Choice (**A**) is correct. When Congress passed the statute saying that all liability of interstate movers would be "governed exclusively" by the contract between the two parties, this manifested Congress's intent to preempt the entire field of regulation of liability of such movers, and to block any non-contract form of recovery (such as recovery in tort). If Lee were permitted to recover under Pink tort law, the results would be at odds with this clear congressional intent to occupy the field. This is, therefore, a classic illustration of the supremacy of federal law over conflicting state law.

(B) is wrong because (in part) the Obligation of Contracts Clause blocks the *states* from modifying contracts in some circumstances, and does not serve as any kind of a limit on when *Congress* may modify contracts. (Also, no contract is being modified here, so even if the state had said by statute what Congress said here, there would be no obligation-of-contracts problem.)

(C) is wrong, because (in part) the Full Faith and Credit Clause does not act as a limit on what Congress may do (and in any event no state is refusing to enforce another court's judgment, which is what the FF&C Clause requires states to do).

(D) is wrong because nothing in constitutional law prevents Congress from authorizing private parties to "contract out of . . . liability for [their] own negligence," assuming Congress was acting pursuant to some enumerated power (such as, here, the power to regulate interstate commerce).

Answer 36

Choice (**C**) is correct. The question, of course, is whether the federal regulation on radon detectors preempts the state regulation. The issue is always one of intent: If the federal government did not intend to preempt the state, or to occupy the entire field, then the state regulation will survive if it does not violate any independent constitutional prohibition. Here, there are strong clues that neither Congress nor the EPA intended to displace more-rigorous state regulation of radar detection: The federal government has not chosen to actually license radon testers, and the EPA is merely purporting to give useful information to the public, not to "regulate." Furthermore, it appears that a radon tester can comply simultaneously with both the federal "reasonably accurate" standard and the more-rigorous Magenta standard. All of this justifies the conclusion that the EPA's maintenance of its reasonably-accurate-methods list was not intended to displace more-rigorous state licensing standards.

(A) is wrong because (among other reasons) the Full Faith and Credit Clause applies only to require a state to honor the statutes and judgments of *another state*, not those of the federal government.

(B) is wrong because, for the reasons described above, the EPA's list was not intended to displace or preempt more-rigorous state licensing methods, so the Supremacy Clause never came into action.

(D) is wrong because the fact that what is being regulated cannot "move in interstate commerce" does not dispose of the issue of whether federal regulation has preempted the state regulation. For instance, Congress could have (but did not) authorized the EPA to enact radon-testing regulations that would displace any more-stringent state regulation; in doing so Congress could have used its commerce power based on the fact that radon *detectors* move in or affect interstate commerce even though the basement areas being measured do not themselves move in interstate commerce.

Answer 37

Choice (**C**) is correct. Congress has the power to consent to state conduct that would, in the absence of congressional consent, violate the dormant commerce clause. That's what has happened here. And the usual rule prohibiting Congress from enacting a statute overruling a constitutional decision of the U.S. Supreme Court does not apply here: Congress is not "overruling" the Court's judgment, it's simply changing the law for future cases, which is an action that is within the legislative power of Congress and that doesn't encroach on the Court's power to decide cases.

(A) is wrong because this is one area in which Congress may reverse the impact of prior Supreme Court decisions. In many areas of constitutional law (e.g., the meaning of the equal protection, due process and free speech guarantees), Congress does not have power to prospectively overrule decisions of the Supreme Court. But that is not true of the Court's decisions in some other areas. In particular, Congress has the power to authorize state conduct that would otherwise violate the dormant commerce clause, and the fact that the Supreme Court has already held that particular state conduct violates the dormant commerce clause does not negate this power.

(B) is wrong because it mischaracterizes what the statute did. The congressional statute permitting any state to regulate the degree of light reflectiveness of the exteriors of trucks using the state's highways did not overrule the U.S. Supreme Court's judgment. If the Court had, for example, awarded damages or attorney's fees to the prevailing party in that earlier suit, those awards would remain in effect after Congress enacted the statute, and Congress would not have had the power to reverse those litigant-specific outcomes. But here, Congress's statute simply changed the law for *future cases*, which is an action that is within the legislative power of Congress and that does not encroach on the Court's judicial power to decide cases within its jurisdiction.

(D) is wrong because it relies on a non-existent source of congressional power. While the Constitution gives Congress the power to *appropriate money* to promote the general welfare of the United States (i.e., to "tax and spend" for the general welfare), it does not give Congress the power generally to enact *regulatory*-type statutes on the basis that they promote the general welfare.

Since there is no taxing or spending being done by the statute here, the concept of "general welfare" is irrelevant.

Answer 38

Choice (**B**) is correct. The Redville rule, by requiring higher limo prices for interstate trips than would be set by the market, might well be an undue burden on interstate commerce (and thus a violation of the dormant commerce clause) if there were no federal legislation on the subject. But Congress has the power to allow state regulation that would otherwise violate the dormant commerce clause, and that's what happened here: Congress gave the city containing the airport the right to set limo rates without respect to the rates' effect on commerce, so there is no dormant commerce clause problem.

(A) is wrong because it incorrectly explains the correct result. If Congress had not specifically allowed the city in which any specified airport is located to regulate limos serving that city, Redville would be acting unconstitutionally by burdening interstate commerce. That is, as a general principle it is not correct to say that a city has exclusive regulatory authority over all transportation to and from an airport located within the city. (Under the dormant commerce clause, no city or state may intentionally discriminate against, or unduly burden, interstate commerce, even if that commerce relates to a facility located within the city or state that's doing the regulating.) Only the special congressional authorization validates the Redville regulation.

(C) is wrong because what Redville is doing here is regulating, not "taking." Only if a regulation destroys all economic value of a business will it be deemed to be a Fifth Amendment "taking" for which compensation must be paid. And there's no evidence that the regulation here will destroy all economic value of the plaintiff's business. Furthermore, even in the exceptionally unlikely event that a court would conclude that there had been a taking, the proper remedy would be an order that Redville pay "just compensation," not a decree holding the regulation itself invalid.

(D) is wrong because Congress has authorized the regulation in question. If Congress had not expressly authorized the type of regulation at issue here (limo rates for airport traffic, imposed by the city where the airport is located), this choice would likely be correct, because the uniform-rate regulation probably would unduly burden (and discriminate against) out-of-state-based limo companies. But Congress always has the power to authorize what would otherwise be a violation of dormant-commerce-clause principles, and that's what it has done here.

Answer 39

Choice (**B**) is correct. In the absence of congressional action, the state rule here probably would be a violation of the dormant commerce clause (what the question calls the "negative implications of the Commerce Clause"), because it discriminates against out-of-state growers. But Congress may use its commerce power to permit states to discriminate against interstate commerce. The federal statute here explicitly authorizes states to enact state-of-origin labeling requirements on imported citrus fruit.

(A) is incorrect, because the balancing argument would work only if: (1) Congress had not enacted a statute authorizing the state regulation at issue; and (2) the state law did not discriminate against interstate commerce. In this case, however, neither of these conditions is satisfied: Congress *has* authorized state-of-origin labeling requirements on imported citrus fruit, and the state law *is* discriminatory.

(C) is incorrect, because the state law *does* discriminate against out-of-state citrus growers, in that the law requires that all citrus fruit "imported" into the state be stamped with the state of origin, while the law imposes no such requirement on citrus fruit grown within the state.

(D) is incorrect, because although this argument correctly paraphrases the burden on the state to justify a law that discriminates against interstate commerce, the argument would be less likely to succeed than the "Congress authorized it" argument: In the absence of congressional authorization, the burden on a state to justify its discriminatory regulation is a heavy one, and states only rarely succeed in carrying it. Here, the availability of less-discriminatory alternatives (e.g., requiring in-state growers, not just out-of-staters, to stamp the state's two-letter code on the fruit) makes it unlikely that the state would win with this argument.

Answer 40

Choice (**C**) is correct. The operations of the federal government are indeed immune from state regulation, no matter how reasonable the state regulation, and even though the regulation is a generally-applicable one that treats the federal government no differently than anyone else. Since the office building is owned by and operated by the federal government, this regulatory immunity applies.

(A) is wrong, because even though the regulation of pollution may be a legitimate state police power concern, that regulation must give way to federal regulatory immunity.

(B) is wrong because, even if regulation of pollution is a joint concern of the federal and state governments, and even though both governments can regulate private parties (assuming that the state regulation is not inconsistent with the federal regulation), it does not follow that the state can regulate the federal government—under the principles of regulatory immunity, the state cannot do so.

(D) is wrong because there is no "de minimis" exception to the principle that states may regulate pursuant to their inherent police power. (The sole problem here is the federal immunity from regulation, which applies whether the asserted violation of the state's regulation is de minimis or not.)

Answer 41

Choice (C) is correct—the federal government, including the operations of federal agencies, are essentially immune from state regulation. Notice that the answer does not use the word "immunity"—it's up to you to recognize that when the choice says "may not be regulated," what's being referred to is the concept of immunity.

(A) is incorrect, because of federal immunity; note that if there were no federal immunity involved (e.g., the entity being regulated was a private company pursuing its own interests), this choice would be correct, at least if the regulation were challenged on equal protection grounds.

(B) is wrong because the Tenth Amendment has no relevance here. The Tenth Amendment does not restrict the powers of the federal government as long as the latter is not purporting to require the state to enact laws or regulations. Here, the Departmetn of Energy ("DOE") isn't requiring the state to enact a federal regulatory program—the DOE is merely pursuing its own regulatory program. And the Tenth Amendment doesn't limit DOE's ability to do that.

(D) is wrong because the Equal Protection Clause would not invalidate this ordinance. The ordinance is an economic regulation, and clearly satisfies the applicable rational-basis test (see the discussion of Choice (A) above). It's only federal immunity from state regulation that causes the ordinance not to be enforceable against the DOE's activities.

Answer 42

Choice (A) is correct. The Blue court issued a valid judgment against the plaintiffs. Therefore, the Red state court was required by the Full Faith and Credit Clause to enforce that judgment, even though the only solvent defendant in the Blue proceeding is the state of Red itself. The constitutional requirement of Full Faith and Credit does not recognize any exception just because the state in which enforcement is sought happens to itself be the defendant against which the original judgment was issued. (By the way, it's important that all the defendants admitted jurisdiction in the original Blue proceedings—if the Blue courts had not had jurisdiction, the defendants could make a "collateral attack" on the original judgment in Red court, and full faith and credit would not have applied.)

(B) is wrong because it gives an incorrect reason for the current result. A state may, without violating the Equal Protection Clause, cap (or even abolish entirely) its liability for torts by its employees or agents. The correct reason Red must pay the judgment is as given in (A).

(C) is wrong because (1) although a state does, as a general rule, have the right to enforce a public policy limiting its tort liability, this right does not derive from the Tenth Amendment; and (2) in any event, a state's obligation to enforce an out-of-state judgment under the Full Faith and Credit Clause takes priority over the state's own public policy, at least where the out-of-state judgment came after all defendants had a full and fair opportunity to litigate in a court that had jurisdiction over them.

(D) is wrong because the Red courts must enforce the Blue court's judgment, regardless of whether a Red court would have reached the same conclusion on the merits as the Blue court did about whether Red as employer is liable for these torts by its agents.

Answer 43

Choice **(C)** is correct. The Full Faith & Credit (FF&C) Clause prohibits state courts from re-litigating cases in which the courts of another state have rendered final judgment. Even if the first court should have applied the second court's laws under standard conflict rules, the FF&C Clause bars the second court from re-hearing the case. (If the State B courts had not had jurisdiction over the man, and the jurisdiction issue had not been litigated or waived, the FF&C Clause might not bar the State A courts from hearing the new suit. But the facts tell us that the man "defended" on the merits, thus waiving any claim he might have had that the State B courts lacked jurisdiction over him.) Accordingly, the court in State A was required to dismiss the suit.

(A) is incorrect, because the FF&C Clause prevents the court in State A from re-litigating the merits, and the fact that the woman drove the car to State A has no effect on the constitutional analysis.

(B) is, similarly, wrong because the location of the car has no effect on the constitutional analysis.

(D) is wrong because the movement of the car across state lines did not create a federal question.

Answer 44

Choice **(C)** is correct. This is a classic illustration of a state regulation in the economic or social-welfare area, where no fundamental right is involved. (Insurers don't have a fundamental right to adopt any particular pricing mechanism.) Since the "one price for all" scheme is rationally related to achieving one or more legitimate state objectives (e.g., promoting a sense of fairness and non-discrimination among insurance customers living in a particular county, or avoiding race-based redlining), the scheme does not violate the insurer's due process rights.

(A) is wrong for the same reason (C) is right—the company may have a due process right not to be irrationally deprived of its desired pricing mechanism, but the requirement of uniform pricing here is not irrational.

(B) is wrong, because the statute does not unduly burden interstate commerce (it only applies to policies written in-state, and it does not discriminate against out-of-state insurers).

(D) is wrong, because federal courts do not have a duty to abstain from passing on the case until the state courts have had an opportunity to pass on the constitutionality of this state statute. When a litigant believes that a state statute violates the federal Constitution, the litigant may sue immediately in federal court for a determination that this is so, as long as the requirements of justiciability (e.g., ripeness, actual injury to the plaintiff, etc.) are met. In other words, there is no sense in which state courts get "first shot" to determine the federal constitutionality of a state statute.

Answer 45

Choice (**B**) is correct. The Supreme Court has held that parental notification requirements constitute an undue burden on the minor's right to abortion, and thus violate the minor's substantive right to due process, unless there is a satisfactory judicial bypass procedure. Such a procedure must allow a court to approve an abortion for a minor without parental notification if the court finds either that: (1) the minor is sufficiently mature and informed to make an independent decision to obtain an abortion; or (2) the abortion would be in the minor's best interest. Because no such bypass procedure is included in the statute at issue, the court will hold the statute unconstitutional.

(A) is wrong because, although it is true that the statute at issue is unconstitutional, this answer misstates the basis for this conclusion—the Supreme Court has held that a short waiting period does not constitute an undue burden on a woman's right to an abortion.

(C) is wrong, because the rights of parents to supervise the health care of their minor children do not always prevail over the individual rights of their children—as discussed above, the Court has held that parental notification requirements violate a minor's right to an abortion unless there is a satisfactory judicial bypass procedure, which is not included in the statute at issue.

(D) is wrong, because the Court has held that parental notification requirements are an undue burden, and violate a minor's right to an abortion, unless there is a satisfactory judicial bypass procedure.

Answer 46

Choice (**C**) is correct. The Court held in *Webster v. Reproductive Health Services* (1989) that a state could constitutionally forbid the use of all public facilities and publicly-employed staff in abortions, without thereby violating the substantive due process right to abortion. If the state forbade all facilities in the state—public or private—from performing abortions, that would be an unconstitutional "undue burden" on abortion, but the availability of private-facility abortions here prevents an undue burden from occurring. And the fact that the state here is allowing the use of public facilities for those abortions necessary to save the life of the mother makes it even more clear that the regulation is constitutional. (Probably under *Webster* such an exception is not even required.)

(A) is wrong because the Court has held (in *Webster*, supra) that the availability of private-facility abortions means that a ban on the use of public facilities does not impermissibly interfere with the right of abortion.

(B) is wrong because the Court has held (in *Harris v. McRae* (1980)) that government's refusal to fund abortions for patients who cannot afford them does not constitute an interference with the constitutionally-protected right to abortion.

(D) is wrong because the Court no longer uses the privilege/right distinction in deciding cases involving the exercise of the important constitutional interests, and it is certainly not the case that the state may condition access to public facilities for an abortion "on any basis it chooses." (For instance, the state could not say that it will fund abortions at state-owned facilities for white women but not black women.)

Answer 47

Choice (**C**) is correct. Since the government had previously agreed that the teacher could only be fired if she were shown not to have had "good behavior," she had a due process "property" interest in maintaining her job. The Supreme Court has held that once a person has a property interest in a job or benefit, only the courts, not the government, may prescribe the procedures that are to be used to terminate that job or benefit. So the fact that the statute provides only for a post-discharge hearing does not mean that this is all that the teacher is due. Instead, the Court has held that the job holder is entitled to a hearing before the termination (or at least before the termination of salary). *Cleveland Bd. of Ed. v. Loudermill* (1985). Since the statute here did not give the teacher such a pre-termination hearing, the statute was unconstitutional. And the statute did not get saved by the government's holding a hearing three months after the termination.

(A) is wrong because it is not true that a claim that a state statute is unconstitutional is not ripe until all state-court remedies have been exhausted. When a litigant believes that a state statute violates the federal Constitution, the litigant may sue immediately in federal court for a determination that this is so, as long as the requirements of justiciability are met. And although it's true that one of the requirements of justiciability is that the case be "ripe," ripeness merely means that the plaintiff has already suffered, or imminently faces, actual injury.

(B) is wrong for at least two reasons: (1) not all state employees have the right not to be dismissed except for good cause (and this choice implies that all of them do); and (2) even if an employee such as the teacher here had a right not to be dismissed except for good cause, the burden of proof on the government would be just a preponderance-of-the-evidence standard, not the hard-to-satisfy "beyond a reasonable doubt" standard.

(D) is wrong because the Supreme Court has held that, where a state employee has a right to hold her job during good behavior, the employee is entitled not only to a pre-dismissal statement of reasons but a pre-dismissal hearing (and the fact that the statute provides only for a post-dismissal hearing does not change the constitutional requirement of a pre-dismissal one). Cf. *Loudermill*, supra.

Answer 48

Choice (C) is correct, because the equal protection issue will determine the validity of the restriction under these facts. Restrictions on the use of land are valid as long as they aren't repugnant to law or public policy. The restriction here creates a classification: people aged 21 and over versus those under 21. A classification that determines people's rights — here, the right to occupy land — is the hallmark of an equal protection problem.

However, this question involves one further step, because the restriction here is a private agreement between owners of land in the subdivision, and the Constitution doesn't ban purely private acts of discrimination; some state action is required. What makes this an equal protection issue is that the other lot owners are seeking to have the restriction enforced in court, and such enforcement constitutes state action. Thus, if the restriction is an equal protection violation, the court could not enforce it. You might argue that the classification here addresses who can exercise the fundamental right of procreation, since those living in the subdivision could not have children. In that case, the restriction would be subject to strict scrutiny, and would thus almost certainly be invalid. What this shows is that an analysis of the restriction under the Equal Protection Clause would determine its validity, and this is the only argument of these four that will determine the lawfulness of the restriction. Thus, Choice (C) is the best response.

(A) is wrong, because the distinction between realty and personalty would be irrelevant here. The restriction here addresses who may own or occupy the land. Thus, it doesn't matter how the land is occupied, whether it's realty, personalty, a gingerbread house, or a giant shoe, as long as the restriction is lawful. The distinction of realty versus personalty would be relevant, say, to whether or not the mobile home were considered a fixture, or, alternatively, for probate purposes in determining who is entitled to the mobile home (if the decedent has willed personalty to one person and realty to someone else). The distinction isn't relevant to this restriction; the only distinction involved here is between people aged 21 and over, and those under 21. Thus, the realty versus personalty distinction won't be the issue deciding the case, making (A) not the best response.

(B) is wrong, because the restriction here wouldn't be unlawful because it's a restraint on alienation. A deed restriction is only an invalid restraint on alienation if landowners could not sell their lots as restricted. Otherwise, property is frequently sold with restraints, like easements and restrictions on use. Here, the property owners could clearly sell their lots to adults without children. Thus, it's not the restriction's impact on alienation that would make it unlawful. As a result, it's not the alienation issue that would decide this case. Since (B) states otherwise, it's not the best response.

(D) is wrong, because if the restriction were valid, it needn't be expressly repeated verbatim in the carpenter's deed in order to bind him. As long as the property holder has, at the very least, constructive notice of the restriction, it doesn't matter that it doesn't appear in his own deed. For instance, real covenants and equitable servitudes are binding as long as they appear somewhere in the chain of title, even if they are completely absent from the current owner's deed. Here, the carpenter's deed specifically references the plat for the subdivision; thus, he had notice of the restriction, and, if the restriction were lawful, it would be binding on the carpenter even without its being repeated verbatim in his deed. Since Choice (D) discusses an issue that will not be determinative under these facts, it's not the best response.

Answer 49

Choice (**B**) is correct. The city here is engaging in economic regulation, and no suspect class or fundamental right is involved. The "even plausibly justifiable" standard is a good summary of the extreme deference that courts give to government choices in the economic-regulatory area where no suspect class or fundamental right is at issue. Grandfather schemes in which people with longtime track records of pursuing an activity are treated more favorably than newcomers to that activity are a good illustration of classifications that are very likely to be upheld.

(A) is wrong because it incorrectly applies strict scrutiny; strict scrutiny would be appropriate for a regulation that intentionally disfavored a suspect class (e.g., persons of a particular race) or substantially impaired a fundamental right (e.g., the right to vote), but the classification here does not do either of these things.

(C) is wrong because the grandfather scheme here would not be found to be so "tenuous" or "underinclusive" as to fail the easy-to-satisfy rational-basis test.

(D) is wrong as a statement of law; so long as no suspect class or fundamental right is impaired, grandfather clauses are usually found valid, and are certainly not "per se violations" of equal protection.

Answer 50

Choice (**D**) is correct. Note that the only plausible ground for plaintiff's attack is the Equal Protection Clause — government is saying that certain groups of four or more people can live together without a permit and others can't. Persons convicted of crimes have not been held to constitute either a suspect or a quasi-suspect class for equal protection purposes. Therefore, the zoning board's denial of the permit discriminated against neither a suspect class nor a quasi-suspect class. Nor did it unduly burden the exercise of a fundamental right (since housing has not been held to be a fundamental right for equal protection purposes). The denial therefore triggers rational basis scrutiny.

(A) is wrong because housing has been held not to be a fundamental right for equal protection purposes. *Lindsey v. Normet* (1972). Therefore, the strict scrutiny standard articulated in this choice would not be appropriate.

(B) is wrong because convicts have never been held to be a semi-suspect class. (The only semi-suspect classes recognized by the Court to date are gender and illegitimacy.) Nor does housing have any special equal protection status as a "basic subsistence right." Therefore, the intermediate standard of review (which this choice correctly describes as the "substantially related to an important state interest" test) would not apply here.

(C) is wrong because convicts do not constitute a suspect class for equal protection purposes. Therefore, while this would be the correct test if the legislative classification involved a suspect class (e.g., race or national origin), it is not the correct test for this case.

Answer 51

Choice **(B)** is correct. What makes this question slightly challenging is that you're expecting a choice that uses the phrase "equal protection" (since the government is treating members of one race differently than those of other races). But the key is that the way equal protection principles apply to the federal government is via the Fifth Amendment's Due Process Clause—the Supreme Court held, in *Bolling v. Sharpe* (1954), that the equal protection principles of the Fourteenth Amendment apply to actions of the federal government through incorporation into the Due Process Clause of the Fifth Amendment. The new security measures presumptively violate equal protection because they contain a racial classification: The new measures apply only to individuals of one race. A court therefore would uphold the measures only if the government could prove that they are necessary to serve a compelling public interest, a standard that the government typically cannot meet and would be very unlikely to meet here.

(A) is wrong because the statute here would be a proper exercise of the commerce power, if it did not violate the Due Process Clause. The Commerce Clause grants Congress plenary power to regulate the safety of air travel because airlines are instrumentalities of interstate commerce.

(Instead, the problem is that the new security measures presumptively violate equal protection, as made applicable to the states via the Fifth Amendment's Due Process Clause. See Choice (B) for more details.)

(C) is wrong because the Privileges and Immunities Clause of Article IV prohibits only actions by states that improperly discriminate against the citizens of other states. The Clause does not apply to actions of the federal government.

(D) is wrong because the Privileges or Immunities Clause of the Fourteenth Amendment prohibits *states* from depriving individuals of the privileges or immunities of United States citizenship. The U.S. Supreme Court has never applied the Clause to actions of the federal government.

(Furthermore, even where state rather than federal action is at issue, be skeptical of any choice that finds a governmental action unconstitutional on the grounds that it violates the Fourteenth Amendment's Privileges or Immunities Clause. That Clause protects only the privileges and immunities of "national citizenship." There are very few privileges and immunities of national citizenship, mainly the right to vote in national elections, the right to travel physically from state to state, and the right not to be discriminated against by virtue of one's having recently moved to the state from a different state.)

Answer 52

Choice **(C)** is correct, because the prosecution's dismissal of jurors solely on racial grounds violates the defendant's equal protection rights. A state may not permit litigants (including litigants who are state actors, such as prosecutors) to exclude jurors based solely on racial grounds. This constitutes a violation of the other litigant's equal protection rights. *Batson v. Ky.* (1986). And that's especially true where the exclusion is based upon the reasoning that "the jurors would decide the case solely on racial considerations," as the prosecution is claiming here.

(A) is wrong, because the director's race wouldn't matter. Prosecutors may not use peremptory challenges to dismiss potential jurors based solely on the race of the juror. (See the discussion of Choice (C) above.) That's true regardless of whether the litigant who is raising the equal protection argument (here, the director) is or isn't a member of the race being discriminated against.

(B) is wrong, because the use of peremptory challenges to dismiss potential jurors based solely on the juror's race is automatically deemed to be a denial of an impartial jury. The use of peremptory challenges based solely on the race of the potential jurors violates equal protection. *Batson v. Ky.*, supra. The litigant who is objecting to the practice doesn't have to make a specific showing that this exclusion denied her an impartial jury — the mere fact of intentional exclusion suffices to create an equal protection violation.

(D) is wrong, because "fair cross-section of the community" is not the appropriate legal standard. When a litigant excludes potential jurors based solely on racial grounds, the other litigant's equal protection rights have been violated. (See the discussion of Choice (C) above.) A litigant has the right to an "impartial" jury, and a jury of her peers. But there is no right to a jury consisting of "a fair cross-section of the community."

Answer 53

Choice **(D)** is correct. The issue here is the validity of the school's gender-based classification, under which students who are mothers of an infant can use the day-care center but students who are fathers of an infant cannot. For such a gender-based classification, the court uses intermediate-level scrutiny, under which, as Choice (D) recites, the defendant (the government) bears the burden of showing that its classification is "substantially related" to the fulfillment of an "important governmental interest." *Craig v. Boren* (1976). Notice that the standard is the same for a male plaintiff who is disadvantaged by the classification as it would be for a female plaintiff who was disadvantaged.

(A) would be correct if the classification were one that did not involve a suspect or semi-suspect class or fundamental interest (e.g., a garden-variety economic or social-welfare regulation); but since gender is a semi-suspect category, the standard in Choice (A) is insufficiently demanding.

(B) is incorrect mainly because, when the classification is based on gender, the use of semi-strict scrutiny means that the government bears the burden of persuasion. (Also, the key phrases "narrowly drawn as possible" and "substantial governmental interest" are not quite right.)

(C) is wrong because, while it correctly places the burden of persuasion on the government defendant, this choice recites the standard for strict rather than semi-strict scrutiny.

Answer 54

Choice **(D)** is correct. Direct impairments of the right to vote, based on a person's race or color, may violate the Fifteenth Amendment, even where Congress has not passed a statute banning the impairment.

(A) is wrong because the Thirteenth Amendment bars only slavery. Congress has the power to ban the "badges and incidents" of slavery under this Amendment, and voting rules that have a racially discriminatory impact might qualify as a badge-or-incident, but Congress has not used its power here (since we're told that there is no applicable federal statute).

(B) is wrong because the Due Process Clause does not directly address voting rights, so any due process violation would be far more tenuous than the Thirteenth Amendment claim. (There might be a valid Fourteenth Amendment *equal protection* claim, but *that's not one of the choices.*)

(C) is wrong because the Fourteenth Amendment's Privileges or Immunities Clause is interpreted to protect only the rights of "national" (not state) citizenship, and the right to vote in a local election is not a right of national citizenship, at least where the local government is not discriminating against those who recently moved there.

Answer 55

Choice **(C)** is correct. Ballot restrictions that are so severe that minor-party and independent candidates have no realistic opportunity to get on the ballot are given strict scrutiny, under both the Equal Protection Clause and the First Amendment's Freedom of Association Clause. *Williams v. Rhodes* (1968). The statute here is such a restriction, because it makes it completely impossible (not just somewhat harder) for someone who fails to get a major-party nomination to then run as an independent or minor-party candidate in the general election, no matter how much public support that person can demonstrate. Consequently, the choice here, by articulating strict scrutiny as the standard, is correct.

(A) is incorrect because, although it correctly articulates the strict-scrutiny standard, it incorrectly says that the plaintiff who is challenging the government bears the burden of persuasion; in those scenarios triggering strict scrutiny, the burden of persuasion is on the government.

(B) is wrong because it incorrectly uses the easy-to-satisfy mere-rationality standard, when what is at issue is a serious impairment of the fundamental right to be a candidate (and the right of voters to choose the best candidate).

(D) is wrong because, for the reasons stated above, the court would apply the strict scrutiny standard on these facts.

Answer 56

Choice **(C)** is correct, because access to the ballot is protected by the Equal Protection Clause of the Fourteenth Amendment. In particular, the Court has strictly scrutinized state burdens that seem to protect major parties at the expense of new parties, minor parties and independent candidates, especially where the disadvantaged voters and/or candidates are racial minorities. See, e.g., *Williams v. Rhodes* (1968). While the equal protection argument might not win (the restrictions here on candidates from new parties are much less severe than the ones struck down in *Williams*, and might not even trigger strict scrutiny), it is the only argument of the four presented that has even a reasonable chance of success.

(A) is wrong because while speech is protected by the First Amendment, access to the ballot is protected by the Fourteenth Amendment. A political party's argument that it is being denied ballot access might theoretically be based on freedom-of-association concepts. But the Court has tended to decide such ballot-access cases on equal protection grounds, not on First Amendment grounds. On the facts here, the state is not saying that people may not get together to join the new political party that is the plaintiff here; the state is merely making it tough for that party to get on the ballot. Since the essence of the party's claim is that the state is preferring the two established parties over newcomer parties, that's really an "unequal treatment" claim, i.e., an equal protection claim.

(B) is wrong because, while the members of the new political party are racial minorities, the issue in this question is access to the ballot, not the badges and incidents of slavery. The Thirteenth Amendment, § 1, provides that "neither slavery nor involuntary servitude, except as a punishment for a crime . . . shall exist in the United States." Section 2 allows Congress to pass "all laws necessary and proper for abolishing all badges and incidents of slavery." While the members of the new party that is the plaintiff here are racial minorities, the connection between a state's making it hard for a minority-based party to get on the ballot and the institution of slavery would almost certainly be held to be too attenuated to constitute a Thirteenth Amendment violation.

(D) is wrong because the Fifteenth Amendment prohibits the federal and state governments from denying any citizen the *right to vote* for reasons of race or color, and the state statute here isn't inhibiting anyone's right to vote; it's directed at who may be on the ballot. Traditionally, the Court has viewed ballot-access restrictions as implicating only the Equal Protection Clause, not the Fifteenth Amendment right to vote.

Answer 57

Choice **(C)** is correct. First, education is not a fundamental right for equal protection purposes. *San Antonio Sch. Dist. v. Rodriguez* (1973). Second, wealth classifications are not a suspect category. This choice therefore correctly asserts that (1) no fundamental right or suspect classification is involved in this case; and (2) where this is true, the plaintiff must bear the very difficult burden of proving that there is no rational relationship between the classification being used and any legitimate state interest. (By the way, it is very unlikely that the plaintiffs would win under this test; a school-funding scheme relying principally on local property taxes was upheld against rational-basis equal protection attack in *San Antonio Sch. Dist. v. Rodriguez*, supra.)

(A) is wrong because classifications based on wealth are not "inherently suspect" for equal protection purposes, so such classifications do not have to satisfy the strict scrutiny standard that this choice articulates.

(B) is wrong because the Court has held that education (or at least the right to have a public education that goes beyond minimally-adequate standards) is not a fundamental right for equal protection purposes; therefore, the strict scrutiny standard articulated by this choice would not apply.

(D) is wrong because it articulates an intermediate level of scrutiny, and that level is only used in cases involving semi-suspect classifications (e.g., ones based on gender).

Answer 58

Choice **(D)** is correct, because without the showing of "rough proportionality" specified in this choice, the ordinance violates the Takings Clause. *Dolan v. City of Tigard* (1994) holds that when a city conditions a building permit on some "give back" by the owner, there must be a "rough proportionality" between the burdens on the public that the building permit would bring about, and the benefits to the public from the give-back. There's nothing in the facts to suggest that the city ever made the required showing here. (Indeed, the facts tell us that city officials presented no evidence of any sort, so they certainly didn't produce evidence either about the size of the public burden from allowing the coffeehouse or the size of the corresponding benefit from the new child care facility they were requiring here.)

(A), (B), and (C) are all wrong because they misstate the burden of proof and the standard. When a city demands a "give back" in return for approving construction, the city, not the owner, bears the burden of proof as to rough proportionality (and this burden is probably

CONSTITUTIONAL LAW ANSWERS

somewhere between the easy-to-satisfy "rational relation" test of Choice (A) and the strict scrutiny of Choice (D)).

Answer 59

Choice **(B)** is correct. When a state (or subdivision of a state, like a city and its municipally-owned operations) regulates a right that is "fundamental to national unity," and does so in a way that disadvantages out-of-staters, that regulation will essentially be subject to strict scrutiny under the Article IV Privileges and Immunities (P&I) Clause. (Among other things, the state must show that the discrimination against non-residents bears a "substantial relation-ship" to the problem the state is attempting to solve.) Practice of one's business or profession is a right "fundamental to national unity" for P&I purposes.

The case here is on all fours with *New Hampshire v. Piper* (1985), where the Court held that New Hampshire's attempt to restrict the right to practice law to state residents violated the Article IV P&I Clause. Applying *Piper*, since there's no showing that out-of-state doctors are the peculiar source of any special problem that the hospital is trying to solve, the restriction violates the P&I Clause.

(By the way, there's no exception under the P&I Clause for activities in which the city or state is a "market participant," as there is under the dormant commerce clause. *United Bldg. and Constr. Trades Council v. Camden* (1984). So the fact that the city owns the hospital that's making the rule doesn't help it, as it would against a Commerce Clause attack.)

(A) is wrong because the legislature of state Red was not trying to punish the doctor. A bill of attainder is a legislative act that attempts to inflict punishment without a judicial trial upon individuals who are designated by name or in terms of past conduct. The constitutional pro-hibition against a bill of attainder would not be helpful to the doctor because the hospital here merely took the purely regulatory action of changing the residency requirement for practicing medicine at the hospital — no public entity named the doctor as a criminal, or attempted to punish or stigmatize her, which is what a bill of attainder would have done.

(C) is wrong because the doctor would have to show that the licensing requirement was not rationally related to a legitimate government interest, a showing the doctor probably couldn't make. The Due Process Clause of the Fourteenth Amendment provides that no state shall make or enforce any law which shall deprive any person of life, liberty, or property, with-out due process of law. When a fundamental right is not involved, substantive due process requires only that a law be "rationally related" to the achievement of a "legitimate government interest." So to win on due process, the doctor would have to prove that Red's new residency requirement was not rationally related to some legitimate government purpose. This standard is very lenient and easy-to-satisfy. Here, for instance, the hospital could plausibly claim that it wants to have on staff only doctors who live very nearby, and that it's entitled to use state of residence as a proxy for nearby-ness. Although the fit between means and end isn't very tight under this rationale, it's almost certainly tight enough to meet the extremely lenient rational-relation standard.

(D) is wrong because state Red was not legislating against past acts. The Ex Post Facto Clauses, Article I, § 9 and § 10, prohibit both the federal government and the state, respectively, from passing legislation that retroactively alters the criminal law as to offenses or punishments, in a substantially prejudicial manner. A retroactive change in civil regulations, such as licensing requirements, cannot violate the prohibition, since the prohibition applies only to "penal," i.e., punitive, measures. Here, the facts make it clear that the hospital was not making a rule penalizing past acts, but was instead making residency a requirement to practice medicine in state Red going forward.

Answer 60

Choice (**A**) is correct. The provision is a *bill of attainder*. A bill of attainder is a law that provides for the punishment of a particular person without trial. The challenged provision satisfies this definition because it deprives two named professors of their salaries, and thus, their employment—a court would almost certainly hold that the purpose of the provision was punitive rather than purely regulatory. (Notice that this correct choice never uses the phrase "bill of attainder," even though that's the key to the analysis. This is typical of the MBE: When a particular doctrine with an unusual name is the key to solving the problem, the examiners will often go out of their way to phrase the correct choice in terms of how the doctrine functions, rather than giving the doctrine's name—they fear that giving the doctrine's name will spot the issue for you, and make the problem too easy. So it's up to you to notice that this is a bill of attainder, and that as such, the law has the problem specified in Choice (A)).

(B) is wrong because, while it is true that the court is likely to strike down the provision, this answer misstates the basis for this conclusion. The fact that the professors' conduct pre-existed the state law would be significant if the state law provided for a criminal penalty—it would then be unconstitutional as an *ex post facto* law in violation of Article I, Section 10, Clause 1 of the Constitution. The Ex Post Facto Clause, however, does not apply to laws attaching civil consequences to past conduct, which is what the present law does.

(C) is wrong because the Eleventh Amendment provides for state sovereign immunity from certain kinds of adjudications. It does not extend legislative authority of any kind to the states.

(D) is wrong because the Full Faith and Credit Clause (Article IV, Section 1 of the Constitution) does not insulate state laws from constitutional challenge. It merely requires state courts to accord due authority to the laws of other states, something that is not at issue here.

Answer 61

Choice (**C**) is correct. Although the state does some regulation of the insurance industry (for solvency), the state is not sufficiently involved with the operations of the insurance company here to satisfy the requirement—applicable to any equal protection claim—that there be "state action." Notice that the choice never uses the phrase "state action"—it's up to you to spot the state action issue and to notice that this choice's use of the phrase "not applicable to the actions of these . . . companies" captures the state-action concept.

(A) is wrong for several reasons, including most basically the fact that it ignores the state-action requirement for any equal protection claim. (The fact that the *state police* are arguably failing to give equal protection is irrelevant, since the police aren't a party and aren't tightly associated with a party.)

(B) and (D) are wrong, similarly, because they too ignore the state-action requirement for equal protection claims. (If the state-action requirement were satisfied—if, for instance, the state expressly required burglary-insurance rates to be adjusted based on local crime rates—then (D) would be the best answer because it correctly expresses the idea that a governmental classification that does not involve a suspect class or fundamental right needs to be supported only by a rational basis.)

Answer 62

Choice (**B**) is correct. The Thirteenth Amendment permits Congress to forbid the "badges and incidents" of slavery. This power has been interpreted by the Court to include the power to forbid even private acts of racial discrimination against black people, on the theory that such discrimination is the relic of slavery.

(A) is wrong because Congress does not have any "authority to enact laws for the general welfare" (only the power to "tax and spend" for the general welfare).

(C) is wrong because this might be an explanation of why the statute couldn't be supported by Congress's commerce power, but the Thirteenth Amendment power allows Congress to forbid even purely local racial discrimination (i.e., discrimination that does not involve interstate commerce).

(D) is wrong because if Congress's action falls within a specific grant of power (here, the Thirteenth Amendment grant), the Tenth Amendment acts as a limitation only in the highly specialized case of Congress's attempt to take over state lawmaking mechanisms.

Answer 63

Choice (**D**) is correct. The tax applies only to films that show some form of sexual intercourse. This means that the regulation is content-based (it treats different forms of expression differently depending solely on the message being conveyed). Therefore, the court will apply strict scrutiny to it. (Notice, by the way, that the tax is not limited to films that would be "obscene" — not all portrayals of sexual intercourse would be obscene; if only obscene films were taxed, probably strict scrutiny would *not* be used.)

Choice (A) is wrong because a tax is not a "prior restraint"; a legislative act imposes a prior restraint only where government forbids the doing of the act in advance (e.g., a statute forbidding showing of a film without first paying a license fee). Since the tax here kicks in only after the showing of the film, it is not a prior restraint.

Choice (B) is wrong because the regulation here is a content-based regulation on expression, and such a restraint is evaluated based on strict scrutiny, not the easy-to-satisfy rational- relation test.

Choice (C) is wrong because an equal protection attack on a legislative classification that does not involve a suspect or semi-suspect class or fundamental right is evaluated based on the easy-to-satisfy rational-relation standard, and the tax here would likely pass that standard.

Answer 64

Choice (**D**) is correct, because it correctly identifies both the level of the burden of proof, and the party on which it is placed. Here, the law limits the First Amendment, the fundamental right to free speech in a public place — the capitol steps. The right to such speech is not absolute; it can be limited, for instance, by valid "time, place, and manner" regulations. In order to be valid as such a regulation:

1. The law must be ***neutral as to the content*** of the speech;

2. It must ***further a significant government interest*** that is not capable of accomplishment by less restrictive means; and

3. There must be ***alternative media of communication*** available.

Thus, the law must promote a significant governmental interest; Choice (D) correctly recognizes this. Furthermore, it places the burden on the correct party. Once a law is shown to adversely impact a First Amendment right, the burden is on the state to prove that the statute is valid. Since Choice (D) correctly identifies the burden and the party on which it will be placed, it's the best response.

(A) is wrong, because it both places the burden on the wrong party, and it misstates the level of scrutiny the statute will undergo. Here, the law limits the First Amendment, the fundamental right to free speech in a public place — the capitol steps. The right to such speech is not absolute; it can be limited, for instance, by valid "time, place, and manner" regulations. In order to be valid as such a regulation:

1. The law must be neutral as to the content of the speech;

2. It must further a significant government interest that is not capable of accomplishment by less restrictive means; and

3. There must be alternative media of communication available.

Thus, the law must promote a significant governmental interest; Choice (A) understates the interest required by stating that the law need only meet the rational basis test. The rational basis test is used for economic and social legislation, not laws limiting First Amendment rights (among others).

Furthermore, Choice (A) misplaces the burden of proof. Once a law is shown to adversely impact a First Amendment right, the burden is on the state to prove that the statute is valid. Since (A) puts the burden on the wrong party, and misstates that burden, it's not the best response.

(B) is wrong, because although it correctly states the burden of proof, it places it on the wrong party. Here, the law limits the First Amendment, the fundamental right to free speech in a public place — the capitol steps. The right to such speech is not absolute; it can be limited, for instance, by valid "time, place, and manner" regulations. In order to be valid as such a regulation:

1. The law must be neutral as to the content of the speech;

2. It must further a significant government interest that is not capable of accomplishment by less restrictive means; and

3. There must be alternative media of communication available.

Here, Choice (B) correctly identifies this burden — it just places that burden on the wrong party. All the owner needs to prove is that his First Amendment rights were adversely impacted by the law. Then, it's up to the state to prove that the statute is valid. Since (B) misplaces this burden, it's not the best response.

(C) is wrong, because although it correctly identifies that the state bears the burden of proof, it understates that burden. Here, the law limits the First Amendment, the fundamental right to free speech in a public place — the capitol steps. The right to such speech is not absolute; it can be limited, for instance, by valid "time, place, and manner" regulations. In order to be valid as such a regulation:

1. The law must be neutral as to the content of the speech;

2. It must further a significant government interest that is not capable of accomplishment by less restrictive means; and

3. There must be alternative media of communication available.

Thus, the law must promote a significant governmental interest; Choice (C) understates the interest required by stating that the law need only meet the rational basis test. The rational basis test is used for economic and social legislation, not laws limiting First Amendment rights (among others).

Although Choice (C) understates the burden, it does place it on the correct party. Once a law is shown to adversely impact a First Amendment right, the burden is on the state to prove that the statute is valid. However, since Choice (C) understates the state's burden, it's not the best response.

Answer 65

Choice (**D**) is correct. While the First Amendment does indeed give the media a privilege to cover newsworthy events, that privilege does not extend to the broadcasting of a performance where this would deprive the performer of the commercial value of that performance. The fact pattern here is on all fours with *Zacchini v. Scripps-Howard Broadcasting* (1997).

(A) is wrong, because while the First Amendment does give a privilege for press coverage of newsworthy events, that privilege does not extend to a broadcast that takes so much of an act that it deprives the performer of much of the commercial value of the act.

(B) is wrong because news broadcasts are not "absolutely privileged"; rather, they receive a qualified privilege, subject to a number of limits (including, here, the limit that the broadcast not appropriate so much of a performance that the commercial value of the performance is taken from the performer).

(C) is wrong, because the Due Process Clause of the Fourteenth Amendment protects only against a taking by a government, and any taking here was by a private party (the TV station), not by the government.

Answer 66

Choice (**B**) is correct. The Supreme Court has repeatedly held that even if a city is using its zoning powers to limit or prohibit a speech-related activity, the regulation is acceptable if the city is reasonably targeting the secondary effects of that speech (e.g., crime or lower property values) rather than targeting the expressive content of that speech. See, e.g., *Erie v. Pap's A.M.* (2004) (city may completely ban "nude dancing" to combat the bad secondary effects of such). Since the government is targeting the secondary effects rather than the message, the regulation is to be evaluated based on the test for content-neutral time, place and manner regulations, which as this choice suggests makes such regulations valid as long as they are designed to serve a substantial governmental interest and do not unreasonably limit alternative avenues of expression. Since the interest in preventing blight is "substantial," and since adult uses are permitted in alternative venues (areas zoned commercial), these requirements are easily satisfied.

(A) is wrong because it falsely asserts that the city may use its zoning powers to forbid particular messages based on their content. Such a content-based regulation would have to be strictly scrutinized, and would almost certainly be struck down.

(C) is wrong because it badly misstates the law: Cities may indeed use their zoning regulations to prevent operators of adult theaters and the like from choosing their location, as long as the city is acting reasonably to combat the perceived negative secondary effects of the business, rather than out of distaste for the content of the messages transmitted by the business.

(D) is wrong because it exactly misstates present law; cities may (not "may not") "zone property in a manner calculated to protect property from the likely adverse secondary effects of adult theaters and bookstores." *Erie v. Pap's*, supra.

Answer 67

Choice (**A**) is correct, because the ordinance here is a content-neutral one that allows reasonable alternatives for the type of expression at issue. The Court has held that a city may confine sexually explicit land uses (like "adult theaters") to a single part of town, as part of a content-neutral attempt to regulate the bad "secondary effects" (e.g., increased crime, declining property values) of such uses. *Renton v. Playtime Theatres* (1986). The ordinance here is exactly on point with *Renton*. (By the way, a 2000 case, *Erie v. Pap's A.M.*, seems to go even further, apparently holding that a city may combat the secondary effects of adult activity like nude dancing by completely *banning* the activity, not just limiting it to a defined zone.) The key to the analysis is that the city is (supposedly) not engaging in "content based" discrimination, because it's attacking not the "message" of the adult activity, but merely its "secondary effects" (bad effects not associated with the precise message, like extra crime). Therefore, this is to be analyzed as a time-place-and-manner restriction (valid if it is substantially related to an important government objective, and it leaves open reasonable alternatives for the same type of expression) rather than as a content-based restriction (subject to strict scrutiny and almost certainly struck down).

(B) is wrong because adult entertainment *is* protected by the First and Fourteenth Amendments. Certain types of expression, while not directly suppressible on the grounds of their content, have been treated by the Court as being inherently less valuable, so that they may be regulated more extensively than speech close to the "core" of the First Amendment values, such as political speech. This less-favored category of speech includes speech that is "indecent," such as the adult entertainment here. So the zoning ordinance here is constitutional, but not for the reason stated. While not afforded the full protection of speech at the core of the First Amendment, such as political speech, public adult sexual expression is protected to some extent.

(C) is wrong because non-obscene adult entertainment may nonetheless be regulated despite its First Amendment protection. It's true that, as Choice (C) suggests, some adult entertainment as defined in the zoning ordinance is non-obscene, and may therefore not be banned on obscenity grounds. But as described in Choice (A) above, because of the "secondary effects" associated with adult entertainment (e.g., extra crime and declining property values), the city may make a time-place-and-manner regulation of such adult entertainment, by limiting it to a particular area of the city (or even banning it completely from the city limits).

(D) is wrong because there are allowable reasons for regulating speech beyond protecting "a community's residential neighborhoods." As Choice (A) above describes, a city may confine sexually explicit land uses like "adult theaters" to a single part of town, as part of a content-neutral attempt to regulate the bad "secondary effects" of such uses. The secondary effects that may be combatted are not limited to (though they may include) declining quality of the community's residential neighborhoods. (For instance, a city might ban adult entertainment from the core business district because such entertainment increases street crime, reduces commercial property values, etc.) So Choice (D) is wrong because it dramatically understates the bad secondary effects that a city is per

Answer 68

Choice **(D)** is the best response, because the operator's ordinance is a content-based restriction on core political speech, and cannot survive strict scrutiny. The city would not be permitted to simply ban all citizens from displaying political bumper sticks on their cars (that would be a content-based restriction on core political speech, which would be strictly scrutinized, and struck down because no compelling governmental interest has been shown). What the government cannot do directly, it cannot do indirectly by conditioning a government benefit (a cab license) on the licensee's agreement not to exercise the speech right in question. And nothing about the taxicab-licensing process changes the fact that the restriction cannot survive strict scrutiny: There is no indication of any meaningful risk that members of the public might incorrectly think that the slogans were attributable to council members, and even if there were such risk, avoiding it would hardly rise to the level of a "compelling" interest.

(A) is wrong because the ordinance is unconstitutional and the driver has not waived his rights to challenge it. It is presumptively unconstitutional for the government to place burdens on speech because of its content. To justify such content-based regulation of speech, the government must show that the regulation is necessary to achieve a compelling state interest and is narrowly defined to achieve that end. The fact that the city has not made display of all political messages a crime, and has instead used its power to deny a hack license as a "club" to induce some people (cab drivers) to "voluntarily" surrender their right to transmit those messages, is no defense. And the fact that the driver knew of the condition when he applied for his license would not cause him to lose standing to contest this clear unconstitutionality.

(B) is wrong because calling a government-bestowed benefit a "privilege" does not entitle the government to condition that benefit on the beneficiary's renunciation of the right to constitutionally-protected speech. As a general matter (subject to some exceptions not relevant here), government may not condition the receipt of a government-conferred benefit upon the beneficiary's willingness to forego the exercise of some constitutional right. So, for instance, government can't say, "We hereby fire any public employee who is a member of the Communist Party," if government wouldn't have the power under the First Amendment to ban Communist Party membership. *Elfbrandt v. Russell* (1966). Here, since the display of political messages on bumper stickers is protected by the First Amendment, the city cannot condition a government-bestowed "privilege" (a cab license) on the driver's willingness to forego the right to make such a display.

(C) is wrong because the ordinance is merely a regulation, not a "taking." The Fifth Amendment provides that private property shall not be taken for public use without paying just compensation to the owner. If the city confiscated cab licenses so that, say, it could operate all cabs itself for profit — and then refused to pay the former license-holders anything — the licensees might have a "taking" argument. But here, what is occurring is merely regulation, and it's regulation of a sort that falls far short of denying the licensee all economically viable use of his property (the standard for when a "taking" is deemed to have occurred). Therefore, the Takings Clause has not been violated.

Answer 69

Choice (B) is correct. The facts here are very similar to those of *Rankin v. McPherson*, where the Court held that: (1) the clerk's statement supporting a recent assassination attempt (of President Reagan) was indeed on a matter of "public concern"; and (2) the fact that the clerk had no policy-making role and that his statement had little negative impact on his job effectiveness made it unreasonable to dismiss him for that statement.

Choice (A) is wrong because even a "permanent" public employee (i.e., one with a property right in his post) may have his job taken without just compensation, as long as procedures constituting due process are followed. In other words, what the Due Process Clause guarantees on these facts is that the clerk's job won't be taken arbitrarily or capriciously, not that the job won't be taken "without just compensation" (a standard that would more properly be applied to the taking of tangible real or personal property rather than a job).

Choice (C) is wrong because the Court has held (in *Rankin*, supra) that although the government has an interest in having loyal and supportive employees, this interest does not outweigh the employee's interest in commenting on matters of public concern, where the comment does not undermine the employee's effectiveness in light of the non-policy-making and limited scope of the employee's job (which, like the job here, was clerical).

Choice (D) is wrong because: (1) the Court does not use the right/privilege distinction in First Amendment public employment cases; and (2) even if the Court did believe that public employment was a "privilege" rather than a "right," the Court would almost certainly view the case as justiciable.

Answer 70

Choice **(A)** is correct. When a public employee speaks on a matter that is arguably one of public concern, the employee gets limited protection against dismissal or discipline. However, where the content of the speech interferes with the speaker's proper performance of his job (or indicates that the speaker has underlying attitudes that would interfere with job perfor-mance), the balance is tipped heavily toward the employer's right to discharge or discipline the employee. Here, given that the inspector is required to enforce the building codes, and given that he has publicly stated that he does not even try to do this core job function on account of his attitudes towards slum dwellers, the city council was clearly justified in firing him.

Choice (B) is wrong because it is overbroad; even a government employee may make public comments inconsistent with current governmental policy, if the speaker is not in a public role and/or the comments do not interfere with the speaker's ability to perform his job adequately.

Choice (C) is wrong because, although the comments may have been "lawful" and on a "mat-ter of public concern," these two facts do not give the speaker immunity from being punished for the comments, for the reasons given above in the discussion of the correct choice.

Choice (D) is wrong because the fact that the comments were published in a newspaper that was in turn protected by the First and Fourteenth Amendments, is irrelevant to the question of whether the speaker may be punished; as described above, government may discharge a government employee for making statements (even ones published in a First-Amendment-protected newspaper) that seriously interfere with the employee's proper performance of his job.

Answer 71

Choice **(C)** is correct, because there is no constitutional principle requiring the government to divulge information it possesses. The suit here is claiming that some constitutional prin-ciple (presumably the First Amendment) is violated by the statute. This amounts to a claim that government is sometimes required by the First Amendment to divulge information that it possesses. However, the Supreme Court has never squarely found that the First Amendment ever requires the release of government information.

The First Amendment does, however, prevent government from imposing a "prior restraint," that is, from prohibiting private individuals (including the media) from publishing informa-tion that they possess, except in the most extraordinary instances (e.g., troop movements in time of war). So if the statute did prohibit a newspaper from publishing information it already possessed about the businessman (or about the prosecution's decision not to prosecute him), the statute would almost certainly violate this prohibition on prior restraints. Since (C) is the only choice that distinguishes between compelling the disclosure by the government of information it holds, and publication of privately-held information that originally comes from government records, it is the correct choice.

(A) is wrong because the answer doesn't address the issue the court would address. This choice sounds as though it would be relevant in defending against an equal protection claim, but it is irrelevant to defending against a First Amendment claim. For instance, if the statute prohibited newspapers from publishing the name of any person prosecuted and not convicted, the fact that it treated those who are acquitted the same as those against whom filed charges are dropped would be completely irrelevant—the statute would still be a prior restraint that violated the First Amendment.

(B) is wrong because even if the press doesn't have greater rights than citizens generally, this would not be a defense against the claim here. First, it's not clear whether the press has greater rights than those of citizens generally—the Court has never definitively decided this. Second, even if the press didn't have greater rights, that wouldn't necessarily help the state defend the statute; for instance, a court might hold that anyone—newspaper or private citizen—had the right to compel disclosure of this information. So the argument is irrelevant to the attack that's been made here.

(D) is wrong because it represents a more extreme position than the Court has ever endorsed. There are a few Court cases (e.g., *Richmond Newspapers v. Virginia* (1989)) that seem to suggest that the press may have some limited right of access to certain types of government-controlled information (e.g., contents of certain trials), if the state interest in non-disclosure is weak. So Choice (D), by indicating that no legislative objective is ever too weak to justify a sealing of governmental records, probably goes too far.

Answer 72

Choice **(B)** is correct. This choice correctly states the three-part *Lemon v. Kurtzman* (1970) test for government action that is alleged to benefit some religious interest. On the facts here, the statute passes all three parts: There is no evidence that the city's decision to operate the cemetery under these rules was intended to benefit religious groups; the primary effect of the cemetery operation is not to benefit those who put religious monuments on their plot; and the city's work in maintaining the religious monuments is so incidental to the overall operation of the cemetery—and so comparable to the work needed to maintain non-religious monuments—that there is no excessive entanglement between government and religion.

(A) is wrong because the amount of government funds spent is not dispositive; if the city was intending to benefit only religion (e.g., by providing a $20 reimbursement to the first 100 people who bought a piece of religious jewelry), the fact that only a "small amount" of city funds was spent would not save the expenditure from being a violation of the Establishment Clause.

(C) is wrong because it misstates the test for Establishment Clause violations; a city may maintain a "religious object" if the maintenance is part of a religiously-neutral program that is not intended to, and does not have the primary effect of, benefiting religion.

(D) is wrong because, if the government acts neutrally as to religion (as it has done here), there is no Establishment Clause violation whether the government has pursued a compelling interest or not.

Answer 73

Choice **(D)** is correct. Government may take generally-applicable actions that advance important public interests, without giving an exemption to those whose religious beliefs are thereby burdened. The facts tell us that the rules against overnight camping and campfires are "consistently enforced" because of "very great dangers," so the "generally applicable" and "advancement of important public interests" standards are met here. The fact that the superintendent doesn't like cults doesn't matter, because there is no indication that his decision to deny the permit here was motivated by anything other than a desire to enforce these generally-applicable rules.

(A) is wrong, for the same reason that (D) is right: Government may impose a generally-applicable rule to promote an important interest, even if government knows that its enforcement of that rule will interfere with religious conduct.

(B) is wrong because the Park Service's action did not "purposely and invidiously discriminate" against the group—what was being enforced was a generally-applicable rule that was not enacted for anti-religious purposes.

(C) is wrong because it misstates the law governing the Establishment Clause as well as the facts—if non-religious groups were permitted to take the same general type of action in question (here, overnight camping and campfires), which they are not, then it would not be a violation of the Establishment Clause for the government to allow a religious group to do the same thing (and, indeed, it would probably be a violation of the Free Exercise Clause for the government *not* to allow the religious group to do the same thing that the non-religious groups are permitted to do).

Answer 74

Choice (**B**) is correct, because it impliedly recognizes that the statute is a reasonable restriction on the free exercise of religion. The "free exercise" part of the First Amendment's Religion Clause guarantees the right to free exercise of religion. However, as with the First Amendment rights of speech, assembly, and association, this right is not absolute. Instead, reasonable regulation is permissible. And, in fact, if government enacts a "neutral law of general applicability" that forbids a certain type of conduct, the free exercise clause "does not relieve an individual of the obligation to comply" with that neutral law. *Employment Div. v. Smith*, 494 U.S. 872 (1990).

Here, the statute which the priest was convicted of violating is a "neutral" and "generally applicable" law prohibiting cruelty to animals — in other words, it does not forbid particular conduct if done as part of a religious observance while allowing the conduct if not religiously-motivated. (If the law made that distinction, it would not be a "generally applicable" law, and the rationale of *Employment Div. v. Smith* wouldn't apply, so the law would violate the free exercise right.) Therefore, the fact that the priest was motivated to perform the act by a sincere religious belief *would* not furnish a defense.

(A) is wrong, because a belief in Satan *could* enjoy constitutional protection, and (A) makes the blanket statement that it cannot. The "free exercise" part of the First Amendment's Religion Clause guarantees the right to free exercise of religion. In order to gain protection a religious belief must be held in good faith, and it must parallel an orthodox religious belief; it cannot be merely a political or philosophical view. *United States v. Seeger* (1965). Thus, a belief in Satan could constitute a religious belief. If the priest, in fact, had a religious belief in Satan, and the statute here violated the priest's right to the free exercise of religion (e.g., by forbidding *any* worship of Satan), his conviction would be overturned. Since (A) doesn't recognize this, it's not the best response.

(C) is wrong, because applying this statute to the priest would not violate his right to freedom of religion. The "free exercise" part of the First Amendment's Religion Clause guarantees the right to free exercise of religion. However, as is further explained in the discussion of Choice (B), the free exercise clause does not relieve a person of the obligation to obey a valid, neutral, and "generally applicable" prohibition of particular conduct. Since the prohibition on animal cruelty constitutes such a neutral and generally applicable prohibition, the priest's conviction does not violate his freedom of religion.

Incidentally, note that while the conduct of religion can be regulated, the beliefs themselves cannot. The right to *hold* religious beliefs is considered absolute. But since the priest is not being punished for believing in Satan, his conviction does not violate this principle.

(D) is wrong, because it does not apply the correct test to these facts.

The statute here impacts the priest's exercise of his religious beliefs. Thus, the "free exercise" part of the First Amendment's Religion Clause, guaranteeing the right to free exercise of religion, is called into question. This right, as with the First Amendment rights of speech, assembly, and association, is not absolute.

However, as is further explained in the discussion of Choice (B), the free exercise clause does not relieve a person of the obligation to obey a valid, neutral, and "generally applicable" prohibition of particular conduct. Since the prohibition on animal cruelty constitutes such a neutral and generally applicable prohibition, the priest's conviction does not violate his freedom of religion. *Employment Div. v. Smith*, 494 U.S. 872 (1990). So even if the court believed that the cult members' belief in the need for pain-inducing animal cruelty was "reasonable" (not a likely conclusion by the court), under *Employment Div. v. Smith* the priest would not be relieved of the obligation to obey the anti-animal-cruelty statute.

Answer 75

Choice (**A**) is correct. The plaintiff does not meet the requirement of "injury in fact." He clearly has not been injured yet; the real question is whether he faces sufficiently imminent injury from the residency requirement. A court would likely hold that because the plaintiff has not yet even made the decision to run, and could not be injured unless he decided to run, any threatened injury to him is too uncertain and speculative to meet the requirement that prospective injury be reasonably concrete and imminent. The fact that the chairman has joined the suit does not change this, since the chairman (and the chairman's party) would not be injured unless some actual candidate was blocked by the residency requirement, and there is no such candidate now.

(B) is wrong because: (1) the absence of a case or controversy would prevent the court even from getting to the issue of whether there was a substantial federal constitutional question in the case; and (2) the fact that something is a local election does not prevent it from presenting a substantial federal constitutional question (for instance, an unduly long residency requirement probably *would* constitute a violation of an actual candidate's equal protection rights).

(C) is wrong because, while the residency restriction might well constitute an equal protection violation of the rights of an actual candidate, the plaintiff's lack of actual-candidate status prevents him from raising a case or controversy.

(D) is wrong because there is no basis (certainly not a federal constitutional basis) for the court to conclude that "substantially complying," rather than fully complying, with the residency requirement here would be sufficient.

Answer 76

Choice (**C**) is correct. Because the only person whose rights have been arguably affected by the new statute is the friend, who is not a claimant, there is no live case or controversy between the litigants, so standing rules prevent the court from hearing it.

(A) is wrong because the lack of standing prevents the court from deciding the case on its merits even though the plaintiff is claiming that the Constitution has been violated (which would of course raise a federal question if there were a case or controversy before the court).

(B) is wrong because, if there were not any standing problem, the question of the constitutionality of the statute would not be a nonjusticiable political question (a category limited to a few special situations, none of which applies here).

(D) is wrong, because the Eleventh Amendment bars only suits seeking money damages against states, and the suit here is seeking a declaratory judgment rather than money damages.

Answer 77

Choice is (**C**) is correct. This is a classic ripeness issue: Economy does not know that it will certainly (or even more-probably-than-not) need another rate increase in less than the now-required two-year minimum. All we know is that Economy "may" need the increase sometime in the next 18 months. Therefore, it is highly uncertain for now whether Economy will ever be harmed by the statute, making it likely that the court would dismiss the action as unripe.

(A) is wrong because the case is not ripe for decision (see the discussion of Choice (C)), so the court will never reach the constitutional merits. (Also, it's highly doubtful that a relatively brief moratorium on rate increases would violate the due process rights of a utility.)

(B) is wrong for the same reason as (A): The case is not ripe for decision (see the discussion of Choice (C)), so the court will never reach the constitutional merits.

(D) is wrong, because the federal judicial power extends to any case raising an issue under the federal Constitution or a federal statute, and the fact that the controversy involves state- regulated utility rates does not prevent that controversy from raising a federal issue. For example, if a state utility commission were to prevent a utility from ever raising its rates again, this would raise a serious taking-without-just-compensation constitutional issue.

Answer 78

Choice **(A)** is correct. The Eleventh Amendment generally forbids the federal courts from entertaining damage suits against states, and Congress cannot override this ban even when it is acting pursuant to some enumerated power (e.g., the Commerce Clause). But there is one exception: When Congress is using its special powers to enforce the post-Civil War amendments (the Thirteenth, Fourteenth and Fifteenth), it may authorize damage suits against the states that would otherwise be barred by the Eleventh Amendment. That is what's happening here.

(B) is wrong because it is overbroad. As a general rule Congress, even where it is acting pursuant to some power given to it by a specific provision in the Constitution, may not override the state immunity from federal-court damage suits conferred by the Eleventh Amendment; enforcement of the post-Civil War amendments represents the only exception to this rule.

(C) is wrong for essentially the same reason: The Eleventh Amendment *does* generally limit the power of Congress (not just the power of the federal judiciary) to modify the sovereign-immunity of the states, but the Supreme Court has held that in the special case in which Congress is enforcing the post-Civil War amendments this general limitation on Congress's power does not apply. *Fitzpatrick v. Bitzer* (1976).

(D) is wrong because it is a flat misstatement of law: The Supreme Court has held that the Eleventh Amendment protects a state from federal-court damage suits even where the suit is brought by a citizen of a different state. *Hans v. Louisiana* (1890).

CONTRACTS

CONTRACTS QUESTIONS BY TOPIC

CHAPTER 1

OFFER AND ACCEPTANCE

I. VALIDITY OF PARTICULAR KINDS OF OFFERS

A. Public offers and advertisements

Question 1

On November 1, the following notice was posted in a privately operated law school:

> The faculty, seeking to encourage legal research, offers to any student at this school who wins the current National Obscenity Law Competition the additional prize of $500. All competing papers must be submitted to the Dean's office before May 1.

(The national competition is conducted by an outside agency, unconnected with any law school.) A student read this notice on November 2, and thereupon intensified his effort to make his paper on obscenity law, which he started in October, a winner. The student also left on a counter in the dean's office a signed note saying, "I accept the faculty's $500 Obscenity Competition offer." This note was inadvertently placed in the student's file and never reached the dean or any faculty member personally. On the following April 1, the above notice was removed and the following substituted therefore:

> The faculty regrets that our offer regarding the National Obscenity Law Competition must be withdrawn.

The student's paper was submitted through the dean's office on April 15. On May 1, it was announced that the student had won the National Obscenity Law Competition and the prize of $1,000. The law faculty refused to pay anything.

Assuming that the faculty's notice of November 1 was posted on a bulletin board or other conspicuous place commonly viewed by all persons in the law school, such notice constituted a

(A) preliminary invitation to deal, analogous to newspaper advertisements for the sale of goods by merchants.

(B) contractual offer, creating a power of acceptance.

(C) preliminary invitation, because no offeree was named therein.

(D) promise to make a conditional, future gift of money.

II. THE ACCEPTANCE

A. Method of acceptance

1. Offer invites either promise or performance

a. Acceptance by shipment of non-conforming goods

Question 2

A retailer ordered from a produce wholesaler 500 bushels of No. 1 Royal Fuzz peaches, at a specified price, "for prompt shipment." The wholesaler promptly shipped 500 bushels, but by mistake shipped No. 2 Royal Fuzz peaches instead of No. 1. The error in shipment was caused by the negligence of the wholesaler's shipping clerk.

Which of the following best states the retailer's rights and duties upon delivery of the peaches?

(A) The wholesaler's shipment of the peaches was a counteroffer and the retailer can refuse to accept them.

(B) The wholesaler's shipment of the peaches was a counteroffer but, since peaches are perishable, the retailer, if it does not want to accept them, must reship the peaches to the wholesaler in order to mitigate the wholesaler's losses.

(C) The retailer must accept the peaches because a contract was formed when the wholesaler shipped them.

(D) Although a contract was formed when the wholesaler shipped the peaches, the retailer does not have to accept them.

b. Accommodation shipment

Question 3

A retailer faxed the following signed message to his long-time widget supplier: "Urgently need blue widgets. Ship immediately three gross at your current list price of $600." Upon receipt of the fax, the supplier shipped three gross of red widgets to the retailer, and faxed to the retailer the following message: "Temporarily out of blue. In case red will help, am shipping three gross at the same price. Hope you can use them."

Upon the retailer's timely receipt of both the shipment and the supplier's fax, which of the following best describes the rights and duties of the retailer and the wholesaler?

(A) The retailer may accept the shipment, in which case he must pay the wholesaler the list price, or he must reject the shipment and recover from the wholesaler for total breach of contract.

(B) The retailer may accept the shipment, in which case he must pay the wholesaler the list price, or he may reject the shipment, in which case he has no further rights against the wholesaler.

(C) The retailer may accept the shipment, in which case he must pay the wholesaler the list price, less any damages sustained because of the nonconforming shipment, or he may reject the shipment and recover from the wholesaler for total breach of contract, subject to the wholesaler's right to cure.

(D) The retailer may accept the shipment, in which case he must pay the wholesaler the list price, less any damages sustained because of the nonconforming shipment, or he may reject the shipment provided that he promptly covers by obtaining conforming widgets from another supplier.

2. Notice of acceptance of unilateral contract

Question 4

A hardware distributor located on the West Coast gave its customer, a hardware retailer who was relocating to the East Coast, the following signed "letter of introduction" to a hardware manufacturer based on the East coast:

> This will introduce you to my good friend and former customer, who is a retailer and will be seeking to arrange the purchase of hardware inventory from you on credit. If you will let him have the goods, I will make good any loss up to $25,000 in the event of his default.

The retailer presented the letter to the manufacturer, who then sold and delivered $20,000 worth of hardware to the retailer on credit. The manufacturer promptly notified the distributor of this sale.

Which of the following is NOT an accurate statement concerning the arrangement between the distributor and the manufacturer?

(A) It was important to enforceability of the distributor's promise to the manufacturer that it be embodied in a signed writing.

(B) By extending the credit to the retailer, the manufacturer effectively accepted the distributor's offer for a unilateral contract.

(C) Although the distributor received no consideration from the retailer, the distributor's promise is enforceable by the manufacturer.

(D) The distributor's promise is enforceable by the manufacturer whether or not the manufacturer gave the distributor seasonable notice of the extension of credit to the retailer.

III. ACCEPTANCE VARYING FROM OFFER

A. UCC view

1. "Additional" term in acceptance

a. Both parties are merchants

i. Does the proposed term materially alter the contract?

Question 5

On June 1, a wholesaler received a purchase-order form from a retailer and new customer, in which the latter ordered 1,000 anti-recoil widgets for delivery no later than August 30 at a delivered total price of $10,000, as quoted in the wholesaler's current catalog. Both parties are merchants with respect to widgets of all types. On June 2, the wholesaler mailed to the retailer its own form, across the top of which the wholesaler's president had written, "We are pleased to accept your order." This form contained the same terms as the retailer's form except for an additional printed clause in the wholesaler's form that provided for a maximum liability of $100 for any breach of contract by the retailer.

As of June 5, when the retailer received the wholesaler's acceptance form, which of the following is an accurate statement concerning the legal relationship between the wholesaler and the retailer?

(A) There is no contract, because the liability-limitation clause in the wholesaler's form is a material alteration of the retailer's offer.

(B) There is no contract, because the retailer did not consent to the liability-limitation clause in the wholesaler's form.

(C) There is an enforceable contract whose terms include the liability-limitation clause in the wholesaler's form, because liquidation of damages is expressly authorized by the Uniform Commercial Code.

(D) There is an enforceable contract whose terms do not include the liability-limitation clause in the wholesaler's form.

2. Contract by parties' conduct

a. "Acceptance by conduct" can occur in non-UCC contracts

Question 6

A developer, needing a water well on one of his projects, met several times about the matter with a well driller. Subsequently, the driller sent the developer an unsigned typewritten form captioned "WELL DRILLING PROPOSAL" and stating various terms the two had discussed but not agreed upon, including a "proposed price of $5,000." The form concluded, "This proposal will not become a contract until signed by you [the developer] and then returned to and signed by me [the driller]."

The developer signed the form and returned it to the driller, who neglected to sign it but promptly began drilling the well at the proposed site on the developer's project. After drilling for two days, the driller told the developer during one of the developer's daily visits that he would not finish unless the developer would agree to pay twice the price recited in the written proposal. The developer refused, the driller quit, and the developer hired a substitute driller to drill the well to completion for a price of $7,500.

In an action by the developer against the driller for damages, which of the following is the probable decision?

(A) The developer wins, because his signing of the driller's form constituted an acceptance of an offer by the driller.

(B) The developer wins, because the driller's commencement of performance constituted an acceptance by the driller of an offer by the developer and an implied promise by the driller to complete the well.

(C) The driller wins, because he never signed the proposal as required by its terms.

(D) The driller wins, because his commencement of performance merely prevented the developer from revoking his offer, made on a form supplied by the driller, and did not obligate the driller to complete the well.

IV. DURATION OF THE POWER OF ACCEPTANCE

A. Irrevocable offers

1. "Firm offers" under the UCC

Question 7

On December 15, a lawyer received from a stationer an offer consisting of its catalog and a signed letter stating, "We will supply you with as many of the items in the enclosed catalog as you order during the next calendar year. We assure you that this offer and the prices in the catalog will remain firm throughout the coming year." On January 15, having at that time received no reply from the lawyer, the stationer notified the lawyer that, effective February 1, it was increasing the prices of certain specified items in its catalog.

Is the price increase effective with respect to catalog orders the stationer receives from the lawyer during the month of February?

(A) No, because the stationer's original offer, including the price term, became irrevocable under the doctrine of promissory estoppel.

(B) No, because the stationer is a merchant with respect to office supplies; and its original offer, including the price term, was irrevocable throughout the month of February.

(C) Yes, because the stationer received no consideration to support its assurance that it would not increase prices.

(D) Yes, because the period for which the stationer gave assurance that it would not raise prices was longer than three months.

a. Effect of firm offer if not by a merchant

Question 8

On November 1, Debbit, an accountant, and Barrister, a lawyer, contracted for the sale by Debbit to Barrister of the law books Debbit had inherited from his father. Barrister agreed to pay the purchase price of $10,000 when Debbit delivered the books on December 1.

On November 10, Barrister received a signed letter from Debbit that stated: "I have decided to dispose of the book stacks containing the law books you have already purchased. If you want the stacks, I will deliver them to you along with the books on December 1 at no additional cost to you. Let me know before November 15 whether you want them. I will not sell them to anyone else before then." Debbit was not a merchant with respect to either law books or book stacks.

On November 12 Debbit told Banister that he had decided not to part with the stacks. Will this communication operate as a legally effective revocation of his offer to deliver the stacks?

(A) Yes, because Barrister had a pre-existing obligation to pay $10,000 for the law books.

(B) Yes, because Debbit was not a merchant with respect to book stacks.

(C) No, because Debbit had given a signed assurance that the offer would be held open until November 15.

(D) No, because by delaying his acceptance until November 14, Barrister detrimentally relied on Debbit's promise not to sell the stacks to anyone else in the meantime.

2. Part performance or detrimental reliance

a. Where offer was for a unilateral contract

Question 9

While waiting in line to open an account with a bank, a customer read a poster on the bank's wall that said, "New Customers! $25 FOR 5 MINUTES. If you stand in line for more than five minutes, we will pay you $25! We like happy customers! (This offer may be withdrawn at any time.)" The customer started timing his wait and just as five minutes was about to pass, the bank manager tore the poster down and announced, "The $25 stand-in-line promotion is over." The customer waited in line for 10 more minutes before being served.

In the customer's action against the bank for $25, will the customer prevail?

(A) No, because the bank withdrew its offer before the customer completed the requested performance.

(B) No, because the bank's statement was a nonbinding gift promise.

(C) Yes, because the bank could not revoke its offer once the customer had commenced performance.

(D) Yes, because the customer's presence in line served as notice to the bank that he had accepted.

CONSIDERATION

I. THE BARGAIN ELEMENT

A. Promises to make gifts

1. Existence of condition

a. Mixture of bargain and gift

Question 10

Rollem, an automobile retailer, had an adult daughter, Betsy, who needed a car in her employ-ment but had only $3,000 with which to buy one. Rollem wrote to her, "Give me your $3,000 and I'll give you the car on our lot that we have been using as a demonstrator." Betsy thanked her father and paid him the $3,000. As both Rollem and Betsy knew, the demonstrator was reasonably worth $10,000. After Betsy had paid the $3,000, but before the car had been delivered to her, one of Rollem's sales staff sold and delivered the same car to a customer for $10,000. Neither the salesperson nor the customer was aware of the transaction between Rollem and Betsy.

Does Betsy, after rejecting a tendered return of the $3,000 by Rollem, have an action against him for breach of contract?

(A) Yes, because Rollem's promise was supported by bargained-for consideration.

(B) Yes, because Rollem's promise was supported by the moral obligation a father owes his child as to the necessities of modern life.

(C) No, because the payment of $3,000 was inadequate consideration to support Rollem's promise.

(D) No, because the salesperson's delivery of the car to the customer made it impossible for Rollem to perform.

II. THE "DETRIMENT" ELEMENT

A. Generally

1. Motives irrelevant

Question 11

A small-business owner encourages "wellness" on the part of his employees and supports var-ious physical-fitness programs to that end. Learning that one of his employees was a dedicated jogger, the business owner promised to pay the jogger a special award of $100 if she could and would run one mile in less than six minutes on the following Saturday. The jogger thanked him, and did in fact run a mile in less than six minutes on the day specified. Shortly thereafter, however, the business owner discovered that for more than a year the jogger had been running at least one mile in less than six minutes every day as a part of her personal fitness program. He refused to pay the $100.

In an action by the jogger against the business owner for breach of contract, which of the fol-lowing best summarizes the probable decision of the court?

(A) The business owner wins, because it is a compelling inference that the business owner's promise did not induce the jogger to run the specified mile.

(B) The business owner wins, because the jogger's running of the specified mile was beneficial, not detrimental, to her in any event.

(C) The jogger wins, because running a mile in less than six minutes is a significantly demanding enterprise.

(D) The jogger wins, because she ran the specified mile as requested, and her motives for doing so are irrelevant.

B. Pre-existing duty rule

1. Modification to contract terms

Question 12

On May 1, a landowner telegraphed an investor, "Will sell you any or all of the lots in Grove subdivision at $5,000 each. Details follow in letter." The letter contained all the necessary details concerning terms of payment, insurance, mortgages, etc., and provided, "This offer remains open until June 1." On May 2, after the investor had received the telegram but before he had received the letter, the investor telegraphed the landowner, "Accept your offer with respect to lot 101." Both parties knew that there were 50 lots in the Grove subdivision and that they were numbered 101 through 150.

On May 3, the landowner telephoned the investor, saying that because he had just discovered that a shopping center was going to be erected adjacent to the Grove subdivision, he would "have to have $6,000 for each of the lots, including lot 101." During the telephone call, the investor agreed to pay him $6,000 for lot 101. On May 6, the investor telegraphed, "Accept your offer with respect to the rest of the lots." Assuming that the two contracts were formed and that there is no controlling statute, the investor will most likely be required to pay

(A) only $5,000 for each of the 50 lots.

(B) only $5,000 for lot 101, but $6,000 for the remaining 49 lots.

(C) $6,000 for each of the 50 lots.

(D) $6,000 for lot 101, but only $5,000 for the remaining 49 lots.

Question 13

An accountant entered into a contract with a painter by the terms of which the painter was to paint the accountant's office for $1,000 and was required to do all of the work over the following weekend so as to avoid disruption of the accountant's business.

If the painter had started to paint on the following Saturday morning, he could have finished before Sunday evening. However, he stayed home that Saturday morning to watch the final game of the World Series on TV, and did not start to paint until Saturday afternoon. By late Saturday afternoon, the painter realized that he had underestimated the time it would take to finish the job if he continued to work alone. The painter phoned the accountant at her home and accurately informed her that it was impossible to finish the work over the weekend unless he hired a helper. He also stated that to do so would require an additional charge of $200 for the work. The accountant told the painter that she apparently had no choice but to pay "whatever it takes" to get the work done as scheduled.

The painter hired a helper to help finish the painting and paid the helper $200. The accountant has offered to pay the painter $1,000. The painter is demanding $1,200.

How much is the painter likely to recover?

(A) $1,000 only, because the accountant received no consideration for her promise to pay the additional sum.

(B) $1,000 only, because the accountant's promise to pay "whatever it takes" is too uncertain to be enforceable.

(C) $1,200, in order to prevent the accountant's unjust enrichment.

(D) $1,200, because the impossibility of the painter's completing the work alone discharged the original contract and a new contract was formed.

a. **Where modification is a response to unanticipated circumstances**

Question 14

A contractor contracted with a warehouse owner to construct for $500,000 a warehouse and an access driveway at highway level on the owner's property. Shortly after commencing work on the driveway, which required for the specified level some excavation and removal of surface material, the contractor unexpectedly encountered a large mass of solid rock. The contractor informed the owner (accurately) that because of the rock the driveway as specified would cost at least $20,000 more than figured, and demanded for that reason a total contract price of $520,000. Since the owner was expecting warehousing customers immediately after the agreed completion date, he signed a writing promising to pay the additional $20,000. Following timely completion of the warehouse and driveway, which conformed to the contract in all respects, the owner refused to pay the contractor more than $500,000.

What is the maximum amount to which the contractor is entitled?

(A) $500,000, because there was no consideration for the owner's promise to pay the additional $20,000.

(B) $500,000, because the owner's promise to pay the additional $20,000 was exacted under duress.

(C) $520,000, because the modification was fair and was made in the light of circumstances not anticipated by the parties when the original contract was made.

(D) $520,000, provided that the reasonable value of the contractor's total performance was that much or more.

2. **Duty owed to third person rather than to promisor**

Question 15

A burglar stole Collecta's impressionist painting valued at $400,000. Collecta, who had insured the painting for $300,000 with Artistic Insurance Co., promised to pay $25,000 to Snoop, a full-time investigator for Artistic, if he effected the return of the painting to her in good condition. By company rules, Artistic permits its investigators to accept and retain rewards from policyholders for the recovery of insured property. Snoop, by long and skillful detective work, recovered the picture and returned it undamaged to Collecta.

If Collecta refuses to pay Snoop anything, and he sues her for $25,000, what is the probable result under the prevailing modern rule?

(A) Collecta wins, because Snoop owed Artistic a pre-existing duty to recover the picture if possible.

(B) Collecta wins, because Artistic, Snoop's employer, had a pre-existing duty to return the recovered painting to Collecta.

(C) Snoop wins, because Collecta will benefit more from return of the $400,000 painting than from receiving the $300,000 policy proceeds.

(D) Snoop wins, because the pre-existing duty rule does not apply if the promisee's (Snoop's) duty was owed to a third person.

3. Agreement to accept part payment of debt

a. Disputed debt

Question 16

In a written contract, an architect agreed to draw up the plans for and to supervise construction of a client's new house. In return, the client agreed to pay the architect a fee of $10,000 to be paid upon the house's completion. After completion, the client claimed erroneously but in good faith that the architect's plans were defective. The client orally offered to pay the architect $7,500 in full settlement of the claim for the fee. The architect orally accepted that offer despite the fact that the reasonable value of his services was in fact $10,000. The client paid the architect $7,500 pursuant to their agreement.

The architect subsequently sued the client for the remaining $2,500. In a preliminary finding, the trier of fact found that there were no defects in the architect's plans.

Will the architect be likely to prevail in his action against the client for $2,500?

(A) Yes, because payment of $7,500 cannot furnish consideration for the architect's promise to surrender his claim.

(B) Yes, because the oral agreement to modify the written contract is not enforceable.

(C) No, because the architect's promise to accept $7,500 became binding when the client made the payment.

(D) No, because the architect's acceptance of partial payment constituted a novation.

b. Cashing of check tendered as settlement

Question 17

A client consulted a lawyer about handling the sale of the client's building, and asked the lawyer what her legal fee would be. The lawyer replied that her usual charge was $100 per hour, and estimated that the legal work on behalf of the client would cost about $5,000 at that rate. The client said, "Okay; let's proceed with it," and the lawyer timely and successfully completed the work. Because of unexpected title problems, the lawyer reasonably spent 75 hours on the matter and shortly thereafter mailed the client a bill for $7,500, with a letter itemizing the work performed and time spent. The client responded by a letter expressing his good-faith belief that the lawyer had agreed to a total fee of no more than $5,000. The client enclosed a check in the amount of $5,000 payable to the lawyer and conspicuously marked, "Payment in full for legal services in connection with the sale of [the client's] building." Despite reading the "Payment in full . . ." language, the lawyer, without any notation of protest or reservation of rights, endorsed and deposited the check to her bank account. The check was duly paid by the client's bank. A few days later, the lawyer unsuccessfully demanded payment from the client of the $2,500 difference between the amount of her bill and the check, and now sues the client for that difference.

What, if anything, can the lawyer recover from the client?

(A) Nothing, because the risk of unexpected title problems in a real-property transaction is properly allocable to the seller's attorney and thus to the lawyer in this case.

(B) Nothing, because the amount of the lawyer's fee was disputed in good faith by the client, and the lawyer impliedly agreed to an accord and satisfaction.

(C) $2,500, because the client agreed to an hourly rate for as many hours as the work reasonably required, and the sum of $5,000 was merely an estimate.

(D) The reasonable value of the lawyer's services in excess of $5,000, if any, because there was no specific agreement on the total amount of the lawyer's fee.

Question 18

Ames had painted Bell's house under a contract which called for payment of $20,000. Bell, contending in good faith that the porch had not been painted properly, refused to pay anything.

On June 15, Ames mailed a letter to Bell stating, "I am in serious need of money. Please send the $20,000 to me before July 1." On June 18, Bell replied "I will settle for $18,000 provided you agree to repaint the porch." Ames did not reply to this letter.

Thereafter, Bell mailed a check for $18,000 marked "Payment in full on the Ames-Bell painting contract as per letter dated June 18." Ames received the check on June 30. Because he was badly in need of money, Ames cashed the check without objection and spent the proceeds but has refused to repaint the porch.

After cashing the check Ames sued Bell for $2,000. Ames probably will

(A) succeed if he can prove that he had painted the porch according to specifications.

(B) succeed, because he cashed the check under economic duress.

(C) not succeed, because he cashed the check.

(D) not succeed, because he is entitled to recover only the reasonable value of his services.

4. Other settlements

Question 19

A lifeguard saved the life of a woman who thereafter changed her will to leave the lifeguard $1,000. However, upon her death she had no property except an undivided interest in real estate held in tenancy by the entirety of her husband. The property had been purchased by her husband from an inheritance.

After the woman died, her husband signed and delivered to the lifeguard the following instrument: "In consideration of the lifeguard's saving my wife's life and his agreement to bring no claims against my estate based on her will, I hereby promise to pay the lifeguard $1,000." Upon the woman's husband's death, the lifeguard filed a claim for $1,000. The husband's executor contested the claim on the ground that the instrument was not supported by sufficient consideration. On which of the following theories would it be most likely that the lifeguard could recover?

(A) The husband and the lifeguard have made a compromise.

(B) The husband must give restitution for benefits it would be unjust to retain.

(C) The husband is bound by promissory estoppel.

(D) The husband executed a binding unilateral contract.

III. ILLUSORY, ALTERNATIVE AND IMPLIED PROMISES

A. Implied promises

Question 20

A buyer, who was a representative of a bank, contracted in writing with a shareholder, who owned all of a corporation's outstanding stock, to purchase all of her stock at a specified price per share. At the time this contract was executed, the buyer said to the shareholder, "Of course, our commitment to buy is conditioned on our obtaining approval of the contract from the bank's board of directors." The shareholder replied, "Fine. No problem."

The board orally approved the contract, but the shareholder changed her mind and refused to consummate the sale on two grounds: (1) when the agreement was made there was no consideration for her promise to sell; and (2) the board's approval of the contract was invalid. If the buyer sues the shareholder for breach of contract, is the buyer likely to prevail?

(A) Yes, because the buyer's promise to buy, bargained for and made in exchange for the shareholder's promise to sell, was good consideration even though it was expressly conditioned on an event that was not certain to occur.

(B) Yes, because any possible lack of consideration for the shareholder's promise to sell was expressly waived by the shareholder when the agreement was made.

(C) No, because mutuality of obligation between the parties was lacking when the agreement was made.

(D) No, because the condition of the board of director's approval of the contract was an essential part of the agreed exchange and was not in a signed writing.

IV. REQUIREMENTS AND OUTPUT CONTRACTS

A. Requirements and output contracts generally

1. UCC approach

Question 21

Responding to County's written advertisement for bids, Tyres was the successful bidder for the sale of tires to County for County's vehicles. Tyres and County entered into a signed, written agreement that specified, "It is agreed that Tyres will deliver all tires required by this agreement to County, in accordance with the attached bid form and specifications, for a one-year period beginning September 1, 2005." Attached to the agreement was a copy of the bid form and specifications. In the written advertisement to which Tyres had responded, but not in the bid form, County had stated, "Multiple awards may be issued if they are in the best interests of County." No definite quantity of tires to be bought by County from Tyres was specified in any of these documents.

In January 2006, Tyres learned that County was buying some of its tires from one of Tyres's competitors. Contending that the Tyres-County agreement was a requirements contract, Tyres sued County for the damages caused by County's buying some of its tires from the competitor.

If the court concludes that the Tyres-County contract is an agreement by County to buy its tire requirements from Tyres, Tyres probably will

(A) recover under the Contracts Clause of the United States Constitution.

(B) recover under the provisions of the Uniform Commercial Code.

(C) not recover, because the agreement lacks mutuality of obligation.

(D) not recover, because the agreement is indefinite as to quantity.

a. Obligation to behave in good faith in setting output or requirements

Question 22

Under a written agreement a manufacturer of pastries promised to sell its entire output of baked buns at a specified unit price to a bakery, for one year. The bakery promised not to sell any other supplier's baked buns. Shortly after making the contract, and before the manufacturer had tendered any buns, the bakery decided that the contract had become undesirable because of a sudden, sharp decline in its customers' demand for baked buns. It renounced the agreement, and the manufacturer sues for breach of contract.

Which of the following will the court probably decide?

(A) The bakery wins, because mutuality of obligation was lacking in that the bakery made no express promise to buy any of the manufacturer's baked buns.

(B) The bakery wins, because the agreement was void for indefiniteness of quantity and total price for the year involved.

(C) The manufacturer wins, because the bakery's promise to sell at retail the manufacturer's baked buns exclusively, if it sold any such buns at all, implied a promise to use its best efforts to sell bakery's one-year output of baked buns.

(D) The manufacturer wins, because under the applicable law both parties to a sale-of-goods contract impliedly assume the risk of price and demand fluctuations.

PROMISES BINDING WITHOUT CONSIDERATION

I. PROMISSORY ESTOPPEL

A. Possible applications

1. Promise to perform business service

a. Promise to make a loan

Question 23

Dominique obtained a bid of $10,000 to tear down her old building and another bid of $90,000 to replace it with a new structure in which she planned to operate a sporting goods store. Having only limited cash available, Dominique asked Hardcash for a $100,000 loan. After reviewing the plans for the project, Hardcash in a signed writing promised to lend Dominique $100,000 secured by a mortgage on the property and repayable over ten years in equal monthly installments at 10% annual interest. Dominique promptly accepted the demolition bid and the old building was removed, but Hardcash thereafter refused to make the loan. Despite diligent efforts, Dominique was unable to obtain a loan from any other source.

Does Dominique have a cause of action against Hardcash?

(A) Yes, because by having the building demolished, she accepted Hardcash's offer to make the loan.

(B) Yes, because her reliance on Hardcash's promise was substantial, reasonable, and foreseeable.

(C) No, because there was no bargained-for exchange of consideration for Hardcash's promise to make the loan.

(D) No, because Dominique's inability to obtain a loan from any other source demonstrated that the project lacked the financial soundness that was a constructive condition to Hardcash's performance.

CHAPTER 4
MISTAKE

I. MUTUAL MISTAKE

A. Three requirements for avoidance

1. Allocation of risk by parties

Question 24

A breeder bought a two-month-old registered boar at auction from a farmer for $800. No express warranty was made. Fifteen months later, tests by experts proved conclusively that the boar had been born incurably sterile. If this had been known at the time of the sale, the boar would have been worth no more than $100.

In an action by the breeder against the farmer to avoid the contract and recover the price paid, the parties stipulate that, as both were and had been aware, the minimum age at which the fertility of a boar can be determined is about 12 months. Which of the following will the court probably decide?

(A) The breeder wins, because the parties were mutually mistaken as to the boar's fertility when they made the agreement.

(B) The breeder wins, because the farmer impliedly warranted that the boar was fit for breeding.

(C) The farmer wins, because the breeder assumed the risk of the boar's sterility.

(D) The farmer wins, because any mistake involved was unilateral, not mutual.

II. REFORMATION AS REMEDY FOR ERROR IN EXPRESSION

A. Generally

1. Reformation not a remedy for underlying disagreement about deal

Question 25

A landowner and a prospective buyer, standing on a parcel owned by the landowner, orally agreed to its sale and purchase for $5,000, and orally marked its bounds as "that line of trees down there, the ditch that intersects them, the fence on the other side, and that street on the fourth side."

In which of the following is the remedy of reformation most appropriate?

(A) As later reduced to writing, the agreement by clerical mistake included two acres that are actually beyond the fence.

(B) The buyer reasonably thought that two acres beyond the fence were included in the oral agreement but the landowner did not. As later reduced to writing, the agreement included the two acres.

(C) The buyer reasonably thought that the price orally agreed upon was $4,500, but the landowner did not. As later reduced to writing, the agreement said $5,000.

(D) The buyer reasonably thought that a dilapidated shed backed up against the fence was to be torn down and removed as part of the agreement, but the landowner did not. As later reduced to writing, the agreement said nothing about the shed.

PAROL EVIDENCE AND INTERPRETATION

I. TOTAL AND PARTIAL INTEGRATIONS

A. The parole evidence rule generally

Question 26

Stirrup, a rancher, and Equinox, a fancier of horses, signed the following writing: "For $55,000, Stirrup will sell to Equinox a gray horse that Equinox may choose from among the grays on Stirrup's ranch."

Equinox refused to accept delivery of a gray horse timely tendered by Stirrup or to choose among those remaining, on the ground that during their negotiations Stirrup had orally agreed to include a saddle, worth $100, and also to give Equinox the option to choose a gray or a brown horse. Equinox insisted on one of Stirrup's brown horses, but Stirrup refused to part with any of his browns or with the saddle as demanded by Equinox.

If Equinox sues Stirrup for damages and seeks to introduce evidence of the alleged oral agreement, the court probably will

(A) admit the evidence as to both the saddle and the option to choose a brown horse.

(B) admit the evidence as to the saddle but not the option to choose a brown horse.

(C) admit the evidence as to the option to choose a brown horse but not the promise to include the saddle.

(D) not admit any of the evidence.

II. SITUATIONS WHERE PAROL EVIDENCE RULE DOES NOT APPLY

A. Existence of a condition on effectiveness of contract

Question 27

Buyer, Inc., contracted in writing with Shareholder, who owned all of XYZ Corporation's outstanding stock, to purchase all of her stock at a specified price per share. At the time this contract was executed, Buyer's contracting officer said to Shareholder, "Of course, our commitment to buy is conditioned on our obtaining approval of the contract from Conglomerate, Ltd., our parent company." Shareholder replied, "Fine. No problem."

Later, Shareholder was willing and ready to consummate the sale of her stock to Buyer, but the latter refused to perform on the ground (which was true) that Conglomerate had firmly refused to approve the contract. If Shareholder sues Buyer for breach of contract and seeks to exclude any evidence of the oral condition requiring Conglomerate's approval, the court will probably

(A) admit the evidence as proof of a collateral agreement.

(B) admit the evidence as proof of a condition to the existence of an enforceable obligation, and therefore not within the scope of the parol evidence rule.

(C) exclude the evidence on the basis of a finding that the parties' written agreement was a complete integration of their contract.

(D) exclude the evidence as contradicting the terms of the parties' written agreement, whether or not the writing was a complete integration of the contract.

Question 28

A landowner and a landscape architect signed a detailed writing in which the landscape architect agreed to landscape and replant the landowner's residential property in accordance with a design prepared by the architect and incorporated in the writing. The landowner agreed to pay $10,000 for the work upon its completion. The landowner's spouse was not a party to the agreement, and had no ownership interest in the premises.

Shortly before the agreement was signed, the landowner and the architect orally agreed that the writing would not become binding on either party unless the landowner's spouse should approve the landscaping design. If the landowner's spouse disapproves the design and the landowner refuses to allow the architect to proceed with the work, is evidence of the oral agreement admissible in the architect's action against the landowner for breach of contract?

(A) Yes, because the oral agreement required approval by a third party.

(B) Yes, because the evidence shows that the writing was intended to take effect only if the approval occurred.

(C) No, because the parol evidence rule bars evidence of a prior oral agreement even if the latter is consistent with the terms of a partial integration.

(D) No, because the prior oral agreement contradicted the writing by making the parties' duties conditional.

III. INTERPRETATION

A. Extrinsic evidence in the case of ambiguous terms

Question 29

Responding to County's written advertisement for bids, Tyres was the successful bidder for the sale of tires to County for County's vehicles. Tyres and County entered into a signed, written agreement that specified, "It is agreed that Tyres will deliver all tires required by this agreement to County, in accordance with the attached bid form and specifications, for a one-year period beginning September 1, 2005." Attached to the agreement was a copy of the bid form and specifications. In the written advertisement to which Tyres had responded, but not in the bid form, County had stated, "Multiple awards may be issued if they are in the best interests of County." No definite quantity of tires to be bought by County from Tyres was specified in any of these documents.

In January 2006, Tyres learned that County was buying some of its tires from one of Tyres's competitors. Contending that the Tyres-County agreement was a requirements contract, Tyres sued County for the damages caused by County's buying some of its tires from the competitor.

If County defends by offering proof of the advertisement concerning the possibility of multiple awards, should the court admit the evidence?

(A) Yes, because the provision in the written agreement, "all tires required by this agreement," is ambiguous.

(B) Yes, because the advertisement was in writing.

(C) No, because of the parol evidence rule.

(D) No, because it would make the contract illusory.

IV. TRADE USAGE, COURSE OF PERFORMANCE, AND COURSE OF DEALING

A. Used to interpret even a complete integration

Question 30

A radio manufacturer and a retailer, after extensive negotiations, entered into a final, written agreement in which the manufacturer agreed to sell and the retailer agreed to buy all of the retailer's requirements of radios, estimated at 20 units per month, during the period January 1, 2004, and December 31, 2006, at a price of $50 per unit. A dispute arose in late December 2006, when the retailer returned 25 non-defective radios to the manufacturer for full credit after the manufacturer had refused to extend the contract for a second three-year period.

In an action by the manufacturer against the retailer for damages due to the return of the 25 radios, the manufacturer introduces the written agreement, which expressly permitted the buyer to return defective radios for credit but was silent as to the return of non-defective radios for credit. The retailer seeks to introduce evidence that during the three years of the agreement it had returned, for various reasons, 125 non-defective radios, for which the manufacturer had granted full credit. The manufacturer objects to the admissibility of this evidence.

The trial court will probably rule that the evidence proffered by the retailer is

(A) inadmissible, because the evidence is barred by the parol evidence rule.

(B) inadmissible, because the express terms of the agreement control when those terms are inconsistent with the course of performance.

(C) admissible, because the evidence supports an agreement that is not within the relevant statute of frauds.

(D) admissible, because course-of-performance evidence, when available, is considered the best indication of what the parties intended the writing to mean.

CONDITIONS, BREACH, AND OTHER ASPECTS OF PERFORMANCE

I. EXPRESS CONDITIONS

A. Satisfaction of a party

Question 31

A photographer and a customer entered a contract in writing on November 1, the essential part of which read as follows: "The photographer to supply the customer with 200 personalized Christmas cards on or before December 15, 2010, bearing a photograph of the customer and his family, and the customer to pay $100 thirty days thereafter. Photograph to be taken by the photographer at the customer's house. Cards guaranteed to be fully satisfactory and on time." Because the customer suddenly became ill, the photographer was unable to take the necessary photograph of the customer and his family until the first week of December. The final week's delay was caused by the photographer's not being notified promptly by the customer of his recovery. Before taking the photograph of the customer and his family, the photographer advised the customer that he was likely to be delayed a day or two beyond December 15 in making delivery because of the time required to process the photograph and cards. The customer told the photographer to take the photograph anyway. The cards were finally delivered by the photographer to the customer on December 17, the photographer having diligently worked on them in the interim. Although the cards pleased the rest of the family, the customer refused to accept them because, as he said squinting at one of the cards at arm's length without bothering to put on his reading glasses, "The photograph makes me look too old. Besides, the cards weren't delivered on time."

In an action by the photographer against the customer, which of the following would be the customer's best defense?

(A) The cards, objectively viewed, were not satisfactory.

(B) The cards, subjectively viewed, were not satisfactory.

(C) The cards were not delivered on time.

(D) The customer's illness excused him from further obligation under the contract.

B. Need to check whose duty was conditional

1. Right to waive condition

Question 32

In a writing signed by both parties on December 1, a buyer agreed to buy from a seller a gasoline engine for $1,000, delivery to be made on the following February 1. Through a secretarial error, the writing called for delivery on March 1, but neither party noticed the error until February 1. Before signing the agreement, the buyer and seller orally agreed that the contract of sale would be effective only if the buyer should notify the seller in writing not later than January 2 that the buyer had arranged to resell the engine to a third person. Otherwise, they agreed orally, "There is no deal." On December 15, the buyer entered into a contract with a third person to resell the engine to the third person at a profit.

On December 16, the buyer notified the seller by telephone of the buyer's resale agreement with the third person, and explained that a written notice was unfeasible because the buyer's secretary was ill. The seller replied, "That's okay. I'll get the engine to you on February 1, as we agreed." Having learned, however, that the engine had increased in value about 75% since December 1, the seller renounced the agreement on February 1.

If the buyer sues the seller on February 2 for breach of contract, which of the following concepts best supports the buyer's claim?

(A) Substantial performance.

(B) Nonoccurrence of a condition subsequent.

(C) Waiver of condition.

(D) Novation of buyers.

a. Waiver by receiving and keeping benefit

Question 33

Ohner and Planner signed a detailed writing in which Planner, a landscape architect, agreed to landscape and replant Ohner's residential property in accordance with a design prepared by Planner and incorporated in the writing. Ohner agreed to pay $50,000 for the work upon its completion.

At Ohner's insistence, the written Ohner-Planner agreement contained a provision that neither party would be bound unless Ohner's law partner, an avid student of landscaping, should approve Planner's design. Before Planner commenced the work, Ohner's law partner, in the presence of both Ohner and Planner, expressly disapproved the landscaping design. Nevertheless, Ohner ordered Planner to proceed with the work, and Planner reluctantly did so. When Planner's performance was 40% complete, Ohner repudiated his duty, if any, to pay the contract price or any part thereof.

If Planner now sues Ohner for damages for breach of contract, which of the following concepts best supports Planner's claim?

(A) Substantial performance.

(B) Promissory estoppel.

(C) Irrevocable waiver of condition.

(D) Unjust enrichment.

II. CONSTRUCTIVE CONDITIONS

A. Waiver of constructive condition

Question 34

Bitz, an amateur computer whiz, agreed in writing to design for the Presskey Corporation, a distributor of TV game systems, three new games a year for a five-year period. The writing provided, in a clause separately signed by Bitz, that "No modification shall be binding on Presskey unless made in writing and signed by Presskey's authorized representative."

Because of family problems, Bitz delivered and Presskey accepted only two game designs a year for the first three years; but the games were a commercial success and Presskey made no objection. Accordingly, Bitz spent substantial sums on new computer equipment that would aid in speeding up future design work. In the first quarter of the fourth year, however, Presskey terminated the contract on the ground that Bitz had breached the annual-quantity term.

In Bitz's suit against Presskey for damages, the jury found that the contract had been modified by conduct and the trial court awarded Bitz substantial compensatory damages.

Is this result likely to be reversed on appeal?

(A) Yes, because the contract's no-oral-modification clause was not expressly waived by Presskey.

(B) Yes, because the contract's no-oral-modification clause was a material part of the agreed exchange and could not be avoided without new consideration.

(C) No, because the contract's no-oral-modification clause was unconscionable as against an amateur designer.

(D) No, because Presskey by its conduct waived the annual-quantity term and Bitz materially changed his position in reasonable reliance on that waiver.

III. SUBSTANTIAL PERFORMANCE

A. Material breach in contracts for the sale of goods

1. "Perfect tender" rule under the UCC

a. Rule not applied very strictly

Question 35

Computers, Inc., contracted in writing with Bank to sell and deliver to Bank a mainframe computer using a new type of magnetic memory, then under development but not perfected by Computers, at a price substantially lower than that of a similar computer using current technology. The contract's delivery term was "F.O.B. Bank, on or before July 31." Computers tendered the computer to Bank on August 15, and Bank rejected it because of the delay.

If Computers sues Bank for breach of contract, which of the following facts, if proved, will best support a recovery by Computers?

(A) The delay did not materially harm Bank.

(B) Computers believed, on the assumption that Bank was getting a "super deal" for its money, that Bank would not reject because of the late tender of delivery.

(C) Computers' delay in tender was caused by a truckers' strike.

(D) A usage in the relevant trade allows computer sellers a 30-day leeway in a specified time of delivery, unless the usage is expressly negated by the contract.

2. Right to cure lack of perfect tender

Question 36

In a signed writing, a buyer contracted to purchase a 25-foot travel trailer from an RV dealer for $15,000, cash on delivery no later than June 1. The buyer arrived at the dealer's sales lot on Sunday, May 31, to pay for and take delivery of the trailer, but refused to do so when he discovered that the spare tire was missing.

The dealer offered to install a spare tire on Monday when its service department would open, but the buyer replied that he did not want the trailer and would purchase another one elsewhere.

Which of the following is accurate?

(A) The buyer had a right to reject the trailer, but the dealer was entitled to a reasonable opportunity to cure the defect.

(B) The buyer had a right to reject the trailer and terminate the contract under the perfect tender rule.

(C) The buyer was required to accept the trailer, because the defect could be readily cured.

(D) The buyer was required to accept the trailer, because the defect did not substantially impair its value.

IV. EXCUSE OF CONDITIONS

A. Where a party hinders the occurrence of a condition

1. Implied promise of cooperation

Question 37

A fugitive was wanted for murder. The authorities offered the following reward: "$20,000 to anyone who provides information leading to the arrest and conviction of this fugitive." A private detective knew of the reward, located the fugitive, and brought him to the authorities, who arrested him. The authorities then determined that while the fugitive had, in fact, committed the crime, he had been directed to commit the crime by his boss. The authorities and the fugitive then agreed that in exchange for the fugitive's testimony against his boss, all charges against the fugitive would be dropped. The fugitive testified and was released. The authorities refused to pay the reward to the private detective on the ground that the fugitive was never convicted.

Would the private detective be likely to prevail in a breach of contract action against the authorities?

(A) No, because the private detective failed to notify the authorities that he had accepted the reward offer.

(B) No, because the express conditions set out in the reward were not met.

(C) Yes, because the authorities' agreement with the fugitive was against public policy.

(D) Yes, because the authorities themselves prevented the conviction of the fugitive.

Chapter 7

ANTICIPATORY REPUDIATION AND OTHER ASPECTS OF BREACH

I. ANTICIPATORY REPUDIATION

A. What constitutes repudiation

1. Statement of grudging willingness to perform

Question 38

Broker needed a certain rare coin to complete a set that he had contracted to assemble and sell to Collecta. On February 1, Broker obtained such a coin from Hoarda in exchange for $1,000 and Broker's signed, written promise to re-deliver to Hoarda "not later than December 31 this year" a comparable specimen of the same kind of coin without charge to Hoarda. On February 2, Broker consummated sale of the complete set to Collecta.

On October 1, the market price of rare coins suddenly began a rapid, sustained rise; and on October 15 Hoarda wrote Broker for assurance that the latter would timely meet his coin-replacement commitment. Broker replied, "In view of the surprising market, it seems unfair that I should have to replace your coin within the next few weeks."

Having received Broker's message on October 17, Hoarda sued Broker on November 15 for the market value of a comparable replacement-coin as promised by Broker in February. The trial began on December 1.

If Broker moves to dismiss Hoarda's complaint, which of the following is Broker's best argument in support of the motion?

(A) Broker did not repudiate the contract on October 17, and may still perform no later than the contract deadline of December 31.

(B) Even if Broker repudiated on October 17, Hoarda's only action would be for specific performance because the coin is a unique chattel.

(C) Under the doctrine of impossibility, which includes unusually burdensome and unforeseen impracticability, Broker is temporarily excused by the market conditions from timely performance of his coin-replacement obligation.

(D) Even if Broker repudiated on October 17, Hoarda has no remedy without first demanding in writing that Broker retract his repudiation.

Question 39

On June 1, a seller and a buyer contracted in writing for the sale and purchase of the seller's cattle ranch (a large single tract), and to close the transaction on December 1.

On October 1, the buyer told the seller, "I'm increasingly unhappy about our June 1 contract because of the current cattle market, and do not intend to buy your ranch unless I'm legally obligated to do so." If the seller sues the buyer on October 15 for breach of contract, the seller will probably

(A) win, because the buyer committed a total breach by anticipatory repudiation on October 1.

(B) win, because the buyer's October 1 statement created reasonable grounds for the seller's insecurity with respect to the buyer's performance.

(C) lose, because the parties contracted for the sale and conveyance of a single tract, and the seller cannot bring suit for breach of such a contract prior to the agreed closing date.

(D) lose, because the buyer's October 1 statement to the seller was neither a repudiation nor a present breach of the June 1 contract.

II. OTHER ASPECTS OF REPUDIATION

A. Retraction of repudiation

1. Final acts

a. Cancellation followed by new contract with someone else

Question 40

On June 1, a seller and a buyer contracted in writing for the sale and purchase of the seller's cattle ranch, and to close the transaction on December 1. The buyer unequivocally repudiated the contract on August 1. On August 15, the seller urged the buyer to change her mind and proceed with the scheduled closing on December 1. On October 1, having heard nothing further from the buyer, the seller sold and conveyed his ranch to a third party — a rancher — without notice to the buyer. On December 1, the buyer attempted to close under the June 1 contract by tendering the full purchase price to the seller. The seller rejected the tender.

If the buyer sues the seller for breach of contract, the buyer will probably

(A) win, because the seller failed seasonably to notify the buyer of any pending sale to the rancher.

(B) win, because the seller waived the buyer's August 1 repudiation by urging her to retract it on August 15.

(C) lose, because the buyer did not retract her repudiation before the seller materially changed his position in reliance thereon by selling the ranch to the rancher.

(D) lose, because acceptance of the purchase price by the seller was a concurrent condition to the seller's obligation to convey the ranch to the buyer on December 1.

B. Special UCC rules

1. Party has choice of remedies

Question 41

Broker needed a certain rare coin to complete a set that he had contracted to assemble and sell to Collecta. On February 1, Broker obtained such a coin from Hoarda in exchange for $1,000 and Broker's signed, written promise to re-deliver to Hoarda "not later than December 31 this year" a comparable specimen of the same kind of coin without charge to Hoarda. On February 2, Broker consummated sale of the complete set to Collecta.

On October 1, the market price of rare coins suddenly began a rapid, sustained rise; and on October 15 Hoarda wrote Broker for assurance that the latter would timely meet his coin-replacement commitment. Broker replied, "In view of the surprising market, it seems unfair that I should have to replace your coin within the next few weeks."

After receiving Broker's message on October 17, Hoarda telephoned Broker, who said, "I absolutely will not replace your coin until the market drops far below its present level." Hoarda then sued Broker on November 15 for the market value of a comparable replacement-coin as promised by Broker in February. The trial began on December 1.

If Broker moves to dismiss Hoarda's complaint, which of the following is Hoarda's best argument in opposing the motion?

(A) Hoarda's implied duty of good faith and fair dealing in enforcement of the contract required her to mitigate her losses on the rising market by suing promptly, as she did, after becoming reasonably apprehensive of a prospective breach by Broker.

(B) Although the doctrine of anticipatory breach is not applicable under the prevailing view if, at the time of repudiation, the repudiatee owes the repudiator no remaining duty of performance, the doctrine applies in this case because Hoarda, the repudiatee, remains potentially liable under an implied warranty that the coin advanced to Broker was genuine.

(C) When either party to a sale-of-goods contract repudiates with respect to a performance not yet due, the loss of which will substantially impair the value of the contract to the other, the aggrieved party may in good faith resort to any appropriate remedy for breach.

(D) Anticipatory repudiation, as a deliberate disruption without legal excuse of an ongoing contractual relationship between the parties, may be treated by the repudiatee at her election as a present tort, actionable at once.

CHAPTER 8

STATUTE OF FRAUDS

I. SURETYSHIP

A. Main purpose rule

Question 42

A father and his adult daughter encountered an old family friend on the street. The daughter said to the friend, "How about lending me $1,000 to buy a used car? I'll pay you back with interest one year from today." The father added, "And if she doesn't pay it back as promised, I will." The friend thereupon wrote out and handed to the daughter his personal check, payable to her, for $1,000, and the daughter subsequently used the funds to buy a used car. When the debt became due, both the daughter and the father refused to repay it, or any part of it.

In an action by the friend against the father to recover $1,000 plus interest, which of the following statements would summarize the father's best defense?

(A) He received no consideration for his conditional promise to the friend.

(B) His conditional promise to the friend was not to be performed in less than a year from the time it was made.

(C) His conditional promise to the friend was not made for the primary purpose of benefiting himself (the father).

(D) The loan by the friend was made without any agreement concerning the applicable interest rate.

II. SATISFACTION BY A MEMORANDUM

A. UCC

1. Confirmation as sufficient memorandum

Question 43

A skiing retailer, in a telephone conversation with a glove manufacturer, ordered 12 pairs of vortex-lined ski gloves at the manufacturer's list price of $600 per dozen "for delivery in 30 days." The manufacturer orally accepted the offer, and immediately faxed to the ski shop this signed memo: "Confirming our agreement today for your purchase of a dozen pairs of vortex-lined ski gloves for $600, the shipment will be delivered in 30 days." Although the retailer received and read the manufacturer's message within minutes after its dispatch, she changed her mind three weeks later about the purchase and rejected the conforming shipment when it timely arrived.

On learning of the rejection, does the manufacturer have a cause of action against the retailer for breach of contract?

(A) Yes, because the gloves were identified to the contract and tendered to the retailer.

(B) Yes, because the manufacturer's faxed memo to the retailer was sufficient to make the agreement enforceable.

(C) No, because the agreed price was $600 and the retailer never signed a writing evidencing a contract with the manufacturer.

(D) No, because the retailer neither paid for nor accepted any of the goods tendered.

REMEDIES

I. EQUITABLE REMEDIES

A. Two types

1. Specific performance as remedy

Question 44

A landowner owned a lot in fee simple. For a consideration of $5,000, the landowner gave a buyer a written option to purchase the lot for $300,000. The option was assignable. For a consideration of $10,000, the buyer subsequently gave an option to a speculator to purchase the lot for $325,000. The speculator exercised his option.

The buyer thereupon exercised his option. The buyer paid the agreed price of $300,000 and took title to the lot by deed from the landowner. Thereafter, the speculator refused to consummate his purchase. The buyer brought an appropriate action against the speculator for specific performance, or, if that should be denied, then for damages. The speculator counterclaimed for return of the $10,000. In this action, the court will

(A) grant money damages only to the buyer.

(B) grant specific performance to the buyer.

(C) grant the buyer only the right to retain the $10,000.

(D) require the buyer to refund the $10,000 to the speculator.

B. Limitations on equitable remedies

1. Requirement that money damages be inadequate remedy

Question 45

Elda, the aged mother of Alice and Barry, both adults, wished to employ a live-in companion so that she might continue to live in her own home. Elda, however, had only enough income to pay one-half of the companion's $2,000 monthly salary. Learning of their mother's plight, Alice and Barry agreed with each other in a signed writing that on the last day of January and each succeeding month during their mother's lifetime, each would give Elda $500. Elda then hired the companion.

Alice and Barry made the agreed payments in January, February, and March. In April, however, Barry refused to make any payment and notified Alice and Elda that he would make no further payments.

Assume that there is a valid contract between Alice and Barry and that Elda has declined to sue Barry. Will Alice succeed in an action against Barry in which she asks the court to order Barry to continue to make his payments to Elda under the terms of the Alice-Barry contract?

(A) Yes, because Alice's remedy at law is inadequate.

(B) Yes, because Alice's burden of supporting her mother will be increased if Barry does not contribute his share.

(C) No, because a court will not grant specific performance of a promise to pay money.

(D) No, because Barry's breach of contract has caused no economic harm to Alice.

2. Difficulty of enforcement

a. Personal service contract

Question 46

On November 15, a carpenter in a signed writing contracted with a homeowner for an agreed price to personally remodel the homeowner's kitchen according to specifications provided by the homeowner, and to start work on December 1. The carpenter agreed to provide all materials for the job in addition to all of the labor required.

On November 26 the carpenter without legal excuse repudiated the contract, and the homeowner, after a reasonable and prolonged effort, could not find anyone to remodel his kitchen for a price approximating the price agreed to by the carpenter. If one year later the homeowner brings an action for specific performance against the carpenter, which of the following will provide the carpenter with the best defense?

(A) An action for equitable relief not brought within a reasonable time is barred by laches.

(B) Specific performance is generally not available as a remedy to enforce a contractual duty to perform personal services.

(C) Specific performance is generally not available as a remedy in the case of an anticipatory repudiation.

(D) Specific performance is not available as a remedy where even nominal damages could have been recovered as a remedy at law.

II. EXPECTATION DAMAGES

A. Formula for calculating

1. Breaching supplier of services

Question 47

A homeowner and a contractor entered into a contract for the construction of a home for the price of $300,000. The contractor was to earn a profit of $10,000 for the job. After the contractor had spent $45,000 on labor and materials, including $5,000 on oak flooring not yet installed, the homeowner informed the contractor that the homeowner had lost his job and could not pay for any services. The homeowner told the contractor to stop working immediately. The reasonable market value of the labor and materials provided by the contractor at that point, including the oak flooring, was $40,000. The contractor used the $5,000 worth of oak flooring on another job.

In an action by the contractor against the homeowner for damages, which of the following would be the largest amount of damages recoverable by the contractor?

(A) $40,000, the reasonable value of the services the contractor had provided.

(B) $40,000, the contractor's construction costs.

(C) $50,000, the contractor's construction costs of $45,000 plus the $10,000 profit minus the $5,000 saved by reusing the oak flooring on another job.

(D) $55,000, the contractor's construction costs of $45,000 plus the $10,000 profit.

Question 48

A contractor agreed to build a power plant for a public utility. A subcontractor agreed with the contractor to lay the foundation for $200,000. The subcontractor supplied goods and services worth $150,000, for which the contractor made progress payments aggregating $100,000 as required by the subcontract. The subcontractor then breached by refusing unjustifiably to perform further. The contractor reasonably spent $120,000 to have the work completed by a third party.

The subcontractor now sues the contractor for the reasonable value of benefits conferred, and the contractor counterclaims for breach of contract.

Which of the following should be the court's decision?

(A) The subcontractor recovers $50,000, the benefit conferred on the contractor for which the subcontractor has not been paid.

(B) The subcontractor recovers $30,000, the benefit the subcontractor conferred on the contractor minus the $20,000 in damages incurred by the contractor.

(C) The contractor recovers $20,000, the excess over the contract price that was paid by the contractor for the performance it had bargained to receive from the subcontractor.

(D) Neither party recovers anything, because the subcontractor committed a material, unexcused breach and the contractor received a $50,000 benefit from the subcontractor for which the subcontractor has not been paid.

B. "Reasonable certainty"

1. Profits from a new business

Question 49

Swatter, a baseball star, contracted with the Municipal Symphony Orchestra. Inc., to perform for $5,000 at a children's concert, as narrator of "Peter and the Wolf." Shortly before the concert, Swatter became embroiled in a highly publicized controversy over whether he had cursed and assaulted a baseball fan. The orchestra canceled the contract out of concern that attendance might be adversely affected by Swatter's appearance.

Swatter sued the orchestra for breach of contract. His business agent testified without contradiction that the cancellation had resulted in Swatter's not getting other contracts for performances and endorsements.

The trial court instructed the jury, in part, as follows: "If you find for the plaintiff, you may award damages for losses which at the time of contracting could reasonably have been foreseen by the defendant as a probable result of its breach. However, the law does not permit recovery for the loss of prospective profits of a new business caused by breach of contract."

On Swatter's appeal from a jury verdict for Swatter, and judgment thereon, awarding damages only for the $5,000 fee promised by the orchestra, the judgment will probably be

(A) affirmed, because the trial court stated the law correctly.

(B) affirmed, because the issue of damages for breach of contract was solely a jury question.

(C) reversed, because the test for limiting damages is what the breaching party could reasonably have foreseen at the time of the breach.

(D) reversed, because under the prevailing modern view, lost profits of a new business are recoverable if they are established with reasonable certainty.

C. Breaching seller of property

Question 50

On April 1, Owner and Buyer signed a writing in which Owner, "in consideration of $100 to be paid to Owner by Buyer," offered Buyer the right to purchase Greenacre for $100,000 within 30 days. The writing further provided, "This offer will become effective as an option only if and when the $100 consideration is in fact paid." On April 20, Owner, having received no payment or other communication from Buyer, sold and conveyed Greenacre to Citizen for $120,000. On April 21, Owner received a letter from Buyer enclosing a cashier's check for $100 payable to Owner and stating, "I am hereby exercising my option to purchase Greenacre and am prepared to close whenever you're ready." Owner explained that he had already sold the property to Citizen. Buyer brought suit against Owner for breach of contract.

Assume that Buyer prevails in the breach of contract suit against Owner. Which of the following is Buyer entitled to recover?

(A) Nominal damages only, because the remedy of specific performance was not available to Buyer.

(B) The fair market value, if any, of an assignable option to purchase Greenacre for $100,000.

(C) $20,000, plus the amount, if any, by which the fair market value of Greenacre on the date of Owner's breach exceeded $120,000.

(D) The amount, if any, by which the fair market value of Greenacre on the date of Owner's breach exceeded $100,000.

III. SUITS IN QUASI-CONTRACT

A. Breaching plaintiff

1. Construction cases

a. Lesser of "cost to owner" and "change in value to owner"

Question 51

In a single writing, a painter contracted with a farmer to paint three identical barns on the farmer's rural estate for $2,000 each. The contract provided for the farmer's payment of $6,000 upon the painter's completion of the work on all three barns. The painter did not ask for any payment when the first barn was completely painted, but she demanded $4,000 after painting the second barn. The farmer rightfully refused the painter's demand for payment. The painter then immediately terminated the contract without painting the third barn. What is the painter entitled to recover from the farmer?

(A) Nothing, because payment was expressly conditioned on completion of all three barns.

(B) The painter's expenditures plus anticipated "profit" in painting the first two barns, up to a maximum recovery of $4,000.

(C) The reasonable value of the painter's services in painting the two barns, less the farmer's damages, if any, for the painter's failure to paint the third barn.

(D) The amount that the combined value of the two painted barns has been increased by the painter's work.

2. UCC gives partial restitution to breaching buyer

a. Exception for actual damages proved by seller

Question 52

Hydro-King. Inc., a high-volume, pleasure-boat retailer, entered into a written contract with Zuma, signed by both parties, to sell Zuma a power boat for $12,000. The manufacturer's price of the boat delivered to Hydro-King was $9,500. As the contract provided, Zuma paid Hydro-King $4,000 in advance and promised to pay the full balance upon delivery of the boat.

The contract contained no provision for liquidated damages. Prior to the agreed delivery date, Zuma notified Hydro-King that he would be financially unable to conclude the purchase; and Hydro-King thereupon resold the same boat that Zuma had ordered to a third person for $12,000 cash.

If Zuma sues Hydro-King for restitution of the $4,000 advance payment, which of the following should the court decide?

(A) Zuma's claim should be denied, because, as the party in default, he is deemed to have lost any right to restitution of a benefit conferred on Hydro-King.

(B) Zuma's claim should be denied, because, but for his repudiation, Hydro-King would have made a profit on two boat-sales instead of one.

(C) Zuma's claim should be upheld in the amount of $4,000 minus the amount of Hydro-King's lost profit under its contract with Zuma.

(D) Zuma's claims should be upheld in the amount of $3,500 ($4,000 minus $500 as statutory damages under the UCC).

IV. LIQUIDATED DAMAGES

A. Reasonableness of estimated amount

Question 53

A sea captain owns an exceptionally seaworthy boat that she charters for sport fishing at a $500 daily rate. The fee includes the use of the boat with the sea captain as the captain, and one other crew member, as well as fishing tackle and bait. On May 1, a customer agreed with the captain that the customer would have the full-day use of the boat on May 15 for himself and his family for $500. The customer paid an advance deposit of $200 and signed an agreement that the deposit could be retained by the captain as liquidated damages in the event the customer canceled or failed to appear.

At the time of contracting, the captain told the customer to be at the dock at 5 a.m. on May 15. The customer and his family, however, did not show up on May 15 until noon. Meantime, the captain agreed at 10 a.m. to take a replacement customer and her family out fishing for the rest of the day. The replacement had happened to come by and inquire about the possibility of such an outing. In view of the late hour, the captain charged the replacement $400 and stayed out two hours beyond the customary return time. The original customer's failure to appear until noon was due to the fact that he had been trying to charter another boat across the bay at a lower rate and had gotten lost after he was unsuccessful in getting such a charter.

Which of the following is an accurate statement concerning the rights of the parties?

(A) The captain can retain the $200 paid by the customer, because it would be difficult for the captain to establish her actual damages and the sum appears to have been a reasonable forecast in light of anticipated loss of profit from the charter.

(B) The captain is entitled to retain only $50 (10% of the contract price) and must return $150 to the customer.

(C) The captain must return $100 to the customer in order to avoid her own unjust enrichment at the customer's expense.

(D) The captain must return $100 to the customer, because the liquidated-damage clause under the circumstances would operate as a penalty.

V. DAMAGES IN SALES CONTRACTS

A. Where goods not accepted

1. Seller's damages for breach

a. Lost profits

i. "Lost volume" seller

Question 54

By the terms of a written contract signed by both parties on January 15, a computer retailer agreed to sell a specific ICB personal computer to a buyer for $3,000, and the buyer agreed to pick up and pay for the computer at the retailer's store on February 1. The buyer unjustifiably repudiated on February 1. Without notifying the buyer, the retailer subsequently sold at private sale the same specific computer to another buyer, who paid the same price ($3,000) in cash. The ICB is a popular product; the retailer can buy from the manufacturer more units than it can sell at retail.

If the retailer sues the buyer for breach of contract, the retailer will probably recover

(A) nothing, because it received a price on resale equal to the contract price that the buyer had agreed to pay.

(B) nothing, because the retailer failed to give the buyer proper notice of the retailer's intention to resell.

(C) the retailer's anticipated profit on the sale to the buyer plus incidental damages, if any, because the retailer lost that sale.

(D) $3,000 (the contract price), because the buyer intentionally breached the contract by repudiation.

CONTRACTS INVOLVING
MORE THAN TWO PARTIES

I. ASSIGNMENT

A. Contract terms prohibiting assignment

Question 55

In a written contract, a seller agreed to deliver to a buyer 500 described chairs at $20 each, F.O.B. seller's place of business. The contract provided that "neither party will assign this contract without the written consent of the other." The seller placed the chairs on board a carrier on January 30. On February 1, the seller said in a signed writing, "I hereby assign to my bank all my rights under the seller-buyer contract." The seller did not request and did not get the buyer's consent to this transaction. On February 2, the chairs while in transit were destroyed in a derailment of the carrier's railroad car.

In an action by the bank against the buyer, the bank probably will recover

(A) $10,000, the contract price.

(B) the difference between the contract price and the market value of the chairs.

(C) nothing, because the chairs had not been delivered.

(D) nothing, because the seller-buyer contract forbade an assignment.

B. Assignee vs. obligor

Question 56

Under the terms of a written contract, a contractor agreed to construct for a homeowner a garage for $10,000. Nothing was said in the parties' negotiations or in the contract about progress payments during the course of the work. After completing 25% of the garage strictly according to the homeowner's specifications, the contractor assigned his rights under the contract to a banker as security for an $8,000 loan. The banker immediately notified the homeowner of the assignment. The contractor thereafter, without legal excuse, abandoned the job before it was half-complete. The contractor subsequently defaulted on the loan from the banker. The contractor has no assets. It will cost the homeowner at least $8,000 to get the garage finished by another builder.

If the banker sues the homeowner for $8,000, which of the following will the court decide?

(A) The banker wins, because the contractor-homeowner contract was in existence and the contractor was not in breach when the banker gave the homeowner notice of the assignment.

(B) The banker wins, because the banker as a secured creditor over the contractor is entitled to priority over the homeowner's unsecured claim against the contractor.

(C) The homeowner wins, because his right to recoupment on account of the contractor's breach is available against the banker as the contractor's assignee.

(D) The homeowner wins, because his claim against the contractor arose prior to the contractor's default on his loan from the banker.

Question 57

On March 1, Mechanic agreed to repair Ohner's machine for $5,000, to be paid on completion of the work. On March 15, before the work was completed, Mechanic sent a letter to Ohner with a copy to Jones, telling Ohner to pay the $5,000 to Jones, who was one of Mechanic's creditors. Mechanic then completed the work.

Which of the following, if true, would best serve Ohner as a defense in an action brought against him by Jones for $5,000?

(A) Jones was incapable of performing Mechanic's work.

(B) Mechanic had not performed his work in a workmanlike manner.

(C) On March 1, Mechanic had promised Ohner that he would not assign the contract.

(D) Jones was not the intended beneficiary of the Ohner-Mechanic contract.

C. Rights of successive assignees of the same claim

Question 58

A tortfeasor tortiously injured a victim in an auto accident. While the victim was consequently hospitalized, the tortfeasor's liability insurer settled with the victim for $5,000. The victim gave the insurer a signed release and received a signed memorandum wherein the insurer promised to pay the victim $5,000 by check within 30 days. When the victim left the hospital two days later, the hospital demanded payment of his $4,000 stated bill. The victim thereupon gave the hospital his own negotiable promissory note for $4,000 payable to the hospital's order in 30 days, and also, as security, assigned to the hospital the insurer's settlement memorandum. The hospital promptly assigned for value the settlement memorandum and negotiated the note to a bank, which took the note as a holder in due course. Subsequently, the victim misrepresented to the insurer that he had lost the settlement memorandum and needed another. The insurer issued another memorandum identical to the first, and the victim assigned it to a furniture company to secure a $5,000 credit sale contract. The furniture company immediately notified the insurer of this assignment. Later it was discovered that the hospital had mistakenly overbilled the victim by an amount of $1,000 and that the tortfeasor was an irresponsible minor.

In view of the tortfeasor's age and irresponsibility when the insurer issued his liability policy, can the bank and the furniture company recover on their assignments?

(A) Neither can recover because the victim, the assignor, is a third-party beneficiary of the liability policy whose rights thereon can be no better than the tortfeasor's.

(B) Neither can recover unless the insurer knowingly waived the defense of the tortfeasor's minority and irresponsibility.

(C) Neither can recover because the liability policy and settlement thereunder are unenforceable on account of the tortfeasor's minority.

(D) Either the bank or the furniture company, depending on priority, can recover as an assignee (or subassignee) on the victim's claim, because the victim's claim arose from the insurer's settlement agreement, and that settlement was valid.

II. DELEGATION OF DUTIES

A. Delegatee's liability

1. Assignment of "the contract"

a. Delegator remains liable

Question 59

Gyro, an expert in lifting and emplacing equipment atop tall buildings, contracted in a signed writing to lift and emplace certain air-conditioning equipment atop Tower's building. The contract contained a clause providing for per diem damages if Gyro did not complete performance by a specified date, and a clause providing that "time is of the essence." Another clause provided that any subsequent agreement for extra work under the contract must be in writing and signed by both parties.

With ample time remaining under the contract for commencement and completion of his performance, Gyro notified Tower that he was selling his business to Copter, who was equally expert in lifting and emplacing equipment atop tall buildings, and that Copter had agreed to "take over the Gyro-Tower contract."

Tower orally agreed with Gyro to accept Copter's services. Copter performed on time but negligently installed the wrong air-conditioning equipment.

Will Tower succeed in an action against Gyro for damages for breach of contract?

(A) Yes, because Tower did not agree to release Gyro from liability under the Gyro-Tower contract.

(B) Yes, because Tower received no consideration for the substitution of Copter for Gyro.

(C) No, because by accepting the substitution of Copter for Gyro, Tower effected a novation, and Gyro was thereby discharged of his duties under the Gyro-Tower contract.

(D) No, because the liquidated-damage clause in the Gyro-Tower contract provided only for damages caused by delay in performance.

III. THIRD-PARTY BENEFICIARIES

A. When beneficiary may sue

1. Intended beneficiaries may sue

Question 60

A written contract was entered into between an investor and a winery. The contract provided that the investor would invest $1 million in the winery for its capital expansion and, in return, that the winery, from grapes grown in its famous vineyards, would produce and market at least 500,000 bottles of wine each year for five years under the investor's label.

The contract included provisions that the parties would share equally the profits and losses from the venture and that, if feasible, the wine would be distributed by the winery only through a specific distributor of fine wines. Neither the investor nor the winery had previously dealt with the distributor. The distributor learned of the contract two days later from reading a trade newspaper. In reliance thereon, it immediately hired an additional sales executive and contracted for enlargement of its wine storage and display facility. If the winery refuses to distribute the wine through the distributor and the distributor then sues the winery for breach of contract, is it likely that the distributor will prevail?

(A) Yes, because the winery's performance was to run to the distributor rather than to the investor.

(B) Yes, because the investor and the winery could reasonably foresee that the distributor would change its position in reliance on the contract.

(C) No, because the investor and the winery did not expressly agree that the distributor would have enforceable rights under their contract.

(D) No, because the investor and the winery, having no apparent motive to benefit the distributor, appeared in making the contract to have been protecting or serving only their own interests.

Question 61

Elda, the aged mother of Alice and Barry, both adults, wished to employ a live-in companion so that she might continue to live in her own home. Elda, however, had only enough income to pay one-half of the companion's $2,000 monthly salary. Learning of their mother's plight, Alice and Barry agreed with each other in a signed writing that on the last day of January and each succeeding month during their mother's lifetime, each would give Elda $500. Elda then hired the companion.

Alice and Barry made the agreed payments in January, February, and March. In April, however, Barry refused to make any payment and notified Alice and Elda that he would make no further payments.

Will Elda succeed in an action for $500 brought against Barry after April 30?

(A) Yes, because by making his first three payments, Barry confirmed his intent to contract.

(B) Yes, because Elda is an intended beneficiary of a contract between Alice and Barry.

(C) No, because a parent cannot sue her child for breach of a promise for support.

(D) No, because Alice and Barry intended their payments to Elda to be gifts.

2. Incidental beneficiaries may not sue

Question 62

A landowner was land-rich by inheritance but money-poor, having suffered severe losses on bad investments, but still owned several thousand acres of unencumbered timberland. He had a large family, and his normal, fixed personal expenses were high. Pressed for cash, he advertised a proposed sale of standing timber on a choice 2,000-acre tract. The only response was from a logging company, which operated a large, integrated construction enterprise. The logging company, after inspection of the advertised tract, offered a fair price for the timber rights in question, and the landowner accepted the offer. The 2,000-acre tract was an abundant wild-game habitat and had been used for many years, with the landowner's permission, by area hunters. The logging company's performance of the timber contract would destroy this habitat. Without legal excuse and over the landowner's strong objection, the logging company repudiated the contract before commencing performance. The landowner could not afford to hire a lawyer and take legal action, and made no attempt to assign any cause of action he might have had against the logging company.

If the logging company is sued for breach of the contract by the landowner's next-door neighbor, whose view of a nearby lake is obscured by the standing timber, the neighbor will probably

(A) lose, as only an incidental beneficiary, if any, of the logging company-landowner contract.

(B) lose, as a maintainer of nuisance litigation.

(C) prevail, as a third-party intended beneficiary of the logging company-landowner contract.

(D) prevail, as a surrogate for the landowner in view of his inability to enforce the contract.

B. Discharge or modification by the original parties

Question 63

On May 4, Mater and Nirvana Motors both signed a single document evidencing a contract for the sale by Nirvana to Mater, "as a wedding gift for Mater's son Gilbert," a new Mark XX Rolls-Royce sedan, for $180,000 cash on delivery. On May 5, Mater handed Gilbert a photocopy of this document. In reliance on the prospective gift, Gilbert on May 20 sold his nearly new Cheetah (an expensive sports car) to a dealer at a "bargain" price of $50,000 and immediately informed Mater and Nirvana that he had done so.

On May 25, however, Mater and Nirvana Motors by mutual agreement rescinded in a signed writing "any and all agreements heretofore made between the undersigned parties for the sale-and-purchase of a new Mark XX Rolls-Royce sedan." Later that day, Nirvana sold for $190,000 cash to another buyer the only new Mark XX Rolls-Royce that it had in stock or could readily obtain elsewhere. On June 1, Gilbert tendered $180,000 in cash to Nirvana Motors and demanded delivery to him "within a reasonable time" of a new Mark XX Rolls-Royce sedan with all available equipment.

Nirvana rejected the tender and denied any obligation.

If Gilbert sues Nirvana for breach of contract, which of the following will the court probably decide?

(A) Gilbert wins, because his rights as an assignee for value of the May 4 Mater-Nirvana contract cannot be cut off by agreement between the original parties.

(B) Gilbert wins, because his rights as a third-party intended beneficiary became vested by his prejudicial reliance in selling his Cheetah on May 20.

(C) Nirvana wins, because Gilbert, if an intended beneficiary at all of the Mater-Nirvana contract, was only a donee beneficiary.

(D) Nirvana wins, because it reasonably and prejudicially relied on its contract of mutual rescission with Mater by selling the only readily available new Mark XX Rolls-Royce sedan to another buyer.

Question 64

On March 1, Zeller orally agreed to sell his land, Homestead, to Byer for $46,000 to be paid on March 31. Byer orally agreed to pay $25,000 of the purchase price to Quincy in satisfaction of a debt which Zeller said he had promised to pay Quincy.

On March 10, Byer dictated the agreement to his secretary but omitted all reference to the payment of the $25,000 to Quincy. Neither Byer nor Zeller carefully read the writing before signing it on March 15. Neither raised any question concerning omission of the payment to Quincy.

In an action by Quincy against Byer for $25,000, which of the following, if proved, would best serve Byer as a defense?

(A) There was no consideration to support Zeller's antecedent promise to pay Quincy the $25,000.

(B) On March 5, before Quincy was aware of the oral agreement between Zeller and Byer, Zeller agreed with Byer not to pay any part of the purchase price to Quincy.

(C) Whatever action Quincy may have had against Zeller was barred by the statute of limitations prior to March 1.

(D) Before he instituted his action against Byer, Quincy had not notified either Byer or Zeller that he had accepted the Byer-Zeller arrangement for paying Quincy.

C. Defenses against the beneficiary

1. Promisor may invoke conditions to his duty

Question 65

Kabb, the owner of a fleet of taxis, contracted with Petrol, a dealer in petroleum products, for the purchase and sale of Kabb's total requirements of gasoline and oil for one year. As part of that agreement, Petrol also agreed with Kabb that for one year Petrol would place all his advertising with Ada Artiste, Kabb's wife, who owned her own small advertising agency. When Artiste was informed of the Kabb-Petrol contract, she declined to accept an advertising account from the Deturgid Soap Company because she could not handle both the Petrol and Deturgid accounts during the same year.

For this question only, assume the following facts. During the first month of the contract, Kabb purchased substantial amounts of his gasoline from a supplier other than Petrol, and Petrol thereupon notified Artiste that he would no longer place his advertising with her agency.

In an action against Petrol for breach of contract, Artiste probably will

(A) succeed, because she is a third-party beneficiary of the Kabb-Petrol contract.

(B) succeed, because Kabb was acting as Artiste's agent when he contracted with Petrol.

(C) not succeed, because the failure of a constructive condition precedent excused Petrol's duty to place his advertising with Artiste.

(D) not succeed, because Artiste did not provide any consideration to support Petrol's promise to place his advertising with her.

IMPOSSIBILITY, IMPRACTICABILITY, AND FRUSTRATION

I. IMPOSSIBILITY OF PERFORMANCE

A. Three classes

1. Destruction of subject matter

Question 66

On June 1, a seller agreed, in a writing signed by both the seller and the buyer, to sell an antique car to a buyer for $20,000. The car was at the time on display in a museum in a different city and was to be delivered to the buyer on August 1. On July 15, before the risk of loss had passed to the buyer, the car was destroyed by fire without fault of either party. Subsequent to the contract but before the fire, the car had increased in value to $30,000. The seller sued the buyer for the contract price of $20,000, and the buyer counterclaimed for $30,000.

Which of the following will the court conclude?

(A) Both claims fail.

(B) Only the seller's claim prevails.

(C) Only the buyer's claim prevails.

(D) Both claims prevail.

2. Supervening illegality

Question 67

Mermaid owns an exceptionally seaworthy boat that she charters for sport fishing at a $500 daily rate. The fee includes the use of the boat with Mermaid as the captain, and one other crew member, as well as fishing tackle and bait. On May 1, Phinney agreed with Mermaid that Phinney would have the full-day use of the boat on May 15 for himself and his family for $500. Phinney paid an advance deposit of $200 and signed an agreement that the deposit could be retained by Mermaid as liquidated damages in the event Phinney canceled or failed to appear.

On May 15 at 1 a.m., the Coast Guard had issued offshore "heavy weather" warnings and prohibited all small vessels the size of Mermaid's from leaving the harbor. This prohibition remained in effect throughout the day. Phinney did not appear at all on May 15, because he had heard the weather warnings on his radio.

Which of the following is an accurate statement?

(A) The contract is discharged because of impossibility, and Phinney is entitled to return of his deposit.

(B) The contract is discharged because of mutual mistake concerning an essential fact, and Phinney is entitled to return of his deposit.

(C) The contract is not discharged, because its performance was possible in view of the exceptional seaworthiness of Mermaid's boat, and Phinney is not entitled to return of his deposit.

(D) The contract is not discharged, and Phinney is not entitled to return of his deposit, because the liquidated-damage clause in effect allocated the risk of bad weather to Phinney.

II. IMPRACTICABILITY

A. Modern view of impracticability

1. Allocation of risk by parties

a. Implicit allocation

i. Risk of technological breakthrough

Question 68

A computer company contracted in writing with a bank to sell and deliver to the bank a mainframe computer using a new type of magnetic memory, then under development but not perfected by the computer company, at a price substantially lower than that of a similar computer using current technology. The contract's delivery term was "F.O.B. the bank, on or before July 31."

After making the contract with the bank, the computer company discovered that the new technology it intended to use was unreliable and that no computer manufacturer could yet build a reliable computer using that technology. The company thereupon notified the bank that it was impossible for the company or anyone else to build the contracted-for computer "in the present state of the art." If the bank sues the computer company for failure to perform its contract, the court will probably decide the case in favor of

(A) the computer company, because its performance of the contract was objectively impossible.

(B) the computer company, because a contract to build a machine using technology under development imposes only a duty on the builder to use its best efforts to achieve the result contracted for.

(C) the bank, because the law of impossibility does not apply to merchants under the applicable law.

(D) the bank, because the computer company assumed the risk, in the given circumstances, that the projected new technology would not work reliably.

ii. Foreseeability and relative expertise

Question 69

For an agreed price of $20 million, a builder contracted with a developer to design and build on the developer's commercial plot a 15-story office building. In excavating for the foundation and underground utilities, the contractor encountered a massive layer of granite at a depth of 15 feet. By reasonable safety criteria, the building's foundation required a minimum excavation of 25 feet. When the contract was made, neither the developer nor the contractor was aware of the subsurface granite, for the presence of which neither party had hired a qualified expert to test.

Claiming accurately that removal of enough granite to permit the construction as planned would cost him an additional $3 million and a probable net loss on the contract of $2 million, the contractor refused to proceed with the work unless the developer would promise to pay an additional $2.5 million for the completed building.

If the developer refuses and sues the contractor for breach of contract, which of the following will the court probably decide?

(A) The contractor is excused under the modern doctrine of supervening impossibility, which includes severe impracticability.

(B) The contractor is excused, because the contract is voidable on account of the parties' mutual mistake concerning an essential underlying fact.

(C) The developer prevails, because the contractor assumed the risk of encountering subsurface granite that was unknown to the developer.

(D) The developer prevails, unless subsurface granite was previously unknown anywhere in the vicinity of the developer's construction site.

III. FRUSTRATION OF PURPOSE

A. Factors to be considered

1. Foreseeability

a. Allocation of risks by parties

Question 70

On August 1, Geriatrics, Inc., operating a "lifetime care" home for the elderly, admitted Ohlster, who was 84 years old, for a trial period of two months. On September 25, Ohlster and Geriatrics entered into a written lifetime care contract with an effective commencement date of October 1. The full contract price was $20,000, which, as required by the terms of the contract, Ohlster prepaid to Geriatrics on September 25. Ohlster died of a heart attack on October 2.

In a restitutionary action, can the administratrix of Ohlster's estate, a surviving sister, recover on behalf of the estate either all or part of the $20,000 paid to Geriatrics on September 25?

(A) Yes, because Geriatrics would otherwise be unjustly enriched at Ohlster's expense.

(B) Yes, under the doctrine of frustration of purpose.

(C) No, because Ohlster's life span and the duration of Geriatrics' commitment to him was a risk assumed by both parties.

(D) No, but only if Geriatrics can show that between September 25 and Ohlster's death it rejected, because of its commitment to Ohlster, an application for lifetime care from another elderly person.

IV. RESTITUTION AND RELIANCE WHERE THE PARTIES ARE DISCHARGED

A. Restitution

1. Time for measuring benefit

Question 71

A lawyer entered into a contract with a painter by the terms of which the painter was to paint the lawyer's office for $1,000 and was required to do all of the work over the following weekend so as to avoid disruption of the lawyer's business. The painter commenced work on Saturday morning, and had finished half the painting by the time he quit work for the day. That night, without the fault of either party, the office building was destroyed by fire.

Which of the following is an accurate statement?

(A) Both parties' contractual duties are discharged, and the painter can recover nothing from the lawyer.

(B) Both parties' contractual duties are discharged, but the painter can recover in quasi-contract from the lawyer.

(C) Only the painter's contractual duty is discharged, because the lawyer's performance (payment of the agreed price) is not impossible.

(D) Only the painter's contractual duty is discharged, and the painter can recover his reliance damages from the lawyer.

MISCELLANEOUS DEFENSES

I. MISREPRESENTATION

A. Non-disclosure

1. Failure to correct other party's basic mistake

Question 72

An heir, who knew nothing about horses, inherited a thoroughbred colt whose disagreeable behavior made him a pest around the barn. The heir sold the colt for $1,500 to an experienced racehorse-trainer who knew of the heir's ignorance about horses. At the time of sale, the heir said to the trainer, "I hate to say it, but this horse is bad-tempered and nothing special." Soon after the sale, the horse won three races and earned $400,000 for the trainer.

Which of the following additional facts, if established by the heir, would best support his chance of obtaining rescission of the sale to the trainer?

(A) The heir did not know until after the sale that the trainer was an experienced racehorse-trainer.

(B) At a pre-sale exercise session of which the trainer knew that the heir was not aware, the trainer clocked the horse in record-setting time, far surpassing any previous performance.

(C) The horse was the only thoroughbred that the heir owned, and the heir did not know how to evaluate young and untested racehorses.

(D) At the time of the sale, the heir was angry and upset over an incident in which the horse had reared and thrown a rider.

II. UNCONSCIONABILITY AND ADHESION CONTRACTS

A. Unconscionability

1. Remedies for unconscionability

Question 73

A landholder was land-rich by inheritance but money-poor, having suffered severe losses on bad investments, but still owned several thousand acres of unencumbered timberland. He had a large family, and his normal, fixed personal expenses were high. Pressed for cash, he advertised a proposed sale of standing timber on a choice 2,000-acre tract. The only response was an offer by a logger, the owner of a large, integrated construction enterprise, after inspection of the advertised tract. The logger offered to buy, sever, and remove the standing timber from the advertised tract at a cash price 70% lower than the regionally prevailing price for comparable timber rights. The landholder, by then in desperate financial straits and knowing little about timber values, signed and delivered to the logger a letter accepting the offer.

If, before the logger commences performance, the landholder's investment fortunes suddenly improve and he wishes to get out of the timber deal with the logger, which of the following legal concepts affords his best prospect of effective cancellation?

(A) Bad faith.

(B) Equitable estoppel.

(C) Unconscionability.

(D) Duress.

CONTRACTS ANSWERS

References to "Rest. 2d" are to the *Second Restatement of Contracts*, to "Farnsworth" are to E.A. Farnsworth, *Contracts* (3d Ed. Aspen, 1999), and to "W&S" are to White & Summers, *Uniform Commercial Code* (5th Ed. West, 2000).

Answer 1

Choice **(B)** is correct,, because it accurately states that the notice fulfills the requirements of a public offer. A public offer requires sufficient definiteness to qualify as an offer at all. The key factors to consider are whether it contains the language of an offer, and a quantity term. (If it *doesn't*, it will be considered merely an invitation for offers.) Here, the offer was specific as to quantity—only one student could win—and it contains the language of a promise—"The faculty . . . offers." As such, the notice creates an offer for a unilateral contract, which any student could accept by winning the competition, having completed performance with knowledge of the offer.

(A) is wrong, because the notice was sufficiently definite to constitute an offer. The key here is distinguishing a public offer from an invitation for offers, which most ads are. The distinction is important because a public offer creates a power of acceptance in offerees, such that if an offeree accepts, a binding contract will be formed. An invitation for offers, on the other hand, doesn't give anyone the power to create a binding contract.

The thing that normally makes an ad an invitation instead of an offer is that it is indefinite, specifically in terms of the lack of language of a promise and quantity. That's not the case here. The notice is specific as to quantity (only one student could win), price ($500), and is worded as a promise ("The faculty . . . offers"). As such, it creates an immediate power of acceptance in any student, such that if a student wins the competition, having completed performance with knowledge of the offer, the faculty will be bound. (Note that the offer is for a unilateral contract, since it can only be accepted by performance, not a return promise.) Since Choice (A) mischaracterizes the notice as only an invitation to deal, it's not the best response.

(C) is wrong, because failure to identify the offeree, in the context of a public offer, would not destroy the offer. While a typical offer must identify the offeree, a public offer (like the offer of a reward) cannot, by dint of its nature, identify the offeree. However if the communication is sufficiently definite (i.e., it contains the language of an offer, and a quantity term), it's an offer nonetheless. The November 1 notice satisfied these requirements.

(D) is wrong because the promise made by the faculty in the notice was a *bargain* promise, not a *conditional* promise to make a gift. This is an important distinction, because a conditional promise to make a gift is not enforceable, whereas a bargain promise, when it's in the form of an offer (as here), creates the power of acceptance in an offeree.

The difference between the two turns on whether the parties consider fulfilling the condition as the "price" of accepting the promise; if they do, it's an enforceable, bargain promise. If not, it's a conditional promise to make a gift. Say the facts were different, and there had been no November 1 notice; instead, the first the student heard from the school was a note he received from the law school dean after winning the contest, saying, "Congratulations on winning the obscenity contest. I have a check from the school for $500 for you, and I'll give it to you if you come to my office at 2 p.m." This is a conditional promise, because the dean intended to make a gift, and the student's going to the office couldn't be construed as a bargained-for "price" of the promise to pay $500. Under the facts as they are in the question, however, things are entirely different. It's clear that both the faculty and the student considered the condition stated—winning the contest—as the bargained-for performance by which the offer of $500 could be accepted. Thus, the promise was a bargain promise for a unilateral contract, which the student accepted by winning the contest (having completed performance with knowledge of the offer). Since (D) mischaracterizes the promise, it's not the best response.

Answer 2

Choice (D) is correct. The retailer's order was an offer. The wholesaler's shipment of goods in response to the offer was an acceptance, even though what the wholesaler shipped was non-conforming goods. That's so because UCC § 2-206(1)(b) says that "an order or other offer to buy goods for prompt or current shipment shall be construed as inviting *acceptance . . .* by the prompt or current *shipment* of conforming or *non-conforming goods*[.]" buyer who receives non-conforming goods has the right to reject those goods, sending them back to the seller or holding them for the seller's pickup. That's because UCC § 2-601 says that, subject to some limitations not applicable here, "If the goods or the tender of delivery fail in any respect to conform to the contract, the buyer may (a) reject the whole; or (b) accept the whole; or (c) accept any commercial unit or units and reject the rest." So the retailer could reject all or some of the bushels.

(A) is wrong because the wholesaler's shipment was not a counteroffer, since nothing in the facts surrounding the shipment indicated that the wholesaler was rejecting the retailer's offer (its order). Instead, the wholesaler's shipment was an acceptance (as well as a breach).

(B) is wrong because: (1) the wholesaler's shipment was not a counteroffer (for the reason described in the analysis of Choice (A)); and (2) under UCC § 2-602(2), if the retailer wants to reject rather than accept the peaches, it is merely required "after rejection to hold [the goods] with reasonable care at the seller's disposition for a time sufficient to permit the seller to remove them." So despite the peaches' perishability, all that the retailer has to do is to promptly notify the wholesaler, "We don't want the peaches because they don't conform; we'll hold them for you to pick up."

(C) is wrong because, although a contract was indeed formed when the wholesaler shipped the peaches, their non-conformity to the retailer's order entitled the retailer to reject the goods rather than accept them.

Answer 3

Choice (B) is correct. This was an accommodation shipment under UCC § 2-206(1)(b)—in the words of that section, the supplier "seasonably notifie[d] the buyer that the shipment [was] offered only as an accommodation to the buyer." Therefore, the supplier's shipment did not constitute an acceptance. Instead, it was a counteroffer to sell three gross of red widgets. At that point, the retailer could choose between accepting the red and paying for them, or rejecting the red, in which case there would be no contract (because there never was an accepted offer).

(A) is wrong because when a seller makes an accommodation shipment, the buyer has the right to reject the shipment but does not have the right to recover for breach. That's because the shipment is not an acceptance but instead a counteroffer, and the buyer's rejection of the goods constitutes a rejection of the counteroffer, with the result that there is no breach by the seller for which the buyer could recover.

(C) is wrong for two reasons: (1) if the retailer accepts the shipment, he cannot deduct any damages because of the nonconformity (since this type of accommodation shipment constitutes a counteroffer rather than acceptance, making the buyer's decision to keep the goods an acceptance of the goods as shipped, meaning that the nonconformity to the original order is irrelevant); and (2) if the retailer rejects the shipment, he has simply rejected the supplier's counteroffer, and there is no breach for which the retailer can deduct.

(D) is wrong for two reasons: (1) if the retailer accepts the shipment, he cannot deduct any damages because of the nonconformity (for the reasons described in the analysis of Choice (C) above); and (2) if the retailer rejects the shipment, he may do so without covering by obtaining conforming widgets from someone else. (He may, for instance, decide that he doesn't need widgets of any color after all.)

Answer 4

Choice (D) is correct (i.e., the statement in this choice is *not* accurate). When the distributor wrote the letter and induced the customer to present the letter to the manufacturer, the distributor was making an offer for a unilateral contract — that is, it's clear that the distributor was expecting the manufacturer to accept (if he accepted at all) by extending the credit, rather than promising the distributor that he would extend the credit. When the manufacturer extended the credit, this was an acceptance of the distributor's offer by performance, so the distributor's guarantee of repayment came into effect. However, because of the requirement that an offeree who accepts an offer for a unilateral contract must ordinarily give prompt notice of acceptance to the offeror, if the manufacturer had not given the distributor prompt notice of the sale (which the facts say he did), the distributor's guarantee duty would have been discharged. Notice that it was up to you to spot the fact that this was an offer for a unilateral contract — the facts don't highlight this, and if you hadn't noticed it yourself, you would probably not have seen why notice by the manufacturer was important.

(A) is wrong because the statement is correct: The distributor's promise would not have been enforceable had it not been embodied in a signed writing. That's because the distributor's offer was a promise to "answer for the debt of another." As such, it fell within the suretyship provision of the Statute of Frauds, and was therefore required to be in a writing signed by the party to be charged (the distributor).

(B) is wrong because the statement is correct: As the discussion of Choice (D) describes, the distributor's offer was an offer for a unilateral contract (i.e., one to be accepted by performance rather than return promise), and the manufacturer accepted that offer by doing the requested act, i.e., extending credit to the retailer.

(C) is wrong because the statement is correct. It's true that the distributor received no consideration from the customer. However, the distributor received consideration *from the manufacturer* — the distributor bargained to have the manufacturer give credit to the customer, and got the performance he bargained for. (The fact that the performance ran to the customer rather than to the distributor [the promisor] does not prevent it from being consideration to support the distributor's promise.) The customer was a third-party beneficiary of the distributor's promise, and in a third-party beneficiary arrangement the fact that the third-party beneficiary does not give consideration to the promisor does not make any difference.

Answer 5

Choice (D) is correct. Under the UCC, a purported acceptance document will not be prevented from operating as a true acceptance even though it states terms that are additional to or different from those in the offer. UCC § 2-207(1). Therefore, the wholesaler's form with the "We are please to accept" language on it operated as an acceptance even though it contained an additional term (the liability cap). On the other hand, the liability cap was an "additional" term (i.e., a term dealing with a subject that was not covered in the retailer's offer). When the offeror and offeree are both merchants, § 2-207(2) says that an additional term is to be construed as a "proposal for addition to the contract," and becomes part of the contract unless (1) "the offer expressly limits acceptance to the terms of the offer" (which didn't happen here), (2) the additional term "materially alter[s]" the contract, or (3) the offeror promptly notifies the offeree that the offeror objects to the additional term. Here, event (2) has occurred: A liability cap would almost certainly be considered by a court to be a "material alteration" of an offer that did not contain any cap. Therefore, a contract was formed but it did not include the liability cap.

(A) is wrong because, as explained in more detail in Choice (D) above, while the liability-limitation clause was indeed a material alteration of the offer, this fact did not prevent the wholesaler's form from constituting an acceptance. (The wholesaler's form meshed sufficiently with the retailer's offer form, and contained sufficient words of acceptance, that it was a "definite . . . expression of acceptance" under UCC § 2-207(1) even though it contained the additional term.)

(B) is wrong because a contract was formed as soon as the wholesaler sent its form, and whether the retailer eventually did or did not expressly consent to the liability-limitation clause wouldn't matter to the issue of whether a contract was formed. (As explained in the discussion of Choice (D), the liability-limitation clause, since it was a material alteration, didn't become part of the contract even if the retailer remained silent.)

(C) is wrong because, while it correctly says that a contract is formed, it is incorrect in stating that the liability-limitation clause would become part of the contract. It's true that a liquidation-of-damages clause can, if the parties agree on it and it is reasonable, be enforced under the UCC. But such a clause won't enter the contract unless the parties somehow agree on the clause, and here, because the proposed clause was a material alteration, the retailer won't be presumed to have agreed from the mere fact that the clause was present on the wholesaler's acceptance and the retailer remained silent.

Answer 6

Choice (**B**) is correct. The driller's "proposal" was not an offer, because it could not be accepted by the unilateral act of the recipient (since by its terms it could not become a contract until it was not only signed by the developer, the recipient, but also signed by the driller). When the developer signed the form and returned it to the driller, the developer was making an offer on the terms described in the form. The driller could have accepted the offer by signing, but didn't in fact sign. However, when the driller started work, his conduct of doing the work described in the form, at the appropriate place, constituted an acceptance by conduct. This acceptance-by-conduct included a promise (albeit an implied one) to complete the work as described in the offer document (the form that the driller didn't sign).

(A) is wrong because, although it lists the correct result, it explains it on an incorrect legal theory. The driller's form could not be an offer, because the provision requiring both signatures meant that the unsigned form as dispatched by the driller did not empower the recipient (the developer) to unilaterally complete the deal (i.e., accept) by signing. Therefore, the developer's signature created an offer, not an acceptance. (And acceptance did not occur until the driller accepted by conduct.)

(C) is wrong because, although the driller never accepted by signature, he did accept by his conduct of starting the well drilling.

(D) is wrong because it misstates the effect of the driller's commencement of performance. That commencement of performance served as an acceptance of the contract, and thereby obligated the driller to complete his side of the deal.

Answer 7

Choice **(B)** is correct. This was a firm offer that met the requirements of UCC § 2-205, since it was (1) by a merchant; (2) in a letter signed by the offeror; and (3) it promised that the offeror would sell all items at the catalog price for a year (a promise to hold the offer open). It's true that this promise of irrevocability didn't legally extend beyond three months (despite what it said), but the three months was enough to cover February.

(A) is wrong because, while the doctrine of promissory estoppel says that detrimental reliance by the offeree may render an offer temporarily irrevocable, here there is no indication that the lawyer detrimentally relied on the stationer's offer.

(C) is wrong because the UCC does not require consideration for an offer to be irrevocable. The whole point of § 2-205's firm-offer provision is that qualifying offers by merchants will be irrevocable even though not supported by consideration.

(D) is wrong because, while the maximum period of irrevocability for firm orders under UCC § 2-205 is three months, when an offer that otherwise meets the firm-offer requirements promises more than three months' irrevocability, the offer will nonetheless be irrevocable for three months.

Answer 8

Choice **(B)** is correct. An offer is revocable unless some special circumstance makes it irrevocable. The contract here is covered by the UCC, making § 2-205's firm-offer provision potentially applicable. However, § 2-205 applies only to "an offer by a merchant." We are told that Debbit is not a merchant with respect to either lawbooks or book stacks. Therefore, his offer was not a firm offer and could be revoked at any time. Consequently, his statement on November 12 that he had decided not to part with the stacks was a legally operative revocation.

(A) is wrong because Barrister's pre-existing obligation to pay $10,000 for the law books is irrelevant on the issue of whether Debbit's offer about the stacks was irrevocable. Debbit's offer was an offer to modify the contract, and that offer was not rendered irrevocable merely because Barrister had previously given consideration (his promise to pay $10,000) to support Debbit's prior promise to sell the law books.

(C) is wrong because an offer is not rendered irrevocable merely because the offer is signed and states that it is irrevocable. Under the UCC, a signed offer that says it will be irrevocable will be so under some circumstances, but as explained above those circumstances include a requirement that the offeror be a merchant.

(D) is wrong because Barrister did not in fact detrimentally rely. If Barrister *had* detrimentally relied on Debbit's promise not to sell the stacks to someone else, this reliance might indeed have caused the offer to become temporarily irrevocable. But a mere delay in accepting is not the sort of detrimental reliance that will suffice for temporary irrevocability.

Answer 9

Choice **(C)** is correct. Where an offer invites acceptance by performance, the offeree's beginning of performance creates an option contract, which precludes the offeror from revoking its offer.

See Rest. 2d, § 45. The customer's beginning to wait in line created the option contract, which couldn't be revoked as long as the customer continued to wait. Notice that this fact pattern is exactly like the famous law-school hypothetical, "I'll pay you $10 if you cross the Brooklyn Bridge," where once the offeree starts to cross, the offeror can't revoke while the offeree is still trying to finish. You might think that the "This offer may be withdrawn at any time" language would change the result; but a court would likely interpret this to apply only to customers who hadn't yet started to wait on line at the moment the offer was withdrawn. See, e.g., Rest. 2d § 45, Comment b, saying that the "option contract" effect "yields to a manifestation of intention which makes reliance unjustified. A reservation of power to revoke *after performance has begun* means that as yet there is no promise and no offer"; the reservation of power to revoke here was not a reservation to revoke "after performance [i.e., waiting on line] has begun," so the right-to-withdraw language would be interpreted to be inapplicable to the customer here.

(A) is wrong because the bank's offer was an offer for a unilateral contract (i.e., an offer that was to be accepted by a performance rather than by a promise), and an offer for a unilateral contract becomes temporarily irrevocable once the offeree has begun to perform. See Choice (C).

(B) is wrong because the consideration required for an enforceable contract is present. The bank's promise to pay the customer $25 and the customer's standing in line constituted a bargained-for exchange. See Rest. 2d, § 71: A performance is consideration if it is "bargained for," and a performance is bargained for if it is "sought by the promisor [here, the bank] in exchange for his promise and is given by the promisee [the customer] in exchange for that promise."

(D) is wrong because it misstates the legal significance of the customer's presence in line. The offer here was an offer for a unilateral contract, that is, an offer that was to be accepted by performance (waiting in line for more than 5 minutes). Therefore, while the customer's mere presence in line constituted the *beginning* of performance, it did not constitute full performance (i.e., standing in line for more than five minutes), which was the only way the customer could accept. It's true that one who accepts an offer for a unilateral contract must sometimes give notice of acceptance-by-performance; but that's true only where the offeror would not otherwise know of the performance (which is not the case here). And in any event, the required notice would be notice of completed performance, not notice of the beginning of performance.

Answer 10

Choice (**A**) is correct. Where a transaction is a mixture of a bargain and a gift, the consideration requirement is satisfied. That is the case where, as here, one party promises to sell the other an item at a deep discount from market. Since Rollem was unquestionably bargaining for Betsy's payment of $3,000, the fact that this payment was much less than the market price does not prevent Betsy's payment from being consideration for Rollem's promise.

(B) is wrong as a matter of consideration doctrine, because a promise that is made on account of moral obligation is not supported by consideration. Furthermore, it is doubtful that contract law would regard a father as having any sort of obligation, even a moral one, to supply his adult daughter with a car.

(C) is wrong because contract law does not consider the adequacy of consideration, as long as the bargain and detriment of elements are satisfied. So here, since Rollem clearly bargained for Betsy's $3,000, the fact that this amount was arguably "inadequate" won't matter.

(D) is wrong because the defense of impossibility would not apply on these facts. Where a seller, acting through his agent, sells the contracted-for goods to someone else, this action will be viewed as being voluntary on the seller's part, and therefore not the sort of involuntary event to which the impossibility doctrine applies.

Answer 11

Choice **(D)** is correct. The only way the business owner can conceivably win is if he can show that his promise was not supported by consideration. But the business owner bargained for the jogger's act of running the six-minute mile. Since the business owner received the bargained act, the consideration requirement was satisfied. The jogger's motives in doing the act—including the fact that she would have done the act anyway without the business owner's request—are indeed irrelevant, as this choice states.

(A) is wrong because it would not matter even if the business owner's promise did not induce the jogger to run the mile. The business owner bargained for a six-minute mile to be run by the jogger, and got it; that's all that matters. So the fact that the jogger would have run that mile on that day anyway is irrelevant.

(B) is wrong because even in courts still interpreting the consideration doctrine to include a requirement that the promisee undergo a "detriment," all that is required is a "legal detriment." "Legal detriment" is really shorthand for "any act, forbearance or promise." The fact that the requested act, forbearance or promise would be of "benefit" to the promisee is irrelevant. Since the jogger performed the requested act, the fact that the doing of that act may have been a benefit to her health therefore doesn't matter.

(C) is wrong because it explains the correct result with incorrect reasoning. Since the jogger performed the requested act, she satisfies the "act, forbearance or promise" aspect of the consideration requirement whether or not the requested act was "significantly demanding" for her.

Answer 12

Choice **(B)** is correct, because it correctly applies the common-law rules on irrevocability and modifications to these facts. First, you have to determine whether the common law or the UCC will control. Since it's the sale of land that's involved, not a transaction in goods, the common law will control.

Second, you have to analyze what each communication does. The first is the landowner's May 1 telegram to the investor. It is sufficiently definite to constitute an offer to sell any or all lots in the subdivision for $5,000 each. The investor's May 2 telegram to the landowner constituted an acceptance as to lot 101 at $5,000, and probably implicitly rejected the offer as to the other 49 lots. As a result, the landowner's offer as to all the other lots terminated, because his original offer to keep the offer open until June 1 was not supported by consideration, so it was revocable. Even if the investor's acceptance as to lot 101 didn't terminate the offer, the landowner's subsequently raising the price to $6,000 did revoke the original offer and created a new one, at $6,000.

Thus, the price on the latter 49 lots was $6,000. The original lot, number 101, had a price of $5,000, because the investor originally accepted at that price. Once the investor accepted at $5,000, there was a contract formed as to lot 101. The subsequent change to $6,000 was thus a modification, and since there was no consideration, the modification as to lot 101 is unenforceable under the pre-existing duty rule. As a result, the contract price is $5,000 for lot 101 and $6,000 for the rest.

This question indicates why it's so important to segregate UCC and non-UCC cases before you analyze them. Here, the rule on modifications under the UCC is very different from the common law. Under UCC § 2-209, modifications are valid without consideration as long as they are in good faith. At common law, consideration is required under the "pre-existing duty" rule. As to irrevocability, at common law, consideration is required to form an option contract; under UCC § 2-205, merchants can make irrevocable, or "firm" offers, without consideration.

Both of these would lead you astray on these facts. However, since B correctly applies the common-law rules, it's the best response.

(A) is wrong, because it ignores the fact that only lot 101 is subject to the $5,000 offer—the remaining lots will cost $6,000. The landowner's May 1 telegram to the investor was sufficiently definite to constitute an offer to sell any or all lots in the subdivision for $5,000 each. The investor's May 2 telegram to the landowner constituted an acceptance as to lot 101 at $5,000, and probably implicitly rejected the offer as to the other 49 lots. As a result, the landowner's offer as to all the other lots terminated, because his original offer to keep the offer open until June 1 was not supported by consideration, so it was revocable. Even if the investor's acceptance as to lot 101 didn't terminate the offer as to the other 49, the landowner's subsequently raising the price to $6,000 did revoke the original offer and created a new one, at $6,000. Thus, the price on the latter 49 lots was $6,000. Any contract for these 49 (which we're told was created) would thus have been at $6,000, not $5,000.

(C) is wrong, because it ignores the fact that lot 101 will only cost $5,000, although this choice is correct in stating that the other 49 will be $6,000 each. The landowner's May 1 telegram to the investor was sufficiently definite to constitute an offer to sell any or all lots in the subdivision for $5,000 each. The investor's May 2 telegram to the landowner constituted an acceptance as to lot 101 at $5,000. The landowner's subsequent change to $6,000 was thus an attempted modification of a completed contract as to lot 101, and since there was no consideration for the modification, at common law the modification as to lot 101 was unenforceable under the pre-existing duty rule. As a result, the contract price remained $5,000 for lot 101. Therefore, this choice is incorrect in implying that the contract price for lot 101 is $6,000.

(D) is wrong, because it doesn't correctly state the price as to either lot 101 or the remaining 49 lots—in fact, it has the prices reversed. Since it's the sale of land that's involved, not a transaction in goods, the common law (not the UCC) will control.

The landowner's May 1 telegram to the investor was sufficiently definite to constitute an offer to sell any or all lots in the subdivision for $5,000 each. The investor's May 2 telegram to the landowner constituted an acceptance as to lot 101 at $5,000, and probably rejected the offer as to the other 49 lots. As a result, the landowner's offer as to all the other lots terminated, because his original offer to keep the offer open until June 1 was not supported by consideration, so it was revocable. Even if the investor's acceptance as to lot 101 didn't terminate the offer, the landowner's subsequently raising the price to $6,000 did revoke the original offer and created a new one, at $6,000, for the other 49 lots.

Thus, the price on the latter 49 lots was $6,000. The original lot, number 101, had a price of $5,000, because the investor originally accepted at that price. Once the investor accepted at $5,000, there was a contract formed as to lot 101. The subsequent change to $6,000 was thus an attempted modification as to lot 101, and since there was no consideration for that modification, the modification was unenforceable under the pre-existing duty rule. As a result, the contract price is $5,000 for lot 101 and $6,000 for the rest.

If you chose this response, you probably mistakenly believed the modification as to lot 101 was valid, but that the original offer as to the other lots was irrevocable. Since neither one of these is true, due to operation of the common-law rules on modifications (not valid without consideration) and irrevocable offers (no irrevocability without consideration), (D) is completely wrong.

Answer 13

Choice **(A)** is correct. If parties to an existing contract agree to modify the contract for the sole benefit of one of them, the modification will usually be unenforceable in non-UCC cases, for lack of consideration. That's because of the pre-existing duty rule: When one party to an existing contract makes an additional promise, and the other party merely promises to do what she is already required to do, the former's promise is not supported by consideration. A primary function of the pre-existing duty rule is to refuse to reward "hold-up" behavior by a provider of services, who in the middle of the contract refuses to complete performance unless he gets a better price or other improved terms. That's exactly what happened here: The painter has unfairly extracted the $200 promise from the accountant when it's too late for the accountant to get a substitute. So the accountant's promise will be unenforceable unless some exception to the pre-existing duty rule applies. Two common exceptions are that: (1) there were unanticipated circumstances that made the painter's request for more money not unreasonable, or (2) the painter agreed to do some additional duty beyond what he was already required to do. But neither of these exceptions (or any other) applies here, so the pre-existing duty rule applies and the accountant's promise is unenforceable for lack of consideration.

(B) is wrong because the accountant's promise is not too uncertain. The parties were not agreeing to a charge of "whatever it takes"—they were instead agreeing to a charge of $200, with the accountant's "whatever it takes" remark being more in the nature of a side commentary (e.g., "I'm agreeing to the $200 because I would in fact agree to whatever it took to get you to finish the work.").

(C) is wrong because letting the accountant escape from her $200-extra-compensation promise would not lead to her unjust enrichment. The painter is only doing exactly what he always agreed to do for exactly the price the two parties agreed to, so depriving him of his unfairly extracted extra $200 would not constitute unjust enrichment to the accountant.

(D) is wrong because a party's inability to complete performance due to that party's own delay or poor planning does not constitute the sort of extraordinary and unanticipated occurrence to which the impossibility doctrine applies. In general, only "external" events (e.g., an act of God, a strike, etc.) will qualify for the impossibility defense.

Answer 14

Choice (C) is correct. Although the general rule is that a modification solely benefiting one party is unenforceable due to lack of consideration, there is a very important exception: If the modification is "*fair and equitable* in view of *circumstances not anticipated by the parties* when the contract was made," the modification will be binding without consideration. That is the case here: the large amount of rock was a "circumstance not anticipated by the parties when the contract was made," and the $20,000 seems to have been a fair estimate of the increased cost to the contractor in performing. Therefore, the fact that the contractor gave no consideration for the owner's promise to pay the extra $20,000 (the contractor merely promised to do what he was already obligated to do, i.e., build the warehouse and driveway) is irrelevant.

(A) is wrong because, although it is true that there was no consideration for the owner's promise to pay the additional $20,000, the absence of consideration does not matter for the reason explained in the discussion of Choice (C).

(B) is wrong because the contractor's request for the extra $20,000 would not be deemed by a court to have constituted duress. If no rock had been discovered, and the contractor had demanded the extra $20,000 merely because he knew that the owner was time-sensitive and vulnerable, this choice would probably be correct in result and reasoning. But because the facts make it clear that the $20,000 *was* merely an adjustment on account of the unanticipated cost of excavating the rock, no duress will be found.

(D) is wrong because it gives the wrong explanation for the correct result. Even if the reasonable value of the contractor's total performance was $520,000 or greater, the contractor would not receive the extra $20,000 if the increase was due to the owner's desperation to have the project completed on time rather than due to an unanticipated circumstance (the rock)—in that case the requirement of consideration would render the modification unenforceable regardless of the "value" of the total performance.

Answer 15

Choice (D) is correct. If the promisee merely does or promises to do what the promisee is already legally obligated *to the promisor* to do, under the pre-existing duty rule that performance or return promise does not serve as consideration for the promisor's promise. But this rule does not apply where the promisee does or promises to do something that is already legally owed not to the promisor but to some *third person*. This exception applies here, since Snoop (the promisee) does not owe any contractual duty to the promisor (Collecta), merely to a third party (Artistic).

(A) is wrong because, while Snoop indeed owed Artistic a pre-existing duty to recover the picture if possible, no duty was owed to the promisor (Collecta), and that's what matters, as explained in the discussion of Choice (D) above.

(B) is wrong because the fact that Artistic may have had a pre-existing duty to return the recovered painting to Collecta is irrelevant, since it is not Artistic that was the promisee of Collecta's promise of a bonus (Snoop was). For the pre-existing duty rule to apply it must be the promisee who has the pre-existing duty (and who owes that duty to the promisor).

(C) is wrong because it states an irrelevant fact. The issue is whether the pre-existing duty rule applies, and the fact that the promisor would receive some net benefit if the promisee performed the act he was already legally obligated to perform does not render the pre-existing rule inapplicable. (Virtually *every* time the promisor makes a promise in return for the promisee's performance of an already-owed duty, the promisor expects to do better than if the promisee didn't perform, otherwise the promisor wouldn't be making the promise; yet the pre-existing duty rule applies to these situations.)

Answer 16

Choice (C) is correct. It's true that under the pre-existing duty rule, as a general matter a party who promises to accept less than the amount or other performance he is owed has not received consideration for that promise. So, for instance, a creditor with an unquestionably-valid liquidated claim who agrees to accept partial payment won't be bound. But all courts recognize an important exception to this rule, in order to encourage settlements: Where either (a) the creditor's claim (or a defense to it) is in fact of *uncertain validity*; or (b) the debtor honestly *believes* that the claim may be invalid (or that the debtor's defense may be valid), then the creditor's agreement to take partial payment *is* supported by consideration, namely the debtor's promise to pay a lesser amount. And that's true even if it later turns out that the claim was valid and/or the defense was invalid. See Rest. 2d, § 74. (In this situation, the settlement agreement is an "executory accord," which becomes a completed "accord-and-satisfaction" when the agreed-upon partial payment is made, thereby extinguishing the creditor's original claim for the whole amount.)

That's exactly what happened here: The client believed in good faith (even though, as it turned out, erroneously) that she had a valid defense, based on the defectiveness of the architect's performance. Her agreement to pay the architect's claim in return for a $2,500 discount was thus a surrender of her good-faith potential defense, and that surrender furnished consideration for the architect's return promise to give the discount. Therefore, the architect's promise to give the discount was binding on him, as an executory accord that became a completed accord-and-satisfaction at the moment the client paid the $7,500.

(A) is wrong because of the special rule validating compromises of claims that are disputed in good faith. The rule of *Foakes v. Beer*, which is a specific application of the pre-existing duty rule, provides that a promise to accept partial payment of a liquidated and undisputed debt is invalid for a lack of consideration. The rule does not apply, however, where there is a compromise of a claim disputed in good faith. This exception applies even if it later becomes apparent that the reason for disputing the claim was invalid. See the analysis of Choice (C) for more information.

(B) is wrong for two reasons. First, there is nothing in these facts that makes the Statute of Frauds applicable, as this choice suggests. Oral contracts are valid unless the situation falls within one of the enumerated Statute of Frauds categories, which this one does not. Oral modifications are ordinarily binding as long as neither the original contract nor the contract-as-modified falls within the Statute of Frauds. And the fact that the original contract was in writing does not change this. If the written contract had contained a "No Oral Modifications" clause, then this clause *would* have been enforceable to make an oral modification (such as a modification of the price) unenforceable. But there is no indication in these facts that a N.O.M. clause was present. Furthermore, even if there *was* a N.O.M. clause, it's likely that the court would conclude that full performance (the payment of the agreed-upon lesser sum, and its acceptance by the architect) caused the N.O.M. clause to become ineffective.

Second, even if the original contract *had* been within the Statute of Frauds, full performance by both parties—the architect's doing of the work, and the client's payment to the agreed-upon lesser sum—would have caused the Statute of Frauds to disappear as a defense anyway. (See Rest. 2d, § 145.)

(D) is wrong because the facts here did not involve a novation. A novation arises where either one or both of the parties to a contract is replaced by a *third party*. See Rest. 2d, § 280. The architect's acceptance of payment does not constitute a novation, since neither the client nor the architect was replaced by a third party.

Answer 17

Choice (**B**) is correct. UCC § 3-311 deals with the effect of a creditor's cashing of an "in full settlement" partial-payment check. To get the protection of § 3-311 (i.e., to have the creditor's cashing of the check constitute full settlement), the debtor must show that: (1) the check or accompanying written communication contained a "conspicuous statement to the effect that the instrument was tendered as full satisfaction of the claim," (2) the underlying claim was either "unliquidated" or "subjected to a bona fide dispute," and (3) the debtor acted in good faith. Here, all of these requirements are met, since: (1) we're told that the check was "conspicuously marked, 'Payment in full'"; (2) the parties had a real dispute about whether the $5,000 initially quoted by the lawyer was merely a non-binding estimate or a binding cap; and (3) we're expressly told that the client's letter expressed his "good-faith belief" that the lawyer had quoted the $5,000 as a cap. Therefore, when the lawyer cashed the check, her doing so constituted an implied agreement to an accord and satisfaction of her claim, under § 3-311. Note that this result would still occur even if the lawyer had placed a notation of protest or of reservation-of-rights on the check before cashing it.

(A) is wrong for two reasons: (1) the "rule of law" it purports to state about the risk of loss probably would not be accurate even in the absence of the lawyer's cashing the partial-payment check; and (2) under UCC § 3-311, the cashing of that check constituted a settlement, for the reasons stated in the discussion of Choice (B) above.

(C) is wrong because it is not clear that the $5,000 figure quoted by the lawyer was merely an estimate—in the absence of the check-cashing, a court might well have found that the client reasonably understood the figure to be a firm cap (i.e., an upper bound) on the amount that the lawyer would charge, in which case the cap would have been deemed part of the contract.

(D) is wrong for two reasons: (1) there may indeed have been a specific agreement on the total amount of the lawyer's fee (the facts are indeterminate about whether this would be true, in the absence of the partial-check-cashing); and (2) when the lawyer cashed the check, the case became governed by UCC § 3-311, not the parties' original agreement, whatever that was.

Answer 18

Choice **(C)** is correct. Under UCC § 3-311, a creditor who cashes a partial-payment check offered in full settlement will be deemed to have accepted an "accord and satisfaction," and lose his right to sue for the balance, if: (1) the check or accompanying communication contained a "conspicuous statement to the effect that the instrument was tendered as full satisfaction of the claim," (2) the claim was either "unliquidated" or was "subject to a bona fide dispute," and (3) the debtor acted in good faith. (This provision applies even to contracts for services rather than goods.) All 3 requirements imposed by § 3-311 are met here: (1) the "payment in full" legend on the check was a "conspicuous statement" that the check was tendered in full payment; (2) the prior letter shows that there was a dispute about whether the painting was done correctly; and (3) there's no indication that Bell didn't act in good faith.

(A) is not the best response, because Ames' cashing of the check was an accord and satisfaction under UCC § 3-311, as described above. Therefore, Ames can't recover even if he did paint the porch according to specs.

(B) is not the best response, because (1) it ignores the fact that UCC § 3-311 treats the cashing of the check as an agreement to settle; and (2) "economic duress" is not a defense or a relevant factor, at least where the duress does not come from the other party to the contract.

(D) is not the best answer, because it states an irrelevant factor. If Ames had not cashed the check, he could have recovered the $2,000 (the remaining contract price) if he had been able to show he had fulfilled the contract. But by cashing the partial-payment check, he cut off his right to sue for the contract price. And that's true no matter what the relationship was between the contract price and the value of the services rendered. (If you chose this response, you may have been thinking of quasi-contractual recovery, where a non-substantially performing plaintiff's damages are measured by the reasonable value of his services. But this concept doesn't apply here, not only because of the check-cashing but because there's no indication that Ames indeed failed to substantially perform, or if so, that the services were worth only $18,000.)

Answer 19

Choice **(A)** is correct, because it provides the lifeguard's best argument for recovery: an enforceable contract. A valid contract requires an offer, acceptance, and consideration (or a substitute for consideration, like promissory estoppel). Consideration is the sticky point here. Consideration requires a bargained-for exchange, and detriment to the promisee or benefit to the promisor. Here, as to the promise to pay, the husband is the promisor and the lifeguard is the promisee. Courts generally hold that if A promises not to sue B on a claim (even a claim that is of questionable validity), in exchange for B's promise to make payment, A's promise not to sue is consideration for B's promise to pay. Therefore, the court will probably hold that the lifeguard's release of his claim against the husband's estate (whether the claim would have proved valid or not) was consideration for the husband's promise. (Courts disagree about what happens when the person surrendering the claim has doubts about its validity, but there's no indication here that the lifeguard had doubts about the validity of his potential claim against the husband's estate, and in any event the "compromise" theory is the only one of the choices that could possibly allow the lifeguard to recover.)

Incidentally, note that the lifeguard's saving the woman's life wouldn't be consideration, because it wasn't bargained for; he saved the woman before his agreement with the husband (or the woman, for that matter). If the husband's promise were solely in return for the lifeguard's saving the woman's life, then, it wouldn't be enforceable. It's the compromise that makes it enforceable.

(B) is wrong, because the husband has not received any unjust benefits and, even if he had, restitution would not apply to these facts. Restitution is a remedy under which the parties are returned to their position before the contract was formed, in order to avoid an outcome in which one of the parties receives unjust benefits. Restitution is measured by the value rendered to defendant. Here, the *husband* hasn't benefitted unjustly (at least in money terms) from the lifeguard's saving the wife's life. In any case, the lifeguard has a valid claim at law (for breach of contract, since his agreement with the husband was enforceable, as discussed in Choice (A) above), so the equitable remedy of unjust enrichment (available only if a legal remedy is unavailable) would not be necessary to fix the problem.

(C) is wrong, because it misstates the facts: The husband would not be bound by promissory estoppel, because he'd be bound by a valid contract. Promissory estoppel is a substitute for consideration, used to avoid injustice. It is triggered by a gratuitous promise that is likely to, and does, induce detrimental reliance in the promisee. The first reason promissory estoppel doesn't apply here is that there's an enforceable contract, and the court will award the plaintiff promissory estoppel only in the absence of an enforceable promise. The second reason is that there's no indication that the promisee (the lifeguard) relied in any substantial way on the promise of payment (since he knew that he could still bring a legal claim against the husband's estate, for the reasons discussed in Choice (A) above).

(D) is wrong because it mischaracterizes the facts: The contract was bilateral, not unilateral. An offer for a bilateral contract seeks acceptance in the form of a promise; one for a unilateral contract seeks acceptance by performance. Here, the husband's document says he was promising to pay $1,000 in return for the lifeguard's return agreement (read: promise) not to sue. Thus, since the husband sought and received an (implicit) return promise, the resulting contract was bilateral.

Answer 20

Choice **(A)** is correct, because a promise to perform an act is sufficient consideration to support a contract even if the duty to perform that act is made expressly conditional on the happening of another event. For a contract to be binding, each party must give bargained-for consideration to the other. In the case of a bilateral contract, such as the one in this problem, the consideration on each side may take the form of a promise. Here, the buyer has promised to pay for the shareholder's stock, while the shareholder has promised to sell the buyer all of her stock. Although the buyer's promise is expressly conditioned on receiving the board's approval, an event that is not certain to occur, the buyer's promise is still adequate as consideration. The shareholder may argue that the buyer had the opportunity to avoid the contract by not seeking the board's approval, rendering the buyer's promise illusory and thus not consideration for the shareholder's return promise to sell. However, the express language of a condition will often be deemed to create an implied promise on the part of the promisor to use his best efforts to cause the condition to occur. A court would likely hold that the buyer impliedly promised to use its best efforts to obtain approval of the contract, making that implicit promise part of the consideration for the shareholder's return promise to sell if board approval occurred.

(B) is not the best response, because the buyer *has* provided consideration for the shareholder's promise to sell. Consideration may consist of a promise to either take any affirmative act or forbear any legal right. Here, in exchange for the shareholder's promise to sell, the buyer has implicitly promised not only to buy if board approval occurred, but also to use his best efforts in seeking approval of the contract, making that implicit promise part of the consideration for the shareholder's return promise to sell if board approval occurred. As a result, this is a bilateral contract: one in which the bargained-for exchange is one promise for another. Since the buyer has provided consideration, there is no need for the shareholder to have waived any possible lack of consideration.

(C) is not the best response, because the parties entered into a valid bilateral contract. For a contract to be binding, each party must give bargained-for consideration to the other. In the case of a bilateral contract, such as the one in this problem, the consideration on each side may take the form of a promise. The shareholder may argue that the buyer had the chance to avoid the contract by not seeking the board's approval, rendering the buyer's promise illusory and thus not consideration for the shareholder's return promise to sell. However, the express language of a condition will often create an implied promise on the part of the promisor to use his best efforts to cause the condition to occur. A court would likely hold that the buyer impliedly promised to use his best efforts in seeking approval of the contract, making that implicit promise part of the consideration for the shareholder's return promise to sell if board approval occurred. So there is no lack of mutuality of obligation—each party has promised to do something in return for the other's promise to do something.

(D) is not the best response, because there is no requirement that an express condition be in a signed writing. Generally, a signed writing will only be required if the contract falls within the Statute of Frauds. However, an agreement to purchase shares of stock does not fall within the Statute of Frauds, so there is no requirement that any part of this contract be in writing. (Note that shares of stock are not "goods" within the meaning of Article 2 of the UCC since they are not tangible items.) Since the contract is not within the Statute of Frauds, the fact that the condition requiring the board's approval is not included within the signed writing will not cause the contract to fail.

Answer 21

Choice (**B**) is correct. The UCC, in § 2-306(1), makes requirements contracts valid, and interprets such agreements to cover "such actual . . . requirements as may occur in good faith, except that no quantity unreasonably disproportionate to any stated estimate or in the absence of a stated estimate to any normal or otherwise comparable prior . . . requirements may be . . . demanded." Given that the question tells you to assume that the Tyres-County contract is interpreted to represent an obligation by County to buy all its requirements for tires from Tyres, the contract is valid as a requirements contract under § 2-306(1).

(A) is wrong because the Contracts Clause of the U.S. Constitution would not furnish the basis of recovery for Tyres. The Contracts Clause limits the circumstances in which a government may use its legislative powers to alter the terms of contracts. But here, County is not trying to alter the terms of its contract; it is merely hoping to persuade the court to find the contract invalid under general contract principles. Such an argument does not implicate the Contracts Clause.

(C) is wrong because the agreement *does* have mutuality of obligation—Tyres is required to supply all of the reasonable requirements of County for tires at the prices stated in the attachments, and in return County is obligated to purchase all of its tires exclusively from Tyres. (If the agreement were interpreted to mean merely that County would "order whatever tires it decides to order" from Tyres, then the lack-of-mutuality argument might work; but you're told that the contract is interpreted by the court to be a true requirements contract.)

(D) is wrong because the agreement is not indefinite as to quantity. It's true that the contract does not specify a particular number of tires, but a contract that specifies that "all of the buyer's requirements" for a particular type of item are to be purchased from the seller is deemed to be sufficiently definite as to quantity.

Answer 22

Choice **(C)** is correct. This was an output contract, as well as a requirements contract. Under UCC § 2-306(2), "A lawful agreement by either the seller or the buyer for exclusive dealing in the kind of goods concerned imposes unless otherwise agreed an obligation by the seller to use best efforts to supply the goods and *by the buyer to use best efforts to promote their sale.*" This was an exclusive-dealing contract (all requirements and output contracts are exclusive-dealing contracts); therefore, since the parties did not otherwise agree, § 2-306(2) imposed on the bakery the "obligation . . . to use best efforts to promote [the goods'] sale." When the bakery renounced the agreement without having even bought any buns yet, it breached this best-efforts-to-promote obligation.

(A) is wrong because, even though the bakery made no express promise to buy any of the manufacturer's buns, under § 2-306(2), the bakery was implicitly obligated to make best efforts to promote the sale of buns so that the bakery would need some of them.

(B) is wrong because, under § 2-306(1), "A term which measures the quantity by the output of the seller . . . means such actual output . . . as may occur in good faith[.]" This section has the effect of providing a quantity (or at least, a method for determining quantity), saving the output contract here from indefiniteness.

(D) is wrong because it does not speak to the main issue in the case. It's essentially true that both buyer and seller "impliedly assume the risk of price and demand fluctuations," but the question here is whether buyer could rely on the sudden reduction in its own customers' demand to escape the contract. UCC § 2-306(2) in effect allocates this risk, by saying that the buyer in both a requirements and output contract must use good faith to promote sale of the goods, effectively negating the bakery's ability to discontinue the product line here without any promotional effort.

Answer 23

Choice **(B)** is correct. Hardcash has made a promise, but no contract has come into existence. (If Hardcash's promise is viewed as an offer, it was never accepted, since Dominique never actually bound herself to take the loan, as is further described in the discussion of Choice (A) below.) Therefore, Dominique will have to recover on a promissory estoppel theory or not at all. Under promissory estoppel, "A promise which the promisor should *reasonably expect to induce action or forbearance* on the part of the promisee or a third person and which *does induce* such action or forbearance is *binding if injustice can be avoided* only by enforcement of the promise." Rest. 2d, § 90. Dominique meets all of the requirements for promissory estoppel: (1) Hardcash made a promise of the loan; (2) Hardcash should reasonably have expected that Dominique would rely on the availability of the loan, by demolishing the old structure (Hardcash knew that Dominique had gotten both bids, an indication of the likelihood that she would rely by doing the demolition); (3) Dominique did indeed rely by demolishing, and reasonably so; and (4) at least some type of enforcement of the loan promise will be required to avoid injustice, since otherwise Dominique will be left without the use of the old building and with a loss of the funds used for the demolition. (Notice that the phrase "promissory estoppel" is not used in this choice—you have to notice that that's the basis for the choice, something that you're clued in to from the reference to "reliance.")

(A) is wrong because Dominique's act of having a building demolished was not an acceptance of the offer. It's not so clear that Hardcash's promise was an "offer" at all, but even if it was,

Hardcash did nothing to authorize Dominique to "accept" the offer by demolishing the old building—any acceptance of a loan offer would, under these circumstances, have to be by Dominique's taking some action vis-à-vis Hardcash (e.g., signing loan papers and promising to repay the loan, or at least paying some sort of commitment fee).

(C) is wrong because the absence of bargained-for consideration does not matter. The whole point of the promissory estoppel doctrine, which as described above applies here, is that there does not need to be consideration for the promise. In other words, promissory estoppel here is a substitute for consideration.

(D) is wrong because the project's financial soundness was not a constructive condition to Hardcash's obligation to make the loan. Hardcash could of course have made his loan promise conditional upon Dominique's demonstration to his satisfaction that the project was financially sound; but the facts give no suggestion that Hardcash did this, and there is no reason for the court to infer such a condition out of thin air.

Answer 24

Choice **(C)** is correct. Since the facts tell us that the farmer made no express warranty, the only way the breeder can avoid the contract is if he successfully invokes the doctrine of mutual mistake. The UCC is silent on the subject of mistake, so the matter is left to the common law. A good summary of the common law on mutual mistake is given by the Second Restatement: "Where a mistake of both parties at the time a contract was made as to a basic assumption on which the contract was made has a material effect on the agreed exchange of performances, the contract is voidable by the adversely affected party *unless he bears the risk of the mistake*[.]" Rest. 2d §152(1). Even if the fertility of the boar was a "basic assumption" on which the contract was made (which it probably wasn't, since both parties knew that fertility couldn't yet be determined), the breeder will lose if the court concludes that he "bore the risk of the mistake." The facts tell us that both parties knew that the boar's fertility could not yet be known at the time of the sale. Therefore, the breeder was *consciously aware of his ignorance* about the boar's fertility, and a party who is consciously aware of his ignorance of fact X will be found to bear the burden of fact X's turning out to be true and damaging. Therefore, the breeder will be found to bear the risk of the boar's turning out to be sterile.

(A) is wrong, because the doctrine of mutual mistake will not apply on these facts. As is described more fully in the discussion of Choice (C), a party cannot invoke the doctrine of mutual mistake if he is found to have borne the risk of the type of mistake in question. A party who proceeds with conscious ignorance of whether a particular "bad" fact is true will be found to have borne the risk of that fact. Since the breeder knew that he didn't (and indeed couldn't) know the boar's fertility status at the time of sale, he'll be found to have borne the risk of infertility, making the mutual mistake doctrine inapplicable.

(B) is wrong, because no implied warranty was made. A seller is deemed to make an implied warranty of fitness for a particular purpose only where the buyer relies on the seller's "skill or judgment to select or furnish suitable goods." UCC § 2-315. Since both parties knew that fertility could not yet be known, and since there is no indication that the farmer said anything to indicate to the breeder that the farmer believed the boar would likely be good for breeding, there is no evidence of the breeder's reliance on the farmer's selection skills. Therefore, the farmer did not make an implied warranty of fitness for breeding.

(D) is not the best response, because no "mistake" was made (whether unilateral or mutual), and because even the existence of a unilateral mistake here would not support recovery. The same requirements are imposed for unilateral mistake as for mutual mistake (see the discussion of Choice (C) above for the latter), but in addition, either of two things must be shown: (1) that the mistake is such that enforcement of the contract would be unconscionable, or (2) that the other party had reason to know of the mistake or his fault caused the mistake. The breeder could not prove a mutual mistake was made, because, as described in the discussion of Choice (C) above, the breeder knew that he didn't know anything about the boar's fertility, and thus bore the risk of any mistake. Furthermore, the breeder cannot show either of the two additional elements needed to prove unilateral mistake: (1) the deal was not unconscionable, since unconscionability is very rare in commercial settings, and since the price here was implicitly set by market conditions, and factored in the risk of infertility; and (2) the farmer did not have reason to know of the mistake—it was impossible for either party to have known the fertility of a two-month-old boar.

Answer 25

Choice (**A**) is correct. If the parties orally agree on a deal, but mistakenly prepare and execute a document which incorrectly reflects that oral agreement, either party may obtain a court order for reformation (i.e., a re-writing of the document). That's what would happen in this choice, since both parties agreed on what acreage was to be covered by the agreement, and a clerical mistake caused the document to diverge from the oral agreement.

Choices (B), (C), and (D) are all wrong for the same reason: The parties did not in fact have a meeting of the minds about a key issue, so reformation to match their "actual" (subjective) agreement is not possible. In this situation, discharge for mutual mistake, rather than reformation, is the appropriate remedy.

Answer 26

Choice (**B**) is correct. The key to this question is to correctly categorize the writing: Is it a complete integration or a partial one? In deciding such a question, courts give a lot of weight to the nature of the document itself: The more extensive and formal, the more likely it is to have been intended to be a complete integration. Here, the fact that the writing consists of just one very informal sentence strongly suggests that it was intended as only a partial integration; since there is no evidence pointing in the other direction, a court would almost certainly conclude that the writing was only a partial integration. Therefore, it can be supplemented, but cannot be contradicted, by a prior or simultaneous oral understanding. The alleged saddle agreement merely supplements the writing, since the writing doesn't purport to cover the issue of accessories; therefore, evidence of the saddle agreement will be admissible. The oral agreement to choose a brown horse, on the other hand, is directly at odds with the writing, since the writing specifies that Equinox is permitted to choose from among gray horses, and does not mention any right to choose a brown horse; therefore, the oral agreement on brown horses will be excluded as a contradiction even though the writing is only a partial integration.

Choices (A), (C), and (D) are wrong because they are inconsistent with the above analysis.

Answer 27

Choice (**B**) is correct. When the parties to a written contract agree orally that the enforceability of the contract is subject to a condition, proof of the existence of that condition does not fall within the parol evidence rule.

(A) is wrong because, although there is indeed a "collateral agreement" exception to the parol evidence rule (an exception discussed immediately below in the main text), that exception is not applicable here. The collateral agreement exception allows proof of an oral "side" agreement in which the parties agreed to a separate exchange, as long as the alleged side agreement is not inconsistent with the total integration. But the "approval required" condition here was not a collateral agreement; rather, it was a condition to the enforceability of the main agreement, so the collateral-agreement exception does not apply.

(C) is wrong because, even though the parties' written agreement here was probably a complete integration of their contract, proof of an oral condition to the contract's enforceability is nonetheless allowed, as described in the discussion of Choice (B).

(D) is wrong because, although this formulation is essentially a correct statement of the parol evidence rule on provisions that contradict the writing (under which even a partial rather than complete integration may not be contradicted by a prior or simultaneous oral understanding), the rule does not apply to a condition to the enforceability of the contract.

Answer 28

Choice **(B)** is correct. Ordinarily, the parol evidence rule bars proof of an oral clause offered to supplement or contradict a completely integrated writing (which the writing here probably was). But an oral agreement that the writing will simply *not be legally enforceable at all* unless some condition precedent is satisfied is *not* barred by the parol evidence rule. This exception applies here: The owner's spouse's approval of the design was a condition precedent to the enforceability of the agreement, so that oral condition, and its non- satisfaction, may be proved.

(A) is wrong because it gives an incorrect reason for the correct result. It is not the fact that a third party's approval was required that makes evidence of the oral agreement admissible in the face of the parol evidence rule; it's the fact that the oral agreement established a condition precedent to the writing's enforceability that exempts proof of the oral agreement from the rule.

(C) is wrong for two reasons: (1) it misstates the "partial integration" branch of the parol evidence rule (under which an oral agreement that supplements rather than contradicts a partial integration *is* admissible); and (2) the parol evidence rule simply doesn't apply to an orally-agreed-upon condition to the writing's enforceability, as analyzed in Choice (B) above.

(D) is wrong because, while it correctly summarizes the branch of the parol evidence rule that bars oral understandings that contradict any sort of integration (partial or complete), it fails to reflect the fact that the parol evidence rules simply doesn't apply to an orally-agreed-upon condition to the writing's enforceability, as analyzed in Choice (B) above.

Answer 29

Choice **(A)** is correct. All courts agree that if a term is found by the trial court to be ambiguous — capable of more than one meaning — extrinsic evidence on the meaning the parties attached to the term must be allowed, notwithstanding the parol evidence rule. The phrase "all tires required by this agreement" is indeed ambiguous, as this choice suggests: A reader looking only at the contract document itself (including the attachments) would not know whether the phrase meant merely "whatever quantities of tires that County decides to order during the contract term" or instead the far meatier "all County's tire requirements during the contract term." Since the advertisement was effectively part of the parties' negotiations — it disclosed to Tyres what County was thinking at the outset — it fairly bears on what the parties intended by the ambiguous phrase.

(B) is wrong because the fact that the advertisement was in writing is irrelevant. This choice incorrectly implies that the only materials barred by the parol evidence rule are prior or simultaneous oral understandings between the parties. Prior *writings* agreed to or exchanged between the parties are also excluded by the parol evidence rule, if offered to add terms to, or contradict terms in, a final writing.

(C) is wrong because of the "ambiguity" exception to the parol evidence rule, described in the discussion of Choice (A) above.

(D) is wrong because it makes a conclusion that does not logically follow from its premise. It is true that if County is permitted to put in proof of the advertisement, the consequence will likely be that the contract would be held illusory (since County would be promising only to "buy whatever we decide to buy"), and County's illusory promise would not furnish consideration for Tyres' return promise. But the fact that an item of proffered evidence would, if admitted, tend to prove that a contract is unenforceable does not mean that the parol evidence rule requires exclusion of that piece of evidence.

Answer 30

Choice (**D**) is correct. Even where the writing is a complete integration, as it is here, the court will look to course-of-performance evidence to determine what the parties meant as to a point on which the writing is ambiguous. This is true in both sales and non-sales cases. Thus, in sales governed by UCC Article 2, § 2-208(1) says that "Where the contract for sale involves repeated occasions for performance by either party with knowledge of the nature of the performance and opportunity for objection to it by the other, any course of performance *accepted or acquiesced in without objection* shall be *relevant to determine the meaning* of the agreement." Here, the evidence proffered by the retailer—that the manufacturer permitted him to return undamaged radios for credit earlier during the course of the present contract—fits § 2-208(1) exactly, since the retailer is claiming that the manufacturer's knowing acquiescence in the retailer's repeated requests for a credit for non-defective returned goods was a course of performance, admissible to show that the parties intended the writing to mean that such returns are allowed.

(A) is wrong because, as further explained in Choice (D) above, even though the writing here is a complete integration, the proffered evidence is course-of-performance evidence, which is admissible notwithstanding the parol evidence rule to show the meaning of the agreement.

(B) is wrong because it states an irrelevant point. It's true that the express terms control if those terms are inconsistent with the course of performance; thus UCC § 2-208(2) says that "The express terms of an agreement and any . . . course of performance, as well as any course of dealing and usage of trade, shall be construed wherever reasonable as consistent with each other; but when such construction is unreasonable, *express terms shall control course of performance* and course of performance shall control both course of dealing and usage of trade[.]" But here, there *is* no express term dealing with the retailer's right to return non-defective goods for credit (the writing is silent on this point), so the priority of express terms over the course of performance simply doesn't apply.

(C) is wrong because it relies on an irrelevant fact. The retailer is not trying to show an "agreement" to modify the original agreement—if he were, then there might be a Statute of Frauds issue. Instead, he's trying to show what the original written agreement *meant* (by the use of course-of-performance evidence), and his ability to do that has nothing to do with the Statute of Frauds.

Answer 31

Choice is (**B**) is correct, because the customer's dissatisfaction, if in good faith, would relieve him of performing under the contract, and would thus be a good defense. Whether satisfaction is objective or subjective depends on the subject matter of the contract. In a construction or manufacturing contract, a satisfaction clause will require the satisfaction of a reasonable person. But if personal taste or judgment is involved (e.g., cosmetic surgery, paintings, and the like), only subjective satisfaction is required. Here, since a portrait photograph is involved, the customer's personal, subjective satisfaction is all that's required; as long as he operates in good faith, he can reject performance and avoid liability under the contract, even if the photograph is objectively satisfactory. As Choice (B) points out, this would, as a result, be a good defense for the customer.

(A) is wrong, because arguing that the cards are objectively unsatisfactory wouldn't help the customer, for two reasons. First, as is described in Choice (B), if personal taste or judgment is involved, only subjective satisfaction is required. Second, the facts tell you that the rest of the family was pleased; it was only the customer who was displeased. So even if the standard *were* objective satisfaction, the fact that the family was satisfied would tend to rebut the argument that the cards are objectively unsatisfactory.

(C) is wrong, because the customer waived the condition that the cards be delivered on time, so arguing that he should be excused from performance due to the delay would not help him.

Under the contract, time was probably made "of the essence" by expressly providing that the cards must be delivered "on time." Even if the contract hadn't specifically provided for delivery on time, the fact that the cards were Christmas cards, and Christmas was fast approaching, suggests that time was of the essence. As a result, under normal circumstances, any delay would be considered a major breach, relieving the customer of the duty to perform under the contract. However, conditions can be excused by waiver, and that's what happened here. When the photographer told the customer that the customer's inability to have his picture taken earlier would mean a delay in the completion date, by telling the photographer to go ahead and take the picture anyway, the customer was waiving delivery on December 15th, and thereby excusing the delivery-on-time express condition. Thereafter, the customer could not rely on breach of the condition as a defense.

(Even if the customer had *not* expressly waived the condition, his subsequent failure to notify the photographer of his recovery would excuse the delivery-on-time condition, since, had the customer notified the photographer immediately of his recovery, the photographer could have performed on time. Thus the customer's own wrongful conduct prevented the condition from occurring, blocking him from avoiding liability by relying on failure of the condition.)

(D) is wrong, because the customer's illness wouldn't excuse him from performing under the contract. If the customer's illness had prevented him from performing under the contract, then he would have a valid impossibility defense, and would avoid liability under the contract. But that's not what the facts here tell you. The photographer's final delivery of the pictures was only two days late, and the customer's delay in giving notice of his recovery lasted one week. Thus, it's not the customer's illness that caused the delay, but his failure to promptly notify the photographer of his recovery. Therefore, as described in (C), the customer's failure to call the photographer in a timely way acted as a waiver of the on-time condition.

Answer 32

Choice (**C**) is correct. It was a condition precedent to the enforceability of the contract that the buyer give written notice to the seller by Jan. 2 that the buyer had found a buyer. However, when the buyer explained the difficulty with a written notice to the seller on Dec. 16, the seller's "That's okay" response clearly indicated to the buyer that the seller would not insist on the written notice. This oral response constituted a waiver of the condition, i.e., a knowing intent to abandon the benefit of the condition.

(A) is wrong because the requirement of a writing by Jan. 2 was an express condition to the enforceability of the contract. Complete, not just substantial, compliance with an express condition is normally required. Since the oral notice did not completely comply with the requirement of a written notice, the fact that it may have constituted substantial performance will not help the buyer.

(B) is wrong because: (1) the condition here was a condition precedent (the condition had to be satisfied before the contract would ever become enforceable), not a condition subsequent (i.e., something that if not satisfied would "unenforce" the previously enforceable contract); and (2) even in the unlikely event that the condition was found to be a condition subsequent, its nonoccurrence could only help the seller, not the buyer.

(D) is wrong because the concept of a novation has nothing to do with these facts. A novation occurs when the two original parties to a contract — an obligor and an obligee — agree that a stranger can be substituted for the original obligor. So, for instance, if the seller and the buyer agreed that the third person would substitute for the buyer as the party who was under contract to buy the engine from the seller, a novation would have occurred. But on the actual facts here, no substitution of either of the original parties to the contract has occurred, so there is no novation.

Answer 33

Choice (**C**) is correct. When the circumstances indicate that a condition is intended for the protection of just one party, that party is always free to waive the condition. Such a waiver can occur by implication. That's what happened here: the "partner must approve" provision was an express condition intended for the benefit of Ohner, and Ohner had the power to waive it, expressly or implicitly. When Ohner ordered Planner to proceed notwithstanding the partner's disapproval, this was an implied waiver of the condition. At the moment the waiver occurred, Ohner had the power to retract it (i.e., reinstate the condition). But once Planner began the work, this was a material change in position by Planner in reliance on the waiver, and that reliance made the waiver non-retractable, i.e., irrevocable.

(A) is wrong because: (1) the doctrine of substantial performance helps a plaintiff recover "on the contract," and here there would *be* no contract if the non-occurrence of the partner-approval condition is not somehow excused (which it is by operation of the doctrine of waiver, as described in the analysis of Choice (C) above); and (2) Planner has done only 40% of the work, and such a small portion would not be considered "substantial performance."

(B) is wrong because the promissory estoppel doctrine, even where it applies, makes the promise enforceable only to the extent "necessary to avoid injustice," and here, injustice could be avoided by awarding Planner just the value of 40% partial performance (a reliance or restitution measure). Planner is suing for breach of the contract, and would like to be able to recover his full "contract," i.e., expectation damages, which would give him a greater recovery than the reliance or restitution damages that are all that promissory estoppel would allow.

(D) is wrong because unjust enrichment would yield a lesser recovery than a waiver-of-condition theory, since unjust enrichment will get Planner just the relatively small amount by which he has increased the value of Ohner's property, whereas waiver will permit recovery "on the contract," i.e., for full expectation damages.

Answer 34

Choice (**D**) is correct. The beneficiary of a constructive condition may be found to have waived the condition. Such a waiver may be implied rather than express. Here, when Presskey accepted the two game-designs a year without protest for three years, this constituted an implied waiver of the minimum-quantity term, at least as to the already-completed three years. Then, when Bitz spent the substantial sums on new computer equipment, this probably constituted a material change of position in reasonable reliance on this waiver. While it is probably not the case that no reasonable jury could have found for *Presskey* on these facts (for instance, a reasonable jury could probably have found that Bitz's reliance expenditure was not reasonable), a reasonable jury could have found for Bitz, so an appellate affirmance would be proper. (Note that the question doesn't ask you to predict who would win at trial, merely to predict whether Presskey could get a reversal of the jury verdict, a harder task for Presskey to accomplish.)

(A) is wrong because, while a no-oral-modification clause will normally be enforced, such a clause does not prevent enforcement of an oral or implicit waiver where the conditions for waiver are satisfied, as they are here. (The difference between modification and waiver is that a true modification—which was forbidden by the n.o.m. clause—could not have been prospectively retracted, whereas Presskey's waiver could have been retracted by it until Bitz changed position in reasonable reliance on it.)

(B) is wrong because it does not apply on these facts—as described in the discussion of Choice (A) above, what happened here was a waiver rather than an avoidance of the no-oral-modification clause's effect, and a waiver is not prevented by a n.o.m. clause.

(C) is wrong because the no-oral-modification clause would not be unconscionable on these facts. It is rare for a clause in a commercial (as opposed to consumer) contract to be ruled unconscionable. To be unconscionable, the clause would have to either be shockingly unfair substantively, or very unfair from a procedural perspective. N.O.M. clauses are quite routine, and the one here would not be found to be either substantively or procedurally unfair. The fact that Bitz was supposedly an "amateur" designer would not change this result, especially since what he was performing was a series of commercial services.

Answer 35

Choice (**D**) is correct. For one-shot (i.e., non-installment) sales contracts like the one here, UCC § 2-601 states what is, in effect, a perfect tender rule: "[I]f the goods or the tender of delivery fail *in any respect* to conform to the contract, the buyer may (a) reject the whole[.]" So Computers will lose unless it finds a defense that is not inconsistent with the perfect-tender rule of § 2-601. Section 1-205(3) says that "[A]ny usage of trade in the vocation or trade in which [the parties] are engaged or of which they are or should be aware *give[s] particular meaning to and supplement[s] or qualif[ies] terms* of an agreement." So if Computers can indeed show that under trade usage in the purchase of computers, an apparently fixed delivery date really means "plus or minus 30 days on either side of the specified date," the contract will be interpreted in light of this usage. In other words, § 2-601 will still entitle Bank to reject if delivery were untimely, but the delivery won't in fact be deemed untimely because of the trade usage.

(A) is wrong because as described in the analysis of Choice (D) above, the UCC essentially requires tenders to be perfect (and "perfect" includes timely delivery), so that a defense based on lack of material harm won't work.

(B) is wrong because the goodness of the deal Bank was getting would not entitle Computers to relief from the perfect-tender rule. As described further in Choice (D) above, UCC § 2-601 essentially applies the perfect tender rule to non-installment contracts. Under § 2-601, there is no room for an argument that because the deal was an unusually good one for the buyer, the buyer loses its right to reject for late delivery or other non-conformity.

(C) is wrong because a trucker's strike would not give Computers a cause of action for breach. The fact that the contract stated "F.O.B. Bank" hurts Computers' ability to rely on the truckers' strike. Section 2-319(1)(b) says that "when the [shipment] term is F.O.B. the place of destination, the seller must at his own expense *and risk* transport the goods to that place and there tender delivery of them . . . ." So a court would probably hold that use of the F.O.B. destination clause shifted to Computers the risk of a problem with Computers' choice of delivery methods. The defense of commercial impracticability might conceivably help Computers escape *monetary liability* (a damages award against it) for breach, but the section wouldn't allow it to insist that Bank must take delivery late; the best that Computers could reasonably hope for is for both parties to be *discharged*, not for an affirmative recovery for breach against Bank.

Answer 36

Choice (**A**) is correct. The case is governed by the UCC, since a trailer, though large, is still an item of personal property and thus constitutes "goods," the sale of which is covered by Article 2. To begin our analysis, if we assume that the contracted-for trailer was one with a spare tire, the buyer was permitted to reject the tendered trailer for lack of the tire. That's because § 2-601 says that in a single-shot (non-installment) contract, "unless otherwise agreed . . . if the goods or the tender of delivery fail *in any respect* to conform to the contract, the buyer may (a) reject the whole [.]" So no matter how minor the defect, the buyer was entitled to insist that it be cured before he was required to accept the trailer. But it does not follow that the defect entitled the buyer to cancel the contract. That's because § 2-508(1) says that "where any tender or delivery by the seller is rejected because non-conforming and the time for performance has not yet expired, the seller may seasonably notify the buyer of his intention to cure and may then within the contract time make a conforming delivery." Here, the time for performance would not expire until the end of business on Monday, June 1, and the dealer was proposing to cure the problem on Monday, i.e., within the contract time. Therefore, the dealer met the notification requirement of § 2-508(1), and had the right to try to make the actual cure up until the end of June 1.

(B) is wrong because, while § 2-601 in theory applies the perfect tender rule — which would allow the buyer to reject and terminate immediately — that rule is subject to the seller's right under § 2-508(1) to give notice of intent to cure within the contract period and to then make the cure.

(C) is wrong because the buyer was not required to accept the trailer on May 31, with the defect still uncured. And that was true no matter how easy and probable a timely cure appeared to be. Instead, the buyer was permitted to suspend his performance (i.e., his acceptance and payment), wait and see whether the dealer promptly cured the defect as promised, and if it didn't, make a final rejection.

(D) is wrong because the buyer was *not* required to accept the trailer given the defect, despite the fact that the defect did not substantially impair the trailer's value. If the tendered goods are defective, no matter how small the defect is (assuming it indeed amounts to a true "defect" as opposed to a permissible variation under relevant trade usage), the buyer may reject the goods if the defect is not cured. To put it another way, there is no doctrine of "substantial performance" with respect to the seller's obligations under a single-shot (non-installment) contract for the sale of goods.

Answer 37

Choice (**D**) is correct. A performance that is subject to an express condition cannot become due unless the condition occurs or its nonoccurrence is excused. The detective's entitlement to the award was subject to two conditions — the arrest and conviction of the fugitive. The first, the arrest, was satisfied when the detective delivered the fugitive to the authorities. The second, the conviction, did not occur. Its nonoccurrence is excused, however, under the doctrine of prevention, which requires that a party refrain from conduct that prevents or hinders the occurrence of a condition. See Farnsworth, §8.6, p. 544: "The duty of good faith and fair deal-ing that is usually imposed requires at least that a party do nothing to prevent the occurrence of a condition of that party's duty." The authorities had it in their power to obtain a conviction, and would ordinarily have done so by routine procedures; the fact that they chose to give up a conviction in order to get the fugitive's testimony against the boss brings the case within this rule that a party whose conduct prevents the occurrence of a condition cannot then claim the benefit of that non-occurrence. See also Rest. 2d § 245, Comment a.

(A) is wrong because it cites a requirement that does not apply to these facts. It's true that in an offer for a unilateral contract, an offeree who accepts by rendering the requested perfor-mance is often required to give notice of that acceptance. But the offeree's duty to give notice of acceptance applies only if the offeree has reason to know that the offeror would not learn of the requested performance with reasonable certainty and promptness after that performance has occurred. That's not the case here, since the offeror learned of the performance when the detective took the fugitive to the authorities, i.e., at the very time the requested performance occurred. Rest. 2d, § 54(2).

(B) is wrong because it overlooks the doctrine of excuse of conditions. The general rule is that a party's performance does not become due until all express conditions to it have occurred or are excused. In this case, the detective's entitlement to the award was subject to two con-ditions, one of which (conviction of the fugitive) was excused under the doctrine of preven-tion, which requires that a party refrain from conduct that prevents or hinders the occurrence of a condition. See the discussion of Choice (D) for more about the doctrine of excuse of conditions.

(C) is wrong because it's unresponsive to the question. That's so because this choice relates to the enforceability of the agreement between the fugitive and the authorities rather than the enforceability of the purported contract between the authorities and the detective. The dispos-itive issue is the effect of the nonoccurrence of an express condition. As discussed further in (D) above, that nonoccurrence was excused by the authorities' preventing the conviction by making the plea deal.

Answer 38

Choice **(A)** is correct. To constitute a repudiation, a party must clearly bring home to the other party that he will be unable or unwilling to perform. Mere expression of doubts about performance, or statements that performance would be burdensome or unfair, will usually not constitute a sufficiently clear indication of an impending non-performance. Therefore, Broker's statement that it "seems unfair" that he should have to honor the contract in a timely manner probably did not constitute a repudiation. It is not certain that Broker will succeed with this argument, but of the four presented, it is the one that has by far the best chance of success for him.

(B) is wrong because it is a flat misstatement of law. While Hoarda would probably be *entitled* to seek specific performance due to the coin's status as a unique chattel, the plaintiff is always free to decline to seek a remedy of specific performance and to instead seek money damages if these can be proved with sufficient certainty (and there is no indication here that they could not be).

(C) is wrong because the facts here would not support the temporary impossibility defense. The defense of impossibility is not available to a party if a court would conclude that the agreement implicitly placed on that party the risk of the type of event that has occurred. The market prices of rare coins are constantly fluctuating, sometimes severely, and a court would almost certainly conclude that Broker, when he undertook to replace Hoarda's coin within a defined period, implicitly took the risk that the price of doing so would increase sharply. This result is especially likely in view of the fact that Broker was in the business of buying and selling such coins.

(D) is wrong because when one party repudiates, the other is not required to demand (in writing or otherwise) that the repudiation be retracted. It is true that the repudiatee has the *right* to demand a retraction, but the repudiatee may instead elect to treat the repudiation as final and immediately sue upon it.

Answer 39

The correct choice is **(D)**, because the buyer stated she would buy the ranch if legally obligated to do so. An anticipatory repudiation is a clear statement by a party, made before performance under a contract is due, that the party does not intend to perform. For a statement by the promisor to constitute a repudiation, it must appear to the promisee that the promisor is quite unlikely to perform. It is not enough that the promisor states vague doubts about her willingness or ability to perform. The buyer's statement here does not meet these requirements: She has not made it clear that she probably won't perform—indeed, just the contrary, since she's indicated that she *will* perform if legally required to do so.

An anticipatory repudiation is treated as if it were a present breach. But since the statement here is not an anticipatory repudiation, and since there is no other present breach (the time for performance won't arrive until December), there has been no breach, and the seller will lose if the case is decided before December.

(A) is wrong because the buyer stated she would buy if legally obligated to do so. As described in the discussion of Choice (D) above, the buyer's statement did not meet the requirements for an anticipatory repudiation, because the buyer indicated that she would perform if required to do so.

(B) is wrong because the seller has not yet requested assurances. A party to a contract has the right to demand reasonable assurances when the other party to a contract gives an ambiguous indication of not performing. If the latter fails to provide these assurances, this failure will itself be considered a repudiation and a breach. The buyer's October 1 statement indeed created reasonable grounds for the seller's insecurity with respect to the buyer's performance. However, before the seller could claim repudiation and sue for breach of contract, he was obligated to request assurances from the buyer. If the buyer then did not give the seller the requested assurances, the seller could treat this failure as a repudiation. However, under these facts, the seller has not yet requested assurances, so the seller cannot successfully claim that a breach has occurred.

(C) is wrong because a seller can bring suit prior to closing if the buyer anticipatorily repudiates. One of the major purposes of the anticipatory repudiation doctrine is that it allows the repudiatee to bring an immediate suit for breach, before the time for performance has arrived. So if the buyer had anticipatorily repudiated, the seller could bring an immediate suit, and Choice (C) would be an incorrect statement. Beyond this problem, of course, there is the additional difficulty (for the seller) that the buyer's words "I won't perform unless legally obligated" are not an anticipatory repudiation, for the reasons described in the discussion of Choice (D) above.

Answer 40

Choice **(C)** is correct. A repudiation may be retracted until the aggrieved party has either (i) sued for breach, (ii) changed his position materially in reliance on the repudiation, or (iii) stated that he regards the repudiation as final. Rest. 2d § 256(1). Under these facts, the buyer had from August 1, when she unequivocally repudiated the contract, to October 1 to retract her unequivocal repudiation. The buyer didn't do so. The buyer's right to retract her repudiation and perform under the contract ended when the seller materially changed his position in reliance on the repudiation, by selling to the rancher. The fact that the seller initially urged the buyer to change her mind does not alter the analysis—under the modern view, the repudiatee's exhortation to the repudiator to perform does not "reinstate the contract," and does not impair the repudiatee's subsequent right to cancel the contract or change position in reliance on the repudiation.

(A) is wrong because the seller had no obligation to notify the buyer that the seller was viewing the contract as being in material breach. A repudiation may be retracted until the aggrieved party has done any of three things (see the discussion of Choice (C) above), one of which is to materially change position in reliance on the repudiation. While the seller had the *right* to notify the buyer that the seller was viewing the contract as terminated and preparing to sell to someone else (and such a notice would have immediately ended the buyer's right to retract the repudiation, under the third branch of the Restatement test cited above), the seller did not have the *obligation* to give this notice before changing position.

(B) is wrong because the seller did not waive the repudiation by urging performance. Under the modern view, the repudiatee's exhortation to the repudiator to perform does not "reinstate the contract," and does not impair the repudiatee's right to cancel the contract or change position in reliance on the repudiation.

(D) is wrong because this choice misstates the law both as to a repudiation and a non-repudiation scenario. For instance, suppose that the buyer never repudiated and tendered the contract price on December 1, and the seller refused either to accept the money or convey the ranch—in that scenario the buyer would win, whereas the language of Choice (D) says that the buyer would lose. Beyond that, of course, the fact that the buyer had repudiated long before December 1 entitled the seller to cancel the contract and convey to someone else, making the buyer's later tender of the contract price (and whether the seller accepted that tender) irrelevant.

Answer 41

Choice (C) is correct. This is a sale-of-goods case, so the UCC's special anticipatory repudiation provision, § 2-610, applies. That section says that "when either party repudiates the contract with respect to a performance not yet due the loss of which will substantially impair the value of the contract to the other, the aggrieved party may . . . (b) resort to any remedy for breach[.]" This section applies to these facts, and almost perfectly matches the phrasing in Choice (C): Broker has repudiated his obligation to deliver a replacement coin by Dec. 31; this repudiation has substantially impaired the value of the contract to Hoarda (since Broker's insistence on waiting for prices to come down means that the delay may be infinite, and will expose Hoarda to an ever-increasing financial loss if prices continue to mount); and a suit for the market value of the promised coin is an authorized "remedy for breach" in the circumstances.

(A) is wrong because Hoarda had no duty to mitigate her losses in the rising market by suing promptly. UCC § 2-610(a) gives Hoarda the right to "for a commercially reasonable time await performance by the repudiating party." So Hoarda could have waited a while, and didn't *have to* mitigate her damages by bringing suit immediately (although for the reasons described in Choice (C) she had the *right* to bring such an immediate suit).

(B) is wrong because, while it is true that in non-UCC cases, the repudiatee cannot bring suit prior to the time for the performance if the repudiatee has no remaining duty of performance, this special rule does not apply to UCC cases. Therefore, it wouldn't matter whether Hoarda did or did not have a surviving implied warranty that the coin she advanced to Broker was genuine.

(D) is wrong because, while this choice correctly states that the repudiatee may bring suit at once, the choice incorrectly states that this action would be for a "present tort." When the doctrine of anticipatory repudiation allows suit, the suit is a form of breach-of-contract action, not a tort suit.

Answer 42

Choice (C) is correct. The daughter is the primary obligor on the debt to the friend. The father, by promising to make the payment if the daughter doesn't, has promised to "answer for the debt of another," making him a surety. Since the father's promise is oral, it is rendered unenforceable by the suretyship provision of the Statute of Frauds, unless some exception makes it inapplicable. The most important exception to the suretyship provision is the main purpose rule. But here, the fact that the father's promise was not made for the "primary purpose" (i.e., "main purpose") of benefiting the father's own economic interests means that the main purpose rule does not apply, making the suretyship provision applicable. (Notice that nowhere in this choice do the examiners mention either the Statute of Frauds, the concept of suretyship, or the significance of the fact that the promise was oral—it's up to you to notice that the reference to the absence of "primary purpose" means that the suretyship provision will apply.)

(A) is wrong because the father *did* receive consideration for his conditional promise—the friend's making of the loan to the daughter. Consideration need not be given to the promisor, but can instead be given to a third party, as long as the promisor bargained for it.

(B) is wrong because it refers to the not-performable-within-one year provision of the Statute of Frauds, and that provision does not apply to the father's promise here. The reason is that there is a special exception under which "the one-year provision does not apply to a contract which is *performed on one side at the time it is made, such as a loan of money,* nor to any contract which has been fully performed on one side, whether the performance is completed within a year or not." Rest. 2d, § 130, Comment d. Since the friend has fully performed on his side by making the loan, the full performance removed the entire contract from the one-year provision.

(D) is wrong because the law will supply a reasonable interest rate under the circumstances, so that the contract (and the father's promise) will not be void for indefiniteness. As long as the term omitted by the parties' agreement is not so basic as to prevent them from having had a meeting of the minds, the court will supply the missing term by implication. Here, since the friend cares mainly about getting his principal back, he can stipulate that the interest rate was 0%, and the court will certainly be willing to apply that rate to save the contract from indefiniteness.

Answer 43

Choice (B) is correct. Normally, a contract for the sale of goods having a value of more than $500 is not enforceable unless memorialized in a writing signed by the party against whom enforcement is sought, here, the retailer. However, there is an important exception for confirmations sent between merchants. According to UCC § 2-201(2), "Between merchants if within a reasonable time a writing in confirmation of the contract and sufficient against the sender is received and the party receiving it has reason to know its contents, it satisfies the requirements of [the Statute of Frauds] against such party unless written notice of objection to its contents is given within 10 days after it is received." So here, even though the retailer didn't sign anything, the confirmation makes the contract good against her under § 2-201(2), because: (1) the retailer and the manufacturer are both merchants; (2) the manufacturer signed the confirmation, so that the confirmation would have been binding against the manufacturer; (3) the retailer had "reason to know [the confirmation's] contents" (because she read it); and (4) the retailer did not indicate her objection to the memorandum's contents within 10 days after receiving it.

(A) is wrong because the fact that the goods were "identified to the contract" is irrelevant to the enforceability of the contract—even if the retailer had canceled before the goods were shipped (or even before the goods were identified within the manufacturer's plant as being the ones that would be shipped to the retailer), the manufacturer would still have been entitled to sue for breach if more than 10 days had passed since the retailer received the confirmation. (The MBE examiners are probably trying to fool you into thinking of § 2-709, under which the fact that the goods have been identified to the contract will entitle the seller to sue for the full contract price if the seller cannot resell them at a reasonable price—but this provision doesn't turn an otherwise-unenforceable contract into an enforceable one; it merely governs the measure of damages for an already-enforceable contract.)

(C) is wrong because the retailer is liable despite never having signed a writing, due to her receipt of a confirmation and her lack of objection to it, as described in the discussion of Choice (B) above.

(D) is wrong because the fact that the retailer never paid for or accepted any of the goods is irrelevant—the retailer is bound by virtue of the fact that she received a signed confirmation and failed to object to it, and this is true regardless of whether she paid for or accepted any of the goods.

Answer 44

Choice **(B)** is correct, because it correctly identifies that the buyer is entitled to the remedy he wanted: specific performance.

Understanding why specific performance is the appropriate remedy requires that you analyze the facts with two rules in mind: first, specific performance is an equitable remedy, requiring as a prerequisite that there be no adequate remedy "at law" (i.e., money damages). This occurs, typically, where the subject is unique—e.g., a piece of land or an antique—and/or the money value is not ascertainable. Second, in land sale contracts, when the seller refuses to convey the property, the buyer can seek specific performance. That's pretty straightforward. But the rule that's less obvious is that if the *buyer* refuses to carry out the sale, the *seller* can usually compel performance—even though the buyer will only be paying money, as he would in a damages claim!

With that in mind, look closely at what happens in these facts. The buyer has an option to buy the lot for $300,000. He then makes an irrevocable offer to the speculator to purchase the lot for $325,000. The speculator exercises his option, meaning the buyer is bound to exercise his own option. The buyer exercises his option, pays the $300,000, and takes the deed to the lot. Only at that point does the speculator renege on the deal. Thus, what you have is the buyer holding the title to the lot, and the speculator refusing to carry out an enforceable duty— paying a stipulated amount and taking title to the lot. Thus, what's involved is a land sale contract—a classic specific performance situation! Note that the reason money damages are inadequate in a case like this—where the buyer refuses to carry out a land sale contract—is the seller's difficulties of proof. In a damages action, the damage would consist of the difference between the market value of the property and the contract price (plus consequential damages, like expenses of finding another buyer). So the seller would have to establish the market value of the land at the time of the breach, and that might be a speculative and hard-to-prove amount. Specific performance relieves the seller of this burden of proof: All he has to show is the contract price.

(A) is wrong, for the reason explained in (B): The buyer/re-seller is entitled to specific performance, because money damages would be inadequate due to difficulties of proof.

(C) is wrong because it understates the buyer's recovery; he's entitled to specific performance of the option contract, for the reasons discussed in (B). If the buyer is unable to recover the exercise price specified under his contract with the speculator, the buyer will be out of pocket for the amount he spent to buy the lot from the original seller.

(D) is wrong because it ignores entirely the fact that the speculator breached the contract with the buyer, and thus the buyer will be entitled to some kind of remedy. In fact, the buyer will be entitled to the remedy he requested—specific performance.

Answer 45

Choice **(A)** is correct. Alice's request that the court order Barry to continue making his payments is a request for a decree of specific performance. The principal requirement that Alice must satisfy in order to get this (or any) form of equitable relief is to show that legal relief—i.e., an award of money damages—would not be adequate to protect her. One reason for which an award of money damages might not be adequate is that the amount of the damage award cannot be computed with reasonable accuracy. Here, we don't know how long Elda will live, so the number of payments that Barry will end up being legally obligated to make is unknown. Therefore, the court cannot accurately assess a single amount as a damage award that represents the certain present value of Barry's obligation, and an award of "$500 per month for the rest of Elda's life" is a more accurate solution.

(B) is wrong because, while the burden on Alice will indeed increase by virtue of Barry's non-performance, this fact alone would not entitle Alice to a decree of specific performance rather than an award of damages. Alice will have to show that money damages are not an adequate remedy, and the reason that this is true is as discussed in the analysis of Choice (A).

(C) is wrong because it is a misstatement of law—there simply is no rule that courts will not grant specific performance of a promise to pay money. (Indeed, where the contract calls for a series of payments in return for some sort of ongoing performance, a decree that the payments be made as scheduled is likely to be *preferable* to a one-shot award of money damages, because the decree better protects the defendant's interest in getting the ongoing return performance in exchange for his payments.)

(D) is wrong because there is no requirement that a plaintiff show economic harm from the defendant's breach. Often the promisee in a third-party beneficiary scenario does not suffer economic harm if the promisor fails to render the promised performance to the third-party, but such promises are nonetheless enforceable by the promisee. It's true that there is a requirement that the defendant's promise have been supported by *consideration*; but here, the consideration for Barry's promise was Alice's return promise to pay her half of each monthly payment, so the fact that Alice herself is suffering no economic harm from Barry's breach of his payment obligation does not mean that Barry's promise lacked consideration.

Answer 46

Choice **(B)** is correct. Courts will usually not grant specific performance of an individual's duty to perform personal services, because of the difficulties in supervising the defendant's ongoing performance, and the distastefulness of ordering what amounts to involuntary servitude. Here, for instance, if the court grants an order compelling the carpenter to do the work at the contracted-for price and in the contracted-for time period, the court may have to make constant decisions about whether the carpenter is keeping up to the schedule and doing the work according to specifications, so that the court risks becoming enmeshed in burdensome project details, which the court probably will conclude is not a sensible use of judicial resources. Also, the court may have to imprison the carpenter if he doesn't perform, a consequence that seems somewhat like slavery.

(A) is wrong because the requirements for laches have not been satisfied here. It is true that if a plaintiff who is seeking equitable relief unjustifiably "sleeps on his rights," the defense of laches may preclude recovery. But here, there seem to be two reasons why laches would not apply: (1) we are told that the homeowner made a "reasonable and *prolonged* effort" to find a substitute, suggesting that the homeowner spent most or all of the one-year gap between repudiation and suit in reasonable efforts to mitigate, making the gap not unjustifiable; and (2) there is no evidence that the carpenter has been prejudiced by the delay, a usual requirement for laches.

(C) is wrong as a statement of law: When a plaintiff suffers from the defendant's anticipatory repudiation, all standard contract remedies are typically available to him, even though the time for performance has not yet arrived. So a decree of specific performance may be issued, though typically the decree would not require performance until the contractually-specified time for it.

(D) is wrong as a statement of law. It is true that a decree of specific performance, like other equitable relief, will not be granted where damages would provide an adequate remedy. But the availability of nominal damages alone will typically not be an adequate remedy, and that is certainly the case here, where the homeowner's actual damages will be more than nominal.

Answer 47

Choice (C) is correct. $50,000 represents the contractor's expectation measure of recovery and gives the contractor the benefit of the bargain—this amount would place the contractor in the position he would have been in but for the breach. It is also the greatest amount the contractor is able to recover. The general expectation formula permits the contractor to recover $50,000 and can be computed as follows:

General expectation formula = Loss In Value + Other Loss – Cost Avoided – Loss Avoided:

> LIV = the difference between the performance the non-breaching party should have received under the contract and what was actually received, if anything, in this case, $300,000 less $0.

> OL = consequential and incidental damages, if any, in this case, $0.

> CA = the additional costs the non-breaching party can avoid by rightfully discontinuing performance under the contract as a result of the other party's breach, in this case, $290,000 less $45,000.

> (Full performance would have cost the contractor $290,000, since he would have made $10,000 on a $300,000-revenue contract. But the contractor has already incurred $45,000 of this $290,000, leaving $245,000.)

> LA = the beneficial effects of the breach due to the non-breaching party's ability to salvage or reallocate resources that otherwise would have been devoted to performing under the contract, in this case, $5,000 (the oak flooring that can be reused).

So $300,000 + $0 – $245,000 – $5,000 = $50,000.

Rest. 2d, § 347; Farnsworth, § 12.9.

(A) is wrong, because it does not put the contractor in the position he would have been in had the contract been fulfilled. The $40,000 figure is an attempt to calculate the contractor's *restitution* recovery, measured by the benefit conferred on the owner. See Rest. 2d, § 371. That measure would yield the smallest amount of recovery, since it would not allow the contractor to recover damages related to the benefit of the bargain. "Innocent" (i.e., non-breaching) plaintiffs like the contractor usually have the option of suing for restitution damages where this would produce a higher recovery than the expectation measure, but restitution wouldn't produce a higher recovery here. Furthermore, the $40,000 amount is incorrect even as a restitution amount, since it fails to deduct the $5,000 worth of oak flooring the contractor used on another job (making the real benefit conferred on the owner $35,000).

(B) is wrong, because it too (like the measure in (A)) fails to put the contractor in the position he would have been in had the contract been fulfilled. $40,000 represents the contractor's *reliance* measure of recovery; that measure fails to take into account the contractor's benefit of the bargain, i.e., the profit the contractor anticipated making on the project. Reliance damages would consist of the contractor's unreimbursed expenses for labor and materials, $45,000, less the salvage value of the oak flooring, $5,000, which indeed equals $40,000, as this choice suggests. Cf. Rest. 2d, § 349. But nothing in this scenario would cause the contractor to seek damages based on the reliance principle and forgo his (larger) expectation measure of recovery. Rest. 2d, §§ 349, 347.

(D) is wrong because it's too generous to the contractor. A $55,000 damages recovery will place the contractor in a better position than he would have been in but for the breach, because it fails to take into account the "loss avoided" (see the discussion of Choice (C))—the beneficial effects to the contractor from the breach, due to the contractor's ability to salvage or reallocate resources that otherwise would have been devoted to performing under the contract. Here the loss avoided is the $5,000 worth of oak flooring that the contractor used on another job.

Answer 48

Choice (C) is correct. The standard measure of contract damages is the expectation measure, which attempts to put the plaintiff in the position he would have been in had the contract been performed. Here, performance meant that the contractor would have a foundation, at a total cost to it of $200,000. The contractor paid the subcontractor $100,000, then paid another $120,000 to the replacement subcontractor, for a total of $220,000. So the contractor is $20,000 worse off than had the subcontractor performed. The contractor will need to recover this $20,000 in order to be in the position that performance would have left it.

(A) is wrong because the subcontractor's restitutionary recovery must be computed after subtracting breach damages owed by the subcontractor. A materially-breaching plaintiff may recover in quasi-contract for the value to the defendant of the rendered performance. But this recovery must be computed on a "net" basis, by subtracting from the unpaid-for value rendered to the defendant any damages caused by the breach. So in this case, if the contractor had been able to finish the work for, say, $10,000 (so that it would have spent a total of $130,000), the subcontractor would have been entitled to recover in quasi-contract the $50,000 difference between the $150,000 value that it rendered to the contractor and the $100,000 the contractor had made in progress payments (since the subcontractor's breach would not have caused any damages to the contractor). But on the actual facts here, even if the subcontractor recovered nothing in quasi-contract, the contractor would still have been damaged by $20,000 (as analyzed in Choice (C)). So the subcontractor obviously can't recover anything in quasi-contract, since each dollar given to it would just make the contractor's net damages worse. Instead, the subcontractor owes the contractor the $20,000 needed to make the contractor whole. Furthermore, in many jurisdictions a plaintiff who "wilfully" breaches isn't even eligible for a quasi-contract recovery, so in such a jurisdiction we wouldn't even get to the point of calculating whether the subcontractor was entitled to anything.

(B) is wrong because this computation would not leave the contractor whole. The contractor has $20,000 in damages (see Choice (C)) only on the assumption that the contractor doesn't have to pay the subcontractor anything in the litigation on a quasi-contract theory. If the subcontractor recovered $50,000, the contractor's net damages would mount to $70,000 from the original $20,000.

(D) is wrong because this computation, too, would not leave the contractor whole. The overriding principle is that the contractor, as a non-breaching counterclaimer, gets expectation damages to put it in the net position it would have been in had the contract been performed. If the subcontractor didn't have to pay anything (and didn't receive anything), the contractor would be $20,000 worse off than if the contract had been performed.

Answer 49

Choice **(D)** is correct. While it is true that any item of damages must be proved with reasonable certainty in order to be recovered, there is no fixed rule of law that prospective profits from a new business may not be recovered in a breach of contract action. Since the judge's instructions prevented the jury from even considering the possibility that some elements of Swatter's lost performance and endorsement income might be proven with reasonable certainty, the instruction was incorrect and not harmless. (For instance, Swatter might have been able to show that he got a certain amount of performance or endorsement revenue each year prior to Orchestra's cancellation, and that this dropped to $0 in the following year without any other explanation; such proof, if made, would likely have satisfied the requirement of reasonable certainty.)

(A) is wrong because the instruction was incorrect, for the reason discussed in Choice (D) above.

(B) is wrong as a matter of law — although the jury computes the damages, the judge can and must instruct the jury on the legal principles applicable to that computation (although here, the judge did so incorrectly).

(C) is wrong because, while it is true that contract damages are generally limited to those which the defendant could reasonably have foreseen, there is an additional requirement that each item of damages be proved with reasonable certainty, and this choice does not contain that important additional limitation.

Answer 50

Choice **(D)** is correct, because it correctly reflects the standard measure of damages for breach: expectation damages. In awarding expectation damages, the court attempts to put the plaintiff in the position she would have been in had the contract been performed by the defendant. Normally, this means that the plaintiff is awarded the profits she would have made had the contract been performed. That's the case here. Choice (D) best states this principle: In giving Buyer "the amount, if any, by which the fair market value of Greenacre on the date of [the] breach exceeded [the contract price]," the court will be giving Buyer the "benefit of her bargain," i.e., the profit she would have been able to make immediately by reselling the property.

(A) is wrong because nominal damages—which are a small sum that is fixed without regard to the amount of harm—are awarded only when a right of action for breach exists but no harm has been done or is provable. Here, Buyer has suffered provable harm (the contract-market differential). The fact that an equitable remedy (injunction) isn't available doesn't mean that Buyer didn't suffer provable harm, and doesn't prevent Buyer from collecting expectation damages.

(B) is wrong because the value of an assignable option would not be a measure of Buyer's expectation interest in this case. When Buyer sent the $100, she was exercising the option, and thus binding herself to purchase the property. Prior to that moment, it's possible that the measure of damages *would* be the value of the option (less the $100 price to "buy" that option). But once Buyer exercised by sending the $100, the option was no longer significant—there was a contract fully binding on both sides, and the usual measure of damages for a buyer whose seller breaches the contract of sale (benefit of the bargain) applied.

(C) is wrong because it incorrectly implies that the market value on the day of the sale to Citizen was at least $120,000. If the sale price to Citizen were the definitive proof of the market value of the property, this choice might be an accurate formulation. But that sale price is not legally dispositive, merely *evidence* of the fair market value. For instance, the sale to Citizen might have been at a price that the court finds to be greater than the actual market value on that day. In that event, guaranteeing Buyer a minimum recovery of $20,000 would be legally incorrect. (True, it seems unlikely that anyone would pay greater than the then "fair market value" on the day of sale. But the point is that the legal standard is "fair market value less plaintiff's contract price," not "the lesser of (1) the price paid by the third party minus the plaintiff's contract price or (2) the fair market value minus the plaintiff's contract price.")

Answer 51

Choice (**C**) is correct. Where a defaulting plaintiff has rendered some performance of value to the defendant, but has not substantially performed, the plaintiff may not recover "on the contract." But she may recover on a *quasi-contract* or *quantum meruit* ("as much as he deserved") theory—the court uses its equity-like powers to prevent unjust enrichment of the defendant. If the farmer didn't have to pay anything, he'd be unjustly enriched (at least with respect to the two painted barns, putting aside his damage from not getting the agreed-upon painting of the third barn) by the "value" to him of the painting of two barns. So the court would start by awarding the painter this value. But then, the farmer would be entitled to be made whole for the damages to him from not getting all three barns painted for the agreed-upon $6,000. So the court would compute how much it would now cost the farmer to get that single barn painted. If that cost would be $2,000 or less, the farmer's damages would be zero. But if it would cost more, then the difference would be deducted from the painter's quasi-contract "value of the services of painting two barns" recovery.

(A) is wrong because even though the painting of all three barns was an express condition of payment under the contract, the court can and would still award a quasi-contract recovery, as described above.

(B) is wrong because the painter is only entitled to a quasi-contract recovery, not to recover "on the contract." So any formula keyed to the painter's anticipated "profit" is irrelevant—it's the value to the defendant, not the profit that would have been made by the breaching plaintiff, that is the starting point. (Profits that would have been made by the plaintiff are relevant only where it's the defendant, not the plaintiff, who breached.)

(D) is wrong because this formula doesn't take into account the farmer's right to deduct damages for the painter's failure to paint the third barn. (The court might indeed use the increase in the value of the two painted barns as the measure of the "reasonable value" of the painter's services, but the court would deduct from this number the farmer's damages from the failure to paint the third barn.)

Answer 52

Choice (C) is correct. The UCC controls. Section 2-718 deals with a repudiating buyer's right to restitution of any deposit. Section 2-718(2) states the general rule that if there is no liquidated damages clause in the contract (and there is none here), the seller must return all but 20% of the total contract price or $500, whichever amount is smaller. However, § 2-718(3) says that the buyer's right to restitution is subject "to offset to the extent that the seller establishes (a) a right to recover damages under the provisions of this Article other than [the liquidated damages provision]." So to the extent that Hydro-King can prove actual damages greater than $500, it need refund only the amount of the deposit less these greater actual damages. That's precisely the formulation listed in Choice (C). (We don't know what Hydro-King's lost profits actually will be, because we don't know whether it is a "lost volume" seller, or instead can only get fewer of the power boats in question than it has customers for, in which case it would not have suffered any actual lost profits. But whatever amount represents its actual lost profits, Hydro-King gets to keep that amount, as this choice specifies.)

(A) is wrong because it directly conflicts with § 2-718(2), which entitles even a defaulting buyer to restitution of his deposit less either the seller's actual damages or the lesser of 20% of the contract price and $500.

(B) is wrong for two reasons: (1) we don't actually know whether Hydro-King is indeed a "lost volume seller" as this choice suggests it is—if Hydro-King had more customers wanting to buy that particular model boat than it could get boats from the manufacturer, Hydro-King didn't lose a net sale; and (2) even if Hydro-King lost a net sale, its damages were only $2,500, so it can't keep the entire $4,000 as this choice asserts it can.

(D) is wrong because, while it correctly states the result that would occur under § 2-718(2) if Hydro-King couldn't prove any actual damages, it ignores the fact that Hydro-King can keep that part of the deposit representing its actual damages from the lost sale if this amount is greater than $500.

Answer 53

Choice (A) is correct. Even in a court that has a relatively tough standard for the enforceability of litigated damages clauses, the court will enforce the clause if *both* of the following are true: (1) the forecast was a reasonable estimate of likely damages at the time the contract was entered into; and (2) the party seeking to enforce the clause has suffered actual damages that are hard to calculate accurately. Here, these two conditions are satisfied: (1) at the time the contract was made, the captain faced a real risk that the customer would fail to show up at the last minute, and that she would be unable to get another charter for that same day; therefore, a deposit of 40% of total contract price was a reasonable forecast of likely damages, especially since most of the captain's costs for a one-day charter are fixed (cost of boat) so that if she doesn't do the trip she recoups relatively little expense; (2) while the captain has collected $400 from the replacement as well as $200 from the customer, giving her a total for the day of $600 (i.e., $100 more than she would have gotten from the customer alone if the contract had been fulfilled), she had to stay out two hours beyond the customary return time, so some of her $100 "surplus" may have been due to this extra-long day rather than being a windfall; consequently, the captain's actual damages are indeed hard to calculate accurately after-the-fact.

(B) is wrong because it is a misstatement of law. In non-sales cases, there is no single formula that determines the outer bounds of permissible liquidated damages, as this choice suggests that there is. The examiners may have been trying to trick you into thinking of the formula applied in UCC cases, under which if the buyer of goods makes a deposit and then breaches (e.g., by canceling), and the contract does not contain a liquidated damages clause, the buyer gets back any part of his deposit in excess of "20% of the value of the total [contract price] or $500, whichever is smaller" if the seller does not establish actual damages. § 2-718(2)(b). Since this is a contract for the sale of services rather than goods, this provision does not apply (and the 10% amount in the choice doesn't match up with the UCC percentage anyway).

(C) is wrong because, while it arguably describes a treatment that puts the captain in the same position she would have been in had the contract been performed (she has collected $600 for the day from the combination of the customer and the replacement, versus $500 if the customer contract had been performed, so she arguably needs to give back $100), this choice ignores the liquidated damages clause. So long as the liquidated damages clause meets the rules for enforceability of such clauses, the fact that the clause gives the person trying to use it some slight benefit over the actual damage amount that a court might compute is irrelevant.

(D) is wrong because the liquidated damages clause here would not operate as a penalty. As long as such a clause at least meets the two-part test described in Choice (A), it by definition does not constitute a penalty. In other words, the "penalty" label is simply a shorthand method of stating that the clause doesn't pass the two-part test, which the clause here does pass.

Answer 54

Choice **(C)** is correct. The retailer is a "lost volume" seller, that is, one who can obtain as many items from a supplier as she can sell. UCC § 2-708(2), which doesn't expressly mention lost-volume sellers but is designed for them, gives such sellers the profit that the seller would have made from full performance by the buyer, together with any incidental damages.

(A) is wrong because § 2-708(2) gives a lost-volume seller such as the retailer its lost profits regardless of the amount of the resale-contract differential. Indeed, the whole point of § 2-708(2) is to prevent a lost-volume seller from being limited to a $0 or very small resale-contract differential.

(B) is wrong because notice of intent to resell is not required where the recovery is on a lost-volume basis. When the seller elects the remedy of "cover"—i.e., the right to resell and collect the difference between the resale price and the (higher) contract price—and the resale is at a private sale, the seller *is* required to give the buyer "reasonable notification of his intention to resell." § 2-706(3). However, the retailer is *not* recovering on this resale/contract-price basis (since that basis would give him $0). Instead, he's recovering his lost profits as a lost-volume seller under § 2-708(2), and no advance notice is required for such a recovery.

(D) is wrong because the damages available to a lost volume seller are not the contract price. The retailer is entitled to its lost profits and any incidental damages suffered. Awarding the retailer the contract price would over-compensate it, since it has not had to bear the expense of buying the computer from the manufacturer.

Answer 55

Choice **(A)** is correct, because it correctly identifies that the bank will be able to recover the entire contract amount. Arriving at this result requires resolving three major issues: (1) whether the assignment to the bank was valid, (2) whether the risk of loss had passed to the buyer by the moment of destruction; and (3) the measure of damages in these circumstances.

First, the assignment was valid, even though the contract expressly prohibited assignment without the other party's permission. Under UCC § 2-210(4), if there are no circumstances indicating the contrary, a provision prohibiting assignment "of the contract" is deemed to bar only the delegation of duties, not the assignment of contractual rights. (Furthermore, under UCC § 9-406, the right to receive payment cannot be prohibited from assignment—so even if the circumstances *had* indicated a contrary intent, the clause barring assignment would not have prevented the seller's assignment of his right to payment.) So the seller was permitted to make—and did make—an assignment to the bank of all his rights (i.e., the right to payment). (The bank as assignee would still be subject to any defenses that the buyer would have had against the seller, but as discussed in the next paragraph, there are no such defenses, because the risk of loss passed to the bank.)

Second, the risk of loss had passed to the buyer by the moment of destruction, because of the "F.O.B. seller's place of business" term. Under that term, the risk of loss passed to the buyer as soon as the seller placed the chairs on board the carrier. Since the chairs were destroyed after the seller did so, while the chairs were in transit, the buyer will bear the loss. Therefore, the bank, as assignee of the seller's rights, gets to collect the purchase price just as the seller would have been entitled to do had he not made the assignment. (Note that the seller and the buyer could have distributed the loss as they saw fit—if they provided "F.O.B. buyer's place of business," the seller would have borne the risk of loss until the goods had arrived at the buyer's business).

Third, you have to figure out what the measure of damages would be. The bank steps into the seller's shoes, because the assignment was valid and the seller complied with all contractual obligations. UCC § 2-709(1) says that "when the buyer fails to pay the price as it becomes due the seller may recover, together with any incidental damages . . . (a) the [contract] price of . . . conforming goods lost or damaged within a commercially reasonable time after risk of their loss has passed to the buyer[.]" So had there been no assignment, the seller would have been entitled to the full contract price. The bank, standing in the shoes of the seller, is entitled to receive this same amount.

(B) is wrong, because it does not use the correct formula in determining the bank's damages. The bank steps into the seller's shoes, because the assignment was valid and the seller complied with all contractual obligations. (Both of these propositions are further explained above.) As explained in the last paragraph of the discussion of Choice (A), the bank is entitled to recover the full contract price. Choice (B), by restricting the bank to the contract/market differential, would leave the bank woefully undercompensated: For instance, if as would likely be the case the contract price was equal to the market price, the differential would leave the bank (standing in the seller's shoes) with $0 recovery, yet the buyer would be deemed to have received and accepted (by virtue of the F.O.B. clause) conforming goods.

(C) is wrong, because it fails to recognize that the buyer will be liable even though the chairs hadn't been delivered. Determining who's responsible for the loss—the seller or the buyer—depends on determining whether the risk of loss had passed from the seller to the buyer. The relevant term is the F.O.B. term—here, that term specifies the seller's place of business. Thus, once the seller placed the goods on board the carrier, the risk of loss passed to the buyer. In other words, the goods are deemed to have been delivered, even though they never got to the buyer's place of business.

If the term had been "F.O.B. buyer's place of business," Choice (C) would be right, because the buyer wouldn't bear the risk of loss until the chairs reached him.

(D) is wrong, because it doesn't recognize that the seller had the right to assign his rights under the contract despite the contract prohibition. Here, it's true that the seller and the buyer agreed not to "assign the contract" without the written consent of the other party. But under UCC § 2-210(4), absent circumstances indicating the contrary, a provision prohibiting assignment "of the contract" is deemed to bar only the delegation of duties, not the assignment of contractual rights. So the seller was permitted to make (and did make) an assignment to the bank of all his rights (i.e., the right to payment). (Furthermore, under UCC § 9-406, the right to receive payment cannot be prohibited from assignment—so even if the circumstances had indicated a contrary intent, the clause barring assignment would not have prevented the seller's assignment of his right to payment.)

Answer 56

Choice (C) is correct. Generally, an assignee "stands in the shoes of his assignor." That is, the assignee generally takes subject to all defenses, set-offs, and counterclaims that the obligor could have asserted against the assignor. Here, therefore, the banker as assignee of the contractor's rights stands in the contractor's shoes, and is vulnerable to any counterclaim or defense to which the contractor would have been vulnerable if it was the contractor that was suing the homeowner. If the contractor had not made the assignment and had sued the homeowner for the $10,000 contract price (or any part of it), the homeowner could have raised the counterclaim or defense for damages for breach due to the contractor's abandonment, and used that counterclaim/defense as a set-off, i.e., to reduce any amount which the homeowner would otherwise owe. Consequently, the homeowner can make this same counterclaim or defense when sued by the banker as the contractor's assignee. (The homeowner could not achieve an affirmative recovery against the banker, but the homeowner isn't trying to do that here, just reduce the amount he owes the banker.)

(A) is wrong because it does not matter either that the contractor-homeowner contract was already in existence at the time of the notice of assignment or that the contractor was not yet in breach at that time. In a suit by the assignee against the obligor, the obligor can raise any defenses or counterclaims that it could have raised against the assignor, regardless of when those defenses or counterclaims came into existence. (If you selected this choice, you may have been thinking about the rules on *modification*, under which the giving of notice of assignment by the assignee to the obligor will deprive the obligor and assignor of the subsequent right to modify the contract if the assignor has fully performed.)

(B) is wrong because it states a completely fictitious rule of law. It is true that the homeowner's claim is unsecured and that the banker's is secured; this fact might prevent the homeowner from getting and collecting an *affirmative recovery* against the contractor (since the banker's secured claim would take priority over the homeowner's later-acquired judgment for the affirmative recovery). But what the homeowner cares about here is using its claim as a set-off (something that can reduce the banker's recovery against the homeowner), and the homeowner's claim is fully operative as a set-off even though the set-off claim is in a sense "unsecured."

(D) is wrong because, while it states the correct result, it gives the wrong reason. Whether or not the homeowner's claim against the contractor arose prior to the contractor's default on the loan from the banker, the homeowner gets to raise against the banker any defense he could use against the contractor (for reasons described in the discussion of Choice (C) above).

Answer 57

Choice (B) is correct. An assignment of contractual rights is the transfer of that right to another. It requires assignor's intent to transfer, identification of the rights to be assigned, and assignee's acceptance (which is normally presumed if the assignment is beneficial). Under the contract here, Mechanic's *"right"* under the contract was to receive payment from Ohner. Thus, his letter to Jones and Ohner would serve to transfer the right to payment to Jones. This makes Jones the assignee, Mechanic the assignor, and Ohner the obligor. The result of the transfer is that Jones "stands in Mechanic's shoes" as to the right to payment. As a result, any defenses under the contract that Ohner could assert against Mechanic, he can assert against Jones. Thus, Mechanic's failure to perform under the contract would be a defense Ohner could successfully assert against Jones.

(A) is not the best response, because Jones's ability to do Mechanic's work is irrelevant to Jones's recovery. If you chose this response, you either confused an assignment of rights with a delegation of duties, or assumed that Mechanic assigned the *contract*, not just the right to payment, which would involve a presumption that the duties were delegated as well. Most "impersonal" duties can be delegated, and Mechanic's duty to repair the machine probably *could* be delegated, barring facts indicating that Ohner had a particular interest in receiving performance from Mechanic. Rest. 2d § 318(2). However, a delegation or an assignment is *not* valid where it materially increases the risk that Ohner will not receive return performance. Rest. 2d § 317 (2). Where Jones can't perform the work, such a delegation would be invalid. However, since only an assignment of right to payment is involved here, Choice (A) isn't the best response.

(C) is not the best response, because the prohibition against assignment would not be upheld. UCC § 9-406(d) provides that a party may assign its right to payment even though the contract under which payment is due prohibits assignment. Here, the proposed answer stipulates that Mechanic promised not to assign the contract. Nonetheless, applicable law would permit Mechanic to assign the right to collect Ohner's payment.

(D) is not the best response, because Jones's not being a third party beneficiary would *not* be determinative of his recovery. This choice suggests that the only way Jones can recover is as an intended beneficiary to the contract. While it's true that an intended beneficiary has enforceable rights under a contract, so does an assignee.

Answer 58

Choice **(D)** is correct, because it identifies the central reason why the insurer will be liable to the bank or the furniture company, whichever assignee has priority. The rights of either the bank or the furniture company stem from the victim-insurer settlement agreement. In order to be valid, a contract requires consideration, which is a bargained-for exchange and either a benefit to the promisor or a detriment to the promisee (and typically both). Under these facts, the victim had a good-faith belief in the validity of his claim against the insurer. Thus, the settlement agreement between them, whereby the victim surrendered his claim, was supported by consideration. Since the insurer's settlement promise (to pay the victim $5,000) was not conditional on the tortfeasor's policy's being valid as against the insurer, the fact that the insurer might have had a chance to void the policy pre-settlement on the grounds of the tortfeasor's minority (an unlikely chance anyway) is irrelevant, and the settlement was binding on the insurer.

Then, because the right to receive payment was assignable, the victim validly assigned his right to either the bank or the furniture company (depending on which had priority). As assignee, the bank or the furniture company assumed the victim's rights under the contract, and could enforce the insurer's promise to pay.

(A) is wrong because the victim's rights under the contract with the insurer have nothing to do with the tortfeasor. The rights of either the bank or the furniture company stem from the victim-insurer settlement agreement. The victim had a good-faith belief in the validity of his claim against the insurer. Thus, the settlement agreement between them, whereby the victim surrendered his claim, was supported by consideration. Since the insurer's settlement promise (to pay the victim $5,000) was not conditional on the tortfeasor's policy's being valid as against the insurer, the fact that the insurer might have had a chance to void the policy pre-settlement on the grounds of the tortfeasor's minority (an unlikely chance anyway) is irrelevant, and the settlement was unconditionally binding on the insurer. Then, the victim was entitled to assign whatever right to payment he had under the contract, and that's what he did. His rights did not spring from any beneficiary status under the insurer-tortfeasor agreement; since (A) states otherwise, it's wrong.

(B) is wrong because the insurer will be liable under its contract with the victim, regardless of the tortfeasor's ultimate irresponsibility. The victim had a good-faith belief in the validity of his claim against the insurer. Thus, the settlement agreement between them, whereby the victim surrendered his claim, was supported by consideration. Since the insured's settlement promise (to pay the victim $5,000) was not conditional on the tortfeasor's policy's being valid as against the insurer, the fact that the insurer might have been able to void the policy pre-settlement on the grounds of the tortfeasor's minority (an unlikely chance anyway) is irrelevant, and the settlement was unconditionally binding on the insurer. Thus this choice is not correct in saying that the insurer is liable only if it "knowingly waived the defense of the tortfeasor's minority and irresponsibility." (The victim's unconditional right to payment was thus properly assigned to either the bank or the furniture company, whichever had priority.)

(C) is wrong because the tortfeasor's minority is not relevant to either the bank's or the furniture company's rights as assignees of the victim's rights. The victim had a good-faith belief in the validity of his claim against the insurer. Therefore the settlement agreement between them, whereby the victim surrendered his claim, was supported by consideration. Since the insured's settlement promise (to pay the victim $5,000) was not conditional on the tortfeasor's policy's being valid as against the insurer, the fact that the insurer might have had a chance to avoid the policy pre-settlement on the grounds of the tortfeasor's minority (an unlikely chance anyway) is irrelevant, and the settlement was unconditionally binding on the insurer. As assignee, the bank or the furniture company assumed the victim's rights under the contract, and could enforce the insurer's promise to pay.

Answer 59

Choice **(A)** is correct. The sale of the business by Gyro to Copter was both an assignment of rights under the Gyro-Tower contract and a delegation of duties under it. When a delegation occurs, the delegator (here, Gyro) remains liable to the obligee (here, Tower) unless the obligee *expressly releases* the delegator and agrees to look solely to the delegate (Copter); if this occurred it would be a "novation." The mere fact that the obligee agrees to the delegation does not by itself constitute a novation or release the delegator from liability. Here, therefore, although Tower agreed to the delegation (i.e., agreed to accept performance from Copter), he did not agree to a novation and therefore did not release Gyro.

(B) is wrong because: (1) an obligee's assent to a delegation does not require consideration; and (2) even though Tower validly assented to Copter's doing the work, this did not release Gyro from liability, for the reason explained in the analysis of Choice (A).

(C) is wrong because the mere fact that an obligee assents to a delegation does not effect a novation. Instead, a novation is deemed to occur only when the obligee expressly agrees to release the obligee and look solely to the delegate; there was therefore no novation here. (If there *had* been a novation, it would indeed have served to discharge Gyro, as this choice suggests.)

(D) is wrong because the fact that the liquidated-damages clause covered only delay damages does not mean that damages for other breaches (e.g., timely but non-conforming work) cannot be recovered. A liquidated damages clause that is restricted to a certain type of breach leaves common-law damages intact for other types of breach.

Answer 60

Choice **(D)** is correct, because it recognizes the central reason the distributor can't recover under the contract: It is an incidental beneficiary, and thus it has no rights under the contract. When two parties enter into a contract, there are two types of beneficiaries that may be created: intended beneficiaries and incidental beneficiaries. Only intended beneficiaries have enforceable rights under the contract. Most courts determine whether a beneficiary is intended by looking at the intent of the promisee (the original contracting party to whom the promise in question was made). If the promisee intends (even though it is not his sole or even primary intent) that the third party receive benefit from the promisor's performance, the third party is an intended beneficiary; if not, he has no enforceable rights under the contract. (Some courts also look secondarily to the intent of the promisor.)

Here, there is no sign that either the investor or the winery had any intent to benefit the distributor: The facts instead suggest that these original parties intended to distribute through the distributor in order to ensure that the wine was distributed correctly, and thus the use of the distributor was intended solely to benefit the *parties themselves*, not the distributor. This prevents the distributor from being an intended beneficiary.

(A) is wrong, because it attaches too much importance to the fact that the winery's performance would run to the distributor. Only intended beneficiaries have enforceable rights under the contract. Courts determine whether a beneficiary is intended mainly by looking at the intent of the promisee (the one to whom the duty in question is owed), and sometimes secondarily at the intent of the promisor. It's true that in assessing this intent, one of the factors is whether the promisor's performance is to run directly to the third party; this factor points towards a finding that the beneficiary was intended. But this "to whom performance runs" factor is at best a "tie-breaker" to be used when the other evidence of intent-to-benefit is unclear or evenly-balanced. Here, all the indications are that the winery and the investor specified this particular distributor only to benefit their own business interests, not to benefit the distributor. So the fact that performance would run to the distributor is not needed as a tie-breaker, and therefore doesn't change the outcome.

(B) is wrong, because reasonable foreseeability of reliance is not an adequate basis on which the distributor could recover. In order to recover, the distributor would have to have been an intended beneficiary under the winery-investor contract. It is the intent of the original parties (principally the promisee of the performance in question) that determines whether the distributor was an intended beneficiary. Thus, the mere foreseeability of the distributor's reliance wouldn't be enough to give him enforceable rights under the contract; only the intent of the original parties would matter.

Reliance can be relevant in the third-party beneficiary context, but only in determining when the intended beneficiary's rights "vest." (Before vesting, but not after, the parties can modify or rescind the contract without the beneficiary's consent.) If the distributor had been an intended beneficiary, then his rights would have vested as soon as he detrimentally relied on the contract. But here, he never attained intended-beneficiary status, so his reliance never became relevant to any issue in the case.

(C) is wrong, because it overstates what's necessary to create an intended beneficiary. The distributor could, in theory, have enforceable rights under the contract without there being an express provision in the contract. Courts determine whether a beneficiary is intended by looking at whether the original parties (principally the promisee, the one to whom the promise in question is made) intended to benefit the beneficiary. But that intent can be inferred from the circumstances—it does not have to be explicitly agreed upon by the original parties. Since (C) asserts that an express agreement to benefit the third party is required, it's wrong.

Answer 61

Choice **(B)** is correct. The issue is whether Elda was an intended beneficiary of the Alice-Barry contract; if she was, she can sue, and if she wasn't, she can't. It's pretty clear from the context that Alice (the promisee of Barry's promise) desired to help her mother; therefore, Elda is an intended beneficiary of Barry's promise even though Alice was also motivated by a desire not to pay for the companion entirely by herself. In other words, Alice's "mixed motives" don't disqualify Elda from being an intended beneficiary, as long as one of Alice's motives was to help Elda. The fact that performance by Barry (payment of $500 per month) was to be rendered directly to Elda, rather than to Alice, also pushes the classification toward a finding that Elda was an intended beneficiary.

(A) is wrong because Barry's making of the first three payments is irrelevant—from the conduct and motivation of the parties in making the contract, we know that Elda was an intended beneficiary (as discussed in Choice (B) above), so Elda would have been entitled to sue Barry for non-payment even if he had not made any prior payments.

(C) is wrong because it ignores the significance of the three-party context. In a two-party scenario in which all that happens is that a child promises to pay for the parent's support, this promise may indeed be unenforceable for lack of consideration. But in a three-party case like this one, the law of third-party beneficiaries can change the result. Here, each of the children's promises supplies consideration for the other child's return promise; therefore, lack of consideration is not a problem even though Elda is not herself giving consideration.

(D) is wrong because, while it is true that Alice and Barry both intended their payments to be gifts, this fact does not prevent Elda from being an intended beneficiary, who therefore gets the right to sue either promisor for breach. The whole idea of a "donee beneficiary" (as opposed to a "creditor beneficiary") is that a person to whom the promisee intends to make a gift becomes an intended beneficiary (of the "donee" sub-category).

Answer 62

Choice **(A)** is correct. Incidental beneficiaries cannot enforce a contract if one of the original parties to it defaults. Since there will often be many people indirectly or even directly benefited by any given contractual performance, the term "incidental beneficiary" is used to describe those persons who would benefit by the performance but who were not intended by the original parties to be benefited. Here, the landowner's neighbor's rights under the landowner-logging company contract are those of an incidental beneficiary, at best—neither the landowner nor the logging company intended to confer any benefit (and certainly not the benefit of an improved view) upon the neighbor when they made the contract. Therefore, the neighbor cannot recover against the logging company for breach.

(B) is wrong because the fact that a suit is "nuisance litigation" will not be a ground on which the defendant to the suit can win. Instead, if the defendant wins "on the merits," the fact that the suit was so meritless as to have been a nuisance might be grounds for the original defendant to win a tort-like recovery from the original plaintiff in a second suit, brought by the original defendant for wrongful use of civil proceedings. So here, the fact that the neighbor was bringing a "nuisance litigation" would be irrelevant to whether the neighbor would win.

(C) is wrong because the neighbor was not an intended beneficiary. For a third party to be an intended beneficiary, the circumstances must indicate that at least one of the original parties intended to give the beneficiary the benefit of the intended promise. Here, this is not so, for the reasons described in Choice (A) above.

(D) is wrong because no rights were transferred to the neighbor to allow him to sue as a surrogate. The neighbor cannot claim to be a surrogate standing in to enforce the landowner's rights under the contract unless he can show some relation to the contract. The facts state that the landowner has made no attempt to assign to his neighbor any cause of action he might have against the logging company; nor do the facts state any other legal relationship between the landowner and his neighbor that might be the basis for some sort of surrogacy.

Answer 63

Choice **(B)** is correct. Gilbert is an intended beneficiary of the Mater-Nirvana agreement, since Mater made it clear that her primary purpose in entering into the contract was to provide a wedding gift for Gilbert. The original parties' power to modify the contract without the beneficiary's consent terminates if the beneficiary, before he receives notification of the discharge or modification, does any of three things: (1) materially *changes his position in justifiable reliance* on the promise; (2) brings suit on it; or (3) manifests assent to it at the request of either of the original parties. Here, Gilbert did the first of these, by selling his old car at a discount, in justifiable reliance on the forthcoming gift. Once he did that, both Mater and Nirvana lost the ability to modify the contract without Gilbert's consent. Therefore, Gilbert has the right to sue the promisor, Nirvana, for breach.

(A) is wrong because Gilbert is not an "assignee for value" of the Mater-Nirvana contract; he's a third-party beneficiary of it. He's not an "assignee" at all (neither of the original parties assigned him any right), and he's certainly not an assignee "for value," since he didn't pay or give anything of value to either of the original parties.

(C) is wrong because, although Gilbert is indeed a donee beneficiary, that status did not prevent his rights from "vesting" when he changed position in reliance on the agreement. (Donee beneficiaries and creditor beneficiaries have the same rights regarding modifications by the original parties.)

(D) is wrong because Nirvana's reliance on the rescission is irrelevant. The promisor under a third-party beneficiary contract is expected to know the rules governing such contracts, and those rules include the rule that a beneficiary who detrimentally relies on the contract gets an immediate vesting.

Answer 64

Choice **(B)** is correct. An intended beneficiary to a contract only has enforceable rights under that contract when his rights "vest." Before the rights vest, the beneficiary can't stop the parties from modifying or rescinding the contract. Under the modern/Restatement view, a beneficiary's rights vest when any of these three events occurs: (1) the beneficiary manifests assent to the promise; (2) the beneficiary sues to enforce the promise; or (3) the beneficiary justifiably relies on the promise to his detriment. Thus, if Byer and Zeller eliminated the Quincy payment provision before Quincy even found out about the contract, Quincy couldn't possibly have either "manifested assent" (#1 above), "sued to enforce the promise" (#2) or "justifiably relie[d]" (#3). That meant that Quincy's rights could not yet have vested as of the moment the original two parties to the contract (Byer and Zeller) modified the contract, and not-yet-vested beneficiary rights may be rescinded or modified by the original parties at any time.

(A) is not the best response, because a promise by one of the original contracting parties to make payment to a third-party beneficiary does not need separate consideration from the beneficiary. The only consideration that's relevant under the Byer-Zeller contract is whether there was consideration to support the contract itself, and there was such—Byer received Zeller's promise to convey the property as consideration for his, Byer's, promise to make the $46,000 in total payments.

(C) is not the best response, because any time-bar of Quincy's right to sue Zeller is not relevant to *Byer's* duty to pay Quincy. As discussed in (A), there does not need to be separate consideration for one contracting party's promise to pay some of the contract price to a third party beneficiary. Therefore, Quincy can recover under the Byer-Zeller agreement if he was an intended beneficiary (or an assignee). Thus, it wouldn't matter if Zeller had an enforceable debt to Quincy or not—Zeller could be giving Quincy money as a gift and Quincy would *still* have enforceable rights. (The only significance of the debt is that it would make Quincy a *creditor* beneficiary instead of a *donee* beneficiary, but that distinction rarely matters today, and doesn't matter on these facts.)

(D) is not the best response, because Quincy's notifying the parties of his acceptance of the agreement wouldn't be relevant to his ability to prevail. An intended beneficiary can (as long as his rights haven't previously been cut off by one of the events described in (B) above) sue the promisor without having first notified either of the two original parties that the beneficiary was "accepting." If Quincy had given such a notice, that notice would serve to "vest" his rights (it would be a "manifestation of assent"). But even absent such a manifestation, the bringing of suit would vest Quincy's rights, if the original parties hadn't modified or rescinded the rights first.

Answer 65

Choice (**C**) is correct. It is true that Artiste was a third-party beneficiary of the Kabb-Petrol agreement. Therefore, if Petrol had breached the agreement by unjustifiably failing to place all of his advertising with Artiste, Artiste would have been able to recover against him for breach. However, when the original parties to an agreement each make a promise to the other, each party's substantial performance of his own promise is generally a constructive condition to the other party's obligation to perform any subsequent duties. Therefore, when Kabb failed to perform his obligations early in the contract by not purchasing all his gas from Petrol, this was not only a breach of the Kabb-Petrol agreement but also operated as the non-occurrence of a constructive condition to Petrol's subsequent duty to continue using Artiste as his sole source for advertising. Therefore, Petrol's notice to Artiste that he would not use her for any further advertising was neither an anticipatory repudiation nor a present breach, so that there is nothing for Artiste to recover on.

(A) is wrong because, although Artiste is in fact a third-party beneficiary of the Kabb-Petrol contract, this does not help her because Petrol committed no breach, for the reasons explained above.

(B) is wrong because even if Kabb is viewed as having been Artiste's agent when he obtained the promise from Petrol that Petrol would buy advertising exclusively from Artiste, this will not entitle Artiste to recover—Petrol's duty to Artiste was dependent upon Kabb's first not materially breaching any prior obligations to Petrol, and as described above Kabb *did* breach.

(D) is wrong because there *was* consideration for Petrol's promise to place all his advertising with Artiste. It's true that *Artiste* did not give consideration for this promise, but there is no rule that says that the beneficiary of a promise must be the one who supplies the consideration—a third-party can supply it. Here, Kabb, by promising to buy all his gas from Petrol, was supplying consideration for Petrol's return promise to place advertising with Artiste.

Answer 66

Choice (**A**) is correct. UCC § 2-613 provides that where goods that are "identified at the time the contract was made" are totally destroyed before the risk of their loss has passed to the buyer and without the fault of either party, the contract is "avoided," and each party is relieved of its respective obligation to perform. Section 2-501 lists various ways that particular goods will be deemed "identified," one of which is that at the time of contract formation the parties agreed that what was being sold was a particular already-existing and identified item. Since the parties here agreed that what was being sold was the particular antique car on display in the museum, that car was deemed "identified" to the contract. Therefore, § 2-613 applied, and both parties' obligations were discharged by the total destruction of the car. Therefore, no claim under the contract could be asserted by either party.

(B), (C), and (D) are all wrong because (A) is correct — the total destruction of the car caused the contract to be discharged, and any claims asserted under it to be void. See the analysis of Choice (A) for more details.

Answer 67

Choice (**A**) is correct. The Coast Guard's prohibition had the force of law, so that prohibition constituted "supervening illegality," a form of impossibility. When the defense of impossibility applies, the court will normally cancel the contract and attempt to put the parties in the position they were in before the contract was made. Doing so in this case will require that Phinney get his deposit back.

(B) is wrong because "mutual mistake" is deemed to occur only when the parties are mistaken about some fact that exists at the time of the contract. Where some supervening event renders performance impossible, the case is treated as involving impossibility, not mutual mistake (although the legal effect is pretty much the same — the contract is canceled and the parties are restored to their pre-contract position to the extent possible).

(C) is wrong because the Coast Guard's prohibition made the performance impossible. Where a supervening rule of law would make it illegal for a party to perform, the fact that the party is physically capable of performing does not prevent the impossibility doctrine from applying. Therefore, the fact that the boat was extra seaworthy did not make performance possible.

(D) is wrong because the liquidated-damages clause did not allocate the risk of a supervening illegality to Phinney. Indeed, a liquidated damages clause normally does not allocate risk at all — it merely specifies what the amount of damages should be if, based on other contract provisions, a breach should occur. Here, there was no breach, so the liquidated-damages clause plays no role.

Answer 68

Choice (**D**) is correct. The computer company's defense would have to be based on the UCC's version of the doctrine of commercial impracticability. Section 2-615(a) says that "[d]elay in delivery or nondelivery in whole or in part by a seller . . . is not a breach of his duty under a contract for sale if performance as agreed has been made impracticable by the occurrence of a contingency the non-occurrence of which was a basic assumption on which the contract was made . . . ." So if the computer company can convince the court that the non-occurrence of the unreliability of the new technology was a "basic assumption" behind the contract, the company would get off the hook.

The problem for the computer company is that in determining whether the non-occurrence of a condition (let's call it "condition X") was a "basic assumption," the court will look to whether the parties implicitly or explicitly allocated to one party the risk of the non-occurrence of condition X. If the party seeking to use commercial impracticability was allocated this risk during the negotiations, that party can't use the defense. And such allocation need not be explicit in the contract—the court can infer it from the circumstances. Where one party (the seller) undertakes to manufacture a device reliant on what both parties know will be new and untested technology, a court would almost certainly infer that that party, not the buyer, implicitly bore the risk that the anticipated technological breakthrough would fail to materialize.

(A) is wrong because, as described in the analysis of Choice (D) above, even if performance by the computer company was objectively impossible, this won't get the company off the hook, because it would be found to have assumed the risk that the anticipated breakthrough would not materialize.

(B) is wrong because it is simply not a correct statement of the law. When a seller contracts to build and deliver a machine incorporating new and heretofore untested technology, the seller has a binding obligation to deliver it, unless the court finds that the parties intended to excuse performance in the event the technology does not come through. There's nothing in these facts to indicate that the parties intended such an excuse here. On the contrary, a court would almost certainly find (as detailed in the analysis of Choice (D) above) that the computer company assumed the risk that it would be unable to make the needed breakthrough.

(C) is wrong because it is an incorrect statement of law: The defense of impossibility *does* essentially apply to merchants under the UCC, in the form of the commercial impracticability defense. It's true that the UCC doesn't use the word "impossibility." But § 2-615 gives a defense called "excuse by failure of presupposed conditions," a defense that is usually referred to as "commercial impracticability." (However, as detailed above, the computer company won't be able to successfully use the impracticability defense on these facts.)

Answer 69

Choice **(C)** is correct. The doctrine of commercial impracticability can cover situations in which a pre-existing fact of which the parties were unaware at the time of contracting becomes known later, and renders performance impracticable. However, the impracticability defense will not apply where the party asserting it is found to have expressly or impliedly borne the risk of the event in question. Here, two facts strongly militate against the builder's being excused under the doctrine: (1) in any substantial excavation project, there is a very foreseeable risk of finding unexpectedly large rock deposits, and the more foreseeable the risk, the less likely it is to be excusable under the impracticability doctrine; and (2) the builder as a professional builder has more experience with the business risks involved in excavation than does a typical owner, so it makes economic sense to put the risk of an excavation-related surprise (or the burden of negotiating a clause dealing specifically with that risk) on the builder rather than on the owner.

(A) is wrong because, as described in the analysis of Choice (C), the doctrine of impracticability does not apply where the party seeking to use the doctrine is found to have impliedly borne the risk of the event in question, as the builder would be found to have done here.

(B) is wrong because, while mutual mistake might apply here just as impracticability might apply, the doctrine of mutual mistake will not apply where the party seeking to assert it would be found to have borne the risk of that type of mistake, and the builder would be found to have borne that risk here.

(D) is wrong because the builder would be found to have borne the risk of subsurface granite even if such granite was previously unknown in the vicinity of the construction site—as further explained in the analysis of Choice (C) above, a builder will normally be found to have borne the risk of unfavorable sub-surface conditions.

Answer 70

Choice (**C**) is correct. The contract will be enforced as written (i.e., no restitutionary recovery) unless the estate can come up with a legal theory why it shouldn't be. The only plausible theory is frustration of purpose. But the frustration defense will not be recognized where the parties are found to have expressly or implicitly allocated the risk of the event in question. Here, a court would almost certainly conclude that given Ohlster's advanced age, he took the risk that he would die before obtaining substantial benefits from the contract, and Geriatrics took the opposite risk that he would live so long that the deal would be a very bad one for Geriatrics.

(A) is wrong because, although Geriatrics has clearly been "enriched," a court would be unlikely to hold that the enrichment was unjust, in view of the substantial risk that Geriatrics took that Ohlster would live a very long time.

(B) is wrong because the doctrine of frustration of purpose will not apply where the party seeking to use it is found to have impliedly borne the risk of the event in question, and the court will probably make such a finding here, as detailed in the discussion of Choice (C) above.

(D) is wrong because Geriatrics will win even if it cannot show that it rejected some other lifetime-care application on account of its deal with Ohlster—the contract will be enforced as written unless some defense applies, and no defense applies here.

Answer 71

Choice (**B**) is correct. First, since the continued existence of the office being painted was a major assumption on which the contract was based, the destruction of the office will cause both parties to be contractually discharged. Second, when contractual duties are discharged on account of impossibility, a party who has partly performed will generally be permitted to recover in quasi-contract for restitution, i.e., for the value of the benefit conferred on the other party. Therefore, the painter will be permitted to recover for the value of the painting that he had done as of the moment of the fire.

(A) is wrong because, as discussed in the analysis of Choice (B) above, a party who has partly performed by the time of the event causing the discharge is permitted to recover in quasi-contract for the value of his partial performance.

(C) is wrong because the lawyer's performance is discharged not because *it* is impossible, but because the performance which the lawyer was to receive in exchange for her own performance (a paint job) is impossible. When performance of one side of the agreed exchange is rendered impossible, the other side is discharged so as to prevent either side from being unjustly enriched.

(D) is wrong because: (1) both parties' contractual duties (not just the painter's) are discharged; and (2) the painter's damages would be measured by a restitution concept (value conferred on the lawyer just before the fire) rather than by a reliance concept.

Answer 72

Choice (**B**) is correct. Normally, even where one party knows that the other is making a mistake about a basic assumption, the former's non-disclosure of the relevant fact will not constitute a misrepresentation that the relevant fact does not exist. But the non-disclosure *will* constitute a misrepresentation that the mistaken fact does not exist—and will be grounds for rescission—if it amounts to a "failure to act in good faith and in accordance with reasonable standards of fair dealing." Rest. 2d, §161(b). Where the non-discloser learns of the true fact through improper or questionable means, the court is likely to find a failure to act in good faith. Here, since the horse was the heir's property at the time the trainer secretly timed it in the exercise session, the case is analogous to the Restatement's example of a mining company trespassing on the seller's property to gain mineral-deposit information; a court would therefore likely conclude that the trainer's timing session pushed the entire transaction into the bad-faith category.

(A) is wrong because the trainer's undisclosed experience as a trainer would not alter the general principle that one party's failure to disclose that the other party is making a mistake about a basic assumption does not constitute the sort of misrepresentation that would allow the "innocent" party to rescind. The test is whether the non-discloser's failure to correct the other's mistake constitutes bad faith, and a court would be unlikely to conclude that the non-discloser's failure to disclose his own credentials pushes the entire situation over into the bad-faith column.

(C) is wrong because the party with superior knowledge is normally not required to correct the other party's mistake about even a basic assumption where that assumption is due to the latter's lack of diligence or knowledge — "if the other [party] is indolent, inexperienced or ignorant, or if his judgment is bad or he lacks access to adequate information, his adversary is not generally expected to compensate for these deficiencies. A buyer of property, for example, is not ordinarily expected to disclose circumstances that make the property more valuable than the seller supposes." Rest. 2d, § 161, Comment d.

(D) is wrong because it cites a completely irrelevant fact. The trainer had no obligation to correct what he knew to be the heir's mistake as to a basic assumption, unless the failure to correct amounted to bad faith or a failure to follow reasonable standards of fair dealing. The fact that the mistaken party was angry does not push the more knowledgeable party's lack of disclosure into the bad-faith category, especially where (as here) there is nothing to indicate that the more-knowledgeable party even knew about the other's anger.

Answer 73

Choice (C) is correct. The test for unconscionability is whether in light of the general commercial background and the commercial needs of the particular parties, the contract is so one-sided as to be unconscionable. Here, there are two facts that support an unconscionability claim: (1) a purchase price that was 70% below market; and (2) the landholder's lack of knowledge about timber values. It is not certain that the landowner will prevail with the unconscionability claim as the basis for rescission, but of the four choices it is the only one that could plausibly work for him.

(A) is wrong because the logger has not behaved in bad faith. A buyer who proposes a very below-market price has not thereby behaved in bad faith. In any event, "bad faith" in some abstract sense is not grounds for canceling a transaction to which the other party has agreed, in the absence of misrepresentation or unconscionability.

(B) is wrong because the logger did not make a misrepresentation, which is necessary for equitable estoppel. Equitable estoppel is a doctrine applied by courts of equity to allow one party to rescind when the other misrepresents a fact on which the first party justifiably and detrimentally relies. Here, the landholder would have to show that the logger misrepresented something, and it's not likely that the landholder could make that showing.

(D) is wrong because the landholder can't show coercion. The defense of duress will rarely be successful where one party merely takes economic advantage of the other's pressing need to enter the contract. For the concept of duress to work for the landholder, he would have to argue that the logger coerced him into entering the contract. There are no facts here to show coercion — all the logger did was take advantage of the landholder's scant knowledge about timber values and his pressing need for immediate money, and that's not the same thing as coercion.

CRIMINAL LAW AND PROCEDURE

CRIMINAL LAW QUESTIONS BY TOPIC

Chapter 1

ACTUS REUS AND *MENS REA*

I. *ACTUS REUS*

A. Omissions

1. Existence of legal duty

a. Special relationship

Question 1

Kathy, a two-year-old, became ill with meningitis. Jim and Joan, her parents, were members of a group that believed fervently that if they prayed enough, God would not permit their child to die. Accordingly, they did not seek medical aid for Kathy and refused all offers of such aid. They prayed continuously. Kathy died of the illness within a week.

Jim and Joan are charged with murder in a common-law jurisdiction.

Their best defense to the charge is that

(A) they did not intend to kill or to harm Kathy.

(B) they were pursuing a constitutionally protected religious belief.

(C) Kathy's death was not proximately caused by their conduct.

(D) they neither premeditated nor deliberated.

II. *MENS REA*

A. "Knowingly"

1. Knowledge of attendant circumstances

Question 2

Dart is charged with the statutory offense of "knowingly violating a regulation of the State Alcoholic Beverage Control Board" and specifically that he knowingly violated regulation number 345-90 issued by the State Alcoholic Beverage Control Board. That regulation prohibits the sale of alcoholic beverages to any person under the age of 18 and also prohibits the sale of any alcoholic beverage to a person over the age of 17 and under the age of 22 without the presentation of such person's driver's license or other identification showing the age of the purchaser to be 18 or older.

The evidence showed that Dart was a bartender in a tavern and sold a bottle of beer to a person who was 17 years old and that Dart did not ask for or see the purchaser's driver's license or any other identification.

Which of the following, if found by the jury, would be of the most help to Dart?

(A) The purchaser had a driver's license that falsely showed his age to be 21.

(B) Dart had never been told he was supposed to check identification of persons over 17 and under 22 before selling them alcohol.

(C) Dart did not know that the regulations classified beer as an alcoholic beverage.

(D) Dart mistakenly believed the purchaser to be 24 years old.

2. "Practically certain" standard for unintended effects

Question 3

A man decided to steal a car he saw parked on a hill. When he got in and started the engine, the car began rolling down the hill. The man quickly discovered that the car's brakes did not work. He crashed through the window of a store at the bottom of the hill.

The man was charged with larceny of the car and with the crime of knowingly damaging the store's property. At trial, the judge instructed the jury that if the jury found both that the man was guilty of larceny of the car and that the damage to the store was the result of that larceny, then it should also find him guilty of malicious damage of property.

The man was convicted on both counts. On appeal, he argued that the conviction for malicious damage of property should be reversed because the instruction was not a correct statement of the law.

Should the man's conviction be affirmed?

(A) Yes, because his intent to steal the car provides the necessary mental element.

(B) Yes, because he was committing a felony.

(C) No, because the instruction wrongly described the necessary mental state.

(D) No, because it would violate double jeopardy to convict the man of two crimes for a single act.

B. "Recklessly"

1. Must be aware of risk

Question 4

A state statute provides: "Aggravated robbery of the elderly consists of robbery committed against a victim who is 65 years of age or older." Another state statute provides that when a criminal statute does not designate a necessary mental state, the mental state required is recklessness. A third state statute provides that a person acts recklessly if the person "consciously disregards a substantial and unjustified risk that the material element exists or will result from the person's conduct."

The evidence at a criminal trial showed that the defendant robbed a 66-year-old man outside a senior citizens' center. The defendant testified truthfully that the robbery had occurred on a dark night, that she had had no idea how old the victim was and had not cared how old the victim was, and that she had intended to rob whomever she encountered.

Could the defendant properly be convicted of aggravated robbery of the elderly?

(A) No, because the only evidence on the issue showed that the defendant did not know, nor could she reasonably have known, the victim's age.

(B) No, because there was no evidence of a substantial risk that the victim was age 65 or older.

(C) Yes, because the evidence was clear that the victim was 66 years old, and the statute is designed to protect the elderly.

(D) Yes, because the jury could find that there was no justification for the defendant's conduct and that she was willing to take the risk that the victim was age 65 or older.

C. Strict liability

1. Factors affecting whether offense can be a strict liability offense

Question 5

Which of the following is most likely to be found to be a strict liability offense?

(A) A city ordinance providing for a fine of not more than $200 for shoplifting.

(B) A federal statute making it a felony to possess heroin.

(C) A state statute making it a felony to fail to register a firearm.

(D) A state statute making the sale of adulterated milk a misdemeanor.

D. Vicarious liability

1. Constitutionality

a. Where D has no control over offender

Question 6

Morten was the general manager and chief executive officer of the Woolen Company, a knitting mill.

Morten delegated all operational decision making to Crouse, the supervising manager of the mill. The child labor laws in the jurisdiction provide, "It is a violation of the law for one to employ a person under the age of 17 years for full-time labor." Without Morten's knowledge, Crouse hired a number of 15- and 16-year-olds to work at the mill full time. He did not ask their ages and they did not disclose them. Crouse could have discovered their ages easily by asking for identification, but he did not do so because he was not aware of the law and believed that company policy was to hire young people.

If the statute is interpreted to create strict liability and Morten is convicted of violating it, his contention that his conviction would violate the federal Constitution is

(A) correct, because it is a violation of due process to punish without a voluntary act.

(B) correct, because criminal liability is personal and the Woolen Company is the employer of the children, not Morten.

(C) incorrect, because regulatory offenses are not subject to due process limitations.

(D) incorrect, because he was in a position to exercise control over the hiring of employees for Woolen Company.

CHAPTER 2

RESPONSIBILITY

I. THE INSANITY DEFENSE

A. Tests for insanity

1. M'Naghten "right from wrong" rule

Question 7

A mental patient suffered from the delusion that he was a special agent of God. He frequently experienced hallucinations in the form of hearing divine commands. The mental patient believed that God told him several times that the local Roman Catholic bishop was corrupting the diocese into heresy, and that the bishop should be "done away with." The patient, a devout Catholic, conceived of himself as a religious martyr. He knew that shooting bishops for heresy is against the criminal law. He nevertheless carefully planned how he might kill the bishop. One evening the patient shot the bishop, who was taken to the hospital, where he died two weeks later.

The mental patient told the police he assumed the institutions of society would support the ecclesiastical hierarchy, and he expected to be persecuted for his God-inspired actions. A psychiatrist examined the patient and found that he suffered from schizophrenic psychosis, that in the absence of this psychosis he would not have shot the bishop, and that because of the psychosis the patient found it extremely difficult to determine whether he should obey the specific command that he do away with the bishop or the general commandment "Thou shalt not kill." The patient was charged with murder. If the patient interposes an insanity defense and the jurisdiction in which he is tried has adopted only the *M'Naghten* test of insanity, then the strongest argument for the defense under that test is that

(A) The patient did not know the nature of the act he was performing.

(B) The patient did not know that his act was morally wrong.

(C) The patient did not know the quality of the act he was performing.

(D) The patient's acts were the product of a mental disease.

II. INTOXICATION

A. Voluntary intoxication

Question 8

During an altercation between two men at a company picnic, the victim suffered a knife wound in his abdomen and the defendant was charged with assault and attempted murder. At his trial, the defendant seeks to offer evidence that he had been drinking at the picnic and was highly intoxicated at the time of the altercation.

In a jurisdiction that follows the common-law rules concerning admissibility of evidence of intoxication, the evidence of the defendant's intoxication should be

(A) admitted without limitation.

(B) admitted subject to an instruction that it pertains only to the attempted murder charge.

(C) admitted subject to an instruction that it pertains only to the assault charge.

(D) excluded altogether.

B. Involuntary intoxication

Question 9

A defendant was charged with battery, defined as at common law. At trial, an expert witness testified for the defense that the defendant, an athlete, was under the influence of a performance-enhancing drug at the time he committed the battery and that he would not have done so had he not been so influenced. The defendant asked for an instruction to the effect that if the jury believed that he was influenced by the drug at the time of the crime and would not have committed it otherwise, it had to acquit him.

Which of the following circumstances would most aid the defendant's argument in favor of such an instruction?

(A) Evidence that the defendant is addicted to this drug and has an overwhelming urge to consume it.

(B) Evidence that the defendant's coach, who gave him the drug, told him it was only an aspirin.

(C) Evidence that the victim of the assault taunted the defendant about his use of the drug immediately before the assault.

(D) Expert testimony that a reasonable person, on consuming this drug, may experience uncontrollable rages.

CHAPTER 3
JUSTIFICATION AND EXCUSE

I. DURESS

A. Not available for homicide

Question 10

Smith joined a neighborhood gang. At a gang meeting, as part of the initiation process, the leader ordered Smith to kill Hardy, a member of a rival gang. Smith refused, saying he no longer wanted to be part of the group. The leader, with the approval of the other members, told Smith that he had become too involved with the gang to quit and that they would kill him if he did not accomplish the murder of Hardy. The next day Smith shot Hardy to death while Hardy was sitting on his motorcycle outside a restaurant.

Smith is charged with first-degree murder. First-degree murder is defined in the jurisdiction as the intentional premeditated killing of another. Second-degree murder is all other murder at common law.

If Smith killed Hardy because of the threat to his own life, Smith should be found

(A) not guilty, because of the defense of duress.

(B) not guilty, because of the defense of necessity.

(C) guilty of first-degree murder.

(D) guilty of second-degree murder.

II. SELF-DEFENSE

A. Degree of force

1. Deadly force

Question 11

Ralph and Sam were engaged in a heated discussion over the relative merits of their favorite professional football teams when Ralph said, "You have to be one of the dumbest persons around." Sam slapped Ralph. Ralph drew a knife and stabbed Sam in the stomach. Other persons then stepped in and stopped any further fighting. Despite the pleas of the other persons, Sam refused to go to a hospital or to seek medical treatment. About two hours later, he died as the result of a loss of blood. Ralph was charged with the murder of Sam. At trial, medical evidence established that if Sam had been taken to a hospital, he would have survived.

At the end of the case, Ralph moves for a judgment of acquittal or, in the alternative, for an instruction on the elements of voluntary manslaughter.

The court should

(A) grant the motion for acquittal.

(B) deny the motion for acquittal, but instruct on manslaughter because there is evidence of adequate provocation.

(C) deny both motions, because Ralph failed to retreat.

(D) deny both motions, because malice may be proved by the intentional use of a deadly weapon on a vital part of the body.

B. Effect of mistake as to need for self-defense

1. Reasonable mistake

Question 12

While walking home one evening, Harold, an off-duty police officer, was accosted by Jones, a stranger. Jones had been drinking and mistakenly thought Harold was a man who was having an affair with his wife. Intending to frighten Harold but not to harm him, Jones pulled out a knife, screamed obscenities, and told Harold he was going to kill him. Frightened and reasonably believing Jones was going to kill him and that using deadly force was his only salvation, Harold took out his service revolver and shot and killed Jones. Harold is charged with murder.

Harold's claim of self-defense should be

(A) sustained, because Harold reasonably believed Jones was planning to kill him and that deadly force was required.

(B) sustained, because the killing was in hot blood upon sufficient provocation.

(C) denied, because Jones did not in fact intend to harm Harold and Harold was incorrect in believing that he did.

(D) denied, because Harold was not defending his home and had an obligation to retreat or to repel with less than deadly force.

Question 13

In which of the following situations would the defendant's mistake most likely constitute a defense to the crime charged?

(A) A local ordinance forbids the sale of alcoholic beverages to persons under 18 years of age. Relying on false identification, the defendant sells champagne to a 16-year-old high school student. The defendant is charged with illegal sale of alcoholic beverages.

(B) Mistaking the defendant for a narcotics suspect, an undercover police officer attempts to arrest him. The defendant, unaware that the person who has grabbed him is an officer, hits him and knocks him unconscious. The defendant is charged with assault.

(C) The defendant, aged 23, has sexual intercourse with a 15-year-old prostitute who tells the defendant that she is 18. The defendant is charged with the felony of statutory rape under a statute that makes sexual relations with a child under 16 a felony.

(D) Relying on erroneous advice from his attorney that, if his wife has abandoned him for more than a year, he is free to marry. The defendant remarries and is subsequently charged with bigamy.

III. ENTRAPMENT

A. "Predisposition" test

Question 14

Kingsley was prosecuted for selling cocaine to an undercover police agent. At his trial, he testified that he only sold the drugs to the agent, whom Kingsley knew as "Speedy," because Speedy had told him that he (Speedy) would be killed by fellow gang members unless he supplied them with cocaine. The prosecution did not cross-examine Kingsley. As rebuttal evidence, however, the prosecutor introduced records, over Kingsley's objection, showing that Kingsley had two prior convictions for narcotics-related offenses. The court instructed the jury concerning the defense of entrapment and added, also over Kingsley's objection but in accord with state law, that it should acquit on the ground of entrapment only if it found that the defendant had established the elements of the defense by a preponderance of the evidence. Kingsley was convicted.

On appeal, Kingsley's conviction should be

(A) reversed, because it was an error for the court to admit the evidence of his prior convictions as substantive evidence.

(B) reversed, because it was a violation of due process to impose on the defense a burden of persuasion concerning entrapment.

(C) reversed, for both of the above reasons.

(D) affirmed, because neither of the above reasons constitutes a ground for reversal.

ATTEMPT

I. IMPOSSIBILITY

A. Factual impossibility

1. Not accepted

a. Combined with accomplice liability

Question 15

A woman promised to pay $10,000 to a hit man if he would kill her neighbor in any manner that could not be traced to her. The hit man bought a gun and watched the neighbor's house for an opportunity to shoot him. One evening, unaware of the hit man's presence, the neighbor tripped as he was walking toward his house, falling and hitting his head against the front steps. Believing that the neighbor was unconscious, the hit man ran over to him and shot him twice in the chest.

When the woman learned of the neighbor's death, she paid the hit man $10,000. A medical examiner determined that the neighbor was already dead when the hit man shot him.

The crimes below are listed in descending order of seriousness.

What is the most serious crime for which the woman properly could be convicted?

(A) Murder.

(B) Attempted murder.

(C) Conspiracy.

(D) Solicitation.

b. Robbery cases where V is not intimidated

Question 16

Robert walked into a store that had a check-cashing service and tried to cash a $550 check which was payable to him. The attendant on duty refused to cash the check because Robert did not have two forms of identification, which the store's policies required. Robert, who had no money except for the check and who needed cash to pay for food and a place to sleep, became agitated. He put his hand into his pocket and growled, "Give me the money or I'll start shooting." The attendant, who knew Robert as a neighborhood character. did not believe that he was violent or had a gun. However, because the attendant felt sorry for Robert, he handed over the cash. Robert left the check on the counter and departed. The attendant picked up the check and found that Robert had failed to endorse it.

If Robert is guilty of any crime, he is most likely guilty of

(A) robbery.

(B) attempted robbery.

(C) theft by false pretenses.

(D) larceny by trick.

B. "True legal" impossibility

1. Where intended acts could never have constituted the offense

Question 17

Arnold decided to destroy an old warehouse that he owned because the taxes on the structure exceeded the income that he could receive from it. He crept into the building in the middle of the night with a can of gasoline and a fuse and set the fuse timer for 30 minutes. He then left the building. The fuse failed to ignite, and the building was not harmed.

Arson is defined in this jurisdiction as "The intentional burning of any building or structure of another, without the consent of the owner." Arnold believed, however, that burning one's own building was arson, having been so advised by his lawyer.

Has Arnold committed attempted arson?

(A) Yes, because factual impossibility is no defense.

(B) Yes, because a mistake of law even on the advice of an attorney is no defense.

(C) No, because his mistake negated a necessary mental state.

(D) No, because even if his actions had every consequence he intended, they would not have constituted arson.

CHAPTER 5

CONSPIRACY

I. *MENS REA* FOR CONSPIRACY

A. Intent to commit the object crime

Question 18

Two criminals planned to break into a federal government office to steal food stamps. One of them telephoned the defendant one night and asked whether the defendant wanted to buy some "hot" food stamps. The defendant, who understood that "hot" meant stolen, said, "Sure, bring them right over." The two criminals then successfully executed their scheme. That same night they delivered the food stamps to the defendant, who bought them for $500. The defendant did not ask when or by whom the stamps were stolen. All three were arrested. The two criminals entered guilty pleas in federal court to a charge of larceny in connection with the theft. The defendant was brought to trial in the state court on a charge of conspiracy to steal food stamps.

On the evidence stated, the defendant should be found

(A) guilty, because when a new confederate enters a conspiracy already in progress, he becomes a party to it.

(B) guilty, because he knowingly and willingly aided and abetted the conspiracy and is chargeable as a principal.

(C) not guilty, because although the defendant knew the stamps were stolen, he neither helped to plan nor participated or assisted in the theft.

(D) not guilty, because the two criminals had not been convicted of or charged with conspiracy, and the defendant cannot be guilty of conspiracy by himself.

II. THE CONSPIRATORIAL OBJECTIVE

A. Substantive liability without "aiding and abetting"

Question 19

Two brothers operated an illicit still. They customarily sold to anyone unless they suspected the person of being a revenue agent or an informant. One day when the older brother was at the still alone, he was approached by a man who asked to buy a gallon of liquor. The man was in fact a revenue officer. After the older brother had sold him the liquor, the officer revealed his identity. The older brother grabbed a pistol from his desk drawer, and shot and wounded the officer. The older brother had kept the pistol, unbeknownst to the younger brother, in case someone should try to rob the still. After the shooting, other revenue agents, hiding nearby, overpowered and arrested the older brother.

Shortly thereafter, the younger brother came on the scene. The revenue agents in hiding had been waiting for him. One of them approached him and asked to buy liquor. The younger brother was suspicious and refused to sell. The revenue agents nevertheless arrested him.

The two brothers were charged with conspiracy to violate revenue laws, illegal selling of liquor, and battery of the officer.

On the charge of battery, which statement concerning the two brothers is true?

(A) Neither is guilty.

(B) Both are guilty.

(C) The older brother is guilty but the younger one is not, because the conspiracy had terminated with the arrest of the older one.

(D) The older brother is guilty but the younger one is not, because the older one's act was outside the scope of the conspiracy.

III. PLURALITY

A. Inconsistent disposition

1. Common-law view

Question 20

A young man, who was 18 years old, and his 14-year-old girlfriend, made plans to meet in the young man's apartment to have sexual intercourse, and they then carried out their plan. The girlfriend later told her mother about the incident. The young man was charged with statutory rape and conspiracy to commit statutory rape.

In the jurisdiction, the age of consent is 15, and the law of conspiracy is the same as at common law. The young man was convicted of both charges and given consecutive sentences. On appeal, he contends that his conspiracy conviction should be reversed. That conviction should be

(A) affirmed, because he agreed with his girlfriend to commit the crime.

(B) reversed, because the girlfriend could not be a conspirator to this crime.

(C) reversed, because the crime is one that can only be committed by agreement and thus Wharton's Rule bars conspiracy liability.

(D) reversed, because one cannot conspire with a person too young to consent.

2. Modern/Model Penal Code "unilateral" view

Question 21

A foreign diplomat discovered that a small person could enter a jewelry store by crawling through an air vent. The diplomat became friendly with a woman in a bar who he believed was small enough to crawl through the air vent. Without telling her that he was a diplomat, he explained how she could get into the jewelry store. She agreed to help him burglarize the store. Someone overheard their conversation and reported it to the police. Shortly thereafter, the police arrested the diplomat and the woman. Both were charged with conspiracy to commit burglary.

Before trial, the diplomat moved to dismiss the charge against him on the ground that he was entitled to diplomatic immunity. The court granted his motion. The woman then moved to dismiss the conspiracy charge against her.

The jurisdiction has adopted the Model Penal Code version of conspiracy.

Should the woman's motion to dismiss the conspiracy charge against her be granted?

(A) No, because the diplomat's defense does not negate any element of the crime.

(B) No, because the woman was not aware of the diplomat's status.

(C) Yes, because a conspiracy requires two guilty participants.

(D) Yes, because but for the diplomat's conduct, no conspiracy would have occurred.

IV. PUNISHMENT

A. Cumulative sentencing allowed

Question 22

Jackson and Brannick planned to break into a federal government office to steal food stamps. Jackson telephoned Crowley one night and asked whether Crowley wanted to buy some "hot" food stamps. Crowley, who understood that "hot" meant stolen, said, "Sure, bring them right over." Jackson and Brannick then successfully executed their scheme. That same night they delivered the food stamps to Crowley, who bought them for $500. Crowley did not ask when or by whom the stamps were stolen. All three were arrested. Jackson and Brannick entered guilty pleas in federal court to a charge of larceny in connection with the theft. Crowley was never charged with anything.

If Jackson and Brannick are charged with conspiracy to steal the stamps in the state court, they should, on the evidence stated, be found

(A) not guilty, because the charge of conspiracy is a lesser included offense in the charge of larceny.

(B) not guilty, because to charge them with conspiracy after their conviction of larceny would constitute double jeopardy.

(C) not guilty, because the state prosecution is barred by the prosecution in federal court.

(D) guilty, because they planned and conspired to steal the stamps.

ACCOMPLICE LIABILITY AND SOLICITATION

I. ACCOMPLICES—THE ACT REQUIREMENT

A. Liability for aiding and abetting

1. When words alone are enough

Question 23

A young man met the victim, whom he hated, in the street outside a bar and began to push him around. The defendant, an older man who also hated the victim, stopped to watch and shouted to the young man, "Kill him." The young man stabbed and killed the victim.

On a charge of murdering the victim, the defendant is

(A) not guilty, because his words did not create a "clear and present danger" not already existing.

(B) not guilty, because a person's mere presence and oral encouragement, whether or not he has the requisite intent, will not make him guilty as an accomplice.

(C) guilty, because, with the intent to have the young man kill the victim, the defendant shouted encouragement to the young man.

(D) guilty, because he aided and abetted the murder through his mere presence plus his intent to see the victim killed.

2. Failure to intervene

Question 24

Bill and Chuck hated Vic and agreed to start a fight with Vic and, if the opportunity arose, to kill him. Bill and Chuck met Vic in the street outside a bar and began to push him around. Ray and Tom, who also hated Vic, stopped to watch. Ray threw Bill a knife. Tom, who made no move and said nothing, hoped that Bill would kill Vic with the knife. Chuck held Vic while Bill stabbed and killed him.

On a charge of murdering Vic, Tom is

(A) not guilty, because mere presence, coupled with silent approval and intent, is not sufficient.

(B) not guilty, because he did not tell Bill ahead of time that he hoped Bill would murder Vic.

(C) guilty, because he had a duty to stop the killing and made no attempt to do so.

(D) guilty, because he was present and approved of what occurred.

II. ACCOMPLICES — MENTAL STATE REQUIRED

A. Mental state needed for a crime where reckless indifference suffices

Question 25

In a jurisdiction that has abolished the felony-murder rule, but otherwise follows the common law of murder, a woman and a man, both armed with automatic weapons, went into a bank to rob it. The man ordered all the persons in the bank to lie on the floor. When some were slow to obey, the woman, not intending to hit anyone, fired about 15 rounds into the air. One of these ricocheted off a stone column and struck and killed a customer in the bank.

The woman and the man were charged with murder of the customer. Which of the following is correct?

(A) The woman can be convicted of murder, because she did the act of killing, but the man cannot be convicted of either murder or manslaughter.

(B) Neither can be guilty of murder, but both can be convicted of manslaughter based upon an unintentional homicide.

(C) The woman can be convicted only of manslaughter, but the man cannot be convicted of murder or manslaughter.

(D) Both can be convicted of murder.

III. GUILT OF THE PRINCIPAL

A. Conviction of principal for use of innocent agent

Question 26

Grace, while baby-sitting one night, noticed that Sam, who lived next door, had left his house but that the door did not close completely behind him. Grace said to Roy, the 11-year-old boy she was baby-sitting with, "Let's play a game. You go next door and see if you can find my portable television set, which I lent to Sam, and bring it over here." Grace knew that Sam had a portable television set and Grace planned to keep the set for herself. Roy thought the set belonged to Grace, went next door, found the television set, and carried it out the front door. At that moment, Sam returned home and discovered Roy in his front yard with the television set. Roy explained the "game" he and Grace were playing. Sam took back his television set and called the police.

Grace is

(A) not guilty of larceny or attempted larceny, because Roy did not commit any crime.

(B) not guilty of larceny but guilty of attempted larceny, because she never acquired possession of the television set.

(C) guilty of larceny as an accessory to Roy.

(D) guilty of larceny by the use of an innocent agent.

HOMICIDE AND OTHER CRIMES AGAINST THE PERSON

I. MURDER—GENERALLY

A. Intent-to-kill murder

1. Ill-will unnecessary

Question 27

Suffering from painful and terminal cancer, Willa persuaded Harold, her husband, to kill her to end her misery. As they reminisced about their life together and reaffirmed their love for each other, Harold tried to discourage Willa from giving up. Willa insisted, however, and finally Harold held a gun to her head and killed her.

The most serious degree of criminal homicide of which Harold can be legally convicted is

(A) no degree of criminal homicide.

(B) involuntary manslaughter.

(C) voluntary manslaughter.

(D) murder.

B. Intent-to-do-serious-bodily-injury murder

1. "Serious bodily injury" defined

Question 28

At a party for coworkers at Defendant's home, Victim accused Defendant of making advances toward his wife. Victim and his wife left the party. The next day at work, Defendant saw Victim and struck him on the head with a soft-drink bottle. Victim fell into a coma and died two weeks after the incident.

This jurisdiction defines aggravated assault as an assault with any weapon or dangerous implement and punishes it as a felony. It defines murder as the unlawful killing of a person with malice aforethought or in the course of an independent felony.

Defendant may be found guilty of murder

(A) only if the jury finds that Defendant intended to kill Victim.

(B) only if the jury finds that Defendant did not act in a rage provoked by Victim's accusations.

(C) if the jury finds that Defendant intended either to kill or to inflict serious bodily harm.

(D) if the jury finds that the killing occurred in the course of an aggravated assault.

C. "Reckless indifference to value of human life," i.e. ,"depraved heart" murder

Question 29

Phillips bought a new rifle and wanted to try it out by doing some target shooting. He went out into the country to an area where he had previously hunted. Much to his surprise, he noticed that the area beyond a clearing contained several newly constructed houses that had not been there before. Between the houses there was a small playground where several children were playing. Nevertheless, Phillips nailed a paper target to a tree and went to a point where the tree was between himself and the playground. He then fired several shots at the target. One of the shots missed the target and the tree and hit and killed one of the children in the playground.

Phillips was convicted of murder. He appealed, contending that the evidence was not sufficient to support a conviction of murder.

The appellate court should

(A) affirm the conviction, as the evidence is sufficient to support a conviction of murder.

(B) reverse the conviction and remand for a new trial, because the evidence is not sufficient for murder but will support a conviction of voluntary manslaughter.

(C) reverse the conviction and remand for a new trial, because the evidence is not sufficient for murder but will support a conviction of involuntary manslaughter.

(D) reverse the conviction and order the case dismissed, because the evidence is sufficient only for a finding of negligence and negligence alone cannot support a criminal conviction.

Question 30

Jack, a bank teller, was fired by Morgan, the president of the bank. Jack decided to take revenge against Morgan, but decided against attempting it personally, because he knew Morgan was protected around the clock by bank security guards. Jack knew that Chip had a violent temper and was very jealous. Jack falsely told Chip that Chip's wife, Elsie, was having an affair with Morgan. Enraged, Chip said, "What am I going to do?" Jack said. "If it were my wife, I'd just march into his office and blow his brains out." Chip grabbed a revolver and rushed to the bank. He walked into the bank, carrying the gun in his hand. One of the security guards, believing a holdup was about to occur, shot and killed Chip.

If charged with murder of Chip, Jack should be found

(A) guilty, based upon extreme recklessness.

(B) guilty, based upon transferred intent.

(C) not guilty, because he did not intend for Chip to be shot by the security guard.

(D) not guilty, because he did not shoot Chip and he was not acting in concert with the security guard.

Question 31

A statute in the jurisdiction defines murder in the first degree as knowingly killing another person after deliberation. Deliberation is defined as "cool reflection for any length of time no matter how brief." Murder in the second degree is defined as "all other murder at common law except felony murder." Felony murder is murder in the third degree. Manslaughter is defined by the common law.

At 2 a.m., Duncan held up an all-night liquor store using an assault rifle. During the holdup, two police cars with flashing lights drove up in front of the store. In order to create a situation where the police would hesitate to come into the store (and thus give Duncan a chance to escape out the back) Duncan fired several rounds through the front window of the store. Duncan then ran out the back but upon discovering another police car there, surrendered quietly. One of the shots he fired while in the store struck and killed a burglar who was stealing items from a closed store across the street.

The most serious degree of criminal homicide Duncan is guilty of is

(A) murder in the first degree.

(B) murder in the second degree.

(C) murder in the third degree.

(D) manslaughter.

Question 32

At a party, a defendant and a victim agreed to play a game they called "spin the barrel." The victim took an unloaded revolver, placed one bullet in the barrel, and spun the barrel. The victim then pointed the gun at the defendant's head and pulled the trigger once. The gun did not fire. The defendant then took the gun, pointed it at the victim, spun the barrel, and pulled the trigger once. The gun fired, and the victim fell over dead.

A statute in the jurisdiction defines murder in the first degree as an intentional and premeditated killing or one occurring during the commission of a common-law felony, and murder in the second degree as all other murder at common law. Manslaughter is defined as a killing in the heat of passion upon an adequate legal provocation or a killing caused by gross negligence. The most serious crime for which the defendant can properly be convicted is

(A) murder in the first degree, because the killing was intentional and premeditated and, in any event, occurred during commission of the felony of assault with a deadly weapon.

(B) murder in the second degree, because the defendant's act posed a great threat of serious bodily harm.

(C) manslaughter, because the defendant's act was grossly negligent and reckless.

(D) no crime, because the victim and the defendant voluntarily agreed to play a game and each assumed the risk of death.

Question 33

A motorist, while intoxicated, drove his car through a playground crowded with children just to watch the children run to get out of his way. His car struck one of the children, killing her instantly.

Which of the following is the best theory for finding the motorist guilty of murder?

(A) Transferred intent.

(B) Felony murder, with assault with a deadly weapon as the underlying felony.

(C) Intentional killing, since he knew that the children were there and he deliberately drove his car at them.

(D) Commission of an act highly dangerous to life, without an intent to kill but with disregard of the consequences.

1. Great recklessness required

a. Omission to act

Question 34

Trelawney worked at a day care center run by the Happy Faces Day Care Corporation. At the center, one of the young charges, Smith, often arrived with bruises and welts on his back and legs. A statute in the jurisdiction requires all day care workers to report to the police cases where there is probable cause to suspect child abuse and provides for immediate removal from the home of any suspected child abuse victims. Trelawney was not aware of this statute. Nevertheless, he did report Smith's condition to his supervisor, who advised him to keep quiet about it so the day care center would not get into trouble for defaming a parent. About two weeks after Trelawney first noticed Smith's condition, Smith was beaten to death by his father. Trelawney has been charged with murder in the death of Smith. The evidence at trial disclosed, in addition to the above, that the child had been the victim of beatings by the father for some time, and that these earlier beatings had been responsible for the marks that Trelawney had seen. Smith's mother had been aware of the beatings but had not stopped them because she was herself afraid of Smith's father.

Trelawney's best argument that he is NOT guilty of murder is

(A) he was not aware of the duty-to-report statute.

(B) he lacked the mental state necessary to the commission of the crime.

(C) his omission was not the proximate cause of death.

(D) the day care corporation, rather than Trelawney, was guilty of the omission, which was sanctioned by its supervisory-level agent.

II. FELONY MURDER

A. "Inherently dangerous" felony

1. The list of "inherently dangerous" felonies: arson, burglary, rape, robbery, and kidnapping

Question 35

In which of the following situations is the defendant most likely to be guilty of common-law murder?

(A) During an argument in a bar, a drunk punches the defendant. The defendant, mistakenly believing that the drunk is about to stab him, shoots and kills the drunk.

(B) While committing a robbery of a liquor store, the defendant accidentally drops his revolver, which goes off. The bullet strikes and kills a customer in the store.

(C) While hunting deer, the defendant notices something moving in the bushes. Believing it to be a deer, the defendant fires into the bushes. The bullet strikes and kills another hunter.

(D) In celebration of the Fourth of July, the defendant discharges a pistol within the city limits in violation of a city ordinance. The bullet ricochets off the street and strikes and kills a pedestrian.

2. Requirement that felony be independent of the killing

Question 36

Which of the following is LEAST likely to be the underlying felony in a prosecution for felony murder?

(A) Arson.

(B) Manslaughter.

(C) Attempted rape.

(D) Burglary.

B. Causal relationship

1. Robberies, burglaries and gunfights

a. Victim or police officer kills bystander

Question 37

Steve, in desperate need of money, decided to hold up a local convenience store. Determined not to harm anyone, he carried a toy gun that resembled a real gun. In the store, he pointed the toy gun at the clerk and demanded money. A customer who entered the store and saw the robbery in progress pulled his own gun and fired at Steve. The bullet missed Steve but struck and killed the clerk.

Steve was charged with felony murder.

His best argument for being found NOT guilty is that he

(A) did not intend to kill.

(B) did not commit the robbery because he never acquired any money from the clerk.

(C) did not intend to create any risk of harm.

(D) is not responsible for the acts of the customer.

2. Arson

Question 38

Shore decided to destroy his dilapidated building in order to collect the insurance money. He hired Parsons to burn down the building. Parsons broke into the building and carefully searched it to make sure no one was inside. He failed, however, to see a vagrant asleep in an office closet. He started a fire. The building was destroyed and the vagrant died from burns a week later. Two days after the fire, Shore filed an insurance claim in which he stated that he had no information about the cause of the fire.

If Shore is guilty of felony murder, it is because the vagrant's death occurred in connection with the felony of

(A) arson.

(B) fraud.

(C) conspiracy.

(D) burglary.

C. Accomplice liability of co-felons

1. "In furtherance" test

Question 39

Dawson was charged with felony murder because of his involvement in a bank robbery. The evidence at trial disclosed that Smith invited Dawson to go for a ride in his new car, and after a while asked Dawson to drive. As Smith and Dawson drove around town, Smith explained to Dawson that he planned to rob the bank and that he needed Dawson to drive the getaway car. Dawson agreed to drive to the bank and to wait outside while Smith went in to rob it. As they approached the bank, Dawson began to regret his agreement to help with the robbery. Once there, Smith got out of the car. As Smith went out of sight inside the bank, Dawson drove away and went home. Inside the bank, Smith killed a bank guard who tried to prevent him from leaving with the money. Smith ran outside and, finding that his car and Dawson were gone, ran down an alley. He was apprehended a few blocks away. Dawson later turned himself in after hearing on the radio that Smith had killed the guard.

The jurisdiction has a death penalty that applies to felony murder.

Consistent with the law and the Constitution, the jury may convict Dawson of

(A) felony murder and impose the death penalty.

(B) felony murder but not impose the death penalty.

(C) bank robbery only.

(D) no crime.

III. MANSLAUGHTER

A. **Voluntary manslaughter**

1. **Requirements for voluntary manslaughter, generally**

   a. **Defenses available**

      i. **Voluntary intoxication**

      Question 40

      A state statute defines murder in the first degree as "knowingly causing the death of another person after deliberation upon the matter." Second-degree murder is defined as "knowingly causing the death of another person." Manslaughter is defined as at common law. Deliberation is defined as "cool reflection for any length of time, no matter how brief." The defendant, despondent and angry over losing his job, was contemplating suicide. He took his revolver, went to a bar, and drank until he was very intoxicated. A customer on the next stool was telling the bartender how it was necessary for companies to downsize and become more efficient in order to keep the economy strong. The defendant turned to him and said, "Why don't you shut the hell up." The customer responded, "This is a free country and I can say what I want," all the while shaking his finger at the defendant. The finger-shaking, combined with the defendant's already bad disposition and the alcohol, enraged the defendant. Trembling with fury, he snatched his revolver from his pocket and shot and killed the customer.

      What crime did the defendant commit?

      (A) Manslaughter, because there was a reasonable explanation for his becoming enraged.

      (B) Murder in the first degree, because deliberation can take place in an instant.

      (C) Murder in the first degree, because he contemplated taking a human life before becoming intoxicated.

      (D) Murder in the second degree, because he knowingly caused the customer's death without deliberation.

      ii. **Lack of proximate cause**

      Question 41

      A high school student's teacher told her that she was going to receive a failing grade in history, which would prevent her from graduating. Furious, she reported to the principal that the teacher had fondled her, and the teacher was fired. A year later, still unable to get work because of the scandal, the teacher committed suicide. The student, remorseful, confessed that her accusation had been false.

If the student is charged with manslaughter, her best defense would be that she

(A) committed no act that proximately caused the teacher's death.

(B) did not intend to cause the teacher's death.

(C) did not act with malice.

(D) acted under extreme emotional distress.

B. Involuntary manslaughter

Question 42

A state adopted the following statute: "VEHICULAR MANSLAUGHTER. Whoever in the course of driving a motor vehicle as defined in the Vehicle Code is criminally negligent in driving such vehicle or omits to do anything that is his duty to do and shows a wanton and reckless disregard for the safety of other persons and as a result of such act or omission causes the death of a human being is guilty of vehicular manslaughter."

Vehicular manslaughter is punishable by a sentence of not more than ten years in the state prison or not more than one year in the county jail. A defendant, driving along at a reasonable rate of speed, was distracted by a child carrying a silver balloon. He went through a boulevard stop light and killed a pedestrian. He is charged with vehicular manslaughter. Of the following proposed definitions of criminal negligence, which is most favorable to the defendant?

(A) Criminal negligence is something more than the slight negligence necessary to support a civil action for damages. It means disregard for the consequences of the act and indifference to rights of others.

(B) Any person who drives a motor vehicle should realize the danger to others. If he fails to respond to surrounding circumstances, he is criminally negligent. Criminal negligence involves reckless disregard for the lives or safety of others.

(C) To find the defendant guilty of criminal negligence, the jury must find as a fact that he intentionally did something he should not have done or intentionally failed to do something which he should have done under circumstances that demonstrate a conscious disregard of a known danger that his conduct would produce the result which it did produce.

(D) Criminal negligence is something more than the slight negligence usually required for tort liability. It is something less than the wanton misconduct required for civil liability under the guest statute. It is, of course, conduct that demonstrates something less than the abandoned and malignant heart required for murder.

Question 43

A father was fired from his job. Too proud to apply for unemployment benefits, he used his savings to feed his family. When one of his children became ill, he did not seek medical attention for the child at a state clinic because he did not want to accept what he regarded as charity. Eventually, weakened by malnutrition, the child died as a result of the illness. The father has committed

(A) murder.

(B) involuntary manslaughter.

(C) voluntary manslaughter.

(D) no form of criminal homicide.

IV. ASSAULT AND BATTERY

A. Assault

1. Intent required for

Question 44

Statutes in the jurisdiction define criminal assault as "an attempt to commit a criminal battery" and criminal battery as "causing an offensive touching."

As a defendant was walking down the street, a gust of wind blew off his hat. The defendant reached out, trying to grab his hat, and narrowly missed striking the plaintiff in the face with his hand.

If charged with criminal assault, the defendant should be found

(A) guilty, because he caused the plaintiff to be in apprehension of an offensive touching.

(B) guilty, because he should have realized he might strike someone by reaching out.

(C) not guilty, because he did not intend to hit the plaintiff.

(D) not guilty, because he did not hit the plaintiff.

2. Duty to retreat

Question 45

A defendant was charged with assault and battery in a jurisdiction that followed the "retreat" doctrine, and he pleaded self-defense. At his trial, the evidence established the following: a man and his wife were enjoying a drink at a tavern when the defendant entered and stood near the door. The wife whispered to her husband that the defendant was the man who had insulted her on the street the day before. The husband approached the defendant and said, "Get out of here, or I'll break your nose." The defendant said, "Don't come any closer, or I'll hurt you." When the husband raised his fists menacingly, the defendant pulled a can of pepper spray from his pocket, aimed it at the husband's face, and sprayed. The husband fell to the floor, writhing in pain.

Should the defendant be convicted?

(A) No, because he had no obligation to retreat before resorting to non-deadly force.

(B) No, because there is no obligation to retreat when one is in an occupied structure.

(C) Yes, because he failed to retreat even though there was an opportunity available.

(D) Yes, because the husband did not threaten to use deadly force against him.

V. RAPE

A. Rape defined

1. Without consent

a. Mistake no defense

Question 46

A statute provides: A person commits the crime of rape if he has sexual intercourse with a female, not his wife, without her consent.

Dunbar is charged with the rape of Sally. At trial, Sally testifies to facts sufficient for a jury to find that Dunbar had sexual intercourse with her, that she did not consent, and that the two were not married. Dunbar testifies in his own defense that he believed that Sally had consented to sexual intercourse and that she was his common-law wife.

At the conclusion of the case, the court instructed the jury that in order to find Dunbar guilty of rape, it must find beyond a reasonable doubt that he had sexual intercourse with Sally without her consent.

The court also instructed the jury that it should find the defendant not guilty if it found either that Sally was Dunbar's wife or that Dunbar reasonably believed that Sally had consented to the sexual intercourse, but that the burden of persuasion as to these issues was on the defendant.

The jury found Dunbar guilty, and Dunbar appealed, contending that the court's instructions on the issues of whether Sally was his wife and whether he reasonably believed she had consented violated his constitutional rights.

Dunbar's constitutional rights were

(A) violated by the instructions as to both issues.

(B) violated by the instruction as to whether Sally was his wife, but not violated by the instruction on belief as to consent.

(C) violated by the instruction on belief as to consent, but not violated by the instruction as to whether Sally was his wife.

(D) not violated by either part of the instructions.

VI. KIDNAPPING

A. Definition of kidnapping

1. Asportation

a. M.P.C. "substantial distance" rule

Question 47

A driver stopped at a red light in his home state. A stranger opened the passenger door, got in, and pointed a gun at the driver. The stranger then directed the driver to keep driving. They drove several miles, crossed into a neighboring state, and drove several more miles. When they reached a remote location, the stranger ordered the driver to pull over. The stranger then robbed the driver of his wallet and cash, and ordered him out of the car. The stranger drove off in the driver's car.

The stranger is charged with kidnapping in the neighboring state, which has adopted the Model Penal Code.

Could the stranger properly be convicted of kidnapping in the neighboring state?

(A) Yes, because the driver was transported under threat of force in the neighboring state.

(B) Yes, because the driver in effect paid ransom for his release.

(C) No, because any kidnapping took place in the driver's home state.

(D) No, because the restraint was incidental to the robbery.

2. Confinement must be against V's will

Question 48

John asked Doris to spend a weekend with him at his apartment and promised her they would get married on the following Monday. Doris agreed and also promised John that she would not tell anyone of their plans. Unknown to Doris, John had no intention of marrying her. After Doris came to his apartment, John told Doris he was going for cigarettes. He called Doris's father and told him that he had his daughter and would kill her if he did not receive $100,000. John was arrested on Sunday afternoon when he went to pick up the $100,000. Doris was still at the apartment and knew nothing of John's attempt to get the money.

John is guilty of

(A) kidnapping.

(B) attempted kidnapping.

(C) kidnapping or attempted kidnapping but not both.

(D) neither kidnapping nor attempted kidnapping.

THEFT CRIMES

I. LARCENY

A. Trespassory taking

1. Larceny by trick

a. Intent to steal required

Question 49

Smith asked Jones if he would loan him $500, promising to repay the amount within two weeks. Jones loaned him the $500. The next day Smith took the money to the race track and lost all of it betting on horse races. He then left town for six months. He has not repaid Jones.

Smith has committed

(A) both larceny by trick and obtaining money by false pretenses (although he can only be convicted of one offense).

(B) larceny by trick only.

(C) obtaining money by false pretenses only.

(D) neither larceny by trick nor obtaining money by false pretenses.

B. Personal property

1. No minimum value

Question 50

David entered the county museum at a time when it was open to the public, intending to steal a Picasso etching. Once inside, he took what he thought was the etching from an unlocked display case and concealed it under his coat. However, the etching was a photocopy of an original that had been loaned to another museum. A sign over the display case containing the photocopy said that similar photocopies were available free at the entrance. David did not see the sign.

Burglary in the jurisdiction is defined as "entering a building unlawfully with the intent to commit a crime."

David may be convicted of:

(A) burglary and larceny.

(B) burglary and attempted larceny.

(C) larceny.

(D) larceny and attempted larceny.

C. Intent to steal

1. Claim of right

a. Grievance not enough

Question 51

The defendant worked as the cashier in a restaurant. One night after the restaurant had closed, the defendant discovered that the amount of cash in the cash register did not match the cash register receipt tapes. He took the cash and the tapes, put them in a bag, gave them to the manager of the restaurant, and reported the discrepancy. The manager immediately accused him of taking money from the register and threatened to fire him if he did not make up the difference. The manager placed the bag in the office safe. Angered by what he considered to be an unjust accusation, the defendant waited until the manager left the room and then reached into the still open safe, took the bag containing the cash, and left.

The defendant is guilty of

(A) larceny.

(B) embezzlement.

(C) either larceny or embezzlement but not both.

(D) neither larceny nor embezzlement.

D. Carrying away ("asportation")

Question 52

A man who had become very drunk left a bar and started to walk home. Another patron of the bar, who had observed the man's condition, followed him. The patron saw the man stumble and fall to the ground near an alley. The patron then began to pull out a gun but saw that the man had passed out asleep in the gutter. The patron reached into the man's pocket, grabbed his wallet, and started to walk away. When the patron heard police officers approaching, he dropped the wallet and ran off.

The crimes below are listed in descending order of seriousness.

What is the most serious crime for which the patron properly could be convicted?

(A) Robbery.

(B) Larceny.

(C) Attempted robbery.

(D) Attempted larceny.

E. Concurrence of taking and intent

Question 53

A customer asked to see an expensive watch in a jewelry store. In conversation with the clerk, the customer falsely claimed to be the son of the mayor. When handed the watch, he asked if he could put it on, walk around a bit so he could see how it felt on his wrist, and then briefly step outside to observe it in natural light. The clerk agreed, saying, "I know I can trust someone like you with the merchandise." The customer walked out of the store wearing the watch and never returned. A week later, the clerk was at a gathering when she spotted the customer wearing the watch. She told him that he must either pay for the watch or give it back.

He hissed, "I'll knock your block off if you mess with me." Intimidated, the clerk backed off. The following list of crimes is in descending order of seriousness.

What is the most serious crime the customer committed?

(A) Robbery.

(B) Larceny.

(C) False pretenses.

(D) Embezzlement.

1. Continuing trespass

Question 54

An executive of an accounting firm was fired and told to immediately leave the building where she worked. The executive went home, but she returned that night to retrieve personal items from her office. When she discovered that her key no longer opened a door to the building, she forced the door open and went to her former office. To avoid attracting attention, she did not turn on any lights. In the dark, she knew that she was taking some items that were not hers; she planned to sort these out later and return them.

Upon arriving home, she found that she had taken a record book and some financial papers that belonged to the firm. After thinking it over and becoming angrier over being fired, she burned the book and papers in her fireplace.

The jurisdiction has expanded the crime of burglary to include all buildings.

What crime(s) has the executive committed?

(A) Burglary and larceny.

(B) Burglary, but not larceny.

(C) Larceny, but not burglary.

(D) Neither larceny nor burglary.

II. BURGLARY

A. Breaking

Question 55

Sam told Horace, his neighbor, that he was going away for two weeks and asked Horace to keep an eye on his house. Horace agreed. Sam gave Horace a key to use to check on the house.

Horace decided to have a party in Sam's house. He invited a number of friends. One friend, Lewis, went into Sam's bedroom, took some of Sam's rings, and put them in his pocket.

Which of the following is true?

(A) Horace and Lewis are guilty of burglary.

(B) Horace is guilty of burglary and Lewis is guilty of larceny.

(C) Horace is guilty of trespass and Lewis is guilty of larceny.

(D) Lewis is guilty of larceny and Horace is not guilty of any crime.

B. Entry

Question 56

A woman decided to steal a necklace that belonged to her neighbor. She knew where the neighbor kept the necklace because she had been in the neighbor's house on many occasions when the neighbor had taken off the necklace and put it away in a jewelry box in the bathroom. One night, the woman went to the neighbor's house. The neighbor was away and the house was dark. The woman opened the bathroom window, saw the jewelry box on the counter, and started to climb inside. As her leg cleared the window sill, the neighbor's cat let out a loud screech. Terrified, the woman bolted back outside and fled.

The crimes below are listed in descending order of seriousness. What is the most serious crime committed by the woman?

(A) Burglary.

(B) Attempted burglary.

(C) Attempted larceny.

(D) No crime.

III. ROBBERY

A. Requirement of taking by force or fear

Question 57

A defendant was tried for robbery. The victim and an eyewitness were the only witnesses called to testify. The victim testified that the defendant threatened her with a knife, grabbed her purse, and ran off with it. The eyewitness testified that he saw the defendant grab the victim's purse and run away with it but that he neither saw a knife nor heard any threats. On this evidence, the jury could properly return a verdict of guilty of

(A) robbery only.

(B) larceny only.

(C) either robbery or larceny.

(D) both robbery and larceny.

1. Threat to third person

Question 58

A husband and wife were walking to their car one evening after having seen a movie. As they were passing a dark alleyway, a defendant leaped out brandishing a gun. He pushed the wife against the wall of a nearby building, held the gun to her head, and demanded money from the man. The husband handed over his cash. The defendant grabbed the cash and ran away.

Which of the following, listed in descending order of seriousness, is the most serious crime for which the defendant may be convicted?

(A) Robbery from the husband.

(B) Larceny from the husband.

(C) Assault on the husband and his wife.

(D) Assault on the wife.

IV. ARSON

A. Nature of offense

1. Act posing great risk of fire

a. Failure to take action

i. D's failure to put out fire D started

Question 59

Defendant was upset because he was going to have to close his liquor store due to competition from a discount store in a new shopping mall nearby. In desperation, he decided to set fire to his store to collect the insurance. While looking through the basement for flammable material, he lit a match to read the label on a can. The match burned his finger and, in a reflex action, he dropped the match. It fell into a barrel and ignited some paper. Defendant made no effort to put out the fire but instead left the building. The fire spread and the store was destroyed by fire. Defendant was eventually arrested and indicted for arson.

Defendant is

(A) guilty, if he could have put out the fire before it spread and did not do so because he wanted the building destroyed.

(B) guilty, if he was negligent in starting the fire.

(C) not guilty, because even if he wanted to burn the building there was no concurrence between his *mens rea* and the act of starting the fire.

(D) not guilty, because his starting the fire was the result of a reflex action and not a voluntary act.

CRIMINAL LAW ANSWERS

References to "LaFave" are to Wayne LaFave, *Principles of Criminal Law* (Thomson/West, 2003). References to "LaFave Criminal Law" are to Wayne LaFave, *Criminal Law* Hornbook (3d Ed., West, 2000). References to "M.P.C." are to the *Model Penal Code.*

Answer 1

Choice **(A)** is correct. Murder is the unlawful killing of another person with malice aforethought. "Malice aforethought" is a term of art that encompasses any of several mental states, mainly the intent to kill, the intent to cause serious bodily harm, reckless indifference to the value of human life, and intent to commit one of a specified list of dangerous felonies (e.g., robbery or burglary). The defendants did not possess any of the required mental states. They come closest to having had "reckless indifference to the value of human life" (also known as a "depraved heart"), but most courts hold that that mental state exists only when the defendant *consciously disregards a known risk*—since the defendants honestly (although perhaps unreasonably) believed that God would protect their child, a court would be unlikely to find that they had the requisite conscious disregard of a high risk of harm.

(B) is wrong, because all persons must obey criminal prohibitions requirements of general applicability, even if obeying that rule of law offends the person's religious beliefs. Therefore, even if the defendants' religious beliefs required them to avoid seeking medical assistance for a sick child, they did not have a constitutionally-protected right to do so.

(C) is wrong, because even though Jim and Joan did not take any affirmative action that proximately contributed to Kathy's death, their failure to act did proximately cause the death. Since parents have a duty to *act affirmatively to care for a minor child*, their failure to act could expose them to criminal liability. And their failure to act would be deemed "conduct."

(D) is wrong because not all forms of common-law murder require premeditated or deliberative conduct. For example, a death that is caused by reckless indifference to the value of human life might well occur without any premeditation or deliberative conduct. In any event, the defendants' failure to seek medical attention probably was "premeditated" or "deliberative," in the sense that their rejection of offers of medical help indicates that they devoted conscious thought to whether to seek such help.

Answer 2

Choice **(D)** is correct. Dart did not "knowingly" violate a regulation if he did not think that the requirements of the regulation were required to be applied in the situation he encountered. Dart believed the purchaser was 24 years old; therefore, he did not think that either of the provisions of the regulation applied: the prohibited sale to a purchaser under 18 and the requirement to check identification of a purchaser over the age of 17 and under the age of 22. The fact that his belief was mistaken is not relevant.

(This scenario is different from the "ignorance of the law" scenario incorrectly asserted in Choices (B) and (C). Here, defendant is mistaken about the underlying facts the existence of which trigger the law, not mistaken about what type of conduct the law prohibits. And a defendant who is mistaken about the underlying facts the existence of which make the conduct illegal won't be said to have "knowingly" violated the statute, according to the prevailing interpretation.)

(A) is wrong because, even though the purchaser had a false driver's license showing him to be 21, Dart never asked to see the license, and he was therefore in violation of the part of the regulation requiring that he do so (for purchasers over the age of 17 and under the age of 22). The fact that the purchaser was indeed of age and could purchase the beer does not affect a finding that Dart "knowingly" violated that part of the regulation.

(B) is wrong because it's argument is based on the theory that ignorance of what conduct the law proscribes can be a defense. It can't—as a general principle, if the defendant intended to perform act X, and act X is proscribed by a valid statute, it's not a defense that the defendant didn't know that performing act X was against the law. In other words, the maxim "ignorance of the law is no excuse" is for the most part a true statement.

(C) is wrong for the same reason as (B)—it amounts to a defense based on defendant's ignorance that a particular act (selling beer to a minor) was against the law.

Answer 3

Choice (**C**) is correct. The man could be convicted only if he was found to have "knowingly damag[ed]" the store's property. For the man to have knowingly damaged the property, the jury would have to have found, beyond a reasonable doubt, that he either intended to damage the property, or knew that such damage was *practically certain* to result from his actions. See, e.g., Model Penal Code § 2.02(b)(i): "A person acts knowingly with respect to a material element of an offense when: . . . (ii) if the element involves a result of his conduct, he is aware that it is practically certain that his conduct will cause such a result." Here, the judge's instruction is asserting that the man's mere act of stealing the car constitutes "knowingly damaging" the store's property as long as the damage resulted from the theft. For the instruction to be correct, it would have to require "concurrence"—that is, it would have to require that the guilty act and the guilty state of mind occurred at the same time. The guilty act here is the theft, which occurred at the moment the man started the engine and caused the car to make a small movement. So the guilty state of mind would have to be present at that same moment. At that start-the-engine-and-first-move-the-car moment, the man did not know that damage to the store was "practically certain" to occur, because the man had not yet even discovered that the brakes didn't work (and if the brakes *had* worked, the damage to the store wouldn't have occurred). So the requirement of concurrence wouldn't be satisfied. At the later moment when the man learned the brakes didn't work, he may then have known that damage to the store was practically certain to occur, but by that moment the larceny had already occurred, and it was too late for the requirement of concurrence to be satisfied.

(A) is wrong because it ignores the requirement that the man have "knowingly damaged" the store's property. To have knowingly damaged the store's property, the man would have had to know (at the time he stole the car by causing it to move) that damage to the store was practically certain to occur. And he didn't have that knowledge at that time, as is further described in Choice (C).

(B) is wrong because the man's commission of a felony is not enough to supply the intent necessary for the crime of knowingly damaging the store's property. To have "knowingly" damaged property, the man must have known, at the relevant time, that damage to the property was "practically certain" to occur. And the judge's instruction made the relevant time be the time at which the man committed larceny (since that's the time of the voluntary act, which is what has to have temporal concurrence with the guilty state of mind). As is further described in Choice (C), at the moment of larceny the man did not yet know that damage to the store's property was practically certain.

(D) is wrong because double jeopardy does not preclude conviction of two distinct crimes with separate legal elements. *Blockburger v. United States* (1932).

If one of the two crimes was a *lesser included offense* of the other, then conviction of both would violate double jeopardy. But here, the elements are clearly different. For instance, the mental state needed here for larceny was an intent to steal the property of another (the car) by taking it away, whereas the mental state needed for malicious damage to the store's property was either intent to cause that damage, or knowledge that the damage was practically certain to occur. Therefore, neither crime is defined in a way that makes it a lesser included offense of the other, so double jeopardy doesn't apply.

Answer 4

Choice (D) is correct, because the jury could properly find that the defendant recklessly disregarded the risk that the victim was over 65. The issue is whether the defendant was "reckless" with respect to the risk that the victim was over 65. The statute says that she was reckless if and only if she "consciously disregard[ed] a substantial and unjustified risk" that the victim was over 65. By this formulation, the terms "substantial" and "unjustified" are to be measured objectively: Would a reasonable observer believe that the risk of the victim's being over 65 was substantial and unjustified? A reasonable jury could answer yes on both of these points: (1) a significant portion of the population is over 65, so the risk that any given person would be over 65 could certainly be found to be "substantial" (and a "substantial" risk is not one that is necessarily greater than 50-50, just one that is of non-trivial probability); (2) in view of the utter lack of social utility in the defendant's behavior, the jury could properly conclude that it was "unjustified" for the defendant to run the risk that the victim would be over 65.

But the analysis isn't finished yet: It must also be the case that a reasonable jury could conclude that the defendant "*consciously disregarded*" the risk that the victim was over 65. Here, we know various things about the defendant's mental state with regard to the victim's age, from her testimony and other circumstances: (1) the crime took place outside a senior citizen center; (2) the defendant couldn't really see the victim (and knew she couldn't see him) because of the darkness; (3) the defendant didn't have any opinion or knowledge about the victim's age; and (4) even if the defendant *had* known that the victim was elderly, she still would have robbed him, since she intended to rob "whomever she encountered." Taken together, this package of circumstances and knowledge would justify a reasonable jury in concluding that, beyond a reasonable doubt, the defendant "consciously disregarded" (rather than merely "was unaware of") the risk that the victim was over 65.

(A) is wrong, because it incorrectly incorporates the element of knowledge into the standard. What matters is whether the defendant was "reckless" as to the risk of the victim's being over 65. This choice asserts that the requisite mental state was not present because the defendant neither knew nor "reasonably could have known" the victim's age. But recklessness is defined in the statute as "conscious disregard [of] a substantial and unjustified *risk*" of the element in question. So a person can be reckless as to an element even if the person neither knows nor could reasonably have known that the element was present. Since this choice incorrectly requires at least a possibility that the defendant "knew" the victim's age, it cannot be the best choice.

(B) is wrong, because it is false as a factual matter. In finding the elements of a crime, the jury is entitled to make reasonable inferences. Therefore, in deciding whether there was a "substantial risk" that the victim was over 65, the jury was entitled to make reasonable inferences from the totality of the circumstances as known to the defendant. And that's true even if (as here), there was no direct evidence in the case about just how great the possibility was that this particular victim was over 65. Where a robbery takes place immediately outside of a senior citizens center, and in the dark, it is reasonable for the jury to infer that there is a "substantial risk" that the victim may be over 65. (A risk can be "substantial" even though it has less than a 50/50 chance of eventuating; all that's required is that the risk be more than remote.)

(C) is wrong, because, although it reaches the right result, it does so without incorporating the elements that go into a finding of recklessness. The defendant can be convicted only if the jury finds, beyond a reasonable doubt, that the defendant behaved "recklessly" with regard to the risk that the victim was over 65. Such a finding of recklessness in turn requires that the jury find that the defendant "consciously disregarded a substantial and unjustified risk" that the victim was over 65. This choice relies on two facts, which even when taken together do not establish the required recklessness as to age. First, the fact that the victim was in fact over 65 only very weakly supports the inference that the defendant "consciously disregarded" the risk that the victim was over 65. For instance, given the fact that the episode occurred in the dark, it may never have occurred to the defendant that the victim was over 65. Second, the fact that the statute's purpose was to protect the elderly doesn't have any bearing on whether the defendant had the required conscious disregard of the victim's age. (It's only the defendant's testimony that she knew that she didn't know the victim's age, didn't care about that age, and would have robbed him regardless of his age, that justifies the conclusion that she "consciously disregarded" the age issue; and none of these aspects of the testimony is referred to in this choice.)

Answer 5

Choice (D) is correct, because it most closely fits the classic attributes of a strict liability offense. Note that the question here asks which crime is *most likely* to be found a strict liability offense. Thus, you must consider the elements of a strict liability crime, and see which choice is the best fit. This requires comparing choices, since all of them will have some elements of a strict liability offense.

The purpose of strict liability crimes is to help the prosecution where the mental element will be difficult to prove, or the harm caused is such that it's worth convicting people who lack "guilty minds." Strict liability crimes generally have the following attributes: (1) they are regulatory in nature; (2) they do not involve serious penalties; (3) they involve serious harm to the public; and (4) it's easy to determine the true facts. In fact, statutes regulating food, drugs and misbranded articles, as well as hunting license requirements and the like, are all common forms of valid strict liability statutes. Furthermore, making such a crime a strict liability crime would not be consistent with the purposes of strict liability: that is, to help the prosecution where the mental element will be difficult to prove, or the harm caused is such that it's worth convicting people who lack "guilty minds." (D) involves the sale of adulterated milk. The seriousness of the harm to the public, the fact that it's a misdemeanor instead of a felony, and the difficulty of proof of a "guilty mind" all make it a candidate for strict liability. Since (D) recognizes this, and none of the other choices are as satisfactory, (D) is the best response.

(A) is wrong, because it's highly unlikely shoplifting would be regarded a strict liability crime, even if the statute did not specify which *mens rea* it would require. Strict liability crimes generally have the following attributes: (1) they are regulatory in nature; (2) they do not involve serious penalties; (3) they involve serious harm to the public; and (4) it's easy to determine the true facts. Here, what would make this statute a less-than-perfect candidate for strict liability is that shoplifting is a type of larceny, and thus a court would likely imply a *mens rea* requirement—that is, the intent to steal. Furthermore, shoplifting is not regulatory in nature (e.g., firearms registration, hunting license requirements, and the like), and so is not a likely strict liability offense. Most importantly, another choice—(D)—represents a crime that is a classic strict liability offense.

(B) is wrong, because it's unlikely that possessing heroin, as a felony, would be a strict liability crime, even if the statute did not mention a *mens rea*. Strict liability crimes generally have the following attributes: (1) they are regulatory in nature; (2) they do not involve serious penalties; (3) they involve serious harm to the public; and (4) it's easy to determine the true facts. Here, the crime is a *felony*, so it's unlikely it would be a strict liability crime.

Furthermore, making such a crime a strict liability crime would not be consistent with the purposes of strict liability: that is, to help the prosecution where the mental element will be difficult to prove, or the harm caused is such that it's worth convicting people who lack "guilty minds." A "possession" statute would be aimed at people who knowingly possess heroin. Thus, the statute in Choice (B) would be an unlikely candidate for strict liability, making (B) not the best response.

(C) is wrong, though it's close. Strict liability crimes generally have the following attributes: (1) they are regulatory in nature; (2) they do not involve serious penalties; (3) they involve serious harm to the public; and (4) it's easy to determine the true facts. The thing that makes this choice difficult is that firearms registration statutes are classic strict liability offenses. *However,* the wrinkle here is that it's a *felony*—so with a stiff potential penalty (more than one year in jail), courts will generally read the statute defining the crime so as to include a *mens rea* element.

Answer 6

Choice (**D**) is correct. Crouse was acting as Morten's agent in running Woolen Company. If a defendant principal had no control over whether the agent committed the crime, it might indeed be a violation of the defendant's due process rights for him to be convicted based on a vicarious-liability theory; but where the principal had control over the agent's conduct, vicarious liability does not pose a due process or other constitutional issue. Since Morten (the principal) had the ability to exercise control over how Crouse (the agent) ran the company, he may constitutionally be held responsible for the criminal acts Crouse performed within the scope of his agency.

(A) is wrong because due process allows punishment of an individual (call him "D") who has not committed a voluntary act in some circumstances. For instance, if D had the legal right and responsibility to supervise the behavior of another person (call him "A") and did not do so, it would not be a violation of due process for the state to impose vicarious criminal responsibility on D. Therefore, vicarious criminal liability of an employer or supervisor for failing to prevent the criminal acts of a worker in furtherance of the job does not violate due process.

(B) is incorrect because hiring the children was a criminal act on the part of Crouse. Therefore Morten, who was Crouse's supervisor and could have prevented him from doing such hiring, can be held criminally liable for Crouse's crimes that were committed within the scope of his employment.

(C) is wrong because due process limits *do* apply even to regulatory offenses. For example, some courts have found that imprisonment for unknowingly committing regulatory offenses can violate due process.

Answer 7

Choice (**B**) is correct. Here, it's key to appreciate what the "best" defense will be: It must be the one that correctly states the *M'Naghten* Rule and best corresponds to the facts given. Under *M'Naghten*, a person is legally insane if, at the time of committing the crime, he was acting under a defect of reason, caused by a disease of the mind, such that he either (1) was unable to understand the nature and quality of his actions, OR (2) if he did know the nature and quality, he was unable to know that what he was doing was wrong. The "wrong" referred to here is interpreted by most courts to refer to legally wrong, not morally wrong; however, some courts hold that the inability to know one's act was morally wrong is enough to declare one insane. Under the facts in this question, you aren't told which of these two interpretations the jurisdiction follows—"legal" wrong or "moral" wrong. Since there's a chance it could follow the "moral" wrong option, the mental patient could be exonerated due to insanity: It's clear that he could not appreciate the moral wrongness of his action even though he fully realized it was legally wrong. Since there's a possibility that (B) could exonerate the mental patient, and the other three options do not offer strong defenses, (B) is the best response.

(A) is wrong because although, if it were true, it would exonerate the mental patient under the *M'Naghten* Rule, it does not apply to these facts. As described in (B) above, under *M'Naghten*, a person is legally insane if, at the time of the crime, he was acting under a defect of reason, caused by a disease of the mind, such that he either was unable to understand the nature and quality of his actions, or if he did know the nature and quality, he was not able to know that what he was doing was wrong. Choice (A), in using the term "nature," is referring to the "nature and quality" part of *M'Naghten*; thus, this choice is theoretically correct in stating that the inability to know the nature of the act performed would exonerate the patient. However, the nature of the act performed refers to the physical consequences of the act — for instance, a man who hit his wife in the head with a baseball bat, believing her head was a baseball, would have the requisite inability to understand. This is clearly not applicable to these facts, because the patient knew that shooting the bishop was likely to kill him. Thus, the patient *did* appreciate the nature and quality of his act, and the statement in Choice (A) cannot exonerate him.

(C) is wrong because although, if it were true, it would exonerate the mental patient under the *M'Naghten* Rule, it does not apply to these facts. Choice (C) is essentially a restatement of Choice (A) and is incorrect on the same grounds. Choice (C), in using the term "quality," is referring to the "nature and quality*"* part of *M'Naghten*, which refers to the physical consequences of the act. This is clearly not applicable to these facts, because the mental patient knew that shooting the bishop was likely to kill him, meaning that he appreciated the physical consequences of his act.

(D) is wrong, because it is not a correct statement of the *M'Naghten* Rule — thus, even if the mental patient's acts were the product of a mental disease, as this choice states, he would not be exonerated under *M'Naghten*. The rule (D) states is the Durham Rule, which is followed by a small minority of jurisdictions. Under *M'Naghten*, even if the patient's acts were the product of a mental disease, he wouldn't be exonerated unless he also satisfied either the "nature and quality" or "knowledge of wrong" element, as described in Choice (B) above.

Answer 8

Choice (**A**) is correct, because evidence of intoxication might negate the requisite intent for both crimes. When the defendant is charged with a crime that requires purpose or intent, evidence of voluntary intoxication may be offered to establish that the intoxication may have prevented the defendant from formulating the requisite intent. Each of the crimes charged here requires a particular intent. Assault requires an intent to cause bodily harm. Attempted murder requires an intent to kill. If the defendant was intoxicated, this fact might (would not necessarily, but might) indicate that he could not or did not form the required intent. Therefore, the evidence is relevant to both crimes, and must be admitted unconditionally (i.e., not subject to any limiting instruction).

(B), (C), and (D) are all wrong because they are inconsistent with the above analysis.

Answer 9

Choice (**B**) is correct, because it would support the defense of involuntary intoxication. First, although the defendant ingested a "drug" rather than alcohol, the defense he is raising is commonly called the defense of "intoxication." There are two varieties of intoxication defense, "voluntary intoxication" and "involuntary intoxication." The main circumstance covered by the involuntary intoxication defense is where the intoxication has "resulted from an *innocent* *mistake* by the defendant as to the *character of the substance taken*, as when another person has tricked him into taking the liquor or drugs." LaFave, § 4.10(g), p. 419. That's the case postulated by this choice, since the defendant's honest belief that what he was taking was aspirin would support the conclusion that he did not knowingly take a substance that would intoxicate him.

Once the defendant has established that his intoxication was involuntary, he would be entitled to an acquittal if the intoxication either prevented him from having the required mental state, or deprived him of the ability to *conform his conduct* to the requirements of the law. See, e.g., Model Penal Code § 2.08(4): "Intoxication that (a) is not self-induced [i.e., that is involuntary] . . . is an affirmative defense if by reason of such intoxication the actor at the time of his conduct lacks substantial capacity either to appreciate its criminality [wrongfulness] or to *conform his conduct to the requirements of law*." Here, the other evidence suggests that even if the drug did not negate the defendant's intent to strike another, it may have caused him to lose the ability to conform his conduct to the law (i.e., his ability to resist the urge to strike). So if the defendant can show that his intoxication was involuntary, he will be entitled to the requested instruction.

Choice (A) is wrong, because voluntary intoxication would not be a defense to battery. A defendant who argues that his addiction to a drug has compelled him to consume that drug is nonetheless raising a version of the "voluntary intoxication" defense. If voluntary intoxication directly negates the required mental state, then in most states the defense will work. But battery is a crime that can be committed not only with the mental state of "intent to strike another," but also with the mental state of *recklessness* as to the risk of striking another. LaFave, § 4.10(a), p. 414. Nearly all courts hold that recklessness cannot be negated by voluntary intoxication. Id. Therefore, courts generally hold that voluntary intoxication is no defense to battery.

Choice (C) is wrong, because even if the taunting occurred, this would not make a legal difference. If there were no intoxication issue in the case, the fact that the victim taunted the defendant would not constitute a defense to a battery charge—a person is expected to have enough self-control not to strike another in response to taunts or insults. Nor would the voluntary intoxication defense change this result—as explained in Choice (A), voluntary intoxication is no defense to battery, and that's true whether or not taunting by the victim is also present. Since under this choice there is nothing to make the intoxication involuntary rather than voluntary, the intoxication defense would not work.

Choice (D) is wrong, because uncontrollable rages would not constitute a defense if the intoxication was voluntary. Voluntary intoxication is no defense to battery, and that's true no matter what the effects of the intoxicant are. Why? Because battery can be committed without the intent to strike another, if the defendant *recklessly disregarded* the risk of striking another. The defendant's voluntary taking of an intoxicant that produces rages would not be deemed to negate recklessness (and, indeed, the taking would itself probably *constitute* recklessness). Therefore, the voluntary intoxication would not negate all possible mental states for battery. Since under this choice there is nothing to make the intoxication involuntary rather than voluntary, the intoxication defense would not work.

Answer 10

Choice (**C**) is correct. Smith should be convicted of first-degree murder because he intentionally and with premeditation killed Hardy. From the facts given, it is clear that Smith intended to kill Hardy when he shot him. In addition, since Smith waited a full day between being told to kill Hardy and doing so, he had a reasonable amount of time to deliberate. If a defendant has a reasonable amount of time to think about the decision to kill, the homicide will be considered premeditated, supporting a conviction of murder in the first degree. (As discussed below in the analysis of Choices (A) and (B), no defense applies to this situation.)

(A) is wrong because what we care about is whether the duress defense will work, and it won't, for two reasons. First, duress is generally not allowed as a defense when the defendant is charged with the intentional killing of another—i.e. murder or voluntary manslaughter. Second, Smith was not in imminent danger when he killed Hardy, and duress only applies when the defendant believes that if he does not commit a criminal act he will suffer immediate or imminent death or serious bodily injury. The gang leader certainly made threats that Smith could reasonably believe would have resulted in his own death. However, there is no indication in the facts given that Smith was in fear of *imminent* death; at worst, Smith had fear of some future harm, which is insufficient to support a claim of duress.

(B) is wrong for two reasons. First, necessity is generally not allowed as a defense when the defendant is charged with the intentional killing of another—i.e., murder or voluntary manslaughter. Second, the gang leader's threat was not the type of influence to which the defense of necessity applies. This question illustrates the distinction between the defenses of duress and necessity. Duress is available when the threat of harm comes from the threat or use of force by a third party. Necessity is available when the threat of harm is caused by non-human events—for example, sickness or weather. Since the gang leader is a person, rather than a force of nature, necessity is not a proper defense.

(D) is wrong because, although Smith has met all the elements required for a conviction of second-degree murder, he would be more properly convicted of the more serious first-degree murder, as discussed in (C) above.

Answer 11

Choice (C) is **incorrect**, because the issue of retreat would never even arise. Before the duty to retreat (in a jurisdiction imposing it) could ever make a difference, D would have to be entitled to use deadly force in self-defense. Here, Sam's slap neither caused Ralph serious bodily harm nor gave Ralph reason to fear serious bodily harm in the near future. Therefore, Ralph was not privileged to respond with deadly force. Since the duty to retreat (even if the jurisdiction imposes it) only makes a difference where defendant would otherwise be entitled to use deadly force, Ralph's loss of the motion of acquittal couldn't be due to his "fail[ure] to retreat."

(A), (B), and (D) were all accepted by the examiners as correct answers; none of them is clearly wrong.

Answer 12

Choice (A) is correct. Harold's claim of self-defense is valid because he reasonably believed that his life was in danger and that the use of deadly force was required to save his own life. Self-defense is a complete defense to a charge of murder. For the defense to be applicable, the defendant must believe that he had to use force to protect himself from the danger. The belief must meet both an objective and a subjective test: The defendant must actually believe that he was in danger (subjective) and that belief must be reasonable (objective). Here, we are told that Harold reasonably believed that Jones was going to kill him, so both the objective and subjective tests are satisfied.

Even if a claim of self-defense is valid, the court must still determine if the degree of force used was excessive. One may only use deadly force in self-defense if one reasonably believes that (1) the attack carries the threat of death or serious bodily harm, and (2) nothing less than deadly force is likely to repel the threat. Here, Harold's reasonable belief was that Jones intended to kill him, and Harold believed that deadly force would be his "only salvation," so these two requirements regarding deadly force are satisfied.

The fact that Harold was mistaken (but reasonably so) on this point does not deprive him of the defense of self-defense, or of the right to use deadly force.

(B) is wrong because "provocation" is not an element of self-defense. Self-defense is a complete defense, which applies when a defendant uses a reasonable level of force in response to a reasonably feared threat. Provocation, on the other hand, is a partial defense that applies when a defendant uses force because something causes him to lose self-control. A defense based on provocation would not be used if the defendant was entitled, as Harold is here, to assert the complete defense of self-defense.

(C) is wrong because, when analyzing self-defense claims, it is the defendant's state of mind, not the victim's that is important. The issue is not whether Jones actually intended to harm Harold, but rather whether Harold was reasonable in his (admittedly mistaken) belief that James intended to attack.

(D) is wrong because the obligation to retreat is only triggered when the defendant believes that he may retreat to complete safety. Here, Harold believed that his "only salvation" was the use of deadly force, which indicates that he did not believe that retreat was possible. Even if Harold were mistaken in his belief, so long as that mistake was reasonable, he had no obligation to retreat. (Note: Only some states require that a defendant retreat before using deadly force in self-defense. And, by the way, retreat is *never* required before the use of *non-deadly* force in self-defense.)

Answer 13

Choice (**B**) is correct, because the right to use self-defense is not lost where the defendant makes a reasonable mistake about the need for self-defense on the present occasion. The defense of self-defense states that an individual who is not the aggressor may use such force as reasonably appears necessary to protect himself from the imminent use of unlawful force upon himself. The defendant does not lose the defense merely because he is reasonably mistaken about some aspect of the situation, such as the legality of the force being used against him. So here, the fact that the defendant mistakenly (but not unreasonably, so far as we're aware from the facts) believes that the person who has grabbed him is not privileged to do so, does not cause the defendant to lose the right to use a reasonable level of force to resist the attack.

(A) is wrong, because the offense here is a "public welfare" offense, and is thus probably a strict liability crime. "Public welfare" offenses are generally interpreted to be strict liability offenses, because they generally involve a relatively low penalty and are not regarded by the community as involving significant moral impropriety. Ordinances forbidding the sale of alcohol to minors generally fall into this public welfare-offense category. Consequently, such ordinances typically do not recognize the defense of mistake (even reasonable mistake).

(C) is wrong, because statutory rape is a strict liability crime. Most statutory rape statutes impose strict liability. In particular, they reject the defense of "I didn't know she was underage," precisely because that defense is so often asserted and so hard for the prosecution to rebut.

(D) is wrong, because reliance on mistaken advice about how a crime is defined is not a defense to most crimes, and certainly not to the crime of bigamy. There are crimes that are defined to require a "knowing" violation. (Income-tax evasion falls into this category, for instance.) For such a crime, the fact that the defendant reasonably relied on counsel's advice that the proposed conduct was legal would be a defense.

But most crimes are *not* defined to make knowledge of illegality an element of the crime. Bigamy is like most crimes in this respect—a mistaken (even reasonably mistaken) belief that the law treats abandonment as being the automatic equivalent of a divorce does not furnish a defense. The colloquial expression "ignorance of the law is no excuse" is in fact a generally correct statement, and it's correct on the facts here.

Answer 14

Choice (**D**) is correct. Neither of the reasons listed in (A) and (B) constitutes a ground for reversal.

(A) is wrong because where entrapment is at issue, the prosecution must prove that the defendant was disposed to commit the criminal act prior to first being approached by government agents. This may be done by showing the defendant's prior crimes that are related to or similar to the instant offense. (Generally, evidence of a person's other crimes or acts is inadmissible to show action in conformity with the person's character. FRE 404(b). However, such other-crimes evidence would be admissible here to show that a defense [entrapment] now being asserted lacks merit.)

(B) is wrong because entrapment is an affirmative defense. A defendant may constitutionally be required to bear both the burden of coming forward with some evidence as to an affirmative defense, and the burden of non-persuasion (by a preponderance of the evidence) as to such a defense.

(C) is wrong because neither of the reasons constitutes a ground for reversal, as explained in (A) and (B).

Answer 15

Choice (**B**) is correct. Let's start with *murder*. One theory under which the woman might be guilty of murder would be on an accomplice theory, that she aided and abetted the hit man to commit murder—if he is substantively liable for murder, so is she as his accomplice. But the hit man is *not* guilty of murder, because, as a factual matter, he did not cause the neighbor's death. (You cannot cause the death of another by taking an action after the other is already dead.) Since the hit man is not guilty of murder, the woman can't be guilty of it either, on an accomplice theory. What about the woman's guilt of murder as a principal? Well, she can't be guilty of murder unless she played some causal role in bringing about the death; since the neighbor would have died in exactly the same way if the woman had not recruited the hit man, the woman was not a cause-in-fact of the death, and therefore cannot be liable for murder as a principal.

Now, what about *attempted murder*? The woman has certainly tried to bring about a murder, and has caused various acts to occur towards fulfillment of that objective (e.g., the hit man's lying in wait). So she is guilty of attempted murder unless some special doctrine helps her. The only doctrine that's even of remotely plausible help to her here is the defense of *"factual impossibility"*—can either the woman or the hit man succeed with the argument that "It was impossible for us to kill the neighbor since he was already dead, making an attempted-murder conviction improper"? The answer is no: The factual impossibility defense is *rejected* by virtually every modern court. That is, where a defendant had an intent to commit crime X, and took actions that would have led to a completed crime X if external reality had been as the defendant mistakenly believed it to be, the fact that the defendant could never have succeeded in completing crime X because external reality made such success impossible does not constitute a defense. Clearly the hit man's actions and intent here were such that had the facts been as the hit man believed (i.e., the neighbor was only unconscious, not dead), the hit man would have been guilty of murder. Therefore, the hit man is guilty of attempted murder, and the factual impossibility defense won't work to save him. Since the woman urged the hit man to take the action he took, and since the woman, too, had an intent to kill, she is guilty of attempted murder on an accomplice theory. The factual impossibility defense doesn't work any better for her as an accomplice than it does for the hit man as a principal.

(A) is wrong because the woman cannot be guilty of murder, since the hit man did not in fact cause the neighbor's death. See Choice (B) for further analysis of why this is so.

(C) is wrong because the woman can be convicted of attempted murder, which the question tells us is a more serious crime than conspiracy. (But the woman can also be convicted of conspiracy to commit murder, since she agreed with another to try to bring about a murder.)

(D) is wrong because the woman can be convicted of attempted murder, which the question tells us is a more serious crime than solicitation. (But the woman can also be convicted of solicitation, since she tried to persuade another to commit a crime.)

Answer 16

Choice **(B)** is correct. For a defendant to be convicted of attempting a particular substantive crime, he must have had the intent to do acts which, if they had been carried out, would have resulted in the commission of that crime. Robert pretended to have a gun and threatened to shoot the attendant if he didn't hand over the money. The fact that Robert's threat was not real (because he didn't have a gun) or taken seriously by the attendant would not negate Robert's intent to cause the attendant to be afraid and to cause him to hand over the money. Therefore, it is possible that he would be guilty of attempted robbery. Although this is not entirely clear from the circumstances of the case (he might be able to defend on the grounds that he wasn't trying to take "property of another" since he was giving equal value in the form of the check), of the choices given, this would be the most likely crime he would be guilty of if he were guilty of any crime.

(A) is wrong because property was not taken by using force or by putting the owner in fear. The elements of robbery are that (1) property is taken from the person or presence of the owner; and (2) the taking is accomplished by using force or putting the owner in fear. A threat of harm will suffice. It is not required that the victim be afraid, only that he be placed in apprehension of harm. However, since the attendant knew Robert as a neighborhood character and did not believe that he was violent or had a gun, he was not placed in apprehension of harm under these circumstances.

(C) is wrong because it is required that the person intend to defraud and that his misrepresentation cause the person to whom it was made to pass title to the property. The elements of the crime are: (1) a false representation (2) of a material present or past fact (3) which causes the person to whom it is made (4) to pass title to (5) his property to the misrepresenter who (6) knows that his representation is false, and intends to defraud. Robert pretended to have a gun and threatened to shoot. He did make a misrepresentation (that he had a gun), but he intended to make a transaction, where he would relinquish his check in return for getting money. The fact that he did not endorse the check is not proof of his intent to defraud because it might have been a careless mistake. Also, his misrepresentation did not cause the attendant to give him the cash—the attendant knew he didn't have a gun and merely felt sorry for him.

(D) is wrong because of the same reasons that Robert is not guilty of the crime of false pretenses, as discussed in Choice (C). Robert did not have the intent to defraud nor was the property turned over as a result of the fact that Robert pretended to have a gun and threatened to use it. Larceny by trick differs from false pretenses in that it requires only that possession has passed (not title) and also requires that the property be converted in some way as to deprive its owner of much of its utility. It does not apply in this situation.

Answer 17

Choice (**D**) is correct. Arnold is not guilty of attempted arson because, even if his actions had their desired result, a crime would not have been committed. This question involves the issue of legal impossibility, which applies when a defendant is mistaken about what type of conduct a statute prohibits. A defendant is not guilty of attempt when, had the attempt been successful, no crime would have been committed, regardless of whether the defendant in fact believed he was committing a crime. Although Arnold intended to burn the warehouse down, believing that doing so would be a crime, had everything gone as planned, he still wouldn't have committed arson because the statute specifies that an owner can't be guilty of burning his own building.

(A) is wrong because Arnold's mistake was about the law, not about a fact. Factual impossibility arises when some fact, unknown to the defendant, makes it impossible to complete the crime that the defendant intended to commit. Factual impossibility is not accepted as a defense to attempt. For example, had Arnold believed the warehouse to belong to someone else while it in fact belonged to him, he would be guilty of attempted arson despite the fact that had he succeeded in burning the building, the completed act would not have been arson. In that example Arnold would be guilty of attempt because, had the facts been as he believed them to be, his actions would have been a crime. In the problem itself, Arnold was not mistaken about any material fact. He knew that he owned the warehouse and he knew that he was trying to burn it down. Therefore factual impossibility is not at issue.

(B) is wrong because, while it is true that mistake of law is not a defense, Arnold's mistake wouldn't help him in any event. This "defense" is tried (unsuccessfully) by those who have committed a criminal act, but believed their actions not to have been prohibited, as a means to show they lacked the *mens rea* to commit the crime. Arnold's situation is the opposite. He believed his act to be a crime when it was not prohibited by the statute. Therefore his mistake would not tend to negate the *mens rea* required for arson.

(C) is wrong because mental state is independent of any outside factual or legal circumstances. The mental state required for arson, as defined in the given statute, is intent to burn. Arnold certainly intended to burn the warehouse, so he possessed the required mental state to commit arson.

Answer 18

Choice (**C**) is correct, because it arrives at the correct response, and correctly analyzes the central reason why the defendant will be acquitted. A conspiracy requires an agreement between at least two people, the intent to enter into such an agreement, and the intent to achieve the agreement's unlawful objective. Here, the defendant didn't have the intent to enter into an agreement to steal food stamps, or the intent to steal food stamps; he only had the intent to buy stolen food stamps. As a result, he was not part of a conspiracy to actually steal the food stamps. Had he actually helped to plan or participated in or assisted the theft, these acts would be evidence of his agreement to take part in the conspiracy; but he didn't. Since (C) correctly identifies that the defendant won't be guilty, and the central reason why he'll be exonerated, it's the best response.

(A) is wrong, because although it states a correct rule of law, it does not apply to these facts, and arrives at an incorrect result. Choice (A) states as a given that the defendant has entered the conspiracy. This overlooks the central issue under these facts: whether or not the defendant actually entered the conspiracy. A conspiracy requires an agreement, an intent to enter into such an agreement, and the intent to achieve the agreement's objectives. Here, the defendant did not conspire to actually steal the food stamps, because he didn't intend to steal the food stamps and didn't agree to enter into a plan to effect the stealing of the food stamps. As a result, he can't be liable for conspiracy to steal the food stamps, and thus (A) cannot be the best response.

(B) is wrong, because it mischaracterizes the facts, and arrives at an incorrect result. The defendant did not knowingly and willingly aid and abet the *theft;* he had no agreement regarding the theft, no intent to enter into such an agreement, and no intent to steal the food stamps. He merely agreed to buy stolen goods. As a result, his involvement is too late for him to be considered a conspirator with respect to stealing the food stamps, since he only agreed to buy them once they actually were stolen. Since (B) misstates the facts, and cites an argument which would not, in fact, result in the defendant being convicted, it cannot be the best response.

(D) is wrong, because it misstates the law. A conspiracy requires that there be an agreement between at least two people, but it doesn't require that they all be charged with conspiracy. Beyond the agreement requirement, conspiracy requires that the defendant had intended to enter such an agreement, and had the intent to achieve the agreement's unlawful objective (at common law, a conspiracy could alternatively involve a lawful ultimate act, to be done unlawfully). If you chose this response, you may have mistaken these facts for a situation where there are two parties to a conspiracy who are both charged with conspiracy, and one is acquitted.

The rule under those circumstances is that the other could not be convicted, because it takes at least two guilty parties to have a conspiracy (likewise, with a conspiracy of three persons, all of whom are charged with conspiracy, if two are acquitted, the third would have to be also). However, the facts here state that *only the defendant has been charged*. Thus, this rule would not apply. Since (D) misstates the law, it's not the best response.

Answer 19

Choice (D) is correct. The key here is identifying *the scope of the conspiracy.* Under the facts given, the older brother is clearly liable for battery, since a battery is the unlawful application of force to the person of another, resulting in bodily injury or offensive touching. There was no excuse or justification for his doing so. However, if the conspiracy to make and sell liquor had a scope large enough to include the shooting, the *younger* brother would be liable as well. That's because at common law, one co-conspirator is liable for any substantive crimes committed by another co-conspirator, if the crimes were "within the scope of the conspiracy." But for this purpose, the scope of a conspiracy includes only crimes that (1) were committed in furtherance of the conspiracy's objectives; and (2) were *"natural and probable consequences"* of the conspiracy, viewed from the position of the non-committing conspirator prior to the commission of the crime in question (i.e., crimes the commission of which were reasonably foreseeable to the non-committing conspirator). Here, the goal of the conspiracy was to make and sell liquor, not to shoot revenue agents. There are no facts to suggest that from the younger brother's perspective, shooting revenue agents would or might be part of the liquor-selling venture. (The younger brother is similarly innocent as an aider-and-abetter, since he didn't procure, counsel or command the older brother to shoot the officer; in fact, the younger brother didn't intend for the older brother to shoot the officer at all.)

(A), (B), and (C) are wrong because each is inconsistent with the above analysis.

Answer 20

Choice (B) is correct. Members of a protected class cannot be members of a conspiracy to commit the crime that is designed to protect that class of people. At common law (as the facts specify to be the relevant law of conspiracy) if only two people are involved, the person who is not in the protected class cannot be guilty of criminal conspiracy on the basis of an agreement with a member in the protected class, since there must be at least two members of the conspiracy (this is the "plurality" requirement). The girl, as a 14-year-old, was part of the class the statute was designed to protect, and so could not be a member of a conspiracy to commit the crime. Because, under these facts, there are only two parties involved and one could not be a party to a conspiracy, the man could not be guilty of conspiracy either, under the common-law approach. (Under the Model Penal Code's "unilateral" approach, by contrast, as long as two people agreed to commit a crime, the fact that one was a member of the protected class would not prevent the other from being convicted.)

(A) is wrong because, as described in the analysis of (B) above, where two people are charged with common-law conspiracy and one is not guilty because she is a member of the protected class, the other cannot be guilty either.

(C) is wrong because Wharton's Rule does not apply to offenses that can possibly be committed by a single person. Wharton's Rule says that where an offense is defined so as to necessarily require the guilty participation of more than one person, and no more than the logically minimum number of participants are involved, a charge of conspiracy to commit that offense cannot be brought, because every substantive violation would logically include a conspiracy. (Example: There can be no conspiracy to commit adultery, if just one man and one woman are charged.) However, statutory rape is not an offense so defined that more than one person's knowing and guilty participation is required. It's true that two people must be "involved," but by definition one of those two is a minor who cannot give consent. In other words, the overage person can be (and usually is) the only person guilty of the substantive crime of statutory rape. Therefore, the crime is not the type of "two or more participants logically required" crime to which Wharton's Rule applies.

(D) is wrong because the answer incorrectly states the law. Conspiracy is an agreement between two or more persons to accomplish some criminal or unlawful purpose. The man's conviction should be reversed, but not for the reason given, which is a misstatement of the law. One can conspire with someone too young to consent, provided the person below the age of consent meets the mental requirements for the substantive crime that is the object of the conspiracy. For instance, the man could conspire with the girl to commit robbery or some other crime. What the man could not do is conspire with the girl to commit statutory rape, because the girl is a member of the class the law is intended to protect (as described in the analysis of Choice (B)).

Answer 21

Choice (**A**) is correct. Model Penal Code § 5.03(1), by defining conspiracy as requiring agreement by the defendant but not by two or more persons, adopts a *"unilateral"* interpretation of conspiracy. Where the unilateral interpretation is applied, as long as one defendant meets all requirements for conspiracy (e.g., guilty mind plus agreement with another), that defendant may be convicted even though no other defendant could be convicted. (Furthermore, the woman might lose even in some jurisdictions that follow the common-law *bilateral* interpretation rather than the M.P.C.'s unilateral interpretation. That's because in many such jurisdictions, the fact that one co-conspirator has a special "personal" defense, like the diplomatic immunity here, does not prevent conviction of a co-conspirator who does not benefit from that defense. See LaFave, Criminal Law, § 6.5(g).)

(B) is wrong because it cites an irrelevant fact. The woman would not be entitled to dismissal even if she knew of the diplomat's status, because the diplomat's capacity to be convicted of the crime would be irrelevant in a jurisdiction that adopted a unilateral view of conspiracy. And the M.P.C. adopts a unilateral view.

(C) is wrong because it misstates the M.P.C.'s definition of conspiracy. Section 5.03(1) of the M.P.C., which defines conspiracy, does not require that there be two guilty participants. All that the M.P.C. requires is that (1) there be two persons who appear to agree to pursue a criminal objective, and (2) the particular defendant being prosecuted have a guilty mind. So if X and Y appear to agree to a conspiratorial objective, the fact that Y has some personal defense (such as the diplomatic immunity here) does not prevent X from being convicted, as long as X meets all the requirements for conspiracy (e.g., a guilty mind, and absence of any personal defense).

(D) is wrong because the "but-for" factor that it cites is irrelevant. The woman can properly be convicted because, regardless of the diplomat's immunity, she agreed to commit a crime. See M.P.C. § 5.03(1). The fact that the diplomat's conduct was a but-for cause of the conspiracy is irrelevant. (If the diplomat had been acting as an agent of the government, and in order to get a conviction for the government had persuaded the woman to agree to a crime that she would not have agreed to without the diplomat's suggestion, then the woman might have a valid *entrapment* defense. But there is no suggestion in these facts that that's what happened here.)

Answer 22

Choice **(D)** is correct. Conspiracy is a distinct offense which is *not* merged into the crime which is the object of the conspiracy. A conspiracy requires an agreement between at least two people, an intent to enter into such an agreement, and the intent to achieve the agreement's unlawful objective (or, at common law, a lawful ultimate act to be done unlawfully). The conspiracy is complete once the agreement is entered into, at common law (the modern rule is to require an act in furtherance of the conspiracy); it does not encompass the ultimate act.

(A) is wrong for the same reason that (D) is correct: Conspiracy is a distinct offense that is *not* merged into the crime which is the object of the conspiracy. If you chose this response, it could be because you confused conspiracy with attempt. Attempt is merged into the completed crime, so that the accused can only be convicted of attempt OR the completed offense, but not both. But conspiracy is a separate and distinct offense, which doesn't merge into the completed crime.

(B) is wrong because it misstates the law, and arrives at an incorrect result: In fact, conspiracy is a separate and distinct offense from the crime which is the object of the conspiracy. Thus, being tried for it after pleading guilty to larceny would not be considered double jeopardy. Double jeopardy only attaches when two prosecutions meet two requirements: They must be based on the same conduct, AND proof of the facts needed for one must necessarily include proof of all facts needed for the other. Conspiracy focuses on the agreement aspect, and is complete once the agreement is made; larceny requires the actual larcenous taking of the stamps (without requiring any prior agreement between the participants).

(C) is wrong because it misstates the law. The facts in this problem suggest that the latter prosecution would not be barred. A state prosecution after a federal prosecution would be forbidden under two circumstances: double jeopardy, or a kind of collateral estoppel because the earlier, federal prosecution was resolved in defendant's favor due to a factual finding that would bar a later conviction in state court (e.g., an alibi was upheld). Neither of these exist under these facts. Larceny and conspiracy are two separate and distinct crimes, and the proof that would be necessary for them would be largely different. Double jeopardy would not attach to the federal larceny conviction (see the discussion of this point in Choice (B) above), and there is nothing under these facts to suggest that resolution of any factual issue precludes conviction in the later state prosecution.

Answer 23

Choice **(C)** is correct. One is liable for a crime, as an accomplice, if he procures, counsels, or commands the commission of that crime. Naturally, this would require that he intend that the crime be committed. Here, the defendant's liability would rest on his statement "Kill him." Intent could be established by presumption, since a person of sufficient intelligence to understand the nature of his actions is presumed to intend the natural and probable consequences of his actions. Here, the defendant encouraged the young man to kill the victim, so it could be said that the defendant intended that the young man kill the victim. Furthermore, his statement would be considered counseling or commanding the commission of the crime of murder. As a result, the defendant will be liable as an accomplice for murder.

(A) is wrong because it arrives at the wrong result, and it applies the wrong rule to these facts. The "clear and present danger" test is the test used to determine the validity, for First Amendment purposes, of a law designed to forbid advocacy of unlawful conduct. It provides that advocacy can only be forbidden if its aim is to produce or incite imminent illegal action, and it is likely to produce or incite such action. Whether the defendant's speech is protected by the First Amendment is not the issue here; instead, the issue is whether the defendant can be held liable for murder for encouraging the young man to kill the victim. Since (A) does not apply the correct rule, and, beyond that, arrives at the wrong result, it's wrong.

(B) is wrong because it's too broad. Given the requisite intent, "mere presence and oral encouragement" *are* sufficient to make the defendant guilty as an accomplice. An accomplice is one who procures, counsels, or commands the commission of a crime. Choice (B) asserts that "mere presence and oral encouragement" are insufficient to make one liable as an accomplice; however, under the definition of accomplice, encouragement would constitute "counseling" or "commanding," and so, if accompanied by an intent that the person being encouraged commit the underlying crime, would create accomplice liability.

(D) is wrong because although it arrives at the correct result, the reasoning it gives would not be sufficient to hold the defendant liable for murder. It's not the defendant's presence and his intent that make him liable, as (D) suggests—rather, it's his act of encouraging the killing that makes him liable. Mere presence wouldn't make him liable, since, in general, one is not obligated to act affirmatively for the benefit of others; furthermore, his intent is not sufficient to create liability, since intent is merely a state of mind and, with nothing more, it's not criminal (until it produces action to bring about the desired results). It's the defendant's active encouragement—"Kill him"—that makes him liable.

Answer 24

Choice (**A**) is correct. Under these facts, Tom has done nothing to subject himself to liability. The most promising element for liability is the fact that he *hoped* Bill would kill Vic. However, even though he hoped that Bill would kill Vic, all that demonstrates is that Tom had a state of mind that, with nothing more, is not criminal. His failure to aid Vic would not subject him to liability because the law imposes no general duty to act affirmatively for the benefit of others, in the absence of some special pre-existing relationship between the defendant and the victim (e.g., defendant's negligence created the peril, or a special relationship mandates affirmative acts [parent and child, for instance]). Liability for murder would have required that Tom do *something*—either helping to plan Vic's murder, or aiding it in some other way—to make him liable under a conspiracy or accomplice theory. Under these facts, no such action exists.

(B) is wrong because although it arrives at the correct result, the reasoning it offers would not exonerate Tom. This choice suggests that Tom could only be liable if he told Bill ahead of time that he hoped Bill would murder Vic. This is both too narrow and too broad a statement of the applicable law. First, merely stating "I hope you kill Vic" might not be enough to make Tom liable, if he didn't plan the killing with Bill (conspiracy) or aid in any way (accomplice liability). (If the "I hope you kill . . ." statement amounted to active encouragement, and helped bring about the killing, that might be enough for accomplice liability; but a mere statement on a prior occasion, without any showing of a causal link to the actual killing, wouldn't be enough.) Second, prior encouragement isn't the only way Tom could be liable; had he encouraged Bill at the scene of the crime (e.g., by shouting "Kill him" at the pivotal moment), he would be liable for murder as an accomplice.

(C) is wrong because it arrives at an incorrect result, and misstates the law. As a general rule, an individual has no duty to act affirmatively for the benefit of others. Although certain relationships between the defendant and the one in peril change this (e.g., defendant's negligence created the peril, or a special relationship mandates affirmative acts [parent-child, for instance]), no such facts exist in this question. Since no duty to aid exists, and Tom did nothing to plan or aid in committing the killing, he cannot be liable for murder.

(D) is wrong because it arrives at an incorrect result, and misstates the law. In order to be found guilty of murder, Tom would have to undertake some type of activity—be it planning or aiding in the killing. Mere presence and tacit approval are insufficient for liability as a conspirator or as an accomplice. Presence is not sufficient for liability, since, as a general rule, the law imposes no duty to act affirmatively for the benefit of others. Even coupling presence with tacit approval is insufficient, since approval is a mere state of mind which, with nothing more, is not criminal.

Answer 25

Choice **(D)** is correct, because the woman acted with a reckless indifference and because the man was her accomplice.

Let's first discuss the woman's guilt. The mental state for murder, in a jurisdiction that has abolished the felony-murder rule, is any of the following: (1) intent to kill; (2) intent to inflict great bodily harm; or a (3) reckless indifference to an unjustifiably high risk to human life.

Here, a court would probably (though not certainly) hold that a person who (1) brings automatic weapons with her to a bank robbery; and then (2) fires those weapons into the ceiling, with lots of people around, meets the standard for "reckless indifference to an unjustifiably high risk to life." Bear in mind that (1) the woman's conduct is of as little redeeming social utility as it can be (so that a lower degree of risk to others should suffice for "reckless indifference" than if the woman were pursuing some socially-worthwhile goal, e.g., speeding to the hospital with her deathly ill child); and (2) any reasonable person ought to know of the large danger of ricocheting bullets, especially where the bullets are fired in a bank containing stone columns and lots of people. Since the woman has proximately caused a death, while satisfying one of the mental-state requirements for common-law murder, she's guilty of murder.

Now, on to the man: A person who intentionally aids, abets or encourages another to commit substantive crime X is himself guilty of substantive crime X as an accomplice. The accomplice needs, however, to have the (or a) mental state required for crime X. So here, the question is whether the man can be guilty of murder as an accomplice to the woman's commission of murder.

If a court is willing to find that the woman had the "reckless indifference" mental state that will suffice for murder, the court will probably also find that the man had that mental state. (This is not certain—the man might have strongly believed that neither he nor the woman would fire the weapons, in which case it wouldn't be logically inconsistent for the court to conclude that the woman, by not only carrying but firing her automatic weapon, met the reckless-indifference standard, but that the man didn't. *Probably*, however, the court would conclude that one who carries automatic weapons into a bank robbery, and who accompanies a co-felon who he knows is also carrying such weapons, has behaved with the requisite reckless indifference to the great danger of death from the joint conduct. In that event the man would be found to meet the reckless-indifference standard.)

There is the further question of whether the man meets the *actus reus* requirement for reckless-indifference murder. The man has clearly given knowing assistance to the woman's commission of this recklessly-dangerous armed bank robbery. Therefore, his assistance to her, in what we've concluded is murder by her, will also be deemed to be the *actus reus* for accomplice liability in that murder by her. Since he's satisfied both the mental-state requirement for reckless-indifference murder and the *actus reus* requirement for reckless-indifference murder (knowing assistance to a person who herself commits reckless-indifference murder), the man is guilty of being an accomplice to the substantive crime of reckless-indifference murder. That makes him, too, guilty of the substantive crime of reckless-indifference murder. Whew!

(A), (B), and (C) are all wrong, because each of them fails to recognize at least one defendant's guilt of murder.

Answer 26

Choice **(D)** is correct. Larceny is the: (1) taking, and (2) carrying away, of the (3) tangible property, (4) of another, (5) by trespass or without consent, (6) with the intent to steal it. Anyone who intentionally acts through an innocent agent is classified as a principal. Grace is guilty of larceny, even though she herself did not take the television set. She knowingly created a mistake of fact in the mind of Roy, and intentionally induced him to commit acts satisfying the first five elements of the crime of larceny. Since Roy was an innocent agent who acted at the behest of Grace, Roy's acts will be ascribed to Grace as if she had done them herself. Grace herself satisfies the sixth requirement (intent to steal the item). Therefore, Grace is guilty of larceny.

(A) is wrong because as an innocent agent of Grace's, Roy's actions are imputed to Grace. It's true that Roy did not commit any crime. But as an innocent agent, his acts are ascribed to the principal. Therefore, his own innocence is irrelevant to whether Grace is guilty. See the analysis in Choice (D) above.

(B) is wrong because Grace's innocent agent acquired possession. When a person intentionally causes an innocent agent to perform an act, the agent's act is attributed to the principal. So once Roy took and carried away possession of the set, this act is ascribed to Grace as if she had done it herself. Therefore, it's not accurate to say, as this choice does, that Grace "never acquired possession."

(C) is wrong because Roy was not guilty of larceny, and Grace is a principal, not an accessory. A principal is one who with the requisite mental state, actually engages in the act or omission that causes the criminal result. An accessory is one who aids or counsels a principal in the completion of a crime. If Roy had been a principal, then Grace would probably have been an accessory. In this case, however, Grace is not guilty as an accessory, because she was the principal. Roy acted without criminal intent after being misled by Grace. Therefore (as explained more fully in the analysis of Choice (D) above), Roy was an innocent agent and Grace a principal in this crime.

Answer 27

Choice **(D)** is correct. Intent-to-kill murder requires that the defendant have the desire to bring about the death of another. Harold intended to kill Willa, held a gun to her head, and succeeded in killing her. He is guilty of murder.

There is no exception in the doctrine of common-law murder for "mercy killings."

Choices (A), (B), and (C) are wrong for the reason that (D) is right—this is murder.

Answer 28

Choice (C) is correct. Defendant can be convicted of murder if he intended either to kill or inflict serious bodily harm when he hit Victim with the soft-drink bottle. Murder is the unlawful killing of another person with malice aforethought. "Malice aforethought" is a term of art that encompasses several mental states, including the intent to kill and the intent to cause serious bodily harm. Therefore, if the jury finds that Defendant intended either to kill Victim or to inflict serious bodily harm to Victim, then Defendant would have had the requisite *mens rea* to be found guilty of murder.

(A) is wrong because it is too restrictive. While it is true that intent to kill is one mental state that can support a murder conviction, it is not the only one. As discussed above, several other mental states are included in "malice aforethought." Since Choice (A) states that "Defendant may be found guilty of murder *only* if the jury finds that Defendant intended to kill Victim" it improperly omits the possibility of conviction based on a different mental state.

(B) is wrong because it is an incomplete statement of the "heat of passion" defense. A defendant who acted in the heat of passion when he killed may be entitled to have his crime reduced from murder to voluntary manslaughter. But "heat of passion" will result in a conviction of voluntary manslaughter rather than murder only if four conditions have been met: (1) the defendant acted in response to a provocation that would have caused a reasonable person to lose self-control (an objective test); (2) the defendant did, in fact, act while in the "heat of passion" (a subjective test); (3) there was no time between the provocation and the act for a reasonable person to "cool off" (objective); and (4) the defendant did not, in fact, "cool off" (subjective). Here, even if the jury were to accept that Defendant acted in a rage brought on by Victim's provocation, only the subjective elements would have been proven. Defendant would still have to show that Victim's accusations were enough to make a *reasonable person* lose his self-control (unlikely) and that the full day that elapsed between the accusations and the attack was an insufficient amount of time for a *reasonable person* to cool off (very unlikely). Since Choice (B) omits the subjective elements of the partial defense, it is an incorrect statement of the law.

(D) is wrong because it is an inaccurate application of the felony-murder rule. The felony-murder rule states that if a defendant, in the process of committing certain dangerous felonies, kills another person, he is guilty of murder. The *mens rea* required to commit the underlying felony is used to supply the mental state required for murder. However, in order for the felony-murder rule to apply, the felony must be *independent* of the killing. In this case, Defendant's aggravated assault with the soft-drink bottle was a lesser included offense in the homicide, and can therefore not be used as the underlying felony for purposes of the felony-murder rule.

Answer 29

Choice (A) is correct. A defendant is guilty of murder if he has acted with reckless indifference to the value of human life. (Cf. MPC § 201.2(1)(b).) Phillips deliberately shot in the direction of the playground. Although Phillips did not intend to shoot into the playground (he was aiming for the target), the fact that he put the target in between himself and the playground (where several children were playing) is enough to show that he had a reckless indifference to human life (sometimes called a "depraved heart").

(B) is wrong because, in order to be guilty of voluntary manslaughter, it is required that the defendant either (1) acted in response to a provocation that would be sufficient to cause a reasonable person to lose his self-control; or (2) made an unreasonable mistake about the need for self-defense. The facts presented here don't fall within either of these scenarios.

(C) is wrong because Phillips' intent was more than just reckless. Shooting into the path of a small playground demonstrates an extreme indifference to the value of human life, which will suffice for murder (as further discussed in (A) above). Therefore, this choice's statement that the evidence is "not sufficient for murder" is incorrect.

(D) is wrong because it falsely asserts that the evidence supports only a finding of negligence. In fact, as is explained in (A), the evidence supports a finding of extreme indifference to the value of human life, which will in turn support a murder conviction.

Answer 30

Choice (**A**) is correct. Jack should be found guilty of Chip's murder because he knowingly put Chip into a situation where Chip was very likely to be shot. Murder is the unlawful killing of another person with malice aforethought. "Malice aforethought" includes several mental states, including reckless indifference to the value of human life. Reckless indifference tends to be found in situations where the defendant was aware of a very high risk of death to the victim. Jack was so aware of the risk in this case that he was fearful to go after Morgan himself. Jack manifested reckless indifference to the value of Chip's life by sending Chip into the bank, gun in hand, knowing that the bank was staffed with armed security guards. Further, Jack's encouragement was the legal cause of Chip's death because the risk he created (getting shot by a security guard) was the actual means of death.

(B) is wrong because it is a misapplication of transferred intent. When a defendant intends a harmful result to one victim, but, while trying to affect that harm, causes similar harm to a different victim, the doctrine of transferred intent allows the intent to harm the intended victim to be transferred to the harming of the actual victim. However, transferred intent only applies when the actual result of an act only differs from the intended result in that a different victim was harmed. That is, the same action as intended causes the same type of harm as intended, but to a victim that was unintended. Here, Jack intended that Chip would fire a gun, killing Morgan. Thus, Jack's intent can only be transferred to a victim shot by Chip. Since it was the security guard who shot Chip, the act was fundamentally different from the one intended, so the doctrine of transferred intent will not apply.

(C) is wrong because intent is not always required to support a murder conviction. As discussed above, reckless disregard for the value of the victim's life is a sufficient mental state for murder. Although Jack did not intend for the security guard to shoot and kill Chip, he was certainly aware of the high risk that it would happen.

(D) is wrong because Jack's creation of the very high risk to Chip's life is sufficient to find him guilty of murder. When the *mens rea* for murder is reckless indifference to the value of the victim's life, the defendant needs neither to personally kill the victim nor be an accomplice of the killer—so long as Jack created a situation in which he knew Chip would be at an unreasonably high risk of death, he can be convicted of murder.

Answer 31

Choice (**B**) is correct. Duncan has committed murder in the second degree because he fired a gun toward an area where he knew others were located. Murder at common law is the unlawful killing of another with "malice aforethought," which includes, among other states of mind, a reckless indifference to the value of human life (sometimes called a "depraved heart"). Duncan, knowing that police officers were stationed outside the front of the store, fired several times through the front window. In doing so, he demonstrated a disregard for the lives of those standing outside since the gunfire created an obvious lethal risk to them. The fact that the person actually killed by one of the shots was unknown to Duncan is irrelevant since the "depraved heart" mental state does not require any particular victim to be in the defendant's mind at the time of his act.

(A) is wrong because Duncan lacked the required mental state to commit first-degree murder. The statute that defines first-degree murder in this jurisdiction requires that the defendant "knowingly" kill another person. "Knowingly" would be interpreted to require that the actor either intend a particular result, or be aware that his act will almost certainly cause that result. When Duncan fired his gun, he did not specifically intend either to hit or to kill anyone, or know with near-certainty that someone would be killed. Thus, it cannot be said that Duncan knowingly killed another, as required for first-degree murder.

(C) is wrong because felony murder is not the most serious degree of homicide of which Duncan is guilty. As discussed above, Duncan is guilty of murder in the second degree, which is a more serious crime than felony murder, which is defined here as murder in the third degree. Duncan is guilty of felony murder because, during the course of committing robbery (an independent, dangerous felony), Duncan caused the death of another.

(D) is wrong because, as discussed above, Duncan is guilty of the more serious crime of second-degree murder. Duncan would be guilty of involuntary manslaughter because firing a gun toward a known group of people was grossly negligent, risking serious bodily harm or death to those standing outside.

Answer 32

Choice (**B**) is correct, because the defendant's actions fit the requirements for the "reckless indifference to the value of human life" variety of murder, which is second-degree murder in this jurisdiction.

The act here cannot be first-degree murder. It is not "intentional and premeditated killing" murder, because there's no evidence that the defendant desired to kill the victim. And it can't be "killing during the commission of a common-law felony" murder, because assault or battery are generally deemed to be lesser included offenses that can't be bootstrapped into felony-murder. (Indeed, it's not even clear that assault or battery existed here, since there's not much evidence that the defendant had any of the possible mental states for assault or battery — she apparently didn't desire to hurt the victim or even cause him fear of bodily harm.)

On the other hand, the facts do fit the definition of murder of the "extreme indifference to the value of human life" (or "depraved heart") variety. The defendant has intentionally or recklessly disregarded what she knows is an extremely high risk of death or serious bodily harm to the victim. Since extreme-indifference murder is a form of common-law murder, and since it doesn't fall within one of the two types of first-degree murder in this jurisdiction (intent-to-kill and in-the-course-of-a-common-law-felony), it's second degree.

(A) is wrong, because the defendant's actions do not fit the given definition for first-degree murder. See the analysis of Choice (B) for why this is so.

(C) is wrong, because the defendant's actions match the requirements for second-degree murder, a more serious crime than manslaughter. The analysis in Choice (B) shows why the defendant qualifies for extreme-indifference second-degree murder.

(D) is wrong, because assumption of risk is a defense in torts but normally not in criminal law. Consent of the victim is no defense in criminal law unless the consent negates an element of the offense. The victim's consent does not negate an element of the crime of murder, because murder is defined as a killing under any of several mental states, and none of the versions of murder is defined to include lack of the victim's consent as an element of the crime. (For instance, if husband kills his pain-ridden dying wife at her urging, her consent would not be a defense to a "mercy killing" murder prosecution of husband.)

Answer 33

Choice **(D)** is correct. The key here is that the defendant had no intent to kill or cause a serious injury. Murder is an unlawful killing with malice aforethought. "Malice aforethought" is a term of art, and can be satisfied by various mental states: (1) intent to kill; (2) intent to do serious bodily injury; (3) intent to commit one of various dangerous felonies (producing felony murder); or (4) acting with reckless disregard of the value of human life (producing "depraved-heart" murder). Depraved heart murder occurs where Defendant engages in conduct which, at the least, a reasonable person would realize creates an extremely high degree of risk to human life, and which results in death. Choice (D), with its language "without an intent to kill but with disregard of the consequences," coupled with "an act highly dangerous to life," essentially reflects this rule.

(A) is wrong because it misapplies the doctrine of transferred intent. The transferred intent doctrine applies where a person intending to commit a crime against one person accidentally commits a crime against another. His intent will be "transferred" from the person he intended to harm to the person he actually harmed (e.g., D tries to shoot A to death and instead kills B). What's missing under these facts is the defendant's intent to kill in the first place—he doesn't intend to kill or even injure anyone. If anything, he intends for the children to run out of the way and not be injured. Since he has no criminal intent, it can't be transferred.

(B) is wrong because the felony is not sufficiently "independent" from homicide to be covered by the felony-murder rule. The felony-murder rule is as follows: Where a killing is committed during the course of certain "dangerous" felonies (or an attempt at such), the homicide is considered murder, even though there is no intent to kill or cause great bodily harm. Such "dangerous" felonies typically include rape, kidnapping, mayhem, arson, robbery, and burglary. The dangerous felony must be reasonably "independent" of the killing. Assault with a deadly weapon would itself require an intent to do serious bodily harm or to kill, so the "independence" required by the felony- murder rule would be lacking.

(C) is wrong because the reasoning it states is insufficient to convict the defendant of intentional killing. While intentional killing is sufficient for murder, intent must be one of two types: Either the actor must consciously desire a result, regardless of the likelihood his conduct will cause it; or, alternatively, he must know the result is practically certain to result from his conduct, regardless of whether he wants it to happen. Thus, under the facts in this question, the defendant would have to want to kill the children, or know he was practically certain to kill one if he drove toward them. Thus, (C) is incorrect in asserting that knowing the children were there and deliberately driving at them would be sufficient to convict the defendant—in addition, he'd have to know that driving at them would result in one being killed. In fact, the defendant believes they will run to get out of the way—he doesn't know he's practically certain to kill one.

Answer 34

Choice **(B)** is correct. Violation of a statute might serve as a basis for a criminal conviction if the statute imposes upon the defendant a duty of care that the defendant has not met. The statute clearly imposed upon Trelawney the duty to report suspected child abuse. In order to be guilty of murder, it must be shown that a defendant had "malice aforethought." Malice aforethought includes various mental states: intent to kill, intent to do serious bodily injury, reckless indifference to human life, or intent to commit a felony. The only possible qualifying mental state here is reckless indifference to human life. But since Trelawney thought about the abuse issue, and brought the issue to his supervisor's attention, he's unlikely to be found to have manifested the required reckless indifference to the value of human life. In any event, that's his only plausible argument from among those listed.

(A) is wrong because ignorance of the duty to report is not an excuse. Criminal liability for omissions can arise where there is a statute imposing on the defendant a distinct duty to act. Here, the statute imposed a duty of care on day care workers to report to the police where there is probable cause to suspect child abuse. Generally, the fact that the defendant did not know that the law imputes a legal duty in a certain situation will not constitute a defense. Therefore, Trelawney's ignorance of the law is not a good argument to use in defending him from a murder charge.

(C) is wrong because Trelawney's omission *was* sufficiently related to Smith's death. It is required that the act (in this case, omission) and the harm were sufficiently related that the act is a proximate cause of the harm. Criminal law generally insists upon a substantially closer connection between the defendant's act and the ensuing harm, than that of tort law. An act is the proximate cause if it is "not too remote or accidental in its occurrence to have a [just] bearing on the actor's liability or on the gravity of his offense." M.P.C. § 2.03(2)(b). Since a report of the earlier abuse by Trelawney would likely have induced the state to remove Smith from exposure to his father, Trelawney's failure to report the beating by the father can easily be said to have proximately caused (i.e., been closely related to) the death of Smith at the hands of the father.

(D) is wrong because the statute imposes a duty on day care workers, regardless of what their superiors may have sanctioned. Any duty or criminal behavior attributable to the supervisor would not prevent conviction of Trelawney for violation of his duty.

Answer 35

Choice **(B)** is correct, because it represents the facts under which the defendant is most likely to be guilty of murder. The key here is realizing that common-law murder does not require *intent.* Murder is an unlawful killing with malice aforethought. Malice is satisfied by either intent to kill or do serious bodily injury, depraved heart, or felony murder. The most applicable category here is *felony murder*.

Felony murder is a killing committed during the course of an *"inherently dangerous"* felony (or an attempt to commit such a crime), even though there is *no intent* to kill or cause serious bodily harm. That's exactly the case here. The list of felonies considered inherently dangerous at common law typically contains just five crimes: *arson, burglary, rape, robbery* and *kidnapping.* Robbery is on this list, and the facts explicitly state that the defendant killed a customer "while committing a robbery." Even though the killing was accidental, felony murder does not require intent, so this fact will not exonerate the defendant. Since the defendant satisfies the elements of felony murder, (B) is the best response.

(A) is wrong, because the defendant would most likely be liable for manslaughter, not murder. While the defendant is unlikely to be exonerated from *any* liability, he'd likely be liable only for manslaughter, not murder, under the imperfect self-defense doctrine. Under that doctrine, the defendant will be liable for manslaughter instead of murder, when he intentionally kills another, if either: (1) the defendant was the aggressor in a fight (and therefore not entitled to a self-defense claim), or (2) the defendant honestly but unreasonably believed deadly force was necessary. While the facts in Choice (A) don't stipulate who started the fight or if the belief was reasonable, the facts do indicate that at most the defendant will likely be liable only for manslaughter. Since the question is looking for the choice most likely representing common-law murder, Choice (A) is not the best response.

(C) is wrong, because the defendant would be unlikely to be liable for common-law murder. Common-law murder is an unlawful killing with malice aforethought. While "malice" can be satisfied by depraved heart murder, "depraved heart" occurs when the defendant engages in extremely negligent conduct, which a reasonable man would realize creates a very high degree of risk to human life, and which results in death. While the defendant's action in Choice (C) was negligent, it is unlikely to be considered serious enough to satisfy depraved heart murder. After all, he was in the woods, hunting deer. Were there other facts—for instance, the woods were crawling with hunters—the result might be different. As the facts are, the defendant's negligence simply would not rise to the level of depraved heart murder, but would likely be criminal negligence manslaughter. Also, the defendant did not intend to kill the other hunter and was not committing a felony, so his conduct does not satisfy other types of malice, and he cannot be guilty of common-law murder. As a result, (C) is not the best response.

(D) is wrong, because the defendant's act is not serious enough to be characterized as common-law murder. Murder is an unlawful killing with malice aforethought. Malice can be intent to kill or do serious bodily injury, depraved heart, or felony murder. There are two facts of particular note here: first, the city ordinance; and second, the culpability of the defendant regardless of the ordinance. The ordinance gives rise to the issue of felony murder. However, violation of a city ordinance is typically a misdemeanor, not a felony, so felony murder could not apply. Analyzing the defendant's act without the ordinance requires focusing on depraved heart murder, since there's clearly no intent here. "Depraved heart" exists when the defendant engages in extremely negligent conduct, which a reasonable man would realize creates a very high degree of risk to human life and results in death. Here, the defendant was aiming at the street, and the bullet bounced up and killed a pedestrian. While this was undoubtedly negligent, without more facts it would be difficult to say that it was *extremely* negligent. For instance, if the pedestrian were part of a crowd, it *would* be; if he were alone, and the angle of the ricochet were unusual, it would be closer to a "freak" accident. As it stands, there are insufficient facts to conclude that the defendant would likely be guilty of murder. Rather, his conduct would most likely satisfy requirements for criminal-negligence manslaughter or misdemeanor manslaughter. Since he won't likely be guilty of murder, (D) isn't the best response.

Answer 36

Choice (**B**) is correct, because it's the only choice that posits an underlying felony that is not independent of the killing to which the felony-murder doctrine would be applied.

Felony murder requires an underlying felony that is inherently dangerous to human life, but the felony has to be sufficiently "independent" from the homicide to which the felony-murder doctrine is going to be applied. Such qualifying (i.e., independent) crimes traditionally include rape, robbery, arson, burglary, and kidnapping. Here, manslaughter *is* a homicide, so it *cannot* be "independent" from that homicide. The same would go for a crime like aggravated battery that led to the battery victim's death. Since the question here asks the least likely basis for felony murder, and (B) is the *only* choice that would *not* be amenable to felony murder, (B) is the best response.

(A) is wrong, because arson is one of the most likely felonies to form a basis for felony murder. Felony murder requires an underlying felony that is inherently dangerous to life, which does not require personal violence. The most common such crimes are rape, robbery, arson, burglary, and kidnapping. Arson is considered sufficiently "independent" from homicide to be covered by the felony-murder rule. If you chose this response, you may have mistakenly read "least" likely for "most" likely, since most MBE questions ask for the choice "most" likely to do something. However, since the question here asks for the *least* likely basis for felony murder, (A) isn't the best response.

(C) is wrong, because rape is a valid underlying crime for felony murder. Felony murder requires an underlying felony that is inherently dangerous to human life, while remaining sufficiently "independent" from homicide (including, traditionally, rape, robbery, arson, burglary, and kidnapping). The traditional test is to exclude those crimes requiring personal violence, but it would be a misnomer to say rape doesn't require personal violence. Nonetheless, rape is one of the traditional bases of felony murder, due to its independence from homicide. Note that the fact that only an attempt is involved here does not change the result, since the felony-murder rule encompasses attempts. Since the question here asks for the least likely basis for felony murder, (C) is not the best response.

(D) is wrong, because burglary is a likely basis for felony murder. Felony murder requires an underlying felony that is inherently dangerous to human life, while remaining sufficiently "independent" from homicide, typically because the crime is said not to require personal violence. Such crimes include, traditionally, rape, robbery, arson, burglary, and kidnapping. Since the question here asks for the least likely basis for felony murder, (D) isn't the best response.

Answer 37

Choice **(D)** is correct. The felony-murder rule provides that if the defendant, while he is in the process of committing a felony (such as robbery), kills another (even accidentally), the killing is murder. However, if the killing that took place during commission of the felony was by an innocent party (the customer) and he killed an innocent party (the clerk), then a court may well hold that the robber would not be responsible for the shooting (though this is not at all certain).

(A) is wrong because, in a jurisdiction recognizing felony murder, it is not required that the defendant have the intent to kill, as long as he had the intent to commit a felony (in this case, robbery).

(B) is wrong because for felony-murder liability, it is not necessary that the defendant be successful in his commission of the felony, merely that the murder occurred in the process of an attempt to commit the felony.

(C) is wrong because where the defendant had the intent to commit one of the specified dangerous felonies that will support felony murder, that's the only intent the defendant needs to have. So the fact that the defendant didn't intend to "create any risk of harm" is irrelevant.

Answer 38

Choice **(A)** is correct. If Shore is guilty of felony-murder, it will be because the vagrant's death occurred during the commission of arson. The felony-murder rule allows the intent to commit a felony to supply the *mens rea* required for murder when the felony is the proximate cause of the killing. The rule states that when a defendant commits a felony that is inherently dangerous, and in so doing causes the death of another, the killing is murder. A felony is considered inherently dangerous if death is a foreseeable result of the crime. Here, the underlying felony was arson, which is an inherently dangerous crime because it inherently carries with it the risk to human life. Shore is responsible for the results of the fire because, although he did not personally start the fire that resulted in the vagrant's death, he is guilty of arson as an accomplice since he hired Parsons to burn the building. Additionally, for the felony-murder rule to apply, the felony must be independent of the killing. This requirement is met here because the purpose of starting the fire was not to harm the vagrant, but only to destroy the building.

Choices (B) and (C) are wrong because neither fraud nor conspiracy is an inherently dangerous felony, and therefore cannot be the underlying felony for a felony-murder conviction.

(D) is wrong because Shore has not committed burglary. Burglary requires the unlawful breaking and entering of a building of another with the intent to commit a crime once inside. Although Parsons "broke" into the building, he did so with the consent of the building's owner. As a result, Parsons's presence in the building was lawful, despite his means of entry and intent to commit arson.

Answer 39

Choice (**B**) is correct. The felony-murder rule provides that if the defendant, while he is in the process of committing a dangerous felony (such as robbery), kills another (even accidentally), the killing is murder. Dawson, by driving Smith to the bank, serving as lookout, and agreeing to drive the getaway car, was an accomplice to bank robbery. Once Dawson performed those "accomplice" services, in a way that contributed to Smith's carrying out the robbery, Dawson became substantively liable for robbery too. After that, any killing by Smith that could be said to be a "natural and probable" result of the felony will be attributable to Dawson under the felony-murder doctrine.

With respect to the death penalty, the Supreme Court has held that the Eighth Amendment prohibits the use of the death penalty on a defendant "who does not kill himself, attempt to kill, or intend that a killing take place or that lethal force may be employed." *Enmund v. Florida* (1982). Therefore, the death penalty may not be imposed upon Dawson, who did not himself kill, attempt to kill or intend that a killing take place or that lethal force be used.

(A) is wrong because the death penalty may not be imposed under these circumstances, as discussed in the explanation of (B).

(C) is wrong because Dawson may be convicted of felony-murder due to the fact that he is responsible for his co-felon's killing of the bank guard that was committed in furtherance of the felony, as discussed in the explanation of (B).

(D) is wrong because (1) Dawson is guilty of bank robbery on an accomplice theory; and (2) he may be convicted of felony-murder, as discussed in the explanation of (B).

Answer 40

Choice (**D**) is correct, because the defendant did "knowingly cause the death of another person," and his intoxication did not preclude the mental state required for second-degree murder. Voluntary, self-induced intoxication may negate the required mental state in specific intent crimes. It is generally held, however, that intoxication cannot further reduce the homicide from second-degree murder down to manslaughter. See LaFave, Criminal Law § 9.5(b).

(A) is wrong, because there was no reasonable explanation for the defendant becoming enraged. To qualify as manslaughter, the defendant's act must be in response to a provocation sufficiently strong that a reasonable person would have been caused to lose self-control enough to kill. The victim's comments and action of shaking his finger at the defendant are not enough to cause a reasonable person to lose self-control to such an extent that he kills. Furthermore, the defendant's intoxication did not preclude the mental state required for second-degree murder. Voluntary self-induced intoxication may negate the required mental state in specific intent crimes. It is generally held, however, that intoxication cannot further reduce the homicide from second-degree murder down to manslaughter. See LaFave, Criminal Law § 9.5(b).

(B) is wrong because, even if this statement were true, the defendant's intoxicated anger prevented the kind of "cool reflection" required for deliberation. See, e.g., LaFave, Substantive Criminal Law § 14.7(a): A "killer may, in a particular situation, be incapable of that cool reflection called for by the requirement of premeditation and deliberation, as where his capacity to premeditate and deliberate is prevented by emotional upset, [or] by intoxication . . . ." Here, the defendant was "[t]rembling with fury" due to his "bad disposition and alcohol," which provides strong evidence that he was not capable of cool reflection.

(C) is wrong, because the defendant did *not* deliberate upon taking the life "of another person" (as required by the statute) prior to becoming intoxicated. Instead, he was contemplating suicide, which would not qualify as murder in the first degree under the statute.

Answer 41

Choice **(A)** is correct, because the facts of the case make proximate cause the best defense. Manslaughter is death caused by criminal negligence. Proximate cause is that which in a natural and continuous sequence, unbroken by any intervening cause, produces injury and without which the injury would not have occurred. The student can plausibly try to show at trial that the teacher was depressed about other things as well, not just the lack of work, so that the firing was not sufficiently closely causally related to the death to meet the requirement of proximate cause. And the student can argue that a death by suicide is not a "natural and probable consequence" of being fired or falsely accused, which is the standard for proximate cause in many jurisdictions.

Finally, the relatively long time period—about a year—between false accusation and death tends to weaken the causal connection. Indeed, notice that the facts say that the suicide occurred "a year later." If there was slightly *more* than a year between false accusation and death, then the common-law "year and a day" rule —by which a death happening more than a year and a day after the *actus reus* would be conclusively deemed not to be the proximate result of the act—might apply. (Some jurisdictions apply this rule to manslaughter cases, not just murders.)

There is no guarantee that this proximate-cause defense will work—indeed, perhaps it's not even "more likely than not" to work. But of the four choices, it's the only one that has a plausible chance. (For why each of the others won't work, read the discussions of those choices below.)

(B) is wrong, because the student's actual intent would not be an issue in an involuntary manslaughter case. The prosecution here would have to be for involuntary manslaughter, not voluntary manslaughter. Involuntary manslaughter is generally defined as death caused by gross criminal negligence (or, sometimes, "recklessness").

The fact that the student did not intend to cause the teacher's death could not possibly be a defense here, because the student's subjective intent would not be the issue where the question is whether she acted with gross negligence or recklessness about the risk of death. Instead, the issue is whether a reasonable person in the student's position would have known that a false accusation like the one she made posed a great risk of the teacher's eventual suicide. (Indeed, intent-to-cause-death is almost *never* present in successful prosecutions for involuntary manslaughter, because if it were present, the case would be a murder prosecution instead.)

(C) is wrong, because malice is relevant to the wrong state of mind. As described in Choice (B) above, the relevant mental state in this involuntary manslaughter prosecution is gross negligence or recklessness. The fact that the student lacked "malice" is not relevant at all. (It's relevant to some types of murder, as in the phrase "with malice aforethought," used to describe the mental state for garden-variety intent-to-kill murder.)

(D) is wrong, because the student's emotional distress would be relevant to sentencing, but not to whether she is guilty of the substantive crime. "Extreme emotional distress" is not generally a substantive defense to crime. Instead, it can be a mitigating factor at sentencing. Even if extreme distress *were* in theory a defense, it would not apply here, where making a false sexual-misconduct accusation would hardly be an excusable response to being upset about a failing grade.

Answer 42

Choice **(C)** is correct, because it introduces the strongest subjective element into the definition of criminal negligence.

The key here is that the question is asking the most favorable definition for the defendant, not the most reasonable definition. The way to determine this is to identify the response that creates the most difficult standard to meet, since that's the definition under which the defendant will most likely be exonerated. To do that, you should identify the standard that has the strongest subjective element—and that's choice (C).

This choice states that criminal negligence requires the defendant (1) to intentionally do something he shouldn't have done or (2) to intentionally fail to do something he should have done, each of which requires a conscious disregard of a known danger. Therefore, Choice (C) makes it unlikely that the defendant will be convicted—while his behavior was probably negligent from an objective viewpoint, he probably did not consciously disregard a known danger.

(A) is wrong, because it does not offer a definition that's particularly helpful to the defendant. By merely stating that criminal negligence is something more than slight negligence, the defendant here is left open to liability, because he clearly disregarded the consequences of his act (whether consciously or not)—not watching where he was going—and displayed indifference to the rights of others. That's a definition less favorable to him than (C), which in effect requires a *conscious* disregard of consequences and the rights of others.

(B) is wrong, because it is not favorable to the defendant. The failure to respond to surrounding circumstances would cook the defendant's goose, because that's what he did—he failed to respond to the stop light. Furthermore, the concept of reckless disregard might be interpreted to contain only an objective element, that the individual undertook an unjustifiable risk, whether he was conscious of the risk or not. That interpretation would make it easier to convict the defendant than the Choice (C) standard, which incorporates a requirement of conscious disregard of risk.

(D) is wrong, because it offers a definition under which the defendant would likely be found guilty. A definition favorable to the defendant would provide as strict a definition as possible of criminal negligence. By characterizing criminal negligence as something more than slight negligence in tort, but less than wanton misconduct, Choice (D) virtually invites a guilty verdict, since the defendant's conduct in ignoring a stop light and killing a pedestrian on a crosswalk could easily be characterized as gross negligence. The best thing for the defendant is to offer a definition that includes as strong a subjective element as possible (e.g., a definition that requires at least conscious disregard of the risk), which Choice (C) does far better than (D).

Answer 43

Choice (**B**) is correct, because it correctly identifies that the father will be guilty of involuntary manslaughter. Remember the process of elimination you should go through when you encounter a homicide problem. First, look at murder as a possibility. A murder is an unlawful killing (neither justifiable nor excusable) with malice aforethought. While malice doesn't require intent, it can be satisfied by "depraved heart," that is, the actor disregards an unreasonably high risk of harm to human life. Here, the father's omission would not rise to this level of negligence (since depraved heart is generally viewed objectively). Since he won't be guilty of murder, the next possibility is involuntary manslaughter, of which the father *will* be guilty.

Specifically, the father will be guilty of criminal negligence manslaughter (the other type, unlawful act manslaughter, is a manslaughter that occurs as a result of or during a *malum in se* misdemeanor or a felony that is not sufficient for). Predictably, criminal negligence manslaughter is manslaughter that occurs through gross or criminal negligence (either by act or omission). Criminal negligence is a somewhat stricter standard than tortious negligence, which requires a higher degree of unreasonability. (However, criminal negligence, like tortious negligence, is generally judged objectively.) Under the facts here, the father knew the child was ill, but refused to seek help at a state clinic solely because of his pride. This kind of conduct could easily be considered a criminally negligent omission, especially in view of the father's fiduciary relationship with his children. Since (B) best characterizes the facts here, it's the best response.

(A) is wrong, because the father's conduct would not qualify as murder. Common-law murder is an unlawful killing (neither justifiable nor excusable) with malice aforethought. While malice aforethought does not require ill-will, it would require either intent to kill, knowledge that death or unreasonably high risk of injury will result, or intent to commit a felony. While the father will be culpable for failing to get medical attention for his child, this would not rise to the level of intent or knowledge of an unreasonably high risk of injury. As a result, (A) is not the best response.

(C) is wrong, because the father's conduct would not qualify as voluntary manslaughter. Voluntary manslaughter is essentially murder except it is committed under adequate provocation (e.g., heat of passion). Under the facts here, the father didn't commit a murder. Common-law murder is an unlawful killing (neither justifiable nor excusable) with malice aforethought. While malice aforethought does not require ill-will, it would require either intent to kill, knowledge that death or unreasonably high risk of injury will result, or intent to commit a felony. While the father will be culpable for failing to get medical attention for his child, this would not rise to the level of intent or knowledge of an unreasonably high risk of injury.

In any case, even if the father's conduct did rise to the level of murder, he wasn't provoked, so he couldn't be guilty of voluntary manslaughter. As a result, (C) is not the best response.

(D) is wrong, because the father *will* be guilty of involuntary manslaughter. In fact, the father will be guilty of involuntary manslaughter of the criminal negligence type. Criminal negligence manslaughter is manslaughter that occurs through gross or criminal negligence (either by act or omission). Under the facts here, the father knew the child was ill, but refused to seek help at a state clinic solely because of his pride. This kind of conduct could easily be considered a criminally negligent omission, especially in view of the father's fiduciary relationship with his children.

If you chose this response, it could be because you placed too much importance on the fact that the child died as a result of the illness. *However,* a "killing" takes place whenever a death is hastened by any time at all (e.g., killing someone who was to be executed in five minutes could still be murder, if the requisite *mens rea* existed). The facts here state that the child's death was hastened because he was weakened by malnutrition. Thus, the father is guilty of some form of homicide, making (D) not the best response.

Answer 44

Choice (**C**) is correct, because it arrives at the correct result, and focuses on the reason why the defendant won't be guilty—because he didn't intend to cause an offensive touching.

The criminal assault statute in this problem requires an attempt to commit a criminal battery. Attempt has two elements: intent, and an overt act done in furtherance of the intent, beyond mere preparation. Here, the defendant had no intent to touch the plaintiff in any way; he was trying to retrieve his hat. Since he didn't intend to touch the plaintiff, he couldn't be liable for any crime that explicitly or implicitly requires intent. Since intent is an element of attempt, he can't be liable. Since (C) correctly identifies that this is the element that will exonerate the defendant, it's the best response.

(A) is wrong, because it ignores the intent element of the crime, and it reaches the wrong result. The statute under which the defendant was charged, the criminal assault statute, would require that the defendant attempted to cause an offensive touching. Attempt has two elements: intent, and an overt act done in furtherance of the intent, beyond mere preparation. Under these facts, this would mean that the defendant would have to have intended to cause an offensive touching. However, the facts indicate the only thing the defendant intended to touch was his hat, not the plaintiff. Since he didn't intend to touch the plaintiff, he couldn't be found guilty of a crime involving attempt, which is what the criminal assault statute requires. Since (A) stops short of what would be required to convict the defendant, it's not the best response.

(B) is wrong, because it arrives at the wrong result, and offers a standard of culpability that is *lower* than the standard in the statute given. The statute under which the defendant was charged, the criminal assault statute, would require that the defendant attempted to cause an offensive touching. Attempt has two elements: intent, and an overt act done in furtherance of the intent, beyond mere preparation. Choice (B) suggests that the defendant should be culpable for merely *negligent* behavior—because he *should have realized* harm might result from his act. This is not sufficient for attempt, since attempt requires intent. Since (B) would hold the defendant liable for assault without intent, it's not the best response.

(D) is wrong, because although it offers the right result, it requires *more* than the actual statute requires. The criminal assault statute only requires *an attempt* to cause an offensive touching. D suggests that an *actual* touching is required. If you chose this response, it could be because you mistakenly believed the defendant was charged with criminal battery—if he *had* been charged with criminal battery, a touching would have been required. As it is, a criminal assault only requires an attempt to commit a criminal battery, and so (D) is not the best response.

Answer 45

Choice **(A)** is correct, because the defendant did not intend to use deadly force, and thus could not have had any duty to retreat. The defendant may utilize the defense of self-defense when he (i) is resisting unlawful force, (ii) does not use excessive force, (iii) does not use deadly force unless the danger being resisted was also deadly force, (iv) is not the aggressor (unless he was a non-deadly aggressor confronted with the unexpected use of deadly force), and (v) was not in a position from which he could retreat with complete safety (or else the attack took place in the defendant's dwelling or the defendant used only non-deadly force). Here, all the elements are met. The husband, through both his physical and verbal action, threatened unlawful force. The defendant did not use excessive force. The defendant did not intend to use deadly force (since he had no reason to believe that the pepper spray would inflict death or serious bodily injury on the husband). And the defendant was not the aggressor. Furthermore, because the defendant did not intend to use deadly force, he was not under any obligation to retreat.

(B) is wrong, because it misstates the retreat rule. The defendant may utilize the defense of self-defense when he (i) is resisting unlawful force, (ii) does not use excessive force, (iii) does not use deadly force unless the danger being resisted was also deadly force, (iv) is not the aggressor (or else is a non-deadly aggressor confronted with the unexpected use of deadly force), and (v) was not in a position from which he could retreat with complete safety (or else the attack took place in the defendant's dwelling or the defendant used only non-deadly force). Here, the defendant was not in his dwelling, and stating that an exception exists for all "occupied structures" is too broad. Instead, the reason that the defendant did not have to retreat is that the defendant did not intend to use deadly force (i.e., pepper spray).

(C) is wrong, because it misstates the retreat rule. The defendant may utilize the defense of self-defense when he (i) is resisting unlawful force, (ii) does not use excessive force, (iii) does not use deadly force unless the danger being resisted was also deadly force, (iv) is not the aggressor (or else is a non-deadly aggressor confronted with the unexpected use of deadly force), and (v) was not in a position from which he could retreat with complete safety (or else the attack took place in the defendant's dwelling or the defendant used only non-deadly force). Here, the answer choice is too broad: a person utilizing self-defense does not have to retreat whenever an opportunity is available if he is using non-deadly force. Thus, the reason that the defendant did not have to retreat is that the defendant did not intend to use deadly force (i.e., pepper spray).

(D) is wrong, because a response of non-deadly force is justified where the defender reasonably believes the other is about to inflict unlawful bodily harm, which need not be deadly harm.

The defendant may utilize the defense of self-defense when he (i) is resisting unlawful force, (ii) does not use excessive force, (iii) does not use deadly force unless the danger being resisted was also deadly force, (iv) is not the aggressor (or else is a non-deadly aggressor confronted with the unexpected use of deadly force), and (v) was not in a position from which he could retreat with complete safety (or else the attack took place in the defendant's dwelling or the defendant used only non-deadly force). Here, the husband threatened unlawful force, so the defendant was entitled to defend himself using reasonable force. The defendant responded to the threat of a punch with non-deadly force (i.e., pepper spray), so his use of force was justified. As this answer choice implies either that self-defense may only be used in response to deadly force or that this defendant used deadly force, it is wrong.

Answer 46

Choice **(B)** is correct. As a criminal defendant, the Due Process Clause guarantees that Dunbar carries no burden to prove or disprove any element of the crime of which he is charged. The prosecution carries the burden of persuasion as to every element of the crime. Dunbar only has a burden of persuasion as to any affirmative defense he may raise. Dunbar has been charged with rape, which in this jurisdiction (as at common law) is defined as a defendant's (1) having sexual intercourse with a female, (2) not his wife, (3) without her consent. This means that the prosecutor must prove each one of those elements and that Dunbar has no burden of persuasion as to any of them. The judge is required to give an instruction that does not unduly saddle Dunbar with any burden regarding any element of the crime. Let's examine each of the judge's instructions separately.

The judge's instruction that the jury should find Dunbar not guilty if it found that Sally was Dunbar's wife, and that Dunbar carried the burden of persuasion on this issue, violated Dunbar's constitutional rights. The issue of whether Sally was Dunbar's wife is an element of the crime, so Dunbar could never be required to bear the burden to prove or disprove it — it must be solely the prosecution's burden to prove that Sally was not Dunbar's wife. Therefore, the judge's instruction improperly shifted the burden of persuasion on this issue from the prosecution to Dunbar, in violation of his due process rights.

On the other hand, the judge's instruction that the jury should find Dunbar not guilty if it found that Dunbar reasonably believed Sally had consented to the sexual intercourse, and that the burden was on Dunbar to persuade the jury of that fact, did *not* violate Dunbar's constitutional rights. Dunbar's belief as to consent at the time is not an element of rape, so the prosecution does not have to prove that Dunbar knew Sally did not consent in order to convict him. (If this jurisdiction follows the majority rule, Dunbar's mistake about consent, even if reasonable, would be no defense to the charge of rape. In that case, the judge's instruction would be in error, but in a way that would be likely to cause a jury to acquit Dunbar, not convict him. Even if the defendant's reasonable belief as to consent was recognized by the jurisdiction as an affirmative defense, the defendant could constitutionally be required to bear the burden of producing evidence to support that defense, and the burden of persuasion by a preponderance of the evidence as to it.)

(A) is wrong because it incorrectly states that Dunbar's rights were violated by the instruction on reasonable belief.

(C), like (A), is wrong because it incorrectly states that Dunbar's rights were violated by the instruction on reasonable belief.

(D) is wrong by not stating that Dunbar's rights were violated by the instruction on whether Sally was his wife.

Answer 47

Choice **(A)** is correct. First, notice that the question was carefully set up to involve two states: the victim's home state, and the neighboring state. The reason the examiners set it up this way is that they wanted to be able to ask you whether that part of the episode that involved transporting the victim into and within the neighboring state was part of the crime—for instance, if the crime of kidnapping was defined in such a way that the crime here was over as soon as the stranger got in the car and drove the first few miles with the victim, then there would be no kidnapping in the neighboring state, only in the home state. But the M.P.C. does not define kidnapping in such a narrow way. The M.P.C. (like nearly all states) defines kidnapping to require either transporting of the victim (usually called "asportation") or secret imprisonment of the victim. The M.P.C. then says that asportation occurs only if the defendant either (1) "removes" the victim from his "place of residence or business," or (2) moves the victim "a *substantial distance* from the vicinity where he is found." M.P.C. § 212.1. The Commentary says that the "substantial distance" requirement is designed to "preclude kidnapping convictions based on trivial changes of location having no bearing on the evil at hand" (e.g., a rapist who forces his victim a few steps into a parked car does not commit kidnapping).

Here, the stranger's act of forcing the driver to transport himself "several miles" to the state border, then several more miles, clearly meets the "substantial distance" requirement. And since the description of the crime makes it clear that the stranger wanted to abandon the driver in a secluded location, the transporting was not a "trivial change [] of location having no bearing on the evil at hand." So the part of the episode that occurred in the neighboring state was definitely part of the crime, under the definition of kidnapping in the M.P.C. (and indeed, under the definitions of virtually every state).

(B) is wrong because it reaches the correct conclusion by incorrect reasoning. First, it is hard to characterize the proceeds of the robbery as "ransom." But more importantly, the propriety of a kidnapping conviction does not turn on whether ransom was paid. The M.P.C. defines kidnapping to mean either the moving of a person "a substantial distance," or the "unlawful confine[ment]" of a person "for a substantial period in a place of isolation," so long as the moving or confinement is done with *any of a variety of purposes* (e.g., holding for ransom, holding as a hostage, facilitating commission of any felony or flight thereafter, inflicting any bodily injury, etc.). M.P.C. § 212.1. Here, the stranger carried out the "moving" ("asportation," as it's usually called) for the purpose of later committing robbery, a felony. So whether the driver did or did not pay ransom is irrelevant. (Indeed, kidnapping is like burglary, in the sense that as long as the defendant confines or transports with one of the forbidden purposes, the crime is complete as soon as the confinement or moving-a-substantial-distance occurs, even if the purpose is never fulfilled. So here, once the stranger transported the driver into the neighboring state, the crime was complete even if the stranger had then abandoned his plan of robbing the driver of his car and wallet.)

(C) is wrong because the stranger properly could be convicted of kidnapping in both states. The movement in the neighboring state was more than incidental to the robbery, and would constitute kidnapping there as well as in the driver's home state. That's especially true since the underlying felony of robbery—the "purpose" for which the transportation occurred—happened in the neighboring state. For more about why the crime is deemed to have occurred in both states, see the analysis of Choice (A).

(D) is wrong because the restraint was not incidental to the robbery. It's true that the M.P.C. defines kidnapping in such a way that where a restraint and/or a transporting is for a brief time or distance, and is truly incidental to the "main" crime intended by the defendant, kidnapping will not be deemed to have occurred. So, for instance, a rapist who forces his victim into a parked car or dark alley does not commit kidnapping. M.P.C. § 212.1, Commentary. But here, the stranger caused the driver to be transported several miles to the state border, then another several miles, all for the purpose of getting him to a secluded location where the car could be stolen. Under these facts, the restraint (and the transporting) were *not* incidental to the robbery.

Answer 48

Choice (**D**) is correct. John is guilty of neither kidnapping nor attempted kidnapping. Let's examine each crime separately.

John has not committed kidnapping because Doris was free to leave his apartment at any time. Kidnapping is the (1) unlawful confinement of another person, (2) accompanied by either the moving or secreting away of that person. Although John may have tricked Doris into spending the weekend at his apartment, he did nothing to confine her once she got there. Confinement occurs when the victim is either forced to remain where she does not wish to remain or compelled to go where she does not wish to be. Doris desired to be at John's apartment and could have left had she so chosen, so she was not confined. The lack of confinement negates the first element of kidnapping, so John has not committed the crime. (And the fact that Doris' presence was brought about by John's trickery about his intent to marry her won't matter—he hasn't confined her, and that's all that matters.)

John is not guilty of attempted kidnapping because he did not intend for his actions to confine Doris to his apartment. In order to find John guilty of attempt, the prosecution would have to show that John intended to commit each element of the crime. In this case, John didn't intend to confine, so he can't have attempted to kidnap.

Choices (A), (B), and (C) are all wrong because they each state that John is guilty of either kidnapping or attempted kidnapping, which cannot be true if there has been no confinement and no attempt to confine.

Answer 49

Choice (**D**) is correct. Let's take the crimes one at a time. First, larceny by trick is a form of larceny, in which the initial possession by the defendant is not only wrongful (which is required for any form of larceny), but is caused by fraud or deceit (as opposed to, say, by force). The fact pattern does not indicate that Smith had any intention other than the intent to repay the loan, when he asked to borrow money from Jones. Therefore, he did not intend to "steal" at the moment he received the money, which would be required for larceny by trick.

Next, obtaining money by false pretenses occurs when the defendant makes a false representation of a material present or past fact, which causes the person to whom it is made to pass title to his property to the defendant, who knows that his representation is false, and intends to defraud. So for this offense, the defendant must be proved to have knowingly made a false representation that causes the victim to pass title to his property. There is no indication that when Smith promised to repay the $500 within two weeks, Smith was intentionally making a false representation about his intent—for all we know, he indeed believed that he would be willing and able to repay the loan on schedule. Therefore, Smith did not have the mental state required at the time title to the money was passed (if, indeed, title rather than mere possession is deemed to have passed at the moment of the loan), and can't be guilty of false pretenses no matter what his post-loan state of mind may have been.

(A), (B), and (C) are all wrong, because each would make Smith guilty of at least one crime (either larceny by trick or false pretenses, or both) and he cannot be convicted of either for the reasons discussed in Choice (D).

Answer 50

Choice **(C)** is correct. For this choice to be correct, David must have committed larceny. Larceny is the (1) trespassory (2) taking and (3) carrying away (4) of the personal property (5) of another with (6) the intent to steal. David's actions fulfill all of the elements: (1) he had no permission to take the document, (2) he took it, (3) and removed it from its case, (4) and (5) the document was property that didn't belong to him, and (6) he intended to steal it. David's mistaken belief that the photocopy was in fact a valuable Picasso original is irrelevant. The value of the item he stole would be relevant to the degree of larceny of which David is guilty, but the common-law definition of larceny has no minimum value threshold. Also irrelevant is the fact that David could have lawfully obtained a duplicate for free—it's true that he could legally have taken one of the copies at the entrance, but he had no permission to take the copy in the display case.

(A) is wrong because David is not guilty of burglary. As defined in the given statute, burglary requires two elements: (1) entering a building unlawfully, (2) with the intent to commit a crime. It is indisputable that David intended to commit a crime once inside the museum since we are told that he entered "intending to steal a Picasso etching." However, David's entry wasn't unlawful. When he entered the museum, it was open to all members of the public, including David. The fact that a criminal purpose motivated his entry does not make that entry "unlawful." For the purposes of burglary, entry is only unlawful if the defendant entered a building, or remained in a building, in which he had no permission to be. Since David's entry to the museum was lawful, he has not committed burglary.

(B) is wrong for the same reason that (A) is wrong: David is not guilty of burglary.

(D) is wrong because although David could be convicted solely of attempted larceny, under the majority approach he cannot be convicted of both larceny and attempted larceny. On these facts, attempted larceny is a lesser included offense within larceny (only one act of "taking" is charged), so if the court convicts him of larceny, it cannot separately also convict him of attempted larceny.

Answer 51

Choice **(A)** is correct. Larceny is the (1) trespassory (2) taking and (3) carrying away of (4) personal property (5) of another (6) with intent to steal. The defendant took the restaurant's money from the safe with the intent to steal it, so he is guilty of larceny. The fact that the defendant felt (properly or not) aggrieved by the false accusation is irrelevant. If the defendant had had a genuine belief that he had a "claim of right" to money or property in the defendant's possession, and had taken the money in satisfaction of that claim, this might be a defense to larceny; but the defendant didn't have that belief here—he was just feeling aggrieved.

(B) is wrong because the defendant took the money from the office safe. Embezzlement is the (1) fraudulent (2) conversion of (3) the property (4) of another (5) by one who is already in lawful possession of it. The element missing here is the one requiring lawful possession. The defendant, as cashier, had lawful possession of the money while he was working the cash register and putting it into a bag in order to give it to the manager (so if he had taken it and carried it away with intent to steal at that point, it would have been embezzlement). But once the bag was put into the office safe, the defendant did not have lawful possession of it any more. Therefore, when he took it from the safe he could not be guilty of embezzlement.

(C) is wrong because the defendant is not guilty of embezzlement, as discussed in Choice (B). (Also, at common law, larceny and embezzlement are defined in mutually exclusive ways, so it could not be the case that the prosecution had a choice of which crime to charge on any given state of facts.)

(D) is wrong because the defendant is guilty of larceny, as discussed in Choice (A).

Answer 52

Choice **(B)** is correct, because, even though the patron possessed the wallet briefly, his conduct satisfied all of the elements of larceny. Larceny is (i) the trespassory (ii) taking and (iii) carrying away of (iv) personal property (v) of another with (vi) intent to steal. All the elements are satisfied here. The taking away element requires movement of only a slight distance, so it was satisfied even though the patron discarded the wallet shortly after taking it.

(A) is wrong, because the taking was not accomplished by using force or putting the owner in fear. Robbery is defined as larceny committed with two additional elements: (i) the property is taken from the person or presence of the owner and (ii) the taking is accomplished by using force or putting the owner in fear. As the victim here was passed out, the taking was not accomplished by using force or putting the owner in fear. Thus, while all the elements of larceny are met, it is not a robbery.

(C) is wrong, because the patron could be convicted of the more serious crime of larceny. Thus, even assuming the patron could be convicted of attempted robbery, this offense is not the most serious possible crime of conviction, so this response is incorrect.

(D) is wrong, because the patron could be convicted of the more serious crime of larceny. Thus, even assuming the patron could be convicted of attempted larceny, this offense is not the most serious possible crime of conviction, so this response is incorrect.

Answer 53

Choice **(B)** is correct, because the customer obtained possession of, but not title to, the watch by lying about a present fact. In order to commit common- law larceny, the customer must meet each of the following six elements: (1) the trespassory (2) taking and (3) carrying away of (4) personal property (5) of another (6) with intent to steal. Here all the elements were met by the customer's actions, unlike the other three crimes listed.

(A) is wrong, because the customer did not take the watch by force or threat of force. Robbery is defined as larceny with two additional elements: (1) the property is taken from the person or presence of the owner; and (2) the taking is accomplished by using force or putting the owner in fear. Here, the taking itself was not accomplished by putting the owner in fear, as the customer had already accomplished the theft when he threatened the clerk. Thus, this is a larceny, as the customer obtained possession of, but not title to, the watch by lying about a present fact.

(C) is wrong, because the customer did not obtain title to the watch. In order to commit false pretenses, the customer must meet each of the following six elements: (1) a false representation of a (2) material present or past fact (3) that causes the person to whom it is made (4) to pass title to (5) his property to the misrepresenter, who (6) knows that his representation is false and intends to defraud. While the customer knows that his representation is false and intends to defraud, he does not obtain title to the watch. Thus, this is a larceny, as the customer obtained possession of, but not title to, the watch by lying about a present fact.

(D) is wrong, because the customer was never in lawful possession of the watch. In order to commit embezzlement, the customer must meet each of the following five elements: (1) a fraudulent (2) conversion of (3) the property (4) of another (5) by one who is already in lawful possession of it. Here, there was a trespassory taking, so the customer was never in lawful possession of the watch. Thus, this is a larceny, as the customer obtained possession of, but not title to, the watch by lying about a present fact.

Answer 54

Choice **(C)** is correct, because the theory of continuing trespass made the executive guilty of larceny when she burned the materials.

First, let's consider whether the executive is guilty of *burglary*. Burglary is: (1) the breaking, (2) and entering, (3) of the dwelling, (4) of another, (5) at night time, (6) with the intent to commit a felony within. (Here, the statute has eliminated requirement (3).) No burglary occurred, because element (6) was missing. The time for measuring the existence of an "intent to commit a felony within" is the moment of the breaking and entering. Here, at the time of the breaking and entering, the executive intended to retrieve only her own personal property. So she did not have a felonious intent at the requisite moment. The fact that she *later* formed such an intent (when she was home, and decided to destroy what she knew was the property of another) doesn't count—the only thing that counts is the intent at the moment of breaking and entering.

Now, let's consider whether the executive committed *larceny*. Larceny is: (1) the taking and (2) carrying away of (3) the tangible property (4) of another, (5) by trespass or without consent, (6) with the intent to permanently deprive the other of his interest in the property. During the entire session at the office building, the executive never satisfied element (6): Since she intended to return any property not belonging to her that she might grab in the dark, she did not act "with the intent to permanently deprive the other of his interest in the property."

But the doctrine of "*continuing trespass*" applies, to make the executive guilty of trespass as soon as she burned the book and papers. Under the continuing trespass doctrine, applied by most courts, one who takes another's property, knowing that it is not his own but intending to return it, commits a "trespassory taking" at that moment; that original trespassory taking, although not coinciding with an intent to steal, is deemed to continue until the taker *does* form such an intent, at which point the larceny is complete. LaFave, § 8.5, p. 817. Here, the executive knew while in the office that she was taking property that was not her own and that she was unauthorized to take; at that moment, she had a trespassory intent, even though she had no present intent to steal and was thus not yet guilty of larceny. Then, at the moment she burned these materials at home, she had the intent to deprive the owner permanently of his interest in the property; that intent now coincided with the continuing trespass, making her guilty of larceny at the moment of burning.

(A), (B), and (D) are all wrong, because each of them is directly inconsistent with the above analysis, either by stating that burglary was present (Choices (A) and (B)) or by stating that larceny was not present (Choice (D)).

Answer 55

Choice **(D)** is correct. First, let's examine whether either Horace or Sam committed burglary. The answer is that neither did. Burglary is the breaking and entering of the dwelling of another at night with intent to commit a felony. Breaking does not occur when one is invited into a house. Since Horace had a key to the premises and had permission to enter the house, there was no breaking. Furthermore, the facts do not indicate that Horace had the intention to commit a felony at the time he entered the premises (or at any time, for that matter); therefore, this requirement is not met either. As to Lewis, he was let into the premises by one who was authorized to be there (and presumably, who was authorized to let in others). Therefore, Lewis, too, did not "break." (Nor is there any indication that Lewis had the intent to commit a felony *at the time* he entered the premises—for all we know this intent might have been formed later, when he noticed the jewelry.) Therefore, Lewis is not guilty of burglary either.

Lewis is guilty of larceny because he took property belonging to another (Sam's rings) and "carried them away" (by putting them in his pocket); a jury could infer that he did this because he meant to steal them. Horace hasn't taken any property belonging to another or intended to; deciding to have a party in someone else's house, when one has the right to be in the house, is not any particular crime, theft or otherwise.

Now, let's examine whether Horace is guilty of trespass, the only crime other than burglary about which any of the choices asserts Horace to be guilty. Horace is not guilty of trespass, because at all times he was permitted to be in Sam's house, under Sam's invitation. (If Sam had expressly told him not to have a party, by having a party Horace might have exceeded the scope of the invitation, and thus become guilty of trespass. But under the actual facts, he had no reason to believe that the invitation did not include the right to have a party, or to invite others to the house.)

(A) is wrong because neither defendant is guilty of burglary, as explained in the discussion of Choice (D) above.

(B) is wrong because Horace is not guilty of burglary, as explained in the discussion of Choice (D) above.

(C) is wrong, because Horace is not guilty of trespass, since at all times he was permitted to be in Sam's house, and did not exceed the scope of his invitation (as is further explained in the last paragraph of the discussion of Choice (D) above).

Answer 56

Choice is (A) is correct. Common-law burglary is defined as the breaking and entering of the dwelling house of another in the nighttime with the intent to commit a felony. LaFave, Criminal Law, § 8.13, at p. 883. The woman satisfies this definition because she unlawfully entered the neighbor's house at night with intent to commit a felony therein (larceny). The "breaking" element is satisfied because the woman opened a window—there is no requirement that the breaking occur by means of force, or that the premises have been secured, such as by a lock. Id. at 884. The "entering" element is more questionable on these facts, but the woman's actions satisfy this element as well. See LaFave, Criminal Law, § 8.13(b), at p. 886 (to constitute burglary it is "sufficient if any part of the actor's person intruded, even momentarily, into the structure. Thus it has been held that the intrusion of a part of a hand in opening a window, or the momentary intrusion of part of a foot in kicking out a window, constituted the requisite entry.").

(B) is wrong because the woman's action proceeded beyond the point of attempted burglary to the completed crime of burglary, as discussed in the analysis of Choice (A) above.

(C) is wrong because, while the woman may have been guilty of attempted larceny, that crime arguably would merge into, and in any event was less serious than, the burglary crime.

(D) is wrong because the woman is guilty of burglary, since she unlawfully entered the neighbor's house at night with intent to commit a felony (larceny), as more fully discussed in the analysis of Choice (A) above.

Answer 57

Choice **(C)** is correct, because it correctly identifies that the jury could find the defendant guilty of either robbery or larceny, but not both. There are two keys here: One is realizing that larceny is a *lesser included offense* to robbery; the second is that the jury could properly decide either way on the use of force and fear (the knife and the threats).

The jury, as finder of fact, could believe or disbelieve any testimony. The key fact here involves the use of the knife and the threats: If the jury believes the victim, it would find the defendant guilty of robbery; if it doesn't, which would be reasonable since the eyewitness wasn't aware of the knife or threats, then it would find the defendant guilty of larceny. Robbery requires a larceny from a person or a person's presence, by either force or fear. The use of the knife and/or the threats in the act described in these facts would thus satisfy robbery. Larceny is the trespassory taking and carrying away of another's personal property with intent to steal. The act described in these facts is sufficient for larceny, if the knife and threats were not used. Note, however, that the jury couldn't properly find the defendant guilty of *both* robbery and larceny, since larceny is a lesser included offense of robbery (requiring proof of some, but not all, of the elements of robbery, and no other elements). Since (C) correctly identifies that the jury could find the defendant guilty of either robbery or larceny but not both, it's the best response.

(A) is wrong, because it is too narrow: The jury could also properly return a verdict of guilty of larceny. The key here is whether the jury believes the defendant used the knife and/or made the threats, because this will determine whether or not it finds him guilty of robbery or larceny. Larceny requires a trespassory taking and carrying away of another's personal property with intent to steal. Robbery additionally requires that the larceny be from a person or in the presence of a person, by either force or fear. The jury, as the finder of fact, would be entitled—under these facts—to believe the victim, and find that force and fear were used, making the defendant liable for robbery, or not to believe the victim (due to the eyewitness's testimony) and find that only a larceny took place. Since (A) incorrectly limits the jury to robbery only, it's not the best response.

(B) is wrong, because it is too narrow: The jury could also properly return a verdict of guilty of robbery. The key here is whether the jury believes the defendant used the knife and/or made the threats, because this will determine whether or not it finds him guilty of robbery or larceny. Larceny requires a trespassory taking and carrying away of another's personal property with intent to steal. Robbery additionally requires that the larceny be from a person or in the presence of a person, by either force or fear. The jury, as the finder of fact, would be entitled—under these facts—to believe the victim, and find that force and fear were used, making the defendant liable for robbery, or not to believe the victim (due to the eyewitness's testimony) and find only a larceny took place. Since (B) limits the jury to finding larceny only, it's not the best response.

(D) is wrong, because the jury *could not* properly find the defendant guilty of both robbery and larceny, since larceny is a lesser included offense of robbery. A lesser included offense is one which requires proof of some but not all of the elements of another offense, and no other elements. Larceny requires a trespassory taking and carrying away of another's personal property with intent to steal. Robbery requires larceny from a person or the presence of a person, by either force or fear. As a result, the defendant *could not* properly be convicted of both charges. Furthermore, the jury could properly find that the defendant did not use a knife or threats. Since robbery requires the use of either force or fear, if the jury didn't believe the victim's testimony about those two factors, it couldn't find the defendant guilty of robbery. Since (D) incorrectly states that the jury could properly find the defendant guilty of both robbery and larceny, it's not the best response.

Answer 58

Choice (**A**) is correct, because it identifies the most serious crime, of these four, for which the defendant can be convicted. Robbery is a larceny from a person accomplished with violence or intimidation. (Larceny is a trespassory taking and carrying away of personal property of another, with intent to steal it.) The wrinkle here is that the victim, the husband, has not acted out of fear for himself, and the violence was not directed at him. However, the rule is that the threat required for robbery can be made to relatives or a companion of the victim. The question tells you that robbery is the most serious crime of the four choices, and asks for the most serious crime for which the defendant can be convicted. The facts here satisfy robbery, making (A) the best response.

(B) is wrong, because although the defendant could be convicted of larceny, he could be convicted of a more serious crime — robbery. Larceny requires a trespassory taking and carrying away of personal property, of another, with intent to steal it. These elements are satisfied by the facts here. Specifically, it would be called "larceny from the person." However, these facts *also* indicate two *additional* elements, which raise the "larceny from the person" to robbery: the use of force or fear. What may have tricked you into choosing this response is that the force was directed at *the wife,* not the victim (the husband). However, the rule is that the threat of harm will qualify even if the person threatened to be harmed is a relative or companion of the victim rather than the victim himself. Since these facts meet the threat requirement, the defendant will be guilty of robbery from the husband. Since he'll be liable for a more serious crime than larceny, and the question asks for the most serious crime for which he can be convicted, (B) is not the best response.

(C) is wrong, because the defendant will be liable for robbery, a more serious crime than assault. Criminal assault can take one of two forms: either an attempt to commit a battery, or the intentional and physical creation of fear of imminent bodily harm in the mind of the victim. Under these facts, the defendant would be liable for assault on the husband and wife for the period of time when he leaped out of the dark alleyway brandishing a gun. However, he will *also* be liable for *at least* battery on the wife, and robbery from the husband. If you chose this response, you overlooked the robbery. The defendant will be liable for robbery from the husband, because his act satisfies all the elements: a larceny from a person or a person's presence, by either force or fear. Here, the threat against the wife is sufficient for the force or fear element of robbery, since the force or fear *can* be directed at the victim's relative or companion. Since the defendant satisfies the robbery elements — the question tells you that robbery is a more serious crime than assault — and the question asks for the most serious crime for which the defendant can be convicted, (C) is not the best response.

(D) is wrong, because the defendant will be liable for a more serious crime than assault. Criminal assault can take one of two forms: either an attempt to commit a battery, or the intentional and physical creation of fear of imminent bodily harm in the mind of the victim. Under these facts, the defendant would be liable for assault on the wife for the period of time when he leaped out of the dark alleyway brandishing a gun. However, the defendant will also be liable for more serious crimes, as well: assault on *both* the husband and wife, larceny from the husband, and robbery from the husband. The defendant's act satisfies all the elements of robbery: a larceny from a person or a person's presence, by force or fear. Here, the threat against the wife is sufficient for the force or fear element, since the force or fear can be directed at the victim's relative or companion. Since the defendant satisfies the robbery elements — the question tells you robbery is a more serious crime than assault — and the question asks for the most serious crime for which the defendant can be convicted, (D) is not the best response.

Answer 59

Choice (**A**) is correct. Ordinarily, a defendant has no affirmative obligation to avoid harm, only an obligation to refrain from doing harm. But where a defendant brings about a risky situation, then he does have a duty to use reasonable efforts to avoid the harm. So once Defendant dropped the match (even if only reflexively), he had an affirmative obligation to stop the fire. When he didn't, and his mental state matched a state that will suffice for arson (intent to burn), he became guilty of arson.

(**B**) is wrong because mere negligence doesn't suffice for arson—it's a crime that requires either an intent to burn, or (in some states) recklessness with regard to the risk of burning.

(**C**) is incorrect, because there *was* concurrence. Even if Defendant behaved non-negligently in lighting a match in the first instance, and involuntarily in dropping it, once the fire started he had the obligation to make reasonable efforts to stop it, because he had caused the peril in the first place. Once he simultaneously failed to perform that duty to stop the peril and desired that the bad result defining the crime (burning) occur, he met the concurrence requirement.

(**D**) is wrong because, while Defendant may have started the fire reflexively, once he failed to put it out while under a duty to do so, this was a voluntary act.

CRIMINAL PROCEDURE QUESTIONS BY TOPIC

Chapter 1

CONSTITUTIONAL CRIMINAL PROCEDURE GENERALLY

I. STATE PROCEDURES AND THE FEDERAL CONSTITUTION

A. State protections going beyond those of the federal constitution

Question 1

After a liquor store was robbed, the police received an anonymous telephone call naming a store employee as the perpetrator of the robbery. Honestly believing that their actions were permitted by the U.S. Constitution, the police talked one of the employee's neighbors into going to the employee's home with a hidden tape recorder to engage him in a conversation about the crime. During the conversation, the employee admitted committing the robbery. The employee was charged in state court with the robbery. He moved to suppress the recording on the grounds that the method of obtaining it violated his constitutional rights under both the state and federal constitutions. Assume that a clear precedent from the state supreme court holds that the conduct of the police in making the recording violated the employee's rights under the state constitution, and that the exclusionary rule is the proper remedy for this violation.

Should the court grant the employee's motion?

(A) No, because the employee's federal constitutional rights were not violated, and this circumstance overrides any state constitutional provisions.

(B) No, because the police were acting in the good-faith belief that their actions were permitted by the federal Constitution.

(C) Yes, because the making of the recording violated the state constitution.

(D) Yes, because use of the recording would violate the neighbor's federal constitutional rights.

ARREST; PROBABLE CAUSE; SEARCH WARRANTS

I. AREAS AND PEOPLE PROTECTED BY THE FOURTH AMENDMENT

A. Guests

1. Guest staying in hotel room

Question 2

A federal officer had probable cause to believe a woman had participated in a bank robbery. Two days after the robbery, the woman checked into a local hotel room. When the woman left for the evening, the hotel manager opened the hotel room door so the officer could enter the room and look inside. The officer did not find any of the stolen money but did see, lying open on the bed, the woman's diary. The diary contained an entry describing the woman's involvement in robbing the bank.

The woman was charged in federal court with bank robbery. She moved to suppress the diary.

Should the court suppress the diary?

(A) Yes, because the officer had no warrant.

(B) Yes, because admitting the diary would violate the woman's privilege against self- incrimination.

(C) No, because the hotel manager had actual authority to allow the officer into the hotel room.

(D) No, because the officer reasonably relied on the hotel manager's apparent authority to allow the officer into the hotel room.

II. THE "PLAIN VIEW" DOCTRINE

A. Aerial observation

Question 3

Police received an anonymous tip that Tusitala was growing marijuana in her backyard, which was surrounded by a 15-foot high, solid wooden fence. Officer Boa was unable to view the yard from the street, so he used a police helicopter to fly over Tusitala's house. Boa identified a large patch of marijuana plants growing right next to the house and used this observation to obtain a search warrant.

Tusitala is prosecuted for possession of marijuana and moves to suppress use of the marijuana in evidence.

The court should

(A) grant the motion, because the only purpose of Boa's flight was to observe the yard.

(B) grant the motion, because Tusitala had a reasonable expectation of privacy in the curtilage around her house and the police did not have a warrant.

(C) deny the motion, because a warrant is not required for a search of a residential yard.

(D) deny the motion, because Tusitala had no reasonable expectation of privacy from aerial observation.

III. PROBABLE CAUSE GENERALLY

A. Only evidence heard by magistrate used

1. Incorrect affidavit

a. Honest police error

Question 4

On October 22, a police officer submitted an application for a warrant to search 217 Elm Street for cocaine. In the application, the officer stated under oath that he believed there was cocaine at that location because of information supplied to him on the morning of October 22 by Susie Schultz. He described Schultz as a cocaine user who had previously supplied accurate information concerning the use of cocaine in the community and summarized what Schultz had told him as follows: The previous night, October 21, Schultz was in the defendant's house at 217 Elm Street. The defendant gave her cocaine. Schultz also saw three cellophane bags containing cocaine in the defendant's bedroom.

The warrant was issued and a search of 217 Elm Street was conducted on October 22. The search turned up a quantity of marijuana but no cocaine. The defendant was arrested and charged with possession of marijuana. The defendant moved to suppress the use of the marijuana as evidence, contending that Susie Schultz was not in 217 Elm Street on October 21 or at any other time.

If, after hearing evidence, the judge concludes that the statement in the application attributed to Susie Schultz is incorrect, the judge should grant the motion to suppress

(A) because the application contains a material statement that is false.

(B) because of the false statement and because no cocaine was found in the house.

(C) only if he also finds that Susie Schultz's statement was a deliberate lie.

(D) only if he also finds that the officer knew the statement was false.

Chapter 3

WARRANTLESS ARRESTS AND SEARCHES

I. SEARCH INCIDENT TO ARREST

A. Protective sweep

1. Can't search too-small spaces

Question 5

The police had, over time, accumulated reliable information that a rock singer operated a large cocaine-distribution network, that he and his accomplices often resorted to violence, and that they kept a small arsenal of weapons in his home.

One day, the police received reliable information that a large brown suitcase with leather straps containing a supply of cocaine had been delivered to the singer's home and that it would be moved to a distribution point the next morning. The police obtained a valid search warrant to search for and seize the brown suitcase and the cocaine and went to the singer's house.

The police knocked on the singer's door and called out, "Police. Open up. We have a search warrant." After a few seconds with no response, the police forced the door open and entered. Hearing noises in the basement, the police ran down there and found the singer with a large brown suitcase with leather straps. They seized the suitcase and put handcuffs on the singer. A search of his person revealed a switchblade knife and a .45-caliber pistol.

The police then fanned out through the house, looking in every room and closet. They found no one else, but one officer found an Uzi automatic weapon in a box on a closet shelf in the singer's bedroom.

In addition to charges relating to the cocaine in the suitcase, the singer is charged with unlawful possession of weapons.

The singer moves pretrial to suppress the use as evidence of the Uzi automatic weapon. The singer's motion to suppress should be

(A) granted, because the search exceeded the scope needed to find out if other persons were present.

(B) granted, because once the object of the warrant—the brown suitcase—had been found and seized, no further search of the house is permitted.

(C) denied, because the police were lawfully in the bedroom and the weapon was immediately identifiable as being subject to seizure.

(D) denied, because the police were lawfully in the house and had probable cause to believe that weapons were in the house.

II. AUTOMOBILE SEARCHES

A. Two special exceptions

1. Field search for contraband

Question 6

Police received information from an undercover police officer that she had just seen two men (whom she described) in a red pickup truck selling marijuana to schoolchildren near the city's largest high school. A few minutes later, two police officers saw a pickup truck fitting the description a half block from the high school. The driver of the truck matched the description of one of the men described by the undercover officer.

The only passenger was a young woman who was in the back of the truck. The police saw her get out and stand at a nearby bus stop. They stopped the truck and asked the driver to exit the car; they then searched the driver's person. In the pocket of the driver's jacket, the police found a small bottle of pills that they recognized as narcotics. They arrested the driver and handcuffed him to the back of the police car. The police then broke open a locked toolbox attached to the flatbed of the truck and found a small sealed envelope inside. They opened it and found marijuana. They also found a quantity of cocaine in the glove compartment.

After completing their search of the driver and the truck, the police went over to the young woman and searched her purse. In her purse, they found a small quantity of heroin. Both the driver and the young woman were arrested and charged with unlawful possession of narcotics.

If the driver moves to suppress the use as evidence of the marijuana and cocaine found in the search of the truck, the court should

(A) grant the motion as to both the marijuana and the cocaine.

(B) grant the motion as to the marijuana but deny it as to the cocaine.

(C) deny the motion as to the marijuana but grant it as to the cocaine.

(D) deny the motion as to both the marijuana and the cocaine.

III. CONSENT SEARCHES GENERALLY

A. Consent generally

Question 7

Police officers received a tip that drug dealing was occurring at a certain ground-floor duplex apartment. They decided to stake out the apartment. The stakeout revealed that a significant number of people visited the apartment for short periods of time and then left. A man exited the apartment and started to walk briskly away. The officers grabbed the man and, when he struggled, wrestled him to the ground. They searched him and found a bag of heroin in one of his pockets. After discovering the heroin on the man, the police decided to enter the apartment. They knocked on the door, which was opened by the woman who lived there. The police asked if they could come inside, and the woman gave them permission to do so. Once inside, the officers observed several bags of heroin on the living room table. The woman is charged with possession of the heroin found on the living room table. She moves pretrial to suppress the heroin on the ground that it was obtained by virtue of an illegal search and seizure.

Should the woman's motion be granted?

(A) No, because the tip together with the heroin found in the man's pocket provided probable cause for the search.

(B) No, because the woman consented to the officers' entry.

(C) Yes, because the officers' decision to enter the house was the fruit of an illegal search of the man.

(D) Yes, because the officers did not inform the woman that she could refuse consent.

B. D need not know he can refuse consent

1. Where D is unaware of police's motive in requesting consent

Question 8

Larson was charged with the murder of a man who had been strangled and whose body was found in some woods near his home. Larson suffers from a neurological problem that makes it impossible for him to remember an occurrence for longer than 48 hours.

After Larson was charged, the police visited him and asked if they might search his home. Larson consented. The police found a diary written by Larson. An entry dated the same day as the victim's disappearance read, "Indescribable excitement. Why did no one ever tell me that killing gave such pleasure to the master?"

Larson was charged with murder. His attorney has moved to exclude the diary from evidence on the ground that its admission would violate Larson's privilege against self-incrimination. Counsel has also argued that Larson could not give informed consent to the search because more than 48 hours had passed since the making of the entry and hence he could not remember the existence of the incriminating entry at the time he gave his consent. There is no evidence that the police officers who secured Larson's consent to the search were aware of his memory impairment.

With regard to the diary, the court should

(A) admit it, because Larson's consent was not obtained by intentional police misconduct and Larson was not compelled to make the diary entry.

(B) admit it, pursuant to the good-faith exception to the exclusionary rule.

(C) exclude it, because Larson was not competent to consent to a search.

(D) exclude it, because use of the diary as evidence would violate Larson's privilege against self-incrimination.

IV. INSPECTIONS AND WEAPONS SEARCHES

A. Searches in schools

1. Where law enforcement agency is involved

Question 9

The police suspected that Yancey, a 16-year-old high school student, had committed a series of burglaries. Two officers went to Yancey's high school and asked the principal to call Yancey out of class and to search his backpack. While the officers waited, the principal took Yancey into the hall where she asked to look in his backpack. When Yancey refused, the principal grabbed it from him, injuring Yancey's shoulder in the process. In the backpack, she found jewelry that she turned over to the officers.

Yancey was charged with the burglaries, and moves to suppress the use of the jewelry.

The court should

(A) deny the motion on the ground that the search was incident to a lawful arrest.

(B) deny the motion on the ground that school searches are reasonable if conducted by school personnel on school grounds on the basis of reasonable suspicion.

(C) grant the motion on the ground that the search was conducted with excessive force.

(D) grant the motion on the ground that the search was conducted without probable cause or a warrant.

CONFESSIONS AND POLICE INTERROGATION

I. VOLUNTARINESS

A. Voluntariness generally

1. Involuntariness requires police coercion

Question 10

Dan entered the police station and announced that he wanted to confess to a murder. The police advised Dan of the *Miranda* warnings, and Dan signed a written waiver. Dan described the murder in detail and pinpointed the location where a murder victim had been found a few weeks before. Later, a court-appointed psychiatrist determined that Dan was suffering from a serious mental illness that interfered with his ability to make rational choices and to understand his rights and that the psychosis had induced his confession.

Dan's confession is

(A) admissible, because there was no coercive police conduct in obtaining Dan's statement.

(B) admissible, because Dan was not in custody.

(C) inadmissible, because Dan's confession was a product of his mental illness and was therefore involuntary.

(D) inadmissible, because under these circumstances, there was no valid waiver of *Miranda* warnings.

II. WHAT CONSTITUTES INTERROGATION

A. Volunteered statements

1. Voluntary custodial statements

Question 11

A grand jury indicted Alice on a charge of arson, and a valid warrant was issued for her arrest. Paul, a police officer, arrested Alice and informed her of what the warrant stated. However, hoping that Alice might say something incriminating, he did not give her *Miranda* warnings. He placed her in the back seat of his patrol car and was driving her to the police station when she said, "Look. I didn't mean to burn the building; it was an accident. I was just burning some papers in a wastebasket."

At the station, after being given *Miranda* warnings, Alice stated she wished to remain silent and made no other statements.

Alice moved to suppress the use of her statement to Paul as evidence on two grounds: first, that the statement was acquired without giving *Miranda* warnings, and second, that the police officer had deliberately elicited her incriminating statement after she was in custody.

As to Alice's motion to suppress, the court should

(A) deny the motion.

(B) grant the motion only on the basis of the first ground stated.

(C) grant the motion only on the basis of the second ground stated.

(D) grant the motion on either ground.

B. Police allow situation to develop

1. Police set up situation

Question 12

The police suspected that Yancey, a 16-year-old high school student, had committed a series of burglaries. They arrested Yancey, took him to the station, and gave him Miranda warnings. Yancey asked to see a lawyer. The police called Yancey's parents to the station. When Yancey's parents arrived, the police asked them to speak with Yancey. They put them in a room and secretly recorded their conversation with a concealed electronic device. Yancey broke down and confessed to his parents that he had committed the burglaries.

Yancey was charged with the burglaries.

Yancey moves to suppress the use of the statement Yancey made to his parents.

The best argument for excluding it would be

(A) Yancey was in custody at the time the statement was recorded.

(B) the police did not comply with Yancey's request for a lawyer.

(C) once Yancey had invoked his right to counsel, it was improper for the police to listen to any of his private conversations.

(D) the meeting between Yancey and his parents was arranged by the police to obtain an incriminating statement.

LINEUPS AND OTHER IDENTIFICATION PROCEDURES

I. THE PRIVILEGE AGAINST SELF-INCRIMINATION IN IDENTIFICATION PROCEDURES

A. General rule as to when privilege applies to ID procedures

Question 13

A defendant was lawfully arrested without a warrant for bank robbery. He was not given *Miranda* warnings, but was immediately taken to a police station where he and five other men were placed in a lineup to be viewed by the bank teller. Each man was required to say the words spoken by the bank robber: "Give me all your money. I've got a gun." After all the men in the lineup spoke those words, the teller identified the defendant as the robber.

The defendant subsequently moved to suppress the testimony of the teller, claiming the lineup violated his privilege against self-incrimination. At a suppression hearing, the teller testified that she had not gotten a good look at the robber's face, because the robber had been wearing a hat pulled down over most of his face, but that she was certain the defendant was the robber because she had recognized his voice at the lineup.

Should the defendant's motion be granted?

(A) No, because being required to speak at the lineup, while compelled, was not testimonial or communicative.

(B) No, because testimony of a witness based on firsthand observation is not subject to exclusion as the fruit of the poisonous tree.

(C) Yes, because the defendant was compelled to speak at the lineup, and this compelled speech led to the witness's identification testimony.

(D) Yes, because the defendant was never informed that he could refuse to make a statement and that any statement could be used as evidence against him.

B. Courtroom identifications

Question 14

Devlin was charged with murder. Several witnesses testified that the crime was committed by a person of Devlin's general description who walked with a severe limp. Devlin in fact walks with a severe limp. He objected to a prosecution request that the court order him to walk across the courtroom in order to display his limp to the jury to assist it in determining whether Devlin was the person that the witnesses had seen.

Devlin's objection will most likely be

(A) sustained, because the order sought by the prosecution would violate Devlin's privilege against self-incrimination.

(B) sustained, because the order sought by the prosecution would constitute an illegal search and seizure.

(C) denied, because the order sought by the prosecution is a legitimate part of a proper courtroom identification process.

(D) denied, because a criminal defendant has no legitimate expectation of privacy.

CHAPTER 6

FORMAL PROCEEDINGS

I. GRAND JURY PROCEEDINGS

A. Self-incrimination and immunity

Question 15

A state grand jury investigating a murder learned that the key suspect might have kept a diary. The grand jury issued a subpoena duces tecum requiring the suspect to produce any diary. The subpoena made clear that the grand jury was seeking only the diary and not any testimony from the suspect. The suspect refused to produce the diary, citing the privilege against self-incrimination.

Under what circumstances, if any, could the grand jury compel production of the diary over the suspect's Fifth Amendment privilege?

(A) It may compel production without granting immunity because the suspect was not compelled to write a diary.

(B) It may compel production only if the suspect is granted use and derivative use immunity from the act of production.

(C) It may compel production only if the suspect is granted transactional immunity.

(D) It may not compel production of a private diary under any circumstances.

B. Attorney's presence in grand jury room

Question 16

A federal grand jury was investigating drug trafficking in the jurisdiction. It subpoenaed a witness to testify, and the prosecutor advised the witness that he had a Fifth Amendment privilege not to testify if he so chose. The witness asked that his counsel be allowed to advise him inside the grand jury room, but the prosecutor refused to allow the attorney inside. The witness, after speaking with his attorney outside the grand jury room, decided to testify and ended up making self-incriminating statements.

The witness subsequently was indicted for drug crimes. The indictment was based on the witness's grand jury testimony and on evidence seized in an unconstitutional search of the witness's home.

The witness moved to dismiss the indictment.

Should the court dismiss the indictment?

(A) Yes, because the witness was denied his constitutional right to advice of counsel.

(B) Yes, because the indictment was based upon illegally seized evidence.

(C) No, because the witness waived his constitutional rights by testifying.

(D) No, because the witness had no right to counsel inside the grand jury room and the illegally seized evidence did not affect the validity of the indictment.

C. Use of illegally-obtained evidence

Question 17

Suspecting that a husband had slain his wife, police detectives persuaded one of the husband's employees to remove a drinking glass from the husband's office so that it could be used for fingerprint comparisons with a knife found near the body. The fingerprints matched. The prosecutor announced that he would present comparisons and evidence to the grand jury. The husband's lawyer immediately filed a motion to suppress the evidence of the fingerprint comparisons to bar its consideration by the grand jury, contending that the evidence was illegally acquired.

The motion should be

(A) granted, because, if there was no probable cause, the grand jury should not consider the evidence.

(B) granted, because the employee was acting as a police agent and his seizure of the glass without a warrant was unconstitutional.

(C) denied, because motions based on the exclusionary rule are premature in grand jury proceedings.

(D) denied, because the glass was removed from the husband's possession by a private citizen and not a police officer.

II. THE TRIAL

A. Burden of proof in criminal cases

1. General rules of allocation

a. Burden as to proving elements of the crime

i. Standard of proof

Question 18

A state statute provides as follows: "In all criminal cases, whenever the Constitution permits, the burden of proof as to a defense claimed by the defendant shall rest on the defendant, and the magnitude of the burden shall be as great as the Constitution permits."

The same state defines the crime of forcible rape as follows: "Forcible rape consists of sexual penetration inflicted on an unconsenting person by means of force or violence. Consent of the victim is a complete defense to a charge of rape."

At a defendant's trial for forcible rape, he testified that the alleged victim had consented to having sexual intercourse with him.

How should the trial judge instruct the jury regarding the issue of consent?

(A) The burden of proving that the victim consented, by a preponderance of the evidence, rests on the defendant.

(B) The burden of proving that the victim consented, by clear and convincing evidence, rests on the defendant.

(C) The burden of proving that the victim consented, by proof beyond a reasonable doubt, rests on the defendant.

(D) The burden of proving that the victim did not consent, by proof beyond a reasonable doubt, rests on the prosecution.

b. Burden as to proving affirmative defenses

Question 19

A defendant was charged with murder. His principal defense was that he had killed in "hot blood" and should be guilty only of manslaughter. The judge instructed the jury that the state must prove guilt beyond a reasonable doubt, that the killing was presumed to be murder, and that the charge could be reduced to manslaughter, and the defendant accordingly found guilty of this lesser offense, if the defendant showed by a fair preponderance of the evidence that the killing was committed in the heat of passion on sudden provocation. The defendant was convicted of murder. On appeal, he now seeks a new trial and claims error in the judge's instructions to the jury.

The defendant's conviction will most probably be

(A) affirmed, because the judge carefully advised the jury of the state's obligation to prove guilt beyond a reasonable doubt.

(B) affirmed, because the defendant's burden to show hot blood was not one of ultimate persuasion but only one of producing evidence to rebut a legitimate presumption.

(C) reversed, because the instruction put a burden on the defendant, which denied him due process of law.

(D) reversed, because presumptions have a highly prejudicial effect and thus cannot be used on behalf of the state in a criminal case.

B. Motion for directed verdict

1. Standard for granting

Question 20

State Y employs the Model Penal Code or American Law Institute test for insanity, and requires the state to prove sanity, when it is in issue, beyond a reasonable doubt. At Askew's trial for murder, he pleaded insanity. The state put on an expert psychiatrist who had examined Askew. He testified that, in his opinion, Askew was sane at the time of the murder. Askew's attorney did not introduce expert testimony on the question of sanity. Rather, he presented lay witnesses who testified that, in their opinion, Askew was insane at the time of the murder. At the end of the trial, each side moves for a directed verdict on the question of sanity.

Which of the following correctly describes the judge's situation?

(A) She may grant a directed verdict for the defense if she believes that the jury could not find the prosecution to have proved sanity beyond a reasonable doubt.

(B) She may grant a directed verdict for the prosecution if she believes that Askew's witnesses on the insanity question are not believable.

(C) She may not grant a directed verdict for the defense, because the state had expert testimony and the defense only lay witnesses.

(D) She may grant a directed verdict for the prosecution if she is convinced by their experts that Askew was sane beyond a reasonable doubt.

C. A witness's Fifth Amendment privilege against self-incrimination

Question 21

In an action to recover for personal injuries arising out of an automobile accident, a plaintiff calls a bystander to testify. Claiming the privilege against self-incrimination, the bystander refuses to answer a question as to whether she was at the scene of the accident. The plaintiff moves that the bystander be ordered to answer the question. The judge should allow the bystander to remain silent only if

(A) the judge is convinced that she will incriminate herself.

(B) there is clear and convincing evidence that she will incriminate herself.

(C) there is a preponderance of evidence that she will incriminate herself.

(D) the judge believes that there is some reasonable possibility that she will incriminate herself.

D. D's Confrontation Clause rights

1. Confession implicating someone else, used during joint trial

Question 22

Smith and Penn were charged with murder. Each gave a confession to the police that implicated both of them. Smith later retracted her confession, claiming that it was coerced.

Smith and Penn were tried together. The prosecutor offered both confessions into evidence. Smith and Penn objected. After a hearing, the trial judge found that both confessions were voluntary and admitted both into evidence. Smith testified at trial. She denied any involvement in the crime and claimed that her confession was false and the result of coercion. Both defendants were convicted.

On appeal, Smith contends her conviction should be reversed because of the admission into evidence of Penn's confession.

Smith's contention is

(A correct, unless Penn testified at trial.

(B) correct, whether or not Penn testified at trial.

(C) incorrect, because Smith testified in her own behalf.

(D) incorrect, because Smith's own confession was properly admitted into evidence.

III. SENTENCING

A. Sentencing generally

Question 23

During the course of a car chase in which two police officers tried to apprehend and arrest the driver and passenger for bank robbery, one of the officers fired, first a warning shot and then at the car. He struck the passenger sitting next to the driver.

The driver was caught five minutes later. The passenger died from loss of blood. The driver was charged with the murder of the passenger. The jury found the driver guilty of the murder of the passenger. Before passing sentence, the judge heard argument by both parties. The prosecutor introduced the criminal record of the driver, showing two prior felony convictions. Defense counsel admitted the correctness of the record. The court imposed the maximum sentence of life imprisonment. On appeal, the appellate court should hold that this sentence

(A) violated the driver's right to due process, in that it deprived him of a fair and unbiased tribunal.

(B) was in error because the introduction of new evidence after the trial deprived the driver of a fair trial.

(C) was not in error.

(D) deprived the driver of the right to confront the witness against him.

IV. DOUBLE JEOPARDY

A. When jeopardy attaches

Question 24

A defendant was charged with manslaughter. At the preliminary hearing, the magistrate dismissed the charge on the grounds that the evidence was insufficient. The prosecutor then brought the case before a grand jury. After hearing the evidence presented by the prosecutor, the grand jury refused to return an indictment. The prosecutor waited a few months until a new grand jury had been impaneled and brought the case before that grand jury, which returned an indictment charging the defendant with manslaughter. The defendant moves to dismiss the indictment on double jeopardy grounds.

Should the motion be granted?

(A) No, because jeopardy had not attached.

(B) No, because there has been no conviction or acquittal.

(C) Yes, because any proceeding after the preliminary hearing would violate double jeopardy.

(D) Yes, because bringing the case before the second grand jury was a violation of double jeopardy.

B. Overlapping offenses

1. Where lesser included offense is tried first

Question 25

Donald was arrested in Marilyn's apartment after her neighbors had reported sounds of a struggle and the police had arrived to find Donald bent over Marilyn's prostrate body. Marilyn was rushed to the hospital where she lapsed into a coma. Despite the explanation that he was trying to revive Marilyn after she suddenly collapsed, Donald was charged with attempted rape and assault after a neighbor informed the police that she had heard Marilyn sobbing, "No, please no, let me alone."

At trial, the forensic evidence was inconclusive. The jury acquitted Donald of attempted rape but convicted him of assault. While he was serving his sentence for assault, Marilyn, who had never recovered from the coma, died. Donald was then indicted and tried on a charge of felony murder. In this common-law jurisdiction, there is no statute that prevents a prosecutor from proceeding in this manner, but Donald argued that a second trial for felony murder after his original trial for attempted rape and assault would violate the Double Jeopardy Clause.

His claim is

(A) correct, because he was acquitted of the attempted rape charge.

(B) correct, because he was convicted of the assault charge.

(C) incorrect, because Marilyn had not died at the time of the first trial and he was not placed in jeopardy for murder.

(D) incorrect, because he was convicted of the assault charge.

2. Where prosecution is unable to try both charges at once

Question 26

On May 1, 2007, a car driven by the defendant struck a pedestrian. On July 1, 2007, with regard to this incident, the defendant pleaded guilty to reckless driving (a misdemeanor) and was sentenced to 30 days in jail and a fine of $1,000. She served the sentence and paid the fine.

On April 1, 2008, the pedestrian died as a result of the injuries she suffered in the accident. On March 1, 2011, a grand jury indicted the defendant on a charge of manslaughter of the pedestrian. On May 15, 2011, the trial had not begun and the defendant filed a motion to dismiss the indictment on the ground of double jeopardy, in that her conviction of reckless driving arose out of the same incident, and on the ground that the three-year statute of limitations for manslaughter had run.

The defendant's motion should be

(A) granted only on double jeopardy grounds.

(B) granted only on statute of limitations grounds.

(C) granted on either double jeopardy grounds or statute of limitations grounds.

(D) denied on both grounds.

CRIMINAL PROCEDURE ANSWERS

References to "L&I" are to LaFave & Israel, *Criminal Procedure*
Hornbook (2d Ed., West, 1992).

Answer 1

Choice (**C**) is correct, because a state may grant broader rights under its own constitution than are granted by the federal Constitution. Thus, even though the secret recording of a conversation by a government informant does not violate the Fourth Amendment, the state may extend their rule beyond the federal guarantee. As the "clear" precedent here held "that the conduct of the police in making the recording violated the employee's rights under the state constitution, and that the exclusionary rule is the proper remedy for this violation," then the court should grant the employee's motion.

(A) is wrong, because, although the initial premise is correct (the employee's federal constitutional rights were not violated), the latter premise is not, as a state may grant broader rights under its own constitution than are granted by the federal Constitution. Thus, even though the secret recording of a conversation by a government informant does not violate the Fourth Amendment, the state may extend their rule beyond the federal guarantee. As the "clear" precedent here held "that the conduct of the police in making the recording violated the employee's rights under the state constitution, and that the exclusionary rule is the proper remedy for this violation," then the court should grant the employee's motion.

(B) is wrong, because it is irrelevant. Regardless of the belief of the police officers regarding the legality of their action under the federal Constitution, the precedent under the state constitution will control here. A state may grant broader rights under its own constitution than are granted by the federal Constitution. Thus, even though the secret recording of a conversation by a government informant does not violate the Fourth Amendment, the state may extend their rule beyond the federal guarantee. As the "clear" precedent here held "that the conduct of the police in making the recording violated the employee's rights under the state constitution, and that the exclusionary rule is the proper remedy for this violation," then the court should grant the employee's motion.

(D) is wrong, because it is incorrect legally. The secret recording of a conversation by a government informant does not violate the Fourth Amendment. Furthermore, the precedent under the state constitution will control here. A state may grant broader rights under its own constitution than are granted by the federal Constitution. As the "clear" precedent here held "that the conduct of the police in making the recording violated the employee's rights under the state constitution, and that the exclusionary rule is the proper remedy for this violation," then the court should grant the employee's motion.

Answer 2

Choice (**A**) is correct. The Fourth Amendment protects places as to which a person has a reasonable expectation of privacy. One of those places is a person's dwelling, even a temporary dwelling like a hotel room. See, e.g., *Minnesota v. Olson* (1990) (overnight social guest has reasonable expectation of privacy in the home in which she is staying); *Stoner v. California* (1964) (hotel guest is to be treated like any other tenant, and management may not consent to a search of the guest room prior to check-out). Before the police may enter a place as to which a suspect has a reasonable expectation of privacy, the police must (1) have probable cause to suspect a crime; and (2) have a search or arrest warrant, or benefit from some exception to the warrant requirement. Here, although requirement (1) (probable cause) was satisfied, the police did not have a search or arrest warrant, and there was nothing in the facts to suggest any exception to the warrant requirement. For example, although there is an exception to the warrant requirement for "exigent circumstances," no such circumstances were presented here, since the woman was out for the evening and thus did not pose an imminent threat to destroy evidence. (If the police were worried that she would destroy evidence as soon as she returned, they could have posted an officer outside the room to prevent her re-entry, while they sought a warrant.)

Nor did the permission from the hotel manager override the woman's right not to have her premises searched without a warrant, for the reasons described in the analysis of Choices (C) and (D).

(B) is wrong because, although it reaches the right outcome, it does so on incorrect reasoning. The privilege against self-incrimination protects a person against being required by government to make an incriminating communication. Since the woman made the diary entries without being required to do so by government, the later seizure of that diary could not violate her privilege. (If she had been required by subpoena to *produce*, say, "any diary or other communication in which you discuss the alleged crime," then this probably *would* have violated her privilege, since it would in effect require her to communicate the information, "This is a diary that I wrote," a communication that would tend to incriminate her. But here, since the police seized the diary without requiring the woman to produce it or authenticate it, there is no self-incrimination problem.)

(C) is wrong because the hotel manager did not have actual authority to allow the officer into the hotel room. "Actual authority" is a concept of agency law: If the principal intentionally confers on the agent the right to do something, the agent is said to have actual authority to do that thing. So if the woman had indicated (either expressly or by implication) to the hotel management that it was OK for management to enter and search her room at any time, the management would have had actual authority to conduct its own search, and also authority to consent to the police search. In another context, suppose that D was an employee of X Corp. and had an office at corporate headquarters; if the understanding was that X Corp. had the right as owner of the office to search its contents at any time, then X Corp. would have had actual authority to permit the police to make such a search, and that permission would have overridden D's reasonable expectation of privacy in the office.

But here, hotel management had at most actual authority to enter for the *limited purposes* of cleaning, trash removal, and the like, not for the purpose of making a search of the guest's belongings. Therefore, the manager did not have actual authority to consent to the police search. See *Stoner v. California* (1964) (hotel guest is to be treated like any other tenant, and management may not consent to a search of the guest room prior to check-out).

(D) is wrong, because the hotel manager did not have apparent authority to allow the officer into the hotel room. "Apparent authority," like "actual authority," is a concept from agency law—if the principal puts the agent in such a position that the world reasonably infers that the agent has actual authority to do Act X, then the agent is deemed to have apparent authority to do X even though the agent does not have actual authority to do X.

Here, the defendant hotel guest (the principal) probably has, merely by checking into the room and not indicating otherwise, conferred on hotel management (the agent) apparent authority to enter for *limited purposes* like cleaning. But the guest has not conferred apparent authority on management to search the room, or to give consent to law enforcement to search the room—that's because renting a hotel room is not commonly understood to confer such authority on hotel management. Since hotel management did not have apparent authority to consent to the search, the police's reliance on what they thought was apparent authority was not reasonable, and therefore not effective. Consequently, the defendant's basic reasonable expectation of privacy in her temporary hotel dwelling prevailed, and was enough to make the warrantless entry a Fourth Amendment violation, as further described in Choice (A).

Answer 3

Choice **(D)** is correct. Where objects on private property can be seen from public places, observation by the police does not constitute a Fourth Amendment search. The fact that a police officer who obtains the "plain view" does so from a contorted or otherwise unusual position does not prevent the "plain view" doctrine from applying, assuming that the policeman is in a place where he has a prior right to be. *Harris v. U.S.* (1968). If the police use an aircraft to view the defendant's property from the air and the aircraft is in public, navigable, airspace, anything the police can see with the naked eye from that airspace falls within the "plain view" doctrine. Even a view taken by the police from a helicopter flying only 400 feet above the ground still fell within the "plain view" doctrine according to a five-Justice majority in *Florida v. Riley* (1989). Therefore, the search of Tusitala's yard from an aerial view was valid, and the subsequent issuance of a warrant to seize the marijuana observed in the search was valid.

(A) is wrong because the purpose of the flight was irrelevant, as long as the police officer was in a place where he had a prior right to be. There is nothing to indicate that the officer was not allowed to be in the airspace above Tusitala's property.

(B) is wrong because, although Tusitala had a reasonable expectation of privacy in his yard from ground-level observation due to his erection of a 15-foot high fence, this expectation of privacy did not extend to aerial observation, as explained in the discussion of (D).

(C) is wrong because if a person has a reasonable expectation of privacy in his yard, then a warrant would be required to enter it. In this case, ground-level observation of Tusitala's yard, which was enclosed by a 15-foot high fence, would require a warrant; by contrast, aerial observation of the yard would not require a warrant.

Answer 4

Choice **(D)** is correct. The exclusionary rule provides that evidence obtained by violating the defendant's constitutional rights may not be introduced by the prosecution, at least for purposes of providing direct proof of the defendant's guilt. The exclusionary rule does not bar evidence that was obtained by officers acting in reasonable reliance on a search warrant issued by a proper magistrate but ultimately found to be unsupported by probable cause. *U.S. v. Leon* (1984). This good-faith exception will not apply if the officer who prepared the affidavit on which the warrant is based knows that the information in it is false or recklessly disregards its truth or falsity. Therefore, the motion to suppress should be granted under these circumstances.

(A) is wrong because it is irrelevant that there was a false material statement in the application, as long as the police officers acted in reasonable reliance upon it. The informant was described as a cocaine user who had previously supplied accurate information concerning the use of cocaine in the community; she also supplied detailed information about how she came upon the information which she supplied to the police. It was reasonable for the police to rely on the warrant that was based on this information offered by this informant. And under *U.S. v. Leon*, supra, the evidence obtained by reasonable reliance on a search warrant is not excludible even though there was not in fact probable cause for issuance of the warrant. (See the analysis of Choice (D) above.)

(B) is wrong because not only is it irrelevant that there was a false statement in the application, but it is also irrelevant that no cocaine was found in the house, as long as the police officers acted in reasonable reliance upon the warrant. There was reasonable reliance on the warrant as explained in the discussion of Choice (A).

(C) is wrong because the nature of the false statement is irrelevant, as long as the police officers acted in reasonable reliance upon the warrant. There was reasonable reliance on the warrant, as explained in the discussion of Choice (A).

Answer 5

Choice **(A)** is correct. Incident to a lawful arrest in an arrestee's home, the officers executing the warrant may conduct a "protective sweep" of all or part of the premises, if they have a "reasonable belief" that another person who might be dangerous to the officers may be present *in the areas swept. Maryland v. Buie* (1990). So here, the police had the right to search the house for accomplices. The Uzi, however, was found in a box on a closet shelf. Clearly the weapon was neither in plain sight nor in a place where a person could be found. Therefore, the protective-sweep exception doesn't apply. Since the search warrant covered only the brown suitcase (which the police had already seized), their search of the closet could not be justified on the grounds that they were executing the search warrant either.

(B) is wrong because the answer misstates the applicable law: The police had the right to search the house for accomplices. As is described in the analysis of Choice (A) above, the police had the right to check protectively for other persons. Therefore, this choice—since it says that no further search of the house was permitted once the suitcase was seized—is inconsistent with the officers' right to make the protective search (which may be made at any time that the police are still on the premises and are thus vulnerable to a sudden attack from someone who might be hiding).

(C) is wrong because the weapon was not in an area that could be searched. It's true that the police were lawfully in the bedroom (under their right to make a protective sweep—see Choice (A)). But while they were in the bedroom, the police were only permitted to look in places where a person might be hiding. They therefore weren't allowed to look in small boxes, as they did here.

(D) is wrong because, while the police knew that there might well be weapons in the house, they would have needed a warrant in order to look for such weapons at the top of the closet. There are two requirements that must be satisfied before a house may be searched for a particular item, unless there is some applicable exception: (1) probable cause to believe that the item will be found; and (2) a warrant to search for it. Here, since the facts tell us that the police had gotten reliable information that the singer and his accomplices "kept a small arsenal of weapons in [the singer's] home," requirement (1) was satisfied as to the weapons. But although the police procured a search warrant, that warrant did not cover the weapons, only the brown suitcase. Therefore, the fact that the police were already in the home, and the further fact that they had probable cause to believe that the weapons would or might be found, were not enough to permit them to look either in the bedroom or in the closet. And while their need to make a "protective sweep" justified them in looking in the bedroom, this need did not, as described in the discussion of Choice (A), authorize them to search in a small box on a shelf, since no one could have been hiding there.

Answer 6

Choice **(D)** is correct. The court should deny the driver's motion to suppress both types of evidence since the search that allowed the police to find the drugs was conducted properly. Generally, the Fourth Amendment requires that police have a warrant to search a person or location. There are many exceptions to this rule, several of which involve the searches of automobiles. In particular, the police could search the driver's car without a warrant if they had probable cause to believe that it contained contraband or evidence of a crime. *California v. Carney* (1985). Since the officers who stopped the car were informed by another officer that, only a few minutes earlier, the occupants of the truck had been observed selling marijuana, the arresting officers had probable cause to search the driver's person for drugs. Once they found drugs on the driver, they then had probable cause (which they may even have had before the stop) to believe that the truck would contain drugs. Given that belief, they were entitled to search the car for drugs, without first getting a warrant.

Once we have determined that the search was allowed, we need to check whether the scope of the search was proper. When the police stop a vehicle and have probable cause to believe that contraband is contained in it, they may search any container that could possibly contain the object of the search. *U.S. v. Ross* (1982). Since the officers were searching the driver's truck for evidence of a recent drug sale, the object of the search was marijuana, which can be stored in very small containers. Both the glove compartment of the truck and the toolbox in the flatbed were large enough to contain the drugs, so the police could lawfully search them without a warrant.

Notice that this is *not* a case in which the driver is benefited by *Arizona v. Gant* (2009), where the Court held that the mere fact that a driver has been arrested for, say, a traffic violation does not automatically entitle the police to do a complete search of the passenger compartment. Here, by the time the police started their search of the truck itself (as opposed to the driver's person), they already had probable cause to believe that the truck would contain evidence of narcotics possession, the offense for which they had arrested the driver. So they were entitled to search the truck's passenger compartment for drugs. That probable cause to believe that drugs would be found in the car makes the constitutional difference. For instance, suppose the police had merely stopped the truck for, say, a traffic violation, arrested the driver for that violation and handcuffed him, and then did a search of the passenger compartment incident to arrest, without any probable cause to believe that drugs or contraband would be found within the truck. In this situation, *Gant* would have made the search of the truck illegal. But here, since the police already had appropriately obtained probable cause to suspect that the truck would contain drugs prior to the moment when they started the truck search, *Gant* is irrelevant, and the search was proper.

Choices (A), (B), and (C) are incorrect because they wrongly conclude that the police improperly searched either the glove compartment or the toolbox.

Answer 7

Choice (**B**) is correct. The woman's consent justified the officers' entry. When a person consents to the entry of law enforcement officers into an area as to which the person would otherwise have a justifiable expectation of privacy, that consent validates the police entry, and nullifies any need for either probable cause or a search warrant if such a need existed prior to the consent. Once the police then make their consented-to entry, the "plain view" doctrine entitles them to seize any item whose contraband or evidentiary nature is obvious, as long as when they have the view the police are standing in a place where they have a right to be. *Harris v. U.S.* (1968). Since the woman consented to the officers' entry into her house, and since the officers spotted the heroin while standing in a place to which the consent applied, there could not have been either an illegal search or an illegal seizure.

(A) is wrong because, while this answer correctly states that the woman's motion to suppress the heroin should not be granted, it misstates the legal basis for this conclusion. Even assuming there was probable cause to search the home, a warrant would have been required for entry had the woman not consented. See, e.g., *Payton v. New York* (1980).

(C) is wrong because the search of the man, even assuming it was improper, did not violate the *woman's* rights and therefore provides no basis for suppressing evidence found in her house. That is, the woman did not have "standing" to assert a violation of the constitutional rights of a third party. Cf. *Minnesota v. Carter* (1998) (discussing standing requirements for third-party constitutional claims).

(D) is wrong because there is no requirement that officers inform individuals of their right to refuse consent. See *Schneckloth v. Bustamonte* (1973). Therefore, the consent was valid.

Answer 8

Choice (**A**) is correct. The police may make a constitutional warrantless search if they receive the consent of the individual whose premises, effects or person are to be searched. The police did not deceive Larson nor make any misrepresentations in order to obtain his consent. Nor did they compel him to make the diary entry, a requirement in order for him to claim that his Fifth Amendment privilege against self-incrimination was violated, as discussed more fully in the analysis of (D). Therefore, the diary should be admitted.

(B) is wrong because the "good faith" exception to the exclusionary rule does not apply in this context, nor is it even necessary to rely on an exception, since the search and seizure were valid. The exclusionary rule provides that evidence obtained by violating the defendant's constitutional rights may not be introduced by the prosecution, at least for purposes of providing direct proof of the defendant's guilt. The exclusionary rule does not bar evidence that was obtained by officers acting in reasonable reliance on a search warrant issued by a proper magistrate but ultimately found to be unsupported by probable cause ("good faith" exception). *U.S. v. Leon* (1984). There was no warrant issued in this case; therefore, the concept is misapplied here. In addition, the diary is admissible without reliance on an exception to the exclusionary rule, because of Larson's consent, as discussed in the explanation to (A).

(C) is wrong because Larson's disability did not affect his ability to understand the nature of his consent. It's true that Larson could not remember things that happened more than 48 hours previously, so that he did not remember making the diary entry. However, what is relevant is that he was fully competent to understand the consequences of his consent to a present search of his home. Therefore, the consent was valid.

(D) is wrong because the police did not compel the production of the diary, nor would evidence of a diary entry be considered "testimonial or communicative." The Fifth Amendment privilege against self-incrimination protects against compulsion to give "testimonial or communicative" evidence. Larson consented to the search without any compulsion on the part of the police. Additionally, Larson's earlier writing of the diary was not intended as a communication (the fact pattern does not indicate that it was intended to be anything other than a private writing meant to be read only by Larson) and would therefore not be covered under the privilege for that reason as well.

Answer 9

Choice (**D**) is correct. School officials may search the person and property of a student without a warrant if there is "reasonable ground for suspecting that the search will turn up evidence that the student has violated or is violating either the law or the rules of the school." *New Jersey v. T.L.O.* (1985). However, this rule almost certainly doesn't apply where the school authorities are performing the search at the express request of the police. Consequently, the usual requirement of probable cause for a search, plus the requirement of a search warrant, apply if there is no other applicable exception to these requirements. There is no such exception to either of these requirements on these facts.

(A) is wrong because a search incident to an arrest must be made incident to a valid arrest, supported by probable cause. The facts do not offer a basis on which probable cause could have been found, only a vague reference that the police "suspected" Yancey. Additionally, the search here happened before the arrest; a valid search incident to an arrest occurs after the arrest has been made.

(B) is wrong because, while it's true that school officials may search the person and property of a student without a warrant if there is "reasonable ground for suspecting that the search will turn up evidence that the student has violated or is violating either the law or the rules of the school," (*N.J. v. T.L.O.,* supra) this rule doesn't apply here. That's because the principal was acting at the specific behest of the police. Consequently, the search had to meet the same requirements as a police search (including satisfaction of the warrant requirement), and the "reasonableness" of the search wouldn't be enough to validate it.

(C) is wrong because there is no "excessive force" basis for excluding the fruits of a search.

Answer 10

Choice (**A**) is correct. Dan's confession is admissible because it was made voluntarily after he had validly waived his Fifth Amendment right against self-incrimination. A confession may only be introduced against a defendant if it meets two criteria. First, the defendant must have made the confession voluntarily. This hurdle is very easy to clear since a statement is considered "voluntary" unless there is evidence of police coercion. Nothing the police did in this situation forced Dan to confess, so his statement was voluntary. (As discussed in Choice (C) below, the Supreme Court has held that a suspect's mental illness, standing alone, will not result in a statement being considered involuntary.) Second, the confession must be made in accordance with the decision in *Miranda,* which requires that the suspect be given "*Miranda* warnings" and have validly waived them before he is questioned by law enforcement authorities. A waiver of the Fifth Amendment right against self-incrimination and the Sixth Amendment right to have counsel present at questioning is valid only if it is made "knowingly and intelligently." To meet this standard, the prosecution must show that (1) the suspect knew what his rights were when he waived them, and (2) he understood that he was giving up those rights. "Intelligence," for the purposes of waiver analysis, has nothing to do with whether the suspect was making a wise decision. Dan was given his *Miranda* warnings and signed a written waiver of his rights before confessing. Since there is no evidence that he was coerced into signing the waiver, the waiver was valid and the confession is admissible against him.

(B) is wrong because Dan was in custody when he confessed. A defendant is in custody when police action has restricted his "freedom of action in any significant way." The "reasonable suspect" test is used to determine if a defendant is in custody. The issue is whether a reasonable person in the suspect's position would believe that he would be allowed to leave. Dan had already walked into a police station and announced that he wanted to confess to murder. Since a reasonable person would believe that the police would not let him simply walk out of the station after making such an announcement, Dan was in custody at that point.

(C) is wrong because Dan's mental illness did not render either his confession or his waiver of his *Miranda* rights involuntary. The issue is not whether the decision to confess was rational, but rather whether it was made of Dan's free will. The Supreme Court has held that a mentally ill suspect's decision to confess and waive his *Miranda* rights, no matter how irrational, is voluntary absent police coercion. *Colorado v. Connelly,* 479 U.S. 157 (1986).

(D) is wrong because Dan's waiver of his *Miranda* rights was valid. As discussed above, a suspect's mental illness does not render his waiver invalid. Additionally, it should be noted that express, written waivers are almost always valid, absent some evidence of police trickery or coercion.

Answer 11

Choice (**A**) is correct. The court should deny Alice's motion to suppress her statement because she wasn't being interrogated when she said it. Alice argues that her statement should be suppressed on two different grounds, so we should examine them separately.

First, Alice claims that because her statement was given before she had been read her *Miranda* warnings, it should not be admissible. Therefore, the question becomes, at what point must a police officer give a suspect *Miranda* warnings? *Miranda* only applies if three requirements have been met: (1) the defendant has been taken into custody, (2) the confession was given in response questioning, and (3) the interrogation was conducted by the police. If all three conditions are met, then any confession may not be admitted unless the police have informed the defendant that she had the right to remain silent, that anything she said could be used against her in a court of law, that she had the right to have an attorney present at questioning, and that if she could not afford an attorney, one would be appointed for her before questioning if she wished. In this case, Alice, having been arrested and put into a police car, was certainly in custody, since a defendant is considered in custody for *Miranda* purposes when a reasonable suspect in her position would not believe she was free to leave. But although Paul believed that Alice might say something incriminating while in the patrol car, he neither said nor did anything to her other than what was required to arrest her and take her into custody. Since, as discussed below, Paul did nothing that was reasonably likely to elicit an incriminating response from Alice, there was no "interrogation" that would trigger Alice's right to be read her *Miranda* warnings.

Second, Alice claims that Paul had deliberately elicited the incriminating statement she made while in the patrol car. The *Miranda* Court specifically said that "volunteered statements of any kind are not barred by the Fifth Amendment and their admissibility is not affected by our holding." The question now becomes what, if anything, did Paul do that would be considered an "interrogation," rendering Alice's statement non-voluntary? The Supreme Court has held that, in addition to direct questioning of a suspect, an interrogation has taken place whenever the police do anything that they should know is reasonably likely to elicit an incriminating response from the suspect. Here, Alice argues that arresting her for arson and putting her in the patrol car was enough to be the functional equivalent of questioning. However, that police conduct was insufficient to constitute interrogation without some further act by Paul, since "officers do not interrogate a suspect simply by hoping that he will incriminate himself." *Arizona v. Mauro* (1987).

Choices (B), (C), and (D) are wrong because they contradict the analysis given above.

Answer 12

Choice (**D**) is correct. Once Yancey asked for a lawyer, no "interrogation" could occur until the police provided one. Interrogation, for purposes of *Miranda*, occurs "whenever a person in custody is subjected to either express questioning or its functional equivalent . . . words or actions on the part of police that the police should know are reasonably likely to elicit an incriminating response from the suspect." *Rhode Island v. Innis* (1980).

If the police conduct merely consists of arranging a situation in which the police believe it likely that the defendant may volunteer an incriminating remark, there is no interrogation, because "officers do not interrogate a suspect simply by hoping that he will incriminate himself." *Arizona v. Mauro* (1987). However, if the arrangement involves sending in a trusted person to speak to the defendant alone and secretly recording the conversation, this would likely constitute interrogation. The police asked Yancey's parents to speak to him and then listened in secretly. This is a situation where the police should know it is reasonably likely that an incriminating remark will be elicited. Therefore, interrogation occurred and the statement should be suppressed because it was obtained in violation of Yancey's *Miranda* rights.

(A) is wrong because, regardless of the fact that Yancey was in custody at the time, it still needs to be established that Yancey was interrogated in order for the statement to be suppressed. This is the case, as discussed in the explanation to Choice (D).

(B) is wrong because the police don't have to provide a lawyer as long as the suspect is not interrogated. The essence of the warning about an attorney is not that a suspect has an automatic right to have the police provide him with a lawyer while they hold him in custody — all the police must do is to choose between providing a lawyer or questioning, so they are always free to defer their questioning until some later date if they can't (or don't want to) provide a lawyer. Therefore, the fact that a lawyer was not procured is not significant by itself. It is significant because, despite the fact that a lawyer was not procured, Yancey was subject to interrogation, as explained in the discussion of Choice (D).

(C) is wrong because it is not true that the police may not listen to any of Yancey's private conversations. The argument for exclusion of the statement is based on the fact that Yancey's *Miranda* rights were violated because he was in custody and was subjected to interrogation despite his request for an attorney. The police were permitted to eavesdrop on Yancey's conversations while he was in custody, as long as the statements he made were not in response to interrogation (or the equivalent of interrogation) by them.

Answer 13

Choice (**A**) is correct. The privilege against self-incrimination extends only to compelled "testimonial" communications. Compulsory physical-identification procedures, like being forced to give fingerprints, blood samples, voice prints, and the like, have been held not to be "testimonial," because the accused is not being asked to make statements that have communicative value. See, e.g., *United States v. Hubbell* (2000): "Thus, even though the act may provide incriminating evidence, a criminal suspect may be compelled . . . to make a recording of his voice." So here, the defendant could properly be required to utter the words spoken by the bank robber, since those words were being used merely to help the victim identify which of the men in the lineup was the robber, not for the communicative value of the words being spoken.

(B) is wrong because it is both overbroad and not applicable to these facts. Why is it overly broad? There is some testimony based on first-hand observation that *is* subject to exclusion as the fruit of the poisonous tree: If a law enforcement officer gets the opportunity to make a first-hand observation as the direct result of police illegality, then his testimony based on that observation will be excludable as fruit of the poisonous tree. So, for instance, if the officer breaks into D's house without a warrant and without probable cause, and while there secretly listens to D making a confession of crime to D's wife, the officer would not be permitted to testify to what he heard, because his first-hand observation is the fruit of the poisonous tree (the illegal break-in).

Nor is the statement in this choice applicable to these facts — since the teller's testimony here is based on the teller's own first-hand observation, and the teller got that observation without any improper law-enforcement procedures, the principle stated in this choice would not apply even if it was an accurate statement of the law.

(C) is wrong for the same reason that Choice (A) is right: The privilege against self-incrimination extends only to compelled "testimonial" communications, and being compelled to supply a voice sample or other form of physical identification is not testimonial.

(D) is wrong because *Miranda* did not apply to these facts. *Miranda* warnings are designed to protect the suspect's ability to exercise his privilege against self-incrimination. The need to supply

Miranda warnings is therefore triggered only when the suspect is being subjected to custodial "interrogation," meaning that the suspect in custody is being asked questions in an attempt to elicit communications. When the defendant here was asked to repeat the words from the holdup, he was not being asked to communicate or give "testimonial"-type information, but rather, to supply a form of physical identification. Therefore, *Miranda* warnings were not required.

Answer 14

Choice **(C)** is correct. The Fifth Amendment protects only against the compulsion of "communications" or "testimony" (privilege against self-incrimination) and not against "compulsion which makes a suspect or accused the source of 'real or physical evidence'." *Schmerber v. California* (1966). In *U.S. v. Wade* (1967), the Court said that the privilege did not apply to a defendant forced to appear in a lineup and to speak for identification. Similarly, the displaying of a defendant's limp would not be covered by the privilege because it is a legitimate part of a proper courtroom identification process.

(A) is wrong because, as described in the explanation of Choice (C), the privilege against self-incrimination would not apply to these facts.

(B) is wrong because no search or seizure has been conducted under circumstances where the defendant is being asked to do something as part of a proper courtroom identification process.

(D) is wrong because every person has a legitimate expectation of privacy, regardless of one's status as a criminal defendant. In addition, this situation is not one where there has been an invasion of a person's legitimate expectation of privacy—Devlin is not in a place where he has the reasonable expectation of privacy (the courtroom), nor is his affliction a private matter (since it is readily apparent when he walks).

Answer 15

Choice **(B)** is correct. The confusing thing about this question is that at first glance, the Fifth Amendment privilege against self-incrimination doesn't seem to play any role at all. What the privilege protects against is government's compelling a person to make a testimonial communication, and it's hard to see what testimonial communication is being compelled here. After all, the government didn't compel the suspect to keep a diary (if he indeed kept one). But the Fifth Amendment has *also* been held to protect against orders compelling a person to *produce* (i.e., deliver to the government) a document or other thing, if the act of production would have testimonial significance by, say, *authenticating* the document or thing. So here, the government, by issuing the subpoena, is in effect saying to the suspect, "If you have kept a diary, give us that diary, and we'll know from the fact that you gave it to us that you are conceding that it is indeed something you wrote." So the suspect's mere act of complying with the subpoena would amount to implied testimony that the diary was written by him.

Because of the above analysis, the government may compel production only if it gives the suspect some sort of immunity against the testimonial consequences of being required to produce the diary. Of the two sorts of immunity—transactional and use—mere use immunity, the narrower of the two, suffices for Fifth Amendment purposes. So here, as this choice indicates, the government would have to give "use and derivative use immunity from the act of production"; what this means is that the diary would be admissible, but only as long as the government had some other, wholly-independent, way to prove to the jury that this was a diary kept by the suspect. For instance, the prosecution might have a friend or relative of the suspect testify that she saw the suspect keep a diary with a cover that matches this one, and/or that the witness now recognizes the handwriting as belonging to the suspect—that way, the government would not be relying in any way on the suspect's act of turning over this particular diary in order to show that the diary was kept by the suspect.

(A) is wrong because it ignores the problem that if the suspect complies by producing his diary, this mere act of production will itself tend to authenticate the diary, and thus be implicitly testimonial. See Choice (B) for more about this problem.

(C) is wrong because use immunity is enough to protect against violations of the Fifth Amendment. It's true that transactional immunity (which in this case would mean that the suspect would not be prosecuted for any crime described in the diary) would also suffice to avoid the Fifth Amendment problem. But that sort of immunity is overkill — it's more than the Constitution requires. As is further explained in Choice (B), the less-broad "use immunity" would be enough. Use immunity in this case would mean that the government must prove the diary's authenticity (i.e., that it was written by the suspect) by means wholly unconnected to the fact that the suspect produced it in response to the subpoena.

(D) is wrong because the suspect's limited privilege against self-incrimination here (the privilege not to have his act of producing the diary in response to the subpoena be used as proof of the diary's authenticity) is adequately protected by either use immunity or transactional immunity. See the analysis in Choice (B) for more about this. So the government *can* compel the production of this private diary.

Answer 16

Choice (**D**) is correct. First, a grand jury witness does not have a constitutional right to counsel inside a grand jury room. *U.S. v. Mandujano* (1976). Second, the Fourth Amendment exclusionary rule does not apply to the presentation of evidence before a federal grand jury. Therefore, such a grand jury can properly issue an indictment based on illegally-obtained evidence. *U.S. v. Calandra* (1974).

(A) is wrong because a grand jury witness does not have a constitutional right to counsel inside a grand jury room. And that is true even if the lawyer is "retained" rather than court-appointed. *U.S. v. Mandujano* (1976). (By the way, it's not even clear that the prosecutor was constitutionally required to let the witness leave the grand jury room to consult his lawyer, as the prosecutor did here.)

(B) is wrong because the Fourth Amendment exclusionary rule does not apply to the presentation of evidence before a federal grand jury. See the discussion of this issue in the analysis of Choice (D).

(C) is wrong because although it reaches the right outcome, it does so on reasoning that is less good than the reasoning in Choice (D). It's certainly the case that the witness indeed had a Fifth Amendment right to decline to testify, and that the witness waived that right by testifying voluntarily after learning that he had the right. (His having consulted with his lawyer outside the jury room further reinforces the idea that he voluntarily waived his right not to testify.) But this waiver does not really explain why the court will refuse to dismiss the indictment. That's because the indictment was based not only on the testimony but also on the evidence from the unconstitutional search, and even unconstitutionally-obtained evidence can be considered by a grand jury in reaching its decision to indict. (See Choice (D) for more about this.) In other words, even if the witness had not waived his right not to testify, the indictment would likely have been issued anyway, and properly so. Therefore, any waiver by the witness is not the best explanation of why the court refused to dismiss the indictment.

Answer 17

Choice (**C**) is correct. A grand jury may hear and use *any* piece of evidence regardless of its admissibility, including hearsay and illegally-obtained evidence. Therefore, there are no grounds to seek the suppression of any particular piece of evidence by a grand jury, and the filing of a motion to suppress before the grand jury proceeding was premature.

(A) is wrong because it misstates the law and does not address the relevant issue. During its deliberations, the grand jury may review *all* evidence available to it to determine whether there is sufficient evidence to justify a trial. In particular, the fact that the police's seizure of the glass may have been illegal (which it would have been if the police had not had probable cause and/or had not gotten a search warrant) would not matter, because even illegally-seized evidence may be considered by the grand jury, as discussed in Choice (C) above.

(B) is wrong because even if the seizure was unconstitutional, the grand jury was entitled to consider the evidence. By the way, on the underlying merits it probably *is* the case that: (1) the employee was acting as a police agent (he was doing what they requested him to do); (2) the husband probably had a reasonable expectation of privacy in the glass located in his office (at least if it was his private office, rather than a part of the office space that he shared with employees); and (3) whether or not the police had probable cause to suspect the husband, they were required to get a search warrant before seizing an item as to which he had a reasonable expectation of privacy. But none of this matters here, because even if the seizure was a violation of the husband's Fourth Amendment rights, the grand jury was still entitled to consider the seized item, as described in the discussion of Choice (C) above.

(D) is wrong because it arrives at the correct result, but for the wrong reason. The reason the motion should be denied is because it was filed at the wrong time. Whether or not the employee was considered a private citizen when he obtained the drinking glass will become relevant only when a motion is properly made at a later point. (However, it is likely that in a pre-*trial* suppression hearing, a court would conclude that the employee *was* acting as a government agent, in which case the evidence would be inadmissible at trial since it was obtained without a search warrant, and its seizure therefore violated the husband's Fourth Amendment rights.)

Answer 18

Choice (**D**) is correct. The state statute includes lack of consent as an element of the offense. (We know that because the statute defines forcible rape as penetration inflicted on an "unconsenting person.") Therefore, constitutional due process requires the state to prove that element (and *every* element) of the crime beyond a reasonable doubt. *Patterson v. New York* (1977). What makes this question mildly confusing is that the statute also says "Consent of the victim is a complete defense to a charge of rape"—this might lead you to believe that the victim's consent is an affirmative defense. (The defendant may be constitutionally required to bear both the burden of production and the burden of persuasion with respect to an affirmative defense.) But once the state defined lack of consent as an element of the crime, as it did here, the state was no longer free to classify lack of consent as an affirmative defense, if the consequence of that classification was to impose on the defendant either the burden of coming forward with some evidence of lack of consent, or the burden of persuading the jury that the victim consented.

(A), (B), and (C) are all wrong because they are inconsistent with the principle—correctly expressed in (D)—that the prosecution bears the burden of proving lack of consent because the crime is defined so as to make lack of consent an element of the crime rather than an affirmative defense.

Answer 19

Choice (**B**) is correct, because it correctly identifies precisely why the instructions were correct: The burden of ultimate persuasion remained with the prosecution, and the defendant only bore the burden of rebutting a presumption of murder.

First, take a close look at what's going on here. The defendant was charged with murder—that is, the killing of another, with malice aforethought. The burden of persuasion is on the prosecution to prove every element of the crime beyond a reasonable doubt. This burden does not shift throughout the trial. The burden of production, or "going forward," requires only that a party introduce enough evidence on an issue such that a reasonable jury could infer the fact alleged. If the defendant wants to claim an affirmative defense—like self-defense or provocation—he will have the burden of going forward.

The judge's instructions create a rebuttable presumption that a killing is murder; he lays the burden of ultimate persuasion on the prosecution, to prove every element of the crime beyond a reasonable doubt; and he establishes that the defendant can rebut the presumption of murder by producing evidence that shows, by a fair preponderance, that the killing was committed under adequate provocation. Note that this doesn't shift the burden of persuasion from the prosecution to the defendant, because that would violate the defendant's due process rights. Instead, it requires only that, once the state has borne its burden of proving every element beyond a reasonable doubt, the defendant has the burden of producing evidence on his affirmative defense; he must show it was more likely than not that he was adequately provoked.

(A) is wrong, because it does not address with sufficient precision, unlike Choice (B), exactly why the defendant's conviction will be upheld. Choice (A) ignores entirely the defendant's burden of going forward, which is significant, due to the potential due process violation placing a burden on a criminal defendant could create. As a result, (A) is not the best response.

The judge's instructions create a rebuttable presumption that a killing is murder; he lays the burden of ultimate persuasion on the prosecution, to prove every element of the crime beyond a reasonable doubt; and he establishes that the defendant can rebut the presumption of murder by producing evidence that shows, by a fair preponderance, that the killing was committed under adequate provocation. Note that this doesn't shift the burden of persuasion from the prosecution to the defendant, because that would violate the defendant's due process rights. Instead, it requires only that, once the state has borne its burden of proving every element beyond a reasonable doubt, the defendant has the burden of producing evidence on his affirmative defense; he must show it was more likely than not that he was adequately provoked. This reflects a fair distribution of the burden between the prosecution and the defendant, and so the defendant's conviction will be upheld.

What Choice (A) does is to address only the state's burden of ultimate persuasion. It does not address the defendant's burden of production at all.

(C) is wrong, because the defendant was not denied due process of law, and, because the judge correctly identified the burdens of proof for both the state and the defendant, the conviction will be upheld. Due process requires fairness of process in circumstances when one is being deprived of life, liberty, or property. Here, if the defendant were required to prove his *innocence,* he'd be denied due process. However, he's only required to introduce enough evidence to create a reasonable doubt in the minds of the jury that he was adequately provoked. This is only a burden of going forward, and is thus considered fair.

The burden of persuasion is on the prosecution, to prove every element of the crime beyond a reasonable doubt. This burden does not shift throughout the trial. The burden of production, or "going forward," requires only that a party introduce enough evidence on an issue such that a reasonable jury could infer the fact alleged. If the defendant wants to claim an affirmative defense—like self-defense or provocation—he will have the burden of going forward.

The judge's instructions create a rebuttable presumption that a killing is murder; he lays the burden of ultimate persuasion on the prosecution, to prove every element of the crime beyond a reasonable doubt; and he establishes that the defendant can rebut the presumption of murder by producing evidence that shows, by a fair preponderance, that the killing was committed under adequate provocation. Note that this doesn't shift the burden of persuasion from the prosecution to the defendant, because that would violate the defendant's due process rights. Instead, it requires only that, once the state has borne its burden of proving every element beyond a reasonable doubt, the defendant has the burden of producing evidence on his affirmative defense; he must show it was more likely than not that he was adequately provoked. Since (C) mistakenly states that the defendant's due process rights were violated by the jury instructions, it's not the best response.

(D) is wrong, because it misstates the law: presumptions *can,* in fact, be used by the state in a criminal case. First, a little background. There are two types of burdens of proof: the burden of persuasion and the burden of going forward. The burden of persuasion is on the prosecution, to prove every element of the crime beyond a reasonable doubt. This burden does not shift throughout the trial. The burden of production, or "going forward," requires only that a party introduce enough evidence on an issue such that a reasonable jury could infer the fact alleged. If the defendant wants to claim an affirmative defense—like self-defense or provocation—he will have the burden of going forward.

A rebuttable presumption has the effect of shifting the burden of "going forward" to the party adversely effected by the presumption. It does not shift the burden of persuasion, which cannot shift throughout the trial. Contrary to what Choice (D) states, there are many, rebuttable presumptions that operate validly on behalf of the state in a criminal case. For instance, as a general rule, people who commit crimes are sane, conscious, sober, and not operating under duress. These are, as a general rule, presumptions that operate in favor of the state, such that it need not prove in a criminal case *any* of these elements—that is, unless the defendant introduces evidence on any of these elements, or in fact any justification or excuse or affirmative defense. Thus, if the defendant introduces no evidence on any presumed fact, the jury can, but doesn't have to, find that those facts exist. However, if the defendant meets the burden of going forward—that is, introduces enough evidence to create a reasonable doubt about a presumed fact in the minds of the trier of fact—then the state must prove the challenged fact beyond a reasonable doubt. There's nothing legally repugnant about any of this; the only presumptions that couldn't operate in the state's favor are those that address the ultimate issue of proof of a crime's elements. As a result, Choice (D)'s statement, that presumptions cannot operate in favor of a state in a criminal case, is incorrect, making (D) not the best response.

Answer 20

Choice (**A**) is correct. When an insanity defense is raised, if the case is tried before a jury, the jury will have the task of deciding the merits of the defendant's insanity defense, just as it will decide the other factual issues in the case. Here, where the state must prove sanity beyond a reasonable doubt, a verdict should be granted for the defense if and only if the judge believes that a reasonable jury could not find the prosecution to have proved sanity beyond a reasonable doubt.

(B) is wrong because the judge's determination of the credibility of the witnesses is not relevant. It is up to the jury to determine the credibility of the witnesses and to decide the factual issue of sanity. In fact, granting a directed verdict for the prosecution on any element of the case would deprive defendant of his constitutional Sixth Amendment right to a jury trial.

(C) is wrong because the jury need not weigh an expert witness's testimony more heavily than that of a lay witness. The jury is always free to disregard or disbelieve any witness's evaluation of the defendant's condition.

(D) is wrong because the determination is made by the jury. In order to grant a directed verdict in favor of the prosecution, it is not necessary that the judge be convinced that Askew was sane, only that a jury could be convinced of Askew's sanity (beyond a reasonable doubt).

Answer 21

Choice (**D**) is correct, because it correctly states the standard. In both federal and state courts, a witness's proper invocation of the privilege against self-incrimination is judged under the "reasonable possibilities" test. Under it, the court must find reasonable grounds for believing the witness is subject to criminal liability (not civil liability or public disgrace), and that his answer will at least provide a link to evidence which may incriminate him, in order to allow him to remain silent. *Hoffman v. U.S.* (1951). Since Choice (D) correctly states this rule, it's the best response.

(A) is wrong, because it overstates the actual standard. In both federal and state courts, a witness's proper invocation of the privilege against self-incrimination is judged under the "reasonable possibilities" test. Under it, the court must find reasonable grounds for believing the witness is subject to criminal liability (not civil liability or public disgrace), and that his answer will at least provide a link to evidence which may incriminate him, in order to allow him to remain silent. Choice (A) states a standard that is much stricter than the actual standard. As a result, it's not the best response.

(B) is wrong, because it overstates the standard. In both federal and state courts, a witness's proper invocation of the privilege against self-incrimination is judged under the "reasonable possibilities" test. Under it, the court must find reasonable grounds for believing the witness is subject to criminal liability (not civil liability or public disgrace), and that his answer will at least provide a link to evidence that may incriminate him, in order to allow him to remain silent. Choice (B) states a standard that is much stricter than the real standard. As a result, it's not the best response.

(C) is wrong, because it overstates the standard. In both federal and state courts, a witness's proper invocation of the privilege against self-incrimination is judged under the "reasonable possibilities" test. Under it, the court must find reasonable grounds for believing the witness is subject to criminal liability (not civil liability or public disgrace), and that his answer will at least provide a link to evidence that may incriminate him, in order to allow him to remain silent. Choice (C) states a standard that is slightly more strict than the real standard. As a result, it's not the best response.

Answer 22

Choice (**A**) is correct. The Sixth Amendment gives any criminal defendant "the right . . . to be confronted with the witnesses against him." The Confrontation Clause has two main components: (1) the right to compulsory process; and (2) the right to cross examine hostile witnesses. The Confrontation Clause prevents, in some circumstances, the use of one person's out-of-court confession against another. The Supreme Court has held that *A*'s Confrontation Clause rights are violated if the confession of *B*, his non-testifying co-defendant, naming *A* as a co-participant in the crime, is introduced at their joint trial. This is true even if the jury is instructed to consider the confession only against *B*, not *A. Bruton v. U.S.* (1968). The *Bruton* principle applies where the defendant who allegedly confessed declines to take the stand. If the confessor takes the stand and denies having made the confession — and perhaps even if he takes the stand and acknowledges the confession, but then opens himself up to the other defendant's cross-examination about it — there is probably no Confrontation Clause problem. Therefore, if and only if Penn testified at trial, Smith's appeal would be denied because his Confrontation Clause rights would not have been denied.

(B) is wrong because whether or not Smith's Confrontation Clause rights were denied does depend upon whether or not Penn testified. If Penn testified, then Smith's rights would not have been violated, as discussed in the explanation of Choice (A).

(C) is wrong because whether or not *Smith* testified is irrelevant. Smith's Confrontation Clause rights give him the right to cross examine hostile witnesses. Therefore, it is relevant whether or not *Penn* testifies, as he is a hostile witness that Smith has a right to cross examine.

(D) is wrong because the fact that Smith's confession was properly admitted has no bearing on whether his Confrontation Clause rights have been violated by admission of a co-defendant's confession. He is afforded the right to cross examine hostile witnesses, a right which has been denied to him in these circumstances.

Answer 23

Choice **(C)** is correct, because it correctly identifies that the prior convictions can be introduced at the sentencing hearing. In imposing sentences, the judge can rely on a wide variety of evidence, including hearsay, reports that are not cross-examined, and the like. (Somewhat different rules apply to "unusual" sentencings — e.g., the death penalty — as well as to sentencing guidelines that let the judge increase the maximum punishment based on the judge's factual findings. But neither of these factors is present here.) Prior convictions are relevant to sentencing since they bear on the likelihood of a defendant's rehabilitation. Since (C) correctly identifies that the convictions will be admissible, it's the best response.

(A) is wrong, because it misstates the law: The driver was not deprived of a fair and unbiased tribunal. At a sentencing hearing, the judge is entitled to take into account prior convictions, as a means of determining the likelihood of the defendant's rehabilitation, among other things (somewhat different rules apply to "unusual" sentencings — e.g., the death penalty).

(B) is wrong, because the driver was not deprived of a fair trial by the delay in introducing the prior convictions. In a usual sentencing hearing, the judge may take into account a broad spectrum of evidence, including hearsay, non-cross-examined reports, and prior convictions (somewhat different rules apply to "unusual" sentencings — e.g., the death penalty). If anything, introducing the prior convictions at trial would have been fraught with pitfalls, since prior convictions can be a very dangerous form of character evidence (the jury is likely to grant them undue weight). As a result, introducing the prior convictions at the sentencing hearing for the first time does not deprive the driver of a fair trial.

(D) is wrong, because it misstates the law. The driver was not entitled to confront witnesses against him in this sentencing hearing, because a usual sentence was imposed (e.g., the death penalty was not being considered). In imposing a "usual" sentence, a judge can rely on hearsay evidence as well as reports that are not cross-examined. *Williams v. N.Y.* (1949).

Answer 24

Choice **(A)** is correct, because jeopardy does not attach at either a preliminary hearing or at grand jury proceedings. Instead, jeopardy attaches in a jury trial when the jury is sworn in and in a bench trial when the court begins to hear evidence. Thus, neither the preliminary hearing nor the initial grand jury will prevent the prosecutor from bringing charges against the defendant.

(B) is wrong, since neither conviction nor acquittal is required for jeopardy to attach. Instead, jeopardy attaches in a jury trial when the jury is sworn in and in a bench trial when the court begins to hear evidence. Thus, neither the preliminary hearing nor the initial grand jury will prevent the prosecutor from bringing charges against the defendant.

(C) is wrong, because it is not the case that jeopardy attaches to "any" proceeding after the preliminary hearing. Jeopardy does not attach at either a preliminary hearing or at grand jury proceedings. Instead, jeopardy attaches in a jury trial when the jury is sworn in and in a bench trial when the court begins to hear evidence. Thus, neither the preliminary hearing nor the initial grand jury will prevent the prosecutor from bringing charges against the defendant.

(D) is wrong, because the double jeopardy clause does not bar a grand jury from returning an indictment when a prior grand jury refused to do so. Jeopardy does not attach at either a preliminary hearing or at grand jury proceedings. Instead, jeopardy attaches in a jury trial when the jury is sworn in and in a bench trial when the court begins to hear evidence. Thus, neither the preliminary hearing nor the initial grand jury will prevent the prosecutor from bringing charges against the defendant.

Answer 25

Choice (**A**) is correct. When a person is tried for offense *A*, then whether he is convicted or acquitted, the Double Jeopardy Clause prevents him from being later tried of an offense B of which offense A was a lesser included offense. So Donald can base his double jeopardy claim on, and only on, an offense that was a lesser included-offense within the felony-murder charge. Courts and legislatures generally restrict application of the felony-murder doctrine to certain dangerous felonies. The doctrine does apply to rape (a crime of which Donald was acquitted), but generally does not apply to assault (a crime of which Donald was convicted). So the acquittal on the rape charge triggers double jeopardy, but the conviction on the assault charge does not.

(B) and (D) are wrong because generally, the felony-murder doctrine does not apply to assault. Therefore, the assault charge could not be a lesser included offense within the felony-murder charge, making the assault charge irrelevant for double jeopardy purposes.

(C) is wrong because it overlooks the fact that an acquittal on lesser-included-offense A will block a trial for greater-offense-B. Therefore, even though Donald couldn't have yet been prosecuted for felony murder at the time his rape trial started (because Marilyn was still alive), the rape trial invoked Donald's double jeopardy rights. (If Donald had been *convicted* at the rape trial, the fact that the felony-murder charge couldn't have been tried yet would negate his double jeopardy claim; but given that the rape trial led to his acquittal, the fact that the felony-murder charge couldn't have been tried when the rape trial started probably *won't* negate Donald's use of double jeopardy.)

Answer 26

Choice (**D**) is correct, because neither provides a valid ground for dismissal.

The double jeopardy guarantee of the Fifth Amendment states that a person cannot be tried twice for the same offense. The guarantee also bars the government from trials for two different crimes if one is a "lesser included offense" of the other. However, there are two exceptions to the lesser-included-offense doctrine. One of those exceptions is that if the government could not have tried the second crime at the time it tried the first, due to circumstances beyond the government's control, and the defendant is convicted of the first crime the lesser-included-offense doctrine doesn't apply. That's what happened here: By the time of the original trial (or, actually, guilty plea) on reckless driving, the pedestrian hadn't yet died, so no manslaughter prosecution was possible. Therefore, double jeopardy doesn't apply.

Nor does the statute of limitations bar the manslaughter prosecution. The statute of limitations doesn't start to run until all facts necessary for prosecution have occurred. Here, the pedestrian's death was one such fact, and it occurred less than three years before the indictment, so the statute of limitations hadn't run by the date of indictment (which was the event that satisfied the statute).

(A), (B), and (C) are wrong, since each of them asserts that at least one of the two grounds was valid, and neither was (as shown in the discussion of Choice (D)).

EVIDENCE

EVIDENCE QUESTIONS BY TOPIC

Chapter 1
BASIC CONCEPTS

I. CONDITIONS FOR ADMITTING EVIDENCE

A. Relevant

1. Definition

Question 1

In a prosecution for aggravated battery, a police officer testified that when he arrested the defendant, he took a knife from the defendant and delivered it to the medical examiner. The medical examiner testified that the knife blade was consistent with the victim's wound but admitted on cross-examination that any number of other knives could also have caused the wound.

Should the judge grant a motion to strike the medical examiner's testimony?

(A) No, because the probative worth of this evidence is for the jury to assess.

(B) Yes, because in light of the medical examiner's admission, his testimony has insufficient probative value.

(C) Yes, because the medical examiner could not state the probability that the wound was caused by the defendant's knife.

(D) Yes, because the probative value is substantially outweighed by the danger of unfair prejudice.

Question 2

A defendant's house was destroyed by fire and she was charged with arson. To prove that the defendant had a motive to burn down her house, the government offered evidence that the defendant had fully insured the house and its contents.

Should the court admit this evidence?

(A) No, because the probative value of the evidence of insurance upon the issue of whether the defendant intentionally burned her house down is substantially outweighed by the dangers of unfair prejudice and confusion of the jury.

(B) No, because evidence of insurance is not admissible upon the issue of whether the insured acted wrongfully.

(C) Yes, because evidence of insurance on the house has a tendency to show that the defendant had a motive to burn down the house.

(D) Yes, because any conduct of a party to the case is admissible when offered against the party.

Question 3

The bus in which a passenger was riding was struck from the rear by a taxi. He sued the taxi company for a claimed neck injury. The taxi company claimed the impact was too slight to have caused the claimed injury and introduced testimony that all passengers had refused medical attention at the time of the accident. The passenger called a doctor from a local hospital to testify that three persons (otherwise proved to have been on the bus) were admitted to the hospital for treatment of severe neck pain within a week after the accident. The trial judge should rule the doctor's testimony

(A) admissible, because a doctor is properly qualified as an expert in medical matters.

(B) admissible if other testimony established a causal connection between the other passengers' pain and the accident.

(C) inadmissible, because the testimony to neck pain is hearsay, not within any exception.

(D) inadmissible, because the testimony is not the best evidence of the other passengers' pain and the passengers are not shown to be unavailable.

2. Exclusion

Question 4

Deeb was charged with stealing furs from a van. At trial, Wallace testified she saw Deeb take the furs.

The jurisdiction in which Deeb is being tried does not allow in evidence lie detector results. On cross-examination by Deeb's attorney, Wallace was asked, "The light was too dim to identify Deeb, wasn't it?" She responded. "I'm sure enough that it was Deeb that I passed a lie detector test administered by the police." Deeb's attorney immediately objects and moves to strike.

The trial court should

(A) grant the motion, because the question was leading.

(B) grant the motion, because the probative value of the unresponsive testimony is substantially outweighed by the danger of unfair prejudice.

(C) deny the motion, because it is proper rehabilitation of an impeached witness.

(D) deny the motion, because Deeb's attorney "opened the door" by asking the question.

Question 5

A defendant is tried on a charge of driving while intoxicated. When the defendant was booked at the police station, a videotape was made that showed him unsteady, abusive, and speaking in a slurred manner. If the prosecutor lays a foundation properly identifying the tape, should the court admit it in evidence and permit it to be shown to the jury?

(A) Yes, because it is an admission.

(B) Yes, because its value is not substantially outweighed by unfair prejudice.

(C) No, because the privilege against self-incrimination is applicable.

(D) No, because specific instances of conduct cannot be proved by extrinsic evidence.

B. Offering testimonial evidence

1. Testimony by trial judge

Question 6

A defendant was charged with murder. While walking down the hallway during a recess in the defendant's trial, the judge overheard the defendant say to his attorney, "So what if I did it? There's not enough proof to convict." Upon the judge's reporting the incident to counsel, the prosecutor called the judge as a witness in the trial.

Is the judge's testimony regarding the defendant's statement admissible?

(A) Yes, as the statement of a party-opponent.

(B) Yes, because the defendant's statement, although otherwise privileged, was made without reasonable efforts to preserve confidentiality.

(C) No, because the statement was a privileged attorney-client communication.

(D) No, because a judge may never testify in a trial over which he or she is presiding.

C. Making and responding to objections

1. Hearing outside of presence of jury

Question 7

A defendant was on trial for burglary. The prosecutor called the arresting officer to testify that shortly after the arrest the defendant had orally admitted her guilt to him. Before the officer testified, the defendant objected that no *Miranda* warning had been given, and she requested a hearing outside the presence of the jury to hear evidence on that issue.

How should the court proceed?

(A) The court should grant the request, because the hearing on the admissibility of the confession must be conducted outside the presence of the jury.

(B) The court may grant or deny the request, because the court has discretion whether to conduct preliminary hearings in the presence of the jury.

(C) The court should deny the request and rule the confession inadmissible, because only signed confessions are permitted in criminal cases.

(D) The court should deny the request and rule the confession admissible, because it is the statement of a party-opponent.

CIRCUMSTANTIAL PROOF: SPECIAL PROBLEMS

I. CHARACTER EVIDENCE

A. Character is essential element of case

1. Other aspects of other-crimes evidence

a. Rule 403 balancing

Question 8

Decker, charged with armed robbery of a store, denied that he was the person who had robbed the store.

In presenting the state's ease, the prosecutor seeks to introduce evidence that Decker had robbed two other stores in the past year.

This evidence is

(A) admissible, to prove a pertinent trait of Decker's character and Decker's action in conformity therewith.

(B) admissible, to prove Decker's intent and identity.

(C) inadmissible, because character must be proved by reputation or opinion and may not be proved by specific acts.

(D) inadmissible, because its probative value is substantially outweighed by the danger of unfair prejudice.

II. METHODS OF PROVING CHARACTER: REPUTATION, OPINION, AND PROOF OF SPECIFIC ACTS

A. FRE

1. D's good-character evidence

a. Prosecution's right of rebuttal

Question 9

The defendant, who was charged with the crime of assaulting a victim, admitted striking the victim. However, the defendant claimed to have acted in self-defense when he was attacked by the victim, who was drunk and belligerent. The defendant offered testimony of his employer, who proposes to testify that he has known and employed the defendant for 10 years and knows the defendant's reputation among the people with whom he lives and works to be that of a peaceful, law-abiding, nonviolent person.

The trial judge should rule this testimony

(A) admissible, because it is relevant to show the improbability of the defendant's having committed an unprovoked assault.

(B) admissible, because it is relevant to a determination of the extent of punishment if the defendant is convicted.

(C) not admissible, because whether the defendant is normally a person of good character is irrelevant to the specific charge.

(D) not admissible, because it is irrelevant without a showing that the defendant's employer was one of the persons among whom the defendant lived and worked.

Question 10

The defendant was charged with the crime of assaulting the victim. He admitted striking the victim, but claimed to have acted in self-defense when he was attacked by the victim, who was drunk and belligerent after a football game.

The defendant offered testimony of defendant's employer that he had known and employed the defendant for twelve years and knew the defendant's reputation among the people with whom he lived and worked to be that of a peaceful, law-abiding, nonviolent person. The trial judge admitted this testimony.

On cross-examination of the employer, the state's attorney asked the employer if he had heard that the defendant often engaged in fights and brawls. The trial judge should rule the question

(A) admissible, because evidence of the defendant's previous fights and brawls may be used to prove his guilt.

(B) admissible, because it tests the employer's knowledge of the defendant's reputation.

(C) inadmissible, because it seeks to put into evidence separate, unrelated offenses.

(D) inadmissible, because no specific time or incidents are specified and inquired about.

III. LIABILITY INSURANCE

A. General rule

1. Offered for other purposes

Question 11

A passenger is suing a defendant for injuries suffered in the crash of a small airplane, alleging that the defendant had owned the plane and negligently failed to have it properly maintained. The defendant has asserted in defense that he never owned the plane or had any responsibility to maintain it. At trial, the passenger calls a witness to testify that the witness had sold to the defendant a liability insurance policy on the plane.

The testimony of the witness is

(A) inadmissible, because the policy itself is required under the original document rule.

(B) inadmissible, because of the rule against proof of insurance where insurance is not itself at issue.

(C) admissible to show that the defendant had little motivation to invest money in maintenance of the airplane.

(D) admissible as some evidence of the defendant's ownership of or responsibility for the airplane.

IV. SETTLEMENTS AND PLEA BARGAINS

A. Settlements generally

Question 12

Carr, a driver, ran into and injured Pedersen, a pedestrian. Pedersen has sued Carr, alleging that Carr, while drunk, struck Pedersen who was in a duly marked crosswalk. Pedersen's counsel wishes to prove that after the accident Carr went to Pedersen and offered $1,000 to settle Pedersen's claim.

The trial judge should rule this evidence

(A) admissible as an admission of a party.

(B) admissible as an admission to show Carr's liability, provided the court gives a cautionary instruction that the statement should not be considered as bearing on the issue of damages.

(C) inadmissible since it is not relevant either to the question of liability or the question of damages.

(D) inadmissible because even though it is relevant and an admission, the policy of the law is to encourage settlement negotiations.

EXAMINATION AND IMPEACHMENT OF WITNESSES

I. PRESENT RECOLLECTION REFRESHED AND OTHER TECHNIQUES

A. Does not constitute evidence

Question 13

A defendant is sued for hitting a pedestrian with his car. On the evening of the day of the accident, a person who had been a passenger in the defendant's car wrote a letter to the passenger's sister in which he described the accident. When the passenger testified at trial, he stated that he could not remember some details of the accident. The pedestrian's counsel now seeks to show him the letter to assist him in his testimony on direct examination. The trial judge should rule this

(A) permissible, under the doctrine of present recollection refreshed.

(B) permissible, under the doctrine of past recollection recorded.

(C) objectionable, because the letter was not a spontaneous utterance.

(D) objectionable, because the letter is a self-serving declaration insofar as the passenger is concerned.

II. IMPEACHMENT BY PRIOR BAD ACTS

A. Federal Rule

1. May bring out on cross

a. Applies to any witness

Question 14

In an automobile negligence action by Popkin against Dwyer, Juilliard testified for Popkin. Dwyer later called Watts, who testified that Juilliard's reputation for truthfulness was bad.

On cross-examination of Watts, Popkin's counsel asks, "Isn't it a fact that when you bought your new car last year, you made a false affidavit to escape paying the sales tax?"

This question is

(A) proper, because it will indicate Watts's standard of judgment as to reputation for truthfulness.

(B) proper, because it bears on Watts's credibility.

(C) improper, because character cannot be proved by specific instances of conduct.

(D) improper, because one cannot impeach an impeaching witness.

III. IMPEACHMENT BY PRIOR INCONSISTENT STATEMENT

A. General rule

Question 15

Davidson and Smythe were charged with burglary of a warehouse. They were tried separately. At Davidson's trial, Smythe testified that he saw Davidson commit the burglary. While Smythe is still subject to recall as a witness, Davidson calls Smythe's cellmate, Walton, to testify that Smythe said, "I broke into the warehouse alone because Davidson was too drunk to help."

This evidence of Smythe's statement is

(A) admissible as a declaration against penal interest.

(B) admissible as a prior inconsistent statement.

(C) inadmissible, because it is hearsay not within any exception.

(D) inadmissible, because the statement is not clearly corroborated.

B. Special rules from FRE 613

1. "Extrinsic evidence," and the "explain or deny" and "interrogate" rules

Question 16

Perez sued Dawson for damages arising out of an automobile collision. At trial, Perez called Minter, an eyewitness to the collision. Perez expected Minter to testify that she had observed Dawson's automobile for five seconds prior to the collision and estimated Dawson's speed at the time of the collision to have been 50 miles per hour. Instead, Minter testified that she estimated Dawson's speed to have been 25 miles per hour.

Without finally excusing Minter as a witness, Perez then called Wallingford, a police officer, to testify that Minter had told him during his investigation at the accident scene that Dawson "was doing at least 50."

Wallingford's testimony is

(A) admissible as a present sense impression.

(B) admissible to impeach Minter.

(C) inadmissible, because Perez may not impeach his own witness.

(D) inadmissible, because it is hearsay not within any exception.

a. Application to hearsay declarants

Question 17

A defendant is charged with the murder of a victim. The prosecutor introduces testimony of a police officer that the victim told a priest, administering the last rites, "I was stabbed by [the defendant]. Since I am dying, tell him I forgive him." Thereafter, the defendant's attorney offers the testimony of a witness that the day before, when the victim believed he would live, he stated that he had been stabbed by a person other than the defendant.

The testimony of the witness is

(A) admissible under an exception to the hearsay rule.

(B) admissible to impeach the dead declarant.

(C) inadmissible, because it goes to the ultimate issue in the case.

(D) inadmissible, because it is irrelevant to any substantive issue in the case.

IV. IMPEACHMENT BY CONTRADICTION; THE "COLLATERAL ISSUE" RULE

A. Collateral issue rule

Question 18

A plaintiff sued a defendant for injuries the plaintiff received in an automobile accident where the defendant was the driver. The plaintiff claimed the defendant was negligent in exceeding the posted speed limit of 35 m.p.h. A bystander who saw the accident testified as an eyewitness for the plaintiff and stated on cross-examination that the defendant was wearing a green sweater at the time of the accident. At the start of the defendant's case, the defendant testified that he was going 30 m.p.h. The defendant's counsel then called a second witness, who also observed the accident, to testify solely that the defendant's sweater was blue. The second witness's testimony is

(A) admissible as substantive evidence of a material fact.

(B) admissible as bearing on the bystander's truthfulness and veracity.

(C) inadmissible, because it has no bearing on the capacity of the bystander to observe.

(D) inadmissible, because it is extrinsic evidence of a collateral matter.

HEARSAY

I. DEFINITION

A. Definition

1. Hearsay may be by the present witness

a. Statement about what declarant previously said

Question 19

Pawn sued Dalton for injuries received when she fell down a stairway in Dalton's apartment building. Pawn, a guest in the building, alleged that she caught the heel of her shoe in a tear in the stair carpet. Pawn calls Witt, a tenant, to testify that Young, another tenant, had said to him a week before Pawn's fall: "When I paid my rent this morning, I told the manager he had better fix that torn carpet."

Young's statement, reported by Witt, is

(A) admissible, to prove that the carpet was defective.

(B) admissible, to prove that Dalton had notice of the defect.

(C) admissible, to prove both that the carpet was defective and that Dalton had notice of the defect.

(D) inadmissible, because it is hearsay not within any exception.

B. Illustrations of hearsay

Question 20

In a jurisdiction without a Dead Man's Statute, a plaintiff's estate sued a defendant claiming that the defendant had borrowed from the plaintiff $10,000, which had not been repaid as of the plaintiff's death. The plaintiff was run over by a truck. At the accident scene, while dying from massive injuries, the plaintiff told a police officer to "make sure my estate collects the $10,000 I loaned to the defendant."

The officer's testimony about the plaintiff's statement is

(A) inadmissible, because it is more unfairly prejudicial than probative.

(B) inadmissible, because it is hearsay not within any exception.

(C) admissible as an excited utterance.

(D) admissible as a statement under belief of impending death.

II. SPECIAL ISSUES

A. "Truth of matter asserted"

1. Verbal acts

Question 21

In a suit based on a will, inheritance of $1 million depended upon whether the wife had survived her husband when both died in the crash of a small airplane. An applicable statute provided that, for purposes of distributing an estate after a common disaster, there was a rebuttable presumption that neither spouse had survived the other. A witness was called to testify that as she approached the plane she heard what she thought was a woman's voice saying, "I'm dying," although by the time the two occupants were removed from the wreckage they were both dead.

Is the witness's testimony admissible?

(A) No, because the matter is governed by the presumption that neither spouse survived the other.

(B) No, because the witness's testimony is too speculative to support a finding.

(C) Yes, because the hearsay rule does not apply to statements by decedents in actions to determine rights under a will.

(D) Yes, because it is relevant and not otherwise prohibited.

HEARSAY EXCEPTIONS AND EXCLUSIONS

I. ADMISSIONS

A. Personal admissions

Question 22

A plaintiff sued a defendant for injuries plaintiff received in an automobile accident. The plaintiff claims the defendant was negligent in (a) exceeding the posted speed limit of 35 m.p.h., (b) failing to keep a lookout, and (c) crossing the center line. The defendant testified in his own behalf that he was going 30 m.p.h. On cross-examination, the plaintiff's counsel did not question the defendant with regard to his speed. Subsequently, the plaintiff's counsel calls an officer to testify that, in his investigation following the accident, the defendant told him he was driving 40 m.p.h. If offered to prove that the defendant exceeded the posted speed limit, the officer's testimony is

(A) admissible as a prior inconsistent statement.

(B) admissible as an admission.

(C) inadmissible, because it lacks a foundation.

(D) inadmissible, because it is hearsay not within any exception.

Question 23

A defendant ran into and injured the plaintiff, a pedestrian. The plaintiff alleges that the defendant, while drunk, struck the plaintiff, who was in a duly marked crosswalk. A police officer investigated the accident, and plaintiff's counsel wants to introduce testimony of the investigating police officer that the defendant told the officer, "I think this was probably my fault."

The trial judge should rule this testimony

(A) admissible as a part of the res gestae.

(B) admissible as an admission of a party.

(C) inadmissible, because it includes a conclusion of law that the declarant was not qualified to make.

(D) inadmissible, because it constitutes an opinion rather than an admission of specific facts.

1. Question may not say "admission"

Question 24

A defendant was on trial for perjury for having falsely testified in an earlier civil case that he knew nothing about a business fraud. In the perjury trial, the defendant again testified that he knew nothing about the business fraud. In rebuttal, the prosecutor called a witness to testify that after the civil trial was over, the defendant admitted to the witness privately that he had known about the fraud.

Is the witness's testimony in the perjury trial admissible?

(A) Yes, but only to impeach the defendant's testimony.

(B) Yes, both to impeach the defendant's testimony and as substantive evidence of the perjury.

(C) No, because it is hearsay not within any exception.

(D) No, because it relates to the business fraud and not to the commission of perjury.

Question 25

The defendant was prosecuted for homicide. He testified that he shot in self-defense. In rebuttal, a police officer testified that he came to the scene in response to a telephone call from the defendant. The officer offers to testify that he asked, "What is the problem here, sir?" and the defendant replied. "I was cleaning my gun and it went off accidentally."

The offered testimony is

(A) admissible, as an excited utterance.

(B) admissible, to impeach the defendant and as evidence that he did not act in self-defense.

(C) inadmissible, because of the defendant's privilege against self-incrimination.

(D) inadmissible, because although it tends to expose the declarant to criminal liability, it is not supported by corroborating circumstances.

II. SPONTANEOUS, EXCITED, OR CONTEMPORANEOUS UTTERANCES (INCLUDING STATEMENTS ABOUT PHYSICAL OR MENTAL CONDITION)

A. Statements made for purposes of medical diagnosis or treatment

1. The statement may include references to the cause of the bodily condition

Question 26

A plaintiff sued a ladder manufacturer for injuries he suffered to his neck and back when a rung of the ladder on which he was standing gave way. When the plaintiff's back and neck continued to be very sore after more than two weeks, his treating physician sent him to an orthopedist for an evaluation. Though the orthopedist did not treat the plaintiff, he diagnosed an acute cervical strain. At trial, the plaintiff called the orthopedist to testify that in response to the orthopedist's inquiry about how the plaintiff had injured his back, the plaintiff told him, "I was standing near the top of a 15-foot ladder when I abruptly fell, landing hard on my back, after which the ladder toppled onto my neck."

Should the statement be admitted?

(A) Yes, because the plaintiff is present and can be cross-examined about it.

(B) Yes, because it was made for the purpose of medical diagnosis or treatment.

(C) No, because it was not made to a treating physician.

(D) No, because it relates to the inception or the cause of the injury rather than the plaintiff's physical condition.

Question 27

In a civil action for personal injury, Payne alleges that he was beaten up by Dabney during an altercation in a crowded bar. Dabney's defense is that he was not the person who hit Payne. To corroborate his testimony about the cause of his injuries, Payne seeks to introduce, through the hospital records custodian, a notation in a regular medical record made by an emergency room doctor at the hospital where Payne was treated for his injuries. The notation is: "Patient says he was attacked by Dabney."

The notation is

(A) inadmissible, unless the doctor who made the record is present at trial and available for cross-examination.

(B) inadmissible as hearsay not within any exception.

(C) admissible as hearsay within the exception for records of regularly conducted activity.

(D) admissible as a statement made for the purpose of medical diagnosis or treatment.

B. Declaration of present mental, emotional, or physical condition

1. State of mind directly in issue

Question 28

In a prosecution of Dale for murdering Vera, Dale testified that the killing had occurred in self-defense when Vera tried to shoot him. In rebuttal, the prosecution seeks to call Walter, Vera's father, to testify that the day before the killing, Vera told Walter that she loved Dale so much she could never hurt him.

Walter's testimony is

(A) admissible within the hearsay exception for statements of the declarant's then existing state of mind.

(B) admissible, because Vera is unavailable as a witness.

(C) inadmissible as hearsay not within any exception.

(D) inadmissible, because Vera's character is not an issue.

2. Offered to prove subsequent event

Question 29

Prine sued Dover for an assault that occurred March 5 in California. To support his defense that he was in Utah on that date, Dover identifies and seeks to introduce a letter he wrote to his sister a week before the assault in which he stated that he would see her in Utah on March 5.

The letter is

(A) admissible, within the state of mind exception to the hearsay rule.

(B) admissible, as a prior consistent statement to support Dover's credibility as a witness.

(C) inadmissible, because it lacks sufficient probative value.

(D) inadmissible, because it is a statement of belief to prove the fact believed.

3. Need for inference

Question 30

Daggett is prosecuted for the murder of Vales, whose body was found one morning in the street near Daggett's house. The state calls Witt, a neighbor, to testify that during the night before the body was found he heard Vales's wife scream, "You killed him! You killed him!"

Witt's testimony is

(A) admissible as a report of a statement of belief.

(B) admissible as a report of an excited utterance.

(C) inadmissible, because it reports a privileged spousal communication.

(D) inadmissible on spousal immunity grounds, but only if the wife objects.

III. PAST RECOLLECTION RECORDED

A. Exception under the FRE

1. Four requirements

Question 31

A plaintiff sued a defendant for wrongful death arising out of a traffic collision between the plaintiff's decedent and the defendant. At trial, the investigating traffic officer authenticated a tape recording of her shift-end dictation of comments used in preparing the written report of her factual findings. She testified that the tape recording was accurate when made and that she currently had no clear memory of the details of the investigation.

Is the tape recording admissible as evidence?

(A) Yes, under the past recollection recorded exception to the hearsay rule.

(B) Yes, under the public records exception to the hearsay rule.

(C) No, because it is hearsay and is a police report being offered against the defendant in a wrongful death case.

(D) No, because the police report itself is the best evidence.

IV. RECORDS OF REGULARLY CONDUCTED ACTIVITY (a/k/a "BUSINESS RECORDS")

A. Person supplying info

1. Consumer complaints or reports

Question 32

Plaza Hotel sued Plaza House Hotel for infringement of its trade name. To establish a likelihood of name confusion, Plaintiff Plaza Hotel offers a series of memoranda which it had asked its employees to prepare at the end of each day listing instances during the day in which telephone callers, cab drivers, customers, and others had confused the two names.

The memoranda should be

(A) excluded, because they are more unfairly prejudicial and confusing than probative.

(B) excluded, because they are hearsay not within any exception.

(C) admitted, because they are records of regularly conducted business activity.

(D) admitted, because they are past recollection recorded.

V. PUBLIC RECORDS AND REPORTS

A. Public records and reports

1. Federal Rule

a. Matters observed under duty

Question 33

A plaintiff sued his insurance company for the full loss of his banquet hall by fire. The insurance company defended under a provision of the policy limiting liability to 50 percent if "flammable materials not essential to the operation of the business were stored on the premises and caused a fire." The insurance company called the keeper of the city fire inspection records to identify a report prepared and filed by the fire marshal as required by law, indicating that shortly before the fire, the fire marshal had cited the plaintiff for storing gasoline at the banquet hall.

Is the report admissible?

(A) No, because it is hearsay not within any exception.

(B) No, because the proceeding is civil, rather than criminal.

(C) Yes, as a public record describing matters observed as to which there was a duty to report.

(D) Yes, as a record of regularly conducted activity, provided the fire marshal is unavailable.

B. Absence of public record

Question 34

In an arson prosecution the government seeks to rebut the defendant's alibi that he was in a jail in another state at the time of the fire. The government calls a witness to testify that he diligently searched through all the records of the jail and found no record of the defendant's having been incarcerated there during the time the defendant specified.

The testimony of the witness is

(A) admissible as evidence of absence of an entry from a public record.

(B) admissible as a summary of voluminous documents.

(C) inadmissible, because it is hearsay not within any exception.

(D) inadmissible, because the records themselves must be produced.

VI. DECLARATIONS AGAINST INTEREST

A. Generally

Question 35

The defendant, a man, has been charged with murdering the victim. The defendant defends on the grounds that the murder was really committed by a particular woman, who has since died. The defendant offers a properly authenticated photocopy of a transcript of a deposition in a civil suit brought against the woman by the victim's family for the victim's death, in which the woman said, "Yes, I killed him because I hated him." The civil suit was brought because the woman was known to have quarreled with and disliked the victim. Upon proper objection by the prosecution, the statement should be

(A) admitted as a declaration against interest.

(B) admitted as former testimony by a person now unavailable.

(C) inadmissible as hearsay not within any exception.

(D) inadmissible, because the original rather than a photocopy must be offered.

Question 36

Pamela sued Driver for damages for the death of Pamela's husband Ronald, resulting from an automobile collision that had occurred a week before the death. At trial, Driver calls Ronald's doctor to testify that the day before his death, Ronald, in great pain, said, "It was my own fault; there's nobody to blame but me."

The doctor's testimony should be admitted as

(A) a statement against interest.

(B) a dying declaration.

(C) a statement of Ronald's then existing state of mind.

(D) an excited utterance.

PRIVILEGES

I. THE ATTORNEY-CLIENT PRIVILEGE

A. Generally

1. Client

Question 37

Pace sues Def Company for injuries suffered when Pace's car collided with Def Company's truck. Def's general manager prepared a report of the accident at the request of the company's attorney in preparation for the trial, and delivered the report to the attorney. Pace demands that the report be produced.

Will production of the report be required?

(A) Yes, because business reports are not generally privileged.

(B) No, because it is privileged communication from the client to the attorney.

(C) No, because such reports contain hearsay.

(D) No, because such reports are self-serving.

B. Professional relationship

1. Fee arrangements not covered by privilege

Question 38

A defendant was on trial for tax evasion. The IRS, seeking to establish the defendant's income by showing his expenditures, called on the defendant's attorney to produce records showing only how much the defendant had paid his attorney in fees.

Should the demand for the attorney's fee records be upheld?

(A) Yes, because it calls for relevant information not within the attorney-client privilege.

(B) Yes, because the attorney-client privilege cannot be invoked to conceal evidence of a crime.

(C) No, because the records are protected by the attorney-client privilege.

(D) No, because the records are protected by the attorney work-product doctrine.

II. THE PRIVILEGE AGAINST SELF-INCRIMINATION

A. Negative inference allowed in civil cases

Question 39

A plaintiff sued an individual defendant for injuries suffered in a collision between the plaintiff's car and the defendant's truck while the defendant's employee was driving the truck. The plaintiff sought discovery of any accident report the employee might have made to the defendant, but the defendant responded that no such report existed. Before trial, the defendant moved to preclude the plaintiff from asking the defendant in the presence of the jury whether he destroyed such a report, because the defendant would then invoke his privilege against self-incrimination.

Should the court allow the plaintiff to ask the defendant about the destruction of the report?

(A) No, because a report that was prepared in anticipation of litigation is not subject to discovery.

(B) No, because no inference may properly be drawn from invocation of a legitimate privilege.

(C) Yes, because a party in a civil action may not invoke the privilege against self-incrimination.

(D) Yes, because the defendant's destruction of the report would serve as the basis of an inference adverse to the defendant.

Chapter 7
REAL AND DEMONSTRATIVE EVIDENCE, INCLUDING WRITINGS

I. AUTHENTICATION

A. Authentication of writings and recordings

1. Signature or handwriting

a. Authentication by non-expert

Question 40

When a man entered a bank and presented a check for payment, the bank teller recognized the signature on the check as a forgery because the check was drawn on the account of a customer whose handwriting she knew. The bank teller called the police. Before the police arrived, the man picked up the check from the counter and left.

The man was charged with attempting to cash a forged check. At trial, the prosecutor called the bank teller to testify that the signature on the check was forged.

Is the bank teller's testimony admissible?

(A) Yes, because a bank teller is by occupation an expert on handwriting.

(B) Yes, because it is rationally based on the bank teller's perception and is helpful to the jury.

(C) No, because the bank teller was at fault in allowing loss of the original by failing to secure the check.

(D) No, because it is not possible for either the jury or an expert to compare the signature on the missing check with a signature established as genuine.

b. Authentication by comparison with exemplar

Question 41

Parker sues Dix for breach of a promise made in a letter allegedly written by Dix to Parker. Dix denies writing the letter.

Which of the following would NOT be a sufficient basis for admitting the letter into evidence?

(A) Testimony by Parker that she is familiar with Dix's signature and recognizes it on the letter.

(B) Comparison by the trier of fact of the letter with an admitted signature of Dix.

(C) Opinion testimony of a nonexpert witness based upon familiarity acquired in order to authenticate the signature.

(D) Evidence that the letter was written in response to one written by Parker to Dix.

2. Phone conversation

a. Incoming calls

Question 42

In a narcotics conspiracy prosecution against Daly, the prosecutor offers in evidence a tape recording of a telephone call allegedly made by Daly. A lay witness is called to testify that the voice on the recording is Daly's. Her testimony to which of the following would be the LEAST sufficient basis for admitting the recording?

(A) She had heard the same voice on a similar tape recording identified to her by Daly's brother.

(B) She had heard Daly speak many times, but never over the telephone.

(C) She had, specifically for the purpose of preparing to testify, talked with Daly over the telephone at a time after the recording was made.

(D) She had been present with Daly when he engaged in the conversation in question but had heard only Daly's side of the conversation.

II. THE "BEST EVIDENCE" RULE FOR RECORDED COMMUNICATIONS

A. Communications covered

1. Other "real" evidence not covered

Question 43

Poole sued Darrel for unlawfully using Poole's idea for an animal robot as a character in Darrel's science fiction movie. Darrel admitted that he had received a model of an animal robot from Poole, but he denied that it had any substantial similarity to the movie character. After the model had been returned to Poole, Poole destroyed it.

In order for Poole to testify to the appearance of the model, Poole

(A) must show that he did not destroy the model in bad faith.

(B) must give advance notice of his intent to introduce the oral testimony.

(C) must introduce a photograph of the model if one exists.

(D) need do none of the above, because the "best evidence rule" applies only to writings, recordings, and photographs.

Question 44

A plaintiff sued a defendant for injuries suffered in a car accident allegedly caused by brakes that had been negligently repaired by the defendant. At a settlement conference, the plaintiff exhibited the brake shoe that caused the accident and pointed out the alleged defect to an expert, whom the defendant had brought to the conference. No settlement was reached. At trial, the brake shoe having disappeared, the plaintiff seeks to testify concerning the condition of the shoe.

The plaintiff's testimony is

(A) admissible, because the defendant's expert had been able to examine the shoe carefully.

(B) admissible, because the plaintiff had personal knowledge of the shoe's condition.

(C) inadmissible, because the brake shoe was produced and examined as a part of settlement negotiations.

(D) inadmissible, unless the plaintiff establishes that the disappearance was not his fault.

B. Proving the contents

Question 45

A defendant was charged with burglary. At trial, a police officer testified that, after the defendant was arrested and agreed to answer questions, the officer interrogated him with a stenographer present, but that the officer could not now recall what the defendant had said. The prosecutor presented the officer with a photocopy of the stenographic transcript of the interrogation. The officer, after looking at it, was prepared to testify that he recalled that the defendant admitted to being in the area of the burglary. The defendant objected to the officer's testimony on the ground that it violated the "original document" rule (also known as the "best evidence" rule).

Should the officer's testimony concerning the defendant's recorded confession be admitted?

(A) No, because a photocopy cannot be used without a showing that the original is unavailable.

(B) No, because the stenographer has not testified to the accuracy of the transcript.

(C) Yes, because a photocopy is a duplicate of the original.

(D) Yes, because the prosecutor is not attempting to prove the contents of the document.

III. SUMMARIES OF VOLUMINOUS WRITINGS

A. Summaries generally

Question 46

A lawyer worked steadily on a case for a client over a five-year period, with the billing agreed to be on particular amount charge per hour worked. The lawyer kept regular timesheets showing, for any day on which he worked on the matter, how long he worked and which of various activities (phone calls, letter-writing, etc.) he performed on that day. In the lawyer's suit against the client for non-payment, the lawyer did not offer into evidence the actual timesheets. Instead, in preparation for trial, the lawyer used the timesheets to create a summary showing, for each week, how much time the lawyer spent on each of the activity types. Then, at trial, the lawyer offered these weekly summaries, together with his testimony about how he had prepared them. If the client properly objects, the judge should hold that the summaries are

(A) inadmissible for any purpose, because the underlying timesheets from which they were prepared were not offered into evidence.

(B) inadmissible as substantive evidence, but usable as non-admitted materials to refresh the lawyer's present recollection.

(C) admissible as substantive evidence of hours worked, if the underlying timesheets were made available to the client prior to trial.

(D) admissible as substantive evidence only if the underlying timesheets were lost through no fault of the lawyer.

OPINIONS, EXPERTS, AND SCIENTIFIC EVIDENCE

I. EXPERT WITNESSES

A. Basis for expert's opinion

1. Inadmissible evidence

a. Proponent and expert can't disclose

Question 47

Phillips purchased a suit of thermal underwear manufactured by Makorp from synthetic materials. While he was attempting to stamp out a fire, Phillips' thermal underwear caught fire and burned in a melting fashion up to his waist. He suffered a heart attack a half hour later. In a suit against Makorp, Phillips alleged that negligence and breach of warranty caused both the burn and the heart attack. Phillips testified to the foregoing.

Dr. Jones, a physician, having listened to Phillips' testimony, is called by Phillips and asked whether, assuming the truth of such testimony, Phillips' subsequent heart attack could have resulted from the burns. His opinion is

(A) admissible as a response to a hypothetical question.

(B) admissible because the physician's expertise enables him to judge the credibility of Phillips' testimony.

(C) inadmissible, because a hypothetical question may not be based on prior testimony.

(D) inadmissible, because an expert's opinion may not be based solely on information provided by lay persons.

B. Opinion about defendant's mental state

Question 48

On trial for murdering her husband, the defendant testified that she acted in self-defense. The defendant calls an expert psychologist to testify that under hypnosis the defendant had described the killing, and that in the expert's opinion the defendant had been in fear for her life at the time of the killing.

Is the expert's testimony admissible?

(A) Yes, because the expert was able to ascertain that the defendant was speaking truthfully.

(B) Yes, because it reports a prior consistent statement by a witness (the defendant) subject to examination concerning it.

(C) No, because reliance on information tainted by hypnosis is unconstitutional.

(D) No, because it expresses an opinion concerning the defendant's mental state at the time of the killing.

CHAPTER 9
BURDENS OF PROOF, PRESUMPTIONS, AND OTHER PROCEDURAL ISSUES

I. PRESUMPTIONS

A. Effect of presumptions in federal civil cases

1. Instructions to jury

Question 49

In litigation on a federal claim, Plaintiff had the burden of proving that Defendant received a notice. Plaintiff relied on the presumption of receipt by offering evidence that timely notice was addressed to Defendant, properly stamped, and mailed. Defendant, on the other hand, testified that she never received the notice.

Which of the following is correct?

(A) The jury must find that the notice was received.

(B) The jury may find that the notice was received.

(C) The burden shifts to Defendant to persuade the jury of nonreceipt.

(D) The jury must find that the notice was not received, because the presumption has been rebutted and there is uncontradicted evidence of nonreceipt.

II. JUDGE-JURY ALLOCATION

A. Issues of fact

1. Technical exclusionary rule

a. Rules of evidence not binding

Question 50

In a prosecution of Drew for forgery, the defense objects to the testimony of West, a government expert, on the ground of inadequate qualifications. The government seeks to introduce a letter from the expert's former criminology professor, stating that West is generally acknowledged in his field as well qualified.

On the issue of the expert's qualifications, the letter may be considered by

(A) the jury, without regard to the hearsay rule.

(B) the judge, without regard to the hearsay rule.

(C) neither the judge nor the jury, because it is hearsay not within any exception.

(D) both the judge and the jury, because the letter is not offered for a hearsay purpose.

Question 51

In a prosecution of the defendant for murder, the government seeks to introduce a properly authenticated note written by the victim that reads: "[the defendant] did it." In laying the foundation for admitting the note as a dying declaration, the prosecution offered an affidavit from the attending physician that the victim knew she was about to die when she wrote the note.

The admissibility of the note as a dying declaration is

(A) a preliminary fact question for the judge, and the judge must not consider the affidavit.

(B) a preliminary fact question for the judge, and the judge may properly consider the affidavit.

(C) a question of weight and credibility for the jury, and the jury must not consider the affidavit.

(D) a question of weight and credibility for the jury, and the jury may properly consider the affidavit.

JUDICIAL NOTICE

I. ADJUDICATIVE FACTS

A. Must take if requested, and may take without a request

1. Discretionary notice

Question 52

In state-court contract litigation between Pixley and Dill, a fact of consequence to the determination of the action is whether Pixley provided Dill with a required notice at Dill's branch office "in the capital" of the state where the suit is taking place. Pixley introduced evidence that he gave notice at Dill's office in the city of Capitan. Although Capitan is the state's capital, Pixley failed to offer proof of that fact.

Which of the following statements is most clearly correct with respect to possible judicial notice of the fact that Capitan is the state's capital?

(A) The court may take judicial notice even though Pixley does not request it.

(B) The court may take judicial notice only if Pixley provides the court with an authenticated copy of the statute that designates Capitan as the capital.

(C) If the court takes judicial notice, the burden of persuasion on the issue of whether Capitan is the capital shifts to Dill.

(D) If the court takes judicial notice, it should instruct the jury that it may, but is not required to, accept as conclusive the fact that Capitan is the capital.

EVIDENCE ANSWERS

All answers assume that the Federal Rules of Evidence ("FRE") are in force as to all issues. "ACN" refers to "Advisory Committee Notes" to a particular Federal Rule of Evidence. "M&K" refers to Mueller & Kirkpatrick, *Evidence* Hornbook (Aspen, 3d Ed., 2003).

Answer 1

Choice **(A)** is correct. This evidence has some probative value, because it links the knife in defendant's possession to the type of knife that could have caused the victim's wound. The evidence is not very strong, because other knives could also have caused the wound. But how much weight to give to the evidence is a decision for the jury. FRE 401 requires only that evidence "(a) has any tendency to make a fact more or less probable than it would be without the evidence; and (b) the fact is of consequence in determining the action." Thus to be relevant, evidence need only have *some* probative value in establishing a fact. The Advisory Committee's Note to Rule 401 quotes the famous statement "A brick is not a wall," making the point that evidence is admissible even if it is only a single brick that is a part of a large wall of evidence establishing a party's case.

(B) is wrong because evidence meets the relevancy requirement of FRE 401 if it "(a) has any tendency to make a fact more or less probable than it would be without the evidence; and (b) the fact is of consequence in determining the action." The medical examiner's testimony meets this minimal standard of probativity. And it is probative of a material fact—whether this knife was the crime weapon.

(C) is wrong because no statement of probability is required for admissibility. The medical examiner's testimony does not have to establish that defendant's knife caused the wound by any particular standard of proof, such as beyond a reasonable doubt, by clear and convincing evidence, or by a preponderance of the evidence—it's up to the jury to assess the value of the evidence in determining guilt. The testimony only needs to have some unspecified-but-minimal probative value to be admissible.

That's shown by FRE 401, under which evidence is deemed to have probative value, and to be admissible (assuming it doesn't violate some other specific prohibition), if it "(a) has any tendency to make a fact more or less probable than it would be without the evidence; and (b) the fact is of consequence in determining the action."

(D) is wrong because it mischaracterizes the evidence here. It's true that FRE 403 requires a weighing of probative value against unfair prejudice, as this choice suggests. That rule establishes what might be described as a presumption of admissibility: Evidence meeting Rule 401's definition of relevance is admissible unless its probative value is "*substantially* outweighed" by the danger of unfair prejudice. Here, the medical examiner's testimony does not appear to pose *any* significant degree of unfair prejudice, let alone enough to "substantially outweigh" the probative value of that testimony.

Answer 2

Choice **(C)** is correct. This is a relevance problem. The main issue is whether the evidence meets the general relevance standard of FRE 401. Under that rule, evidence is relevant as long as it "(a) has any tendency to make a fact more or less probable than it would be without the evidence; and (b) the fact is of consequence in determining the action." Thus, evidence that has only the slightest probative value can be admitted under this rule. While evidence that the property is insured is not conclusive that the defendant committed arson (many people fully insure their houses), it is relevant to the issue of whether the defendant would have had a financial incentive or motive to commit the arson—the defendant might be able to generate cash more quickly by burning down the house and collecting insurance proceeds than by attempting to sell the house. This evidence meets the minimal probativity standard of FRE 401.

(There is a special rule concerning the admissibility of evidence of insurance, but that rule doesn't bar the evidence here; see the discussion of Choice (B) for more about this.)

(A) is wrong because although the probative value of this evidence on the issue of whether defendant intentionally burned her house down is not particularly strong, it is somewhat probative of the issue of possible motive, so it meets the easy-to-satisfy probativity standard of FRE 401 (quoted in the discussion of Choice (C) above). FRE 403 provides that relevant evidence should be admitted unless its probative value is "substantially outweighed" by the dangers of unfair prejudice, confusion, or waste of time. Here, the evidence of insurance is probably not unfairly prejudicial at all (in the sense that it does not have an undue tendency to produce decision on an improper basis such as emotion); in any event, whatever small prejudicial tendency the evidence might have is certainly not enough to "substantially outweigh" the probative value of the evidence.

(B) is wrong because although it is true that FRE 411 bars evidence of insurance to establish that the insured acted negligently or otherwise wrongfully, such evidence is admissible for *other purposes*, and proof of motive is such a purpose. (In this respect, Rule 411 is similar to Rule 404(b), under which evidence of past conduct cannot be admitted to prove a propensity to engage in such conduct but can be admitted for other purposes, such as to prove motive.)

(D) is wrong because there is no such broad rule that any conduct of a party may be admitted against that party.

Answer 3

Choice (**B**) is correct, because it correctly identifies that, if a causal connection is provided, the other instances will be admissible. The passenger is offering evidence of other injuries from the bus accident to prove that his own injuries were caused by the accident. The problem posed by such evidence is its relevance. In order for such evidence to be admissible, the material circumstances must be *substantially identical*, and the proponent of the evidence (here, the passenger) must establish the similarity.

In this question, you're told that it's already been proven that the other three passengers were involved in the same accident. Thus, the only "missing link" that the passenger must prove is that their injuries came from the same accident, since this will provide the "substantial similarity" that relevance requires. Choice (B) recognizes and resolves this issue, by focusing on the causal connection between the other passengers' injuries and the accident.

(A) is wrong, because the doctor's expert status is not relevant to the issue of admissibility here. The passenger is offering evidence of other injuries from the bus accident to prove that his own injuries were caused by the accident. The problem posed by such evidence is its relevance; in order for such evidence to be admissible, the material circumstances must be "substantially similar," and the proponent of the evidence (here, the passenger) must establish the similarity. The only "missing link" that the passenger must prove is that their injuries came from the same accident, since this will provide the "substantial similarity" that relevance requires.

The doctor's expertise matters only if he is going to give expert testimony about medical matters. So if the doctor's testimony proposed to address, say, the similarity of the injuries between the passenger and the other three passengers, the doctor's expert status would be relevant. But that's not what's been asked of him here: Instead, all the doctor has been asked is whether three other passengers from the same bus accident were admitted to the hospital that week for treatment of severe neck pain, a question that would not require expert testimony.

(C) is wrong, because the testimony here does not involve hearsay. Hearsay is an out-of-court statement offered to prove the truth of its assertion. Here, there's no out-of-court statement; the doctor is being asked whether or not three other bus passengers were admitted to the hospital for treatment of neck pain within a week of the accident. This doesn't involve recounting any out-of-court statement, and one quick way for you to identify this is that there's no out-of-court declarant.

(D) is wrong, because it misapplies the "best evidence" rule. The Best Evidence Rule applies only when the terms of a writing (or recording or photograph) are being proven. FRE 1002. It doesn't require that the "best evidence" for every issue be offered. Since no writing (or recording or photograph) is involved here, there's no "best evidence" rule issue.

Answer 4

Choice (**B**) is correct. FRE 403 provides: "The court may exclude relevant evidence if its probative value is substantially outweighed by a danger of one or more of the following: *unfair prejudice*, confusing the issues, misleading the jury, undue delay, wasting time, or needlessly presenting cumulative evidence." The fact pattern tells us that the jurisdiction excludes evidence of lie detector results, indicating that the jurisdiction questions the reliability of the test and considers evidence of the test results to be of low probative value. "Unfair" prejudice means "an undue tendency to suggest decision on an improper basis . . . ." Advisory Committee Note to FRE 403. It is reasonable to assume that some members of a jury may regard the results of a lie detector test as more scientific than they actually are, and consequently give the test too much weight. Therefore, in this jurisdiction, the danger of unfair prejudice would substantially outweigh the (low) probative value of the lie detector test.

(A) is wrong because, although the motion would be granted, it would not be for the stated reason. Leading questions are generally permissible on cross examination. FRE 611(c).

(C) is wrong because, even apart from the FRE 403 problem discussed in Choice (B), the reasoning supporting this answer mischaracterizes the concept of "rehabilitation." Once a witness has been impeached, rehabilitation is brought out through separate testimony that is offered by counsel representing the party who is a proponent of the impeached witness's testimony. It is incorrect to characterize the witness's own response to opposing counsel's "impeaching" question as "rehabilitation" of that witness's credibility.

(D) is wrong because (1) the motion would be granted for the reason discussed in Choice (B); and (2) the reasoning supporting this answer misapplies the concept of "opening the door." A topic which is otherwise off-limits to an opposing party is considered "opened for questioning" once it has been introduced by the other party—the rationale is that if the topic has been "opened" by one party it would be unfair to prohibit the opposing party from addressing it. In this case, the question "The light was too dim to identify Deeb, wasn't it?" is not even arguably related to the topic of Wallace's passing a lie detector test, so there is no unfairness in not allowing Wallace to talk about the lie detector test.

Answer 5

Choice (**B**) is correct. To answer this question, you have to deal with two issues: (1) is the evidence relevant?; and (2) if the answer to (1) is "yes," does any principle prevent the admission of the evidence?

With respect to (1), FRE 401 says that "Evidence is relevant if: (a) it has any tendency to make a fact more or less probable than it would be without the evidence; and (b) the fact is of consequence in determining the action." Whether the defendant was intoxicated is certainly a "fact . . . of consequence in determining the action," so part (b) of the relevance test is easily satisfied. And the fact that the videotape shows the defendant being "unsteady, abusive, and speaking in a slurred manner" clearly makes it more likely that the defendant was intoxicated than if the videotape were not presented, so part (a) is satisfied, making the evidence relevant.

With respect to (2), there must not be any principle that makes this piece of evidence inadmissible despite its relevance. The only plausible candidate for such a principle is FRE 403, which says that "The court may exclude relevant evidence if its *probative value is substantially outweighed* by a danger of one or more of the following: unfair prejudice, confusing the issues, misleading the jury, undue delay, wasting time, or needlessly presenting cumulative evidence." Since Choice (B) refers to the balance between probative value and negative consequences like unfair prejudice, FRE 403 has to be analyzed. The defendant's best argument would be that the tape would result in "unfair prejudice" substantially outweighing the tape's probative value. But the court would almost certainly conclude that any such prejudice would not be "unfair"—the tape accurately depicts the defendant's state, and there is nothing unfair about the depiction.

(A) is wrong, because it does not correctly characterize the facts. This choice suggests that the defendant's acts would be considered hearsay, but would be admissible nonetheless under the "admissions" hearsay exclusion. Hearsay is an out-of-court statement offered to prove the truth of its assertion. The problem here is that the videotape does not contain any assertion the truth of which is being proven by the videotape. While conduct can be considered an admission if, from it, one can reasonably infer that the actor is conscious of his guilt, this is not the case here; the defendant's conduct is non-assertive (i.e., not intended to communicate).

(C) is wrong, because the privilege against self-incrimination would not apply to these facts. The privilege against self-incrimination is a testimonial privilege; it only allows a person the right not to be compelled to testify as to matters that might tend to incriminate him. Here, there's no testimony involved—the evidence being offered is an out-of-court videotape of the defendant, but the defendant is not "testifying" in the video (nor has he apparently been "compelled" to do anything). As a result, the videotape is not covered by the privilege.

(D) is wrong, because it both misstates the facts and misstates the law. This choice states an ostensible rule of law, but refers to two ideas, neither of which applies here.

The "specific instances of conduct" part suggests that character evidence is involved here—the examiners are trying to make you think of the rule (FRE 405(a)) that prohibits proving someone's character trait by specific prior instances of that character trait, to show that he probably acted in conformity with that trait on the present occasion. However, the evidence here suggests that the defendant was drunk on *this* occasion, not another one, so it's not character evidence of the sort that's covered by the no-specific-instances rule.

The "extrinsic evidence" part is designed to make you think of the rule that even in those situations where someone's character trait *can* be proven by specific instances of prior conduct, that proof must come in the form of cross-examination of an already-testifying witness, not by means of a new witness or a new piece of documentary evidence. (This is a common-law rule, carried forward by negative implication in FRE 405(a).) But since no character-trait evidence is being offered here (see the prior paragraph), the reference to extrinsic evidence is irrelevant.

Answer 6

Choice (**D**) is correct. Although the judge is being asked to recount an out-of-court statement made by a party that is offered against that party, admissibility here does not turn on the hearsay rule. Regardless of whether the evidence is admissible under the hearsay rule, FRE 605 provides that "The presiding judge may not testify as a witness at the trial." Thus, the judge cannot offer any testimony of any kind, no matter how probative and important his testimony.

(A) is wrong because even though the statement is the admission of a party-opponent and would be otherwise admissible non-hearsay under FRE 801(d)(2)(A), FRE 605 says that the presiding judge cannot be called as a witness to testify about anything.

(B) is wrong because, although it is true that reasonable efforts were not made by the defendant and his attorney to preserve confidentiality, this means only that the communication was not privileged—it does not mean the statement is necessarily admissible. The problem here is that under FRE 605, the statement cannot be proven through the testimony of the presiding judge because that rule bars the presiding judge from offering any testimony of any kind. The defendant's lack of efforts to preserve confidentiality mean that the statement probably *would* be admissible if someone other than the presiding judge had heard it and been asked to testify about it.

(C) is wrong because, although it reaches the right outcome, it uses incorrect reasoning. The statement would *not* be privileged. That's because reasonable efforts were not made by the defendant and his attorney to preserve confidentiality, since the statement was made in a hallway open to the public in a voice loud enough to be overheard.

Answer 7

Choice (**A**) is correct. The admissibility of the officer's testimony turns on two issues: (1) whether a *Miranda* warning had to be given to the defendant before her confession can be admitted; and (2) whether the judge's determination of the first issue must be preceded by a hearing conducted in front of or outside the hearing of the jury. With respect to the first question, *Miranda* warnings must be given before a confession made by a person under arrest can be admitted. Since the defendant contends that no *Miranda* warnings were given, she is entitled to a hearing on the issue. The rule resolving the second question is contained in FRE 104(c), which says that a "hearing [that involves] the admissibility of a confession" must be conducted "so that the jury cannot hear it." (Note that this provision goes on to say that hearings on all *other* preliminary matters shall be conducted outside the presence of the jury *only* when either justice requires or when a criminal defendant is a witness and requests a hearing outside of the jury's presence.) Thus under FRE 104(c), the hearing must be conducted outside the presence of the jury.

(B) is wrong because FRE 104(c) mandates that the admissibility of confessions "must" be conducted out of the hearing of the jury. So the trial court has no discretion in this matter.

(C) is wrong because oral confessions, like signed written confessions, are admissible in criminal cases, assuming that any required *Miranda* warnings were given.

(D) is wrong because it ignores the effect of *Miranda*. It's true that a confession of a criminal defendant is an out-of-court statement made by a party-opponent, which makes it non-hearsay under FRE 801(d)(2)(A) and thus admissible—as a matter of evidence law—to prove the truth of the matter asserted within that statement. But the rules of evidence cannot alter the *constitutional* requirement that *Miranda* warnings must be given before a confession made by a person under arrest is admissible.

Answer 8

Choice **(D)** is correct. Although evidence of Decker's previous two robberies may arguably be relevant as to whether Decker robbed the store in the present case, its probative value is low and dwarfed by the prejudicial value of the evidence. FRE 403 says that relevant evidence may be excluded "if its probative value is substantially outweighed by the danger of one or more of the following: unfair prejudice[.]" "Unfair" prejudice means "an undue tendency to suggest decision on an improper basis. . . ." Advisory Committee Note (ACN) to FRE 403. The probative value of the evidence is pretty low, since the other acts don't bear very strongly on whether Decker is the robber in the present case (there's no indication that the m.o.'s are all that similar, for instance—see Choice (B) below). Conversely, there's a large risk that if the evidence were admitted, some members of the jury would likely regard it as more probative than it actually is, and consequently give the evidence too much weight.

(A) is wrong because the general rule is that "Evidence of a person's character or character trait is not admissible to prove that on a particular occasion the person acted in accordance with the character or trait." FRE 404(a)(1). There are some exceptions, but none applies here. This choice asserts a rule—admissibility of character-trait evidence to prove action in conformity with the trait on the present occasion—that is the exact opposite of the real rule of 404(a).

(B) is wrong for two reasons. First, the previous robberies are probably not sufficiently probative of Decker's identity or his intent (the latter isn't even an issue in this case). It's true that evidence of other acts may be admissible for purposes other than to show action in conformity with a person's character, and that two of these acceptable purposes are to prove identity and intent. FRE 404(b)(2). But generally, when other acts are offered to prove identity, the prosecution's theory is that the other acts by the accused are so similar in method to the crime charged that all bear his "signature" (thus justifying the inference that if the defendant committed the prior acts, he also must have committed the present one). Here, the other robberies aren't similar enough to meet this "signature" standard.

Secondly, this evidence poses an extremely high risk of prejudice, far outweighing its limited probative value, and is thus excludible under FRE 403 (see the discussion of Choice (D) above).

(C) is wrong because (1) it at least slightly misstates the law; and (2) more importantly, it gives an explanation that is inapplicable here. While it's true that, in general, character or a trait of character must be proved by reputation or opinion evidence, not specific-acts evidence (FRE 405(a)), there are some scenarios in which specific-acts evidence *is* admissible (e.g., where a character trait is an "essential element of a charge, claim or defense"—see FRE 405(b)). But the bigger problem is that what the prosecution is offering here is not, strictly speaking, character evidence—the prosecution is not offering the evidence to show that Decker has a character or tendency to commit robbery; rather, it's trying to qualify for one or more of the "other purposes than character" exceptions mentioned by 404(b), e.g., identity.

Answer 9

Choice **(A) is the best choice**, because it correctly applies the "Mercy Rule" to these facts. The problem under these facts is that the evidence offered is *character* evidence, which is, as a very general rule, inadmissible. However, Choice (A) correctly identifies that the "Mercy Rule" will operate to make this evidence admissible. Under the "Mercy Rule," in criminal cases only, the defendant may offer evidence (presumably favorable) of his own character in the form of reputation or opinion, if the evidence is pertinent to an issue in the case. See FRE 404(a): "Evidence of a person's character or character trait is not admissible to prove that on a particular occasion the person acted in accordance with the character or trait . . . [except that (2)] . . . in a criminal case: (A) a defendant may offer evidence of the defendant's pertinent trait[.]" The character evidence here is in the form of reputation, and, by tending to prove that the defendant is a non-violent, peace-loving person, it is pertinent to an issue in the case (whether the defendant is likely to have committed an unprovoked assault).

(B) is wrong, because the evidence is substantively admissible on the issue of the defendant's guilt (see the discussion of Choice (A) above), not merely on the issue of punishment. In fact, evidence offered solely for purposes of sentencing would not generally not be admissible during the guilt phase of the trial. But once the defendant was found guilty, in the sentencing phase, the judge can rely on evidence that would be inadmissible at trial (e.g., hearsay not within any exception). *Williams v. N.Y.* (1949).

(C) is wrong, because it doesn't recognize that the "Mercy Rule" will make the evidence admissible. As a general rule, evidence of a person's character, offered to prove he acted in conformity with that character on the present occasion, is inadmissible. FRE 404(a)(1). However, under the "Mercy Rule," in criminal cases only, the defendant may offer pertinent evidence of his own character, in the form of reputation or opinion. See the discussion of Choice (A) above for more details.

(D) is wrong, because it raises a threshold issue of competency that is not at issue under these facts. Under FRE 602 and 603, a witness is competent to testify if he has personal knowledge of the matter on which he will testify, and he declares that he will testify truthfully, by oath or affirmation. As the defendant's employer, it could fairly be assumed that the employer is, in fact, competent to testify about the defendant's reputation for peacefulness. Furthermore, since reputation testimony by definition only requires that the witness be familiar with the subject's *reputation* (not, for instance, familiar with specific acts by the defendant demonstrating the character trait in issue), it would not be necessary to prove that the witness lived or worked with the defendant.

Answer 10

Choice **(B)** is correct. The question will be admissible to impeach the employer as a reputation witness. The problem here is that the evidence the prosecutor is seeking is character evidence. Choice (B) offers a way to overcome this problem. Under these facts, the employer is testifying as a reputation witness on the defendant's behalf; that is, he's testifying that the defendant is known as a peaceful, nonviolent person. This evidence is admissible under FRE 404(1), which allows an accused to offer evidence of his own "pertinent trait of character." Then, FRE 405(a) says that where evidence of a "person's character or character trait is admissible" (which the evidence here is, as described in the prior sentence), "On cross-examination of the character witness, the court may allow an inquiry into relevant specific instances of the person's conduct." So once the employer gave the testimony favorable to the defendant about the defendant's peaceable reputation, the prosecution was entitled to make "inquiry into relevant specific instances of [the defendant's] conduct." The specific instances being inquired about (frequent engaging in fights and brawls) are "relevant," because if the employer didn't know about these instances, his testimony about the defendant's reputation for peaceability would be of questionable accuracy. (If the employer didn't know these true facts, is he really knowledgeable about the defendant's reputation on this subject?)

(A) is wrong because it is unduly broad. Since the defendant offered favorable reputation evidence of his peaceability as he was permitted to do under 404(a)(1), the prosecution was permitted to rebut that evidence. The rebuttal evidence was in fact substantively admissible to prove that the defendant was not peaceable, and therefore probably wasn't acting in self-defense. However, this choice suggests that independent (extrinsic) evidence of the fights would have been admissible. In fact, only questioning of the defendant's character witness (the employer) was permissible, on account of FRE 405(a)—the prosecution couldn't have introduced extrinsic proof of the defendant's previous fights (e.g., by testimony from a different witness who observed them), and his choice falsely implies that such evidence could have been admitted.

(C) is wrong because it fails to identify that the evidence can be brought out on the cross of the employer, as further discussed in Choice (B).

(D) is wrong because, while impeachment of a reputation witness with specific instances is possible, the specific instances need not be identified as precisely as (D) suggests. Under FRE 404(a), a reputation witness (of which the employer is one) may be questioned about specific instances bearing on the reputation, since *not* knowing such information reflects on the witness's *competence* to testify as to the person's reputation in the community. However, the testimony here is specific enough to constitute specific acts; it clearly does not amount to opinion or reputation testimony.

Answer 11

Choice (**D**) is correct. The FRE (like the common law) provide that evidence that a person carried or did not carry liability insurance is not admissible on the issue of whether that person acted negligently. (See FRE 411, first sentence.) This rule bars such evidence when it is offered by a plaintiff to suggest that because the defendant was insured, the defendant was probably careless. However, the rule does not apply where the evidence is offered for some other purpose, "such as proving . . . agency, ownership, or control." (FRE 411, second sentence.) That's what's happening here—the evidence is being used to show that because the defendant bought a liability policy on the plane, he had ownership or control of it.

(A) is wrong because the terms of the policy are not at issue, only the policy's existence. It's true that FRE 1002, entitled "Requirement of the original" (and commonly called the Best Evidence Rule (BER)) says that in proving the terms of a writing or a recording, the original must normally be produced. Here, the BER would apply if the terms of the insurance policy were in question. But the terms are not in question here—the witness's testimony involves only the existence of the policy, not its terms, so the BER does not apply.

(B) is wrong because it misstates the rule about proof of insurance. The rule against proof of liability insurance is not a general rule against "proof of insurance where insurance is not itself the issue" (as this choice asserts). Instead, the rule, embodied in FRE 411, prohibits proof of a liability policy's existence when *offered to prove negligence*. (But as the discussion of Choice (D) explains, Rule 411 does not apply here, because the proof of the policy's existence is not being offered to prove negligence.)

(C) is wrong because it inaccurately asserts that the evidence is being offered to suggest the defendant was probably careless, an assertion that, if true, would result in the evidence's being *in*admissible. FRE 411, first sentence, says that "Evidence that a person was or was not insured against liability is not admissible to prove whether the person acted negligently or otherwise wrongfully." Since this choice suggests that the evidence is being offered to show that an insured plane owner would be less likely to properly maintain the plane, it's treating the evidence as a method of asserting the defendant's negligence, a use that would fly squarely in the face of FRE 411.

Answer 12

Choice (**D**) is correct. This choice correctly characterizes the statement as relevant and an admission, and correctly concludes that the evidence will be inadmissible due to public policy considerations. What's being proffered is a settlement offer by Carr. But under FRE 408, admissions in conjunction with settlement negotiations are inadmissible to prove negligence, liability, or a claim's value. That's the case here.

(A) is wrong because FRE 408 says that statements in conjunction with settlement offers are inadmissible to prove negligence, liability, or a claim's value. So even though Carr's statement would otherwise be admissible as an admission by a party-opponent, the special rule of FRE 408 makes it inadmissible.

(B) is wrong because a limiting instruction would not make the evidence here admissible. FRE 408 makes the statement inadmissible as a statement in connection with a settlement negotiation, and that's true if it's offered to prove liability, not just if it's offered to prove damages. So the limiting instruction wouldn't get around the FRE 408 problem.

(C) is wrong because it misstates the facts — the settlement offer *is* relevant. The settlement offer could be taken to mean that Carr acknowledges his own guilt. Thus, it's relevant to the issue of fault. The problem is that the evidence is barred by the special settlement-offers rule of FRE 408, not that it fails to be relevant to any issue in the case.

Answer 13

Choice (**A**) is correct. Under the doctrine of present recollection refreshed, any item may be used to refresh the witness's memory, including leading questions, documents, or objects. If the witness, having seen the refreshing object, can testify from memory, the item will not be considered evidence. See FRE 612, implicitly allowing the present recollection refreshed technique, subject to certain limitations (which don't affect the outcome here). (If the witness *cannot* testify from memory even after reviewing the item, then the item may be admissible as a past recollection recorded, if the situation meets the requirements of FRE 803(5), which the situation here has not yet been shown to do). Here, all you're told is that the pedestrian's counsel is seeking to show the letter to the passenger to help the passenger testify. This "refreshment" is valid under the present recollection refreshed technique.

(B) is wrong, because the doctrine of past recollection recorded has not yet been shown to apply to these facts. Under FRE 803(5), a document is only admissible as a past recollection recorded if it meets these requirements: (A) it "is on a matter the witness once knew about but *now cannot recall well enough to testify fully and accurately*"; (B) it "was made or adopted by the witness when the matter was fresh in the witness's memory"; and (C) it "accurately reflects the witness's knowledge."

At the point in time you're asked about, the letter does not yet qualify for the doctrine. The proponent wants to show the witness the letter "to assist him in his testimony on direct examination." That's a classic use of the present recollection refreshed technique, in which the document does not become evidence. So applying the doctrine of past recollection recorded here would be "jumping the gun" — it should only be used as a last resort if the revivifying document does not, in fact, jog the witness's memory (and in that case, the document itself would be evidence, not merely used "to assist [the witness] in his testimony," which is the use that you're asked to evaluate.)

(C) is wrong, because it ignores the fact that the letter can be used to refresh the passenger's memory, and because there is no "spontaneous utterance" exception to the hearsay rule.

Choice (C) implicitly recognizes that there's a hearsay problem with the letter itself. Hearsay is an out-of-court statement offered to prove the truth of its assertion. Here, the out-of-court declarant is the passenger himself. However, the letter isn't being offered into evidence at all — it's merely being used to refresh the passenger's memory. As a result, its use does not need to satisfy a hearsay objection—the letter may be used as non-evidence, under the doctrine of present recollection refreshed.

Further, the phrase "spontaneous utterance" is not a recognized exception to the hearsay rule under the FRE. Situations qualifying for what the common law might have called the "spontaneous utterance" exception are approximately covered, in the FRE, under either the present sense impression or the excited utterance exceptions. But under the FRE, the letter would not qualify either as a present sense impression or an excited utterance, due to its lack of temporal proximity to the accident (since it was not written until the evening of the day of the accident).

(D) is wrong, because the self-serving nature of the letter would not prevent its being used to refresh the passenger's memory. Choice (D) misses the mark in at least two respects. First, it suggests that the letter itself is being offered as evidence. In fact, it's not—all that's happening is that the pedestrian's counsel is seeking to show the passenger the letter to help him with his testimony.

Second, even if the letter *were* being offered into evidence, the self-serving nature of the letter wouldn't be a problem, because the self-serving nature of any evidence affects its credibility, not its admissibility. Instead, if the letter itself was being offered, there'd be a hearsay problem, since it would be an out-of-court statement offered to prove the truth of what it contains—namely, the passenger's recollections of the accident.

Answer 14

Choice **(B)** is correct. A witness's credibility may be impeached by evidence of specific instances of conduct reflecting on his truthfulness, but only by the cross-examiner's making "inquiry" into those specific instances during the cross-examination of that witness. FRE 608(b). Since Watts is on the stand and being cross-examined, the question about his prior act of dishonesty meets these requirements (it's probative of his general truthfulness, and what Popkin's counsel is doing is merely making "inquiry" into the act). The fact that Watts is a witness called solely to give impeachment testimony, as opposed to substantive or occurrence-type testimony, doesn't matter—*any* witness may be impeached by inquiry into specific past conduct of the witness that is probative of untruthfulness.

(A) is wrong because Watts is not being asked about the reputation testimony, but is instead being impeached on account of his own bad acts. So what Watts' standard is for judging reputation is not what the question is about.

(C) is wrong because there is an exception to the general rule that, for the purpose of attacking a witness's character for truthfulness, specific instances of conduct may not be proved by extrinsic evidence. The judge may, in her discretion, allow such evidence if it is brought out through cross examination of the witness whose credibility is being attacked and if the bad acts are probative of truthfulness or untruthfulness. FRE 608(b). Watts is being cross-examined with evidence of his falsifying an affidavit to avoid paying sales tax on the sale of a new car. The act is probative of untruthfulness and is being brought out on cross-examination. Therefore, the question is proper even though it involves a specific instance of the witness's past conduct.

(D) is wrong because it states a non-existent rule: There is no rule against "impeaching an impeaching witness."

Answer 15

Choice **(B)** is correct. Under FRE 613(b), when a witness testifies at trial, evidence of his prior inconsistent statement is admissible to impeach his credibility (if a foundation is laid either before or after the impeachment where the witness has an opportunity to explain or deny the statement and where the opposite party has the opportunity to interrogate the witness). Since Smythe is "still subject to recall as a witness," the foundation can be laid. In addition, some types of prior inconsistent statements are not barred by the hearsay rule and may be admitted as substantive proof of the matters contained in the statement—i.e., those made in an earlier trial or proceeding, where the declarant spoke under oath and subject to perjury penalties. FRE 801(d)(1). Since Smythe's statement was not under oath, it may not be admitted substantively. Therefore, the statement is admissible as a prior inconsistent statement, but only for impeachment purposes. (Note that this answer is correct because Smythe is a non-party in this action. If Smythe were on trial here, his prior statement would be admissible for substantive purposes, as an admission.)

(A) is wrong because the declarant is available. Under FRE 804(b)(3), the requirements for the declaration-against-interest exception are: (1) the declaration must be against the declarant's pecuniary or proprietary interest when made; (2) the declarant must be unavailable; and (3) the declarant must have had first-hand knowledge of the facts asserted in the declaration. The fact pattern indicates that Smythe is still subject to recall as a witness when Walton is testifying about Smythe's prior statement, so he is available.

(C) is wrong because, although it is correct in identifying the statement as hearsay not within any exception, it does not recognize that the statement would still be admissible for impeachment purposes.

(D) is wrong because the statement is admissible, and the requirement of corroboration does not apply in the context of a prior inconsistent statement, but rather, to the hearsay exception for declarations against interest. FRE 804(b)(3), which provides for the hearsay exception for declarations against interest, denies the exception for a statement "offered in a criminal case as one that tends to expose the declarant to criminal liability," unless the statement "is supported by corroborating circumstances that clearly indicate its trustworthiness[.]" This is the source of the language in (D), but it does not apply here. If the declarant was unavailable and the exception was applied, then corroboration *would* be required.

Answer 16

Choice (**B**) is correct. Under FRE 613(b), when a witness testifies at trial, extrinsic evidence of his prior inconsistent statement is admissible to impeach his credibility, so long as the witness has an opportunity to explain or deny the statement and the opposite party has the opportunity to interrogate the witness about it. Wallingford's testimony as to Minter's statement at the accident scene—"the driver (defendant) was doing at least 50"—is inconsistent with Minter's previous testimony at trial that the defendant's speed was 25 miles per hour. The fact pattern indicates that Minter was not excused as a witness and that therefore there exists the opportunity for him to explain or deny the statement and to be interrogated on it by the opposite party (Dawson).

(A) is wrong because the statement was not made close enough to the time of the accident. FRE 803(1) provides for the hearsay exception of a present sense impression, defined as a statement "describing or explaining an event or condition, *made while or immediately after the declarant perceived it.*" Minter's statement was made to the police officer during the investigation of the accident scene so it was not made immediately after viewing the collision.

(C) is wrong because "Any party, including the party that called the witness, may attack the witness's credibility." FRE 607.

(D) is wrong because what Minter said to the Officer is not hearsay. The out-of-court statement at issue is Minter's statement to the officer, "Dawson was doing at least 50." But the statement is not being offered to prove that Dawson really was doing at least 50—it's merely being used to cast doubt on the credibility of Minter's in-court statement that Dawson was doing 25. If the statement to the officer *were* being offered as substantive evidence, i.e., to prove that Dawson really was "doing at least 50," then it *would* be inadmissible hearsay.

Answer 17

Choice (**B**) is correct. The victim's initial statement about the defendant was hearsay, but was properly admitted under FRE 804(b)(2)'s "dying declaration" exception, because it was made by a person now unavailable to testify, believing he was about to die, concerning personal knowledge of the cause of death, and the statement is offered at either a criminal homicide trial or a civil wrongful death suit. Since that statement came in, the victim's prior inconsistent statement (about the stabber being a different person, not the defendant) can be used to *impeach his credibility*, since hearsay declarants can be impeached. See FRE 806: "When a hearsay statement . . . has been admitted in evidence, the declarant's credibility may be attacked, and then supported, by any evidence that would be admissible for those purposes if the declarant had testified as a witness."

Note that this impeaching evidence would not be admissible *substantively*, since it does not fulfill the requirements of 801(d)(1)(A)'s prior-inconsistent-statement hearsay exclusion—the prior inconsistent statement is only admissible substantively if the statement was made under oath, at a prior proceeding, subject to perjury, with the declarant now being the testifying witness; here, the victim's statement about the third person was not made under oath or at a proceeding, so it's admissible *only* for impeachment.

(A) is wrong, because the witness's testimony does not fit an exception to the hearsay rule; it's inadmissible hearsay. In particular, the statement does not fit the most obvious exception, the "dying declaration" exception to the hearsay rule, because the victim did not have an impending sense of death when he made the statement. FRE 804(b)(2). The rationale behind the exception is that no one wants to die with a lie on his lips; where a person thinks he's going to live, this is not applicable. (Also, the statement will not be admissible substantively as a prior inconsistent statement, for the reasons discussed in Choice (B) above.)

(C) is wrong because the FRE do not condition the admissibility of a statement on whether it addresses an "ultimate issue." See FRE 704(a).

(D) is wrong, because the testimony *is* relevant to a substantive issue in the case. A piece of evidence is logically relevant if it tends to prove or disprove a material fact. FRE 401. If the victim's prior statement about the third person being the stabber is true, it will tend to prove that the victim was lying about the defendant's stabbing him, and thus make it less likely that the defendant is guilty of murder. As a result, it's extremely relevant!

Answer 18

Choice (**D**) is correct. The defendant's counsel is attempting to impeach the bystander with evidence that is not from the bystander's own mouth—in other words, by "extrinsic" evidence. Evidence that only discredits a witness, without bearing on any substantive issues in the case, is called "collateral," and in most instances is not admissible if it is extrinsic. Evidence that discredits the witness by showing that the witness gave incorrect testimony in the present case about an immaterial issue falls into this category of inadmissible extrinsic evidence on collateral matters. The FRE do not specifically recite this rule, but it is a common-law rule that is universally observed by courts following the FRE. Here, the issues in the case involve only the driving behavior of the defendant. The color of his sweater is not a material issue; all the second witness's testimony will serve to do is slightly discredit the bystander by contradiction. So it's a classic illustration of the "no extrinsic evidence on collateral matters" rule.

(A) is wrong because it mischaracterizes the facts: The color of the defendant's sweater is not a material fact (it doesn't relate to any of the substantive issues in the case). It is instead a "collateral" matter—relevant only to discredit a witness, the bystander. As such, it will not be admissible, under the common-law rule against extrinsic evidence on collateral matters, applicable as a "gap filler" to cases governed by the FRE.

(B) is wrong because the testimony here could not be admitted on the subject of the bystander's truthfulness and veracity. It's true that the testimony has some bearing on the bystander's truthfulness, because it contradicts his testimony (and thus raises the question, "If he is lying or mistaken on this point, isn't he likely to be lying or mistaken about some really important fact in his testimony?") But because the contradiction about the color of the sweater does not touch on any substantive issue in the case, and does not bear on other issues considered highly important aspects of witness veracity (e.g., presence of bias), its impeachment effect is considered minor, and not worth the trouble of calling a separate witness. Therefore, it falls within the general common-law rule that extrinsic impeachment evidence on a collateral matter is not allowed.

(C) is wrong because it misstates the facts—the testimony would (or at least might) bear on the bystander's ability to observe. Any contradiction of witness 1's testimony by witness 2 about a matter that witness 1 said he observed would or might bear on witness 1's ability to observe. But where the contradiction is on a point that does not matter substantively, and is not on some other kind of issue that is considered important to credibility (e.g., bias on the part of witness 1), the contradiction is excludable based on the common-law rule barring extrinsic evidence (i.e., evidence from a separate witness or document) on a collateral matter.

Answer 19

Choice (**D**) is correct. Young's statement, "I told the manager he had better fix that torn carpet," is an "out-of-court statement" being offered to "prove the truth of the matter asserted," that Young told the manager about the needed repair and that, therefore, the manager knew of the ripped carpet. In other words, Young's out-of court-statement "I told the manager X" is being offered to show that Young, the declarant, indeed told the manager X. So the statement is inadmissible hearsay if offered for that purpose. FRE 801. (Notice that this would be hearsay whether or not X was itself true.) And there is no other plausible purpose for which it is being offered on these facts.

(A) is wrong because the statement is inadmissible to prove that the carpet was defective, because it is hearsay not within any exception, as discussed in Choice (D). The statement can't tend to prove that the carpet was defective unless the trier first believes that Young made the statement about a defect to the manager; so the statement "Young told me he had told the manager X" would be offered to prove that Young indeed told the manager X, and that would be an offer to prove the truth of the matter asserted.

(B) is wrong because the statement is inadmissible hearsay, as explained in the discussion of (D). Young's statement "I told the manager thus-and-such" is being offered to prove that Young, the declarant, indeed told the manager thus-and-such. So even if the statement is not being offered to prove that Young's statement to the manager was true (and instead offered to merely prove "notice" to the manager of a fact that might or might not be true), Young's statement to Witt that Young had previously made the statement to the manager is inadmissible hearsay.

(C) is wrong because, as discussed in (D), the statement is inadmissible for both these purposes.

Answer 20

Choice (**B**) is correct. First, let's look at whether the statement was hearsay. It's clearly an out-of-court declaration. And, the statement includes the plaintiff's assertion that he's owed

$10,000 by the defendant, offered to prove that the defendant does indeed owe this money. So the statement easily fits within the definition of hearsay—out-of-court statement offered to prove the truth of the matter asserted. Now, does some exception apply? No. The two most plausible ones are the excited utterance exception (not applicable because the statement doesn't relate to the exciting event—see the discussion of Choice (C) below) and the dying declaration exception (not applicable because the statement doesn't relate to the cause of impending death—see the discussion of Choice (D) below).

(A) is wrong because the statement here is not especially prejudicial, so it's unlikely that the statement's probative value would be found to be "substantially outweighed" by its prejudicial effect, as FRE 403's balancing test requires as a basis for exclusion.

(C) is wrong because FRE 803(2)'s excited-utterance exception applies to "a statement *relating to a startling event or condition*, made while the declarant was under the stress of excitement that it caused." As you can see from the italicized phrase, the statement has to relate to the startling event. The plaintiff's comment here relates solely to the debt, not to the startling event (the truck accident).

(D) is wrong because the plaintiff's comment did not concern the cause or circumstance of his death. FRE 804(b)(2)'s dying-declaration exception applies to (in a civil case or homicide prosecution) "a statement that the declarant, while believing the declarant's death to be imminent, made *about its cause or circumstances*." Since the plaintiff's statement related only to the collection of the debt, not to the truck accident that was about to cause his death, it doesn't qualify.

Answer 21

Choice (**D**) is correct. The witness is testifying as to what she heard someone say outside of the courtroom. But this is not hearsay, because although the witness is recounting an out-of-court statement, that statement is not being offered to prove the truth of the matter asserted therein, i.e., that the declarant was, in fact, dying. Rather, the statement is being offered to prove only that it was made, because that fact has independent legal significance. As such, it is classified as a verbal act, i.e., an operative fact that gives rise to legal consequences. Thus, the statement does not constitute hearsay as defined by FRE 801(c) and, therefore, is not barred by FRE 802. And it is relevant as it helps establish that the wife survived the husband.

(A) is wrong because under the majority common-law "bursting bubble" rule, which is followed by FRE 301, a presumption disappears when sufficient counterproof is offered about the presumed fact. Here the testimony of the witness, although not conclusive, is sufficient to rebut the presumption that neither spouse survived the other and to support a jury finding that the wife outlived the husband. Therefore, the presumption is no longer controlling, and the witness's testimony is admissible.

In any event, regardless of how (or even whether) the bursting bubble rule applies, the witness's testimony would be admissible—in all jurisdictions, the party who does not benefit from a presumption is always entitled to submit otherwise-competent evidence rebutting the existence of the presumed fact.

(B) is wrong because the testimony is not "too speculative." A witness need not be absolutely certain of matters about which the witness testifies. Here the testimony is based on the perception and memory of a lay witness, and thus satisfies the FRE 701 standard that lay testimony be "(a) rationally based on the witness's perception; [and] (b) helpful to clearly understanding the witness's testimony or to determining a fact in issue[.]"

(C) is wrong because it presumes that the statement is hearsay. But the statement is not hearsay under FRE 801(c), because it is not being offered to prove the truth of the matter asserted. Instead, the statement is an operative fact being offered to prove that the woman was alive at the time she made the statement; so the mere existence of the statement (regardless of its "truth value") is relevant on the issue of whether the speaker survived her husband, even if by only a few minutes.

Answer 22

Choice **(B)** is correct, because it correctly identifies the statement as an admission, and declares it admissible on that basis. The plaintiff is offering the defendant's out-of-court statement to prove that the defendant was speeding. Since the statement is being offered to prove the truth of its assertion, the statement is hearsay. However, the statement will be admissible under the admission exclusion to the hearsay rule. FRE 801(d)(2) gives a hearsay exclusion for a statement that is "offered against an opposing party and . . . (A) was made by the party in an individual or representative capacity[.]" Since the statement was made by the defendant, and is being offered against him, it qualifies for this 801(d)(2)(A) exclusion for personal admissions.

(A) is wrong, because the hearsay exception for prior inconsistent statements does not apply on these facts. We're told that the statement is being offered for the substantive purpose of proving that the defendant was speeding (not merely for the statement's impeachment value of showing that the defendant told a different story previously and is therefore not worthy of having his trial testimony believed). FRE 801(d)(1) gives a hearsay exclusion for certain prior inconsistent statements by the witness, namely, where "The declarant testifies and is subject to cross-examination about a prior statement, and the statement: (A) is inconsistent with the declarant's testimony and was *given under penalty of perjury at a trial, hearing, or other proceeding or in a deposition*[.]" But there is no indication that the defendant's prior statement being recited in the officer's testimony was given at a "trial, hearing, or other proceeding or in a deposition[.]" Therefore, it doesn't qualify for the exclusion for prior inconsistent statements by a witness. (Instead, it can come in for substantive purposes as an admission, as described in Choice (B).)

(C) is wrong, because it implicitly mischaracterizes the basis on which the officer's testimony will be admissible. The central problem here addresses hearsay. Hearsay is an out-of-court statement offered to prove the truth of its assertion. Since the officer's testimony is offered to prove that the defendant was speeding, it is being offered as substantive evidence.

This choice implicitly (and wrongly) characterizes the officer's testimony as being offered for its impeachment value only. The choice appears to be referring to the common-law requirement that before a witness could be impeached by showing that he made a prior inconsistent statement, a foundation had to be laid by showing the witness the statement, or disclosing its contents to him. But FRE 613(a) does away with this requirement of a foundation ("When examining a witness about the witness's prior statement, a party need not show it or disclose its contents to the witness.") So the lack of a foundation here would not prevent the plaintiff from using the prior statement for impeachment only, if that was the plaintiff's purpose (which the facts tell us it was not—the statement was offered for its substantive value).

(D) is wrong, because it fails to realize that the testimony will be admissible as an admission. This choice correctly reflects the fact that the defendant's statement to the officer is being offered to prove the truth of the matter asserted in the statement, and would thus normally be hearsay. What Choice (D) fails to realize is that the testimony is an admission, rendered non-hearsay by FRE 801(d)(2), as explained in the discussion of Choice (B) above.

Answer 23

Choice **(B)** is correct. This choice implicitly recognizes that there's a hearsay problem under these facts. Hearsay is an out-of-court statement offered to prove the truth of its assertion. Here, the out-of-court declarant is the defendant: "I think this was probably my fault." The statement is being offered to prove that the defendant *was* at fault, so it's hearsay, and it will only be admissible if it fits a hearsay exception or exclusion.

FRE 801(d)(2) gives a hearsay exclusion for a "statement [that] is offered against an opposing party and: (A) was made by the party in an individual or representative capacity[.]" Since the statement was made by the defendant in an individual capacity, and is being offered against him, it qualifies for the admission exclusion.

(A) is wrong, because res gestae as a concept is not recognized by the Federal Rules. At common law, res gestae represented the group of spontaneous hearsay declarations that were collectively considered admissible because of their proximity to an act or event. What would be the res gestae at common law is essentially covered, in the Federal Rules, by the categories of declarations of present bodily or mental state, excited utterances, and present sense impressions. Even if res gestae as a concept were recognized by the Federal Rules, it wouldn't apply here, because the defendant made the statement at the police station, so it wouldn't be sufficiently proximate to the accident to be part of what the common law would have called res gestae.

(C) is wrong, because it misstates the law. This choice suggests that the defendant's statement will not be admissible because it includes a conclusion of law, namely, that he'll be legally liable for causing the accident. However, admissions by a party, introduced against that party, are not disqualified from admissibility merely because they state a conclusion of law.

(D) is wrong, because the fact that the statement included an opinion is irrelevant. This choice suggests that the defendant's statement will not be admissible because it includes an opinion as to a conclusion of law, rather than a statement about specific facts. However, admissions by a party, introduced against that party, are not disqualified from admissibility merely because they state an opinion and do not refer to specific facts.

Answer 24

Choice **(B)** is correct. First, let's consider the statement's admissibility as substantive evidence of the perjury. The witness is testifying about an out-of-court statement. If the statement is offered to prove the truth of its contents, i.e., that the declarant knew about the fraud, this would meet the hearsay definition of FRE 801(c). But the declarant is the defendant in this case, and the declarant's statement is being offered against him. Consequently, the statement is a party admission and, therefore, FRE 801(d)(2)(A) says that it is deemed not hearsay. Since it is not hearsay, it is admissible to prove the truth of its contents (i.e., as substantive evidence of the perjury).

The statement is also admissible to impeach the declarant's testimony, since it is a prior statement that is inconsistent with the declarant/defendant's testimony at the present (perjury) trial. Rule 613, which deals with prior inconsistent statements, makes them generally admissible for impeachment, subject to some exceptions that are not relevant here. In fact, where, as here, the prior inconsistent statement was made by one who is a party opponent in the present proceeding, Rule 613(b) allows use of "extrinsic evidence" (which is what the prosecutor's witness's statement is) of the prior inconsistent statement even if the maker of the prior statement (here, the defendant) is not given an opportunity to "explain or deny" the prior statement.

(A) is wrong because although the testimony is certainly admissible to impeach the defendant's testimony, it can *also* be used substantively as an admission by a party-opponent under FRE 801(d)(2)(A), as the analysis of Choice (B) demonstrates.

(C) is wrong because, under FRE 801(d)(2)(A), a statement of a party-opponent that is offered against that party is deemed to be not hearsay.

(D) is wrong because, although the statement made to the witness does relate to the prior business fraud, it also relates to the present perjury charge. That's because the prior statement demonstrates that the defendant in fact *did* know about the fraud, despite his testimony in two trials that he did not know of it. Thus the statement is relevant to prove that the defendant's trial testimony was knowingly false and hence constituted perjury.

Answer 25

Choice **(B)** is correct. First, let's consider whether it's admissible substantively, i.e., to prove that the defendant did not act in self-defense. The police officer's testimony that the defendant had told him, "I was cleaning my gun and it went off accidentally," is an "out-of-court statement" offered to "prove the truth of the matter asserted," so it would on its face be hearsay if it's being used as evidence that the defendant did not act in self-defense. However, admissions of a party-opponent are treated as non-hearsay statements and are admissible under FRE 801(d)(2)(A). Next, once a statement is available substantively because it's non-hearsay (or falls within a hearsay exception), it can also be used for impeachment purposes. (A separate provision, FRE 613(b), allows for impeachment by a prior inconsistent statement, but use of this provision is necessary only when the witness is a non-party — if the witness that is the target of impeachment is a party, as here, then it's simpler to use FRE 801(d)(2)(A) to get the statement in for both impeachment and substantive purposes.)

(A) is wrong because the fact that a statement is an excited utterance matters only if the statement is hearsay. As described in Choice (B), under the FRE admissions by a party opponent are hearsay "exclusions" — i.e., non-hearsay — so the statement was never hearsay in the first place, and does not need a hearsay exception in order to be admitted. Furthermore, it's doubtful that the defendant's statement would qualify as an excited utterance even if offered by, rather than against, him (so that the statement was not a non-hearsay party-admission). FRE 803(2) defines the excited-utterance hearsay exception this way: "a statement relating to a startling event or condition made *while the declarant was under the stress of excitement that it caused.*" Here, there's no affirmative indication that the statement was being uttered under the stress of excitement from the shooting (though we don't know for sure).

(C) is wrong because application of the Fifth Amendment privilege of self-incrimination that "no person . . . shall be compelled in any criminal case to be a witness against himself . . ." applies only where there is some element of compulsion that brought about (or threatens to bring about) the statement. So statements at a trial or other proceeding (e.g., a grand jury hearing or deposition) where the defendant is required to testify are covered. Similarly, statements made in response to custodial interrogation are covered if the *Miranda* warnings weren't given, because *Miranda* is a method of preventing Fifth Amendment violations. But the defendant's out-of-court statement here did not fall into either of these two categories. In particular, it is not covered by the *Miranda* anti-self-incrimination policy, because the defendant was not in custody at the time he made the statement, and no other element of compulsion was present. (Also, even a statement by a defendant that was given in custody in violation of *Miranda* may be used to impeach the defendant's contrary trial testimony; *Harris v. N.Y.* (1971).)

(D) is wrong because the principle cited does not apply in the context of admissions, but rather, to the declaration-against-interest hearsay exception. FRE 804(b)(3), which provides for that exception, says that where a statement is "offered in a criminal case as one that tends to expose the declarant to criminal liability," the exception applies only if the statement "is supported by corroborating circumstances that clearly indicate its trustworthiness." But even where the quoted "corroboration" language applies to make the statement ineligible for the declaration-against-interest exception (which would be so here), that ineligibility doesn't prevent the statement from being admissible as an admission against a party-opponent, as described in the discussion of Choice (B).

Answer 26

Choice (**B**) is correct. The witness orthopedist is testifying about an out-of-court statement to prove the truth of the contents of that statement. So the statement meets the definition of hearsay under FRE 801(c). (Although the declarant is a party to the case, the statement is being offered by that party, so is not a party admission within FRE 801(d)(2)(A).) But this hearsay statement fits within the exception codified at FRE 803(4) for statements made for the purpose of (and reasonably *pertinent to*) *medical diagnosis* or treatment, where the statement describes "medical history; past or present symptoms or sensations; their inception; or their general *cause*." Both of these requirements are met: The plaintiff's statement relates to the cause of his injury, and the cause of his injury is relevant to the orthopedist's diagnosis. Moreover, Rule 803(4) allows not only statements made to treating physicians, but also statements made to other doctors for evaluation or diagnosis. So the fact that the orthopedist never treated the plaintiff doesn't affect admissibility of the statement. And, by the way, this exception applies regardless of whether or not the declarant is unavailable to testify at trial.

(A) is wrong because the choice gives an incorrect reason for the correct outcome. The statement is an admissible statement for purposes of medical diagnosis or treatment under FRE 803(4). While it is true that the plaintiff is present and presumably could be cross-examined about the statement, this exception to the hearsay rule does not depend on the declarant's being present—the statement would be admissible even if the plaintiff were not present to testify or be cross-examined.

(C) is wrong because FRE 803(4) does not require that the statement be made to a treating physician—the Rule also admits statements made to a non-treating doctor for purposes of diagnosis. The Rule is specifically designed to admit statements such as this, where an injured party is seeking a diagnosis and opinion from a medical specialist.

(D) is wrong because FRE 803(4) expressly permits the introduction of statements concerning the cause of injury when that information is pertinent to diagnosis or treatment. Thus it is admissible under FRE 803(4).

(If the statement related to *fault*—e.g., "I fell when D tripped over the base of the ladder"—then the part of the statement relating to fault would likely *not* be covered by the 803(4) exception.)

Answer 27

Choice (**B**) is correct. The out-of-court statement (the note in the file) is being offered to prove that Payne really was attacked by Dabney. That's a hearsay use, since the out-of-court statement about what "the Patient" said about the cause of the injuries is being offered to prove that these really *were* the causes. No hearsay exception applies—see the discussion of the other three answers for why some of the possible exceptions don't apply. In particular, notice that this is a two-level hearsay problem; the outer level is an out-of-court statement (the notation) by the E.R. doctor, and the inner level is the oral statement by the patient that was supposedly being recorded. Unless each of the levels is shown to fall within a hearsay exception, the entire notation must be excluded. And the inner level does not fall within any exception.

(A) reaches the right conclusion, but for the wrong reasons. There is no hearsay exception that applies merely because the person who records an out-of-court declaration (here, the doctor who records a patient's out-of-court declaration) is available for cross-examination.

(C) is wrong because this is a two-level hearsay problem, and this choice only deals with the outer level. If the notation concerned solely a fact personally observed by the E.R. doctor (e.g., "I measured Patient's blood pressure and found it to be 130/80"), the notation probably *would* be admissible as a record of regularly conducted activity. But here, the notation is a quotation of someone else's statement (Payne's), so Payne's statement is the "inner" level of hearsay, and that statement does not fall within any hearsay exception.

(D) is wrong, because the statement does not fall under the purpose-of-medical-diagnosis-or-treatment exception, since the identification of the attacker was not pertinent to the diagnosis or treatment of Payne's injuries. Under FRE 803(4), statements describing "symptoms or sensations" or "their inception or their general cause," are admissible if *"reasonably pertinent to . . . medical diagnosis or treatment."* Payne's statements to his doctor that he was attacked and how he was attacked might well be admissible under FRE 803(4) on the theory that they were "reasonably pertinent to medical diagnosis or treatment." However, a statement *identifying his attacker* will not help in treatment or diagnosis in any way, and is therefore inadmissible under this exception.

Answer 28

Choice **(A)** is correct. When the mental state of a declarant is directly at issue in a case, statements of the declarant's then existing state of mind are admissible under FRE 803(3) to prove the declarant's mental state pre-dating or post-dating the statement. Here, Vera's statement, that she loved Dale and she could never hurt him, is being offered to prove the truth of the matter asserted, that she could not hurt him, and that therefore, the next day, it is unlikely that she would have been the first aggressor in the encounter with Dale. This evidence would counter Dale's claim that he acted in self-defense.

(B) is wrong because the declarant's availability is immaterial when a statement is being offered under the exception for a then existing state of mind under FRE 803(3).

(C) is wrong because the statement is admissible under the then existing state of mind hearsay exception provided by FRE 803(3), as explained in the discussion of Choice (A).

(D) is wrong because (1) the statement is admissible and (2) it does not reflect on Vera's "character," but rather, her state of mind, as further discussed in Choice (A).

Answer 29

Choice **(A)** is correct. A statement is admissible to prove that a plan, design, or intention of the declarant was in fact carried out by the declarant, under the hearsay exception for a statement concerning a declarant's present mental, emotional or physical condition. FRE 803(3). That provision allows for the introduction of a statement showing that the declarant had the intent to take a certain action, in order to prove that the declarant did in fact eventually take that action where whether that act took place is an issue in the case. Here, Dover's stated intention to meet his sister in Utah on March 5 is admissible to prove that he in fact was in Utah on March 5; therefore, it is evidence that he did not commit an assault in California on that same day.

(B) is wrong because the general rule is that evidence offered to bolster the character of a witness is not admissible. Under FRE 801(d)(1)(B), a statement consistent with the declarant's testimony may only be "offered to rebut an express or implied charge that the declarant recently fabricated it or acted from a recent improper influence or motive in so testifying." The fact pattern does not indicate that those circumstances occurred here.

(C) is wrong because the letter is admissible and it, in fact, has sufficient probative value. It makes the factual proposition that Dover was not in California on March 5 more likely than it would be without the evidence.

(D) is wrong because the letter is admissible and the concept stated does not apply. It's true that FRE 803(3) provides for an exception for the declarant's then existing mental, emotional or physical condition, "but not including a statement of memory or belief to prove the fact remembered or believed unless it relates to the . . . declarant's will." But, here, the letter is not a statement of belief about past actions or events. It is a stated intention to do something in the future, as explained in the discussion of (A).

Answer 30

Choice (B) is correct. The wife's statement is hearsay, an "out-of-court statement" offered to "prove the truth of the matter asserted"—that Daggett was the killer. FRE 801. FRE 803(2) provides for the excited utterance exception to the hearsay rule—"a statement relating to a startling event or condition made while the declarant was under the stress of excitement that it caused." The screamed exclamation, "You killed him! You killed him!" would qualify—the fact that there was a scream strongly suggests that Vale's wife was responding to some event that (1) startled her, (2) convinced her that her husband had been killed (the event), and (3) induced her to make the statement (showing causation between the startling event, and the statement).

(A) is wrong because it relies on a concept that doesn't exist. There is no hearsay exception provided for a "statement of belief." Indeed, FRE 803(3) indicates just the contrary, since it gives a hearsay exception for "A statement of the declarant's then existing state of mind . . . but *not* including a statement of memory or belief to prove the fact remembered or believed[.]"

(C) is wrong because the evidence would not be barred by the confidential spousal communications privilege. If the wife thought her husband was dead, she could not have been intending to communicate with him (barring communications with the other world, which are presumably not protected by the privilege).

(D) is wrong because the evidence is not barred by the adverse testimony privilege. The privilege applies only to testimony against the spouse of the declarant. So there are two problems here: (1) the husband (the declarant's spouse) is not on trial; and (2) this out-of-court startled exclamation would not be deemed to be "testimonial" for purposes of the adverse-testimony privilege, even if it were used by the prosecution against the husband.

Answer 31

Choice (A) is correct. The tape recording is evidence of an oral out-of-court statement that is being offered to prove the truth of the contents of that statement. Thus it is hearsay under FRE 801(c). But it also satisfies the requirements of FRE 803(5), the past recollection recorded exception to the hearsay rule. Under that rule, a record is admissible if it "(A) is on a matter the witness once knew about but now cannot recall well enough to testify fully and accurately; (B) was made or adopted by the witness when the matter was fresh in the witness's memory; and (C) accurately reflects the witness's knowledge."

So here all four of the requirements embedded in FRE 803(5) are met: (1) we know that the "witness once knew about" requirement is satisfied because we're told that she was the investigating officer, and was dictating an account of what she had learned first-hand; (2) we know she "now cannot recall [the matter] well enough to testify fully and accurately" because we're explicitly told in the facts that she "currently ha[s] no clear memory of the details"; (3) we know that she "made [the record] when the matter was fresh in [her] memory" from the fact that she made the tape recording at the end of the very shift in which she learned the underlying facts to which the recording pertained; and (4) we know the record "accurately reflects the witness's knowledge" because the facts tell us that the witness "testified that the tape recording was accurate when made." Accordingly, under FRE 803(5), the recording is admissible evidence (in the sense that it can be played for the jury, although not taken into the jury room as an exhibit).

(B) is wrong because although the officer's formal written report would qualify as a public record under FRE 803(8), the informal dictated comments she made to help her prepare the report would not. To be admissible under 803(8), the material must fall within one of clauses (A)(i), (A)(ii), or (A)(iii) of 803(8). All of these apply to "a record or statement of a *public office*." Let's see why none of these clauses applies:

Clause (A)(i) of 803(8) covers reports of "the office's activities." The clause is interpreted to refer to records of the internal activities of the agency, not to its inquiries into events occurring in the outside world. So the recording here does not qualify, since it's not about the police department, but about real-world non-police activities.

Clause (A)(ii) of 803(8) covers a public office's record or statement setting out "a matter observed while under a legal duty to report, but not including, in a criminal case, a matter observed by law-enforcement personnel." (A)(ii) is generally interpreted to cover only material that is "more concrete and simple than interpretive or evaluative" (see M&K, § 8.50, p. 862), so it would not apply to the dictated notes here, which clearly have an evaluative component. (Who caused the accident, which the officer didn't personally witness?)

Clause (A)(iii) of 803(8) covers public records or statements offered "in a civil case or against the government in a criminal case," if the record or statement consists of "factual findings from a legally authorized investigation." The fact that this is a civil action does not bar (A)(iii) use here. But (A)(iii) by its terms covers "factual *findings*," and the preliminary, informal tape-recording here would not be construed to have produced such "factual findings" (a phrase that has the connotation of final and formal conclusions), especially given that the traffic officer knew that she would later use her recording in order to prepare her eventual "written report of her factual findings." (The written report is a document that *would* satisfy clause (A)(iii).)

So none of the three clauses of 803(8) applies.

(C) is wrong because although the tape recording is hearsay, it fits the hearsay exception of FRE 803(5) as a past recollection recorded. This choice's reference to a "police report being offered against the defendant in a wrongful death case" is an attempt to trick you into thinking that the prohibition in 803(8), clause (A)(iii), applies. As is covered in more detail in the analysis of Choice (B) above, 803(8)'s public-records hearsay exception says, in clause (A)(iii), that "factual findings resulting from an investigation made pursuant to authority granted by law" are admissible only in civil actions and against the government in criminal cases, not against the accused in a criminal case. And there is some (though weak) authority that where factual findings by law enforcement officials are prohibited by 803(8)(A)(iii) (i.e., where the findings are proposed to be used by the government against the accused), not only can't Rule 803(8) be used, but neither can other exceptions, like past recollection recorded. But even in a court following this minority authority, the 803(8)(A)(iii) prohibition wouldn't apply here, since the prohibition doesn't apply in a civil case, even one involving wrongful death.

(D) is wrong because the tape recording was made prior to the written report and was used as a basis for the written report. The recording is not being offered to prove the content of the written report, so its admission does not violate the best evidence/original document rule of FRE 1002. (If the officer gave courtroom testimony that the previous day, she had listened to the recording and here is what it said, then this testimony *would* violate the original document rule of FRE 1002, because the recording itself would have to be offered as the best evidence of what the recording's contents were.)

Answer 32

Choice **(B)** is correct — this is hearsay not within any exception. Each memorandum contains a statement of the form, "Person X confused Plaza Hotel with Plaza House Hotel," offered to prove that the person indeed had this confusion. So each memo is being offered to prove the truth of the matter asserted in it (that confusion existed). Unless some hearsay exception applies, the memos must be excluded under the hearsay rule. No exception applies, including the exceptions mentioned in Choices (C) and (D).

(A) is wrong for two reasons. First, under FRE 403, evidence is excludable based on the relative probative value and prejudice only if the probative value is "*substantially* outweighed" by the danger of unfair prejudice or confusion, and the formulation here omits the word "substantially," incorrectly suggesting that if unfair prejudice and confusion is slightly greater than probative value, exclusion must occur. Second, the court would never even get to the issue of balancing probative value against prejudice, because the evidence is hearsay not within any exception. (FRE 403 only matters in the case of otherwise-admissible evidence.)

(C) is wrong, because this choice refers to what is commonly known as the "business records" exception, and the requirements for that exception are not met here. FRE 803(6) provides for the business record hearsay exception if "(A) the record was made at or near the time by — or from information transmitted by — someone with knowledge; (B) the record was kept in the course of a regularly conducted activity of a business, organization, occupation, or calling, whether or not for profit; (C) making the record was a regular practice of that activity; (D) all these conditions are shown by the testimony of the custodian or another qualified witness, or by a certification that complies with Rule 902(11) or (12) or with a statute permitting certification; and (E) neither the source of information nor the method or circumstances of preparation indicate a lack of trustworthiness." The memos here don't satisfy clause (E) — the circumstances of preparation (anticipation of litigation, and the hotel's strong self-interest) make the records untrustworthy.

(D) is wrong, because several of the prerequisites laid out in FRE 803(5) for past recollection recorded have not been satisfied. For instance, there is no sponsoring witness who is testifying, as to each memorandum, that the memo is "on a matter the witness once knew about but cannot now recall well enough to testify fully and accurately." (803(5)(A)). Similarly, there is no sponsoring witness who is testifying that the memo was "made or adopted by the witness when the matter was fresh in the witness's memory" (803(5)(B)).

Answer 33

Choice **(C)** is correct. The report is an out-of-court written statement offered to prove the truth of its contents, so it meets the hearsay definition of FRE 801(c). Nevertheless, it is admissible because it falls within the hearsay exception for "public records and reports" codified at FRE 803(8). Under Clause (A)(ii) of this rule, a report made by a public official or agency concerning "a matter observed while under a legal duty to report, but not including, in a criminal case, a matter observed by law-enforcement personnel" is admissible, as long as "neither the source of information nor other circumstances indicate a lack of trustworthiness" (Clause (B)). All of the requirements embedded in Clauses (A)(ii) and (B) are met: (1) The fire marshal is a public official; (2) we know that the report concerned a matter that the marshal "observed," since the fact that he issued the citation indicates that he observed gasoline being stored in the banquet hall; and (3) we know that the report concerned something observed "while under a legal duty to report," because the facts tell us that the report was prepared and filed "as required by law." As to the "lack of trustworthiness" proviso, there is no suggestion of any reason to believe that the report's contents are untrustworthy. Thus, the report meets the requirements of the FRE 803(8) public records exception to the hearsay rule, making it admissible.

(A) is wrong because this report is admissible as a public record under FRE 803(8). See the analysis of Choice (C) for why this is so.

(B) is wrong because the fact that this is a civil case does not make the report inadmissible. Public records are admissible in both civil and criminal cases. In fact, they are more broadly admissible in civil cases than in criminal cases, because law enforcement reports are generally not admissible against criminal defendants. See the analysis of Choice (C) for why the report here is admissible as a public record.

(D) is wrong because it incorrectly states how the regularly-conducted-activity exception works. This choice is correct in suggesting that the hearsay exception for records of regularly conducted activity contained in FRE 803(6) (commonly called the "business records" exception) would likely apply to this report. But the choice is incorrect in stating that the exception will apply only if the fire marshal is unavailable to testify. The 803(6) business-records exception, like all the exceptions contained in FRE 803, does not require a showing of the unavailability of the declarant (here, the fire marshal).

Answer 34

Choice **(A)** is correct, because this type of "absence of a public record" evidence is admissible and falls within a hearsay exception given by FRE 803(10).

The fact that the records are silent here is a form of hearsay: The records are an out-of-court statement, and they're offered to say, in essence, "Because the records don't say that the defendant was incarcerated on a particular date, he was not in fact incarcerated on that date." So the silence would not, strictly speaking, be admissible unless there were a hearsay exception to cover the situation.

But there *is* such an exception. FRE 803(10), entitled "Absence of a public record," gives a hearsay exception for "Testimony . . . that a diligent search failed to disclose a public record or statement," if the testimony is admitted to prove that "(B) a matter did not occur or exist, if a public office regularly kept a record or statement for a matter of that kind." Here, we know that if the defendant had been incarcerated at a particular jail on a particular date, there would be a record at the jail to that effect. So the proffered testimony that a search of the jail's collected attendance records showed no such record meets the requirements of FRE 803(10). (Notice, by the way, that the witness need not be an employee of the jail, or even of the government—anyone who testifies that he conducted a diligent search of the relevant records can testify to the absence of the record in question.)

(B) is wrong, because the witness was testifying about only the absence of a single record, not the contents of voluminous records. FRE 1006, entitled "Summaries to prove content," says that "The proponent may use a summary, chart, or calculation to prove the content of voluminous writings, recordings, or photographs that cannot be conveniently examined in court." Here, however, while the records the witness searched might be voluminous, the subject of his search was a single record, which he didn't find. The witness was therefore not summarizing "the content of voluminous writings."

(C) is wrong, because there is a hearsay exception for the absence of official records. As described in the analysis of Choice (A) above, FRE 803(10) gives a hearsay exception for the absence of an official record. Consequently, the testimony here is not hearsay.

(D) is wrong, because testimony about the absence of an official record receives a hearsay exception, and the records containing the omission need not be produced. FRE 803(10), allowing testimony that a particular official record was not found after diligent search, does not include any requirement that the records that were searched be produced.

It's true that apart from hearsay issues, when the affirmative contents of a document are offered the document itself must normally be offered under the Best Evidence Rule (BER) (the FRE's general formulation of which occurs in Rule 1002). But the BER is not deemed applicable to the "absence of a record" situation—testimony that a diligent search has not turned up the record is all that is required, and the mass of searched records need not be produced.

Answer 35

Choice **(A)** is correct. First, this is hearsay: The declarant's statement "I killed him" is being offered to show that she did indeed kill him. But FRE 804(b)(3) (one of the declarant-unavailable exceptions) gives a hearsay exception for a statement by a now-unavailable witness which "when made, . . . was so contrary to the declarant's proprietary or pecuniary interest or had so great a tendency to invalidate the declarant's claim against someone else or to expose the declarant to civil or criminal liability" that "a reasonable person in the declarant's position would have made [the statement] only if the person believed it to be true[.]" Where, as here, the statement is "offered in a criminal case as one that tends to expose the declarant to criminal liability," 804(b)(3)(B) adds the further requirement that the statement be "supported by corroborating circumstances that clearly indicate its trustworthiness." Here, the fact that the woman was known to have quarreled with and disliked the victim, and the fact that the victim's family chose to bring civil suit against the woman, supply the required corroborating circumstances to indicate the statement's trustworthiness.

(B) is wrong because, although there is indeed an exception for former testimony given under oath at a trial or other proceeding, the exception applies only if the testimony is "now offered against a party who had—or, in a civil case, whose predecessor in interest had—an opportunity and similar motive to develop it by direct, cross-, or redirect examination." See FRE 804(b)(1)(B). Since the party against whom the testimony is now being offered is the government, the statement could qualify only if the government had the opportunity and similar motive to "develop" (i.e., undermine) the woman's testimony in the earlier civil suit; because the prosecution was not part of that suit, this requirement is not satisfied.

(C) is wrong because, while the statement is indeed hearsay, the declaration-against-interest exception applies, as described in Choice (A) above.

(D) is wrong because, although the Best Evidence Rule does indeed sometimes require an original, FRE 1003 says that "a duplicate is admissible to the same extent as the original unless a genuine question is raised about the original's authenticity or the circumstances make it unfair to admit the duplicate." There is no indication on these facts that either of these problems is present.

Answer 36

Choice **(A)** is correct. There are three requirements for the declaration-against-interest exception to the hearsay rule: (1) the declarant must be unavailable; (2) the declaration must have been against the declarant's pecuniary or proprietary interest when made; and (3) the circumstances must be such that declarant would not have made the statement unless he believed it to be true. All of these requirements are fulfilled regarding the statement made by the now-deceased Ronald: (1) he's dead and thus unavailable; (2) he exposed himself to tort liability by acknowledging responsibility for the accident; and (3) there is no apparent reason why he'd acknowledge responsibility if he didn't think he was in fact at fault.

(B) is wrong, because the dying declaration exception applies only where the declarant believes that his own death is imminent. See FRE 804(b)(2). The statement here was made by Ronald the day before he died, and there is no indication that at the time, Ronald believed that his death was "imminent."

(C) is wrong, because of the timing element. FRE 803(3) gives a hearsay exception for "A statement of the declarant's then-existing state of mind," but says that the exception does not apply to "a statement of memory or belief to prove the fact remembered or believed unless it relates to the validity or terms of the declarant's will." Here, Ronald's statement is a statement about a fact remembered or believed (that the accident, which had happened nearly a week before, was caused by Ronald's own fault), so the exception doesn't apply.

(D) is wrong because FRE 803(2)'s excited utterance exception applies only to "a statement relating to a startling event or condition, *made while the declarant was under the stress of excitement that it caused.*" There is no evidence that Ronald, at the time of his visit to the doctor, was still under the stress of excitement from the accident itself, which had happened almost a week before. The excited utterance exception is usually held to apply only to the immediate aftermath of the startling event.

Answer 37

Choice (B) is correct. A communication is subject to attorney-client privilege if it is a communication from the client to the attorney, made in confidence, concerning legal representation. A corporation is subject to the same privilege as an individual, and the general manager would be within the scope of the privilege under the modern "performance of duties" test, under which the privilege extends to any employee's communication if it was within his duties, and it was offered to advance the legal interests of the corporation. So the communication here is within the attorney-client privilege. A companion "work product immunity," in force as a matter of common law in nearly all jurisdictions, gives an immunity from discovery or other "production" for materials that would be inadmissible at trial due to the attorney-client privilege.

(A) is not the best response because it does not correctly characterize the facts and law. A communication of *any* kind, business report or not, is subject to attorney-client privilege if it is a communication from the client to the attorney, made in confidence, concerning legal representation. Here, the report fits this description—the general manager made the report about the accident, intended that it be read only by the attorney, and it was made in preparation for trial. And apart from admissibility at trial, the "work product immunity" for direct client-attorney communication prevents the client (Def Co.) from having to produce it in discovery.

(C) is not the best response because (1) it ignores the central reason the report will be non-producible—it is covered by the work-product immunity; and (2) it falsely asserts that because the report is or might be inadmissible, it need not be produced. As to (1), what makes the report non-producible is the attorney-client privilege and companion "work product immunity," not the presence of hearsay. As to (2), even materials that would not be admissible at trial because they contain hearsay are producible in discovery, if they are reasonably likely to lead to discoverable evidence. (And it's not so clear that the report wouldn't be admissible if it were not for the attorney-client work-product immunity problem; for instance, the report and the statements in it might all be admissible as non-hearsay admissions by a party-opponent or its agents.)

(D) is wrong because the self-serving nature of the report won't prevent the opposite party (the adversary of the report's author) from offering it. If Def Company were offering the report as a business record under FRE 803(6), the fact that the "source of information [or] the method or circumstances of preparation indicate a lack of trustworthiness" (803(6)(E)) would be fatal. But where the adversary of the preparer of the record or report is offering it against the preparer, the report can come in as an admission, and the document's self-serving nature won't matter.

Answer 38

Choice **(A)** is correct. The attorney-client privilege applies only to confidential communications made for the purpose of facilitating legal representation of the client. Courts have uniformly held that the details of fee arrangements, including the amount paid by the defendant in fees, are not communications made for the purpose of facilitating representation, and are therefore not covered by the privilege. See M&K, § 5.19, p. 356.

(B) is wrong because it gives an incorrect explanation of the correct outcome. The attorney-client privilege *can* be invoked even where it conceals evidence of a *past* crime. (The examiners are trying to make you think of the "crime or fraud" exception, by which communications are not covered by the privilege if they are made for the purpose of accomplishing or concealing a *future* crime or fraud.)

(C) is wrong because the attorney-client privilege applies only to confidential communications made for the purpose of facilitating legal representation of the client. The amount the defendant paid in legal fees does not qualify as such a communication, as is described in the analysis of Choice (A).

(D) is wrong because the work-product doctrine provides a qualified immunity for only those materials prepared by an attorney or client in anticipation of litigation, such as witness statements, investigative reports, or trial memoranda. Documents showing the amount a client has paid or will pay to his attorney for legal representation are not deemed to be prepared "in anticipation of litigation," so they are outside the protection of the work-product doctrine.

Answer 39

Choice **(D)** is correct. If a party destroys evidence, it is proper for the jury to draw an inference that the evidence was adverse to that party. It's true that the Supreme Court has held that in a *criminal* case, neither the judge nor the prosecution can encourage a jury to draw an inference of guilt from a defendant's invocation of her privilege against self-incrimination; *Griffin v. California* (1965). But it's proper for the jury to draw an adverse inference in a *civil* case from a party's assertion of the privilege against self-incrimination. Thus, the court should allow the question to be asked, because it is proper regardless of how the defendant responds.

(A) is wrong because although it is true that a report prepared in anticipation of litigation may qualify as work product, the work-product immunity is not absolute. Documents that are work product are still subject to discovery upon a showing of substantial need and the inability to obtain the substantial equivalent of the materials by other means. Moreover, a claim of work-product immunity must be asserted before, and ruled on by, the court—a party cannot simply destroy the material and claim work-product protection. Finally, here the plaintiff would not be asking the defendant to produce the report for the jury to see; the plaintiff would only ask whether such a report had been destroyed.

(B) is wrong because although the Supreme Court has held that neither the judge nor the prosecution can encourage a jury to draw an inference of guilt from a defendant's invocation of her privilege against self-incrimination in a *criminal* case, *Griffin v. California* (1965), it is proper for the jury to draw an adverse inference in a *civil* case from a party's assertion of the privilege against self-incrimination.

(C) is wrong because the privilege against self-incrimination may be asserted in both civil and criminal cases.

Answer 40

Choice (**B**) is correct. The witness teller, who has not been qualified as a handwriting expert, is offering her lay opinion as to the genuineness of the signature on the check. FRE 701 allows lay opinion testimony in general when it is "rationally based on the witness's perception" *and* is "helpful to clearly understanding the witness's testimony or to determining a fact in issue[.]" These requirements are met here. Additionally, FRE 901(b)(2) provides that the authenticity of a document can be established by "a nonexpert's opinion that handwriting is genuine, based on a familiarity with it that was not acquired for the current litigation." This requirement is met here, since the facts tell us that the witness/teller already, at the time of the episode, knew the signature of the bank customer on whose account the check was drawn. This knowledge made it possible for her to recognize the signature on the check as a forgery, and to testify with first-hand knowledge that the signature on the check presented was different from the signature of the owner of the account. Thus, the testimony is permitted.

(A) is wrong because there is nothing in the fact pattern to suggest that the bank teller is an expert on handwriting—merely working as a bank teller would not give a person such expertise.

(C) is wrong because it misstates the application of the original document rule. This choice is premised on a plausible idea: that because what is being proved is the contents of a writing (namely, the signature on a check), the original of that writing must be produced. FRE 1002's implementation of the original documents rule (a/k/a the Best Evidence Rule) indeed says that "An original writing, recording, or photograph is required in order to prove its content unless these rules or a federal statute provides otherwise." So if the original of the check had been available to the prosecution, the prosecution's failure to present that original, and to have the teller testify about the check's contents instead, would indeed have been a violation of FRE 1002. But FRE 1004(a) grants an exception to the original documents rule where "all the originals are lost or destroyed, and not by the proponent acting in bad faith[.]" The proponent here is the prosecution (not the bank teller), so even if the teller had acted in bad faith in not securing the check, the FRE 1004(a) exception would still have applied. In any event, on the facts here, there is no evidence that the teller behaved in bad faith (or was even at fault) by not securing the check before the defendant could grab it and run away with it.

(D) is wrong because having an expert (or even the jury members themselves) compare an exemplar established as genuine with the disputed signature is not the only way to establish whether a signature is forged or authentic. It's true that FRE 901(b)(3) permits authentication of a document via "a comparison with an authenticated specimen by an expert witness or the trier of fact." However, this is not the only method authorized by FRE 901. FRE 901(b)(2) permits authentication by "a nonexpert's opinion that handwriting is genuine, based on a familiarity with it that was not acquired for the current litigation." The testimony here satisfies that method, since the teller got her familiarity with the real account-holder's signature in a way that pre-dated the litigation.

Answer 41

Choice (**C**) is correct (i.e., the choice is *not* an acceptable method of authentication). FRE 901(b)(2) allows authentication by "a nonexpert's opinion that handwriting is genuine, based on a familiarity with it that was not acquired for the current litigation." The fact pattern indicates that the nonexpert acquired familiarity in order to authenticate the signature; therefore, this would not serve as a sufficient basis for admitting the letter into evidence.

(A) is wrong because a nonexpert who is already familiar with a signature may testify as to its genuineness as provided by FRE 901(b)(2) and discussed in the explanation to (C). It is irrelevant that the nonexpert is a party to the litigation.

(B) is wrong because handwriting may be authenticated by the use of exemplars, in which case it is up to the jury to compare the exemplar with the offered writing to determine its genuineness.

(D) is wrong, because evidence that the letter (relying on its contents and other circumstances) was written as a reply to one already authenticated is a method of authentication falling under the category of "distinctive characteristics of the item, taken together with all the circumstances." FRE 901(b)(4).

Answer 42

Choice **(A)** is the best response, because under this alternative, the lay witness is not *personally familiar* with Daly's voice, and thus the recording wouldn't be admissible with this testimony alone. The rule is that a voice can be authenticated by any person who recognizes it. FRE 901(b)(5) allows authentication by means of "an opinion identifying a person's voice—whether *heard firsthand or through mechanical or electronic transmission or recording*—based on hearing the voice at any time under circumstances that connect it with the alleged speaker." Here, the only thing linking the lay witness and Daly's voice is an assurance by Daly's brother that a recorded voice was Daly's; the witness herself has no personal familiarity with it. (Thus, if Daly's brother were lying or mistaken, the lay witness's testimony would be useless.) Since (A) states the only basis on which the lay witness *couldn't* authenticate the tape, of these four choices, it's the best response.

(B) is wrong because the fact that the witness had never heard Daly speak over the telephone would be irrelevant. FRE 901(b)(5) allows authentication by means of "an opinion identifying a person's voice—whether heard firsthand or through mechanical or electronic transmission or recording—based on hearing the voice at any time under circumstances that connect it with the alleged speaker." Here, the lay witness satisfies this requirement because she had heard the voice many times. The rule doesn't require that the witness be familiar with the voice in the form in which it must be authenticated (here, a tape recording).

(C) is wrong because the lay witness could authenticate the recording on this basis, since any person who recognizes a voice can authenticate it. FRE 901(b)(5) (quoted in full in (A) above) allows lay testimony identifying a voice based upon "hearing the voice *at any time* under circumstances that connect it with the alleged speaker." This language means that familiarity acquired in anticipation of litigation does not disqualify the witness. (This makes the situation different from handwriting, as to which 901(b)(2) allows lay testimony only if "based on a familiarity with it that was not acquired for the current litigation.")

(D) is wrong because it represents possibly the *best* basis on which the lay witness *could* authenticate the recording. Not only would she be able to recognize the voice, but she'd be familiar with the very conversation that was recorded. Nothing in 901(b)(5) would come close to ruling out an identification of the speaker on a tape as having been the person whose side of the taped conversation the witness heard in person.

Answer 43

Choice **(D)** is correct. Under FRE 1002, the Best Evidence Rule applies only to writings recordings, and photographs.

Since the Best Evidence Rule doesn't apply to models, the original model need not be produced, and Poole may testify to its appearance without adhering to any of the requirements laid out in Choices (A), (B), and (C).

Answer 44

Choice **(B)** is correct. Where a witness has personal knowledge about a fact, the witness is ordinarily entitled to testify about that fact. Here, the plaintiff has personal knowledge about the condition of the shoe, and is therefore entitled to testify about that condition, unless some other rule blocks the testimony. There is no such other rule that applies here.

(A) is wrong because the fact that the defendant's expert was able to examine the shoe carefully is irrelevant. Even if the defendant's expert had not been able to examine the shoe, the plaintiff would still have been permitted to testify about his personal knowledge of the condition.

(C) is wrong because the fact that a physical object was present during settlement negotiations does not mean that testimony about the object's condition becomes inadmissible. It is true that FRE 408(a) makes inadmissible settlement offers, as well as "conduct or a statement made during" settlement negotiations, if offered to "prove or disprove the validity or amount of a disputed claim." But FRE 408(b) carefully states that the court may admit such settlement-related conduct or statements *"for another purpose"* than proving or disproving the validity or amount of the disputed claim. The fact that the plaintiff displayed the shoe during a settlement conference doesn't mean that the plaintiff's testimony about the shoe's condition is being offered to "prove or disprove the validity or amount of a disputed claim" as prohibited by 408(a); therefore, it's 408(b) that controls, to make 408's ban on settlement-related conduct or statements inapplicable.

(D) is wrong because the plaintiff does not bear the burden of establishing that the disappearance was not his fault. If the item had been a document, and its "contents" were sought to be proved, the FRE's implementation of the Best Evidence Rule would mean that the fact that the person seeking to testify about the contents was responsible in bad faith for the document's disappearance would cause the testimony to be excluded. (See FRE 1004: "An original is not required, and other evidence of the contents of a writing . . . is admissible if (a) all the originals are lost or destroyed, and not by the proponent acting in bad faith[.]") But no such rule applies to items of *physical evidence* that are *not writings*, recordings, or photographs (i.e., to items that are not subject to the Best Evidence Rule). The court probably has discretion to exclude testimony about an item of real evidence whose disappearance has been shown to have been procured by the intentional wrongdoing of the proponent of the testimony. But even so, it certainly is not the case that the burden would be placed on the party who will be testifying to make an affirmative showing that that party was not responsible for the disappearance.

Answer 45

Choice **(D)** is correct. The prosecutor is trying to prove what the defendant said, not what the transcript says. Accordingly, FRE 1003, the Best Evidence Rule, is not relevant. (It would be different, for example, if this was a contract and the parties differed over the wording of a clause in the contract—then the Best Evidence Rule *would* apply.) In this case, the copy of the transcript is properly used under FRE 612 to revive the officer's recollection.

Notice, by the way, that neither this choice nor any part of the question uses the phrase *"present recollection refreshed,"* even though that's the doctrine that controls the outcome. It's up to you to recognize that refreshment of recollection is what's occurring, and that it's being done properly here. Under the doctrine of present recollection refreshed, any item may be used to refresh the witness's memory, including leading questions, documents, or objects. If the witness, having seen the refreshing object, can testify from memory, the item will not be considered evidence. See FRE 612, implicitly allowing the present recollection refreshed technique, subject to certain limitations (which don't affect the outcome here). Here, the officer is going to testify (from his memory, after refreshing it from the transcript) to his recollection that the defendant admitted being nearby, so the recollection-refreshed doctrine applies.

(A) is wrong because the prosecutor is trying to prove what the defendant said, not what the transcript says. Accordingly, the Best Evidence Rule is not relevant. By the way, even assuming that the Best Evidence Rule applied here, this choice is not an accurate statement of the law. Under FRE 1003, a duplicate can be admissible without any showing that the original is unavailable. A showing of unavailability is required only if the party is seeking to introduce something other than a duplicate (e.g., oral testimony) to prove the contents of a document. See FRE 1004.

(B) is wrong because this is not a case of past recollection recorded; if it were, the prosecutor would have to show that the stenographer accurately recorded what the defendant said. In this case, the officer is testifying to his own (present) recollection of what the defendant said, that recollection having been revived by looking at the transcript. Therefore, the relevant doctrine is "present recollection refreshed." That doctrine is embodied in FRE 612, under which a document used only to refresh the recollection of the witness does not have to be accurate or reliable, because the document is not being admitted into evidence. So here, the copy of the transcript is being properly used to refresh the officer's recollection, and the officer's testimony is the evidence.

(C) is wrong because, although FRE 1003 supports the admission of photocopies with some exceptions, this option assumes that the Best Evidence Rule applies here, which it doesn't. The prosecutor is trying to prove what the defendant said, not what the transcript says. The transcript here is being used to refresh the officer's recollection under Federal Rule of Evidence 612, so Rule 1003 (the FRE's version of the Best Evidence Rule) is not relevant.

Answer 46

Choice **(C)** is correct. FRE 1006 says that "The proponent may use a *summary*, chart, or calculation to prove the content of *voluminous writings*, recordings, or photographs that cannot be conveniently examined in court." The individual timesheets here meet the "voluminous writings" standard, since they would be almost daily over a five-year timeframe, a stack that would be hard for the judge or jury to examine in court. FRE 1006 also says that "The proponent must make the originals or duplicates available for examination or copying, or both, by other parties at a reasonable time and place." So the fact that the underlying timesheets were made available to the client prior to trial, as specified in this choice, is a necessary condition for the summaries' admission under FRE 1006. By the way, the summaries: (1) become evidence (i.e., they're not just non-evidentiary testimonial aids); and (2) substitute for the underlying originals, which means that those originals must be independently admissible. Here, the underlying timesheets are hearsay, but they fall within FRE 803(6)'s business records exception.

(A) is wrong because the summary-of-voluminous-writings provision of FRE 1006 applies as described in Choice (C) above, and that provision does not require that the underlying writings being summarized be offered into evidence (although they may be).

(B) is wrong because, under FRE 1006, the summaries can come in as substantive evidence, as described in Choice (C) above.

(D) is wrong because the summaries can come in under FRE 1006 even if the underlying timesheets have not been lost. If you picked this choice, you may be thinking of FRE 1004(1), under which the Best Evidence Rule can be satisfied by something other than the original writing or a duplicate thereof (e.g., a summary) if "all the originals are lost or have been destroyed, and not by the proponent acting in bad faith[.]" But FRE 1006 provides an independent means of getting summaries into evidence (one that does not depend on loss of originals), and that means 1006 is available here as discussed in Choice (C) above.

Answer 47

Choice (**A**) is the best response because it correctly identifies that the testimony here is admissible as a response to a hypothetical question. Expert testimony is appropriate where the court determines that "the expert's scientific, technical, or other specialized knowledge will help the trier of fact to understand the evidence or to determine a fact in issue[.]" FRE 702(a). Here, Dr. Jones' testimony will address the causation issue—whether or not flaming underwear could cause a heart attack. Dr. Jones' status as an expert entitles him to offer opinion evidence that would be inadmissible coming from a lay witness, and to rely on information unavailable to a lay witness. The related issue is whether Dr. Jones may rely on the testimony presented at trial. The answer is yes: FRE 703 says that "an expert may base an opinion on facts or data in the case that the expert *has been made aware of* or personally observed." So data supplied at the hearing—whether in the form of testimony of other witnesses or a hypothetical posed by the questioner (here, it's a combination of both)—may be the basis for the expert opinion, since it's data that the expert "has been made aware of."

(B) is wrong because Jones's status as a physician wouldn't give him expert status in determining credibility. As a threshold matter, credibility itself is not a "fact," and expert testimony is only available to assist the trier of fact to understand evidence or to determine a fact in issue. FRE 702. Beyond that, a physician's expertise gives him the ability to offer opinion testimony on medical matters; it's irrelevant to assessing the credibility of testimony, since one's status as a doctor doesn't make him a better judge of witness credibility than anyone else.

(C) is wrong because it states an incorrect rule. FRE 703 says that "an expert may base an opinion on facts or data in the case that the expert *has been made aware of* or personally observed." This language allows the expert to offer an opinion based on the "data" included in a hypothetical question. And the hypothetical question for this purpose can be based on prior trial testimony and on the assumption that that prior testimony is truthful. (That's in fact a very common way for a proponent of expert testimony to proceed.)

(D) is wrong because it states an incorrect rule. An expert may base his opinion on "facts or data in the case that the expert has been made aware of." FRE 703. Neither this nor any other provision prevents the expert from basing his opinion solely on information provided by lay persons.

Answer 48

Choice (**D**) is correct. FRE 704(b) says that "In a criminal case, an expert witness must not state an opinion about whether the defendant did or did not have a mental state or condition that constitutes an element of the crime charged or of a defense. Those matters are for the trier of fact alone." The proposed testimony here—that the defendant had the mental state required for a defense (the defense of self-defense)—falls squarely within this prohibition.

(A) is wrong because the statement is not admissible, whether or not the expert believed that the defendant was speaking truthfully. As described in Choice (D) above, FRE 704(b) bars the proposed testimony. Additionally, the vast majority of courts have rejected the admission of statements made under hypnosis. This is true whether the statement is offered as substantive evidence or for its bearing on the credibility of the witness's live testimony at trial.

(B) is wrong because, as described in Choice (D), the statement is expressly barred by FRE 704(b). If it weren't barred by 704(b), it might well be admissible under FRE 801(d)(1)(B), which defines as non-hearsay, and thus allows, a prior statement if "the declarant testifies and is subject to cross-examination about [the] prior statement, and the statement . . . (B) is consistent with the declarant's testimony and is offered to rebut an express or implied charge that the declarant recently fabricated it or acted from a recent improper influence or motive in so testifying[.]" It's not clear from the facts here that the prosecution is making an "express or implied charge" that the defendant has "recently fabricated" her assertion that she acted in fear for her life, but if the court were convinced that there was such a charge (and if the defendant was willing to testify after the expert did and be cross-examined about the declaration), and if FRE 704(b) didn't intervene, the statement here would be admissible under 801(d)(1)(B).

(C) is wrong because use of the hypnosis-induced out-of-court statement by the defendant would not violate her constitutional rights. If hypnosis-induced testimony were introduced *against* a criminal defendant, this usage might conceivably violate the defendant's criminal rights. (If the statement were induced from a third-party witness who was not available for cross-examination at trial, for instance, use of the testimony might violate the defendant's Confrontation Clause rights.) But use *by* a criminal defendant could never violate the Constitution—whose rights would be violated? (The state itself, in the form of the prosecution, does not have "constitutional rights" vis-à-vis the defendant.)

Answer 49

Choice (**B**) is correct. Under FRE 301, once the opponent of the presumption comes up with enough evidence of the presumed fact's non-existence that a jury could reasonably find that the presumed fact does not exist, the presumption disappears from the case in the sense that there is no effect on the burden of persuasion. When this happens, the court may instruct the jury that it *may* infer the existence of the presumed fact from proof of the basic fact, but the jury is not required to so infer. In this case, Defendant's testimony, "I never got the notice," is enough to entitle a reasonable jury to find that the presumed fact (receipt) does not exist. Therefore, the presumption of receipt has disappeared and the plaintiff still has the burden of persuasion regarding the issue of receipt of the notice. But notwithstanding the disappearance of the presumption, the jury is still entitled to conclude that notice was received from proof of the basic fact that notice was given. Therefore, this choice is accurate in saying that the jury may infer, but is not required to infer, that the notice was received.

(A) is wrong because, as noted in the explanation of (B), once the presumption disappears from the case, the court may instruct the jury that it *may* infer the existence of the presumed fact from proof of the basic facts, but it is *not required* that the jury do so.

(C) is wrong because, as explained in (B), the presumption has no effect on the burden of persuasion; it "remains on the party who had it originally" (FRE 301), which, in this case, is the plaintiff.

(D) is wrong because, as discussed in (B), the jury may infer the existence of the presumed fact from proof of the basic fact (i.e., jury may find that the notice was received) even though the presumption has disappeared from the case.

Answer 50

Choice (**B**) is correct. Questions of whether a person is qualified to be a witness (whether expert or lay) are to be decided by the judge. In doing so, the judge may take into account inadmissible evidence (except with respect to privileges). FRE 104(a).

(A), (C), and (D) are wrong because each is inconsistent with the above explanation.

Answer 51

Choice (**B**) is correct. Both parts of this answer are true. As to the first part, before a declaration can be found to be an admissible "dying declaration," some preliminary questions of fact must be answered. In particular, it must be determined whether the declarant was indeed aware of her impending death. Under the FRE, the jury decides issues like this, of conditional relevance, but it is the judge who makes the initial decision of admissibility, in determining whether a reasonable jury could find that the preliminary fact exists: "When the relevance of evidence depends on whether a fact exists, proof must be introduced *sufficient to support a finding* that the fact does exist." FRE 104(b). In other words, if the judge decides that there is enough evidence that a jury could reasonably find (that's what the phrase "sufficient to support a finding" means) that there was an awareness of impending death, he will let the jury hear the declaration, even though he may personally believe that it is less likely than not that there was such awareness.

As to the second part, the judge's ability to consider the affidavit, FRE 104(a) says that "The court must decide any preliminary question about whether a witness is qualified, a privilege exists, or evidence is admissible. In so deciding, the court is *not bound by evidence rules*, except those on privilege." The affidavit is relevant to the issue of whether the declarant was aware of her impending death. It's true that the affidavit is hearsay (it's an out-of-court statement offered to prove the truth of the matter asserted, i.e., that the victim knew or believed she was dying). And this hearsay does not fall within any exception. But under 104(a), the judge may consider this inadmissible hearsay to make her preliminary ruling on the admissibility of the note.

(A) is wrong because, although it correctly states that the admissibility of the note is a preliminary fact question for the judge, it incorrectly states that the judge must not consider the affidavit. As described in the discussion of Choice (B) above, the judge may consider inadmissible hearsay when resolving a preliminary question about the admissibility of other evidence.

(C) is wrong because, although it is true that the jury must not consider the affidavit, the admissibility of the note is not a question for the jury. It will be up to the jury to determine what weight and credibility to give the evidence of the note once it has been admitted.

(D) is wrong because the jury cannot consider the affidavit (it is hearsay) and also because the admissibility of the note is not a question for the jury. It will be up to the jury to determine what weight and credibility to give the evidence of the note once it has been admitted.

Answer 52

Choice **(A)** is correct. First, the location of the state capital is a fact that is *"generally known within the trial court's territorial jurisdiction."* FRE 201(b)(1). So the fact that Capitan is the capital is appropriate for judicial notice. Second, FRE 201(c)(1) provides that a court "may take judicial notice on its own." So the court may take notice here without a request from either party.

(B) is wrong because judicial notice of an appropriate fact may be taken without submission of formal evidence that the fact is true.

(C) is wrong because, in a civil case, once there is judicial notice, the issue is decided and the jury is not permitted to weigh the evidence in order to come to its own conclusion. See FRE 201(f): In a civil case, "the court *must* instruct the jury to accept the noticed fact as *conclusive.*"

(D) is wrong because in a civil case the jury is required to accept as conclusive the judicially noticed fact, as discussed in (C).

REAL PROPERTY

REAL PROPERTY QUESTIONS BY TOPIC

CHAPTER 1
ADVERSE POSSESSION

I. "HOSTILE" POSSESSION

A. Boundary disputes

Question 1

Twenty-five years ago a seller conveyed Lot 1 to a buyer by a warranty deed. The seller at that time also executed and delivered an instrument in the proper form of a deed, purporting to convey Lot 2 to the buyer. The seller thought she had title to Lot 2 but did not; therefore, no title passed by virtue of the Lot 2 deed. Lot 2 consisted of three acres of brushland adjoining the west boundary of Lot 1. The buyer has occasionally hunted rabbits on Lot 2, but less often than annually. No one else came onto Lot 2 except occasional rabbit hunters.

Twenty years ago, the buyer planted a row of evergreens in the vicinity of the opposite (east) boundary of Lot 1 and erected a fence just beyond the evergreens to the east. In fact both the trees and the fence were placed on Lot 3, owned by a neighbor, which bordered the east boundary of Lot 1. The buyer was unsure of the exact boundary, and placed the trees and the fence in order to establish his rights up to the fence. The fence is located ten feet within Lot 3.

Now, the buyer has had his property surveyed and the title checked and has learned the facts.

The period of time to acquire title by adverse possession in the jurisdiction is 15 years.

The buyer consulted his lawyer, who properly advised that, in an appropriate action, the buyer would probably obtain title to

(A) Lot 2 but not to the ten-foot strip of Lot 3.

(B) the ten-foot strip of Lot 3 but not to Lot 2.

(C) both Lot 2 and the ten-foot strip of Lot 3.

(D) neither Lot 2 nor the ten-foot strip of Lot 3.

II. CONTINUITY OF POSSESSION

A. Continuity of possession generally

1. Temporary or seasonal gaps in possession

Question 2

Brown owned Blackacre, a tract of undeveloped land. Blackacre abuts Whiteacre, a tract of land owned by Agency, the state's governmental energy agency. At Whiteacre, Agency has operated a waste-to-electricity recycling facility for 12 years. Blackacre and Whiteacre are in a remote area and Whiteacre is the only developed parcel of real estate within a ten-mile radius. The boundary line between Blackacre and Whiteacre had never been surveyed or marked on the face of the earth.

During the past 12 years, some of the trucks bringing waste to the Agency facility have dumped their loads so that the piles of waste extend from Whiteacre onto a portion of Blackacre. However, prior to the four-week period during each calendar year when the Agency facility is closed for inspection and repairs, the waste piles are reduced to minimal levels so that during each of the four-week closures no waste was, in fact, piled on Blackacre. Neither Brown nor any representative of Agency knew the facts about the relation of the boundary line to the waste piles.

The time for acquiring title by adverse possession in the jurisdiction is ten years.

Last year, Brown died, and his son, Silas, succeeded him as the owner of Blackacre. Silas became aware of the facts, demanded that Agency stop using Blackacre for the piling of waste, and, when Agency refused his demand, brought an appropriate action to enjoin any such use of Blackacre in the future.

If Agency prevails in that action, it will be because

(A) the facts constitute adverse possession and title to the portion of Blackacre concerned has vested in Agency.

(B) Brown's failure to keep himself informed as to Agency's use of Blackacre and his failure to object constituted implied consent to the continuation of that use.

(C) the interest of the public in the conversion of waste to energy overrides any entitlement of Silas to equitable remedies.

(D) the power of eminent domain of the state makes the claim of Silas moot.

FREEHOLD ESTATES

I. THE FEE SIMPLE

A. Fee simple defeasible

1. Fee simple determinable

Question 3

A grantor executed an instrument in the proper form of a warranty deed purporting to convey a tract of land to his church. The granting clause of the instrument ran to the church "and its successors forever, so long as the premises are used for church purposes." The church took possession of the land and used it as its site of worship for many years. Subsequently, the church wanted to relocate and entered into a valid written contract to sell the land to a buyer for a substantial price. The buyer wanted to use the land as a site for business activities and objected to the church's title. The contract contained no provision relating to the quality of title the church was bound to convey. There is no applicable statute. When the buyer refused to close, the church sued the buyer for specific performance and properly joined the grantor as a party.

Is the church likely to prevail?

(A) No, because the grantor's interest prevents the church's title from being marketable.

(B) No, because the quoted provision is a valid restrictive covenant.

(C) Yes, because a charitable trust to support religion will attach to the proceeds of the sale.

(D) Yes, because the grantor cannot derogate from his warranty to the church.

2. Fee simple subject to condition subsequent

Question 4

A landowner owned land in fee simple. A small house on the land was occupied, with the landowner's oral permission, rent-free, by the landowner's son and the son's college classmate. The son was then 21 years old.

The landowner, by properly executed instrument, conveyed the land to "my beloved son, his heirs and assigns, upon the condition precedent that he earn a college degree by the time he reaches the age of 30. If, for any reason, he does not meet this condition, then the land shall become the sole property of my beloved daughter, her heirs and assigns." At the time of the conveyance, the son and the classmate attended a college located several blocks from the land. Neither had earned a college degree.

One week after the delivery of the deed to the son, the son recorded the deed and immediately told the classmate that he, the son, was going to begin charging the classmate rent since "I am now your landlord." There is no applicable statute.

The son and the classmate did not reach agreement, and the son served the appropriate notice to terminate whatever tenancy the classmate had. The son then sought, in an appropriate action, to oust the classmate.

Who should prevail?

(A) The son, because the conveyance created a fee simple subject to divestment in the son.

(B) The son, because the landowner's conveyance terminated the classmate's tenancy.

(C) The classmate, because the landowner's permission to occupy preceded the landowner's conveyance to the son.

(D) The classmate, because he is a tenant of the landowner, not of the son.

II. THE LIFE ESTATE

A. Duties and powers of life tenant

1. Duties

a. No right to commit waste

Question 5

Alice owned a commercial property, Eastgate, consisting of a one-story building rented to various retail stores and a very large parking lot. Two years ago, Alice died and left Eastgate to her nephew, Paul, for life, with remainder to her godson, Richard, his heirs and assigns. Paul was 30 years old and Richard was 20 years old when Alice died. The devise of Eastgate was made subject to any mortgage on Eastgate in effect at the time of Alice's death.

When Alice executed her will, the balance of the mortgage debt on Eastgate was less than $5,000. A year before her death, Alice suffered financial reverses; and in order to meet her debts, she had mortgaged Eastgate to secure a loan of $150,000. The entire principal of the mortgage remained outstanding when she died. As a result, the net annual income from Eastgate was reduced not only by real estate taxes and regular maintenance costs, but also by the substantial mortgage interest payments that were due each month.

Paul was very dissatisfied with the limited benefit that he was receiving from the life estate. When, earlier this year, Acme, Inc., proposed to purchase Eastgate, demolish the building, pay off the mortgage, and construct a 30-story office building, Paul was willing to accept Acme's offer. However, Richard adamantly refused the offer, even though Richard, as the remainderman, paid the principal portion of each monthly mortgage amortization payment. Richard was independently wealthy and wanted to convert Eastgate into a public park when he became entitled to possession.

When Acme realized that Richard would not change his mind, Acme modified its proposal to a purchase of the life estate of Paul. Acme was ready to go ahead with its building plans, relying upon a large life insurance policy on Paul's life to protect it against the economic risk of Paul's death. Paul's life expectancy was 45 years.

When Richard learned that Paul had agreed to Acme's modified proposal, Richard brought an appropriate action against them to enjoin their carrying it out.

There is no applicable statute.

The best argument for Richard is that

(A) Acme cannot purchase Paul's life estate, because life estates are not assignable.

(B) the proposed demolition of the building constitutes waste.

(C) Richard's payment of the mortgage principal has subrogated him to Paul's rights as a life tenant and bars Paul's assignment of the life estate without Richard's consent.

(D) continued existence of the one-story building is more in harmony with the ultimate use as a park than the proposed change in use.

b. Duty to pay current operating expenses

i. Duty to pay taxes

Question 6

Ody, owner of Profitacre, executed an instrument in the proper form of a deed, purporting to convey Profitacre "to Leon for life, then to Ralph in fee simple." Leon, who is Ody's brother and Ralph's father, promptly began to manage Profitacre, which is valuable income-producing real estate. Leon collected all rents and paid all expenses, including real estate taxes. Ralph did not object, and this state of affairs continued for five years until 2007. In that year, Leon executed an instrument in the proper form of a deed, purporting to convey Profitacre to Mona. Ralph, no admirer of Mona, asserted his right to ownership of Profitacre. Mona asserted her ownership and said that if Ralph had any rights he was obligated to pay real estate taxes, even though Leon had been kind enough to pay them in the past. Income from Profitacre is ample to cover expenses, including real estate taxes.

In an appropriate action to determine the rights of the parties, the court should decide

(A) Leon's purported deed forfeited his life estate, so Ralph owns Profitacre in fee simple.

(B) Mona owns an estate for her life, is entitled to all income, and must pay real estate taxes; Ralph owns the remainder interest.

(C) Mona owns an estate for the life of Leon, is entitled to all income, and must pay real estate taxes; Ralph owns the remainder interest.

(D) Mona owns an estate for the life of Leon and is entitled to all income; Ralph owns the remainder interest, and must pay real estate taxes.

c. Duty to pay mortgage interest and principal

Question 7

A testator owned in fee simple a farm of 300 acres. He died and by will duly admitted to probate devised the farm to his surviving widow, for life with remainder in fee simple to his three children, two daughters and a son. All three children survived the testator.

At the time of the testator's death, there existed a mortgage on the farm that the testator had given ten years before to secure a loan for the purchase of the farm. At his death, there remained unpaid $40,000 in principal, payable in installments of $4,000 per year for the next ten years. In addition, there was due interest at the rate of 10% per annum, payable annually with the installment of principal. The widow took possession and out of a gross income of $50,000 per year realized $25,000 net after paying all expenses and charges except the installment of principal and interest due on the mortgage.

The daughters wanted the three children, including the son, to each contribute one-third of the amounts needed to pay the mortgage installments. The son objected, contending that the widow should pay all of these amounts out of the profits she had made in operation of the farm. When foreclosure of the mortgage seemed imminent, the son sought legal advice.

If the son obtained sound advice relating to his rights, he was told that

(A) his only protection would lie in instituting an action for partition to compel the sale of the life estate of the widow and to obtain the value of the son's one-third interest in remainder.

(B) he could obtain appropriate relief to compel the widow personally to pay the sums due because the income is more than adequate to cover these amounts.

(C) he could be compelled personally to pay his share of the amounts due because discharge of the mortgage enhances the principal.

(D) he could not be held personally liable for any amount but that his share in remainder could be lost if the mortgage installments are not paid.

FUTURE INTERESTS

I. POSSIBILITY OF REVERTER; RIGHT OF RE-ENTRY

A. Possibility of reverter and right of re-entry

1. Possibility of reverter

Question 8

Twenty years ago, a landowner who owned Blackacre, a one-acre tract of land, duly delivered a deed of Blackacre "to School District so long as it is used for school purposes." The deed was promptly and properly recorded. Five years ago, the landowner died, leaving Sonny as his only heir at law. The landowner left a duly probated will, by which he left "all my Estate" to his friend, who was a doctor.

Last month, School District closed its school on Blackacre and for valid consideration duly executed and delivered a quitclaim deed of Blackacre to a developer, who planned to use the land for commercial development. The developer has now brought an appropriate action to quiet title against the son, the doctor and School District.

The only applicable statute is a provision in the jurisdiction's probate code which provides that any property interest which is descendible is devisable.

In such action, the court should find that title is now in

(A) the developer.

(B) the son.

(C) the doctor.

(D) School District.

II. REMAINDERS

A. Contingent remainders

Question 9

A testator owned a tract of land in fee simple. By will duly admitted to probate after his death, the testator devised the land to "any wife who survives me with remainder to such of my children as are living at her death."

The testator was survived by his widow and by three children, who were an accountant, a lawyer, and a doctor. Thereafter, the lawyer died and by will duly admitted to probate devised his entire estate to his friend. The accountant and the doctor were the lawyer's heirs at law.

Later the widow died. In an appropriate lawsuit to which the accountant, the doctor, and the friend are parties, title to the land is at issue.

In such lawsuit, judgment should be that title to the property is in

(A) the accountant, the doctor, and the friend, because the earliest vesting of remainders is favored and reference to the surviving wife's death should be construed as relating to time of taking possession.

(B) the accountant, the doctor, and the friend, because the provision requiring survival of children violates the Rule Against Perpetuities since the surviving wife might have been a person unborn at the time of writing of the will.

(C) the accountant and the doctor, because the lawyer's remainder must descend by intestacy and is not devisable.

(D) the accountant and the doctor, because the remainders were contingent upon surviving the life tenant.

Question 10

A testator owned a tract of land in fee simple. The testator wrote and executed, with the required formalities, a will that devised the tract to "my daughter for life with remainder to my descendants per stirpes." At the time of writing the will, the testator had a husband and no descendants living other than her two children, the daughter named in the will and a son.

The testator died and the will was duly admitted to probate. The testator's husband pre-deceased her, but she was survived by her daughter, her son, four grandchildren, and one great-grandchild. The testator's two children were the testator's sole heirs at law. The testator's children brought an appropriate action for declaratory judgment as to title of the tract. Guardians ad litem were appointed and all other steps were taken so that the judgment would bind all persons interested whether born or unborn. In that action, if the court rules that the daughter has a life estate in the whole of the tract and that the remainder is contingent, it will be because the court chose one of several possible constructions and that the chosen construction

(A) related all vesting to the time of writing of the will.

(B) related all vesting to the death of the testator.

(C) implied a condition that remaindermen survive the daughter.

(D) implied a gift of a life estate to the son.

1. Unborn or unascertained

a. Remainder "to A and her heirs or assigns" is vested

Question 11

A grantor owned a tract of land in fee simple. By warranty deed he conveyed the land to his nephew for life "and from and after the death of my nephew to my niece, her heirs and assigns."

Subsequently the niece died, devising all of her estate to the niece's boyfriend. The niece was survived by a cousin, her sole heir-at-law.

Shortly thereafter the nephew died, survived by the grantor, the niece's boyfriend, and the niece's cousin.

Title to the land now is in

(A) the grantor, because the contingent remainder never vested and the grantor's reversion was entitled to possession immediately upon the nephew's death.

(B) the boyfriend, because the vested remainder in the niece was transmitted by her will.

(C) the cousin, because she is the niece's heir.

(D) either the grantor or the cousin, depending upon whether the destructibility of contingent remainders is recognized in the applicable jurisdiction.

III. THE RULE AGAINST PERPETUITIES (RAP)

A. Applicability of Rule to various estates

1. Options to purchase land

a. Right of first refusal

Question 12

A grantor owned two tracts of land, one of 15 acres and another of five acres. The two tracts were a mile apart.

Fifteen years ago, the grantor conveyed the smaller tract to a grantee. The grantor retained the larger tract. The deed to the grantee contained, in addition to proper legal descriptions of both properties and identifications of the parties, the following:

> I, the grantor, bind myself and my heirs and assigns that in the event that the larger tract that I now retain is ever offered for sale, I will notify the grantee and his heirs and assigns in writing, and the grantee and his heirs and assigns shall have the right to purchase the larger tract for its fair market value as determined by a board consisting of three qualified expert independent real estate appraisers.

With appropriate references to the other property and the parties, there followed a reciprocal provision that conferred upon the grantor and her heirs and assigns a similar right to purchase the smaller tract, purportedly binding the grantee and his heirs and assigns.

Ten years ago, a corporation acquired the larger tract from the grantor. At that time, the grantee had no interest in acquiring the larger tract and by an appropriate written document released any interest he or his heirs or assigns might have had in the larger tract.

Last year, the grantee died. The smaller tract passed by the grantee's will to his daughter. She has decided to sell the smaller tract. However, because she believes the corporation has been a very poor steward of the larger tract, she refuses to sell the smaller tract to the corporation even though she has offered it for sale in the local real estate market.

The corporation brought an appropriate action for specific performance after taking all of the necessary preliminary steps in its effort to exercise its rights to purchase the smaller tract.

The daughter asserted all possible defenses.

The common-law Rule Against Perpetuities is unmodified in the jurisdiction.

If the court rules for the daughter, what is the reason?

(A) The provision setting out the right to purchase violates the Rule Against Perpetuities.

(B) The grantee's release 10 years ago operates as a waiver regarding any right to purchase that the corporation might have.

(C) The two tracts of land were not adjacent parcels of real estate, and thus the right to purchase is in gross and is therefore unenforceable.

(D) Noncompliance with a right to purchase gives rise to a claim for money damages, but not for specific performance.

CONCURRENT OWNERSHIP

I. JOINT TENANCY

A. Severance

1. Conveyance by one joint tenant

Question 13

By warranty deed, Marta conveyed Blackacre to Beth and Christine "as joint tenants with right of survivorship." Beth and Christine are not related. Beth conveyed all her interest to Eugenio by warranty deed and subsequently died intestate. Thereafter, Christine conveyed to Darin by warranty deed.

There is no applicable statute, and the jurisdiction recognizes the common-law joint tenancy.

Title to Blackacre is in

(A) Darin.

(B) Marta.

(C) Darin and Eugenio.

(D) Darin and the heirs of Beth.

a. Motive for severance irrelevant

Question 14

A brother and sister owned a large tract of land in fee simple as joint tenants with rights of survivorship. While the sister was on an extended safari in Kenya, the brother learned that there were very valuable coal deposits within the land, but he made no attempt to inform his sister. Thereupon, the brother conveyed his interest in the land to his wife, who immediately reconveyed that interest to the brother. The common-law joint tenancy is unmodified by statute.

Shortly thereafter, the brother was killed in an automobile accident. His will, which was duly probated, specifically devised his one-half interest in the property to his wife.

The sister then returned from Kenya and learned what had happened. The sister brought an appropriate action against the brother's wife, who claimed a one-half interest in the property, seeking a declaratory judgment that she, the sister, was the sole owner of the land.

In this action, who should prevail?

(A) The brother's wife, because the brother and sister were tenants in common at the time of the brother's death.

(B) The brother's wife, because the brother's will severed the joint tenancy.

(C) The sister, because the joint tenancy was reestablished by the brother's wife's reconveyance to the brother.

(D) The sister, because the brother breached his fiduciary duty as her joint tenant.

2. Rights of creditors of deceased joint tenant

Question 15

A brother and sister owned a parcel as joint tenants, upon which was situated a two-family house. The brother lived in one of the two apartments and rented the other apartment to a tenant. The brother got in a fight with the tenant and injured him. The tenant obtained and properly filed a judgment for $10,000 against the brother.

The statute in the jurisdiction reads: "Any judgment properly filed shall, for ten years from filing, be a lien on the real property then owned or subsequently acquired by any person against whom the judgment is rendered."

The sister, who lived in a distant city, knew nothing of the tenant's judgment. Before the tenant took any further action, the brother died. The common-law joint tenancy is unmodified by statute.

The sister then learned the facts and brought an appropriate action against the tenant to quiet title to the land.

The court should hold that the tenant has

(A) a lien against the whole of the property, because he was a tenant of both the brother and the sister at the time of the judgment.

(B) a lien against the brother's undivided one-half interest in the land, because his judgment was filed prior to the brother's death.

(C) no lien, because the sister had no actual notice of the tenant's judgment until after the brother's death.

(D) no lien, because the brother's death terminated the interest to which the tenant's lien attached.

II. TENANCY IN COMMON

A. Tenancy in common

1. Conveyance by one co-tenant

a. Grant of mortgage or judgment lien

Question 16

A mother owned a two-family apartment house on a small city lot not suitable for partition-in-kind. Upon the mother's death, her will devised the property to "my son and my daughter."

A week ago, a creditor of the son obtained a money judgment against the son, and properly filed the judgment in the county where the property is located. A statute in the jurisdiction provides: Any judgment properly filed shall, for ten years from filing, be a lien on the real property then owned or subsequently acquired by any person against whom the judgment is rendered.

The son needed cash, but the daughter did not wish to sell the property. The son commenced a partition action against the daughter and the creditor.

Assume that the court properly ordered a partition by judicial sale.

After the sale, the creditor's judgment will be a lien on

(A) all of the property.

(B) only a one-half interest in the property.

(C) all of the proceeds of sale of the property.

(D) only the portion of the proceeds of sale due the son.

CHAPTER 5
LANDLORD AND TENANT

I. TORT LIABILITY OF LANDLORD AND TENANT

A. Landlord's liability

1. Common law

a. Assignment of interest by L

Question 17

Les leased a barn to his neighbor, Tom, for a term of three years. Tom took possession of the barn and used it for his farming purposes. The lease made Les responsible for structural repairs to the barn, unless they were made necessary by actions of Tom.

One year later, Les conveyed the barn and its associated land to Lottie "subject to the lease to Tom." Tom paid the next month's rent to Lottie. The next day a portion of an exterior wall of the barn collapsed because of rot in the interior structure of the wall. The wall had appeared to be sound, but a competent engineer, on inspection, would have discovered its condition. Neither Lottie nor Tom had the barn inspected by an engineer. Tom was injured as a result of the collapse of the wall.

Les had known that the wall was dangerously weakened by rot and needed immediate repairs, but had not told Tom or Lottie. There is no applicable statute.

Tom brought an appropriate action against Les to recover damages for the injuries he sustained. Lottie was not a party.

Which of the following is the most appropriate comment concerning the outcome of this action?

(A) Tom should lose, because Lottie assumed all of Les's obligations by reason of Tom's attornment to her.

(B) Tom should recover, because there is privity between lessor and lessee and it cannot be broken unilaterally.

(C) Tom should recover, because Les knew of the danger but did not warn Tom.

(D) Tom should lose, because he failed to inspect the barn.

II. TRANSFER AND SALE BY LESSOR; ASSIGNMENT AND SUBLETTING BY LESSEE

A. Generally allowed

1. Distinguish assignment from sublease

Question 18

A landlord leased an apartment to a tenant by written lease for two years ending on the last day of a recent month. The lease provided for $700 monthly rental. The tenant occupied the apartment and paid the rent for the first 15 months of the lease term, until he moved to a new job in another city. Without consulting the landlord, the tenant moved a friend into the apartment and signed an informal writing transferring to the friend his "lease rights" for the remaining nine months of the lease. The friend made the next four monthly $700 rental payments to the landlord. For the final five months of the lease term, no rent was paid by anyone, and the friend moved out with three months left on the lease term. The landlord was on an extended trip abroad, and did not learn of the default and the vacancy until last week. The landlord sued the tenant and the friend, jointly and severally, for $3,500 for the last five months' rent.

What is the likely outcome of the lawsuit?

(A) Both the tenant and the friend are liable for the full $3,500, because the tenant is liable on privity of contract and the friend is liable on privity of estate as assignee.

(B) The friend is liable for $1,400 on privity of estate, which lasted only until he vacated, and the tenant is liable for $2,100 on privity of contract and estate for the period after the friend vacated.

(C) The friend is liable for $3,500 on privity of estate and the tenant is not liable, because the landlord's failure to object to the friend's payment of rent relieved the tenant of liability.

(D) The tenant is liable for $3,500 on privity of contract and the friend is not liable, because a sublessee does not have personal liability to the original landlord.

B. Running of benefit and burden

1. Purchase options in leases

Question 19

Lanny, the owner of Whiteacre in fee simple, leased Whiteacre to Ten for a term of ten years by a properly executed written instrument. The lease was promptly and properly recorded. It contained an option for Ten to purchase Whiteacre by tendering $250,000 as purchase price any time "during the term of this lease." One year later, Ten, by a properly executed written instrument, purported to assign the option to Oscar, expressly retaining all of the remaining term of the lease. The instrument of assignment was promptly and properly recorded.

Two years later, Lanny contracted to sell Whiteacre to Jones and to convey a marketable title "subject to the rights of Ten under her lease." Jones refused to close because of the outstanding option assigned to Oscar.

Lanny brought an appropriate action against Jones for specific performance.

If judgment is rendered in favor of Lanny, it will be because the relevant jurisdiction has adopted a rule on a key issue as to which various state courts have split.

Which of the following identifies the determinative rule or doctrine upon which the split occurs, and states the position favorable to Lanny?

(A) In a contract to buy, any form of "subject to a lease" clause that fails to mention expressly an existing option means that the seller is agreeing to sell free and clear of any option originally included in the lease.

(B) Marketable title can be conveyed so long as any outstanding option not mentioned in the purchase contract has not yet been exercised.

(C) Options to purchase by lessees are subject to the Rule Against Perpetuities.

(D) Options to purchase contained in a lease cannot be assigned separately from the lease.

C. Agreement by the parties about transfer

1. Generally enforced

a. Condemnation awards

Question 20

Six years ago, a landlord and a tenant entered into a ten-year commercial lease of land. The written lease provided that if a public entity using the power of eminent domain condemned any part of the land, the lease would terminate and the landlord would receive the entire condemnation award. Thereafter, the city condemned approximately two-thirds of the land.

The tenant notified the city and the landlord that an independent appraisal of the value of the tenant's possessory interest established that it substantially exceeded the tenant's obligation under the lease and that the tenant was entitled to share the award. The appraisal was accurate. In an appropriate action among the landlord, the tenant, and the city as to the right of the tenant to a portion of the condemnation award, for whom will the court likely find?

(A) The landlord, because the condemnation superseded and canceled the lease.

(B) The landlord, because the parties specifically agreed as to the consequences of condemnation.

(C) The tenant, because the landlord breached the landlord's implied warranty of quiet enjoyment.

(D) The tenant, because otherwise the landlord would be unjustly enriched.

CHAPTER 6

EASEMENTS AND SERVITUDES

I. CREATION OF EASEMENTS

A. Easement by prescription

1. Adverse use

Question 21

Oxnard owned Goldacre, a tract of land, in fee simple. At a time when Goldacre was in the adverse possession of Amos, Eric obtained the oral permission of Oxnard to use as a road or driveway a portion of Goldacre to reach adjoining land, Twin Pines, which Eric owned in fee simple. Thereafter, during all times relevant to this problem, Eric used this road between Goldacre regularly for ingress and egress between Twin Pines and a public highway.

Amos quit possession of Goldacre before acquiring title by adverse possession. Without any further communication between Oxnard and Eric, Eric continued to use the road for a total period, from the time he first began to use it, sufficient to acquire an easement by prescription. Oxnard then blocked the road and refused to permit its continued use. Eric brought suit to determine his right to continue use of the road. Eric should

(A) win, because his use was adverse to Amos and once adverse it continued adverse until some affirmative showing of a change.

(B) win, because Eric made no attempt to renew permission after Amos quit possession of Goldacre.

(C) lose, because his use was with permission.

(D) lose, because there is no evidence that he continued adverse use for the required period after Amos quit possession.

II. SCOPE OF EASEMENTS

A. Development of dominant estate

1. Remedy for misuse

Question 22

A large tract of land was owned by a religious order. On the land, the order erected a large residential building where its members reside. The land is surrounded by rural residential properties and its only access to a public way is afforded by an easement over a strip of land 30 feet wide. The easement was granted to the order by deed from a neighbor, who owned one of the adjacent residential properties. The order built a driveway on the strip, and the easement was used for 20 years without incident or objection.

Last year, as permitted by the applicable zoning ordinance, the order constructed a 200-bed nursing home and a parking lot on their land, using all of the land that was available for such development. The nursing home was very successful, and on Sundays visitors to the nursing home overflowed the parking facilities on the land and parked all along the driveway from early in the morning through the evening hours. After two Sundays of the resulting congestion and inconvenience, the neighbor erected a barrier across the driveway on Sundays preventing any use of the driveway by anyone seeking access to the order's land. The order objected.

The neighbor brought an appropriate action to terminate the easement.

The most likely result in this action is that the court will hold for

(A) the neighbor, because the order excessively expanded the use of the dominant tenement.

(B) the neighbor, because the parking on the driveway exceeded the scope of the easement.

(C) the order, because expanded use of the easement does not terminate the easement.

(D) the order, because the neighbor's use of self-help denies her the right to equitable relief.

III. REPAIR AND MAINTENANCE OF EASEMENTS

A. Dominant owner's rights

Question 23

Two adjacent, two-story, commercial buildings were owned by a landowner. The first floors of both buildings were occupied by various retail establishments. The second floors were rented to various other tenants. Access to the second floor of each building was reached by a common stairway located entirely in Building 1. While the buildings were being used in this manner, the landowner sold Building 1 to an accountant by warranty deed which made no mention of any rights concerning the stairway. About two years later the landowner sold Building 2 to a lawyer. The stairway continued to be used by the occupants of both buildings. The stairway became unsafe as a consequence of regular wear and tear. The lawyer entered upon the accountant's building and began the work of repairing the stairway. The accountant demanded that the lawyer discontinue the repair work and vacate the accountant's building. When the lawyer refused, the accountant brought an action to enjoin the lawyer from continuing the work.

Judgment should be for

(A) the accountant, because the lawyer has no rights in the stairway.

(B) the accountant, because the lawyer's rights in the stairway do not extend beyond the normal life of the existing structure.

(C) the lawyer, because the lawyer has an easement in the stairway and an implied right to keep the stairway in repair.

(D) the lawyer, because the lawyer has a right to take whatever action is necessary to protect himself from possible tort liability to persons using the stairway.

Question 24

Maria is the owner and possessor of Goodacre, on which there is a lumber yard. Maria conveyed to Reliable Electric Company the right to construct and use an overhead electric line across Goodacre to serve other properties. The conveyance was in writing, but the writing made no provision concerning the responsibility for repair or maintenance of the line. Reliable installed the poles and erected the electric line in a proper and workmanlike manner. Neither Maria nor Reliable took any steps toward the maintenance or repair of the line after it was built. Neither party complained to the other about any failure to repair. Because of the failure to repair or properly maintain the line, it fell to the ground during a storm. In doing so, it caused a fire in the lumber yard and did considerable damage. Maria sued Reliable Electric Company to recover for damages to the lumber yard. The decision should be for

(A) Maria, because the owner of an easement has a duty to so maintain the easement as to avoid unreasonable interference with the use of the servient tenement by its lawful possessor.

(B) Maria, because the owner of an easement is absolutely liable for any damage caused to the servient tenement by the exercise of the easement.

(C) Reliable Electric Company, because the possessor of the servient tenement has a duty to give the easement holder notice of defective conditions.

(D) Reliable Electric Company, because an easement holder's right to repair is a right for his own benefit, and is therefore inconsistent with any duty to repair for the benefit of another.

1. Limited right to contribution

Question 25

Beach owned a tract of land called Blackacre. An old road ran through Blackacre from the abutting public highway. The road had been used to haul wood from Blackacre. Without Beach's permission and with no initial right, Daniel, the owner of Whiteacre, which adjoined Blackacre, traveled over the old road for a period of 15 years to obtain access to Whiteacre, although Whiteacre abutted another public road. Occasionally, Daniel made repairs to the old road.

The period of time to acquire rights by prescription in the jurisdiction is ten years.

After the expiration of 15 years, Beach conveyed a portion of Blackacre to Carrol. The deed included the following clause: "together with the right to pass and repass at all times and for all purposes over the old road." Carrol built a house fronting on the old road. After the conveyance, Beach has used the road once or twice per year. Daniel almost never uses the road anymore.

The road was severely damaged by a spring flood, and Carrol made substantial repairs to the road. Carrol asked Daniel and Beach to contribute one-third each to the cost of repairing the flood damage. They both refused, and Carrol brought an appropriate action to compel contribution from Beach and Daniel.

In this action, Carrol will

(A) lose as to both defendants.

(B) win as to both defendants.

(C) win as to Beach, but lose as to Daniel.

(D) win as to Daniel, but lose as to Beach.

IV. TRANSFER AND SUBDIVISION OF EASEMENTS

A. Transfer of benefit

1. Transfer of easements appurtenant

Question 26

Olwen owned 80 acres of land, fronting on a town road. Two years ago, Olwen sold to Buck the back 40 acres. The 40 acres sold to Buck did not adjoin any public road. Olwen's deed to Buck expressly granted a right-of-way over a specified strip of Olwen's retained 40 acres, so Buck could reach the town road. The deed was promptly and properly recorded.

Last year, Buck conveyed the back 40 acres to Sam. They had discussed the right-of-way over Olwen's land to the road, but Buck's deed to Sam made no mention of it. Sam began to use the right-of-way as Buck had, but Olwen sued to enjoin such use by Sam.

The court should decide for

(A) Sam, because he has an easement by implication.

(B) Sam, because the easement appurtenant passed to him as a result of Buck's deed to him.

(C) Olwen, because Buck's easement in gross was not transferable.

(D) Olwen, because Buck's deed failed expressly to transfer the right-of-way to Sam.

V. LICENSES

A. Definition

1. Where agreement is oral

Question 27

A landowner orally gave his neighbor permission to share the use of the private road on the landowner's land so that the neighbor could have more convenient access to the neighbor's land. Only the landowner maintained the road. After the neighbor had used the road on a daily basis for three years, the landowner conveyed his land to a grantee, who immediately notified the neighbor that the neighbor was not to use the road. The neighbor sued the grantee seeking a declaration that the neighbor had a right to continue to use the road.

Who is likely to prevail?

(A) The grantee, because an oral license is invalid.

(B) The grantee, because the neighbor had a license that the grantee could terminate at any time.

(C) The neighbor, because the grantee is estopped to terminate the neighbor's use of the road.

(D) The neighbor, because the neighbor's use of the road was open and notorious when the grantee purchased the land.

VI. EQUITABLE SERVITUDES/RESTRICTIVE COVENANTS

A. Intent to benefit plaintiff's parcel

Question 28

A landowner owned a large tract of land. During the landowner's lifetime, he conveyed the eastern half of the tract to his son, and the western half to his daughter. The two halves of the tract were located in different municipalities. Each of the conveyances, which were promptly and properly recorded, contained the following language:

> The parties agree for themselves and their heirs and assigns that the premises herein cnveyed shall be used only for residential purposes; that each lot created within the premises herein conveyed shall contain not less than five acres; and that each lot shall have not more than one single-family dwelling. This agreement shall bind all successor owners of all or any portion of the tract, and any owner of any part of the tract may enforce this covenant.

After the landowner's death, the landowner's son desired to build houses on one-half acre lots in his half of the tract, as authorized by current applicable zoning and building codes in its municipality. The area surrounding the son's half of the tract was developed as a residential community with homes built on one-half acre lots. The western half of the tract was in a residential area covered by a zoning code that allowed residential development only on five-acre tracts of land. In an appropriate action brought by the daughter to enjoin the son's proposed construction on one-half acre lots, the court will find the quoted restriction to be

(A) invalid, because of the change of circumstance in the neighborhood.

(B) invalid, because it conflicts with the applicable zoning code.

(C) valid, but only so long as the original grantees from the landowner own their respective tracts.

(D) valid, because the provision imposed an equitable servitude.

B. Running of benefit and burden

Question 29

A landowner owned five adjoining, rectangular lots, numbered 1 through 5 inclusive, all fronting on Main Street. All of the lots are in a zone limited to one- and two-family residences under the zoning ordinance. Two years ago, the landowner conveyed Lots 1, 3, and 5. None of the three deeds contained any restrictions. Each of the new owners built a one-family residence.

One year ago, the landowner conveyed Lot 2 to a developer. The deed provided that each of the developer and the landowner, as well as their respective heirs and assigns, would use Lots 2 and 4 respectively only for one-family, residential purposes. The deed was promptly and properly recorded. The developer built a one-family residence on Lot 2. Last month, the landowner conveyed Lot 4 to an investor. The deed contained no restrictions. The deed from the landowner to the developer was in the title report examined by the investor's lawyer. The investor obtained a building permit and commenced construction of a two-family residence on Lot 4. The developer, joined by the owners of Lots 1, 3, and 5, brought an appropriate action against the investor to enjoin the proposed use of Lot 4, or, alternatively, damages caused by the investor's breach of covenant. Which is the most appropriate comment concerning the outcome of this action?

(A) All plaintiffs should be awarded their requested judgment for injunction because there was a common development scheme, but award of damages should be denied to all.

(B) The developer should be awarded an appropriate remedy, but recovery by the other plaintiffs is doubtful.

(C) Injunction should be denied, but damages should be awarded to all plaintiffs, measured by diminution of market value, if any, suffered as a result of the proximity of the investor's two-family residence.

(D) All plaintiffs should be denied any recovery or relief because the zoning preempts any private scheme of covenants.

Question 30

A realty company developed a residential development, which included single-family dwellings, town houses, and high-rise apartments for a total of 25,000 dwelling units.

Included in the deed to each unit was a covenant under which the grantee and the grantee's "heirs and assigns" agreed to purchase electrical power only from a plant the realty company promised to build and maintain within the development. The realty company constructed the plant and the necessary power lines. The plant did not supply power outside the development. An appropriate and fair formula was used to determine price. After constructing and selling 12,500 of the units, the realty company sold its interest in the development to an investor. The investor operated the power plant and constructed and sold the remaining 12,500 units. Each conveyance from the investor contained the same covenant relating to electrical power that the realty company had included in the 12,500 conveyances it had made. A woman bought a dwelling unit from its former resident, who had purchased it from the realty company. Subsequently, the woman, whose lot was along the boundary of the development, ceased buying electrical power from the investor and began purchasing power from an outside electric company, which provided such service in the area surrounding the development. Both the electric company and the investor have governmental authorization to provide electrical services to the area. The investor instituted an appropriate action against the woman to enjoin her from obtaining electrical power from the outside electric company. Assume that the jurisdiction follows the traditional rule for the running of covenants. If judgment is for the woman, it most likely will be because

(A) the covenant does not touch and concern the land.

(B) the mixture of types of residential units is viewed as preventing one common development scheme.

(C) the covenant is a restraint on alienation.

(D) there is no privity of estate between the woman and the investor.

1. Requirement that subsequent grantee be on notice of burden

Question 31

In 2000, Oscar, owner of a 100-acre tract, prepared and duly recorded a subdivision plan called Happy Acres. The plan showed 100 one-acre lots, and said that these lots would be "single-family, no mobile homes allowed."

In 2001, Oscar sold 60 of the lots to individual purchasers. Each deed referred to the recorded plan and also contained the following clause: "No mobile homes shall be erected on any lot within Happy Acres." Sarah was one of the original purchasers from Oscar.

In 2006, Oscar sold the remaining 40 lots to Max by a deed which referred to the plan and contained the restriction relating to mobile homes. Max sold the 40 lots to individual purchasers, whose deeds from Max did not include the mobile-home restriction. One of those purchasers was Joe, who did not know of the no-mobile-homes restriction in any prior deeds within Happy Acres. Joe then placed a mobile home on his lot. Sarah now brings an action against Joe to force him to remove the mobile home. The result of this action will be in favor of

(A) Sarah, because the restrictive covenant in her deed runs with the land.

(B) Sarah, because the presence of the mobile home may adversely affect the market value of her land.

(C) Joe, because his deed did not contain the restrictive covenant.

(D) Joe, because he is not a direct but a remote grantee of Oscar.

Question 32

Able, owner of Blackacre and Whiteacre, two adjoining parcels, conveyed Whiteacre to Baker and covenanted in the deed to Baker that when he, Able, sold Blackacre he would impose restrictive covenants to prohibit uses that would compete with the filling station that Baker intended to construct and operate on Whiteacre. The deed was not recorded.

Baker constructed and operated a filling station on Whiteacre and then conveyed Whiteacre to Dodd, who continued the filling station use. The deed did not refer to the restrictive covenant and was promptly and properly recorded.

Able then conveyed Blackacre to Egan, who knew about Able's covenant with Baker to impose a covenant prohibiting the filling station use but nonetheless completed the transaction when he noted that no such covenant was contained in Able's deed to him. Egan began to construct a filling station on Blackacre.

Dodd brought an appropriate action to enjoin Egan from using Blackacre for filling station purposes.

If Dodd prevails, it will be because

(A) Egan had actual knowledge of the covenant to impose restrictions.

(B) Egan is bound by the covenant because of the doctrine of negative reciprocal covenants.

(C) business-related restrictive covenants are favored in the law.

(D) Egan has constructive notice of the possibility of the covenant resulting from the circumstances.

C. Developer's building plan

1. Plan filed without restriction

Question 33

A fee-simple landowner lawfully subdivided his land into 10 large lots. The recorded subdivision plan imposed no restrictions on any of the 10 lots. Within two months after recording the plan, the landowner conveyed Lot 1 to a buyer, by a deed that contained no restriction on the lot's use. There was then a lull in sales. Two years later, the real estate market in the state had generally improved and, during the next six months, the landowner sold and conveyed eight of the remaining nine lots. In each of the eight deeds of conveyance, the landowner included the following language: "It is a term and condition of this conveyance, which shall be a covenant running with the land for the benefit of each of the 10 lots [with an appropriate reference to the recorded subdivision plan], that for 15 years from the date of recording of the plan, no use shall be made of the premises herein conveyed except for single-family residential purposes." The buyer of Lot 1 had actual knowledge of what the landowner had done. The landowner included the quoted language in part because the zoning ordinance of the municipality had been amended a year earlier to permit professional offices in any residential zone. Shortly after the landowner's most recent sale, when he owned only one unsold lot, the buyer of Lot 1 constructed a one-story house on Lot 1 and then conveyed Lot 1 to a doctor. The deed to the doctor contained no reference to any restriction on the use of Lot 1. The doctor applied for an appropriate certificate of occupancy to enable her to use a part of the house on Lot 1 as a medical office. The landowner, on behalf of himself as the owner of the unsold lot, and on behalf of the other lot owners, sued to enjoin the doctor from carrying out her plans and to impose the quoted restriction on Lot 1.

Who is likely to prevail?

(A) The doctor, because Lot 1 was conveyed without the inclusion of the restrictive covenant in the deed to the first buyer and the subsequent deed to the doctor.

(B) The doctor, because zoning ordinances override private restrictive covenants as a matter of public policy.

(C) The landowner, because the doctor, as a successor in interest to the first buyer, is estopped to deny that Lot 1 remains subject to the zoning ordinance as it existed when Lot 1 was first conveyed by the landowner to the first buyer.

(D) The landowner, because with the first buyer's knowledge of the facts, Lot 1 became incorporated into a common scheme.

VII. MODIFICATION AND TERMINATION OF COVENANTS AND SERVITUDES

A. Modification and termination generally

1. Effect of passage of time

Question 34

A grantor owned in fee simple two adjoining lots, Lots 1 and 2. He conveyed in fee simple Lot 1 to an investor. The deed was in usual form of a warranty deed with the following provision inserted in the appropriate place:

> Grantor, for himself, his heirs and assigns, does covenant and agree that any reasonable expense incurred by grantee, his heirs and assigns, as the result of having to

repair the retaining wall presently situated on Lot 1 at the common boundary with Lot 2, shall be reimbursed one-half the costs of repairs; and by this provision the parties intend a covenant running with the land.

The investor conveyed Lot 1 in fee simple to a housewife by warranty deed in usual and regular form. The deed omitted any reference to the retaining wall or any covenant. Fifty years after the grantor's conveyance to the investor, the housewife conveyed Lot 1 in fee simple to a student by warranty deed in usual form; this deed omitted any reference to the retaining wall or the covenant.

There is no statute that applies to any aspect of the problems presented except a recording act and a statute providing for acquisition of title after ten years of adverse possession.

All conveyances by deeds were for a consideration equal to fair market value.

The deed from the grantor to the investor was never recorded. All other deeds were promptly and properly recorded.

Lot 2 is now owned by the grantor's son, who took by intestate succession from the grantor, now dead.

The student expended $3,500 on the retaining wall. Then he obtained all of the original deeds in the chain from the grantor to him. Shortly thereafter, the student discovered the covenant in the grantor's deed to the investor. He demanded that the grantor's son pay $1,750, and when the son refused, the student instituted an appropriate action to recover that sum from the son. In such action, the son asserted all defenses available to him.

If judgment is for the grantor's son, it will be because

(A) the student is barred by adverse possession.

(B) the investor's deed from the grantor was never recorded.

(C) the student did not know about the covenant until after he had incurred the expenses and, hence, could not have relied on it.

(D) the student's expenditures were not proved to be reasonable and customary.

CHAPTER 7
LAND SALE CONTRACTS, MORTGAGES, AND DEEDS

I. LAND SALE CONTRACTS

A. Statute of Frauds

Question 35

Ozzie owned and occupied Blackacre, which was a tract of land improved with a one-family house. His friend, Victor, orally offered Ozzie $50,000 for Blackacre, the fair market value, and Ozzie accepted. Because they were friends, they saw no need for attorneys or written contracts and shook hands on the deal. Victor paid Ozzie $5,000 down in cash and agreed to pay the balance of $45,000 at an agreed closing time and place.

Before the closing, Victor inherited another home and asked Ozzie to return his $5,000. Ozzie refused, and, at the time set for the closing, Ozzie tendered a good deed to Victor and declared his intention to vacate Blackacre the next day. Ozzie demanded that Victor complete the purchase. Victor refused. The fair market value of Blackacre has remained $50,000.

In an appropriate action brought by Ozzie against Victor for specific performance, if Ozzie loses, the most likely reason will be that

(A) the agreement was oral.

(B) keeping the $5,000 is Ozzie's exclusive remedy.

(C) Victor had a valid reason for not closing.

(D) Ozzie remained in possession on the day set for the closing.

B. Marketable title

1. Time for measuring marketability

a. Effect of outstanding mortgage

Question 36

A landowner mortgaged the land to a bank to secure his preexisting obligation to the bank. The mortgage was promptly and properly recorded. The landowner and a buyer then entered into a valid written contract for the purchase and sale of the land, which provided for the transfer of "a marketable title, free of encumbrances." The contract did not expressly refer to the mortgage.

Shortly after entering into the contract, the buyer found another property that much better suited her needs and decided to try to avoid her contract with the landowner. When the buyer discovered the existence of the mortgage, she asserted that the title was encumbered and that she would not close. The landowner responded by offering to provide for payment and discharge of the mortgage at the closing from the proceeds of the closing. The buyer refused to go forward, and the landowner brought an appropriate action against her for specific performance.

If the court holds for the landowner in this action, it will most likely be because

(A) the mortgage is not entitled to priority because it was granted for preexisting obligations.

(B) the doctrine of equitable conversion supports the result.

(C) the landowner's arrangements for the payment of the mortgage fully satisfied the landowner's obligation to deliver marketable title.

(D) the existence of the mortgage was not the buyer's real reason for refusing to close.

Question 37

Venner, the owner of Greenacre, a tract of land, entered into an enforceable written agreement with Brier providing that Venner would sell Greenacre to Brier for an agreed price. At the place and time designated for the closing. Venner tendered an appropriate deed, but Brier responded that he had discovered a mortgage on Greenacre and would not complete the transaction, because Venner's title was not free of encumbrances, as the contract required. Venner said that it was his intent to pay the mortgage from the proceeds of the sale, and he offered to put the proceeds in escrow for that purpose with any agreeable, responsible escrowee. The balance due on the mortgage was substantially less than the contract purchase price. Brier refused Venner's proposal. Venner began an appropriate legal action against Brier for specific performance. There is no applicable statute in the jurisdiction where Greenacre is located.

Venner's best legal argument in support of his claim for relief is that

(A) as the seller of real estate, he had an implied right to use the contract proceeds to clear the title being conveyed.

(B) the lien of the mortgage shifts from Greenacre to the contract proceeds.

(C) under the doctrine of equitable conversion, title has already passed to Brier and the only issue is how the purchase price is to be allocated.

(D) no provision of the contract has been breached by Venner.

C. Remedies for failure to perform

1. Damages

a. Where no earnest money deposit

Question 38

Able was the owner of Blackacre, an undeveloped city lot. Able and Baker executed a written document in which Able agreed to sell Blackacre to Baker and Baker agreed to buy Blackacre from Able for $200,000; the document did not provide for an earnest money down payment. Able recorded the document, as authorized by statute.

Able orally gave Baker permission to park his car on Blackacre without charge prior to the closing. Thereafter, Baker frequently parked his car on Blackacre.

Another property came on the market that Baker wanted more than Blackacre. Baker decided to try to escape any obligation to Able.

Baker had been told that contracts for the purchase and sale of real property require consideration and concluded that because he had made no earnest money down payment, he could refuse to close and not be liable. Baker notified Able of his intention not to close and, in fact, did refuse to close on the date set for the closing. Able brought an appropriate action to compel specific performance by Baker.

If Able wins, it will be because

(A) Baker's use of Blackacre for parking constitutes part performance.

(B) general contract rules regarding consideration apply to real estate contracts.

(C) the doctrine of equitable conversion applies.

(D) the document was recorded.

2. Specific performance

a. Breaching buyer

Question 39

Adam entered into a valid written contract to sell Blackacre, a large tract of land, to Betsy. At that time, Blackacre was owned by Adam's father, Fred; Adam had no title to Blackacre and was not the agent of Fred.

After the contract was executed and before the scheduled closing date. Fred died intestate, leaving Adam as his sole heir. Shortly thereafter, Adam received an offer for Blackacre that was substantially higher than the purchase price in the contract with Betsy. Adam refused to close with Betsy although she was ready, willing, and able to close pursuant to the contract.

Betsy brought an appropriate action for specific performance against Adam.

In that action, Betsy should be awarded

(A) nothing, because Adam had no authority to enter into the contract with Betsy.

(B) nothing, because the doctrine of after-acquired title does not apply to executory contracts.

(C) judgment for specific performance, because Adam acquired title prior to the scheduled closing.

(D) judgment for specific performance, to prevent unjust enrichment of Adam.

3. Deposit

a. Where deposit is a reasonable estimate of damages

Question 40

Three months ago, Bert agreed in writing to buy Sam's single-family residence, Liveacre, for $110,000. Bert paid Sam a $5,000 deposit to be applied to the purchase price. The contract stated that Sam had the right at his option to retain the deposit as liquidated damages in the event of Ben's default. The closing was to have taken place last week. Six weeks ago, Bert was notified by his employer that he was to be transferred to another job 1,000 miles away. Bert immediately notified Sam that he could not close, and therefore he demanded the return of his $5,000. Sam refused, waited until after the contract closing date, listed with a broker, and then conveyed Liveacre for $108,000 to Conner, a purchaser found by the real estate broker. Conner paid the full purchase price and immediately recorded his deed. Conner knew of the prior contract with Bert. In an appropriate action, Bert seeks to recover the $5,000 deposit from Sam.

The most probable result will be that Sam

(A) must return the $5,000 to Bert, because Sam can no longer carry out his contract with Bert.

(B) must return the $5,000 to Bert, because Bert was legally justified in not completing the contract.

(C) must return $3,000 to Bert, because Sam's damages were only $2,000.

(D) may keep the $5,000 deposit, because Bert breached the contract.

D. Equitable conversion

1. Effect of pending contract

Question 41

On September 1, a seller and a buyer executed an agreement for the sale of real property, closing scheduled for November 1. The jurisdiction in which the property is located recognizes the principle of equitable conversion and has no statute pertinent to this problem.

The seller died before closing, and his will left his personal property to his son and his real property to his daughter. Assuming that there has been no breach of the agreement by either party (or that party's successor in interest), which of the following is correct?

(A) Death, an eventuality for which the parties could have provided, terminates the agreement if they did not so provide.

(B) The daughter is entitled to the proceeds of the sale when it closes, because the doctrine of equitable conversion does not apply to these circumstances.

(C) The son is entitled to the proceeds of the sale when it closes.

(D) Title was rendered unmarketable by the seller's death.

2. Risk of loss

Question 42

Landover, the owner in fee simple of Highacre, an apartment house property, entered into an enforceable written agreement with VanMeer to sell Highacre to VanMeer. The agreement provided that a good and marketable title was to be conveyed free and clear of all encumbrances. However, the agreement was silent as to the risk of fire prior to the closing, and there is no applicable statute in the state where the land is located. The premises were not insured. The day before the scheduled closing date, Highacre was wholly destroyed by fire. When VanMeer refused to close, Landover brought an action in specific performance. If Landover prevails, the most likely reason will be that

(A) the failure of VanMeer to insure his interest as the purchaser of Highacre precludes any relief for him.

(B) the remedy at law is inadequate in actions concerning real estate contracts and either party is entitled to specific performance.

(C) equity does not permit consideration of surrounding circumstances in actions concerning real estate contracts.

(D) the doctrine of equitable conversion applies.

Question 43

A seller owned a single-family house. A buyer gave the seller a signed handwritten offer to purchase the house. The offer was unconditional and sufficient to satisfy the Statute of Frauds, and when the seller signed an acceptance an enforceable contract resulted.

The house on the land had been the seller's home, but he had moved to an apartment, so the house was vacant at all times relevant to the proposed transaction. Two weeks after the parties had entered into their contract, one week after the buyer had obtained a written mortgage lending commitment from a lender, and one week before the agreed-upon closing date, the house was struck by lightning and burned to the ground. The loss was not insured because, three years earlier, the seller had let his homeowner's insurance policy lapse after he had paid his mortgage debt in full. The handwritten contract was wholly silent as to matters of financing, risk of loss, and insurance. The buyer declared the contract voided by the fire, but the seller asserted a right to enforce the contract despite the loss. There is no applicable statute. If a court finds for the seller, what is the likely reason?

(A) The contract was construed against the buyer, who drafted it.

(B) The lender's written commitment to make a mortgage loan to the buyer made the contract of sale fully binding on the buyer.

(C) The risk of loss falls on the party in possession, and constructive possession passed to the buyer on the contract date.

(D) The risk of loss passed to the buyer on the contract date under the doctrine of equitable conversion.

II. MORTGAGES AND INSTALLMENT CONTRACTS

A. Nature of mortgage

1. Sale of mortgaged property

a. Assumption by buyer

Question 44

Several years ago, a man purchased a building, financing a large part of the purchase price by a loan from a bank that was secured by a mortgage. The man made the installment payments on the mortgage regularly until last year. Then the man persuaded an investor to buy the building, subject to the mortgage to the bank. They expressly agreed that the investor would not assume and agree to pay the man's debt to the bank. The man's mortgage to the bank contained a due-on-sale clause stating, "If the mortgagor transfers his/her interest without the written consent of the mortgagee first obtained, then at the mortgagee's option the entire principal balance of the debt secured by this mortgage shall become immediately due and payable." However, without seeking the bank's consent, the man conveyed the building to the investor, the deed stating in pertinent part, "subject to a mortgage to" the bank and giving details and recording data.

The investor took possession of the building and made several mortgage payments, which the bank accepted. Now, however, neither the investor nor the man has made the last three mortgage payments. The bank has brought an appropriate action against the investor for the amount of the delinquent payments. In this action, judgment should be for

(A) the investor, because she did not assume and agree to pay the man's mortgage debt.

(B) the investor, because she is not in privity of estate with the bank.

(C) the bank, because the man's deed to the investor violated the due-on-sale clause.

(D) the bank, because the investor is in privity of estate with the bank.

Question 45

A man borrowed money from a bank and executed a promissory note for the amount secured by a mortgage on his residence. Several years later, the man sold his residence. As provided by the contract of sale, the deed to the buyer provided that the buyer agreed "to assume the existing mortgage debt" on the residence.

Subsequently, the buyer defaulted on the mortgage loan to the bank, and appropriate foreclosure proceedings were initiated. The foreclosure sale resulted in a deficiency.

There is no applicable statute.

Is the buyer liable for the deficiency?

(A) No, because even if the buyer assumed the mortgage, the seller is solely responsible for any deficiency.

(B) No, because the buyer did not sign a promissory note to the bank and therefore has no personal liability.

(C) Yes, because the buyer assumed the mortgage and therefore became personally liable for the mortgage loan and any deficiency.

(D) Yes, because the transfer of the mortgage debt to the buyer resulted in a novation of the original mortgage and loan and rendered the buyer solely responsible for any deficiency.

Question 46

Ashton owned Woodsedge, a tract used for commercial purposes, in fee simple and thereafter mortgaged it to First Bank. She signed a promissory note secured by a duly executed and recorded mortgage. There was no "due on sale" clause, that is, no provision that, upon sale, the whole balance then owing would become due and owing. Ashton conveyed Woodsedge to Beam "subject to a mortgage to First Bank, which the grantee assumes and agrees to pay." Beam conveyed Woodsedge to Carter "subject to an existing mortgage to First Bank." A copy of the note and the mortgage that secured it had been exhibited to each grantee.

After Carter made three timely payments, no further payments were made by any party. In fact, the real estate had depreciated to a point where it was worth less than the debt.

There is no applicable statute or regulation.

In an appropriate foreclosure action, First Bank joined Ashton, Beam, and Carter as defendants. At the foreclosure sale, although the fair market value for Woodsedge in its depreciated state was obtained, a deficiency resulted.

First Bank is entitled to collect a deficiency judgment against

(A) Ashton only.

(B) Ashton and Beam only.

(C) Beam and Carter only.

(D) Ashton, Beam, and Carter.

2. Redemption of mortgage

a. Who has right to redeem

Question 47

A brother and sister owned a property in fee simple as tenants in common, each owning an undivided one-half interest. The two joined in mortgaging the property to an investor by a properly recorded mortgage that contained a general warranty clause. The brother became disenchanted with land-owning and notified his sister that he would no longer contribute to the payment of installments due to the investor. After the mortgage was in default and the investor made demand for payment of the entire amount of principal and interest due, the sister tendered to the investor, and the investor deposited, a check for one-half of the amount due the investor. The sister then demanded a release of her undivided one-half interest. The investor refused to release any interest in the property. The sister promptly brought an action against the investor to quiet title to an undivided one-half interest in the property.

In such action, the sister should

(A) lose, because the investor's title had been warranted by an express provision of the mortgage.

(B) lose, because there was no redemption from the mortgage.

(C) win, because the sister is entitled to marshalling.

(D) win, because the cotenancy of the mortgagors was in common and not joint.

3. Priorities (allocation of foreclosure proceeds)

a. Judgment lien creditor's status

i. Two-property scenario

Question 48

A businessman owned a hotel, subject to a mortgage securing a debt he owed to a bank. The businessman later acquired a nearby parking garage, financing a part of the purchase price by a loan from a financing company, secured by a mortgage on the parking garage. Two years thereafter, the businessman defaulted on the loan owed to the bank, which caused the full amount of that loan to become immediately due and payable. The bank decided not to foreclose the mortgage on the hotel at that time, but instead properly sued for the full amount of the defaulted loan. The bank obtained and properly filed a judgment for that amount. A statute of the jurisdiction provides: "Any judgment properly filed shall, for ten years from filing, be a lien on the real property then owned or subsequently acquired by any person against whom the judgment is rendered." There is no other applicable statute, except the statute providing for judicial foreclosure of mortgages, which places no restriction on deficiency judgments. Shortly thereafter, the bank brought an appropriate action for judicial foreclosure of its first mortgage on the hotel and of its judgment lien on the parking garage. The financing company was joined as a party defendant, and appropriately counterclaimed for foreclosure of its mortgage on the parking garage, which was also in default. All procedures were properly followed and the confirmed foreclosure sales resulted in the following: The net proceeds of the sale of the hotel to a third party were $200,000 less than the bank's mortgage balance. The net proceeds of the sale of the parking garage to a fourth party were $200,000 more than the financing company's mortgage balance.

How should the $200,000 surplus arising from the bid on the parking garage be distributed?

(A) It should be paid to the bank.

(B) It should be paid to the businessman.

(C) It should be paid to the financing company.

(D) It should be split equally between the bank and the financing company.

III. DEEDS

A. Formalities

1. Identification of parties

Question 49

A landowner owned a valuable parcel of land located in York County. The landowner executed a document in the form of a warranty deed of the parcel, which was regular in all respects except that the only language designating the grantees in each of the granting and *habendum* clauses was: "The leaders of all the Protestant Churches in York County." The instrument was acknowledged as required by statute and promptly and properly recorded. The landowner told his lawyer, but no one else, that he had made the conveyance as he did because he abhorred sectarianism in the Protestant movement and because he thought that the leaders would devote the asset to lessening sectarianism.

The landowner died suddenly and unexpectedly a week later, leaving a will that bequeathed and devised his entire estate to his cousin. After probate of the will became final and the administration on the landowner's estate was closed, the cousin instituted an appropriate action to quiet title to the parcel and properly served as defendant each Protestant church situated in the county.

The only evidence introduced consisted of the chain of title under which the landowner held, the probated will, the recorded deed, the fact that no person knew about the deed except the landowner and his lawyer, and the conversation the landowner had with his lawyer described above.

In such action, judgment should be for

(A) the cousin, because there is inadequate identification of grantees in the deed.

(B) the cousin, because the state of the evidence would not support a finding of delivery of the deed.

(C) the defendants, because a deed is *prima facie* valid until rebutted.

(D) the defendants, because recording established delivery *prima facie* until rebutted.

Question 50

A vendee entered into a valid written contract to purchase a large tract of land from a vendor for its fair market value of $50,000. The contract was assignable by the vendee. The vendee duly notified the vendor to convey title jointly to the vendee and "Charles," Charles being the vendee's friend whom the vendee had not seen for many years.

When the vendee learned that Charles would have to sign certain documents in connection with the closing, she prevailed upon her brother to attend the closing and pretend to be Charles. The vendee and her brother attended the closing, and the vendor executed an instrument in the proper form of a deed, purporting to convey the property to "[the vendee] and Charles, as tenants in common." The brother pretended that he was Charles, and he signed Charles's name to all the required documents. The vendee provided the entire $50,000 consideration for the transaction. The deed was promptly and properly recorded.

Unknown to the vendee or her brother, Charles had died several months before the closing. Charles's will, which was duly probated, devised "all my real estate to my nephew" and the residue of his estate to the vendee.

The vendee and the nephew have been unable to agree as to the status or disposition of the property. The nephew brought an appropriate action against the vendor and the vendee to quiet legal title to an undivided one-half interest in the property.

The court should hold that legal title to the property is vested

(A) all in the vendor.

(B) all in the vendee.

(C) one-half in the vendee and one-half in the vendor.

(D) one-half in the vendee and one-half in the nephew.

B. Delivery of deed

1. Delivery to agent of grantee

Question 51

When a homeowner became ill, he properly executed a deed sufficient to convey his home to his nephew, who was then serving overseas in the military. Two persons signed as witnesses to qualify the deed for recordation under an applicable statute. The homeowner handed the deed to his nephew's friend and said, "I want [the nephew] to have my home. Please take this deed for him." Shortly thereafter, the nephew's friend learned that the homeowner's death was imminent. One day before the homeowner's death, the nephew's friend recorded the deed. The nephew returned home shortly after the homeowner's death. The nephew's friend brought him up to date, and he took possession of the home. The homeowner died intestate, leaving a daughter as his sole heir. She asserted ownership of his home. The nephew brought an appropriate action against her to determine title to the home. The law of the jurisdiction requires only two witnesses for a will to be properly executed.

If the court rules for the nephew and against the daughter, what is the most likely explanation?

(A) The deed was delivered when the homeowner handed it to the nephew's friend.

(B) The delivery of the deed was accomplished by the recording of the deed.

(C) The homeowner's death consummated a valid gift causa mortis to the nephew.

(D) The homeowner's properly executed deed was effective as a testamentary document.

2. Revocability of delivery

Question 52

Ogle owned Greenacre, a tract of land, in fee simple. Five years ago, he executed and delivered to Lilly an instrument in the proper form of a warranty deed that conveyed Greenacre to Lilly "for and during the term of her natural life." No other estate or interest or person taking an interest was mentioned. Lilly took possession of Greenacre and has remained in possession.

Fifteen months ago, Ogle died, leaving a will that has been duly admitted to probate. The will, *inter alia,* had the following provision:

"I devise Greenacre to Mina for her natural life and from and after Mina's death to Rex, his heirs and assigns, forever."

Administration of Ogle's estate has been completed. Mina claims the immediate right to possession of Greenacre. Rex also asserts a right to immediate possession.

In an appropriate lawsuit to which Lilly, Mina, and Rex are parties, who should be adjudged to have the right to immediate possession?

(A) Lilly, because no subsequent act of Ogle would affect her life estate.

(B) Mina, because Ogle's will was the final and definitive expression of his intent.

(C) Mina, because Lilly's estate terminated with the death of Ogle.

(D) Rex, because Lilly's estate terminated with Ogle's death and all that Ogle had was the right to transfer his reversion in fee simple.

C. Covenants for title in warranty deed

1. Present vs. future covenants

Question 53

Seller owned Blackacre, improved with an aging four-story warehouse. The warehouse was built to the lot lines on all four sides. On the street side, recessed loading docks permitted semi-trailers to be backed in. After the tractors were unhooked, the trailers extended into the street and occupied most of one lane of the street. Over the years, as trailers became larger, the blocking of the street became more severe. The municipality advised Seller that the loading docks could not continue to be used because the trailers blocked the street; it gave Seller 90 days to cease and desist.

During the 90 days, Seller sold and conveyed Blackacre by warranty deed for a substantial consideration to Buyer. The problem of the loading docks was not discussed in the negotiations.

Upon expiration of the 90 days, the municipality required Buyer to stop using the loading docks. This action substantially reduced the value of Blackacre.

Buyer brought an appropriate action against Seller seeking cancellation of the deed and return of all monies paid.

Such action should be based upon a claim of

(A) misrepresentation.

(B) breach of the covenant of warranty.

(C) failure of consideration.

(D) mutual mistake.

D. Undisclosed condition in house

Question 54

Able, who owned Blackacre, a residential lot improved with a dwelling, conveyed it for a valuable consideration to Baker. The dwelling had been constructed by a prior owner. Baker had inspected Blackacre prior to the purchase and discovered no defects. After moving in, Baker became aware that sewage seeped into the basement when the toilets were flushed. Able said that this defect had been present for years and that he had taken no steps to hide the facts from Baker. Baker paid for the necessary repairs and brought an appropriate action against Able to recover his cost of repair.

If Baker wins, it will be because

(A) Able failed to disclose a latent defect.

(B) Baker made a proper inspection.

(C) the situation constitutes a health hazard.

(D) Able breached the implied warranty of habitability and fitness for purpose.

RECORDING ACTS

I. WHAT INSTRUMENTS MUST BE RECORDED

A. What instruments must be recorded

1. Contract of sale

Question 55

Able was the owner of Greenacre, a large tract of land. Able entered into a binding written contract with Baker for the sale and purchase of Greenacre for $125,000. The contract required Able to convey marketable record title.

Baker decided to protect his interest and promptly and properly recorded the contract.

Thereafter, but before the date scheduled for the closing, Charlie obtained and properly filed a final judgment against Able in the amount of $1 million in a personal injury suit. A statute in the jurisdiction provides: "Any judgment properly filed shall, for ten years from filing, be a lien on the real property then owned or subsequently acquired by any person against whom the judgment is rendered."

The recording act of the jurisdiction authorizes recording of contracts and also provides: "No conveyance or mortgage of real property shall be good against subsequent purchasers for value and without notice unless the same be recorded according to law."

There are no other relevant statutory provisions.

At the closing, Baker declined to accept the title of Able on the ground that Charlie's judgment lien encumbered the title he would receive and rendered it unmarketable. Able brought an appropriate action against Baker for specific performance of the contract and joined Charlie as a party.

In this action, the judgment should be for

(A) Able, because in equity a purchaser takes free of judgment liens.

(B) Able, because the contract had been recorded.

(C) Baker, because Able cannot benefit from Baker's action in recording the contract.

(D) Baker, because the statute creating judgment liens takes precedence over the recording act.

II. WHO IS PROTECTED BY THE RECORDING ACT

A. Who is a bona fide purchaser (BFP)?

Question 56

Devlin was the owner of a large subdivision. Parnell became interested in purchasing a lot but could not decide between Lot 40 and Lot 41. The price and fair market value of each of those two lots was $50,000. Parnell paid Devlin $50,000, which Devlin accepted, and Devlin delivered to Parnell a deed which was properly executed, complete, and ready for recording in every detail except that the space in the deed for the lot number was left blank. Devlin told Parnell to fill in either Lot 40 or Lot 41 according to his decision and then record the deed. Parnell visited the development the next day and completely changed his mind, selecting Lot 25. He filled in Lot 25 and duly recorded the deed. The price of Lot 25 and its fair market value was $75,000.

Before Devlin had time to learn of Parnell's actions, Parnell sold Lot 25 to Caruso for $60,000 by a duly and properly executed, delivered, and recorded warranty deed. Caruso knew that Devlin had put a price of $75,000 on Lot 25, but he knew no other facts regarding the Devlin-Parnell transaction. Caruso's attorney accurately reported Parnell's record title to be good, marketable, and free of encumbrances. Neither Caruso nor his attorney made any further investigation outside the record. Devlin brought an appropriate action against Caruso to recover title to Lot 25. If Devlin loses, the most likely basis for the judgment is that

(A) the Statute of Frauds prevents the introduction of any evidence of Devlin's and Parnell's agreement.

(B) recording of the deed from Devlin to Parnell precludes any question of its genuineness.

(C) as between Devlin and a bona fide purchaser, Devlin is estopped.

(D) the clean hands doctrine bars Devlin from relief.

B. The "gave value" requirement

1. Judgment creditors

Question 57

A seller owned a piece of land in fee simple, as the land records showed, when he contracted to sell the land to a buyer. Two weeks later, the buyer paid the agreed price and received a warranty deed. A week thereafter, when neither the contract nor the deed had been recorded and while the seller remained in possession of the property, a creditor of the seller properly filed a money judgment against the seller. The creditor knew nothing of the buyer's interest.

A statute in the jurisdiction provides: "Any judgment properly filed shall, for ten years from filing, be a lien on the real property then owned or subsequently acquired by any person against whom the judgment is rendered."

The recording act of the jurisdiction provides: "No conveyance or mortgage of real property shall be good against subsequent purchasers for value and without notice unless the same be recorded according to law."

The creditor brought an appropriate action to enforce her lien against the property in the buyer's hands.

If the court decides for the buyer, it will most probably be because

(A) the doctrine of equitable conversion applies.

(B) the jurisdiction's recording act does not protect creditors.

(C) the seller's possession gave the creditor constructive notice of the buyer's interest.

(D) the buyer was a purchaser without notice.

Question 58

Able conveyed Blackacre to Baker by a warranty deed. Baker recorded the deed four days later. After the conveyance but prior to Baker's recording of the deed, Smollett properly filed a judgment against Able.

The two pertinent statutes in the jurisdiction provide the following: 1) any judgment properly filed shall, for ten years from filing, be a lien on the real property then owned or subsequently acquired by any person against whom the judgment is rendered, and 2) no conveyance or mortgage of real property shall be good against subsequent purchasers for value and without notice unless the same be recorded according to law.

The recording act has no provision for a grace period.

Smollett joined both Able and Baker in an appropriate action to foreclose the judgment lien against Blackacre.

If Smollett is unsuccessful, it will be because

(A) Able's warranty of title to Baker defeats Smollett's claim.

(B) Smollett is not a purchaser for value.

(C) any deed is superior to a judgment lien.

(D) four days is not an unreasonable delay in recording a deed.

C. Recording first in a race or race-notice state

Question 59

A landowner owned a piece of land in fee simple of record on January 10. On that day, a bank loaned the landowner $50,000 and the landowner mortgaged the property to the bank as security for the loan. The mortgage was recorded on January 18.

The landowner conveyed the property to an investor for a valuable consideration on January 11. The bank did not know of this, nor did the investor know of the mortgage to the bank, until both discovered the facts on January 23, the day on which the investor recorded his deed from the landowner.

The recording act of the jurisdiction provides: "No unrecorded conveyance or mortgage of real property shall be good against subsequent purchasers for value without notice, who shall first record." There is no provision for a period of grace and there is no other relevant statutory provision.

The bank sued the investor to establish that its mortgage was good against the property.

The court should decide for

(A) the investor, because he paid valuable consideration without notice before the bank recorded its mortgage.

(B) the investor, because the bank's delay in recording means that it is estopped from asserting its priority in time.

(C) the bank, because the investor did not record his deed before the mortgage was recorded.

(D) the bank, because after the mortgage to it, the landowner's deed to the investor was necessarily subject to the mortgage.

III. PURCHASER MUST TAKE "WITHOUT NOTICE"

A. Notice to subsequent claimants

1. Record notice

a. Imputed knowledge

i. Mortgage and note

Question 60

A landowner executed and delivered a promissory note and a mortgage securing the note to a mortgage company, which was named as payee in the note and as mortgagee in the mortgage. The note included a statement that the indebtedness evidenced by the note was "subject to the terms of a contract between the maker and the payee of the note executed on the same day" and that the note was "secured by a mortgage of even date." The mortgage was promptly and properly recorded. Subsequently, the mortgage company sold the landowner's note and mortgage to a bank and delivered to the bank a written assignment of the note and mortgage. The assignment was promptly and properly recorded. The mortgage company retained possession of both the note and the mortgage in order to act as collecting agent. Later, being short of funds, the mortgage company sold the note and mortgage to an investor at a substantial discount. The mortgage company executed a written assignment of the note and mortgage to the investor and delivered to him the note, the mortgage, and the assignment. The investor paid value for the assignment without actual knowledge of the prior assignment to the bank and promptly and properly recorded his assignment. The principal of the note was not then due, and there had been no default in payment of either interest or principal.

If the issue of ownership of the landowner's note and mortgage is subsequently raised in an appropriate action by the bank to foreclose, the court should hold that

(A) the investor owns both the note and the mortgage.

(B) the bank owns both the note and the mortgage.

(C) the investor owns the note and the bank owns the mortgage.

(D) the bank owns the note and the investor owns the mortgage.

B. Purchaser from one without notice

1. Donee who takes from person protected by act

Question 61

A grantor who owned a parcel conveyed it by quitclaim deed as a gift to a woman, who did not then record her deed. Later, the grantor conveyed the parcel by warranty deed to a man, who paid valuable consideration, knew nothing of the woman's claim, and promptly and properly recorded. Next, the woman recorded her deed. Then the man conveyed the parcel by quitclaim deed to his nephew as a gift. When the possible conflict with the woman was discovered, the nephew recorded his deed.

The parcel at all relevant times has been vacant unoccupied land.

The recording act of the jurisdiction provides:

"No unrecorded conveyance or mortgage of real property shall be good against subsequent purchasers for value without notice, who shall first record." No other statute is applicable.

The nephew has sued the woman to establish who owns the parcel.

The court will hold for

(A) the nephew, because the woman was a donee.

(B) the nephew, because the man's purchase cut off the woman's rights.

(C) the woman, because she recorded before the nephew.

(D) the woman, because the nephew was a subsequent donee.

2. Status of one who lends to a person protected by act

Question 62

Five years ago, an investor who owned a vacant lot in a residential area borrowed $25,000 from a friend and gave the friend a note for $25,000 due in five years, secured by a mortgage on the lot. The friend neglected to record the mortgage. The fair market value of the lot was then $25,000.

Three years ago, the investor discovered that the friend had not recorded his mortgage and in consideration of $50,000 conveyed the lot to a buyer. The fair market value of the lot was then $50,000. The buyer knew nothing of the friend's mortgage. One month thereafter, the friend discovered the sale to the buyer, recorded his $25,000 mortgage, and notified the buyer that he held a $25,000 mortgage on the lot.

Two years ago, the buyer needed funds. Although she told her bank of the mortgage claimed by the investor's friend, the bank loaned her $15,000, and she gave the bank a note for $15,000 due in two years secured by a mortgage on the lot. The bank promptly and properly recorded the mortgage. At that time, the fair market value of the lot was $75,000.

The recording act of the jurisdiction provides: "No conveyance or mortgage of real property shall be good against subsequent purchasers for value and without notice unless the same be recorded according to law."

Both notes are now due and both the investor and the buyer have refused to pay. The lot is now worth only $50,000.

What are the rights of the investor's friend and the bank in the lot?

(A) Both mortgages are enforceable liens and the friend's has priority because it was first recorded.

(B) Both mortgages are enforceable liens, but the bank's has priority because the buyer was an innocent purchaser for value.

(C) Only the friend's mortgage is an enforceable lien, because the bank had actual and constructive notice of the investor's fraud.

(D) Only the bank's mortgage is an enforceable lien, because the buyer was an innocent purchaser for value.

CHAPTER 9
RIGHTS INCIDENT TO LAND

I. NUISANCE

A. Private nuisance

1. Failure to abate the nuisance

Question 63

A homeowner and his neighbor own adjacent lots in fee simple. The homeowner has kept the lawns and trees on his property trimmed and neat. His neighbor "lets nature take its course" on her property. As a result, the neighbor's lawn is a tangle of underbrush, fallen trees, and standing trees that are in danger of losing limbs. Many of the trees on the neighbor's land are near the homeowner's property. In the past, debris and large limbs have been blown from the neighbor's property onto the homeowner's. By local standards the neighbor's lot is an eyesore that depresses market values of real property in the vicinity, but its condition violates no applicable laws or ordinances.

The homeowner demanded that his neighbor keep the trees near his property trimmed. The neighbor refused. The homeowner brought an appropriate action against his neighbor to require her to abate what he alleges to be a nuisance. In the lawsuit, the only issue is whether the condition of the neighbor's property constitutes a nuisance. The strongest argument that the homeowner can present, if factually correct, is that the condition of his neighbor's lot

(A) has an adverse impact on real estate values.

(B) poses a danger to the occupants of the homeowner's lot.

(C) violates community aesthetic standards.

(D) cannot otherwise be challenged under any law or ordinance.

II. WATER RIGHTS

A. Drainage of surface waters

1. When one party wants to get rid of the water

Question 64

A rancher and a farmer own adjacent tracts of rural land. For the past nine years, the rancher has impounded on her land the water that resulted from rain and melting snow, much of which flowed from the farmer's land. The rancher uses the water in her livestock operation. Recently, the farmer increased the size of his farming operation and built a dam on his land near the boundary between the two tracts. Because of the dam, these waters no longer drain from the farmer's land onto the rancher's land. There is no applicable statute. The rancher sued the farmer to restrain him from interfering with the natural flow of the water onto her land.

Who is likely to prevail?

(A) The farmer, because he has the right to use all of the water impounded on his land.

(B) The farmer, because the rancher's past impoundment of water estops her from asserting the illegality of the farmer's dam.

(C) The rancher, because she has acquired riparian rights to use the water.

(D) The rancher, because the farmer is estopped to claim all of the surface water on his land.

III. AIR RIGHTS

A. Other air-rights issues

1. Right to sunlight

Question 65

Pauline and Doris own adjacent parcels of land. On each of their parcels was a low-rise office building. The two office buildings were of the same height.

Last year Doris decided to demolish the low-rise office building on her parcel and to erect a new high-rise office building of substantially greater height on the parcel as permitted by the zoning and building ordinances. She secured all the governmental approvals necessary to pursue her project.

As Doris's new building was in the course of construction, Pauline realized that the shadows it would create would place her (Pauline's) building in such deep shade that the rent she could charge for space in her building would be substantially reduced.

Pauline brought an appropriate action against Doris to enjoin the construction in order to eliminate the shadow problem and for damages. Pauline presented uncontroverted evidence that her evaluation as to the impact of the shadow on the fair rental value of her building was correct. There is no statute or ordinance (other than the building and zoning ordinances) that is applicable to the issues before the court.

The court should

(A) grant to Pauline the requested injunction.

(B) award Pauline damages measured by the loss of rental value, but not an injunction.

(C) grant judgment for Doris, because she had secured all the necessary governmental approvals for the new building.

(D) grant judgment for Doris, because Pauline has no legal right to have sunshine continue to reach the windows of her building.

Question 66

The plaintiff and the defendant own adjoining lots in the central portion of a city. Each of their lots had an office building. The defendant decided to raze the existing building on her lot and to erect a building of greater height. The defendant received all governmental approvals required to pursue her project. There is no applicable statute or ordinance (other than those dealing with various approvals for zoning, building, etc.).

The defendant constructed her new building without incident. However, when it was completed, the plaintiff discovered that the shadow created by the new higher building placed the plaintiff's building in such deep shade that her ability to lease space was diminished and that the rent she could charge and the occupancy rate were substantially lower. Assume that these facts are proved in an appropriate action the plaintiff instituted against the defendant for all and any relief available.

Which of the following is the most appropriate comment concerning this lawsuit?

(A) The plaintiff is entitled to a mandatory injunction requiring the defendant to restore conditions to those existing with the prior building insofar as the shadow is concerned.

(B) The court should award permanent damages, in lieu of an injunction, equal to the present value of all rents lost and loss on rents for the reasonable life of the building.

(C) The court should award damages for losses suffered to the date of trial and leave open recovery of future damages.

(D) Judgment should be for the defendant, because the plaintiff has no cause of action.

REAL PROPERTY ANSWERS

References to "Rest. 2d" are to the *Second Restatement of Property*.

Answer 1

Choice (**B**) is correct. Courts generally hold that one who possesses an adjoining landowner's land, under the mistaken belief that he has only possessed up to the boundary of his own land, meets the requirement of "hostile" possession and can become an owner by adverse possession. This is especially likely where the possessor has both planted and fenced in the land in question, since such actions are very likely to bring home to the record owner that the possessor is asserting an adverse claim. So the buyer is highly likely to be found to have gained title to the 10-foot strip of Lot 3 by adverse possession. On the other hand, the buyer has not met the requirement for "continuous" possession of Lot 2. The requirement of "continuous" position does not mean that the possessor must be physically on the property 100% of the time. However, a court would almost certainly require more than the very occasional rabbit-hunting at issue here in order to conclude that the buyer had "continuously" occupied Lot 2.

(A), (C), and (D) are wrong because they are inconsistent with the above analysis.

Answer 2

Choice (**A**) is correct. Agency will win on an adverse possession claim if its possession was open, notorious, visible, hostile and continuous. The requirement of hostility would likely be deemed satisfied, because in a boundary dispute an owner who openly occupies the adjacent parcel under the mistaken belief it is his own is typically found to meet the hostility requirement. The only other requirement that is seriously in issue here is whether Agency's possession was "continuous," in the light of the annual four-week period in which there was no trespass. A court would likely hold that this brief respite each year did not prevent the possession from being continuous, because Agency was treating Blackacre exactly the same way it treated its own adjacent portion of Whiteacre—doing annual cleanup that happened to have the unanticipated effect of removing the trespass. It is not certain that a court would conclude that the continuity requirement was met, but adverse possession is the only one of the choices that would plausibly yield a victory for Agency.

(B) is wrong because the only way in which Brown could be found to have given an implied consent to Agency's use would be if Brown's silence was found to have created either a license or an easement. A license is by its nature a revocable right of use, so even if Brown's silence had created a license by implication, Brown or his successor would be entitled to revoke the license at will, and Silas's suit would constitute such a revocation. As for an easement, easements must generally satisfy the statute of frauds. It is true that an easement by "estoppel" can be created, but this occurs only when the owner of the servient tenement allows a use of his land while he knew or should have known that the user would change position in reliance; here there has been no meaningful reliance by Agency, so this theory would not work.

(C) is wrong because Agency can win only if it obtained legal title to the part of Blackacre in question, and no degree of "public interest" in waste-conversion could ever give Agency title to the property by operation of law.

(D) is wrong because it concerns the wrong area of law. Agency is not trying to obtain title to the relevant portion of Blackacre through eminent domain (i.e., it is not trying to obtain title by paying just compensation). Instead, it is acting under "color of title" as if it already owned the portion of Blackacre concerned. Hence, the problem calls for an adverse possession analysis, not an eminent domain analysis.

Answer 3

Choice **(A)** is correct. The warranty deed conveyed a fee simple determinable title to the church, and the grantor retained the future interest (a possibility of reverter). Such a reverter becomes possessory immediately upon the occurrence of the limitation. A title is unmarketable when a reasonable person would not purchase it. This buyer plans to use the land as a site for business purposes, which would cause the limitation to occur and the title to be forfeited automatically to the grantor. That possibility is easily enough to render the title unmarketable.

(B) is incorrect. Although this answer correctly states that the church is unlikely to prevail, it misstates the legal basis for this conclusion. The quoted provision creates a fee simple determinable title in the church (because the title in this case will be automatically forfeited to the grantor if the land is not used for church purposes), not a restrictive covenant. A restrictive covenant involves a promise regarding the use of the land and is not the title itself (though the existence of a restrictive covenant barring non-church uses would, like the determinable fee here, be enough to render title unmarketable).

(C) is wrong because it cites an irrelevant fact. The "so long as . . ." clause created a possibility of reverter, making the church's title unmarketable. The clause will not create a trust for the benefit of religion, as this choice asserts (and even if it did, that wouldn't prevent the possibility of reverter from operating to divest the buyer of title if he were forced to close on the sale).

(D) is wrong because it's gibberish. The choice seems to be asserted that the grantor can't have a possibility of reverter because such an interest would be inconsistent with the warranty deed that grantor gave. But that's flatly untrue—the warranty deed just asserts that whatever title grantor is conveying, he has (and in this case, he gave a lesser interest than he had, i.e., reserved a possibility of reverter to himself).

Answer 4

Choice **(D)** is correct. The conveyance to the son was a gift of a fee simple subject to the condition precedent that the son get a college degree prior to turning 30. Until the son got the degree, the conveyance did not create any present possessory interest in him (and the possessory interest remained in the landowner, with an executory interest in the daughter ready to spring out of the landowner if the son turned 30 without getting the degree). Therefore, the classmate continued to be a tenant of the landowner, not of the son, with the result that the son did not have the right to terminate the classmate's tenancy or oust him.

(A) is wrong because the phrase "upon the condition precedent . . ." in the landowner-to-son conveyance made the gift a fee simple subject to a condition precedent, not a fee simple subject to divestment. (If the gift had read, "to my son and his heirs, but if my son turns 30 without having obtained a college degree, then to my daughter," then the son *would* indeed have had a fee simple subject to divestment, and the son would have won the case, making this choice correct.)

(B) is wrong because a conveyance by the owner will not normally terminate a tenancy, even where the conveyance is a transfer of a fee simple absolute or a fee simple subject to divestment; furthermore, in this case the conveyance was of a fee simple subject to a condition precedent, so it was even further from terminating the classmate's tenancy.

(C) is wrong because the fact that the permission to occupy was both oral and rent-free establishes that it was a tenancy at will (or else a license); therefore, it could be terminated at any time by either party acting unilaterally. Consequently, although this choice correctly states the result that the classmate wins, it does not correctly state the reason this is so.

Answer 5

Choice (**B**) is correct. Ordinarily, a life tenant may not demolish a structure on the premises, even in order to build a bigger structure at his own expense that would render the future interest more valuable; such a demolition is classified as waste. Courts have recognized a narrow exception where changes in the character of the neighborhood have deprived the property in its present form of "reasonable productivity or usefulness," but this would probably not be found to have occurred here, since the structure is being used for retail stores and produces meaningful rent. (The problem is the substantial mortgage that eats up the rents, not the lack of any reasonably-productive use.) It is not certain that Richard would win with this argument (since Paul might succeed in establishing the no-reasonably-productive-use-in-present-form exception), but this is the only one of the four listed arguments that might plausibly produce a victory for Richard.

(A) is wrong because life estates are completely assignable, without the consent of the holder of the future interest; the assignee simply receives a life estate *per autre vie*.

(C) is wrong because Richard's payment of the mortgage principal does not change his rights; even without such payments he would be entitled to veto a demolition and replacement of the premises unless the narrow exception described in (B) applied.

(D) is wrong because the maintenance of "harmony" with the use envisioned by the future interest holder is not a relevant factor in the decision about whether the proposed use violates the latter's rights; the issue is whether the proposed use would or would not constitute "waste," and harmony with the future holder's desires is not part of the waste analysis.

Answer 6

Choice (**C**) is correct. When Leon, the life tenant, purported to convey the fee simple to Mona, this conveyance had the effect of conveying all of Leon's interest in the property, i.e., his life tenancy. Therefore, Mona had a life estate *per autre vie*, i.e., an estate for the life of Leon. Once Mona stepped into Leon's shoes as life tenant, she had the right to collect all income from the property, but also the obligation to pay all current operating expenses including real estate taxes. Ralph always had a remainder interest following Leon's life estate, and Ralph's interest was not changed in any way by Leon's conveyance of his own interest to Mona.

(A) is wrong because a life tenant's attempt to convey a fee simple does not cause the life estate to be forfeited; such a conveyance merely transfers to the grantee the entirety of the grantor's interest (i.e., the life tenancy).

(B) is wrong because what Mona received is precisely what Leon had, namely an estate for the life of Leon.

(D) is wrong because real estate taxes are the responsibility of the life tenant, not the remainderman.

Answer 7

Choice (**D**) is correct. The general rule about personal liability for mortgage payments as between present and future interests is that neither party has personal liability, except to the extent that party is receiving net operating income from the property. Since the son as remainderman gets no operating income from the property, he has no personal liability to make any mortgage payments. However, if neither he nor anyone else makes all required mortgage payments, the property will presumably be lost to foreclosure, in which case the son's remainder interest will be lost. Therefore, the son has the right (which he may well want to exercise), but not the obligation, to contribute his one-third share of whatever mortgage payments that the widow is unable or unwilling to make.

(A) is wrong because the holder of a future interest generally does not have the right to bring a partition action to compel the sale of the possessory estate (here, the widow's life estate).

(B) is wrong because it overstates the widow's obligation; the widow probably does have a personal obligation to pay her fairly-allocated share of the mortgage payments (based on the relative value of the widow's life estate versus the remainder), up to the amount of net income she's receiving, but this choice incorrectly suggests that she would be personally liable to pay the *entire* installments rather than just her share if the net income were large enough.

(C) is wrong because the son, as a remainderman, has no personal liability to make mortgage payments at all (since he is not getting any operating income out of which to pay them).

Answer 8

Choice **(C)** is correct. When the landowner conveyed to School District, School District got a fee simple determinable (a fee simple that would automatically end if the property ever ceased to be used for school purposes). The landowner retained a possibility of reverter, which is what the grantor retains following a fee simple determinable, if the fee simple determinable doesn't specify what happens upon failure of the condition. In virtually all states, a possibility of reverter can be inherited under the intestacy statute (i.e., it is "descendible"). The probate provision here tells us that if the interest is descendible, it is also devisable (i.e., can be left by will). Since we know that the possibility of reverter is descendible, we therefore know that it is also devisable. Since the landowner left a will devising his entire estate to the doctor, the reverter will pass by devise (i.e., by the will), not by inheritance. That's because of the basic rule that where a particular item of property is covered by a valid bequest in a will, the item will pass by will rather than by intestacy. Therefore, the reverter goes to the doctor under the will.

(A) is wrong because once School District closed its school, its interest in Blackacre was automatically extinguished, and there was nothing left to pass to the developer via the quitclaim deed.

(B) is wrong because the son's status as heir (i.e., as taker under the intestacy statute) was irrelevant given that the reverter here was bequeathed under the will, and was therefore not available to be passed by inheritance.

(D) is wrong because once School District closed its school, its interest was automatically extinguished.

Answer 9

Choice **(D)** is correct. The terms of the bequest made it clear that only a child who survived the testator's wife would take. Each child had a contingent remainder as of the testator's death. When the lawyer died before his mother (the widow) died, the lawyer's contingent remainder was nullified without ever becoming vested, leaving nothing to pass to the lawyer's friend by devise. At the widow's death, the contingent remainders in the accountant and the doctor vested (and, simultaneously, became possessory).

(A) is wrong for the same reason (D) is right: The remainders were intended by the testator to be contingent unless and until the remaindermen survived the widow, at which time they would vest. So when the lawyer died, his contingent remainder was destroyed by his failing to have survived the widow, and he had no interest to pass to the friend.

(B) is wrong because under the common-law approach to the Rule against Perpetuities, the time for evaluating a will is when the testator *dies*, *not* when the will was *executed*. At the time the testator died, his widow (and, indeed, his children as well) were necessarily already in existence, and could therefore serve as measuring lives. So there was no risk that the remainder to the testator's children would vest beyond "measuring lives plus 21 years," making the gift to those children valid contingent remainders.

(C) is wrong as a matter of law: Some remainders can indeed descend by intestacy. *Example*: O bequeaths "to A for life, then to B." Assume B is living at O's death, but dies intestate before A, and with C as his heir at law. At B's death, the vested remainder in B passes by intestacy to C, and C will have a fee simple once B dies.

Answer 10

Choice **(C)** is correct, because if no condition that the remaindermen survive the daughter was implied, the remainder would be vested rather than contingent. A remainder is contingent if it is subject to a condition precedent (other than the mere expiration of the preceding estate) that must be satisfied before the remainder can become a present interest. A common type of condition precedent is the requirement that the holder of the remainder survive the holder of the previous estate (often a life estate), and that is what we might have here. There are two most plausible interpretations of what the testator meant by "my descendants": (1) "all of my descendants existing and identifiable at the moment of my own death" (when the remainder is being created); or (2) "all of my descendants in existence when the remainder becomes possessory" (i.e., all descendants who survive the daughter). If interpretation (1) is chosen by the court, the remainder would be vested, because at the moment of the testator's death we would know everyone who was to take, and if any later pre-deceased the daughter, their heirs could take. If interpretation (2) is chosen, we would not know who takes until the daughter dies, at which point we would look to which descendants of the testator survived the daughter; in that event, the remainder would be contingent as of the testator's death (because at the moment when the testator created the interest by dying, we don't know who will take). So it is only if the court selects interpretation (2) (imputing a condition that the remaindermen must survive the daughter in order to take) that the remainder would be deemed contingent at the present time.

(A) is wrong because if vesting occurred at the moment the will was written, the remainder would be vested as of the testator's death, not contingent. This choice is referring to the possibility that the court would conclude that the bequest's reference to "my descendants" meant "anyone who is my descendant viewed as of the moment when I am writing this will." If this were the interpretation, then at the moment of the will-writing, we would know everyone who could take (they're all identifiable, and their remainder interests would vest immediately even though the remainder would not become possessory until the daughter died). In that event, the remainder would be vested, not contingent.

(B) is wrong because if all vesting were related to the testator's death, the remainder would be vested, not contingent, at that moment. The vesting/contingent determination is to be made at the moment the interest (the remainder) is created. That moment of creation is the testator's death. Saying that "all vesting is [related] to the death of the testator," as this choice does, is equivalent to saying that to be a "descendant," a person just has to survive the testator, not the daughter. In that scenario, at the moment of the testator's death, the remaindermen would be fully identifiable, and would be certain to take once the daughter died. So on this analysis, all remainder holders would be vested (because fully identified as of the moment of creation of the interest, and certain to take), not contingent.

(D) is wrong because an interpretation giving a remainder life estate to the son wouldn't automatically make that remainder contingent. Even in the unlikely event the court implied a life estate remainder to the son, we still wouldn't know whether that remainder was vested or contingent, since we wouldn't know whether there was a requirement that the son survive the daughter (it would be contingent if there were a survival requirement, vested if there were not). In other words, reading in a remainder for life to the son doesn't fully answer the vested/contingent question — of the four choices, only the choice that implies a surviving-the-daughter condition (Choice (C)) does that.

Answer 11

Choice (**B**) is correct. The remainder to "my niece, her heirs and assigns" was a remainder to the niece in fee simple. Since the niece was alive and identifiable at the time of the grantor's deed, the remainder to the niece was vested. A vested remainder can be left by will. Therefore, the remainder passed by the will to the boyfriend.

(A) is wrong because the remainder was never contingent, not even for an instant.

(C) is wrong because a vested remainder can be passed by will, and the will here devised the remainder to the boyfriend; therefore, the fact that the niece's cousin was the niece's heir at law is irrelevant.

(D) is wrong because the remainder here was vested, not contingent; therefore, the doctrine of destructibility of contingent remainders is irrelevant.

Answer 12

Choice (**A**) is correct. Each of the original parties granted a reciprocal right of first refusal to the other and the other's heirs and assigns. A right of first refusal provides that if the owner ever decides to sell the property, the one holding the right of first refusal has the right to purchase it. A right of first refusal is therefore a conditional option to purchase, and it is analyzed for Rule Against Perpetuities (RAP) issues like other purchase options that are "in gross" (i.e., not associated with a lease). Courts are split as to whether to apply the RAP to rights of first refusal or other options in gross. We don't know here that the RAP will definitely be applied to such interests, but we do know that *if* it's applied, the daughter will win (and the question is asking what the reason will be if the daughter wins). Why will the daughter win? Because the RAP invalidates an interest unless it can be said with certainty at the time of creation that that interest will vest or fail to vest within 21 years. Here, the right of first refusal extended to the heirs and assigns of the original parties, so the decision to exercise the right *might* occur more than 21 years after a life in being at the time the right was granted. (For instance, the grantor's great-grandchild might try to exercise the right as against the grantee's great-grandchild.) The RAP in this jurisdiction is unmodified by statute — therefore, the right of first refusal is deemed void as of the time it was created, and the court will not wait to see whether anyone tries to exercise that right more than 21 years after a life in being. Consequently, the right is already invalid, even though only 15 years have passed since the right was created.

(B) is wrong because the fact that the grant*ee* chose not to exercise *his* right of first refusal has no effect on whether the grant*or* can exercise the reciprocal right of first refusal regarding the land originally owned by the grantee. That is, even if the grantee's decision not to exercise the right 10 years ago was a waiver of any subsequent right of first refusal on the part of the grantee or his heirs (which it almost certainly was), there would be no reason why that decision should act as a waiver by the grantor or her heirs as to the reciprocal right held by them.

(C) is wrong because it misstates the effect of the fact that the option is "in gross." An option "in gross" is an option that is not associated with a lease to the option-holder of the property to which the option applies. So the right of first refusal here is indeed an option in gross, as the choice suggests. But the choice is wrong for two reasons: (1) an option in gross is enforceable as long as the time period during which it can be enforced is not longer than the RAP period (i.e., not longer than lives in being plus 21 years); and (2) the fact that the parcels are not adjacent is irrelevant to the analysis. (That is, even if the two parcels *were* adjacent, the option would still be in gross because there is no lease.)

(D) is wrong because it misstates the remedies for breach of a right of first refusal. A holder of a purchase option is entitled to a decree of specific performance, under which the other party will be compelled to make the sale in return for the payment of the option's strike price. A right of first refusal is a conditional option to purchase. Once the condition is satisfied (by the other party's decision to sell), the holder of the option has the same right to a decree of specific performance as would the holder of an unconditional purchase option.

Answer 13

Choice (**C**) is correct. When Beth conveyed her interest to Eugenio, this act caused a severance, destroying the joint tenancy immediately and leaving Eugenio and Christine as tenants in common. When Christine conveyed her interest to Darin, he stepped into Christine's shoes, becoming a tenant in common with Eugenia.

Choices (A), (B), and (D) are wrong because they are inconsistent with the above analysis.

Answer 14

Choice (**A**) is correct. When the brother conveyed his interest in the property to his wife, this conveyance acted as an immediate severance, transforming the joint tenancy into a tenancy in common between the wife and the sister. When the wife immediately reconveyed to the brother, the brother and sister were tenants in common. When the brother died, his interest as a tenant in common passed back to his wife, making her a tenant in common with the sister.

(B) is wrong because the joint tenancy was severed before the brother's will took effect (at the moment the brother conveyed to his wife).

(C) is wrong because once the joint tenancy was broken by the conveyance from the brother to his wife, it could only be reestablished by a new conveyance joined in by both tenants in common, i.e., the wife and the sister (or, later, the brother and sister).

(D) is wrong because a conveyance by either joint tenant severs the joint tenancy regardless of whether the conveying joint tenant had or breached any fiduciary obligation to the other.

Answer 15

Choice (**D**) is correct. Since the tenant's judgment was only against the brother, the tenant's judgment lien was only against the brother's real property, not the sister's real property. That real property consisted of the brother's joint tenancy interest. At the moment of the brother's death, that joint tenancy interest ceased to exist, and there was nothing left for the judgment lien to be a lien against.

(A) is wrong because the basis for the tenant's judgment (and thus for his judgment lien) was the brother's having injured him in the fight; since this had nothing to do with the tenant's having been a tenant of both brother and sister, it did not create any lien against the sister's interest in the property.

(B) is wrong because it inaccurately characterizes the brother's interest: It was a joint tenancy, not an "undivided one-half interest" (a phrase that would be used to describe a tenancy in common). Therefore, the fact that the judgment was filed while the brother was still alive is irrelevant, because the brother's joint tenancy ceased to exist at the moment he died.

(C) is wrong because it cites an irrelevant factor; even if the sister had had actual notice of the judgment while the brother was still alive, there would be no lien after the brother died for the reasons described in the discussion of (D).

Answer 16

Choice **(D)** is correct. The mother's will had the effect of giving the property to the son and the daughter as tenants in common, with an undivided one-half interest going to each. (A conveyance "to *A* and *B*," without further specification, creates a tenancy in common with equal shares.) At the time the creditor got his money judgment against the son, that judgment became a lien only against real property owned by the son, and the son's real property consisted of his undivided one-half interest. When the partition by judicial sale occurred, the son's interest in the property became sole ownership of one-half of the proceeds, and the creditor's lien became a lien solely on that share of the proceeds.

Choices (A), (B), and (C) are wrong because they are inconsistent with the above analysis.

Answer 17

Choice **(C)** is correct. A landlord generally does not have tort liability for accidents that arise out of a dangerous condition on the property. For example, a landlord has no duty to inspect the property to discover dangerous conditions. But the landlord does have liability if he *knows* of the danger, or is in possession of facts that would reasonably have led a person in his position to know of the danger, and the tenant does not know of the danger. Les met this requirement because the facts tell us that he had "known that the wall was dangerously weakened by rot and needed immediate repairs." When Les assigned to Lottie, Les remained liable until Lottie actually discovered the condition and had a reasonable opportunity to fix it. Since Lottie had only owned the property for one day before the accident, and had not learned of the condition, liability had not yet passed to Lottie, and thus remained with Les, at the moment of the accident.

(A) is wrong because, while Lottie took "subject to" the lease, she did not assume Les's obligations to Tom, and her receipt of a payment from Tom did not change this. By the rule discussed in the prior paragraph, Lottie would not become liable for the condition until she learned of it and had time to fix it (unless she expressly assumed liability for conditions not known to her, which didn't happen here).

(B) is wrong because a landlord is liable to the tenant for failing to disclose a known dangerous condition. That liability persists regardless of whether landlord and tenant remain in privity of estate (and ends only when the successor on the landlord side becomes liable, which could only have been when the successor learned of the condition and had a chance to fix it).

(D) is wrong because, where a landlord is actually aware of a dangerous condition, and the tenant is not aware, the landlord is liable regardless of whether the tenant could have (or even reasonably should have) inspected the premises. In other words, the tenant has no duty to inspect, at least in a scenario where the landlord has actual knowledge of the danger.

Answer 18

Choice **(A)** is correct. An assignment arises when a tenant transfers all or some of the leased premises to another for the remainder of the lease term, retaining no interest in the assigned premises. In this case, prior to the agreement with the friend, the tenant had privity of contract with the landlord because of the lease. The tenant also had privity of estate because the tenant was in possession of the apartment. Subsequently, an assignment arose when the tenant transferred the premises to the friend for the remainder of the lease term of nine months. The friend was then in privity of estate with the landlord as to all promises that run with the land, including the covenant to pay rent. (When the friend moved out, this did not end the privity of estate, because the friend did not assign to someone else, and simply abandoned the premises. See Rest. 2d (Landlord & Tenant), § 16.1, Illustr. 24.) The tenant was not released by the landlord, however, and thus remained liable on privity of contract.

(B) is incorrect, because the friend entered privity of estate with the landlord when he received the assignment, and this privity of estate remained with the friend until the end of the lease because the friend made no assignment. Therefore, the friend remained liable on privity of estate for the period after he vacated. Furthermore, because the landlord never released the tenant, the tenant remained liable for the full $3,500 on privity of contract.

(C) is incorrect, because the landlord never released the tenant, thereby keeping the tenant liable on privity of contract based on the original lease. (There was no express release, and a release would not be implied merely because the landlord accepted rent from the friend.)

(D) is incorrect, because this choice assumes that the friend was a sublessee, which he was not. A sublease arises when a tenant transfers the right of possession to all or some of the leased premises to another for a time less than the remaining time of the lease, or when the tenant retains some other interest in the premises. Here, the tenant transferred all the remaining time of the lease to the friend and retained no other interest. Accordingly, this was an assignment and not a sublease. As an assignee, the friend was in privity of estate with the landlord as to all promises that run with the land, including the covenant to pay rent.

Answer 19

Choice **(D)** is correct. Courts disagree about whether a purchase option embodied in a lease may be assigned independently of the lease. Since Lanny is arguing that his title is marketable, the position that purchase options cannot be assigned independently of the lease is favorable to Lanny (because that position, if upheld, would certainly mean that Oscar could not exercise the option, and might even mean that Ten had rendered the option invalid by purporting to assign it independently of the lease).

(A) is wrong because, even if the contract's "subject to a lease" language meant what this choice says it means (that Lanny is committing to sell free and clear of any option), Lanny would still lose: He would not in fact be able to sell free and clear of the purchase option now purportedly held by Oscar.

(B) is wrong because the existence of a purchase option renders title unmarketable, even though the option has not yet been exercised. (If the rule were otherwise, the buyer would be paying full dollar for property that might be "called away" from him by exercise of the option at any time, perhaps at a below-market price.)

(C) is wrong because: (1) purchase options embodied in leases are typically not subjected to the Rule against Perpetuities; and (2) even if the option here *were* subject to the Rule, the option would not thereby be rendered invalid (since the option must be exercised during the lease term, and the lease terms falls within "lives in being plus 21 years").

Answer 20

Choice **(B)** is correct. The lease between the landlord and the tenant specifically addressed what would happen if a public entity condemned any part of the land under its power of eminent domain. That agreement between the parties controls. Thus, the court will find for the landlord: The lease will terminate and the landlord will receive the entire condemnation award.

(A) is wrong because the specific terms of the lease supersede the condemnation, not vice versa. If the lease had been silent on the issue of condemnation, then the result would have depended on whether the condemnation was of all the property, or of just part. (With a total condemnation and a lease silent on this point, the leasehold and all the tenant's duties under the lease would have been terminated, and the tenant would have been entitled to share in the condemnation award only to the extent that the fair market value of his leasehold exceeded his obligations under the lease. Had the city condemned just part of the property, in most courts the tenant would have been required to continue paying the full rent, but would have been entitled to a portion of the condemnation award to compensate him for the portion of the leasehold no longer available to him.) However, this "default" rule for handling a condemnation award will, in all courts, not be applied if the parties have specified a different treatment, as they did here.

(C) is wrong because it misstates the law. The taking of all or part of the leased land, or the taking of some interest in it—say an easement—by eminent domain does not constitute a breach of the landlord's covenant of quiet enjoyment of the premises because it occurs through no fault of the landlord.

(D) is wrong because there has been no unjust enrichment. Had the lease not provided for the consequences of condemnation, the lease would have remained in force, and the tenant would, to prevent unjust enrichment of the landlord, have gotten either a pro-rata reduction of rent, some portion of the award (if the lease was below-market), or both. But the fact that the parties expressly agreed that the landlord would keep the entire award means that there is no unjust enrichment when the agreed-upon outcome is enforced.

Answer 21

Choice (C) is correct, because it correctly identifies the reason Eric will lose: His use of Goldacre was not "adverse," i.e., non-permissive. The key facts here are that Eric had oral permission from Oxnard *originally* to use the road across Goldacre, and Amos quit possession of Goldacre before acquiring title by adverse possession. What does this mean? That Eric's use of Goldacre was never adverse to the interests of the landowner, and that Amos never had any enforceable rights to Goldacre. In order to gain an easement by prescription, one's use of another's property must be actual, open and notorious, continuous for the statutory period, exclusive, and hostile and adverse (non-permissive). Here, the facts specifically state that Eric had Oxnard's oral permission to use the road across Goldacre. The red herring here is the presence of Amos. However, Amos is merely in possession of Goldacre. The facts state that he quit possession before he acquired title to it. Thus, the elements of an easement by prescription would apply to Eric vis-à-vis Oxnard, *not* Eric vis-à-vis Amos.

(A) is wrong because it focuses on the wrong fact. Here, it doesn't matter if Eric's use is adverse to Amos, because Amos is not the landowner—*Oxnard* is. Eric's use is not adverse to Oxnard, because the facts state that Oxnard granted Eric oral permission to use the road across Goldacre. An easement by prescription requires use of another's property that is actual, open and notorious, continuous for the statutory period, exclusive, and hostile and adverse. "Hostile and adverse" means non-permissive in this context. Here, since Eric's use was with the permission of the landowner the entire time, his use was *never* adverse. Since (A) does not recognize this, it's not the best response.

(B) is wrong because it falsely suggests that Amos's quitting possession of Goldacre is relevant. It is not, because an easement by prescription is gained by adverse use against the *landowner,* not the *possessor.* Eric could only gain an easement by prescription if his use of Goldacre *as against Oxnard* was actual, open and notorious, continuous for the statutory period, exclusive, and non-permissive.

(D) is wrong because it focuses on a basically irrelevant fact. What matters is whether Eric had the requisite open and hostile use *as against the true owner*, Oxnard. If Eric hadn't originally gotten permission from Oxnard, his time of use of the driveway while Amos was in adverse possession of the overall tract would count against Oxnard. So the problem is not that Eric didn't use the driveway long enough once Amos left, it's that Eric's entire use of the driveway (even when Amos was there) wasn't adverse as against Oxnard.

Answer 22

Choice (**C**) is correct. The expanded use of the easement here—especially the parking along the driveway at all hours—probably does represent excessive use going beyond the intended scope of the easement. However, a court would almost certainly limit the remedy to an injunction against further violations, or to damages for the two past violations, and would not order a forfeiture of the easement. That's because forfeitures are drastic remedies, and will be awarded in excessive-use situations only if no other remedy will be adequate, which would not be the case for the violations here.

(A) is wrong because, while the order has indeed probably excessively expanded their use of the easement, the court would not order the easement forfeited as a remedy, for the reasons stated above.

(B) is wrong for the same reason (A) is wrong.

(D) is wrong because a court would not grant the neighbor the extreme remedy of forfeiture whether or not she had used self-help.

Answer 23

Choice (**C**) is correct. At the time of the conveyance by the landowner to the lawyer, the lawyer received an implied easement to use the stairs for access to Building 2. (The three requirements for an easement by implication were met here: (1) the land was "severed" from common ownership when the landowner kept Building 2 while selling Building 1; (2) the use of the stairway for access to Building 2 existed prior to this severance; and (3) the easement was and is reasonably necessary to enjoyment of Building 2.) The holder of the easement (the lawyer) therefore had an implied right to maintain the property used in the easement, given that the maintenance was compatible with the intended use of the easement and did not unreasonably interfere with the servient owner's (the accountant's) use of the servient estate.

(A) is wrong because the lawyer *does* have rights in the stairway, namely an implied easement.

(B) is wrong because the lawyer as easement holder has the right to maintain or repair the structure indefinitely, not just for the normal life of the original staircase.

(D) is wrong because it misstates the reason for the lawyer's repair right, which is that the lawyer has an implied easement; if the lawyer did not have an implied easement, he would probably not face tort liability for failing to correct the stairway danger on property belonging to another, at least if he asked the owner (the accountant) to do the work and the owner refused.

Answer 24

Choice (**A**) is correct. Reliable has an expressly-created easement for constructing and using overhead electric lines. Since Reliable was given the right to use Maria's land, it's the "dominant" tenement holder (and Maria is the "servient" tenement holder, since it's her land that's burdened by the easement). The rule on maintaining easements is that the dominant tenement holder has both the *right* and the *duty* to use reasonable care to maintain the easement. Thus, Reliable would have the *right* to enter Maria's land and repair the line and poles, as necessary, and Maria could not object to this interference. However, Reliable also had the duty to use reasonable care to maintain the equipment so it did not pose an unreasonable danger to Maria's land, and the utility, by failing to maintain the line at all, did not fulfill that duty. As a result, Maria will be able to recover for damages to the lumber yard.

(B) is wrong because although it arrives at the correct result, it misstates the responsibility of the dominant tenement holder. There is no doctrine that states that an easement owner is strictly liable for damage caused to the servient tenement by the exercise of the easement. Instead, the dominant holder merely has the obligation to use reasonable care to maintain the easement in such a way that it does not damage the servient property. If the accident had happened without the lack of due care by Reliable (which is not the way it happened), Reliable would not be liable to Maria.

(C) is wrong because it misstates the duty of the servient tenement holder, and arrives at the wrong result. In general, the dominant holder has the obligation to use reasonable care to maintain the easement so that it does not pose unreasonable risk to the servient parcel. This obligation includes an obligation to inspect. So the mere fact that Maria didn't give notice of the problem doesn't save Reliable from liability. (Indeed, an electric utility ought to be able to recognize maintenance issues more easily than a non-utility customer.)

(D) is wrong because it fails to recognize Reliable Electric's duty to Maria. The holder of an easement has both the *right* and the *duty* to take reasonable steps to maintain the easement.

Answer 25

Choice (**A**) is correct. Carrol is the owner of the dominant tenement (i.e., the owner of the easement), and Beach is the owner of the servient tenement. Beach, as the servient owner, has no obligation to contribute one-third of Carrol's repair expenditures. Beach may have *some* obligation of reimbursement, based on the intensity and frequency of his bridge use versus Carrol's, but certainly not a one-third-of-total-cost obligation, since Beach clearly does not represent one-third of the total usage of the bridge. As to Daniel, he may well have obtained an easement by prescription. But even if he has done so, he, too, has no obligation to reimburse Carrol for one-third of the latter's expenditures, because Daniel, like Beach, rarely makes use of the bridge, and has at most an obligation to reimburse for his small pro rata share of total usage.

Choices (B), (C), and (D) are wrong because they are inconsistent with the above analysis.

Answer 26

Choice (**B**) is correct. What we have here is an easement appurtenant, because the easement is for the benefit of a particular parcel (the back 40 acres). An easement appurtenant passes to the new holder of the dominant tenement automatically, even if the deed to the dominant tenement does not mention the easement.

(A) is wrong, because the easement here is an express easement, not one by implication. Furthermore, even if the easement here *were* an easement by implication, it would automatically pass together with the dominant tenement.

(C) is wrong because the easement here is appurtenant, not in gross. That is, it is clear from the surrounding circumstances that the easement is being used to benefit a particular parcel (the back 40 acres), not to benefit Buck irrespective of Buck's ownership of those 40 acres. So while many courts indeed hold that an easement in gross is not transferable if the document creating it is silent on the issue, this principle won't apply to the facts here.

(D) is wrong because, as described in the answer to (B) above, an easement appurtenant will pass together with the dominant tenement, even if the deed conveying the dominant tenement does not mention the easement.

Answer 27

Choice **(B)** is correct. A license is permission to use the land of another. It is ordinarily revocable, and is not subject to the Statute of Frauds. In this case, because the neighbor had the landowner's permission to use the road and did not expend any money, property, or labor pursuant to the agreement (i.e., the neighbor did substantially rely on the continued availability of the license), the neighbor had a license that was revocable—and effectively revoked—by the grantee.

(A) is incorrect because, while this option correctly states that the grantee will prevail, it misstates the reason why this is so. A license (unlike an easement) is not subject to the Statute of Frauds; it may be oral, written, or implied.

(C) is incorrect because for estoppel to apply to make a license (which is ordinarily revocable) irrevocable, the neighbor must have expended money, property, or labor pursuant to the agreement. In this case, the landowner alone maintained the road. The neighbor's use of the land by permission, without expense, was therefore a revocable license that was effectively revoked by the grantee.

(D) is incorrect. An open and notorious use of the road suggests a claim for an easement by prescription. However, the use was with permission, which prevents a prescriptive claim. (Also, the use was for just three years, making it extremely unlikely that the statutory period for adverse possession-type claims could have run.) Instead, the neighbor's use of the land was a license that was effectively revoked by the grantee.

Answer 28

Choice **(D)** is correct. Where a promise regarding land use is a negative one—i.e., one forbidding certain uses—the promise is called an "equitable servitude." An equitable servitude is not enforceable by the owner of a particular parcel unless the original parties intended to benefit that particular parcel. The language in the deeds from the landowner to his son and from the landowner to his daughter specifically provided that "any owner of any part of the tract may enforce the covenant"; the fact that the daughter's parcel was part of the tract shows that that parcel was intended to be benefitted by the restriction. Since the daughter's parcel was intended to be benefitted, and since equitable servitudes are generally enforceable, the daughter wins.

(A) is wrong because the change in local land use does not mean that the court will not enforce the servitude. There can be extreme circumstances in which a change of land use throughout an entire neighborhood might lead a court to conclude that it should no longer enforce an equitable servitude; but the mere fact that uses inconsistent with the servitude are now prevalent in adjacent parcels would not be enough. That's especially true where, as here, some of the parcels near plaintiff (i.e., any parcel on the western side of the municipal line) are used in a way that is consistent with the restriction.

(B) is wrong, because the fact that a use forbidden by a servitude is allowed by local zoning codes won't cause a court to refuse enforcement of an otherwise valid restriction unless the *entire area* in question has changed in such a way that enforcement would be of little value. So where, as here, use patterns on the western side are still five-acre minimums, the fact that the zoning code applicable to the eastern side is inconsistent with five-acre-minimums would not induce the court to relax the enforcement of the servitude.

(C) is wrong, because courts will enforce an equitable servitude against a subsequent owner of burdened land who took with actual or constructive notice. So if, for instance, the son sold to a buyer, that buyer would be deemed to have constructive notice of the restriction (it's in her chain of title). Consequently, the landowner's daughter could get an injunction against the buyer even though the buyer was not an "original grantee."

Answer 29

Choice **(B)** is correct. The plaintiff owner of a parcel can't gain enforcement of either a covenant at law or an inequitable servitude against a defendant who is the "downstream" owner of a burdened parcel (i.e., one who took after the burden was imposed), unless: (1) there was an intent by the original parties to benefit the parcel now owned by the plaintiff; *and* (2) the defendant was on actual or constructive notice of the nature of the restriction at the time she took. In the case of the suit by the developer on behalf of Lot 2, both of these requirements are satisfied: (1) the landowner-to-developer deed made it clear that both Lots 2 and 4 were being both burdened and benefited by mutual single-family-only restrictions (so the requisite intent to benefit Lot 2 is present); and (2) the investor was on constructive (and probably actual) notice of the restriction on the lot she was buying at the time she bought because it was mentioned in the landowner-to-developer deed that was part of the investor's title report (and, indeed, from this the investor knew that that restriction was intended to benefit Lot 2). Therefore, the developer will likely be entitled to his choice of an injunction and damages (i.e., to recover on the equitable servitude or, alternatively, for breach of covenant at law).

The owners of Lots 1, 3, and 5, by contrast, cannot satisfy either of these requirements: (1) nothing indicates that at the time the landowner conveyed these three lots, he was intending (then or ever) to create any equitable restrictions on any of his five lots, so the present owners of the three lots cannot show that their parcels were ever intended to be benefited; and (2) the investor, at the time she took, was not on notice that Lots 1, 3, and 5 were to be benefited by any restriction on the parcel she was buying. So these owners are unlikely to get any relief against the investor.

(A) is wrong because there was no common development scheme at the time Lots 1, 3, and 5 were conveyed. It's true that had there been in place, at the time Lots 1, 3, and 5 were conveyed, a "plan of development" (say, a filed subdivision plat) showing an intent to keep the whole development single-family residential, the owners of Lots 1, 3, and 5 might succeed with an "implied reciprocal servitude" argument, that the landowner implicitly promised them that he'd burden his remaining lots consistently with this plan and that the investor should have known of this promise and be required to honor it. But the facts do not indicate that any such plan existed at the time the landowner sold Lots 1, 3, and 5.

(C) is wrong because, as noted in the analysis of Choice (B), owners cannot recover damages (i.e., recover on a covenant at law) unless they can show that there was an intent to give their parcels the benefit of the restrictive promise, an intent which is absent as to Lots 1, 3, and 5. The fact that the landowner later developed such a purpose to burden his remaining lots doesn't help—there must have been an intent-to-burden at the time when the landowner still owned the lots in question.

(D) is wrong because the existence of a zoning scheme that allows the activity in question doesn't trump a stricter scheme of covenants. If the zoning scheme was stricter, it would prevail (landowners can't by mutual agreement cause strict zoning rules to be relaxed). But the converse is not true—indeed, the whole idea of restrictive covenants is that they can be used to forbid uses that are allowed by the zoning rules.

Answer 30

Choice (**A**) is correct. The covenant here is ostensibly a "real" covenant, which is a promise related to land that is enforceable by (and against) subsequent holders of the land. Traditionally, for a covenant to be "real" (i.e., to be enforceable by and against subsequent landholders) (1) the original parties must have intended that the covenant run with the land, (2) the covenant must "touch and concern" the land, (3) the Statute of Frauds must be satisfied, and (4) privity of estate must exist. Choice (A) correctly focuses on the touch-and-concern requirement. A covenant does not touch and concern the land if it doesn't change the value, use, or utility of the land. Most typically, covenants that touch and concern the land are building restrictions, although even payments to homeowner's associations can qualify. However, a mere agreement to purchase electricity from the realty company's facility would traditionally not be considered to touch and concern the residential owner's land; therefore, it couldn't "run with" the land, and, as a result, the woman would not be bound by it without her personally covenanting to do so. Since, of the four answer choices presented, Choice (A) correctly identifies the most likely basis on which the woman will prevail, it's the best response. (Note that, under the modern trend, as represented by § 3.2 of the Third Restatement (Servitudes), the covenant need not fulfill the touch-and-concern requirement in order to run. But you're told that the jurisdiction follows the "traditional rule" for the running of covenants, and touch-and-concern is part of the traditional set of rules.)

(B) is wrong because it misstates the law, and, in any case, does correctly characterize these facts. The covenant here, if it is enforceable at all, is a "real covenant," whose requirements are summarized in the discussion of Choice (A) above. The requirement to which Choice (B) refers is not for a real covenant, but for an "implied reciprocal servitude." An implied reciprocal servitude is a means by which a subsequent property owner can be bound by a covenant that is not present in his own deed (or in the deed of his predecessor(s)), but that is present in deeds from the same grantor to prior purchasers of different parcels, typically in the same subdivision. That isn't the case here, since the covenant appeared in the deed to the woman's predecessor. So there is no place for the doctrine of implied reciprocal servitudes. In any case, even if the doctrine applied, the fact that not all the dwellings were of the same type would not prevent a common development scheme from existing.

(C) is wrong, because it does not focus on the correct issue, and, in any case, misstates the law. Restraints on alienation are not per se invalid; for instance, promissory restraints are valid, as in the case of prohibitions against subletting and assignment in landlord-tenant agreements. Restraints are viewed narrowly by courts, but they can be valid. While the covenant here would be a restraint on alienation, it would not be invalid for that reason, since if the covenant touched and concerned the land, it would be enforceable as a "real" covenant.

(D) is wrong, because it is factually incorrect. There *is* privity between the woman and the investor, because most states hold that privity exists if both interests ultimately come from a common grantor (here, the realty company). Instead, the problem here is the touch-and-concern element traditionally required for a real covenant, as discussed in Choice (A).

Answer 31

Choice (**A**) is correct. A restrictive covenant will normally run with the land, i.e., be enforceable by subsequent grantees of the benefitted parcels, and against subsequent grantees of the burdened parcels, if the original parties intended that it run. The existence of the filed subdivision plat with the restriction, and the fact that Oscar took the trouble to insert the restriction in all his deeds, establish that he and his grantees intended the burden and benefit of the restriction to run. Meanwhile, Joe, as a subsequent grantee, will only be bound by the restrictive covenant if he was on actual or constructive notice when he took. "Constructive" notice includes "record" notice. Here, Joe was on record notice of the restriction. That's true because although Joe's deed did not itself refer to the no-mobile-homes restriction, that restriction was present in a prior recording in his chain of title (the Oscar-Max deed). And a purchaser is deemed to be on record notice of any restrictions in his chain of title. Intuitively, this makes sense—Joe's lawyer could have and should have found the Oscar-to-Max deed, and noticed the restriction. (Or, the lawyer could have and should have noticed that the lot was part of a filed subdivision plat that contained the restriction.)

(B) is wrong because the fact it cites is irrelevant to the issues here. The mere fact that the presence of mobile homes would adversely affect the value of Sarah's land does not mean that Sarah has a legally cognizable right to forbid their presence. As a general principle, the owner of land may put the land to any lawful use he chooses, without regard to the impact on the market value of other, neighboring properties. Thus, even if (B) were true, it would not provide a sound basis for Sarah to prevail.

(C) is wrong because it does not correctly cite the rule on restrictive covenants (or "equitable servitudes," as they are also called). Restrictive covenants will bind subsequent purchasers of the land as long as the original parties intended that the agreement will run with the land, and the subsequent purchaser had actual or constructive notice of the restriction. Here, Joe had constructive notice (namely, record notice) of the restriction, as further explained in (A). Therefore, the fact that Joe's own deed did not contain the covenant is irrelevant.

(D) is wrong because as long as the restriction was intended to run with the land, the fact that the person sought to be bound is a remote grantee of the original, covenanting party—here, Oscar—is irrelevant. That's what the fact that the covenant or restriction "runs with the land" *means*—the restriction binds remote grantees who take with actual or constructive (including record) notice.

Answer 32

Choice **(A)** is correct. Dodd can win only if Egan is found to have been bound by Able's promise to Baker that Able would impose a restriction on Blackacre when he sold it. A subsequent purchaser of a use-restricted parcel can be bound by the restriction only if he had some sort of *notice* of the restriction at the time he took. Egan did not have *record* notice of the restriction because (1) the restriction was not contained in the Able-to-Egan deed by which Egan took Blackacre; and (2) even if the Able-to-Baker deed to Whiteacre was held to be within Egan's chain of title (which it wouldn't be), that wouldn't give Egan notice, because the Able-to-Baker deed was not recorded, so Egan couldn't have discovered the restriction by tracing back title to Whiteacre in the public records. Therefore, the only way Egan could have received the required notice (and thus lose) is if he had actual notice or some form of *constructive* notice not involving record notice. (A), by referring specifically to Egan's "actual knowledge" of the restriction, is the only choice that satisfies the notice-to-Egan requirement. And as we know from the statement of facts, Egan indeed had such actual knowledge.

(B) is wrong because, while the doctrine of negative reciprocal covenants might apply to restrict Whiteacre, Egan wouldn't be bound by that restriction if he didn't have some form of notice, and this choice does not refer to the notice problem.

(C) is wrong because, like (B), it fails to refer to the key point, notice to Egan.

(D) is wrong because, while Egan might indeed lose if he had constructive notice of the possibility of the restriction, such constructive notice was not present in the facts here: The mere fact that Able sold Whiteacre to Baker and that Baker put a filling station on the property would not suggest to a reasonable purchaser of the adjacent Blackacre parcel that Able would likely have restricted Blackacre by giving Baker a non-compete. (Otherwise any purchaser of a commercially-zoned parcel would have to check into the facts surrounding his seller's sale of any other nearby parcel, to make sure that the seller didn't give a non-compete, too large a burden on buyers to make sense.)

Answer 33

Choice (**A**) is correct. To be binding, a restrictive covenant must be placed on property *at the time it is conveyed.* Here, neither the deed to the first buyer nor the deed to the doctor contains the restrictive covenant. The burden cannot be attached to Lot 1 at a later time by someone who has no interest in Lot 1, even if that person (here, the landowner) purports to be acting on behalf of the entire subdivision. Therefore, the doctor may proceed with her plan to use part of the property as a medical office.

(B) is incorrect, because although this option correctly concludes that the doctor will prevail, it misstates the reason why this is so. Zoning ordinances do not automatically override a private restrictive covenant. The stricter of either the zoning ordinance or the covenant will prevail. In this case, the doctor will prevail because the restrictive covenant was not in the deed to the first buyer of Lot 1, nor was it in the deed to the doctor.

(C) is incorrect. Public land use controls and private land use controls are separate issues. Zoning may be changed. In this case, the zoning was changed a year after the first buyer purchased Lot 1. The doctor's use of Lot 1 is governed by the zoning in existence during the time of the doctor's ownership, and the previous zoning of the property is irrelevant. The doctor may proceed with her plan to use part of the property as a medical office, because the restrictive covenant was not in the deed to the first buyer of Lot 1, nor was it in the deed to the doctor.

(D) is incorrect. To be binding, a restrictive covenant must be placed on property at the time when it is conveyed. The first buyer's learning of the covenant two years after he acquired it is irrelevant, and does not incorporate Lot 1 into the common scheme of the subdivision; nor does the actual knowledge of any subsequent buyer of Lot 1 (even knowledge acquired before he took) have any effect. A common-scheme argument might prevail as to subsequent purchasers of other lots in the subdivision who took from the landowner after the landowner had already burdened other parcels with the restriction. As to Lot 1, however, the doctor may proceed with her plan to use part of the property as a medical office, because the restrictive covenant was not in the deed to the first buyer, nor was it in the deed to the doctor.

Answer 34

Choice (**D**) is correct. When the grantor conveyed Lot 1 to the investor, the grantor burdened Lot 2 with the covenant to reimburse the owner of Lot 1 for wall-repair expenses. This covenant was enforceable, and ran with the land on both the burden and benefit side. Even though more than 50 years have passed, no event has occurred (e.g., change of circumstances rendering fulfillment of the covenant's purposes impossible) that would cause the covenant to be extinguished, and the mere passage of time does not suffice to end the covenant. The fact that the covenant ran with the land on the benefit side means that the student as present owner of the benefited lot gets to enforce the covenant; this running of the benefit side occurs even though the deed to convey the benefited parcel to the student did not mention the covenant or the wall (since mention of the covenant in the deed to the benefited lot is simply not a requirement). The running of the covenant on the burden side means that the obligation of payment attached to the grantor's son's interest in Lot 2. Therefore, the only way the student can lose is if his expenditures were not reasonable and customary (in which case they would not be covered by the terms of the covenant, even though the covenant is still enforceable).

(A) is wrong because nothing occurred to cause the doctrine of adverse possession to affect title to the benefited lot (Lot 1) while that lot was held by either the investor, the housewife, or the student. For instance, no action by any owner of Lot 2 could even arguably have constituted the requisite hostile, notorious, open, and continuous possession of the wall so as to wipe out the covenant governing repairs.

(B) is wrong because the fact that the investor's deed from the grantor for Lot 1 was not recorded had no effect on anyone who ever had an interest in Lot 2. It's true that the grantor, by conveying Lot 1 to the investor, simultaneously created a covenant burdening Lot 2, which was an interest in Lot 2. But a grantee's failure to record under a recording act has no effect on the rights as between the original grantor and grantee; therefore, in a contest between the grantor and the investor, the investor's failure to record his covenant against Lot 2 would not prevent the investor from recovering reimbursement from the grantor while the grantor still owned Lot 2. The interesting question is whether the investor's failure to record can be taken advantage of by the grantor's son as the grantor's successor. In other words, is the grantor's son a "subsequent purchaser without notice" who can take advantage of the fact that the deed creating the covenant never appeared in his chain of title? The answer is that because recording acts invariably protect only "purchasers for value," and because the son took by intestate succession (and thus did not give value for his interest), the son is *not* a purchaser for value and thus *cannot* take advantage of the recording act. (If the son had purchased for value and without notice of the covenant, he *would* have been free of the covenant on account of the investor's failure to record.)

(C) is wrong because the owner of a parcel benefited by an affirmative covenant does not lose the benefit merely because he did not act in reliance on the covenant's existence.

Answer 35

Choice (**A**) is correct. The Statute of Frauds applies to all contracts for the sale of land, or for the sale of an interest in land. Therefore, such a contract will not be enforced unless it is in writing. There are a few exceptions to this rule (e.g., where there has been part performance in reliance on an oral agreement), but none of those exceptions applies here.

(B) is wrong because it is not the case that the seller's exclusive remedy for breach is to keep the deposit; often, a court will order the buyer to specifically perform even where the seller has a deposit. (Furthermore, unless the parties have agreed that the deposit will be the exclusive measure, the seller will be entitled to recover his actual damages from the buyer's breach if these are greater than the deposit.)

(C) is wrong because the fact that Victor inherited a different home is not a valid reason for not closing; the doctrine of frustration of purpose occasionally applies to land-sale contracts, but would virtually never apply where the only event alleged to have frustrated the buyer's purpose is that he found or acquired other property he liked better.

(D) is wrong because Ozzie's anticipated one-day delay in vacating would not have been a material breach, unless the agreement or the circumstances indicated that time was of the essence. There's no indication that that happened here. Therefore, the one-day delay would not have deprived Ozzie of his otherwise-existing right to obtain specific performance.

Answer 36

Choice (**C**) is correct. Unless the sale contract specifies otherwise, the seller's title is not required to be marketable until the date set for the closing. The fact that there is an outstanding mortgage on the property, therefore, does not entitle the buyer to cancel the contract, as long as the seller has the right and probable ability to pay off the mortgage at the closing.

(A) is wrong because the fact that the mortgage was granted for pre-existing obligations (as opposed, say, to being a purchase money mortgage) is irrelevant to the issue of whether the seller's title is marketable. For instance, if the seller were not paying off the mortgage at the closing, the mortgage would indeed be an encumbrance rendering title unmarketable, even though it was granted to secure the seller's pre-existing obligation to the mortgagee.

(B) is wrong because the doctrine of equitable conversion is used to pass the risk of loss to the buyer under a purchase contract, and has nothing to do with whether the seller's title is marketable.

(D) is wrong because a purchaser's "real reason" (i.e., motive) for refusing to close is irrelevant to whether the purchaser has the right to so refuse. For example, if the seller's title had been unmarketable, the buyer would have been entitled to refuse to close even though her real reason for refusing was something entirely unrelated to the quality of the seller's title.

Answer 37

Choice (**A**) is correct. This choice correctly identifies that Venner can use the sale proceeds to pay off the mortgage, and thus force Brier to honor the contract. Where, as is usually the case, the seller in a land-sale contract covenants to deliver the property free and clear of encumbrances, the presence of a mortgage would be an encumbrance rendering the title unmarketable. But you're told here that the proceeds will cover the mortgage. When that's the case, the seller has an implied right to use the proceeds of the sale to pay off the mortgage. When you think about it, this rule comports with what you'd expect to happen, since many homeowners, in real life, couldn't sell their home if this weren't the case.

(B) is wrong because it misstates the law. Although it's possible that the law of the jurisdiction may make the mortgage payable from the proceeds, and the mortgage agreement itself may insist on payoff if the property is conveyed, the "rule" stated in this choice wouldn't cause the mortgage to be removed from Greenacre — and that's the central problem here. Instead, the key is that the seller gets to use the sale proceeds to pay off the mortgage simultaneously with the closing of title.

(C) is wrong because the doctrine of equitable conversion would not apply to these facts. The doctrine of equitable conversion addresses the period between the signing of the land sale contract and the closing. Under the doctrine, the vendor has a personal property interest in the property, between the signing of the contract and the closing, in the form of the balance of the purchase price owed to him; the vendee is considered the beneficial owner of the property. The doctrine wouldn't help with the problem here, which is that Venner can't deliver marketable title unless he can remove the mortgage.

(D) is wrong because it states an insufficient ground on which Venner could prevail. Of course, his underlying argument must be that he hasn't breached the contract, because if he had, he wouldn't be entitled to specific performance. However, Choice (D), in and of itself, doesn't provide a rule allowing Venner to use the proceeds to pay off the mortgage, and enforce the contract. Only Choice (A) does this.

Answer 38

Choice (**B**) is correct. It is likely, though not absolutely certain, that Abel will be able to obtain specific performance (the court will have to be satisfied that money damages would not give him an adequate remedy). But one thing that *is* certain is that Baker will fail with his lack-of-consideration argument, because the general contract principle that an exchange of promises meets the consideration requirement applies to real estate contracts. Able has made a promise (to convey in return for the purchase price), and Baker has made a return promise (to pay the purchase price in return for title), so standard consideration requirements are easily satisfied. The fact that there was no earnest money deposit is completely irrelevant to the consideration issue — an earnest money deposit is not required, and where present is merely a form of liquidated-damages clause.

(A) is wrong because the contract, since it is in writing and meets the consideration requirement, would be binding even if Baker had not parked on the property and therefore arguably partly performed. (If the contract had been oral, Baker's parking might supply him with an argument for application of the part-performance exception to the Statute of Frauds, but even here, he would probably lose because the parking was not really part "performance.")

(C) is wrong because equitable conversion, where applicable, vests "equitable title" in the vendee under a land sale contract (thus passing the risk of loss to the vendee), and neither equitable title nor risk of loss is at issue on these facts.

(D) is wrong because a vendor under a land sale contract can recover for breach (including specific performance if money damages would not be an adequate remedy) whether the contract was recorded or not — recording is merely relevant to the vendee's rights vis-à-vis later grantees from the vendor (by giving the world constructive notice of the pending transfer), not to the vendee's rights vis-à-vis the vendor.

Answer 39

Choice (**C**) is correct. The purchaser under a land-sale contract will normally be entitled to a decree of specific performance if the seller is able but unwilling to perform. Here, the fact that Adam did not have title at the time he signed the contract is irrelevant; the contract called for him to make a conveyance at the scheduled closing date, and he is able to do that. The case therefore falls within the familiar principle that the time for measuring whether a seller has marketable title is the time for closing, not some earlier date.

(A) is wrong because the fact that Adam did not have authority to sell the land at the moment of signing is irrelevant; he has title by now (prior to the scheduled closing date), and that's all that matters for purposes of specific performance.

(B) is wrong because the doctrine of after-acquired title is not necessary for a decree of specific performance here; all that matters is that Adam has title by the time scheduled for performance.

(D) is wrong because specific performance is used for breach of contract where (as here) damages would be an inadequate remedy, and the concept of unjust enrichment is not needed or relevant to whether specific performance should be decreed.

Answer 40

Choice (**D**) is correct. The contract provision concerning the deposit was a liquidated damages clause. In most courts, a liquidated damages clause is enforceable if it was a reasonable estimate (viewed *either* as of the time the contract was made or at the time of suit) of the damages that the seller would likely incur if the buyer breached. Here, an estimate, as of the time the contract was signed, that the seller would sustain $5,000 in damages if there was a breach on a $110,000 contract, seems reasonable. The fact that the seller ended up with a slightly smaller-than-predicted loss of $2,000 (not counting any incidental expenses to the seller from having to re-list the property or wait for a later sale) does not change the reasonableness of the time-of-contract estimate; in fact, the $5,000 estimate is probably also reasonable viewed as of the time of suit.

(A) is wrong because Sam's present inability to carry out his contract with Bert was caused by Bert's breach, and therefore does not nullify Sam's ability to rely on the liquidated damages clause.

(B) is wrong because Bert's need to transfer is not the sort of extraordinary event that would excuse Bert's nonperformance.

(C) is wrong because, as explained in (D), the liquidated damages clause will be enforced here, even though it differs from the seller's actual damages.

Answer 41

Choice (C) is correct. Under the doctrine of equitable conversion, during the period between the land sale contract and the conveyance, the purchaser is considered the equitable owner of the property, and the seller is deemed to have a personal property interest in the purchase price. Therefore, if the seller dies before the conveyance takes place, the one entitled to his personal property is entitled to the purchase price. (The one entitled to his real property only gets a bare legal title, which she must convey to the purchaser when the purchaser performs his duty under the contract, i.e., turns over the cash.) Under these facts, the son is entitled to the seller's personalty, so he gets all the cash from the sale, and the daughter is out of luck.

(A) is wrong, because death does not terminate a land sale contract. As long as the land sale contract is specifically enforceable, if the vendor dies before the conveyance takes place, the one to whom he willed his personal property is entitled to the purchase price when the conveyance takes place. This is part of the doctrine of equitable conversion. If you chose this response, it could be because you thought the situation was covered by the rule that terminates an *offer* on the death or insanity of either the offeror or the offeree. That rule is not involved here, since there's an enforceable contract already in place.

(B) is wrong because it arrives at the wrong conclusion and states, wrongly, that the doctrine of equitable conversion does not apply to these circumstances. In fact, the doctrine of equitable conversion *does* apply to these circumstances, and its operation means that the person entitled to the seller's personal property—his son—is entitled to the purchase price. Under the doctrine of equitable conversion, during the period between the land sale contract and the conveyance, the purchaser is considered the beneficial owner of the property, and the seller has a personal property interest in the purchase price. If the seller dies before the conveyance takes place, the one entitled to his personal property is entitled to the purchase price. (The one entitled to his real property only gets a bare legal title, which he must convey to the purchaser when the purchaser performs his duty under the contract, i.e., turns over the cash.)

(D) is wrong, because it misstates the rule of law, and, in any case, the concept of marketable title is irrelevant to these facts.

Title is not rendered unmarketable by the seller's death. A marketable title is one that, viewed objectively, is free from reasonable doubt in both law and fact, and that the reasonable buyer would accept without fear of litigation. The conveyance of marketable title is an implied covenant in land sale contracts. (However, the terms of the deed will control once the deed is conveyed and accepted; thus, if a quitclaim deed is conveyed, there will be no remaining obligation to provide marketable title.) Here, the mere fact that the seller died would not render the title unmarketable. Since the doctrine of equitable conversion is followed in the jurisdiction, there's no question that the one entitled to the seller's personal property—his son—will be entitled to the purchase price. Thus, there is no reasonable doubt as to law and fact, and there should be no reasonable fear of litigation. Therefore, the title is not unmarketable.

Answer 42

Choice **(D)** is correct. Under the doctrine of equitable conversion, the vendee is considered the beneficial owner of the property after the sales contract takes effect, leaving the vendor with a personal property interest in the property, in the form of the balance of the purchase price the vendee owes him. This common-law doctrine is followed by most states. In a state following equitable conversion, the vendee is required to close, even though the structures on the property have been destroyed. (But the vendee gets the benefit of any insurance policy the vendor may have had on the structure.)

(A) is wrong because it relies on a fact which is irrelevant: VanMeer's failure to insure the property is not dispositive of Landover's ability to recover the purchase price. Whether VanMeer did or did not buy insurance (which he could have — he had an insurable interest as soon as he signed the contract), Landover would still be able to force a closing, if and only if the jurisdiction applies equitable conversion (see Choice (D) above).

(B) is wrong because although it is a correct statement of the law, it would be insufficient, under these facts, to result in a decision for Landover. (B) is correct in that, in general, remedies at law (e.g., damages) are inadequate in actions where real estate is involved, since real estate is "unique." In such situations, specific performance is an appropriate remedy. However, specific performance is an *equitable* remedy, meaning that equitable considerations will be taken into account to determine if it's appropriate. Choice (D) is just such a consideration — the doctrine of equitable conversion. Conversely, if the jurisdiction does not apply equitable conversion, Landover won't be able to force a closing even though his remedy at law is inadequate.

(C) is wrong because it misstates the law. Specific performance is an equitable remedy. Equitable remedies are granted by determining whether the remedy will be just in the circumstances. As a result, the circumstances surrounding the contract *are* considered.

Answer 43

Choice **(D)** is correct. Under the equitable conversion doctrine, courts treat the signing of the contract as vesting equitable ownership of the land in the purchaser. (Conversely, the seller is treated as becoming the equitable owner of the purchase price.) Not all courts apply the doctrine of equitable conversion (though most do). When a court does apply the doctrine, the main result is that the risk of loss is deemed to belong to the equitable owner of the land, i.e., the buyer. So where, as here, the contract is unconditional and silent as to the risk of loss, if equitable conversion applies, the buyer will be deemed to bear the risk of loss and cannot cancel the contract.

(A) is wrong because it relies on an irrelevant fact. It does not matter who drafted the contract if it is silent as to risk of loss and there is no applicable statute. By contrast (and as further described in the analysis of Choice (D) above), it *does* matter whether the court applies the doctrine of equitable conversion. If the doctrine applies (as it does in the majority of courts), the risk of loss is deemed to pass to the buyer as soon as the contract is signed, assuming that the contract is silent on the risk-of-loss issue. If equitable conversion does not apply, the court will apply the minority common-law rule, under which the risk of loss remains with the seller until the closing.

(B) is wrong because it relies on an irrelevant fact. The contract became binding when the seller accepted the buyer's offer. The facts state that the offer to purchase was unconditional, so the buyer was obligated to purchase the house whether or not he got a loan commitment. In a jurisdiction applying equitable conversion, the buyer was thus the equitable owner as of the time seller signed an acceptance and, as of that moment, the buyer bore the risk of loss.

(C) is wrong because possession does not pass to the buyer until closing, absent a contrary provision in the contract of sale. On the other hand, equitable ownership passes on the signing of the contract, and that is enough to transfer the risk of loss to the buyer if the jurisdiction applies the doctrine of equitable conversion (as described above in the analysis of Choice (D)).

Answer 44

Choice (**A**) is correct, because the investor would have to assume the man's mortgage to be liable under it. When a person buys a mortgaged property without assuming the mortgage, the buyer has no liability on the mortgage. That's true even if the mortgage contains a due-on-sale clause. The clause will be enforced (and will entitle the mortgagee to accelerate the mortgage), but the clause won't cause the buyer to be deemed to have assumed the mortgage, and therefore won't require the buyer to pay for any missed payments.

(B) is wrong, because privity of estate is not an issue in mortgage cases. Privity of estate makes a difference in cases involving covenants at law. Absence of privity of estate may mean that a successor to the covenantor won't be bound. But a mortgage is not a covenant running with the land, so privity of estate doesn't matter.

(C) is wrong, because the violation of the due-on-sale clause didn't make the investor personally liable on the mortgage. A due-on-sale clause allows a lender to demand full payment of the remainder of an existing loan if the mortgagor transfers any interest in the property securing the loan without the lender's consent. The violation of the due-on-sale clause would give the bank grounds for a case against the man, and grounds to accelerate the mortgage, but not grounds to obtain a personal judgment against the investor. The investor did not assume the man's debt to the bank, and the violation of the due-on-sale clause does not change this fact.

(D) is wrong, because a mortgage is not a covenant running with the land, making privity of estate irrelevant. Privity of estate makes a difference in cases involving covenants running with land. A covenant running with the land is simply a contract between two parties, which, because it meets certain technical requirements, has the additional quality that it is binding against one who later buys the promisor's land. In determining whether a covenant runs with the land, one of the requirements is that there be privity of estate between the parties.

However, a mortgage is not a covenant running with the land. Therefore, the existence or non-existence of privity of estate as between the bank and the investor is irrelevant—the bank would only prevail against the investor if the investor expressly assumed the mortgage that existed between the man and the bank, which she didn't.

Answer 45

Choice (**C**) is correct. When a buyer assumes the seller's mortgage, the buyer becomes primarily liable for the mortgage debt. (The seller is secondarily liable, assuming there is no release.) The lender may therefore sue the buyer for the deficiency when a foreclosure sale is not sufficient to discharge the debt. (Contrast this to the situation where the buyer takes "subject to the mortgage." In that situation, the buyer would not be personally liable for the mortgage debt or for a deficiency judgment after foreclosure.)

When a buyer knowingly receives a deed that recites that the buyer is assuming the mortgage and intends to be bound, assumption occurs even though the buyer has not signed the deed. (Here, where the buyer previously signed the contract, which called for assumption, it's even more clear that the buyer will be deemed to have assumed even though he never signed the deed.)

(A) is wrong because it misstates the law. When a buyer agrees to "assume" a mortgage, this language is always interpreted to mean that if the lender forecloses and is left with a deficiency judgment, the lender can recover that deficiency from the assuming buyer without first trying to recover it from the original borrower. In other words, the assuming buyer becomes "primarily liable" for the mortgage debt and for any deficiency after foreclosure sale.

(B) is wrong because it was not necessary for the buyer to sign a promissory note to be liable. Once the buyer assumed the mortgage, he became primarily liable on the mortgage and thus is liable for the deficiency. (And the fact that the buyer didn't sign the deed doesn't prevent him from being deemed to have assumed, as long as the buyer knew the deed contained an assumption provision; see Choice (C) for more about this.)

(D) gives the right result but the wrong rationale. The buyer's assumption of the mortgage is not the same as a novation. With a novation, the bank agrees to *substitute* the personal liability of the buyer for that of the original debtor and *releases* the original debtor. Nothing in the facts suggests the bank's involvement in the transaction at all, let alone its willingness to release the original borrower.

Answer 46

Choice (**B**) is correct. Ashton is personally liable because she signed the original promissory note. Beam is personally liable because he assumed the mortgage by means of the document that conveyed to him (and the fact that Beam may not have signed the deed won't matter, as long as he was aware of the assumption language in the deed and intended to be bound by it.) First Bank can recover even though it was not a party to the Beam-to-Ashton promise, because First Bank would be found to be an intended beneficiary (and thus a third party beneficiary who may recover) of that promise. Carter is not personally liable, because a person who receives a conveyance stating that the transfer is "subject to" an outstanding mortgage does not, without more, assume (i.e., become personally liable for) the mortgage. Carter's lack of liability did not change by virtue of the fact that he made several timely payments; only an express promise of assumption by Carter (made either to Ashton, Beam or First Bank) could have rendered him personally liable.

(A), (C), and (D) are wrong to the extent that they are inconsistent with the above analysis.

Answer 47

Choice (**B**) is correct. The mortgage attached to the entire property, and payment of 1/2 the total amount therefore did not "free up" a 1/2 undivided interest. The investor as mortgagee has a lien on the *entire property*. That is, the investor received a security interest on the full property—and the concomitant right upon default to conduct a judicial sale of the full property to get her debt repaid—regardless of whether one party paid that party's full share. A.L.P. § 16.172. In other words, the investor is entitled to say, "Who paid what is between the two of you—I've got the right to have the whole property sold at foreclosure if any part of my loan is in default and the default is not wholly cured." That's what happened here. (The sister's remedy is a suit in contribution against the brother for 1/2 the amount she paid to the investor.)

(A) is wrong, because the investor did not have title to the property. A mortgage is a security interest in a property securing a loan. The fact that the mortgage instrument contained a clause in which the brother and sister warranted that they owned the property free of encumbrances (which is what the general warranty clause did) is irrelevant to the issue of whether the sister is entitled to quiet title.

(C) is wrong, because the equitable doctrine of marshaling does not apply to these facts. Marshaling is the ranking of assets in a certain order toward the payment of debts. The concept arises in equity, and means that where there are two creditors, with the senior one having two funds to satisfy his debt, that senior creditor must resort first to the fund which is not subject to demand of the junior creditor. The concept is misapplied to this fact pattern, because the doctrine would be one a second mortgagee invoked to protect his interest from the first mortgagee's foreclosure. Under these facts there is only one mortgage on the property, and as a party who joined with the brother in making the mortgage on the property, the sister would not be able to have her interest released.

(D) is wrong, because the sister would lose even if the cotenancy was joint. Joint tenancy differs from tenancy in common only with respect to the right of survivorship, which exists as to the former but not the latter. There is no difference in the legal analysis here between the joint-tenancy and tenancy-in-common scenarios.

Answer 48

Choice (A) is correct. The foreclosure sale of the bank's mortgage on the hotel was insufficient to pay the businessman's debt to the bank. The bank had received a judgment against the businessman for the entire amount of the defaulted loan. This lien was properly recorded and applied to all property owned by the businessman during the following ten-year time period, including the parking garage. After the financing company was paid in full from the funds generated by the foreclosure sale of its mortgage on the parking garage, the additional funds generated by that sale would be paid to the bank not as a deficiency judgment, but because of the unsatisfied amount of the prior money judgment.

(B) is incorrect. The judgment lien was properly filed against the businessman. Therefore, the garage was subject not only to the loan of the financing company, but also to the judgment lien as a second priority. The businessman would be entitled to surplus proceeds only if both liens had been fully paid.

(C) is incorrect. The foreclosure sale of the financing company's mortgage on the parking garage was sufficient to pay the businessman's debt to the financing company in full. The fact that the garage was sold for more money than was owed under the garage mortgage is irrelevant to the amount owed to the financing company — a mortgagee doesn't receive any part of the "surplus" after its mortgage has been paid in full.

(D) is incorrect for the same reason that (C) is incorrect.

Answer 49

Choice (A) is correct. In order to be valid, a deed must identify the grantee(s) with reasonable precision. Here, the grantees are "the leaders of all the Protestant churches in York County." It may be possible to identify with acceptable confidence all Protestant churches in the county, but it is unlikely that the "leader" of each church can be identified, given the imprecision of the term "leader" in the context of a church (is it the minister, or is it the president of the congregation, or is it the entire board of directors of the organization?). Where a deed does not identify the grantee with acceptable precision, the deed will be treated as if it had never been made. That would mean that the landowner died still holding title, which passed to the cousin.

(B) is wrong because the fact that the deed was recorded furnishes a strong presumption that delivery occurred (i.e., that the grantor intended the deed to take effect immediately, which is all that "delivery" means).

(C) is wrong because, while it may be true that a deed is presumed valid, the lack of an acceptably-precise designation of grantees here would be sufficient to rebut the presumption of validity.

(D) is wrong because, while recording will indeed create a *prima facie* (but rebuttable) case that delivery occurred, the problem here is not delivery but imprecision in the designation of the grantees.

Answer 50

Choice (**C**) is correct. Because Charles was dead at the time of the purported conveyance to the vendee and Charles as tenants in common, the deed's attempt to pass an interest to him was not effective (i.e., the deed was "void" as to him). Therefore, no interest passed through to his estate or via his estate to his nephew. The "Charles" portion of the tenancy in common therefore remained in the vendor. The deed was effective as to the vendee's interest, however, since she was correctly named and the deed was delivered to and accepted by her; therefore, she has the tenancy in common interest that the vendor intended to convey to her.

Choices (A), (B), and (D) are wrong because they are inconsistent with the above analysis.

Answer 51

Choice (**A**) is correct. An inter vivos gift (i.e., one made during the giver's lifetime) may be made of real estate. The gift is deemed made when "delivery" occurs, accompanied by the requisite donative intent. Here, the homeowner had the requisite donative intent as shown by his words. Delivery occurred when the homeowner physically handed the deed to the nephew's friend as the agent of the nephew; this was delivery because it is clear from the homeowner's words that he intended the gift to take place immediately rather than at some future time. Acceptance is presumed if the gift is beneficial. Once delivery occurred, the homeowner could not recall the gift.

(B) is wrong, because although the recording of a deed may create a presumption of delivery, here the delivery occurred prior to the recordation of the deed (at the moment the homeowner physically handed the deed to the nephew's friend as the agent of the nephew, with the intent to pass the title).

(C) is wrong, because a gift causa mortis may only be made of personal property. In addition, the gift was not made in view of pending death from a stated peril (the facts only note that the homeowner was ill).

(D) is wrong, because a testamentary document takes effect at the death of the testator and must have been executed with the requisite testamentary intent. Here, the homeowner wanted the nephew to have title immediately and thus delivered the deed to the nephew's friend; the homeowner did not want to postpone delivery until his death.

Answer 52

Choice (**A**) is correct. When Ogle delivered the deed to Lilly, she received a life estate, and nothing Ogle did thereafter could undo or modify that life estate. Therefore, the clause in Ogle's will leaving a life estate to Mina did not affect Lilly's life estate. (Instead, Mina got an executory life estate that would not start until Lilly's death.)

(B) is wrong because of the principle stated in Choice (A) above. (C) and (D) are wrong because of this same principle; notice that a grantor (here, Ogle) can create a life estate in the grantee, and the grantor's death does not act to terminate that life estate, as Choices (C) and (D) suggest that it would.

Answer 53

Choice (**A**) is correct. By concealing the fact that the present use was the subject of current enforcement proceedings, Seller would likely be found liable on a fraudulent misrepresentation theory. It is not certain that such a claim will succeed—the case may be found to fall within the general rule that nondisclosure is actionable only if the party who failed to disclose had an affirmative duty to do so, and that there was no such duty here. But the more likely result is that Seller will be found liable for his intentional nondisclosure. One ground for such a result is that a party to a business transaction is under a duty to disclose "facts basic to the transaction, if the [defendant] knows that the other is about to enter into it under a mistake as to [those facts], and that the other, because of the relationship between them, customs of the trade or other objective circumstances, would reasonably expect a disclosure of those facts." Rest. 2d (Torts) § 551(2)(e). Here, Buyer has a good chance of establishing that under the customs of the real estate trade, where a seller offers a properly for a particular use (warehousing with large trucks), which he knows the buyer intends to continue, the buyer would reasonably expect a disclosure that the legality of that present use is being contested by a governmental authority.

(B) is wrong, because the covenant of warranty protects the grantee only against an eviction or disturbance, due to absence of title or to an encumbrance. So the facts here fail to support a claim for breach of the warranty covenant in two respects: (1) the problem with using the loading docks was not a problem with title or an encumbrance (merely a problem that the existing use violated city rules), and (2) more fundamentally, Buyer has not been evicted or even threatened with eviction (he can stay on the property forever as long as he doesn't unload trailers in a way that blocks the street).

(C) is wrong, because each party gave a promise in consideration for the other's promise in the original contract of sale. In any event, any problem with consideration would have been eliminated, because any contract rights would have been deemed merged into the deed.

(D) is wrong, because any "mistake" was certainly not "mutual"—Seller knew all along that the present use was the subject of current enforcement proceedings.

Answer 54

Choice (**A**) is correct. An increasing number of courts now impose liability on a home seller who is aware of a material defect and who fails to disclose it to a buyer, where the defect is a latent one that cannot easily be found by an inspection. It is by no means certain that a court would find for Baker on this ground, but of the four possibilities this is the only one that offers Baker even a plausible chance of success.

(B) is wrong because Baker's having made a proper inspection, by itself, would not be enough to ensure him a victory. For instance, if the defect had been a "patent" one (one that ought to have been discovered by a reasonable inspection), virtually no courts would impose liability.

(C) is wrong because, while the fact that the condition constitutes a health hazard is a factor making liability slightly more likely, the key factor leading to liability is that the defect was latent (not readily discoverable), a factor that this choice does not refer to at all.

(D) is wrong because courts virtually never hold that the seller of a "used" house built by someone else makes an implied warranty of habitability or fitness for particular purpose; since the facts tell us that a prior owner built the house, this rule precludes liability on warranty-of-habitability grounds.

Answer 55

Choice (**B**) is correct. In most states, a land-sale contract is recordable, and the facts here tell us that this is so for the state in question (by telling us that Baker "properly recorded the contract"). Once the contract was recorded, it created an interest in land on the part of the vendee (namely, the right to buy on the stated terms) that was superior to any later-created interest in the property. Therefore, Baker's right to purchase was superior to the later-filed judgment lien obtained by Charlie. Consequently, Able would be deemed to have marketable title, because notwithstanding the judgment lien he was capable of conveying the property free and clear to Baker.

(A) is wrong because it states the right result, but for the wrong reason. A purchaser would not always take free of a judgment lien; for instance, a purchaser would not take free of a judgment lien that was filed before the purchase contract. It is only the fact that the sale contract was recorded before the judgment lien was filed that lets the purchaser here take free of the lien.

(C) is wrong because Able can indeed benefit from Baker's action in recording. The issue is whether Able can convey marketable title to Baker, and the fact that Baker recorded means that Able can do this; there is no rule that one party cannot benefit from the other's action in recording.

(D) is wrong because it is a misstatement of law. The statute creating judgment liens merely describes that a judgment lien is an interest in property; the statute does not say anything about priorities, a subject that is left to the recording act. Under the recording act, an early-filed interest in land (here, the vendee's rights under the sale contract) takes priority over a later-filed interest (here, the judgment lien).

Answer 56

Choice (C) is correct. The goal of recording statutes is to protect subsequent bona fide purchasers and incumbrancers—those who pay value and take without notice of prior conveyances, in good faith. Here, Caruso is a bona fide purchaser, because he has no notice of any defects in the chain of title. The price he paid, $60,000, was a bargain compared to what Devlin asked previously, but this would not in and of itself negate his bona fide purchaser status, since it would still constitute "value" and would not, barring other facts, indicate something untoward was involved. Since the chain of title indicates that Parnell was conveying marketable title, Caruso was not obligated to look further. Choice (C) goes on to suggest that Devlin is "estopped" from denying the validity of the deed. An estoppel occurs, in facts like these, when one has done or omitted to do something, and is as a result forbidden from pleading or proving an otherwise-important fact. Here, Devlin's carelessness in allowing Parnell to fill in the deed will lead to his being bound by the resultant deed—he'll be "estopped" from denying its validity.

(A) is wrong because the Statute of Frauds would *not* prevent proof of Devlin's and Parnell's oral agreement. Devlin is trying to show that the deed he signed has the wrong lot number on it, due to Parnell's wrongdoing. That's not a contracts problem, and the Statute of Frauds applies only to contracts. Except for the estoppel problem (discussed in (C)), Devlin would be able to show that the deed as filed was not genuine (i.e., was a forgery as to the lot number). And that would be true even though Devlin's proof would consist of proof of an oral agreement. So the Statute of Frauds wouldn't be relevant.

(B) is wrong because it states an incorrect rule of law: Recording a deed does not preclude any question as to its genuineness. The mere act of recording would not, for instance, make a fraudulent deed genuine. The upshot, nonetheless, might be that, *despite* the fact that a deed is incorrect, *the bona fide purchaser may still prevail,* on grounds of estoppel. But (B) states as a concrete rule that recording a deed means its genuineness cannot be questioned, and this is incorrect.

(D) is wrong because it misstates the facts: Devlin's hands are not "unclean." Under the equitable doctrine of "unclean hands," one who has acted "unconscionably," or in a morally reprehensible manner, cannot recover. Here, at most Devlin has behaved negligently; there is no basis on which to attach any bad faith to his behavior. If anything, he was gullible in trusting

Parnell to fill in the blank in the deed as instructed; but the creation of the agency did not involve wrongdoing. If anyone, it's Parnell who's the wrongdoer.

Answer 57

Choice **(B)** is correct. Where the language of the recording act is ambiguous about whether judgment creditors are covered (e.g., where, as here, "purchasers for value" are what are covered), most courts have interpreted the statute so as not to cover the judgment creditor. There is no guarantee that a court would interpret the statute in this anti-creditor way, but that's at least a possibility, and of the four choices this is the most likely explanation for an anti-creditor result. (Remember, you're not asked to say how the case will come out—you're merely asked to say what the most likely rationale will be *if* the case is decided for the buyer.)

(A) is wrong because the doctrine of equitable conversion has nothing to do with any issue presented by this question. Equitable conversion, where the court chooses to apply it, makes a vendor under a land-sale agreement the "equitable seller," and the vendee the "equitable buyer." The main consequence of the doctrine's application is that risk of loss passes to the buyer upon the signing of the contract, even though the seller still holds the legal title.

(C) is wrong, because the seller's possession would not suggest the seller had sold the property to the buyer. Under a recording statute like the one here, a subsequent bona fide purchaser (i.e., a person who gives valuable consideration and has no actual or constructive notice of the prior instrument) prevails over a prior grantee who failed to record. If the creditor was trying to become covered by the recording act, and *the buyer* had been in possession at the time the creditor filed her lien, the fact that the buyer (not the seller, who was the record owner) was in possession at the date of lien filing might have been enough to cause the buyer to lose, since this possession might have put her on inquiry notice that the seller was perhaps no longer the owner. But the fact that *the seller* was still in possession didn't put the buyer on notice of anything, so it's irrelevant on these facts.

(D) is wrong, because recording acts protect the second, not the first, purchaser in certain circumstances. Here, it would be the creditor (who can argue that she "purchased" by filing her lien), not the buyer, who is trying to get the protection of the recording act. It is the person seeking the protection of the recording act (the second purchaser), not the person resisting application of the act (the first purchaser) who needs to be "without notice." So here, the notice status of the creditor might well matter (if the recording act otherwise applied to judgment lien creditors). But the notice status of the buyer, the first "purchaser," does not matter at all.

Answer 58

Choice **(B)** is correct. Smollett could win only if he were protected by the recording act. This is so because without the recording act's protection, Smollet would have to lose since Baker received his conveyance before Smollett filed his lien (meaning that Able no longer had any interest in the property at the moment Smollett's judgment became a lien on Able's "property" by means of Smollett's filing). In most jurisdictions, if the recording act protects only "purchasers for value," a judgment creditor will not be deemed to be a "purchaser." So if Smollett were found not to be a purchaser, and therefore not to receive any protection from the recording act, he would lose. It is not certain that the recording act here would be interpreted so as to not protect lien creditors, but of the four choices, this is the only one that could plausibly yield a defeat for Smollett.

(A) is wrong because Able's warranty of title to Baker might help Baker in a suit against Able, but would not help Baker in a suit against Smollett. Where a party (here, Baker) doesn't record immediately (or within the applicable grace period if any), nothing in that party's deed can save her from losing to a subsequent purchaser for value who is protected by the recording act. (That's the purpose of recording acts—to protect subsequent purchasers for value, and to allow them to rely on the record as of the time of the subsequent purchase.)

(C) is wrong because it is a gross misstatement of law, especially the law of the jurisdiction in question here. The first statute cited in the question gives a filed judgment a lien against all real property then owned by the judgment debtor; so if the judgment had been filed before the conveyance to Baker, the judgment lien would indeed be superior to Baker's deed (which this choice says could never happen).

(D) is wrong because, when a recording act does not have a grace period, the purchaser takes the risk of a subsequent purchaser's gaining rights in the gap between the first conveyance and a recording of that conveyance, no matter how small this gap is. (If there *had* been a grace period of more than four days, this choice would have been a good explanation of why Smollett would lose.)

Answer 59

Choice (**C**) is correct. This is a race notice statute, since it says that it protects only "subsequent purchasers for value without notice, *who shall first record.*" Therefore, the investor could only obtain the protection of the recording statute if he recorded before the prior interest (the bank's mortgage) was recorded. Since the bank recorded on Jan. 18 and the investor on Jan. 23, the investor did not satisfy the record-first requirement. Therefore, the recording act does not apply, and the bank wins under the common-law principle that the first-in-time conveyance takes priority over the second conveyance.

(A) is wrong because, while the investor's paying valuable consideration and taking without notice prior to the bank's recording were *necessary* elements for him to be covered by the recording act, they were not *sufficient* elements—he was also required to record first.

(B) is wrong because there is no principle of estoppel by which a party who delays in recording loses the right to rely on the recording act; the only risk taken by the delaying party is that during the delay, a subsequent purchaser may meet the requirements for protection under the recording act.

(D) is wrong because it gives an incorrect explanation for the correct result: After the bank received its mortgage, it would still lose to a subsequent purchaser for value without notice who beat it to the recording office.

Answer 60

Choice (**B**) is correct. The bank was the first grantee of both the note and the mortgage, so the bank is the owner unless the recording act somehow gave the investor superior title. When the bank promptly recorded the assignment to it of the note and mortgage, the bank complied with all requirements of the recording act. Therefore, no later assignment by the mortgage company to the investor (or anyone else) could take priority, under the recording act, over the assignment to the bank. The fact that the investor paid value for his assignment, and without actual notice of the prior assignment to the bank, doesn't change any of this—the investor is deemed to be on notice of what a proper record search would have indicated, and here a search of the mortgage company in the records would have disclosed the prior assignment to the bank. Similarly, the fact that the mortgage company kept possession of the note and mortgage after assigning these to the bank makes no difference; the investor as second grantee cannot take priority over a prior conveyance that was properly recorded.

(A), (C), and (D) are wrong because they are inconsistent with the above analysis.

Answer 61

Choice (**B**) is correct. The man met all the requirements of the recording statute: He took for value, he took without notice of the prior conveyance, and he recorded before the prior conveyance was recorded. Once the man met those requirements, his interest cut off all rights of the prior grantee (the woman) who didn't record first. The man therefore had the ability to pass a valid title to his nephew, even though the nephew did not take for value, and even though the nephew was on record notice of the woman's claim at the time he took (since by then the woman had recorded).

(A) is wrong because it is not the woman's status as a donee that causes her to lose, it is the fact that she did not record before a subsequent BFP (the man) recorded. Remember that under recording acts, it is never significant whether the *first* grantee took for value; it only matters whether the *subsequent* grantee, who is trying to take advantage of the recording act, took for value.

(C) is wrong because the fact that the woman recorded before the nephew cannot save her; once a subsequent grantee (the man) took for value and without notice and then recorded first, a person downstream from that subsequent grantee (the nephew) wins against the original late-filing grantee regardless of whether the downstreamer took for value, took without notice, or recorded first.

(D) is wrong because the fact that the nephew did not give value doesn't matter; as with Choice (C), once the subsequent grantee (the man) got the protection of the recording act, it doesn't matter whether a person downstream from him gave value, recorded first, or took without notice.

Answer 62

Choice (**D**) is correct. This is a complicated fact pattern, but the essential information is that the buyer purchased the lot from the investor before the friend recorded his mortgage. Thus, (1) the buyer was a bona fide purchaser (BFP) for value and is protected by the recording statute; and (2) the bank who lent to the buyer is also protected despite the fact that the buyer knew of the prior mortgage when it lent.

The jurisdiction's recording act is a "notice" statute because it provides, "No conveyance or mortgage of real property shall be good against subsequent purchasers for value and without notice *unless same be recorded according to law.*" A notice statute protects only a subsequent taker who takes for value and without notice of the prior conveyance or mortgage. (Because this is a pure notice rather than race-notice statute, the subsequent taker doesn't have to have recorded before the prior grantee or mortgagee records.) Notice can be actual, record, or inquiry. The facts do not indicate that the buyer had actual notice of the friend's mortgage. Since the friend had not recorded the mortgage at the time the buyer purchased the lot, the buyer did not have record notice. Finally, the property is a vacant lot; so even if the buyer had inspected the property, she would not have been put on inquiry notice of the friend's mortgage. Thus, the buyer is a BFP (i.e., she took without any kind of notice) and receives the protection of the recording act. Therefore, the friend's lien is unenforceable against the buyer (or against anyone who deals with her, as we'll see in a minute).

The bank's mortgage, on the other hand, *is* an enforceable lien against the property, because the buyer is a party to the mortgage and the bank promptly and properly recorded the mortgage. (Even if you did not know this, you would be able to pick the correct answer by eliminating the other three choices, which all rely on the friend's having an enforceable lien.)

And the fact that the bank made its loan while having notice (both actual and record) of the prior mortgage to the friend does not prevent the bank's mortgage from being a valid first lien—that's because the buyer took free of the friend's mortgage for the reasons described above, and once the buyer had this free-and-clear title she was entitled to place a first mortgage on it (or re-sell it) regardless of the state of knowledge possessed by the new mortgagee (or new buyer). If the rule were otherwise, an innocent buyer would never be able to take out a first mortgage or re-sell, if the holder of a prior interest who didn't record promptly eventually recorded, as happened here.

(A) is wrong because, for the reasons explained in the analysis of Choice (D), the friend did not have an enforceable lien against the property. Thus, the fact that the friend recorded before the bank is irrelevant.

(B) is wrong because, for the reasons explained in the analysis of Choice (D), the friend did not have an enforceable lien against the property. This answer choice misstates the significance of the buyer's being an innocent purchaser for value. The buyer's BFP status protects her from the enforcement of the friend's lien; it does not affect the "priority" of the liens (since there is only one valid lien, the bank's).

(C) is wrong because, for the reasons explained in the analysis of Choice (D), the friend did not have an enforceable lien against the property. The friend recorded too late to prevent the buyer from being a BFP; so, the fact that the buyer later learned of the friend's mortgage is of no consequence—the buyer took free of the friend's mortgage. Once the buyer had this free-and-clear title, she was entitled to place a first mortgage on it (or sell it) regardless of the state of knowledge possessed by the new mortgagee (or new buyer). Such a rule is necessary to protect the innocent buyer's financing and resale market. See the analysis of Choice (D) for more about this.

Answer 63

Choice (**B**) is correct. Normally, an owner's refusal to abate a naturally-occurring condition on his land will not be deemed to be a nuisance. But nearly all courts have long recognized an exception for trees that pose the risk of falling on the public highway, and some courts have extended this exception to trees that pose a risk of physical danger to those on adjacent non-highway property. A court would not necessarily find that the risk of danger from the fallen trees makes the condition a nuisance, but of the four choices this is the only one that could plausibly lead to a finding of nuisance.

(A) is wrong because, while impact on real estate values might a reason for holding that a *man-made* feature poses a nuisance, it would not be grounds for overruling the usual rule that failure to abate a naturally-occurring condition is a nuisance.

(C) is wrong for the same reason as (A): While a violation of community aesthetic standards might be a reason for holding that a man-made feature poses a nuisance, it would not be grounds for overruling the usual rule that failure to abate a naturally-occurring condition is not a nuisance.

(D) is wrong because the fact that a condition cannot be challenged by any other law or ordinance does not mean that the court will find it to constitute a nuisance—the homeowner will have to show that the conditions here cause him a substantial interference with his use and enjoyment of his property, and the fact that the condition doesn't violate a law or ordinance doesn't say anything about whether the homeowner can meet this standard.

Answer 64

Choice (**A**) is correct. This water is diffuse surface water. Although there are three different views regarding the way an owner may *expel* such water if he doesn't want it, there is only one view about whether the owner may impound it if he does want it: The rule is that an owner such as the farmer may impound all such water, at least in the absence of any malice (and there is none here).

(B) is wrong because although this option correctly concludes that the farmer will prevail, it misstates the reason why this is so. At least in the absence of malice, either landowner may impound diffuse surface waters, and that would be true even if the other party hadn't also previously impounded (so that the doctrine of estoppel doesn't apply).

(C) is wrong because water from melting snows and rain is diffuse surface water. Riparian waters are waters with defined beds and banks, such as streams, rivers, and lakes, and a riparian owner is one whose land borders such waters. Here, the only water at issue is diffuse surface water, and the rule for such waters is as stated in the discussion of Choice (A).

(D) is wrong because as described above, either party may impound surface waters that are on his own land, and the doctrine of estoppel would not apply to change this general rule.

Answer 65

Choice **(D)** is correct. A landowner has no legal right to have sunlight continue to reach her building. For example, it is not a nuisance for one owner to block another owner's access to sunlight, even if the consequence of the blockage is to reduce the latter building's rental or market value.

Since Doris has done nothing wrong, both (A) and (B) are incorrect.

Although (C) states the right result, the fact that Doris secured all necessary government approvals is not dispositive; for instance, if the government-approved building built by Doris had released noxious odors that substantially impaired the value of Pauline's building, the fact that Doris had obtained all necessary permits would not be a defense to Pauline's nuisance suit.

Answer 66

Choice **(D)** is correct. A landowner has no legal right to have sunlight continue to reach her building. Therefore, it is not a nuisance or other violation for one owner to block another owner's access to sunlight, even if the consequence of the blockage is to reduce the latter building's rental or market value.

Since the defendant has done nothing wrong, (A), (B), and (C) are all incorrect.

TORTS

TORTS QUESTIONS BY TOPIC

CHAPTER 1

INTENTIONAL TORTS AGAINST THE PERSON

I. BATTERY

A. Intent

1. Intent to create apprehension of contact

Question 1

A golfer was annoyed that his caddie was joking about the golfer's bad last shot. The golfer swung his newly-purchased golf club in the direction of the caddie's head, intending to frighten the caddie but not to hit him. The caddie started to duck to avoid the blow. The golfer stopped his swing so that the club would not have hit the caddie, except that due to the club manufacturer's negligence the club head flew off and hit the caddie in the top of the head, seriously injuring him. The caddie will be able to recover for:

(A) assault but not battery.

(B) battery but not assault.

(C) assault and battery.

(D) neither battery nor assault.

Question 2

Peter and Donald were in the habit of playing practical jokes on each other on their respective birthdays. On Peter's birthday, Donald sent Peter a cake containing an ingredient that he knew had, in the past, made Peter very ill. After Peter had eaten a piece of the cake, he suffered severe stomach pains and had to be taken to the hospital by ambulance. On the way to the hospital, the ambulance driver suffered a heart attack, which caused the ambulance to swerve from the road and hit a tree. As a result of the collision, Peter suffered a broken leg.

In a suit by Peter against Donald to recover damages for Peter's broken leg, Peter will

(A) prevail, because Donald knew that the cake would be harmful or offensive to Peter.

(B) prevail, only if the ambulance driver was negligent.

(C) not prevail, because Donald could not reasonably be expected to foresee injury to Peter's leg.

(D) not prevail, because the ambulance driver's heart attack was a superseding cause of Peter's broken leg.

2. D must intend contact

Question 3

Plaintiff, a jockey, was seriously injured in a race when another jockey, Daring, cut too sharply in front of her without adequate clearance. The two horses collided, causing Plaintiff to fall to the ground, sustaining injury. The State Racetrack Commission ruled that, by cutting in too sharply, Daring committed a foul in violation of racetrack rules requiring adequate clearance for crossing lanes. Plaintiff has brought an action against Daring for damages in which one count is based on battery.

Will Plaintiff prevail on the battery claim?

(A) Yes, if Daring was reckless in cutting across in front of Plaintiff's horse.

(B) Yes, because the State Racetrack Commission determined that Daring committed a foul in violation of rules applicable to racing.

(C) No, unless Daring intended to cause impermissible contact between the two horses or apprehension of such contact by Plaintiff.

(D) No, because Plaintiff assumed the risk of accidental injury inherent in riding as a jockey in a horse race.

3. D must intend contact with a "person"

Question 4

Peavey was walking peacefully along a public street when he encountered Dorwin, whom he had never seen before. Without provocation or warning, Dorwin picked up a rock and struck Peavey with it. It was later established that Dorwin was mentally ill and suffered recurrent hallucinations.

If Peavey asserts a claim against Dorwin based on battery, which of the following, if supported by evidence, will be Dorwin's best defense?

(A) Dorwin did not understand that his act was wrongful.

(B) Dorwin did not desire to cause harm to Peavey.

(C) Dorwin did not know that he was striking a person.

(D) Dorwin thought Peavey was about to attack him.

B. Harmful or offensive contact

1. Contact beyond level consented to

Question 5

A professional football player signed a written consent for his team's physician to perform a knee operation. After the player was under a general anesthetic, the physician asked a world-famous orthopedic surgeon to perform the operation. The surgeon's skills were superior to the physician's, and the operation was successful.

In an action for battery by the player against the surgeon, the player will

(A) prevail, because the player did not agree to allow the surgeon to perform the operation.

(B) prevail, because the consent form was in writing.

(C) not prevail, because the surgeon's skills were superior to the physician's.

(D) not prevail, because the operation was successful.

C. Extends to personal effects

1. Indirect contact

Question 6

A customer ordered some merchandise from a retail store. After a dispute about payment, the store turned the account over to a bill collector. The bill collector called at the customer's house at 7 p.m. on a summer evening while many of the customer's neighbors were seated on their porches. When the customer opened the door, the bill collector, who was standing just outside the door, raised an electrically amplified bullhorn to his mouth. In a voice that could be heard a block away, the bill collector called the customer a "deadbeat" and asked him when he intended to pay his bill to the store. The customer, greatly angered, slammed the door shut. The door struck the bullhorn and jammed it forcibly against the bill collector's face. As a consequence, the bill collector lost some of his front teeth.

If the bill collector asserts a claim of battery against the customer, will the bill collector prevail?

(A) Yes, because the customer had not first asked the bill collector to leave the property.

(B) Yes, if the customer knew that the door was substantially certain to strike the bullhorn.

(C) No, if the bill collector's conduct triggered the customer's response.

(D) No, because the bill collector was an intruder on the customer's property.

II. ASSAULT

A. Actual contact or apprehension of contact

Question 7

A host pointed an unloaded revolver at her guest, threatening to shoot him. The guest knew that the revolver was not loaded, and that the ammunition for the revolver was stored in a locked basement closet, two stories below where the two were then standing.

In an action brought by the guest against the host for assault, will the guest prevail?

(A) No, because the host did not intend to shoot her guest.

(B) No, because the host did not put her guest in apprehension of an imminent contact.

(C) Yes, because the ammunition was accessible to the host.

(D) Yes, because the host threatened her guest with a revolver.

B. Imminence of contact

Question 8

Pocket, a bank vice president, took substantial kickbacks to approve certain loans that later proved worthless. Upon learning of the kickbacks, Dudd, the bank's president, fired Pocket, telling him, "If you are not out of this bank in ten minutes, I will have the guards throw you out bodily." Pocket left at once.

If Pocket asserts a claim against Dudd based on assault, will Pocket prevail?

(A) No, because the guards never touched Pocket.

(B) No, because Dudd gave Pocket ten minutes to leave.

(C) Yes, if Dudd intended to cause Pocket severe emotional distress.

(D) Yes, because Dudd threatened Pocket with a harmful or offensive bodily contact.

III. INTENTIONAL INFLICTION OF EMOTIONAL DISTRESS ("IIED")

A. "Extreme and outrageous"

Question 9

Poe ordered some merchandise from Store. When the merchandise was delivered, Poe decided that it was not what he had ordered, and he returned it for credit. Store refused to credit Poe's account, continued to bill him, and, after 90 days, turned the account over to Kane, a bill collector, for collection.

Kane called at Poe's house at 7 p.m. on a summer evening while many of Poe's neighbors were seated on their porches. When Poe opened the door, Kane, who was standing just outside the door, raised an electrically amplified bullhorn to his mouth. In a voice that could be heard a block away, Kane called Poe a "deadbeat" and asked him when he intended to pay his bill to Store. Poe, greatly angered, slammed the door shut. Poe's neighbors teased him on and off for several weeks about being a deadbeat, causing him severe embarrassment.

If Poe asserts a claim based on intentional infliction of emotional distress against Kane, will Poe prevail?

(A) Yes, because Kane's conduct was extreme and outrageous.

(B) Yes, because Kane was intruding on Poe's property.

(C) No, unless Poe suffered physical harm.

(D) No, if Poe still owed Store for the merchandise.

B. Actual severe distress

Question 10

Dumont, a real estate developer, was trying to purchase land on which he intended to build a large commercial development. Perkins, an elderly widow, had rejected all of Dumont's offers to buy her ancestral home, where she had lived all her life and which was located in the middle of Dumont's planned development. Finally, Dumont offered her $250,000. He told her that it was his last offer and that if she rejected it, state law authorized him to have her property condemned.

Perkins then consulted her nephew, a law student, who researched the question and advised her that Dumont had no power of condemnation under state law. Perkins had been badly frightened by Dumont's threat, and was outraged when she learned that Dumont had lied to her.

If Perkins sues Dumont for damages for emotional distress, will she prevail?

(A) Yes, if Dumont's action was extreme and outrageous.

(B) Yes, because Perkins was frightened and outraged.

(C) No, if Perkins did not suffer emotional distress that was severe.

(D) No, if it was not Dumont's purpose to cause emotional distress.

Question 11

Dayton operates a collection agency. He was trying to collect a $400 bill for medical services rendered to Pratt by Doctor.

Dayton went to Pratt's house and when Martina, Pratt's mother, answered the door, Dayton told Martina he was there to collect a bill owed by Pratt. Martina told Dayton that because of her illness, Pratt had been unemployed for six months, that she was still ill and unable to work, and that she would pay the bill as soon as she could.

Dayton, in a loud voice, demanded to see Pratt and said that if he did not receive payment immediately, he would file a criminal complaint charging her with fraud. Pratt, hearing the conversation, came to the door. Dayton, in a loud voice, repeated his demand for immediate payment and his threat to use criminal process.

If Pratt asserts a claim against Dayton, based on infliction of emotional distress, will Pratt prevail?

(A) Yes, if Pratt suffered severe emotional distress as a result of Dayton's conduct.

(B) Yes, unless the bill for medical services was valid and past due.

(C) No, unless Pratt suffered physical harm as a result of Dayton's conduct.

(D) No, if Dayton's conduct created no risk of physical harm to Pratt.

C. Suits by public figures

Question 12

Doe, the governor of State, signed a death warrant for Rend, a convicted murderer. Able and Baker are active opponents of the death penalty. At a demonstration protesting the execution of Rend, Able and Baker carried large signs that stated, "Governor Doe, Murderer." Television station XYZ broadcast news coverage of the demonstration, including pictures of the signs carried by Able and Baker. If Doe asserts against XYZ a claim for damages for intentional infliction of emotional distress, will Doe prevail?

(A) Yes, if the broadcast showing the signs caused Doe to suffer severe emotional distress.

(B) Yes, because the assertion on the signs was extreme and outrageous.

(C) No, unless Doe suffered physical harm as a consequence of the emotional distress caused by the signs.

(D) No, because XYZ did not publish a false statement of fact with "actual malice."

INTENTIONAL INTERFERENCE WITH PROPERTY

I. TRESPASS TO LAND

A. Intent

1. Involuntary entry onto land of another

Question 13

A car driven by Dan entered land owned by and in the possession of Peter, without Peter's permission.

Which, if any, of the following allegations, without additional facts, would provide a sufficient basis for a claim by Peter against Dan?

I.   Dan intentionally drove his car onto Peter's land.

II. Dan negligently drove his car onto Peter's land

III. Dan's car damaged Peter's land.

(A) I only.

(B) III only.

(C) I, II, or III.

(D) Neither I, nor II, nor III.

2. Effect of mistake

Question 14

David built in his backyard a garage that encroached two feet across the property line onto property owned by his neighbor, Prudence. Thereafter, David sold his property to Drake. Prudence was unaware, prior to David's sale to Drake, of the encroachment of the garage onto her property. When she thereafter learned of the encroachment, she sued David for damages for trespass.

In this action, will Prudence prevail?

(A) No, unless David was aware of the encroachment when the garage was built.

(B) No, because David no longer owns or possesses the garage.

(C) Yes, because David knew where the garage was located, whether or not he knew where the property line was.

(D) Yes, unless Drake was aware of the encroachment when he purchased the property.

II. CONVERSION

A. Forced sale

Question 15

Dower, an inexperienced driver, borrowed a car from Puder, a casual acquaintance, for the express purpose of driving it several blocks to the local drug store. Instead, Dower drove the car, which then was worth $12,000, 100 miles to Other City. While Dower was driving in

Other City the next day, the car was hit by a negligently driven truck and sustained damage that will cost $3,000 to repair. If repaired, the car will be fully restored to its former condition.

If Puder asserts a claim against Dower based on conversion, Puder should recover a judgment for

(A) $12,000.

(B) $3,000.

(C) $3,000 plus damages for the loss of the use of the car during its repair.

(D) nothing, unless Dower was negligent and his negligence was a substantial cause of the collision.

CHAPTER 3

DEFENSES TO INTENTIONAL TORTS

I. SELF-DEFENSE

A. Degree of force

Question 16

In a plaintiff's action for battery, the evidence established that the plaintiff was bad-tempered and, the defendant knew, carried a gun and used it often; that the plaintiff struck the defendant first; that during the altercation, the plaintiff repeatedly tried to get to his gun; and that the blows inflicted upon the plaintiff by the defendant resulted in the plaintiff being hospitalized.

Which finding of fact would be most likely to result in a verdict for the defendant?

(A) The defendant used no more force than he actually believed was necessary to protect himself against death or serious bodily harm.

(B) The defendant used no more force than he reasonably believed was necessary to protect himself against death or serious bodily harm.

(C) The defendant, in fact, feared death or serious bodily harm.

(D) The defendant was justified in retaliating against the plaintiff because the plaintiff struck the first blow.

B. Injury to third person

Question 17

In the course of a bank holdup, Robber fired a gun at Guard. Guard drew his revolver and returned the fire. One of the bullets fired by Guard ricocheted, striking Plaintiff.

If Plaintiff asserts a claim against Guard based upon battery, will Plaintiff prevail?

(A) Yes, unless Plaintiff was Robber's accomplice.

(B) Yes, under the doctrine of transferred intent.

(C) No, if Guard fired reasonably in his own defense.

(D) No, if Guard did not intend to shoot Plaintiff.

II. DEFENSE OF OTHERS

A. General rule

1. Unreasonable mistake

Question 18

A pedestrian was crossing a street at a crosswalk. A jogger who was on the sidewalk nearby saw a speeding automobile heading in the pedestrian's direction. The jogger ran into the street and pushed the pedestrian out of the path of the car. The pedestrian fell to the ground and broke her leg.

In an action for battery brought by the pedestrian against the jogger, will the pedestrian prevail?

(A) Yes, because the jogger could have shouted a warning instead of pushing the pedestrian out of the way.

(B) Yes, if the pedestrian was not actually in danger and the jogger should have realized it.

(C) No, because the driver of the car was responsible for the pedestrian's injury.

(D) No, if the jogger's intent was to save the pedestrian, not to harm her.

III. NECESSITY

A. Private necessity

1. Compensation for actual damage

Question 19

Husband and Wife, walking on a country road, were frightened by a bull running loose on the road. They climbed over a fence to get onto the adjacent property, owned by Grower. After climbing over the fence, Husband and Wife damaged some of Grower's plants which were near the fence. The fence was posted with a large sign, "No Trespassing."

Grower saw Husband and Wife and came toward them with his large watchdog on a long leash. The dog rushed at Wife. Grower had intended only to frighten Husband and Wife, but the leash broke, and before Grower could restrain the dog, the dog bit Wife.

If Grower asserts a claim against Wife and Husband for damage to his plants, will Grower prevail?

(A) Yes, because Wife and Husband entered on his land without permission.

(B) Yes, because Grower had posted his property with a "No Trespassing" sign.

(C) No, because Wife and Husband were confronted by an emergency situation.

(D) No, because Grower used excessive force toward Wife and Husband.

NEGLIGENCE GENERALLY

I. THE REASONABLE PERSON

A. Physical and mental characteristics

1. Children

Question 20

Dora, who was eight years old, went to the grocery store with her mother. Dora pushed the grocery cart while her mother put items into it. Dora's mother remained near Dora at all times. Peterson, another customer in the store, noticed Dora pushing the cart in a manner that caused Peterson no concern. A short time later, the cart Dora was pushing struck Peterson in the knee, inflicting serious injury.

If Peterson brings an action, based on negligence, against Dora, Dora's best argument in defense would be that

(A) Dora exercised care commensurate with her age, intelligence, and experience.

(B) Dora is not subject to tort liability.

(C) Dora was subject to parental supervision.

(D) Peterson assumed the risk that Dora might hit Peterson with the cart.

B. Anticipating conduct of others

1. Anticipating negligence by the other

a. Inadequate parental supervision

Question 21

An eight-year-old girl went to the grocery store with her mother. The girl pushed the grocery cart while her mother put items into it. The girl's mother remained near the girl at all times. The plaintiff, another customer in the store, noticed the girl pushing the cart in a manner that caused the plaintiff no concern. A short time later, the cart the girl was pushing struck the plaintiff in the knee, inflicting serious injury.

If the plaintiff brings an action, based on negligence, against the girl's mother, will the plaintiff prevail?

(A) Yes, if the girl was negligent.

(B) Yes, because the girl's mother is responsible for any harm caused by the girl.

(C) Yes, because the girl's mother assumed the risk of her child's actions.

(D) Yes, if the girl's mother did not adequately supervise the girl's actions.

2. Anticipating criminal or intentionally tortious acts by the other

Question 22

A light company is the sole distributor of electrical power in a city. The company owns and maintains all of the electric poles and equipment in the city. The light company has complied with the National Electrical Safety Code, which establishes minimum requirements for the installation and maintenance of power poles. The Code has been approved by the federal and state governments.

The light company has had to replace insulators on its poles repeatedly because unknown persons repeatedly shoot at and destroy them. This causes the power lines to fall to the ground. On one of these occasions, a 5-year-old boy wandered out of his parents' yard, intentionally touched a downed wire, and was seriously burned.

If a claim on the boy's behalf is asserted against the light company, the probable result is that the boy will

(A) recover, if the light company could have taken reasonable steps to prevent the lines from falling when the insulators were destroyed.

(B) recover, because a supplier of electricity is strictly liable in tort.

(C) not recover, unless the light company failed to exercise reasonable care to stop the destruction of the insulators.

(D) not recover, because the destruction of the insulators was intentional.

Question 23

A construction company was digging a trench for a new sewer line in a street in a high-crime neighborhood. During the course of the construction, there had been many thefts of tools and equipment from the construction area. One night, the construction company's employees neglected to place warning lights around the trench. A delivery truck drove into the trench and broke an axle. While the delivery driver was looking for a telephone to summon a tow truck, thieves broke into the delivery truck and stole $350,000 worth of goods. The delivery company sued the construction company to recover for the $350,000 loss and for $1,500 worth of damage to its truck. The construction company stipulated that it was negligent in failing to place warning lights around the trench, and admits liability for damage to the truck, but denies liability for the loss of the goods.

On cross-motions for summary judgment, how should the court rule?

(A) Deny both motions, because there is evidence to support a finding that the construction company should have realized that its negligence could create an opportunity for a third party to commit a crime.

(B) Grant the construction company's motion, because no one could have foreseen that the failure to place warning lights could result in the loss of a cargo of valuable goods.

(C) Grant the construction company's motion, because the criminal acts of third persons were a superseding cause of the loss.

(D) Grant the delivery company's motion, because but for the construction company's actions, the goods would not have been stolen.

a. Premises liability

Question 24

The plaintiff and a salesman, who were strangers to each other, were passengers sitting in adjoining seats on an airline flight. There were many empty seats on the aircraft.

During the flight, a flight attendant served the salesman nine drinks. As the salesman became more and more obviously intoxicated and attempted to engage the plaintiff in a conversation, the plaintiff chose to ignore the salesman. This angered the salesman, who suddenly struck the plaintiff in the face, giving her a black eye. If the plaintiff asserts a claim for damages against the airline based on negligence, the plaintiff will

(A) not recover, because a person is not required by law to come to the assistance of another who is imperiled by a third party.

(B) not recover, if the plaintiff could easily have moved to another seat.

(C) recover, because a common carrier is strictly liable for injuries suffered by a passenger while aboard the carrier.

(D) recover, if the flight attendants should have perceived the salesman's condition and acted to protect the plaintiff before the blow was struck.

C. Actual negligence by D

Question 25

A plaintiff always brought her lunch to eat in the office. One Saturday afternoon the plaintiff went to a local self-service grocery, and bought a can of corned beef. The can had printed on its label "A Product of Beef Company." The company was a reputable supplier of beef products. On Sunday evening, the woman prepared a sandwich for lunch the next day, using the can of corned beef she had bought on Saturday. When the plaintiff bit into her sandwich at lunch time the next day, a large sliver of bone concealed in the corned beef slice pierced between her teeth, broke one off, and came to rest deep in the roof of her mouth. This accident caused her to suffer severe pain and to incur medical expenses of $700.

The plaintiff brought two claims for damages: one against the local grocery and the other against Beef Company. The claims were tried together. At the trial, the plaintiff proved all of the above facts leading up to her injury as well as the elements of her damage. Beef Company proved that it had not processed and packed the corned beef, but that such had been done by its regular and independent supplier, Meat Packing Company. Beef Company further proved that it had never obtained from Meat Packing Company defective meat products, and that it had no way of knowing that the can contained any dangerous material. The grocery proved that it had no way of knowing the content of the can was likely to cause harm, and that it had sold the products of Beef Company for a number of years without ever having been told by a customer that the products were defective. Both defendants agreed by stipulation in open court that Meat Packing Company had been guilty of negligence in packing the corned beef containing the sliver of bone. The jurisdiction still follows common-law contributory negligence.

If the plaintiff's claim against the grocery is based on a negligence theory, the plaintiff will

(A) recover, because the negligence of Meat Packing Company follows passage of title of the product to the grocery.

(B) recover, because the grocery is liable for the negligence of Meat Packing Company since they are joint venturers.

(C) not recover, because there was no evidence that the grocery failed to exercise due care in selling her the corned beef.

(D) not recover, because she was guilty of contributory negligence when she selected the can containing the sliver of bone.

1. D's failure to supervise customers or others

Question 26

Cara, who was eight years old, went to the grocery store with her mother. Cara pushed the grocery cart while her mother put items into it. Cara's mother remained near Cara at all times. Penny, another customer in the store, noticed Cara pushing the cart in a manner that caused

Penny no concern. A short time later, the cart Cara was pushing struck Penny in the knee, inflicting serious injury.

If Penny brings an action, based on negligence, against the grocery store, the store's best defense will be that

(A) a store owes no duty to its customers to control the use of its shopping carts.

(B) a store owes no duty to its customers to control the conduct of other customers.

(C) any negligence of the store was not the proximate cause of Penny's injury.

(D) a supervised child pushing a cart does not pose an unreasonable risk to other customers.

Question 27

Ohner owns the Acme Hotel. When the International Order of Badgers came to town for its convention, its members rented 400 of the 500 rooms, and the hotel opened its convention facilities to them. Badgers are a rowdy group, and during their convention they littered both the inside and the outside of the hotel with debris and bottles. The hotel manager knew that objects were being thrown out of the hotel windows. At his direction, hotel employees patrolled the hallways telling the guests to refrain from such conduct. Ohner was out of town and was not aware of the problems which were occurring. During the convention, as Smith walked past the Acme Hotel on the sidewalk, he was hit and injured by an ashtray thrown out of a window in the hotel. Smith sued Ohner for damages for his injuries.

Will Smith prevail in his claim against Ohner?

(A) Yes, because a property owner is strictly liable for acts on his premises if such acts cause harm to persons using the adjacent public sidewalks.

(B) Yes, if the person who threw the ashtray cannot be identified.

(C) No, because Ohner had no personal knowledge of the conduct of the hotel guests.

(D) No, if the trier of fact determines that the hotel employees had taken reasonable precautions to prevent such an injury.

II. MALPRACTICE

A. Malpractice generally

1. When expert testimony is or isn't needed

Question 28

Two lawyers are the only members of a law partnership in a small town that has only one other lawyer in it. Both attorneys do a substantial amount of personal injury work. A client was severely and permanently injured in an automobile collision when struck by an automobile driven by a motorist. The client employed the law partnership to represent her in obtaining damages for her injuries. At the time the client employed the partnership, the statute of limitations had six weeks to run on her claim. The complaint was prepared but not filed. Each lawyer thought that the other lawyer would file the complaint. The statute of limitations ran out on the client's claim against the motorist.

The client has filed suit against both lawyers for negligence. That case is on trial with a jury in a court of general jurisdiction.

In order to establish a breach of standard of care owed to her by the two lawyers, the client

(A) must have a legal expert from the same locality testify that the defendants' conduct was a breach.

(B) must have a legal expert from the same state testify that the defendants' conduct was a breach.

(C) can rely on the application of the jurors' common knowledge as to whether there was a breach.

(D) can rely on the judge, as an expert in the law, to advise the jury whether there was a breach.

III. VIOLATION OF STATUTE

A. Statute must apply to facts

1. Legislature's intent to protect against the particular type of risk at issue

Question 29

A pedestrian started north across the street in a clearly marked north-south crosswalk with the green traffic light in her favor. The pedestrian was in a hurry, and so before reaching the north curb on the street, she cut to her left diagonally across the street to the east-west crosswalk and started across it. Just after reaching the east-west crosswalk, the traffic light turned green in her favor. She proceeded about five steps further across the street to the west in the crosswalk, when she was struck by a car approaching from her right that she thought would stop, but did not. The car was driven by a driver, 81 years of age, who failed to stop his car after seeing that the traffic light was red against him. As a result of the impact, the pedestrian suffered a broken leg.

The pedestrian has filed suit against the driver. The driver's attorney has alleged that the pedestrian violated a state statute requiring that pedestrians stay in crosswalks, and that if the pedestrian had not violated the statute she would have had to walk 25 feet more to reach the impact point and therefore would not have been at a place where she could have been hit by the driver. The pedestrian's attorney ascertains that there is a statute as alleged by the driver, that his measurements are correct, that there is a state statute requiring observance of traffic lights, and that the driver's license expired two years prior to the collision. The jurisdiction follows pure comparative negligence.

The violation of the crosswalk statute by the pedestrian should not reduce her recovery in an action against the driver because

(A) the driver violated the traffic light statute at a later point in time than the pedestrian's violation.

(B) pedestrians are entitled to assume that automobile drivers will obey the law.

(C) the pedestrian was hit while in the crosswalk.

(D) the risks that the statute was designed to protect against probably did not include an earlier arrival at another point.

IV. *RES IPSA LOQUITUR*

A. P's failure to exclude other causes

1. Object falling from window

Question 30

Landco owns and operates a 12-story apartment building containing 72 apartments, 70 of which are rented. Walker has brought an action against Landco alleging that while he was walking along a public sidewalk adjacent to Landco's apartment building a flower pot fell from above and struck him on the shoulder, causing extensive injuries. The action was to recover damages for those injuries.

If Walker proves the foregoing facts and offers no other evidence explaining the accident, will his claim survive a motion for directed verdict offered by the defense?

(A) Yes, because Walker was injured by an artificial condition of the premises while using an adjacent public way.

(B) Yes, because such an accident does not ordinarily happen in the absence of negligence.

(C) No, if Landco is in no better position than Walker to explain the accident.

(D) No, because there is no basis for a reasonable inference that Landco was negligent.

B. Effect of *res ipsa* on burden of production

1. Where *res ipsa* is not mentioned in question

Question 31

As a shopper was leaving a supermarket, an automatic door that should have opened outward opened inward, striking and breaking the shopper's nose. The owner of the building had installed the automatic door. The lease, pursuant to which the supermarket leased the building, provided that the supermarket was responsible for all maintenance of the premises.

The shopper sued the supermarket. At trial, neither the shopper nor the supermarket offered any testimony, expert or otherwise, as to why the door had opened inward. At the conclusion of the proofs, both the shopper and the supermarket moved for judgment.

How should the trial judge rule?

(A) Grant judgment for the shopper, because it is undisputed that the door malfunctioned.

(B) Grant judgment for the supermarket, because the shopper failed to join the owner of the building as a defendant.

(C) Grant judgment for the supermarket, because the shopper failed to offer proof of the supermarket's negligence.

(D) Submit the case to the jury, because on these facts negligence may be inferred.

C. Rebuttal evidence

1. Where rebuttal shows some other explanation

Question 32

Defendant left her car parked on the side of a hill. Two minutes later, the car rolled down the hill and struck and injured Plaintiff.

In Plaintiff's negligence action against Defendant, Plaintiff introduced into evidence the facts stated above, which are undisputed. Defendant testified that, when she parked her ear, she turned the front wheels into the curb and put on her emergency brakes, which were in good working order. She also introduced evidence that, in the weeks before this incident, juveniles had been seen tampering with cars in the neighborhood. The jury returned a verdict in favor of Defendant, and Plaintiff moved for a judgment notwithstanding the verdict.

Plaintiff's motion should be

(A) granted, because it is more likely than not that Defendant's negligent conduct was the legal cause of Plaintiff's injuries.

(B) granted, because the evidence does not support the verdict.

(C) denied, because, given Defendant's evidence, the jury was not required to draw an inference of negligence from the circumstances of the accident.

(D) denied, if Defendant was in no better position than Plaintiff to explain the accident.

ACTUAL AND PROXIMATE CAUSE

I. CAUSATION IN FACT

A. "But-for" test

1. Must be tied to D's negligence

a. Rescue scenarios

Question 33

Desmond fell while attempting to climb a mountain, and lay unconscious and critically injured on a ledge that was difficult to reach. Pearson, an experienced mountain climber, was himself seriously injured while trying to rescue Desmond. Pearson's rescue attempt failed, and Desmond died of his injuries before he could be reached.

Pearson brought an action against Desmond's estate for compensation for his injuries. In this jurisdiction, the traditional common-law rules relating to contributory negligence and assumption of risk remain in effect.

Will Pearson prevail in his action against Desmond's estate?

(A) Yes, if his rescue attempt was reasonable.

(B) Yes, because the law should not discourage attempts to assist persons in helpless peril.

(C) No, unless Desmond's peril arose from his own failure to exercise reasonable care.

(D) No, because Pearson's rescue attempt failed and therefore did not benefit Desmond.

2. Successive incidents, allocation of causation as between

Question 34

A driver drove his car into an intersection and collided with a fire engine that had entered the intersection from the driver's right. The accident was caused by negligence on the driver's part. As a result of the accident, the fire engine was delayed in reaching a homeowner's house, which was entirely consumed by fire. The homeowner's house was located about ten blocks from the scene of the accident.

If the homeowner asserts a claim against the driver, what would the homeowner recover?

(A) The part of his loss that would have been prevented if the collision had not occurred.

(B) The value of his house before the fire.

(C) Nothing, if the driver had nothing to do with causing the fire.

(D) Nothing, because the driver's conduct did not create an apparent danger to the homeowner.

II. PROXIMATE CAUSE—FORESEEABILITY

A. How tested on the MBE

Question 35

Doe negligently caused a fire in his house, and the house burned to the ground. As a result, the sun streamed into Peter's yard next door, which previously had been shaded by Doe's house. The sunshine destroyed some delicate and valuable trees in Peter's yard that could grow only in the shade. Peter has brought a negligence action against Doe for the loss of Peter's trees. Doe has moved to dismiss the complaint.

The best argument in support of this motion would be that

(A) Doe's negligence was not the active cause of the loss of Peter's trees.

(B) Doe's duty to avoid the risks created by a fire did not encompass the risk that sunshine would damage Peter's trees.

(C) the loss of the trees was not a natural and probable consequence of Doe's negligence.

(D) Peter suffered a purely economic loss, which is not compensable in a negligence action.

III. PROXIMATE CAUSE—INTERVENING CAUSES

A. Foreseeability rule

Question 36

A driver's car sustained moderate damage in a collision with a car driven by a sightseer. The accident was caused solely by the sightseer's negligence. The driver's car was still drivable after the accident. Examining the car the next morning, the driver could see that a rear fender had to be replaced. He also noticed that gasoline had dripped onto the garage floor. The collision had caused a small leak in the gasoline tank.

The driver then took the car to a mechanic, who owns and operates a body shop, and arranged with the mechanic to repair the damage. During their discussion the driver neglected to mention the gasoline leakage. Thereafter, while the mechanic was loosening some of the damaged material with a hammer, he caused a spark, igniting vapor and gasoline that had leaked from the fuel tank. The mechanic was severely burned.

The mechanic has brought an action to recover damages against the driver and the sightseer. The jurisdiction has adopted a pure comparative negligence rule in place of the traditional common-law rule of contributory negligence.

In this action, will the mechanic obtain a judgment against the sightseer?

(A) No, unless there is evidence that the sightseer was aware of the gasoline leak.

(B) No, if the mechanic would not have been harmed had the driver warned him about the gasoline leak.

(C) Yes, unless the mechanic was negligent in not discovering the gasoline leak himself.

(D) Yes, if the mechanic's injury was a proximate consequence of the sightseer's negligent driving.

B. Foreseeable intervening causes

1. "Second collision" scenarios

Question 37

While driving at a speed in excess of the statutory limit, Dant negligently collided with another car, and the disabled vehicles blocked two of the highway's three northbound lanes. When Page approached the scene two minutes later, he slowed his car to see if he could help those involved in the collision. As he slowed, he was rear-ended by a vehicle driven by Thomas. Page, who sustained damage to his car and was seriously injured, brought an action against Dant to recover damages. The jurisdiction adheres to the traditional common-law rules pertaining to contributory negligence.

If Dant moves to dismiss the action for failure to state a claim upon which relief may be granted, should the motion be granted?

(A) Yes, because it was Thomas, not Dant, who collided with Page's car and caused Page's injuries.

(B) Yes, if Page could have safely passed the disabled vehicles in the traffic lane that remained open.

(C) No, because a jury could find that Page's injury arose from a risk that was a continuing consequence of Dant's negligence.

(D) No, because Dant was driving in excess of the statutory limit when he negligently caused the first accident.

C. Responses to defendant's actions

1. Escape

Question 38

While Driver was taking a leisurely spring drive, he momentarily took his eyes off the road to look at some colorful trees in bloom. As a result, his car swerved a few feet off the roadway, directly toward Walker, who was standing on the shoulder of the road waiting for a chance to cross. When Walker saw the car bearing down on him, he jumped backwards, fell, and injured his knee.

Walker sued Driver for damages, and Driver moved for summary judgment. The foregoing facts are undisputed.

Driver's motion should be

(A) denied, because the record shows that Walker apprehended an imminent, harmful contact with Driver's car.

(B) denied, because a jury could find that Driver negligently caused Walker to suffer a legally compensable injury.

(C) granted, because the proximate cause of Walker's injury was his own voluntary act.

(D) granted, because it is not unreasonable for a person to be distracted momentarily.

D. Third person's failure to discover, warn about or avoid the danger

Question 39

A motorist was driving north on an interstate highway at about 50 miles per hour when a tractor-trailer rig, owned and driven by a trucker, passed her. The tractor was pulling a refrigerated meat trailer fully loaded with beef carcasses hanging freely from the trailer ceiling. When the trucker cut back in front of the motorist, the shifting weight of the beef caused the trailer to overturn. The motorist was unable to avoid a collision with the overturned trailer and was injured.

The trailer had been manufactured by a trailer company. A number of truckers had complained to the trailer company that the design of the trailer, which allowed the load to swing freely, was dangerous. An alternative design could have been used, at little extra financial or functionality cost to the trailer company, that would have avoided the load-swinging problem. The trucker knew of the dangerous propensity of the trailer. A restraining device that could be installed in the trailer would prevent the load from shifting and was available at nominal cost. The trucker knew of the restraining device but had not installed it. The jurisdiction has adopted a pure comparative fault rule in strict liability cases.

If the motorist asserts a claim based on strict liability in tort against the trailer company, she will

(A) recover, unless the motorist was negligently driving when the truck overturned.

(B) recover, because the trucker's knowledge of the dangerous propensity of the trailer does not relieve the trailer company of liability.

(C) not recover, because there was no privity of contract between the motorist and the trailer company.

(D) not recover if the trucker was negligent in failing to install the restraining device in the trailer.

CHAPTER 6
JOINT TORTFEASORS

I. JOINT LIABILITY

A. Joint-and-several liability generally

1. Meshing with P's comparative negligence

Question 40

Jones, who was driving his car at night, stopped the car and went into a nearby tavern for a drink. He left the car standing at the side of the road, projecting three feet into the traffic lane. The lights were on and his friend, Peters, was asleep in the back seat. Peters awoke, discovered the situation, and went back to sleep. Before Jones returned, his car was hit by an automobile approaching from the rear and driven by Davis. Peters was injured.

Peters sued Davis and Jones jointly to recover the damages he suffered resulting from the accident. The jurisdiction has a pure comparative negligence rule and has abolished the defense of assumption of risk. In respect to other issues, the rules of the common law remain in effect.

Peters should recover

(A) nothing, if Peters was more negligent than either Davis or Jones.

(B) nothing, unless the total of Davis's and Jones's negligence was greater than Peters's.

(C) from Davis and Jones, jointly and severally, the amount of damages Peters suffered reduced by the percentage of the total negligence that is attributed to Peters.

(D) from Davis and Jones, severally, a percentage of Peters's damages equal to the percentage of fault attributed to each of the defendants.

II. CONTRIBUTION

A. Contribution generally

1. Amount

Question 41

While driving his car, Plaintiff sustained injuries in a three-car collision. Plaintiff sued the drivers of the other two cars, D-1 and D-2, and each defendant crossclaimed against the other for contribution. The jurisdiction has adopted a rule of pure comparative negligence and allows contribution based upon proportionate fault. The rule of joint-and-several liability has been retained.

The jury has found that Plaintiff sustained damages in the amount of $100,000, and apportioned the causal negligence of the parties as follows: Plaintiff 40%, D-1 30%, and D-2 30%.

How much, if anything, can Plaintiff collect from D-1, and how much, if anything, can D-1 then collect from D-2 in contribution?

(A) Nothing, and then D-1 can collect nothing from D-2.

(B) $30,000, and then D-1 can collect nothing from D-2.

(C) $40,000, and then D-1 can collect $10,000 from D-2.

(D) $60,000, and then D-1 can collect $30,000 from D-2.

Question 42

The plaintiff sustained personal injuries in a three-car collision caused by the concurrent negligence of the three drivers, who consisted of the plaintiff, Donald, and Drew. In the plaintiff's action for damages against Donald and Drew, the jury apportioned the negligence 30% to the plaintiff, 30% to Donald, and 40% to Drew. The plaintiff's total damages were $100,000. Assume that a state statute provides for a system of pure comparative negligence, joint-and-several liability of concurrent tortfeasors, and contribution based upon proportionate fault.

If the plaintiff chooses to execute against Donald alone, she will be entitled to collect at most

(A) $70,000 from Donald, and then Donald will be entitled to collect $40,000 from Drew.

(B) $30,000 from Donald, and then Donald will be entitled to collect $10,000 from Drew.

(C) $30,000 from Donald, and then Donald will be entitled to collect nothing from Drew.

(D) nothing from Donald, because Donald's percentage of fault is not greater than that of the plaintiff.

III. INDEMNITY

A. Negligent vs. intentional tortfeasor

Question 43

David owned a shotgun that he used for hunting. David knew that his old friend, Mark, had become involved with a violent gang that recently had a shoot-out with a rival gang. David, who was going to a farm to hunt quail, placed his loaded shotgun on the back seat of his car. On his way to the farm, David picked up Mark to give him a ride to a friend's house. After dropping off Mark at the friend's house, David proceeded to the farm, where he discovered that his shotgun was missing from his car. Mark had taken the shotgun and, later in the day, Mark used it to shoot Paul, a member of the rival gang. Paul was severely injured.

Paul recovered a judgment for his damages against David, as well as Mark, on the ground that David was negligent in allowing Mark to obtain possession of the gun, and was therefore liable jointly and severally with Mark for Paul's damages. The jurisdiction has a statute that allows contribution based upon proportionate fault and adheres to the traditional common-law rules on indemnity.

If David fully satisfies the judgment, David then will have a right to recover from Mark

(A) indemnity for the full amount of the judgment, because Mark was an intentional tortfeasor.

(B) contribution only, based on comparative fault, because David himself was negligent.

(C) one-half of the amount of the judgment.

(D) nothing, because David's negligence was a substantial proximate cause of the shooting.

I. EMOTIONAL DISTRESS

A. Emotional distress without physical impact

1. General rule of no recovery where no bodily harm

a. Exceptions

i. Negligent handling of corpse

Question 44

Ann's three-year-old daughter, Janet, was killed in an automobile accident. At Ann's direction, Janet's body was taken to a mausoleum for interment. Normally, the mausoleum's vaults are permanently sealed with marble plates secured by "tamper-proof" screws. After Janet's body was placed in the mausoleum, however, only a fiberglass panel secured by caulking compound covered her vault. About a month later, Janet's body was discovered in a cemetery located near the mausoleum. It had apparently been left there by vandals who had taken it from the mausoleum.

As a result of this experience, Ann suffered great emotional distress.

If Ann sues the mausoleum for the damages arising from her emotional distress, will she prevail?

(A) No, because Ann experienced no threat to her own safety.

(B) No, unless the mausoleum's behavior was extreme and outrageous.

(C) Yes, if the mausoleum failed to use reasonable care to safeguard the body.

(D) Yes, unless Ann suffered no physical harm as a consequence of her emotional distress.

Question 45

John's father, Jeremiah, died in Hospital. Hospital maintains a morgue with refrigerated drawers a bit larger than a human body. Jeremiah's body was placed in such a drawer awaiting pickup by a mortician. Before the mortician called for the body, a Hospital orderly placed two opaque plastic bags in the drawer with Jeremiah's body. One bag contained Jeremiah's personal effects, and the other contained an amputated leg from some other Hospital patient. It is stipulated that Hospital was negligent to allow the amputated leg to get into Jeremiah's drawer. The mortician delivered the two opaque plastic bags to John, assuming both contained personal effects. John was shocked when he opened the bag containing the amputated leg. John sued Hospital to recover for his emotional distress. At the trial, John testified that the experience had been extremely upsetting, that he had had recurring nightmares about it, and that his family and business relationships had been adversely affected for a period of several months. He did not seek medical or psychiatric treatment for his emotional distress.

Who should prevail?

(A) John, because of the sensitivity people have regarding the care of the bodies of deceased relatives.

(B) John, because hospitals are strictly liable for mishandling dead bodies.

(C) Hospital, because John did not require medical or psychiatric treatment.

(D) Hospital, because John suffered no bodily harm.

b. Recovery by an "at risk" plaintiff

i.   Where P suffers bodily harm

Question 46

Palko is being treated by a physician for asbestosis, an abnormal chest condition that was caused by his on-the-job handling of materials containing asbestos. His physician has told him that the asbestosis is not presently cancerous, but that it considerably increases the risk that he will ultimately develop lung cancer.

Palko brought an action for damages, based on strict product liability, against the supplier of the materials that contained asbestos. The court in this jurisdiction has ruled against recovery of damages for negligently inflicted emotional distress in the absence of physical harm.

If the supplier is subject to liability to Palko for damages, should the award include damage for emotional distress he has suffered arising from his knowledge of the increased risk that he will develop lung cancer?

(A) No, because Palko's emotional distress did not cause his physical condition.

(B) No, unless the court in this jurisdiction recognizes a cause of action for an increased risk of cancer.

(C) Yes, because the supplier of a dangerous product is strictly liable for the harm it causes.

(D) Yes, because Palko's emotional distress arises from bodily harm caused by his exposure to asbestos.

II.   PURE ECONOMIC LOSS

A. Traditional rule

1. Rationale

Question 47

Star, who played the lead role in a television soap opera, was seriously injured in an automobile accident caused by Danton's negligent driving. As a consequence of Star's injury, the television series was canceled, and Penn, a supporting actor, was laid off.

In an action against Danton, can Penn recover for his loss of income attributable to the accident?

(A) Yes, because Danton's negligence was the cause in fact of Penn's loss.

(B) Yes, unless Penn failed to take reasonable measures to mitigate his loss.

(C) No, unless Danton should have foreseen that by injuring Star he would cause harm to Penn.

(D) No, because Danton's liability does not extend to economic loss to Penn that arises solely from physical harm to Star.

OWNERS AND OCCUPIERS OF LAND

I. TRESPASSERS

A. General rule of liability to

Question 48

A bright nine-year-old child attended a day care center after school. The day care center was located near a man-made duck pond on the property of a corporation. During the winter, the pond was used for ice skating when conditions were suitable. At a time when the pond was only partially frozen, the child sneaked away from the center and walked out onto the ice covering the pond. The ice gave way, and the child fell into the cold water. He suffered shock and would have drowned had he not been rescued by a passerby. At the time of the incident, the pond was clearly marked with signs that stated, "THIN ICE—NO SKATING." When the child left the day care center, the center was staffed with a reasonable number of qualified personnel, and the center's employees were exercising reasonable care to ensure that the children in their charge did not leave the premises. The jurisdiction follows a rule of pure comparative negligence.

In a suit brought on the child's behalf against the corporation, who is likely to prevail?

(A) The child, because the corporation owes a duty to keep its premises free of dangerous conditions.

(B) The child, because the pond was an attractive nuisance.

(C) The corporation, because the danger of thin ice may reasonably be expected to be understood by a nine-year-old child.

(D) The corporation, because the day care center had a duty to keep the child off the ice.

B. Exceptions to general rule

1. Discovered trespassers

Question 49

Prad entered Drug Store to make some purchases. As he was searching the aisles for various items, he noticed a display card containing automatic pencils. The display card was on a high shelf behind a cashier's counter. Prad saw a sign on the counter that read, "No Admittance, Employees Only." Seeing no clerks in the vicinity to help him, Prad went behind the counter to get a pencil. A clerk then appeared behind the counter and asked whether she could help him. He said he just wanted a pencil and that he could reach the display card himself. The clerk said nothing further. While reaching for the display card, Prad stepped sideways into an open shaft and fell to the basement, ten feet below. The clerk knew of the presence of the open shaft, but assumed incorrectly that Prad had noticed it.

Prad sued Drug Store to recover damages for the injuries he sustained in the fall. The jurisdiction has adopted a rule of pure comparative negligence, and it follows traditional common-law rules governing the duties of a land possessor.

Will Prad recover a judgment against Drug Store?

(A) No, because Prad was a trespasser.

(B) No, unless Prad's injuries resulted from the defendant's willful or wanton misconduct.

(C) Yes, because the premises were defective with respect to a public invitee.

(D) Yes, if the clerk had reason to believe that Prad was unaware of the open shaft.

2. Children

Question 50

Davis has a small trampoline in his backyard which, as he knows, is commonly used by neighbor children as well as his own. The trampoline is in good condition, is not defective in any way, and normally is surrounded by mats to prevent injury if a user should fall off. Prior to leaving with his family for the day, Davis leaned the trampoline up against the side of the house and placed the mats in the garage.

While the Davis family was away, Philip, aged 11, a new boy in the neighborhood, wandered into Davis's yard and saw the trampoline. Philip had not previously been aware of its presence, but, having frequently used a trampoline before, he decided to set it up, and started to jump. He lost his balance on one jump and took a hard fall on the bare ground, suffering a serious injury that would have been prevented by the mats.

An action has been brought against Davis on Philip's behalf to recover damages for the injuries Philip sustained from his fall. In this jurisdiction, the traditional common-law rules pertaining to contributory negligence have been replaced by a pure comparative negligence rule.

In his action against Davis, will Philip prevail?

(A) No, if children likely to be attracted by the trampoline would normally realize the risk of using it without mats.

(B) No, if Philip failed to exercise reasonable care commensurate with his age, intelligence, and experience.

(C) No, because Philip entered Davis's yard and used the trampoline without Davis's permission.

(D) No, because Philip did not know about the trampoline before entering Davis's yard and thus was not "lured" onto the premises.

II. LICENSEES

A. Social guests

Question 51

At the trial of an action against Grandmother on behalf of Patrick, the following evidence has been introduced. Grandson and his friend, Patrick, both aged eight, were visiting at Grandmother's house when, while exploring the premises, they discovered a hunting rifle in an unlocked gun cabinet. They removed it from the cabinet and were examining it when the rifle, while in Grandson's hands, somehow discharged. The bullet struck and injured Patrick. The gun cabinet was normally locked. Grandmother had opened it for dusting several days before the boys' visit, and had then forgotten to relock it. She was not aware that it was unlocked when the boys arrived.

If the defendant moves for a directed verdict in her favor at the end of the plaintiff's case, that motion should be

(A) granted, because Grandmother is not legally responsible for the acts of Grandson.

(B) granted, because Grandmother did not recall that the gun cabinet was unlocked.

(C) denied, because a firearm is an inherently dangerous instrumentality.

(D) denied, because a jury could find that Grandmother breached a duty of care she owed to Patrick.

III. INVITEES

A. Duty of due care

1. Effect of warning

a. Torts by third persons

Question 52

Supermarket is in a section of town where there are sometimes street fights and where pedestrians are occasionally the victims of pickpockets and muggers. In recognition of the unusual number of robberies in the area, the supermarket posted signs in the store and in its parking lot that read:

> Warning: There are pickpockets and muggers at work in this part of the city. Supermarket is not responsible for the acts of criminals.

One evening, Lorner drove to Supermarket to see about a special on turkeys that Supermarket was advertising. She decided that the turkeys were too large and left the store without purchasing anything. In the parking lot, she was attacked by an unknown man who raped her and then ran away.

If Lorner sues Supermarket, the result should be for the

(A) plaintiff, if Supermarket failed to take reasonable steps to protect customers against criminal attack in its parking lot.

(B) plaintiff, because Supermarket is liable for harm to business invitees on its premises.

(C) defendant, if the warning signs were plainly visible to Lorner.

(D) defendant, because the rapist was the proximate cause of Lorner's injuries.

CHAPTER 9
DAMAGES

I. PUNITIVE DAMAGES

Question 53

While driving his open-bed truck with a friend in the open bed, the driver swerved, throwing his friend to the pavement. The friend sustained severe injuries. The friend had often ridden in the open bed of the driver's truck, and on some of those occasions the driver had swerved to frighten his friend. The friend sued the driver to recover both compensatory damages for his injuries and punitive damages.

Which cause of action would NOT permit the friend to recover punitive damages?

(A) Assault.

(B) Battery.

(C) Negligence.

(D) Recklessness.

Chapter 10
VICARIOUS LIABILITY

I. EMPLOYER-EMPLOYEE RELATIONSHIP

A. Torts by non-employees (e.g., guests and customers)

Question 54

Perkins and Morton were passengers sitting in adjoining seats on a flight on Delval Airline. There were many empty seats on the aircraft.

During the flight, a flight attendant served Morton nine drinks. As Morton became more and more obviously intoxicated and attempted to engage Perkins in a conversation, Perkins chose to ignore Morton. This angered Morton, who suddenly struck Perkins in the face, giving her a black eye.

If Perkins asserts a claim for damages against Delval Airline based on battery, she will

(A) prevail, because she suffered an intentionally inflicted harmful or offensive contact.

(B) prevail, if the flight attendant acted recklessly in continuing to serve liquor to Morton.

(C) not prevail, because Morton was not acting as an agent or employee of Delval Airline.

(D) not prevail, unless she can establish some permanent injury from the contact.

STRICT LIABILITY

I. WILD OR DANGEROUS ANIMALS

A. Non-trespass liability

1. Wild animals

Question 55

A homeowner owned a large poisonous snake, which had been defanged and was kept in a cage. A storm damaged the homeowner's house and the snake's cage, allowing it to escape. During the cleanup after the storm, a volunteer worker came across the snake. The worker tried to run away from the snake and fell, breaking his arm.

In a suit by the worker against the homeowner based on strict liability in tort to recover for his injury, will the worker prevail?

(A) No, because the snake's escape was caused by a force of nature.

(B) No, because the worker should have anticipated an injury during his volunteer work.

(C) Yes, because the homeowner did not take adequate precautions to secure the snake.

(D) Yes, because the worker's injury was the result of his fear of the escaped snake.

II. ABNORMALLY DANGEROUS ACTIVITIES

A. Common scenarios

1. Nuclear reactor

Question 56

As a result of an accident at the NPP nuclear power plant, a quantity of radioactive vapor escaped from the facility and two members of the public were exposed to excessive doses of radiation. According to qualified medical opinion, that exposure will double the chance that these two persons will ultimately develop cancer. However, any cancer that might be caused by this exposure will not be detectable for at least ten years. If the two exposed persons do develop cancer, it will not be possible to determine whether it was caused by this exposure or would have developed in any event.

If the exposed persons assert a claim for damages against NPP shortly after the escape of the radiation, which of the following questions will NOT present a substantial issue?

(A) Will the court recognize that the plaintiffs have suffered a present legal injury?

(B) Can the plaintiffs prove the amount of their damages?

(C) Can the plaintiffs prove that any harm they may suffer was caused by this exposure?

(D) Can the plaintiffs prevail without presenting evidence of specific negligence on the part of NPP?

2. Construction activities

Question 57

Innes worked as a secretary in an office in a building occupied partly by her employer and partly by Glass, a retail store. The two areas were separated by walls and were in no way connected, except that the air conditioning unit served both areas and there was a common return-air duct.

Glass began remodeling, and its employees did the work, which included affixing a plastic surfacing material to counters. To fasten the plastic to the counters, the employees purchased glue, with the brand name Stick, that was manufactured by Steel, packaged in a sealed container by Steel, and retailed by Paint Company.

In the course of the remodeling job, one of Glass's employees turned on the air conditioning and caused fumes from the glue to travel from Glass through the air conditioning unit and into Innes's office. The employees did not know that there was common ductwork for the air conditioners. Innes was permanently blinded by the fumes from the glue.

The label on the container of glue read, "DANGER. Do not smoke near this product. Extremely flammable. Contains Butanone, Tuluol and Hexane. Use with adequate ventilation. Keep out of the reach of children."

The three chemicals listed on the label are very toxic and harmful to human eyes. Steel had received no reports of eye injuries during the ten years that the product had been manufactured and sold.

If Innes asserts a claim against Glass, the most likely result is that she will

(A) recover, because a user of a product is held to the same standard as the manufacturer.

(B) recover, because the employees of Glass caused the fumes to enter her area of the building.

(C) not recover, because Glass used the glue for its intended purposes.

(D) not recover, because the employees of Glass had no reason to know that the fumes could injure Innes.

B. Requirement that D "carry out" the activity

1. D uses an independent contractor

Question 58:

Landco purchased a large tract of land intending to construct residential housing on it. Landco hired Poolco to build a large in-ground swimming pool on the tract. The contract provided that Poolco would carry out blasting operations that were necessary to create an excavation large enough for the pool. The blasting caused cracks to form in the walls of Plaintiff's home in a nearby residential neighborhood.

In Plaintiff's action for damages against Landco, Plaintiff should

(A) prevail, only if Landco retained the right to direct and control Poolco's construction of the pool.

(B) prevail, because the blasting that Poolco was hired to perform damaged Plaintiff's home.

(C) not prevail, if Poolco used reasonable care in conducting the blasting operations.

(D) not prevail, if Landco used reasonable care to hire a competent contractor.

CHAPTER 12

PRODUCTS LIABILITY

I. NEGLIGENCE

A. Classes of defendants

1. Manufacturers

Question 59

A bicycle company manufactured a bicycle that it sold to a retail bicycle dealer, which in turn sold it to a cyclist. Shortly thereafter, while the cyclist was riding the bicycle along a city street, he saw a traffic light facing him turn from green to amber. He sped up, hoping to cross the intersection before the light turned red. However, the cyclist quickly realized that he could not do so and applied the brake, which failed. To avoid the traffic that was then crossing in front of him, the cyclist turned sharply to his right and onto the sidewalk, where he struck a pedestrian. Both the pedestrian and the cyclist sustained injuries. The jurisdiction has retained common-law joint-and-several liability.

If the pedestrian asserts a claim based on negligence against the bicycle company and it is found that the brake failure resulted from a manufacturing defect in the bicycle, will the pedestrian prevail?

(A) Yes, because the bicycle company placed a defective bicycle into the stream of commerce.

(B) Yes, if the defect could have been discovered through the exercise of reasonable care by the bicycle company.

(C) No, because the pedestrian was not a purchaser of the bicycle.

(D) No, if the cyclist was negligent in turning onto the sidewalk.

2. Retailers

Question 60

Parents purchased a new mobile home from Seller. The mobile home was manufactured by Mobilco and had a ventilating system designed by Mobilco with both a heating unit and an air conditioner. Mobilco installed a furnace manufactured by Heatco and an air conditioning unit manufactured by Coolco. Each was controlled by an independent thermostat installed by Mobilco. Because of the manner in which Mobilco designed the ventilating system, the first time the ventilating system was operated by Parents, cold air was vented into Parents' bedroom to keep the temperature at 68°F. The cold air then activated the heater thermostat, and hot air was pumped into the bedroom of Child, the six-month-old child of Parents. The temperature in Child's room reached more than 170°F before Child's mother became aware of the condition and shut the system off manually. As a result, Child suffered permanent physical injury.

Child, through a duly appointed guardian, has asserted a claim against Seller based solely on negligence. The minimum proof necessary to establish Seller's liability is that the ventilating system

(A) was defective.

(B) was defective and had not been inspected by Seller.

(C) was defective and had been inspected by Seller, and the defect was not discovered.

(D) was defective, and the defect would have been discovered if Seller had exercised reasonable care in inspecting the system.

II. WARRANTY

A. Express warranties

1. UCC scenarios

Question 61

At a country auction, Powell acquired an antique cabinet that he recognized as a "Morenci," an extremely rare and valuable collector's item. Unfortunately, Powell's cabinet had several coats of varnish and paint over the original finish. Its potential value could only be realized if these layers could be removed without damaging the original finish. Much of the value of Morenci furniture depends on the condition of a unique oil finish, the secret of which died with Morenci, its inventor.

A professional restorer of antique furniture recommended that Powell use Restorall to remove the paint and varnish from the cabinet. Powell obtained and read a sales brochure published by Restorall, Inc., which contained the following statement: "This product will renew all antique furniture. Will not damage original oil finishes."

Powell purchased some Restorall and used it on his cabinet, being very careful to follow the accompanying instructions exactly. Despite Powell's care, the original Morenci finish was irreparably damaged. When finally refinished, the cabinet was worth less than 20% of what it would have been worth if the Morenci finish had been preserved.

If Powell sues Restorall, Inc., to recover the loss he has suffered as a result of the destruction of the Morenci finish, will Powell prevail?

(A) Yes, unless no other known removal technique would have preserved the Morenci finish.

(B) Yes, if the loss would not have occurred had the statement in the brochure been true.

(C) No, unless the product was defective when sold by Restorall, Inc.

(D) No, if the product was not dangerous to persons.

III. STRICT PRODUCT LIABILITY

A. Retailers and other non-manufacturers

1. Retailer's fate linked to manufacturer's fate

Question 62

A secretary worked in an office in a building occupied partly by her employer and partly by a retail glass store. The two areas were separated by walls and were in no way connected, except that the air conditioning unit served both areas and there was a common return-air duct.

The glass store began remodeling, and its employees did the work, which included affixing a plastic surfacing material to counters. To fasten the plastic to the counters, the employees purchased glue, with the brand name Stick, that was manufactured by a glue manufacturer, packaged in a sealed container by that glue manufacturer, and retailed to the glass store by a paint company.

In the course of the remodeling job, one of the glass store's employees turned on the air conditioning and caused fumes from the glue to travel from the glass store through the air conditioning unit and into the secretary's office. The glass store employees did not know that there was common ductwork for the air conditioners. The secretary was permanently blinded by the fumes from the glue.

The label on the container of Stick glue read, "DANGER. Do not smoke near this product. Extremely flammable. Contains Butanone, Tuluol, and Hexane. Use with adequate ventilation. Keep out of the reach of children."

The three chemicals listed on the label are very toxic and harmful to human eyes. The glue manufacturer had received no reports of eye injuries during the ten years that the product had been manufactured and sold.

If the secretary asserts a claim against the paint company, the most likely result is that she will

(A) recover, if she can recover against the glue manufacturer.

(B) recover, because the secretary was an invitee of a tenant in the building.

(C) not recover unless the paint company was negligent.

(D) not recover, because the glue came in a sealed package.

B. Bystanders and other non-user plaintiffs

Question 63

In preparation for a mountain-climbing expedition, Alper purchased the necessary climbing equipment from Outfitters, Inc., a retail dealer in sporting goods. A week later, Alper fell from a rock face when a safety device he had purchased from Outfitters malfunctioned because of a defect in its manufacture. Thereafter, Rollins was severely injured when he tried to reach and give assistance to Alper on the ledge to which Alper had fallen. Rollins's injury was not caused by any fault on his own part.

If Rollins brings an action against Outfitters, Inc., to recover damages for his injuries, will Rollins prevail?

(A) No, unless Outfitters could have discovered the defect by a reasonable inspection of the safety device.

(B) No, because Rollins did not rely on the representation of safety implied from the sale of the safety device by Outfitters.

(C) Yes, unless Alper was negligent in failing to test the safety device.

(D) Yes, because injury to a person in Rollins's position was foreseeable if the safety device failed.

IV. DESIGN DEFECTS

A. Negligence predominates

1. Reasonable alternative design

Question 64

A 16-year-old student purchased an educational chemistry set made by a manufacturer. The student invited his classmate to assist him in a chemistry project. Referring to a library chemistry book on explosives and finding that the chemistry set contained all of the necessary chemicals, the student and the classmate agreed to make a bomb. During the course of the project, the student carelessly knocked a lighted Bunsen burner into a bowl of chemicals from the chemistry set. The chemicals burst into flames, injuring the classmate.

In a suit by the classmate against the manufacturer, based on strict liability, the classmate will

(A) prevail, if the chemistry set did not contain a warning that its contents could be combined to form dangerous explosives.

(B) prevail, because manufacturers of chemistry sets are engaged in an abnormally dangerous activity.

(C) not prevail, because the student's negligence was the cause in fact of the classmate's injury.

(D) not prevail, if the chemistry set was as safe as possible, consistent with its educational purposes, and its benefits exceeded its risks.

2. Component makers

Question 65

A married couple purchased a new mobile home from a retailer of such homes. The mobile home was assembled by a manufacturer and had an "HVAC" (heating, ventilating, and air conditioning) system designed by that manufacturer. The HVAC system contained both a furnace and an air conditioner, neither of which was made by the manufacturer—the furnace was made by a heating company and the air conditioner was made by a cooling company. The manufacturer selected and installed the furnace and the air conditioner into the overall HVAC unit. The furnace and the air conditioner were each controlled by an independent thermostat installed by the manufacturer. Because of the manner in which the manufacturer designed the HVAC system, the first time the system was operated by the couple, cold air was vented into the couple's bedroom to keep the temperature at 68°F. The cold air then activated the heater thermostat, and hot air was pumped into the bedroom of the couple's six-month-old child. The temperature in the child's room reached more than 160°F before the child's mother became aware of the condition and shut the system off manually. As a result, the child suffered permanent physical injury.

The child, through a duly appointed guardian, has asserted claims against the manufacturer, the heating company, and the cooling company (but not the retailer), all of which claims are based on strict liability in tort. The child will probably recover against

(A) the manufacturer only, because the ventilating system was defectively designed by it.

(B) the heating company only, because it was the excessive heat from the furnace that caused the child's injuries.

(C) the manufacturer and the heating company only, because the combination of the manufacturer's design and the heating company's furnace caused the child's injuries.

(D) the manufacturer, the heating company, and the cooling company, because the combination of the manufacturer's design, the heating company's furnace, and the cooling company's air conditioning unit caused the child's injuries.

V. DUTY TO WARN

A. Unknown and unknowable dangers

1. Adequacy of warning

Question 66

Peter, who was 20 years old, purchased a new, high-powered sports car that was marketed with an intended and recognized appeal to youthful drivers. The car was designed with the capability to attain speeds in excess of 100 miles per hour. It was equipped with tires designed and tested only for a maximum safe speed of 85 miles per hour. The owner's manual that came with the car stated that "continuous driving over 90 miles per hour requires high-speed-capability tires," but the manual did not describe the speed capability of the tires sold with the car.

Peter took his new car out for a spin on a straight, smooth country road where the posted speed limit was 55 miles per hour. Intending to test the car's power, he drove for a considerable distance at over 100 miles per hour. While he was doing so, the tread separated from the left rear tire, causing the car to leave the road and hit a tree. Peter sustained severe injuries.

Peter has brought a strict product liability action in tort against the manufacturer of the car. You should assume that pure comparative fault principles apply to this case.

Will Peter prevail?

(A) No, because Peter's driving at an excessive speed constituted a misuse of the car.

(B) No, because the car was not defective.

(C) Yes, if the statement in the manual concerning the tires did not adequately warn of the danger of high-speed driving on the tires mounted on the car.

(D) Yes, unless Peter's driving at a speed in excess of the posted speed limit was negligence per se that, by the law of the jurisdiction, was not excusable.

VI. WHO MAY BE A DEFENDANT

A. Services

Question 67

A dentist was anesthetizing a patient's gum before pulling a tooth. Although the dentist used due care, the hypodermic needle broke off in the patient's gum, causing injury. The needle broke because of a manufacturing defect that the dentist could not have detected.

Is the patient likely to recover damages in an action against the dentist based on strict products liability and malpractice?

(A) No, on neither basis.

(B) Yes, based on malpractice, but not on strict products liability.

(C) Yes, based on strict products liability, but not on malpractice.

(D) Yes, on both bases.

NUISANCE

I. PRIVATE NUISANCE

A. Interference with use or enjoyment of land

Question 68

Electco operates a factory that requires the use of very high voltage electricity. Paul owns property adjacent to the Electco plant where he has attempted to carry on a business that requires the use of sensitive electronic equipment. The effectiveness of Paul's electronic equipment is impaired by electrical interference arising from the high voltage currents used in Electco's plant. Paul has complained to Electco several times, with no result. There is no way that Electco, by taking reasonable precautions, can avoid the interference with Paul's operation that arises from the high voltage currents necessary to Electo's operation.

In Paul's action against Electco to recover damages for the economic loss caused to him by the electrical interference, will Paul prevail?

(A) Yes, because Electco's activity is abnormally dangerous.

(B) Yes, for loss suffered by Paul after Electco was made aware of the harm its activity was causing to Paul.

(C) No, unless Electco caused a substantial and unreasonable interference with Paul's business.

(D) No, because Paul's harm was purely economic and did not arise from physical harm to his person or property.

B. Unreasonableness

1. Noise and unattractive sights

Question 69

Palmco owns and operates a beachfront hotel. Under a contract with City to restore a public beach, Dredgeco placed a large and unavoidably dangerous stone-crushing machine on City land near Palmco's hotel. The machine creates a continuous and intense noise that is so disturbing to the hotel guests that they have canceled their hotel reservations in large numbers, resulting in a substantial loss to Palmco.

Palmco's best chance to recover damages for its financial losses from Dredgeco is under the theory that the operation of the stone-crushing machine constitutes

(A) an abnormally dangerous activity.

(B) a private nuisance.

(C) negligence.

(D) a trespass.

CHAPTER 14

DEFAMATION

I. DEFAMATORY COMMUNICATION

A. Opinion

1. Liability for statement of opinion

Question 70

Doe, the governor of State, signed a death warrant for Rend, a convicted murderer. Able and Baker are active opponents of the death penalty. At a demonstration protesting the execution of Rend, Able and Baker carried large signs that stated, "Governor Doe — Murderer." Television station XYZ broadcast news coverage of the demonstration, including pictures of the signs carried by Able and Baker. If Governor Doe asserts a defamation claim against XYZ, will Doe prevail?

(A) Yes, because the signs would cause persons to hold Doe in lower esteem.

(B) Yes, if Doe proves that XYZ showed the signs with knowledge of falsity or reckless disregard of the truth that Doe had not committed homicide.

(C) No, unless Doe proves he suffered pecuniary loss resulting from harm to his reputation proximately caused by the defendants' signs.

(D) No, if the only reasonable interpretation of the signs was that the term "murderer" was intended as a characterization of one who would sign a death warrant.

II. PUBLICATION

A. Requirement of publication generally

1. Must be intentional or negligent

Question 71

Drew, the owner of a truck leasing company, asked Pat, one of Drew's employees, to deliver $1,000 to the dealership's main office. The following week, as a result of a dispute over whether the money had been delivered, Drew instructed Pat to come to the office to submit to a lie detector test.

When Pat reported to Drew's office for the test, it was not administered. Instead, without hearing Pat's story, Drew shouted at him, "You're a thief," and fired him. Drew's shout was overheard by several other employees who were in another office, which was separated from Drew's office by a thin partition. The next day, Pat accepted another job at a higher salary. Several weeks later, upon discovering that the money had not been stolen, Drew offered to rehire Pat.

In a suit for slander by Pat against Drew, Pat will

(A) prevail, because Pat was fraudulently induced to go to the office for a lie detector test, which was not, in fact, given.

(B) prevail, if Drew should have foreseen that the statement would be overheard by other employees.

(C) not prevail, if Drew made the charge in good faith, believing it to be true.

(D) not prevail, because the statement was made to Pat alone and intended for his ears only.

2. Must be understood

Question 72

Able and Baker are students in an advanced high school Russian class. During an argument one day in the high school cafeteria, in the presence of other students, Able, in Russian, accused Baker of taking money from Able's locker.

In a suit by Baker against Able based on defamation, Baker will

(A) prevail, because Able's accusation constituted slander per se.

(B) prevail, because the defamatory statement was made in the presence of third persons.

(C) not prevail, unless Able made the accusation with knowledge of falsity or reckless disregard of the truth.

(D) not prevail, unless one or more of the other students understood Russian.

III. FAULT

A. Constitutional decisions

1. Private figures

a. P must prove at least negligence

i.   D must have had serious doubts about statement's truth

Question 73

Allen and Bradley were law school classmates who had competed for the position of editor of the law review. Allen had the higher grade point average, but Bradley was elected editor, largely in recognition of a long and important note that had appeared in the review over her name.

During the following placement interview season, Allen was interviewed by a representative of a nationally prominent law firm. In response to the interviewer's request for information about the authorship of the law review note, Allen said that he had heard that the note attributed to Bradley was largely the work of another student.

The firm told Bradley that it would not interview her because of doubts about the authorship of the note. This greatly distressed Bradley. In fact the note had been prepared by Bradley without assistance from anyone else.

If Bradley asserts a claim against Allen based on defamation, Bradley will

(A) recover, because Allen's statement was false.

(B) recover, if Allen had substantial doubts about the accuracy of the information he gave the interviewer.

(C) not recover, unless Bradley proves pecuniary loss.

(D) not recover, because the statement was made by Allen only after the interviewer inquired about the authorship of the note.

TORTS ANSWERS

"Rest. 2d" refers to the *Restatement (Second) of Torts.*

Answer 1

Choice **(C)** is correct. This is both assault and battery. Here, we're concerned just with battery. Battery occurs when the defendant, with the intention of causing either a harmful or offensive contact or an imminent apprehension of such a contact, causes a harmful contact with the plaintiff. Rest. 2d, §13. The golfer had the requisite intention to induce apprehension of an imminent harmful or offensive contact, even though the golfer did not in fact intend to make such a contact. Since a harmful contact with the caddie's person resulted, the required result for battery also occurred, so all elements of battery have been satisfied. The fact that the club manufacturer's negligence was a but-for cause of the harmful contact won't act as a superseding cause; in intentional torts (as opposed to negligence, for instance), an intervening act caused by negligence won't supersede unless it is totally bizarre and unforeseeable, and a clubhead flying off is unusual but not unforeseeable (especially in the case of a newly-purchased club). Cf. Rest. 2d, §16, Illustr. 2. Notice, by the way, that if what had resulted was merely an "offensive" but not harmful contact (e.g., a light tap on the caddie's head), this would not be enough for battery — whereas the intent for battery can be to create an apprehension of either a harmful or offensive contact, the result required for battery must be harmful, not merely offensive. See Rest. 2d, § 13(b).

Choices (A), (B), and (D) are wrong because they are inconsistent with the above analysis.

Answer 2

Choice **(A)** is correct. Battery is the intentional infliction of a harmful or offensive bodily contact. Rest. 2d §§ 13, 18. Once it is established that the defendant intended to commit a harmful or offensive touching and such a contact occurred, the defendant is liable for any consequences which ensue, even though he did not intend them, and in fact could not reasonably have foreseen them.

(B) is wrong because the issue of proximate cause, not Driver's negligence, is determinative of Donald's liability. Donald is liable if his tortious conduct was the (or "a") proximate cause of Peter's injury, and that's true regardless of whether the ambulance driver was also negligent.

(C) is wrong because it is both legally and factually incorrect. Peter's suit would have to be either for battery or negligence, and in neither of these cases does foreseeability supply a defense. In a suit for battery, the tortfeasor will be liable for virtually every result stemming directly or even somewhat indirectly from his conduct, however unlikely it might have seemed at the time of his act that this result would follow. Rest. 2d, § 435B. In a negligence suit, the defendant will be held liable only for those consequences that were at least somewhat foreseeable.

(D) is wrong because an accident in the ambulance on the way to the hospital that would cause Peter injury was not so unexpected that it would be a superseding cause. Only an intervening cause that is so unlikely as to be bizarre will be deemed "superseding." Negligence of rescue professionals and medical professionals is sufficiently foreseeable (even if unlikely) that it will almost never be deemed superseding.

Answer 3

Choice **(C)** is correct. Battery is the intentional infliction of a harmful or offensive bodily contact. An assault is the intentional causing of an apprehension of harmful or offensive contact. The intent necessary for a battery is the intent to make contact with the plaintiff or the intent to commit an assault with a resulting accidental "harmful or offensive contact." A battery may be committed not only by a contact with the plaintiff's body, but also by contact with anything that is so closely identified with her body that contact with it is as offensive as contact with the body would be. Rest. 2d § 18, Comment c. Therefore, Plaintiff will not prevail on the battery claim unless Daring intended to cause either contact between the horses or apprehension of such by Plaintiff.

(A) is wrong because a reckless intent is not sufficient to be liable for battery. If Daring acted recklessly (i.e., in deliberate disregard of a high probability that the result would occur) this is a broader mental state than what is required in a case of battery—that the defendant must desire a certain outcome and also know with substantial certainty that the result will occur.

(B) is wrong because the fact that Daring violated the racing rule requiring adequate clearance for crossing lanes by itself does not show that he had the requisite intent to be liable for battery. Only if the intent as described in (C) was present, may Daring be liable for battery.

(D) is wrong because the doctrine of assumption of risk would not apply in this context, where the injury was intentional. A plaintiff is said to have assumed the risk of certain harm if he has voluntarily consented to take his chances that that harm will occur. Within the context of sports, if the risk of the sort of injury that occurred is inherent in the sport or activity, then the plaintiff will be blocked from recovering based on application of the doctrine. However, courts now hold that, in co-participant sports, although *ordinary carelessness* is inherent in the game, a defendant who *intentionally* injures a participant will be held liable and the doctrine will not apply.

Answer 4

Choice (C) is correct. Battery is the intentional infliction of a harmful or offensive bodily contact. Rest. 2d § 13. An insane person is capable of forming the intent to do a harmful act, and the fact that the insanity may have been the cause of the intent is irrelevant. Rest. 2d § 895J. However, if Dorwin didn't know he was striking a person, then he in fact did not have the requisite intent to inflict a harmful or offensive bodily contact on Peavey. Therefore, this would be his best defense in Peavey's claim for battery.

(A) is wrong because it is irrelevant whether or not Dorwin understood that his act was wrongful; he only needed to intend to cause an offensive bodily contact in order to be liable for battery.

(B) is wrong because it is not required that Dorwin wished to cause harm to the plaintiff, only that he wished to inflict an offensive contact, i.e., one damaging to a "reasonable sense of dignity."

(D) is wrong because if Dorwin struck Peavey because he mistakenly and unreasonably thought Peavey was about to attack him, he still had the requisite intent to inflict an offensive bodily contact on Peavey. And although a reasonable mistake about the need for self-defense will be a defense to battery, an unreasonable mistake will not. Here, the facts indicate that if Dorwin believed Peavey was attacking him, that belief was based on Dorwin's hallucinations, which would make the mistake "unreasonable." (Courts apply an objective standard for reasonableness of mistake, i.e., a standard that does not take into account the defendant's particular mental peculiarities or defects.)

Answer 5

Choice (**A**) is correct. The essence of battery is lack of consent, and the plaintiff did not consent to the surgeon's performing the operation. Consent is a defense to a tortious interference with a plaintiff's person or property. Even if the plaintiff gives actual consent to some type of invasion of his interests, the defendant will not be privileged if she goes substantially beyond the scope of consent and invades the plaintiff's interests in a way that is substantially different than what was consented to. Under these facts, the plaintiff specifically consented in writing to having the operation performed by the team physician. The team physician's decision to have the surgeon perform the operation exceeded the scope of the plaintiff's original consent. It doesn't matter that the surgeon was a world famous orthopedic surgeon with skills better than the team physician's, or that he successfully performed the operation—the plaintiff's consent applied to the team physician, not to the surgeon.

(B) is wrong because the written consent form was for the team physician, not for the surgeon, to perform the operation. A patient's consent is read relatively strictly, and for the reasons discussed in (A) above would not be found to apply to the surgeon, only to the team physician. The fact that the consent form was in writing would not change the fact that the operation here exceeded the scope of the consent.

(C) is wrong because even if the plaintiff gives actual consent to some type of invasion of his interests, the defendant will not be privileged if she goes substantially beyond the scope of consent and invades the plaintiff's interests in a way that is substantially different than what was consented to. Here, the plaintiff's consent was for the team physician personally to perform the surgery, not for the team physician or "anyone as good as or better than the team physician." Therefore, the surgeon's performance of the operation exceeded the scope of the consent, and the surgeon's better skills didn't change this fact.

(D) is wrong because the success of the surgery is not a defense. Here the plaintiff specifically consented in writing to the team physician's performing the surgery. The surgeon's performance of that surgery, whatever its outcome, went substantially beyond the scope of the plaintiff's consent. The outcome of the surgery, successful or not, is not a defense to the surgeon's operating without consent.

Answer 6

Choice (**B**) is correct. A prima facie claim of battery includes proof that defendant intended to bring about a harmful or offensive contact with plaintiff's person. It's not clear from these facts that the customer intended to bring about a harmful or offensive contact with the bill collector's person. Intent can take one of two forms: either a desire that a certain result will come about, or the *substantial certainty* that it will, regardless of one's desire that it do so. Thus, if the customer knew that the door was substantially certain to hit the bullhorn, he could be said to have *intended* that the contact with the bullhorn happen even if he didn't desire that contact.

By the way, the customer need not have intended that the bullhorn in turn hit the bill collector's teeth or some other part of his body. The tort of battery occurs when the defendant intends to bring about, and in fact brings about, a harmful or offensive touching "of another's person." The "person" of another includes not only the other's body, but any item so connected with the body as to be regarded as part of the other's essence, such as clothing or something that the other person is holding. Certainly where the bill collector was not only holding the bullhorn but placing it near his lips, the customer's intent to create a contact that was merely with the bullhorn would suffice even if the customer did not intend the bullhorn to hit or harm the bill collector's mouth. (Also, the fact the contact was intended to be between the *door* and the bullhorn rather than between the customer's body and the bullhorn would not matter—as long as the customer intended to bring about a contact with the bill collector's "person," the fact that there was some intermediate object, the door, in between the customer and the bill collector's person wouldn't change things.)

(A) is wrong because this might have been battery even if the customer *had* first asked the bill collector to leave. This choice is referring to the defense of property, which requires a request to desist, unless it would be dangerous or futile, before physical force is used. The problem with applying this to these facts is that even if the customer *had* asked the bill collector to leave first, the physical force the customer used would be considered excessive and thus beyond the scope of his privilege making him liable for battery.

(C) is wrong because it does not offer a valid defense to battery. This option suggests that verbal provocation is a valid defense to battery. In fact, it's not. If the facts were different, and the bill collector's taunts had prompted the customer to *kill* him, the conduct may be enough to reduce murder to manslaughter (due to provocation), but that's criminal law. Instead, in tort law, provocation would have to rise to the level of justifying self defense to be a valid defense. And mere words—however offensive—cannot be a justification for what would otherwise be a battery.

(D) is wrong because the fact it offers is not determinative of the bill collector's recovery. This option suggests that the bill collector's trespasser status gave the customer the privilege to use the force he used. While there *is* a defense based on defense of property, there are two principal reasons it wouldn't apply here. First, a valid defense on this basis requires a request to desist, unless it would be dangerous or futile, before physical force is used. Under these facts there's no evidence of such a request. Second, the privilege would only entitle the customer to use *reasonable* force. Putting out a couple of teeth would exceed the scope of the customer's privilege, and constitute a battery (if the act were intentional).

Answer 7

Choice **(B)** is correct, because the plaintiff did not have apprehension of imminent bodily contact. Assault is the intentional causing of an imminent apprehension of harmful or offensive contact. Thus, assault requires an *effect*: The plaintiff must either actually undergo a harmful or offensive contact or be put in immediate apprehension of such a contact. Here, the apprehension of harm is missing, as the guest knew that the revolver was not loaded and that the ammunition was in "a locked basement closet, two stories below where the two were then standing."

(A) is wrong, because it chooses the wrong legal basis for the conclusion. Assault is the intentional causing of an imminent apprehension of harmful or offensive contact. Here, the host may have intended to cause the guest apprehension of getting shot, even if the host did not intend to shoot the guest. The better choice here focuses on the guest's missing apprehension of harm, as the guest knew that the revolver was not loaded and that the ammunition was in "a locked basement closet, two stories below where the two were then standing."

(C) is wrong, because the harm was not imminent. Assault is the intentional causing of an imminent apprehension of harmful or offensive contact. Here, the host could not quickly retrieve ammunition from a "locked basement closet, two stories below where the two were standing." The better choice here focuses on the guest's missing apprehension of harm, as the guest knew that the revolver was not loaded and the ammunition was far away.

(D) is wrong, because a threat alone is not enough to cause an assault unless the apprehension of bodily contact is imminent. Thus, assault requires an *effect*: The plaintiff must either actually undergo a harmful or offensive contact or be put in immediate apprehension of such a contact. Here, the apprehension of harm is missing, as the guest knew that the revolver was not loaded and that the ammunition was in "a locked basement closet, two stories below where the two were then standing."

Answer 8

Choice **(B)** is correct. An assault is the intentional causing of an apprehension of harmful or offensive contact. It must appear to the plaintiff that the harm being threatened is imminent. Threats of future harm cannot constitute assaults, and the courts have taken a relatively strict view requiring a short period between the making of the threat and the time when, according to the threat, the harm will take place. Rest. 2d § 29, Comment c. A threatened harm ten minutes later would be considered a future harm, and not an assault.

(A) is wrong because an assault results in an apprehension of contact. It is not necessary that the plaintiff actually be touched.

(C) is wrong because the intent to cause severe emotional distress is not an element of the crime of assault. The question asks if the plaintiff would "prevail" in a claim for assault, and plaintiff would have been able to prevail (i.e., recover some damages) for impairment of his interest in "dignity," even without any showing of emotional distress, if the "imminence" requirement discussed in (B) had been satisfied.

(D) is wrong because, as discussed in the explanation of (B), threats of future harm are not actionable.

Answer 9

Choice **(A)** is correct. An intentional infliction of emotional distress claim has four elements: (1) extreme and outrageous conduct of defendant; (2) defendant's intent to cause plaintiff to suffer emotional distress; (3) causation; and (4) severe distress on the plaintiff's part. Thus, the element Choice (A) states—the extreme and outrageous conduct—is the lynchpin of an emotional distress claim. In fact, where creditors are concerned, a pattern of abuse, hounding and extreme conduct can form the basis for an emotional distress claim, *even if* the plaintiff really owes the money! The conduct here—especially the use of the bullhorn to embarrass Poe in front of his neighbors—rises to the level of the required outrageousness.

(B) is wrong because, while Kane's invading Poe's property *might* contribute to the outrageousness of his conduct, it's not a necessary element. If Kane had gone up to Poe in a restaurant and undertaken the same behavior, it would have constituted emotional distress. Where creditors are concerned, severe abuse, hounding and otherwise-outrageous conduct will form the basis for an emotional distress claim (whereas garden-variety phone calls, even rude ones, won't).

(C) is wrong because, while plaintiff must show that he suffered severe emotional distress, the distress need not be accompanied by, or lead to, physical injury or bodily harm. For instance, plaintiff's embarrassment and humiliation, if severe enough, can constitute the requisite severe distress.

(D) is wrong because it's not relevant to Poe's claim. Even if Poe actually *did* owe the store money, this would not preclude his recovery on an emotional distress claim. If you chose this response, you may have been thinking of a defamation claim, where truth *is* a defense. Thus, if Poe actually owed money and Kane called him a "deadbeat" in the hearing of others, even if Poe proved special damages Kane would have a valid defense to defamation—Poe's actually being a deadbeat. However, the claim here is for emotional distress, and truth is not a defense to that tort.

Answer 10

Choice (C) is correct. In order to prevail in a case of intentional infliction of emotional distress, the plaintiff must show that the defendant's conduct was extreme and outrageous and that she, in fact, suffered severe emotional distress. If Perkins did not suffer emotional distress that was severe, she will not prevail.

(A) is wrong because the plaintiff must not only show that the defendant's conduct was extreme and outrageous, but also that she, in fact, suffered severe emotional distress. The facts state that Perkins was badly frightened and outraged; however, this does not indicate that she suffered severe emotional distress. Therefore, Perkins is not certain to prevail merely by showing "extreme and outrageous" conduct, as this choice suggests.

(B) is wrong because, as discussed in the explanation of Choice (A), the fact that Perkins was frightened and outraged does not indicate that she suffered severe emotional distress, as required in a claim for intentional infliction of emotional distress.

(D) is wrong because the plaintiff is not required to show that the defendant's purpose was to cause emotional distress. The plaintiff may recover if she can show that the defendant either intended to cause severe emotional distress or acted recklessly with respect to the risk of plaintiff's emotional distress (i.e., in deliberate disregard of a high probability that the distress would occur).

Answer 11

Choice (A) is correct. In order to prevail in a case of intentional infliction of emotional distress, the plaintiff must show that the defendant's conduct was extreme and outrageous and that she, in fact, suffered severe emotional distress. The conduct must be ". . . so outrageous in character, and so extreme in degree, as to go beyond all possible bounds of decency, and to be regarded as atrocious, and utterly intolerable in a civilized community." Rest. 2d § 46, Comment d. In determining whether the defendant's conduct is sufficiently outrageous, the court will take into account the particular characteristics of the plaintiff and the relationship between her and the defendant. Pratt has been ill for six months and unable to work, apparently in a physically frail or mentally frail condition. As a bill collector, Dayton's conduct, repeatedly screaming at Pratt (even when she came to the door) and threatening to file criminal fraud charges against her, while aware of her poor state of health, would rise to the level of extreme and outrageous. Therefore, if Pratt suffered severe emotional distress, she would prevail.

(B) is wrong because Pratt would not prevail unless she showed that she suffered severe emotional distress as a result of Dayton's extreme and outrageous behavior, an element missing from this choice. In any case, it is irrelevant whether or not the $400 bill was indeed valid and past due, since Dayton's conduct would be deemed extreme and outrageous regardless of the validity of the debt.

(C) is wrong because whether or not the plaintiff suffers physical harm is not determinative. As long as the conduct is extreme and outrageous, plaintiff is not required to show that she suffered physical harm in order to recover for intentional infliction of emotional distress.

(D) is wrong because whether or not the defendant's conduct created risk of physical harm is irrelevant in a case for intentional infliction of emotional distress. In order to prevail in a case of intentional infliction of emotional distress, the plaintiff must show that the defendant's conduct was extreme and outrageous and that she, in fact, suffered severe emotional distress.

Answer 12

Choice (D) is correct in its emphasis on two distinct, and important, points. First is the issue of defendant's mental state. In the case of a *defamation* suit, the media defendant must have acted with knowledge of the statement's falsity or with reckless disregard of its truth ("actual malice"). *New York Times Co. v. Sulllivan* (1964).The Supreme Court has made the *New York Times* standard *also* applicable to actions against public figures for intentional infliction of emotional distress (IIED): The defendant must have acted with "actual malice" (i.e., with intent or reckless disregard) with respect to the accuracy of the statement. *Hustler Magazine v. Falwell* (1988). Second, in an IIED case involving a public figure, as in a defamation case, the defendant must have made a provably false statement of fact, as opposed, for instance, to a statement of opinion. Here, any reasonable reader of the sign who took into account the political context of its display (death-penalty protest) would have understood that Able and Baker were making statements of opinion, not provably-false statements of fact. Therefore, XYZ couldn't be liable for either defamation or IIED for repeating those non-factually-false statements.

(A) is wrong because the plaintiff must show a provable false statement made with actual malice (not merely that plaintiff suffered severe emotional distress) as described in (D).

(B) is wrong because the plaintiff must show a provable false statement made with actual malice (not merely that defendant's conduct was extreme and outrageous) as described in (D).

(C) is wrong because whether or not the plaintiff suffers physical harm is not determinative. Most modern courts do not require physical harm—merely severe emotional distress—for claims of intentional infliction of emotional distress. In any event, plaintiff won't recover for the reasons described in (D).

Answer 13

Choice (**A**) is correct, because it recognizes that only Choice I contains an allegation which by itself would provide the plaintiff with a sufficient basis for relief.

I. A trespass to land can occur when the defendant enters the plaintiff's land, or causes another person or an object to enter the plaintiff's land. If a defendant intentionally drives his car onto plaintiff's land, he has committed a trespass, and the plaintiff is entitled to nominal damages regardless of whether any harm has occurred. Rest. 2d §163. This answer choice contains an allegation that would provide the plaintiff with a sufficient basis for relief.

II. If the plaintiff relies on a negligence theory in a trespass case, he must prove not only that the defendant was in fact negligent, but also that he (the plaintiff) suffered actual damages. Rest. 2d § 165. The facts do not indicate that the plaintiff suffered any harm; therefore, this answer choice does not contain an allegation that would provide the plaintiff with a sufficient basis for relief.

III. To be liable for trespass, entry on another's land must be intentional, negligent, or pursuant to the carrying out of an "abnormally dangerous activity." Rest. 2d § 166. Although the facts do indicate that Dan's car damaged Peter's land, he would not be liable for trespass unless one of those three conditions applied. Therefore, the allegation by itself would not provide the plaintiff with a sufficient basis for relief.

(B), (C), and (D) are all wrong, because each is somehow inconsistent with the above analysis.

Answer 14

Choice (**C**) is correct. A trespass to land can occur when the defendant enters the plaintiff's land, or causes another person or an object to enter the plaintiff's land. A "continuing trespass" is one where the object stays on the land. If a defendant intentionally enters onto the plaintiff's land, the plaintiff is entitled to nominal damages regardless of whether any harm has occurred. David built the garage, so his intentional actions caused an object to enter onto Prudence's land and constituted a continuing trespass. The fact that he may not have known where the property line was and so was unaware of the encroachment is irrelevant.

(A) is wrong because it implies that there is no liability for trespass if a defendant enters onto the land and is unaware that he is trespassing. If the defendant enters onto the plaintiff's land thinking that it is his own, or thinking erroneously that he is entitled to be there, he has still committed an intentional trespass.

(B) is wrong because David committed the tort and is liable for it regardless of whether or not he has current ownership of the trespassing object.

(D) is wrong because David committed an act that constituted trespass and he is liable for it. That's true even if the new owner knew of the encroachment—once David built the encroaching structure he had committed trespass (which was an ongoing tort as long as he owned the structure), and nothing that happened at or after the time of sale by David could retroactively change this fact.

Answer 15

Choice (**A**) is correct. Conversion occurs when the defendant so substantially interferes with the plaintiff's possession or ownership of property that it is fair to require the defendant to pay the property's full value. Rest. 2d § 222A. One must consider the extent and duration of the defendant's exercise of control over the object, the defendant's good faith, the harm done to the property, and the inconvenience and expense caused to the plaintiff. The defendant had permission to drive the plaintiff's car several blocks and instead drove 100 miles to Other City and continued to drive it in Other City the following day. There does not appear to be any good faith exhibited by the defendant. The car sustained $3,000 in damages (1/4 of its total value). Considering these facts, it is fair to require that the defendant pay the full value of the car as damages for conversion.

(B) and (C) are wrong because they incorrectly assert that plaintiff's recovery would provide only for repair of the car and loss of use of the car (as in a claim of trespass to chattels). The suit here is for conversion, and in conversion plaintiff recovers the full value of the item (viewed as of the moment before the taking).

(D) is wrong because in a claim of conversion, the issue of who was at fault in damaging the plaintiff's property (once the defendant committed a substantial interference with it) is irrelevant. In other words, if the car was the subject of conversion, then the defendant is responsible to pay for its full value regardless of whether it was physically damaged (or by whom).

Answer 16

Choice (**B**) is correct. The facts show that the plaintiff hit the defendant and the defendant hit him back. So the defendant committed a battery, but he may be privileged because he was acting in self-defense. The question is whether the force used by the defendant was justified. Choice (B) states the test correctly: The defendant is not liable if he "used no more force than he reasonably believed was necessary to protect himself against death or serious bodily harm." The most important point about this answer is the word "reasonably." Claims of self-defense are not judged by asking whether the defendant thought he was using necessary force. The test is whether the amount of force was reasonable under the circumstances. Only then does the defendant get the benefit of the self-defense privilege. See Rest. 2d § 63 and Comment i.

(A) is wrong because it focuses on whether the defendant "actually" believed that the force he used was necessary. As explained in the discussion of Choice (B) above, the legal test is not whether the defendant acted in good faith, or according to "actual" beliefs. The legal test is whether he acted reasonably—and reasonableness is judged by the trier of fact, not by the defendant. If the defendant did not act reasonably, he loses the privilege no matter how strongly he believed that the force he used was necessary. See Rest. 2d § 63 and Comment i.

(C) is wrong because, like Choice (A), it focuses on what was going through the defendant's mind—on whether he "in fact" feared death or serious bodily harm. But an authentic fear of death is not enough to support the self-defense privilege. The force used by the defendant must be reasonable under the circumstances. The reasonableness of the force used by the defendant is an objective judgment made by the trier of fact. See Rest. 2d § 63 and Comment i.

(D) is wrong because being hit first does not necessarily entitle the defendant to respond with force. First, note the suggestion in this choice that the defendant was "retaliating." The privilege of self-defense does not create a right to "retaliate" or "get even." It is strictly a privilege to protect oneself against present or future attack. In this case the facts obviously do suggest that the defendant faced an ongoing threat. But in that case the outcome depends on the reasonableness of the defendant's use of force in reply to that threat—it does not depend on the fact that the plaintiff hit him first. See Rest. 2d § 63 and Comment g.

Answer 17

Choice (**C**) is correct. In a situation where the defendant is entitled to use reasonable force in his self-defense, and does so, the fact that he injures an innocent bystander does not prevent the use of force from being privileged (as long as the defendant did not act negligently in choosing to shoot, and in how he shot). That's what this choice says.

(A) is wrong because Plaintiff will not prevail if the defendant's actions were privileged, which they would be if the defense of self-defense applied. And that's true regardless of whether Plaintiff was Robber's accomplice or was instead an innocent bystander (as discussed in the explanation of (C)).

(B) is wrong because Guard's actions may have been privileged, and if so, he will not be liable for battery despite application of the transferred intent doctrine. The doctrine of transferred intent provides that as long as the defendant held the necessary intent with respect to one person, he will be held to have committed an intentional tort against any other person who he happens to injure. Ordinarily this would mean that if Guard had the requisite intent to commit battery against Robber he would also be deemed to have had the requisite intent to commit battery against Plaintiff who was injured by accident. However, if Guard was acting in self-defense, his actions were privileged, in which case Plaintiff would not prevail, as discussed in the explanation of Choice (C).

(D) is wrong because it cites a fact that will not be dispositive. According to the transferred intent doctrine, as explained in the discussion of (B), Guard could be held liable for battery of Plaintiff even if he didn't intend to shoot Plaintiff, as long as he had the requisite intent to shoot Robber. (Instead, the outcome will depend on whether Guard qualifies for the defense of self-defense.)

Answer 18

Choice (**B**) is correct, because the defense of "defense of others" would be negated if the jogger's belief about the danger was unreasonable. Since the jogger has intentionally caused a harmful or offensive contact with another, he's liable for battery unless he has a defense. The only defense that plausibly applies here is "defense of others." That is, just as a person has the right to use self-defense to save himself from harm, he has that right with respect to another person who is threatened with harm (even a stranger, under the modern view).

However, the defense-of-others defense, like the right of self-defense, requires that both the actor's belief that danger exists, and his belief that the proposed conduct is a good way to deal with the danger, be reasonable. If the jogger should have realized that the pedestrian was not in fact in danger, this requirement for the defense-of-others defense would not exist.

(A) is wrong, because the fact that an alternative method of dealing with the danger might have solved the problem does not automatically mean that the jogger's method was unreasonable. As described in the analysis of Choice (B) above, the jogger was entitled to the defense of defense of others unless either his choice of methods, or his belief in the pedestrian's peril, was unreasonable. The mere fact that the alternative method of shouting a warning might have solved the problem doesn't mean that the jogger's approach was unreasonable. (For one thing, pushing the pedestrian to the ground merely threatened minor injury, whereas if she were hit she might well be killed or seriously injured. For another, the jogger could reasonably have believed that the pedestrian wouldn't hear his shout, that she wouldn't know that she was the one being shouted at, or that there wasn't time for her to react if she did hear.)

(C) is wrong, because the jogger might be jointly and severally liable with the driver. The speeding driver would clearly be *a* cause of the injury, and would therefore likely be jointly and severally liable with the jogger if the jogger was liable. But this fact wouldn't save the jogger from liability, if the jogger's choice of methods (or his belief in the danger) were unreasonable. Always remember that a given injury can have multiple causes, and can thus lead to multiple tortfeasors (even if they did not act in concert) being held jointly liable.

Here, the jogger's liability (as discussed in the analysis of Choice (B) above) would turn on the reasonableness of his belief in the danger, not on the existence of some other jointly acting cause.

(D) is wrong, because the jogger's intent to save the pedestrian wouldn't immunize him if his belief in the danger was unreasonable. As is discussed in the analysis of Choice (B) above, the jogger only qualifies for the defense of defense of others if his belief in the existence of the danger, and his choice of methods, were reasonable. Since Choice (D) ignores this fact, and focuses only on the genuineness of the jogger's desire to save the pedestrian, it is incorrect.

Answer 19

Choice (**A**) is correct. This choice correctly identifies the basis on which Husband and Wife will be liable: Although their entry was privileged, it was not authorized, so they'll be liable for any damage they cause. The charging bull created the necessity that created the privilege to enter Grower's land. However, private necessity is a *qualified* privilege, requiring that the entrant pay for any damage caused. While (A) does not explicitly mention necessity, it does identify the essential reason Husband and Wife will be liable, so it's the best response.

(B) is wrong because it's not relevant. Without a "No Trespassing" sign, Wife and Husband would still be liable as trespassers if their entry wasn't authorized or justified; and with it, they wouldn't be liable if their entry *was* authorized or justified. In fact, under these facts Husband and Wife were privileged to enter Grower's property due to necessity: They were escaping from a bull. The reason they'll be liable for the damage to the plants is because necessity is only a *qualified* privilege, meaning any loss caused must be compensated. The existence of a "No Trespassing" sign is thus irrelevant to Husband and Wife's liability.

(C) is wrong because, although it correctly characterizes the facts, it ignores the fact that Husband and Wife will be liable for the damage to the plants. Husband and Wife entered Grower's land under a privilege of private necessity: They were being chased by a bull. However, the defense of private necessity is a *qualified* one, requiring that any loss caused be compensated. If you chose this response, it could be that you confused private necessity with *public* necessity, which involves a threat to the public necessitating entry (e.g., burning down a house to stop the spread of a fire). Most courts hold that public necessity is an *absolute* defense, such that the entrant will *not* be liable for damage caused. However, that's not the case here—the threat is only to Husband and Wife. As a result, they'll be liable for the damaged plants.

(D) is wrong because it cites an irrelevant fact. Even if Husband and Wife have a viable assault claim against Grower (which is doubtful—he was probably using reasonable measures to protect his property, and was not negligent in failing to foresee that the leash might break), the assault claim wouldn't be a defense against Grower's claim for the damage to the plants. The damage to the plants had already occurred by the time the dog rushed at Wife, so the couple's liability for that damage must rise or fall without reference to the dog's later actions or Grower's role in enabling those actions.

Answer 20

Choice **(A)** is correct. Children are not held to the level of care which would be exercised by a reasonable adult. A child must merely conform to the conduct of a "reasonably careful person of the same age, intelligence, and experience." Rest. 3d (Liab. For Phys. Harm), § 10(a).

(B) is wrong because children are subject to liability for intentional torts and also for negligence. Dora is eight years old—capable of negligence, and subject to liability using the "reasonable person" standard discussed in (A). Traditionally, children under seven have been deemed incapable of negligence; under modern cases, only children under the age of five are usually deemed incapable of negligence. Rest. 3d (Liab. For Phys. Harm, § 10(b)). Children are also subject to liability for intentional torts if it can be proven that they had the requisite intent. So there is no principle by which an eight-year-old would get immunity from tort law, as this choice asserts.

(C) is wrong because a parent's duty to supervise her child is separate from the duty of the child to not cause intentional or negligent harm to others. The fact that Dora was supervised (or should have been supervised) would not relieve her of tort liability for her actions.

(D) is wrong because the assumption-of-risk doctrine would not apply in this context. Assumption of risk applies when a plaintiff has voluntarily consented to take his chances that harm will occur. A grocery store is not a dangerous place where one expects to get struck in the knee and suffer serious injury. Nor was Peterson alerted to a possible danger, because Dora was not pushing the cart in a manner that caused her concern.

Answer 21

Choice **(D)** is correct. The issue is whether and when a parent has a duty to supervise a child. The Restatement says: "A parent is under a duty to exercise reasonable care so as to control his minor child as to prevent it from intentionally harming others or from so conducting itself as to create an unreasonable risk of bodily harm to them, if the parent (a) knows or has reason to know that he has the ability to control his child, and (b) knows or should know of the necessity and opportunity for exercising such control." Rest. 2d § 316. Since the girl's mother was with her when she was pushing the cart in the supermarket the mother had the duty to control the girl's actions if they caused an unreasonable risk of harm to others.

(A) is wrong because the parent's duty is independent and is not affected by the fact that the child is or is not subject to liability for her own actions. Rest. 2d § 316, Comment c. So even if the child was negligent, the mother wouldn't be liable (e.g., vicariously liable) as long as the mother didn't fail to make reasonable supervision of the child.

(B) is wrong because it is too broad a statement. There is a duty to exercise reasonable care to prevent intentional harm or an unreasonable risk of harm if and only if "the parent (a) knows or has reason to know that he has the ability to control his child, and (b) knows or should know of the necessity and opportunity for exercising such control." Rest. 2d § 316. And a parent has no vicarious liable for her child's torts, whether that tort consists of negligence or an intentional tort.

(C) is wrong because it misapplies the assumption-of-risk concept. Assumption of risk applies when a plaintiff has voluntarily consented to take her chances that harm will occur and is therefore barred from recovery under traditional common-law principles. Here, whether the mother was or wasn't tolerating a risk to a third person, the assumption-of-risk concept wouldn't apply to the mother's liability to the third person.

Answer 22

Choice **(A)** is correct. First, although the question doesn't mention it, Choice A suggests that the claim is for negligence. It couldn't be an intentional tort since there's clearly no intent; however, what is trickier is to eliminate the possibility of strict liability, since transmitting electricity over ordinary electric lines might (though probably wouldn't (see the discussion of Choice (B) below) be considered ultrahazardous. However, even in the unlikely case that the electric transmission here did qualify for strict liability, the required proximate cause element for strict liability would be missing, since the result—people shooting out insulators, causing the line to fall to the ground and causing injury there—would be sufficiently outside the risk inherent in electricity transmission to prevent strict liability from applying.

Once you've concluded that the claim is one for negligence, you need to see what the boy would have to prove in order to succeed. He'd have to show that (1) the light company failed to exercise such care as a reasonable person in its position would have exercised, (2) this was a breach of the duty to prevent the foreseeable risk of injury to anyone in the boy's position; and (3) this breach proximately caused the boy's damages. As to (2), where danger from the negligence or intentional wrongdoing of *third persons* is reasonably foreseeable to the defendant, the defendant's failure to take reasonable steps to prevent the wrongdoing, or the danger from the wrongdoing, will constitute a breach of the duty of care.

Element (3), causation, is also a serious issue in this case. That is, if the boy is to prevail, he must show what *specifically* the light company failed to do that it reasonably could have done, and that if done would likely have prevented the harm. This choice asserts liability "if the light company could have taken reasonable steps to prevent the lines from falling when the insulators were destroyed." That's a conditional but true statement—we don't know whether the company could in fact have taken reasonable (practical) steps to prevent the lines from falling when the insulators were shot out, but if such steps *were* practical, the company would have breached its ordinary duty of due care, proximately causing the boy's harm. This choice also doesn't assert that failure to take such steps to prevent falling lines was the *only* way to prevent the harm. Therefore, the fact that the company might have had other possible methods to avoid the harm (e.g., reinforcing the insulators or other parts of the lines so that shooting the insulators wouldn't cause the lines to fall) doesn't prevent this choice from correctly specifying one practical way of handling the problem the absence of which proximately caused the harm.

(B) is wrong, because for the company to be strictly liable, that liability would have to be premised upon either product liability or liability for conducting an abnormally dangerous activity, and neither applies here. Strict product liability applies only when a person "sells or otherwise distributes" a defective "product." Those who sell "services" as distinguished from "products" are not subject to strict product liability. Rest. 3d (Prod. Liab.), §19. While some courts have held that electricity becomes a "product" when it passes through the customer's own electric meter, virtually none have held that electricity constitutes a product rather than a service when it is part of the high voltage transmission system on its way to the customer. Id., §19, Comm. d. So when the accident happened here, the light company was supplying a service not a product, and has no strict product liability. With respect to strict liability for carrying on an abnormally dangerous activity, the provision of electricity, even through high-powered transmission lines, is generally not considered abnormally dangerous, because it can (and usually is) carried on with considerable safety if customary precautions are taken. (Furthermore, even in the unlikely case that the electric transmission here *did* qualify for the abnormally-dangerous form of strict liability, the required scope-of-risk element for strict liability would be missing, as described in the last sentence of the first paragraph of the discussion of Choice (A) above.)

So the light company will not be strictly liable on either theory.

(C) is wrong, because the word "unless" causes the choice to ignore an additional potential source of liability for the light company. It's true that the light company's failure to take reasonable steps to stop the destruction of the insulators would make it liable in negligence. But even if the light company *had* taken all reasonable steps to stop this destruction, if those steps had been unsuccessful and the company failed to also take a second available approach to the problem—by failing to use reasonable care to prevent the lines from falling when the insulators were destroyed, assuming those steps would likely have succeeded—this failure would be a separate, legally-sufficient act of negligence, making this choice wrong in stating that the company could *only* be liable if it failed to stop the destruction itself.

(D) is wrong because a person who maintains property in a condition dangerous to the public can be liable for negligently failing to secure the property even against intentional wrongdoing (not just negligence) by a third party.

Answer 23

Choice **(A)** is correct, because this response recognizes the exception for when a negligent tortfeasor may be liable for the criminal acts of a third party. When a tortfeasor should have realized the likelihood of the crime at the time of his negligence, he may be liable for the criminal acts of a third party. The issue of foreseeability is generally a question for the jury, so we must look closely at the facts of this question. Here, we are informed that this was a "high-crime neighborhood" and "there had been many thefts of tools and equipment from the construction area." Thus, there is enough evidence of foreseeability that this issue should go to the jury. Also note that the evidence must be overwhelming for the judge to take the issue away from the jury by granting summary judgment for the defendant. Here, the evidence was not overwhelming based on the criminal activity at the construction site.

(B) is wrong, because enough facts of criminality in the neighborhood exist such that it might have been foreseeable that a damaged vehicle would be vulnerable to theft. While normally a negligent tortfeasor will not be liable for the criminal acts of a third party, an exception exists. When a tortfeasor should have realized the likelihood of the crime at the time of his negligence, he may be liable for the criminal acts of a third party. The issue of foreseeability is generally a question for the jury, so we must look closely at the facts of this question. Here, we are informed that this was a "high-crime neighborhood" and "there had been many thefts of tools and equipment from the construction area." Thus, there is enough evidence of foreseeability that this issue should go to the jury. Also note that the evidence must be overwhelming for the judge to take the issue away from the jury by granting summary judgment for the defendant. Here, the evidence was not overwhelming based on the criminal activity at the construction site.

(C) is wrong, because this response states the general rule, but the exception to the rule applies here. While normally a negligent tortfeasor will not be liable for the criminal acts of a third party, an exception exists. When a tortfeasor should have realized the likelihood of the crime at the time of his negligence, he may be liable for the criminal acts of a third party. The issue of foreseeability is generally a question for the jury, so we must look closely at the facts of this question. Here, we are informed that this was a "high-crime neighborhood" and "there had been many thefts of tools and equipment from the construction area." Thus, there is enough evidence of foreseeability that this issue should go to the jury. Also note that the evidence must be overwhelming for the judge to take the issue away from the jury by granting summary judgment for the defendant. Here, the evidence was not overwhelming based on the criminal activity at the construction site.

(D) is wrong, because whether the theft by a third party was foreseeable is a jury question. While normally a negligent tortfeasor will not be liable for the criminal acts of a third party, an exception exists. When a tortfeasor should have realized the likelihood of the crime at the time of his negligence, he may be liable for the criminal acts of a third party. The issue of foreseeability is generally a question for the jury, so we must look closely at the facts of this question. While we are informed that this was a "high-crime neighborhood" and "there had been many thefts of tools and equipment from the construction area," this is not enough evidence for a judge to conclude, as matter of law, that if a vehicle was left unattended a third party would commit a theft. This is a factual dispute that would be resolved by the jury, thus mandating that the motion be denied.

Answer 24

Choice **(D)** is correct. A business operator whose premises are open to third persons owes a duty of reasonable care to those on the premises to make reasonable efforts to control the behavior of others on the premises, so as to prevent them from causing bodily harm. Therefore, if the flight attendants should have perceived that the salesman posed an unreasonable risk of bodily harm to the plaintiff, and should have realized that they could or might be able to protect the plaintiff, the airline (the business operator) will be liable for negligence because its employees did not intervene. The defendant's employees (the flight attendants) seem to have had the power to intervene—even if only by cutting off the drinks, or moving either the plaintiff or the salesmen. Therefore, under the doctrine of respondeat superior, the airline would be vicariously liable for this failure to intervene if the attendants should have recognized the danger and acted to avoid it.

(A) is wrong because, while this choice correctly states the general rule, there is an exception where some special relationship exists between the defendant and the plaintiff, such as where the defendant operates business premises open to the public on which the plaintiff is present at the defendant's invitation (in which case the defendant owes a duty of care to make reasonable efforts to prevent harm to the plaintiff). This "business premises" exception applies here, as discussed in the explanation of Choice (D).

(B) is wrong, because whether or not the plaintiff could have easily changed her seat does not change the fact that the flight attendants had a duty to act reasonably to protect her from foreseeable harm. The plaintiff's failure to change seats would have been at most comparative negligence, which would have reduced but not eliminated the plaintiff's recovery (so that plaintiff would still have "recovered," though not the full amount of her damages).

(C) is wrong because breach of the duty of reasonable care may result in negligence liability of a common carrier, but a common carrier is not strictly liable for injuries to its passengers, as this choice asserts.

Answer 25

Choice **(C)** is correct, because it correctly identifies why the grocery won't be liable: It wasn't negligent. As in any negligence claim, a product liability suit predicated on negligence requires proof that (1) the defendant failed to exercise such care as a reasonable person in his position would have exercised, (2) the failure was a breach of the duty to prevent the foreseeable risk of harm to anyone in the plaintiff's position, and (3) this breach caused the plaintiff's damages. The details of the duty vary depending on whether the defendant is a manufacturer, wholesaler, or retailer. As a retailer, the grocery would be liable for its own affirmative negligence in handling products. For instance, a retailer does have a responsibility to inspect for defects if it has any reason to believe the product is likely to be defective (e.g., a broken seal, or past defective products from the source in question).

Here, the grocery was not affirmatively negligent, and since the defect was inside the can, there was nothing to trigger the grocery's duty to inspect. Thus, it cannot be liable for negligence

(A) is wrong, because it misstates the law: Negligence does not, in fact, follow passage of title. As a retailer, the grocery would only be liable for its own affirmative negligence in handling the product. For instance, a retailer does have a responsibility to inspect for defects if it has any reason to believe the product is likely to be defective (e.g., a broken seal, or past defective products from the source in question). Here, the grocery was not affirmatively negligent, and since the can itself was not defective, the local grocery did not breach a duty by failing to inspect. Since negligence requires a failure to exercise due care, the grocery can't be liable for negligence on these facts.

If you chose this response, you may have been thinking of strict liability, although the reasoning in Choice (A) isn't an accurate statement of that doctrine, either. However, under strict liability, the defendant is liable if the product was dangerously defective when it left his control, even if he had nothing at all to do with its defective condition. Thus, under strict liability, the local grocery *would* get tagged with liability (since if the product was ever dangerously defective, it had that status when it left the grocery). But the claim here is for negligence, not strict liability.

(B) is wrong, because it mischaracterizes the facts. A joint venture is similar to a partnership, but generally it is entered into for a limited time and purpose. The two identifying elements are a common purpose and a mutual right of control. (B) is theoretically correct as an abstract statement of law: One joint venturer is liable for the torts committed by the other if the torts are committed in the scope of the venture (most joint venture cases involve automobile trips). Here, there was no mutual right of control between the Meat Packing Company and the grocery, so the grocery can't be liable for the Meat Packing Company's negligence on a joint-venture theory.

(D) is wrong, because the reasoning does not support a contributory negligence defense. Contributory negligence, where it still applies, is a defense to a negligence claim if it meets this standard: A plaintiff's conduct must fail to meet the standard of care for his own protection, and that failure must cause his harm. Here, there was nothing to trigger any alarm in the plaintiff, since the can looked fine. So the plaintiff could not have been contributorily negligent.

Answer 26

Choice (**D**) is correct. Grocery store shoppers are invitees—members of the public who come onto land held open to them and who do so for the purpose for which the land is held open. Such people reasonably expect that the premises have been made safe for them, and the owner must exercise reasonable care for the safety of such people. Reasonable care by the owner may require that she exercise control over third persons on the premises. But the fact pattern indicates that Cara's mother was near her at all times and that the plaintiff herself was not concerned by Cara's pushing of the grocery cart. Under these circumstances, it does not appear that Cara posed an unreasonable risk to the grocery shoppers. Therefore, the store acted reasonably and should not be held responsible for her actions.

(A) is wrong because, as discussed in Choice (D), a store *does* owe a duty of reasonable care to provide for the safety of its invitees—this duty would likely include reasonable attempts to protect customers from various harms that might foreseeably result from shopping carts.

(B) is wrong because, as discussed in Choice (D), a store *does* owe a duty of reasonable care to provide for the safety of its invitees, and this might include trying to protect them from harm posed by other customers. For instance, had Cara been an unsupervised cart-pushing menace about whom customers had complained, then the store, under its duty of reasonable care, would have had to control her actions for the safety of its invitees. However, the store did not act unreasonably under the circumstances presented in the fact pattern, as discussed in the explanation of Choice (D).

(C) is wrong because on the facts here, "lack of negligence" (Choice (D)) is more convincing than "lack of proximate" cause. If Cara had posed a foreseeable risk of injury to Penny, while on the store's premises and using an instrument (the cart) belonging to the store, the store's failure to intervene *would* be a proximate cause of Penny's injuries. (By using the phrase "the proximate cause" instead of "a proximate cause," this choice incorrectly suggests that there can be only one proximate cause. If the store negligently failed to supervise Cara or intervene to take the cart away from her, both the store's failure and Cara's conduct would be proximate causes.)

Answer 27

Choice **(D)** is correct. The most likely basis on which Ohner would be liable is vicarious liability for the negligence of his employees in failing to take reasonable precautions for the safety of passersby. The facts here tell you that hotel employees patrolled the hallways, telling the guests to refrain from destructive conduct (of the type which injured Smith). It's clear that the employees couldn't *stop* guests from misbehaving, so it's possible that such patrols would be considered reasonable precautions to prevent injuries like Smith's. Negligence requires *unreasonable* conduct, so if the employees were *reasonable* in their behavior, there could be no basis for negligence, and Ohner would not be liable.

(A) is not the best response, because it misstates the law, and arrives at an incorrect result. Without more, a property owner is *not* strictly liable for acts on his premises vis-à-vis *any* adjacent property, public or private. Instead, in order to be strictly liable, the owner (or his employees) will have to engage in some activity that involves strict liability—e.g., an ultra-hazardous activity, like blasting.

(B) is wrong because it assumes the applicability of a doctrine that doesn't in fact apply to these facts. The examiners are probably trying to trick you into thinking that *res ipsa loquitur* applies—they are guessing that you'll remember that the doctrine originated in a case in which a barrel of flour fell from an upper-story window and injured a passerby. But *res ipsa* applies only where the accident is of a type that ordinarily would not occur without the negligence of the defendant. That, in turn, means that the doctrine usually doesn't apply where, even though we don't know exactly who was negligent, we have reason to believe that the tortfeasor was someone other than the defendant. Here, even if we don't know who threw the ashtray, it's likely that it was thrown by a Badger, and not by (or in the face of negligence by) a hotel employee. So *res ipsa* wouldn't apply, and the lack of precise identification of the thrower won't matter.

(C) is not the best response, because it turns on an irrelevant fact. If Ohner's employees were negligent within the scope of their employment and Smith was injured as a result, Ohner would be liable on the basis of respondeat superior *regardless* of whether he had personal knowledge of his guests' behavior.

Answer 28

Choice **(C)** is correct, because it correctly states that expert testimony will not be necessary to determine whether the two attorneys breached their standard of care. This is a bit of a tricky question, because to answer it correctly, you must be able to eliminate some distractors dealing with the tort law principles governing standards of care for professionals.

Under these facts, all the jury must do is determine whether the two attorneys filed the suit within the period authorized by the statute of limitations. Although this is not an Evidence question, the law of evidence bears on whether expert testimony was required on this matter. According to Federal Rule of Evidence (FRE) 702, expert testimony is used where the court determines that "scientific, technical, or other *specialized knowledge* will assist the trier of fact to understand the evidence or to determine a fact in issue." The timeliness issue here is not a matter that would require the kind of sophistication that would trigger the need for expert testimony; all an expert would do, really, is point to a deadline on a calendar. Since the jury can "understand" and "determine" the issue of timeliness of filing without "specialized knowledge," expert testimony was not needed, making Choice (C) the best response.

(A) is wrong, because it erroneously suggests that expert testimony is necessary to determine breach of the standard of care, and, beyond that, it misstates the standard by which the two attorneys would be judged. Under FRE 702, expert testimony is only necessary where the court determines that "scientific, technical, or other specialized knowledge will assist the trier of fact to understand the evidence or to determine a fact in issue." Determining whether the two attorneys missed their deadline would not be the kind of matter necessarily meriting expert testimony. Furthermore, the standard against which lawyers are judged is the minimum common skill of members in good standing in their profession. The "locality" requirement that Choice (A) mentions is an old concept, which is only one factor for juries to consider in modern cases determining if the actor behaved reasonably in the circumstances; and even when this rule was applied, it was applied generally to general medical practitioners. Since Choice (A) does not state the correct result or the correct standard, it's not the best response.

(B) is wrong, because it erroneously suggests that expert testimony is necessary to determine breach of the standard of care, and, beyond that, it misstates the standard by which the two attorneys would be judged. Under FRE 702, expert testimony is only necessary where the court determines that "scientific, technical, or other specialized knowledge will assist the trier of fact to understand the evidence or to determine a fact in issue." Determining whether the two attorneys missed their deadline would not be the kind of matter necessarily meriting expert testimony, because all that needs to be determined is if the two attorneys made the deadline. Furthermore, the standard against which lawyers are judged is the minimum common skill of members in good standing in their profession. Thus, the "statewide" standard Choice (B) suggests would not be appropriate for the two attorneys. Since Choice (B) misses both of these points, it's not the best response.

(D) is wrong, because the judge is not competent as a witness in a case, and even if he were, expert testimony is not appropriate here. Even though the judge is (hopefully) an expert on the law, he cannot testify as to whether the two attorneys breached their duty, since that is a matter of fact, not law, and thus it's a matter for the jury to decide. The judge cannot offer expert testimony, because judges are not competent witnesses. FRE 605.

Even if the judge could offer expert testimony, it's not merited here. Under FRE 702, expert testimony is only necessary where the court determines that "scientific, technical, or other specialized knowledge will assist the trier of fact to understand the evidence or to determine a fact in issue." Determining whether the two attorneys missed their deadline would not be the kind of matter meriting expert testimony, because all that needs to be determined is whether the two attorneys complied with the deadline. Since Choice (D) mistakenly states that the judge can testify as an expert witness, and it states the expert testimony is needed on a matter where it's not, Choice (D) is not the best response.

Answer 29

Choice **(D)** is correct, because it identifies the argument most likely to stop the statutory standard of care from constituting comparative fault that would reduce the pedestrian's claim against the driver.

The pedestrian's violating the crosswalk statute could reduce her recovery if it established comparative negligence *per se*. Here is the general rule on negligence *per se*: "an actor is negligent if, without excuse, the actor ***violates a statute*** that is designed to ***protect against the type of accident the actor's conduct causes***, and if the accident victim is within the class of persons the statute is designed to protect." Rest. 3d (Liab. For Phys. Harm) §14.

Where it is the defendant who is claiming that the plaintiff has committed "comparative negligence *per se*," the standard is still the one quoted above, except that the violator of the statute and the "accident victim" are the same person. Here, the crosswalk statute would be very unlikely to be found to have been "designed to protect against the type of accident" that the plaintiff's violation caused. Crosswalk statutes are generally designed to avoid the risk of an immediate collision occurring in the non-crosswalk portion of the street, where drivers are not expecting a pedestrian to be walking. Such a statute would be unlikely to be found to have been designed to reduce the risk that a pedestrian might, by jaywalking, arrive earlier at some other point where the accident then occurs but wouldn't have occurred had there been no jaywalking. To put it in terms of scope of risk, jaywalking does not increase the risk that the jaywalker will, after the jaywalking is complete, be hit somewhere else by a car. (To see this principle in a typical *defendant*-negligence-per-se setting, suppose D drives over the speed limit at 1:00 PM, and therefore arrives at a particular crosswalk at 1:25 PM instead of 1:30, where, while driving carefully, he hits the pedestrian P—the fact that D's 1:00 PM speed-limit violation made the 1:25 PM accident factually possible doesn't mean that D will be negligent per se, because the 1:00 PM speeding did not increase the risk of a later non-speeding collision down the road.)

(A) is wrong, because the timing of the violations will not be relevant as to whether the pedestrian's violation of the crosswalk statute should count against her. As discussed in Choice (D), the pedestrian was not comparatively negligent per se. Therefore, the fact that the driver's violation occurred later than the pedestrian's legally-irrelevant crosswalk violation does not make any difference.

(B) is wrong, because the reasoning it states would not be sufficient to bar application of the statute against the pedestrian. Even though one may assume that others will obey the law, this doesn't give one a license to act unreasonably regarding one's own safety. Looked at another way, the pedestrian had no more right to rely on the driver than the driver had to rely on her. So if the pedestrian's violation had constituted comparative negligence per se, her abstract entitlement to assume that the driver would obey the traffic-light statute wouldn't prevent the pedestrian from having the comparative-negligence-per-se doctrine reduce her recovery. (Rather, the pedestrian avoids negligence per se for the reason discussed in Choice (D).)

(C) is wrong, because it provides an insufficient basis on which to prevent application of the crosswalk statute to establish the pedestrian's comparative negligence per se. If the earlier crosswalk violation had satisfied the requirements for application of comparative negligence per se, the fact that the pedestrian was later, at the time of the accident, in the crosswalk wouldn't help her. (But comparative negligence per se *doesn't* apply against the pedestrian, for the reason discussed in Choice (D).)

Answer 30

Choice (**D**) is correct. Walker's only hope of prevailing would be *res ipsa loquitur*, since there's no direct proof of negligence by Landco or anyone for whose conduct Landco is responsible. The doctrine of *res ipsa loquitur* allows the plaintiff to point to the fact of the accident, and to create an inference that, even without a precise showing of how the defendant behaved, the defendant was probably negligent. The courts generally agree on four requirements before the doctrine may be applied: (1) there must be no direct evidence of the defendant's conduct; (2) the event must be of a kind which ordinarily does not occur except through negligence; (3) the instrument which caused the injury must have been, at the relevant time, in the exclusive control of the defendant; and (4) plaintiff must show that her injury was not due to her own action. It is questionable whether at least two of these requirements are fulfilled. Requirement (3) would require that the flower pot have been in the exclusive control of Landco, which is not the case (given that 70 of the 72 apartments have been rented to third persons for whose behavior Landco would not be vicariously liable). Requirement (2) would require proof that a flower pot usually does not fall without negligence, which is not true. Therefore, the doctrine of *res ipsa loquitur* could not be applied here.

(A) is wrong because: (1) a landowner is not strictly liable for injuries from an artificial condition to persons on an adjacent public way (only required to use reasonable care to prevent such injuries); and (2) there's no evidence here that Landco failed to use reasonable care in trying to prevent such accidents (since flowerpots on windowsills are not all that dangerous, and in any event there's no evidence that Landco even knew of the particular flowerpot, or had any practical right to have the pot taken off the sill by what was probably a tenant who was not under Landco's direct control).

(B) is wrong because, as discussed in (D), it is possible for a flower pot to fall and for it not to be due to negligence. Furthermore, even if the falling pot was due to someone's negligence, that someone was probably not Landco (since 70 of 72 apartments were rented to outsiders), and was not someone for whose acts Landco was vicariously responsible. (A landlord is not vicariously liable for torts committed by a tenant.) So the statement in this choice is both probably untrue as a factual matter, and legally irrelevant.

(C) is wrong because this factor wouldn't make a difference. It's true that some courts (though probably no longer a majority) will apply *res ipsa loquitur* only if the plaintiff can show that a true explanation of the events is more readily accessible to the defendant than to the plaintiff. But apart from this factor, the plaintiff must show that the type of accident usually doesn't happen without someone's negligence, and that the defendant was probably in exclusive control of the instrumentality that caused the accident. As is further discussed in (D), the plaintiff can't meet either of these requirements.

Answer 31

Choice (**D**) is correct. In a case like this, where there is no evidence to show why an accident happened, the underlying issue is whether the plaintiff can use the doctrine of *res ipsa loquitur*. *Res ipsa* allows a jury to find a defendant negligent even without specific evidence of what the defendant did wrong. In other words, where the doctrine applies, it deems the plaintiff to have fulfilled her burden of production as to the element of negligence, and thus entitles the plaintiff to get to the jury on this element. For the doctrine to apply, there are two basic requirements: the accident must be one that ordinarily does not occur unless someone was negligent; and the defendant has to be responsible for the thing, or "instrumentality," that caused the harm. In this case it seems fair to suppose that automatic doors usually do not open the wrong way unless somebody responsible for the doors has been negligent. And it also is fair to say that the defendant supermarket is responsible for the doors, since the market is put in charge of ongoing maintenance by its lease. Therefore *res ipsa loquitur* applies. The case should go to a jury, which can decide whether or not to give a verdict to the plaintiff on the basis of those inferences. See Rest. 2d, § 328D.

Notice that neither the correct choice nor any other portion of the question *mentions the doctrine* of *res ipsa* by name — it's up to you to notice that the doctrine applies, and that it's central to the outcome.

(A) is wrong because the mere malfunction of the door does not require judgment against the supermarket. A reasonable jury *could* decide that the door malfunctioned without any negligence by the supermarket; perhaps the door was examined just as often as due care requires, and failed for some reason that inspections could not detect. As explained in the discussion of Choice (D), *res ipsa loquitur* would likely apply here, but that doctrine would not cause a judge to declare the plaintiff the winner — at most it would cause the judge to give the case to the jury to decide. *Res ipsa loquitur allows* a jury to find for a plaintiff, but it doesn't *require* it. This also is not a case to which strict liability applies; it does not involve an abnormally dangerous activity or the sale of a defective product.

(B) is wrong because a plaintiff is not required to join all parties as defendants who might have been responsible for an accident. Any defendant can be sued individually. (The supermarket is free to join the building's owner as a third-party defendant if it thinks the owner should pay some or all of the damages.) See Rest. 2d § 882. It's true that *res ipsa loquitur* is only available when it's clear that the defendant had responsibility for the instrument that caused the harm, and it's also true that the owner of the building originally installed the door in this case. See Rest. 2d § 328D and Comment g. But the ongoing responsibility for the door was assigned by contract to the supermarket. Since the door had been working in the months before the accident, its failure in the plaintiff's case seems likely to have been the result of negligence by the party in charge of maintaining it: the defendant.

(C) is wrong because it is not always necessary for a plaintiff to offer evidence of the defendant's negligence. Proof of that kind is *usually* the plaintiff's responsibility, but not always: as explained in the discussion of Choice (D) above, the doctrine of *res ipsa loquitur* sometimes lets a plaintiff reach a jury without any evidence of how the defendant was negligent. The jury will be permitted to find for the plaintiff in such a case if the accident is one that usually occurs only when someone was negligent, and if the defendant had responsibility for (that is, control over) the instrumentality that caused the harm. Rest. 2d § 328D.

Answer 32

Choice (C) is correct. The doctrine of *res ipsa loquitur* allows the plaintiff to point to the fact of the accident, and to create an inference that, even without a precise showing of how the defendant behaved, the defendant was probably negligent. The consequence of the doctrine's application is that the plaintiff has met her burden of production. The defendant may counter with evidence that rebuts any or all of the elements required for *res ipsa* (e.g., by showing other possible causes not involving the defendant's negligence). It will then be up to the jury to decide whether the defendant's evidence is enough to negate the inference of negligence stemming from application of *res ipsa*. Here, the defendant provided enough evidence (proper use of the emergency brakes and evidence of juveniles tampering with cars in the neighborhood) that a jury was not required to infer negligence of the defendant from the fact that the defendant parked her car and two minutes later it rolled down the hill.

(A) and (B) are wrong because, as discussed in the explanation of (C), there was enough evidence provided by the defendant to entitle a reasonable jury to conclude that it should not apply *res ipsa*, i.e., that it should not infer negligence. This fact will be dispositive, since the verdict-loser's motion for a JNOV should be granted only if there was not enough evidence to permit a reasonable jury to find for the verdict-winner.

(D) is wrong because it focuses on a factor that won't be dispositive. It's true that some courts (though probably no longer a majority) hold that in order for the plaintiff to benefit from *res ipsa loquitur*, the plaintiff must show that a true explanation of the events is more readily accessible to the defendant than to the plaintiff. But the court probably wouldn't apply this rule, and even if it did, the plaintiff will lose because the defendant came up with enough evidence that a reasonable jury could find that the inference of negligence by the defendant was unjustified.

Answer 33

Choice (**C**) is correct. A rescuer who sustains injuries can recover from the rescuee, if the rescuee acted negligently in putting himself in the position of needing rescue. But if the rescuee did not act negligently (or any negligence did not contribute directly to the arising of the peril), then the rescuer would not be permitted to recover, even though the peril was the proximate cause and cause in fact of the harm to the rescuer.

(A) is wrong because, even if Pearson's rescue attempt was reasonable, if it was not in response to a danger caused by the Desmond's negligence, then Pearson would not prevail in an action against defendant for his injuries.

(B) is wrong because, even if rescue attempts should be encouraged, if Pearson's rescue attempt was not in response to a danger caused by the Desmond's negligence, then Pearson would not prevail in an action against defendant for his injuries.

(D) is wrong because, even though Desmond didn't benefit from the rescue attempt, he would still be liable to the rescuer if the rescue attempt was in response to Desmond's own negligence in putting himself in need of rescue.

Answer 34

Choice (**A**) correct, because it correctly states exactly what damages the defendant will be responsible for. You're told under these facts that the defendant was negligent. Thus, he'll be liable for any damages flowing from that negligence. Here, the plaintiff's' house was already on fire when the accident occurred; thus, that portion of the damage is not attributable to the defendant. By negligently hitting a fire truck on its way to a fire, the defendant created the foreseeable risk of loss to whoever's house the fire truck was heading. Here, the damages the defendant caused—for which he'll be liable—are the part of the loss that would have been prevented had the accident not occurred. Since (A) correctly states this, it's the best response.

(B) is wrong, because it overstates the damages the plaintiff will be able to recover from the defendant. The facts here tell you that the defendant was negligent. As a result, he'll be liable for those damages caused by his negligence. Here, the plaintiff's' house was already on fire *before* the defendant's negligence occurred, so the defendant *couldn't* be responsible for the whole house. Even if the defendant hadn't been negligent at all, the firefighters would only have been able to salvage part of the house, and it's only that portion for which the defendant would be liable. Since (B) ignores this, it's not the best response.

(C) is wrong, because the defendant will be liable for damages even if he had no hand in starting the fire. By negligently hitting a fire truck on its way to a fire, the defendant created the foreseeable risk of loss to whoever's house the fire truck was heading. Here, the damages the defendant caused—for which he'll be liable—is the part of the loss that would have been prevented had the accident not occurred.

Of course, whoever *started* the fire will be liable *as well*, and the defendant's negligence would not exonerate the arsonist (since the defendant's negligence would be considered a foreseeable intervening cause of the plaintiff's damages). However, what's at issue here is *the defendant's* liability, and not having started the fire would not exonerate the defendant. Since (C) states otherwise, it's not the best response.

(D) is wrong, because it doesn't correctly analyze the issue of causation on these facts. Due to his negligence, the defendant will be liable for all damages flowing from his act. Here, the defendant's negligence prevented the fire truck from reaching the fire. Thus, the part of the plaintiff's loss that would have been prevented had the accident not occurred is a direct result of the defendant's negligence, since it would not have occurred "but for" the defendant's negligence. Thus, it's not necessary that the defendant's negligence created an "apparent danger" to the plaintiff. Since (D) states otherwise, it's not the best response.

Answer 35

Choice (**B**) is correct. Doe's liability extends to foreseeable damages from a fire. It was not foreseeable that a fire would damage trees by depriving them of the structure that was sustaining them by providing shade. Had the trees burned down, this *would* be a foreseeable consequence of the fire, but that was not the case here.

(A) is wrong because Doe's negligence did in fact cause the loss of the trees, albeit in an unexpected manner.

(C) is wrong because the loss of trees *is* a natural and probable consequence of a fire. The manner in which Peter's trees were lost was not foreseeable, however, which is why Choice (B) is the correct answer.

(D) is wrong because Peter suffered property damage, which is compensable in a negligence action. Examples of pure economic loss are loss of profits or wages. Property damage does not fall under this category.

Answer 36

Choice (**D**) is correct. Under the prevailing view of proximate cause, the defendant's negligent conduct is the (or a) proximate cause of the plaintiff's injury if (and only if) the general type of harm that occurred to the plaintiff was a reasonably foreseeable consequence of the defendant's negligent action. Choice (D) articulates this standard. We cannot definitively say on these facts that the mechanic's injury was in fact a proximate consequence of the sightseer's negligent driving—but *if* it was a proximate consequence, the mechanic would be entitled to at least partial recovery from the sightseer, under pure comparative-negligence principles. By the way, the fact that the accident might have been avoided by a warning from the driver won't get the sightseer off the hook (see the discussion of Choice (B) for why). If the driver's failure to mention the leak constituted negligence by him, this would *reduce* the sightseer's share of the judgment under comparative negligence, but it wouldn't eliminate the sightseer's liability.

(A) is wrong because the sightseer's liability arises out of his negligent driving, not his awareness of the gasoline leak. If it was a foreseeable consequence of that negligent driving that some repairer of the other party's car might be hurt as a result, the sightseer will be liable even though he never knew precisely in what way his negligence created the special danger to the repairer. In other words, liability depends on the foreseeable consequences of the negligently-caused event (the accident), not from whether the negligent actor was or wasn't aware of how the danger arose.

(B) is wrong because the lack of such a warning would not be deemed to have broken the causal link between the sightseer's negligent driving and the injury to the mechanic. In general, a third party's failure to discover or warn of a danger caused by the defendant will not insulate the defendant from negligence liability, even if a warning would have eliminated the danger. Especially in a comparative-negligence jurisdiction such as the one here, even if the driver's failure to mention the leak was negligence, a court would almost certainly conclude that this failure was not a "superseding cause," and was merely co-negligence (which would serve to reduce the sightseer's liability to the mechanic but not eliminate it).

(C) is wrong because even had the mechanic negligently failed to discover the danger, he would still be entitled to recovery. In a pure comparative negligence jurisdiction such as the one here, the plaintiff's negligent failure to discover a danger caused by the defendant will *not eliminate* the defendant's liability, merely *reduce* it. Since the sightseer would be otherwise liable to the mechanic if the accident was a proximate consequence of the sightseer's negligent driving (see Choice (D)), this result would still be true in the face of the mechanic's negligent failure to discover the danger.

Answer 37

Choice **(C)** is correct. Dant's initial negligence brought about the condition in which lanes were blocked, and in which other drivers might slow down to rubberneck. The fact that other drivers might behave in this way (and that one of the slowing drivers might in turn cause a second accident) was relatively foreseeable. At the least, a reasonable jury *could* find (even if it need not find) that the causal connection between Dant's initial negligence and the second accident was not so far-fetched or attenuated that the second accident (and Thomas's negligence) should be regarded as a superseding cause. Remember, a second event must be very, very bizarre and hard to foresee before it will be deemed superseding.

(A) is wrong because, although Dant did not collide with Page's car, Dant's negligence proximately caused Page's injuries, as discussed in Choice (C).

(B) is wrong because, even if Page could have safely passed the disabled vehicles, it is probably not the case that his not doing so would constitute contributory negligence. This jurisdiction adheres to the traditional common-law rules pertaining to contributory negligence, under which the plaintiff will be barred from recovering if he was contributorily negligent. Page's action in slowing down his car when he saw that an accident had blocked two lanes of traffic, and his intention to see if he could help, were probably reasonable under the circumstances. Therefore, he was not contributorily negligent.

(D) is wrong because it doesn't address the key factor. Dant was clearly negligent in causing the first accident — that's not disputed. The interesting question is whether the connection between the first accident and the second one involving Page was so attenuated that the second (or Page's negligence in bringing about the second) should be viewed as superseding. Since this choice doesn't refer to this key issue, it's not the best answer.

Answer 38

Choice **(B)** is correct. When *A* puts *B* in peril, it's typically quite foreseeable that *B* will try to escape the peril. Therefore, if *A* acted negligently in putting *B* in peril, *A* will be liable for injury to *B* that occurs during *B*'s foreseeable efforts to escape the peril. Here, it's completely foreseeable that one in Walker's position might jump backwards to escape the oncoming car, and thereby be injured. That's all that this choice is asserting.

(A) is wrong because Driver's actions were negligent and apprehension of an imminent harmful contact is the definition of an assault, an intentional tort.

(C) is wrong because, when *A* is put in peril by *B*'s negligence, *A*'s efforts to escape the peril — unless they are truly bizarre and unforeseeable — won't act as superseding causes. So while Walker's injury may have been due in part to his "voluntary act" of jumping backward, this certainly doesn't prevent Driver's negligence from also being a proximate cause of the injury. (Remember that there can be, and often are, multiple proximate causes for a given event.) Given that Walker's behavior in jumping wasn't even negligent, it's even less likely that his behavior would let Driver off the hook on proximate-cause grounds.

(D) is wrong because, although sometimes it may not be unreasonable for a person to be distracted momentarily, in this case it was unreasonable. In assessing reasonableness, courts do a cost-benefit analysis. Here, a driver's looking at "colorful trees in bloom" during a "leisurely spring drive" is certainly not an event whose social value outweighs the major risk to others.

Answer 39

Choice **(B)** is correct. First, the trucking company's failure to use a reasonably available alternative design constituted strict product liability of the defective-design variety. See Rest. 3d (Prod. Liab.) § 2(b), defining a product as being "defective in design" (and thus giving rise to strict product liability) "when the *foreseeable risks of harm posed* by the product *could have been reduced or avoided by the adoption of a reasonable alternative design* by the seller or other distributor, or a predecessor in the commercial chain of distribution, and the omission of the alternative design *renders the product not reasonably safe.*"

A sticky point here is the effect of the trucker's realization that the truck was dangerous, and his failure to buy and install the restraining device. But as Choice (B) states, this will not relieve the trailer company of liability toward the motorist. If a manufacturer produces a defectively dangerous product, the manufacturer will virtually never be absolved of responsibility merely because some person further down the distributive chain (e.g., a distributor or an end-user) either negligently fails to discover the danger or does discover the danger but fails to take available steps to remedy it (e.g., by installing a readily-available and cheap safety device).

(A) is wrong, because it incorrectly suggests that the motorist will only recover if she wasn't driving negligently. First, under these facts, there's no evidence the motorist was driving negligently—you're told that the motorist was driving 50 m.p.h. on an interstate, and that she was unable to avoid colliding with the truck. But more importantly, even if the motorist was driving negligently, she could still recover. You're told that the jurisdiction has adopted comparative fault for strict liability cases. So the most that could happen is that the motorist's fault would cause her recovery to be *reduced*, not eliminated. (You're asked whether the motorist can "recover," and a recovery reduced by comparative-fault principles is still a recovery.)

(C) is wrong, because it imposes a privity requirement where, in fact, there isn't one. There is no privity requirement in strict product liability cases, so a bystander who is injured by a defectively dangerous product can recover against the manufacturer, even though the bystander and the manufacturer have no contractual or other pre-existing relationship.

(D) is wrong, because even if the trucker was negligent, this will not relieve the trailer company of strict product liability. As the discussion of Choice (B) describes, a manufacturer will virtually never be absolved of responsibility merely because some person further down the distributive chain (e.g., a distributor or an end-user) either negligently fails to discover the danger or does discover the danger but fails to take available steps to remedy it.

Answer 40

Choice **(C)** is correct. If more than one person is a proximate cause of the plaintiff's harm, and the harm is indivisible, then under the traditional common-law rule, each defendant is liable for the entire harm. Davis and Jones would be jointly and severally liable. In a pure comparative fault system, the plaintiff is allowed to recover even if his fault is greater than that of the defendant. The plaintiff's recovery is reduced by a proportion equal to the ratio between his own fault and the total fault contributing to the accident. Therefore, Peter's recovery would be the amount of damages suffered reduced by the percentage of the total negligence that is attributed to him. And Peter can recover that entire amount of "net" damages from either defendant.

(A) and (B) are wrong because in a pure comparative fault system, the plaintiff is allowed to recover even if the percentage of his fault is greater than that of either defendant or greater than the fault of both defendants combined.

(D) is wrong because the harm is indivisible; therefore, the defendants are jointly and severally liable (each defendant is liable for the entire harm).

Answer 41

Choice **(D)** is correct. In a pure comparative negligence jurisdiction, the plaintiff is allowed to recover even if his fault is greater than that of the defendant. The plaintiff's recovery is reduced by a proportion equal to the ratio between his own negligence and the total negligence contributing to the accident. Under the rule of joint-and-several liability, if two defendants acted separately to produce an indivisible harm to the plaintiff, then each can be required to pay 100% of the plaintiff's damages. (Of course, plaintiff can recover only one satisfaction.) A defendant who is required to pay more than her fair share can recover the balance from the other. So here, Plaintiff can collect the full $60,000 (the total damage for which Plaintiff himself is not responsible) from either defendant; the defendant who pays the whole $60,000 may in turn collect from the other that portion representing the overpayment. Since D-1 has paid $60,000 when his fair share was only $30,000, he can recover the $30,000 overpayment from D-2.

(A) is wrong because, in a pure comparative negligence jurisdiction, the plaintiff is allowed to recover even if he is at fault and even if his fault is greater than that of the defendant. (A) incorrectly supposes that Plaintiff will not be able to collect damages because of his own fault.

(B) is wrong because it does not allow for Plaintiff to collect the full amount of damages owed to him ($60,000) from one defendant (even though each defendant's proportional share of the damages is $30,000) as provided under the rule of joint-and-several liability. See the discussion of Choice (D).

(C) is wrong because it limits Plaintiff's recovery to the amount of his own negligence (40% of $100,000). In a pure comparative negligence jurisdiction, the plaintiff is allowed to recover even if his fault is greater than that of the defendant. The plaintiff's recovery is reduced by a proportion equal to the ratio between his own negligence and the total negligence contributing to the accident. (In this case the computation produces $100,000 reduced by 40%, or a net of $60,000.)

Answer 42

Choice **(A)** is correct. Under the rule of joint-and-several liability, if two or more defendants are joint tortfeasors, the plaintiff may sue and collect from either of them or all of them. In a comparative fault system, the plaintiff's recovery is reduced by a proportion equal to the ratio between her own fault and the total fault contributing to the accident. If the plaintiff's total damages were $100,000, her damages will be reduced by 30% (her percentage of fault) for a total of $70,000. Where the negligence has been apportioned between the two defendants (at 30% for Donald and 40% for Drew), yet they were joint tortfeasors, the plaintiff may collect the total amount of damages from one defendant and then that defendant may later seek reimbursement ("contribution") from the other defendant for his share of the damages award. So the plaintiff can collect $70,000 from Donald (i.e., the full percentage of fault represented by all parties other than plaintiff), but Donald will then be able to collect $40,000 from Drew for the latter's share of the damages.

(B) is wrong because it allows Donald to be liable for only his proportion of the damages, which is not the case in a jurisdiction applying joint-and-several liability. This choice also allows Donald to recover $10,000 from Drew; however, in the case that Donald paid only $30,000, he would not be entitled to contribution, since he is responsible for at least his percentage of fault ($30,000). In other words, a defendant bringing a third-party contribution action against another joint tortfeasor is entitled to contribution only if he pays more than his percentage of fault.

(C) is wrong because it allows for Donald to be liable for only his proportion of the damages, which is not the case in a jurisdiction applying joint-and-several liability.

(D) is wrong because, in a pure comparative fault system, the plaintiff is allowed to recover even if his fault is greater than that of the defendant (indeed, even if the plaintiff's fault is greater than that of all defendants put together).

Answer 43

Choice **(A)** is correct. If there is a great difference in the degree of culpability of the defendants, the court will shift the financial responsibility for a tort from the less-culpable to the more-culpable one, by the use of the doctrine of indemnity. In this case, where Mark was an intentional tortfeasor (causing severe injury with a gun) and David was merely a negligent one (in allowing Mark to obtain possession of the gun), David will have the right to indemnity, i.e., the right to recover from Mark the full amount of the judgment that David paid.

(B) is wrong because, as stated in (A), David will be indemnified for the full amount of damages he paid, because of the great difference in the degree of culpability of the defendants.

(C) is wrong because it incorrectly implies that the parties are equally culpable and it does not recognize that David will be indemnified for the full amount of damages because of the great difference in the degree of culpability of the defendants.

(D) is wrong because, despite the fact that David's negligence was a proximate cause of the injury, David will be indemnified by Mark for the full amount of damages.

Answer 44

Choice **(C)** is correct. Most courts allow recovery for pure emotional distress, even if unaccompanied by bodily harm, where the defendant has negligently handled the corpse of the plaintiff's relative. This answer choice correctly applies this rule.

(A) is wrong because, although it is generally true that a plaintiff who does not suffer any physical impact or even threat to her own safety can't recover in negligence for emotional distress, there are exceptions. One exception is where the plaintiff has suffered emotional distress due to the defendant's mishandling of a corpse belonging to the plaintiff's close relative.

(B) is wrong because, although it is necessary to show that the defendant's behavior was extreme and outrageous in a suit for intentional infliction of emotional distress, this is not required to be proven in a case of negligent infliction of emotional distress. And by inference, what Ann is alleging here is negligent, not intentional, infliction of emotional distress.

(D) is wrong because a claim for negligent mishandling of a corpse is one of the few special situations where courts have allowed damages for pure emotional suffering despite the fact that the defendant has suffered no physical harm.

Answer 45

Choice (**A**) is correct. Most courts allow recovery for negligent infliction of emotional distress when there has been a negligent mishandling of a corpse. The fact pattern indicates that the Hospital was negligent in its care of the body. Where the facts are such that it can confidently be believed that there has been actual mental distress (i.e., where mental distress would be the normal human reaction), courts ignore the ban on recovery for purely mental harm in a claim for negligent infliction of emotional distress.

(B) is wrong because it misstates the law—neither hospitals nor any other class of defendant is strictly liable for mishandling dead bodies. What's special about dead bodies is that when they're *negligently* mishandled, a close relative of the body can recover for emotional distress that's not accompanied by bodily harm (something that is not usually the case in negligence actions).

(C) is wrong because, in the case of a claim for negligent mishandling of a corpse, it is not necessary that the plaintiff seek treatment for his distress. Where such mishandling occurs, courts are confident in inferring that a close relative of the corpse would indeed have suffered actual mental distress from the mishandling.

(D) is wrong because a claim for negligent mishandling of a corpse is a situation where courts have allowed damages for pure emotional suffering despite the fact that the defendant has suffered no physical harm.

Answer 46

Choice (**D**) is correct. Palko is an at-risk plaintiff, one who by virtue of his exposure to a particular substance, has suffered an increased likelihood of a particular disease. Even in jurisdictions disallowing recovery for pure emotional distress (unaccompanied by bodily harm) for negligently-inflicted harm or harm caused by a defective product, a plaintiff may recover for emotional distress as an "add on" if the plaintiff has also suffered bodily harm. That's true here—Palko's asbestosis is bodily harm, so he can add recovery for emotional distress due to the increased cancer risk on top of it to his recovery from the already-existing (though perhaps minor) bodily harm from asbestosis.

(A) is wrong because, in a suit for negligent infliction of emotional distress, it is not required that the emotional distress be the cause of a physical condition; it is possible that physical harm can cause compensable emotional distress, as is the case here.

(B) is wrong as a matter of law. If plaintiff had not already suffered bodily harm (the abnormal chest condition called asbestosis), this choice would be correct—many courts don't recognize a cause of action for "increased risk of cancer" even against a tortfeasor who has brought about that increased risk. But where plaintiff has already been injured—and asbestosis is an injury, i.e., a form of bodily harm regardless of whether it later produces cancer—virtually all courts allow the injured plaintiff to "tack on" a recovery for emotional distress due to the injury. And distress at the knowledge of increased cancer risk is no different, for this purpose, from any other distress.

(C) is wrong because it misses the issue. True, a supplier of a defectively dangerous product is strictly liable for the "harm" it causes. But the key question is, what *is* the harm that's compensable? (D) is a better explanation of why plaintiff will recover from harm that might seem to be purely intangible.

Answer 47

Choice **(D)** is correct. The general rule is that even if D negligently causes physical harm or property harm to *A*, D will not be liable for pure economic harm to *B*, where the latter harm stems from the harm to *A*. There is an exception if *B* was in the zone of physical danger. In many courts, there is a second exception if *B* watched physical harm to *A*, at least where *B* and *A* are close relatives. But here, neither exception applies. So the default rule applies: Since Penn was never placed at physical risk, and didn't witness the physical risk or injury to Star, Penn can't recover for his pure economic loss. (The theory behind this principle is that if such pure-economic-loss recovery were allowed, negligence liability would extend too far, and lawsuit costs would go through the roof.)

(A) and (B) are wrong, because neither recognizes the key issue, which is discussed in Choice (D).

(C) is wrong because it cites an irrelevant factor. Even if Danton had been able to foresee that by injuring Star he would cause harm to Penn, Danton would still not be liable, because the harm to Penn here is purely economic. In other words, this choice, like Choices (A) and (B), fails to deal with the key issue, liability for pure economic harm.

Answer 48

Choice **(C)** is correct. As a general rule, a landowner owes no duty to a trespasser to make her land safe. There are several exceptions, but none of those exceptions applies here. The exception that comes closest to applying is that an owner may have a duty of reasonable care to a trespassing child, if the owner has maintained an "attractive nuisance." But for reasons described in the analysis of Choice (B) below, this exception does not apply here.

(A) is wrong because the duty of a landowner to trespassers to keep the property free of dangerous artificial conditions exists only where the owner has reason to know that trespassers are in dangerous proximity to the condition and that they are unlikely to appreciate the risk. Even then, the duty is only to exercise reasonable care to warn trespassers of the danger, which was done here.

(B) is wrong because, while it is true that an owner may be liable to a trespasser if the owner has maintained an "attractive nuisance," the condition here was not an attractive nuisance. For a condition on land to be considered an attractive nuisance, there must be evidence that the possessor had reason to know that children were likely to trespass, as well as evidence that the plaintiff did not appreciate the risk involved. No such evidence is mentioned in the facts; for instance, there is no suggestion that children often stray from the day care center, and there is no reason to believe the child was not aware of the danger (since we're told he was a "bright nine-year-old" and that the danger was well-marked).

(D) is wrong because, while this answer correctly states that the corporation will prevail, it misstates the legal basis for this conclusion. Even if the day care center had a duty to keep children from the ice, the corporation could also be liable if it was negligent. That is, if *A* is negligent as to a risk, the fact that *B* was also negligent as to the same risk is unlikely to save *A* from liability.

Answer 49

Choice **(D)** is correct. Normally, a shopper in a store would be considered an invitee—a member of the public who comes onto land held open to him and who does so for the purpose for which the land is held open. Such people reasonably expect that the premises have been made safe for them. A visitor who is an invitee as to one part of the premises may become a trespasser if he goes beyond the part of the land held open to him. When Prad went behind the counter despite seeing the sign "No Admittance, Employees Only," he might be found to have been a trespasser. But even if that's true, when the clerk saw him in that position, he was a "discovered trespasser," and as such the store had an obligation to warn him of dangers known to it and likely unknown to Prad. Therefore, if the clerk had reason to believe that Prad was unaware of the open shaft (and given that the facts tell us the *clerk* knew about the open shaft), Drug Store will be liable for the clerk's failure to warn Prad of the danger.

(A) is wrong because Prad was a licensee when he was behind the cashier's counter, as explained in the discussion of Choice (D).

(B) is wrong because liability arose from breach of the owner's duty to warn Prad of a danger that it should reasonably anticipate that Prad may not discover. Willful or wanton conduct is not required.

(C) is wrong because this is not a claim for strict liability. Premises are not "defective." Liability arises here, if at all, from negligence principles, not from strict liability. So the key issue is whether the clerk should have realized that Prad didn't know about the open shaft (as discussed in Choice (D)).

Answer 50

Choice (**A**) is correct. A trespassing child may sue for harm suffered from an injurious condition on the defendant's land. The only plausible basis for Philip to recover would be the special rule under which a landowner will be liable for an artificial condition that is highly dangerous to trespassing children. The requirements set forth in Rest. 2d, § 339 for such liability are that: (1) the place where the condition exists must be (as the owner knows) one on which children are likely to trespass; (2) there is, as the owner knows, an unreasonable risk of death or serious bodily harm to such children from the condition; (3) the children because of their youth do not discover the condition or don't recognize the risk from it; (4) the utility of maintaining the condition is slight compared with the risks to the children involved; and (5) the owner fails to exercise reasonable care. Choice (A) correctly addresses requirement (3), that the child, because of his youth, either did not discover the condition or did not realize the danger posed by it.

(B) is wrong because, if Philip failed to exercise reasonable care, this would merely reduce his recovery, but not block it altogether. The facts indicate that the traditional common-law rules pertaining to contributory negligence (which would block recovery by a negligent plaintiff) have been replaced by a pure comparative negligence rule (where the plaintiff's recovery is reduced by a proportion equal to the ratio between his own fault and the total fault contributing to the accident). Therefore, if Philip was negligent, his recovery would be reduced, but not eliminated as this choice implies.

(C) is wrong because a duty is owed to child trespassers as long as certain requirements are met, as discussed in the explanation of Choice (A).

(D) is wrong because most modern courts reject the requirement that the child must have been attracted by the particular condition which ends up injuring him (the "attractive nuisance" doctrine).

Answer 51

Choice (**D**) is correct. Patrick was a licensee, a person who has the owner's consent to be on the owner's property, but who does not have a business purpose for being there, or anything else entitling him to be there apart from the owner's consent. When the plaintiff is a licensee, the defendant does not have a "duty to inspect" for dangers. But if the defendant knows of a dangerous condition, the defendant has a duty to take reasonable precautions to make the premises safe. In this case, a reasonable jury could find that since Grandmother knew of the danger from guns, she had a duty to take reasonable care to keep the cabinet locked.

(A) is wrong because, even though there may not be a special duty arising from the Grandmother-Grandson relationship, a duty did arise for Grandmother, as owner of the premises and the gun cabinet, to use reasonable care in safeguarding the guns. She is therefore liable for the foreseeable consequences of her breach of this duty regardless of whether it was Grandson or some other child who got his hand on the gun.

(B) is wrong because if Grandma did not recall that the gun cabinet was unlocked, this is evidence of her unreasonable behavior. Reasonable care would require that an owner of a gun cabinet be extremely vigilant in making sure that the cabinet is locked, especially when there are young children exploring the premises.

(C) is wrong because it relies on an inappropriate concept. The concept of an "inherently dangerous instrumentality" might apply to strict product liability, or to strict liability for conducting an abnormally dangerous activity. But it would not apply to a negligence suit. In other words, plaintiff can't win unless defendant was negligent—it's not enough that defendant possessed an inherently dangerous instrumentality (if, indeed, a gun is such). Also, guns can themselves be locked (trigger guards), so the factual accuracy of this choice is questionable as well.

Answer 52

Choice (A) is correct. Grocery store shoppers are invitees—members of the public who come onto land held open to them and who do so for the purpose for which the land is held open. Such people reasonably expect that the premises have been made safe for them, and the owner must exercise reasonable care for the safety of such people. Reasonable care by the owner will typically require that she attempt to exercise control over third persons on the premises. A storekeeper, for instance, will generally be required to take reasonable security measures to prevent attacks or thefts against her customers.

(B) is wrong because Supermarket is liable for harm caused to its invitee only if it has breached a duty of reasonable care to that invitee. Choice (B) asserts a blanket rule of liability, and is therefore incorrect.

(C) is wrong because Supermarket's duty requires that it use reasonable efforts to control third persons on the premises. Issuing a warning does not necessarily satisfy this duty.

(D) is wrong because if Supermarket breached its duty in failing to protect Lorner against the rapist, it is liable for injuries inflicted by the rapist that were a foreseeable result of breach of that duty. Note that an event may have multiple proximate causes; so here, the fact that the rapist was a proximate cause of Lorner's injuries doesn't prevent Supermarket's negligence (in failing to use adequate security measures) from also being a proximate cause of those injuries.

Answer 53

Choice (C) is correct, because punitive damages are not available in ordinary negligence cases. Since this is the only cause of action listed that would NOT allow punitive damages, it is the best response.

(A) is wrong, because punitive damages are available to victims of intentional torts. Ordinary negligence cases, however, do not allow for punitive damages.

(B) is wrong, because punitive damages are available to victims of intentional torts. Ordinary negligence cases, however, do not allow for punitive damages.

(D) is wrong, because punitive damages may be available to victims of reckless conduct. Ordinary negligence cases, however, do not allow for punitive damages.

Answer 54

Choice **(C)** is correct. The doctrine of vicarious liability provides that in some special relationships, such as that of employer-employee, the tortious act of an employee may be imputed to his employer. As a result, the latter will be held liable, even though its own conduct may have been completely blameless. In order for Delval Airline to be liable for the battery perpetrated by Morton, there would have to be such a relationship between Morton and the airline. Since, as (C) correctly recites, Morton was not acting as an agent or employee of Delval, vicarious liability would not be applied.

(A) is wrong because the fact that Perkins suffered a battery by itself doesn't justify imposing liability on Delval for the battery.

(B) is wrong because the airline has not committed battery here. Battery is, of course, an intentional tort, so the airline can be liable for that intentional tort (as opposed to liable in negligence) only if the airline or someone for whom the airline is directly responsible had the requisite intent to commit a harmful or offensive contact. Since Morton wasn't the airline's agent or employee, this requirement of intent isn't satisfied. The fact that the airline may have been *reckless* in facilitating Morton's intentional tort won't be enough, because a reckless mental state on the part of the airline won't suffice for battery. (Whereas a business owner can be liable in *negligence* for failing to stop someone else's negligent or intentional tort, there's no comparable principle whereby a business owner becomes liable for intentional tort X merely for recklessly bringing about a third person's commission of X.)

(D) is wrong the because severity of the injury is irrelevant in determining Delval's liability for the conduct of another.

Answer 55

Choice **(D)** is correct, because an owner of a wild animal or an abnormally dangerous animal is strictly liable for harm caused by that animal's dangerous nature. Part of what makes wild animals dangerous is that third persons who encounter the animal may well experience acute fear, whether that fear is well-founded or not as to the particular animal. Rest. 2d Torts, § 507, cmt. g and illus. 1. Here, even though the snake was defanged, the worker had no reason to know this. Therefore, his injury was caused by a foreseeable aspect of the animal's wild and dangerous nature, namely, its tendency to cause fear of being bitten.

(A) is wrong, because owners of dangerous animals are strictly liable even when the harm would not have occurred but for the operation of a force of nature. Thus, the fact that a storm caused the snake to be released, rather than any action on the part of the homeowner, does not limit the homeowner's liability.

(B) is wrong, because an owner of a wild animal or an abnormally dangerous animal is strictly liable for harm caused by that animal's dangerous nature. The contributory negligence of the worker would not be a defense to strict liability, and in any case there is nothing in the facts to indicate that the worker would have reason to foresee the risk of a poisonous snake.

(C) is wrong, because, while this answer correctly states that the worker will prevail, it misstates the legal basis for this conclusion. There is probably not enough evidence here to support a finding of negligence. In any event, whether the owner did or did not take precautions that would be "adequate" (i.e., that would constitute reasonable care), this won't matter — the whole point of strict liability for keeping wild animals is that if the wild animal causes harm in a way that is related to its wildness, the plaintiff does not have to show negligence by the owner. Nor does it matter that the snake was defanged; the worker had no reason to know this, and his injury falls within the risk run by the homeowner because it was caused by the worker's foreseeable reaction to seeing an escaped snake.

Answer 56

Choice (D) is correct. Operation of a nuclear power plant is an ultrahazardous activity. Therefore, NPP can be strictly liable for the accident without any proof by the exposed plaintiff that NPP behaved negligently.

(A) is incorrect because the question of whether doubling the risk of contracting cancer ten years into the future presents a substantial issue, that is, whether the plaintiff's have already suffered a present compensable legal injury.

(B) is incorrect because valuing the damages suffered by a plaintiff who is now healthy but is at an increased risk of contracting a deadly disease, raises the substantial issue of whether the damages are too speculative to calculate at the present time.

(C) is incorrect because causation is a real issue in the case. Plaintiffs ordinarily have the burden of proving harm. At present they have not contracted cancer and have suffered no present harm. So it's a real issue whether any cancer they suffer in the future (the "present value" of which they're trying to recover now) will have been caused by the radiation exposure.

Answer 57

Choice (D) is correct. What we care about here is whether Glass is strictly liable for having carried out an abnormally dangerous activity. The answer is, "no." It's very unlikely the use of the glue here would be considered ultrahazardous, as you can see by considering the four elements that generally make an activity ultrahazardous: (1) the activity involves a high risk of serious harm, (2) there's no way to perform the activity completely safely no matter how much care is taken, (3) the activity is not commonly engaged in in the particular community, and (4) the danger of the activity outweighs its utility to the community. At least element (2) is missing (it's possible to do glueing safely by venting the glue fumes to the outside), and it's doubtful whether element (3) is satisfied either (since remodeling with glue occurs all the time, even if this particular glue brand is not widely used). So the activity isn't ultrahazardous.

Nor were Glass's employees negligent—it's clear from the facts that they did not know about the danger that the fumes would be vented over to Innes, so there's no indication of negligence on their part. And Glass has no strict product liability, because as is further discussed in Choice (A) below, only "sellers" or makers of defective products, not users, have such liability.

(A) is wrong because it states incorrect law. It is not true that a user of a product is held to the same standard as the manufacturer. That's because a manufacturer is strictly liable for selling a defective product, whereas a user is not. (Even if the use occurs in a business context, and even if the use directly injures a third person because the product being used is "defective" and dangerous, the user will be liable only for negligence.)

(B) is wrong because even if the employees of Glass caused the fumes, this does not automatically make Glass strictly liable. Unless either the activity was ultrahazardous, or Glass's employees were negligent, Glass would not be liable even though the employees caused the fumes to enter plaintiff's area of the building.

(C) is wrong because there could be an instance where using a product for its intended purposes still creates liability. For instance, if Glass's use of the product was indeed ultrahazardous, as discussed in the explanation for Choice (D), Glass could have been liable.

Answer 58

Choice **(B)** is correct. Blasting is considered an ultrahazardous activity, giving rise to strict liability. Where one person hires an independent contractor to perform an untrahazardous activity, the hirer is strictly liable, just as the contractor is, even if the hirer used all due care selecting a careful contractor.

(A) is wrong because Landco is responsible for damages caused by Poolco regardless of whether or not Poolco is Landco's employee. The doctrine of vicarious liability provides that in some special relationships, such as that of employer-employee, the tortious act of an employee may be imputed to his employer. As a result, the latter will be held liable, even though its own conduct may have been completely blameless. An employee is one who works subject to the control of the person who has hired him. If the party that caused the damage is not an employee, but an independent contractor, there will generally not be vicarious liability. However, there is an exception—where the work is such that, unless special precautions are taken, there will be a high degree of danger to others. Rest. 2d, §§ 416, 427. That's clearly true of blasting in a residential neighborhood (which is an "ultrahazardous activity" for which the person carrying it out has strict liability). Therefore, Landco, the hiring party, will be liable for the damage caused by Poolco, despite the fact that Poolco is an independent contractor, and even if Landco didn't retain the right to direct and control Poolco's work.

(C) is wrong because the use of reasonable care is irrelevant in a claim for strict liability for an ultrahazardous activity, as this is. (See the discussion of Choice (A) for more about this.)

(D) is wrong because, as the hiring party, Landco will be vicariously liable for harm caused by Poolco based on the abnormal dangerousness of the activity in which Poolco was engaging. See the more extensive discussion of why this is so, in the treatment of Choice (A).

Answer 59

Choice **(B)** is correct. As in any negligence claim, a defendant will be liable for product liability based on negligence if (1) he failed to exercise such care as a reasonable person in his position would have exercised; (2) this was a breach of the duty to prevent the foreseeable risk of injury to anyone in the plaintiff's position, and (3) this breach must have caused the plaintiff's damages. There are four principal ways in which a manufacturer can be negligent: (1) manufacturing flaw, (2) negligent failure to inspect, (3) negligent design, and (4) failure to warn.

Choice (B) is directed at scenario (2): If the bicycle company, using reasonable care in the inspection process, would have discovered the defect, then its not discovering it was negligent. This would satisfy the "breach" element of negligence, and the other three elements—duty, causation, and damages—are not at issue here. Finally, if the bicycle company was negligent, it'll be liable to the pedestrian, since it is reasonably foreseeable that if a cyclist's brakes fail, he will hit a pedestrian.

(A) is wrong, because the element it states would be irrelevant in a product liability claim based on negligence, and it ignores an element negligence requires: fault. As in any negligence claim, a product liability suit based on negligence requires, among other things, that the defendant failed to exercise such care as a reasonable person in his position would have exercised. The mere fact that the bicycle was defective would not be sufficient to establish negligence by the bicycle company, since the defect might have occurred despite the company's total carefulness in design, manufacture and inspection.

If you chose this response, you were probably thinking of a product liability claim based on *strict* liability. Under that theory, a defendant *will* be liable if the product was defectively dangerous when it left his control (in the parlance of Choice A, when the product was "placed in the stream of commerce"). However, you're told here that the basis of the claim is negligence.

(C) is wrong, because the pedestrian needn't be a purchaser in order to prevail. Choice (C) suggests that the pedestrian should lose because, as a non-purchaser, he lacks privity with the bicycle company. This is not the actual rule for a product liability suit based on negligence; in fact, the defendant's duty extends to anyone foreseeably endangered by the product. The scope of the risk posed by failing bicycle brakes includes injury to bystanders whom the rider tries to avoid but can't because of the failure. Thus, as long as the pedestrian can prove that the bicycle company was negligent and this proximately caused his damages, he'll prevail.

(D) is wrong, because even if the cyclist was negligent, this will not prevent the pedestrian from recovering. This choice suggests that if the cyclist's turning onto the sidewalk was negligent, this negligence will constitute a supervening cause, breaking the chain of causation from the bicycle company to the pedestrian. Even in the unlikely case that the cyclist's conduct was considered unreasonable, this negligence wouldn't exonerate the bicycle company. A negligent tortfeasor will only be relieved of liability due to intervening forces if those forces were extremely hard to foresee at the time of the defendant's negligent conduct (here, the negligent manufacture of the bike). Where a bicycle's brakes fail, it's perfectly foreseeable that the failure might combine with negligent riding by the cyclist, so as to cause an accident with a bystander, so the negligent riding (even if it occurred) won't be a superseding event. Nor will the cyclist's negligence *reduce* the pedestrian's recovery from the bicycle company—joint-and-several liability means the pedestrian can recover the full amount of his damages from any co-tortfeasor; it would be up to the bicycle company to recover contribution (a sharing of the damages, in proportion to fault) from the cyclist.

Answer 60

Choice **(D)** is correct. As a retailer, Seller will only be liable in negligence due to its own affirmative negligence. Retailers only have a duty to inspect if they have reason to believe the product is likely to be defective, and even if they do have a duty to inspect, they'll only be liable if an inspection undertaken with reasonable care would have uncovered the defect. This choice mirrors these requirements by comparing Seller's conduct to what a retailer in the exercise of due care would have done.

(A) is wrong because, as a retailer defending a *negligence* action, Seller will only be liable for negligence due to its own affirmative negligence. So the fact that the product was defective isn't close to enough. If you chose this response, you were probably thinking of strict product liability, under which proof of the defect would be the lynchpin of Child's claim. However, you're told the suit has been brought only in negligence, and negligence requires some proof of lack of due care on defendant's part.

(B) is wrong because it, like Choice (A), understates the proof Child's negligence claim will require. Since the action is based solely on negligence, Seller will only be liable due to its own affirmative negligence. Retailers only have a duty to inspect if they have reason to believe the product is likely to be defective, and even if they *do* have a duty to inspect, they'll only be liable if an inspection undertaken with reasonable care would have uncovered the defect. Thus, merely proving a defect and a lack of inspection would be insufficient to pin negligence liability on Seller—Child would also have to prove that a reasonable inspection would have uncovered the defect.

(C) is wrong because it, too, understates the proof Child's negligence claim will require. Child must show both that (1) Seller failed to follow the reasonable standard of care of a retailer, and (2) this failure proximately and actually caused the accident. Seller's mere failure to discover the defect during an inspection that actually occurred would not make Seller negligent unless a reasonable inspection would have uncovered the defect (since without the latter showing, Seller's failure to inspect in a reasonable manner didn't change the outcome, and thus wasn't the proximate cause of the accident).

Answer 61

Choice (**B**) is correct. A seller may expressly represent that her goods have certain qualities. If the goods turn out not to have these qualities, the purchaser may sue for breach of warranty. UCC Sec. 2-313. Had the statement "will not damage original oil finishes" been true, then the loss suffered would not have occurred. In this case, the product is not defective or dangerous to people (it only causes harm to a particular type of furniture). Therefore, a warranty claim is suitable for this kind of case.

(A) is wrong because the fact that no other product would have been safer for use on the furniture is irrelevant when the claim is based on breach of an express warranty, i.e., a warranty stating that the product works on all antique furniture and will not damage original oil finishes. This answer sounds like it's trying to conjure up a design defect claim, where it is relevant that the adoption of a reasonable alternative design is available or not. However, the availability of such a reasonable alternative design is irrelevant here, given the warranty claim.

(C) is wrong because suit for breach of warranty does not require that the product be "defective."

(D) is wrong because the fact that the product is not dangerous to people is irrelevant in this case of breach of warranty.

Answer 62

Choice (**A**) is correct. This choice is correct because: (1) it correctly implies that the only basis on which the glue manufacturer could be liable is on a strict product liability theory; and (2) it correctly asserts that if the glue manufacturer is strictly liable, then the paint company must be as well. Let's take these steps one at a time. As to (1), the glue manufacturer won't be found negligent, since it had no reason to believe that the product posed eye dangers, and since it warned of any danger (e.g., from lack of ventilation) of which it was aware. So if the glue manufacturer were liable, it would have to be on a strict product liability basis. As to (2), if the glue manufacturer were strictly liable, it would have to be because it sold a defectively dangerous product. If the product was defectively dangerous, then the paint company, as a "downstream" re-seller, would have exactly the same liability, since anyone who sells a defectively dangerous product is strictly liable for it. So there's no way the glue manufacturer could be liable without the paint company's also being liable.

(B) is wrong because it doesn't matter whether the secretary was an invitee of a tenant in the building or not. The recovery here would have to be on a strict product liability basis (see the analysis of Choice (A) for why), and any person who is injured by a defect in a defective product can recover against any seller of that product, whether the plaintiff was an invitee at the time of the injury or not. (Indeed, even if the secretary had been a trespasser, she could have recovered against the paint company in strict product liability.)

(C) is wrong because it ignores the possibility that the paint company is strictly liable as a non-negligent seller of a dangerously defective product.

(D) is wrong because it ignores the possibility that the paint company as a seller of a dangerously defective product would be strictly liable even though the product came in a sealed package. Sellers of dangerously defective products are strictly liable for the harm caused by the defect, and that is true even though the seller behaved with all possible care. So the fact that the product came in a sealed package — thus preventing the paint company from recognizing or altering the danger even if it wanted to — is irrelevant to its strict liability.

Answer 63

Choice (**D**) is correct. This is a strict liability claim for a manufacturing defect, i.e., a scenario in which the product has departed from its intended design in a way that makes it unsafe. It must be proven that (1) the product was defective, (2) at the time it left the defendant's hands, and (3) the product caused harm. The causation element will be satisfied in this case if it was foreseeable that the failure of the safety device would invite rescue by a third party (and if the rescue was not performed in a grossly careless manner).

(A) is wrong because the retailer will be subject to strict product liability; and, therefore the reasonableness of his conduct is irrelevant.

(B) is wrong because reliance is irrelevant here. One who is in the business of selling a product which turns out to be dangerously defective has strict product liability, and that's true whether the retailer made any implied or express representation of safety (and whether or not the buyer relied on such a representation if one was made).

(C) is wrong because, in the ordinary case, the product user's failure to discover the defect will not be considered negligence. And even if the user's failure to discover the defect *was* negligence (which it isn't), that negligence would only reduce the plaintiff's recovery, not eliminate it. (The choice asks you whether plaintiff would "prevail," and a recovery reduced by plaintiff's percentage of fault would still constitute "prevailing" in everyday usage.)

Answer 64

Choice (**D**) is correct. Products that conform to their design, and essentially do what the consumer expects them to do, yet are by their very nature inherently dangerous, are products that are "unavoidably unsafe." The chemistry set is such a product. The question to be determined is whether such an unavoidably-unsafe product is "reasonably safe" (because if it isn't, it gives rise to strict products liability, and if it is, it doesn't trigger such liability). The Third Restatement applies a risk-utility approach to such products, finding them defective rather than reasonably safe "when the foreseeable risks of harm posed by the product could have been reduced or avoided by the adoption of a reasonable alternative design by the seller . . . and the omission of the alternative design renders the product not reasonably safe." Rest. 3d (Prod. Liab.) § 2(b). (D) essentially applies this test. That is, the choice turns on whether the set was as safe as possible and its benefits exceeded its risks; if it was, the choice correctly asserts that the classmate would not prevail.

(A) is wrong because the outcome would not turn on whether such a warning was given. The presence or absence of a warning will only determine the outcome of a product-liability case if the warning would have altered the outcome. Here, even if there had been a warning, this would probably not have prevented the knocking over of the Bunsen burner. (Would the student have been less likely to knock over the burner if there had been such a warning and he had read it? Probably not.)

(B) is wrong because when a person manufactures and sells a dangerous product that causes injury post-sale, the act of manufacturing and selling it won't be deemed to be an abnormally dangerous activity. If the explosion had occurred during manufacture, that probably *would* qualify for the abnormally-dangerous-activity form of strict liability (also known as strict liability for "ultrahazardous" activities). But post-manufacture and post-sale, the relevant doctrine is strict product liability.

(C) is wrong because it falsely suggests that the student's negligence would bar the manufacturer's liability to the classmate. There can be multiple causes in fact, and if the chemistry set had been defectively designed (which it wasn't), that defect could (and likely would) have been a cause in fact, just as the student's negligence would also have been. In that scenario, the student's negligence wouldn't even have caused the classmate's recovery from the manufacturer to be reduced, let alone eliminated, because the student's negligence wouldn't have been imputed to the classmate.

Answer 65

Choice (**A**) is correct. The manufacturer is the only one of the three potential defendants who can be liable in strict liability. A person who is engaged in the business of selling products, and who sells a defective product, is subject to liability for harm to persons or property caused by the defect. Rest. 3d (Prod. Liab.) § 1. One type of defect is a "design defect." A design defect occurs "when the foreseeable risks of harm posed by the product could have been reduced or avoided by the adoption of a reasonable alternative design by the seller or other distributor, or a predecessor in the commercial chain of distribution, and the omission of the alternative design renders the product not reasonably safe." Rest. 3d (Prod. Liab.) § 2(b). Here, the manufacturer will be strictly liable because it satisfies the required elements for strict liability: (1) it was in the business of selling products; (2) it sold the product that caused the harm here (the HVAC system); and (3) the HVAC system was "defectively designed," since a better HVAC system was a reasonably available alternative design that could have reduced or avoided the harm, making the omission of such alternative something that rendered the product not reasonably safe.

Neither the heating company nor the cooling company is liable under this test, since neither sold the defectively-designed product (the HVAC system). It's true that the heating company and the cooling company sold *components* that went into the defective HVAC system. But their components were not themselves defective at the time of sale, and these defendants did not do anything that contributed to the "downstream" design defect introduced by the manufacturer (e.g., they didn't give the manufacturer instructions that induced the manufacturer to design the ventilating system in a defective manner). So they cannot be said to have "sold" a "defectively-designed product)."

Since (B), (C), and (D) all treat either the heating company or the cooling company as liable, these choices are wrong for the reasons described in the discussion of Choice (A) above.

Answer 66

Choice (**C**) is correct. In product liability cases, the duty to warn is in effect an extra duty. That is, even if the product would not be defectively dangerous if accompanied by the appropriate warning, absence of such a warning may convert the product into a defectively dangerous product for which there is strict product liability. So here, even if a tire tread that can separate at speeds of 85+ would not have been defectively dangerous if properly warned of, the car manufacturer (which "sold" the tires as part of the original car equipment) would be strictly liable if the manual did not contain an adequate warning of the risk. And it's quite plausible that the manual's failure to specify that the tires that came with the car were not the sort of "high-speed-capability tires" that were required for high speeds would be an actionable failure to warn (especially in light of the fact that the car was designed and marketed based on its ability to go 100+ mph).

(A) is wrong because it is not a misuse of a sports car to drive it at a speed in excess of 100 miles per hour when that was a use intended by the manufacturer who designed the car for high-speed driving and who marketed the car with an intended and recognized appeal to youthful drivers.

(B) is wrong because, as discussed in (C), the car might well be "defective" in light of inadequate warnings about the capabilities of the tires sold with it.

(D) is wrong because if Peter was found to be negligent he could still prevail. The facts state that the jurisdiction applies a pure comparative fault system in strict product liability actions. In a pure comparative fault system, the plaintiff is allowed to recover even if his fault is greater than that of the defendant. The plaintiff's recovery is reduced by a proportion equal to the ratio between his own fault and the total fault contributing to the accident. Therefore, Peter's negligence would not bar recovery in this case, but merely reduce his recovery.

Answer 67

Choice (**A**) is correct, because the plaintiff cannot satisfy his *prima facie* case for either cause of action. To succeed in a strict products liability claim in this context, plaintiff would need to prove that a product was sold in a defective condition that is unreasonably dangerous to the user or consumer. As the dentist was not in the business of selling the product, the plaintiff cannot succeed against the dentist (although the plaintiff could sue the product's manufacturer). To succeed in a malpractice claim in this context, the plaintiff must prove that the dentist did not act with the level of skill and learning commonly possessed by members of the profession in good standing. Here, the dentist used "due care," so the plaintiff cannot satisfy this burden.

(B) is wrong, because the dentist did not depart from a professional standard of care. To succeed in a malpractice claim in this context, the plaintiff must prove that the dentist did not act with the level of skill and learning commonly possessed by members of the profession in good standing. Here, the dentist used "due care," so the plaintiff cannot satisfy this burden.

(C) is wrong, because the dentist is not in the business of selling this product. To succeed in a strict products liability claim in this context, the plaintiff would need to prove that a product was sold in a defective condition that is unreasonably dangerous to the user or consumer. As the dentist was not in the business of selling the product, the plaintiff cannot succeed against the dentist (although the plaintiff could sue the product's manufacturer).

(D) is wrong, because the plaintiff cannot satisfy his *prima facie* case for either cause of action. To succeed in a strict products liability claim in this context, the plaintiff would need to prove that a product was sold in a defective condition that is unreasonably dangerous to the user or consumer. As the dentist was not in the business of selling the product, the plaintiff cannot succeed against the dentist (although the plaintiff could sue the product's manufacturer). To succeed in a malpractice claim in this context, the plaintiff must prove that the dentist did not act with the level of skill and learning commonly possessed by members of the profession in good standing. Here, the dentist used "due care," so the plaintiff cannot satisfy this burden.

Answer 68

Choice (**C**) is correct. Paul can win only on a nuisance theory (not on negligence or strict liability for ultrahazardous activities, as to which see Choice (A) below). So let's analyze whether the requirements for nuisance are satisfied here. A private nuisance is an unreasonable interference with the plaintiff's use and enjoyment of his land. In order to recover for private nuisance, the plaintiff must show (1) that his use and enjoyment of his land was interfered with in a "substantial" way and (2) that the defendant's conduct was negligent, abnormally dangerous, or intentional. The facts state that the effectiveness of Paul's electronic equipment is impaired by electrical interference from Electo's plant. But unless the interference with Paul's business is substantial and unreasonable, Paul cannot prevail.

(A) is wrong because Electo's use of high voltage electricity would not be found to be abnormally dangerous, especially considering the fact that the harm it caused (interference with use of land) was not dangerous. Activities considered "abnormally dangerous" are subject to strict liability. The Second Restatement lists factors to consider when determining whether an activity is abnormally dangerous: (1) it creates a high degree of risk; (2) it poses a risk of serious harm; (3) it cannot be eliminated even by due care; (4) it is uncommon and (5) it is inappropriate at the particular site. Liability is more likely to be imposed where the activity's value to the community is outweighed by its dangerous attributes. Rest. 2d, § 520. Here, factors (3), (4), and (5) cut against liability. Generally, electric utilities are found not to be engaged in an ultrahazardous activity when they maintain power lines.

(B) is wrong because, if the interference with Paul's business was not substantial and unreasonable, then Electo would not be responsible in nuisance for any harm caused to Paul, even that harm of which it was subsequently made aware.

(D) is wrong because there *has* been harm to Paul's property. There has been physical harm to equipment located on his property, from Electo's activity.

Answer 69

Choice **(B)** is correct. A private nuisance is an unreasonable interference with the plaintiff's use and enjoyment of his land. Rest. 2d, § 822. Whereas trespass is an interference with the plaintiff's right of exclusive possession of his property, nuisance is an interference with his right to use and enjoy it. A condition, such as noise, near the plaintiff's property that interferes with his peace of mind would be a nuisance, but not a trespass, since nothing physically entered the property. Palmco might not win on its nuisance theory (the court might hold that the social utility of the beach restoration project outweighs the damage to Palmco's use and enjoyment), but of the theories listed it is the only one that is plausible.

(A) is wrong because, even though operating a stone-crushing machine may very well be an abnormally dangerous activity, and worthy of applying strict liability, the only harm caused thus far is noise. And noise is not the kind of harm that makes using a stone-crushing machine abnormally dangerous (if, indeed, use of such a machine *is* abnormally dangerous).

(C) is wrong because a plaintiff generally cannot recover in negligence for pure economic loss, in the absence of harm to the plaintiff's person or property. No exception to this general rule applies here.

(D) is wrong because trespass liability requires physical entry by the defendant (or by some object under the defendant's control) onto the plaintiff's property. Sound waves are deemed insufficiently physical to give rise to trespass liability.

Answer 70

Choice **(D)** is correct. If a statement could be reasonably interpreted only in one way, then that interpretation must in fact be defamatory in order for a plaintiff to prevail in a case of defamation. Here, the answer states that there is only one reasonable interpretation, that "murderer" means one who would sign a death warrant. Therefore, the statement was pure opinion (that one who signs a death warrant is properly classified as a murderer), not a provably false fact.

(A) is wrong because there must be an element of disgrace connected with the allegation, not a mere lowering of esteem, in order for the statement to be deemed defamatory. Also, to be defamatory a statement must be a provably false statement of fact, and this isn't (for reasons described in the analysis of (D) above).

(B) is wrong because the foundation for the defamation claim must be laid before the constitutional questions are addressed. It is true that when the plaintiff is a public official there is an additional requirement that the defendant make the accusation with knowledge of falsity or reckless disregard of the truth. *New York Times Co. v. Sulllivan* (1964). However, the common-law elements of the claim must be satisfied first. To be defamatory a statement must be a provably false statement of fact, and this isn't (for reasons described in the analysis of (D) above). Therefore Governor Doe would fail in setting out a claim for defamation even before the constitutional issues were addressed.

(C) is wrong because if this is libel, then the plaintiff does not have to show "special harm" of a pecuniary nature, and if it is slander, then it would be categorized as "slander per se." It is unclear whether the sign broadcast on television news would be considered libel (written or printed matter) or slander (oral and all other statements). "Special harm" of a pecuniary nature need not be proven for libelous statements. A statement imputing criminal behavior to the plaintiff that is "punishable by imprisonment" or "regarded by public opinion as involving moral turpitude" is "slander per se" and does not require a showing of special harm either. Rest. 2d § 571. Therefore, however the statement is categorized, pecuniary loss need not be proven in order for the plaintiff to prevail.

Answer 71

Choice (B) is correct. One of the elements of defamation is "publication," i.e., the fact that the defamatory statement was communicated to at least one person other than the plaintiff. Furthermore, plaintiff must show that defendant acted either negligently or intentionally with regard to publication. So if defendant neither knew nor had reason to know that the statement would be heard and understood by someone other than the plaintiff, the publication requirement has not been satisfied, but if defendant did have reason to anticipate such an overhearing, then the requirement has been satisfied.

(A) is wrong because whether or not Pat was fraudulently induced into the office is irrelevant to the determination of his slander suit.

(C) is wrong. Drew could have been negligent in believing in the charge. If Drew was indeed negligent in not verifying the truth of the theft accusation, his "good faith" (i.e., honest belief in the statement's truth) won't shield him. That is, where, as here, the plaintiff is not a public figure, plaintiff may recover for defamation based on a mere showing of negligence regarding the truth, rather than knowledge of falsity or reckless disregard of the truth (which public-figure plaintiffs have to show, as a constitutional matter under *N.Y. Times v. Sullivan* (1964)).

(D) is wrong because if Drew should have foreseen that his statement would be overheard by another person, then the publication element was satisfied, as discussed in the explanation of Choice (C).

Answer 72

Choice (D) is correct. In a common-law claim for defamation, the plaintiff must show that a (1) defamatory statement (2) regarding the plaintiff (3) was communicated to at least one other person (publication) and (4) that the plaintiff's reputation was damaged. In addition, some degree of fault will usually have to be proven. The issue in this fact pattern is whether the statement was published. Able's statement was made in a foreign language, so although there were other students present, it is not clear whether or not the statement was understood (the fact pattern does not, for instance, indicate that the fellow classmates who heard the statement were in the advanced Russian language course). It is therefore unclear whether the "publication" element has been satisfied, and Baker cannot prevail unless it is determined that at least one of the other students understood Able's statement.

(A) is wrong because even if the statement could be categorized as "slander per se," Baker would still have to prove all the other elements of a defamation case; he still needs to show that the statement was indeed understood by at least one other student in the cafeteria in order to fulfill the "publication" element. To ultimately prevail in a case of slander, the plaintiff must usually show special harm of a pecuniary nature unless the statement is categorized as "slander per se." Rest. 2d § 558. A statement imputing criminal behavior to the plaintiff that is "punishable by imprisonment" or "regarded by public opinion as involving moral turpitude" falls under this category. Rest. 2d § 571. However, even if Baker's alleged crime of taking money would fall under the category of slander per se, Baker would still need to overcome the hurdle of proving the publication element, as discussed in the explanation of (D).

(B) is wrong because the "publication" requirement not only requires that the statement be made in the presence of at least one other person, but that the third person understand it and perceive its defamatory aspects. The fact pattern is vague on this matter. Therefore, in order for Baker to prevail, it must be determined that the statement was understood by a third person, as discussed in the explanation of (D).

(C) is wrong because the requirement that the defendant make the accusation with knowledge of falsity or reckless disregard of the truth applies only when the plaintiff is a public official or public figure. *New York Times Co. v. Sulllivan* (1964). Baker, as a student, clearly doesn't qualify as a public figure or public official.

Answer 73

Choice **(B)** is correct. Even under Supreme Court First Amendment-based restrictions, states are permitted to give a private (i.e., non-public-figure) plaintiff the right to win if the plaintiff can show that the defendant made a defamatory falsehood and behaved at least negligently with respect to the statement's truth. Since Bradley is not a public figure, the fact that the defendant entertained substantial doubts about the truth of the statement is more than enough to prove negligence. (In fact, such doubts probably even establish the "reckless disregard of the truth" variety of "actual malice," which Bradley would have to show if he *were* a public figure.)

(A) is wrong because it is not enough to prove that the statement was false. All states require that some degree of fault be proven on the part of the defendant.

(C) is wrong because special harm need not be proven in this case. A plaintiff may generally establish slander only if she can show that she sustained some special harm, usually required to be of a pecuniary nature. However, there are four kinds of utterances, categorized as "slander per se," which, even though they are slander rather than libel, require no showing of special harm. One of these is an allegation that adversely reflects on the plaintiff's fitness to conduct her business, trade, profession, or office. That kind of utterance occurred in this case.

(D) is wrong because it is irrelevant. A defamatory statement is actionable, despite the fact that it came out in a conversation where the subject matter was being inquired into. The defendant may have a privilege to respond to a reasonable inquiry, but the privilege is a qualified one, which is lost if it is abused by defendant's negligence concerning the truth or falsity of the answer.